Dictionary of
AMERICAN
DIPLOMATIC
HISTORY

Dictionary of
AMERICAN DIPLOMATIC HISTORY

SECOND EDITION,
Revised and Expanded

John E. Findling

Greenwood Press
New York • Westport, Connecticut • London

Library of Congress Cataloging-in-Publication Data

Findling, John E.
    Dictionary of American diplomatic history / John E. Findling.—
2nd ed., rev. and expanded.
        p. cm.
    Includes index.
    ISBN 0–313–26024–9 (lib. bdg. : alk. paper)
    1. United States—Foreign relations—Dictionaries.
    2. Ambassadors—United States—Biography—Dictionaries.
    3. Diplomats—United States—Biography—Dictionaries. I. Title.
E183.7.F5   1989
327.73—dc19   88–7701

British Library Cataloguing in Publication Data is available.

Library of Congress Catalog Card Number: 88–7701
ISBN: 0–313–26024–9

First published in 1989

Greenwood Press, Inc.
88 Post Road West, Westport, Connecticut 06881

Printed in the United States of America

∞

The paper used in this book complies with the
Permanent Paper Standard issued by the National
Information Standards Organization (Z39.48–1984).

10 9 8 7 6 5 4 3 2 1

327.73
F494

To My Parents

CONTENTS

Preface   ix

List of Standard Abbreviations   xi

Introduction   xiii

Maps   xix

The United States and European Possessions in North America, 1783
United States Expansion to 1853
Louisiana Purchase, 1803, and Florida Purchase, 1819
United States Collective Defense Arrangements

Organization Charts   xxvii

Department of State
Arms Control and Disarmament Agency
International Development Cooperation Agency
Agency for International Development
Trade and Development Program
Overseas Private Investment Corporation

The Dictionary   3

Appendix A   Chronology of American Diplomatic History   565

Appendix B   Key Diplomatic Personnel Listed by Presidential
             Administration   581

Appendix C   Initiation, Suspension, and Termination of
             Diplomatic Relations   595

Appendix D   Place of Birth   603

Appendix E   Locations of Manuscript Collections and Oral
             Histories   623

Index   637

PREFACE

This work attempts to serve three purposes. First, it provides basic information about nearly six hundred persons associated with U.S. foreign policy from the Revolution through 1988, as well as descriptions or definitions of about six hundred nonbiographical items connected with American diplomacy, ranging from crises to catchwords. The criteria for the selection of the entries in this book are explained in some detail in the Introduction. Additional information is contained in the appendixes following the main body of entries.

Second, wherever appropriate, entries include a statement or comment concerning their historical importance. For biographical entries, I have tried to place the subject in the context of American diplomacy and give a brief estimation of his or her contribution (or lack of one). Diplomatic events, treaties, and other nonbiographical entries are related to the broader picture of U.S. foreign policy, with comment as to their impact on that policy. In this way, readers can derive some notion of the significance of an item without further research.

Third, for those who do wish to probe further, each entry contains a bibliographical citation of varying length. These bibliographical notes are meant to be suggestive rather than exhaustive or comprehensive. I have attempted to strike a balance between easily accessible general works, often available in paperback, and the most recent and highly regarded monographs or biographical studies. In some cases, particularly more obscure individuals or contemporary people and events, I have resorted to other reference works or newspaper sources; often these are the only sources of information available. The Introduction contains a more detailed accounting of some frequently used reference works.

The first edition of this book covered the period up to the end of 1978; this second edition carries diplomatic history forward to mid-1988, thus providing coverage of the last two years of the Jimmy Carter administration and the first seven years of the Ronald Reagan administration. Nearly one hundred new entries have been added, split approximately between biographical and nonbiographical subjects. Perhaps twenty-five or thirty entries, none of which, it is hoped, will be missed, have been deleted. In addition, over four hundred of the original entries have been revised, either in terms of their content or by the citing of new publications in the bibliographies following each entry. Many of the new entries and many of the revisions came from kind suggestions of colleagues. I am grateful to John Carroll, Robert Divine, Al Eckes, Andy Fry, Tom Kennedy, and the late Warren Kuehl for their help.

For this second edition, I received cheerful and friendly assistance from the library staffs of Indiana University Southeast, Indiana University at Bloomington, and the University of Maryland. My editor at Greenwood Press, Cynthia Harris, has been a most cooperative overseer and a source of constant encouragement. A grant-in-aid from Indiana University Southeast enabled me to utilize the cheerful and efficient services of Kimberly Pelle as a research assistant, who helped with appendixes and indexing. Mary Ann Braden, Linda Williams, and Lesley Schulz word processed all the new entries with good humor and promptness, and Mary Goble and Cora Huffines also provided valuable clerical services. As always, my family—Carol and Jamey, and one surviving neurotic cat—bore up wonderfully under the strain of all twelve hundred or so entries, each of which had its own distinctive flavor.

LIST OF STANDARD
ABBREVIATIONS

CB	*Current Biography*
DAB	*Dictionary of American Biography*
FR	*Foreign Relations of the United States*
NCAB	*National Cyclopedia of American Biography*
WWA	*Who's Who in America*
WWWA	*Who Was Who in America*

An asterisk(*) indicates that an individual, issue, or term appears as an entry in this book.

INTRODUCTION

Preparing a dictionary of American diplomatic history calls on one to make many decisions. The first and most important of these is winnowing the more than two thousand U.S. chiefs of mission down to a manageable number of biographical entries and adding a selection of nondiplomatic personnel, businessmen, missionaries, and publicists, including correspondents and broadcasters, who had an impact on diplomatic history. The same process must be undertaken to create the approximately six hundred nonbiographical events contained in this book. How does one decide what should be included and what may safely be left out?

The roster of nearly six hundred biographical entries for this dictionary was drawn first from a perusal of the State Department's publication, *Principal Officers of the Department of State and United States Chiefs of Mission, 1778–1986* (1986). This valuable work lists all U.S. chiefs of mission by country and alphabetically. It enabled the determination of ministers and ambassadors who served in important missions at significant times. All ministers or ambassadors accredited to Great Britain were included, as were all to the Soviet Union after the restoration of diplomatic relations in 1933. Most chiefs of mission to France, Germany, Japan, and China were included, as well as a large share of representatives to nations such as Mexico, Italy, and Spain. Ambassadors to South Vietnam during the U.S. war there, to Chile and Peru during the War of the Pacific, and to Central America and the Caribbean during various periods of U.S. intervention typify the manner in which significant times dictated that a diplomat warranted an entry. Career diplomats, such as Ellis O. Briggs or A. J. D. Biddle, Jr., who held a number of ambassadorships over a period of time, were worthy of an entry, as were individuals whose major place in history lay outside diplomacy but nonetheless headed a legation or embassy. Examples of this latter group include Washington Irving and James Russell Lowell, both well-known literary figures, and William O'Dwyer, better known as mayor of New York City than ambassador to Mexico.

In addition to a wide variety of chiefs of mission, this book contains biographies of a substantial number of people who never headed an embassy or legation yet still had an impact on American diplomacy, among them, members of Congress, and in particular, important chairmen of the Senate Foreign Relations Committee. A number of correspondents or broadcasters, whose careers focused on foreign affairs or who influenced foreign policy through their work, are accorded a place. Several diplomatic historians of the past are included, since their work has had a great influence on how students and scholars interpret diplomatic history. And a few others—philanthropists, presidential advisers, and entrepreneurs—for example, were judged to be worthy of inclusion.

The *Dictionary of American Biography* (*DAB*), which contains biographical information on many of the people mentioned in *Principal Officers*, helped provide the names of people outside formal diplomatic channels, and stood as a beginning point for researching many individuals in this book. In its twenty volumes and eight supplements, the *DAB* presents a wealth of biographical material on thousands of prominent Americans; it is, on the whole, however, more useful for the facts of a subject's life outside his or her diplomatic career. Although a wide variety of authors contributed the essays found in the *DAB*, with varying results in emphasis and quality, most authors tend to overlook a subject's diplomatic endeavors if he or she made contributions in another field such as business or politics. Students should note too that the first twenty volumes of the *DAB* were written in the 1930s; many of the articles are outdated and should be supplemented with more recently published books or articles.

Another biographical reference work frequently used is the *National Cyclopedia of American Biography* (*NCAB*)—over fifty volumes and a multivolume supplement (in which the volumes are indicated by letters) of contemporary biographies. The quality of the biographical entries in the *NCAB* is not very high in the early volumes; they contain numerous errors of fact, so readers should corroborate facts found in the first thirty volumes with other reference sources. The more recent volumes of the *NCAB* are more thorough and reliable.

For scholars interested in collective biography, the obituary page in the *New York Times* should not be overlooked. Most of the subjects included in this dictionary merited a *Times* obituary, and although some were perfunctory and useless, others, particularly on prominent, recent subjects, provided information not found elsewhere. The *New York Times Obituary Index, 1858–1968* and a supplement indexing obituaries through 1980 are convenient research aids.

The editors of *Who's Who in America* (*WWA*) and *Who Was Who in America* (*WWWA*) have taken the word *terse* as their hallmark. Still, these works contain a greater number of entries than any other biographical reference work and often provide basic information not otherwise available. Finally, for individuals prominent since 1940, the longer, insightful articles in *Current Biography* are valuable.

Two other important reference works for diplomatic historians deserve special mention. Published just a few months before the first edition of this work, the *Encyclopedia of American Foreign Policy*, 3 vols. (1978), edited by Alexander DeConde, contains ninety-five articles on various aspects of American diplomacy. These articles, written by acknowledged experts in the field, are long and interpretive, and the subjects covered tend to be more theoretical than most in this volume. In addition, the *Encyclopedia* contains a small section of biographies. In 1983, the *Guide to American Foreign Relations Since 1700*, edited by Richard Dean Burns, was published. This is the first comprehensive bibliography on U.S. diplomatic history since Samuel F. Bemis and Grace G. Griffin's (eds.), *Guide to the Diplomatic History of the United States, 1775–1921* (1935). The listings of Burns's *Guide* are annotated, where appropriate, and extensively cross-indexed.

The publication of historical documents has been something of a growth industry in the last ten years, and students interested in documentary research who have access to large libraries may wish to look into the output of University Publications of America and Scholarly Resources. Both companies have taken advantage of the declassification of World War II and early cold war era documents and have made them (and much else) available on microfiche or microfilm. Unfortunately, the massive quantity of documents in many of the collections makes for a purchase price prohibitively expensive for all but the largest institutions.

Certain classes of individuals were peremptorily eliminated from consideration as entries in this book. Presidents of the United States were not included unless they had a significant diplomatic career as secretary of state and/or as a chief of mission. Thus John Adams, Thomas Jefferson, James Madison, James Monroe, John Quincy Adams, Martin Van Buren, and James Buchanan were included, whereas Theodore Roosevelt, Woodrow Wilson, and Richard Nixon were not. This is not to deny that Roosevelt, Wilson, and Nixon contributed significantly to American diplomatic history but to concede that much has been written and is easily accessible about these (and all other) presidents and that anything included here would be superfluous and superficial. A measure of the diplomatic contribution of any president may be made by consulting the index.

Another class of individuals excluded from consideration are foreign diplomats and statesmen. Admittedly, foreign-born individuals as diverse as Winston Churchill and the Empress Dowager T'zu Hsi of China have played a part in U.S. foreign policy, but the problem is one of limits. Where does one draw the line? It seemed best to draw the line as closely as possible and allow no foreigners in unless, like Albert Gallatin or Henry Kissinger, they had become naturalized citizens.

Many of the same problems of selection and limitation apply to the six hundred or so nonbiographical entries. Entries to be included came from items noted during over fifteen years of teaching, from reading the indexes of countless textbooks and monographs, from suggestions of colleagues, and from sources used to prepare biographical entries. No attempt has been made to present a complete history of most of these nonbiographical entries, many of which are the subject of full-length monographs or more. Instead I have presented basic background information on these items, with some commentary on their significance and bibliographical aids to help students pursue further research.

As with presidents among the biographies, American wars proved too much to include as nonbiographical entries in this book. Each of these wars has been carefully indexed, however, and researchers can pursue the trail of wartime diplomacy by judicious use of the index. Another area excluded from this volume is the post–World War II Department of Defense, its secretaries, and its military activities abroad. Although a number of military conferences with diplomatic overtones and nuclear weapons treaties have been included, much is left out on the grounds that the major portion of defense concerns is not with diplomacy.

The Changing Role of the Chief of Mission

Any student of American diplomatic history will note that the nature of American foreign relations has changed substantially in the two hundred years of independent nationhood. The United States occupies a much different place among the nations of the world now than in the past. Its national interests are different, as are the nations with which it has its most intensive diplomatic relationships.

One indicator of this change in American diplomacy is the altered role of U.S. chiefs of mission. As a scrutiny of the biographical entries in this book will show, American diplomats in the nineteenth century operated with much more independence and authority than do present-day diplomats. Benjamin Bidlack negotiated the treaty named for him with New Granada in 1846; James Gadsden, on his own, arranged for the Gadsden Purchase from Mexico in 1853; and an assortment of ministers to Turkey tried, usually without success, to win privileges and favors for Americans in that country. Biographical accounts of U.S. ministers are replete with accounts of substantial and concrete achievements of this nature.

This process of individualized diplomacy appears to have undergone a change in the late nineteenth and early twentieth centuries. The successful laying of telegraph cables across the Atlantic brought Washington into much closer contact with European capitals, and more and more frequently, major international conferences were called to work out the world's problems. The result was less opportunity for diplomats to make their own diplomatic mark. Nonetheless, some did stand out. George von L. Meyer was, by all accounts, an influential friend of Kaiser Wilhelm; Charles Denby made his presence felt in China during his long tenure there; and Henry Lane Wilson, by aiding Victoriano Huerta at a crucial time, changed the course of Mexican history. But more frequently the sources reveal the frustrations of increasing number of chiefs of mission. Horace Porter, ambassador to France, located, had exhumed, and shipped back to the United States the body of John Paul Jones as his most notable achievement. In Central America, isthmian canal enthusiast William L. Merry was bitterly disappointed to have been shunted aside while negotiations for the canal were conducted in Washington.

This tendency for ambassadors to become highly anonymous diplomatic officials has accelerated since World War II. One can read account after account of cold war diplomacy and seldom come upon the name of an ambassador, unless the account is the ambassador's own memoirs. Airplanes and the advent of summit diplomacy have made the difference. Secretaries of state from James F. Byrnes to George Shultz have spent an inordinate amount of time in foreign travel to consult with foreign counterparts, with the result that ambassadors and their staffs are reduced to the roles of political reporters, facilitators of tourists' problems, and social impresarios. Thus could Walworth Barbour serve twelve years as ambassador to Israel and draw only a handful of notices in the *New York Times* and just fleeting mention in the autobiography of Abba Eban, former Israeli United Nations ambassador and foreign minister. Walter Stoessel, Jr., was sent to Moscow as ambassador to the Soviet Union; he made news only when he became ill, allegedly from microwave radiation beamed into the U.S. embassy. Ambassadors to Great Britain and France need have no diplomatic experience—but wealth, and a great deal of it, is essential to maintain the social obligations of the embassy. From Charles Francis Adams and Thomas F. Bayard at the Court of St. James in the nineteenth century, the United States now requires representatives such as Walter F. Annenberg and Anne Armstrong. This is not to demean Annenberg and Armstrong, who were popular diplomats and served the nation well, but it does illustrate the changing nature of the American ambassador's role.

The Changing Nature of American Diplomatic Events

In the nineteenth century, American diplomacy had the great virtue of simplicity. Secretaries of state as ministers negotiated and signed specific treaties or conventions, which often emerged in history bearing their names as, for example, the Adams-Onís Treaty of 1819. Crises also were clear-cut, bilateral, and usually easily resolved. Slogans and catchwords from that era can be easily described or defined.

In the late nineteenth century, there was a trend for U.S. diplomacy to move away from bilateral treaties and toward more complex international conferences and agreements. The diplomacy of the Webster-Ashburton Treaty of 1842 gave way to the Berlin Conference on the Congo of 1884–1885 or the Tripartite Treaty of 1889 concerning Samoa. Increasing colonial and commercial rivalry accounted for much of this, as did the rise of Germany and the United States to prominence in world affairs. This international conference phase reached its apogee in the Paris Peace Conference in 1919, called to draft the Treaty of Versailles ending World War I, and continued on into the 1920s with an assortment of major conferences, mainly concerned with disarmament, a major element of interwar foreign policy for the United States.

Beginning with World War II, summit diplomacy, carried on by heads of state, has been added to the repertoire of U.S. diplomacy. From Teheran in 1943 to the last Moscow Summit in 1988, these events have dominated headlines when they have occurred and stand as milestones along the path of diplomatic history, with many other events relating to one summit or another.

Another feature of post–World War II diplomacy that stands as a contrast to earlier times is what might be called, for lack of a better term, its fuzziness. The cold war and its indefinite political and strategic objectives, the complexity of a post–cold war multipolar world, the technology of atomic warfare, and the growth of multinational corporations, often engaging in covert foreign activities, all conspire to confound the author of a dictionary or encyclopedia of diplomatic history, who depends on discrete, easily definable items to form his body of entries. Entries such as SALT, NATO, and the International Monetary Fund proved considerably more difficult to describe adequately in the limited space of an entry in this book, a problem amplified by the lack of sound historical studies on the most recent entries. A similar dilemma exists with the movers and shakers of American foreign policy during the post–World War II era. How can one deal adequately with John Foster Dulles or Henry Kissinger in three hundred or four hundred words? One cannot obviously; one can only hint at career highlights and suggest the most important contributions.

The role of multinational corporations is even more difficult to handle. This book contains a number of entries of U.S. business enterprises connected with diplomacy in the nineteenth and early twentieth centuries. It is not too difficult to describe the activities of the Pacific Mail Steamship Company, the Alaska Commercial Company, or United Fruit. But ITT? the major oil companies? the internationally connected banks? Their role abroad is clearly profound economically and possibly politically as well. But the nature of their activities defies easy description, and the decision has been made generally to exclude them from this book.

MAPS

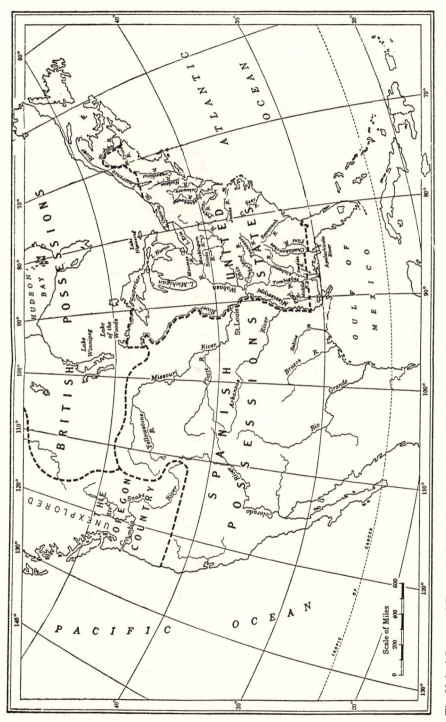

The United States and European Possessions in North America, 1783

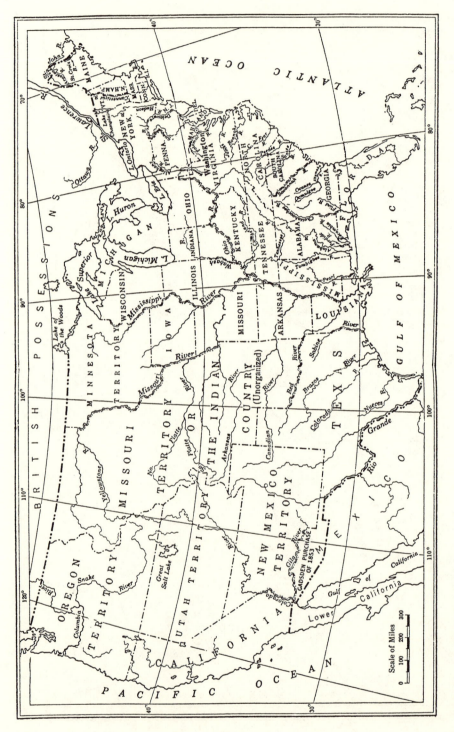

United States Expansion to 1853

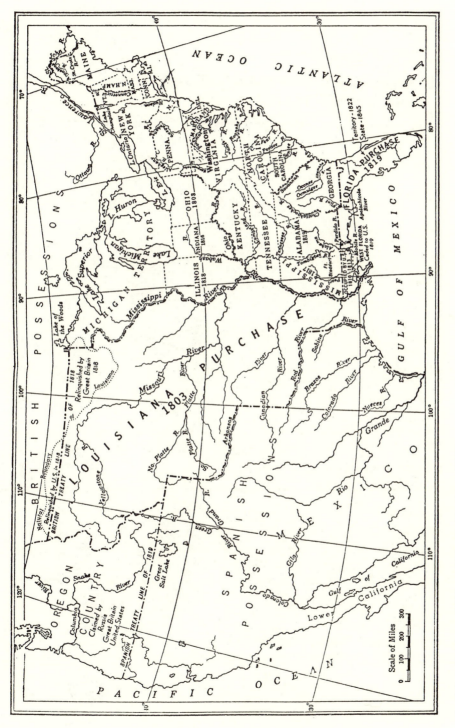

Louisiana Purchase, 1803, and Florida Purchase, 1819

UNITED STATES COLLECTIVE DEFENSE ARRANGEMENTS

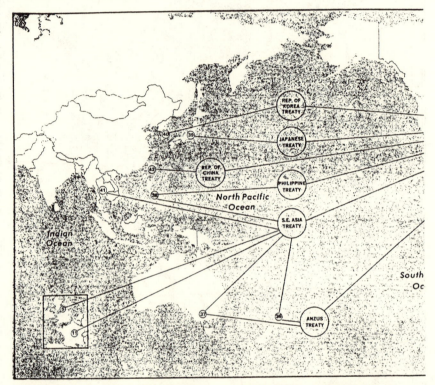

NORTH ATLANTIC TREATY (15 NATIONS)

A treaty signed April 4, 1949, by which "the Parties agree that an armed attack against one or more of them in Europe or North America shall be considered an attack against them all; and . . . each of them . . . will assist the . . . attacked by taking forthwith, individually and in concert with the other Parties, such action as it deems necessary, including the use of armed force . . ."

1	UNITED STATES	9	LUXEMBOURG
2	CANADA	10	PORTUGAL
3	ICELAND	11	FRANCE
4	NORWAY	12	ITALY
5	UNITED KINGDOM	13	GREECE
6	NETHERLANDS	14	TURKEY
7	DENMARK	15	FEDERAL REPUBLIC OF GERMANY
8	BELGIUM		

ANZUS (Australia — New Zealand—United States) TREATY (3 NATIONS)

A treaty signed September 1, 1951, whereby each of the parties "recognizes that an armed attack in the Pacific Area on any of the Parties would be dangerous to its own peace and safety and declares that it would act to meet the common danger in accordance with its constitutional processes."

1 UNITED STATES
36 NEW ZEALAND
37 AUSTRALIA

PHILIPPINE TREATY (BILATERAL)

A treaty signed August 30, 1951, by which the parties recognize "that an armed attack in the Pacific Area on either of the Parties would be dangerous to its own peace and safety" and each party agrees that it will act "to meet the common dangers in accordance with its constitutional processes."

1 UNITED STATES
38 PHILIPPINES

SOUTHEAST ASIA TREATY (7 NATIONS)

A treaty signed September 8, 1954, whereby each party "recognizes that aggression by means of armed attack in the treaty area against any of the Parties . . . would endanger its own peace and safety" and each will "in that event act to meet the common danger in accordance with its constitutional processes."

1 UNITED STATES
5 UNITED KINGDOM
11 FRANCE
36 NEW ZEALAND
37 AUSTRALIA
38 PHILIPPINES
41 THAILAND

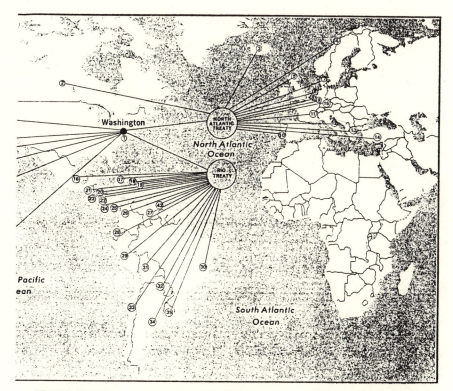

REPUBLIC OF CHINA TREATY (BILATERAL)

A treaty signed December 2, 1954, whereby each of the parties "recognizes that an armed attack in the West Pacific Area directed against the territories of either of the Parties would be dangerous to its own peace and safety . . ." and that each "would act to meet the common danger in accordance with its constitutional processes." The territory of the Republic of China is defined as "Taiwan (Formosa) and the Pescadores."

1 UNITED STATES
42 REPUBLIC OF CHINA (FORMOSA)

JAPANESE TREATY (BILATERAL)

A treaty signed January 19, 1960, whereby each party "recognizes that an armed attack against either Party in the territories under the administration of Japan would be dangerous to its own peace and safety and declares that it would act to meet the common danger in accordance with its constitutional provisions and processes." The treaty replaced the security treaty signed September 8, 1951.

1 UNITED STATES
39 JAPAN

REPUBLIC OF KOREA TREATY (BILATERAL)

A treaty signed October 1, 1953, whereby each party "recognizes that an armed attack in the Pacific area on either of the Parties . . . would be dangerous to its own peace and safety" and that each Party "would act to meet the common danger in accordance with its constitutional processes."

1 UNITED STATES
40 REPUBLIC OF KOREA

RIO TREATY (22 NATIONS)

A treaty signed September 2, 1947, which provides that an armed attack against any American State "shall be considered as an attack against all the American States and . . . each one . . . undertakes to assist in meeting the attack . . ."

1 UNITED STATES	**26 COLOMBIA**
16 MEXICO	**27 VENEZUELA**
17 CUBA	**28 ECUADOR**
18 HAITI	**29 PERU**
19 DOMINICAN REPUBLIC	**30 BRAZIL**
20 HONDURAS	**31 BOLIVIA**
21 GUATEMALA	**32 PARAGUAY**
22 EL SALVADOR	**33 CHILE**
23 NICARAGUA	**34 ARGENTINA**
24 COSTA RICA	**35 URUGUAY**
25 PANAMA	**43 TRINIDAD AND TOBAGO**

ORGANIZATION CHARTS

DEPARTMENT OF STATE

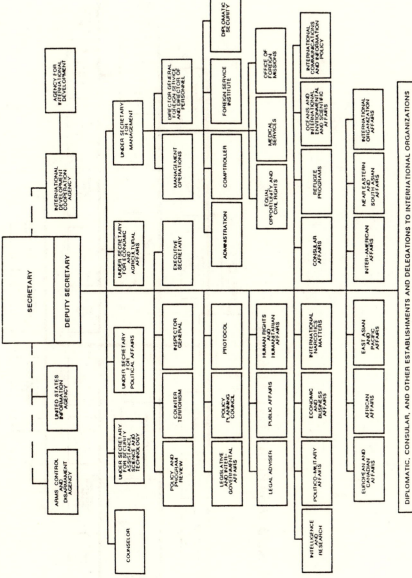

DIPLOMATIC, CONSULAR, AND OTHER ESTABLISHMENTS AND DELEGATIONS TO INTERNATIONAL ORGANIZATIONS

ARMS CONTROL AND DISARMAMENT AGENCY

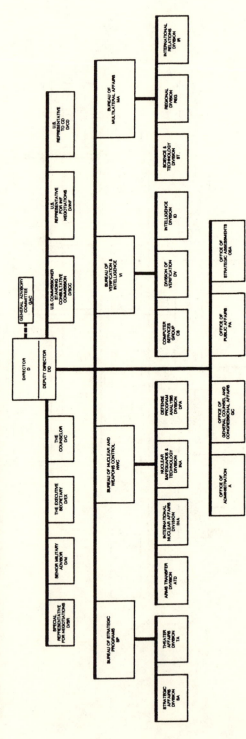

INTERNATIONAL DEVELOPMENT COOPERATION AGENCY

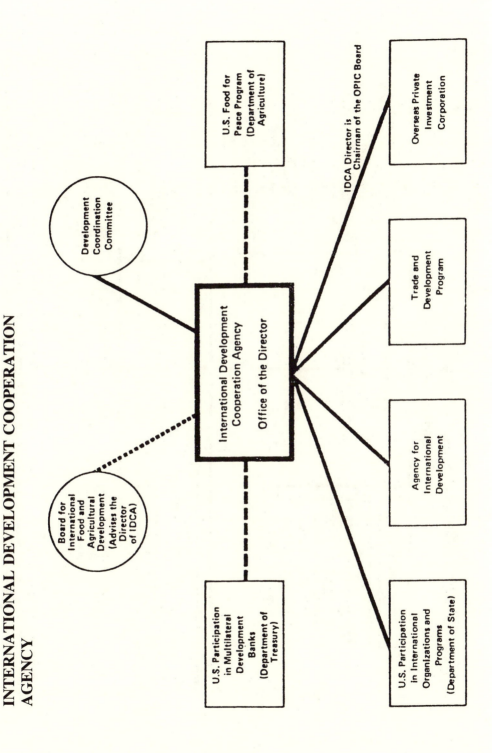

AGENCY FOR INTERNATIONAL DEVELOPMENT

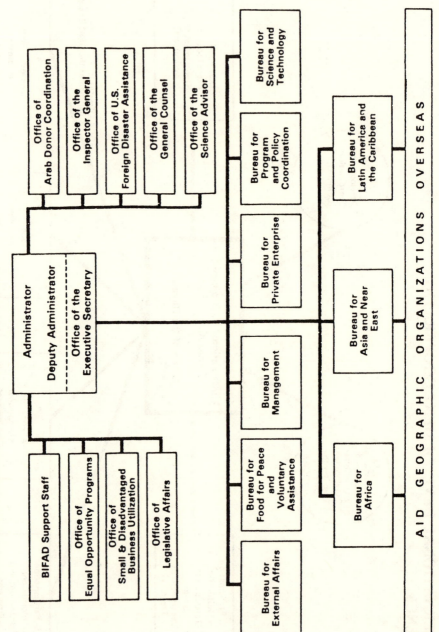

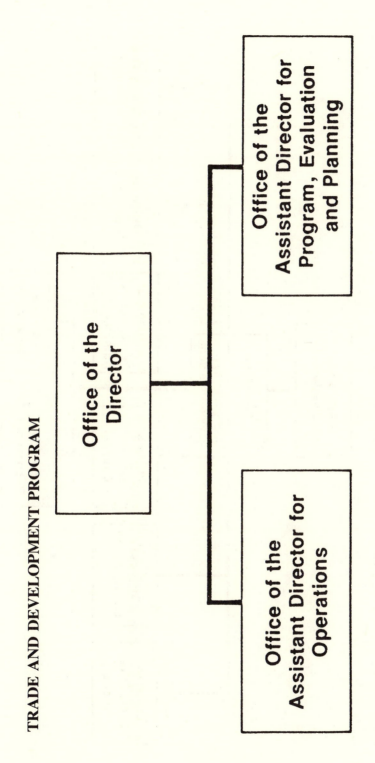

TRADE AND DEVELOPMENT PROGRAM

Office of the Director

Office of the Assistant Director for Program, Evaluation and Planning

Office of the Assistant Director for Operations

OVERSEAS PRIVATE INVESTMENT CORPORATION

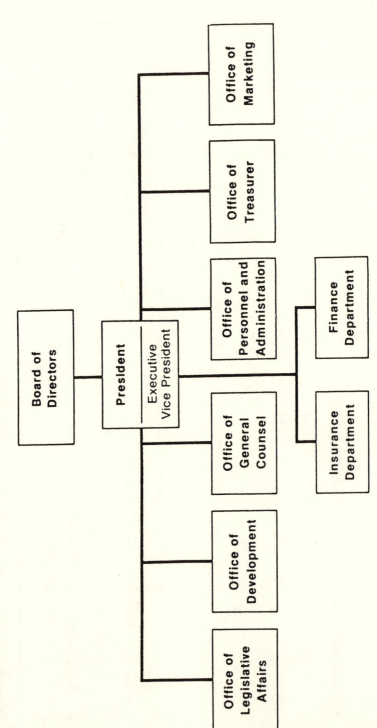

Dictionary of
AMERICAN
DIPLOMATIC
HISTORY

A

ABBOTT, WILLIS JOHN (1863–1934). A journalist and publicist of American foreign policy, Willis J. Abbott is known for his best-selling work, *Panama and the Canal in Picture and Prose* (1913). He was born on March 16, 1863, in New Haven, Connecticut, and graduated from the University of Michigan Law School in 1884. He chose to follow a career in journalism rather than law and went to work for the *New York Times-Democrat* (1884) and the *New York Tribune* (1886), while writing juvenile histories. He married Marie Mack in 1887 and in the same year became co-owner of the *Kansas City Evening News*. When that paper failed in 1889, he moved to Chicago as an editorial writer for the *Evening Mail* (1889–1892) and managing editor of the *Times* (1892–1893). William Randolph Hearst hired Abbott in 1893 to edit the editorial page of the *New York Journal*; at this time he also became involved in Democratic party politics. In 1903 Marie Mack died; two years later he married Verona Maples. After years of writing books such as *Notable Women in History* (1913) and editing for the *Journal* and other papers, Abbott capped his career by becoming editor of the *Christian Science Monitor* (1922–1927), fittingly so, since he had become a devout Christian Scientist. During the 1920s, he was well known as a peace advocate, a supporter of the League of Nations,* and a member of the Foreign Policy Association and the Council on Foreign Relations.* In 1933 he published his memoirs, *Watching the World Go By*, and on May 19, 1934, he died in Brookline, Massachusetts.*DAB*, Supp. 1:1; *New York Times*, May 20, 1934.

ABC MEDIATION (1914). The ABC nations are Argentina, Brazil, and Chile, the most influential nations in South America. In 1914, these powers offered to mediate the dispute between the United States and Mexico that had resulted in the U.S. occupation of Veracruz. After both disputants agreed, delegates from the United States, Mexico, and the ABC powers, as Argentina, Brazil, and Chile became popularly known, met in May 1914 at Niagara Falls. Because of the U.S. insistence that Mexican president Victoriano Huerta resign, nothing concrete was accomplished at the conference, but Rippy notes that it strengthened Pan-American friendship.*FR*, 1914, 488ff; Mecham, J. Lloyd, *A Survey of United States–Latin American Relations* (1965); Rippy, J. Fred, *The United States and Mexico* (1931).

ABC—1 STAFF AGREEMENT (1941). A result of Anglo-American military staff discussions (Joint Staff Conference) held between January and March 1941, this agreement stipulated that if the United States became involved in war with Germany and Japan, the main theater would be Europe. Large numbers of U.S.

forces in Europe would allow British Commonwealth troops to fight in the Far East, where the U.S. Navy would defend Hawaii, the Philippines, Guam, and Wake Island, and where Pacific operations would be coordinated but not jointly commanded. The "Europe first" war strategy had been central to U.S. military thinking since the 1920s and was partly due to lingering suspicions of the political motives behind British military strategy. Some Americans were concerned about British designs to maintain preeminence in European affairs; others disapproved of British efforts to cling to as much of the empire as long as possible. President Franklin D. Roosevelt was known to favor this agreement, although he never gave any formal notice of his assent.Feis, Herbert, *The Road to Pearl Harbor* (1950); McNeill, William H., *America, Britain, and Russia* (1953); Offner, Arnold A., *The Origins of the Second World War* (1975).

ABRAMS, ELLIOTT (b. 1948). One of the most controversial figures in the foreign policy establishment of President Ronald Reagan, Elliott Abrams was born in New York City on January 24, 1948. He earned a B.A. from Harvard in 1969, an M.S. from the London School of Economics in 1970, and a law degree from Harvard in 1973 and went into private law practice in New York. In 1975, he entered federal government service as a special counsel to the Senate Permanent Subcommittee on Investigations. From this position, he moved later that year to the staff of Senator Henry Jackson (D., Washington) as a special counsel and in 1977 to Senator Daniel Patrick Moynihan (D., New York)* as a special counsel, and in 1978 he became chief of staff. After another two years (1979–1980) in private law practice, Abrams joined the Reagan administration as assistant secretary of state for international organization affairs (the youngest assistant secretary in this century), where he supervised United Nations* policy development. In late 1981, he became assistant secretary of state for human rights and humanitarian affairs, when he successfully walked a tightrope between human rights activists left from the Carter administration and Reagan loyalists who preferred to downplay human rights in favor of anti-Communist concerns. Having learned much about Latin America through concern with human rights, Abrams replaced Langhorne Motley as assistant secretary of state for inter-American affairs in 1985. There he soon became the major spokesman for the administration's policies in Central America. He believed strongly that any solution to the Nicaraguan problem had to result from military pressure applied by the contras* and he became an outspoken advocate of their cause. Abrams's involvement in the Iran-contra scandal,* in which he solicited $10 million from the sultan of Brunei and then deliberately misled Congress on this and related activities, badly undermined his credibility with congressional leaders and led to concerted demands for his resignation. Secretary of State George Shultz,* however, stoutly defended Abrams, and he remained in his post. In early 1988, Abrams earned more public criticism when his policy to oust General Manuel Antonio Noriega from power in Panama by means of economic sanctions and diplomatic pressures was unsuccessful.*New York Times*, May 1, 1985, February 4, 1988; *WWA* (1986–1987):7.

ACCESSORY TRANSIT COMPANY, isthmian transportation company. Due to increased transisthmian traffic as a result of the discovery of gold in California, the American Atlantic and Pacific Ship-Canal Company received a Nicaraguan charter in 1849 granting it the exclusive right to transport passengers and cargo across the country. Under this charter, the company operated as the Accessory Transit Company. Disagreements between transit company officials and the American minister, Solon Borland,* and authorities of the Nicaraguan town of Greytown (San Juan del Norte) led to the destruction of the town by the U.S.S. *Cyane* on July 13, 1854. When the filibusterer* William Walker* attempted to gain control of the transit business in 1856, company officials, led by Cornelius Vanderbilt,* allied with opposition factions and forced Walker out of Nicaragua.Findling, John E., *Close Friends, Distant Neighbors* (1987); Parker, Franklin D., *The Central American Republics* (1964); Williams, Mary W., *Anglo-American Isthmian Diplomacy, 1815–1915* (1916); Folkman, David I., *The Nicaragua Route* (1972).

ACCORD. See INTERNATIONAL AGREEMENT.

ACHESON, DEAN GOODERHAM (1893–1971). The influential and controversial secretary of state during the height of cold war* tensions, Dean Acheson was born in Middletown, Connecticut, on April 11, 1893, and graduated from Yale University (1915) and Harvard Law School (1918). After World War I service in the U.S. Navy, he was secretary to Supreme Court justice Louis D. Brandeis from 1918 to 1920, was admitted to the bar in 1921, and became a practicing lawyer. In 1933, he became under secretary of the treasury and in 1941 joined the State Department as an assistant secretary, where he specialized in international economic matters, helping to develop Lend-Lease* and planning various postwar organizations such as the United Nations Relief and Rehabilitation Administration,* the International Monetary Fund,* and the International Bank for Reconstruction and Development.* As assistant secretary of state for congressional relations, he played a major role in winning Senate approval of the United Nations* Charter. In 1945, Acheson became under secretary of state. Having developed an early distrust of Soviet Russia, he worked for the adoption of the Truman Doctrine* and the Marshall Plan* in 1947. In 1949, he succeeded George C. Marshall* as secretary of state. A stalwart anti-Communist, he completed Marshall's European containment* policies with the establishment of the North Atlantic Treaty Organization* (NATO) but still ran into trouble in domestic political circles because of the "loss" of China to the Communists in 1949. From 1950 to 1953, Acheson secured military aid for the French in their struggle against Ho Chi Minh in Indochina, worked on the development of a home government and NATO membership for West Germany, and dealt with the controversies surrounding the conduct of the Korean War. Leaving the State

Department in 1953, Acheson remained a public figure, criticizing the massive retaliation* policy of his successor, John Foster Dulles*, and serving as an adviser to Presidents Kennedy, Johnson, and Nixon. Married to Alice Stanley in 1917, Acheson wrote several important books on foreign affairs, including his memoirs, *Present at the Creation* (1969). He died at his Sandy Springs, Maryland, farm on October 12, 1971.Gardner, Lloyd C., *Architects of Illusion* (1970); Graebner, Norman, "Dean G. Acheson," in Graebner, N., ed., *An Uncertain Tradition* (1961); Isaacson, Walter, and Evan Thomas, *The Wise Men: Six Friends and the World They Made* (1986); Kolko, Joyce, and Gabriel Kolko, *The Limits of Power* (1972); McLellan, David S., *Dean Acheson: The State Department Years* (1976); *New York Times*, October 13, 1971; Rose, Lisle A., *Roots of Tragedy* (1976).

ACHESON-LILIENTHAL REPORT (1946). This report, sometimes referred to as the Acheson-Lilienthal Plan, dealt with atomic energy control and outlined the stages by which that control could be internationalized. According to the plan, the United States would remain in control of its atomic capability during the transition period, since it possessed the world's only atomic bombs, and other nations would have to agree to be licensed and to submit to inspection by an international agency connected with the United Nations.* The Acheson-Lilienthal Report was distrusted by Bernard Baruch,* the U.S. delegate to the United Nations Atomic Energy Commission, and was scrapped in favor of a plan devised by Baruch that was unacceptable to the Soviet Union. The major point of contention with the Baruch Plan was the use of the Security Council veto on atomic energy issues. Baruch thought that major powers should not be able to use the veto on such issues (which would have required a change in the United Nations Charter); opponents said this insistence would ruin the chance for Soviet acceptance of the plan, which it did. However, Gaddis concludes that the Soviets would have accepted only a plan that would have given them full access to technical information about atomic energy and full freedom to use it. The Acheson-Lilienthal Plan was made public in March 1946 and named for Dean Acheson,* then under secretary of state, and David E. Lilienthal, head of the U.S. Atomic Energy Commission.Gaddis, John L., *The United States and the Origins of the Cold War* (1973); LaFeber, Walter, *America, Russia, and the Cold War, 1945–1984* (1985); Lieberman, Joseph I., *The Scorpion and the Tarantula* (1970); Lilienthal, David E., *Journals of David Lilienthal: The Atomic Energy Years* (1964).

ADAMS, BROOKS (1848–1927). Born June 24, 1848, Brooks Adams was the son of diplomat Charles Francis Adams* and the grandson of President John Quincy Adams.* He graduated from Harvard in 1870, served as his father's secretary in the negotiation to settle claims arising from the raiding during the Civil War of the C.S.S. *Alabama** (1871–1872), and was admitted to the bar in 1873. He sought to establish a cyclical theory of history—"The Law of Civilization and Decay"—in which nations would pass through phases alternating between barbarism and civilization. Around 1900, he theorized, the United

States and other Western nations would enter a period of decay unless they could adapt to the changing environment. Among the ways in which the United States could avoid entering this new phase would be to gain control of Asia, where there was great potential energy. Consequently, Adams supported an active Asian policy until 1906. He also favored an Anglo-Saxon alliance to fend off Russia, which he considered dangerous. Later in life, he became a cynic, convinced that the United States had missed its opportunity. He died in Boston, February 13, 1927. Among Adams's writings are *American's Economic Supremacy* (1900) and *The New Empire* (1902).Anderson, Thornton, *Brooks Adams: Constructive Conservative* (1951); Beringause, Arthur F., *Brooks Adams: A Biography* (1955, 1979); *DAB*, 1:38; Donovan, Timothy P., *Henry Adams and Brooks Adams: The Education of Two American Historians* (1961); Ford, Worthington, *Brooks Adams* (1927); LaFeber, Walter, *The New Empire* (1963); *New York Times*, February 14, 1927.

ADAMS, CHARLES FRANCIS (1807–1886). United States minister to Great Britain during the Civil War, Charles Francis Adams was the son of President John Quincy Adams.* Born in Boston on August 18, 1807, he graduated from Harvard in 1825, read law under Daniel Webster,* and was admitted to the bar in 1829, the same year he married Abigail Brooks. During the 1830s, he wrote for the *North American Review*, administered family matters, and edited and published the letters of his grandmother, Abigail Adams. As a Whig, he was elected to the Massachusetts legislature in 1841; as a Free-Soil partisan, he was a vice-presidential candidate in 1848; and as a Republican, he served in the U.S. House of Representatives, 1858–1861. President Abraham Lincoln named Adams minister to Great Britain in 1861, and he proved a cool and effective diplomatic representative during the seven years of his mission. He enjoyed good relations with Foreign Secretary Lord John Russell but not with the prime minister, Lord Palmerston. As advocate for the Union cause during the Civil War, Adams protested the British recognition of Confederate belligerency, succeeded in halting further talks between Russell and Confederate commissioners, eased the widespread distrust in Britain of Secretary of State William H. Seward,* and worked to block the sailing of the Laird rams* from Scotland in 1863. He failed to work out an Anglo-American accord on the Declaration of Paris (1856)* and was unable to stop the sailing of the highly destructive Confederate raider, *Alabama*,* although he did initiate the claims process that ultimately resulted in the Treaty of Washington (1871)* and the subsequent arbitral award to the United States. In general, his tact and correctness, his subtle influence with Russell and members of Parliament, and his avoidance of major errors combined to make his a successful ministry. He returned to the United States in 1868 but in 1871–1872 served on the joint board of arbitration for the *Alabama* claims. After 1872, he retired from public life and worked on family papers, including the diaries of John Quincy Adams and a tribute to Seward. Politically he was involved in the Liberal Republican movement of 1872, preferred the Democrat, Samuel Tilden, in 1876, and ran for governor of Massachusetts as a Democrat that year but lost. Adams died in Boston on November 21, 1886. Adams, Ephraim D., *Great Britain and the American Civil War*, 2 vols. (1925); *DAB*, 1:40; Duberman, Martin B., *Charles Francis Adams* (1961).

ADAMS, EPHRAIM DOUGLASS (1865–1930). E. D. Adams was born in Decorah, Iowa, on December 18, 1865, attended Iowa College (later Grinnell), and graduated from the University of Michigan in 1887. Three years later he received a Ph. D. from Michigan and began a lifelong career teaching and writing history. From 1891 to 1902, Adams was at the University of Kansas; from 1902 to 1930, he taught at Stanford, specializing in American diplomatic history and Anglo-American relations. He wrote several significant books, the most important of which was *Great Britain and the American Civil War* (2 vols., 1925). In 1915, Adams urged Herbert Hoover to preserve the records of the Belgian Relief Commission, which under Hoover's direction provided food and other needed goods for Belgium from 1915 to 1919, and in the latter year he went to Paris to organize historical materials from the war years into a collection that became the Hoover War Library. Adams was twice married: first to May Stevens Breakey, who died in 1916, and then to Florence S. Ober. Elected first vice-president of the American Historical Association in 1929, Adams died September 1, 1930, in Palo Alto, California. *DAB*, Supp., 1:8; Jameson, J. F., "Ephraim Douglass Adams," *Annual Report, American Historical Association, 1930* 1 (1931): 48–49; *New York Times*, September 3, 1930.

ADAMS, JOHN (1735–1826). An important figure in Revolutionary era diplomacy, John Adams was born in Braintree, Massachusetts, on October 19, 1735, graduated from Harvard in 1755, and was admitted to the bar in 1758. He soon became involved in Massachusetts politics, married Abigail Smith in 1764, and was active in pre-Revolutionary protestations of British colonial policy. After service in the Continental Congress, 1774–1777, Adams was selected commissioner to France in late 1777. He returned to Boston in early 1779 but in September was on his way back to France as a member of the delegation appointed to negotiate peace. In December 1780, he was named minister to the Netherlands, where he made useful contacts and achieved diplomatic recognition, a treaty of alliance, and a loan in the spring of 1782. Returning to Paris in October 1782, Adams participated in peace negotiations with the British and was particularly influential in the debt and fisheries questions. From 1785 to 1788, he was minister to Great Britain, attempting, without success, to settle problems arising from the Treaty of Paris (1783),* including the return of slaves taken by British troops during the war, the adjudication of ships seized illegally, and the unfulfilled promise of the British to evacuate forts in the Old Northwest. With negotiations stalemated, Adams spent his time writing a three-volume work, *Defence of the Constitutions* (1787–1988), to influence politics in the United States. From 1789 to 1797, he served as vice-president under George Washington and from 1797 to 1801 was president. During his term, the quasi-war* with France occurred, and Adams managed to overcome the strong political objections of his secretary of state, Timothy Pickering,* and his chief political rival, Alexander Hamilton, to keep the weak United States out of a full-scale war with France. After many years in retirement in Quincy, Massachusetts, Adams died July 4, 1826.Brown, Ralph A., *The Presidency of John Adams* (1975); Chinard, Gilbert, *Honest John Adams* (1933); *DAB*, 1:72; Hutson, James H., *John Adams and the Diplomacy of the American Revolution* (1980); Smith, Page, *John Adams*, 2 vols. (1962–1963, 1968).

ADAMS, JOHN QUINCY (1767–1848). The son of President John Adams,* John Q. Adams was born in Braintree, Massachusetts, on July 11, 1767, educated in Europe and at Harvard, and was admitted to the bar in 1790. A succession of diplomatic appointments began in 1794: minister to the Netherlands (1794–1797), minister to Prussia (1797–1801), minister to Russia (1809–1811), and minister to Great Britain (1815–1817). In the Netherlands during a period of French occupation, Adams's duties were confined to observing and reporting European affairs. He negotiated a treaty with Prussia and visited Silesia. His Russian mission marked the beginning of a period of cordial relations that would prove useful a half-century later during the Civil War. Between his ministries in Russia and Great Britain, Adams served on the peace commission that negotiated the Treaty of Ghent,* ending the War of 1812. After the war, as minister to Great Britain, he worked on a commercial treaty and other problems but without result. President James Monroe* named Adams secretary of state in 1817, and in eight years at that post, he was responsible for the acquisition of Florida through the Adams-Onís Treaty (1819),* the settlement of the U.S.–Canadian boundary through the Convention of 1818,* and for much of the Monroe Doctrine (1823).* After a term as president (1825–1829), in which foreign affairs were of little note, Adams spent most of the rest of his life in Congress, where he was prominent in his opposition to the annexation of Texas and the Mexican War. According to his biographer, Samuel F. Bemis,* John Quincy Adams was at the center of the development of most of the principles of American foreign policy that were established between 1790 and 1830. His ability to take advantage of America's favorable geographic position and his personal qualities—self-discipline, industry, negotiating skill—mark him as the foremost American diplomatist before the Civil War. Adams married Louise Catherine Johnson in 1797 and died in Washington, D. C., while still in Congress, on February 23, 1848. Adams's *Memoirs*, 12 vols. (1874–1877), were edited by his son, Charles Francis Adams.*Bemis, Samuel F., *John Quincy Adams and the Foundations of American Foreign Policy* (1949); *DAB*, 1:84; Kushner, Howard I., *Conflict on the Northwest Coast* (1975); Perkins, Dexter, *The Monroe Doctrine, 1823–26* (1927).

"ADAMS FORMULA," diplomatic principle named for John Quincy Adams. First included in the Adams-Onís Treaty (1819),* this formula held that if one of the treaty powers goes to war with a third nation and the other remains neutral, the property of belligerents that acknowledge this principle shall be protected by the neutral, but the property of belligerents that do not recognize this principle shall be liable to capture.Bemis, Samuel F., *John Quincy Adams and the Foundations of American Foreign Policy* (1949).

ADAMS-ONÍS TREATY (1819). In this treaty, also known as the Transcontinental Treaty, the United States acquired Florida and agreed to a new boundary line between U.S. and Spanish domain through the West to the Pacific Ocean. The United States assumed all American claims against Spain up to a total of $5 million and renounced claims to Texas. The treaty, ratified by the Senate in 1821, gave the United States equal claim with Great Britain to Oregon and thus complemented the Convention of 1818.* The treaty also marked the first recognition by a European power of United States territorial claims to the Pacific coast, hence the name Transcontinental Treaty. According to Bemis, the Adams-Onís treaty, named for Secretary of State John Quincy Adams* and Spanish minister to the United States Juan de Onís, stands as the "greatest diplomatic victory ever won by an American Secretary of State."Bemis, Samuel F., *John Quincy Adams and the Foundations of American Foreign Policy* (1949); Brooks, Philip C., *Diplomacy and the Borderlands* (1939).

ADEE, ALVEY AUGUSTUS (1842–1924). Alvey A. Adee was born in Astoria, New York, on November 27, 1842, and was privately educated, becoming a noteworthy linguist, Shakespearean scholar, and writer. His first diplomatic experience came in 1869–1870, when he served as private secretary to Daniel Sickles,* U.S. minister to Spain. He moved to the legation secretaryship in Madrid, 1870–1878, and then was made chief of the Diplomatic Bureau in Washington. In 1882, he was made third assistant secretary of state and four years later was promoted to second assistant secretary, a post he held until the year of his death. In this post, he frequently served as acting secretary of state; more important, he provided continuity in the department and knowledge of its operations through several presidential administrations. He introduced typewriters into the department in the 1880s and became well known for his memory and his often wry comments on interdepartmental memorandums. As acting secretary of state, Adee was in charge during the Boxer Rebellion (1900),* the peace talks that ended the Russo-Japanese War (1905),* and the Washington Conference (1907).* In 1924, he was promoted to first assistant secretary of state. Adee never married, was an avid cyclist, and was one of the original incorporators of the American National Red Cross. He died in Washington on July 5, 1924.*DAB*, 1:105; DeNovo, John A., "The Enigmatic Alvey A. Adee and American Foreign Relations, 1870–1924," *Prologue* 7 (1975): 69–80; *New York Times*, July 6, 1924.

AFGHANISTAN CRISIS (1979–1988). Soviet troops invaded neighboring Afghanistan in December 1979 to stabilize a leftist regime that had come to power in an April coup. Anti-Soviet resistance developed quickly into a force of some

100,000 pitted against 115,000 Soviet troops and 70,000 loyal Afghan soldiers, secret police, and paramilitary forces. The war dragged on brutally for several years, with large numbers of casualties and as many as 2 ½ million refugees living in camps inside the Pakistan border. Peace talks that began in 1982 proceeded glacially but finally resulted in an agreement, signed April 1988, that provided for Soviet troop withdrawal over a nine-month period beginning in May. For the United States and the Jimmy Carter administration, the invasion caused a fundamental reappraisal of policy toward the Soviet Union, bringing an end to the period of détente.* President Carter reacted by deferring consideration of the SALT II (Strategic Arms Limitation Talks*) ratification, placing an embargo on grain sales to the Soviet Union, boycotting the 1980 Olympic Games scheduled to be held in Moscow, and curtailing other economic and cultural exchanges. In addition, the administration instituted a neocontainment set of values in such areas as military assistance programs and consideration of arms development and the announcement in January 1980 of the Carter Doctrine.* In the 1980 presidential campaign, the Republicans made the Afghanistan invasion an issue, charging that Carter's approach to foreign policy was naive. Under the Ronald Reagan administration, covert aid was sent to Afghan guerrillas, and large amounts of assistance were sent to Pakistan, partly to express gratitude for their burden in handling the refugees and partly to deter Soviet movements in that direction. Amstutz, J. Bruce, *Afghanistan: The First Five Years of Soviet Occupation* (1986); Brown, Seyom, *The Faces of Power* (1983); Collins, Joseph J., *The Soviet Invasion of Afghanistan* (1986); Klass, Rosanna, ed., *Afghanistan: The Great Game Revisited* (1987); *Washington Post*, April 1, 1988.

AFRICAN DEVELOPMENT BANK. One of a number of multinational development banks, the African Development Bank was founded in 1963 and began operations at its Abidjan, Ivory Coast, headquarters in 1966. Until 1982, its membership was limited to regional countries; in that year, non-African countries were admitted. In 1987, there were fifty African members and twenty non-African members, including the United States. In 1985, the bank loaned $1.15 billion for 415 development projects, mainly agricultural. Banks, Arthur S., ed., *Political Handbook of the World 1987* (1987).

AFRICAN INTERNATIONAL ASSOCIATION. Created in 1876 by Leopold II of Belgium, who saw colonial potential in Africa, the African International Association had the announced purpose of furthering exploration and civilization in tropical Africa. King Leopold, with an American, Colonel Henry S. Sanford and Belgian Colonel William Strauch, tried to interest the United States by advertising duty-free entry for American goods to association-controlled ports in the recently acquired Belgian Congo and by offering to pay part of an American consul's salary. Sanford lobbied successfully in 1884 for U.S. recognition of the association, though his activities aroused criticism from European rivals and isolationist newspapers. At the Berlin Congo Conference (1884–1885),* the association received the tacit approval of all major European powers. Fry, Joseph A., *Henry S. Sanford* (1982); Pletcher, David, *The Awkward Years* (1962).

AFRICAN SLAVE TRADE TREATY (1862). This treaty, also known as the Anglo-American Treaty of 1862, pledged Anglo-American cooperation in stopping the African slave trade. It was initiated by Secretary of State William H. Seward* and was viewed by some as pro-abolitionist, anti-Confederate propaganda, but it did help improve Anglo-American relations at a difficult time. Adams, Ephraim D., *Great Britain and the American Civil War* (1925); Henderson, Conway W., "The Anglo-American Treaty of 1862 in Civil War Diplomacy," *Civil War History* 15,4 (1969): 308–319; Van Deusen, Glyndon, *William Henry Seward* (1967).

AGAR, HERBERT SEBASTIAN (1897–1980). A journalist and author who played an important role in cementing the Anglo-American alliance during World War II, Herbert Agar was born in New Rochelle, New York, on September 29, 1897. He received an A.B. degree from Columbia in 1919 and an A.M. (1920) and Ph.D. (1924) from Princeton. Entering the field of journalism, he was London correspondent for the *Louisville Courier-Journal* from 1929 to 1934 and wrote a syndicated column, "Time and Tide," from 1935 to 1939. From 1940 to 1942, Agar was editor of the *Courier-Journal* and an early supporter of U.S. intervention in the war. From 1943 to 1946, as a commander in the U.S. Navy, Agar directed the London bureau of the Office of War Information and was attached to the staff of Ambassador John Winant.* He lived most of the postwar years in England and continued his career as a professional writer. As an author, he won a Pulitzer Prize in 1933 for his study of U.S. presidents, *The People's Choice.* Among his other books are *Land of the Free* (1935), *What Is America?* (1936), *A Time for Greatness* (1942), *The Price of Union* (1950), and *The Darkest Year* (1973). In much of his writing, he extolled the virtues of democratic Great Britain and America's common interests with Britain. Thrice married, Agar died in Sussex, England, on November 24, 1980. *New York Times*, November 25, 1980; *WWWA*, 7 (1977–1981):4.

AGRICULTURE TRADE DEVELOPMENT AND ASSISTANCE ACT (1954). This act, better known as P. L. 480 or Food for Peace, evolved from concern about the abundant commodity surplus that existed in the 1950s. Over the first three years, the act provided $700 million to be loaned to needy countries for food purchases from the United States and an additional $300 million in donations. In 1975, Food for Peace was combined with the general developmental assistance program. Food for Peace is now channeled into Title I, which includes concessional sales and in which other foreign policy considerations may be involved; Title II, which are grants sent to the neediest nations, with much less concern for other foreign policy considerations; and Title III, which is food given or sold for developmental assistance purposes. In recent years, Food for Peace has been funded at slightly over $1 billion annually. Pastor, Robert A., *Congress* *and the Politics of U.S. Foreign Economic Policy, 1929–1976* (1980); Wilhelm, John, and Gerry Feinstein, *U.S. Foreign Assistance: Investment or Folly?* (1984).

AIX-LA-CHAPELLE, CONGRESS OF (1818). In this congress, France, Russia, Austria, Great Britain, and Spain discussed ways of restoring wayward Spanish colonies in the New World to Spain. Great Britain opposed an intervention plan proposed by France and Russia that envisioned regaining colonies by means other than direct military invasion. The United States was viewed as a threat to monarchical Europe, especially at the head of a republican Western Hemisphere. The congress alerted the United States to the fact that American and British policies had much in common, although Britain's Lord Castlereagh later called for the restoration of the colonies to Spain. Whitaker, Arthur P., *The United States and the Independence of Latin America, 1800–1830* (1941).

ALABAMA, **C.S.S.,** Confederate raider. The *Alabama* was built in England in 1862 and commanded by Raphael Semmes. From September 1862 to June 1864, the *Alabama* raided Union shipping, capturing, destroying, or ransoming sixty-four prizes before being sunk by the U.S.S. *Kearsarge* in the English Channel near Cherbourg, France, June 19, 1864. The fact that the ship had been built in England caused severe strains in Anglo-American relations during and after the war, when the United States demanded satisfaction for the so-called *Alabama* claims. In 1871, in the Treaty of Washington,* the United States received $15.5 million in settlement of claims against the *Alabama* and other British-built Confederate raiders. Cook, Adrian, *The Alabama Claims* (1975); Davis, J. C. Bancroft, *Mr. Fish and the Alabama Claims* (1893); *FR* (1862): 204ff.; *FR* (1863): 103ff.; *FR* (1866): 1:44ff.; Merli, Frank J., *Great Britain and the Confederate Navy* (1970); Owsley, Frank L., *King Cotton Diplomacy*, 2d ed. (1959); Van Deusen, Glyndon, *William Henry Seward* (1967).

ALASKA BOUNDARY DISPUTE (1898–1903). This controversy concerned the boundary between Alaska and Canada, originally drawn in the Anglo-Russian Convention (1825)* and neglected until the Klondike gold discoveries in 1896. At that point, the question of who controlled the headwaters of the Lynn Canal, the longest inlet or fjord into the Klondike region, became a matter of dispute, since the nation that controlled the canal would control the commerce of the region. The Hay-Herbert Treaty (1903) established a mixed commission (the Alaska Arbitral Tribunal), which in October 1903 announced a verdict that left the United States in control of the Lynn Canal. The settlement of this dispute removed the last serious obstacle from the Anglo-American rapprochement of the early years of the century. Campbell, Charles S., *Anglo-American Understanding* (1957); Devine, Michael J., *John W. Foster: Politics and Diplomacy in the Imperial Era, 1873–1911* (1981); Tansill, C. C., *Canadian-American Relations, 1875–1911* (1943).

ALASKA COMMERCIAL COMPANY, U.S. sealing company. This company received from the U.S. government in 1870 monopoly rights to harvest fur seals on the Pribilof islands in the Bering Sea and did so from 1870 to 1890. In the mid-1880s, Canadian sealers began to hunt seals from boats outside the three-mile limit. This practice, known as pelagic sealing, hurt the company's profits and the government's royalties and led to arbitration in 1893 in which pelagic limits were established. By this time, the lease of the Alaska Commercial Company had expired, and Pribilof island sealing was being done by the North American Commercial Company. Campbell, Charles S., *Anglo-American Understanding, 1898–1903* (1957).

ALASKA PURCHASE (1867). From 1845 on, American interest increased in the purchase of Russian America, or Alaska. Russia had been interested in selling the territory to the United States since it was virtually indefensible against British advances from Canada. A treaty was discussed in the late 1850s, but the Civil War blocked negotiations for several years. Secret negotiations between Secretary of State William H. Seward* and the Russian minister to the United States, Baron Edouard de Stoeckl, resulted in a treaty, March 30, 1867, for the purchase of Alaska for $7.2 million. Although public reaction was often derisive (the purchase was popularly referred to as Seward's Folly), the Senate ratified the treaty on April 9 by a vote of 37 to 2. Increasing hostility in Congress to the Andrew Johnson administration delayed the House vote to appropriate the purchase money for more than a year. When consummated, the purchase added to the United States an area nearly twice the size of Texas. According to Van Deusen, Seward's biographer, the treaty exemplified Seward's expansionism and vision of the United States as a future world leader. Holbo, Paul S., *Tarnished Expansion: The Alaska Scandal, the Press and Congress, 1867–1871* (1983); Jensen, Ronald J., *The Alaska Purchase and Russian-American Relations* (1975); Kushner, Howard I., *Conflict on the Northwest Coast* (1975); Van Deusen, Glyndon, *William Henry Seward* (1967).

ALDRICH, WINTHROP WILLIAMS (1885–1974). An uncle of Nelson Rockefeller,* Winthrop W. Aldrich was born in Providence, Rhode Island, on November 2, 1885. He graduated from Harvard (1907) and Harvard Law School (1910) and gained admittance to the bar in 1912. From 1912 to 1929, Aldrich practiced law in New York City, except during World War I, when he served in the U.S. Navy. In 1929, he entered the banking business as president of the Equitable Trust Company, a bank partly owned by his brother-in-law, John D. Rockefeller, Jr. A merger in 1930 created the Chase National Bank, then the world's largest, and Aldrich was chairman of the board from 1934 to 1953. A Republican, Aldrich accepted the appointment as ambassador to Great Britain in 1953. He had headed the Allied Relief Fund, and after World War II, as president of the International Chamber of Commerce, he had actively supported the Marshall Plan*; hence he was not unacquainted with Europe's problems when he went to London. The high point of his mission was the Suez crisis (1956),* during which he worked to restore friendly relations in a period of mistrust and suspicion brought on by the U.S. refusal to support the British-French-Israeli invasion of Egypt. Apart from Suez, Aldrich's mission was principally social—he attended the coronation of Queen Elizabeth II—and commercial—he worked to strengthen Anglo-American economic relations. Aldrich resigned his post in 1957 and with his wife, Harriet Alexander Aldrich, lived in retirement, enjoying yachting and supporting Tuskegee Institute. He died in New York City on February 25, 1974. Johnson, Arthur Menzies, *Winthrop W. Aldrich: Lawyer, Banker, Diplomat* (1968); *NCAB*, D:74; *New York Times*, February 26, 1974; *WWWA*, 6 (1974–1976): 4–5.

ALGECIRAS CONFERENCE (1906). This conference stemmed from rivalry between France and Germany over Morocco. France claimed Morocco as a dependency, while Germany insisted on Moroccan independence. Great Britain, then on poor terms with Germany, supported France and opposed German suggestions for a conference. In June 1905, as tensions mounted, President Theodore Roosevelt convinced the French of the desirability of a conference, and the British acceded. The meetings in Algeciras, Spain, lasted from January until March 1906, and Roosevelt was influential behind the scenes in reconciling differences between Germany and France. The conference ended with a compromise agreement over control of the Moroccan police and a Moroccan bank, the key points of conflict. Anderson, Eugene N., *The First Moroccan Crisis, 1904–1906* (1930); Beale, Howard K., *Theodore Roosevelt and the Rise of America to World Power* (1956); *FR* (1906) 2:1470–1513.

ALGIERS CONFERENCE (1943). This World War II conference brought together Winston Churchill and an assortment of Allied military commanders, including Generals George C. Marshall* and Dwight D. Eisenhower. Following the Trident Conference* and the successful conclusion of the North African campaign, the Algiers Conference concerned itself principally with future Allied military moves. Churchill advocated an invasion of the Italian peninsula following the taking of Sicily, but Marshall was concerned that such a move might tie up too many troops and further delay a cross-channel invasion. An alternative plan, the taking of Sardinia and Corsica, was dismissed. The conference, which lasted from May 29 until June 3, resulted in no fixed decisions; rather, it was agreed to wait and see how the battle for Sicily proceeded. Feis, Herbert, *Churchill—Roosevelt—Stalin* (1967); McNeill, William H., *America, Britain, and Russia* (1953).

ALIEN AND SEDITION ACTS (1798). These were a series of four acts passed by Congress in June and July 1798 as a result of troubles with France. The acts were designed ostensibly by the ruling Federalists to halt French intrigues against the United States but were viewed then and now as meant primarily to destroy the political opposition of the Republican party. The Naturalization Act raised from five to fourteen the years of residency required for citizenship; the Alien Enemies Act authorized the deportation of all resident alien citizens of an enemy nation in time of war; the Alien Act extended the power of the government over all aliens in the United States; and the Sedition Act provided criminal punishment for acts of seditious printing, writing, or speaking. The Alien and Sedition Acts were a product of the French crisis and quasi-war* of 1798–1799 and were repealed or allowed to expire under the administration of President Thomas Jefferson. Miller, John C., *Crisis in Freedom: The Alien and Sedition Acts* (1951).

ALLEN, ELISHA HUNT (1804–1883). Born January 28, 1804, in New Salem, Massachusetts, Elisha Allen was graduated from Williams College (1823), read law, and was admitted to the bar in 1825. In 1827, he moved to Maine, where he practiced law in Bangor and in 1836 entered the Maine House of Representatives. In 1840, Allen, a strong advocate of Maine's rights in the northeastern boundary dispute (see Webster-Ashburton Treaty*), was elected as a Whig to the U.S. House for one term. In the late 1840s, he lived in Boston and served in the Massachusetts legislature. The Zachary Taylor administration named Allen consul* in Hawaii in 1850, and for the rest of his life, he was closely associated with Hawaiian affairs. He served as consul only a short while before becoming Hawaiian minister of finance, a position he held until 1857. In that year, he assumed the office of chancellor and chief justice, remaining on the bench for twenty years. In addition, Allen became closely connected with efforts to secure a U.S.–Hawaiian reciprocity treaty, traveling to the United States in 1856–1857 and again in 1864 to urge such a treaty before Congress. Finally, in 1876, his efforts were successful with the ratification of the Hawaiian Reciprocity Treaty* and, after retiring from the Supreme Court of Hawaii the following year, he served as Hawaii's minister to the United States until his death on January 1, 1883, at a presidential New Year's reception in Washington. Allen was twice married: to Sarah Fessenden in 1828 and, after her death in 1845, to Mary Harrod Hobbs in 1857. *DAB*, 1:187; *NCAB*, 27:300.

ALLEN, GEORGE VENABLE (1903–1970). George V. Allen was born in Durham, North Carolina, on November 3, 1903, and was graduated from Duke University (B.A., 1924) and Harvard (M.A., 1929), where he won the Charles Sumner Prize for International Relations. A high school teacher and journalist during the 1920s, he entered the U.S. Foreign Service in 1930 and held a succession of minor posts until becoming chief of the Near Eastern Division in 1942. He was a member of the U.S. delegation to the San Francisco Conference (1945)* and was named ambassador to Iran the following year. In Iran during the Iran crisis (1946),* he played a role in diminishing Soviet influence and improving U.S.-Iranian relations in spite of concern about U. S. hegemony. After two years as assistant secretary of state for public affairs, a forerunner of the U.S. Information Agency (USIA),* from 1948 to 1950, Allen became ambassador to Yugoslavia, a relatively uneventful three-year tour. In 1953, he was appointed ambassador to India and Nepal, where for two years he argued for increased economic aid to those countries. After a year as assistant secretary of state for Near Eastern, South Asian, and African affairs, Allen went to Athens as ambassador to Greece in 1956. In 1958, he returned to Washington to head the USIA, perhaps his most significant post. There he encouraged a policy of emphasizing a "full and fair picture of American life and culture," toning down some of the more blatantly propagandistic efforts of his predecessors. Under his direction, the USIA increased its involvement in international expositions and trade fairs, its teaching of English abroad, and its promotion of cultural over political viewpoints. Following the election of John F. Kennedy in 1960, Allen retired from government service and became president of the Tobacco Institute, defending the industry against reports linking smoking with cancer. In 1966, he was named a career ambassador, an honorific title, and became head of the Foreign Service Institute. He left that post in 1969 and died at his farm near Bahama, North Carolina, on July 11, 1970. Elder, Robert E., *The Information Machine* (1968); Kuniholm, Bruce R., *The Origins of the Cold War in the Near East* (1980); *New York Times*, July 12, 1970; Sheehan, Michael K., *Iran: The Impact of U.S. Interests and Policies, 1951–1954* (1986); Sorenson, Thomas C., *The Word War: The Story of American Propaganda* (1968).

ALLEN, RICHARD VINCENT (b. 1936). President Ronald Reagan's first national security adviser, Richard V. Allen was born New Year's Day, 1936, in Collingswood, New Jersey. He received a B.A. (1957) and an M.A. (1958) from Notre Dame and spent two years teaching in the University of Maryland's overseas program. From 1961 to 1962, Allen taught at Georgia Tech; from 1962 to 1966, he was on the staff of the Center for Strategic and International Studies. After three years at the Hoover Institute (1966–1969), he spent three years in the Richard Nixon administration, on the National Security Council (NSC)* and the White House staff. In 1972, he became president of the Potomac International Corporation in Washington, remaining in that position until 1980. Allen met Ronald Reagan during the 1976 campaign and two years later began advising Reagan on national security issues. After Reagan's election in 1980, Allen was asked to head the NSC, an appointment made in part because of the new president's desire to have a traditional cabinet style of government. The relatively unknown and technocratic Allen suited the idea of lowering the visibility of the NSC from the Carter administration and the mercurial Zbigniew Brzezinski.* But Allen's tenure was brief; within a year, he had earned a reputation as a lackluster administrator who could not bring focus to the overall foreign policy concerns of the White House and who underestimated the political opposition in Congress. His relationship with Secretary of State Alexander Haig* was, at best, uneasy, and when it was discovered that he had accepted $1,000 from three Japanese journalists in return for arranging an interview with first lady Nancy Reagan, Allen was forced to resign, though an investigation cleared him of any wrongdoing. Leaving the administration in January 1982, Allen formed a consulting firm, Richard V. Allen Company, and has been associated with the Heritage Foundation and the Republican National Committee. He married Patricia Ann Mason in 1957 and wrote *Peace or Peaceful Coexistence* in 1966. Barnett, Lawrence I., *Gambling with History* (1983); *New York Times*, January 5–8, 1982; *WWA* (1986–1987):45.

ALLIANCE FOR PROGRESS, Latin American development program. Formally created in August 1961 at a special meeting of the Inter-American Economic and Social Council in Punta del Este, Uruguay, the Alliance for Progress had its roots in Operation Pan-America, a plan devised in 1958 by Brazilian president Juscelino Kubitschek and was, in part, an attempt to provide an alternative to the appeal of Castroism. In the alliance, public funds were used to create conditions in Latin American nations attractive enough to invite private capital, which would be guided by national economic development plans. By 1963, multilateral control over the alliance seemed more desirable to most Latin Americans but was hard for U.S. leaders to accept, given the traditional bilateral relationship of the United States with the other nations of the hemisphere. Under President Lyndon B. Johnson, appropriations for the alliance declined, and so did the mystique surrounding the program (especially after the Cuban missile crisis* made Fidel Castro seem less a threat), and Latin Americans became restive at the alliance's failure to meet their high expectations. Levinson and de Onís concluded that after a decade, the achievements of the alliance were at best spotty and that the program had neither defused revolution nor brought progress in solving basic social and economic problems. Connell-Smith notes a basic contradiction in the Alliance for Progress between its emphasis on social and agrarian reform and its implicit anticommunism: the more anti-Communist a Latin American government is, the less inclined it is to bring about the social and agrarian reform. Connell-Smith, Gordon, *The United States and Latin America* (1974); Levinson, Jerome, and Juan de Onís, *The Alliance That Lost Its Way* (1970); Mecham, J. Lloyd, *A Survey of United States–Latin American Relations* (1965); Rogers, William D., *The Twilight Struggle: The Alliance for Progress and the Politics of Development in Latin America* (1967); Welch, Richard E., *Response to Revolution: The United States and the Cuban Revolution, 1959–1967* (1985).

ALLIED CONTROL COUNCIL, quasi-central government for Germany, 1945–1948. First formally mentioned in an American memorandum on postwar Germany at the Moscow Conference (1943)* as a body to enforce the terms of surrender, the Allied Control Council came to include France at the Dumbarton Oaks Conference (1944)* and was agreed to by Soviet premier Joseph Stalin at the Yalta Conference (1945)*. By this time, the European Advisory Commission had planned for the Allied Control Council to be composed of the commander in chief of each occupation force; thus General Dwight D. Eisenhower, Field Marshal Viscount Bernard Montgomery, and Marshal Georgi Zhukov were the original representatives. At an organizational meeting on June 5, 1945, the Allies declared that the control council would function as a central government for Germany, would take whatever steps were necessary in Germany to ensure future peace and security, and would assume uniformity of action in each zone, with all council decisions to be unanimous. In practice, the council also allocated reparations* and defined the level of industry permitted the Germans. Problems arose by the end of 1945, however, over differing interpretations of, for example, political parties and the confiscation of property. Even more detrimental to the council's functioning was French resistance to every attempt to re-create a central administrative structure for Germany. The Allied Control Council met for the final time in March 1948, heard Soviet accusations that the Western powers were running their zones without Soviet participation and Western accusations that the Soviets were autonomously controlling their zone, and never met again. For most of the life of the council, Lucius Clay* was the U.S. representative. Feis, Herbert, *From Trust to Terror* (1970); Gimbel, John, *The American Occupation of Germany* (1968); McNeill, William H., *America, Britain, and Russia* (1953); Wheeler-Bennett, John W., and Anthony Nicholls, *The Semblance of Peace* (1972).

ALLISON, JOHN MOORE (1905–1978). Born in Holton, Kansas, on April 7, 1905, John Allison graduated from the University of Nebraska in 1927, taught school in Japan, and worked for General Electric in Shanghai until 1930, when he began a diplomatic career at the U.S. consulate in Shanghai. Formally admitted to the Foreign Service in 1932, Allison held minor posts in Kobe (Japan), Tokyo, Dairen, Tsinam, and Nanking, China, and Osaka until 1941, when he was interned by the Japanese for several months. After his release in 1942, he became second secretary of the London embassy, rising to first secretary in 1945. From 1946 to 1951, he served in Washington, with responsibility in Far Eastern affairs, 1952–1953. From 1953 to 1957, he was ambassador to Japan, where he dealt with Mutual Security Agency aid and its role in U.S.-Japanese defense concerns. He signed a Mutual Defense Agreement (1954) as well as three economic agreements and a convention removing extraterritorial status from U.S. troops stationed in Japan. Additionally, Allison handled problems relating to U.S. atomic bomb test fallout. His Japanese tour was followed by ambassadorships in Indonesia (1957–1958) and Czechoslovakia (1958–1960). In Indonesia, he was concerned with President Sukarno's relationship with Communist factions, with Japanese domination of the central government, and with the Indonesia-Dutch conflict over West Irian. His differences with Washington over the extent of a Communist threat and the treatment of Sukarno, to whom he was sympathetic, probably contributed to his transfer to Prague in 1958. There he reassured the Czechs about German rearmament and dealt with problems of compensation to U.S. firms that had lost property in the Communist takeover. Allison retired from the State Department in 1960, taught at the University of Hawaii, and wrote his memoirs, *Ambassador from the Prairie* (1973). He was married twice and died in Honolulu on October 28, 1978. *Washington Post*, October 30, 1978; *WWA* (1958–1959):45.

"ALL-OF-MEXICO" MOVEMENT, an expansionist movement related to the Mexican War. This movement to acquire all of Mexico was generated first in 1846 and again in late 1847 by extremists dissatisfied with efforts toward peace with Mexico. Motivations of those involved ranged from a desire to exact vengeance on the Mexicans to a racist but altruistic sense of regenerating the land and people in the superior traditions of Anglo-Saxon civilization. Stronger in the Northwest and Northeast than in the South, the movement peaked in February 1848 and withered rapidly after the signing of the Treaty of Guadalupe-Hidalgo* became known. Fuller, John D. P., *The Movement for the Acquisition of All Mexico, 1846–1848* (1936); Pletcher, David, *The Diplomacy of Annexation* (1973).

"ALL OREGON," slogan, 1844–1846. "All Oregon" refers to the idea that the United States should acquire the entire Oregon territory that had been jointly claimed with Great Britain since 1818, that is, the territory north to latitude 54°40′. The phrase was mentioned in the Democratic convention of 1844 and in the congressional session of 1844–1845, where a bill calling for the occupation of all of Oregon passed the Senate as a demonstration of Democratic sentiment. In early 1846, the sentiment was revived in the slogan "Fifty-four Forty or Fight!"* Merk, Frederick, *The Monroe Doctrine and American Expansionism* (1966) and *The Oregon Question* (1967).

AMBASSADOR. See **CHIEF OF MISSION.**

AMBRISTER, ROBERT CHRISTY, AND ARBUTHNOT, ALEXANDER, AFFAIR OF (1818). This incident came about when Andrew Jackson, with a large body of troops, invaded Spanish Florida in March 1818 to halt Indian raids into the United States. In April, Ambrister, a young British army captain, was arrested and charged with "assuming command of Indians in war with the United States," and Arbuthnot, an elderly Scottish trader, was arrested on accusations of "exciting" the Indians to war, spying, and giving aid to the enemy. Both were convicted in a court-martial. Arbuthnot was hanged from the yardarm of his own trading ship, and Ambrister fell before a firing squad. The evidence against the two, taken from testimony of witnesses and letters written by Arbuthnot, was so conclusive that the British government raised no protest, despite considerable public uproar. Spain did protest the invasion of its territory, but the Monroe administration effectively used the situation to speed up the negotiations that led to the Adams-Onís Treaty.* Bemis, Samuel F., *John Quincy Adams and the Foundations of American Foreign Policy* (1949); James, Marquis, *Andrew Jackson* (1938); Perkins, Bradford, *Castlereagh and Adams* (1964).

AMERICA FIRST COMMITTEE (1940–1941). A noninterventionist organization in the period immediately preceding World War II, America First was founded in June 1940 through the efforts of R. Douglas Stuart, a Yale law student, General Robert E. Wood, chairman of the board of Sears, Roebuck,

William E. Regnery, a wealthy publisher, and other prominent Americans. America First believed in keeping out of the European war by building a strong defense and avoiding "aid short of war." Members of the organization lobbied strongly among the public and in Congress against measures such as Lend-Lease,* convoying, and repeal of the Neutrality Acts.* According to Cole, America First served to unify noninterventionist sentiment in such a way that President Franklin D. Roosevelt was forced to take a much more cautious approach to U.S. involvement in the war. Immediately following the attack on Pearl Harbor,* the committee stopped all noninterventionist activity and urged its members to give full support to the war. Cole, Wayne S., *America First* (1963) and *Charles A. Lindbergh and the Battle against American Intervention in World War II* (1974); Stenehjem, Michele Flynn, *An American First: John T. Flynn and the America First Committee* (1976).

AMERICAN ASIATIC ASSOCIATION, commercial organization, 1898– c. 1910. This organization was formed in January 1898 by American businessmen who favored a more active China policy. Its purpose was to influence public and congressional opinion by demonstrating China's importance to America's interests and by showing how recent events in China (such as the Sino-Japanese War*) threatened those interests. The textile industry, concerned with finding foreign markets for cotton goods, was especially important in the organization, which remained an influential pro-Asian voice during the Theodore Roosevelt administration. Cohen, Warren I., *American's Response to China* (1971); McKee, Delber L., *Chinese Exclusion and the Open Door* (1977); Young, Marilyn B., *Rhetoric of Empire* (1968).

AMERICAN ATLANTIC AND PACIFIC SHIP-CANAL COMPANY, early isthmian canal company. This company, based in New York, acquired in 1849 a concession to construct a canal across Central America along the route of the San Juan River and Lake Nicaragua. The concession was won through the efforts of Ephraim George Squier,* U.S. chargé d'affaires in Central America. Squier's diplomacy sparked Anglo-American rivalry in Central America that was temporarily resolved by the Clayton-Bulwer Treaty (1850).* Although the company never built a canal, it did operate a transportation line across Nicaragua from 1851 to 1856 under the name of Accessory Transit Company.* Findling, John E., *Close Neighbors, Distant Friends* (1987); Williams, Mary W., *Anglo-American Isthmian Diplomacy, 1815–1915* (1916).

AMERICAN CHINA DEVELOPMENT COMPANY. This American company received a concession in 1898 to build a railroad in China from Canton to Hankow. After spending six years doing little but engaging in stock manipulations and violating its contract by selling a large bloc of its stock to a Belgian-owned concern, the company was threatened with the cancellation of its concession. American banker J. P. Morgan intervened and purchased the Belgian-owned stock, removing that concern, and then, at considerable profit, resold the stock to the Chinese government over the objections of President Theodore Roosevelt. By selling the stock to the Chinese government, Morgan in effect terminated the concession. When sold, the company had built just twenty-eight miles of railroad out of a total of 840 and had amply demonstrated most of the worst features of American business enterprise. Beale, Howard K., *Theodore Roosevelt and the Rise of America to World Power* (1956); Cohen, Warren I., *America's Response to China* (1971).

AMERICAN FOREIGN SERVICE ASSOCIATION. The professional organization of the Foreign Service, the American Foreign Service Association grew out of the reorganization of the American Consular Association in 1924, following the passage of the Rogers Act.* The American Consular Association had been created in 1919. Apart from representing the interests of foreign service personnel, the organization publishes the *American Foreign Service Journal*. Harr, John E., *The Professional Diplomat* (1969); Ilchman, Warren F., *Professional Diplomacy in the United States, 1779–1939* (1961).

AMIENS, TREATY OF (1802). The Treaty of Amiens, signed April 18, 1802, brought about a truce in the Anglo-French or Napoleonic Wars for several months in 1802–1803 and allowed President Thomas Jefferson* to begin the process leading to the purchase of the Louisiana territory from France (Louisiana Purchase*). Darling, Arthur B., *Our Rising Empire* (1940); DeConde, Alexander, *This Affair of Louisiana* (1976).

***AMISTAD* AFFAIR (1839).** The crew of the *Amistad*, a Spanish schooner, mutinied, and the mutineers sailed the ship to Long Island Sound, where it was intercepted by an American ship and taken to New London, Connecticut. Spain demanded the release of the ship and crew, but American officials resisted, stating that the case was already in U.S. courts. This was one of a number of incidents that sullied Spanish-American relations throughout the nineteenth century. Jones, Howard, *Mutiny on the Amistad* (1987); MacCormac, Eugene E., "John Forsyth," in Bemis, Samuel F., ed., *American Secretaries of State and Their Diplomacy*, vol. 4 (1928).

ANDERSON, RICHARD CLOUGH (1788–1826). One of the earliest representatives of the United States in Latin America, Richard C. Anderson was born in Jefferson County, Kentucky, on August 4, 1788, graduated from William and Mary College in 1804, and studied law, both on his own and at William and Mary, until 1809. He practiced law in Louisville, was elected to the Kentucky legislature for five one-year terms between 1812 and 1822, and served two terms in the U.S. House of Representatives (1817–1821). While in Washington, he became known for his sympathy with the Spanish-American revolutions for independence; accordingly, he was named minister to Colombia in 1823, staying two years at the post. He negotiated the first treaty between the United States and a nation of South America: a general treaty of amity, navigation, and commerce, which was ratified in 1825. Early that year his wife, Elizabeth Gwathmey Anderson, died in Colombia, and he resigned his post. The next year, Anderson was chosen U.S. delegate to the Panama Congress* but died July 24, 1826, in Cartagena, Colombia, while en route to the congress. *DAB*, 1:271; *NCAB*, 6:115; Tischendorf, Alfred, and E. Taylor Parks, eds., *Diary and Journal of Richard C. Anderson, 1814–1826* (1964).

ANDREWS, ISRAEL DEWOLF (1813–1871). I. D. Andrews was born in May 1813 near Eastport, Maine. Apparently self-educated, he engaged in trade between Maine and the eastern Canadian provinces and was consul at St. John's, New Brunswick, from 1845 to 1849. In 1849, he was appointed a special agent to gather information on British North American commerce, as Canadian exporters wanted greater U.S. trade to replace business lost when Parliament ended colonial preferences in British markets. After his investigation, Andrews became convinced that reciprocity was the solution to U.S.-Canadian trade problems. In 1853, the Franklin Pierce administration was similarly convinced, and Andrews was again appointed a special agent, this time to gain support in Canada for a reciprocity treaty. Working diligently and often unethically, Andrews spent a great deal of money and was successful in bringing about ratification of an agreement whereby access to American markets would be exchanged for access to Canadian inshore fishing areas, a treaty known as the Reciprocity Treaty of 1854 or the Marcy-Elgin Treaty (1854).* Andrews spent the rest of his life trying, in vain, to collect some $200,000 in claimed expenses from both the U.S. and Canadian governments, finally dying of alcoholism in Boston, February 17, 1871. *DAB*, Supp. 1:29; Masters, D. C., *The Reciprocity Treaty of 1854* (1937); Overman, William D., "I. D. Andrews and Reciprocity in 1854," *Canadian Historical Review*, n.s. 15 (September 1934): 248–63.

ANGELL, JAMES BURRILL (1829–1916). Born near Scituate, Rhode Island, on January 7, 1829, James B. Angell graduated from Brown University (1849), studied further in Paris and Munich (1851–1853), and married Sarah Swope in 1855. He then was editor of the *Providence Journal* for the next six years, giving strong editorial support to Abraham Lincoln. In 1866, he was chosen president of the University of Vermont; five years later, he took the same post at the University of Michigan, staying there until his retirement in 1909. From time to time during his long tenure at Michigan, Angell was called into public service, usually a task involving diplomacy. In early 1880, he directed a U.S. commission (including John F. Swift* and William H. Trescot*) sent to China to negotiate a new immigration treaty limiting but not prohibiting Chinese immigration to America. After the work of the commission was done, Angell stayed on in China as minister for a year (1880–1881). In 1887–1888, he was a member of the Anglo-American Northeastern Fisheries Commission, which negotiated a treaty that was rejected by the Senate. In 1896–1897, Angell served on the Canadian-American Deep Waterways Commission, which reported that deep water communication between the Atlantic Ocean and the Great Lakes was feasible and would be of great value. No action was taken on the report. Later in 1897, Angell was named minister to Turkey and spent an unhappy year there dealing with problems of neutrality during the Spanish-American War and protesting Turkish treatment of U.S. missionaries. His protests cost him favor with the government; he could not get exaquaturs for U.S. consuls, and he resigned. After retiring from the University of Michigan, he published *Reminiscences* (1911) and died April 1, 1916, in Ann Arbor, Michigan. Anderson, David L., *Imperialism and Idealism* (1985); *DAB*, 1:304; *New York Times*, April 12, 1916; Spaulding, E. Wilder, *Ambassadors Ordinary and Extraordinary* (1961); Straus, Oscar S., *Under Four Administrations* (1922).

ANGLO-AMERICAN ARBITRATION TREATY (1911). This treaty originated with a suggestion from President William H. Taft to British Ambassador James Bryce in August 1910; the idea was later taken up by British Foreign Secretary Lord Grey, who invited the submission of a draft treaty. The State Department did this in May 1911, and in August the two countries signed a treaty calling for arbitration of all problems for which the law provided a remedy, such as conflicts over fishing rights and minor boundary disputes, and for a six-member commission to decide in which cases the treaty was to apply. At the same time, a similar treaty was signed with France, a move that aroused opposition from Theodore Roosevelt, who feared the making of such treaties with less honorable nations and from an unconsulted Congress, always jealous of senatorial prerogatives. As a result, the treaties were so heavily amended that President Taft never signed them. Perkins, Bradford, *The Great Rapprochement* (1968); Smith, Daniel, *The Aftermath of War* (1960).

ANGLO-AMERICAN LEAGUE. Founded in July 1898 by a number of prominent Englishmen, the aim of this organization was "to secure the most cordial and constant cooperation" between Great Britain and the United States. Among the founders were the archbishop of Canterbury, Henry Asquith, and Rudyard Kipling. In the United States, a similar but much smaller counterpart, the Anglo-American Committee, was created later in July 1898 by a group including Whitelaw Reid,* William C. Whitney, and Carl Schurz.* These groups reflected the growing Anglo-American rapprochement of the day, as well as the widely held belief in Anglo-Saxon unity and racial superiority. Without having anything to do, the league was defunct by 1903. Campbell, Charles S., *Anglo-American Understanding, 1898–1903* (1957); Perkins, Bradford, *The Great Rapprochement* (1968).

ANGLO-FRENCH NAVAL AGREEMENT (1928). This agreement, made in June 1928 without consultation with the United States, suggested that naval limitations be based on a "global" tonnage maximum, divided into four naval categories as each nation saw fit, replacing the tonnage within particular categories then in effect. The United States was not pleased with either the new tonnage concept or the implications of an exclusive Anglo-French rapprochement, which might some day be directed against the United States. The Rapidan Conference (1929)* helped ease Anglo-American tensions to which this agreement had contributed. Ellis, Ethan L., *Republican Foreign Policy, 1921–1933* (1968).

ANGLO-JAPANESE ALLIANCE (1902). This alliance was suggested by Japan, which wanted to isolate Russia and protect Korea. The treaty, signed with Great Britain January 30, 1902, pledged each party to the conditional defense of the other in the case of a Far Eastern war. On August 12, 1905, the treaty was extended to include Japanese aid in case of an attack on India and to strengthen Japanese protection from Russia. Most Americans favored this alliance as a support to the Open Door* principle and a barrier to Russian encroachment in the Far East. The Anglo-Japanese Treaty was abrogated by the Four Power Treaty (1921).* Collier, Basil, *The Lion and the Eagle* (1972); Perkins, Bradford, *The Great Rapprochement* (1968).

ANGLOPHOBIA. This term is used to indicate extreme dislike of Great Britain, its people, its government, or its policies. It has been recurrent throughout American diplomatic history but was particularly prominent around the time of the War of 1812 and the Oregon Question,* and during the Gilded Age, when Great Britain was viewed as an especially strong military, commercial, or imperial rival. Beale, Howard K., *Theodore Roosevelt and the Rise of America to World Power* (1950); Pletcher, David, *The Diplomacy of Annexation* (1973).

ANGLO-RUSSIAN CONVENTION (1825). Signed at St. Petersburg, Russia, on February 6/18, 1825, this agreement determined the boundary between British and Russian possessions in North America (now Canada and Alaska). The boundary extended northwest from 56° north latitude and 130° west longitude along the summits of coastal mountains to 141° west longitude and along that meridian to the Arctic Ocean. In 1903, the Hay-Herbert Treaty between the United States and Britain created a commission that clarified a number of disputed points in the boundary. Bemis, Samuel F., *John Quincy Adams and the Foundations of American Foreign Policy* (1949).

ANGLO-RUSSIAN TREATY (1942). This treaty was signed on May 26, 1942, after several months of intermittent negotiations among British Foreign Secretary Anthony Eden, Joseph Stalin, and Soviet Foreign Minister V. M. Molotov. British desires to hew to the Atlantic Charter* precluded acceding to Soviet requests for a treaty including a large number of specific postwar guarantees and frontiers. The final draft of the treaty contained a twenty-year postwar alliance ensuring British support of the Soviet Union in the event of renewed German aggression but with no mention of boundaries. The treaty was signed in London by Eden and Molotov and met with the general approval of the United States. Wheeler-Bennett, John W., and Anthony Nicholls, *The Semblance of Peace* (1972).

ANGOLAN CIVIL WAR (1974–   ). After an April 1974 coup in Portugal, movements for independence in the Portuguese colony of Angola gathered momentum, with greater sympathy from the new government in Lisbon. By the spring of 1975, however, a civil war had developed among rival factions: MPLA (Popular Movement for the Liberation of Angola) and FNLA-UNITA (a coalition of the National Front for the Liberation of Angola and the National Union for the Total Independence of Angola). The MPLA was supported by the Soviet Union and Cuba, and increasing numbers of Cuban troops were reported in Angola; the FNLA was supported by the United States, the People's Republic of China, and Zaire; the UNITA by the United States and South Africa. The threat of a Vietnam-style limited war existed in late 1975 if the United States had decided to take a more active role, but Congress voted in January 1976 not to fund further the FNLA-UNITA coalition (the Clark amendment) despite Secretary of State Henry Kissinger's* contention that to do so might slow the advancing MPLA and force a military stalemate. The MPLA eventually wore down its opposition and was recognized as the legitimate government of Angola by most other African states in the spring of 1976. The United States temporarily vetoed the Angola application for United Nations* membership in June 1976 because of the continuing presence of Cuban troops but reversed itself and allowed Angola to join in November 1976. During the Jimmy Carter administration, efforts were made to improve relations with Angola, despite the Cuban troops, but under President Ronald Reagan, a more confrontational policy emerged. In July 1985, Congress, at the Reagan administration's request, repealed the Clark amendment, allowing the administration to funnel $15 million in covert aid to UNITA forces and their leader, Jonas Savimbi. Not only did this policy conform to the Reagan Doctrine,* but also it fit in with the policy of constructive engagement* toward South Africa, in which a friendly South Africa would work with the United States to arrange a coalition government (or even an anti-Communist one) in Luanda after UNITA, with American aid, forced a military stalemate in the Angolan civil war. Baker, Pauline H., "United States Policy in Southern Africa," *Current History* 86, 520 (May 1987): 193–96, 225–27; Marcum, John A., "Angola: Twenty-five Years of War," *Current History* 85, 511 (May 1986): 193–96, 229–31, and "Lessons of Angola," *Foreign Affairs* 54, 4 (April 1976): 407–25; *New York Times*, November 30, 1986.

ANNENBERG, WALTER HUBERT (b. 1908). Ambassador to Great Britain during the administration of President Richard M. Nixon (1969–1974), Walter H. Annenberg was born in Milwaukee on March 13, 1908, and attended the Wharton School of Finance at the University of Pennsylvania, 1927–1928. He joined his father's business, Triangle Publications, as an assistant in the bookkeeping office, eventually rising to head the firm when his father died in 1942. Triangle publishes the *Philadelphia Inquirer*, the *Daily Racing Form, Seventeen*, and *TV Guide*, among others, and owns a radio and television stations. As head of Triangle, Annenberg gained a reputation as a conservative editorialist, pro-

Republican and pro-Israel in his politics, and a philanthropist. His appointment as ambassador to Great Britain in 1969 drew criticism from those who wondered if the conservative and aristocratic Annenberg, inexperienced in foreign affairs, could deal with the British Labour party. After five and a half years in the post, Annenberg's image had improved in his highly social and cultural mission. He won praise for donations to worthy British causes, such as the Royal Opera House and Covent Garden, for commissioning a statue of former Prime Minister Harold Macmillan, and for facilitating a touring exhibit of part of his extensive art collection. Annenberg returned to the United States in 1974 and founded the Annenberg School of Communications at the University of Pennsylvania. He remains active in Triangle Publications and a variety of Philadelphia cultural and philanthropic organizations. *CB* (1970):9–12; Fonzi, Gaston, *Annenberg: A Biography of Power* (1970); *New York Times*, December 30, 1972, October 15, 1974; *WWA* (1986–1987):74.

ANTI-COMINTERN PACT (1936). This was a treaty directed against Soviet Russia, signed by Germany and Japan in 1936 and by Italy the following year. The treaty pledged its signatories to work to halt the spread of domestic communism and "not to do anything to ease the position" of Russia if it attacked another signatory. Although the language of the treaty was vague and somewhat pretentious, assurances were given to the United States and Britain that the pact bore no danger to them. After the signing of this treaty, Hitler felt free to scorn the Brussels Conference (1937)* and began discussions in 1938 of a full alliance with Japan and Italy. However, the expediency to Hitler of the Nazi-Soviet Non-Aggression Pact (1939)* delayed the completion of that alliance until 1940. American diplomacy, shaped at this time by the Neutrality Acts,* came forth with no specific response to the Anti-Comintern Pact. Feis, Herbert, *The Road to Pearl Harbor* (1950); *FR* (1937); 1:605–18; Offner, Arnold A., *The Origins of the Second World War* (1975).

ANTI-IMPERIALISM, political movement, c. 1870–1900. Anti-imperialism was seen as early as the 1870s, when a number of Democrats, notably Carl Schurz,* opposed the expansionist policies of the Grant administration. During the 1890s, anti-imperialists opposed in vain such measures of the McKinley administration as the annexation of Hawaii, the ratification of the peace treaty ending the Spanish-American War, and McKinley's reelection in 1900. Not often united, anti-imperialists based their arguments on, among other things, the need to tend to internal affairs in America, the danger of precipitating costly foreign wars, and the unsuitability of non-Anglo-Saxon people for American civilization and citizenship. The movement died out shortly after 1900 due to the defeat of William Jennings Bryan,* the Roosevelt administration's reluctance to acquire more colonies, and the death of many anti-imperialist leaders. Notable anti-imperialists included Bryan, Schurz, E. L. Godkin, Edward Atkinson, and

Andrew Carnegie.* Beisner, Robert L., *Twelve against Empire: The Anti-imperialists, 1898–1900* (1968); Healy, David, *US Expansionism* (1970).

ANTI-IMPERIALIST LEAGUE, political organization 1898–c. 1900. This organization was begun in late 1898 in several eastern cities by moderate reformers and anti-imperialists, such as Carl Schurz,* E. L. Godkin, Edward Atkinson, and Charles Eliot Norton. In 1899, local organizations were joined in a single American Anti-Imperialist League, which propagandized the country and Congress by holding conferences, sponsoring speakers, and publishing pamphlets and articles opposing America's colonial policy. Andrew Carnegie* funded much of the campaign, and labor, agricultural, and ethnic leaders were active. Although the league was composed primarily of Democrats, a few Republicans participated. Beisner, Robert L., *Twelve against Empire: The Anti-imperialists 1898–1900* (1968); Healy, David *US Expansionism* (1970).

ANZUS TREATY (1951). This treaty, signed September 1, 1951, by Australia, New Zealand, and the United States (hence, its name), provides for consultation when one of the signatories considers itself threatened with respect to territorial integrity, political independence, or Pacific area security. Implicit is the maintenance of the ability to resist collectively any armed attack. The Anzus Treaty is similar in form to the North Atlantic Treaty (1949)* and linked with the Japanese peace settlement. The alliance originally reflected Australian–New Zealand concern about renewed Japanese militarism, and in that way it resembled the Mutual Defense Treaty between the United States and the Philippines. For the United States, however, it represented yet another link in the chain of alliances containing Soviet expansionism. The alliance was badly shaken in 1984 when New Zealand instituted a policy of refusing to allow nuclear-powered ships, or ships carrying nuclear weapons, in its ports. Since it is U.S. policy not to reveal whether a ship has nuclear arms and since many other U.S. ships are nuclear powered, the New Zealand decision represented a fundamental change in the alliance relationship, resulting in a U.S. decision in August 1986 to suspend any treaty obligations to New Zealand. Albinski, Henry S., "Australia and New Zealand in the 1980s," *Current History* 85, 510 (April 1986): 149–54, 182–83; Fifield, Russell H., *Americans in Southeast Asia* (1973); *New York Times*, June 27, 1986; Stark, J. G., *The Anzus Treaty Alliance* (1965); Thakur, Ramesh, *In Defense of New Zealand Foreign Policy Choices in the Nuclear Age* (1986).

ARAB-AMERICAN OIL COMPANY (ARAMCO). After oil was discovered in Bahrain in 1932, the king of Saudi Arabia was prompted to go to the West for help in exploiting his potential oil reserves. In 1933, the Standard Oil Company (California) was granted exploration rights in the eastern half of the country. Oil was first found in 1936, Texaco joined Standard, and a consortial arrangement, involving several oil companies, evolved. The name Aramco first appeared in 1944, and by the 1950s, it was producing 90 percent of Saudi Arabian oil and had assumed considerable importance in U.S. foreign policy, since the United

States had become a net importer of the oil in the previous decade. Company leaders generally followed the Saudi line on foreign policy, opposing the creation of Israel in 1948, for example. With the rise of Arab nationalism and the creation of the Organization of Petroleum Exporting Countries* in the early 1970s, Aramco's difficulties began. By 1980, control of the company was transferred to the Saudi government through nationalization. In the 1980s, Aramco employed 50,000 and had gross receipts of $50 billion; it remains an effective foreign policy lobby for Saudi Arabia in the United States. Anderson, Irvine H., *Aramco, Saudi Arabia, and the United States, 1933–1950* (1981); Emerson, Steven, *The American House of Saud* (1985); Tillman, Seth P., *The United States in the Middle East* (1982).

ARABIC, sinking of (1915). The *Arabic*, a British White Star liner, was sunk in the Irish Channel by German U-boats* in August 1915, four months after the torpedoing of the *Lusitania.** Forty-four lives, including two Americans, were lost, but President Woodrow Wilson counseled patience in spite of urgings made by Colonel Edward M. House* and other advisers for more direct action. The German government disavowed the attack and issued a statement promising warning and precaution on the part of U-boat commanders toward unarmed vessels. The incident was an early test of Wilson's pacifism, and his response reflected the divided state of public opinion at the time, as well as his awareness of U.S. military unpreparedness and his concern over the possibility of collaborative action by German-Americans. *FR* (1915), 2:516ff.; *FR: Lansing Papers*, 1:467–83; May, Ernest, *The World War and American Isolation, 1914–1917* (1959); Millis, Walter, *Road to War: America, 1914–1917* (1935); Smith, Daniel M., *The Great Departure* (1965).

ARAMCO. See ARAB-AMERICAN OIL COMPANY.

ARANJUEZ, TREATY OF (1779). This treaty, or convention, between Spain and France was signed April 12, 1779, and involved Spain in the American Revolution. Spain was promised the restoration of Gibraltar, the expulsion of the British from the Bay of Honduras, and possession of the river and fort of Mobile (Florida), among others, for aiding France against Britain. Direct Spanish aid to America was minimal inasmuch as the Spanish felt a successful American revolution would set a bad example for Spanish colonies in the Western Hemisphere to follow. Bemis, Samuel F., *The Diplomacy of the American Revolution* (1935); Morris, Richard B., *The Peacemakers* (1965).

ARBITRATION, manner of peaceful resolution of conflict. In the process of arbitration, the contentious parties select an impartial agent—an arbiter—or court of arbitration to settle the conflict by compromise or through legal procedures, as agreed to by the parties, who also agree to accept the decision. According to Gamboa, the era of modern arbitration began with the Jay Treaty (1794),* in which the United States and Great Britain utilized the process in the cases of

U.S. ships seized in alleged violation of neutrality.* A major nineteenth-century arbitration procedure was carried out in the *Alabama** claims case (1871) between the United States and Britain. The First Hague Peace Conference (1899)* provided the machinery for arbitration in the Permanent Court of Arbitration.* The interwar period (1919–1939) saw a major international effort to broaden the availability and acceptability of arbitration through the signing of bilateral and multilateral treaties to that effect. Gamboa, Melquiades J., *Elements of Diplomatic and Consular Practice* (1966); Plischke, Elmer, *The Conduct of American Diplomacy* (1967).

ARCADIA CONFERENCE (1941–1942). This conference, held in Washington from December 1941 to January 1942, was attended by Winston Churchill and Lord Beaverbrook, from Great Britain, and President Franklin D. Roosevelt and Harry Hopkins,* from the United States, as well as military leaders from both nations. This was the first conference since the attack on Pearl Harbor* had brought the United States actively into World War II. It was decided to defeat Germany first while undertaking a holding action against Japan (although the Allies would try to prevent Japanese capture of Hawaii, Alaska, Singapore, the Dutch East Indies, the Philippines, Rangoon, and the land route from there to China). Churchill suggested the idea of a North African invasion, which won general approval, but its implementation was delayed for several months. To coordinate military planning, the Allies created Anglo-American Combined Boards and Chiefs of Staff and a combined Far East Command. An important sidelight of this conference was the signing on January 1, 1942, of the United Nations Declaration.* Feis, Herbert, *Churchill—Roosevelt—Stalin* (1967); *FR: The Conferences at Washington, 1941–1942, and Casablanca, 1943*, pp. 3–418.; McNeill, William H., *America, Britain, and Russia* (1953).

ARIAS PLAN (1987). See **ESQUIPULAS II (1987).**

ARMED NEUTRALITY, LEAGUE OF, diplomatic alliance, 1780–1783. During the American Revolution, a number of European neutrals banded together to protect their commerce and hasten peace by the isolation of Great Britain (and other belligerents). A declaration by the prime mover of the league, Empress Catherine of Russia, demanded free navigation of neutral ships, exemption from seizure of contraband in neutral ships' cargoes, acceptance of naval stores as non-contraband, and acceptance of the definition of a blockaded port as one where there is evident physical danger of entry. Members of the league were Russia, the Netherlands, Prussia, Austria, Portugal, Two Sicilies, Denmark, and Sweden. In practice, the league did not operate very effectively, for fear of antagonizing powerful Britain—hence the name "armed nullity," given by critics. Bemis, Samuel F., *The Diplomacy of the American Revolution* (1935); Morris, Richard B., *The Peacemakers* (1965).

ARMOUR, NORMAN (1887–1982). Norman Armour was born October 14, 1887, in Brighton, England, but was educated in the United States at Princeton (B.A. 1909; M.A., 1915) and Harvard (LL.B., 1913) and was admitted to the bar in 1914. He joined the Foreign Service in 1915 and held various minor posts until 1932, when he was appointed minister to Haiti, the first in a long series of ministerial and ambassadorial appointments. In Haiti, Armour negotiated the agreement whereby American occupation forces were withdrawn. His other posts included: minister to Canada, 1935–1938; ambassador to Chile, 1938–1939, where he chaired the U.S. delegation at the Third Pan-American Highway Conference; ambassador to Argentina, 1939–1944, where he was involved in efforts to bring that nation into the Allied camp during World War II; ambassador to Spain, 1944–1946; assistant secretary of state, 1947–1948; ambassador to Venezuela, 1950–1951, where he undertook important oil negotiations; and ambassador to Guatemala, 1954–1955, where he served in the aftermath of the 1954 revolution directed by the Central Intelligence Agency, overthrowing the purportedly Communist government of Jácobo Arbenz. Armour, who married a Swedish princess, Myra Koudacheff, in 1919, retired from the State Department in 1955 and died in New York City on September 28, 1982. *NCAB*, G:178; *New York Times*, August 25, 1954, September 29, 1982; Woods, Randall B., *The Roosevelt Foreign Policy Establishment and the "Good Neighbor": The United States and Argentina, 1941–1945* (1979); *WWA* (1958–1959): 38.

ARMSTRONG, ANNE LEGENDRE (b. 1927). A native of New Orleans, where she was born December 27, 1927, Anne Legendre graduated from Vassar in 1949 and married Tobin Armstrong in 1950. She worked in family ranching interests in southern Texas and became involved in Republican politics, supporting Dwight Eisenhower's candidacy in 1952 and rising through the ranks to become cochair of the party's national committee from 1971 to 1973. She served as a counselor to President Richard M. Nixon from 1972 to 1974 and was a delegate to the United Nations* Food Conference in Rome, 1974. In 1976, President Gerald Ford appointed her ambassador to Great Britain. In her year at that post, she was popular but had little to do with foreign policymaking due to lack of major issues touching on Anglo-American relations and the personal diplomacy of Secretary of State Henry Kissinger.* A foreign policy novice, Armstrong had no clear views on specific U.S. diplomatic issues except a commitment to a general internationalist policy for America. Since 1977, she has been principally involved in private business but has also been a board member and lecturer at the Center for Strategic and International Studies at Georgetown University and since 1981 the chairman of the President's Foreign Intelligence Advisory Board. *CB* (1976):6–9; *New York Times*, January 6, May 29, 1976; *WWA* (1986–1987):86.

ARMSTRONG, JOHN (1755–1843). Born in Carlisle, Pennsylvania, on November 25, 1755, John Armstrong served in the American Revolution under Generals Hugh Mercer and Horatio Gates, worked in Pennsylvania state government after the war, and farmed in New York from 1789 to 1800. In 1789, he married Slida Livingston, the sister of Edward and Robert Livingston,* and through this family connection, he went to the U.S. Senate, 1800–1804, before replacing Robert Livingston as minister to France. From 1804 to 1810, Armstrong tried to win Napoleon's goodwill in order to halt the seizure of U.S. ships. He was also interested in acquiring Florida from Spain and was critical of the administration's timid attitudes, recommending that Florida be taken by force. Although he was often ostracized and officially ignored by the French government, he did receive the controversial Cadore letter* in August 1810, shortly before leaving in protest of the French decrees and shipping policies aimed against the United States. After a disastrous year as secretary of war (1813–1814), which earned him public blame for the British capture of Washington, Armstrong retired from public life and devoted himself to biographical and agricultural writing. He died April 1, 1843, in Red Hook, New York. *DAB*, 1:355; Egan, Clifford L., *Neither Peace nor War: Franco-American Relations, 1803–1812* (1983); Perkins, Bradford, *Prologue to War* (1961); Willson, Beckles, *America's Ambassadors to France, 1777–1927* (1928).

ARTICLE X. For the U.S. Senate, this was the most controversial article in the Covenant of the League of Nations,* employing, as it did, the idea of collective security to stop aggression. Opponents argued that this appeared to supersede the congressional war-making power and that it would compromise American security and take Americans into war all over the world. President Wilson said the commitment was not legal but simply moral. One of the Lodge Reservations* emphasized the necessity of obtaining congressional approval before agreeing to an implementation of Article X. However, the entire Treaty of Versailles* was never ratified, and Article X became a moot question. Bailey, Thomas A., *Woodrow Wilson and the Great Betrayal* (1945); Kuehl, Warren F., *Seeking World Order: The United States and World Organization to 1920* (1969); Osgood, Robert E., *Ideals and Self-Interest in America's Foreign Relations* (1953); Vinson, John C. *Referendum for Isolation: Defeat of Article Ten of the League of Nations Covenant* (1971).

ASIAN DEVELOPMENT BANK. This multinational bank was created in 1966 and has its headquarters in Manila. In 1987, it had forty-seven members, including thirty-two Asian nations. The People's Republic of China joined in 1986 when the designation for Taiwan was changed to "Taipei, China." The non-Asian members include the United States and most of the nations of Western Europe. The bank is funded principally through country subscriptions, with Japan and the United States each contributing 16.7 percent. A subsidiary organization, the Asian Development Fund, provides soft loans and operates on voluntary contributions. Banks, Arthur S., ed., *Political Handbook of the World 1987* (1987).

ATHERTON, ALFRED LEROY, JR. (b. 1921). Born in Pittsburgh on November 22, 1921, Alfred L. Atherton, Jr., graduated from Harvard (B.S., 1941; M.A., 1947), served in World War II, and married Betty Wylie Kittridge in

1946. Joining the Foreign Service in 1947, he served in minor posts in Stuttgart, Bonn, Damascus, Aleppo, and Washington through 1961. In 1962, he was appointed consul in Calcutta, where he spent three years, returning to a succession of State Department administrative posts in 1965. In 1974, Atherton became assistant secretary of state for Near Eastern and South Asian affairs, and in 1978, he was named an ambassador at large. In these two posts, he played a central role in the preliminary talks leading up to the Camp David Accords* and was part of a secret planning group within the Jimmy Carter administration that arranged the meeting between Anwar Sadat and Menachem Begin at Camp David. After Camp David, Atherton went to Egypt as ambassador, remaining there through the first two years of the Ronald Reagan administration and working to carry on the optimistic spirit of Egyptian-Israeli reconciliation. In 1983, he left Cairo to become director-general of the Foreign Service, retiring from the service at the end of 1984. Since that time, Atherton has been involved with the New York City–Cairo sister city committee and the Harkness Fellowship program of the Commonwealth Fund. He was named a career ambassador in 1981. *New York Times*, February 21, 1978; Quandt, William B., *Camp David* (1986); *WWA* (1986–1987): 98.

ATLANTIC CHARTER (1941). Signed August 12, 1941, at a conference held at Argentia, Newfoundland, on Placentia Bay, attended by Winston Churchill and President Franklin D. Roosevelt and various advisers, including Harry Hopkins* and W. Averell Harriman,* the Atlantic Charter was a product of Roosevelt's initiative. This document outlined in general terms a set of principles to guide the Allies in their struggle against nazism. The charter contained eight clauses, among which were a denial of territorial or other aggrandizements, an endorsement of self-determination,* and commitments to the equal access for all to raw materials and to the postwar "abandonment of the use of force." Churchill advocated the creation of an international organization to enforce a "permanent system of general security," and though not spelled out in specific terms, this point was implicitly included. In the United States, congressional critics called the Atlantic Charter a secret alliance, whereas internationalists praised it. On the whole, it had domestic propaganda value by making it easier for the American people to accept the increasing involvement of the United States in the war. Dobson, Alan P., *U.S. Wartime Aid to Britain, 1940–1946* (1986); Feis, Herbert, *Churchill—Roosevelt—Stalin* (1967); Offner, Arnold A., *The Origins of the Second World War* (1975); Wheeler-Bennett, John W., and Anthony Nicholls, *The Semblance of Peace* (1972); Wilson, T. A., *The First Summit: Roosevelt and Churchill at Placentia Bay, 1941* (1969).

ATLANTIC CONFERENCE (1941). This conference, held from August 9 to August 12, 1941, was arranged by Harry Hopkins* and marked the first direct meeting of consequence between President Franklin D. Roosevelt and British Prime Minister Winston Churchill (they had met briefly in London in 1918).

Held at Placentia Bay, Newfoundland, the conference involved the drafting of the Atlantic Charter* and included discussions about Atlantic defense, military disposition, supply allocation, and the state of U.S. belligerency as they related to various Japanese moves in the Pacific. After the conference, there was some disappointment in Britain that the United States seemed no nearer to entering the war. Roosevelt, on the other hand, was encouraged by the meeting, particularly by the fact that he and Churchill had good rapport. This conference is sometimes called the Argentia Conference, after the nearby Newfoundland town on Placentia Bay. Dobson, Alan P., *U.S. Wartime Aid to Britain, 1940–1946* (1986); Feis, Herbert, *The Road to Pearl Harbor* (1950); Lash, Joseph, *Roosevelt and Churchill, 1939–1941* (1976); Offner, Arnold A., *The Origins of the Second World War* (1975); Wilson, T. A., *The First Summit: Roosevelt and Churchill at Placentia Bay, 1941* (1969).

AUSTIN, WARREN ROBINSON (1877–1962). Warren R. Austin was born in Highgate, Vermont, on November 12, 1877, graduated from the University of Vermont (1899), studied law in his father's office, and was admitted to the Vermont bar in 1902. After years of law practice in Highgate (1902–1916) and Burlington (1917–1931), Austin was elected as a Republican to the U.S. Senate in 1931, serving until 1946 and gaining a reputation as a leading prewar internationalist. During World War II, as a member of the Senate Foreign Relations Committee, he attended the Dumbarton Oaks Conference (1944),* helping to formulate the United Nations.* He also served as an adviser to the U.S. delegation at the Mexico City Conference (1945)* and helped frame the Act of Chapultepec. His enthusiasm for the United Nations won him appointment as special ambassador and adviser to that body in 1946 and U.S. representative to the United Nations from 1947 to 1953. His main concern there was blunting Soviet efforts to use the United Nations as a propaganda forum. He served on the Security Council, the Atomic Energy Commission, and the Commission for Conventional Armaments, but his influence was lessened by the limited use Washington made of the United Nations. Austin's optimistic faith in the international organization exceeded that of nearly everyone else in American diplomacy; his support of the North Atlantic Treaty Organization (1949)* reflected a moving away from that optimism. Still, in 1950, he saw United Nations police action in Korea as typifying the real objectives of the organization as a peacekeeper, and he led the U.S. delegation in securing the resolution to send United Nations forces. He was replaced by Henry Cabot Lodge, Jr.,* in 1953 with the incoming Dwight D. Eisenhower administration. A stroke that year forced his retirement from public life until his death in Burlington on December 25, 1962. Austin married Mildred Mary Lucas in 1901 and was for many years a trustee of the University of Vermont. Darilek, Richard E., *A Loyal Opposition in Time of War* (1976); Mazuzan, George T., *Warren R. Austin at the UN, 1946–1953* (1977); *New York Times*, March 28, 1953, December 26, 1962; *NCAB*, G:76; Porter, David L., *The Seventy-sixth Congress and World War II, 1939–1940* (1979); *WWWA*, 4 (1961–1968):43.

AUSTRIAN STATE TREATY (1955). Negotiations to end the state of war between Austria and the victors of World War II began in 1946 in meetings of the Council of Foreign Ministers* and their deputies. Despite an enormous number of meetings, there was no real progress toward a peace treaty until February 1955, when the Soviet Union agreed to separate the Austrian peace from the unresolved issue of a German peace treaty, thus removing a major obstacle to the negotiations. In April 1955, the so-called Moscow Memorandum, an Austro-Soviet agreement, signified further Soviet flexibility; the Soviets agreed to sign a peace treaty and remove occupation forces by the end of the year, release remaining Austrian prisoners of war, and make certain economic concessions in return for Austria's pledge to remain neutral and pay $150 million for the German assets remaining in the country. After this breakthrough, the foreign ministers from the four occupying powers met in Vienna and on May 15, 1955, signed the Austrian State Treaty. The most important point, Austrian neutrality,* was not part of the treaty itself but was incorporated in the Austrian constitution in October. After the signing of the treaty and the neutrality amendment, Austria received diplomatic recognition and became a member of the United Nations* in December 1955. Wheeler-Bennett and Nicholls suggest that Soviet intransigence ended in 1955 because of the example a neutral Austria might set for a possible neutral Germany, because the enhanced image of the Soviet Union from cooperative behavior on the Austrian treaty might help in the more complex German negotiations, and because settlement of the Austrian matter would help improve Soviet relations with Yugoslavia. For the United States, the Austrian State Treaty was something of a cold war* victory, since American policy since 1947 had been directed toward preventing Austria from becoming a Soviet satellite. Bader, William B., *Austria between East and West, 1945– 1955* (1966); Kreisky, Bruno, "Austria Draws the Balance," *Foreign Affairs* 37 (January 1959): 269–78; Wheeler-Bennett, John W., and Anthony Nicholls, *The Semblance of Peace* (1972).

BACON, ROBERT (1860–1919). Born in Jamaica Plain, Massachusetts, on July 5, 1860, Robert Bacon graduated from Harvard in 1880, entered the banking business, and joined J. P. Morgan's firm in 1894. In 1905, he became assistant secretary of state under Elihu Root,* and following Root's resignation in 1909, he served as secretary of state for the final weeks of the Theodore Roosevelt administration. President William Howard Taft appointed Bacon ambassador to France in December 1909, and Bacon remained in that post until January 1912, winning substantial goodwill by arranging for American aid during the Paris flood of 1910 and participating in various cultural and ceremonial events. Bacon served in the Quartermaster Corps during World War I and died on May 29, 1919, in New York City, shortly after his return from Europe. *DAB*, 1:483; *New York Times*, May 30, 1919; Scott, James Brown, *Robert Bacon, Life and Letters* (1923); Willson, Beckles, *America's Ambassadors to France, 1777–1927* (1928).

BAGBY, ARTHUR PENDLETON (1794–1858). Born in Louisa County, Virginia, sometime in 1794, Arthur P. Bagby was educated in the law and admitted to the bar in 1819. By 1821, he lived in Alabama and had embarked on a political career as a democrat that took him through both houses of the Alabama legislature to the governor's chair in 1837. He was reelected governor in 1839, moved to the U.S. Senate in 1841 to fill an unexpired term, and was elected in his own right the following year. In the Senate, he was a supporter of President James K. Polk and the annexation of Texas. In 1848, Polk appointed him minister to Russia, but Bagby spent only five months at the post, arriving in January 1849 and leaving in advance of a Zachary Taylor administration appointee in 1849. No diplomatic issues of importance faced Bagby during these months, and his main concern was the frightful climate of St. Petersburg. After his brief diplomatic excursion, Bagby returned to Alabama, moved to Mobile in 1856, and died there of yellow fever on September 21, 1858. He was married twice and was known for constantly being in great financial difficulties, due largely to his own carelessness and inefficiency. *DAB*, 1:491; *NCAB*, 10:428; Thomas, Benjamin P., *Russo-American Relations, 1815–1867* (1930).

BAGHDAD PACT (1955). This treaty was signed by Turkey and Iraq in early 1955 as mutual protection against potential Soviet danger. It was later signed by Pakistan, Iran, and Great Britain, and in November 1955, a formal organization, the Middle East Treaty Organization, was established. Although not a signatory to the pact, the United States strongly supported it as part of its policy of containment.* The Baghdad Pact was opposed by Egypt and other Arab nations as an intrusion into Arab unity. After a coup in 1958, Iraq withdrew from the alliance, the United States signed bilateral agreements with Pakistan, Turkey, and Iran, and the remaining pact members reorganized themselves as the Central Treaty Organization.* According to Bryson, the Baghdad Pact resulted in Soviet entry into Middle Eastern affairs, the decline of British and French influence in the region, and the heightening of Arab-Israeli tensions, and it contributed to the Suez crisis (1956).* Bryson, Thomas A., *American Diplomatic Relations with the Middle East, 1794–1975* (1977); Gallman, Waldemar, *Iraq under Gen. Nuri* (1964); Hammond, Paul V., *Cold War and Detente* (1975); Spanier, John W., *American Foreign Policy since World War II* (1988).

BAILEY, THOMAS ANDREW (1902–1983). A highly regarded and prolific diplomatic historian, Thomas A. Bailey was born in San Jose, California, on December 14, 1902, and graduated from Stanford (A.B., 1924; A.M., 1925; Ph.D., 1927). In 1925, he embarked on a teaching career at Stanford, retiring to emeritus status in 1968 but remaining active in the profession until his death. The author of seventeen books, including a textbook, *Diplomatic History of American People*, which had gone through ten editions by 1980, and a general U.S. history text, *The American Pageant*, Bailey was known for his wit and use of humorous anecdotes and an ability to be "provocative [while] avoiding the path of the revisionist." Among his most heralded monographs are *Woodrow Wilson and the Lost Peace* (1944) and *Woodrow Wilson and the Great Betrayal* (1945), both pleas for America to join the United Nations,* *The Man on the Street* (1948), a study of public opinion, and *The Pugnacious Presidents* (1980) and *Presidential Saints and Sinners* (181), more anecdotal in character. Bailey, who married Sylvia Dean in 1928, was president of the Organization of American Historians in 1968 and the Pacific branch of the American Historical Association in 1969. He died in Menlo Park, California, on July 26, 1983. *New York Times*, July 29, 1983; *WWWA*, 8 (1982–1985):17

BAILLY-BLANCHARD, ARTHUR (1855–1925). A native of New Orleans, Louisiana, where he was born October 1, 1855, Arthur Bailly-Blanchard began his diplomatic career in 1885 after attending the University of Louisiana Law School and working for *La Petit journal* (New Orleans) as assistant editor. For the first twenty-three years of his diplomatic career, he served in a succession of secretarial posts, to both ministers and special commissions. In 1914, Bailly-Blanchard became minister to Haiti, arriving in that country during a period of extreme political instability. He tried unsuccessfully to interest different revolutionary governments in a convention to establish a U.S. customs receivership before the intervention by U.S. Marines in the summer of 1915. Although he remained at his post until September 1921, he played only a minor role during the occupation. He died in Montreal on August 22, 1925. *FR* (1915–1921), passim;

Munro, D. G., *Intervention and Dollar Diplomacy in the Caribbean, 1900–1921* (1964); *New York Times*, August 25, 1925; *WWWA*, 1 (1897–1942): 45.

BAKER, JAMES MARION (1861–1940). James Marion Baker was born in Lowndesville, South Carolina, on August 18, 1861, was educated at Wofford College, married Mary Adams in 1883, and in 1893 was appointed assistant librarian for the U.S. Senate, a position he held for twenty years. After serving in other government posts from 1913 to 1921, he left government service and practiced law. In 1933, President Franklin Roosevelt named Baker minister to Siam, where he served four years. His major diplomatic effort focused on discussion leading to a revision of the 1920 Treaty of Commerce and Friendship, certain terms of which threatened to discriminate against American nationals living in Siam. However, the beginning of the Sino-Japanese War in 1937 precluded finalization of the treaty revision before Baker's departure. Baker retired to South Carolina and died in Lowndesville on November 21, 1940. *New York Times*, November 22, 1940; *WWWA*, 1 (1897–1942):48.

BALANCE OF POWER, principle of international relations. The concept of balance of power emerged in Europe during the seventeenth century, replacing, to a degree, the supranational power of the pope. Various treaties, beginning with the Peace of Westphalia (1648), invoked the idea of balance of power, which holds that preventing the dangerous growth of power in one nation or combination of nations is desirable. To maintain the balance of power, nations often surrendered conquered territories at the negotiating table. Since the seventeenth century, the balance of power has often been used as a justification for a nation's foreign policies, whether in creating alliances, warding off aggression, or establishing international organizations. Modern technology has wrought a fundamental change in the idea of the balance of power; whereas in the past altered through territorial conquest, it can now be altered through military or technological developments within a state. Henry Kissinger,* a careful student of early diplomacy, based his global view on a modernized variation of the balance of power principle. Campbell, A. E., "Balance of Power," in DeConde, Alexander, ed., *Encyclopedia of American Foreign Policy* (1979); Kissinger, Henry, *American Foreign Policy*, 2d ed. (1974); Savelle, Max, *The Origins of American Diplomacy* (1967).

BALTIMORE AFFAIR (1891). Sailors from the U.S.S. *Baltimore*, a cruiser commanded by Captain W. S. Schley, were on shore leave in Valparaiso, Chile, when they were attacked by a Chilean mob on October 16, 1891. Two deaths and several injuries resulted, and the State Department, in a note written by Acting Secretary Francis W. Wharton, reacted as if the attack had been a deliberate assault on American honor and demanded reparations. Chile was going through a period of revolutionary turmoil at this time; its response to Wharton's note was hostile, and relations were nearly severed. In December 1891, however, a new Chilean foreign minister, Luis Pereira, wrote a more tactful note of apology

and agreed to negotiate the question of reparations, which later were set at
$75,000. Subsequently, the American minister to Chile, Patrick Egan,* and
Chilean officials negotiated a convention calling for arbitration* of mutual claims
of citizens of Chile and the United States. Devine, Michael J., *John W. Foster:
Politics and Diplomacy in the Imperial Era, 1873–1917* (1981); Goldberg, Joyce S., *The
Baltimore Affair* (1986); Lockey, Joseph B., "James Gillespie Blaine," in Bemis, Samuel
F., *American Secretaries of State and Their Diplomacy* (1928), vol. 8.

BANCROFT, EDGAR ADDISON (1857–1925). A native of Galesburg, Illinois, Edgar Addison Bancroft was born November 20, 1857, graduated from
Knox College and Columbia Law School, and practiced law both privately and
with different corporations until 1924. In that year, he was appointed ambassador
to Japan, where he did much to improve relations damaged by the passage of
immigration legislation excluding Japanese from the United States. He served
as ambassador only eight months before dying on July 27, 1925, in Karuizawa
of complications from a duodenal ulcer. Bancroft also won notice as an orator,
especially during World War I, and as chairman of Chicago's Commission on
Race Relations, which investigated that city's race riots in 1919. *DAB*, 1:562; *FR*
(1924), 2:411–13; *New York Times*, July 29, 1925.

BANCROFT, GEORGE (1800–1891). Massachusetts born and Harvard educated, George Bancroft was born in Worcester on October 3, 1800. He taught
at the Round Hill School (Massachusetts), 1823–1831, and began writing his
monumental *History of the United States*, which was eventually published in ten
volumes between 1834 and 1874. He entered Democratic politics in 1845 during
the James K. Polk administration as secretary of the navy. The next year, Bancroft
became minister to Great Britain, holding that post until August 1849. He worked
to allay American fears of British intervention in Mexico and participated in
discussions preparatory to the Clayton-Bulwer Treaty (1850).* After an interval
of nearly twenty years, during which he continued his historical work, he was
appointed minister to Prussia in 1867 and continued after 1871 as minister to
the German Empire until his return to the United States in 1874. While in
Germany, he was able to pursue his academic interests but was not involved in
any significant diplomatic actions. From 1874 until his death in Washington in
1891, Bancroft continued writing and revising his historical studies. Handlin,
Lilian, *George Bancroft: The Intellectual as Democrat* (1984); Howe, M. A. DeWolfe,
The Life and Letters of George Bancroft, 2 vols. (1908); Kaplan, Lawrence S., "The
Brahmin as Diplomat in Nineteenth Century America," *Civil War History* 19, 1 (March
1973): 5–28; Nye, Russel B., *George Bancroft* (1972); Williams, Mary W., *Anglo-
American Isthmian Diplomacy, 1815–1915* (1916); Willson, Beckles, *American Ambas-
sadors to England, 1785–1929* (1929).

BARBARY PIRATES, RELATIONS WITH (c. 1790–1803). Barbary pirates
along Africa's Mediterranean coast had been exacting tribute from foreign nations, including the United States, for years when President Thomas Jefferson*

decided to end the practice. An expedition in 1802 of two frigates and a number of smaller ships failed to subdue the pirates, but the following year, a larger expedition was successful in stabilizing the area and securing the release of American prisoners for a payment of $60,000. Irwin, Ray W., *The Diplomatic Relations of the United States with the Barbary Pirates, 1776–1816* (1931); Peterson, Merrill D., *Thomas Jefferson and the New Nation* (1970); Varg, Paul A., *Foreign Policies of the Founding Fathers* (1963).

BARBOUR, JAMES (1775–1842). James Barbour was born June 10, 1775, in Barboursville, Virginia, and served in the Virginia House of Delegates from 1798 to 1805 and from 1807 to 1812, when he was elected governor of Virginia. In 1815, Barbour began ten years of service in the U.S. Senate, where he was at various times chairman of both the Military Affairs and Foreign Relations committees. During the presidency of John Quincy Adams,* he was secretary of war. In 1828, at his own request, Barbour was appointed minister to Great Britain, but he served less than a year in the post before his replacement by an Andrew Jackson appointee. Barbour, in his brief tenure, began negotiations with Lord Aberdeen on such matters as the abolition of privateering, the laws of blockade* and contraband,* the rights and duties of belligerents and neutrals, and the practice of impressment.* Although no agreements were made, the discussions were cordial. After his diplomatic service, Barbour served briefly in the Virginia House of Delegates and worked in Whig politics until his death in Orange County, Virginia, on June 7, 1842. *DAB*, 1:590; Long, W. S., "Life of James Barbour," *John P. Branch Papers of Randolph-Macon College* 4, 2 (1914): 34–64; Lowery, Charles D., *James Barbour, a Jeffersonian Republican* (1984); Willson, Beckles, *America's Ambassadors to England, 1785–1929* (1929).

BARBOUR, WALWORTH (1908–1982). Born June 4, 1908, in Cambridge, Massachusetts, Walworth Barbour graduated from Harvard in 1930 and joined the State Department as a clerk the following year. He held minor posts in the Middle East and Europe until 1945, when he began a tour in the Division of South European Affairs, rising to division chief in 1948. From 1949 to 1951, he was minister-counselor at the Moscow embassy, but for the next five years he was posted in Washington, first as director of the Office of East European Affairs (1951–1954) and then as deputy assistant secretary of state for European affairs (1954–1956). In 1956, he went with London as minister-counselor of the embassy there. Five years later, he was appointed ambassador to Israel, a post he occupied for twelve years, until his retirement in 1973. Although he had remarkably little to do or say publicly in Israel, he cultivated close relations with most high-ranking political and military leaders and was credited with heading off a number of American-Israeli crises, including a particularly difficult incident when he had to scold Prime Minister Levi Eshkol tactfully for his indiscretion in launching a retaliatory air raid on the Beirut airport shortly after the United States had sent Israel fifty new warplanes. In 1969, Barbour turned down President Richard Nixon's offer to be ambassador to the Soviet Union, electing to stay in Israel. Never married, Barbour lived in Massachusetts after his retirement. He died in Gloucester on July 24, 1982. Eban, Abba, *An Autobiography* (1977); *New York Times*, March 8, 1961, July 26, 1982; *WWWA*, 8 (1982–1983): 21.

BARLOW, JOEL (1754–1812). One of the most prominent literary figures of early America, Joel Barlow was born March 24, 1754, in Redding, Connecticut, graduated from Yale in 1778, and served as a chaplain during the American Revolution. After the war, he was admitted to the bar, published an epic poem, "The Vision of Columbus" (1787), and went to Europe as the agent of the Scioto Company, where he became an expert on French affairs. In 1795, Washington appointed him consul in Algiers, and he worked to secure the release of American prisoners in North Africa. President James Madison* named Barlow minister to France in 1811 with instructions to intercede with Napoleon with respect to violations of the repeal of the Berlin Decree* and Milan Decree,* wherein the French were still capturing American ships and seamen. On December 26, 1812, he died in Zarnowiec, Poland, while returning to France from a fruitless journey to meet Napoleon. *DAB*, 1:609; Egan, Clifford L., *Neither Peace nor War: Franco-American Relations, 1803–1812* (1983); Todd, C. G., *Life and Letters of Joel Barlow* (1886); Willson, Beckles, *America's Ambassadors to France, 1777–1927* (1928).

BARNARD, DANIEL DEWEY (1797–1861). Daniel Dewey Barnard was born in East Hartford, Connecticut, on July 16, 1797, and graduated from Williams College in 1818. Winning admittance to the bar in 1821, Barnard practiced law in Rochester, New York, until 1826. He was elected to the U.S. House of Representatives and served from 1827 to 1829 and 1839 to 1845, practicing law in Albany when out of office. From 1850 to 1853, he was minister to Prussia, where his official duties were so light that his main activity was writing a book, *Political Aspects and Prospects in Europe* (1854), examining the revolutions of 1848. After returning from Prussia, Barnard continued writing and practicing law until his death in Albany on April 24, 1861. *DAB*, 1:617; *NCAB*, 10:70; Nevins, Allan, *Hamilton Fish*, 2 vols. (1957); Penny, Sherry H., *Patrician in Politics* (1974); *WWWA*, historical volume, p. 41.

BARRETT, JOHN (1866–1938). John Barrett was born November 28, 1866, in Grafton, Vermont, graduated from Dartmouth College in 1889, and worked for several Pacific Coast newspapers between 1889 and 1894, winning recognition for articles about his travels to the Far East. A Grover Cleveland Democrat, Barrett was named minister to Siam in 1894 and worked effectively to settle American claims involving several million dollars. He was a journalist in the Far East during the Spanish-American War and in 1903 became a Republican because of his sympathy with that party's foreign policy ideas. President Theodore Roosevelt appointed Barrett minister to Argentina in 1903, to Panama in 1904, and to Colombia in 1905. In Panama and Colombia, he worked to adjust relations among Panama, Colombia, and the United States after the Panamanian revolution. In 1907, Barrett became director-general of the Pan-American Union,* a post he held for thirteen years. An ardent exponent of Pan-Americanism,* he wrote several books on the subject before his death, on October 17, 1938, in Bellows Falls, Vermont. Barrett was married in 1934 to Mary Elizabeth Cady. *DAB*, Supp. 2:25–26; *New York Times*, April 16, 1898, October 1, 1938; Prisco, Salvatore, III, *John Barrett, Progressive Era Diplomat* (1973); Waller, Robert A., "John Barrett: Pan-American Promoter," *Mid-America* 53, 3 (1971): 170–89.

BARRINGER, DANIEL MOREAU (1806–1873). A North Carolinian, Daniel Barringer was born in Poplar Grove on July 30, 1806, and graduated from the state university in 1826. In 1829, he was admitted to the bar and then elected to the state legislature, serving until 1835 and again from 1840 to 1842. He went to the U.S. House of Representatives in 1843 as a Whig, and, with the election of the Whig administration of Zachary Taylor in 1848, he was appointed minister to Spain. In Spain from 1849 to 1853, Barringer pursued without success the standard American policy of trying to acquire Cuba, always a touchy subject with the Spanish, but his knowledge of the language helped him establish cordial relations with the Spanish court and foreign office. After his return from Spain, he continued to be active in North Carolina state politics until his death in White Sulphur Springs, West Virginia, on September 1, 1873. *DAB*, 1:648; *NCAB*, 11:505; *New York Times*, September 2, 1873.

BARTLETT, JOSEPH JACKSON (1834–1893). Born in Binghamton, New York, on November 4, 1834, Joseph J. Bartlett read law in Utica, New York, was admitted to the bar, and practiced law in Binghamton after 1858. He fought for the Union in the Civil War and attained the rank of brevet major general. In 1867, he was named minister to Sweden and Norway, a post he held until 1869. Bartlett traveled widely in Sweden and got along well until becoming involved in a controversy resulting from his suggestion that, in the interests of better U.S.–Russian relations, Russia ought to control certain ports on the northwest coast of Norway. Since Russian designs on Scandinavia were a source of considerable concern to Sweden and Norway, Bartlett found himself in considerably less favor than he had been, and the foreign office in Stockholm officially repudiated his statement. After his return to the United States, Bartlett worked at the Pension Office in Washington. He died January 14, 1893, in Baltimore, Maryland. Heitman, F. B., *Historical Register and Dictionary of the United States Army, 1789–1903*, vol. 1 (1903); Hovde, B. J., *Diplomatic Relations of the United States with Sweden and Norway, 1814–1905* (1920); *The Twentieth Century Biographical Dictionary of Notable Americans* (1904).

BARTON, JAMES LEVI (1855–1936). Born in Charlotte, Vermont, on September 12, 1855, James Levi Barton graduated from Middlebury College (A.B., 1881) and the Hartford Theological Seminary (B.D., 1885), and was sent to Harpoot, Turkey, as a missionary upon his graduation from seminary. In Turkey, he taught at Euphrates College, a Congregationalist institution founded in 1878 by the American Board of Commissioners for Foreign Missions, and he served as president of the college for a brief period in 1893–1894. When his wife, the former Flora Holmes, became ill in 1894, they returned to the United States, and he became the foreign secretary of the American Board, remaining in that post until 1927 and working on behalf of missionary colleges to make them interdenominational and fiscally sound and independent from the support of any one church group. Between 1902 and 1927, Barton raised $33 million to support twenty-one colleges. After World War I, he founded Near East Relief to help that distressed area; the organization provided food to an estimated 12 million people and medical treatment worth an estimated $116 million. Barton was also a member of Woodrow Wilson's Near East Emergency Commission after World War I and attended the Near East Conference at Lausanne in 1921. He wrote several books about missionary work, including two touching on his own career: *Daybreak in Turkey* (1908) and *Story of Near East Relief* (1930). Barton died on July 21, 1936, in Brookline, Massachusetts. *DAB*, Supp. 2:27–28; Goodsell, F. F., *James Levi Barton* (1964); *New York Times*, July 22, 1936.

BARTON, THOMAS PENNANT (1803–1869). Born in 1803 in Philadelphia, Barton was educated privately in Philadelphia and went to France with his family in 1815, spending about fifteen years there. He married Cora Livingston in 1833 and became secretary of the legation in Paris under his father-in-law, Minister Edward Livingston,* the same year. Livingston was engaged in fruitless negotiations over the payment of the so-called French spoliations claims*; in 1835, he demanded his passports and left France, while Barton remained as chargé d'affaires.* From April to November 1835, while Barton was in charge of the legation, the French Chamber of Deputies voted to pay the claims but attached such impossible conditions to the payment that Barton also returned to the United States. After his arrival in the United States, Barton wrote a report to the government and retired with his father-in-law to the family estate in New York. He built an arboretum and assembled one of the finest libraries in the country, achieving prominence as the first important American collector of Shakespearean folios. A man of great refinement and fastidious taste, Barton died in New York City on April 5, 1869. *DAB*, 2:23; Hunt, Charles H., *Life of Edward Livingston* (1864).

BARUCH, BERNARD MANNES (1870–1965). One of America's best-known financiers and philanthropists, Bernard Baruch also played a significant part in U.S. diplomacy. Born in Camden, South Carolina, on August 19, 1870, he moved to New York City at the age of ten and graduated from City College of New York in 1889. After working for a New York glass wholesaler for a short time, Baruch became a stockbroker in 1891 and was extremely successful, purchasing his own seat on the New York Stock Exchange in 1903 and becoming wealthy. He was a keen supporter of Woodrow Wilson, who made him chairman of the War Industries Board in 1918 and shortly after a member of the U.S. delegation to the Paris Peace Conference,* where he contributed to the economic aspects of peacemaking. During the interwar years, Baruch was a frequent consultant to the government, particularly to the Herbert Hoover administration, whose conservative fiscal beliefs he shared. In 1946, Secretary of State James F. Byrnes* appointed him U.S. representative on the United Nations* Atomic Energy Commission, where his main task was to work out a successful plan for the international control of atomic energy. At the time, U.S. policy was reflected in the Acheson-Lilienthal Report,* but Baruch favored a much broader plan for atomic control. The key question was enforcement, according to Baruch, and his plan called for a suspension of the Security Council veto on the imposition of atomic control penalties. This the Soviet delegation would never accept, and the result was no international control of atomic energy at all. Baruch was married in 1897 to Annie Griffen; she died in 1964. He died in New York City on June 20, 1965. Baruch, Bernard, *The Public Years* (1960); Feis, Herbert, *From Trust to Terror* (1970); Grant, James, *Bernard Baruch* (1983); Lieberman, Joseph I., *The Scorpion and the Tarantula* (1970); McLellan, David S., *Dean Acheson: The State Department Years* (1976); *New York Times*, June 21, 1965; Schwartz, Jordan A., *The Speculator* (1981).

BASSETT, EBENEZER DON CARLOS (1833–1908). One of the first blacks in the diplomatic service, Ebenezer Bassett was born on October 16, 1883, in Litchfield, Connecticut, graduated from the Connecticut State Normal School in 1853, and studied further at Yale. From 1853 to 1869, he taught school in New Haven and Philadelphia and also served as the Haitian consul general in New York. In 1869, he was appointed minister to Haiti, a post he held for eight years. There he worked to ensure Haitian neutrality* and noninvolvement while the Ulysses S. Grant administration dickered for Samana Bay in the neighboring Dominican Republic. Bassett also dealt with numerous American claims against Haiti, ultimately settling some forty of them but getting mixed up in a sharp conflict with his successor, John Mercer Langston,* over the legitimacy of the Lazare claim for $500,000 concerning a breach of contract in the establishment of a national bank. Ultimately, the arbiter set aside the $117,500 award when it was concluded that the claim was fradulent. Little is known of Bassett's life after 1877 except that he died in New York in 1908. Miller, Jake C., *The Black Presence in American Foreign Affairs* (1978); Montague, Ludwill Lee, *Haiti and the United States, 1714–1938* (1940); *WWWA*, 1 (1897–1942): 66; Wynes, Charles E., "Ebenezer Don Carlos Bassett, America's First Black Diplomat," *Pennsylvania History* 51 (July 1984): 232–40.

BATCHELLER, GEORGE SHERMAN (1837–1908). Born July 25, 1837, in Batchellerville, New York, George Sherman Batcheller graduated from Harvard in 1857, read law, and was admitted to the New York bar the same year. He was was elected to the New York State Assembly in 1859, served in a New

York regiment during the first years of the Civil War, and in 1863 was named deputy provost marshal general. In 1865, he became inspector general of the New York militia, a post he held until 1868. A Republican, he was a presidential elector for Grant in 1868 and a representative in the New York State Assembly, 1873–1874 and 1886. From 1876 to 1885, Batcheller was a member of the Mixed (International) Tribunal in Egypt. (This court, with a panel of both foreign and native judges, adjudicated cases involving disputes between a foreigner and a local citizen.) In 1889, President Harrison appointed him assistant secretary of war and the next year named him minister to Portugal, where he served until May 1893. While in Portugal, he traveled to the Azores (and became the first foreign diplomat of ministerial rank to visit the islands) to recover the cannon, "Long Tom," salvaged from the American privateer *General Armstrong*, which the British had sunk at the port of Fayal in 1814. Between 1893 and 1897 Batcheller worked in Europe, and in 1897, he presided over the Universal Postal Congress. In 1898, he was reappointed to the Mixed Tribunal on Egypt, and four years later, he became president of the tribunal's court of appeals. Batcheller, who was married to Catherine Phillips Cook, died in Paris, July 2, 1908. *DAB,* 2:41; *FR* (1892): 358–61; *New York Times,* July 3, 1908.

BATTLE, LUCIUS DURHAM (b. 1918). Born in Dawson, Georgia, on June 1, 1918, Lucius Battle graduated from the University of Florida in 1939 and after navy service during World War II received a law degree from the university in 1946. He joined the State Department in 1946, working in the Office of European Affairs for most of the next ten years. From 1949 to 1953, he was a special assistant to Dean Acheson,* and from 1955 to 1956, he was a member of the secretariat of the North Atlantic Treaty Organization.* He left the State Department to be vice-president of Colonial Williamsburg from 1956 to 1961 but returned in the latter year as executive secretary of the department, where he worked on improving liaison with other federal agencies and created an operations center for keeping a constant watch on world events. In 1964, he was named ambassador to the United Arab Republic (Egypt and Syria), at a time when the Lyndon Johnson administration was hardening its attitude toward the United Arab Republic, but Battle successfully cultivated cordial relationships with political leaders there. In 1967, he succeeded Raymond A. Hare* as assistant secretary of state for Near Eastern and South Asian affairs, visiting Egypt in April 1968 for ceremonies at the Nubian site of Abu Simbel and talks with Egyptian leaders. This trip marked the first time an American diplomat had visited Egypt since the breaking of relations in June 1967. Resigning from the State Department in 1968, Battle worked for COMSAT from 1968 to 1980, first as a congressional lobbyist and vice-president for corporate affairs and from 1974 as senior vice-president. From 1980 to 1984, he was chairman of the Foreign Policy Institute at Johns Hopkins University, and, from 1984 to 1987, he was chairman of the American Institute of Islamic Affairs. *New York Times,*

November 28, 1964, January 27, 1967, September 19, 1968, April 20, 1969; *WWA* (1986–1987):170.

BAY OF PIGS INVASION (1961). This was an invasion of Cuba for the purpose of overthrowing the government of Fidel Castro. Planned in 1960 by the Central Intelligence Agency* under the Eisenhower administration, it was carried out April 15, 1961, shortly after John F. Kennedy became president. Some 1,453 Cuban exiles were trained in Central America, but with breakdowns in secrecy and U.S. air support and the lack of an expected uprising from the Cuban people, the invasion was a total disaster. A major foreign policy defeat for the United States, whose complicity was well known, the Bay of Pigs invasion contributed to the Cuban missile crisis* sixteen months later. In December 1962, 1,179 prisoners were ransomed for $53 million worth of pharmaceutical supplies. Aguilar, Luis (intro.), *Operations Zapata: The "Ultrasensitive" Report and Testimony of the Board of Inquiry on the Bay of Pigs* (1981); Bohlen, Charles E., *Witness to History* (1973); Connell-Smith, Gordon, *The United States and Latin America* (1974); Johnson, Haynes, et al., *The Bay of Pigs* (1964); Welch, Richard E., *Response to Revolution: The United States and the Cuban Revolution, 1959–1967* (1985); Wyden, Peter, *Bay of Pigs: The Untold Story* (1979).

BAYARD, THOMAS FRANCIS (1828–1898). A member of one of Delaware's most prominent families, Thomas Francis Bayard was born October 29, 1828, in Wilmington. He was educated at a private school in Flushing, New York, and never attended college but read law and was admitted to the Delaware bar in 1851. From 1851 to 1869, he practiced law in Wilmington and Philadelphia. In 1869, he was elected, as a Democrat, to the U.S. Senate, where he served sixteen years. A presidential hopeful in both 1880 and 1884, Bayard was named secretary of state in 1885 in Cleveland's administration. In the State Department, he pursued negotiations on matters such as the North Atlantic fisheries question, the seizure of Bering Sea sealing vessels, and the Samoan question, but none of them was settled by the end of Cleveland's term. Upon Cleveland's reelection in 1892, Bayard became the first ambassador to Great Britain, where he adopted a temperate stand during the Venezuelan crisis* while disapproving privately of Cleveland's militancy. He also encouraged a European conference to discuss the Monroe Doctrine,* an idea rejected by Secretary of State Richard Olney,* and he made a number of speeches advocating free trade, which led to his censure by the House of Representatives in 1896. Bayard returned to the United States in 1897 and took no further part in public affairs before his death in Dedham, Massachusetts, on September 28, 1898. *DAB*, 2:70; Tansill, C. C., *The Foreign Policy of Thomas F. Bayard, 1885–1897* (1936); *New York Times*, September 29, 1898; Willson, Beckles, *America's Ambassadors to England 1785–1929* (1929).

BAYARD-CHAMBERLAIN TREATY (1888). This agreement, signed by Secretary of State Thomas F. Bayard* and Joseph Chamberlain, special representative of Great Britain, on February 10, 1888, and accepted by President

Cleveland on February 15, dealt with the long-standing fisheries problem between Canada and the United States. The treaty provided for the removal of restrictions on areas where American fishermen could operate, on purchases of bait and other supplies in Canada, and on the transshipment of catches and the travel of crews. In return, the United States agreed to lift duties on Canadian and New-foundland fish products. However, the Senate rejected the treaty by a 27–30 vote on August 21, 1888, because of partisanship and the idea that reciprocity in this case was a sellout to Great Britain. The defeat of the treaty dampened a growing enthusiasm for reciprocity and was a setback for better political and commercial relations with Canada. Shippie, Lester B., "Thomas Francis Bayard," in Bemis, Samuel F., ed., *American Secretaries of State and Their Diplomacy*, vol. 8 (1928); Tansill, C. C., *Canadian-American Relations, 1875–1911* (1943).

BAYLIES, FRANCIS (1783–1852). Born October 16, 1783, in Taunton, Mas-sachusetts, Francis Baylies attended Bristol Academy in Taunton; he then read law and was admitted to the bar in 1811. From 1812 to 1820, he was register of probate in Massachusetts and from 1821 to 1827, he served three terms in Congress, winning distinction as the only New Englander to vote against John Quincy Adams* in the congressionally decided election of 1824. Baylies sat in the Massachusetts legislature from 1827 to 1832, until his appointment as chargé d'affaires* to Buenos Aires. In Argentina only from June to September 1832, he nevertheless played a key role in a Falkland Islands fishing controversy. After Argentine officials on the islands seized the *Harriet** and three other New England fishing vessels for violations of local regulations, President Andrew Jackson responded by sending the U.S.S. *Lexington;* it raided the islands, dispersed the so-called pirates, and detained the responsible officials for trial. When the gov-ernment at Buenos Aires refused to negotiate until apologies were made and indemnities paid, Baylies peremptorily refused and left his post. Diplomatic relations between the two nations were not resumed until 1844. A result of the affair was that, in the absence of the Argentine officials on the islands, British forces occupied them and have exercised control ever since. Baylies's perfor-mance did not win him much credit. Goebel termed him temperamental and unsuited for delicate diplomatic negotiations, and John Quincy Adams called him "one of the most talented and worthless men in New England," a phase quoted by Peterson. Baylies returned to the United States, became a lecturer and historical writer, served another term in the Massachusetts legislature, and died in Taunton on October 28, 1852. *DAB*, 2:75; Goebel, Julius L., *The Struggle for the Falkland Islands* (1927); Klafter, Craig Evan, "United States Involvement in the Falkland Islands Crisis of 1832–1833," *Journal of the Early Republic* 4, 4 (Winter 1984):395–402; Peterson, Harold, *Argentina and the United States, 1810–1960* (1964).

BEALE, EDWARD FITZGERALD (1822–1893). Born in Washington, D.C., on February 4, 1822, Edward Fitzgerald Beale attended Georgetown College before graduating from the U.S. Naval Academy in 1842. He married Mary

Edwards in 1849 and served in the U.S. Navy until 1850, seeing action in the Mexican War and traveling frequently between California and the East. In the 1850s, Beale settled in California as manager of some mining properties and later as surveyor general of California and Nevada (1861–1865). After a five-year respite on a California ranch, Beale bought the Decatur House and moved to Washington, D.C., in 1870. Six years later, President Ulysses S. Grant appointed him minister to Austria-Hungary, a post he held for a year. Relations between the United States and Austria-Hungary had not been cordial since Austrian Prince Maximilian's ill-fated Mexican adventure, but Beale established a good working relationship with Foreign Minister Jules Andrassy and alleviated the diplomatic mistrust. After his return from Vienna, Beale lived in retirement in Washington until his death April 22, 1893. Bonsal, Stephen, *Edward Fitzgerald Beale* (1912); *DAB*, 2:88; Thompson, Gerald, *Edward F. Beale and the American West* (1983).

BEALE, TRUXTUN (1856–1936). The son of General Edward Fitzgerald Beale,* Truxtun Beale was born March 6, 1856, in San Francisco and graduated from Pennsylvania Military College (1874) and Columbia University Law School (1878). He was admitted to the bar in 1878 but returned to California and managed his father's ranch for the next thirteen years. Beale married Harriet Blaine, the daughter of Secretary of State James G. Blaine,* and was named minister to Persia by his father-in-law in 1891 and minister to Greece, Romania, and Serbia the next year. In Persia, he persuaded the shah's government to participate in the World's Columbian Exposition in 1893 and helped arrange the abolition of export duties on goods bound for the fair and import duties on goods bought at the exposition and sent back to Persia. Beale also convinced the government to rescind its prohibition against foreign landownership with respect to American missionaries. He served in Greece fewer than five months before a Grover Cleveland appointee replaced him; there were no significant diplomatic questions at stake. Between 1894 and 1896, Beale traveled extensively in Siberia, Central Asia, and Chinese Turkestan before returning to the United States. After a divorce in 1896, Beale married Marie Oge in 1903. He made front page news in 1916 by fighting in the street in front of New York's Knickerbocker Club with George von L. Meyer.* He died June 2, 1936, at Laurel Farms, his country home near Annapolis, Maryland. *FR* (1892), 355–57; *New York Times* July 22, 1892, January 25, 1916, June 3, 1936, June 12, 1956; *WWWA*, 1 (1897–1942):73.

BEAM, JACOB DYNELEY (b. 1908). Born in Princeton, New Jersey, on March 24, 1908, Jacob D. Beam graduated from his home town university in 1929 and studied at Cambridge in 1929–1930. In 1931, he joined the State Department, serving in minor posts in Europe until 1944, when he became a member of the political advisory staff of SHAEF (Supreme Headquarters, Allied Expeditionary Force), a post he held until 1946. After a succession of other minor posts, Beam became minister-counselor at the Moscow embassy in 1952 and served as chargé d'affaires,* 1952–1953, providing useful information to the State Department at the time of Joseph Stalin's death in March 1953. As ambassador to Poland, 1957–1961, he carried on negotiations with the Chinese Communists in Warsaw and communicated Secretary of State John Foster Dulles's* rejection of the Rapacki Plan for a nuclear-free Central Europe. From 1966 to 1969, Beam was ambassador to Czechoslovakia, and from 1969 to 1973, he was ambassador to the Soviet Union. Although these were important missions, Beam was not personally involved in major issues of policymaking. Beam, who married Margaret Glassford in 1952, retired from the State Department in 1973 and published his memoirs, *Multiple Exposure,* in 1978. *CB* (1959): 30–32; *New York Times,* January 13, 1973.

BEARD, CHARLES AUSTIN (1874–1948). An important American historian, much of whose writing touched on diplomatic matters, Charles A. Beard was born near Knightstown, Indiana, on November 27, 1874. He received a B.A. degree from DePauw in 1898, attended Oxford and Cornell universities, and received graduate degrees from Columbia (A.M., 1903; Ph.D., 1904). For thirteen years (1904–1917), Beard taught history, public law, and politics at Columbia, resigning in protest of the trustees' attempts to stifle criticism of American intervention into World War I. Although he never held another regular teaching position, he remained active in academic life, writing books and articles and holding high office in professional organizations. He became interested in U.S. foreign policy in the 1920s during the debate over the wisdom of American intervention in World War I. Convinced that the intervention had been wrong and that America's national interest was best served by staying out of war and building democracy from within, Beard became an ardent advocate of isolationism* in the 1930s, endorsing the ideas of the America First Committee* and arguing in popular books written after World War II that President Franklin D. Roosevelt had purposely inveigled a Japanese attack on Pearl Harbor* in order to bring the United States into the war with popular support. He married Mary Ritter in 1900; she coauthored some of his works and wrote a biographical study, *The Making of Charles A. Beard* (1955). Beard died in New Haven, Connecticut, September 1, 1948. Among his books concerned with foreign policy are *The Idea of National Interest* (1934), *American Foreign Policy in the Making, 1932–1940* (1946), and *President Roosevelt and the Coming of the War* (1948). *DAB,* Supp. 4:61; Hofstadter, Richard, *The Progressive Historians* (1968); Kennedy, Thomas C., *Charles A. Beard and American Foreign Policy* (1975); Radosh, Ronald, *Prophets on the Right* (1975); *New York Times,* September 2, 1948.

BEAR FLAG REVOLT (1846). The Bear Flag revolt, so named because of the flag used by the revolutionists, occurred in California in May 1846. American settlers, restive under the rule of Mexican General Mariano Vallejo, declared their independence and established an independent republic. John C. Frémont, head of an American exploring expedition in California, brought his men into the movement, which shortly preceded the Mexican War. In the war itself, however, troops from an American fleet commanded by Commodore Robert F. Stockton* did most of the actual conquest of California. Graebner, Norman, *Empire on the Pacific* (1955); Pletcher, David, *The Diplomacy of Annexation* (1973).

BEAULAC, WILLARD LEON (b. 1899). A career diplomat who held ambassadorships in five Latin American nations, Willard Beaulac was born on July 25, 1899, in Pawtucket, Rhode Island, attended Brown University, 1916–1918, and graduated from Georgetown University in 1921 after World War I service in the U.S. Navy. Joining the Foreign Service upon graduation, he served in various consular posts in Latin America until 1933. From 1934 to 1937, Beaulac was assistant chief, Division of Latin American Affairs, and in 1937, he became first secretary of the embassy in Havana. He was promoted to counselor at Havana in 1940 and the next year moved to the same position in Madrid, where he stayed until 1944. In that year, he was appointed ambassador to Paraguay. This mission was followed by ambassadorships to Colombia (1947–1951), Cuba (1951–1953), Chile (1953–1956), and Argentina (1956–1960). In Paraguay, Beaulac helped implement a new program of argricultural, health, and educational aid while attempting, without success, to steer the government toward a more democratic stance. His mission in Colombia included the Ninth International Conference of American States* in Bogotá, 1948, to which he was a delegate. The Cuban years were relatively uneventful, but in Chile, Beaulac played an important role in arrangements for the United States to purchase 100,000 tons of copper to relieve an international surplus and to explore for uranium sources in that South American nation. He went to Argentina shortly after the overthrow of Juan D. Perón, negotiated for the return of the U.S. air mission and for new educational exchange programs. In addition, he hosted Vice-President Richard M. Nixon on his 1958 visit to Argentina. In 1935, Beaulac married Catherine Green and in 1957 wrote *Career Ambassador*, a partially autobiographical book designed mainly to describe the life and work of a typical ambassador. Since his retirement from the State Department in 1960, he has continued to write, publishing *A Diplomat Looks at Aid to Latin America* (1970), *The Fractured Continent* (1980), and *Franco* (1986). *CB* (1958): 11–13.

BEAUPRÉ, ARTHUR MATTHIAS (1853–1919). Born in Illinois, on July 29, 1853, Arthur Matthias Beaupré was educated in public schools in Illinois, read law, and was admitted to the Illinois bar during the 1870s. He entered the printing business, developed an interest in Republican politics, and became clerk of Kane County, Illinois, in 1886, serving in that position for six years. In 1897 the McKinley administration appointed him consul general* to Guatemala and Honduras; two years later, he took the same post in Colombia. Promoted to minister to Colombia in 1903, Beaupré tried to convince the Colombian Congress to ratify the Hay-Herrán Treaty* and was in personal danger after the Panamanian revolution. He served uneventfully as minister to Argentina, 1904–1908, and to the Netherlands and Luxembourg, 1908–1911. In 1911, he was appointed minister to Cuba and survived accusations of enriching himself through graft. He represented President Wilson at the inauguration of Cuban president Mario García Menocal in May 1913 and handled the treaty conveying additional land for the Guantanamo Naval Base to the United States, ratified in the same year. After leaving Cuba in June 1913, Beaupré retired to Chicago until his death on September 13, 1919. *DAB*, 2:110; *FR* (1903), 132–230; Munro, Dana G., *Intervention and Dollar Diplomacy in the Caribbean, 1900–1921* (1964); *New York Times*, September 15, 1919.

BELCHER, TAYLOR GARRISON (b. 1920). Taylor G. Belcher was born on Staten Island, New York, on July 1, 1920. He graduated from Brown University in 1941, served in the navy during World War II, and joined the State Department in 1947, holding minor posts in Mexico City, Glasgow, Washington, Nicosia, and Ottawa until 1964, when he became ambassador to Cyprus, a post he held for five years. In 1969, Belcher was named ambassador to Peru, where his appointment coincided with a Peruvian decision to rescind an expropriation order for W. R. Grace and Company's chemical, paper, and sugar properties, a move that was well received in the United States. On May 31, 1970, Peru was struck by a devastating earthquake. Belcher authorized the first earthquake relief on June 1 and continued to provide valuable information in the days that followed. He left Peru in 1974 and became a State Department counselor. Married to Edith Anthony in 1942, Belcher is closely involved with the Cyprus Relief Fund of America and the Cyprus Children's Fund. Sharp, Daniel A. ed., *U.S. Foreign Policy and Peru* (1972); *New York Times*, August 27, 1969, June 3, 5, 1970; *WWA* (1976–1977): 221.

BELL, ISAAC, JR. (1846–1889). Born November 6, 1846, in New York City, Bell was educated in private schools there. As a youth, he worked as a clerk in the cotton brokerage of Brown Brothers & Company. He moved to Savannah about 1870, pursued the cotton brokerage business, and retired in 1877 as a wealthy man. He then married Jeanette Cordon Bennett, the daughter of newspaper publisher James Gordon Bennett, moved to Newport, Rhode Island, and mingled with his in-laws' social, literary, and Democratic party political friends. In order to solidify his eastern seaboard support, President Grover Cleveland named Bell minister to the Netherlands in 1885. He served in that post for three years and was very popular. His work there consisted mainly of reporting to the State Department on matters such as a campaign for universal suffrage, an increase in petroleum import duties, and a major revision of the constitution. He resigned his position in March 1888 for private business reasons. Returning to Newport, Bell was a delegate to the 1888 Democratic National Convention and campaigned for Cleveland. He died in New York City on January 20, 1889, of pyemia, a form of blood poisoning. *DAB*, 2:155; *FR* (1885–1888), passim; *New York Times*, January 21, 1889.

BELMONT, AUGUST (1816–1890). Born December 8, 1816, in the Rhenish Palatinate, August Belmont was educated in Frankfort, entered the Rothschilds firm in 1831, and came to the United States in 1837 to begin his own banking business as an agent of the Rothschilds. With his European connections, he soon became one of New York's leading bankers. He received American citizenship in 1842 and served as Austria's consul general* in New York from 1843 to 1850. In 1853, the Pierce administration appointed Belmont chargé d'affaires* to the Netherlands; the next year, he became minister to that country and served until 1857. A popular diplomat, his principal achievement was the negotiation of a consular convention with the Dutch. More important diplomatic service was rendered during the Civil War, when he served as an agent for the Union in Spain, where he worked to prevent Spanish recognition of Confederate belligerency. After the Civil War, Belmont remained active in Democratic politics and was an avid art collector and lover of horses and racing, serving as president of the American Jockey Club for many years before his death on November 24, 1890, in New York City, of pneumonia. *DAB*, 2:169; *New York Times*, November 25, 1890.

BELMONT, PERRY (1851–1947). The son of August Belmont,* Perry Belmont was born December 28, 1851, in New York City. He graduated from Harvard in 1872, studied civil law at the University of Berlin, and received a law degree from Columbia in 1876. Entering law practice in New York City, he was elected as a Democrat to the U.S. House of Representatives in 1881 and served four terms, the last two of which he was chairman of the International Affairs Committee. In 1888, near the end of President Grover Cleveland's first term, Belmont was named minister to Spain and served until 1890. At Secretary of State James G. Blaine's* request, he protested the discriminatory duties and fines laid against U.S. vessels in Cuba and Puerto Rico and was successful in securing relief from such fines and in obtaining a refund of excess duties to one ship. After his ministerial service, Belmont continued to be active in Democratic politics, served in the Spanish-American War and in World War I, and became an anti-isolationist during the 1920s, publishing *National Isolation and Illusion* (1925). Belmont continued his father's interest in horses, serving as the first president of the United Hunts Racing Association and of the Turf and Field Club. He wrote his autobiography, *An American Democrat* (1940), and died in Newport, Rhode Island on May 25, 1947. *FR* (1889): 658–81; *New York Times*, September 28, 1889, May 26, 1947.

BEMIS, SAMUEL FLAGG (1891–1973). One of the most prominent of recent U.S. diplomatic historians, Samuel Flagg Bemis was born in Worcester, Massachusetts, on October 20, 1891, and received degrees from Clark University (A.B., 1912; A.M., 1913) and Harvard (A.M., 1915, Ph.D., 1916). He began his teaching at Colorado College in 1917, moved to Whitman College (Washington) in 1920, and then spent the 1923–1924 academic year engaged in research at the Carnegie Institute in Washington, D.C. Bemis began teaching at George Washington University in 1924, went to Harvard ten years later, and in 1945 accepted a position at Yale, where he concluded his teaching career. Bemis was the first major diplomatic historian to adopt a multiarchival research technique and though his work often tended to be defensive of U.S. foreign policy, the research in foreign archives gave it unusual breadth. His major monographs are almost too numerous to mention: *Jay's Treaty* (1923), *Pinckney's Treaty* (1926), *The Diplomacy of the American Revolution* (1935), *The Latin American Policy of the United States* (1943), *John Quincy Adams and the Foundations of American Foreign Policy* (1949), and *John Quincy Adams and the Union* (1956). In addition, he wrote a basic textbook, *A Diplomatic History of the United States* (1936), a basic bibliographical reference work, *Guide to the Diplomatic History of the United States* (1935), prepared with Grace G. Griffen, and edited the first ten volumes of *American Secretaries of State and Their Diplomacy* (1927–1929). Bemis won the Pulitzer Prize for *Pinckney's Treaty* and *John Quincy Adams and the Foundations of American Foreign Policy*. He married Ruth M. Steele in 1919 and died in Bridgeport, Connecticut, on September 26, 1973. *American Historical Review* 79 (June 1974): 922–23 (obituary note by Robert H. Ferrell); *New York Times*, September 28, 1973; *WWWA*, 6 (1974–1976): 29.

BENJAMIN, JUDAH PHILIP (1811–1884). Judah P. Benjamin was born on St. Thomas in the British West Indies on August 6, 1811, and came to the United States as a youth, attending Yale from 1825 to 1827. By 1833, he was practicing law in New Orleans and in the early 1840s was involved in the *Creole* affair.* Successful at law, he also became a wealthy sugar planter and was elected to the U.S. Senate, serving from 1852 to 1861. In the Senate, he supported most expansionist issues, including an isthmian canal across Tehuantepec and commercial development abroad. He resigned in 1861 to serve the Confederacy and after a brief tenure as attorney general and war secretary, he was appointed secretary of state in February 1862, holding that office for the duration of the war. As secretary of state, Benjamin did little but continue the initiatives begun before he entered the office. After the war, he lived in England and became a renowned and busy lawyer for over fifteen years before his death, May 6, 1884, in Paris. *DAB*, 2:181; Evans, Eli N., *Judah P. Benjamin, The Jewish Confederate* (1988); Meade, Robert D., *Judah P. Benjamin, Confederate Statesman* (1943); Neiman, Simon I., *Judah Benjamin* (1963); Osterweis, Rolli, *Judah P. Benjamin, Statesman of the Lost Cause* (1933); Owsley, Frank L., *King Cotton Diplomacy*, 2d ed. (1959).

BENJAMIN, SAMUEL GREENE WHEELER (1837–1914). A son of missionaries, Benjamin was born in Argus, Greece, on February 13, 1837, and spent the first eighteen years of his life in Greece and the Near East, attending schools in Smyrna, Turkey, and learning much of the area's languages, culture, and art. He graduated from Williams College in 1859, taught school, worked as a librarian, painted seascapes, and wrote books and articles during the next twenty years, making frequent transatlantic trips. In 1883, Benjamin, a Republican, was named the first American minister to Persia. He dealt mainly with missionary problems and drafted the diplomatic code used by the American legation in Persia. However, according to Pletcher, he "lacked common sense and set out with an exalted opinion of his own importance [and] . . . soon became suspicious of Russian influence and disgraced himself by petty quarrels with the Russian and German ministers, so that finally he had to be recalled." After his return, he published *Persia and the Persians* (1886) and *The Story of Persia* (1887) and his autobiography, *The Life and Adventures of a Free Lance* (1914). *DAB*, 2:189; *FR* (1883–1884), 702–6; Goode, James J., "A Good Start: The First American Mission to Iran, 1883–5," *Muslim World* 74 (April 1984): 100–118; *New York Times*, July 20, 1914: Pletcher, David, *The Awkward Years* (1962); Yoselon, Abraham, *United States–Persian Relations, 1883–1921* (1956).

BENNETT, WILLIAM TAPLEY, JR. (b. 1917). A native of Griffin, Georgia, where he was born on April 1, 1917, W. Tapley Bennett, Jr., graduated from the University of Georgia in 1937, studied in Germany, 1937–1938, and worked for the National Institute of Public Affairs, 1939–1940, and with the Office of Defense Housing, 1940–1941. He joined the State Department in 1941 and except for army service (1944–1946) held minor posts in Ciudad Trujillo (Santo Domingo), Washington, Vienna, Rome, and Athens until 1964. That year he was appointed ambassador to the Dominican Republic and soon became closely involved in helping the governing junta, led by Donald Reid Cabral, with economic and fiscal policy and many other internal matters. When the Dominican crisis* erupted in 1965, Bennett supported Reid, tried to help his government get additional U.S. aid, and blamed Reid's difficulties on bad luck. By this time, the Lyndon Johnson administration had become unhappy with Bennett's generally "conservative, anti-constitutionalist and self-justifying" reporting and sent former ambassador John Bartlow Martin to Santo Domingo as a special presidential representative to gather information and make contact with groups hostile to Bennett. A particularly controversial matter was Bennett's refusal to negotiate with a group headed by former president Juan Bosch or to mediate among contending parties early in the conflict; the situation worsened, and U.S. intervention was undertaken (at Bennett's recommendation). Leaving the Dominican Republic in 1966, Bennett served uneventful tours as ambassador to Portugal (1966–1969) and as a State Department adviser to Air University at Maxwell Air Force Base (1969–1971). From 1971 to 1977, he was a high-ranking member of the U.S. delegation to the United Nations* and was periodically prominent in debates over an international agreement to combat terrorism. In 1977, he was appointed the U.S. representative to the North Atlantic Treaty Organization.* In 1983, Bennett was named assistant secretary of state for intergovernmental affairs. He retired from the State Department in 1985. Lowenthal, Abraham F., *The Dominican Intervention* (1972); Slater, Jerome, *Intervention and Negotiation* (1970); *New York Times*, March 22, 1966, December 23, 1973, April 14, 18, 1977; *WWA* (1984–1985):239.

BERGER, SAMUEL DAVID (1911–1980). Samuel D. Berger was born in Gloversville, New York, on December 6, 1911, received a Ph.D. from the University of Wisconsin, and did graduate work at Wisconsin and the London School of Economics from 1935 to 1939, becoming a specialist in labor matters. During World War II, he was attached to the Lend-Lease* mission in London and worked as a labor consultant to the British government. In 1945, he joined the State Department as a labor officer attached to the U.S. embassy in London. The previous year he had drafted a memorandum with Arthur Notman outlining the need for a coal allocation organization for Europe; this led to the creation of the European Coal Organization in London in May 1945, with the United States and eight European nations as charter members. The purpose of the organization was to recommend to member governments an equitable allocation of coal, based on reports by members of their needs and supplies available for export. After three years (1950–1953) on the White House staff, Berger was sent to Tokyo as counselor, but a disagreement with visiting Vice-President Richard Nixon about the degree of Communist influence in the Japanese labor movement brought about his transfer to New Zealand. From there, he spent a short time in Athens before his appointment as ambassador to (South) Korea in 1961. During his three years there, General Park Chung Hee assumed power, and Berger successfully served as a moderating influence in the political turmoil that followed. In addition, he played a role in the normalization of diplomatic relations between South Korea and Japan. After a tour in Washington as deputy assistant secretary of state for East Asian affairs, (1965–1968), Berger was named deputy ambassador to (South) Vietnam, a position he held for four years. There his main responsibility concerned the relationship between the United States and the government of Nguyen Van Thieu; he worked with the military to win support for Thieu and consulted frequently with the South Vietnamese president. One important area of consultation was in planning the Laotian incursion (1971).* Berger left Saigon in 1972 and took a position with the Foreign Service Institute. Twice married, he retired in 1976 and died in Washington, D.C., on February 12, 1980. Kwak, Tae-hwon, et al., *U.S.-Korean Relations, 1882–1982* (1982); Samuels, Nathaniel, "European Coal Organization," *Foreign Affairs* 26, 4 (July 1948): 728: *New York Times*, February 23, April 28, 1968, February 9, 1971, March 15, 1972, February 13, 1980; *WWWA*, 7 (1977–1981): 47.

BERING SEA DISPUTE. From the 1870s, American companies had been granted the right by the Treasury Department to harvest seals on the Pribilof Islands on the Bering Sea. In the mid-1880s, Canadian sealers began the practice of pelagic sealing, or hunting seals by boat outside the three-mile limit. Their actions cut into the American companies' profits and led to American seizures of Canadian sealers and diplomatic controversy between Great Britain and the United States. The two nations agreed on arbitration,* and in 1893 an arbitration commission assessed damages against the United States for the seizures but set a sixty-mile limit around the islands in which pelagic sealing was prohibited.

Dissatisfied, the United States pressed for a more favorable arrangement. A review of the arbitration decision in 1898 resulted in the submission of the dispute to a Joint High Commission dealing with an assortment of Anglo-American questions; however, no solution was reached until 1911, when the North Pacific Sealing Convention* was signed. Campbell, Charles S., *Anglo-American Understanding, 1898–1903* (1957); Tansill, C. C., *Canadian-American Relations, 1875–1911* (1943).

BERLE, ADOLF AUGUSTUS, JR. (1895–1971). Born in Boston on January 29, 1895, Adolf A. Berle, Jr., was privately tutored by his father and graduated from Harvard (A.B., 1913; M.A., 1914; LL.B., 1916). He practiced law until 1917, when he joined the army for a year's service in the Caribbean. In 1919, he was a member of the U.S. delegation at the Paris Peace Conference,* dealing primarily with the Middle East and European problems. From 1919 to 1932, he practiced law in New York City; after 1927, he taught at Columbia Law School as well. In 1932, he became part of President-elect Franklin D. Roosevelt's Brain Trust and remained associated with the White House until 1938, when he was named assistant secretary of state for Latin American affairs. In this post, Berle was active in the execution of the Good Neighbor Policy,* attended several Pan-American conferences, and during World War II prepared position papers for Roosevelt on Latin American wartime relations. In 1945, he attended the Mexico City Conference* and helped draft the Act of Chapultepec; by this time, he was ambassador to Brazil, a post he held for a year. Berle was out of government from 1946 to 1960, when President-elect John F. Kennedy asked him to head a task force to study Latin American problems. He did, and the task force recommended support of social reform, trade privileges, and loans, much of which was incorporated into the Alliance for Progress.* From 1961 until his death on February 17, 1971, in New York City, Berle wrote, taught, and practiced law and worked in the New York Liberal party and the Twentieth Century Fund. He was married to Beatrice Bend Bishop in 1927. Berle, Adolf A., Jr., *Power* (1969); *CB* (1961): 48–50; *New York Times*, February 19, 1971; Schwartz, Jordan A., *Liberal: Adolf A. Berle and the Vision of an American Era* (1987); Woods, Randall B., *The Roosevelt Foreign Policy Establishment and the "Good Neighbor": The United States and Argentina, 1941–1945* (1979).

BERLIN, TREATY OF (1889). Sometimes referred to as the Berlin General Act, this treaty, signed June 14, 1889, established a complicated system of tripartite (Germany, United States, Great Britain) control over Samoa, ostensibly maintaining Samoan independence. Designed to end international rivalry over the islands, the protectorate did not work well and was terminated in the Convention of 1899.* The Treaty of Berlin was ratified by the Senate, although opponents vigorously protested the violation of the American tradition of no entangling alliances of a political nature. Dulles, Foster, R., *The Imperial Years* (1956); *FR* (1889), 179–423; Henderson, John B., *American Diplomatic Questions*

(1901); Kennedy, Paul M., *The Samoan Tangle: A Study in Anglo-German-American Relations, 1878–1900* (1974); Ryder, George H., *The Foreign Policy of the United States in Relation to Samoa* (1933).

BERLIN, TREATY OF (1921). After the U.S. Senate rejection of the Treaty of Versailles (1919),* this treaty was signed on August 25, 1921, to bring a formal end to hostilities between the United States and Germany following World War I; ratifications were exchanged November 11, 1921. The treaty provided that the value of confiscated German property in the United States would be applied against American claims and that Americans would have equal treatment with other claimants in claims settlements. The treaty further stated that the United States would bear none of the political or military responsibilities described in the Treaty of Versailles. Jones, Manfred, *The United States and Germany* (1984); Offner, Arnold A., *The Origins of the Second World War* (1975).

BERLIN, TREATY OF (QUADRIPARTITE AGREEMENT ON BERLIN, 1971). This treaty removed the major East-West problem over access to Berlin and in so doing facilitated diplomatic movement toward a general European security conference around the principle of mutual balanced force reduction. Discussion concerning Berlin access had been going on since 1969, when Willy Brandt became West German chancellor. In the treaty, the Soviet Union guaranteed unimpeded access to West Berlin and granted West Berliners the right to visit East Berlin and East Germany thirty days each year. The Western allies, in return, agreed that West Berlin was not "a constituent part" of West Germany and would be governed separately. The West German parliament would no longer meet in West Berlin as it had been occasionally doing. The treaty was signed by the United States, Britain, France, and the USSR on September 3, 1971; by East Berlin and West Berlin on December 17; and by East and West Germany on December 20. Catudal, Honoré M., *The Diplomacy of the Quadripartite Agreement on Berlin* (1978); Gaddis, John L., *Russia, the Soviet Union, and the United States* (1978); Szulce, Tad, *The Illusion of Peace* (1978).

BERLIN BLOCKADE (1948–1949). This major cold war* crisis began in June 1948 when the Soviets cut off all land access to the western sectors of Berlin and its population of 2 million, lying completely within the Russian occupation zone of Germany. General Lucius Clay,* in charge of the American zone, recommended a direct challenge to the blockade, but this idea was passed over in favor of supplying Berlin by means of an airlift. In addition, a counterblockade was imposed on the Soviet zone, denying it needed industrial goods. Soviet officials in West Berlin were harassed—for example, through rigid enforcement of traffic regulations. More threateningly, U.S. planes of a type known as "atomic bombers" were sent to forward bases in Britain to enhance the value of deterrence, but concern about the postwar military weakness of the United States precluded a more aggressive policy in response to the blockade. In May 1949, the Soviets evidently concluded that the blockade was being counterproductive in that the East Germans were becoming restless, while the obvious success of the airlift was having highly positive psychological effects on both the people of Berlin and the nations of the Western alliance. With the signing of the New York Agreement on May 4, the blockade was lifted. According to Gimbel, the blockade was a Soviet response to the Allied decision to begin forming a German government in the western zones in order to stabilize the economy of these zones and, perhaps more important, to ensure West Germany's economic and political alignment with the United States and its allies. The blockade accelerated this process and also contributed to the decision to create the North Atlantic Treaty Organization.* Feis, Herbert, *From Trust to Terror* (1970); *FR* (1948), 2:909–94; Gaddis, John L., *Russia, the Soviet Union, and the United States* (1978); George, Alexander, and Richard Smoke, *Deterrence in American Foreign Policy* (1974); Gimbel, John, *The American Occupation of Germany* (1968); Shlaim, Avi, *The United States and the Berlin Blockade* (1983); Yergin, Daniel, *Shattered Peace* (1977).

BERLIN CONFERENCE (1884–1885). This conference was called by Chancellor Otto von Bismarck of Germany to deal with questions concerning the Congo, including freedom of commerce, freedom of river navigation, and formalities to be observed in the acquisition of African territory. The U.S. delegation was led by minister to Germany John A. Kasson,* who was instructed not to pledge the United States to anything contrary to known policies; the result was that the United States refused to ratify the "General Act." However, the U.S. delegation, usually siding with Belgium's King Leopold II, was influential in discussions leading to freedom of trade, abolition of the slave traffic, and wartime neutralization of the Congo area. In the United States, the Chester Arthur administration met considerable criticism for involving the country in European political matters, contrary to the Monroe Doctrine* and traditional American diplomacy. Brown, Philip M., "Frederick T. Frelinghuysen," in Bemis, Samuel F., ed., *American Secretaries of State and Their Diplomacy*, vol. 8 (1928); Fry, Joseph A., *Henry S. Sanford* (1982); Pletcher, David, *The Awkward Years* (1962); Younger, Edward, *John A. Kasson: Politics and Diplomacy from Lincoln to McKinley* (1958)

BERLIN CRISIS (1958–1962). Precipitated by Soviet fear of West Germany's rearmament and especially its acquisition of nuclear weapons, the Berlin crisis was based on Premier Nikita Khrushchev's insistence in November 1958 that negotiations on European security, a nuclear-free Germany, and the end of the four-power occupation of Berlin had to begin within six months or the Soviet Union would conclude a separate peace treaty with East Germany, which would then control access routes into West Berlin. The deadline was subsequently extended in stages until the end of 1961. Negotiations failed to bring a settlement in 1959, and the Paris summit of 1960, where Berlin talks were scheduled, was sabotaged by the U-2 incident.* In 1961, President John F. Kennedy inherited the situation and asked for immediate defense increases. Khrushchev and Kennedy discussed Berlin at their Vienna meeting in 1961, but to no avail, and in August of that year, the Berlin wall was erected, separating East Berlin from

West Berlin and halting the flow of people out of East Germany. There was no active U.S. response to the wall, which earned Kennedy some criticism, but in retrospect, it did stabilize the situation and tacitly ended the crisis, although some tension lingered until January 1963, when Khrushchev announced that his objectives with respect to Germany had been met, although no European or Berlin settlement had been made. The Berlin crisis, according to Richardson, moved West Germany even closer to the Western alliance and to the United States, since in the Western alliance lay the means for the protection of West Berlin from Soviet or East German harassment. Gaddis, John L., *Russia, the Soviet Union, and the United States* (1978); Morgan, Roger, *The United States and West Germany* (1974); Richardson, James L., *Germany and the Atlantic Alliance* (1966); Schick, Jack, *The Berlin Crisis, 1958–1962* (1974); Slusser, Robert M., *The Berlin Crisis of 1961* (1973).

BERLIN DECREE (November 1806). Napoleon's decree, announced November 21, 1806, placed Great Britain under a state of blockade and forbade all trade in British goods. It was enforced through Napoleon's control of European ports where ships of any nation coming from Britain would be denied entry or would be seized. This decree was followed by the Milan Decree (1807)* and the British Orders-in-Council (1807)* as subsequent measures of economic warfare. For the United States, the largest neutral trading nation, the Berlin Decree had a limiting effect on commerce and placed an impossible barrier in front of the pending Monroe-Pinkney Treaty* with Britain—that the United States, as a treaty condition, pledge its resistance to the decree. Egan, Clifford L., *Neither Peace nor War: Franco-American Relations, 1803–1812* (1983); Horsman, Reginald, *The Causes of the War of 1812* (1962); Perkins, Bradford, *Prologue to War* (1961).

BERMUDA CONFERENCE (1953). Held in December 1953, the Bermuda Conference brought together President Dwight D. Eisenhower, Secretary of State John Foster Dulles,* Prime Minister Winston Churchill, French Premier Joseph Lanier, and French Foreign Minister Georges Bidault. The discussions ranged over European matters, with Dulles warning the French that if they and Germany became enemies again (because of French rejection of the European Defense Community)* and threatened the security of continental Europe, U.S. policy would be "reappraised." General views on other foreign problems were exchanged, but no major agreements were concluded. Hoopes, Townsend, *The Devil and John Foster Dulles* (1973); Wheeler-Bennett, John W., and Anthony Nicholls, *The Semblance of Peace* (1972).

BERN CONFERENCE (1874). The United States participated in this international conference held at Bern, Switzerland, at which the Universal Postal Union was established. Conference participants also agreed on a uniform rate for sending mail overseas (five cents per ounce or the equivalent). Codding, George A., *The Universal Postal Union* (1964); Plesur, Milton, *America's Outward Thrust* (1971).

BERNSTEIN, HERMAN (1876–1935). Herman Bernstein was born on September 21, 1876, in Neustadt-Scherwindt, Russia, near the German border. The family was anticzarist and emigrated to the United States in 1893. Bernstein was educated by his family and became a speaker on the American immigrant experience and a translator of Russian works. In 1908, the *New York Times* sent him to Russia, East Europe, and Germany as an observer of government operations, an assignment that lasted four years. In 1914, he founded *The Day*, a Yiddish daily, and two years later became editor in chief of *American Hebrew*. A Republican, Bernstein was appointed minister to Albania by the Hoover administration in 1930. From Tirana, he reported not only on Albanian affairs but also on the whole Balkan area. He negotiated naturalization and extradition treaties with Albania and received the grand cordon of the Order of Skanderberg from the Albanian government for his work. Bernstein returned from Albania in 1933, served as executive director of the Maimonides Octocentennial Committee, and published a symposium, *Can We Abolish War?* before his death on August 31, 1935, in Sheffield, Massachusetts. *DAB*, Supp. 2:78; *New York Times*, September 1, 1935.

BERRY, BURTON YOST (1901–1985). A native of Fowler, Indiana, Burton Y. Berry was born August 31, 1901, graduated from Indiana University (B.A., 1923; M.A., 1925), and studied further at the University of Paris (1925–1927). He entered the Foreign Service in 1928 and over the next sixteen years held minor posts in Istanbul, Tehran, Athens, Naples, and Cairo. During World War II, as consul general* in Athens, he arranged for humanitarian food distribution while Greece was under Axis occupation. In addition, he was a staff adviser during the war to the U.S. Mediterranean command. From 1944 to 1947, he was the U.S. representative in Romania and a consultant on Romanian postwar affairs to the Council of Foreign Ministers.* In 1947, Berry was made a special assistant to the chief of the aid mission to Greece, helping to implement aid given under the Truman Doctrine (1947).* From 1949 to 1952, he held various administrative posts in Washington, and in 1952, he was appointed ambassador to Iraq. His main duty there was to administer Point Four* aid, which increased 35 percent in 1953; this money was used for equipment and technical services in education and agriculture. Berry was President Eisenhower's special representative to the coronation of King Faisal in 1953. He retired from the State Department in 1956 and pursued his interest in Islamic antiquities. He died in Zurich on August 22, 1985. *New York Times*, June 5, 1953, June 30, 1954, August 26, 1985; *WWA* (1958–1959):226.

BEVERIDGE, ALBERT JEREMIAH (1862–1927). Albert J. Beveridge, born October 6, 1862, in Highland County, Ohio, graduated from DePauw University in 1885, and was admitted to the bar in 1887. He involved himself in Indiana Republican party politics, became well known for his masterful oratorical style, and was elected to the U.S. Senate in 1899, where he emerged quickly as an ardent champion of American expansion. Having favored American involvement in the Spanish-American War, he urged increased American commerce through the development of foreign markets, the maintenance of a large navy, and the spread of American institutions. He was famous for his patriotic orations, which tended toward Anglophobia* and jingoism. He joined the insurgent wing of the party, lost his Senate seat in 1911, and went with Theodore Roosevelt into the Progressive party in 1912. Despite a return to Republicanism, however, he was never again elected to public office. His later years were spent in historical and biographical writing and in opposing American entry into the League of Nations.* He died of heart disease April 27, 1927, in Indianapolis. Bowers, Claude G., *Beveridge and the Progressive Era* (1932); Braeman, John., *Albert J. Beveridge* (1971); Healy, David, *U.S. Expansionism* (1970); *New York Times*, April 28, 1927.

BIDDLE, ANTHONY JOSEPH DREXEL, JR. (1896–1961). Born in Philadelphia on December 17, 1896, A. J. D. Biddle, Jr., graduated from St. Paul's School in 1915 but never attended college. After service in the army during World War I, he was engaged in various private business enterprises, including nightclubs and South African mines, until 1934. An active supporter of Franklin D. Roosevelt, Biddle was named ambassador to Norway in 1935. In 1937, he became ambassador to Poland, accompanying that government into exile in 1939. In 1940, Biddle was named deputy ambassador to France and based in Bordeaux; while there he was the U.S. representative to several governments in exile, including Belgium, the Netherlands, Norway, Yugoslavia, Czechoslovakia, and Greece, between 1941 and 1943. From 1944 to 1955, Biddle was again on active duty with the army, holding various liaison positions with General Dwight D. Eisenhower's headquarters in Europe and serving as an adviser to General Matthew B. Ridgway. After six years as adjutant general of Pennsylvania, 1955–1961, Biddle spent a few months as ambassador to Spain before his death in Washington on November 13, 1961. Biddle was married three times and was known as an excellent tennis player. *NCAB*, 53:14; *New York Times*, November 14, 1961; *WWWA*, 4 (1961–1968): 84.

BIDDLE, JAMES (1783–1848). Born in Philadelphia on February 18, 1783, James Biddle studied at the University of Pennsylvania between 1798 and 1800, but despite some academic talent, entered the navy as a midshipman in 1800. The navy was his life's career, and he rose to the rank of commodore. He served in the Tripoli wars against the Barbary pirates* and was held prisoner for nineteen months following the grounding of the U.S.S. *Philadelphia*. While on leave from the navy, he served on a merchant ship to China in 1807. His gallantry during the War of 1812 contributed to his promotion to captain, and in the years following the war he made several voyages to South America, where he successfully negotiated for the release of U.S. sailors and ships caught up in the Latin American struggle for independence. In 1830, he played a role in the negotiations for the first treaty between the United States and Turkey, and in

1846, he exchanged ratifications and implemented the Treaty of Wang-Hsia*
with China by establishing consulates in four of the five treaty ports stipulated
in the agreement. On the same voyage, he visited Japan, a forerunner to the
visit of Matthew Perry in 1853. After service in the Mexican War, he died at
the family estate, Andalusia, near Philadelphia, on October 1, 1848. *DAB*, 1:240–
41; Long, David F., *Sailor-Diplomat: A Biography of Commodore James Biddle* (1983).

BIDLACK, BENJAMIN ALDEN (1804–1849). Born September 8, 1804, in
Paris, New York, Benjamin Bidlack was educated into the law and was admitted
to the bar about 1825. He practiced law in Luzerne County, Pennsylvania, in
1833 and was editor of the *North Eagle* (Pike County, Pennsylvania) from 1834
to 1841. He served in the Pennsylvania legislature, 1835–1836, and the U.S.
House of Representatives, 1841–1845. In December 1845, he was named chargé
d'affaires* in New Granada and remained there until his death in Bogotá on
February 6, 1849. He was instructed to gather information about isthmian transit
routes and prevent New Granada from granting transit privileges to any other
nation. He went beyond his instructions, however and, in 1846, negotiated a
treaty for U.S. transit rights on the isthmus of Panama in return for U.S. guarantees of isthmian neutrality and New Granada's sovereignty. The agreement
was also a general treaty of amity, navigation, and commerce and was ratified
after the Mexican cession on June 8, 1848. Bidlack negotiated the treaty because
of his concern about British aggression in the Caribbean, French influence in
the isthmus, and his feeling that the time for such a treaty was opportune, as
New Granada felt the need of protection. The treaty stands as the only nineteenth-
century pact in which the United States agreed to defend a Latin American state's
sovereignty at the request of that state. *DAB*, 2:245; *NCAB*, 13:415; Parks, E. Taylor,
Colombia and the United States, 1765–1934 (1935, 1968).

BIG FOUR, name applied to the Council of Four*—Woodrow Wilson, Georges
Clemenceau, David Lloyd George, and Vittorio Orlando—comprising the major
powers at the Paris Peace Conference, 1919.* Originally a Council of Ten* was
established as the principal working body, but Wilson and Clemenceau argued
successfully for the efficiency of a smaller group. Between March and June
1919, the Big Four met once or twice daily. Bailey, Thomas A., *Woodrow Wilson
and the Lost Peace* (1944); Duroselle, Jean-Baptiste, *From Wilson to Roosevelt* (1963);
Walworth, Arthur, *Wilson and His Peacemakers: American Diplomacy at the Paris Peace
Conference* (1986).

"BIG FOUR", diplomatic catchphrase, c. World War II. This term refers to
the United States, Great Britain, the Soviet Union, and China and was first used
in connection with the United Nations Declaration,* January 1, 1942, when these
four nations stood at the head of the list of signatories. China was what McNeill
calls a "courtesy" member, included at the request of the United States out of
sentiment and the potential of a well-organized and politically stable China. The

term "Big Three," referring to the United States, the Soviet Union, and Great Britain, is often seen in connection with wartime diplomatic history. McNeill, William H., *America, Britain, and Russia* (1953).

BIGELOW, JOHN (1817–1911). Born in Malden, New York, on November 25, 1817, John Bigelow graduated from Union College in 1835 and was admitted to the bar in 1838. In 1844, he became a New York State prison inspector, a post he held for three years. In 1848, he was active in the Free-Soil campaign, and the following year he became editor and part-owner of the *New York Evening Post*. In 1861, the Abraham Lincoln administration appointed Bigelow consul in Paris, where he worked to persuade the French that the North was more important commercially than the South. Upon the death of Minister William Dayton* in late 1864, Bigelow became first chargé d'affaires* and then, in April 1865, minister to France. As minister, he conducted negotiations resulting in the removal of the French Imperial Army from Mexico. Bigelow's efforts in uncovering a plot of the French government to supply the Confederacy with four ships were detailed in his book, *France and the Confederate Navy* (1888). Bigelow resigned his ministry in 1866 and lived in Germany from 1870 to 1873. From 1875 to 1877, he was Democratic secretary of state of New York and a close associate of Samuel J. Tilden, of whose estate he was executor. During this period, he also embarked on a literary career, writing biographies of Benjamin Franklin and Tilden, travel books on Jamaica and Haiti, a volume on Swedenborgian philosophy, and his autobiography. Bigelow married Jane Tunis Poultney in 1850 and died in New York on December 19, 1911. Bigelow, John, *Retrospections of an Active Life* 5 vols. (1905–1913); Clapp, Margaret, *Forgotten First Citizen: John Bigelow* (1947; 1968); *DAB*, 2:258; McCullough, David, *The Path between the Seas* (1977); *New York Times*, December 23, 1911; Willson, Beckles, *America's Ambassadors to France, 1777–1927* (1928).

BINGHAM, JOHN ARMOUR (1815–1900). Born January 21, 1815, in Mercer, Pennyslvania, John A. Bingham attended Franklin College (Pennsylvania) for two years, studied law, and was admitted to the bar in 1840. He practiced law in Ohio and then served as district attorney in Tuscarawas County (1846–1849) and as a Republican member of the U.S. House of Representatives (1855–1863). In 1864, he became a major and judge advocate in the Union army; after the war, he helped frame the Fourteenth Amendment and was a special judge advocate in the trial of the Lincoln conspirators. Reelected to the House in 1864, he emerged as a leader in the movement to impeach President Andrew Johnson. In 1873, he was appointed minister to Japan, a post he held for nearly twelve years. There he worked to alter the Convention of 1866, a commercial treaty with Japan signed jointly by the United States, Great Britain, France, and the Netherlands as an expression of the "cooperative" policy. Bingham, however, felt that the cooperative policy was detrimental to both Japanese and American interests, but the treaty revisions he sought were not finalized until several years after he had left Japan. In addition, he mediated a settlement between China and Japan resulting from an armed clash during the Korean revolution in 1884. After his return from Japan, Bingham lived with his wife, Amanda, in Cadiz, Ohio, where he died March 19, 1900. *DAB*, 2:277; Dennett, Tyler, *Americans in Eastern Asia* (1922); *FR* (1885); 553–60; *NCAB*, 9:375; Pletcher, David, *The Awkward Years* (1962).

BINGHAM, ROBERT WORTH (1871–1937). Robert Worth Bingham was born November 8, 1871, in Orange County, North Carolina, and graduated from the family-owned Bingham School in 1888. He attended the Universities of North Carolina and Virginia and received a law degree from the University of Louisville, 1897. In 1896, he married Eleanor E. Miller, who died in 1913; three years later he married Mary Lily Kenan Flagler, the widow of Standard Oil magnate Henry M. Flagler, who soon died and left him $5 million. His third wife was Aleen M. Hilliard. After a career in local Louisville politics, Bingham purchased the *Courier-Journal* and *Louisville Times* newspapers in 1919, and his editorial support of the League of Nations* led to close friendships with Franklin D. Roosevelt and Cordell Hull.* Originally considered for secretary of state, Bingham was appointed ambassador to Great Britain in 1933. His chief objective was to negotiate a reciprocal trade agreement, and although his favoring lower tariffs and closer U.S.-British ties made him popular in London, the treaty was never finalized during his four-year tenure. Bingham differed with Roosevelt and Hull on the issue of pound and dollar stabilization, but his friendship with British leaders served as an effective counter to the growing isolationist* sentiment in the United States. He returned to the United States in November 1937 and died in Baltimore on December 18 of that year. Chandler, David L., *The Binghams of Louisville* (1987); *New York Times*, December 19, 1937; *Courier-Journal* (Louisville), December 19–21, 1937.

BIRCH, THOMAS HOWARD (1875–1929). Thomas H. Birch was born September 5, 1875, in Burlington, New Jersey, had no college education, and joined his father in the carriage-manufacturing business in 1893. He married Helen L. Barr in 1902 and remained in the family business until 1913, meanwhile developing a close friendship with William Jennings Bryan*. Birch is credited with bringing Bryan and Woodrow Wilson together in a conciliatory meeting in 1911. With Wilson's victory in 1912 and his subsequent appointment of Bryan as secretary of state, Birch was soon on the way to Portugal as minister, a post he held until 1922. He was a popular diplomatic representative, acting also as business adviser to several Portuguese ministries. The Portuguese government asked that Birch be kept in his post permanently and gave him the Order of Christ, its highest civilian honor, as well as the Order of the Tower and Sword. When Birch returned to the United States, he organized the Trust Company of North America in New York City, headed a syndicate of Spanish capitalists investing in New York real estate, and founded the Club Vasco da Gama to encourage close U.S.–Portuguese ties. He died February 1, 1929, in New York. *NCAB*, 22:390; *New York Times*, February 2, 1929.

BIZONIA, political and economic arrangement in occupied Germany, 1946–1948. *Bizonia* is a term describing the unifying of the British and American occupation zones in Germany in 1946 in areas such as economic and agricultural policy, food distribution, transportation, and communication. A formal financial agreement, the Bevin-Byrnes Bizonal Fusion Agreement, was signed in December 1946 and went into effect in January 1947. In late 1947 and early 1948, talks were held concerning the creation of a political structure for Bizonia; these discussions evolved into more generalized talks for a West German federal government, a move Gimbel suggests prompted the Berlin blockade.* Feis, Herbert, *From Trust to Terror* (1970); *FR* (1947), 2:909–76; Gimbel, John, *The American Occupation of Germany* (1968).

BLACK, JEREMIAH SULLIVAN (1810–1883). Born January 10, 1810, in Somerset County, Pennsylvania, Jeremiah S. Black attended local schools, read law, and was admitted to the bar in 1830. The following year he became deputy attorney general in Somerset County and in 1842 began a judicial career as a common pleas court judge. In 1851, he was elevated to the Pennsylvania Supreme Court. After six years there, he was appointed U.S. attorney general under President James Buchanan.* Black was secretary of state in Buchanan's cabinet from December 1860 to March 1861, following the resignation of Lewis Cass.* His main duty was to instruct U.S. diplomatic representatives in Europe to do what they could to prevent European recognition of the Confederacy. Most of the rest of his time was spent dealing with the secession crisis. After 1861, Black was a Supreme Court reporter and a practicing lawyer in York, Pennsylvania. He was a member of the Pennsylvania Constitutional Convention, 1872–1873, and represented Samuel J. Tilden before the Electoral Commission in 1877. Black married Mary Forward in 1836 and died in York on August 19, 1883. Brigance, William N., *Jeremiah Sullivan Black* (1934, 1971); *DAB*, 2:310; *NCAB*, 5:5.

BLACK, SHIRLEY TEMPLE (b. 1928). Shirley Temple was born in Santa Monica, California, on April 23, 1928, made her movie debut at age three, and became one of America's most popular movie stars in the 1930s and early 1940s. She retired from her film career in 1947, married Charles Black, her second husband, in 1950, and made occasional television appearances in the 1950s but grew increasingly interested in Republican politics. She lost a race for the U.S. House of Representatives in 1967, but, in 1969, she was named a member of the U.S. delegation to the United Nations,* sitting in the General Assembly. From 1970 to 1972, she was the deputy chairman of the U.S. delegation to the UN Conference on the Environment, and from 1973 to 1974, she served as a member of the U.S. Commission for the UN Educational, Scientific, and Cultural Organization. In 1974, Black's appointment as ambassador to Ghana was criticized in the United States because her Hollywood background was considered inappropriate training for diplomacy, and in Ghana because of its political nature. In the two years at that post, however, she became popular for her opposition to apartheid, support of women's rights, and ability to mix well with Ghanaians and participate in their cultural heritage. She left Ghana in 1976 and became the chief of protocol for the State Department, 1976–1977, where her duties were social and ceremonial. In 1981, she served on the U.S. delegation to the UN commission on African refugee problems. Fasulo, Linda M., *Representing America: Experiences of U.S. Diplomats at the UN* (1984); *New York Times*, July 14, 1976; *Washington Post*, June 11, August 1, 1976; *WWA* (1986–1987):293.

BLACK WARRIOR, AFFAIR OF (1854). The *Black Warrior* was an American coastal steamer that made frequent stops at Havana and informally had been exempted from the standard procedure of making a cargo manifest. But on February 28, 1854, Spanish officials abruptly changed their custom and demanded a manifest without allowing the captain time to prepare one. The ship and its cargo were seized but later released after the payment of a $6,000 fine. The incident caused a diplomatic uproar between Spain and the United States. Minister to Spain Pierre Soulé* was instructed to demand satisfaction, which led to a great flurry of diplomatic correspondence before affairs were settled in May 1855. The incident contributed to the anti-Spanish attitude of the Ostend Manifesto* in October 1854. Janes, Henry L., "The *Black Warrior* Affair," *American Historical Review* 12 (January 1907); Learned, Henry B., "William Learned Marcy," in Bemis, Samuel F., ed., *American Secretaries of State and Their Diplomacy*, vol. 6 (1928).

BLAINE, JAMES GILLESPIE (1830–1893). Probably the most prominent Republican politician in America between the Civil War and 1900, James G. Blaine was twice secretary of state (1881, 1889–1892). Born in West Brownsville, Pennsylvania, on January 31, 1830, he graduated from Washington College in Pennsylvania in 1847, married Harriet Stanwood in 1850, and taught until 1854. In that year, he purchased an interest in the *Kennebec Journal* (Augusta, Maine) and worked on its editorial staff until 1860. He served in the Maine legislature, 1859–1863, the U.S. House of Representatives, 1863–1876 (and was Speaker, 1869–1876), and the U.S. Senate, 1876–1881. He was the Republican candidate for president in 1884 and was conspicuously mentioned for the nomination every election year between 1876 and 1892. In 1881, he was secretary of state in the brief administration of James A. Garfield. In his several months in office, he intervened in the War of the Pacific,* without success, initiated his program of Pan-Americanism,* and involved himself in some acrimonious conflict with Great Britain over a Central American isthmian canal. Eight years later, under President Benjamin Harrison, Blaine had more time to implement his ideas. He moved Pan-Americanism from rhetoric to reality by sponsoring the First International Conference of American States (1889),* which laid the groundwork for the Bureau of American Republics,* and by supporting reciprocal treaty arrangements with Latin American nations. He tried again to persuade Britain to give up its rights under the Clayton-Bulwer Treaty (1850)* and permit the United States to build an isthmian canal; he supported the annexation of Hawaii; and he joined in the movement to suppress the African slave trade. The *Baltimore* affair,* with Chile, flared up in 1891, and Blaine took a tolerant attitude toward the Chileans until Harrison overruled him and adopted a tougher policy. By his second stint as secretary of state, Blaine's health was beginning to fail, and, according to Tyler, his loss in the 1884 presidential election seemed to have robbed him of some of his enthusiasm and self-confidence. Hence, his diplomacy was more conservative and restrained. Finally, worn down by Bright's disease and lung problems, Blaine resigned in late 1892 and died in Washington on January 27, 1893. His congressional career, but not his diplomacy, are recounted in his *Twenty Years of Congress*, 2 vols. (1884–1886). *DAB*, 2:322; Lockey, J. B., "James Gillespie Blaine," in Bemis, Samuel F., ed., *American Secretaries of State and the Diplomacy*, vols. 7–8 (1928); Stanwood, Edward, *James G. Blaine* (1972); *New York Times*, January 28, 1893; Tyler, Alice Felt, *The Foreign Policy of James G. Blaine* (1927).

BLAIR, WILLIAM McCORMICK, JR. (b. 1916). Born in Chicago on October 24, 1916, William McCormick Blair, Jr., graduated from Stanford (B.A., 1940) and the University of Virginia (LL.B., 1947), with his education interrupted by service in the U.S. Army Air Force intelligence in the China-Burma-India theater during World War II. After law school, Blair practiced law in Chicago, became an administrative assistant to Governor Adlai Stevenson* in 1950, and after 1952 continued to work with Stevenson in Democratic party affairs. Reward came with the return of the Democrats to power in 1961; Blair was named ambassador to Denmark. There for three years with no major diplomatic problems to confront, he toured the country widely and enjoyed considerable popularity. From 1964 to 1967, he was ambassador to the Philippines, a tour marked by a controversial incident in 1965 in which two U.S. Marines were accused of shooting two Filipinos on a U.S. military base. Blair, without much evidence, suggested that the Filipinos might have been pilfering mortar shells. The Philippine government demanded jurisdiction over the accused marines and a renegotiation of a 1947 treaty dealing with the legal status of military personnel in the islands. In August 1965, an agreement was signed giving Philippine courts more jurisdiction in this area. In October 1967, Blair retired to private life with his wife, the former Catherine Gerlach, whom he married in 1961. From 1968 to 1972, he was general director of the John F. Kennedy Center in Washington. Since 1972, he has practiced law in Washington, D.C. *New York Times*, December 25, 1964, August 11, 1965, September 23, 1967; *WWA* (1986–1987):257.

BLAKE, MAXWELL (1877–1959). For nearly thirty years, Maxwell Blake was America's diplomatic representative in Morocco, allowing U.S. diplomacy to profit from his long experience in that part of the world. He was born November

15, 1877, in Kansas City, Missouri, attended Scaritt College and the University of Missouri, and married Ruth Maxwell in 1906, the same year he entered the Foreign Service as U.S. consul in Funchal, Madeira. From 1907 to 1910, he was consul at Dunfermline, Scotland, and after a short stint in 1910 as consul general* in Bogotá, he went to Tangier as consul general late that same year. In 1912, he became chargé d'affaires ad interim in Morocco; in 1917, his title was changed to agent and consul general. He left Morocco briefly to serve as consul general in Australia, 1923–1925, but returned to Morocco, 1925–1940, as diplomat agent and consul general. In addition, he was a member of various international commissions relative to Moroccan affairs, including the Tax Urbaines, the Sanitary Council, and the Commission of Public Works. He was on the staff of the U.S. delegation to the Paris Peace Conference, 1919.* In Morocco, Blake observed and wrote valuable reports on the establishment of the French protectorate after 1912 and the dictatorial rule of Marshal Louis H. G. Lyautey, and protected German and Austrian interests during World War I. He recommended the establishment of a condominium for Tangier in the 1920s, when Spain and France were both claiming jurisdiction, and in the 1930s, when the area was in serious economic trouble. The policy of the United States had little direct interest in Morocco, but Blake did what he could to maintain an Open Door Policy* for trade there. He left Morocco in August 1940 and died in January 1959. Hall, Luella J., *The United States and Morocco, 1776–1956* (1971); Stuart, Graham, *The International City of Tangier* (1955); *WWWA*, 3 (1951–1960): 81.

BLANCKÉ, WILTON WENDELL (1908–1971). A native of Philadelphia, where he was born on June 29, 1908, Wilton W. Blancké graduated from Haverford College in 1929 and worked in the advertising business for N. W. Ayer and Company until 1942, spending the last nine years in Ayer's Buenos Aires office. He joined the embassy staff in Buenos Aires in 1942, specializing in political affairs. After the war, he worked in the Office of the Allied Military Government in Berlin, and in 1946, he became a Foreign Service officer. Between 1946 and 1960, he held various staff and consular jobs in Havana, Hanoi, and Vientiane, Laos, as well as a stint as Burmese desk officer in the State Department. In 1960, he became the first U.S. ambassador to the newly independent Congo (Brazzaville) and soon after was accredited to the Central African Republic, Chad, and Gabon. He served at the Congo post until 1963 and at the others until late 1961. After his return from Africa, Blancké was a senior inspector in the Foreign Service, 1963–1965, and consul general, Mexico City, 1965–1966. He retired in 1966 and died March 14, 1971, in Washington, D.C. Blancké was married to Frances Elizabeth Nichol in 1952 and was the author of *The Foreign Service of the United States* (1969). *New York Times*, March 15, 1971; *WWWA*, 5 (1969–1973):66.

BLATCHFORD, RICHARD MILFORD (1798–1875). Blatchford, born in Stratford, Connecticut, on April 23, 1798, was a graduate of Union College (1815); he became the financial agent of the Bank of England in the United

States in 1826 and soon moved to the Bank of the United States in the same capacity. In 1855, he served a term in the New York State Assembly and was active in recruiting Union troops at the outbreak of the Civil War. In August 1862, he was appointed minister to the Papal States and remained at the post from November 1862 until May 1863, keeping close contact with Pope Pius IX and transmitting assurances of the pope's Union sentiments to the State Department. Blatchford went to London in May 1863 and worked with William M. Evarts,* who was there as a special envoy to try to halt the construction of Confederate ships in Great Britain. After the war, he returned to New York City and took an active interest in the public parks of the city before his death in Newport, Rhode Island, on September 4, 1875. *DAB*, 2:359; Stock, Leo Frances, ed., *United States Ministers to the Papal States: Instructions and Despatches, 1848–1868* (1933); *New York Times*, September 5, 1875.

BLISS, ROBERT WOODS (1875–1962). Born in St. Louis on August 5, 1875, Robert Woods Bliss was a graduate of Harvard (1900). In 1901, he became secretary to the governor of Puerto Rico and in 1903 joined the Foreign Service as consul in Venice. Other minor posts followed between 1904 and 1916: in St. Petersburg, Brussels, Buenos Aires, and Paris. From 1916 to 1920, he was counselor* at the Paris embassy, where he dealt principally with alien relief matters. Returning to Washington in 1920, Bliss was named protocol officer for the Washington Conference (1921–1922),* with the rank of third assistant secretary of state. He was minister to Sweden for four uneventful years (1923–1927) and capped his career with appointment as ambassador to Argentina (1927–1933). In Argentina, Bliss was particularly concerned with the escalation of Anglo-American trade rivalry in 1931–1932 and urged the Hoover administration to win Argentine favor by reducing import duties, but nothing was done before Bliss left his post in 1933. From 1942 to 1945, Bliss returned to the State Department as a special consultant and special assistant to the secretary of state. In later years, Bliss lived in Dumbarton Oaks, near Washington D.C., was an art collector, and served on the Harvard University Board of Overseers from 1939 to 1945. He married Mildred Barnes in 1908 and died in Washington on April 19, 1962. *New York Times*, April 20, 1962; Peterson, Harold F., *Argentina and the United States, 1810–1960* (1964); *WWWA*, 4 (1961–1968):94.

BLISS, TASKER HOWARD (1853–1930). Born in Lewisburg, Pennsylvania, on New Year's Eve, 1853, Tasker Howard Bliss attended the University of Lewisburg (now Bucknell) before going to West Point, from which he was graduated in 1875. He then began an army career that included teaching at West Point (1876–1880) and at the Naval War College (1885–1888) and service as military attaché in Madrid (1897–1898). He was chief of the Cuban customs service during the U.S. occupation, 1899–1902, and negotiated the Cuban reciprocity treaty (1902). He served in the Philippines, 1905–1909, and was a military representative on the Supreme War Council in 1917, where he urged the disarmament of Germany. He was a member of the American delegation to the Paris Peace Conference, 1919,* but had relatively little influence in the deliberations and was not highly enthusiastic about the Treaty of Versailles.* From 1920 to 1927, he was governor of the National Soldiers' Home; during most of this time, he was also a member of the editorial board of *Foreign Affairs*. He married Eleanora E. Anderson in 1882 and died in Washington, November 9, 1930. *DAB*, 3:88; *Foreign Affairs* 9 (January 1931): 339–40; *FR: Lansing Papers*, 2:199–306; *New York Times*, November 9, 1930; Palmer, Frederick, *Bliss, Peacemaker: The Life and Letters of General Tasker Howard Bliss* (1934).

BLOCKADE, form of limited warfare. A blockade is a maneuver wherein ports thought to harbor naval or commercial vessels of importance are blocked, physically by ships or, occasionally, symbolically by decree, so that vessels emerging may legally be captured or destroyed if capture is resisted. The first modern blockade was declared by Napoleon in his Berlin Decree* and Milan Decree,* directed at the British Isles. During World War I, Great Britain extended the notion of blockade by requiring ships from neutral ports to submit to search at designated ports. The Germans developed submarine warfare partly as an anti-blockade measure. Blockades, in international law, are acts of war; they must be declared, and notification must be made to neutral countries. Hence, during the Cuban missile crisis,* the United States placed a "quarantine" on Cuba, avoiding the belligerent implications of "blockade." Gamboa, Melquiades J., *Elements of Diplomatic and Consular Practice* (1966); Pratt, William V., "Warfare in the Atlantic," *Foreign Affairs* 19 (July 1941): 729–36.

BLOUNT, JAMES HENDERSON (1837–1903). Born September 12, 1837, in Jones County, Georgia, James Henderson Blount received an A.B. degree from the University of Georgia in 1857, read law, and was admitted to the bar. He served four years as a cavalryman in the Confederate army and from 1873 to 1893 was a U.S. congressman from Georgia. In early 1893, he was appointed a special commissioner to Hawaii to investigate the governmental crisis there in which a group of Americans led by Sanford B. Dole had overthrown Queen Liliuokalani, established a provisional government, and requested annexation. Blount discovered the complicity of the Americans in the revolution and wrote a report advising against annexation. President Grover Cleveland followed the recommendation; the provisional government collapsed, and Blount went on to serve as minister to Hawaii from May to August 1893. After his return, Blount lived with his wife, the former Eugenia Wiley, in Macon, Georgia, where he practiced law until his death on March 8, 1903. *DAB*, 2:388; *FR* (1894), Appx. 2:467–1150; Lanier, Osmos, Jr., "'Paramount' Blount: Special Commissioner to Investigate the Hawaiian Coup, 1893," *West Georgia College Studies in the Social Sciences* 11 (June 1972): 45–55; McWilliams, Tennant S., *The Mission and the Burden: New Southerners Face the World, 1877–1947* (1987); Wriston, H. M., *Executive Agents in American Foreign Relations* (1929).

BLOW, HENRY TAYLOR (1817–1875). Henry T. Blow was born in South-ampton, County, Virginia, on July 15, 1817; he moved to Missouri and graduated from St. Louis University in 1835. He studied law but became involved in the business of lead mining and railroads, opening mines in southwest Missouri and becoming president of the Iron Mountain Railroad. Republican politics beckoned; Blow was a member of the Missouri State Senate (1854–1858), a delegate to the Republican national convention (1860), and a U.S. congressman (1863–1867). In 1861, he was named minister to Venezuela but never served in the post, choosing to run for Congress in 1862. He was elected and served two terms before returning to his mining interests in 1867. In 1869, he was appointed minister to Brazil, where he was popular but served less than two years because of the debilitating climate. From 1871 to 1874, he was active in business in St. Louis and a strong supporter of the Mississippi River bridge project of James B. Eads.* He was married to Minerva Grimsley, fathered twelve children, and died of "congestion of the brain" in Saratoga Springs, New York, on September 11, 1875. *DAB*, 2:391; *New York Times*, September 12–13, 1875; *WWWA*, Historical Volume, p. 61.

BOAL, PIERRE DE LAGARDE (1895–1966). Boal was born in Thonons-les-Baines, France, on September 29, 1895, and served in World War I as a member of the Lafayette Escadrille. He joined the State Department in 1919 and by 1931 had become chief of the West European Division. He was also a secretary or counselor in various posts before his appointment as minister to Nicaragua in 1941. The following year he was appointed ambassador to Bolivia, serving until February 1944. While at La Paz, Boal was accused of trying to impede passage of a Bolivian labor code for miners that was considered pro-labor. He was exonerated by Secretary of State Cordell Hull,* who explained that Boal had only made inquiries regarding the effect of the code on the production costs of strategic materials the United States was then obtaining from Bolivia. Boal retired from the State Department in 1948 and died in Washington on May 24, 1966. *New York Times*, May 25, 1966; *WWWA*, 4 (1961–1968): 97.

BOER WAR (1899–1902). The Boer War took place in southern Africa between British troops and Afrikaaner, or Dutch settlers and represented an effort to bring the Boer Republics (Transvaal, Orange Free State) into the British Empire. The war was unpopular in England and in much of the rest of the world. Many Americans condemned British participation in this war, but there was no official protest due to the comparable war Americans were fighting in the Philippines and the renewed cordiality between the United States and Great Britain. The American government showed no sympathy for the Boer cause, rebuffing Boer attempts to induce the United States to act as mediator. Campbell, Charles S., *Anglo-American Understanding, 1898–1903* (1957); Farwell, Byron, "Taking Sides in the Boer War," *American Heritage* 28 (April 1976): 20–25, 92–97; Ferguson, James H., *American Diplomacy and the Boer War* (1939); Noer, Thomas J., *Briton, Boer and*

Yankee: The United States and South Africa, 1860–1914 (1978); Pakenham, Thomas, *The Boer War* (1979); Perkins, Bradford, *The Great Rapprochement* (1968).

BOGOTÁ CONFERENCE (Ninth International Conference of American States, 1948). This inter-American conference, the first since World War II, proved disappointing to Latin American leaders when their hopes of substantial commitments of U.S. aid were dashed. The conference was significant, however, because the charter of the Organization of American States* was written, setting up a body for regional consultation and a military Advisory Defense Committee. The charter also included standard proscriptions forbidding intervention or the use of economic or political coercion by one state against another, adopted over U.S. objections. The conference was marked by outbreaks of violent rioting, the *Bogotazo*, touched off by the assassination of a well-known Colombian Liberal party leader, Jorge Eliécer Gaitan. Viewed by many as Communist inspired, the *Bogotazo* resulted in a resolution, ''The Preservation and Defense of Democracy in America,'' at the conference and helped usher in a period of strong anticommunism in U.S. policy toward Latin America. Connell-Smith, Gordon, *The United States and Latin America* (1975); *FR* (1948), 9:1–72; LaFeber, Walter, *America, Russia and the Cold War, 1945–1984* (1985).

BOHLEN, CHARLES EUSTIS (1904–1974). The grandson of one-time U.S. minister to France James B. Eustis,* ''Chip'' Bohlen became one of the most prominent post–World War II diplomats. Born in Clayton, New York, on August 30, 1904, he graduated from Harvard in 1927 and joined the Foreign Service the following year. He received early training in Soviet affairs, became a friend of George F. Kennan,* and served in the Moscow embassy in 1934–1935 and again in 1938–1941. An interpreter for President Franklin D. Roosevelt at the Teheran Conference (1943),* Bohlen became a White House liaison officer with the State Department after World War II. A State Department counselor* during the Truman years, he worked as an interpreter and wrote the first draft of the Marshall Plan* speech in 1947. In 1953, Bohlen was named ambassador to the Soviet Union, an appointment that stirred controversy because of the opposition of Senator Joseph McCarthy (R., Wisconsin). In Moscow, Bohlen served mainly as a reporter on internal changes in the Soviet Union after the death of Joseph Stalin, advising Secretary of State John Foster Dulles* that neither one-man rule nor extensive political purges would return. Never close to Dulles, who viewed him as the ''symbol of Yalta appeasement,'' Bohlen was transferred to Manila as ambassador to the Philippines in 1957 and returned to Washington to advise Secretary of State Christian A. Herter* on Soviet affairs in 1959. Bohlen was named ambassador to France in 1962, remaining there until 1968, pursuing his chief task of peacefully coexisting with the imperious President Charles de Gaulle. In 1968, he returned to Washington for a brief stint as deputy under secretary of state (political affairs). In that capacity, he served a short time in early 1969 as secretary of state ad interim. Bohlen, who was married to Avis

Thayer, died in Washington, D.C., on New Year's Day, 1974. A highly influential Soviet affairs adviser for twenty years, he was described as the "classic type of diplomat, and although conventional in style, always ready to accept changes in American policy." Bohlen, Charles E., *Witness to History, 1929–1969* (1973); Isaacson, Walter, and Evan Thomas, *The Wise Men: Six Friends and the World They Made* (1986); *New York Times*, July 24, 1955, January 2, 1974; Ruddy, T. Michael, *The Cautious Diplomat: Charles E. Bohlen and the Soviet Union* (1986); *WWA* (1970–1971):215.

BOKER, GEORGE HENRY (1823–1890). The son of noted financier Charles S. Boker, George Henry Boker was born in Philadelphia on October 6, 1823. He graduated from Princeton and studied law but was never admitted to the bar. He toured Europe after college and then embarked on a literary career, writing poetry and Elizabethan-style plays; during the Civil War, he penned patriotic Union poems. In 1871, the Ulysses S. Grant administration honored him with an appointment as minister to Turkey, where he served from March 1872 to May 1875. In Turkey, he negotiated an extradition treaty and a treaty in which the Turkish government recognized that naturalized Turks were American citizens. In 1875, Boker was named minister to Russia; there he developed a personal friendship with the czar and persuaded the Russian government to participate in the Centennial Exposition. Despite his Republican politics, he was replaced in 1878 by a Rutherford B. Hayes administration appointee. After his diplomatic career, Boker served as president of the Union League of Philadelphia, which he had helped establish, and as president of the Fairmount Park Commission, putting to work his interest in park system development. He died on January 2, 1890, in Philadelphia, of an "affection of that throat." Bradly, Edward S., *George Henry Boker* (1927); *DAB*, 2:415–18; Evans, Oliver H., *George Henry Boker* (1984); *FR* (1872–1878), passim.

BOLAND AMENDMENT. This term refers to any of five separate amendments attached to various defense or intelligence appropriation or authorization bills between 1982 and 1986 generally specifying that no funds could be used by the Department of Defense or the Central Intelligence Agency* or other intelligence agencies for the purpose of overthrowing the Nicaraguan government or supporting the military operations of any group opposed to that government. The wording varied slightly in each version of the amendment. One aspect of the Iran-contra scandal* concerned whether the Boland amendment applied to the National Security Council.* When the last Boland amendment expired in October 1986, Congress voted military aid for the contras.* The amendments were named for Congressman Edward P. Boland (D., Massachusetts), chairman of the House Intelligence Committee. *New York Times*, December 19, 1982, June 17, 1987; *Wall Street Journal*, June 4, 1987.

BONN CONVENTIONS (1952). This group of five conventions, signed May 26, 1952, by the United States, France, Great Britain, and the Federal Republic of Germany, proclaimed German sovereignty except in matters such as German reunification, the status of Berlin, and the presence of foreign (North Atlantic Treaty Organization*) troops. Rees, David, *The Age of Containment* (1968).

BONSAL, PHILIP WILSON (b. 1903). Born in New York City on May 22, 1903, Philip W. Bonsal graduated from Yale in 1924. He worked for AT&T (1926–1935) in Cuba, Spain, and Chile, and for the Federal Communications Commission (1935–1937) before entering diplomatic service in 1938. During the next ten years, Bonsal served in minor posts in Havana, Washington, Madrid, and the Hague. In 1948, he became an adviser to W. Averell Harriman,* working to implement the Marshall Plan,* and was attached to the Paris embassy until 1952. Assigned to Washington, 1952–1954, Bonsal was an adviser at the Geneva Conference in 1954,* and the following year embarked on a series of ambassadorial appointments: Colombia, 1955–1957; Bolivia, 1957–1959; Cuba, 1959–1960; and Morocco, 1961–1962. In Colombia, he earned some notoriety for mingling with the political opposition; in Bolivia, he worked during a period of labor and economic difficulties to avert the growth of Communist influence. He was the last U.S. ambassador to Cuba before relations with the Castro regime were broken, and his experience produced a thoughtful book, *Cuba, Castro and the United States* (1971), advocating a restrained and cautiously liberalized U.S. policy toward the island. Bonsal, who married Margaret Lockett in 1929, retired from the State Department in 1965 and lives in Washington, D.C. *CB* (1959):38–39; Welch, Richard E., *Response to Revolution: The United States and the Cuban Revolution, 1959–1967* (1983); Woods, Randall B., *The Roosevelt Foreign Policy Establishment and the ''Good Neighbor'': The United States and Argentina, 1941–1945* (1979); *WWA* (1976–1977):330.

BOOTH, RALPH HERMAN (1873–1931). Born September 29, 1873, in Toronto, Ralph H. Booth moved to Detroit in 1881 and was educated in public schools there. At fifteen, he went to work for the Detroit National Bank but in 1892 began a newspaper career with the *Detroit Tribune*. He moved to the *Chicago Journal* in 1894 and became that paper's editor in a few years. In 1904, he was back in Detroit as editor and publisher of the *Tribune*, but the following year, he became president and publisher of the *Grand Rapids Herald* and from that point built up a substantial newspaper chain in Michigan, Booth Newspapers. In 1917–1918, he was vice-president of Associated Press. A Republican, Booth was appointed minister to Denmark by the Hoover administration in 1930. In Copenhagen, his home became the center of the city's social life, and his daughter's wedding was the most elaborate event of the season. Booth's warm hospitality was a boon to Danish-American relations. However, he was ill frequently, and on May 11, 1931, he died in Salzburg, Austria, of kidney and heart ailments. Booth was married to Mary M. Batterman in 1906 and was an art collector; he left a large bequest to the Detroit Museum of Art. *New York Times*, June 21, 1931; *WWWA*, 1 (1897–1942):117.

BORAH, WILLIAM EDGAR (1865–1940). For many years a leading Republican senator and chairman of the Foreign Relations Committee, William E. Borah was closely involved in virtually every foreign policy question from World War I until 1940. Born near Fairfield, Illinois, on June 29, 1865, he attended the University of Kansas, 1885–1887, but never graduated. He read law and was admitted to the bar. He moved to Boise, Idaho, set up a criminal law practice, became active in Republican party affairs, and married May McConnell in 1895. By this time he had developed a reputation as an orator, and after a losing race for a House seat in 1896 and one for a Senate seat in 1902, he was elected to the Senate in 1906 and remained there until his death in Washington on January 19, 1940. He was a member of the Foreign Relations Committee from 1913 to 1940 and its chairman from 1925 to 1933. An "irreconcilable"* and opponent of collective security* in the League of Nations* debate, Borah did favor certain peace and outlawry movements in the 1920s although without a great deal of sincerity. He opposed U.S. intervention in Latin America, persistently favored diplomatic recognition of Soviet Russia, was distrustful of European powers, and was unhappy with the various treaties that emerged from the Washington Conference (1921–1922).* In the 1930s, he was less influential because of his age, which helped to make his positions on issues inflexible, and the fact that the Republicans were the minority party after 1933. Furthermore, according to Maddox, many of his foreign policy stands may have been the product of his self-image as a "fearless dissenter" and his lack of trust in the executive branch's handling of foreign affairs. *DAB*, Supp. 2:49; Johnson, Claudius D., *Borah of Idaho* (1936); Maddox, Robert James, *William E. Borah and American Foreign Policy* (1969); McKenna, Marian C., *Borah* (1961); Porter, David L., *The Seventy-sixth Congress and World War II, 1939–1940* (1979); Vinson, John Chalmers, *William E. Borah and the Outlawry of War* (1957).

BORLAND, SOLON (1808–1864). Born September 21, 1808, in Suffolk, Virginia, Borland studied medicine privately in North Carolina and set up a medical practice in Little Rock, Arkansas, in 1832. He practiced in Little Rock for sixteen years, entered Democratic politics, and served five years in the Senate, where he took a considerable interest in foreign affairs. In 1853, he was appointed minister to Central America by the Pierce administration. He worked aggressively to increase American (at the expense of British) influence on the isthmus, evidently favoring American annexation of Central America. He negotiated a commercial treaty with Nicaragua and was involved in an incident in Greytown, Nicaragua, in which he protested the arrest of an American and was slightly injured by a hostile Nicaraguan crowd in Greytown. His protestations to President Pierce brought the U.S.S. *Cyane* to the scene to demand an official apology and

$24,000 in damages. When Nicaraguan officials refused to apologize or pay, the American vessel destroyed the town. Borland left Central America in 1854 and returned to medical practice in Little Rock. When the Civil War began, he organized the Third Arkansas Cavalry, serving first as a colonel and then as a brigadier general. On January 31, 1864, Borland died near Houston, Texas. *DAB*, 2:464; Scroggs, William, *Filibusters and Financiers* (1916); Williams, Mary W., *Anglo-American Isthmian Diplomacy* (1916); Woods, James M., "Expansion as Diplomacy: The Career of Solon Borland in Central America, 1853–1854," *Americas* 40, 3 (January 1984): 399–416.

BORTON DRAFTS (1947). Named for their author, Dr. Hugh Borton, a special assistant to the director of the Office of Far Eastern Affairs in the State Department, the Borton Drafts were efforts to write a Japanese peace treaty. Borton wrote the original draft in March 1947 and made revisions in August 1947 and January 1948. The proposed treaty stressed the prevention of Japan's military resurgence; it forbade Japan to have a military force or even military potential and called for a Council of Ambassadors to oversee Japan for twenty-five years. The State Department and others criticized the Borton Drafts for their vengeful tone and their ignorance of cold war* realities and for leaving Japan defenseless. There was a feeling that the United Nations* would not be able to provide adequate protection for Japan. The Borton Drafts and the reactions to them are significant in revealing the range of State Department attitudes toward the defeated enemy just two years after the end of World War II. Wheeler-Bennett, John A., and Anthony Nicholls, *The Semblance of Peace* (1972).

BOWEN, HERBERT WOLCOTT (1856–1927). Born February 29, 1856, in Brooklyn, Herbert Bowen was educated by a private tutor in Europe, graduated from Yale in 1878, and attended Columbia Law School with Theodore Roosevelt. His diplomatic career began in 1890 with his appointment as a consul to Barcelona; two years later he was promoted to consul general,* remaining in Barcelona until the outbreak of the Spanish-American War. During the war, he was a consultant to the Departments of State and War. Named minister to Persia in 1899, Bowen spent two uneventful years in the Middle East. In 1901, he was appointed minister to Venezuela, a post he held until 1905. In Caracas, he played an important role in the Venezuelan dispute (1902–1903),* when Germany and Great Britain demanded payment of debts and backed up their demands with a naval blockade* and the bombardment of Puerto Cabello. When Venezuelan dictator Cipriano Castro jailed German and British nationals in retaliation, Bowen secured their release. Castro asked Bowen to initiate negotiations to settle the dispute; these talks resulted in the signing of protocols in February 1903, referring the matter to the international tribunal at the Hague, which decided in 1904 in favor of the creditors. President Roosevelt wanted to be the arbitrator at the Hague; when Bowen insisted on the privilege, his indiscretion ultimately cost him his post. After leaving the diplomatic service, Bowen retired to a farm in Connecticut and wrote his memoirs, *Recollections Diplomatic and Undiplomatic*

(1927). Bowen was married twice and died May 29, 1927, in Woodstock, Connecticut. Bowen, H. W., "Queer Diplomacy with Castro," *North American Review* 184 (1907): 577–80; *DAB*, 2:505; Munro, D. G., *Intervention and Dollar Diplomacy in the Caribbean 1900–1921* (1964); *New York Times*, May 30, 1927.

BOWERS, CLAUDE GERNADE (1878–1958). A noted historian, Claude G. Bowers was born November 20, 1878, in Hamilton County, Indiana, and had a high school education. He began his career as a journalist with the *Indianapolis Sentinel* in 1901 and wrote editorials and columns for various papers, including the *New York World* and *New York Journal*, until 1933. A Democrat and noted speaker, he delivered the keynote addresses at the 1920 and 1928 national conventions. In 1933, he began a diplomatic career, serving as ambassador to Spain, 1933–1939, and ambassador to Chile, 1939–1953. In Spain, he reported on the civil war from St. Jean-de-Luz, where the diplomatic community resided, and worked to repatriate Americans who had fallen into the hands of the Franco forces. Opposed to Franco, he was recalled in 1939 so that the United States could grant diplomatic recognition to Franco-led Spain. In Chile, Bowers worked during World War II to persuade the government to break off relations with Axis powers. As a historian, Bowers dealt with Reconstruction (*The Tragic Era*, 1929) and progressivism (*Albert Beveridge and the Progressive Era*, 1932), among other topics. He also wrote accounts of his diplomatic missions (*My Mission to Spain*, 1954; *Chile Through Embassy Windows*, 1958) and an autobiography (*My Life*, 1962), edited by his daughter, Patricia Bowers. Married to Sybil McCaslin in 1911, Bowers spent the last years of his life lecturing and writing; he died in New York City on January 21, 1958. Jones, Kenneth Paul, *U.S. Diplomats in Europe, 1919–1941* (1981); *New York Times*, January 22, 1958; Traina, Richard P., *American Diplomacy and the Spanish Civil War* (1968).

BOWLES, CHESTER BLISS (1901–1986). Born in Springfield, Massachusetts, on April 5, 1901, Chester Bowles graduated from Yale in 1924 and founded a highly successful advertising firm, Benton and Bowles, in 1929. In 1942, he became Connecticut director of the Office of Price Administration and in 1943 went to Washington as a member of the War Production Board, remaining in that post until 1946. His first contact with diplomacy came in 1947 when he was a special assistant to the secretary-general of the United Nations.* Elected governor of Connecticut in 1949, Bowles served one term before his appointment as ambassador to India in 1951. There until March 1953, he worked to secure for India a well-administered U.S. aid program; it came with a $54 million Point Four* grant, which was raised to $200 million just before his departure and then cut back again just after his departure. He returned to public life in 1958 as a U.S. congressman from Connecticut, serving one term. In 1961, he was named under secretary of state in the Kennedy administration but was out of step with the younger administration policy makers who were advocating a more militaristic diplomacy. Later in 1961, Bowles was made an ambassador-at-large, a position in which he made speeches on administration policy, worked on United Nations issues and traveled to the Middle East, Asia, and Africa. In July 1963, he replaced John K. Galbraith* as ambassador to India. His second mission to that country lasted six years and involved much consultation with Jawaharlal Nehru and other Indian leaders over disputes concerning Kashmir and China. He championed increased U.S. military aid for India but without success; India ultimately obtained it from the Soviet Union. Following his retirement in 1969, Bowles wrote his memoirs, *Promises to Keep: My Years in Public Life, 1941– 1969* (1971), and a volume on his second ambassadorship to India, *Mission to India* (1974). The author of several other books on politics and international relations, Bowles married Dorothy Stebbins in 1934 and died in Essex, Connecticut, on May 25, 1986. Burke, Lee H., *Ambassador at Large: Diplomat Extraordinary* (1972); *New York Times*, May 26, 1986; *WWA* (1976–1977):348.

BOWLIN, JAMES BUTLER (1804–1874). Born in Fredericksburg, Virginia, on January 16, 1804, James B. Bowlin was educated to be a lawyer and gained admittance to the Virginia bar in 1826. After seven years of practice in Greenbrier County, Virginia, he moved to St. Louis, where he continued his law practice and gradually became involved in Democratic politics, serving a term in the Missouri legislature (1836–1837) and four terms in the U.S. House of Representatives (1843–1851). From 1855 to 1857, he was minister to New Granada, an uneventful mission. In 1858, however, he went to Paraguay as commissioner to resolve the *Water Witch* affair, concerning a U.S. ship that had sailed into Paraguayan waters in 1853 although ordered not to, and had been fired upon. One person had been killed, and the incident had caused losses to U.S. Consul Edward A. Hopkins and American businessmen, who had been closed down by the government. Bowlin was instructed to demand an apology and indemnification for the sailor killed, reparations for business losses, and ratification of an 1853 navigation treaty or negotiation of a new one. With the assistance of Argentine President Justo José de Urquíza and his adviser, General Tomás Guido, Bowlin successfully completed his mission, which included a new treaty, arbitration* of Hopkins's damage claim, the requisite apology, and a $10,000 idemnity payment. Bowlin returned to his interests in St. Louis in 1859 and died there July 19, 1874. Peterson, Harold F., *Argentina and the United States, 1810–1960* (1964); *WWWA*, Historical Volume, p. 67.

BOXER REBELLION (1900). In an attempt to shore up her weakened regime, the Chinese empress dowager, T'zu Hsi, supported the Boxers ("The Secret Order of the Harmonious Fists"), a secret society, in a terrorist campaign being waged against foreigners in China in the late 1890s. In 1900, having allied the Chinese army with the Boxers, the empress ordered that all foreigners, including the diplomatic corps, be killed. The Legation Quarter in Peking was surrounded and besieged for two months while Japanese and Western troops made their way inland, ultimately saving much of the foreign community. American diplomatic contact with Chinese leaders opposed to the empress resulted in the suppression of the Boxers in such a way that it perpetuated the idea that the terrorist group had been acting without official sanction. This was significant, for it precluded war against the Chinese government, which would certainly have resulted in the partition of the country. The emerging Open Door Policy,* as expressed in the second round of Open Door Notes reiterated this policy of preserving the territorial integrity of China. Cohen, Warren I., *America's Response to China* (1971); Dennett, Tyler, *Americans in Eastern Asia* (1922); *FR* (1900), 77–382.

BRADEN, SPRUILLE (1894–1978). A major figure in U.S.–Latin American relations in the 1930s and 1940s, Spruille Braden was born March 13, 1894, in Elkhorn, Montana, and graduated from Yale in 1914. Between 1914 and 1920, he was involved in various business ventures in Chile, including copper mining and loan negotiations for the government. In addition, he negotiated a large contract between Westinghouse and the Chilean army. He returned to the United States in 1925 to take over and reorganize the Monmouth Rug Company of New Jersey; seven years later, he organized the Rehabilitation Corporation. In 1933, he was delegate to the Seventh Pan-American Conference* in Montevideo, and from 1935 to 1938, he led the U.S. delegation at the Chaco Peace Conference in Buenos Aires. He was named ambassador to Colombia in 1939 and served there until 1942, alerting the Colombian government to the danger to itself and to the Panama Canal of German aviation interests. In 1942, Braden moved to Cuba, where he spent the rest of the war years as ambassador. He was hostile to the Cuban dictator, Fulgencio Batista, and spoke out in ways that Cubans and some State Department officials thought constituted interference in Cuban domestic affairs. By far his most controversial tenure was as ambassador to Argentina in 1945. Although he was there from only May until September, Braden stirred considerable controversy by speaking out publicly in league with forces opposing Juan Perón, then emerging as Argentina's new leader. Braden defended his actions as merely reflecting his strong belief in democracy and inter-American security, but the State Department concluded that his actions were causing resentment among Argentinians and strengthening extremist groups. Braden was brought back to Washington and made assistant secretary of state for American republic affairs, a post he held until 1947, when he resigned under pressure in the wake of a bitter dispute with George Messersmith,* his successor at the Buenos Aires embassy. In private business after 1947, Braden published his memoirs, *Diplomats and Demagogues*, in 1971. Twice married, he died in Los Angeles on January 10, 1978. Gellman, Irwin F., *Roosevelt and Batista* (1973); *NCAB*, F:532; Peterson, Harold F., *Argentina and the United States, 1810–1960*; Ronning, Neale C., and Albert P. Vannucci, ed., *Ambassadors in Foreign Policy* (1987); *New York Times*, January 11, 1978; Welles, Sumner, *Where Are We Heading?* (1946).

BRADLEY, CHARLES WILLIAM (1807–1865). Charles William Bradley was born in New Haven, Connecticut, on June 27, 1807, and graduated from the General Theological Seminary in New York City in 1830. An Episcopalian, he was rector at various churches in Connecticut in the 1830s and 1840s and served a term as Connecticut secretary of state (1846–1847). He traveled abroad from 1847 to 1849 and was appointed consul* at Amoy, China, in 1849. Five years later, he moved to Singapore as consul, and in 1857 he became consul at Ningpo, China. In 1857, he negotiated a treaty with Siam and the following year accompanied the Pei-ho expedition into the interior of China, one of the first Americans to go there. In 1859, Bradley was the senior member of the American Claims Commission dealing with China. He resigned from government service in 1860 to work in the Imperial Chinese Customs at Hankow, where he stayed until 1863. Returning to the United States, Bradley died in New Haven on March 8, 1865. He built a collection of Chinese books, which he bequeathed to the American Oriental Society. *DAB*, 2:568.

BRENTANO, THEODORE (1854–1940). Born March 29, 1854, in Kalamazoo, Michigan, and educated in both Europe and the United States, Theodore Brentano became a lawyer and settled in Chicago, where he was elected judge of the superior court in 1890. He sat on the bench for thirty-one years, and his decisions concerning eminent domain enabled the city to develop its lakefront. In 1922, President Warren G. Harding appointed him the first postwar minister to Hungary. He served for five years, building cordial U.S.–Hungarian relations by his support of the Treaty of the Trianon (1922)* and an Allied loan to Hungary in 1923. Brentano died in Larchmont, New York, on July 2, 1940. *New York Times*, July 3, 1940.

BREST–LITOVSK, TREATY OF (1918). This treaty terminated hostilities between the Central Powers* and Russia, thus marking Russia's exit from World War I. In the treaty, Russia lost control over substantial territory on its western frontier and promised to demobilize and evacuate troops from areas around the Baltic Sea. The signatories promised not to propagandize against each other, to exchange prisoners, or to renew diplomatic relations after ratification. According to Wheeler-Bennett, the treaty negotiations inspired Woodrow Wilson's Fourteen Points* in an effort to prevent a separate peace, and the harsh terms imposed on Russia steeled the will of the Western powers. *FR* (1917), Russia 1:404–77; Wheeler-Bennett, John W., *Brest-Litovsk, The Forgotten Peace, March, 1918* (1938).

BRETTON WOODS CONFERENCE (1944). Also called the United Nations* Monetary and Financial Conference, this meeting was chaired by Secretary of the Treasury Henry Morgenthau. Lasting from July 1 to July 22, 1944, it brought together delegates from most of the Allied nations. From the Bretton Woods Conference came recommendations to establish the International Monetary Fund* (IMF) and the International Bank for Reconstruction and Development* (IBRD). The monetary fund, based largely on the ideas of Harry Dexter White,* was designed to prevent the recurrence of the fiscal war of the 1930s by setting up regulations preventing, among others, competitive currency devaluations for the purpose of international trade advantages. In addition, the IMF would be funded to provide stocks of currencies available to members who needed such currency for international exchange purposes. The IBRD, or World Bank, as it came to be known popularly, was to be funded by IMF members to provide a source of money for nations interested in long-range capital improvements while still promoting private investments. Not intended to begin operation until after a postwar period of adjustment, the IBRD began organizing in June 1946, but its global potential was hindered by the refusal of the Soviet Union to cooperate in either it or the IMF. The United States had hoped that these agencies would help with postwar reconstruction and economic stabilization and lead to a general expansion of world trade. Eckes, Alfred E., *The Search for Solvency* (1975); *FR* (1944), 2:106–35; LaFeber, Walter F., *America, Russia, and the Cold War, 1945–1984* (1985); McNeill, William H., *American, Britain, and Russia* (1953); Van Dormael, Armond, *Bretton Woods* (1978).

BREWSTER, KINGMAN, JR. (1919–1988). Born June 17, 1919, in Long-meadow, Massachusetts, Kingman Brewster graduated from Yale in 1941. After marriage to Mary Louise Phillips in 1942 and service in the naval reserve during World War II, he attended Harvard Law School, receiving a degree in 1948. That year, he became assistant general counsel in the office of the U.S. special representative in Europe; after a year, he returned to the United States and became a research associate in economics at MIT. In 1950, Brewster began teaching law at Harvard; he moved to Yale in 1961 and assumed the duties of provost in addition to his teaching. Three years later, Brewster was chosen president of Yale, a post he held until his appointment as ambassador to Great Britain in 1977. While his Yale presidency had been marked by his controversial sympathy for the anti–Vietnam War movement and civil rights activism, his tenure in London was, by contrast, almost reclusive. Brewster played a public role in the diplomacy concerning the ending of white minority rule in Rhodesia but otherwise confined his activities to the normal administrative, social, and ceremonial functions of the embassy. From 1981 to 1986, Brewster practiced law, and in 1986, he became master of University College at Oxford University. He died November 8, 1988, near Oxford, of a cerebral hemorrhage. He was the coauthor (with William M. Katz) of *Anti-Trust and American Business Abroad* (1959) and the author of *Law of International Transactions and Relations* (1960). *New York Times*, March 17, 1977, March 19, 1979, November 9, 1988; *Washington Post*, April 8, 1977; *WWA* (1986–1987):334.

BRIGGS, ELLIS ORMSBEE (1899–1976). Born December 1, 1899, in Watertown, Massachusetts, Ellis O. Briggs graduated from Dartmouth College in 1921 and taught three years at Robert College in Istanbul before embarking on a career in the State Department. He held minor posts between 1926 and 1944 and then was appointed to a series of eight ambassadorial posts: Dominican Republic (1944–1945), Uruguay (1947–1949), Czechoslovakia (1949–1952), Korea

(1952–1955), Peru (1955–1956), Brazil (1956–1959), Greece (1959–1962), and Spain, for which he was nominated in 1961 but declined for health reasons. In addition, he was minister-counselor in Chunking (1945) and director of the Office of American Republic Affairs and a close adviser to Spruille Braden* (1945–1947). Of these missions, the more significant were: Czechoslovakia, where he was stationed shortly after the Communist coup and played a major role in gaining the release of imprisoned correspondent William Oates but did not help general relations with numerous anti-Communist statements; Korea, where he worked with General Mark Clark in preparing for the armistice ending the Korean conflict and signed a $700 million economic recovery pact; and Brazil, where he negotiated for the acquisition of a missile tracking station on a Brazilian-owned island in the Atlantic Ocean. In retirement, Briggs wrote a book of commentary and reminiscence, *Farewell to Foggy Bottom* (1964), and indulged his love of game bird hunting, which had produced an earlier book, *Shots Heard Round the World* (1957). He married Lucy Barnard in 1928 and died in Gainesville, Georgia, on February 21, 1976. *New York Times*, February 23, 1976.

BRINKMANSHIP, diplomatic catchword of the 1950s. This term was applied to aspects of U.S. diplomacy carried on during John Foster Dulles's* tenure as secretary of state (1953–1959). According to Dulles, it meant "the ability to get to the verge without getting into war." Under this policy, the United States would go to the brink of war to prevent future limited wars or to gain important diplomatic objectives. The adversary would understand clearly the consequences of noncompliance, and, in this context, brinkmanship was linked closely to the presumptive deterrence of massive retaliation, According to Rees, brinkmanship in practice was not so clear-cut as brinkmanship in rhetoric, but applications of it found their way into the diplomacy ending the Korean War and settling the Quemoy-Matsu crises* of 1954 and 1958. Rees, David, *The Age of Containment* (1968); Spanier, John W., *American Foreign Policy since World War II* (1977); Weintal, Edward, *Facing the Brink* (1967).

BRISTOL, MARK LAMBERT (1868–1939). A career officer in the navy, Mark Lambert Bristol is noteworthy for his involvement in U.S.–Turkish affairs. He was born in Glassboro, New Jersey, April 17, 1868, and was an 1887 graduate of the U.S. Naval Academy. By 1913, he had risen to the rank of captain, having seen service in the Spanish-American War and in the Far East. At the end of World War I, he was a member of the International Armistice Commission in Belgium. From 1919 to 1927, Bristol was U.S. high commissioner to Turkey, the principal American representative there at a time when normal relations were broken. His effective diplomacy and cordial relationship with the dominant Nationalist party led to the resumption of normal diplomatic ties, the restoration of trade, and an arrangement for claims considerations. In addition, Bristol was involved in postwar relief work, in evacuating Americans from Smyrna in 1922 during a clash between Greeks and Turks there, and in the Lausanne Conference

(1922) as an American observer. From 1927 to 1929, Bristol was in charge of the Asiatic fleet; he engaged in diplomacy with the Chinese Nationalists, who had recently come to power. He retired in 1932. He was married in 1908 to Helen Beverly Moore and died May 13, 1939, in Washington. *DAB*, Supp. 2:65; *FR* (1919–1927), passim; *New York Times*, May 14, 1939.

BRITISH NORTHWEST COMPANY, fur-trading company. The British Northwest Company (sometimes referred to as the Northwest Company) was headquartered in Fort William (Oregon Territory) after 1803. From this vantage point, the company traded with and influenced Indians, excluded American traders, took over the American fur-trading post of Astoria in 1813, and generally stood as the major British commercial presence in the Oregon Territory. After the Convention of 1818,* which provided for joint occupation of the territory, the Northwest Company remained an important economic enterprise as long as there was an adequate supply of furs. Burt, A. L., *The United States, Great Britain and British North America* (1940).

BROWN, JAMES (1766–1835). James Brown was born September 11, 1766, near Staunton, Virginia, graduated from William and Mary College, and studied law. After becoming a lawyer, he moved to Lexington, Kentucky, in 1789, and served a term as Kentucky secretary of state (1792). Around 1804, Brown moved to New Orleans, where he continued the practice of law while serving as district attorney and secretary of the territory of Orleans. Between 1806 and 1808, he wrote the Civil Code for the Louisiana Territory; from 1813 to 1817 and again from 1819 to 1823, he was a U.S. senator from Louisiana. His knowledge of Louisiana affairs and French prompted his appointment in 1823 as minister to France, where he could refute an anticipated counterclaim to the Louisiana Territory. Although this never materialized in any serious manner, Brown, who served until 1829, dealt with the problems caused by Spain's rebellious American colonies, urged France to halt slave trading, and pressed spoliation claims against the French government. He retired after his return from France and died April 7, 1835, in Philadelphia. *DAB*, 3:126; Willson, Beckles, *America's Ambassadors to France, 1777–1927* (1928).

BROWN, JOHN PORTER (1814–1872). A nephew of Commodore David Porter, John Porter Brown was born in Chillicothe, Ohio, August 17, 1814. In 1835, he joined his uncle, then chargé d'affaires* in Turkey, and held various legation offices in Constantinople the rest of his life. From 1858 to 1872, he was secretary of the legation and served as chargé on nine different occasions. Brown is best remembered for his involvement in the Koszta Affair, concerning a Hungarian refugee named Koszta who came to the United States in 1851, declared his intention to become a U.S. citizen, and then went to Turkey, where he was arrested on orders from the Austro-Hungarian government. Brown felt that Koszta deserved U.S. protection and ordered the U.S. naval commander to demand his surrender by means of an ultimatum. The Austrians relented, turned Koszta over to French authorities; a naval bombardment was prevented, and ultimately Koszta returned to the United States. Brown's actions, though they exceeded his authority, were upheld by the State Department. Brown was also influential in persuading Turkey to send its first diplomatic mission to the United States, in 1850. Brown, who was married to Mary A. P. Brown, acquired a reputation as a fine Oriental scholar, translating various Turkish literary classics into English. He died in Constantinople on April 28, 1872. *DAB*, 3:139; Klay, Andor, *Daring Diplomacy: The Case of the First American Ultimatum* (1957).

BRUCE, DAVID KIRKPATRICK ESTE (1898–1977). The only American to have served as ambassador to all three of the major European nations of Great Britain, France, and Germany, David K. E. Bruce was born in Baltimore on February 12, 1898. He attended Princeton, 1915–1917, but left school to serve in the army during World War I. After the war, he attended law school at both the University of Virginia (1919–1920) and the University of Maryland (1920–1921) and gained admittance to the bar in 1921. A practicing lawyer, tobacco farmer, and state legislator during the interwar years, Bruce married Alisa Mellon, the daughter of Andrew Mellon, in 1926 (they were divorced in 1945) and wrote *Revolution to Reconstruction* (1939), a study of the first sixteen presidents. In 1941, he began a full-time career in public service as an organizer and then European chief of the Office of Strategic Services (OSS). In 1947, he was named assistant secretary of commerce, but the following year saw him in Paris as a Marshall Plan* administrator. His Marshall Plan work in France had helped avert economic catastrophe there and had made him well known, so that his appointment as ambassador to France in 1949 was popularly received. He remained at that post until 1952, and although his strong support of the European Defense Community (EDC),* which France opposed and eventually rejected, earned him criticism from some quarters, he remained an influential diplomat and became well versed in French wines and history. Under the Eisenhower administration, Bruce served first as an American observer at the EDC and then as the American representative to the European Coal and Steel Community before going to Bonn as ambassador to Germany in 1957. His two years in the German post were less publicly fruitful; he worked closely with Konrad Adenauer, to the exclusion of other German political and business leaders. From 1961 to 1969, Bruce was ambassador to Great Britain, relatively placid years in Anglo-American relations. In 1970, he was named to head the U.S. delegation to the Paris peace talks to end the war in Vietnam; although the public talks achieved nothing, Bruce worked behind the scenes to help facilitate the secret talks. In 1972, after President Richard M. Nixon's trip to the People's Republic of China had removed some of the diplomatic barriers, he became the first U.S. liaison officer in Peking, remaining there until 1974, when he returned to the United States to accept his last assignment, that of ambassador to the North Atlantic Treaty Organization,* 1974–1976. Known throughout his career as a versatile, tactful, and knowledgeable diplomat, Bruce married Evangeline Bell in 1945 and died in Washington, D.C., on December 5, 1977. *New York Times*, April 16, 1961, December 6, 1977; *WWA* (1976–1977): 422.

BRUSSELS CONFERENCE (1937). This conference, sponsored by the League of Nations,* was called in November 1937 to seek a peaceful solution to the crisis generated by Japan's invasion of China. Attending were delegations representing the signatory powers to the Nine-Power Treaty (1922)* and other interested nations. The United States, through its delegate, Norman H. Davis,* opposed any coercive measures against Japan and the conference adjourned, having done nothing but verbally chastise Japan for violating the Nine-Power Treaty. Borg suggests that U.S. restraint was due to the fear of heightening isolationism* and anti-British feelings in America, but Feis believes that a good chance to settle the conflict in China was lost at Brussels. Borg, Dorothy, *The United States and the Far Eastern Crisis of 1933–1938* (1964); Feis, Herbert, *The Road to Pearl Harbor* (1950); Wiltz, John E., *From Isolation to War* (1968).

BRUSSELS PACT (1948). Signed March 17, 1948, by Great Britain, France, the Netherlands, Belgium, and Luxembourg, this pact was a fifty-year defensive alliance calling for military coordination of strategies and forces to facilitate cooperation in times of crisis. Similar in form to the Rio Treaty (1947),* the pact was suggested by U.S. Secretary of State George C. Marshall.* Soon after the signing, discussions were held to broaden the alliance by including Italy, Norway, Denmark, Iceland, and Portugal, as well as the United States and Canada. American support of (and participation in) the alliance was seen in the Vandenberg Resolution, passed 64–4 by the Senate in June 1948. The end result was the signing in April 1949 of the North Atlantic Treaty (ratified in July 1949), the basis for the North Atlantic Treaty Organization (NATO).* Feis, Herbert, *From Trust to Terror* (1970); Rees, David, *The Age of Containment* (1968); Wheeler-Bennett, John W., and Anthony Nicholls, *The Semblance of Peace* (1972).

BRYAN, WILLIAM JENNINGS (1860–1925). A three-time candidate for president, William Jennings Bryan's work as secretary of state is overshadowed by his more public political involvements. He was born in Salem, Illinois, on March 19, 1860, graduated from Illinois College (1881; A.M., 1883) and from the Union College of Law (1883), and practiced law in Jacksonville, Illinois, until 1887, when he moved to Lincoln, Nebraska. There politics beckoned, and he went to the U.S. House (1891–1895). He won the Democratic nomination for president in 1896, losing the election to William McKinley. Two subsequent losing presidential races (1900, 1908) and years as a nationally famous Chautauqua speaker gave Bryan an elder-statesman image by 1913 and contributed to his appointment as secretary of state in the Wilson administration. Reflecting Wilsonian idealism, Bryan possessed a simplistic view of world problems and a sincere desire to advance the cause of world peace. As a practical result, he negotiated some thirty cooling-off treaties with various nations and supported China in the face of increasing Japanese pressure seen in the Twenty-one Demands.* On the other hand, he joined Wilson's interventionist program in Latin America for the sake of bringing about political reform and acquiring coaling stations. In 1915, he split with Wilson over the course of American neutrality* and resigned when the president made what he considered a belligerent response to Germany after the *Lusitania* sinking. In the last decade of his life, Bryan was a lecturer and writer and in 1925, won headlines in the Scopes trial, opposing famed lawyer Clarence Darrow on the issue of evolution. He died soon after the trial in Dayton, Tennessee, on July 26, 1925. Challener, Richard, "William Jennings Bryan," in Graebner, Norman, ed., *An Uncertain Tradition* (1961); Clements, Kendrick A., *William Jennings Bryan: Missionary Idealist* (1983); Curti, Merle E., *Bryan and World Peace* (1931); Koenig, L. W., *Bryan* (1971); *New York Times*, July 27, 1925.

BRYAN-CHAMORRO TREATY (1916). Negotiated in 1914 by William Jennings Bryan,* secretary of state, and Nicaraguan minister Emiliano Chamorro, this treaty was similar to the Chamorro-Weitzel Treaty (1913).* It gave the United States an option to build an isthmian canal across Nicaragua and rights to build naval bases at the Gulf of Fonseca and on the Corn Islands. For this, the United States was to pay $3 million. Opposed by Costa Rica and El Salvador, upon whose territory construction would impinge, the treaty was not ratified by the Senate until February 1916. Costa Rica then asked the Central American Court* to nullify the treaty, but the United States and Nicaragua claimed that the treaty was outside the jurisdiction of the court. Nicaragua denounced the treaty establishing the court, which soon went out of existence. The Bryan-Chamorro Treaty was abrogated by mutual consent in 1970. Callcott, Wilfrid H., *The Caribbean Policy of the United States, 1890–1920* (1942); *FR* (1916), 811–98; Munro, Dana G., *Intervention and Dollar Diplomacy in the Caribbean, 1900–1921* (1964).

BRZEZINSKI, ZBIGNIEW (b. 1928). A native of Warsaw, Poland, where he was born March 28, 1928, Zbigniew Brzezinski graduated from McGill University in Montreal (B.A., 1949; M.A., 1950) and Harvard (Ph.D., 1953) and was naturalized as a U.S. citizen in 1958. Following graduation from Harvard, he stayed on there as a research fellow (1953–1956) and professor (1956–1960), before moving to a teaching position at Columbia (1960–1977). An occasional State Department consultant, he was a member of the Policy Planning Staff (1966–1968) and director of the Trilateral Commission (1973–1976), a group established to encourage closer ties among the United States, Western Europe, and Japan. In 1977, President Jimmy Carter appointed Brzezinski special assistant to the president for national security affairs, in which position he functioned also as chairman of the National Security Council.* Sometimes outspoken, he is an acknowledged expert on the problems of communism and in the Carter administration was more pessimistic and negative than Secretary of State Cyrus Vance* on Soviet intentions. Brzezinski reduced the size of the National Security staff from Henry Kissinger's* days and on the whole had less public contact than Kissinger did when he occupied the same position. Since 1981, Brzezinski has been a senior adviser at the Center for Strategic and International Studies at Georgetown University. Brzezinski married Emilie Ann Benes in 1955 and is the author of a number of books on foreign policy, including *Soviet Bloc—Unity and Conflict* (1960); *Ideology and Power in Soviet Politics* (1962); *Between Two Ages* (1970); *The Fragile Blossom* (1971); and his memoirs, *Power and Principle* (1983). *New York Times*, December 17, 1976, February 13, 1977, April 17, 1983; *WWA* (1986–1987):376–77.

BUCARELI AGREEMENT (1923). This agreement, named for the Calle Bucareli, where negotiations took place, culminated over two years of efforts to normalize U.S.-Mexican relations. In the agreement, the Mexican government agreed to negotiate claims arising since 1868, once formal recognition was made; the United States agreed to recognize Mexican title to subsoil minerals, as spelled out in the Mexican Constitution of 1917. After the agreement was signed, the United States established formal diplomatic relations with the government of Alvaro Obregón on August 31, 1923, ending several years of severed relations. However, two Mexican laws passed in 1925 violated the agreement, causing another round of ill-will, but patient diplomacy, especially after the 1927 appointment of the popular Dwight Morrow* as ambassador, brought about renewed cordiality. Cline, Howard F., *The United States and Mexico* (1953); Ellis, L. Ethan, *Republican Foreign Policy, 1921–1933* (1968); *FR* (1923), 2:522–67.

BUCHANAN, JAMES (1791–1868). The fifteenth president of the United States (1857–1861), James Buchanan also played an important part in U.S. foreign policy during the mid-nineteenth century as minister to Russia (1832–1833), secretary of state (1845–1849), and minister to Great Britain (1853–1856). He was born on April 23, 1791, near Mercersburg, Pennsylvania, graduated from Dickinson College in 1809, read law, and was admitted to the bar in 1812. He soon developed a successful law practice and a reputation as a good orator while nurturing a political career that began in the Pennsylvania legislature (1814–1816) and moved on to the U.S. House of Representatives (1821–1831). In 1832, he was appointed minister to Russia; in his one year there, he signed a commercial treaty but spent most of his time learning about world affairs. Buchanan returned and won a seat in the U.S. Senate (1834–1845); with the election of James K. Polk as president, he became secretary of state. He was a hardworking, assertive secretary who lent strong support to the expansionist ideas of the president. He negotiated the Oregon Treaty (1846)* with the British minister, Sir Edward Pakenham, ending a threat of war, and moved to meet British advances in the Yucatán and Central America, thus maintaining the integrity of the Monroe Doctrine.* His role in the diplomacy of the Mexican War was minor, and he was unsuccessful in attempts to purchase Cuba from Spain. In London, Buchanan dealt mainly with problems related to the Clayton-

Bulwer Treaty (1850)* but did not successfully resolve any of them. In addition, he had a minor dispute with Secretary of State William L. Marcy* and the British concerning proper dress at court occasions. In 1854, he joined John Y. Mason* and Pierre Soulé* in signing the Ostend Manifesto.* Many of Buchanan's foreign policy involvements, such as the Clayton-Bulwer Treaty problems, continued into his presidency. After 1861, Buchanan, who never married, lived in retirement at Wheatland, his estate near Lancaster, Pennsylvania, where he died June 1, 1868. *DAB*, 3:207; Horton, Rushmore G., *The Life and Public Services of James Buchanan* (1971); Klein, Philip D., *President James Buchanan* (1962); Smith, Elbert B., *The Presidency of James Buchanan* (1975); Thomas, Benjamin P., *Russo-American Relations, 1815–1867* (1930); Willson, Beckles, *America's Ambassadors to England, 1785–1929* (1929).

BUCHANAN, WILLIAM INSCO (1852–1909). One of America's most knowledgeable Latin American diplomats, William I. Buchanan was born September 10, 1852, near Covington, Ohio, and attended country schools in Ohio. After some years as a traveling salesman, he settled in Sioux City, Iowa, working as a wholesaler and then a theater manager; his success led to his helping direct the Iowa exhibit at the World's Columbian Exposition in 1893. A Democrat, Buchanan was named minister to Argentina in 1894, a position he held for six years. There he dealt mainly with tariff questions, worked to prevent Americans from being forced into Argentine military service, and successfully arbitrated an Argentine-Chilean boundary dispute. The years between 1900 and 1906 saw Buchanan serving as a delegate to the Second and Third International Conferences of American States (1901, 1906)* and spending six weeks as minister to Panama (1903–1904), dealing with sanitary matters. Perhaps his most important contribution came in 1907 when he orchestrated the Washington Conference,* and in 1908–1909 when he worked for the reestablishment of diplomatic relations with Venezuela after the overthrow of Cipriano Castro, negotiating the settlement of outstanding claims against American interests. He died in London, October 16, 1909, while acting as agent for the United States in the arbitration* of the Venezuelan claims. Briggs, John E., "Iowa and the Diplomatic Service," *Iowa Journal of History and Politics* 19 (1921): 321–65; *DAB*, 3:219; Peterson, Harold F., *Diplomat of the Americas* (1976).

BUENOS AIRES CONFERENCE (1910). This was the Fourth International Conference of American States, held from July 12 to August 30, 1910, in Buenos Aires in an atmosphere of anti-American feeling due to the recent wave of U.S. interventions in the Caribbean and Central America. Further acrimony at the conference was the result of numerous conflicts among Latin American republics over boundaries and revolutionary activity. However, the United States blocked consideration of political questions, and these controversial matters were not placed on the agenda. With regard to items that were placed on the agenda, the Bureau of American Republics* was reorganized and renamed the Pan-American

Union,* and its functions were more specifically delineated. Other conference actions were limited to inconsequential discussions of old topics such as arbitration of pecuniary claims, patents and inventions, trademarks and copyrights, the Pan-American railway, and the International Sanitary Convention. Brazil initiated private talks with other nations concerning a resolution of gratitude toward the United States because of the protection of the Monroe Doctrine,* but the idea was quietly abandoned when opposition became apparent. Henry White* was the chairman of the U.S. delegation, which also included John Bassett Moore* and Paul S. Reinsch.* Connell-Smith, Gordon, *The United States and Latin America* (1974); *FR* (1910), 12–61; Inman, Samuel Guy, *Inter-American Conferences* (1965); Mecham, J. Lloyd, *A Survey of United States–Latin American Relations* (1965).

BUENOS AIRES CONFERENCE (1936). This conference, suggested by President Franklin D. Roosevelt after the disruptive Chaco War* and in the light of the worsening European situation and the apparent failure of the League of Nations* to take appropriate action, was an attempt to find a way to maintain Western Hemisphere peace and solidarity. The United States, represented at the conference by Roosevelt and Secretary of State Cordell Hull,* introduced a treaty calling for a common policy of neutrality* during a European war. The treaty failed at the conference as some Latin American members of the League of Nations felt that it would compromise their membership obligations in the league. What was passed, in place of the treaty, was a Consultative Pact, in which the signatories recognized an obligation to consult in the event of a threat to peace but to do no more than that. A related protocol, also passed, restated more strongly the policy of nonintervention adopted at the Montevideo Conference (1933).* The treaty Roosevelt sought at this conference was passed as a General Declaration of Continental Neutrality at the Panama Conference (1939). Mecham, J. Lloyd, *A Survey of United States–Latin American Relations* (1965); Wood, Bryce, *The Making of the Good Neighbor Policy* (1961).

BULLITT, WILLIAM CHRISTIAN (1891–1967). William C. Bullitt was born in Philadelphia January 25, 1891, graduated from Yale (1913), and attended Harvard Law School. After a brief career in journalism, Bullitt joined the State Department in 1917 as chief of the Bureau of Central European Information, where he supplied data on the Russian Revolution for President Wilson. He was a member of the U.S. delegation to the Paris Peace Conference* and was sent on a secret mission to Moscow to confer on relevant peace-related issues but was repudiated by Wilson on his return and resigned in bitterness. Disillusioned with the Treaty of Versailles,* he testified against it before the Senate and spent the years from 1919 to 1933 in private business. In 1933, he played a major role in discussions leading to the Roosevelt-Litvinov Agreements* and was rewarded with the appointment as the first ambassador to the Soviet Union, serving there from 1933 to 1936. Though heartily welcomed there, he soon grew sour on the Soviet system, asked pointed questions on sensitive issues, and became increasingly isolated. He was transferred to France in 1936, where for four years, until the fall of France, he was openly opposed to Hitler and supported the Resistance. Bullitt is most significant for his close relationship with Franklin D. Roosevelt, whom he served as a European adviser, pointing out the need to resist Nazi belligerence. During the war, he was a special representative of the president in North Africa and the Middle East. After 1945, Bullitt was an avid anti-Communist and supporter of Chiang Kai-shek and the Nationalist Chinese. He wrote, with Sigmund Freud, the controversial *Thomas Woodrow Wilson* (1967), a psychohistory poorly received by Wilson scholars and Freud partisans alike. Bullitt died of leukemia February 15, 1967, in Neuilly, France. He was married twice; both marriages ended in divorce. Brownell, Will, and Richard N. Billings, *So Close to Greatness* (1988); Bullitt, Ernesta D., ed., *An Uncensored Diary* (1917); Bullitt, Orville H., ed., *For the President, Personal and Secret: Correspondence between Franklin D. Roosevelt and William C. Bullitt* (1972); Farnsworth, Beatrice, *William C. Bullitt and the Soviet Union* (1967); Gardner, Lloyd C., *Architects of Illusion* (1970); *NCAB*, D:35; *New York Times*, February 16, 1967.

BUNCHE, RALPH JOHNSON (1904–1971). Ralph J. Bunche, the first black American to hold a high post in the United Nations,* was born August 7, 1904, graduated from UCLA (A.B., 1927) and Harvard (A.M., 1928; Ph.D., 1934), and did postdoctoral work (1936–1938). He taught at Howard University from 1928 to 1941 while pursuing his own graduate studies and became an analyst for the War Department's National Defense Program on the eve of World War II. In 1944, he transferred to the State Department, where he was an area expert on Africa and territories. His United Nations involvement began in 1944 when he served as an assistant secretary to the U.S. delegation at the Dumbarton Oaks Conference.* In 1945, he was an adviser to the U.S. delegation at the San Francisco Conference*; the following year, he was a delegate to the first meeting of the General Assembly in London. Bunche became director of the Division of Trusteeship* in the United Nations in 1946 (on loan from the State Department; he became a permanent United Nations official after 1947) and moved to the position of under secretary in 1955 and under secretary-general in 1968. As trusteeship director of the United Nations, he played an important role in preparing for the decolonization movement of the 1950s and 1960s and in mediating an Arab-Israeli settlement, 1948–1949. His main duties as under secretary included directing United Nations peacekeeping forces during and after the Suez crisis* (1956), which he regarded as his most satisfying work, as well as heading the United Nations operation in the Congo crisis (1960),* investigating the civil war in Yemen (1962–1964), and taking charge of the peacekeeping forces in Cyprus (1964) and India and Pakistan (1965). Late in the 1960s, he served as an important adviser to Secretary-General U Thant. Bunche, in failing health for a number of years, retired in June 1971 and died in New York in December of that year. He married Ruth Ethel Harris in 1930, collaborated with Gunnar

Myrdal in writing *An American Dilemma* (1944), and won the Nobel Peace Prize in 1950 for his work on the Palestine accord. Mann, Peggy, *Ralph Bunche: UN Peacemaker* (1975); *New York Times*, December 10, 1971.

BUNDY, McGEORGE (b. 1919). Born in Boston on March 30, 1919, McGeorge Bundy graduated from Yale in 1940 and was a junior fellow at Harvard, compiling a brilliant academic record. During World War II, he served in army intelligence, was an aide to Admiral Alan G. Kirk,* and helped plan the invasions of Sicily and France. After his discharge, Bundy assisted former Secretary of State Henry L. Stimson* in writing his memoirs, *On Active Service in Peace and War* (1948), served briefly as a consultant for the Economic Advisory Commission, and worked as a foreign policy advisor to presidential candidate Thomas E. Dewey and as a political analyst for the Council on Foreign Relations.* In 1949, he joined the political science faculty at Harvard, where he was an extremely popular teacher, and became dean of the faculty in 1953. After working for John F. Kennedy in the 1960 presidential campaign, Bundy became Kennedy's special assistant for national security affairs. According to Halberstam, he was the "traffic cop" in the Kennedy administration, keeping things moving, summarizing situations at meetings, making personnel recommendations, and in general making up for Kennedy's dissatisfaction with Secretary of State Dean Rusk's* passivity. As the main foreign policy adviser for Kennedy and for Lyndon B. Johnson until 1966, Bundy played a major role in the Cuban missile crisis (1962)* and the Dominican intervention (1965)* and in planning the American escalation and bombing in the Vietnam War. In February 1965, he went to Saigon, at the time of the Vietcong attack on the U.S. base at Pleiku, and recommended immediate retaliation. Returning home, he advised "graduated and continuing reprisal" based on the incidence of Vietcong activity. Less a hawk than Walt W. Rostow,* however, Bundy had grown disenchanted with the Vietnam muddle by 1966 and left the administration, becoming president of the Ford Foundation. He married Mary Buckminster Lothrop in 1950, edited a study of Dean Acheson's* foreign policy, *Patterns of Responsibility* (1952), and wrote *The Strength of Government* (1956). In 1979, Bundy left the Ford Foundation and joined the history faculty at New York University. Garraty, John A., ed., *Encyclopedia of American Biography* (1974); Halberstam, David, *The Best and the Brightest* (1972); Karnow, Stanley, *Vietnam: A History* (1983); *WWA* (1986–1987):387.

BUNKER, ELLSWORTH (1894–1984). One of the most prolific U.S. diplomats of the mid-twentieth century, Ellsworth Bunker was born May 11, 1894, in Yonkers, New York, and graduated from Yale in 1916. From 1916 to 1951, he worked for the National Sugar Refining Company, rising to the company presidency in 1940 and to the board chairmanship in 1948. In 1951, he began a diplomatic career with his appointment as ambassador to Argentina, where in a year he restored cordial relations between the Péronistas and the United States.

Next, he was ambassador to Italy, 1952–1953, an uneventful mission. In 1956, he became ambassador to India and Nepal, remaining accredited to India until 1961 and to Nepal until 1959. His forthrightness in India won him the praise of Prime Minister Jawaharlal Nehru and the leading newspapers. His mediation of the Netherlands-Indonesia dispute over West Irian in 1962 earned him a reputation as an effective troubleshooter and led to assignments in problem areas. As a State Department consultant, 1962–1964, he negotiated a settlement of the Panama crisis, 1964. As U.S. representative to the Organization of American States,* he handled the negotiations following the Dominican crisis (1965),* defending U.S. intervention in the Dominican Republic. Bunker was ambassador to (South) Vietnam, 1967–1973, where he worked closely with the government of Nguyen Van Thieu, supported the policy of Vietnamization* and a negotiated settlement to the war, and resigned after the signing of the January 1973 treaty ending U.S. military involvement. Later in 1973, he was named ambassador-at-large; as such, he led the U.S. delegation to Geneva for talks on the Middle East and then in November 1973 began negotiations with Panamanian President Omar Torrijos on a new Panama Canal Treaty. These negotiations, the most complex of his career, culminated in the Panama Canal Treaties* signed on September 7, 1977, and ratified in early 1978 by the U.S. Senate. Bunker was married twice; his second wife was Carol L. Laise, a former ambassador to Nepal and director-general of the Foreign Service. He died September 27, 1984, in Brattleboro, Vermont. Burke, Lee H., *Ambassador at Large: Diplomat Extraordinary* (1972); *CB* (March 1978):12–16; Hung, Nguyen Tien, and Jerrold L. Schecter, *The Palace File* (1986); McMullen, Christopher J., *Mediation of the West New Guinea Dispute, 1962: A Case Study* (1981); *New York Times*, March 31, 1973, February 14, 1977, September 28, 1984; *WWWA* 8 (1982–1985):61.

BUREAU OF AMERICAN REPUBLICS. Created at the Washington Conference (1889),* this agency began operation in 1890 and served primarily to facilitate inter-American commercial relations through the collection and publication of statistics, consular reports, and other matters of use to American businessmen. In 1910, the bureau was replaced by the Pan-American Union,* a much broader-based hemispheric organization. Among the early directors of the bureau were William E. Curtis, William W. Rockhill,* and Frederic Emory. Callcott, Wilfrid H., *The Caribbean Policy of the United States, 1890–1920* (1942); LaFeber, Walter, *The New Empire* (1963); Vivian, James F., "Four Missing Men: Directors of the Bureau of American Republics, 1893–1899," *Inter-American Review of Bibliography* 24 (January–March 1974): 31–49.

BURLINGAME TREATY (1868). Anson Burlingame, former minister to China, negotiated this treaty with the United States on behalf of China. The treaty consisted of eight additional articles to the Treaty of Tientsin* and was of little real significance; the articles simply legalized the conduct of Americans in China and reaffirmed Chinese sovereignty. The treaty and Burlingame's speeches on China at the time of the negotiations wrongly implied that China could and did exercise sovereignty under a centralized government, and, according to Dennett, formed assumptions that would underlie future American relations with China. One article, guaranteeing Chinese immigration to the United States on a most-favored-nation* basis, provoked such opposition that in 1880 a treaty revision was made in which the Chinese agreed that the United States could suspend, but not prohibit, immigration. This led to the passage of Chinese Exclusion Act* in 1882. Anderson, David L., *Imperialism and Idealism* (1985); Cohen, Warren I., *America's Response to China* (1971); Dennett, Tyler, *Americans in Eastern Asia* (1922); Hunt, Michael H., *The Making of a Special Relationship: The United States and China to 1914* (1983).

BURNS, ARTHUR F. (1904–1987). Born in Stanislau, Austria, on April 27, 1904, Arthur Burns came to the United States in 1914 and earned undergraduate and graduate degrees at Columbia University (A.B., 1925; A.M., 1925 Ph.D., 1931). He taught economics at Rutgers from 1927 to 1944 and then was research director of the National Bureau of Economic Research from 1945 to 1953 while simultaneously teaching at Columbia. He continued teaching at Columbia until 1969, meanwhile holding various federal posts concerned with the economy. In 1970, he became the chairman of the Federal Reserve Board of Governors, serving eight controversial years marked by high inflation followed by wage and price controls, a rapid growth in the money supply, and a recession. Between 1978 and 1981, Burns was a scholar at the American Enterprise Institute, returning to government service in the latter year as ambassador to West Germany. In Bonn for four years, Burns cultivated good relations with Chancellor Helmut Schmidt, and his monetary and fiscal knowledge was helpful in the complex economic dealings between the two countries. He rejoined the American Enterprise Institute after his return from Germany and wrote *The United States and Germany* (1986). Married to Helen Bernstein in 1930, Burns died in Baltimore on June 26, 1987. *New York Times*, June 27, 1987; *WWA* (1986–1987):397.

BURT, RICHARD REEVES (b. 1942). Born in Sewell, Chile, on February 3, 1942, of American parents, Richard Burt received a B.A. degree from Cornell in 1969 and a master's from the Fletcher School of Law and Diplomacy in 1972. Prior to joining the State Department in 1981, he was a research associate and assistant director at the International Institute for Strategic Studies in London. An appointee of the Reagan administration, Burt served as director of the Bureau of Politico-Military Affairs and as assistant secretary of state (European and Canadian affairs) before 1985. In these posts, he played a role in various arms control talks, but his moderate views were not always acceptable to conservatives in the administration. In 1985, he was appointed ambassador to West Germany, where he soon established a reputation as an image-conscious, highly visible, candid diplomat. He won praise for his frequent visits to U.S. military bases in Germany and for rekindling ties with the opposition Social Democrat and Green party leaders. In addition, Burt helped plan the U.S. role in the ceremonies for the 750th anniversary of Berlin and for helping win German support for the Intermediate Nuclear Force (INF) Treaty.* In 1985, he married Gahl Lee Hodges. *New York Times*, February 16, 1985, March 16, 1986; *WWA* (1986–1987):402.

BUSH, GEORGE HERBERT WALKER (b. 1924). The son of Senator Prescott Bush (R., Connecticut), George Bush was born in Milton, Massachusetts, on June 12, 1924, and graduated from Yale in 1948 after World War II service as a navy pilot. In 1953, he was a cofounder of the Zapata Petroleum Corporation, which successfully engaged in offshore drilling. After two terms in Congress as a Republican (1967–1971), Bush was appointed ambassador to the United Nations,* where he led U.S. efforts to promote the two-China policy, which failed; Nationalist China was replaced by the People's Republic. Bush left the United Nations in 1973, served a year as chairman of the Republican National Committee before being named chief of the U.S. Liaison Office in Peking, where he replaced David K. E. Bruce.* In 1976, Bush was named director of the Central Intelligence Agency,* holding that position for a year until the incoming administration of President Jimmy Carter appointed its own director. Bush returned to private life as director of the First International Bank of Houston and of First Bancshares of Florida, Inc. In 1980, running on the Republican ticket with Ronald Reagan, he was elected vice-president, serving two full terms and loyally supporting the president's foreign policy agenda. He captured the Republican presidential nomination in 1988 and survived Democratic attempts to link him with the Iran-contra affair* to win the election. He married Barbara Pierce in 1945 and published a campaign autobiography, *Looking Forward*, in 1987. *New York Times*, September 5, November 5, 1974, February 23, 1986; *WWA* (1986–1987):404–5.

BUTLER, NICHOLAS MURRAY (1862–1947). Nicholas Murray Butler, long-time president of Columbia University and internationalist, was born in Elizabeth, New Jersey, on April 2, 1862. He was educated in local public schools and at Columbia, receiving a Ph.D. in 1884. In 1885, he began teaching at his alma mater. Five years later, he was appointed dean, and in 1901 he was chosen president, an office he held until age and blindness forced his retirement in 1945. A conservative Republican, he was a close adviser to Theodore Roosevelt, William Howard Taft, Warren G. Harding, and Calvin Coolidge. He traveled frequently in Europe after 1905 and was well acquainted with European leaders of his time. Butler was a member of the executive committee of the Carnegie Endorsement for International Peace* and from 1925 to 1945 was its president. His major involvement in foreign affairs was with the Kellogg-Briand Pact (1928).* It was his suggestion that the pact be opened to all nations; his efforts in obtaining Pope Pius XI's support for it and in speaking out for its ratification brought him the Nobel Peace Prize in 1931. During the 1930s, he was active in efforts to ease the international economic crisis through regional understandings and colonial systems. He died in New York City on December 7, 1947. Butler, Nicholas Murray, *Across the Busy Years*, 2 vols. (1939–1940); *DAB*, Supp. 4:136; Kuehl,

Warren F., *Seeking World Order: The United States and International Organization to 1920* (1969); *New York Times*, December 7, 1947.

BYRNES, JAMES FRANCIS (1879–1972). Secretary of State (1945–1947) under President Harry S Truman, James F. Byrnes was a native of Charleston, South Carolina, where he was born May 2, 1879. Although he had no college education, he studied law and gained admittance to the bar in 1903. From 1903 to 1907, he edited the *Aiken* (S. C.) *Journal and Review*, but he then turned to law and politics as a career, serving as prosecutor for the Second Circuit of South Carolina (1908–1910) and a U.S. congressman (1911–1925). Defeated for the U.S. Senate in 1924, Byrnes practiced law until 1930, when he won election to that body. A senator for ten years (1931–1941), Byrnes emerged as a Democratic New Deal leader and stepped up to the Supreme Court in 1941. After just a year on the Court, where he was not particularly happy, he resigned to take over the Office of Economic Stabilization (1942–1943) and the Office of War Mobilization (1943–1945). In February 1945, he attended the Yalta Conference* as a personal adviser to President Franklin D. Roosevelt; his notes on the conference later aided Truman. Appointed secretary of state in July 1945, he accompanied Truman to the Potsdam Conference* and as the U.S. member of the Council of Foreign Ministers* attended conferences in Moscow, London, Paris, and New York City in 1945–1946. He represented the United States at the Paris Peace Conference (1946).* Initially Byrnes's policy was based on compromise and openness in order to maintain the wartime alliance. But the principle of compromise soon floundered in the growing hostility between the United States and the Soviet Union after the end of the war. Byrnes's new firmness with the Soviets was evident in the Iran crisis (1946)* and in the making of peace terms with Italy, Romania, Bulgaria, Hungary, and Finland. By early 1947, he was recognized as an important architect of the hardened attitude toward the USSR, which he deemed the best alternative to either acceptance of Soviet expansion or war. In early 1947, Byrnes, whose effectiveness as secretary of state had been limited by his frequent travels, resigned and was succeeded by George C. Marshall.* From 1951 to 1955, he was governor of South Carolina, where he opposed public school desegregation. After 1955, he lived in retirement in South Carolina with his wife, the former Maude Perkins Busch, whom he had married in 1906. Byrnes died in Columbia, South Carolina, on April 9, 1972. Burns, Richard D., "James F. Byrnes," in Graebner, Norman, ed., *An Uncertain Tradition* (1961); Byrnes, James F., *Speaking Frankly* (1947) and *All in One Lifetime* (1958); Clements, Kendrick A., *James F. Byrnes and the Origins of the Cold War* (1982); Curry, George, "James F. Byrnes," in Bemis, Samuel F., ed., *American Secretaries of State and Their Diplomacy*, vol. 14 (1965); Gardner, Lloyd C., *Architects of Illusion* (1970); *New York Times*, April 10, 1972; Ward, Patricia D., *The Threat of Peace: James F. Byrnes and the Council of Foreign Ministers, 1945–1948* (1979).

BYROADE, HENRY ALFRED (b. 1913). A native of Allen County, Indiana, where he was born July 24, 1913, Henry Byroade was a 1937 West Point graduate and earned an M.S. degree from Cornell in 1941. An army officer from 1937 to 1952, he served in the Seabees during World War II and was a military attaché to General George Marshall* during the latter's mission to China, 1945–1946. Promoted to brigadier general in 1946, he oversaw construction of B–29 bases in China and helped direct the Berlin airlift, 1948–1949. Although still in the army, Byroade was named the State Department's director of German affairs in 1949 and remained in that position until 1952, when he left the service. That year, he became assistant secretary of state for Near Eastern, South Asian, and African affairs, where his main concern was trying to ease Arab-Israeli tensions. In 1955, Byroade was named ambassador to Egypt, serving during the early months of the Suez crisis* but losing his post to Raymond Hare* when the Eisenhower administration decided he was too sympathetic to the views of Egyptian president Gamal Abdel Nasser. Following his Egyptian tour, he was ambassador to several other nations: South Africa, 1956–1959; Afghanistan, 1959–1962; Burma, 1963–1969; the Philippines, 1969–1973; and Pakistan, 1973–1977. At most of these posts, Byroade's duties were routine, although in Burma he played a minor role in making contacts with North Vietnam during a U.S. bombing pause in the Vietnam War. Twice married, Byroade spent a year (1962–1963) with the Arms Control and Disarmament Agency. Neff, Donald, *Warriors at Suez* (1981); *New York Times*, January 8, 1950, November 29, 1951, February 8, 1957; *WWA* (1974–1975): 462.

C

CABOT, JOHN MOORS (1901–1981). Born December 11, 1901, in Cambridge, Massachusetts, John M. Cabot graduated from Harvard (A.B., 1923) and Oxford (B.Litt., 1925) before joining the Foreign Service in 1926. He served in minor posts in Callao, Peru; Santo Domingo; Mexico City; Rio de Janeiro; the Hague; Stockholm; Guatemala City; and Washington, D.C., before 1944. In 1945, he became counselor in Buenos Aires; two years later, he went to Belgrade in the same position, where he foresaw Yugoslavia's break with the Soviet Union and advised the State Department to encourage the split. In 1948, Cabot went to Shanghai as consul general*; he was the last to hold that post before the Communist forces prevailed in the civil war. From 1950 to 1952, he was minister to Finland; from 1952 to 1953, he was ambassador to Pakistan, both relatively uneventful tours. After a year in Washington as assistant secretary of state (inter-American affairs), Cabot went to Sweden in 1954 as ambassador, where he won praise for his openness and the public meetings he held throughout the country. He was ambassador to Colombia, 1957–1959, and Brazil, 1959–1961, before moving to the embassy in Warsaw in 1962. As U.S. ambassador to Poland, Cabot led the U.S. negotiating team in talks with representatives from the People's Republic of China in these years prior to the normalization of relations. After a year as deputy commandant of the National War College, 1965–1966, Cabot retired from the Foreign Service. Married to Elizabeth Lewis in 1932, he taught briefly at the Fletcher School of Law and Diplomacy, 1967–1968, and died in Washington, D.C., on February 24, 1981. Cabot wrote a number of books, including *The Racial Conflict in Transylvania* (1926) and *Toward Our Common American Destiny* (1955). *New York Times*, February 28, 1960, October 19, 1962, February 25, 1981; *WWWA*, 7 (1977–1981):91.

CADORE LETTER (1810). On August 4, 1810, Jean, duc de Cadore, French foreign minister, delivered this diplomatic note to U.S. Minister John Armstrong.* In it, Napoleon promised to revoke the Berlin Decree* and Milan Decree* in November 1810 if the British Orders-in-Council* were repealed or if the United States reinstituted sanctions against Britain. The latter happened; nonintercourse was resumed against the British on February 28, 1811. The Cadore letter turned out to be a sham; American ships continued to be seized, and President James Madison* stubbornly refused to change his decision with regard to the British embargo. Egan, Clifford L., *Neither Peace nor War: Franco-American Relations, 1803–1812* (1983); Perkins, Bradford, *Prologue to War* (1961).

CAFFERY, JEFFERSON (1886–1974). Born in Lafayette, Louisiana, on December 1, 1886, Jefferson Caffery graduated from Tulane University in 1906, read law, and was admitted to the bar in 1909. After two years of law practice, he entered the Foreign Service and held minor posts in Caracas, Stockholm, Tehran (where during World War I he represented the interests of various belligerents), Madrid, and Athens. In 1923, he became counselor at the Tokyo embassy and, in the absence of the ambassador, bore most of the brunt of the protests over the Johnson-Reed Act.* After a year (1925–1926) as counselor* in Berlin, Caffery was named minister to El Salvador in 1926, the first in a long series of chief of mission appointments, including minister to Colombia (1928–1933) and ambassador to Cuba (1934–1937), Brazil (1937–1944), France (1944–1949), and Egypt (1949–1955). Because of his political conservatism and pro-business orientation, Caffery found himself embroiled in occasional controversy. In Colombia, he allegedly promoted the granting of a concession to the Mellon oil interests; when the concession was subsequently canceled, National City Bank cut off credit to the Colombian government, also with Caffery's alleged involvement. During his Cuban mission, a U.S.-Cuban reciprocity treaty was passed, and Caffery was criticized for an agreement that seemed to be anti-Cuban. However, the Cuban economy thrived after the implementation of the treaty, Caffery gained the confidence of Cuban dictator Fulgencio Batista, and U.S. influence in Cuban affairs grew. In Brazil, Caffery persuaded President Getúlio Vargas to cast his lot with the Allies during World War II, and in Egypt, despite a fondness for King Farouk, Caffery established good ties with the revolutionary party that overthrew the king. He married Gertrude McCarthy in 1937, retired from the Foreign Service in 1955, and died in Lafayette on April 12, 1974. Dur, Phillip F., "Jefferson Caffery of Louisiana: Highlights of His Career," *Louisiana History 15*, nos. 1, 4 (1974): 9–34, 367–402; Gellman, Irwin F., *Roosevelt and Batista* (1973); *NCAB*, F: 534; *New York Times*, April 15, 1974; Spaulding, E. Wilder, *Ambassador Ordinary and Extraordinary* (1961).

CAIRO CONFERENCE (1943). This World War II conference, code-named SEXTANT, immediately preceded the Teheran Conference (1943)* and was attended by President Franklin D. Roosevelt, British Prime Minister Winston Churchill, and Generalissimo Chiang Kai-shek of China, along with the Anglo-American Combined Chiefs of Staff. Its purpose was twofold: to give Chiang Kai-shek the stature of an important wartime ally and to discuss Far Eastern military strategy and postwar planning. A plan was worked out to open the Burma Road in order to supply China from the south. The conferees also discussed the growing strength of the Chinese Communists. A second phase of this conference met immediately after the Teheran Conference in early December 1943, with Roosevelt and Churchill meeting with Prime Minister Ismet Inonu of Turkey and unsuccessfully trying to persuade him to abandon Turkish neutrality and join the war on the Allied side. Harriman, W. Averell, and Elie Abel, *Special Envoy to Churchill and Stalin, 1941–1946;* McNeill, William H., *America,*

Britain, and Russia (1953); Sainsbury, Keith, *The Turning Point: Roosevelt, Stalin, Churchill and Chiang Kai-shek, 1943* (1985); Wheeler-Bennett, John A., and Anthony Nicholls, *The Semblance of Peace* (1972).

CALHOUN, JOHN CALDWELL (1782–1850). Better known as a U.S. senator and champion of states' rights, John C. Calhoun spent a year as secretary of state in the presidency of John Tyler. Born in what became Abbeville County, South Carolina, on March 18, 1782, he graduated from Yale (1804), studied law at Litchfield, Connecticut, and was admitted to the bar in 1807. He returned to South Carolina where he developed both a plantation in the lowlands and a political career in the South Carolina legislature (1808–1809) and the U.S. House of Representatives (1811–1817). From 1817 to 1825, Calhoun was secretary of war, and from 1825 to 1832, he was vice-president under Presidents John Quincy Adams* and Andrew Jackson. He resigned the vice-presidency in 1832 because of personal and policy differences with Jackson and was elected by the South Carolina legislature to a seat in the U.S. Senate. He became secretary of state in 1844 upon the death of Abel P. Upshur* and remained in that office until the end of John Tyler's presidency. As secretary of state, Calhoun completed work on the treaty for Texas annexation begun by Upshur (which was never ratified) and later aided the congressional joint resolution that did result in the annexation of Texas. He favored a conciliatory policy toward both Mexico and Great Britain and initiated the talks with British Minister Richard Pakenham that led in 1846 to the Oregon Treaty.* After his year in the State Department, Calhoun returned to the Senate, where he became increasingly committed to the doctrine of states' rights. Calhoun married Floride Bonneau Calhoun, his second cousin, in 1811 and died in Washington, while still a senator, on March 31, 1850. Calhoun, John C., *Works*, 6 Vols. (1854–1860); Capers, Gerald S., *John C. Calhoun—Opportunist* (1960); *DAB*, 3:411; Lander, Ernest M., Jr., *Reluctant Imperialists* (1980); Wiltse, Charles M., *John C. Calhoun*, 3 vols. (1944–1951), esp. vol. 3.

CALHOUN, WILLIAM JAMES (1848–1916). Born in Pittsburgh on October 5, 1848, W. J. Calhoun attended Union Seminary in Poland, Ohio, moved to Illinois, read law, and was admitted to the bar in 1875. He practiced law in Danville from 1875 to 1898 and was the western counsel for the Baltimore and Ohio Railroad. In 1897, he was sent to Cuba as a special agent to investigate alleged cruelty in the concentration camps; his report helped influence President William McKinley to go to war with Spain. After a year on the Interstate Commerce Commission, Calhoun returned to law practice, working in Chicago (1900–1905) until his appointment as confidential agent to Venezuela in 1905. There he looked into problems that American concessionaires in the asphalt business were having with the Cipriano Castro government. His success in mollifying these problems led to his selection as minister to China (1909–1913). In China, his work was overshadowed by the activities of the promoters of dollar diplomacy,* but he was able to maintain American influence without intervention through a period of considerable turmoil. Married twice, Calhoun died in Chicago on September 19, 1916. *Chicago Daily Tribune*, September 20, 1916; Crane, David M., and Thomas A. Breslin, *An Ordinary Relationship* (1986); *DAB*, 3:420; *NCAB*, 14:429.

CAMBODIAN INCURSION (1970). This refers to a phase of the war in Vietnam that saw 74,000 U.S. and South Vietnamese troops stage what was called an incursion into Cambodia to root out North Vietnamese and Vietcong forces and supply depots there on the ground that their presence in Cambodia amounted to a foreign invasion of a neutral country. The incursion, which began on April 29, 1970, brought about a highly critical and occasionally violent round of public reaction in the United States, which included the deaths of college students in confrontations at Kent State University and Jackson State College in early May. The stated objectives of the mission were to improve the military position of the South Vietnamese army, enable U.S. troop withdrawal to continue, and help shore up the pro-U.S. Cambodian regime of Lon Nol. After the public criticism, the Nixon administration terminated the Cambodian incursion sooner than planned (by the end of June) and claimed success, which was limited to the capture of some stores of military supplies. The invasion blossomed into a full-scale civil war in Cambodia, however, which ended with a Communist victory and the creation of the state of Kampuchea in 1975. Brandon, Henry, *The Retreat of American Power* (1972); Kissinger, Henry, *The White House Years* (1979); Shawcross, William, *Sideshow: Kissinger, Nixon and the Destruction of Cambodia* (1979); Szulc, Tad, *The Illusion of Peace* (1978).

CAMERON, SIMON (1799–1889). Born March 8, 1799, in Lancaster County, Pennsylvania, Simon Cameron was educated by his mother and a neighbor, who was an Italian poet-librettist. An apprentice printer as a youth, Cameron became editor of the *Bucks County Messenger* in 1821, worked in a Washington printing house, 1822–1824, and bought the *Harrisburg Republican* in 1824. His ownership of the paper soon made him influential in state and national politics and led him into banking and other profitable business ventures. Cameron sat in the U.S. Senate, 1845–1849, became a Republican party leader in Pennsylvania during the 1850s, and returned to the Senate, 1857–1861. President Lincoln appointed him secretary of war in 1861, but, after only a year in the cabinet, he was named minister to Russia and virtually exiled to St. Petersburg because of complaints about his mishandling of the War Department and his advocacy of policies contrary to Lincoln's. Cameron was in Russia only three months (June–September 1862), although he did not formally resign until 1863. While there, he maintained czarist support of the Union, the standard assignment of all U.S. diplomatic representatives in Europe during the Civil War. After the war, Cameron spent ten more years (1867–1877) in the Senate before retiring to his farm at Donegal Springs, near Harrisburg. He was married to Margaret

Brua, and he died at his farm on June 26, 1889. Bradley, Erwin S., *Simon Cameron: Lincoln's Secretary of War* (1966); *DAB*, 3:437.

CAMP DAVID ACCORDS (1978). The result of a process that began in 1974, with the signing of an Israeli-Egyptian disengagement agreement, the Camp David Accords consisted of two documents: a framework for Israeli-Egyptian peace and a framework for a comprehensive Middle East settlement. The document calling for an end to the state of war between Israel and Egypt, the withdrawal of Israeli troops from the Sinai peninsula, and the establishment of "normal and friendly" relations was implemented in the formal Israeli-Egyptian peace treaty, signed in March 1979. Ambassadors were exchanged in February 1980, and Israel removed its last troops from the Sinai in April 1982. The framework for a comprehensive regional peace has never been implemented, largely because of the lack of a solution to the Palestinian question. The Camp David Accords were named for the presidential retreat in the Maryland mountains where President Jimmy Carter mediated the accords between President Anwar Sadat of Egypt and Prime Minister Menachem Begin of Israel in September 1978. This meeting reflected Carter's desire to take a more personally active role in settling Middle East problems, which were a threat to U.S. energy sources and to U.S.-Soviet relations. Camp David was, however, a controversial agreement. Pro-Israeli elements deplored Carter's expression of concern for the Palestinians and the greatly increased amounts of economic and military aid promised to Egypt as part of the arrangement, while the Soviet Union, the Arab League, and the Palestine Liberation Organization* heartily criticized the accords for the enhanced position they provided Israel in both the geopolitics of the region and the security system of the United States. Although Camp David created a better relationship between Egypt and Israel, it did so at the cost of Egyptian influence with its Arab neighbors. Bradley, C. Paul, *The Camp David Peace Process* (1981); Carter, Jimmy, *Keeping Faith* (1982); Quandt, William B., *Camp David* (1986); Rubenberg, Cheryl A., *Israel and the American National Interest* (1986).

CAMPBELL, LEWIS DAVIS (1811–1882). Lewis D. Campbell was born in Franklin, Ohio, on August 9, 1811, worked as an apprentice on the *Cincinnati Gazette* (1828–1831), and then became editor of the *Hamilton* (Ohio) *Intelligencer* in 1831. He was admitted to the bar in 1835 and was a U.S. congressman from Ohio from 1849 to 1859. Service in the Union army as a colonel was followed by his appointment in 1866 as minister to Mexico. Mexico at this time was controlled by the Maximilian regime, and Campbell was instructed by Secretary of State William H. Seward* to go with General William T. Sherman into northern Mexico and make contact with the exiled government of Benito Juárez, which the United States recognized as the legitimate government of Mexico. Failing to reach Juárez, Campbell returned to the United States, set up an office in New Orleans, and, despite Seward's urgings, made no further effort to contact Juárez. Outraged, the Republican leadership in Congress demanded and received Campbell's resignation in 1867. He went back to Ohio, served another term in the House of Representatives (1871–1873), and farmed near Hamilton. He was married to Jane H. Reily and died November 26, 1882, in Hamilton. *DAB*, 3:461; *NCAB*, 13:278.

CANNON, CAVENDISH WELLS (1895–1962). Ambassador to four Mediterranean countries in the 1940s and 1950s, Cavendish Cannon was born February 1, 1895, in Salt Lake City and graduated from the University of Utah in 1915. After service in the marines during World War I, he studied in Paris and Vienna before joining the Foreign Service in 1920. Between 1920 and 1947, Cannon served in a succession of minor posts, including Zurich, Sofia, and Athens. He attended the Moscow Conference (1943)* as an aide to Cordell Hull* and the Potsdam Conference.* In 1947, he received his first ambassadorial post, to Yugoslavia, where he observed Marshal Josip Tito's break with Moscow and handled American relations well in a delicate time. Cannon moved to Syria as minister in 1950, during a time of turmoil in which both his residence and the U.S. Information Service* office were bombed by terrorists. After an uneventful year in Lisbon, 1952–1953, he was named ambassador to Greece, where he successfully negotiated a North Atlantic Treaty Organization* base rights agreement for the United States. His last tour was as ambassador to Morocco, 1956–1958. Cannon then retired and lived with his wife, the former Lily Horsetzky, in Tangier until his death October 7, 1962, near Seville, Spain. *New York Times*, March 26, 1951, December 13, 1954, October 8, 1965.

CARACAS CONFERENCE (TENTH INTERNATIONAL CONFERENCE OF AMERICAN STATES, 1954). This conference, which met from March 1 to March 28, 1954, was dominated by Secretary of State John Foster Dulles,* who introduced a strongly worded anti-Communist resolution, implying that Communist intervention in the Western Hemisphere would call for collective action under the provisions of the Rio Treaty (1947).* After sharp debate, the resolution passed, 17–1, with Guatemala opposing and Argentina and Mexico abstaining. Two months later, a coup engineered by the Central Intelligence Agency* overthrew the Jácobo Arbenz government in Guatemala, which was sympathetic to communism. Although it appeared that the intervention had been undertaken in the light of the Caracas resolution, a meeting of the foreign ministers of the Organization of American States* did not result in the invocation of the resolution. Connell-Smith, Gordon, *The United States and Latin America* (1974); Immerman, Richard H., *The CIA in Guatemala* (1982); Mechan, J. Lloyd, *A Survey of United States–Latin American Relations* (1965).

CARLUCCI, FRANK CHARLES, III (b. 1930). President Ronald Reagan's second secretary of defense, Frank Carlucci came to the Pentagon after a long and varied career in U.S. diplomacy and intelligence. He was born October 18, 1930, in Scranton, Pennsylvania, and graduated from Princeton in 1952. After two years in the U.S. Navy and a year at Harvard Business School, he went to work for the Jantzen Company in Portland, Oregon. In 1956, he joined the State Department and held minor posts in Johannesburg and Kinshasa. In Kinshasa during the Congo crisis (1960–1962),* Carlucci was seriously injured while saving a carload of Americans from a hostile mob. In 1962, he returned to Washington and worked two years at the Congo desk in the State Department. Named chargé d'affaires* to Zanzibar in 1964, he served only a year before being expelled for alleged subversive activities. From 1965 to 1969, he was a political officer in the U.S. embassy at Buenos Aires. In 1969, he returned to the United States and held a succession of nondiplomatic appointments in the Nixon administration: assistant director and director, Office of Economic Opportunity, 1969–1970; associate director and deputy director, Office of Management and the Budget, 1971–1972; and under secretary, Department of Health, Education and Welfare (HEW), 1972–1974, earning a reputation as a good administrator and becoming a close friend of Caspar Weinberger, then secretary of HEW. From 1974 to 1978, Carlucci was ambassador to Portugal, an appointment that reflected Secretary of State Henry Kissinger's* concern with growing Communist influence in the Lisbon government. Although Kissinger wanted to cut off aid to Portugal, Carlucci managed to maintain good relations with government leaders, who remained pro–United States in their policies. After his return from Portugal, Carlucci spent three years (1978–1981) as deputy director of the Central Intelligence Agency,* where he did much to improve morale, and a year (1981–1982) as Weinberger's second in command at the Defense Department. From 1982 to 1986, he was out of government as president of Sears World Trade, but following the revelation of the Iran-contra scandal,* he was brought back to lend respectability to the position of national security adviser. After several months in the White House, Carlucci became secretary of defense upon Weinberger's retirement. *CB* (1981): 49–52; *New York Times*, December 29, 1982, December 3, 1986, August 26–27, November 4, 1987; *WWA* (1986–1987):444.

CARNEGIE, ANDREW (1836–1919). Andrew Carnegie was born in Dumferline, Scotland, on November 25, 1836, and came to Allegheny, Pennsylvania, in 1848. After the Civil War, he built up the largest steel company in the country, earning a vast fortune and retiring in 1901 to a life of philanthropy. By the time of his retirement, he had become a leading foreign affairs spokesman. Carnegie was prominent in the anti-imperialist movement and contributed heavily to the Anti-Imperialist League,* serving as a first vice-president of the organization. His anti-imperialism was based on the expense of maintaining and defending colonies and his feeling that imperialism was damaging to the moral health of America. He was adamantly against the acquisition of the Philippines, but he favored taking Cuba and Puerto Rico and annexing Hawaii because they were closer. Carnegie was also interested in Pan-Americanism,* serving as a delegate to the Washington Conference of 1889* and donating the money to construct the Pan-American Union* building in Washington, D.C. Another major gift established the Carnegie Endowment for International Peace* in 1910. He died August 11, 1919, at his Massachusetts country home. Beisner, Robert L., *Twelve against Empire: The Anti-Imperialists, 1898–1900* (1968); *DAB*, 3:499; Fabian, Larry L., *Andrew Carnegie's Peace Endowment* (1985); Hacker, Louis M., *The World of Andrew Carnegie* (1968); Hendrick, Burton J., *The Life of Andrew Carnegie* (1933; 1969).

CARNEGIE ENDOWMENT FOR INTERNATIONAL PEACE. Founded in 1910 by Andrew Carnegie's* $10 million endowment after persuasive efforts by Hamilton Holt,* Nicholas Murray Butler,* and other internationalists, the Carnegie Endowment strove to abolish war through arbitration* and goodwill. The Carnegie Endowment developed along conservative lines, strongly oriented toward international law and the judicial settlement of conflict, and tried to promote these ends through publications and appeals to other organizations. Its first president was former Secretary of State Elihu Root,* but much of the real work of the endowment was done by James Brown Scott,* who directed the Division of International Law and produced much scholarly research and legal analysis. The Carnegie Endowment sidestepped the League of Nations* controversy in 1910–1920 but later supported league educational activities in the form of grants to scholars, support of college international relations clubs, and subsidization for teaching of courses in international relations. During World War II, the Carnegie Endowment worked with other organizations to win public support for the United Nations.* In recent years, the endowment has published the highly regarded journal, *Foreign Policy*. Divine, Robert A., *Second Chance* (1967); Fabian, Larry L., *Andrew Carnegie's Peace Endowment* (1985); Kuehl, Warren F., *Seeking World Order: The United States and International Organizations to 1920* (1968).

CAROLINE* AFFAIR (1837). In December 1837, the *Caroline*, a supply ship for an incipient American filibustering* expedition into Canada, was sunk on the American side of the Niagara River by a Canadian rebel raiding party. A segment of American public opinion demanded war against Canada, but President Martin Van Buren* sent General Winfield Scott to the area to calm American tempers, while the British put a damper on rebel activity in Canada. Jones. Howard, *To the Webster-Ashburton Treaty* (1977); Pletcher, David, *The Diplomacy of Annexation* (1973).

CARR, WILBUR JOHN (1870–1942). Wilbur J. Carr was born October 31, 1870, near Taylorsville, Ohio. He graduated from the Commercial College of the University of Kentucky (1889) and received a law degree from Georgetown (1894). In 1899, he was awarded an LL.M. degree from Columbian University (now George Washington University). After teaching at Peekskill Military Academy for two years, Carr joined the State Department in 1892 and by 1902 had become chief of the Consular Bureau, where he worked to ensure that consuls were adequately paid and free from political influence. From 1907 to 1909, he became chief clerk of the State Department, and in 1909 he began a fifteen-year tenure as director of the Consular Service. He helped draft the Rogers Act (1924),* combining the consular and diplomatic services, and in the same year was promoted to assistant secretary of state. In this position, he served as the administrative head of the Foreign Service, where he did much to professionalize U.S. diplomatic service. Though he had little background in policymaking, he was several times acting secretary of state and was well regarded for his calm nature and intimate knowledge of departmental procedures. Much of what he did in his thirteen years as assistant secretary was institutionalized in the Foreign Service Act (1946).* As a reward for long and able duty, Carr was named ambassador to Czechoslovakia in 1937 but did little there until he was forced to leave in advance of the German takeover in early 1939. He was married in 1897 to Mary Eugenia Crane, who died in 1911, and in 1917 to Edith Adele Koon. He died in Baltimore, June 26, 1942. Crane, Katherine, *Mr. Carr of State* (1960); *DAB*, Supp. 3:138; *New York Times*, June 27, 1942.

CARTER, BOAKE (HAROLD THOMAS HENRY) (1903–1944). A native of Baku, South Russia, where he was born on September 15, 1903, Boake Carter moved to England as a child, served in a Royal Air Force coast patrol in World War I, and attended public school from 1918 to 1921. After two years as a journalist in Mexico and Central America, where his father had mining interests, Carter took a position with the *Philadelphia Evening Bulletin* and spent the rest of his life in the United States, becoming a citizen in 1933. He broke into radio in 1930 and came into national prominence two years later through covering the sensational Lindbergh kidnapping case. Affiliated with CBS after 1932, he was an influential commentator, interviewing prominent personalities and occasioning some controversy for not checking his facts before broadcasting his stories. Politically, Carter was a staunch isolationist* who maintained that U.S. involvement abroad was meddling and not in the national interest. His persuasive and omniscient-sounding radio voice strengthened extreme isolationist sentiment in the mid-1930s and led to accusations that he favored totalitarianism. Losing his sponsors at CBS in 1938, Carter returned to the air the next year on the Mutual Broadcasting System but with far fewer stations and a newly found religious zeal, a faith he termed "biblical Hebrew." Carter, who married Beatrice Olive Richter in 1924, died November 16, 1944, in Hollywood. His significance lies in his pioneering work as an independent news analyst and commentator. He wrote a number of books, including *Black Shirt, Black Skin* (1935), a popular account of the Italo-Ethiopian War, *I Talk As I Like* (1937), *Why Meddle in the Orient?* (1938), and *Why Meddle in Europe?* (1939). *CB* (1942): 138–41; Culbert, David H., *News for Everyman* (1976); Horowitz, David, *Thirty-three Candles* (1949); *New York Times*, November 17, 1944.

CARTER, HENRY ALPHEUS PEIRCE (1837–1891). A native of Honolulu, Henry A. P. Carter was born August 7, 1837, and attended school in Boston for a short time before entering the mercantile business. In 1862, he became a partner in C. Brewer & Company, which was involved in the development of the Hawaiian sugar industry. Carter was interested in governmental affairs, advocating a system of tariff reciprocity between the United States and Hawaii as a prelude to annexation. In 1874–1875, he was in Washington to negotiate the Hawaiian Reciprocity Treaty* and then traveled to Europe, where he soothed European governments upset at the preferential treatment given the United States and arranged a reciprocity treaty with Germany on terms less favorable than those made with the United States. From 1883 to 1891, Carter was the Hawaiian minister to the United States, defending Hawaiian sugar against U.S. sugar producers and securing in 1887 an extension of the Hawaiian Reciprocity Treaty, known as the Pearl Harbor Treaty,* which granted to the United States the exclusive right to use Pearl Harbor as a coaling and repair station. In 1862, Carter married Sybil Augusta Judd, the daughter of Hawaii's foreign minister. He died in New York City on November 1, 1891. *DAB*, 3:534; Daws, Gavan, *Shoal of Time* (1968); Stevens, Sylvester K., *American Expansion in Hawaii, 1842–1898* (1945).

CARTER DOCTRINE (1980). Announced in January 1980 in the wake of the Soviet invasion of Afghanistan and the beginning of the Iranian hostage crisis,* the Carter Doctrine asserted that the Persian Gulf region was a vital national interest of the United States, which would, if necessary, use force to defend or protect that interest. The creation of the Rapid Deployment Force to provide a quick military response to a crisis in the area soon followed. President Ronald Reagan built on his predecessor's doctrine by attempting to build a barrier from Pakistan to Egypt through military assistance programs, the establishment of U.S. military bases, and even greater support of Israel, while overlooking the destabilizing Palestinian question and other issues of local concern. According to Quandt, the need for such a declaration as the Carter Doctrine had been discussed in the administration for a year before it was announced. Quandt, William B., *Camp David* (1986); Rubenberg, Cheryl A., *Israel and the American National Interest* (1986); *New York Times*, January 24, 1980.

CASABLANCA CONFERENCE (1943). This January 1943 conference was attended by President Franklin D. Roosevelt and British Prime Minister Winston Churchill and their combined chiefs of staff. Soviet Premier Joseph Stalin was invited, but military exigencies kept him in Moscow. Discussions revolved almost entirely around military operations, and several important decisions were made. It was decided to postpone the cross-channel invasion another year, until 1944, and instead proceed with an invasion of Sicily, accelerated bombing of Germany, continued supplying of the Soviet Union and an intensification of both the naval war and the U.S. troop buildup in Great Britain. Other discussions centered on aspects of the Pacific war, the lack of merchant ships, and the political conflict between French leaders Charles de Gaulle and General Henri Giraud. Finally, Roosevelt and Churchill agreed to adopt the concept of unconditional surrender. *FR: The Conferences at Washington, 1941–1942, and Casablanca, 1943*, pp. 487–852; Harriman, W. Averell, and Elie Abel, *Special Envoy to Churchill and Stalin, 1941–1946* (1975), McNeill, William H., *America, Britain, and Russia* (1953).

CASH-AND-CARRY, diplomatic catchword, c. 1930s. This term was first seen in a diplomatic context in neutrality* legislative proposals in November 1935 concerning the arms embargo, trade quotas, and a ban on loans. First suggested by Bernard Baruch,* cash-and-carry required that belligerents trading with American merchants transport their goods in foreign vessels and that title to the goods be transferred (that is, the goods were paid for) before they left American ports. Cash-and-carry was adopted as part of the Neutrality Acts of 1937* and 1939,* although in October 1939 it was limited to the North Atlantic area. It was one of the ways in which U.S. policymakers tried to keep out of European entanglements during the 1930s yet still favor Britain and France, traditional allies, should war come. Divine, Robert A., *The Illusion of Neutrality* (1962); Porter, David L., *The Seventy-sixth Congress and World War II, 1939–1940* (1979); Wiltz, John E., *From Isolation to War, 1931–1941* (1968).

CASS, LEWIS (1782–1866). Secretary of state in the James Buchanan* administration, Lewis Cass was also a minister to France, U.S. senator, and Democratic presidential nominee during a political career that spanned the half-century prior to the Civil War. Born in Exeter, New Hampshire, on October 9, 1782, Cass attended Exeter Academy, read law, and was admitted to the bar in 1802. By this time, he had moved to Ohio, where he set up a law practice, and he served in the Ohio legislature (1806) and as U.S. marshal for the Ohio District (1807–1812). After service in the War of 1812, he was named governor of Michigan Territory in 1813, a position he held until 1831, when he became secretary of war in the cabinet of Andrew Jackson. In 1836, he was appointed minister to France; his six years in Paris are notable for his many anti-British stands on issues. He opposed the French signing of a British-sponsored treaty dealing with the right of search and wrote a controversial pamphlet on the right of search and the slave trade that was implicitly anti-British and led to the French failure to ratify the treaty. This, along with Cass's objection to the Webster-Ashburton Treaty,* earned Cass the enmity of Secretary of State Daniel Webster* and cost him his ministry in 1842. From 1845 to 1848 and from 1849 to 1857, Cass was a member of the U.S. Senate from Michigan; in 1848, he lost the presidency to the Whig candidate, General Zachary Taylor. In 1857, he joined the Buchanan* cabinet as secretary of state, where he won British abandonment of the right-of-search principle and gained a reputation as an expansionist interested in territorial acquisitions in the Caribbean and increased influence in China and in the corresponding reduction of British claims and influence in those areas. In 1860, he resigned over a dispute with Buchanan as to whether the forts in Charleston Harbor should be fortified and whether customs duties should continue to be collected after South Carolina's secession from the Union. In retirement in Michigan, Cass read and wrote history and was an enthusiastic supporter of the Union in the Civil War. Married to Elizabeth Spencer, he died June 16, 1866, in Detroit. *DAB*, 3:562; Dunbar, Willis F., *Lewis Cass* (1970); Willson, Beckles, *America's Ambassadors to France, 1777–1927* (1928); Woodford, Frank B., *Lewis Cass: Last Jeffersonian* (1950).

CASS-YRISARRI TREATY (1857). This treaty, between the United States and Nicaragua and acceded to by Great Britain, granted the United States an "open and neutral transit" through Nicaragua and the right to use troops to protect the route. Felix Belly, a French canal promoter, induced the Nicaraguan government not to ratify the treaty but rather to grant his company a transit concession, which it did. Nicaragua's attitude reflected the anti-American feelings created by the William Walker* filibustering* expedition the preceding year. Einstein, Lewis, "Lewis Cass," in Bemis, Samuel F., ed., *American Secretaries of State and Their Diplomacy*, vol. 6 (1928); Williams, Mary W., *Anglo-American Isthmian Diplomacy, 1815–1915* (1916).

CASTE WAR, YUCATÁN. The Yucatán peninsula of Mexico held attractive potential for annexation to the United States because of its strategic location on the Gulf of Mexico. When Yucatán seceded from Mexico in 1846 and a caste (race) war between Maya Indians and whites broke out, some Americans favored intervention and eventual annexation. In April 1848, Mexican envoy Justo Sierra formally offered the province to the United States, Great Britain, and Spain, but annexationist desire in the United States had faded once the Treaty of Guadalupe-Hidalgo* had been ratified. Neither Britain nor Spain was interested, and the area remained under Mexican control. Pletcher, David, *The Diplomacy of Annexation* (1973); Reed, Nelson, *The Caste War of Yucatan* (1964).

CASTLE, WILLIAM RICHARDS, JR. (1878–1963). Born in Honolulu, June 19, 1878, William R. Castle, Jr., graduated from Harvard (1900), married Margaret Farlow (1902), and worked as an assistant dean at Harvard (1906–1913). From 1915 to 1917, he edited the *Harvard Graduate Magazine*. In 1917, he became director of the Bureau of Communication of the American National Red Cross. In 1919, he entered the State Department as a special assistant, and two years later he was named chief of the Division of West European Affairs. A Republican and acknowledged expert in international affairs, Castle was promoted to assistant secretary of state (1927) and under secretary of state (1931) before leaving the department in 1933. In 1929–1930, he was a special ambassador to Japan during the Naval Arms Conference in London.* He conducted many of the negotiations revolving around the Hoover moratorium* on debt payments and reparations* and foreign acceptance of the plan in 1931. A believer in international cooperation as the route to peace, he supported the Stimson doctrine* on nonrecognition of territorial gains through aggression and opposed diplomatic recognition of the Soviet Union, whose policies he termed "an inciter to war." After 1933, he became a bitter critic of New Deal foreign policy and a staunch isolationist on the eve of World War II. From 1945 to 1952 he served as president of the Garfield Memorial Hospital. He died in Washington on October 13, 1963. *DAB*, Supp. 7:112–13; Ellis, L. Ethan, *Republican Foreign Policy, 1921–33* (1968); Ferrell, Robert H., *American Diplomacy in the Great Depression* (1957); *New York Times*, October 14, 1963; *WWWA*, 4 (1961–1968):161.

CENTRAL AMERICAN COURT OF JUSTICE. Established at the Washington Conference (1907)* in the General Treaty of Peace and Amity, this court was to settle all future Central American disputes. The national legislatures of Guatemala, Honduras, El Salvador, Nicaragua, and Costa Rica each elected one judge for a five-year term, and judges were paid by the court and not by their home governments. Secretary of State Elihu Root* was influential in the creation of the court, which in 1908 helped prevent a Central American war by adjudicating a dispute wherein revolutionaries sheltered in El Salvador tried to overthrow the Honduran government. Although charges against El Salvador were dismissed, the crisis passed peacefully. In 1916, when El Salvador and Costa Rica brought suit against the United States and Nicaragua because of the terms of the Bryan-Chamorro Treaty (1916),* the United States protested. Nicaragua denounced the treaty that had established the court, and it soon ceased to exist. In 1923, a new, less political Central American court was included in the Central American Treaty.* El Salvador, however, refused to ratify that convention, and the court never came to exist. Callcott, Wilfrid H., *The Caribbean Policy of the United States, 1890–1920* (1942); Hudson, Manley O., "The Central American Court of Justice," *American Journal of International Law* 26, 4 (October 1932): 761–68; Karnes, Thomas L., *The Failure of Union* (1961); Munro, Dana G., *The Five Republics of Central America* (1918) and *The United States and the Caribbean Republics, 1921–1933* (1974).

CENTRAL AMERICAN TREATY (1923). This General Treaty of Peace and Amity was the result of a Central American conference held in Washington from December 1922 to February 1923. In it, there was provided a new, less political version of a Central American Court of Justice* and an affirmation not to recognize chiefs of state who achieved power through revolution or who were constitutionally ineligible to hold the office. Costa Rica denounced the treaty in 1934 over controversy concerning the recognition of the Hernández Martínez government in El Salvador. Karnes, Thomas L., *The Failure of Union* (1961); Munro, Dana G., *The United States and the Caribbean Republics, 1921–1933* (1974).

CENTRAL AMERICAN UNION. An often-sought-after goal of Central American leaders since the 1830s, the union of the five republics—Guatemala, Honduras, El Salvador, Nicaragua, and Costa Rica—has proved elusive. The United States generally has favored union in the form of confederation, either for purposes of defense against the British in the 1840s, or for the political stability and economic well-being it would bring. Central American union formed part of Secretary of State James G. Blaine's* concept of Pan-Americanism* and was implicitly encouraged in the Theodore Roosevelt administration through the Washington Conference (1907).* Karnes, Thomas L., *The Failure of Union* (1961); Pletcher, David, *The Awkward Years* (1962).

CENTRAL INTELLIGENCE AGENCY (CIA). The successor to the World War II Office of Strategic Services (OSS) and the postwar National Intelligence Authority, the Central Intelligence Agency was created in the National Security Act (1947). It operates the foreign intelligence–gathering operations of the United States, coordinates the activities of similar branches of other governments, and is officially under the supervision of the National Security Council.* The Central Intelligence Agency Act (1949) exempted the organization from all statutes concerning disclosure of its activities and gave the director power to spend money and utilize personnel without public accounting. The aim of this act was to allow covert operations on a large scale. In the late 1940s and early 1950s, the CIA provided a great deal of needed information on the Soviet Union and East Europe through covert activities. The use of Soviet agents and photographic and electronic intelligence gathering became more common after 1953. Covert activities include the support of internal resistance movements within Communist countries, the subversion of Communist or sympathizing governments, and the countering of Communist propaganda. These kinds of activities have been significant in several major diplomatic events since 1949, including the Guatemalan crisis (1954),* the Bay of Pigs invasion (1961),* the assassination of Ngo Dinh Diem in Vietnam (1963), and the Chilean intervention (1973).* In the 1970s, revelation of CIA activities brought considerable criticism from those who maintain such activities are not in keeping with an open democratic society. Despite that criticism, the CIA operated in the 1980s with substantial alacrity, particularly with respect to its deep and continuing involvement with the Nicaraguan contras* and the role it played, as yet unclear, in the Iran-contra scandal.* Rositzke and others have maintained that the CIA would function more as it was intended and with greater congressional support if it no longer involved itself in psychological, paramilitary, or strategic espionage activities. Among CIA directors, who are appointed by the President and confirmed by the Senate, have been General Walter Bedell Smith,* Allen W. Dulles, the brother of John Foster Dulles,* George Bush,* and William J. Casey. Blum, William, *The CIA: A Forgotten History* (1986); Prados, John, *Presidents' Secret Wars: CIA and Pentagon Covert Operations since World War II* (1986); Ranelagh, John, *The Agency: The Rise and Fall of the CIA* (1986); Rositzke, H., "America's Secret Operations: A Perspective," *Foreign Affairs* 53, 3 (January 1975): 334–51.

CENTRAL POWERS. This was the collective name applied to those nations that fought against Great Britain, France, and their allies in World War I. The Central Powers were Germany, Austria-Hungary, Bulgaria, and Turkey. Bailey, Thomas A., *Woodrow Wilson and the Lost Peace* (1944).

CENTRAL TREATY ORGANIZATION (CENTO), Middle East mutual security alliance, 1959–1979. CENTO was formed in 1959 out of the remnants of the Baghdad Pact* after the withdrawal of Iraq. The alliance comprised Turkey, Iran, Pakistan, and Great Britain, with the United States as a "participating non-member." The United States was interested in associating with CENTO because of its geographical extent and proximity to the Soviet Union but chose not to become a full-fledged member so as to preserve good relations with the Arab states and Israel, nonmembers, and to avoid having to obtain Senate approval, deemed unlikely. Loosely organized, CENTO required its members only to "cooperate for security and defense" and had little in the way of organizational structure. There was, from time to time, considerable controversy over the nonmember status of the United States. After years of almost total inactivity, CENTO was formally dissolved in September, 1979. LaFeber, Walter, *America, Russia, and the Cold War, 1945–1984* (1985); Noble, G. Bernard, "Christian A. Herter," in Ferrell, Robert H., ed., *American Secretaries of State and Their Diplomacy*, vol. 18 (1970).

CENTURY GROUP, interventionist group, 1940–1941. Formed in July 1940, by Lewis W. Douglas,* Herbert Agar,* Bishop Henry Hobson, Francis P. Miller, Whitney Shepherdson, and Admiral William Standley,* this organization believed that the United States should declare war immediately in order to halt Germany's march toward world conquest, which would become all the more likely should Britain fall and its fleet fall into German control. Aware of the need to change public opinion, the group used endorsements, personal influence, news releases, and lobbying tactics to show the folly of isolationism* and the desirability of war. Through the liaison work of Douglas, the Century Group established close relations with the Committee to Defend America by Aiding the Allies* but was generally more militant. The Century Group came up with the idea of the destroyers-for-bases deal at a time when Congress was objecting because the British had asked for the destroyers without offering anything in return. The name came from the Century Association, a private club in New York City where the group, which eventually numbered twenty-eight, held its meetings. Chadwin, Mark L., *The Warhawks* (1968); Divine, Robert A., *The Reluctant Belligerent* (1965).

CHACO WAR (1932–1935). This was a war between Bolivia and Paraguay over control of the Chaco Boreal, an area between the Paraguay River and the Andes Mountains. The United States first became involved in a Neutral Commission that tried, in vain, to negotiate an end to the fighting. In 1934, the war became an issue in early arms embargo discussions as Congress passed an act forbidding the sale of arms to either belligerent. A truce was signed in 1935, and a formal treaty was signed in 1938 giving Paraguay most of the disputed territory. Spruille Braden* headed the U.S. delegation to the peace conference that concluded this war. The war also helped influence President Franklin D. Roosevelt to call for a strict neutrality* treaty at the Buenos Aires Conference

(1936).* Braden, Spruille, *Diplomats and Demagogues* (1971); Divine, Robert A., *The Illusion of Neutrality* (1962); *FR* (1935), 4:1–198; *FR* (1936), 5:35–106; *FR* (1937), 5:4–45; *FR* (1938), 5:89–177; Wood, Bryce, *The Making of the Good Neighbor Policy* (1961).

CHAMORRO-WEITZEL TREATY (1913). This treaty, a forerunner of the Bryan-Chamorro Treaty (1916),* was negotiated in February 1913 by U.S. Minister George T. Weitzel and Nicaraguan Foreign Minister Emiliano Chamorro. The treaty was not ratified before the end of the congressional session in March and was never revived. It was a canal-option treaty in which the United States would pay $3 million for canal rights in Nicaragua, as well as the right to construct naval bases on the Corn Islands and at the Gulf of Fonseca. To Weitzel, the treaty was designed to show continued American confidence in the Adolfo Díaz government, to head off possible foreign canal projects, and to strengthen hemispheric defense. Munro, Dana G., *Intervention and Dollar Diplomacy in the Caribbean, 1900–1921* (1964).

CHAPIN, SELDEN (1899–1963). One of the few American diplomats ever to have been declared persona non grata by the country to which he was accredited, Selden Chapin was a native of Erie, Pennsylvania, where he was born on September 19, 1899. After graduation from the U.S. Naval Academy (1919) and six years of active duty, he entered the Foreign Service in 1925 and held a succession of minor posts in Hankow, Peking, Rome, Quito, San Salvador, Port-au-Prince, Montevideo, and Washington before 1943. In that year, he was appointed counselor at the American diplomatic mission at Algiers and the following year, he became chargé d'affaires* in Algiers and then in Paris. In 1946–1947, he was director of the Office of Foreign Service. His first ambassadorship was to Hungary in 1947, and it was in Budapest in February 1949 that he was declared persona non grata after his criticism of the handling of the trial of Joseph Cardinal Mindszenty. Hungary demanded Chapin's recall. The United States denied the charges against him but replaced him in May 1949 rather than leave the post vacant. Chapin went on to serve in other ambassadorships, largely uneventful: the Netherlands, 1949; Panama, 1953–1955; Iran, 1955–1958; and Peru, 1960–1963. From 1958 to 1960, he was deputy commandant for foreign affairs at the National War College. Chapin, who married Mary Paul Noyes in 1927, died in San Juan, Puerto Rico, on March 26, 1963. *New York Times*, February 18, May 26, 1949, March 28, 1963; *WWWA*, 4 (1961–1968):167.

CHAPULTEPEC CONFERENCE (1945). See **MEXICO CITY CONFERENCE (1945).**

CHARGÉ D'AFFAIRES, embassy or legation official. Normally the second-ranking official at an embassy or legation, the chargé d'affaires takes charge of the mission in the absence of the ambassador or minister. Although not officially accredited to the head of state, he or she is accredited to the foreign minister of the host country and conducts business as usual during his or her incumbency, which is normally of relatively short duration. A chargé d'affaires ad interim conducts embassy or legation business in the intervening period pending the appointment of a new chief of mission. Gamboa, Melquiades J., *Elements of Diplomatic and Consular Practice* (1966); Plischke, Elmer, *The Conduct of American Diplomacy* (1967).

CHESAPEAKE AFFAIR (1807). The U.S.S. *Chesapeake*, a frigate, was fired upon June 22, 1807, in the Atlantic Ocean off Norfolk, Virginia, by the British warship *Leopard*, resulting in three deaths and eighteen wounded. A boarding party from the *Leopard* removed four deserters from the British Navy, three of whom were American, in an act of impressment.* The incident caused a great public outcry against Great Britain in the United States, and many urged war, but President Thomas Jefferson* moved the country toward the Embargo Act* instead. Horsman, Reginald, *The Causes of the War of 1812* (1962); Perkins, Bradford, *Prologue to War* (1961); Spivak, Burton, *Jefferson's English Crises: Commerce, Embargo, and the Republican Revolution* (1979).

CHIEF OF MISSION, diplomatic official. At the Congress of Vienna (1814)* and the Congress of Aix-la-Chapelle (1818),* diplomatic title and rank were established as follows: (1) ambassadors extraordinary and plenipotentiary (AE/P) and papal legates or nuncios; (2) envoys extraordinary, ministers plenipotentiary (EE/MP) and papal internuncios; (3) ministers-resident (M/R); and (4) chargés d'affaires.* Each of these is a chief of mission and must be accredited to a foreign government or international organization. In the United States, chiefs of mission are appointed by the President and confirmed by the Senate. The United States did not use ambassadors until 1893 because of the prevailing feeling that the rank and title were too monarchical. However, the stigma of political and diplomatic inferiority finally induced Congress to legislate the authorization for ambassadors and, immediately, U.S. ministers in France, Germany, Great Britain, Italy, and Russia were raised to ambassadorial status. Now virtually all U.S. chiefs of mission are ambassadors. Gamboa, Melquiades J., *Elements of Diplomatic and Consular Practice* (1966); Jackson, Sir Geoffrey, *Concorde Diplomacy: The Ambassador's Role in the World Today* (1981); Johnson, Richard A., *The Administration of United States Foreign Policy* (1971); Plischke, Elmer, *The Conduct of American Diplomacy* (1967).

CHILD, RICHARD WASHBURN (1881–1935). Richard W. Child was born in Worcester, Massachusetts, on August 5, 1881, attended Milton Academy, and received both an A.B. (1903) and LL.B. (1906) from Harvard. After graduation, he wrote for *Collier's* and other publications before entering law practice in New York in 1915. However, he was more interested in literary pursuits, writing short stories and popular novels and editing *Collier's* (1919–1921). A Republican and a Catholic, Child was well enough regarded to merit appointment as ambassador to Italy in 1921, a position he held for three years. In Italy, he was a great admirer of Benito Mussolini and the efficiency and energy of Italy's Fascist government. He served as an American observer at the Genoa and Lausanne conferences (1922), declaring U.S. adherence to the principle of the Open Door* in the Middle East at the latter conference. Before he left Italy, he convinced Mussolini to write his autobiography and translated it into English. He continued to write popular articles after 1924 and probably raised public interest in foreign affairs with his writing. In 1932, he formed the Republicans for Roosevelt League and was rewarded in 1933 with an appointment as special adviser to Secretary of State Cordell Hull* at the London Economic Conference. The following year, he made a survey of European economic conditions for the State Department. Married four times, Child died of pneumonia in New York on January 31, 1935. Child, Richard W., *A Diplomat Looks at Europe* (1925); *DAB*, Supp. 1:172; *New York Times*, February 1, 1935.

CHILEAN INTERVENTION (1973). This crisis developed after the democratic election in 1970 of Marxist Salvador Allende in Chile. The Central Intelligence Agency (CIA)* had given $700,000 to anti-Allende parties; the International Telephone and Telegraph corporation (ITT) added another $300,000. The fear was that Allende's election would lead to expropriation of American property, as had occurred in Cuba and Guatemala. After covert attempts to invalidate the election in the Chilean congress failed, the CIA's Chilean Task Force continued to operate, expending, according to Prados, over $7.5 million in efforts to bring about Allende's overthrow. In addition, the United States cut off economic aid, blocked development bank loans, and funneled secret aid to the Chilean military. Finally, CIA operatives exploited an economic crisis that was at least partly of Allende's own making; strikes and an alienated middle class badly undermined his popularity, and a military coup overthrew his government in September 1973. During the coup, Allende was killed in the presidential palace in Santiago. Although Secretary of State Henry Kissinger* and U.S. Ambassador Nathaniel Davis* claimed Allende was responsible for his own downfall through the imposition of Socialist policies, U.S. military attachés assisted those who managed the coup. Davis, Nathaniel, *The Last Two Years of Salvador Allende* (1985); Petras, James, and Morris Morely, *The United States and Chile* (1975); Prados, John, *Presidents' Secret Wars* (1986); Sigmund, Paul E., *The Overthrow of Allende and the Politics of Chile, 1965–1976* (1977).

CHINA LOBBY, U.S. political pressure group, c. 1945–1955. The catchphrase *China lobby* was current in the late 1940s and early 1950s and referred to those who supported Chiang Kai-shek and the Nationalist Chinese in the civil war with the Communists in China, who condemned the State Department for having "lost" China after the Nationalists were defeated in 1949, and who later opposed the admission of the People's Republic of China to the United Nations.* The China lobby consisted of a number of organizations and individuals, including Alfred Kohlberg, a wealthy San Francisco businessman, Congressman Walter

Judd (R., Minnesota), and publisher Henry R. Luce. Among the lobby's principal activities were the revelation of an alleged State Department conspiracy to turn China over to Communist control, the public criticism of those who were responsible for U.S. China policy and the China White Paper,* and the encouragement of a foreign policy directed toward the restoration of Chiang to power in mainland China. In 1955, the China lobby was seen in the Committee of One Million (against the Admission of Communist China to the United Nations). Much of the China lobby activity paralleled the anti-Communist activities of Senator Joseph R. McCarthy (R., Wisconsin). Bachrack, Stanley D., *The Committee of One Million: "China Lobby" Politics, 1953–1971* (1976); Cohen, Warren I., "The China Lobby," in DeConde, Alexander, ed., *Encyclopedia of American Foreign Policy* (1979); Kahn, E. J., *The China Hands* (1975); LaFeber, Walter, *America, Russia and the Cold War, 1945–1975* (1976); Purifoy, Lewis McCarroll, *Harry Truman's China Policy* (1976).

CHINA WHITE PAPER, State Department publication, 1949. This controversial publication consisted of a 409-page text and 645 pages of documents, all in defense of U.S. policy in China. The introduction, written by Secretary of State Dean Acheson,* maintained that nothing the United States could have done would have prevented the Communist victory in the Chinese civil war. The idea for the White Paper apparently originated in the State Department's Office of Far Eastern Affairs in late 1948, when the Communist forces in China were well on their way to victory. In an era of heightened emotionalism and cold war* tensions, probably no explanation of the Chinese situation would have satisfied the American public, but the China White Paper was attacked as biased, selective in its choice of documents, and premature in its publication. Much of the compilation of material was done by Ambassador-at-Large Philip C. Jessup* and Acting Assistant Secretary of State for the Far East W. Walton Butterworth. The formal title of the work, seldom used, is *U.S. Relations with China with Special Reference to the Period 1944–1949.* McLellan, David S., *Dean Acheson: The State Department Years* (1976); Stanford University, *The China White Paper* (with an introduction by Lyman P. Van Slyke, 1967).

CHINESE EXCLUSION ACT (1882). The Burlingame Treaty (1868)* had allowed Chinese free immigration to the United States, but the great influx of coolie labor during the 1870s had created much anti-Chinese feeling in California, where most Chinese settled. In 1880, President Rutherford B. Hayes sent a commission to China to negotiate changes in the Burlingame Treaty and found the Chinese conciliatory (because of quarrels with Russia, China valued U.S. friendship) though not agreeable to a complete prohibition of immigration. The next year, Congress passed a bill suspending Chinese immigration for twenty years and denying citizenship to resident Chinese. President Chester Arthur felt that a suspension of immigration for twenty years was tantamount to a prohibition and vetoed the bill. In 1882, he signed a revised version, which placed only a

ten-year moratorium on Chinese immigration. This was the Chinese Exclusion
Act (1882), and it was the first American move to limit the tradition of free
immigration. Hill, Herbert, "Anti-Oriental Agitation and the Rise of Working Class
Racism," *Society* (January-February 1972): 43–54; Hunt, Michael H., *The Making of a
Special Relationship: The United States and China to 1914* (1983); Pletcher, David, *The
Awkward Years* (1962).

CHOATE, JOSEPH HODGES (1832–1917). Perhaps America's most prominent lawyer in the Gilded Age, Joseph H. Choate was born January 24, 1832,
in Salem, Massachusetts, graduated from Harvard (1852) and Harvard Law
School (1854), and was admitted to the bar in 1855. He went to New York and
became a partner in the country's most prominent law firm, Butter, Evarts and
Southmayd, gained a reputation as a noted orator, and took an active part in
Republican politics. As a lawyer, he participated in many famous cases of the
late nineteenth century and presided over the New York state constitutional
convention in 1894. In 1897, he lost a bid for a U.S. Senate seat, but two years
later President William McKinley named him ambassador to Great Britain, replacing John Hay,* who had been named secretary of state. Choate's personality,
speaking ability, and attention to social detail were important factors in strengthening Anglo-American cordiality and resolving various problems. He dealt with
the deadlock of the Joint High Commission on the Alaskan boundary question
(1898) and with Hay worked out an agreement to submit the matter to a tribunal.
He played an important role in persuading the British to accept the abrogation
of the Clayton-Bulwer Treaty* and to acquiesce in the Open Door Policy.* He
remained in London until 1905 and in 1907 led the U.S. delegation to the Second
Hague Conference,* where his leadership and forthright manner of negotiation
were evident throughout. Choate married Caroline Dutchen Sterling in 1861,
was well known as a member of many social and humanitarian organizations,
and died in New York City on May 14, 1917. Ayers, Helen M., *The Contribution
of Joseph H. Choate to Anglo-American Understanding* (1953); *DAB*, 4:83; Marshman,
D. M., Jr., "Four Ages of Joseph Choate," *American Heritage* 26 (April 1975): 33–
40; Martin, Edward S., *Life of Joseph Hodges Choate*, 2 vols. (1920); Perkins, Bradford,
The Great Rapprochement (1968); *New York Times*, May 15, 1917.

CHRISTIANCY, ISAAC PECKHAM (1812–1890). Born in Johnstown, New
York, on March 12, 1812, Isaac P. Christiancy was educated in local schools,
moved to Michigan, read law, and gained admittance to the bar in 1835. He
was prosecuting attorney for Monroe County, Michigan, from 1841 to 1846 and
was elected to the Michigan Senate as a Free-Soil candidate in 1850. A founder
of the Republican party in Michigan, Christiancy edited the *Monroe Commercial*
for two years (1856–1858) before becoming a justice on the Michigan Supreme
Court (1858–1874) and a U.S. senator (1874–1879). In 1879, he was named
minister to Peru. His tendency to quarrel with the U.S. ministers to Chile and
Bolivia damaged Secretary of State William M. Evarts's* attempts to settle the

War of the Pacific.* Christiancy was criticized for overly pro-Peruvian sentiments, for advocating American armed intervention in the war, and for writing
a letter to James G. Blaine* asserting that 50,000 Americans could dominate
Peru and turn it into an American commercial outpost in South America. He
returned from Peru in 1881, at the end of the Hayes administration, and lived
at the home of his daughter in Monroe County. Christiancy was married twice
and died September 8, 1890, in Lansing, Michigan. Barrows, Chester Leonard,
William M. Evarts (1941); *DAB*, 4:96; *NCAB*, 23:348; Millington, Herbert, *American
Diplomacy and the War of the Pacific* (1948); Pike, Frederick B., *Chile and the United
States, 1880–1962* (1963).

CHRISTOPHER, WARREN MINOR (b. 1925). Warren Christopher was born
October 27, 1925, in Scranton, North Dakota, served in the naval reserve during
World War II, and graduated from the University of Southern California (B.S.,
1945) and Stanford (LL.B., 1949). After a year as law clerk for Supreme Court
Associate Justice William O. Douglas, Christopher practiced law in Los Angeles,
serving as a counsel in the office of the under secretary of state, 1961–1965,
and as a deputy attorney general, 1967–1969. In 1977, he was appointed deputy
secretary of state, the top aide to Secretaries of State Cyrus Vance* and Edmund
Muskie.* In this post, he helped in the ratification of the Panama Canal treaties,*
with the sale of sophisticated military supplies to Arab states, and in handling
the delicate problem of redefining the U.S.-Taiwan relationship after the establishment of full diplomatic ties with the People's Republic of China. His most
significant achievement was concluding the negotiations that ended the Iranian
hostage crisis* in 1981. Christopher, noted as a calm, unflappable and effective
negotiator, left government service in 1981 and returned to his California law
practice. Twice married, he has written *Diplomacy, the Neglected Imperative*
(1981) and, with others, *American Hostages in Iran* (1985). *New York Times*,
January 17, 1981; *WWA* (1984–1985):582.

CIA. See CENTRAL INTELLIGENCE AGENCY.

CLARK, JOSHUA REUBEN, JR. (1871–1961). A native of Grantsville, Utah,
J. Reuben Clark, Jr., was born September 1, 1871, and attended the Latter-Day
Saints College (1891–1892) before graduating from the University of Utah (1898)
and receiving a law degree from Columbia (1906). His State Department career
began in 1906 as an assistant solicitor; from 1910 to 1913 he was solicitor.
During World War I, Clark served on the staff of the judge advocate general.
He was a special counsel at the Washington Conference (1921–1922)* and from
1927 to 1928 was special counsel to Ambassador Dwight Morrow* in Mexico,
advising Morrow on the legal ramifications of the oil and agrarian problems of
Americans in Mexico. In 1928, he was appointed under secretary of state and
wrote the Clark Memorandum (first published in 1930), in which he stated that
the Monroe Doctrine* did not apply to purely inter-American relations. In 1930,

he succeeded Morrow as ambassador to Mexico, where he was popular and not beset with any major problems. A Republican, Clark remained in Mexico City until 1933. After leaving the Foreign Service, Clark was director and later president of the Foreign Bondholders Protective Council and was active in the leadership of the Mormon church as a member of the first presidency of the church. He was married in 1898 to Luacine A. Savage, and he died in Salt Lake City on October 6, 1961. Hillam, Ray C., ed., *J. Reuben Clark, Jr., Diplomat and Statesman* (1973); *NCAB*, D:290; *New York Times*, October 7, 1961; *WWWA*, 4 (1961–1968), 171.

CLARK, WILLIAM PATRICK (b. 1931). A long-time friend and confidant of President Ronald Reagan, William P. Clark was born October 23, 1931, in Oxnard, California. He attended Stanford from 1949 to 1951 and, after army service, Loyola Law School in 1955 but never received a degree. He married Joan Brauner in 1955, passed the California bar, and practiced law in Oxnard until 1966, when he joined the administration of Governor Ronald Reagan as chief of staff. In 1969, he was appointed a judge in the Superior Court at San Luis Obispo. Two years later, he went to the Los Angeles Court of Appeals, and in 1973, he was elevated to the California Supreme Court, where he sat until 1981. Joining President Reagan's administration in 1981, Clark's first post was deputy secretary of state, a controversial appointment because he revealed in his Senate confirmation hearing that he knew little about contemporary foreign issues. But he was a quick learner and, more important, a good administrator and mediator who had the confidence of the president. In early 1982, Clark replaced Richard V. Allen* as national security adviser and soon found himself quarreling with Secretary of State Alexander Haig* over the direction of the administration foreign policy. Along with Jeane Kirkpatrick,* Clark favored a harder line toward the USSR and was more critical of Israel than Haig, factors that contributed to the secretary's resignation in June 1982. In late 1983, Clark moved to the Interior Department, replacing the highly controversial secretary, James Watt. He remained there through the Reagan reelection campaign of 1984, leaving the administration in 1985 to pursue part-time law practice in Washington and ranching interests in California. During the Iran-contra scandal,* Clark was an occasional adviser to the embattled administration. Brownstein, Ronald, and Nina Easton, *Reagan's Ruling Class* (1982); *CB* (1982):68–71; *New York Times*, January 5, 1982, January 6, 1985; *WWA* (1984–1985):595.

CLAY, CASSIUS MARCELLUS (1810–1903). A native of Madison County, Kentucky, where he was born October 19, 1810, Cassius M. Clay attended the Jesuit College of St. Joseph in Nelson County, Kentucky, and Transylvania College, and graduated from Yale in 1832. He returned to Kentucky, where he served several terms in the state legislature and one as governor (1849–1853), established an antislavery newspaper (1845), and became a Republican and enthusiastic supporter of Abraham Lincoln. In 1861, his support was rewarded with appointment as minister to Russia. Except for a brief period in 1862–1863, when Simon Cameron* was minister, Clay remained in St. Petersburg until 1869. His main function was to maintain the pro-Union attitude of the government; in this, he was successful, despite his eccentric, jealous behavior and numerous social gaffes. During the Polish insurrection, he communicated U.S. support to Russia and sent information back to Washington about the resources of Alaska, thus aiding the purchase of that territory. At the end of his mission, he retired to his estate, Whitehall, in Madison County, where he grew increasingly eccentric until his death on July 22, 1903. He was twice married and twice divorced and wrote his autobiography, *Life of Cassius M. Clay, Written and Compiled by Himself* (1886). *DAB*, 4:169; Richardson, H. Edward, *Cassius Marcellus Clay* (1976); Robertson, James R., *A Kentuckian at the Court of the Tsars* (1935); Smiley, David L., *Lion of White Hall: Cassius M. Clay* (1962).

CLAY, HENRY (1777–1852). One of America's most prominent congressional leaders before the Civil War and three times candidate for the presidency, Henry Clay was also secretary of state in the administration of President John Quincy Adams (1825–1829). Clay was born in Hanover County, Virginia, on April 12, 1777, studied law on his own, and was admitted to the bar in 1797. That year he moved to Lexington, Kentucky, where he became a leading criminal lawyer, a prominent state and national politician, and a well-known bon vivant. His political career included service in the Kentucky legislature (1803–1806, 1807–1809) and the U.S. Senate (1806–1807, 1831–1842, 1849–1852). In Congress, he gained a reputation as a compromiser, playing influential roles in the Missouri Compromise, the Compromise Tariff of 1833, and the Compromise of 1850. Clay ran unsuccessfully for president in 1824, 1832, and 1844. His diplomatic experience included service on the U.S. peace commission that negotiated the Treaty of Ghent (1814)* and climaxed with his tenure as secretary of state, an appointment he received after throwing his support to John Quincy Adams when the election of 1824 was decided by the House of Representatives. The high points of his rather unexciting term included the Panama Congress (1826),* to which American delegates arrived too late to participate, and the signing of twelve commercial treaties, more than any previous administration. Important agreements were made with Britain, providing for an indemnity payment of $1,204,960 for slaves taken during the War of 1812 and for the joint occupation of Oregon.* As a senator, late in his career, Clay opposed the annexation of Texas and the declaration of war on Mexico, although he supported the prosecution of the war. Married to Lucretia Hart in 1799, Clay died in Washington, D.C., on June 29, 1852. Burton, Theodore E., "Henry Clay," in Bemis, Samuel F., ed., *American Secretaries of State and Their Diplomacy*, vol. 4 (1928); *DAB*, 4:173; Eaton, Clement, *Henry Clay and the Art of American Politics* (1957); Peterson, Merrill D., *The Great Triumvirate: Webster, Clay, and Calhoun* (1987); Van Duesen, Glyndon G., *The Life of Henry Clay* (1937).

CLAY, LUCIUS DUBIGNON (1897–1978). A descendant of Henry Clay* and son of a U.S. senator, Lucius D. Clay was born April 23, 1897, in Marietta, Georgia, and graduated from West Point in 1918. He pursued an army career, teaching at West Point (1924–1928), working as an engineer and administrator, and reaching the rank of general in 1947. During World War II, he was a deputy to James F. Byrnes* at the Office of War Mobilization. Later he was a deputy to General Dwight D. Eisenhower and then to the military government in Germany, where he was in charge of civil affairs. In 1947, Clay became commander in chief of U.S. forces in Europe and military governor of Germany, the position in which he made his most significant contributions to U.S. diplomatic history. Shortly after the end of the war, Clay objected to the harsh, spartan measures for German occupation called for in JCS 1067,* worked to improve the food supply and to end the exploitation of the German people, and advocated the industrial rehabilitation of the country. He was anxious for and optimistic about postwar Soviet cooperation, and in May 1946 he recommended economic unification among the occupation zones and the establishment of a provisional civilian government. At the same time, however, he ordered the dismantling of German industrial facilities in the American zone halted, and by 1947, he had grown suspicious of Soviet aims and more interested in the economic recovery of the western zones and in the creation of a West German state. In 1948–1949, Clay directed the Berlin airlift in response to the Soviet-induced Berlin blockade.* He retired in 1949, wrote of his experiences in *Decision in Germany* (1950), and went to work for the Continental Can Company, serving as chairman of the board from 1950 to 1962. From 1963 to 1973, he was a senior partner in Lehman Brothers, an investment banking house. In 1961–1962, Clay was President John F. Kennedy's special representative in Berlin, there to reassure the people of West Berlin of continued U.S. support. The following year, 1963, he headed a presidential committee investigating the U.S. foreign aid program. The committee concluded that the United States was doing "too much for too many." From time to time, Clay also worked on behalf of the Republican party or in New York City civic affairs. Married in 1918 to Marjorie McKeown, he was known for his stamina, concentration, and memory, particularly in his effective direction of postwar Germany. He died in Chatham, Massachusetts, on April 16, 1978. Baker, John, *Winds of History: The German Years of Lucius Dubignon Clay* (1983); Gardner, Lloyd C., *Architects of Illusion* (1970); Gimbel, John, *The American Occupation of Germany*; (1968); *New York Times*, April 17, 1968; *WWA* (1976–1977):588–89.

CLAYTON, JOHN MIDDLETON (1796–1856). Secretary of state (1849–1850) in the short administration of President Zachary Taylor, John M. Clayton was a native of Dogsborough, Delaware, where he was born July 24, 1796. After graduating from Yale in 1815, he read law, was admitted to the bar in 1819, and became in the next decade a prominent courtroom lawyer in Delaware, serving also in the state legislature (1824–1826) and as Delaware secretary of state (1826–1828). In 1829, Clayton was elected to the U.S. Senate, remaining there until 1836. The following year, he was named chief justice of the Delaware Supreme Court but in 1839 stepped down to become a scientific farmer. From 1845 to 1849, he was again in the U.S. Senate, and in the election of 1848 he gave his support to Taylor's candidacy. As secretary of state, he is best remembered for negotiating the Clayton-Bulwer Treaty (1850)* with Great Britain concerning the neutrality of the Central American isthmus and any future canals built through it. In addition, Clayton worked to prevent filibustering* expeditions to Cuba, initiated the policy toward Japan that led three years later to Commodore Matthew C. Perry's* visit there, and presented Portugal with an ultimatum demanding an indemnity payment for the destruction of a number of U.S. ships. Clayton served one more time in the Senate, 1853–1856, where he was primarily involved in defending the Clayton-Bulwer Treaty. He was married in 1822 to Sarah Ann Fisher, who died in 1825. Clayton died in Dover, Delaware on November 9, 1856. *DAB*, 4:185; *NCAB*, 6:179; Williams, Mary W., "John Middleton Clayton," in Bemis, Samuel F., ed., *American Secretaries of State and Their Diplomacy*, vol. 6 (1928).

CLAYTON, WILLIAM LOCKHART (1880–1966). Born near Tupelo, Mississippi, on February 7, 1880, Will Clayton was educated only through grade seven, at which point he went to work as an assistant to the court clerk in Madison County, Texas. In 1896, he became a stenographer for a cotton broker; he learned the business quickly and by 1902 had become secretary-treasurer of Texas Cotton Products Company, a subsidiary of the American Cotton Company. In 1904, with his brother and brother-in-law, Clayton founded Anderson, Clayton and Company, which grew to become the largest cotton brokerage in the world. During World War I, he served on the War Industries Board and during the Great Depression gave financial backing to the anti–New Deal Liberty League. Interested in foreign affairs and an internationalist, Clayton was a member of the Council on Foreign Relations,* and just before U.S. entry into World War II, he joined the Century Group.* In 1940, he became a vice-president of the Export-Import Bank* and also worked for the Office of the Coordinator of Inter-American Affairs, under the direction of Nelson Rockefeller.* During the war, he held various government positions: deputy administrator, Federal Loan Administration; assistant secretary of commerce; and war surplus administrator. In 1945, Clayton attended the Mexico City Conference,* giving support to the idea of free trade but only with countries having efficient economies. He headed the U.S. economic contingent at the Potsdam Conference (1945)* and worked out a reparations* agreement with the Soviet Union. For postwar Europe, he advocated continued U.S. economic support through the United Nations Relief and Rehabilitation Administration (UNRRA)* and through a continuation of Lend-Lease.* He was influential in arranging a major loan to Great Britain in late 1945 and in winning congressional approval for it. In May 1947, Clayton wrote what Dean Acheson* called the "concrete outline" of the Marshall Plan* while at the same time playing a major role in negotiations in Geneva for a General Agreement on Trade and Tariffs (GATT)* and for an International Trade Organization (ITO).* He left government service in 1948 and returned to Anderson, Clayton and Company. In later years, he was also associated with the Atlantic Union Committee, an organization of internationalists advocating the political, economic, and military union of the free nations of the world to resist Communist economic encroachment. Married in 1902 to Sue Vaughn, Clayton died February 8, 1966, in Houston. Chadwin, Mark L., *The Warhawks* (1968); Dobney, Frederick J., ed., *Selected Papers of Will Clayton* (1971); Gardner, Lloyd C., *Architects of Illusion* (1970); Garwood, Ellen Clayton, *Will Clayton: A Short Biography* (1968); *New York Times*, February 9, 1966.

CLAYTON-BULWER TREATY (1850). Designed to end rivalry between Great Britain and the United States in Central America, this unpopular treaty placed any isthmian canal or other transportation means under joint Anglo-American control, guaranteed its neutrality, and provided for equal tolls for both states' subjects or citizens. No fortifications were permitted, nor was there to be any attempt at domination or colonization in Central America, although a controversial clause left Britain in control of its existing protectorates along the east coast of the isthmus. Disputed throughout the 1850s, the Clayton-Bulwer Treaty was superseded by the Hay-Pauncefote Treaty (1901),* granting the United States the exclusive right to build and operate an isthmian canal. Findling, John E., *Close Neighbors, Distant Friends* (1987); Jones, William Devereux, *The American Problem in British Diplomacy, 1841–1861* (1974); Williams, Mary W., *Anglo-American Isthmian Diplomacy, 1815–1915* (1916).

COEXISTENCE, PEACEFUL, diplomatic catchphrase, c. 1950s. The Soviet Union used this phrase during the 1950s as part of its "New Look" in international relations. Many cold warriors* in the United States did not like the principle behind the phrase but could do nothing about it because the nation could not go to war to defeat its antagonist. At the same time, however, the United States could not sacrifice the principles of its world mission in order to accept publicly the reality of peaceful coexistence. In 1960, George Kennan* published an article in *Foreign Affairs* repudiating the Soviet claim of peaceful coexistence as the basis of its foreign policy. Kennan pointed out that Soviet control of East European nations, Soviet military policies, Soviet government monopolization of foreign trade, and Soviet anti-American propaganda provoked responses in the West that threatened to bring on war and undo peaceful coexistence. Still, peaceful coexistence can develop between two ideologically antagonistic systems, but only if both are prepared to make the necessary policy revisions. Kennan concluded that Moscow expected the West to make all the changes. Carleton, William G., *The Revolution in American Foreign Policy* (1963); Kennan, George F., "Peaceful Coexistence: A Western View," *Foreign Affairs* 38 (January 1960): 171–90.

COLBY, BAINBRIDGE (1869–1950). Born December 22, 1869 in St. Louis, Bainbridge Colby was graduated from Williams College (1890) and New York Law School (1892). He practiced law in New York City from 1892 to 1936, served in the New York State Assembly (1901–1902) as a Republican, but helped found the Progressive party in 1912. After 1912, he became a supporter of Woodrow Wilson, was appointed vice-president of the U.S. Shipping Board in 1917, and was a member of the American Mission to the Interallied Conference (1917).* In early 1920, Colby succeeded Robert Lansing* as secretary of state and spent just under a year in the post. He defended Wilson's position on the League of Nations,* continued the policy of blunting Japanese expansion in Manchuria, which contributed to the set of Pacific-related treaties written at the Washington Conference (1921–1922),* and initiated a policy of nonrecognition of the Soviet Union. He signed a Japanese-American treaty in 1921 permitting the United States to build a cable station on Yap, an island under Japanese mandate. In Latin America, Colby declared that the United States would begin withdrawing occupation forces, made a goodwill tour, and began talks with Mexico that led to the Bucareli Agreement (1923).* After 1921, he continued his law practice, again became a Republican, and helped found the anti–New Deal American Liberty League in the 1930s. Twice married, he died in Bemis Point, New York, on April 11, 1950. *DAB*, Supp. 4:170; *New York Times*, April 12, 1950; Smith, Daniel, *Aftermath of War: Bainbridge Colby and Wilsonian Diplomacy, 1920–21* (1970); Spargo, John, "Bainbridge Colby," in Bemis, Samuel F., ed., *American Secretaries of State and Their Diplomacy*, vol. 10 (1929).

COLD WAR. This common term describes the state of relations between the United States and its allies and the Soviet Union and its allies after World War II. In general, the cold war has been marked by international tension and hostility arising from the economic, diplomatic, social, propagandistic, and even military pressures short of war that have been employed by one side against the other to gain advantage economically, in terms of security, or in terms of world opinion. Different authorities place different dates on the beginning of the cold war and disagree as to when or even whether it has ended. After several years in the 1970s, in which U.S.-Soviet relations were marked by various cooperative ventures in a policy known as détente,* the Soviet invasion of Afghanistan in 1979 and the election of the conservative Ronald Reagan may be said to have ushered in a period of "neo–cold war," lasting at least until the accession of Mikhail Gorbachev to power in the Soviet Union and the successful conclusion of the Intermediate Nuclear Forces (INF) Treaty.* A major historical controversy revolves around the origins of the cold war and which side bears the greater responsibility for having caused it; a wealth of historical writing has been produced on the subject. Alperovitz, Gar, *Atomic Diplomacy* (1965); Gaddis, John Lewis, *The United States and the Origins of the Cold War, 1941–1947* (1972); Gaddis, John Lewis, *The Long Peace* (1987); Herz, Martin, *The Beginnings of the Cold War* (1966); LaFeber, Walter, *America, Russia, and the Cold War, 1945–1984* (1985); Schlesinger,

Arthur J., Jr., "Origins of the Cold War," *Foreign Affairs* 46, 2 (October 1967): 22–52; Spanier, John W., *American Foreign Policy since World War II* (1988).

COLLECTIVE SECURITY. Collective security is an arrangement, usually accomplished by means of a treaty or convention, by which the signatories pledge to cooperate for the maintenance of their mutual security should any one of them be attacked. Article X* of the League of Nations* Covenant included this principle, which proved to be a major impediment to Senate ratification of the Treaty of Versailles (1919).* Many Americans felt that adherence to the notion of collective security might oblige the United States to become involved in military action without congressional consent and in places and at times not of its own choosing. With the creation of the United Nations* in 1945, the United States accepted the principle of collective security, although in practice the collective security machinery of the United Nations has been greatly subordinated to the independent foreign and military policy of the major powers. Since World War I, the meaning of collective security has changed somewhat. In League of Nations days, it was taken to mean a universal peacekeeping alliance; during the cold war,* it referred to the purposes of limited alliances or spheres of influence. The Korean War (1950–1953) was initially seen as a hopeful resurrection of collective security in practice, but the military adventure turned into sour stalemate, frustrating the U.S. public as well as collaborating United Nations members. Gamboa, Melquiades T., *Elements of Diplomatic and Consular Practice* (1966); Stromberg, Roland N., *Collective Security and American Foreign Policy* (1963).

COLONIALISM. Colonialism may be defined as the practice of a nation acquiring control over or title to other territories, called colonies. A first phase of colonialism, from about 1520 to 1760, was motivated mainly by the economic policy of mercantilism. The second phase of colonialism, from 1870 to World War I, also had economic motives, but there was greater concern with such matters as security, national prestige, and racially oriented altruism. Colonialism is closely related to the concept known as imperialism.* Bennett, Edward M., "Colonialism," in DeConde, Alexander, ed., *Encyclopedia of American Foreign Policy* (1979); Hartmann, Frederick H., *The Relations of Nations* (1962); Koebner, Richard, *Empire* (1961).

COMMITTEE OF SECRET CORRESPONDENCE. Formed November 29, 1775, by the Continental Congress, this committee was to correspond "with our friends in Great Britain, Ireland and other parts of the world." Its first action was to direct Arthur Lee* in London to send secret information to America regarding the attitudes of foreign nations toward the rebellious colonies. After April 1777, it was known as the Committee for Foreign Affairs, and in 1781, the secretary of foreign affairs for the Continental Congress assumed the responsibilities of the Committee for Foreign Affairs. Following the adoption of the Constitution in 1789, the Department of State handled foreign affairs. Bemis, Samuel F., *The Diplomacy of the American Revolution* (1935).

COMMITTEE TO DEFEND AMERICA BY AIDING THE ALLIES (CDAAA), internationalist organization, 1940–1941. Created by William Allen White and Clark Eichelberger after the German offensive in May 1940, the Committee to Defend America by Aiding the Allies grew to become a national organization with over three hundred local chapters. Its prime purpose was to lobby and influence public opinion in favor of aid (but not military intervention) to Britain and other allies in the European war to ensure an Axis defeat. The CDAAA cooperated with the Century Group* and other internationalist organizations, such as Fight for Freedom,* in supporting measures such as the bases-for-destroyers deal, Lend-Lease,* and, later, American convoys. By 1941, the CDAAA was edging toward support of intervention. Divine credits the organization, along with European events, as bringing about a major shift in American opinion concerning aid to Britain and ultimately in making entry into the war more palatable. Chadwin, Mark L., *The Warhawks* (1968); Divine, Robert A., *The Reluctant Belligerent* (1965).

CONANT, JAMES BRYANT (1893–1978). James B. Conant was born March 26, 1893, in Dorchester, Massachusetts. He graduated from Harvard (A.B., 1913; Ph.D., 1916) in chemistry, served in the chemical warfare service during World War I, and taught chemistry at Harvard after the war (1919–1933). In 1933, Conant became president of Harvard, a post he occupied for twenty years. Before World War II, he was a member of both the Century Group* and the Committee to Defend America by Aiding the Allies.* In 1940, he traveled to Great Britain to establish a scientific liaison office with the British. During the war, he was an adviser to the National Defense Research Committee, where he helped set policies for the development of the atomic bomb. In 1945, Conant was a member of a committee that advised President Harry S Truman on the actual use of the bomb and on postwar atomic policy; in this capacity, he was an advocate of international control of atomic weapons. In spite of conservative opposition, he was appointed U.S. high commissioner to Germany in 1953, a position that evolved into an ambassadorship in 1955 with the formal assumption by West Germany of foreign policy responsibility. As high commissioner and ambassador, Conant dealt with such matters as the American military presence in Germany, refugees from the Soviet zone, and the reconstruction of Berlin's industrial capacity. He got along well with Chancellor Konrad Adenauer but saw little realistic chance for German reunification. In 1957, he resigned his post and returned to the United States, where he involved himself in the problems of the American public school system. Conant married Grace Thayer Richards in 1921 and died in Hanover, New Hampshire, on February 11, 1978. Chadwin, Mark L., *The Warhawks* (1978); Conant, James B., *My Several Lives* (1970); Lieberman, Joseph I., *The Scorpion and the Tarantula* (1970); *New York Times*, December 26, 1956, February 12, 1978; *NCAB*, D:48.

CONGER, EDWIN HURD (1843–1907). Born near Galesburg, Illinois, on March 7, 1843, Edwin H. Conger graduated from Lombard College (1862) and Albany Law School (1866). In between, he served as a Union officer in the

Civil War. After law school, he practiced law in Galesburg for a short time before moving to Madison County, Iowa, where he became involved in stock raising and banking and began a political career. A Republican, Conger was active in local and state politics for fourteen years before winning election to the U.S. House of Representatives in 1884. He had served three terms when the Benjamin Harrison administration made him minister to Brazil. He stayed three uneventful years until supplanted by a Democratic appointee in 1893 and returned briefly in 1897 at the beginning of the McKinley administration. In early 1898, Conger was appointed minister to China, a more important mission. He was minister until 1905 and in general preserved the Open Door policy* by dampening other foreign moves to exploit or make excessive demands of the Chinese. In Peking during the Boxer Rebellion,* Conger made accurate reports on the situation that were important in hastening the fleet to China and in starting the relief column toward the besieged foreign community. He was a close friend of the empress dowager, which was of assistance in negotiating a commercial treaty that opened Mukden and Antung in Manchuria to foreign trade. In 1905, Conger was named ambassador to Mexico but served only a short time before retiring because of ill health and the high expense of the Mexican embassy. Conger was married to Sarah Pike and died May 18, 1907, in Pasadena, California from the effects of a disease contracted in China. Briggs, John E., "Iowa and the Diplomatic Service," *Iowa Journal of History and Politics* 19 (1921): 321–65; Conger, Sarah P., *Letters from China* (1909); *DAB*, 4:344; Dennis, A. L. P., *Adventures in American Diplomacy, 1896–1906* (1928); *New York Times*, May 19, 1907.

CONGO CONFERENCE. See BERLIN CONFERENCE (1884–1885).

CONGO CRISIS (1960–1962). In 1960, Belgium granted independence to the former Belgian Congo without having prepared the people through the establishment of local governmental institutions or secondary or higher educational institutions during colonial rule. Soon after independence, a problem arose with the secession of the copper-rich Katanga province, under the leadership of Moishe Tshombe, who received substantial tax receipts from Union Minière du Haut Katanga, the largest (and European-owned) mining company in the country. When the Kinshasa government, led by the eccentric Patrice Lumumba, proved unable to deal with this situation, the United Nations* stepped in to try to reunify the Congo diplomatically. When diplomacy failed, troops were sent in to do the job, and in the resulting turmoil, many Belgian nationals and several American missionaries were killed. Because Lumumba had ties with Moscow, the Soviet Union was highly critical of the intervention, which cost Lumumba his life, and the United States was obliged to pay much of the cost when the Soviets (as well as the Belgians and French, among others) refused to contribute. Because Tshombe was anti-Communist, conservatives in the United States were incensed when the Kennedy administration supported the intervention. Tshombe was defeated in early 1962, the Congo was reunited, and United Nations prestige held firm. Jackson, Henry F., *From the Congo to Soweto* (1982); Kalb, Madeleine G., *The Congo Cables* (1982); Mahoney, Richard D., *JFK: Ordeal in Africa* (1983).

CONNALLY RESOLUTION (1943). Named for Senator Tom Connally (D., Texas), this resolution stated that the United States would join an international organization established to maintain peace after World War II. The resolution consisted of three parts: (1) the United States would cooperate with other nations that had signed the United Nations Declaration* in waging the war; (2) the United States would cooperate in securing the peace after the war; and (3) the United States would cooperate in "the establishment and maintenance of an international authority with power to prevent aggression and to preserve the peace of the world." The Connally Resolution was passed by the U.S. Senate, 85–5, on November 5, 1943. In general, according to Divine, the resolution was weakened by its ambiguity and evasiveness on the issue of the use of force to maintain peace. The language of the resolution probably came from a Four-Power Declaration on General Security,* issued by the Moscow Conference of Foreign Ministers,* which had met in late October 1943. A similar resolution, introduced by Congressman J. William Fulbright,* was approved by the House of Representatives at about the same time. Darilek, Richard E., *A Loyal Opposition in Time of War* (1976); Divine, Robert A., *Second Chance* (1967); Wheeler-Bennett, John W., and Anthony Nicholls, *The Semblance of Peace* (1972).

CONSORTIUM LOAN TO CHINA (1911–1913). The original consortium consisted of French, German, and British bankers, who received a concession to build the Hukuang Railroad. The United States used diplomatic pressure to gain admittance to the consortium, which then negotiated with the Chinese a loan to provide money to strengthen and stabilize the Chinese and Manchurian financial situation. Russia and Japan joined the consortium in 1912, and the six powers imposed stringent conditions on the loan arrangement, virtually assuming control of Chinese finances. In 1913, when Woodrow Wilson became president, the United States withdrew from the consortium, choosing instead to protect China and preserve an independent course of action. This marked a significant break with past policy, which for some years had been to cooperate with other powers in Chinese matters. Crane, Daniel M., and Thomas A. Breslin, *An Ordinary Relationship* (1986); Curry, Roy, *Woodrow Wilson and Far Eastern Policy, 1913–1921* (1957).

CONSTRUCTIVE ENGAGEMENT. This term describes the policy employed from 1981 to 1985 by the Reagan administration to induce the government of South Africa to change its apartheid policy. Devised in 1980 by Chester Crocker, who became assistant secretary of state for African affairs, it marked a reversal of the Carter administration's policy of emphasizing human rights and publicly criticizing South Africa. Under constructive engagement, the Reagan administration took a much more conciliatory line toward the Pretoria government, expanding areas of intergovernmental cooperation, supporting South Africa in the United Nations,* and criticizing the African National Congress, the largest black organization in South Africa. The policy appeared to be based on the administration's perception of international relations in an East-West context and the fact that South Africa is anti-Communist and a source of strategically important minerals. Constructive engagement also sought to give the United States more leverage in related southern African issues such as Namibia* and Angola. In 1985, however, President Reagan approved the imposition of limited economic sanctions on South Africa, a sign that constructive engagement, by itself, had not succeeded. Ungar, Sanford J., and Peter Vale, "South Africa: Why Constructive Engagement Failed," *Foreign Affairs* 64, 2 (Winter 1985-1986): 234–58.

CONSUL, diplomatic official. A consul is an official in the Foreign Service charged with attending to the nation's commercial interests, the welfare of its citizens, and other administrative tasks, such as passport issuance, in a foreign post. As with chiefs of mission,* there is a prescribed rank for the consular service: (1) consuls general, who often supervise the subordinate ranks; (2) consuls; and (3) vice-consuls. A consular agent is of still lesser rank and functions much like an employee of the consul; often he or she is a citizen or subject of the country in which the consul is posted. Nations normally agree in a consular convention to exchange consular officers, who are recognized in the country to which they are assigned by documents known as exequaturs, authorizing them to perform their assigned functions. Gamboa, Melquiades J., *Elements of Diplomatic and Consular Practice* (1966); Johnson, Richard A., *The Administration of United States Foreign Policy* (1971); Plischke, Elmer, *The Conduct of American Diplomacy* (1967).

CONSUL GENERAL. See CONSUL.

CONSULAR AGENT. See CONSUL.

CONTADORA GROUP. Representatives from Panama, Mexico, Venezuela, and Colombia met in January 1983 on the island of Contadora off the coast of Panama in an effort to find a comprehensive settlement to the Central American turmoil. A series of meetings in 1983 and 1984 resulted in a draft treaty presented in September 1984 to the leaders of the five nations of Central America. The proposed agreement included provisions to reduce the level of armed conflict, grant political amnesty, and provide for free elections. When Nicaragua, somewhat surprisingly, pronounced the treaty acceptable, the United States allegedly induced its Central American allies (Honduras and El Salvador in particular) to object, and the process stalled, never to regain its momentum, despite encouragement from an association of four major South American countries—the Lima Group—beginning in the summer of 1985. Although the Reagan administration voiced its support for the work of the Contadora Group, critics asserted that the U.S. policy of aiding the contra* movement was inimical to the peace process.

Esquipulas II (1987)* evolved, at least in part, from the unhappy legacy of the Contadora Group. Bagley, Bruce M., ed., *Contadora and the Diplomacy of Peace in Central America* (1987); Findling, John E., *Close Neighbors, Distant Friends* (1987); Martin, Brian G., *The Contadora Process and the Crisis in Central America, 1983–1986* (1986); Purcell, Susan Kaufman, "Demystifying Contadora," *Foreign Affairs* 64, 1 (Fall 1985): 74–95.

CONTAINMENT, U.S. diplomatic policy, post–World War II. A term devised by George F. Kennan* in 1947, containment describes an American foreign policy meant to counter the arrogant and expansionist foreign policy the Soviet Union was perceived as employing. Kennan's hope was that by containing Soviet expansionism in key regions of the world, internal changes would result in Moscow and would lead to a moderation or overthrow of the Communist regime. Originally containment was intended to apply primarily to Europe and be non-military in character, but during the late 1940s and early 1950s, it took on a new character, emerging as a literal encirclement of the Soviet Union (and, after 1949, China) with a network of military alliances including the North Atlantic Treaty Organization (NATO),* the Baghdad Pact,* and the Southeast Asia Treaty Organization (SEATO).* This global containment reached its apogee, militarily and rhetorically, during the tenure of Secretary of State John Foster Dulles* (1953–1959). According to Gaddis, an important "intended follow-up," in Kennan's mind, to containment had to wait until the early 1970s. This involved the recognition and exploitation of the polycentrism in the international Communist movement and the exploration with the Soviet Union of areas where tension might be reduced. Gaddis concluded that an objective of containment had been satisfied in that there was a more stable international environment in the 1970s than there had been in the late 1940s, although the renewal of tensions after 1979 undermined that view in the early 1980s. Since 1985, however, the annual summit conferences between President Ronald Reagan and General Secretary Mikhail Gorbachev and the signing of the Intermediate Nuclear Force Treaty* suggest another shift toward a stable environment. Bernstein, Barton, "Containment," in DeConde, Alexander, ed., *Encyclopedia of American Foreign Policy* (1979); Diebel, Terry L., and John L. Gaddis, eds., *Containment: Concept and Policy* (1985); Gaddis, John L., "Containment: A Reassessment," *Foreign Affairs* 55, 1 (July 1977): 873–87; Kennan, George F., "Containment Then and Now," *Foreign Affairs* 65, 4 (Spring 1987): 885–90; Kennan, George F., *Memoirs, 1925–1950* (1967); Spanier, John, *American Foreign Policy since World War II* (1988); X, Mr. [Kennan, George F.], "The Sources of Soviet Conduct," *Foreign Affairs* 25 (July 1947): 566–82.

CONTINENTAL SYSTEM. This term is used to describe the combination of the Berlin Decree* and Milan Decree* (1806–1807) used by Napoleon in an attempt to destroy British commerce and to prevent trade with Britain. As the name implies, Napoleon controlled ports all over the continent of Europe; the decrees comprising the Continental System ordered the seizure of all British ships or ships of neutrals that had or were planning to trade with Britain. The system was never totally effective but was a factor, along with the British Orders-in-Council,* in bringing about the War of 1812. Perkins, Bradford, *Prologue to War* (1961); Zahniser, Marvin I., "The Continental System," in DeConde, Alexander, ed., *Encyclopedia of American Foreign Policy* (1979).

"CONTINUOUS VOYAGE" DOCTRINE. A "continuous voyage" occurred when a neutral ship carried goods from an enemy colony to an unblockaded enemy home port. The British navy, in the Napoleonic Wars, did not permit continuous voyages from the French West Indies to France after 1800, but insisted that American ships engaged in such trade break the voyage by a stop at an American port with the payment of duties. In the *Essex* decision,* 1805, the British admiralty court decided that the rebating of duties, as was the American practice, made the trip in effect a continuous voyage, and thus contrary to the Rule of the War of 1756,* since such trips were forbidden in peacetime. In the Civil War, the Union invoked similar strictures against British endeavors to ship goods to the Confederacy, and in World War I the British abused the doctrine with the assumption that all goods sent to neutral countries were in reality bound for the Central Powers* and hence subject to seizure. Bemis, Samuel F., *John Quincy Adams and the Foundations of American Foreign Policy* (1949); Borchard, Edwin M., and William P. Lage, *Neutrality for the United States* (1937).

CONTRABAND, goods whose trade is prohibited in wartime or by treaty. Contraband was first defined in the Treaty of Southampton (1625), an Anglo-Dutch alliance. Contraband generally refers to goods useful in war and subject to capture if carried in neutral ships. In the Anglo-American crisis of the 1790s, a dispute arose over whether foodstuffs and naval stores, necessary to civilian life as well as to the military, should be considered contraband. In the Declaration of Paris (1856),* contraband was left undefined, although it has often been defined in bilateral treaties. The Declaration of London (1909) included a detailed list of contraband items, but the declaration was never ratified, and the lack of definition was a hindrance to American shipping in World War I. Borchard, Edwin M., and William P. Lage, *Neutrality for the United States* (1937); *FR* (1914), 2:215–70; Savelle, Max, *The Origins of American Diplomacy* (1967).

CONTRAS. This is the name commonly applied to the Nicaraguan force opposing the Sandinista government that came to power in 1979. The contras were born in 1980 out of the remnants of the National Guard forces of deposed dictator Anastasio Somoza, Jr. In 1981, the Reagan administration decided to conduct covert military operations against Nicaragua, and the Central Intelligence Agency* began to fund and train the rebels, who took on the name *contras*, a shortening of the Spanish word for "counterrevolutionary." President Reagan publicly praised the contras and, with rhetorical extravagance, referred to them as "freedom fighters." Over the next seven years, the contras, a combination of Somoza's guardsmen, disenchanted Sandinistas, and unhappy peasants, grew to perhaps 15,000 and received intermittent funding from Congress and from various private sources. They waged a generally ineffective low-intensity conflict against the Sandinistas, operating from bases in remote parts of Nicaragua or across the Honduran border and frequently quarreling among themselves. Peace talks between the contras and the Sandinistas began in early 1988 after the signing of Esquipulas II* and a suspension of aid from Congress. As of the summer of 1988, these talks had proved fruitless, with the contras demanding extensive political and institutional reforms and the Sandinistas more interested in ending the military conflict and less in reforming themselves out of power. Dickey, Christopher, *With the Contras* (1986); Findling, John E., *Close Neighbors, Distant Friends* (1987); Gleijeses, Piero, "The Reagan Doctrine and Central America," *Current History* 85, 515 (December 1986): 401–4, 435–37.

CONVENTION. See INTERNATIONAL AGREEMENT.

CONVENTION OF 1800, treaty between France and United States. Also known as the Treaty of Môrtefontaine, the Convention of 1800 ended the quasi-war* between the United States and France. The French agreed to the abrogation of the Franco-American Treaty of Amity and Commerce (1778),* and the Americans agreed to the cancellation of all claims against France. In addition, the convention included provisions dealing with neutrals' rights. The main consequence of the treaty was the restoration of harmonious relations with Napoleon's France, a major factor in the Louisiana Purchase* in 1803. American negotiators were Oliver Ellsworth, William R. Davie, and U.S. Minister to France William Vans Murray.* DeConde, Alexander, *The Quasi-War* (1966); Hill, Peter P., *William Vans Murray, Federalist Diplomat* (1971); Varg, Paul A., *Foreign Policies of the Founding Fathers* (1963).

CONVENTION OF 1818, treaty between the United States and Great Britain. This four-part agreement between Britain and the United States settled a number of contentious points. The United States gained permanent fishing rights off New-foundland's southern shore, the Labrador coast, and the Magdalen Islands. The U.S.-Canadian boundary was extended along the line of 49° north latitude from the Lake of the Woods to the Rocky Mountains, leaving the area to the west (Oregon Territory) open for subjects and citizens of both nations for ten years. The two parties agreed to arbitration in the matter of compensation for slaves taken by the British in the recent war, from which American slave owners ultimately received $1,204,960. The commercial convention of 1815 was extended for ten years, but American negotiators were unable to gain acceptable trading rights for Americans in the British West Indies. The British refused to surrender the principle of impressment,* a point the Americans had been eager to win. Nevertheless, the treaty was quickly ratified and stands as a major contribution to Anglo-American friendship. Albert Gallatin* and Richard Rush* signed the convention for the United States on October 20, 1818; the British negotiators were Henry Goulbourn and Frederick John Robinson. Bemis, Samuel

F., *John Quincy Adams and the Foundations of American Foreign Policy* (1949); Perkins, Bradford, *Castlereagh and Adams* (1964).

CONVENTION OF 1899, treaty among the United States, Germany, and Great Britain. This treaty, signed in Washington on December 2, 1899, settled the Samoan question. The Samoan Islands were partitioned between Germany and the United States, and Britain, which had also shared in the joint protectorate established by the Treaty of Berlin (1889),* was compensated with the formerly German Tonga Islands and other concessions in West Africa. The United States received the island of Tutuila, with its excellent harbor at Pago Pago, which pleased the Navy Department. Anti-imperialists protested that the treaty would "blot out . . . a sovereign nation . . . with whom we have treaty relations," but the Senate ratified the treaty January 16, 1900, and a month later President McKinley placed Tutuila under control of the navy. Campbell, Charles S., *Anglo-American Understanding, 1898–1903* (1957); *FR* (1899), 667–71; Henderson, John B., *American Diplomatic Questions* (1901); Ryden, George H., *The Foreign Policy of the United States in Relation to Samoa* (1933).

COOLIDGE, THOMAS JEFFERSON (1831–1920). A descendant of his namesake, Thomas Jefferson Coolidge was born August 26, 1831, in Boston, attended boarding schools in Europe, and was graduated from Harvard in 1850. He entered business, first in the East India trade. In 1857, he became treasurer of Boott Mills, a cotton-spinning industry in New England. Although he maintained connections in the textile industry, his business interests grew to include banking and a stint as president of the Atchison, Topeka, and Santa Fe Railroad. A Republican, Coolidge was first called to public service as a delegate to the Washington Conference (1889).* In 1892, he was appointed minister to France, a post he held for eleven months. He spoke French and got along well with the government, even during the touchy incident in which Captain Borup, a U.S. military attaché, was accused of obtaining and passing to the Germans French military documents, which led to his recall. Coolidge was also linked to a scandal involving the defunct Panama scheme of Ferdinand de Lesseps, in which several Americans allegedly shared in the corruption and plunder. Coolidge recommended the elevation of the mission to an embassy, headed by an ambassador; this was done with his successor. In 1898–1899, he was a member of a Joint High Commission, consisting of representatives from the United States, Great Britain, Canada, and Newfoundland, which investigated various U.S.–Canadian problems such as the Alaskan boundary dispute,* the fisheries question, and the fur-sealing controversy. He returned to Boston after 1899, was active in the development of the Boston park system, and was a benefactor of research in physics. Coolidge married Helty Sullivan Appleton in 1852 and died in Boston on November 17, 1920. *DAB*, 4:395; *T. Jefferson Coolidge, 1831–1920, An Autobiography* (1923); *NCAB*, 12:58; *New York Times*, November 18, 1920; Willson, Beckles, *America's Ambassadors to France, 1777–1927* (1928).

COOMBS, FRANK L. (1853–1934). Born in Napa, California, on December 27, 1853, Frank L. Coombs was graduated with a law degree from Columbian (now George Washington) University in 1875 and gained admittance to the bar the following year. In 1879, he married Belle M. Roper, and from that year until 1884 he was district attorney for Napa County. A Republican, he served several terms in the California state legislature (1887, 1889, 1891–1892, 1893–1897). In 1892, he was named minister to Japan. In the fourteen months he occupied that post, he continued work on the treaty revision question and observed a quarrel between Portugal and Japan, in which Portugal withdrew its consul general* and Japan revoked Portugal's extraterritoriality privileges. According to Treat, Coombs was more sympathetic toward Japan than his predecessor, John F. Swift,* advocating, for example, joint action on immigration and anti-Japanese discrimination problems then current in the United States. He hoped Japan would take voluntary steps to prohibit the emigration of laborers, but no action was taken at that time. After his mission to Japan, Coombs returned to California, where he was state librarian (1898–1899), U.S. attorney for the Northern District (1898–1901), and a U.S. congressman (1901–1903). He died in Napa on October 5, 1934. Treat, Payson J., *Diplomatic Relations between the United States and Japan, 1853–1895*, 2 vols. (1932). *WWWA*, 1 (1897–1942):257.

COOPER, JOHN SHERMAN (b. 1901). Born August 23, 1901, in Somerset, Kentucky, John Sherman Cooper attended Centre College (1918–1919), graduated from Yale (A.B., 1923), and studied at Harvard Law School (1923–1925), gaining admittance to the Kentucky bar in 1928. He embarked on a political career as a Republican with election to the Kentucky legislature. After one term, he became county judge in Pulaski County, Kentucky, a position he held for eight years, until 1938. After military service in Europe during World War II, Cooper remained in Germany after World War II and reorganized the Bavarian judicial system. Returning to Kentucky in late 1945, he spent a short time as a circuit judge before going to the U.S. Senate in 1946. He served three separate periods of time in the Senate: 1946–1948, 1953–1955, and 1957–1973. From 1949 to 1951, Cooper was attached to the U.S. delegation to the United Nations* and was an adviser to Secretary of State Dean Acheson* on North Atlantic Treaty Organization (NATO)* affairs. His Senate career was interrupted in 1955 when he lost to former Vice-President Alben Barkley; the Eisenhower administration then named him ambassador to India. There for less than a year, Cooper used a quiet style of diplomacy to smooth relations ruffled by India's neutralism in the cold war* and leanings toward economic socialism and convinced the administration that India's international stance was sincere and that India deserved longer-term foreign aid commitments from the United States. In 1973, Cooper retired from the Senate but returned to public life the following year as the first U.S. ambassador to East Germany, where his two-year mission was largely organizational and routine, although his reporting on hardening Soviet attitudes toward the West reputedly had an effect on President Gerald R. Ford's foreign policy in 1976. Cooper, who has been married twice, practices law in Washington. *NCAB* 1:376; Schulman, Robert, *John Sherman Cooper: The Global Kentuckian* (1976); *WWA* (1986–1987):573.

CORWIN, THOMAS (1794–1865). Born July 29, 1794, in Bourbon County, Kentucky, Thomas Corwin was a self-educated person who read law and gained admittance to the bar about 1816. He married Sarah Ross, moved to Ohio, and served three terms in the Ohio Assembly. A Whig and supporter of Henry Clay,* the "Wagon Boy of Ohio" was promoted to the U.S. House of Representatives (1831–1841). He then was elected governor of Ohio (1841–1843) and U.S. senator (1845–1850), where he was an opponent of the war with Mexico. President Millard Fillmore appointed Corwin secretary of the treasury in 1850, and after a respite from political office (1853–1859), he returned to the House of Representatives as a Republican for one term (1859–1861). Named minister to Mexico by President Abraham Lincoln in 1861, Corwin had to counter the efforts of Confederate envoy John Pickett* to win Mexican recognition. He urged, without success, U.S. loans to Mexico to prevent European intervention but did negotiate an agreement whereby the United States would assume Mexico's debt interest on a loan basis. This agreement, however, was not ratified. In general, Corwin avoided contact with the Maximilian government and continued to recognize the Juárez government. After the war, he returned to Washington and practiced law for a short time before his death in the capital, December 18, 1865. Auer, J. Jeffery, "Lincoln's Minister to Mexico," *Ohio State Archaeological and Historical Quarterly* 69 (1950): 115–28; *DAB*, 4:465.

COUNCIL OF FOREIGN MINISTERS. At British Prime Minister Winston Churchill's suggestion, the delegations to the Yalta Conference (1945)* agreed that the foreign ministers of the United States, Great Britain, France, and the Soviet Union should meet periodically to deal with the complex problems encountered at Yalta and anticipated in the future. The Council of Foreign Ministers was confirmed at the Potsdam Conference* by means of the Potsdam Protocol, August 2, 1945, and was instructed to draft peace treaties with Italy, Romania, Bulgaria, Hungary, and Finland. After council meetings in London (September 11-October 2, 1945) and Paris (April 25-May 17 and June 15-July 12, 1946), the foreign ministers were able to present draft treaties at the Paris Peace Conference* so that a larger number of nations could deliberate. From the beginning, the United States prevented the council from debating the issue of Japan, over Soviet objections, only one of many differences that emerged among the Allies during these meetings, paralleling the development of the cold war.* The Council of Foreign Ministers meeting in Moscow (March 12-April 24, 1947) confirmed cold war hostilities, as Secretary of State George C. Marshall,* newly appointed and unfamiliar with the issues before the foreign ministers, came away so impressed with Soviet intransigence that the Marshall Plan* soon followed. After 1947, the foreign ministers deadlocked for several years over the matter of an

Austrian State Treaty,* which was not concluded until 1955. After 1955, the Council of Foreign Ministers was supplanted by summit diplomacy and discontinued its meetings, although in 1958, C. L. Sulzberger of the *New York Times* suggested that the council be revived to conduct disarmament talks. Gaddis, John L., *Russia, the Soviet Union, and the United States* (1978); McNeill, William H., *America, Britain, and Russia* (1953); *New York Times*, January 13, 1958; Ward, Patricia Dawson, *The Threat of Peace: James F. Byrnes and the Council of Foreign Ministers, 1945–1946* (1979); Wheeler-Bennett, John W., and Anthony Nicholls, *The Semblance of Peace* (1972).

COUNCIL OF FOUR. This was the name applied to the working body consisting of Woodrow Wilson, Georges Clemenceau, David Lloyd George, and Vittorio Orlando, which dealt with the major problems at the Paris Peace Conference, 1919.* The Council of Four was known, more informally, as the Big Four.* Bailey, Thomas A., *Woodrow Wilson and the Lost Peace* (1944); Duroselle, Jean-Baptiste, *From Wilson to Roosevelt* (1963); *FR* (1919), The Paris Peace Conference, vols. 5–6.

COUNCIL OF TEN. This was the organization initially set up for the working sessions of the Paris Peace Conference, 1919.* Composed of the heads of government and foreign ministers of the United States, Great Britain, France, Italy, and Japan, the council was reduced by the suggestion of Woodrow Wilson and Georges Clemenceau in March 1919 to a Council of Four.* Japan was excluded except in Far Eastern matters, and the foreign ministers met separately to deal with lesser problems. Bailey, Thomas A., *Woodrow Wilson and the Lost Peace* (1944); Duroselle, Jean-Baptiste, *From Wilson to Roosevelt* (1963); *FR* (1919), The Paris Peace Conference, vol. 4.

COUNCIL ON FOREIGN RELATIONS, internationalist organization (1921–). Primarily an educational organization, the Council on Foreign Relations was created in 1921 by a number of prominent business, professional, and government leaders. Its membership was limited to 650, and its function was to create understanding of foreign affairs and foreign policy through meetings, study groups, and discussion. In 1922, the council founded a quarterly journal, *Foreign Affairs*, now the most prestigious foreign policy publication. In 1931, the council also began publishing yearly diplomatic summaries, *The United States in World Affairs*, and has through the years published various other reference works and monographs. Although highly elitist, the organization was important between the wars in converting substantial sectors of American business and governmental leadership to internationalism. By World War II, the original objectives of the council had changed somewhat, as a close relationship between it and the State Department had developed, with several council members serving as advisers or consultants to the government on such matters as planning for the United Nations.* With such connections, the council took on the appearance of having semiofficial statues, which has subsequently never fully been removed.

Council on Foreign Relations, *The Council on Foreign Relations: A Record of Twenty-five Years* (1947); Divine, Robert A., *Second Chance* (1967); Schulzinger, Robert D., *The Wise Men of Foreign Affairs: The History of the Council on Foreign Relations* (1984).

COUNSELOR, diplomatic official. A counselor is the senior diplomatic secretary and occasionally the second-ranking diplomat at an embassy, although more often, in recent years, the second position is held by a Foreign Service officer with the title of minister* or minister-counselor, often referred to as the deputy chief of mission (DCM), and the counselor is the third-ranking officer. The counselor section does political and liaison reporting, coordinates intelligence activities, negotiates political questions too minor to concern the ambassador, and handles politically related and representational matters. The rank of counselor was created in 1916. Gamboa, Melquiades J., *Elements of Diplomatic and Consular Practice* (1966); Johnson, Richard A., *The Administration of United States Foreign Policy* (1971).

COX, SAMUEL SULLIVAN (1824–1889). Samuel S. "Sunset" Cox was born in Zanesville, Ohio, on September 30, 1824, attended Ohio University before graduating from Brown University in 1846, and read law. He practiced law in Cincinnati briefly but, preferring literature and travel, went to Europe in the early 1850s, returned, and wrote *A Buckeye Abroad* (1852). The next year he became owner-editor of the *Ohio Statesman* (Columbus). This led to a political career that saw Cox in the U.S. Congress as an Ohio Democratic congressman from 1857 to 1865, and after an 1866 move to New York, as a congressman from that state from 1869 to 1885 and from 1886 to 1889. As a congressman, he was on the Foreign Affairs Committee and played a part in the settlement of the *Trent* affair (1861).* In 1885, he was appointed minister to Turkey, and, although he spent only a year there, his was an active and constructive mission. Cox watched over American missionaries and schools and negotiated naturalization and extradition treaties, as well as commercial and trademark agreements. He gave active encouragement for U.S. business to come to Turkey to counter growing Russian influence through the Black Sea. Finally, Cox sent informative reports on the rebellion in Eastern Rumelia in 1885, a conflict that threatened to spread into a general European war. A congressman again after his return from Turkey, Cox died September 10, 1889, in New York City. He was married to Julia C. Buckingham and wrote *Three Decades of Federal Legislation* (1885), which covers most of his congressional career, and *Diversions of A Diplomat in Turkey* (1887). *DAB*, 4:482; Lindsay, David, *"Sunset" Cox: Irrepressible Democrat* (1959); *NCAB*, 6:369.

CRANE, CHARLES RICHARD (1858–1939). Charles R. Crane was born in Chicago on August 7, 1858, and spent several years in local public schools before being apprenticed in his father's plumbing company at the age of fourteen. By 1894, he had risen to vice-president of the Crane Company; from 1912 to 1914, he was president before selling his interests to his brother. A Republican in the Theodore Roosevelt–William Howard Taft years, he was nominated minister to China in 1909 but never served due to Japanese objections to a speech in which Crane had predicted a U.S.-Japanese war and to his plan to take with him a militantly anti-Japanese secretary. By 1912, his progressive sympathies had made him a Wilson supporter and a financial backer of *Harper's Weekly*. In 1917, Wilson sent him on a special mission to Russia. Upon his return, he, with Henry Churchill King, was appointed to the Inter-Allied Commission on Mandates in Turkey (the King-Crane Commission)* and wrote a report synthesizing Middle Eastern problems. In 1920–1921, Crane was minister to China, where his major work was with the International Famine Relief Committee. He retired to Woods Hole, Massachusetts, in 1921 and pursued his interest in marine biology, although his frequent travels, contacts with international leaders, and philanthropy kept him in the news. He married Cornelia W. Smith in 1881 and died in Palm Springs, California, on February 15, 1939. *DAB*, Supp. 2:128; Howard, Harry N., *The King-Crane Commission* (1963); *New York Times*, February 16, 1939.

CRAWFORD, WILLIAM HARRIS (1772–1834). Born in Amherst County, on the Virginia frontier, on February 24, 1772, William H. Crawford was privately educated, admitted to the bar, and moved to Georgia where he taught school and then practiced law in Augusta. After his marriage to Susanna Girardin in 1804, Crawford settled on a plantation near Lexington, Georgia, where he prospered and continued a political career begun in the state legislature in 1803. In 1807, he was elected to the U.S. Senate for a term. From 1813 to 1815, he was minister to France. Normal diplomatic relations were impossible because the Napoleonic Wars were at their climax, and Crawford's duties included resolving quarrels among American consuls* over such matters as privateering and prize money, observing the defeat of Napoleon and his attempted comeback, and pressing maritime spoliation claims (one of several successive ministers to deal with that difficult question). After his return, Crawford was secretary of the treasury, 1816–1825, and he was prominently mentioned for the presidency in 1816 and again in 1824. However, a stroke in late 1823 left him partially paralyzed, ruining his presidential chances and forcing his retirement from the national scene. He served as a Georgia judge until 1831 and died September 15, 1834, in Elbert County, Georgia. An edited version of Crawford's diaries written in Paris is found in *Smith College Studies in History* 11, 2 (1925). *DAB*, 4:527; Egan, Clifford L., *Neither Peace nor War: Franco-American Relations, 1803–1812* (1983); Green, Philip J., *William H. Crawford* (1965); Mooney, Chase C., *William H. Crawford, 1772–1834* (1974); *NCAB*, 4:82; Willson, Beckles, *America's Ambassadors to France, 1777–1927* (1928).

CREOLE AFFAIR (1841–1842). In October 1841, the American ship *Creole*, carrying slaves, was cruising along the Atlantic coast when the slaves mutinied and took the ship to the Bahamas, a British colony. The local authorities refused to release the mutineers to the United States, in the absence of treaty provisions to that effect. The dispute led to negotiations between Secretary of State Daniel Webster* and British Minister Lord Ashburton, resulting in a treaty of extradition for certain high crimes (1842). This extradition treaty accompanied the better-known Webster-Ashburton Treaty (1842),* which settled the northeast boundary question. Duniway, Clyde, A., "Daniel Webster," in Bemis, Samuel F., ed., *American Secretaries of State and Their Diplomacy*, vol. 5 (1928); Jones, Howard, *To the Webster-Ashburton Treaty* (1977).

CROMWELL, WILLIAM NELSON (1854–1948). Born in Brooklyn in 1854, William Nelson Cromwell became a founding partner in the law firm of Sullivan and Cromwell, whose lawyers included John Foster Dulles* and Allen W. Dulles. Cromwell worked from 1896 for the New Panama Canal Company* to prevent the Nicaraguan route from being adopted by Congress as the site of an isthmian canal. He lobbied successfully with Philippe Bunau-Varilla, a French engineer who had worked for the New Panama Canal Company and who later was centrally involved in the movement for Panamanian independence, for acceptance by Congress of the rival Panama route and for the purchase of the rights and equipment of the New Panama Canal Company. In 1905, Cromwell was accused by a promoter, Ella Rawls Reader, who was trying to become a fiscal agent for the Dominican Republic, of betraying her plans to the U.S. government, thus preventing her from becoming the fiscal agent, but the Dominican Republic government later said that Reader's proposal had not been seriously considered. In the same year, 1905, Cromwell became the fiscal agent for Panama in the United States, after having accompanied William Howard Taft there the preceding year to negotiate the Taft Agreement.* He remained Panama's fiscal agent until 1937, and died in New York City on July 19, 1948. Dean, Arthur H., *William Nelson Cromwell, 1854–1948* (1957); McCullough, David, *The Path between the Seas* (1977); Munro, Dana G., *Intervention and Dollar Diplomacy in the Caribbean, 1900–1921* (1964); *New York Times*, July 20, 1948; Weisberger, Bernard A., "The Strange Affair of the Taking of the Panama Canal Zone," *American Heritage* (October 1976): 6–11, 68–77.

CRONKITE, WALTER LELAND, JR. (b. 1916). Probably television's most renowned newsman, Walter Cronkite was born November 4, 1916, in St. Joseph, Missouri, and attended the University of Texas (1933–1935). After college, he was a news writer and editor on various papers before becoming a United Press (UP) war correspondent in Europe from 1942 to 1945. Remaining in Europe after the war, Cronkite reopened several UP news bureaus and was bureau manager in Moscow from 1946 to 1948. After a year (1948–1949) of lecturing and freelance writing, he joined CBS-TV as a news correspondent, becoming an anchorman in 1962. In this position he achieved great trust and credibility, promoting a generally pro-administration, cold warrior* viewpoint. In 1968, however, he returned from a trip to Vietnam shortly after the Tet offensive highly disillusioned about the deception of the military hierarchy and the reality of the war as opposed to the official version of the war. In his first attempt at "advocacy journalism," Cronkite urged a negotiated end to the war. His opinion had a great impact on the general public and may have helped convince President Lyndon B. Johnson not to run for reelection in 1968. Cronkite married Mary Elizabeth Maxwell in 1940 and retired as anchorman for "CBS Evening News" in 1981. Since 1981, he has been involved in occasional documentary productions for the network. He has written *Challenges of Change* (1971) and edited *Eye on the World* (1970), a collection of news stories of that year. *CB* (1975):95–98; Gates, Gary Paul, *Air Time: The Inside Story of CBS News* (1978); Karnow, Stanley, *Vietnam: A History* (1983); *WWA* (1986–1987):612.

CROWDER, ENOCH HERBERT (1859–1932). A graduate of West Point (1881) and a career army officer, Enoch Crowder was also a leading figure in early U.S.-Cuban relations. He was born in Edinburgh, Missouri, on April 11, 1859, and after West Point taught military science at the University of Missouri while earning a law degree there. His active duty in the army included service as judge advocate general in the Department of the Platte (1895–1898), a stint in the Philippines (1898–1901), during which he was, for a time, an associate justice of the Philippine Supreme Court, and an observer in the Russo-Japanese War.* Crowder was in Cuba on two separate occasions. From 1906 to 1909, he was a member of the occupation force, acting as minister of state and justice, where, under the aegis of the Platt Amendment,* he brought about economic, legal, and administrative reforms. He was a special presidential representative in Cuba in 1919 and again in 1921–1923, observing elections and the Cuban political scene; this led directly to his selection as the first U.S. ambassador to Cuba (1923–1927). As ambassador, he obtained tariff concessions for U.S. businesses, dealt with several claims cases, and organized relief efforts after the severe hurricane of 1926. After his return in 1927, Crowder practiced law in Chicago until 1931 and died in Washington on May 7, 1932. *DAB*, Supp. 1:210; Lockmiller, David A., *Enoch H. Crowder: Soldier, Lawyer, Statesman* (1955); *NCAB*, A:455; *New York Times*, May 8, 1932.

CRUISE MISSILES, DEPLOYMENT OF. A North Atlantic Treaty Organization* agreement in 1979 provided for the deployment of intermediate-range cruise missiles in Great Britain, Italy, and West Germany, with Pershing II missiles also to be placed in West Germany. In 1983, deployment took place in these countries amid considerable political protest from antinuclear groups and the Soviet Union, which broke off arms negotiations in Geneva. In 1985, Belgium and the Netherlands approved the deployment of cruise missiles on their soil. Arms talks toward an Intermediate Nuclear Forces (INF) Treaty* resumed in 1985 and were successfully concluded in 1987. Under the terms of the INF Treaty, the cruise missiles and Pershing II missiles will be removed from Western

Europe over a three-year period. The treaty is seen as a successful outcome of the U.S. dual-track policy—to deploy missiles and negotiate their elimination simultaneously. Betts, Richard K., *Cruise Missiles* (1981); *New York Times*, December 13, 1979, December 6, 1987, May 8, 1988, May 28, 1988.

CUBAN MISSILE CRISIS (1962). This major U.S.-Soviet confrontation arose with the American discovery in August 1962 that the Soviet Union was placing nuclear missiles in Cuba, well within striking distance of U.S. targets. Feeling his resolve put to the test, President John F. Kennedy responded on October 22, 1962, with a quarantine, an arrangement somewhat like a blockade,* to prevent further Soviet missile delivery to Cuba, along with a blunt public demand that the missiles already in Cuba be dismantled and removed. After several days of high international tension and the exchange of letters between Kennedy and Soviet Premier Nikita Khrushchev, the Soviets agreed on October 28 to stop work on the missile sites and take out the missiles already in place. In return, the United States pledged not to invade Cuba and in a later, secret arrangement removed obsolete missiles from Turkey. The Soviet motivation for introducing the missiles into Cuba seems to have been partly a matter of internal politics, partly due to the desire to gain advantage in the ongoing rivalry with the People's Republic of China, and partly encouraged by a feeling of U.S. weakness drawn from the Bay of Pigs invasion* disaster. For the United States, the outcome of the Cuban missile crisis was viewed as a prestigious diplomatic victory, although it also accelerated a Soviet nuclear arms buildup and hastened the downfall of Khrushchev. Some historians critical of Kennedy's foreign policy have concluded that his quarantine and virtual ultimatum were unnecessarily risky and that the problem could have been solved by means of more conventional diplomacy. According to Gaddis, the Cuban missile crisis demonstrated the deterrent power of nuclear weapons; without them, war might well have occurred. Alexander, George L., and Richard Smoke, *Deterrence in American Foreign Policy* (1974); Dinerstein, Herbert, *The Making of a Missile Crisis: October 1962* (1976); Divine, Robert M., ed., *The Cuban Missile Crisis* (1971); Gaddis, John L., *Russia, The Soviet Union, and the United States* (1978); Hammond, Paul Y., *Cold War and Detente* (1975); Kennedy, Robert F., *Thirteen Days* (1969).

CUBAN RECIPROCITY TREATY (1902). This treaty, signed December 11, 1902, was designed primarily to aid the Cuban sugar industry, whose prosperity the Roosevelt administration believed was important to the political stability of Cuba. Reciprocal tariff cuts were provided for Cuban sugar and other products imported into Cuba. In general, reductions in American duties were greater than those in Cuban tariffs. According to Munro, the treaty was of real economic benefit to Cuba, contributing to a large increase in sugar production, but with the unfortunate later result of creating an overdependence on a one-crop economy. Munro, Dana G., *Intervention and Dollar Diplomacy in the Caribbean, 1900–1921* (1964).

CYPRUS QUESTION (1974–1976). In July 1974, following a Greek-sponsored military coup in Cyprus that deposed the nationalist leader, Archbishop Makarios, the Turkish army invaded the island, ostensibly to protect the Turkish minority within the population. The Turks effected a brutal seizure of the northern third of Cyrus, inflicting many civilian casualties and forcing an ethnic division among native Cypriots. This situation presented a serious dilemma for the United States. On the one hand, the Greek military government, which had come to power in 1967, had proved itself a staunch and loyal ally of the North Atlantic Treaty Organization (NATO).* On the other hand, the Turks were also dependable partners in the NATO alliance. Other complications came from the fact that the Nixon administration (and especially President Nixon) was paralyzed by the Watergate scandal, then in its final weeks. Secretary of State Henry Kissinger,* moreover, was at the time deeply involved in Middle East diplomacy. Since he viewed Makarios as a troublesome nationalist, he vacillated with regard to formulating a U.S. response, claiming "private diplomacy" was at work. Congress, meanwhile, voted an arms embargo against Turkey over Kissinger's objections, but the embargo was partially lifted the next year. By 1976, the situation had stabilized, and in 1983, the Turks created a state out of the territory they continued to occupy. In 1988, economic necessities caused Turkey to agree to United Nations–sponsored reunification talks. Couloumbis, Theodore A., *The United States, Greece, and Turkey: The Troubled Triangle* (1983); Hitchens, Christopher, *Cyprus* (1984); *New York Times*, July 5, 1988; Stern, Laurence, *The Wrong Horse* (1977).

DALLAS, GEORGE MIFFLIN (1792–1864). A Philadelphian, George M. Dallas was born July 10, 1792. He graduated from Princeton in 1810, read law, and was admitted to the bar in 1813. After service in the War of 1812, he served as secretary to Albert Gallatin* on the mission to negotiate the Treaty of Ghent (1814).* After a brief time as a Treasury Department clerk, Dallas returned to private life and practiced law. In 1831, he was elected to the U.S. Senate; in 1833, he began two years as attorney general of Pennsylvania. A Jacksonian Democrat, Dallas was named minister to Russia by President Martin Van Buren in 1837. His two years in Russia were of little importance apart from issues concerning Pacific trade. In 1844, Dallas was elected vice-president in the administration of James Knox Polk, and in 1856 he was appointed minister to Great Britain, his most important diplomatic post. In London, he handled discussions over problems arising from the Clayton-Bulwer Treaty (1850),* especially with regard to British reluctance to vacate areas of Central America along the Caribbean coast. The result of these talks was the Dallas-Clarendon Treaty (1856),* never ratified. Dallas claimed to have persuaded the British to abandon their policy of visit and search of American ships in peacetime, although Willson claims that Dallas contributed little. Dallas's letters written from London have earned him a literary reputation. In 1816, he had married Sophia Nicklin, and on December 31, 1864, he died in Philadelphia. Belohlavek, John M., *George Mifflin Dallas: Jacksonian Patrician* (1977); *DAB*, 5:38; Dallas, Susan, ed., *Diary of George Mifflin Dallas While U.S. Minister to Russia, 1837–39, and to England, 1856–61* (1892); Willson, Beckles, *America's Ambassadors to England, 1785–1929* (1929).

DALLAS-CLARENDON CONVENTION (1856), projected treaty between the United States and Great Britain. Signed by George M. Dallas* and George Villiers, earl of Clarendon, on October 17, 1856, this agreement attempted to solve some of the territorial and jurisdictional questions that had arisen subsequent to the signing of the Clayton-Bulwer Treaty (1850).* The convention set boundaries for the Mosquito Territory and Belize and recognized the free territory of the Bay Islands as part of Honduras, pending an Anglo-Honduran treaty to that effect. Ratification by the Senate failed because of the Bay Islands clause; the American position was that Honduras had always owned the islands. The failure of the Dallas-Clarendon Convention led to strong but unsuccessful agitation in Congress to abrogate the Clayton-Bulwer Treaty. Humphreys, R. A., *The Diplomatic History of British Honduras, 1638–1901* (1961); Williams, Mary W., *Anglo-American Isthmian Diplomacy, 1815–1915* (1916).

DANIELS, JOSEPHUS, JR. (1862–1948). Born May 18, 1862, in Washington, North Carolina, Josephus Daniels, Jr., attended the Wilson (North Carolina) Collegiate Institute, studied law, and was admitted to the bar in 1885. He embarked on a career in journalism, owning and editing various weekly papers in North Carolina. In 1894, he consolidated three papers to form the *Raleigh News and Observer*, which he published for fifty-three years. A prominent Democrat, Daniels supported William Jennings Bryan* and served as secretary of the navy (1913–1921) under Woodrow Wilson. Upon the return of the Democrats to power in 1933, Daniels was named ambassador to Mexico, an appointment initially criticized because of the U.S. intervention at Veracruz during his navy secretaryship. But he soon gained popularity and in eight years in Mexico City dealt ably with a number of serious problems for Americans resulting from Mexican land reform and the expropriation of oil holdings. In the latter area, Daniels's tact prevented the rupture of diplomatic relations and led to a settlement of outstanding Mexican-American disputes in 1941. In 1888, he married Addie Warth Bagley, who died in 1943. On January 15, 1948, Daniels died in Raleigh. Cronon, E. David, *Josephus Daniels in Mexico* (1960); *DAB*, Supp. 4:215; Daniels, Josephus, *Shirt-Sleeve Diplomat* (1947); *New York Times*, January 16, 1948.

DANISH WEST INDIES, ACQUISITION OF (1917). In 1915, the United States began negotiations with Denmark for the purchase of the Danish West Indies, motivated at least partly by fear of German activity in the Caribbean. American Minister to Denmark Maurice F. Egan initiated the talks in Copenhagen, but Secretary of State Robert Lansing* completed the arrangements late in the year. The treaty, signed in early 1916, was not ratified until January 1917, a month after Danish ratification. The purchase price for the three islands (now known as the Virgin Islands) was $25 million. Callcott, Wilfrid H., *The Caribbean Policy of the United States, 1890–1920* (1942); *FR* (1917), 457–707; Tansill, Charles C., *The Purchase of the Danish West Indies* (1932).

DAVIES, JOHN PATON, JR. (b. 1908). One of a number of celebrated China experts following World War II, John Paton Davis was born to missionary parents in Kiating, China, on April 6, 1908. During the 1920s, he studied at Yenching University in Peking but received a B.S. degree from Columbia in 1931, the same year he joined the Foreign Service. From the beginning of his career, he specialized in Chinese affairs, serving at minor posts in Kumming, Peking, Mukden, Hankow, and Chunking before and during World War II. He was an adviser to Generals Joseph Stilwell and Patrick Hurley* during the war, and it was his realistic view of the civil war in China that later torpedoed his diplomatic career. As early as 1944, he believed that the United States should give political recognition to the Communist Chinese as a means of keeping them apart from Moscow, providing that an acceptable coalition government between the Communists and the Nationalist government of Chiang Kai-shek could not be formed. In the early 1950s, the China Lobby* and Hurley accused Davis of disloyalty and demanded his removal from the Foreign Service. By that time, he had served as first secretary in Moscow, on the State Department's Policy Planning Staff, and in West Germany. He was forced to undergo numerous security checks; finally the State Department Loyalty Board recommended his firing in 1954 after testimony by Hurley. Davies went to Peru and for a number of years was in the furniture business in Lima. In 1972, he published *Dragon by the Tail*, a memoir. Kahn, E. J. Jr., *The China Hands* (1972); Lauren, Paul Gordon, ed., *The China Hands' Legacy* (1987); Schoenbaum, Eleanora W., *Political Profiles: The Truman Years* (1978).

DAVIES, JOSEPH EDWARD (1876–1958). Joseph E. Davies was born November 29, 1876, in Watertown, Wisconsin, and graduated from the University of Wisconsin (1898) and its law school (1901). He married Emlen Knight in 1902 and began law practice that year, serving as state's attorney (1902–1906). A Democrat, he was named commissioner of corporations in 1913 and chairman of the Federal Trade Commission in 1915. At the Paris Peace Conference,* Davies was an adviser to President Woodrow Wilson. Defeated for the U.S. Senate in 1918, he returned to private law practice for the next eighteen years. In November 1936, Davies became ambassador to the Soviet Union, a position he held until June 1938. His book, *Mission to Moscow* (1941), recounts his activities in Moscow, which were principally concerned with observations of the internal political situation, the Soviet debt question, and the Soviet Union's views of European and Far Eastern developments. His sympathetic account was made into a movie in 1943 designed to elicit American goodwill toward its wartime ally. Davies also served as ambassador to Belgium and Luxembourg (1938–1939). During World War II, he went on special missions to the USSR (1943) to make preliminary arrangements for the Teheran Conference* and to Britain (1945) to do the same for the Potsdam Conference.* After the war, Davies advocated military preparedness to counter Communist expansion; he was chairman of a commission that studied universal military training (1946). His first wife died in 1935, and he married Marjorie Merriweather Post, from whom he was divorced in 1955. He died May 9, 1958, in Washington. Eagles, Keith D., *Ambassador Joseph E. Davies and American-Soviet Relations, 1937–1941* (1985); Gaddis, John L., *The United States and the Origins of the Cold War* (1972); *New York Times*, May 10, 1958; *WWWA* 3 (1951–1960):210.

DAVIS, ELMER HOLMES (1890–1958). Elmer Davis, the voice of much of middle America in the years just preceding World War II, was born January 13, 1890, in Aurora, Indiana, graduated from Franklin (Indiana) College (A.B., 1910; M.A., 1911), and, as a Rhodes Scholar, from Queen's College, Oxford (B.A., 1912). From 1913 to 1914, he worked on the editorial staff of *Adventure;* in 1914, he began ten years' service on the *New York Times*. From 1924 to 1939, he was a freelance writer, producing popular fiction and essays for magazines such as the *Saturday Evening Post*. In 1939, he became a news analyst for CBS, where his even-toned, reassuring voice brought him high ratings. Davis, a close friend of Stanley K. Hornbeck,* became an interventionist in the spring of 1940 after the German invasion of the Low Countries and joined the Century Group.* His commentaries made good use of sarcasm and humor and paralleled the changing public mood of the nation during these years. He left CBS in 1942 to become director of the Office of War Information. From 1945 to 1953, he was a radio newsman for ABC and after 1954 appeared occasionally as a television commentator. Also, in 1954, he wrote a best-selling series of essays, *But We Were Born Free*. Davis married Florence MacMillan in 1917 and died in Washington on May 18, 1958. Burlingame, Roger, *Don't Let Them Scare You: The Life and Times of Elmer Davis* (1961); Culbert, David H., *News for Everyman* (1976); *New York Times*, May 19, 1958; *WWWA*, 3 (1951–1960): 211.

DAVIS, JOHN CHANDLER BANCROFT (1822–1907). John C. B. Davis was born in Worcester, Massachusetts, on December 29, 1822, and graduated from Harvard in 1847, three years after his admission to the Massachusetts bar. From 1849 to 1852, he was secretary of the legation in London, and from 1854 to 1861 he worked as a correspondent for the *Times* of London. In 1869, President Ulysses S. Grant appointed him assistant secretary of state, and he became deeply involved in the negotiations leading to the Treaty of Washington (1871).* He served as minister to Germany, 1874–1877, and was again appointed assistant secretary of state in 1881 under Secretary of State Frederick T. Frelinghuysen.* During that time, he went on a confidential mission to Britain on the Irish-American question and advocated, without success, the abrogation of the Clayton-Bulwer Treaty (1850).* After his diplomatic career, Davis spent nearly twenty years as reporter for the U.S. Supreme Court and editor of the *United States Reports* volumes of the court, becoming an authority on judicial history. Among his writings is *Mr. Fish and the Alabama Claims* (1893). He died in Washington on December 27, 1907. *DAB*, 5:134; *New York Times*, December 28, 1907; Pletcher, David, *The Awkward Years* (1962).

DAVIS, JOHN WILLIAM (1873–1955). A native of Clarksburg, West Virginia, John W. Davis graduated from Washington and Lee (1892) and received a law degree from the same school in 1895. He was admitted to the bar in 1895 and after two years of teaching law at Washington and Lee entered into law partnership with his father. He became politically active in the Democratic party as well, serving a term in the West Virginia House of Delegates (1899) and a term in the U.S. House (1911–1913) before his appointment as solicitor general in 1913. In 1918, President Woodrow Wilson named Davis ambassador to Great Britain, a post he held until 1921. His appointment came about through his close friendship with Secretary of State Robert Lansing* and his strident anti-Germanism. In London, he reorganized the war-bloated embassy staff, profited from the grateful friendliness of the British government, and advised Wilson during the Paris Peace Conference,* drafting the section of the Versailles Treaty* dealing with the Rhineland. The prestige he gained in Britain contributed to his nomination as the Democratic presidential candidate in 1924. Returning to law practice after 1924, Davis opposed much of the New Deal, helped organize the Liberty League (1935), and supported Republican candidates Wendell Willkie and Dwight Eisenhower. He was married twice, to Julia T. McDonald (1899–1900) and to Ellen G. Bassel (1912–1943), and he died in Charleston, South Carolina, March 24, 1955, not long after representing South Carolina before the Supreme Court in a 1954 school desegregation case. Harbaugh, William H., *Lawyer's Lawyer* (1973); *New York Times*, March 25, 1955; Willson, Beckles, *America's Ambassadors to England, 1785–1929* (1929).

DAVIS, MONNETT BAIN (1893–1953). Born August 13, 1893, in Greencastle, Indiana, Monnett Davis graduated from the University of Colorado in 1917 and served in World War I. He joined the State Department in 1920 and held various consular posts until 1938, when he became first secretary of the Buenos Aires embassy. In 1941, Davis returned to Washington to head the Division of Foreign Service Administration; three years later, he moved to the post of deputy director of the Office of Foreign Service. After the war, Davis was minister to Denmark (1945–1946); consul general* and counselor,* Shanghai (1946); ambassador to Panama (1948–1951); and ambassador to Israel (1951–1953). In Panama he proved helpful in mediating internal political conflicts and averting civil war, and in Israel he advocated a regional defense plan for the Middle East, later seen in the Baghdad Pact.* Davis married Pearl Erhart in 1917 and died in Ramatgan, Israel, on December 26, 1953. *NCAB*, 47:475; *New York Times*, December 27, 1953; *WWWA*, 3 (1951–1960): 213.

DAVIS, NATHANIEL (b. 1925). A native of Boston, where he was born on April 12, 1925, Nathaniel Davis graduated from Brown in 1944, served in the U.S. Navy, and later received an M.A. (1947) and a Ph.D. (1960) from the Fletcher School of Law and Diplomacy at Tufts. He joined the Foreign Service in 1947 and served in minor posts in Prague, Florence, Rome, Moscow, Washington, and Caracas until 1962. In that year, he became acting director of the Peace Corps* in Chile, and later in 1962, he returned to Washington and worked as a Peace Corps administrator until 1965. After a year as minister in Bulgaria (1965–1966) and two years on the staff of the National Security Council* (1966–1968), Davis was named ambassador to Guatemala, serving three relatively uneventful years there. In 1971, he went to Chile as ambassador to try to create a better working relationship with the elected Marxist president, Salvador Allende. Two years later, Allende was overthrown and killed in a military coup, widely believed to have been the work of the Central Intelligence Agency.* Davis, however, in a well-received book, *The Last Two Years of Salvador Allende* (1985), argues that there was practically no U.S. involvement in Allende's fall. Davis left Chile just a month after the coup, becoming director general of the Foreign Service. When, in 1975, he was nominated to be assistant secretary of state for African affairs, there was opposition from the Organization of African

Unity, as well as a number of congressmen. He was confirmed but served less than a year before resigning, apparently because of disagreement with Secretary of State Henry Kissinger* over U.S. policy in the Angolan civil war.* After a tour as ambassador to Switzerland, Davis took a teaching position at the Naval War College. In 1983, he joined the faculty of Harvey Mudd College and is married to Elizabeth Kirksdale Creese. *New York Times*, September 16, 1973, June 23, 1985; *WWA* (1986–1987):662–63.

DAVIS, NORMAN HEZEKIAH (1878–1944). Norman Davis was born August 9, 1878, in Normandy, Tennessee, attended local schools, Vanderbilt, and Stanford, but never graduated from any of them. In 1902, he moved to Cuba, organized the Trust Company of Cuba (1905), and was financially successful. By 1917, he was in New York's international financial circles; success there and with the Treasury Department during the war led to his appointment as under secretary of state in 1920. In that position, he worked on a nonrecognition policy toward the Soviet Union and advocated Pan-Americanism* and improved Anglo-American relations. A Democrat, he left government service in 1921 and became known as a spokesman for disarmament, the League of Nations,* and the World Court.* He was a cofounder of the Council on Foreign Relations* and a frequent contributor to *Foreign Affairs*, as well as a delegate to the Geneva Economic Conference (1927) and the World Disarmament Conference (1932).* In 1933, he joined the Roosevelt administration as a foreign policy adviser and ambassador-at-large. Among his contributions at this time were serving as chairman of the U.S. delegation at both the London Naval Conference (1935–1936)* and the Brussels Conference (1937),* drafting much of Roosevelt's "quarantine" speech (1937), and playing a major role in the International Sugar Conference (1937). During the war years, he headed the Security Committee, an advisory body to the State Department, and advised President Roosevelt on relief matters. In addition, he was chairman of the National American Red Cross (1938–1944), an immense task during World War II. He was married to Mackie Paschall in 1898 and died in Hot Springs, Virginia, on July 2, 1944. *DAB*, Supp. 3:218; *New York Times*, July 2, 1944.

DAVIS, RICHARD HARDING (1864–1916). Born in Philadelphia on April 18, 1864, Richard Harding Davis attended Lehigh and Johns Hopkins universities, chose journalism as a career, and made his mark as a reporter covering the Johnstown (Pennsylvania) flood for the *Philadelphia Press* in 1889. He later worked for the *New York Evening Sun* and for three years was managing editor of *Harper's Weekly*. In 1897, he covered the Turkish-Greek war for the *New York Herald* and *London Times*. He achieved his greatest fame as a war correspondent, although he was also a prolific novelist, writing adventure-style fiction often set during wars or in exotic places. He reported the Spanish-American, Boer,* and Russo-Japanese wars, the Mexican Revolution, and the early years of World War I before his death at his home near Mount Kisco, New

York, on April 12, 1916. His work as a war correspondent during these conflicts was reflected in highly imagistic writing and in the development of a set of beliefs concerning America's role in the world. A friend and supporter of Theodore Roosevelt after reporting on the Rough Riders during the Spanish-American War, Davis shared Roosevelt's conviction that a strong national defense was essential. After 1900, he concerned himself with Latin America, favoring U.S. intervention and feeling that the Latin Americans were generally incompetent to govern themselves. He reported from the front lines in France and Serbia during World War I's opening year and became an outspoken advocate of U.S. entry into the war on the Allied side after the sinking of the *Lusitania*.* Davis was married twice and counted Lloyd Griscom* among his close friends. *New York Times*, April 13, 1916; Osborn, Scott C., and Robert L. Phillips, Jr., *Richard Harding Davis* (1978); *WWWA*, 1 (1897–1942):303.

DAVIS, ROY TASCO (1889–1975). Roy Tasco Davis was born June 24, 1889, in Ewing, Missouri, and graduated from LaGrange College (Missouri) in 1908. In 1910, he received a Ph.B. degree from Brown University. Davis returned to Missouri where he worked briefly as a clerk in the state legislature and as secretary of the state capitol commission before becoming secretary and business manager of Stephens College in 1914, a post he held until his entrance into the State Department in 1921. Between 1921 and 1933, he was minister to Guatemala (1921–1922), to Costa Rica (1922–1929), and to Panama (1929–1933). These were relatively quiet years in Central America; Davis's most notable work was in chairing a Honduras-Guatemala boundary commission in 1928 and acting as an unofficial mediator during the Panama revolution in 1931. Returning to Stephens College in 1933, he held the position of assistant to the president until 1937, when he became president of National Park Seminary. Between 1942 and 1953, he filled various international education posts. With the Republicans' return to the White House in 1953, Davis went to Haiti as ambassador, spending an uneventful four years there before his retirement. He was married in 1913 to Loyce Enloe and died December 27, 1975, in Chevy Chase, Maryland. *NCAB*, E:409; *WWWA*, 6 (1974–1976):105–6.

DAWES, CHARLES GATES (1865–1951). One of America's most prominent and active Republicans in the 1920s, Charles Gates Dawes was born in Marietta, Ohio, on August 27, 1865, graduated from Marietta College (A.B., 1884; A.M., 1887) and Cincinnati Law School (LL.B., 1886), and was admitted to the bar in 1886. He practiced law in Lincoln, Nebraska, 1887–1894, and then became involved in the utility business as the highly successful president of the La Crosse Gas and Light Company and, later, the Northwestern Gas, Light, and Coke Company. His first major political involvement was managing William McKinley's campaign in Illinois in 1896. In the McKinley administration he became comptroller of the currency, 1897–1902. From 1902 to 1921, Dawes was in private business as president of the Central Trust Company and for the next four years was its chairman of the board. During World War I, he was a general on General John J. Pershing's staff, and after the war, he was a member of the Liquidation Board of the War Department. In 1921, the Republican administration of Warren G. Harding named Dawes the first director of the budget. Three years later, as chairman of the Committee of Experts of the Allied Reparations Commission, Dawes was a major impetus behind the design of the Dawes Plan,* a scaling down of reparations* and reorganization of the German financial system that was probably his most conspicuous achievement. After four years (1925– 1929) as vice-president under Calvin Coolidge, Dawes served the Hoover administration as ambassador to Great Britain. He was appointed because of Hoover's conviction that he could be effective in arms reduction talks. Dawes held conferences with British Prime Minister Ramsay McDonald before the London Naval Conference (1930),* to which he was a delegate, and then helped get the resulting treaty ratified by the Senate. In addition, Dawes supported the Hoover moratorium* on international debts and advised the League of Nations* during the Manchurian crisis.* He returned from Britain in 1932 to direct the Reconstruction Finance Corporation. After several months in that post, he resigned and returned to private banking interests in Chicago. He died in Evanston, Illinois, on April 23, 1951. Dawes won the Nobel Peace Prize in 1925 (with Austen Chamberlain of Great Britain) for his work on reparations. He married Caro D. Blymyer in 1889, and wrote and performed music for the piano. *DAB*, Supp. 5:159; Dawes, Charles G., *A Journal of the Great War* (1921), and *Journal as Ambassador to Great Britain* (1939); *New York Times*, April 24, 1951; Timmons, Bascom N., *Portrait of an American: Charles G. Dawes* (1953).

DAWES PLAN (1924). This plan, worked out by a committee headed by Charles Gates Dawes,* was designed to restructure Germany's payment schedule. The committee report, published on April 24, 1924, after four months of work, recommended a reorganization of the German currency and established a schedule of payments beginning at £5 million per year and rising after the fifth year to a maximum of £125 million, guaranteed by railway and industrial bonds and customs, alcohol, sugar, and tobacco taxes. Payment could be made in German marks; transferability was the obligation of the Allied governments. In addition, the Ruhr occupation was to be ended to give Germany economic control of all its territory. Finally, Germany was to receive a £40 million loan for use as a currency reserve and for payment of the first annuity. Secretary of State Charles Evans Hughes* traveled through Europe in 1924 and worked to persuade European leaders to accept the plan, which they did at a conference in London in the summer. The Dawes Plan removed much of the politics from reparations* and contributed to European goodwill, but it failed to set a total amount of borrowing on the part of Germany and was replaced by the Young Plan (1929).* Carr, E. H., *International Relations between the Two World Wars, 1919–1939* (1947); Craig, Gordon A., and Felix Gilbert, eds., *The Diplomats, 1919–1939* (1965); *FR* (1924), 2:1–140; *FR* (1925), 2:133–65; Jonas, Manfred, *The United States and Germany* (1984).

DAWSON, THOMAS CLELAND (1865–1912). A Latin American diplomat known as the "Great Pacificator," Thomas C. Dawson was born July 30, 1865, in Hudson, Wisconsin. He graduated from Hanover College (Indiana) in 1883 and received a law degree from the Cincinnati Law School in 1886. He practiced law in Iowa from 1886 to 1897 and served as assistant attorney general of the state (1891–1894). In 1897, his diplomatic career began with his appointment as legation secretary in Rio de Janeiro, a post he held until 1904. Between 1904 and 1911, Dawson was minister to the Dominican Republic (1904–1907), Colombia (1907–1909), Chile (1909–1910), and Panama (1910–1911). In 1911, he was named resident diplomatic officer in the State Department. One of his most significant contributions came in the Dominican Republic, where he negotiated the convention for U.S. assumption of customs and financial administration. Although the convention was not ratified, a modus vivendi based on it was employed to the same end until a later convention was ratified. While minister to Panama, Dawson went to Nicaragua and negotiated the Dawson Agreements,* settling U.S.-Nicaraguan differences. By the time of his death in Washington on May 1, 1912, Dawson was regarded as the "foremost Latin American diplomat." He married Luiza Guerra Duval in 1900 and wrote a two-volume study, *The South American Republics* (1903–1904). *DAB*, 5:153; Munro, Dana G., *Intervention and Dollar Diplomacy in the Caribbean, 1900–1921* (1964); *New York Times*, May 2, 1912.

DAWSON, WILLIAM, JR. (1885–1972). William Dawson, Jr., was born August 11, 1885, in St. Paul, Minnesota, graduated from the University of Minnesota in 1906, and studied two years at the Ecole des sciences politiques in Paris. In 1908, he entered the consular service, holding posts in St. Petersburg, Barcelona, Frankfurt, Rosario, Montevideo, Danzig, and Munich before 1922. In that year, he became a consul-general-at-large, and in 1925 he began a three-year stint as an instructor at the Foreign Service School. Dawson then was appointed consul general* at Mexico City in 1928, a post he held until 1930, when he was named minister to Ecuador, the first in a series of Latin American missions, which included: minister to Colombia, 1934–1937; minister to Uruguay, 1937–1939; ambassador to Panama, 1939–1941; ambassador to Uruguay, 1941–1946; and U.S. representative to the Pan-American Union* and then to the Organization of American States,* 1947–1948. Of these posts, the ministry in Colombia was perhaps the most significant; Dawson was engaged there in reciprocal trade negotiations and in combating German and Italian economic influence. He married Agnes Ballock Bready in 1926, retired in 1948, and died in Blue Hill, Maine, on July 4, 1972. *CB* (1941):212–213; *New York Times*, July 5, 1972; *WWWA*, 5 (1969–1973):175.

DAWSON AGREEMENTS (1910). Thomas C. Dawson,* an American special envoy, worked out this set of political agreements with the Nicaraguan government of Juan J. Estrada in November 1910. The agreements provided that Estrada would become president for a two-year term, that Adolfo Díaz would be vice-president, that a mixed claims commission would judge unpaid claims against Nicaragua, that the Estrada government would request U.S. help in obtaining a customs-secured loan, and that the murderers of two Americans during the 1909 revolution would be prosecuted. A constitutional convention met in late November, approved the agreements, and elected Estrada and Díaz to their respective offices. Munro, Dana G., *Intervention and Dollar Diplomacy in the Caribbean, 1900–1921* (1964).

DAY, WILLIAM RUFUS (1849–1923). Secretary of state during the Spanish-American War and U.S. Supreme Court justice, William R. Day was born in Ravenna, Ohio, on April 17, 1849, and graduated from the University of Michigan in 1870. Two years later, he had gained admittance to the bar and began a law career in Canton, Ohio, where he became a good friend of county prosecutor William McKinley. Later a legal and political adviser to McKinley, Day accepted the position of assistant secretary of state after McKinley's election to the presidency. However, because of the age and failing health of John Sherman,* the secretary of state, Day was the secretary in all but name during Sherman's thirteen months in office. When the war broke out in April 1898, Sherman resigned, and Day became secretary until the following September, after which he headed the U.S. commission to make peace with Spain. Although he had no diplomatic training, his tact, discreet manner, and careful use of subordinates such as John Bassett Moore* and Alvey A. Adee* served him and the country well. He played a role in securing European neutrality during the war and is credited with drafting the protocol for the Treaty of Paris (1898).* He favored acquisition of the Philippines but also favored paying $20 million for the islands. After concluding the treaty, Day was appointed a judge of the U.S. Court of Appeals (1899) and, four years later, an associate justice of the U.S. Supreme Court. He resigned in 1922 in order to serve on a mixed claims commission for the United States against Germany. Married to Mary Elizabeth Schaefer in 1875, Day died on Mackinac Island, Michigan, on July 9, 1923. *DAB*, 5:163; McLean, Joseph E., *William Rufus Day* (1946); *New York Times*, July 10, 1923; Shippee, L. B., and R. B. Way, "William Rufus Day," in Bemis, Samuel F., ed., *American Secretaries of State and Their Diplomacy*, vol. 9 (1929).

DAYTON, WILLIAM LEWIS (1807–1864). Minister to France during the Civil War, William L. Dayton was born February 17, 1807, in Basking Ridge, New Jersey, and graduated from Princeton in 1825. He read law, was admitted to the bar, and soon achieved an enviable reputation as a "master of common law." He was appointed to the New Jersey Supreme Court in 1838 but retired three years later to return to private practice. From 1842 to 1851, Dayton represented New Jersey in the U.S. Senate, opposing the annexation of Oregon and Texas, and losing his seat to Commodore Robert F. Stockton,* an enthusiastic expansionist. Joining the Republican party soon after its founding, Dayton was its first vice-presidential candidate in 1856 and attorney general of New Jersey from 1857 to 1861. President Lincoln named him minister to France in 1861, a post he held until his sudden death in Paris on December 1, 1864. In France, he established cordial relations with Louis-Napoleon, despite the handicap of knowing little about the French or diplomacy, and was successful in blunting the efforts of Confederate envoy John Slidell.* Dayton managed to stop Confederate use of French ports and French construction of Confederate naval vessels and on the whole enjoyed the confidence of Secretary of State William H. Seward.* Dayton was much aided by working closely with the influential U.S. consul* in Paris, John Bigelow.* *DAB*, 5:166; Willson, Beckles, *America's Ambassadors to France, 1777–1927* (1928).

DEANE, SILAS (1737–1789). Silas Deane was born in Groton, Connecticut, on December 24, 1737, received a B.A. from Yale in 1758, read law, and was admitted to the bar in 1761. After receiving an A.M. from Yale in 1763, he settled down to a law practice for several years before his election to the Connecticut General Assembly in 1772. He became prominent in colonial politics and served in both Continental Congresses before his appointment as colonial agent to France in March 1776. The Committee of Secret Correspondence* instructed him to sound out the French on diplomatic recognition and an alliance. Deane was also to acquire needed war supplies. Benjamin Franklin* arrived in France in December 1776 and quickly overshadowed Deane, especially in the area of treaty negotiations, but Deane, working with Pierre A. C. Beaumarchais, a well-known dramatist and advocate of French aid to the American cause, succeeded in sending eight shiploads of supplies to America and in commissioning a number of foreign military officers for service in America.

In November 1777, Congress recalled Deane because of his overzealous commissioning of French officers for service in the American Revolution. Many of these officers were unqualified, spoke no English, and could not be fitted into the American military hierarchy. The following year, Arthur Lee* alleged that Deane had planned to profit personally from his dealings with Beaumarchais and confirmed Congress's decision to order his recall. Lee's accusations hurt Deane badly and in 1781 he advocated peace without independence and a reconciliation with Britain. These statements were regarded in America as traitorous, and Deane never returned, living in Britain until 1789. On September 23, 1789, while sailing from Britain to Canada, Deane died. In 1842, Congress made a restitution of $37,000 to the heirs of Silas Deane for salary and expenses never paid him. Bemis, Samuel F., *The Diplomacy of the American Revolution* (1935); Clark, G.L., *Silas Deane* (1913); Storch, Neil T., "The Recall of Silas Deane," *Bulletin of the Connecticut Historical Society* 38 (January 1973), 30–32. Stourzh, Gerald, *Benjamin Franklin and American Foreign Policy* (1954).

DECLARATION ON LIBERATED EUROPE, 1945. This statement originated in the U.S. State Department and was accepted by the U.S., Soviet, and British delegations at the Yalta Conference* in February 1945. It declared that

the three major powers would work together to help the nations of Europe liberated from the Axis powers become internally stable and free of distress. The Allies would cooperate in encouraging the formation of representative interim governments and, if necessary, would facilitate elections to choose permanent governments. The declaration provided for Allied consultation before any action was taken. The United States hoped that adherence to the principles espoused in the declaration would end European spheres of influence, but Joseph Stalin did not see it that way, either because he had a different concept of representative government and free elections or because he felt that a truly liberated Eastern Europe would not welcome Soviet supervision. When the Declaration on Liberated Europe proved to have no practical effect in promoting free elections and representative governments in Eastern Europe, the United States chose to resist creation of a closed Soviet sphere of influence there. This resistance, nonmilitary in character, formed a large part of the early cold war.*
Davis, Lynn Etheridge, *The Cold War Begins* (1974); Feis, Herbert, *From Trust to Terror* (1970); *FR, The Conferences at Malta and Yalta, 1945*, pp. 848ff.; Gaddis, John, *The United States and the Origins of the Cold War* (1972); Herring, George C., Jr., *Aid to Russia, 1941–1946* (1973); McNeill, William H., *America, Britain, and Russia* (1953); Sainsbury, Keith, *The Turning Point* (1985).

DE LEON, EDWIN (1818–1891). Born in Columbia, South Carolina, on May 4, 1818, Edwin De Leon graduated from South Carolina College in 1837 and was admitted to the bar three years later. For several years he edited the *Republican*, a Savannah, Georgia, newspaper. In 1850, he moved to Washington, D.C., where he was editor of the *Southern Press* until 1854, when the Pierce administration named him consul general* and diplomatic agent in Egypt. He remained in Egypt until 1861, resigning to enlist in the service of the Confederacy as a publicity agent in Europe. There he was a counterpart of Henry Hotze,* the Confederacy's publicist in Great Britain, and although he was given more money than Hotze, he was not as successful a propagandist. De Leon's major contribution was writing a pamphlet for French consumption, *La Verité sur des états confedérés*. He spent most of his money bribing the French press and ruined his career in 1863 by opening a secret document of Confederate envoy John Slidell,* who thereafter would have nothing to do with him. In February 1864, after a speech critical of the French government, De Leon found his service to the Confederacy terminated. He remained in Europe and Egypt most of the rest of his life but died in New York City on December 1, 1891. De Leon wrote his autobiography, *Thirty Years of Life on Three Continents* (1886), and two books in Egypt and is credited with introducing the telephone into that country. Cullop, Charles P., *Confederate Propaganda in Europe* (1969); Owsley, Frank, *King Cotton Diplomacy*, 2d ed. (1959); Wakelyn, Jon L., *Biographical Dictionary of the Confederacy* (1977).

De LOME LETTER (1898). Enrique Dupuy de Lome was the Spanish minister to the United States, and this famous diplomatic incident centers on a letter he wrote to a friend in Havana in which he characterized President William

McKinley as "weak and a bidder for the admiration of the crowd." The de Lome letter was intercepted in Cuba by a rebel sympathizer and sent back to New York, where it was published in the *Journal* on February 9, 1898. The letter was convincing evidence of the sham of Spain's seemingly conciliatory policy. De Lome resigned; Spain sent a rather ungracious apology, and McKinley was content to consider the incident closed. However, it had done much to swing moderate American opinion toward intervention in Cuba. *FR* (1898), 1007–22; Millis, Walter, *The Martial Spirit* (1931); Morgan, H. Wayne, *America's Road to Empire* (1965).

DELONG, CHARLES E. (c. 1831–1876). Born about 1831, Charles Delong had only a limited education and by 1859 was living in California, where he was a member of the Constitutional Commission that year. He served in the California state legislature and moved to Virginia City in 1863, the year Nevada became a state. At some point, he attracted the notice of someone in the Ulysses S. Grant administration, which named him minister to Japan in 1869. In Japan until 1873, Delong served as an intermediary in efforts by Japan to secure U.S. mediation of a Japanese-Russian territorial conflict over Sakhalin and the Kuril islands. He opposed suggestions of Sino-Japanese alliance (1871) on the ground that Japan would be a formidable enemy should trouble between the United States and China ever develop. Delong, an ardent expansionist on behalf of the Japanese, was recalled in 1873 for his enthusiastic support of punitive Japanese expeditions to Korea and Formosa (which also involved the American adventurer Charles Le Gendre*) and the implicit threat to Chinese security of these expeditions. Delong died in Virginia City on October 26, 1876. Dennett, Tyler, *Americans in Eastern Asia* (1922); *New York Times*, October 27, November 5, 1876.

DENBY, CHARLES (1830–1904). Charles Denby was born June 16, 1830, in Mount Joy, Virginia, and, after attending Georgetown, graduated in 1850 from the Virginia Military Institute. Brief careers in teaching and journalism gave way to the law by 1855. Now a resident of Evansville, Indiana, Denby was elected to the state legislature in 1856 and served in the Civil War until he was wounded at the Battle of Perryville in 1863. From 1863 to 1885, he practiced law in Evansville and maintained his interest and activity in Democratic politics, doubtless a factor in his appointment as minister to China by the Democratic administration of Grover Cleveland. Denby remained in China for thirteen years, developing good relations with Chinese leaders and working hard for a settlement of the Sino-Japanese War (1894–1895)* while at the same time representing Japanese interests in China. In 1898, after his return from China, he was a member of a commission to investigate the conduct of the war with Spain and, in 1899, a member of the U.S.-Philippines Commission. Denby married Martha Fitch in 1858 and died in Jamestown, New York, on January 13, 1904. His experiences in China are described in his book, *China and Her People*, 2 vols. (1906). Anderson, David L., *Imperialism and Idealism* (1985); *DAB*, 5:233; Hunt,

Michael H., *The Making of a Special Relationship: The United States and China to 1914* (1983); *NCAB*, 8:276; *WWWA*, 1 (1897–1942):313.

DENBY, CHARLES, II (1861–1938). The son of Charles Denby,* minister to China (1885–1898), Charles Denby II was born in Evansville, Indiana, on November 14, 1861, and graduated from Princeton in 1882. He studied law in Evansville from 1882 to 1885 before accompanying his father to China as second secretary, rising to first secretary by 1897. In 1897, he entered private business in Tienstin and from 1900 to 1902 was secretary-general of the provisional government established by the Western powers in Tienstin after the Boxer Rebellion.* Denby then served as foreign adviser to the viceroy of the province of Chihli in northern China (1902–1905) and, returning to Washington, as chief clerk of the State Department (1905–1907). In 1907, he became consul general* in Shanghai; two years later, he moved to Vienna as consul general. Temporarily leaving government service in 1914 to become vice-president of the Hupp Motor Car Company in Detroit (1915–1917), Denby returned in 1917 as director of the Bureau of Foreign Agents, part of the War Trade Board. In 1918, he went back to China as a special agent in connection with the War Trade Board. His last public service came as a special representative on the U.S. Shipping Board in China and Japan (1922–1923). He married Martha Orr in 1895 and died in Washington on February 14, 1938. Denby's brother, Edwin, was secretary of the navy in President Warren G. Harding's administration. Hunt, Michael H., *The Making of a Special Relationship: The United States and China to 1914* (1983); *NCAB*, 39:50; *New York Times*, February 15, 1938.

DENNETT, TYLER WILBUR (1883–1949). An educator and important diplomatic historian, Tyler Dennett was born June 13, 1883, in Spencer, Wisconsin, and graduated from Williams College in 1904. In 1908 he received a B.D. from Union Theological Seminary, and in 1924 he received a Ph.D. from Johns Hopkins. From 1909 to 1914 he was a Congregational minister, and from 1914 to 1920 he worked for the Methodist Board of Missions, making two trips to Asia and cultivating an interest in Asian affairs. This resulted in a book, *The Democratic Movement in Asia* (1918), and a shift to an academic career, beginning with research in the State Department Archives preparing background material for the Washington Conference.* In 1922, Dennett published *Americans in Eastern Asia*, which made him the best-known authority on Far Eastern diplomacy. After a two-year teaching stint at Johns Hopkins while finishing his Ph.D., he became chief of the Division of Publications for the State Department (1924–1929) and then the department's historical adviser (1929–1931). In 1931, he returned to teaching, giving courses in international affairs at Princeton until 1934, when he accepted the presidency of Williams College. His three-year tenure at Williams was highly controversial, characterized by conflict with alumni and a dispute over the college's acquisition of property in Williamstown. Among Dennett's other major writings are *Roosevelt and the Russo-Japanese War*

(1925), and *John Hay, from Poetry to Politics* (1934), for which he won a Pulitzer Prize. Dennett married Maybelle Raymond in 1911 and died in Geneva, New York, December 29, 1949. Borg, Dorothy, ed., *Historians and American Far Eastern Policy* (1966); *DAB*, Supp. 4:223; *New York Times*, December 30, 1949.

DENNIS, ALFRED LEWIS PINNEO (1874–1930). The son of a Presbyterian minister, A. L. P. Dennis was born in Beirut on May 21, 1874, and graduated from Princeton in 1893. He attended graduate school at Columbia, receiving a Ph.D. in 1901. He then spent most of the rest of his life teaching history at institutions such as Bowdoin College, the University of Chicago, Harvard, Wisconsin, and Clark University. During World War I, he served with the Military Intelligence Division of the Army General Staff, and in 1919 he was military attaché in London. Dennis wrote much on and was highly regarded in the field of diplomatic history. His best-known work, *Adventures in American Diplomacy, 1896–1906* (1926), details much of the complex diplomacy at the turn of the century. He also contributed "John Hay" to Samuel F. Bemis's *American Secretaries of State and Their Diplomacy* (1929). Among his other works are *The Anglo-Japanese Alliance* (1923) and *Foreign Policies of Soviet Russia* (1924). Married to Mary Boardman Cable in 1899, Dennis died in Worcester, Massachusetts, on November 14, 1930. *American Historical Review* 36 (January 1931): 459; *DAB*, Supp. 1:239; *New York Times*, November 15, 1930.

DÉTENTE. A French word meaning relaxation of tensions, détente characterizes U.S.-Soviet policy as it developed under President Richard M. Nixon and Henry Kissinger.* This policy stresses direct cooperative dealings with former cold war* rivals in areas that were formerly competitive but avoids ideological accommodations. Areas affected by détente include arms control, particularly attempts at slowing down the nuclear arms race (SALT),* easing of Central European (German) tensions, avoidance of direct military confrontation in such areas as the Middle East, and closer economic, social, and cultural ties. According to Spanier, détente did, on the other hand, result in increased U.S. difficulties with North Atlantic Treaty Organization* allies and neglect of the developing nations of the world. Other critics of détente claim that by minimizing U.S.-Soviet differences, U.S. policymakers created a dangerous indifference to Soviet military and diplomatic moves around the world. With the Soviet invasion of Afghanistan in late 1979, the cooperative spirit of détente collapsed, and a period of heightened U.S.-Soviet hostility ensued. Beam, Jacob D., *Multiple Exposure* (1978); Brandon, Henry, *The Retreat of American Power* (1972); Ekirch, Arthur A., Jr., "Detente," in DeConde, Alexander, ed., *Encyclopedia of American Foreign Policy* (1979); Gaddis, John L., "The Rise, Fall, and Future of Detente," *Foreign Affairs* 62, 2 (Winter 1983–1984): 354–77; Garthoff, Raymond L., *Detente and Confrontation: American-Soviet Relations from Nixon to Reagan* (1985); Graebner, Norman A., *Cold War Diplomacy* (1977); Hammond, Paul, *Cold War and Detente* (1974); Spanier, John W., *American Foreign Policy since World War II* (1977).

DEWEY, GEORGE B. (1837–1917). A career navy officer, Dewey was born December 26, 1837, in Montpelier, Vermont, and graduated from the U.S. Naval Academy in 1858. He served under Admiral David G. Farragut during the Civil War and had various land and sea assignments after the war. In January 1898 he took command of the Asiatic squadron, sailed to Hong Kong, and on May 1, 1898, defeated the Spanish fleet at Manila, thereby elevating the United States to a position of power in the Far East. Dewey maintained control at Manila as fleets of other nations arrived and worked with Philippine leader Emilio Aguinaldo to protect the city until U.S. troops arrived to occupy it. Dewey's grand welcome home in 1899 led his friends to suggest he run for the presidency, but Dewey did not find deep popular support for the race. After seventeen years as president of the General Board of the Navy Department, Dewey died January 16, 1917, in Washington. Owing to his experience in the Philippines, Dewey became a fervent advocate of a U.S. naval base at Subig Bay. Challener, Richard D., *Admirals, Generals, and American Foreign Policy, 1898–1914* (1973); *Autobiography of George Dewey* (1913); Healy, Laurin, and Luis Kutner, *The Admiral* (1944); Spector, Ronald, *Admiral of the New Empire* (1974).

DILLON, CLARENCE DOUGLAS (b. 1909). Born in Geneva, Switzerland, on August 21, 1909, Douglas Dillon graduated from Harvard in 1931 and went to work in his father's investment house, Dillon, Read and Company. In 1937, he joined the U.S. and Foreign Securities Corporation, an investment trust founded by Dillon, Read in 1924. The following year he also became associated with its subsidiary, the U.S. and International Securities Corporation. From 1941 to 1945, Dillon was on active naval duty in World War II. Returning from the war, he became chairman of the board of Dillon, Read and Company and also president of U.S. and Foreign Securities Corporation. A Republican, he was active in the 1948 campaign, along with John Foster Dulles,* on behalf of Thomas E. Dewey, writing foreign policy speeches. In 1952, he supported Dwight D. Eisenhower, and when the Eisenhower administration took office in 1953, Dillon became ambassador to France. He arrived in France too late to be directly involved in the Marshall Plan,* nor was he connected with problems of German rearmament or the European Defense Community.* He was, however, highly regarded for his reporting on the complexities of French politics and on lingering problems of Franco-German accord, and he supported "liberal" French settlements for Algeria and other areas of French North Africa. In 1957, he returned to Washington as deputy under secretary of state (economic affairs), becoming under secretary of state in the same area in 1958. There he reorganized the State Department's economic functions to improve coordination between foreign aid and overall foreign policy, a process that cleared the way for the creation of the Inter-American Development Bank.* He also persuaded Common Market and European Free Trade Association members to join in the Organization for Economic Cooperation and Development in 1960, in which the United States and Canada also became members. In 1961, although still a Republican, Dillon joined the Kennedy administration as secretary of the treasury. In this capacity, he headed the U.S. delegation to the Punta del Este Conference (1961),* at which the Alliance for Progress* was established. In 1965, he returned to private life with Dillon, Read and Company and the U.S. and Foreign Securities Corporation. He married Phyllis Chase Ellsworth in 1931; after her death, he married Susan S. Sage. Dillon is active in the New York City cultural and philanthropic endeavors. *Barron's*, February 6, 1984, p. 8; *NCAB*, J:39; *New York Times*, January 18, 1953, September 16, December 23, 1956; *WWA* (1986–1987): 715.

DIMITRY, ALEXANDER (1805–1883). Born February 7, 1805 in New Orleans, Alexander Dimitry graduated from Georgetown College (Washington, D.C.) in 1820, taught at Baton Rouge (Louisiana) College, and in 1830 became the editor of the *New Orleans Bee*. From 1834 to 1842, he was in Washington, D.C., working as a post office clerk, but in 1842, he returned to Louisiana and established a school in St. Charles Parish. Dimitry directed the school until 1847, when he was appointed first state superintendent of schools in Louisiana, a post he held for four years. In 1854, he joined the State Department as a translator, and from 1859 to 1861, he was minister to Costa Rica and Nicaragua. Rivalry with British interests stood as America's major problem in this area, and Dimitry was instructed to cultivate good relations with Central American nations and continue the relative cordiality that had developed between the United States and Britain since 1856 while at the same time urging the British and Nicaraguan governments to resolve their differences in the Mosquito protectorate, on Nicaragua's Caribbean coast. According to Williams, however, Dimitry did not interpret his instructions properly and hindered British efforts to settle the Mosquito conflict. Dimitry resigned at the outbreak of the Civil War and became assistant postmaster-general of the Confederacy. After the war, he spent most of his time in New Orleans, involved in educational matters such as schools for blacks. For a time, he taught at Christian Brothers College, Pass Christian, Mississippi. Dimitry married Mary Powell Mills in 1835 and died in New Orleans on January 30, 1883. *DAB*, 5:313; *NCAB*, 10:176; *New York Times*, January 31, 1883; Williams, Mary W., *Anglo-American Isthmian Diplomacy, 1815–1915* (1916).

DISENGAGEMENT, proposed diplomatic policy, 1950s. In post–World War II international relations, disengagement referred mainly to the neutralization of certain parts of the world, with both the United States and the Soviet Union agreeing to keep hands off those areas. In 1949–1950, George F. Kennan* argued for the neutralization of Central Europe, and in 1958 he reiterated the idea, which, if implemented, would have moved Western and Soviet troops out of Central Europe, including Germany. German reunification, he suggested, might come about in the context of disengagement, with an independent, nonaligned, and rearmed Germany negotiating directly with the USSR. The idea was heartily opposed by Dean Acheson* and John Foster Dulles* as vague, isolationist,* and potentially destructive, since the Soviets would take immediate advantage of the power vacuum in Central Europe. With that kind of opposition, disengagement soon fell out of policy makers' thinking. Acheson, Dean G., "The Illusion of Disengagement," *Foreign Affairs* 36 (April 1958): 371–82; Graebner, Norman, *Cold War Diplomacy* (1977); Kennan, George F., "Disengagement Revisited," *Foreign Affairs* 27 (January 1959): 187–210; LaFeber, Walter, *America, Russia, and the Cold War, 1945–1984* (1985); Robinson, James W., "Disengagement in Europe: An Evaluation for United States Foreign Policy," in Cordier, Andrew W., ed., *Columbia Essays in International Affairs, The Dean's Papers, 1965* (1966).

DIX, JOHN ADAMS (1798–1879). John A. Dix was born July 24, 1798, in Boscaisen, New Hampshire, and was educated at the College of Montreal, where he learned to speak fluent French. From 1812 to 1828, he served in the army, but while in the service he became a lawyer and practiced law in Cooperstown from 1828 to 1830. Dix was New York adjutant general, 1830–1833, and New York secretary of state, 1833–1839. In 1839, he returned to private law practice and two years later took over the editorship of the periodical *Northern Light*. He gave that up in 1843 and in 1845 was elected to the U.S. Senate, serving until 1850. During the 1850s, he again was practicing law privately and was involved in the railroad business. During the Civil War he was a Union general, responsible for administrative work behind the lines in Maryland and New York. In 1866, Dix was appointed minister to France. He remained at that post until 1869, and his mission was highlighted by a sharp controversy with George Bancroft,* U.S. minister to Germany. Dix disliked Bancroft and his pro-German attitudes, refused to get Bancroft tickets for the Paris Exposition of 1867, and reported an anti-French, pro-German speech Bancroft had made in Berlin to the State Department. Bancroft was furious. Dix was also involved in the Cluseret case, dealing with an allegedly naturalized French-American who asked for American protection after getting into trouble for writing offensively about the French government and army. The case led to talks concerning a new naturalization treaty, but nothing substantive was accomplished. Dix returned to New York, served a term as governor (1873–1875), and died in New York City on April 21, 1879. He was married to Catherine Morgan in 1826 and wrote a popular travel book on Madeira, Spain, and Italy. His two-volume *Memories of John Adams Dix* (1883) was compiled by his son, Morgan Dix. *DAB*, 3:325; Willson, Beckles, *America's Ambassadors to France, 1777–1927* (1928).

DODD, WILLIAM EDWARD (1869–1940). A prominent American historian before becoming ambassador to Germany in the 1930s, William E. Dodd was born near Clayton, North Carolina, on October 27, 1869, earned B.S. (1895) and M.S. (1897) degrees at Virginia Polytechnic Institute (V.P.I.), and continued his studies at the University of Leipzig, where he received a Ph.D. degree in 1900. He began a teaching career while at V.P.I. in 1895, but from 1908 until 1933 he was at the University of Chicago; there he became known as one of the foremost authorities on southern history through his writing and teaching. A

Democrat and supporter of Woodrow Wilson, Dodd also wrote on the historical aspects of contemporary problems, and his work reflected his strong belief in democracy. President Franklin D. Roosevelt, looking for a liberal to set an example in Germany, named Dodd ambassador in 1933, after several others had declined. Although Dodd had studied in Germany, his was purely a patronage appointment; he had no diplomatic experience or any ties with the State Department. Dodd spent a miserable four years in Berlin. He did not have good relations with the government, which he regarded as thoroughly undemocratic; he had difficulty living within his income and was frustrated in attempts to reduce embassy expenses; and he spent most of his time lodging protests with the government over its racial policies involving Americans or over discrimination against American holders of Dawes* and Young Plan* bonds. He deplored the fact that neither the United States nor Germany seemed interested in a peace conference, and he became more outspokenly anti-Nazi by the end of his ambassadorship. After his return in 1937, he spoke and wrote in defense of his Berlin mission and exposed Nazi propaganda. His health declined, especially after the death of his wife, Martha Johns Dodd, in 1938, and he died in Round Hill, Virginia, on February 9, 1940. *DAB*, Supp. 2: 152; Dallek, Robert, *Democrat and Diplomat: The Life of William E. Dodd* (1968); Ford, Franklin C., "Three Observers in Berlin," in Craig, Gordon A., and Felix Gilbert, eds., *The Diplomats, 1919–39*, 2 vols. (1953); *New York Times*, February 10, 1940.

DODGE, AUGUSTUS CAESAR (1812–1883). A native of Missouri, Augustus Caesar Dodge was born January 2, 1812, in Saint Genevieve, had scant schooling, and worked with his father in Wisconsin mines as a youth. He fought in Indian wars in 1827 and 1832, moved to the Iowa Territory, married Clara Ann Hertich (1837), and became registrar of the public land office in Burlington (1838–1840) and the territorial representative in Congress (1840–1846). When Iowa became a state, Dodge became one of its first senators (1848–1854). In 1855, he was named minister to Spain after losing his bid to retain his Senate seat. In Madrid, he followed the controversial Pierre Soulé* as U.S. minister and managed to restore some of the cordiality sacrificed by Soulé's zealous questing for the acquisition of Cuba. Dodge tried more subtly but equally unsuccessfully to obtain Cuba, but he did bring about the settlement of the *Black Warrior* affair.* Sharply critical of Spanish government and society, he resigned in 1859. He lost elections for the governorship of Iowa (1859) and for the Senate (1860) and retired to Burlington, where he died November 20, 1883. Briggs, John E., "Iowa and the Diplomatic Service," *Iowa Journal of History and Politics* 19 (1921): 321–65; *DAB*, 5:344; Pelzer, Louis, *Augustus Caesar Dodge* (1908).

DODGE, HENRY PERCIVAL (1870–1936). A native of Boston, H. Percival Dodge was born January 18, 1870, graduated from Harvard (1892) and Harvard Law School (1895), and was admitted to the bar in 1895. He practiced law in Boston for two years and in 1897 went to Europe for further study. In 1899, he joined the Berlin legation as third secretary, rising to first secretary by 1902. Four years later, he moved to Tokyo as first secretary of the legation. Beginning in 1907, Dodge was appointed to a succession of ministries: Honduras and El Salvador, 1908–1909; Morocco, 1909–1910; Panama, 1911–1913; Kingdom of the Serbs, Croats, and Slovenes, 1919–1926; and Denmark, 1926–1930. From 1910 to 1911, he was in Washington as chief of the Division of Latin American Affairs, and during World War I he held a number of special posts, including secretary of the American Commission to the Mediation Conference, United States and Mexico, 1914; representative, American Commission for the Repatriation of Americans in Europe, 1914; in charge of Austro-Hungarian and German interests in France and attached to the U.S. embassy in Paris, 1914–1917; and special representative to Serbia, in charge of the U.S. legation, 1917–1919. Dodge retired in 1930 and died in Zurich, Switzerland, on October 16, 1936. He was married twice: in 1903 to Margaret Riche, who died in an elevator accident in 1919, and in 1922 to Agnes Page-Brown. *NCAB*, 14:428; *WWWA*, 1 (1897–1942): 329.

DOLLAR DIPLOMACY (1909–1913). This policy, devised in the administration of President William Howard Taft and Secretary of State Philander C. Knox,* was directed principally at the Caribbean–Central American area. Dollar diplomacy stressed financial reform through loans and customs receiverships as a way toward political stability and financial solvency. The policy originated as a humane substitute for military intervention but was attacked by critics as a device for the benefit of American bankers and as a way to facilitate American economic exploitation of the region. Employed most actively in Nicaragua, Honduras, Haiti, and the Dominican Republic, dollar diplomacy did not bring profits to the bankers, and in Haiti, the Dominican Republic, and Nicaragua, it did not prevent military intervention. Dollar diplomacy and its effect did, however, create a residue of ill will toward the United States. To a lesser degree, the policy was attempted in China, mainly through the efforts of Willard Straight.* Munro, Dana, G., *Intervention and Dollar Diplomacy in the Caribbean, 1900–1921* (1964); Nearing, Scott, and Joseph Freeman, *Dollar Diplomacy* (1925); Trani, Eugene P., "Dollar Diplomacy," in DeConde, Alexander, ed., *Encyclopedia of American Foreign Policy* (1979).

DOMINICAN CRISIS (1965). On April 24, 1965, a revolution against a military junta headed by Donald Reid Cabral broke out in Santo Domingo, the capital of the Dominican Republic. U.S. military intervention came at the request of U.S. Ambassador W. Tapley Bennett* just four days later, ostensibly to protect American lives and property although in reality to prevent the establishment of what the Johnson administration feared would be a Cuban-style Communist-oriented government under former President Juan Bosch. On May 1, the Organization of American States* met and after intensive U.S. lobbying passed a resolution to create an inter-American peacekeeping force and to send a delegation led by Ellsworth Bunker* to negotiate a settlement. The peacekeeping force remained in the Dominican Republic until September 1966, by which time a stable government under Joaquin Balaguer, another former president, had been elected and recognized by the United States. The intervention badly undermined the improved U.S. image in Latin America developed since the Good Neighbor Policy* and the Alliance for Progress.* To many Latin Americans, it was all too reminiscent of the interventions carried out half a century earlier under the guise of the Roosevelt Corollary.* Some observers have suggested that the Dominican intervention may have been a response by the Johnson administration to setbacks in the Vietnam War as an effort to demonstrate to the rest of the world that the United States was not so totally wrapped up in Vietnam that it could not meet a presumed Communist challenge in some other part of the world. Barnet, Richard J., *Intervention and Revolution* (1968); Bracey, Audrey, *The Resolution of the Dominican Crisis, 1965: A Study in Mediation* (1980); Lowenthal, Abraham F., *The Dominican Intervention* (1972); Martin, John Bartlow, *Overtaken by Events* (1966); Slater, Jerome, *Intervention and Negotiation* (1970); Szulc, Tad, *Dominican Diary* (1965).

DOMINO THEORY, U.S. diplomatic concept, post–World War II. This notion of international relations, usually applied to Southeast Asia, posited that if one nation in that region fell to communism (or anything else, presumably), then inevitably other nations in that region would fall (analogous to a row of dominoes lined up such that if the first is toppled, the remaining ones inevitably fall). The idea dates back to the Truman administration, where it was applied to Greece and Turkey, but it was explicitly and publicly spelled out by President Dwight Eisenhower in April 1954 and continued to be significant in the policymaking and public statements of the Kennedy and Johnson administrations with respect to Southeast Asia. In the 1980s, the Reagan administration and its supporters frequently invoked the domino theory in attempting to win favor for a strong, military-oriented anti-Communist policy in Central America. Fifield, Russell H., *Americans in Southeast Asia* (1973); Findling, John E., *Close Neighbors, Distant Friends* (1987); Graebner, Norman A., *Cold War Diplomacy* (1977); Gregory, Ross, "The Domino Theory," in DeConde, Alexander, ed., *Encyclopedia of American Foreign Policy* (1979); LaFeber, Walter, *America, Russia and the Cold War, 1945–1975*, (1976).

DONELSON, ANDREW JACKSON (1799–1871). A nephew, namesake, and protégé of Andrew Jackson, A. J. Donelson was born near Nashville on August 25, 1799. He graduated from West Point in 1827, studied law at Transylvania College, and was admitted to the bar in 1823. In 1824, he became Andrew Jackson's confidential secretary; when Jackson became president, Donelson was his private secretary. In 1844, President John Tyler appointed Donelson chargé d'affaires* to Texas to negotiate concerning annexation, and he continued in this assignment after James K. Polk was elected president and did a good job, giving Polk and Secretary of State James Buchanan* valuable information and sound advice and enjoying their confidence. As a result, he was made minister to Prussia in 1846, remaining for the duration of Polk's term. In 1851, Donelson became editor of the *Washington Union*, and in 1856 he was Millard Fillmore's running mate on the American party ticket. He opposed the Civil War, was upset at its divisiveness, and lived in retirement on his plantation near Australia, Mississippi. Donelson was married twice and died June 26, 1871, in Memphis. A collection of his letters has been published in the *Tennessee Historical Magazine* 3 (1919): 51–73; 134–62. *DAB*, 5:363; Pletcher, David, *The Diplomacy of Annexation* (1973).

DONNELLY, WALTER JOSEPH (1896–1970). Walter J. Donnelly was born January 9, 1896, in New Haven, Connecticut. He attended local schools before going to the Georgetown University School of Foreign Service (1919–1921) and the University of Caracas (1921). From 1923 to 1929, he worked as a commercial agent for the Department of Commerce and then began a diplomatic career as a commercial attaché under Ambassador Jefferson Caffery* in Bogotá (1929–1933), Havana (1934–1937), and Rio de Janeiro (1937–1942). In 1942, he became embassy counselor* in Brazil and held similar posts in Panama (1945) and Peru (1945–1947). Between 1947 and 1952, Donnelly was ambassador to Costa Rica (1947) and Venezuela (1947–1950); minister to Austria (1950–1951); ambassador to Austria (1951–1952); and high commissioner to West Germany (1952). His major contributions include helping draft the Pan-American mutual defense treaty (Rio Treaty)* at the Rio de Janeiro Conference (1947) and bringing about major changes in the Economic Cooperation Administration in Austria. He left the diplomatic service in 1952 and worked for U.S. Steel (1953–1966). He was married to Maria Helena Samper de Herrera and died in Bogotá on November 12, 1970. In Venezuela, Donnelly is remembered for his efforts to popularize baseball. *New York Times*, November 13, 1970.

DOUGLAS, LEWIS WILLIAMS (1894–1974). Born July 2, 1894, in Bisbee, Arizona Territory, Lewis Douglas graduated from Amherst (1916) and subsequently attended both MIT and the Harvard Law School. After army service during World War I, he taught for two years in the East and then returned to Arizona, where from 1921 to 1923 he engaged in mining and citrus growing. In 1923, he began his political career with a term in the Arizona legislature, followed in 1927 by election to the U.S. House of Representatives. Douglas served three terms in the House (1927–1933) and a year as director of the budget (1933–1934) before returning to private life as vice-president of American Cyanamid Company (1934–1937) and principal and vice-chancellor of McGill University (1937–1940). During World War II, he was deputy war shipping administrator. At the war's end, he became chief adviser to General Lucius Clay,* American high commissioner in Germany. From 1947 to 1950, Douglas was ambassador to Great Britain, his most important post. There he helped shape the Marshall Plan* and win European and congressional acceptance of it. In addition, he played a role in the establishment of the North Atlantic Treaty

Organization* and was chief U.S. representative at the Six Nation Conference on Germany (1948),* which led to the formation of the West German government. In 1949, he lost an eye in a fishing accident. Douglas retired from diplomatic service in 1950 and served as president of the Winston Churchill Foundation and as director of several major banks and corporations. He married Peggy Zinsser in 1921 and died in Tucson on March 7, 1974. Browder, Robert Paul, and Thomas G. Smith, *Independent: A Biography of Lewis W. Douglas* (1986); Feis, Herbert, *From Trust to Terror* (1970); *NCAB*, D:22; *New York Times*, March 8, 1974.

DOUGLASS, FREDERICK (FREDERICK AUGUSTUS WASHINGTON BAILY) (1817?–1895). Born a slave, probably in February 1817, in Tuckahoe, Maryland, Frederick Douglass escaped to freedom and became the most celebrated black public figure in his era. He was educated by the mistress of the house in which he was a servant, went north in 1838, and during the 1840s worked closely with the abolitionist and other reform movements, especially as an orator and founder of the paper, *North Star*, an outlet for reformist writing. During the Civil War, he was active in the recruitment of black troops, and after the war he worked to ensure freed slaves their suffrage and other civil rights. In 1871, he was secretary of a commission sent to Santo Domingo by the Grant administration to investigate annexation possibilities. After lending his support to the candidacy of Benjamin Harrison in 1888, Douglass was appointed minister to Haiti and chargé d'affaires* to Santo Domingo (Dominican Republic) in 1889. At this time, the United States was interested in leasing from Haiti the island of Mole St. Nicolas as a coaling station for the U.S. Navy. Douglass's efforts to negotiate for this island were unsuccessful, and when he was critical of a U.S. show of force to pressure the Haitians, he was accused of excessive sympathy to the Haitian point of view, and his resignation was requested. He returned to the United States in 1891 and died February 20, 1895, in Washington, D.C. Douglass was married to Anna Murray and wrote his autobiography at more than one point in his life, the last version appearing, however, before his mission to Haiti. *DAB*, 5:406; Miller, Jake C., *The Black Presence in American Foreign Affairs* (1978); Montague, Ludwell Lee, *Haiti and the United States, 1714–1938* (1940).

DOWLING, WALTER CECIL (1905–1977). Born August 4, 1905, in Atkinson, Georgia, Walter Dowling graduated from Mercer (Georgia) University in 1925 and worked in a bank until 1931, when he joined the Foreign Service. Between 1931 and 1950, he held minor posts in Oslo, Lisbon, Rome, Rio de Janeiro, and Vienna. In 1950, he was named deputy high commissioner and minister for Austria, remaining there until 1953 and participating in preliminary Austrian peace treaty negotiations. From 1953 to 1955, he was deputy high commissioner in Germany under James B. Conant.* The Eisenhower administration appointed Dowling ambassador to Korea in 1956; there he signed a treaty of friendship, commerce, and navigation to facilitate economic relations but was called home in 1959 as a symbolic protest when President Syngman Rhee induced the passage of acts limiting democracy in Korea, although he returned after a short time. Later that year, however, he left Seoul permanently and returned to Washington as assistant secretary of state for European affairs. Although in this post for only a few months, Dowling played an important role in preparations for the Geneva Foreign Ministers Conference (1959), accompanied Vice-President Richard M. Nixon to the Soviet Union, and facilitated Soviet Chairman Nikita Khrushchev's return visit to the United States. Late in 1959, Dowling was named ambassador to Germany, succeeding David K. E. Bruce* in that post. In a time of crisis, he reassured West Berlin of continued American support. Dowling retired in 1963 because of health reasons. Before his death on July 1, 1977, in Savannah, Georgia, he was director general of the Atlantic Institute in Paris (1963–1969) and taught political science at Mercer University. He married Alice Jernigan in 1930, was a member of the Council on Foreign Relations,* and was involved with various cultural and historical organizations. *CB* (1963): 112–14; New York *Times*, November 7, 1959, July 9, 1977; *WWA* (1976–1977): 842.

DRAGO DOCTRINE (1903). During the Venezuelan dispute (1903),* Dr. Luis M. Drago, Argentine foreign minister, asserted that armed intervention in or territorial occupation of a Latin American nation should not result from matters related to the public finances of that nation. A variation of the doctrine was adopted as an international convention, with U.S. support, at the Second Hague Conference, 1907.* Bemis, Samuel F., *The Latin-American Policy of the United States* (1943); Connell-Smith, Gordon, *The United States and Latin America* (1974).

DRAPER, WILLIAM HENRY, JR. (1894–1974). A native of New York City, where he was born on August 10, 1894, William H. Draper graduated from New York University (B.A., 1916; M.A., 1917), saw army service in World War I, and entered a banking career after the war. In 1927, he joined Dillon, Read and Company, investment bankers, eventually becoming a vice-president. Stationed in Washington during World War II as an economic adviser to the army, Draper went to Germany after the war as an adviser to the army occupation forces. There he played an important part in getting the German economy functioning again by his supervision of German industrial and agricultural production, permitting the manufacture of some heavy goods, such as steel. In 1947, he returned to Washington to be under secretary of the army in the new Department of Defense. In this capacity, he traveled to Japan in 1948 as head of an economic mission that recommended the rebuilding of the Japanese merchant marine. Back in private banking in 1949, Draper reentered public life in 1952 with his appointment as U.S. representative to the North Atlantic Treaty Organization,* special representative of the United States in Europe, and chief of the Mutual Security Agency in Europe. Headquartered in Paris, Draper worked in his joint appointment to coordinate U.S. activities in Europe, keep the Western alliance functioning smoothly, and correct world trade imbalances. He retired in 1953 to private business and to pursue his interest in population control, serving the governing board of International Planned Parenthood and as a U.S. representative on the United Nations Population Commission (1969–1974). Twice married, Draper died in Naples, Florida, on December 26, 1974. Kolko, Joyce, and Gabriel Kolko, *The Limits of Power* (1972); *New York Times*, December 21, 1952, December 27, 1974; *WWWA*, 6 (1974–1976); 119.

DRESEL, ELLIS LORING (1865–1925). A native of Boston, where he was born November 28, 1865, Ellis L. Dresel graduated from Harvard (1887) and Harvard Law School (1892) and entered the practice of law in his native city. In 1915, he was made an attaché to the U.S. embassy in Berlin and put in charge of relations between British prisoners of war and the German government. Sent to Vienna in 1917, he settled the affairs of the U.S. embassy there after the American entry into the war and then went to Switzerland, where for the duration of the war he worked with the Red Cross in caring for American war prisoners. At the Paris Peace Conference (1919),* Dresel headed the political information section and made two inspection tours of Germany. Later that year, he became U.S. commissioner to Germany, and in 1921, his title was changed to chargé d'affaires* as relations grew back to normal. In 1921, Dresel signed the Treaty of Berlin* for the United States that formally ended the war with Germany. He left Germany in 1922 and died September 19, 1925, in Pride's Crossing, Massachusetts. Jonas, Manfred, *The United States and Germany* (1984); *New York Times*, September 21, 1925; *WWWA*, 1 (1897–1942):339.

DROPPERS, GARRETT A. (1860–1927). Garrett Droppers was born April 12, 1860, in Milwaukee, graduated in 1887 from Harvard, and subsequently studied at the University of Berlin. He taught political economy and finance at Tokyo University (1889–1898), was president of the University of South Dakota (1898–1906), and taught at the University of Chicago (1907) and Williams College (1908–1914). He developed a close friendship with a fellow academic and Democrat, Woodrow Wilson, which led to his selection as minister to Greece and Montenegro (1914–1920). Service in this part of Europe during World War I was taxing; Droppers handled Austrian, Bulgarian, and Turkish affairs in Greece and Montenegro, as well as American matters. A particular problem concerned the military obligation of Greeks who had become naturalized Americans, but in 1919 Droppers successfully achieved their exemption from Greek military duty. The burden of Droppers's work probably contributed to a paralytic stroke in 1920 that forced his resignation and return home. He recovered sufficiently to resume teaching at Williams until 1923 and to publish *The Economic History of the Nineteenth Century* in the same year. Droppers was married twice: to Cora A. Rand, who died in 1896, and to her sister, Jean, whom he married in 1897. He died in Williamstown, Massachusetts, July 7, 1927. *NCAB*, 20:16; *New York Times*, August 5, 1914, July 8, 1927.

DUBS, ADOLPH (1920–1979). One of several U.S. ambassadors to have been killed at his post, Adolph Dubs was born in Chicago on August 4, 1920. He graduated from Beloit College in 1942, served in the navy during World War II, and studied at Georgetown after the war. Joining the State Department in 1949, he saw duty in Frankfurt, Monrovia, Ottawa, and Washington before 1961. In that year, he became first secretary and consul in Moscow. In 1963–1964 he spent a year at the National War College. Following that experience, he was chief of the political section and counselor, Belgrade, 1964–1968; country director, USSR, in the State Department, 1968–1972; and minister-counselor, Moscow, 1972–1974. In 1975, he became deputy assistant secretary of state for the Near East and South Asia, a post he held for three years before his first ambassadorial appointment to Afghanistan in 1978. Dubs had been in Kabul only a few months when he was kidnapped by Muslim terrorists and shot to death during a rescue attempt on February 14, 1979. *New York Times*, August 9, 1975, February 15, 1979; *Washington Post*, February 15, 1979; *WWWA*, 7 (1977–1981):165.

DULLES, JOHN FOSTER (1888–1959). Secretary of state under President Dwight D. Eisenhower and one of the most prominent individuals to have held that post, John Foster Dulles was the grandson of one secretary of state (John W. Foster)* and the nephew of another (Robert Lansing).* Born February 25, 1888, in Washington, D.C., he graduated from Princeton in 1908, attended the Sorbonne in Paris, and graduated from George Washington Law School (in 1911, although by a technicality, the degree was not officially granted until 1936). His international experience began early; in 1907, he was secretary to his grandfather at the Second Hague Peace Conference.* In 1911, he began practicing law in New York with the prominent firm of Sullivan and Cromwell, specializing in international law. After serving as an adviser to President Woodrow Wilson at the Paris Peace Conference (1919)* and as a U.S. delegate on the Reparations Commission* and Supreme Economic Council, where he warned against excessive demands on Germany, Dulles's star rose in the legal profession, and his success was assured. Service as a delegate to the Berlin Debt Conference (1933), the San Francisco Conference (1945),* and assorted United Nations* General Assemblies (1946–1948, 1950) kept him in the public eye and contributed to his appointment, as a gesture to bipartisanship, by the Truman administration as special representative to negotiate the Japanese Peace Treaty* (1950–1951) and security treaties with Australia and New Zealand, the Philippines, and Japan. In 1953, Dulles fulfilled his life's ambition by becoming secretary of state. He came to office attacking the prevailing policy of containment* and calling instead for a new policy of liberation,* but the lack of U.S. response to the East German revolt in 1953 and the Hungarian revolt in 1956 belied the sincerity of liberation; a similar attitude was manifested toward Chiang Kai-shek and China. In reality, Dulles extended containment to the Middle East (Baghdad Pact)* and Southeast Asia (SEATO)* and generally opposed violence as a means of foreign policy (by criticizing the joint British-French-Israeli venture in the Suez crisis, 1956).* He was aware of the importance of maintaining domestic support for his policies; hence, he popularized catchwords and made public pronouncements that did not really reflect his actual diplomacy. Of these, the most meaningful are probably *brinkmanship** and *massive retaliation.** In 1958, Dulles developed the Eisenhower Doctrine,* which stated that the United States would use armed force to help any Middle East nation avoid a Communist takeover. Easily the strongest and most visible member of the Eisenhower cabinet, Dulles gained a reputation as an excellent advocate of foreign policy to the administration and Congress, and his frequent travels to different parts of the world made him seem to overshadow the president himself as an American foreign policy leader, although recent research has shown that Eisenhower remained firmly in charge. He wrote two books, *War, Peace and Change* (1939) and *War or Peace* (1950), both of which reflect his belief in the necessity of fair and Christian peace treaties. After a two-year bout with cancer, Dulles died May 24, 1959, in Washington. He married Janet Pomeroy Avery in 1912, and his brother, Allen, achieved a degree of fame as director of the Central Intelligence Agency.* Barnet, Richard J., *Allies* (1984); Gerson, Louis L., "John Foster Dulles," in Ferrell, Robert H., ed., *American Secretaries of State and Their Diplomacy*, vol. 17, (1967); Guhin, Michael, *John Foster Dulles: A Statesman—and His Times* (1972); Morgenthau, Hans J., "John Foster Dulles," in Graebner, Norman, ed., *An Uncertain Tradition* (1961); *New York Times*, May 25, 1959; Toulouse, Mark, *The Transformation of John Foster Dulles* (1986).

DUMBARTON OAKS CONFERENCE (1944). This conference, held at an estate in Georgetown, Washington, D.C., produced the basic framework of the United Nations.* Delegates from thirty-nine nations agreed on the General Assembly, the Security Council, the Secretariat, and an International Court of Justice.* Aware of the reasons for the failure of the League of Nations,* the conferees could not find a way to guarantee continued great power cooperation, but they worked toward that end by not requiring unanimous votes and by lodging peacekeeping activities in the Security Council, where the great powers were to have permanent representation and a veto privilege. Among differences left for later resolution were the need for separate economic and social agencies; an international air force; the place of regional arrangements such as the Pan-American Union* and imperial organizations such as the British Commonwealth; the status of the Soviet Union's sixteen republics; and the application of the Security Council veto. The conference was held in two phases: the first (or Soviet) phase, lasting from August 21 to September 28, and the second (in which a Chinese delegation replaced the Soviets), lasting from September 28 to October 7. Most of the major decisions were made during the first phase. On the whole, Dumbarton Oaks was a successful conference full of optimism for future international cooperation. Many of the differences brought to light at this conference were settled at the Yalta Conference (1945).* The U.S. delegation was headed by Edward R. Stettinius* and Henry P. Fletcher,* a former under secretary of state and a Republican. Divine, Robert A., *Second Chance* (1967); *FR* (1944), 1:614–959; McNeill, William H., *America, Britain, and Russia* (1953); Wheeler-Bennett, John, and Anthony Nicholls, *The Semblance of Peace* (1972).

DUN, EDWIN (1848–1931). Born in Chillicothe, Ohio, in July 1848, Edwin Dun lived in obscurity until 1873 when he went to Japan. In 1874, he became an agricultural adviser to the Japanese Colonization Department. After a decade in that position, he secured a position with the U.S. legation and rose through the ranks to become minister to Japan in 1893, the first career diplomat to reach that plateau in Japan. As minister, Dun concluded the long-negotiated treaty revision (1894) and signed a commercial treaty. He played down American fears of Japanese immigration, observed the Sino-Japanese War,* and transmitted a U.S. offer of good offices to Japan, although Minister Charles Denby* in China played a more important role in the settlement of the conflict. Little is known of Dun's later life. He died May 16, 1931. Dennett, Tyler, *Americans in Eastern Asia* (1922); *WWWA*, 1 (1897–1942): 345.

DURBROW, ELBRIDGE (b. 1903). Born in San Francisco on September 21, 1903, Elbridge Durbrow received a Ph.D. from Yale in 1926 and studied further at Stanford, Dijon, and the Hague. In 1930, he joined the Foreign Service and held a succession of minor posts in Warsaw, Bucharest, Moscow, Naples, Rome, Lisbon, and Washington before returning to Moscow as counselor in 1946. From 1948 to 1950, Durbrow was attached to the National War College; in 1950, he became chief of the Division of Foreign Service Personnel. In 1952, he went to Rome as minister-counselor and became deputy chief of mission under Ambassador Clare Boothe Luce* the following year. From 1957 to 1961, Durbrow occupied his most sensitive position, ambassador to Vietnam. Here he witnessed the beginning of Vietcong terror against the Ngo Dinh Diem regime and became gradually isolated from Diem, whom he openly criticized. In 1961, Durbrow was replaced by Frederick Nolting* in the hope that the change would restore Diem's confidence and trust in the United States. Durbrow became the alternate permanent representative to the North Atlantic Council until 1965, when he took a position as adviser to the commander of Air University, Maxwell Air Force Base. Twice married, Durbrow retired in 1968 and lives in Washington. Halberstam, David, *The Best and the Brightest* (1972); Shadegg, Stephen, *Clare Booth Luce* (1970); *WWA* (1976–1977):872.

E

EADS, JAMES BUCHANAN (1820–1887). Eads, born May 23, 1820, in Lawrenceburg, Indiana, was a self-educated civil engineer. He salvaged steamboats and built the first bridge across the Mississippi River, but he is important in American diplomacy because of his idea for a ship-railway across the isthmus of Tehuantepec in Mexico as an alternative to an isthmian canal. Eads and the directors of the first Maritime Canal Company, Daniel Ammen and Seth L. Phelps,* fought to win congressional support of their respective projects, including a guarantee of profits. This political struggle hurt the chances for a congressional canal bill in the early 1880s. Eads obtained a concession from the Mexican government for his ship-railway project but never succeeded in bringing it to reality, dying in the Bahamas on March 8, 1887. *DAB*, 5: 587; Dorsey, Florence, *Road to the Sea: the Story of James B. Eads and the Mississippi River* (1947); Mack, Gerstle, *The Land Divided* (1944); Pletcher, David, *The Awkward Years* (1962).

EBERHARDT, CHARLES CHRISTOPHER (1871–1965). Born in Salina, Kansas, on July 27, 1871, Charles C. Eberhardt attended Kansas Wesleyan University before entering the lumber business in Salina in 1891. In 1894, he moved to Springfield, Massachusetts, to work for the Massachusetts Mutual Life Insurance Company and from 1902 to 1903 was their agent in Kansas. Eberhardt worked in Mexico City for the Waters-Pierce Oil Company, 1903–1904; by 1906, he had joined the State Department and was U.S. consul* at Iquitos, Peru. From 1908 to 1910, he was consul at Barranquilla. Then followed three assignments as consul-general-at-large: South and Central America, 1910–1919; East Asia, 1919–1922; and East Europe, 1922–1924. In 1925, he was named minister to Nicaragua, his most eventful post. Eberhardt was minister during the revolution that prompted renewed U.S. intervention in Nicaragua in 1926. Absent on leave during much of 1926 when the major coup took place and chargé Lawrence Dennis became overinvolved in domestic affairs, Eberhardt had nothing to do with the actual U.S. intervention but assisted Henry L. Stimson* in negotiating the Peace of Tipitapa (1927).* He supported the idea of a Nicaraguan "Platt Amendment"* that would bring stability at the cost of independence, but the State Department was not receptive to this idea. His ministry was marred by a feud with General Logan Feland, of the marines, over the proper policy toward the Nicaraguan national guard and the role of the U.S. Marines. Eberhardt left Nicaragua in 1930 and spent three uneventful years as minister to Costa Rica (1930–1933). He died February 22, 1965, in Salina. Kamman, William, *A Search for Stability* (1968); *WWWA*, 4 (1961–1968):276.

EDGE, WALTER EVANS (1873–1956). Born in Philadelphia November 20, 1873, and educated in public schools, Walter Edge moved to Atlantic City, New Jersey, at an early age and became a leading citizen of that state, serving twice as its governor. After a brief journalistic career as the owner of the *Atlantic City Press* and *Atlantic City Union*, Edge was elected as a Republican to the state assembly (1910) and senate (1911–1916) before his first term as governor (1917–1919). In 1919, he went to the U.S. Senate, where over the next ten years he became a leading supporter of international trade expansion, sponsoring the Edge Amendment (1919) to the Federal Reserve Act. President Herbert Hoover named Edge ambassador to France in 1929, and he spent the four years of Hoover's presidency in Paris. There he secured American participation in the International Colonial Exposition, a world's fair held in Paris in 1931, conferred with French leaders on problems of the London Naval Conference (1930),* negotiated the Franco-American Moratorium Accord, with the assistance of Secretary of the Treasury Andrew Mellon* (1931), and negotiated another treaty (1932), which eased some of the retributions placed on American interests by the French after the passage of the Smoot-Hawley Tariff (1930).* After his return from France, Edge became an elder statesman of the Republican party, serving another term as governor of New Jersey (1944–1947) and giving strong support to Dwight D. Eisenhower in 1952 and 1956. He was married twice: to Lady Lee Phillips in 1907 and, after her death in 1915, to Camilla Loyall Ashe Sewall in 1922. Walter Edge died in New York City on October 29, 1956. Edge, Walter Evans, *A Jerseyman's Journal: Fifty Years of American Business and Politics* (1948); *New York Times*, October 29, 1956; *WWWA*, 3 (1951–1960):250.

EGAN, PATRICK (1841–1919). One of America's most controversial diplomats, Patrick Egan was born August 18, 1841, in Ballymahon, County Longford, Ireland, and, after a career as a bookkeeper and Irish home rule supporter, emigrated to Lincoln, Nebraska, in 1883. There he was soon successful in the grain and milling business and became a leader of the Irish National League of America. This led to involvement in American politics; in 1888, the year he became a citizen, he was a delegate to the Republican convention. His support of Benjamin Harrison led to his appointment as minister to Chile after Harrison's election, amid accusations that the appointment was the worst sort of spoils abuse. In Chile, Egan's mission was to investigate British influence. To do this, he sided with the Balmaceda government and, as a result, endured intense criticism in the American press after Balmaceda's overthrow for his alleged involvement in Chilean politics. However, Egan managed to establish cordial relations with the new government, negotiating an arbitration* treaty and handling matters in the *Baltimore* affair (1891).* Hardy argues that criticism of Egan was motivated by the anti–James G. Blaine* press, that Egan's performance did not warrant the attacks. Others have concluded that the highly partisan Irishman was the wrong person to send to do diplomatic battle with the British in an important South American nation. Egan returned from Chile in 1893, settled in New York City, and resumed his activity in Irish and American politics, supporting Irish home rule but opposing Irish independence. He died in New York City on September 30, 1919. *DAB*, 6:51; Hardy, Osgood, "Was Egan a 'Blundering Minister'?" *Hispanic American Historical Review* 8 (1928):65–81; Pike, Frederick B., *Chile and the United States, 1880–1962* (1963).

EIGHTH INTERNATIONAL CONFERENCE OF AMERICAN STATES (1938). See **LIMA CONFERENCE (1938).**

EILTS, HERMANN FREDERICK (b. 1922). Born March 23, 1922, in Weissenfels Saale, Germany, Herman Eilts came to the United States in 1926; he received a B.A. from Ursinus College (1942) and an M.A. from Johns Hopkins (1947) and studied further at the Foreign Service Institute and the University of Pennsylvania (1950–1951). He served in World War II and joined the Foreign Service in 1947, holding minor posts in Tehran, Jidda, Aden, Sana (Yemen), and Baghdad until 1956. From 1957 to 1959, Eilts was officer-in-charge, Baghdad Pact* Affairs (Central Treaty Organization),* and from 1959 to 1961, he supervised Arabian peninsula affairs. He spent a year with the National War College (1961–1962), two years as first secretary in the London embassy (1962–1964), and a year as counselor in Tripoli (1964–1965) before his first ambassadorial assignment, to Saudi Arabia (1965–1970), an uneventful tour. After three years with the U.S. Army War College (1970–1973), Eilts returned to the Middle East as ambassador to Egypt (1973–1979). There he formed a close and trusting relationship with President Anwar Sadat and served as a valuable intermediary in negotiations between Egypt and Washington and Egypt and the U.S. embassy in Tel Aviv, Israel, especially during the period of Secretary of State Henry Kissinger's* "shuttle diplomacy" (1974–1975). Eilts married Helen Josephine Brew in 1948. Since 1979 he has taught political science and directed the Center for International Relations at Boston University. Shannon, Elizabeth, "The Ambassadors," *Boston Magazine* 78 (February 1986): 136; *New York Times*, January 28, 1978; *WWA* (1984–1985):930.

EINSTEIN, LEWIS DAVID (1877–1967). A historian and writer as well as a career diplomat, Lewis Einstein was born March 15, 1877, in New York City and received A.B. (1898) and A.M. (1899) degrees from Columbia. Joining the State Department, he held minor posts in Paris and London before promotion to first secretary of the Constantinople legation (1906–1909) and legation secretary, Peking (1909–1911). During this time, he also served as secretary to the U.S. delegation at the Algeciras Conference (1906).* A two-month stint as minister to Costa Rica (1911) was uneventful. In 1915, he was sent to Turkey as a special agent to assist in the protection of entente interests. After a short while, he went to Sofia, Bulgaria, as the American diplomatic representative in charge of British interests but was soon back in Turkey, having left Sofia because of a jurisdictional quarrel with Minister Charles Vopicka.* Einstein remained in

Turkey during World War II, handling the affairs of nations with which Turkey had severed relations. In 1921, Einstein, a Republican, was named minister to Czechoslovakia, a post he held until 1930. Much of his time in Prague was devoted to social affairs and legation accommodations, but he did make useful observations of the Czech political kaleidoscope and dealt with the complex problems of war debts and trade barriers. In 1930, he retired to private life, living in England much of the time and writing. In Turkey, he wrote *Inside Constantinople* (1915) and *A Prophecy of the War* (1918); in retirement, he wrote several volumes of poetry and *Divided Loyalties: Americans in England During the War of Independence* (1933). He also contributed "Lewis Cass" to Samuel F. Bemis, ed., *American Secretaries of State and Their Diplomacy*, vol. 9 (1929). An autobiographical work, *A Diplomat Looks Back* (1968), edited by Lawrence E. Gelfand, was published shortly after Einstein's death in Paris on December 4, 1967. *New York Times*, December 5, 1967.

EISENHOWER, MILTON STOVER (1899–1985). The brother of President Dwight D. Eisenhower, Milton Eisenhower was born in Abilene, Kansas, on September 15, 1899, and graduated from Kansas State University in 1924, after service in the U.S. Student Army Training Corps during World War I and work with the *Abilene Daily Reflector*. He taught briefly at Kansas State after graduation, served a year as a vice-consul in Edinburgh, Scotland, and in 1926 joined the Department of Agriculture, where he remained until 1942. In that year, he became director of the War Relocation Authority, where he was involved with the internment of Japanese-Americans on the West Coast, and then he moved to the associate directorship of the Office of War Information. Eisenhower left government service in 1943 upon his selection as president of Kansas State University, the first of three college presidencies (Pennsylvania State University, 1950–1956; Johns Hopkins, 1956–1967, 1971–1972; emeritus, 1972–1985). In the meantime, public service frequently drew him into the diplomatic arena. In the late 1940s, he worked with the United Nations* Educational, Scientific, and Cultural Organization,* and under his brother's administration (1953–1961), he twice undertook missions to Latin America, making lengthy trips through the region and recommending a more economically generous and considerate U.S. policy toward these hemispheric neighbors. After 1960, Eisenhower served on numerous presidential commissions, including the Atlantic-Pacific Interoceanic Study Commission (1965–1970) and the International Radio Broadcasting Commission (1972–1973). In addition, he had a brief (1968–1969) appointment as a State Department counselor on Latin American affairs. He was married to Helen Elsie Eakin, who preceded him in death. Eisenhower wrote two autobiographical works, *The Wine is Bitter* (1963), on his Latin American experiences, and *The President Is Calling* (1974), and died May 2, 1985, in Baltimore. Ambrose, Stephen E., and Richard H. Immerman, *Milton S. Eisenhower: Educational Statesman* (1983); *CB*, 46 (July 1985):43; *NCAB*, 1:332; *WWA* (1976–77):907.

EISENHOWER DOCTRINE (1958). This statement of diplomatic policy was an outgrowth of a congressional joint resolution (1957) authorizing the president to use U.S. military forces if deemed necessary to defend Middle Eastern nations (that had requested such aid) from overt Communist-inspired aggression. A consequence of the Suez crisis (1956),* the doctrine was formulated by Secretary of State John Foster Dulles* and found favor with the Baghdad Pact* nations, as well as much of the rest of the region. In April 1957, the threat of its implementation helped prop up the Jordanian government of King Hussein during a period of political and economic instability. During the Lebanon crisis* in May 1958, U.S. troops were sent under the provisions of the Eisenhower Doctrine to forestall a threatened Communist coup similar to a recent one in Iraq. But when the coup did not occur, the Eisenhower administration was subjected to criticism at home and further complications in the Middle East, due largely to the fact that the doctrine took little account of Arab nationalism. DeNovo, John A., "The Eisenhower Doctrine," in DeConde, Alexander, ed., *Encyclopedia of American Foreign Policy* (1979); George, Alexander L., and Richard Smoke, *Deterrence in American Foreign Policy* (1974); Gerson, Louis L., "John Foster Dulles," in Ferrell, Robert E., ed., *American Secretaries of State and Their Diplomacy*, vol. 17 (1967); Hammond, Paul Y., *Cold War and Detente* (1975).

EL SALVADOR CIVIL WAR (1979–). Starting about 1972, guerrilla-style violence from the left and paramilitary ("death squad") violence from the right began to disrupt the political life of El Salvador. By 1979, what amounted to a civil war was in process, and a coup led by moderate political elements did not bring calm. In December 1980, the American public was shocked by the brutal murder of three nuns and a lay churchwoman from the United States. When Ronald Reagan took office as president in January 1981, El Salvador was one of the first areas to which he turned his attention. Thinking of Central America in global cold war* terms, the administration sought to end the guerrilla war, thought to be financed by Communist-bloc countries using Cuba and Nicaragua as conduits, by giving massive amounts of economic and military aid and sending fifty-six military advisers to El Salvador. By 1984, the internal political situation had stabilized with the election of José Napoleon Duarte, a moderate, to the presidency, the civil war had settled into a stalemate, despite continuing large amounts of U.S. aid, and Nicaragua had replaced El Salvador as the focus of Reagan's Central American policy. Arnson, Cynthia, *El Salvador: A Revolution Confronts the United States* (1982); Bonner, Raymond, *Weakness and Deceit: U.S. Policy and El Salvador* (1984); Findling, John E., *Close Neighbors, Distant Friends* (1987).

EMBARGO ACT (1807). This act of Congress, signed by President Thomas Jefferson,* forbade American vessels to leave American ports and permitted foreign vessels to leave only with what cargo was then on board. Overland trade with Canada was also prohibited. Brought about through hostility engendered by the *Chesapeake* affair,* the Embargo Act was an attempt to bring about the resumption of normal commercial relations between the United States and nations of Europe. The act was an economic and political failure, causing severe dislocation in many sectors of the American economy and endangering the political fortunes of the Republican party. It was repealed in February 1809, and was replaced with the Non-Intercourse Act.* Egan, Clifford L., *Neither Peace nor War: Franco-American Relations, 1803–1812* (1983); Perkins, Bradford, *Prologue to War* (1961).

EMBARGO ACT (1812). This embargo, a ninety-day general prohibition of trade, was proposed primarily to deprive British troops fighting in the Iberian peninsula of American food and supplies, to clear American ships from the seas, and to convince Americans and British alike that Congress was serious about the problems between the two nations. Lack of firmness on the part of President James Madison,* delay by Congress (the act was not passed until April 4, 1812), and evasion by American merchants blunted the effectiveness of the measure, which was superseded by the declaration of war on June 18. Perkins, Bradford, *Prologue to War* (1961); Spivak, Burton, *Jefferson's English Crises: Commerce, Embargo, and Republican Revolution* (1979).

EMERGENCY QUOTA ACT (1921). An immigration restriction act, this assigned quotas to each nonhemispheric nation based on 3 percent of the foreign-born residents of each nationality in the United States in 1910. An answer to pressure groups arguing against cheap foreign labor and foreign radicalism, this act still let in too many Southern and Eastern Europeans to satisfy many Americans and was replaced by the Johnson-Reed Act (1924).* Ellis, L. Ethan, *Republican Foreign Policy, 1921–1933* (1968); Higham, John, *Strangers in the Land* (1966).

ENDERS, THOMAS OSTROM (b. 1931). A native of Hartford, Connecticut, where he was born November 28, 1931, Thomas O. Enders received a B.A. from Yale in 1953 and graduate degrees from the University of Paris (1955) and Harvard (1957). He joined the Foreign Service in 1958 and held minor posts in Washington, Stockholm, and Belgrade until 1970, when he became deputy chief of mission and then chargé d'affaires* in Phnom Penh, Cambodia. There he headed a civil-military committee that worked to expedite the sending of U.S. air attacks against Communist rebels. This led to some criticism in connection with legal restrictions on U.S. involvement in Cambodia. After another tour in Washington, Enders was appointed ambassador to Canada in 1976, a post he held until 1979, concerning himself mainly with trade matters. After a stint as ambassador to the European Communities, 1979–1981, Enders was appointed assistant secretary of state for inter-American affairs by the Reagan administration. In this position, he became the point man for the administration's Central American policy. Although he tended to see the region's problems in the harsh context of the cold war,* he eventually ran afoul of William Clark* and Jeane Kirkpatrick,* who felt his policies in Central America were too moderate. As a consequence, Enders was transferred to Madrid in 1983, where he spent three uneventful years before leaving the Foreign Service in 1986 to join the New York investment banking firm of Salomon Brothers. Findling, John E., *Close Neighbors, Distant Friends* (1987); Kissinger, Henry, *Years of Upheaval* (1982); *New York Times*, March 26, 1982, May 28, 1983, May 21, 1986; Shawcross, William, *Sideshow: Kissinger, Nixon and the Destruction of Cambodia* (1979); *WWA* (1984–1985):952.

ENGERT, CORNELIUS VAN HEMERT (1887–1985). Born in Vienna, Austria, on New Year's Eve, 1887, Cornelius Engert came to the United States as a child and received both an undergraduate and a law degree from the University of California. After two years of teaching at California, Engert joined the Foreign Service in 1912 and served in minor posts until the 1930s, most of them in the Middle East but also in Europe, Latin America, and China. In 1917, he was interned by the Turks when the United States entered World War I. In 1922, Engert was the first American diplomat to visit Kabul, Afghanistan; twenty years later, he became the first resident minister there (previously the embassy in Iran had handled Afghan relations). He was in Ethiopia in 1936 when it fell to Italy and defended the U.S. legation against vandals. As the U.S. consul general* in Lebanon, 1940–1942, he negotiated a settlement between French Vichy troops and British and Free French forces who were overrunning Vichy positions at great cost of life on both sides. Engert retired from the State Department in 1945 but continued to travel extensively in the Middle East as a representative of the United Nations Relief and Rehabilitation Administration,* 1946–1947, and the International Bank for Reconstruction and Development (World Bank),* 1948–1951. He was married in 1922 to Sara Cunningham; she died in 1972, and he died on May 12, 1985, in Washington. *New York Times*, May 15, 1985; *WWWA*, 8 (1982–1985):127.

ENTENTE CORDIALE. This name was applied to the occasional periods of Anglo-French cordiality and cooperation in foreign affairs following the end of the Napoleonic Wars. One such period was during the 1840s; another was in the years preceding World War I. The term *entente* was also applied to the alliance of Great Britain, France, and Russia during World War I. Renouvin, Pierre, and Jean-Baptiste Duroselle, *Introduction to the History of International Relations* (1964).

ERLANGER AND COMPANY, European banking house, 1860s. One of the most important and influential banking firms on the Continent, Emille Erlanger and Company negotiated with Confederate agent John Slidell* a loan for £5 million in cotton bonds at 8 percent, with at least 34 percent of the proceeds going to Erlanger. Objection on the part of agent James Mason* and the Confederate government in Richmond resulted in an alteration of the terms to £3 million in bonds at 7 percent, with a slightly reduced commission for Erlanger. After some delay, the loan was agreed upon, and the bonds were marketed March 21, 1863. In the end, the Confederacy received about $2.6 million of the $5.5

million contracted for. Confederate military reverses at Vicksburg and Gettysburg badly depressed the value of the bonds. Owsley, Frank L., *King Cotton Diplomacy*, 2d ed. (1959).

ERSKINE AGREEMENTS (1809). The Erskine Agreements consisted of diplomatic notes exchanged April 18–19, 1809, between Secretary of State Robert Smith* and British Minister David Erskine. Erskine pledged the revocation of the 1807 Orders-in-Council,* and Smith agreed to restore commercial ties with Britain. On July 21, 1809, however, Foreign Minister George Canning repudiated the agreements and shortly after replaced Erskine with the hostile Francis James Jackson. Although significant as the "first important executive agreement" in American history, the failure of the Erskine Agreements was a blow to the deteriorating Anglo-American relationship before the War of 1812. Horsman, Reginald, *The Causes of the War of 1812* (1962); Perkins, Bradford, *Prologue to War* (1961).

ESQUIPULAS II (1987). Proposed by Costa Rican President Oscar Arias in February 1987 and substantially modified over the next several months, Esquipulas II was a comprehensive peace settlement for Central America that the presidents of the five isthmian nations signed on August 7, 1987. The plan called for each country to initiate steps toward internal stability through the creation of national reconciliation commissions and toward democratization through the guaranteeing of the freedom of press and assembly. Nations engaged in armed conflict were urged to arrange cease-fires, and all governments were requested to end martial law, grant amnesty to political prisoners, and arrange for democratic elections of domestic legislatures and representatives to a Central American parliament. Armed resistance groups were to be denied aid and the use of neighboring territory, and verification and mediation, where appropriate, could be carried out by the members of the Contadora group* and its South American support group, as well as the secretaries-general of the United Nations* and the Organization of American States.* On January 15, 1988, the Central American presidents met and declared their continuing commitment to Esquipulas II. By mid-1988, some compliance had occurred in each country, although important problems remained, especially in El Salvador, Honduras, and Nicaragua. The Reagan administration gave, reluctantly, a conditional endorsement of the plan, although many observers feel that its continuing support of the Nicaraguan contras* directly undermined the long-term chances for the plan's success. President Arias was awarded the Nobel Peace Prize in 1987 for this plan, which is also known as the Guatemala Accord or the Arias Plan. LASA Commission on Compliance with the Central American Peace Accord, "Extraordinary Opportunities . . . and New Risks," *LASA Forum* 19, 1 (Spring 1988): 1–41; *New York Times*, August 12, 23, 1987.

ESSEX **DECISION (1805).** This was a British Admiralty court decision that restored much of the force of the Rule of the War of 1756* and took away many of the liberties allowed under the *Polly* decision (1800).* Most significant, the burden of proof of legitimate reexport trade now had to be borne by the neutral shipowner rather than the captor. American commercial interests were insulted by the sudden implementation of this new policy, the first step in a program of increasing harassment of American commerce in the years before the War of 1812. Horsman, Reginald, *The Causes of the War of 1812* (1962); Perkins, Bradford, *Prologue to War* (1961).

EUROPEAN DEFENSE COMMUNITY (EDC). After World War II, France had consistently opposed the rearmament of Germany, but in 1950, after the beginning of the Korean War, the United States began to push for German rearmament in order to improve Western European security, and Great Britain seemed to concur. In late 1950, French Prime Minister René Pleven suggested that German rearmament take place gradually within the structure of a European army (the Pleven Plan). French public opinion remained opposed both to this plan and to German membership in the North Atlantic Treaty Organization (NATO).* However, discussions about the Pleven Plan began in 1951 among Belgium, Luxembourg, Italy, France, and West Germany, with the United States joining in later that year. These talks resulted in the signing of a European Defense Community Treaty in May 1952. Opposition to the EDC continued to grow in France in 1952 and 1953, coinciding with the rise of Charles de Gaulle in political importance, while the death of Joseph Stalin in Moscow and the end of the Korean War seemed to make German rearmament less urgent. Secretary of State John Foster Dulles* pressured the French to ratify the treaty, but to no avail. In 1954, with French reverses in Indochina, the EDC appeared to the French as another way in which their military prestige was vanishing. Finally, on August 30, 1954, the French Assembly rejected the treaty. Soon after, Germany was rearmed within the structure of NATO in a new organization, the Western European Union. Carleton, William G., *The Revolution in American Foreign Policy* (1963); Tint, Herbert, *French Foreign Policy since the Second World War* (1972).

EUSTIS, JAMES BIDDLE (1834–1899). James B. Eustis was born in New Orleans on August 21, 1834, received a law degree from Harvard in 1854, and returned to New Orleans to practice law. During the Civil War, he served in the Confederate army and also as secretary to John Slidell,* the Confederate envoy in Paris. Returning to law practice after the war, Eustis entered politics in 1866 with election to the state legislature. In 1876, he became a U.S. senator from Louisiana, serving until 1879 and again from 1885 to 1891. A Democrat and supporter of Grover Cleveland, he was rewarded with the mission to France in 1893 after Cleveland's election. Eustis was the first ambassador to France after Thomas J. Coolidge,* his predecessor, had recommended the upgrading of the legation. He served four years in Paris, confronting problems when a secret code book was stolen from the desk of First Secretary Henry Vignaud*; when the French, in 1895, followed Germany and Belgium in prohibiting the importation of American cattle; when the American consul in the French colony of Madagascar was sentenced to twenty years in prison for conspiring with French enemies; and when the American consul at Bordeaux spoke disparagingly about French wine. Eustis resolved all of these matters while maintaining cordial relations and thus helped secure French neutrality during the Spanish-American War. He practiced law in New York after his return from France and died in Newport, Rhode Island, on September 9, 1899. *DAB*, 6:193; Willson, Beckles, *America's Ambassadors to France, 1777–1927* (1928).

EVARTS, WILLIAM MAXWELL (1818–1901). Secretary of state during the Hayes administration (1877–1881), William M. Evarts was born in Boston on February 6, 1818, was graduated from Yale (1837), attended Harvard Law School, and was admitted to the bar in 1841. He formed a law partnership with Charles E. Butler that lasted sixty years and became one of America's most renowned trial lawyers, playing important roles in the impeachment trial of Andrew Johnson, the Tilton-Beecher scandal, and the disputed Hayes-Tilden election. In 1863, he was sent to England on two occasions to bring an end to Confederate shipbuilding, and in 1871–1872 he was a counsel for the United States in the Geneva Arbitration, which had resulted from the Treaty of Washington (1871).* As secretary of state, he was competent and used good judgment but was not an efficient administrator. He was interested in the growth of foreign commerce and tried to aid it by upgrading the standards of consular appointments and negotiating new commercial treaties with China, Japan, and Samoa. Mexican relations were probably the most critical foreign policy matter. Porfirio Díaz had come to power in 1877 amid nettlesome border raids from Mexico to the United States. Evarts held off recognition of Díaz, hoping for a resolution to the border problems in Mexican acceptance of the U.S. doctrine of "hot pursuit," wherein U.S. troops could cross the border if they were actively pursuing Mexican raiders. Although Mexico never formally agreed to the doctrine of hot pursuit, the climate between the two nations improved, and recognition was granted. Evarts also stated clearly the American desire to build and operate unilaterally an isthmian canal across Central America, directed the negotiation of a treaty with China giving the United States the right to "regulate . . . or suspend" immigration of Chinese laborers, a forerunner of the Chinese Exclusion Act (1882),* and made a major but unsuccessful effort to settle the War of the Pacific (1879–1883),* among Chile, Peru, and Bolivia. In 1881, after leaving the State Department, he was a delegate to the International Monetary Conference in Paris, and from 1885 to 1891 he represented New York in the U.S. Senate. He married Helen Minerva Wardner in 1843 and died in New York City on February 28, 1901. Barrows, Chester L., *William M. Evarts* (1941); *DAB*, 6:215; Dyer, Brainerd, *The Public Career of William M. Evarts* (1933); Millington, Herbert, *American Diplomacy and the War of the Pacific* (1948).

EVERETT, EDWARD (1794–1865). Edward Everett, born April 11, 1794, in Dorchester, Massachusetts, is best known as America's most renowned orator in the mid-nineteenth century. He was, however, also minister to Great Britain (1841–1845) and secretary of state (1852–1853). Everett received B.A. (1811) and M.A. (1914) degrees from Harvard and a Ph.D. (1817) from the University of Göttingen. His oratorial talent was first seen in his pastorate of the Brattle Street Unitarian Church in 1814. From 1819 to 1825, he taught at Harvard, and from 1825 to 1835, he served in the U.S. House of Representatives. He was governor of Massachusetts from 1836 to 1839 and became minister to Great Britain in 1841 through his friendship with Secretary of State Daniel Webster.* He participated in some preliminary talks prior to the negotiation of the Webster-Ashburton Treaty (1842)* and dealt also with the African slave trade matter and the *Caroline* incident.* After three years as president of Harvard (1846–1849), Everett returned to public service as secretary of state under President Millard Fillmore in 1852. He was involved in the Cuban question, rejecting a proposal of Britain and France to guarantee Spanish control of the island. He left office in March 1853, with the change of administration, after only five months on the job. Everett went to the Senate for a short while (1853–1854), resigning in 1854 because of criticism over his failure to vote on the Kansas-Nebraska bill. He became a professional orator, ran for the vice-presidency in 1860 on the Constitutional Union ticket, published his four-volume *Orations and Speeches on Various Occasions* (1853–1868), and died January 15, 1865, in Boston. *DAB*, 6:223; Kaplan, Lawrence S., "The Brahmin as Diplomat in Nineteenth Century America," *Civil War History* 19, 1 (March 1973): 5–28; Willson, Beckles, *America's Ambassadors to England, 1785–1929* (1929).

EXECUTIVE AGREEMENT. An executive agreement is a binding international obligation made between chiefs of state, without legislative sanction. In the United States, it is an agreement made by the president or his representative, without Senate ratification, based on the general prerogatives of the president as the head of state and commander in chief. Plischke notes that while a treaty, since it must be ratified, may depart substantially from existing laws, an executive agreement must conform to law and policies existing prior to the time it is made. In other words, a treaty is, in effect, a new law, but an executive agreement cannot change existing law. Between 1789 and 1939, there were 1,182 executive agreements and 799 treaties, but between 1940 and 1964, 4,358 executive agreements and only 244 treaties were concluded. Among important executive agreements in U.S. diplomatic history are the Rush-Bagot Agreement (1817),* the Root-Takahira Agreement (1908),* the Lansing-Ishii Agreement (1917),* and the various agreements made at the Yalta Conference (1945).* Plischke, Elmer, *Conduct of American Diplomacy* (1967).

EXPORT-IMPORT BANK. This institution was created in March 1934 specifically for the purpose of lending money to U.S. exporters doing business with Cuba in order to promote trade and stimulate a depression-ridden economy. In

1939, at a meeting of Western Hemisphere foreign ministers in Panama, the functions of the bank were broadened to include loans to all Latin American governments, as well as to U.S. exporters, and in September 1940 its total lending authorization was raised from $200 million to $700 million to enable it better to contribute to the resource development, economic stabilization, and orderly marketing procedures of Latin American nations. Operated by the U.S. government and funded by Congress, the bank generally lends money only for purchases from the United States. In 1986 Congress expressed its continuing support for the bank by voting to extend its authority for six years and appropriating $145 million to cover the costs of subsidies. At the same time, the bank was prohibited from making loans to facilitate export sales to Communist countries or Angola. Baron, David M., *The Export-Import Bank* (1983); *New York Times*, March 23, 1986; Rodriguez, Rita M., ed., *The Export-Import Bank at Fifty* (1987).

EXTRATERRITORIALITY. Now quite uncommon, extraterritoriality is a process whereby subjects or citizens of one country are exempt from the legal jurisdiction and courts of another country in which they are living. Based on international custom or treaty provision, it was most frequently applied in China, beginning with Western penetration in the early nineteenth century. During World War II, however, the United States and most European powers abandoned extraterritoriality. The practice of exempting diplomatic agents and their families from local jurisdiction, similar to extraterritoriality, is called *exterritoriality*. FR (1930), 2:353–522; Hyamson, A. M., *A Dictionary of International Affairs* (1947); Plischke, Elmer, *Conduct of American Diplomacy* (1967).

FALKLAND ISLANDS WAR (1982). On December 15, 1965, United Nations* Resolution 2065 was adopted, calling for a peaceful settlement of the 130-year-old dispute between Great Britain and Argentina over the Falkland (or Malvinas) Islands. After years of sporadic and fruitless negotiations, during which the British argued for continued control of the islands because that was the desire of the 2,000 inhabitants while Argentina claimed legal sovereignty, war broke out on April 2, 1982, when Argentine forces invaded the Falklands and seized control of Port Stanley, the capital. The British responded with military force and, after ten weeks of fighting, accepted Argentina's surrender. About 250 British troops and between 700 and 1,000 Argentines were killed in the conflict. The United States initially tried to act as a mediator in the conflict, with Secretary of State Alexander Haig* playing the lead role and shuttling between London and Buenos Aires. After a month, his efforts had failed, and the Reagan administration chose to ally itself with Great Britain. This decision surprised the Argentines, since there had been a significant improvement in U.S.-Argentine relations since Reagan had become president and since Argentina had been supportive of U.S. policy in Central America. Virtually every other Western Hemisphere nation voiced its support for Argentina. In November 1982, the United Nations* adopted another resolution calling for renewed negotiations. Freedman, Lawrence, "The War of the Falkland Islands, 1982," *Foreign Affairs* 61, 1 (Fall 1982): 196–210; Hastings, Max, and Simon Jenkins, *The Battle for the Falklands* (1983); Hoffman, Fritz C., and Olga Mingo Hoffman, *Sovereignty in Dispute: The Falklands/Malvinas, 1493–1982* (1984).

FAREWELL ADDRESS, message of George Washington, 1796. George Washington's final words, September 19, 1796, to his countrymen were written by Alexander Hamilton. The address contained what became, until well into the twentieth century, the fundamental statement of American isolationism*: that there should be "as little political connection [with foreign nations] as possible." Kaufman challenges this traditional view, believing instead that Washington foresaw an expanding United States and that his views of nonentanglement were meant for the present in view of the weakness of the newly independent nation. Kaufman, Burton I., *Washington's Farewell Address: The View from the 20th Century* (1969); Lycan, Gilbert L., *Alexander Hamilton and American Foreign Policy* (1970).

FAULKNER, CHARLES JAMES (1806–1884). Born in Martinsburg, Virginia (now West Virginia), on July 6, 1806, Charles J. Faulkner graduated from

Georgetown University in 1822 and was admitted to the bar in 1829. He practiced law in Martinsburg, married Mary Wagner Boyd in 1833, and served several years in the Virginia legislature, where he helped negotiate a settlement of the Virginia-Maryland boundary dispute. In 1851, he was elected to the U.S. House of Representatives, serving four consecutive terms. President James Buchanan* appointed him minister to France in March 1860, and he served fourteen months before the Lincoln administration appointee, William L. Dayton,* arrived. Faulkner's main contribution was to secure French recognition of American citizenship of French nationals and their exemption from French military service. When Virginia's secession appeared likely in early 1861, he asked to be recalled; he was and was briefly jailed for his Confederate sympathies after his return to the United States. Once released, he went South and became an officer on the staff of General Stonewall Jackson. After the war, he returned to his law practice and active participation in West Virginia politics, serving one more term in the U.S. House of Representatives (1875–1877). He died November 1, 1884, in Boydville, West Virginia. *DAB*, 6:299; McVeigh, Donald R., "Charles James Faulkner in the Civil War," *West Virginia History* 12 (January 1951): 129–41; Rogers, Augustus, ed., *Our Representatives Abroad* (1874); Willson, Beckles, *America's Ambassadors to France, 1777–1927* (1928).

FEIS, HERBERT (1893–1972). Born in New York City on June 7, 1893, Herbert Feis attended City College of New York before graduating from Harvard (A.B., 1916; Ph.D., 1921). From 1920 to 1929, he taught at Harvard, Kansas, and Cincinnati, working during the summers as an adviser to the International Labor Organization.* In 1930, Feis became a staff member of the Council on Foreign Relations.* The following year, he joined the State Department as an economic adviser and was the chief technical adviser to the U.S. delegation at the London Economic Conference (1933). In 1937, he became an international economic adviser in the State Department and, seven years later, went to the War Department for two years (1944–1946) as a special consultant. From 1948 to 1957, Feis was a member of the Institute of Advanced Study at Princeton, except for a short time in 1950–1951, when he was a member of the State Department's Policy Planning Staff. Most of his time after 1946 was devoted to researching and writing books on economic and diplomatic history. Those particularly relevant to diplomacy are *The Diplomacy of the Dollar: First Era, 1919–1932* (1950) and a series of five volumes dealing with World War II and its aftermath: *The Road to Pearl Harbor* (1951), *The China Tangle* (1953), *Churchill-Roosevelt-Stalin* (1957), *Between War and Peace* (1960), and *Japan Subdued* (1961). Others of Feis's books are *Foreign Aid and Foreign Policy* (1964), *1933: Characters in Crisis* (1966), *The Contest over Japan* (1967), *The Birth of Israel* (1969), and *From Trust to Terror* (1970). Feis had special access to State Department records for much of his research, and some critics feel that his writings therefore hewed too closely to an establishment line; Feis himself sharply rejected such criticism. He was married in 1922 to Ruth Stanley-Brown and died March 2, 1972, in Winter Park, Florida. *NCAB*, 57: 481; *New York Times*, March 3, 1972.

FIFTH INTERNATIONAL CONFERENCE OF AMERICAN STATES (1923). See **SANTIAGO CONFERENCE (1923).**

"FIFTY-FOUR FORTY OR FIGHT!" diplomatic slogan, 1846. Not an 1844 campaign slogan, as often believed, this phrase arose out of Senate debates on the Oregon question* and first appeared in early 1846. At that time, Britain and the United States had conflicting claims to the Oregon Territory, which extended along the Pacific coast from 42° north latitude to 54° 40' north latitude, and inland to the Rocky Mountains. Those who adopted the slogan demanded the acquisition of all the Oregon Territory to 54° 40', the northern limit of any American claim. The Oregon Treaty (1846)* divided the territory at 49° north latitude. Miles, Edwin A., "Fifty-four Forty or Fight'—An American Political Legend," *Mississippi Valley Historical Review* (1957); 291–309; Pletcher, David, *The Diplomacy of Annexation* (1973); Van Alstyne, Richard W., *The Rising American Empire* (1960).

FIGHT FOR FREEDOM COMMITTEE (FFF), interventionist organization, 1941. This important organization was founded in April 1941 after several months of preparatory meetings of individuals associated with the Century Group.* Fight for Freedom favored all-out aid to Great Britain short of war, including the use of naval and air power to keep the seas open. Senator Carter Glass (D., Virginia) was the group's titular head, and Bishop Henry W. Hobson was the chairman. Sponsors of FFF included many prominent persons in the arts and government and, particularly, in organized labor. The committee organized on a local level where it was, in a sense, competitive with the Committee to Defend America by Aiding the Allies,* becoming by the summer of 1941 the more dominant of the two groups. Operating through mailings, newspaper advertisements, and public speakers, FFF put interventionist arguments before the American public and enjoyed a cordial relationship with the White House, to the point of following White House instructions at times. In October, FFF began a public campaign for an outright declaration of war on Germany. After the attack on Pearl Harbor* and American entrance into the war, the leaders of FFF felt that its purposes had been achieved and disbanded the group. Chadwin, Mark L., *The Warhawks* (1968).

FILIBUSTER, c. mid-nineteenth century. This term refers to private adventurers who led expeditions of Americans into foreign lands, usually in the Caribbean or Central America, in efforts to colonize, Americanize, and, often, begin a process toward annexation by the United States. The best-known filibustering expeditions are those of John A. Quitman to Cuba, which died aborning, and William Walker* to Nicaragua, a more successful effort resulting in Walker's effective control of the country for several months in 1856–1857. Brown, Charles

H., *Agents of Manifest Destiny* (1980); Carr, Albert Z., *The World and William Walker* (1962); Scroggs, W. O., *Filibusters and Financiers* (1916); Williams, Mary W., *Anglo-American Isthmian Diplomacy, 1815–1915* (1916).

FIRST INTERNATIONAL CONFERENCE OF AMERICAN STATES (1889). See WASHINGTON CONFERENCE (1889).

FISH, HAMILTON (1808–1893). Secretary of state during the two terms of President U.S. Grant, Hamilton Fish is generally considered the leading light of that star-crossed administration. He was born August 3, 1808, in New York City, graduated from Columbia in 1827, and was admitted to the bar in 1830. He entered law practice in partnership with William B. Lawrence, specializing in real estate law. In 1836, Fish married Julia Kean, and, in 1843, he served a term in the U.S. House of Representatives as a Whig. In 1848, he became lieutenant governor, and in 1849–1850 he was governor of New York. From 1851 to 1857, he was a U.S. senator from New York, junior to William H. Seward. During the Civil War, Fish served on the Union Defense Committee and as a U.S. commissioner for the relief of prisoners of war. In 1869, President Grant named him secretary of state, and he came to office reluctantly and with little experience in foreign affairs. In that office, he attempted, without enthusiasm and without success, to annex the Dominican Republic and, according to Nevins, combated a "sentimental imperialism" that would have put a social, financial, and political strain on the United States. His greatest accomplishment may have been settling the *Alabama** claims matter with Great Britain in the Treaty of Washington (1871).* In addition, Fish dealt with the Cuban insurrection as it touched on American claims and the recognition of Cuba, a question that was complicated by the *Virginius* affair (1873).* He also helped prevent the Franco-Prussian War from spreading to the Far East, upheld American rights in China, concluded a reciprocity treaty with Hawaii (1875),* and attempted to promulgate an isthmian canal treaty. He left office in 1877, declined an offer to be chief justice of the Supreme Court, and retired, devoting his time to philanthropic and charitable interests. Fish died on September 7, 1893, at his estate, Glen Clyffe, near Garrison, New York. *DAB*, 6:397; Nevins, Allan, *Hamilton Fish*, 2 vols. (1957); *New York Times*, September 8, 1893.

FISKE, JOHN (1842–1901). John Fiske was born March 30, 1842, in Hartford, Connecticut, and graduated from Harvard in 1863 and Harvard Law School in 1865. An early devotee of Herbert Spencer and social Darwinism,* Fiske began teaching at Harvard in 1869 and turned to public lecturing in 1871. He became an extremely popular writer and speaker, ardently championing Anglo-Saxon expansionism. Fiske firmly believed in the superiority of American political institutions and their spread across the world in a peaceful manner. American industry would create a world of peace, superintended by what Fiske called the "English race." Much of his thought on expansion was published in 1885 in a popular lecture, "Manifest Destiny." Fiske is best known today for his books on early American history, such as *The Critical Period in American History* (1888), *The Beginnings of New England* (1898), and *The American Revolution* (1901). He also wrote an autobiography, *Excursions of an Evolutionist* (1884). Fiske died on Independence Day, 1901, in Gloucester, Massachusetts. *DAB*, 6:420; Fisk, Ethel, *The Letters of John Fiske* (1940); Healey, David, *US Expansionism* (1970); Hofstadter, Richard, *Social Darwinism in American Thought* (1955); LaFeber, Walter, *The New Empire* (1963); *New York Times*, July 5, 1901.

FIUME PROBLEM (1919). Fiume, a port at the north end of the Adriatic Sea, was designated at the Paris Peace Conference* to be part of the new state of Yugoslavia—its only viable port. Italy, however, claimed Fiume, because of its strategic location and economic potential and because 30,000 Italians lived there. President Wilson studied the problem, decided Italy had no case, and nearly sabotaged the conference by stating his position to the Italian people through the press instead of to Vittorio Orlando, the Italian premier. In 1920, Italy and Yugoslavia negotiated a treaty making Fiume a free state; in 1924, a new treaty gave Fiume to Italy and the nearby harbor of Porta Bavos and a fifty-year lease of part of Fiume's harbor to Yugoslavia. Bailey, Thomas A., *Woodrow Wilson and the Lost Peace* (1944); Carr, E. H., *International Relations between the Two World Wars, 1919–1939* (1967).

FIVE-POWER TREATY (1922) . A naval agreement made at the Washington Conference* in February 1922, the Five-Power Treaty established ratios of naval strength (for battleships and aircraft carriers) at 5:5:3:1.75:1.75 for the United States, Great Britain, Japan, France, and Italy, respectively. In addition, the signatories agreed to a ten-year holiday on naval construction and the maintenance of the status quo in the Pacific. Smaller ships and submarines were excluded from these restrictions, although the London Naval Conference* of 1930 set ratios for cruisers. The treaty stopped the worst of a postwar naval arms race and was ratified by the Senate, 67–22, in March 1922. Buckley, Thomas H., *The United States and the Washington Conference, 1921–1922* (1970); Duroselle, Jean-Baptiste, *From Wilson to Roosevelt* (1963); *FR* (1922), 1:53–267.

FLETCHER, HENRY PRATHER (1873–1959). A career diplomat, Henry F. Fletcher was born in Greencastle, Pennsylvania, on April 10, 1873. After attending Chambersburg (Pennsylvania) Academy, he read law and was admitted to the bar in 1894. He worked as a court reporter for seven years (1891–1898) before becoming a Rough Rider in the Spanish-American War. Military service in the Philippines (1899–1901) preceded his entry into diplomatic service. Between 1902 and 1909, he held minor posts at legations in Cuba, China, and Portugal. In 1909, Fletcher, a Republican, was named minister to Chile, where, over seven years, he reestablished cordial relations after a period of hostility brought on by claims disputes and other problems. In 1916, he became minister to Mexico, a delicate mission because of John J. Pershing's punitive expedition then operating in northern Mexico in 1916 and the publication of the Zimmermann telegram* in 1917. In 1919, Fletcher moved to Washington as director of the Division of Latin American Affairs, resigning a year later because of his opposition to the League of Nations.* During the 1920s, Fletcher was minister to Belgium (1922–1924), and Luxembourg (1923–1924) and ambassador to Italy (1924–1929). He was on good terms with Benito Mussolini in Italy and arranged a settlement of the Italian war debt to the United States. In 1928, he was President-elect Herbert Hoover's diplomatic adviser on Hoover's goodwill trip to Latin America and after 1929 served on several special commissions and boards concerned with international relations. In the 1930s, he continued to be active in Republican party matters and in 1944–1945, served as a special adviser to the secretary of state. He married Beatrice Bend in 1917. She died in 1941, and he died on July 10, 1959, in Newport, Rhode Island. *DAB*, Supp. 6:206–7; *New York Times*, July 11, 1959; *WWWA*, 3 (1951–1960):288

FOOD FOR PEACE. See **AGRICULTURE TRADE DEVELOPMENT AND ASSISTANCE ACT (1954).**

FOREIGN ASSISTANCE ACT (1961). First in a series of annual pieces of legislation, the Foreign Assistance Act of 1961 represented the start of a third phase in the history of post–World War II foreign aid, following the Marshall Plan* and the Mutual Security Act.* In this phase, there was a lessening of military aid and the drive to contain communism at all costs and a greater commitment to provide economic aid to help developing nations, many newly independent. The program flourished until 1967, when it was swamped by the escalating costs of the Vietnam War; when it was revived in the Foreign Assistance Act of 1973, foreign aid was oriented more toward multilateral economic assistance through the United Nations* or multinational development banks. In the Foreign Assistance Act of 1961, Congress created the Agency for International Development as the administrative organization to manage assistance programs. An important and controversial part of the Foreign Assistance Act for several years was the Hickenlooper amendment, named for its sponsor, Senator Bourke Hickenlooper (R., Iowa). Adopted in 1962, this provided for the suspension of foreign aid to any country that expropriated U.S. property without prompt and adequate compensation. Debated and amended itself during the 1960s, the Hickenlooper amendment was never actually invoked because disputes were generally settled before invocation was necessary. In 1973, the amendment was made discretionary in its application. Cohen, Bernard C., ed., *Foreign Policy in American Government* (1965); Pastor, Robert A., *Congress and the Politics of Foreign Economic Policy, 1929–1976* (1980); Wilhelm, John, and Gerry Feinstein, *U.S. Foreign Assistance: Investment or Folly?* (1984).

FOREIGN ENLISTMENT ACT (1819). This British act established rules of neutrality* for the British and was applied in the matter of Confederate shipbuilding during the Civil War. It limited belligerent use of British ports and prohibited shipbuilding for belligerents, although this prohibition was interpreted in such a way that the Confederacy could have ships built for it as long as the component parts of military armament were assembled outside the three-mile limit. The act was the basis of several ship detentions and seizures during the war years, most notably the Laird rams.* *FR* (1868) 1:208–308; Merli, Frank J., *Great Britain and the Confederate Navy* (1965).

FOREIGN POLICY ASSOCIATION, internationalist organization. Founded in 1918 by Charles A. Beard,* Herbert Croly, and others as the League of Free Nations Association, this group was dedicated to educating the public on foreign affairs from an objective standpoint, while at the same time remaining sympathetic to the League of Nations.* Changing its name to Foreign Policy Association after the Senate's rejection of the Treaty of Versailles,* the organization claimed over ten thousand members and branches in seventeen states by the end of the 1920s. Quite influential at this time, the Foreign Policy Association sponsored radio discussions and published the weekly *Foreign Policy Bulletin*, a foreign affairs newsletter. Its meetings and publications during World War II helped educate the public on the formation of the United Nations.* The Foreign Policy Association continues to be an important organization, carrying out educational efforts, such as the Great Decisions programs, to promote awareness of contemporary foreign policy issues. Open forums held in New York City feature prominent speakers on contemporary topics. Divine, Robert A., *Second Chance* (1967); *New York Times*, February 2, 1978.

FOREIGN RELATIONS OF THE UNITED STATES: DIPLOMATIC PAPERS, State Department publication, 1861– . These volumes, published every year (except 1869) since 1861, are digests of selected diplomatic correspondence. Currently (1988) publishing the volumes for 1958–1960, the State Department has had such a mass of relevant documentary materials, particularly since World War II, that a thirty-year backlog has resulted. In addition to the annual volume or volumes of correspondence, the department occasionally publishes special appendix volumes for major diplomatic problems, as well as separate volumes for diplomatic events of importance such as the Paris Peace Conference* (thirteen volumes) and most of the conferences among Allied leaders during World War II. For students of U.S. diplomatic history, *Foreign Relations* is an accessible and valuable research tool. Plischke, Elmer, *Conduct of American Diplomacy* (1967).

FOREIGN SERVICE ACT (1946). This act, fostered by Seldin Chapin* and other Foreign Service officers, brought improvements and clarifications to the Rogers Act (1924)*. Designed to maintain the principle of a professional foreign service free from domestic political influence, the Foreign Service Act created new, more rational career categories, provided for periods of mandatory service in Washington, D.C., established the Foreign Service Institute for training Foreign Service officers, included a "selection-out" procedure, clarified "lateral-entry'' provisions, and raised the level of internal administration. Etzold, Thomas H., *The Conduct of American Foreign Relations: The Other Side of Diplomacy* (1977); Harr, John E., *The Professional Diplomat* (1969).

FORMOSA STRAITS CRISES (1954–1955, 1958). See **QUEMOY-MATSU CRISES.**

FORSYTH, JOHN (1780–1841). Born October 22, 1780, in Fredericksburg, Virginia, John Forsyth graduated from the College of New Jersey (now Princeton) in 1799, read law, and was admitted to the bar in 1802. He married Clara Meigs about 1801 and moved to Georgia. He entered politics as attorney general of Georgia (1808–1813), followed by service in the U.S. House of Representatives (1813–1818, 1823–1827) and Senate (1818–1819, 1829–1834) and a term as governor of Georgia (1827–1829). From 1819 to 1823, Forsyth was minister to Spain, where he procured ratification of the Adams-Onís Treaty* while gaining a reputation as "peremptory and impatient," qualities that earned him an official rebuke from the Spanish government. In 1834, he became secretary of state under President Andrew Jackson, continuing in the post during President Martin Van Buren's single term (1837–1841). This was a quiet period in America's foreign relations, and Forsyth's limited accomplishments include dealing with the long-standing French spoliations claims* concerning $5 million in claims dating from the Napoleonic Wars. In return for the payment of these claims, the United States offered to reduce the import duty on French wines. After delays caused by political problems in France, the treaty was successfully concluded. Forsyth also dealt with the matter of Texas annexation, but nothing decisive took place, partly because France was probably opposed to recognition and annexation. Forsyth died in Washington on October 21, 1841, shortly after his retirement from the State Department. His son, John, was minister to Mexico (1856–1858). *DAB*, 6:533; Duckett, Alvin Laroy, *John Forsyth: Political Tactician* (1962); McCormac, E. I., "John Forsyth," in Bemis, Samuel F., ed., *American Secretaries of State and Their Diplomacy*, vol. 4 (1928).

FORT MISSIONS. President Wilson sent this commission of three, headed by former Governor J. Franklin Fort of New Jersey, to the Dominican Republic in August 1914 to seek an end to the civil war there by coercing acceptance of "the Plan of President Wilson," which called for the naming of a provisional president, the holding of elections, and the establishment of a new constitutional government. Otherwise American military intervention would take place. In October, Isidro Jiménez was elected president, and intervention was averted. In January 1915 the commission was ordered to Haiti for much the same reason. Arriving in March, the commissioners stayed only a few days, gathering material to report on the popularity and qualifications of President Guillaume Sam, preparatory to the establishment of an American customs receivership. On the whole, the Fort Missions collected some data that may have been helpful later to the

State Department in its Caribbean policymaking. Munro, Dana G., *Intervention and Dollar Diplomacy in the Caribbean, 1900–1921* (1964).

FOSTER, JOHN WATSON (1836–1917). John Watson Foster was born in Pike County, Indiana, on March 2, 1836, graduated from Indiana University in 1855, attended Howard Law School for a year, and was admitted to the bar in 1857. He returned to Indiana University for an A.M. degree in 1858. In 1859, he married Mary Parke McFerson and began practicing law in Evansville. He fought with the Union army during the Civil War, attaining the rank of brevet brigadier general, and after the war returned to Evansville. There he was editor of the *Evansville Daily Journal* (1865–1869), postmaster (1869–1873), and chairman of the Republican State Committee. His Republican loyalty earned him appointment as minister to Mexico in 1873. In seven years there, he worked harmoniously in the transition period between the Lerdo and Díaz governments. In 1880, Foster was transferred to Russia, where he spent a year engaged mainly in ceremonial duties. Then he spent two years as minister to Spain (1883–1885), highlighted by the negotiation of a reciprocity treaty for Cuban trade that was rejected by the Senate (a similar treaty was ratified in the late 1880s). Under President Benjamin Harrison, Foster was secretary of state for eight months in 1892–1893. He negotiated a Hawaiian annexation treaty that was later withdrawn by President Cleveland and dealt with the Chileans over the *Baltimore* affair.* After 1894, he lived in Washington, traveled frequently and represented the United States in the Alaska boundary dispute (1903)* and on a special mission to Great Britain and Russia (1897). Foster was also one of the first to write extensively on American diplomatic history. Among his works are *A Century of American Diplomacy, 1776–1886* (1900), *American Diplomacy in the Orient* (1903), *Arbitration and the Hague Court* (1904), and his two-volume autobiography, *Diplomatic Memories* (1909). The grandfather of John Foster Dulles,* he died in Washington on November 15, 1917. Castle, Williams R., Jr., "John W. Foster," in Bemis, Samuel F., ed., *American Secretaries of State and Their Diplomacy*, vol. 8 (1928); *DAB*, 6:551; Devine, Michael J., *John W. Foster: Politics and Diplomacy in the Imperial Era, 1873–1917* (1981); *New York Times*, November 16, 1917; Hammersmith, Jack L. "John Watson Foster: A Pacifist after a Fashion" *Indiana Magazine of History* 84 (June 1988): 117–33.

"FOUR POLICEMEN," diplomatic concept, c. World War II. This idea was first brought forth by President Franklin D. Roosevelt at the Teheran Conference (1943)* in discussions of a postwar international organization. As part of such an organization, a body composed of only the United States, Great Britain, the Soviet Union, and China would police the rest of the world to prevent or combat aggression. Joseph Stalin wondered if China had sufficient stature to be a "policeman" and said that smaller nations would not like the plan. Ultimately the idea of the "Four Policemen" became incorporated into a United Nations* dominated by the world's great powers, through permanent membership on the

Security Council. Divine, Robert A., *Second Chance* (1967); Eubank, Keith, *Summit at Teheran* (1985); McNeill, William H., *America, Britain, and Russia* (1953).

FOUR-POWER DECLARATION ON GENERAL SECURITY (1943). Approved at the Moscow Conference,* October 30, 1943, this was a proposal of Secretary of State Cordell Hull* aimed toward postwar cooperation in Europe by means of the establishment of an international organization open to all, an avoidance of the use of military force except for securing peace, and a pledge of mutual cooperation toward postwar arms regulation. The principles of the Four-Power Declaration were echoed in the Connally* and Fulbright resolutions passed in the U.S. Congress and represented an important step for the United States away from its isolationist* tradition and toward a willingness to institutionalize political entanglement on the international scene. McNeill, William H., *America, Britain, and Russia* (1953); Wheeler-Bennett, John W., and Anthony Nicholls, *The Semblance of Peace* (1972).

FOUR-POWER TREATY (1921). One of the treaties that came out of the Washington Conference,* this treaty among Japan, Great Britain, France, and the United States was a mutual guarantee of the Pacific possessions of each and included a pledge to consult if differences arose. The treaty also abrogated the Anglo-Japanese Treaty (1902),* thus satisfying an American diplomatic objective. The Senate ratified the Four-Power Treaty by a 67–27 vote in March 1922. Buckley, Thomas H., *The United States and the Washington Conference, 1921–1922* (1970); Duroselle, Jean-Baptiste, *From Wilson to Roosevelt* (1963); *FR* (1922), 1:1–53.

FOURTEEN POINTS. These represented the summarization of Woodrow Wilson's aims and hopes for a settlement of World War I. Presented publicly for the first time in a speech to Congress, January 8, 1918, they signify the highest expression of what Wilson termed the New Diplomacy and were the basis on which Germany asked for peace. The first four points dealt with such general topics as open diplomacy, freedom of the seas, tariff reductions, and disarmament. The next nine were geographical, a redrawing of the map of Europe by combining the principle of self-determination* with other considerations. Point 14 called for the creation of a League of Nations* to guarantee peace in the future. Bailey, Thomas A., *Woodrow Wilson and the Lost Peace* (1944); Smith, Daniel M., "The Fourteen Points," in DeConde, Alexander, ed., *Encyclopedia of American Foreign Policy* (1979); Walworth, Arthur, *Wilson and His Peacemakers: American Diplomacy at the Paris Peace Conference* (1986).

FOURTH INTERNATIONAL CONFERENCE OF AMERICAN STATES (1910). See **BUENOS AIRES CONFERENCE (1910).**

FRANCIS, DAVID ROWLAND (1850–1927). A prominent Missourian, David R. Francis was born in Richmond, Kentucky, on October 1, 1850. He graduated from Washington University in St. Louis in 1870 and became a commissioner and grain merchant in the city. Successful in business, Francis rose to prominence in civic affairs, serving as mayor of St. Louis (1885–1889) and governor of Missouri (1889–1893). A Democrat, he was secretary of the interior at the end of President Grover Cleveland's second term (1896–1897) but opposed William Jennings Bryan's * Democratic candidacy in 1896 and was out of politics until 1906. He was president of the company that put on the Louisiana Purchase Exposition in St. Louis in 1904, came around to support Bryan in 1908, and was himself defeated for the U.S. Senate in 1910. In 1916, Francis became ambassador to Russia. He arrived in Russia in April 1916 and stayed until November 1918, although normal relations had been broken off after the Bolshevik Revolution in November 1917. Before 1917, he was active in relief work among German and Austrian prisoners of war and represented German and Austrian interests in Russia. After November 1917, he withstood Bolshevik accusations that he was fomenting counterrevolution and appealed to the Russians to stay in the war on the side of the Entente Cordiale.* His health failing in 1918, he went to England for surgery and never returned. He was an adviser to Secretary of State Robert Lansing* at the Paris Peace Conference.* He married Jane Perry in 1876 and died in St. Louis January 15, 1927. *DAB*, 6:577; Francis, David R., *Russia from the American Embassy, April 1916–November 1918* (1921), and *Recollections and Letters* (1928); *New York Times*, January 16, 1927; Stevens, Walter B., *David R. Francis: Ambassador Extraordinary and Plenipotentiary* (n.d.).

FRANKLIN, BENJAMIN (1706–1790). Benjamin Franklin was born January 17, 1706, in Boston. Largely self-educated, Franklin moved to Philadelphia early in life and embarked on a multifaceted career as a journalist, politician, scientist, and inventor. A leader in colonial affairs just prior to the War of Independence, Franklin was named in 1776 one of a commission of three (with Silas Deane* and Arthur Lee*) to negotiate a treaty with France. Already well known in France from earlier travels and work, he succeeded in completing the Franco-American Treaty* in 1778, while at the same time becoming involved in the quarrel between his colleagues, Deane and Lee. In September 1778, Franklin was made sole minister to France, and he visibly enjoyed the pleasures of Parisian life while arranging for loans from the French. Resigning for health reasons in 1781, he was appointed later that year one of three commissioners (with John Jay* and John Adams*) to negotiate the treaty for peace with Great Britain and was chiefly responsible for initiating early discussions of the treaty terms. Franklin was also named minister to Sweden in 1782 but never presented his credentials to the Swedish court, although he did negotiate a treaty with Sweden while he was in Paris in 1783. A delegate to the Constitutional Convention in 1787, Franklin died in Philadelphia on April 17, 1790. Bemis, Samuel F., *The Diplomacy of the American Revolution* (1957); *DAB*, 6:585; Morris, Richard B., *The Peacemakers* (1965); Stourzh, Gerald, *Benjamin Franklin and American Foreign Policy* (1954); Willson, Beckles, *America's Ambassadors to France, 1777–1927* (1928).

FREE SHIPS, FREE GOODS, diplomatic maxim developed in the seventeenth and eighteenth centuries. Under this maxim, small-navy powers, generally neutral carriers in wartime, could make treaties with belligerents to allow enemy goods to pass freely, though neutral goods on enemy ships were subject to confiscation. The idea, strongly supported by the United States in its early national history, was usually ignored by large-navy powers. The idea was included in the principles of the League of Armed Neutrality. Bemis, Samuel F., *The Diplomacy of the American Revolution* (1935); DeConde, Alexander, *The Quasi-War* (1966).

FREEDOM OF THE SEAS. This diplomatic principle of the United States dates from the Revolutionary War (Plan of 1776)* and embodies the following points: free ships, free goods,* except for contraband* of war; unfree (belligerent) ships make unfree goods; neutral ships may freely carry noncontraband goods to ports of belligerents; contraband consists of "warlike instruments" but not naval stores of food; and a blockade* must include the physical presence of the blockader's ships. These points were often disputed by Great Britain and others, but they were included in nearly all early American treaties and have remained a basic tenet of American diplomacy. Bemis, Samuel F., *John Quincy Adams and the Foundations of American Foreign Policy* (1949); Rappaport, Armin, "Freedom of the Seas," in DeConde, Alexander, ed., *Encyclopedia of American Foreign Policy* (1979).

FRELINGHUYSEN, FREDERICK THEODORE (1817–1885). Secretary of state under President Chester A. Arthur (1881–1885), Frederick T. Frelinghuysen was born August 4, 1817, in Millstone, New Jersey. He graduated from Princeton (1836), read law, and was admitted to the bar in 1839. He practiced law in Newark and gradually became involved in politics, first as attorney general of New Jersey (1861–1866) and then as a U.S. senator (1866–1869, 1871–1877). A Republican, he advocated the removal of Andrew Johnson from the presidency and was a member of the Hayes-Tilden Electoral Commission in 1877. In 1881, Frelinghuysen replaced James G. Blaine* as secretary of state when Arthur succeeded James A. Garfield. He reversed the American policy of involvement in attempting to settle the War of the Pacific,* pressed for abrogation of the Clayton-Bulwer Treaty,* and negotiated the Frelinghuysen-Zavala Treaty* for an isthmian canal through Nicaragua. He generally supported improved commercial relations abroad, initiated diplomatic relations with Korea, and concluded the Pearl Harbor Treaty* with Hawaii (ratified in 1887). In addition, he sent delegates to the Berlin Conference on the Congo (1884–1885)* and mediated the Mexican-Guatemalan boundary dispute. Frelinghuysen was known as a patient and cautious negotiator who left no serious problems for his successor. He married Matilde E. Griswold in 1842 and died in Newark on May 20, 1885, just ten weeks after leaving office. Brown, P. M., "Frederick T. Frelinghuysen," in Bemis, Samuel F., ed., *American Secretaries of State and Their Diplomacy*, vol. 8 (1928); *DAB*, 7:15; Fletcher, David, *The Awkward Years* (1962).

FRELINGHUYSEN-ZAVALA TREATY (1884). This was a proposed isthmian canal treaty between the United States and Nicaragua, in which a two-and-one-half-mile-wide canal zone would have become a U.S. protectorate. The United States promised to complete a canal within ten years, with facilities and tax relief granted by the Nicaraguan government. Nicaragua would have received a $4 million loan, equal representation on the six-man directorate, and one-third of the canal's net profits. Also, Nicaragua would have retained certain jurisdiction over the canal zone in peacetime; American powers in wartime were not specified. Soon after his inauguration in March 1885, however, President Grover Cleveland withdrew the treaty from the Senate, out of consideration of the Clayton-Bulwer Treaty* and opposition to what he considered an unhealthy treaty relationship with Nicaragua. Pletcher, David, *The Awkward Years* (1962).

FRENCH SPOLIATION CLAIMS (1829–1831). These claims resulted from damages inflicted on the neutral commerce of the United States during the Napoleonic Wars. Minister William Cabell Rives* was instructed in 1829 to negotiate a treaty wherein a flat sum would be paid. Negotiations were interrupted by the July Revolution of 1830 and had to be started again with the new government. On July 4, 1831, a treaty was signed, providing for a French payment of 25 million francs to the United States and a U.S. payment of 1.5 million francs to France, each in recompense for claims. A long delay ensued, however, before French payments were actually made. Bassett, John Spencer, "Martin Van Buren," in Bemis, Samuel F., ed., *American Secretaries of State and Their Diplomacy,* vol. 4, (1928); Willson, Beckles, *American Ambassadors to France, 1777–1927* (1928).

FULBRIGHT, JAMES WILLIAM (b. 1905). One of the most influential chairmen of the Senate Foreign Relations Committee in the twentieth century, J. William Fulbright was born in Sumner, Missouri, on April 9, 1905, but soon moved to Arkansas, where he graduated from the state university (1925) and then, receiving a Rhodes Scholarship, went to Oxford (B.A., 1928; M.A., 1931). After completing his education with a law degree from George Washington University, Fulbright was a Justice Department lawyer for a year before beginning a teaching career, briefly at George Washington and then at the University of Arkansas (1935–1939). From 1939 to 1941, he was president of that university. In 1942, he was elected to the U.S. House of Representatives where he introduced the Fulbright Resolution endorsing collective security* and saw it passed in September 1943. In 1944, he attended an international conference in London, helping to plan what became known as the United Nations Educational, Social, and Cultural Organization. That fall, he won election to the Senate, where he remained the rest of his political career, until 1974. From 1949 to 1974, he served on the Foreign Relations Committee; the last fifteen years, he chaired the committee. An internationalist throughout his career, he championed the United Nations* after World War II, favored the North Atlantic Treaty Organization,* and opposed the anti-Communist purges of Senator Joseph McCarthy (R., Wisconsin). He was interested in the recovery of Western Europe and supported the policy of containment,* although he disliked the reliance on nuclear deterrence and military power that keynoted U.S. diplomacy in the 1950s, considering it too inflexible to deal with a changing and often revolutionary world. Another major concern of Fulbright was the relationship between the executive and legislative branches concerning foreign policymaking; he was particularly bothered by excessive and irresponsible use of executive power. Considered for secretary of state by John F. Kennedy in 1961, Fulbright actively discouraged his selection, preferring to remain in the Senate. Although he was the Senate floor leader for the Tonkin Gulf Resolution (1964),* he soon concluded he had been misled by the executive branch about the war in Vietnam and became by 1965 one of the country's foremost opponents of the war. He believed that the U.S. commitment to Vietnam was grounded in the myth of an international Communist monolith and an excessive dose of U.S. moralism—he called it the "arrogance of power"—and advocated instead a conciliatory policy wherever possible toward the Soviet Union and the idea of a neutralized Southeast Asia. Defeated in the Arkansas Democratic primary in 1974, Fulbright now practices law in Washington. He married Elizabeth Kremer Williams in 1932 and has written several books on foreign policy issues, including *Old Myths and New Realities* (1964) and *The Arrogance of Power* (1966). Brown, Eugene, *J. William Fulbright, Advice and Dissent* (1985); *CB* (1955):217–19; Coffin, Tristram, *Senator Fulbright: Portrait of a Public Philosopher* (1966); Halberstam, David, *The Best and the Brightest* (1972); Trask, David F., "J. William Fulbright and the Crisis of American Power," in Merli, Frank J., and Theodore A. Wilson, eds., *Makers of American Diplomacy*, vol. 2 (1974); *WWA* (1986–1987):966.

G

GADSDEN, JAMES (1788–1858). A native of Charleston, South Carolina, James Gadsden was born May 15, 1788, and graduated from Yale in 1806. He served in the army from 1811 to 1821 and is credited with seizing the correspondence that led to the conviction of the British subjects Ambrister and Arbuthnot* for collaborating with Indians against Americans in 1818. Gadsden also negotiated the Treaty of Fort Moultrie, removing the Seminoles to southern Florida. In 1835, he became president of the Louisville, Cincinnati, and Charleston Railroad, a position he held for ten years, during which time he became an ardent southern nationalist and supporter of a transcontinental railroad along the southern route from New Orleans to California. In 1853, because of his friendship with Jefferson Davis, secretary of war, Gadsden was appointed minister to Mexico. His principal mission was to purchase land for a southern rail route, and he received authority to buy as much territory as he could for $50 million. In the end, however, the Gadsden Purchase (1853)* transferred to the United States a relatively small amount of land for $10 million. He remained in Mexico until 1856, dealing inconclusively with Indian and boundary matters and fearful of the anti-American European influences in Mexico. Married to Susanna Gibbs Host, James Gadsden died in Charleston, South Carolina, on December 26, 1858. *DAB*, 7:83; Garber, P. N., *The Gadsden Treaty* (1923); *NCAB*, 12:68; Rippy, J. F., *The United States and Mexico* (1925).

GADSDEN PURCHASE (1853), a piece of territory, approximately 45,000 square miles, comprising present-day southern Arizona and New Mexico, through which ran the best route for a southern transcontinental railroad. The territory was sold to the United States by the Mexican government of Santa Anna for $10 million, and the treaty purchasing it was negotiated by the U.S. minister to Mexico, James Gadsden,* a railroad man from South Carolina. The Gadsden Purchase completed the contiguous continental expansion of the United States. Garber, Paul N., *The Gadsden Purchase* (1923); Pletcher, David, *The Diplomacy of Annexation* (1973).

GALBRAITH, EVAN GRIFFITH (b. 1928). Evan Galbraith was born in Toledo, Ohio, on July 2, 1928, and graduated from Yale (1950) and Harvard Law School (1953). From 1953 to 1957, he was in the naval reserves and was attached to the Central Intelligence Agency.* Except for a year as a special assistant in the Commerce Department, he was engaged in private legal and banking work until 1981. In his career, he had worked in London and Paris for many years and developed solid conservative Republican credentials as a friend of William F. Buckley and a cofounder of *National Review*, a conservative political journal. Consequently, the incoming Reagan administration named Galbraith ambassador to France. He served four years in Paris and, by his own account, worked hard to influence French public opinion toward support of Reagan's foreign policy, especially with regard to Nicaragua, Grenada, and the Siberian gas pipeline, a project to bring natural gas from the Soviet Union to Western Europe that the United States opposed. In general, Galbraith was a strong opponent of détente* and a believer in the evil nature of the USSR. Not long before he left Paris, he stirred considerable controversy by strongly criticizing the State Department and the Foreign Service, asserting that a diplomat's role is to promote the president's viewpoints, that the State Department is too deeply involved in the making of foreign policy, and that Foreign Service officers are too concerned about career advancement to involve themselves in anything controversial or confrontational. Political appointees, Galbraith said, could represent the president better. Twice married, Galbraith has been writing and lecturing since 1985. In 1987, he published *Ambassador in Paris: The Reagan Years*, a memoir. *New York Times*, February 13, 1985; *WWA* (1986–1987):977.

GALBRAITH, JOHN KENNETH (b.1908). One of the foremost economists in mid-twentieth-century America, John Kenneth Galbraith was born on a farm near Iona Station, Ontario, on October 15, 1908, graduated from the University of Toronto (B.S., 1931) and the University of California (M.S., 1933; Ph.D., 1934) and embarked on a teaching career. He taught at Harvard from 1934 to 1939 (except for a year's research at Cambridge in 1937), at Princeton from 1939 to 1940, resigning to work for the federal government during World War II. From 1943 to 1948, he sat on the editorial board of *Fortune* magazine, but in 1949, he returned to the classroom of Harvard, where he remained until 1975, except for a two-year stint (1961–1963) as ambassador to India. Sympathetic to India, as his *Ambassador's Journal* (1969) shows, Galbraith sought to increase U.S. military and economic aid to the country, advising the government on economic development matters. He helped keep a leash on India during its border war with China (1962) and sided with the Indian viewpoint on the takeover of Goa. He often differed with State Department policy and thought Secretary of State Dean Rusk* to be inflexible and overly cautious. Returning from India in 1963, Galbraith continued his teaching and writing. Among his books on political and economic theory and history are *The Affluent Society* (1958), *The New Industrial State* (1967), *Money* (1977), *The Anatomy of Power* (1983), and *A View from the Stands* (1986). He has written two autobiographical works, *Annals of an Abiding Liberal* (1981) and *A Life in Our Times* (1983), and a work of fiction, *The Triumph: A Novel of Modern Diplomacy* (1968). He married Catherine Atwater in 1937, and since 1984, he has been president of the American Academy of Arts and Sciences. *CB* (1975):150–54; Galbraith, John K., "Rival Economic Theories in India," *Foreign Affairs* 36 (July 1958): 587–96; *New York Times*, February 18, 1973; *WWA* (1986–1987):977.

GALLATIN, ALBERT (1761–1849). Best known as secretary of the treasury under Presidents Thomas Jefferson* and James Madison,* Albert Gallatin had a long political career that included important ventures in early American diplomacy. Born in Geneva, Switzerland, on January 29, 1761, Gallatin attended Geneva Academy in 1779 before coming to the United States the following year. He initially settled in Maine but soon moved to Boston and there found a patron and friend who secured for him some land in Pennsylvania. He went to Pennsylvania, attended the state constitutional ratification convention, and in 1790 was elected to the state legislature. He was elected to the U.S. Senate in 1793 but was denied his seat because he had not been a citizen the required nine years. From 1795 to 1801, he served in the U.S. House of Representatives; in the latter year, upon Jefferson's election, he became secretary of the treasury. In 1813, Gallatin left the Treasury Department and went to Russia to discuss a mediation offer in connection with the War of 1812. That same year, he was appointed to the peacemaking commission that negotiated the Treaty of Ghent (1814),* ending the war. In this context, Gallatin's significance lay largely in his ability to harmonize the disparate membership of the U.S. delegation. In 1815, he became minister to France, spending eight relatively inconsequential years at that post. He dealt with the indemnity question, attempting unsuccessfully to win payment of the French spoliation claims* resulting from U.S. ship seizures under the Berlin Decree* and Milan Decree.* In 1818, he aided Richard Rush,* minister to Britain, in negotiating the Convention of 1818,* and in 1826, he replaced Rufus King* as minister to Great Britain. In his year at this post, he renewed the Convention of 1818 in 1827, eased some difficulties with Britain over commerce and problems with the navigation acts, and signed conventions with the British referring the disputed Maine boundary to a "friendly sovereign" and providing indemnity for slaves taken by the British during the War of 1812. After returning from Europe, Gallatin served as president of the National Bank (1831–1839), was a founder of City University of New York (1831), and pursued interests in history and ethnology. Maintaining an interest in public affairs, he opposed war with Mexico and the threatened war with Great Britain over the Oregon Territory. He married Hannah Nicholson in 1793 and died in Astoria, Long Island, on August 12, 1849. *DAB*, 12:103; Gallatin, James, *A Great Peacemaker, the Diary of James Gallatin* (1914); Walters, Raymond, *Albert Gallatin: Jeffersonian Financier and Diplomat* (1957); Willson, Beckles, *America's Ambassadors to England, 1785–1929* (1929), and *America's Ambassadors to France, 1777–1927* (1928).

GALLMAN, WALDEMAR J. (1899–1980). Born in Wellsville, New York, on April 27, 1899, Waldemar Gallman graduated from Cornell in 1921 and studied at Georgetown Law School. He joined the Foreign Service in 1922 and served in minor posts in Havana, San José, Quito, Riga, and Warsaw before becoming consul at Danzig in 1934. By 1941, he was assistant chief of the Division of European Affairs at the State Department. Gallman spent the World War II years at the London embassy as first secretary, counselor,* and minister, successively between 1942 and 1945. In 1948, he was named ambassador to Poland. In 1951, he was transferred to South Africa. His most important tour was in Iraq, where he served from 1954 to 1958. In Baghdad, he was an intermediary in the Baghdad Pact* negotiations and urged formal U.S. adherence to the alliance, without success, although he coordinated U.S. liaison with the regional council created by the pact. Gallman published an insightful book, *Iraq under Gen. Nuri* (1964), based on his Iraqi years and his close ties with the man who was prime minister there from 1954 to 1958. Following his departure from Iraq, Gallman was director-general of the Foreign Service, 1959–1961, and then taught at George Washington University. From time to time, he served as an adviser to the Foreign Service Training Institute and a consultant to the Asia Foundation before his death on June 28, 1980. *New York Times*, June 30, 1980; *WWWA*, 7 (1977–1981):213.

GARRETT, JOHN WORK (1872–1942). John W. Garrett was born in Baltimore on May 19, 1872, and graduated from Princeton in 1895. He spent six years in the banking business before entering the Foreign Service as legation secretary at the Hague (1901–1905). This assignment was followed by others of a similar nature in Luxembourg, Berlin, and Rome. Between 1910 and 1914, Garrett had uneventful missions as minister to Venezuela (1910–1911) and minister to Argentina (1911–1914). In 1914, Garrett was dispatched to Paris to assist with the additional duties brought on by the war. He aided Americans stranded in Switzerland and Bordeaux and was in charge of the welfare of German and Austrian civilian prisoners of war in France. In 1917, when the United States entered the war, Garrett became minister to the Netherlands and Luxembourg, where he countered German propaganda relative to U.S. requisitions of Dutch ships in U.S. harbors and negotiated a prisoner-of-war treaty with German government representatives. Garrett left the Low Countries in 1919 and in 1921–1922 served as secretary-general of the Washington Conference.* His last diplomatic assignment was as ambassador to Italy (1929–1933), where he had difficulty maintaining even relations because of Italy's Fascist policies. Garrett married Alice Warder in 1908, took an active part in Republican politics during the 1920s, and died in Baltimore on June 26, 1942. *NCAB*, A:336; *New York Times*, June 27, 1942.

GAUSS, CLARENCE EDWARD (1887–1960). American ambassador to China during most of World War II, Clarence E. Gauss was born in Washington, D.C., on January 12, 1887, and educated by private tutors and in local public schools. In 1903, he began working as a stenographer and shorthand reporter, and three years later he joined the State Department, holding minor posts in China (1907–1909, 1912–1931) and Washington (1931–1933). Sent back to

China in 1933 as counselor* and chargé d'affaires* in Peking, he stayed two years before moving to his one major European assignment, counselor and consul general,* Paris (1935). But the following year, he was back in China as consul general at Shanghai (1936–1940). There he reported on the progress of the Sino-Japanese War after its outbreak in 1937. In 1940, he was appointed minister to Australia but stayed there only a year before returning one more time to China as ambassador, an appointment that signified a new, firm policy toward Japan. American policy toward China after 1941 was to keep the Chinese in the war and maintain Chinese confidence in the United States. Problems arose when Chiang Kai-shek requested a huge ($500 million) loan from the United States; Gauss opposed it on the grounds that Chiang's government was inefficient and unable to make good use of the money, but the loan was granted anyway. His influence in America's China policy declined after the military mission headed by General Joseph W. Stilwell arrived in 1942. Gauss, who believed in the necessity of basic economic and political reforms and strongly opposed Chinese communism, finally left his post in 1944 out of frustration. The military was bypassing the embassy, he was not getting a full measure of information from Washington, and by 1944, he had been virtually supplanted by special envoy Patrick J. Hurley.* Gauss retired from the State Department in 1945 and became a director of the Export-Import Bank.* He married Rebecca Louise Barker in 1917 and died April 8, 1960, in Los Angeles. *CB* (1941):318–19; Durrence, James L., "Ambassador Clarence E. Gauss and United States Relations with China, 1941–44" (Ph.D. diss., University of Georgia, 1971); *NCAB*, F:365; *New York Times*, April 9, 1960.

GAVIN, JAMES MAURICE (b. 1907). James M. Gavin was born in Brooklyn on March 22, 1907, joined the army at the age of seventeen, and, despite the lack of formal high school education, graduated from West Point in 1929. Until 1958, he served as an active duty army officer, attached to the army air force during World War II. There, as commander of the Eighty-second Airborne, he was involved in the D-Day invasion and compiled a superb combat record. After the war, Gavin served several months with the occupation forces in Berlin. He retired in 1958 because of his opposition to the Eisenhower-Dulles* "new look" military policy based on massive retaliation* and a deemphasis on conventional weapons. He became executive vice-president of Arthur D. Little, rising to president in 1960. President John F. Kennedy named Gavin ambassador to France in 1961, a controversial appointment because of Gavin's lack of fluency in French, his lack of wealth necessary to maintain the social responsibilities of the embassy, and French President Charles de Gaulle's known antipathy toward generals other than himself. In France, he advocated increased U.S. aid toward an improved French nuclear capability, expecting, in return, a fuller commitment toward the North Atlantic Treaty Organization* from de Gaulle. The Kennedy administration, however, opposed Gavin's advocacy on the grounds that nuclear proliferation enhanced the likelihood of nuclear war. This difference of opinion probably contributed to Gavin's resignation in 1962. From 1964 to 1977, he was chairman of the board of Arthur D. Little and has served as a director of several other corporations. He married Jean Emert Duncan in 1948 and has written several books, including *War and Peace in the Space Age* (1958), advocating military mobility and flexibility rather than massive retaliation, *France and the Civil War in America* (1962), and *On to Berlin* (1978). Biggs, Bradley, *Gavin* (1980); *CB* (1961):169–171; *New York Times*, August 1, 16, 1962; *WWA* (1986–1987):996.

GEARY ACT (1892). Named for Congressman Thomas J. Geary (D., California), this act of Congress extended the Chinese Exclusion Act of 1882* and made Chinese residents show proof of their right to be in the United States. Generally speaking, skilled and unskilled laborers and miners were excluded, while teachers, students, merchants, tourists, and public officials were exempt from the provisions of the act. Violators could receive one year at hard labor, followed by deportation. In 1893, an act modified the exclusion law by broadening the scope of the term *laborer*, and in 1894 another act extended the prohibition of Chinese laborer immigration for ten years and precisely defined the classes of admissible Chinese. Dennett, Tyler, *Americans in Eastern Asia* (1922); McKee, Delber L., *Chinese Exclusion and the Open Door* (1977); May, Ernest R., and James C. Thomson, Jr., eds., *American-East Asian Relations: A Survey* (1972).

GENERAL AGREEMENT ON TARIFFS AND TRADE (GATT). The passage of this agreement was the main business of the International Trade and Employment Conference (1947) which met for five months in Geneva, Switzerland, to work out general tariff reductions and to draft a preliminary charter for an International Trade Organization*. Will Clayton* headed the U.S. delegation, although he was simultaneously engaged in preparatory work for implementation of the Marshall Plan*. In the end, 23 nations at Geneva wrote 122 mutual tariff reduction agreements. At the same time, arrangements for further tariff reductions (or increased preferences, as it was termed) on a limited basis were allowed if they accompanied a scheme leading to a regional free trade or common market organization.

Since 1947, there have been eight rounds of multinational negotiations for further tariff reductions, bringing about a generally liberalized international trade environment. Of these, the most significant was the Kennedy Round* (1963–1967) which brought about large tariff reductions among major trading nations. From 1972 to 1979, annual negotiations comprising the Tokyo Round dealt with a very comprehensive range of trade issues, including subsidies, licensing procedures, an anti-dumping code, and government procurement. In 1986, the Uruguay Round of negotiations began. Scheduled to conclude in 1990, these talks concern not only tariffs, but also foreign investment, intellectual property rights, and trade in services. In addition to periodic rounds of negotiation, special committees review on a continuing basis adherence to prior agreements and relevant national legislation. GATT has ninety-six contracting parties, with a number of other states maintaining pending applications. Ashworth, William, *A Short History of the International Economy Since 1850* (1975); Banks, Arthur S., ed., *Political Handbook of the World, 1988* (1988); Bergsten, C. Fred, "The New Economies and U.S. Foreign Policy," *Foreign Affairs* 50 (January 1972): 199–222; Dobney, Frederick, ed., *Selected Papers of Will Clayton* (1971); *FR* (1948), 1:802–947; *FR* (1949), 1:657–728; Kolko, Joyce, and Gabriel Kolko, *The Limits of Power* (1972).

GENEVA ACCORDS (1954). The Geneva Accords is the collective term for the series of agreements on Indochina at the Geneva Conference (1954).* The accords were complex in documentation but included a cease-fire for Vietnam with a provisional demarcation line at roughly 17° north latitude, provisions for French withdrawal from the North and Viet Minh withdrawal from the South, limitations on the presence of foreign troops in Vietnam and a prohibition on the introduction of new troops, a cease-fire and troop withdrawal for Laos and Cambodia, the establishment of an International Supervisory Commission (with representatives from India, Canada, and Poland) to implement the cease-fire, and provisions for unification elections for Vietnam in July 1956. The United States did not sign the accords but issued a formal unilateral declaration, "taking note" of them, generally agreeing with them, and pledging not to disturb them with threats or force and to support self-determination in Vietnam. The South Vietnamese did not sign the accords either but issued a "statement of action" to guarantee the rights of the Vietnamese people. According to Randle, the United States gained from the accords by remaining militarily uninvolved in Vietnam, thus saving money and making President Dwight D. Eisenhower's fiscal conservatism more credible and avoiding Third World* criticism for having assisted actively in a colonial war. However, the psychological impact of the "loss" of North Vietnam was a negative item, as was the strain on the NATO alliance. A subsequent related development was the creation later in 1954 of the Southeast Asia Treaty Organization (SEATO).* Fifield, Russel H., *Americans in Southeast Asia* (1973); Kahin, George T. and John W. Lewis, *The United States in Vietnam* (1967); Karnow, Stanley, *Vietnam: A History* (1983); Randle, Robert F., *Geneva 1954* (1969).

GENEVA ARMS CONVENTION (1925). This meeting, formally called the International Conference for the Supervision of the International Trade in Arms and Munitions, resulted in a treaty providing for the licensing of arms and munitions exports, with nations to make quarterly reports on exports (in peacetime only). The United States was represented by Congressman Theodore Burton (R., Ohio) and Ambassador to Switzerland Hugh S. Gibson,* but the Senate did not ratify the treaty until June 1935, when it was approved in connection with discussion concerning the creation of a National Munitions Control Board. Divine, Robert A., *The Illusion of Neutrality* (1962).

GENEVA CONFERENCE (1954). The Geneva Accords,* dealing with Indochina, were the main outcome of this conference, which met from May 8 to July 21, 1954. Attending were delegates from the United States, the Soviet Union, the People's Republic of China, Great Britain, France, India, the Republic of Vietnam, the Democratic Republic of Vietnam, Laos, and Cambodia. The conference also had a Korean phase, beginning on April 26 and running past May 8, but attempts to bring about the unification of that country reached an impasse in June. W. Bedell Smith* headed the U.S. delegation. Karnow, Stanley, *Vietnam: A History* (1983); Randle, Robert F., *Geneva 1954* (1969); Rees, David, *The Age of Containment* (1968).

GENEVA CONFERENCE (1961–1962). This conference was called in early 1961 to settle the complexities of the Laotian crisis (1960–1962).* Delegates from fourteen nations met from May 1961 to July 1962 before final agreement on the Declaration on the Neutrality of Laos. Under a coalition government (headed by Prince Souvanna Phouma), Laos would be a neutral state, joining no military alliances, permitting no construction of foreign military bases, and separating itself from the protective guarantees of the Southeast Asia Treaty Organization.* The nations at the conference signed another document guaranteeing Laotian neutrality* and pledging the withdrawal of any foreign troops from the country within seventy-five days. The lengthy duration of the conference was due in large part to the difficulty Souvanna Phouma and his colleagues in the coalition, leftist Prince Souphanouvong and rightist Prince Boun Oum, had in reaching agreement on the internal structure of government and who should control which cabinet post. American diplomatic pressure and renewed activity of the Pathet Lao, a Communist dominated insurgent movement, hastened their agreement. The final declaration was signed July 21, 1962, guaranteeing Laotian neutrality and creating an International Control Commission (Canada, India, Poland) to supervise the settlement. W. Averell Harriman* headed the U.S. delegation and was the dominant voice at the conference. Fall, Bernard B., *Anatomy of a Crisis* (1969); Goldstein, Martin E., *American Policy toward Laos* (1973); Hilsman, Roger, *To Move a Nation* (1967); Poole, Peter A., *The United States and Indochina from FDR to Nixon* (1973); Stevenson, Charles A., *The End of Nowhere* (1972).

GENEVA CONVENTIONS (1949). Adopted at the International Red Cross Conference in Geneva, Switzerland, these four conventions pertain to aspects of international conduct during wartime. They are conventions for (1) treating wounded and sick in the field; (2) laws of maritime warfare; (3) the treatment of prisoners of war; and (4) the protection of civilians in time of war. Three of these were revisions of earlier, pre–World War II conventions. Most nations of the world, including the United States, have ratified them. Mallison, W. Thomas, and Sally V. Mallison, *The Palestine Problem* (1986); Wheeler-Bennett, John W., and Anthony Nicholls, *The Semblance of Peace* (1972).

GENEVA NAVAL CONFERENCE (1927). After the Washington Conference,* a new naval construction race developed around categories of ships other than capital ships, particularly cruisers. Delegations met at Geneva from June 20 to August 4, 1927, and included naval experts, who had not participated in the Washington Conference. The main question dealt with tonnage ratios for cruisers. Great Britain insisted on the doctrine of "absolute need," based on defense necessities without concern for other nations or for mathematical formulas. The United States and Britain disagreed on the priority of discussing the number of cruisers or tonnage limits. After lengthy debate and hardening attitudes on all sides, the conference adjourned in failure, with the United States and Britain each unwilling to yield to the other. Naval construction continued, although in 1930 the London Naval Conference* set tonnage limits on various classes of smaller ships. Ellis, L. Ethan, *Republican Foreign Policy, 1921–1933* (1968); *FR* (1927), 1:1–158.

GENEVA PROTOCOL (PROTOCOL FOR THE PACIFIC SETTLEMENT OF INTERNATIONAL DISPUTES). This was a proposed agreement among members of the League of Nations* in 1924 that the League's Council should submit all legal disputes to the World Court*; if the council could not agree on whether a dispute was submissible, the matter would be referred to a committee of arbitrators for a binding decision. The protocol also provided that matters of domestic jurisdiction, formerly outside the covenant, were to be reconciled under Article XI and that a disarmament conference would meet in June 1925, after which the other provisions in the protocol would take effect. Any impact the protocol might have had was nullified in March 1925, when Great Britain rejected it. Secretary of State Charles Evans Hughes* saw in the protocol a potential for concert against the United States or an obstacle to U.S. neutral rights and did not favor it. Carr, E. H., *International Relations Between the Two World Wars, 1919–1939* (1967); Craig, Gordon A., and Felix Gilbert, *The Diplomats, 1919–1939*, vol. 1 (1965); Dexter, Byron, *Years of Opportunity: The League of Nations, 1920–1926* (1967).

GENEVA SUMMIT CONFERENCE (1955). Inspired by Winston Churchill after Stalin's death in 1953, this conference (the only "summit" of the 1950s) reflected his belief that East-West relations could be helped by direct contact with Stalin's successors. By 1955, conciliatory events such as the Austrian State Treaty (1955)* and the resolution of the Trieste question between Italy and Yugoslavia had improved the climate enough to make the summit possible. Meeting from July 18 to 23, 1955, delegations from the United States, Great Britain, France, and the Soviet Union discussed the issues of German reunification, European security, disarmament, and East-West contacts. The main result was a joint directive to the foreign ministers, scheduled to meet in the fall, to consider the same questions. A major stumbling block was the Soviet insistence on the dismantling of the North Atlantic Treaty Organization* before an agreement on German reunification could be reached. The high point of the Geneva summit conference may have been President Dwight D. Eisenhower's declaration that the United States would never wage aggressive war and his call for "open skies"—aerial reconnaissance. The foreign ministers did meet in October–November 1955 but deadlocked over all issues, ending the optimistic spirit of the Geneva summit. Gerson, Louis L., "John Foster Dulles," in Ferrell, Robert H., ed., *American Secretaries of State and Their Diplomacy*, vol. 17 (1967); Rees, David, *The Age of Containment* (1968).

GENEVA SUMMIT CONFERENCE (1985). Held November 19–21, 1985, this was the first of four summit conferences held between President Ronald Reagan and Party Secretary Mikhail Gorbachev of the Soviet Union. The initiative came from the president, who wanted to meet the relatively young new Soviet leader. Gorbachev accepted in order to strengthen his own political position and gauge the U.S. attitude toward arms control. This was a summit where process and style far outweighed substance; there was no structured agenda and no concrete result but rather a general agreement to move ahead on arms talks. President Reagan avoided any firm commitments on arms reduction or his Strategic Defense Initiative (SDI),* a spaced-based missile defense system; both leaders agreed that there would be future summits. *New York Times*, November 22, 1985; Wehlmiller, Gordon W., and Dusko Doder, *U.S.-Soviet Summits* (1986).

GENTLEMEN'S AGREEMENT (1907). This agreement was worked out by Secretary of State Elihu Root* and Japanese Foreign Minister Tadasu Hayashi in February 1907 to alleviate tensions in California brought on by the increasing numbers of Japanese immigrants and the decision of the San Francisco school board to segregate the school system. According to the terms of the agreement, Japanese laborers would no longer move from Hawaii to the American mainland, and Japan would continue to deny passports to skilled or unskilled laborers for travel to Hawaii or the United States. The agreement was completed in February 1908, with Japanese acceptance of various administrative regulations designed to implement its terms. The Gentlemen's Agreement ended most Japanese immigration to the United States, the most troublesome aspect of Japanese-American relations. The Johnson-Reed Immigration Act (1924)* ended immigration altogether, creating what the Japanese considered a breach of the Gentlemen's Agreement. For that reason, Japan abrogated the agreement on June 30, 1924.Ellis, L. Ethan, *Republican Foreign Policy, 1921–1933* (1968); *FR* (1924); 2:333–411; Neu, Charles E., *An Uncertain Friendship* (1967).

GERARD, JAMES WATSON, III (1867–1951). American ambassador to Germany on the eve of World War I, James W. Gerard was born in Geneseo, New York, on August 25, 1867, was graduated from Columbia University (A.B., 1890; A.M., 1891), attended New York Law School, and was admitted to the bar in 1892. He entered private law practice in New York City, saw service in the Spanish-American War, married Mary Daly in 1901, and became a successful lawyer who moved in high society. In 1908, he became a New York Supreme Court justice and in 1913 took a leave from the bench to accept appointment as ambassador to Germany. In his ambassadorship, which lasted until America's entry into the war in 1917, Gerard looked after British interests and Allied prisoners in Germany, negotiated a successful Belgian relief agreement that won praise from Herbert Hoover, and, most important, reported on German activities and policies to the U.S. government. Gerard was an advocate of preparedness, and when his reports stressed German hostility toward U.S. munitions sales to Britain and France and rumors of German intervention in Latin America, President Woodrow Wilson came to the conclusion that the ambassador was "gullible and unreliable" as a reporter. Gerard returned to the United States late in 1916 bearing a German suggestion that Wilson make another peace attempt and predicting unrestricted submarine warfare before long. His prediction was correct, and he never returned to Berlin. He became a speaker on the Liberty Bond circuit and, after the war, a firm advocate of the League of Nations.* Gerard remained active in Democratic party circles and held advisory and ceremonial posts under Presidents Franklin Roosevelt and Harry Truman. He died in Southampton, Long Island, on September 6, 1951. He recorded his impressions of Germany in *My Four Years in Germany* (1917) and *Face to Face with Kaiserism* (1918). *DAB*, Supp. 5:241; *New York Times*, September 7, 1951.

GHENT, TREATY OF (1814), treaty ending the War of 1812. After five months of difficult negotiations, British and American diplomats agreed to a status quo antebellum arrangement, with points of contention to be worked out later (Rush-Bagot Agreement, 1817*; Convention of 1818*). No mention was made of impressment* or questions concerning neutrals' rights; the only goal secured was peace. Historians generally agree that the Treaty of Ghent and the subsequent agreements marked a positive change in Anglo-American relations and allowed the United States the freedom necessary to pursue internal development for the next forty-five years. American negotiators were John Quincy Adams,* Henry Clay,* Albert Gallatin,* James A. Bayard, and Jonathan Russell*; British representatives were Lord James Gambier, Henry Goulbourn, and Dr. William Adams. Bemis, Samuel F., *John Quincy Adams and the Foundations of American Foreign Policy* (1949); Engleman, Fred, *The Peace of Christmas Eve* (1962); Walters, Raymond, Jr., *Albert Gallatin: Jeffersonian Financier and Diplomat* (1957).

GIBSON, HUGH SIMONS (1883–1954). Hugh Gibson was born August 16, 1883, in Los Angeles and, after schooling by private tutors, graduated from the Ecole libre des sciences politiques in Paris in 1907. He entered the Foreign Service, holding minor posts in Tegucigalpa, London, Havana, Brussels, Paris, and Washington from 1908 to 1919. In Brussels, he was involved, with Minister Brand Whitlock,* in the attempt to save the life of Edith Cavell, the British nurse who was executed by the Germans for collaborative activities. From 1918 to 1919, he distributed food in Europe as director-general of the American Relief Administration, under Herbert Hoover. In 1919, he was named minister to Poland, the first of several ministerial and ambassadorial appointments. His five years in Poland (1919–1924) consisted mainly of war relief work and were followed by appointments as minister to Switzerland (1924–1927), ambassador to Belgium and minister to Luxembourg (1927–1933, 1937–1938), and ambassador to Brazil (1933–1936). In Switzerland, Gibson played an important role as an observer of League of Nations* activities and was chairman of the U.S. delegation at the Geneva Naval Conference (1927).* He also was a delegate to the London Naval Conference (1930)* and acting chairman of the World Disarmament Conference (1932).* While ambassador to Brazil, he acted as U.S. representative on the body that mediated a settlement of the Chaco War* (1935). He retired in 1938 and devoted his time to writing such books as *The Problems of Lasting Peace* (with Herbert Hoover) (1942), *The Road to Foreign Policy* (1944), and *The Basis of Lasting Peace* (with Hoover) (1945). He was married in 1922 to Ynis Reyntiens, and he died in Geneva, Switzerland, on December 12, 1954.Jones, Kenneth Paul, *U.S. Diplomats in Europe, 1919–1941* (1981); *New York Times*, December 13, 1954; *WWWA*, 3 (1951–1960):322.

GIFFORD, WALTER SHERMAN (1885–1966). Born in Salem, Massachusetts, on January 10, 1885, Walter S. Gifford was a 1905 graduate of Harvard who began a business career with the Western Telephone Company, a subsidiary of American Telephone and Telegraph Company. In 1908, he joined the parent company and rose through the corporate hierarchy, becoming chief statistician in 1911, controller in 1918, vice-president for finance in 1919, executive vice-president in 1923, president in 1925, and chairman of the board in 1945. Known as an efficiency expert, Gifford was principally responsible for AT&T's substantial growth from 1925 until 1950. In 1950, President Harry Truman appointed him ambassador to Great Britain. Gifford's duties at this mission were largely social; the most important political problem was winning British acceptance of the peace treaty with Japan. In general, he opposed requests for foreign aid unless they clearly served both British and U.S. interests. Gifford was married twice, served several years on the Harvard Board of Overseers, and, after 1953, lived in retirement until his death in New York City on May 7, 1966. *NCAB*, H:28; *New York Times*, May 8, 1966; *WWWA*, 4 (1961–1968): 356.

GILBERT, SEYMOUR PARKER (1892–1938). An expert on reparations after World War I, Seymour Parker Gilbert was born October 13, 1892, in Bloomfield, New Jersey, and was an outstanding student at Rutgers (A.B., 1912; A.M., 1916) and Harvard Law School (LL.B., 1915). After college, he was briefly a law clerk in New York City. In 1918 he became counsel for the Treasury Department, and two years later was appointed assistant secretary of the treasury in charge of fiscal matters. From 1921 to 1923, he was under secretary of the treasury, winning a reputation as a hard, diligent worker. A brief interval, 1923–

1924, saw Gilbert back in private law practice and marrying Louise Ross Todd. In 1924, however, he was back in public life as agent-general for reparations* payments, a post he held until it was abolished in 1930 with the implementation of the Young Plan.* The position had originated with the Dawes Plan (1924),* and Gilbert's duties were to decide whether payments should be converted to foreign currencies or invested in Germany and to advise the German government on financial matters. His task was made easier by his ability to get along well with German leaders. His work was written up in *The Execution of the Experts Plan* (9 vols., 1924–1930). In 1927, Gilbert began urging another review of reparations liability, which was accomplished in the Young Plan, which established the Bank of International Settlements. Gilbert turned down an offer to head this bank and continue administering reparations. Instead, he returned to private life as a partner in J. P. Morgan & Company and, later, as a director of Bankers Trust Company. Gilbert died February 23, 1938, in New York City of cardionephritis. *DAB*, Supp. 2:234; *NCAB*, 28:331.

GOOD NEIGHBOR POLICY, phase in U.S.–Latin American relations, c. 1930–1945. Preceded by a period (1920–1933) termed by Dean Acheson* and quoted in Wood as "renunciation of domination," the Good Neighbor Policy began to take shape during the Hoover administration and was more clearly defined under the Roosevelt administration. Involved in the policy was a formal abandonment of U.S. intervention and a call for the recognition of equality among American republics and of their collective and individual responsibilities. The formal beginning of the Good Neighbor Policy may be said to have been Secretary of State Cordell Hull's* signing in 1933 of the Convention on the Rights and Duties of States, which declared that no state has the right to intervene in the affairs of another. Difficulties arose when they did not always cooperate, as with Mexico in the expropriation of U.S. oil properties. The Good Neighbor Policy paid dividends during World War II when most Latin American nations cooperated with U.S. hemispheric defense measures. After the war, however, U.S. diplomacy concentrated on Europe, and the Good Neighbor Policy was, to all intents, a policy of the past. Curry, E. R., *Hoover's Dominican Diplomacy and the Origins of the Good Neighbor Policy* (1979); Mecham, J. Lloyd, *A Survey of United States–Latin American Relations* (1965); Wood, Bryce, *The Making of the Good Neighbor Policy* (1961) and *The Dismantling of the Good Neighbor Policy* (1985); Woods, Randall B., *The Roosevelt Foreign Policy Establishment and the "Good Neighbor"* (1979).

GORE-McLEMORE RESOLUTIONS (1915–1916). This was an effort by neutralists in Congress, led by Senator Thomas P. Gore (D., Oklahoma) and Congressman Jeff McLemore (D., Texas), to express congressional sentiment against Americans' traveling on belligerent ships subject to U-boat* attack. Their objective was to remove this as a pretext for American entrance into the war. President Woodrow Wilson opposed the resolutions, exerted pressure on congressional leaders, and the Gore-McLemore Resolutions were tabled. The imbroglio showed Wilson's dominance over Congress, but the resolutions did indicate the presence of a significant pacifist faction. May, Ernest, *The World War and American Isolation, 1914–1917* (1959).

GRACE, WILLIAM RUSSELL (1832–1904). Born May 10, 1832, in Queenstown, Ireland, William R. Grace had no formal education but spent his early years at sea. In the 1850s, he settled in Peru and, with his brother, built up a firm of ship chandlers. By 1865, he was living in New York, where he organized W. R. Grace and Company, a mercantile operation that supplied materials for the Peruvian railway system, advised the Peruvian government, and equipped the army for the War of the Pacific (1879–1883).* When Peru lost the war, the government owed Grace a great deal of money. A settlement was reached with the Grace-Donoughmore contract (1890), which gave Grace a "virtual mortgage" on the nation. Grace cancelled the debt but received concessions in silver, guano, oil, and railroads and formed the Peruvian Corporation to exploit the concessions. In 1895, a new company, William R. Grace and Company, was chartered. With it, Grace made important banking and commercial connections throughout Latin America and joined with his previously (1891) established steamship operations. Grace was a late entrant in the Nicaragua canal chase, offering to build an isthmian canal in 1899, but he was not successful and may not have been seriously interested. A Republican, Grace was mayor of New York City from 1880 to 1888, winning a reputation as an anti-Tammany reformist. He died, probably in New York City, March 21, 1904. *DAB*, 7:463; Dunn, R. W., *American Foreign Investments* (1926); Grace, Joseph Peter, *W. R. Grace, 1832–1904, and the Enterprises He Created* (1953).

GRADY, HENRY FRANCIS (1882–1957). Born February 12, 1882, in San Francisco, Henry Grady attended a number of universities, receiving a bachelor's degree from St. Mary's (Baltimore) in 1907 and a doctorate from Columbia in 1927. He taught at City College of New York and Columbia (1917–1918) and after government service during and just after World War I resumed teaching at the University of California in 1921. During the next sixteen years, he offered courses in international trade, published *British War Finances, 1914–1918* (1927), and from 1928 to 1937 served as dean of the College of Commerce. In 1937, Grady reentered government service as vice-chairman of the U.S. Tariff Commission. Two years later, he was named assistant secretary of state, where his main contribution was a tour of the Far East in 1941 to seek out sources of strategic materials and find ways to divert them from the Axis. From 1941 to 1947, he was president of the American President Lines; in 1947 he left that post to become ambassador to India. After a year there (part of the time serving also as minister to Nepal), he was transferred to Greece, where his major responsibility was administering the Marshall Plan.* In 1950–1951, Grady was ambassador to Iran, working there to minimize the harmful effects of the seizure of the British oil properties at Abadan. After his return from Iran in 1951, Grady continued to dabble in Democratic politics, advising Adlai Stevenson* and joining in a move to recall Senator Joseph McCarthy (R.-Wisconsin). In 1917, Grady married Lucretia del Valle, and on September 14, 1957, he died on a ship while cruising between Hong Kong and Japan. *New York Times*, September 15, 1957; *WWWA*, 3 (1951–1960):337.

GRAHAM, JOHN (1774–1820). Born in Dumfries, Virginia, in 1774, John Graham graduated from Columbia College (1790) and moved to Mason County, Kentucky. He married Susan Hill, served a term in the Kentucky legislature (1800–1801), and was named secretary of the legation in Madrid. In 1803 he returned from Spain and the following year became secretary of the newly acquired territory of Orleans, where he investigated Aaron Burr's activities. From 1807 to 1817, Graham was chief clerk in the State Department, serving under Secretaries James Madison* and James Monroe* and playing a particularly important role in developing policies toward Latin America. From March 4 to March 10, 1817, he was secretary of state ad interim. In 1817, he was sent with Caesar Rodney and Theodorick Bland to Buenos Aires to look into independence prospects among Spanish-American colonies. Their report, however, was inconclusive because of disagreements among them. Appointed minister to Portugal in 1819, Graham stayed less than a year, returning to the United States in failing health and dying in Washington on August 6, 1820. *DAB*, 7:477; *NCAB*, 11:317; Whitaker, Arthur P., *The United States and the Independence of Latin America, 1800–1830* (1964).

GREAT WHITE FLEET, name applied to the U.S. Navy on its world cruise, 1907–1909. President Theodore Roosevelt sent the U.S. battleship fleet on this cruise to demonstrate the improbability of a Japanese-American conflict, to promote goodwill at the various ports of call, and, perhaps most important, to present a tangible demonstration of American naval strength. The voyage went smoothly and efficiently; the navy gained much practical information, and the diplomatic objectives appeared to have been met, although there is evidence that Japan may have used the show of American naval strength to accelerate its own naval buildup. Beale, Howard K., *Thedore Roosevelt and the Rise of America to World Power* (1956); Challener, Richard D., *Admirals, Generals and American Foreign Policy, 1898–1914* (1973); Hart, Robert A., *The Great White Fleet: Its Voyage around the World, 1907–1909* (1965); Reckner, James R., *Teddy Roosevelt's Great White Fleet* (1988).

GREATER EAST ASIA CO-PROSPERITY SPHERE. This term describes a futuristic program formulated by Japanese political and military leaders in the year before World War II. After conquering China, Japan would install a puppet regime and integrate the Chinese economy into its own. The term succeeded the "New Order in East Asia," and to some more aggressive Japanese leaders the sphere went beyond China to include the Netherlands Indies and French Indochina, projections that, by 1940, began to cause the U.S. considerable concern.

Lebra, Joyce C., ed., *Japan's Greater East Asia Co-prosperity Sphere in World War II* (1975); Wiltz, John, *From Isolation to War* (1968).

GREEN, BENJAMIN EDWARDS (1822–1907). Born February 5, 1822, in Elkton, Kentucky, Benjamin E. Green graduated from Georgetown College (1838) and studied law at the University of Virginia, after which he practiced law in New Orleans. In 1843, he was appointed legation secretary in Mexico City, and from March to September 1844, he was chargé d'affaires,* effectively managing negotiations at a difficult time in U.S.-Mexican relations. He dealt with the boundary question, a claims convention, and the Mier expedition, and he broached the likelihood that the United States would annex Texas, stating that an annexation treaty was necessary for the United States because of British intrigues over slavery and should not be taken as a threat to Mexico. In 1845, he returned to law practice in Washington, D.C., and in 1848, he was employed by the Mexican government to handle the indemnity payments from the United States stipulated in the Treaty of Guadalupe-Hidalgo (1848).* In 1849, President Zachary Taylor sent Green on a mission to the West Indies to attempt to purchase Cuba and arrange with the Dominican Republic for an American naval station at Samaná Bay. Unsuccessful in both ventures, his diplomatic career ended. Green spent his later years involved with industrial development in antebellum Georgia and iron manufacturing for the Confederacy. After the Civil War, he married Lizzie Waters (1866) and was something of an entrepreneur and financial writer. He died near Dalton, Georgia, on May 12, 1907. *DAB*, 7:538; Reynolds, Curtis R., "The Deterioration of Diplomatic Relations, 1843–1845," in Faulk, Odie G., and Joseph A. Stout, Jr., eds., *The Mexican War: Changing Interpretations* (1973); Tansill, Charles C., *The United States and Santo Domingo, 1798–1873* (1938).

GREEN, JOHN CLEVE (1800–1875). An American merchant with important ties to the Far East, John Green was born April 4, 1800, in Maidenhead, New Jersey, and attended Lawrenceville School. His first employment was with N.L.&G. Griswold, New York merchants in foreign trade; he married Sarah Griswold and spent most of the time between 1823 and 1833 working on Griswold ships. In 1833, Green joined Russell & Company, America's largest China trader, and rose to head the firm in a year, profiting from the greatly increased trade that resulted when the East India Company's monopoly on opium ended. He retired from Russell & Company in 1839 after the Chinese suppressed the opium trade and was succeeded by Robert W. Forbes. Returning to the United States, he continued active in business as an importer of Chinese goods, a banker, and an investor in railroads. He garnered a large fortune, much of which went to philanthropic ends, among which was the John C. Green School of Science at Princeton. Green died April 29, 1875, in New York City. *DAB*, 7:551; *NCAB*, 2:336.

GREEN, MARSHALL (b. 1916). Born in Holyoke, Massachusetts, on January 27, 1916, Marshall Green graduated from Yale in 1939 and became private secretary to the U.S. ambassador to Japan, Joseph Grew,* for the next two years. After service in the naval reserve from 1942 to 1945, Green embarked on a career in the Foreign Service, serving in minor posts in Wellington, Washington (where he was acting officer in charge of Japanese affairs, 1947–1950), and Stockholm before 1955. He was attached to the National War College for a year and then became a regional planning officer for the Far East, 1956–1959, and an acting deputy assistant secretary of state, 1959–1960. Posts in Seoul, Hong Kong, and another Washington tour preceded his first ambassadorial appointment, to Indonesia, 1965–1969, a relatively uneventful mission. From 1969 to 1973, Green was back in Washington as assistant secretary of state for East Asia and Pacific affairs. In 1973, he was named ambassador to Australia, a post in which he performed well in soothing relations that had been ruffled because of the U.S. policy in Vietnam and the coming to power of the Australian Labour party, which opposed that policy. In addition, Green facilitated Australian participation in U.S. defense facilities, neutralized objections to a U.S. base on Diego Garcia in the Indian Ocean, and emphasized cordiality in areas of common concern, such as policy toward Japan. Married to Lispenard Seabury Crocker in 1942, Green left Australia in 1975, took on a number of special assignments as a career ambassador, and retired from the diplomatic service in 1979. Barclay, Glen St. I., *Friends in High Places: Australian-American Diplomatic Relations since 1945* (1985); Siracusa, Joseph M., "Ambassador Green, America, and Australia: The Making of a New Relationship," *World Review* 14 (October 1975): 17–25; *WWA* (1986–1987):1100.

GREENVILLE, TREATY OF (1795). This treaty, between the United States and western Indian tribes, was a result of General Anthony Wayne's victory at the Battle of Fallen Timbers (1794). In the treaty, the Indians ceded large parts of present-day Ohio and Indiana to the United States and accepted American protection in place of former British protection. The treaty also provided that Indian traders procure a license from the American government. The treaty was in part a consequence of Jay's Treaty (1794)* and helped usher in a period (1795–1805) of improved Anglo-American relations. Bemis, Samuel F., *John Quincy Adams and the Foundations of American Foreign Policy* (1949); Burt, A. L., *The United States, Great Britain, and British North America* (1940).

GRENADA INTERVENTION (1983). Twelve days after a coup on the Caribbean island of Grenada on October 13, 1983, the United States launched an invasion of 1,900 troops plus 300 policy and military personnel from neighboring islands to remove those who had recently come to power. The ostensible reason for this intervention was concern about the safety of 1,000 U.S. citizens on Grenada, most of them medical students, but clearly the Reagan administration was also concerned with increased ties between Grenada and Cuba and the construction of a long runway at the local airport that could accommodate large military aircraft. The invasion succeeded in its purpose within a week, at a reported cost of 18 U.S. dead and 106 wounded. By mid-December, all U.S. combat troops had left Grenada. Controversy arose over whether the security concerns and the danger to Americans were serious enough to warrant overt military force and whether the operation would have a negative impact on the larger framework of U.S.–Latin American relations, especially in the light of general disapproval from most North Atlantic Treaty Organization* allies, the Organization of American States (OAS),* and Eastern bloc nations. Some believed that the Grenada invasion was meant in part as a warning to the Sandinista government of Nicaragua. Critics contended that the intervention, with the use of military force, lacked legal justification based on the charters of the United Nations* and the OAS, while defenders of the operation pointed to the commonly accepted tenet of international law allowing intervention to protect nationals or restore order, as well as the fact that the intervention had apparently been requested by the Organization of Eastern Caribbean States and had generally been welcomed by the people of Grenada. Dunn, Peter M., and Bruce W. Watson, *American Intervention in Grenada* (1985); Gilmore, William C., *The Grenada Intervention: Analysis and Documentation* (1984); O'Shaughnessy, Hugh, *Grenada Revolution, Invasion, and Aftermath* (1984); *New York Times*, October 26, 28, November 1, 14, 1983.

GRESHAM, WALTER QUINTIN (1832–1895). A native of Indiana, Walter Q. Gresham was born near Lanesville on March 17, 1832, attended Indiana University for a year, and, after reading law, was admitted to the bar in 1854. He began a law partnership in Corydon, Indiana, with Thomas C. Slaughter, married Matilda McGrain in 1858, sat in the state legislature as a Republican, 1860–1861, served in the Union army, becoming a major general and a friend of Ulysses S. Grant, and, after the war, returned to private law practice in New Albany and continued to be active in Republican politics. During the Arthur administration, Gresham was postmaster general (1883–1884). A circuit court judge after 1884, Gresham was mentioned for the presidency in 1888 but in 1892 became a Democrat because he favored free trade and the maintenance of the gold standard. President Grover Cleveland, who shared those views, appointed him secretary of state in 1893. In the State Department, he opposed the annexation of Hawaii because of the illegitimacy of the provisional government and the reports of special commissioner James H. Blount.* In addition, he brought about British withdrawal from Corinto, Nicaragua, with the pledge of an indemnity payment, helped facilitate an end to the Sino-Japanese War,* and dealt with problems such as the Bering Sea sealing controversy, difficulties with Italy over the lynching of Italians in Colorado, and the consequences to the United States of an insurrection in Brazil. Gresham died, rather unexpectedly, in Washington on May 28, 1895, and was succeeded by Richard Olney.* *DAB*, 7:607; Gresham, Matilda McGrain, *Life of Walter Quintin Gresham, 1832–1895*, 2 vols.

(1919); Schuyler, Montgomery, "Walter Quintin Gresham," in Bemis, Samuel F., ed., *American Secretaries of State and Their Diplomacy*, vol. 8 (1928).

GREW, JOSEPH CLARK (1880–1965). One of America's most prominent career diplomats in the first half of the twentieth century, Joseph C. Grew was born into a wealthy Boston family on May 27, 1880. He graduated from Harvard (1902) and after traveling in Europe and the Far East entered the Foreign Service in 1904. Between 1904 and 1916, he held minor posts in Cairo, Mexico City, St. Petersburg, Berlin (twice), and Vienna. During World War I, he was in Washington, and he accompanied the U.S. delegation to the Paris Peace Conference* as a secretary. In 1920, he was appointed minister to Denmark, where his main task was to gather information about Russia. In 1921, he moved to Switzerland, covertly gathered League of Nations documents relevant to U.S. interests and forwarded them to the State Department, and was a delegate to the Lausanne Conference (1922–1923).* From 1924 to 1927, Grew was in Washington as under secretary of state, where he was instrumental in taking the Foreign Service out of domestic politics. Five years as ambassador to Turkey (1927–1932) were uneventful and preceded his most important assignment, ambassador to Japan. In Japan for nearly ten years (1932–1941), he established cordial relations with Japanese leaders, kept well informed on Japanese affairs, and tried to avert war, advising against economic sanctions until 1940 and warning of a possible assault on Pearl Harbor as early as January 1941. Returning home after the outbreak of war, Grew served again as under secretary of state in 1945 and briefly as secretary of state ad interim in 1945, the year he retired. In retirement, he was board chairman of the Free Europe Committee, which administered Radio Free Europe. He married Alice de Vermandois Perry in 1905. She died in 1959, and he died in Manchester, Massachusetts, on May 25, 1965. His experiences in Japan are told in his *Ten Years in Japan* (1944); a broader autobiography is *Turbulent Era* (1952). Heinrichs, Waldo H., Jr., *American Ambassador: Joseph C. Grew and the Development of the U.S. Diplomatic Tradition* (1966); Kolko, Gabriel, *The Politics of War* (1968); *New York Times*, May 27, 1965.

GRIFFIS, STANTON (1887–1974). A cultural impresario who also served as ambassador to three countries on three continents, Stanton Griffis was born in Boston on May 2, 1887. After graduation from Cornell in 1910 and apart from army service in World War I, Griffis worked as a fruit grower, a stockbroker, and chairman of the Madison Square Garden Corporation. In the 1930s, he developed a talent for reorganizing and restoring the financial soundness of failing businesses and was involved in a variety of cultural enterprises—Brentano's Books, Paramount Pictures, and several Broadway shows. During World War II, Griffis worked as chief of the Motion Picture Bureau in the Office of War Information. After the war, he embarked on a series of ambassadorial appointments. In Poland, 1947–1948, he helped arrange the flight to safety of government opponent Stanislaw Mikolajczyk; in Egypt, 1948–1949, he organized Arab relief activities during the turbulent period following the creation of Israel; in Argentina, 1949–1951, he earned some criticism by being overly conciliatory toward the regime of Juan Péron, but he did succeed in getting the dictator to sign the Rio Treaty.* In his final post, Spain, he initiated a new degree of cordiality with the Francisco Franco government, which led to the establishment of U.S. bases in Spain. Retiring from diplomatic life in 1952, he wrote a witty memoir, *Lying in State* (1952), and organized American Friends of Spain in 1953. Thrice married, he died in New York City on August 29, 1974, as a result of injuries suffered in a fire in his apartment. *New York Times*, August 30, 1974; *WWWA*, 6 (1974–1976):168–69.

GRISCOM, LLOYD CARPENTER (1872–1959). Born in Riverton, New Jersey, on November 4, 1872, Lloyd C. Griscom graduated from the University of Pennsylvania (1891), attended New York Law School, and was admitted to the New York bar in 1896. While studying law, Griscom spent some time in London as secretary to Ambassador Thomas F. Bayard* and in Central America, traveling with author and war correspondent Richard Harding Davis* (*Three Gringoes in Central America*). In 1897, he became an assistant district attorney in New York City but moved to Arizona and lived there, 1897–1898, until he went into active service in the Spanish-American War. After the war, he reentered diplomatic service as first secretary of the legation in Constantinople. There from 1899 to 1901, he was chargé d'affaires* for fifteen months and dealt with an Armenian indemnity claim, obtaining $90,000 for the Armenians while maintaining goodwill toward the United States. In 1901, Griscom married Elisabeth Duer Bronson and began a series of ministerial and ambassadorial posts: Persia (1901–1902), Japan (1902–1906), Brazil (1906–1907), and Italy (1906–1909). In Persia, he traveled widely investigating various trade routes and found a better and cheaper way to get U.S. products into the country. He was in Japan during the Russo-Japanese War,* maintained U.S. neutrality,* transmitted President Theodore Roosevelt's offer to mediate a peace settlement, and hosted visiting dignitaries Alice Roosevelt and William Howard Taft. In Brazil, Griscom hosted Secretary of State Elihu Root,* en route to the Rio de Janeiro Conference (1906),* and in Italy he organized relief efforts for the 1908 earthquake in Messina. He returned to New York City in 1909 and practiced law in New York City, maintaining an involvement in Republican party politics. During World War I, he was a liaison officer on General John J. Pershing's staff and, after the war, became board chairman of the *Tallahassee Democrat*. He died February 8, 1959, in Thomasville, Georgia. Dennis, A. L. P., *Adventures in American Diplomacy, 1896–1906* (1928); Griscom, Lloyd C., *Diplomatically Speaking* (1940); *NCAB*, 12:196; *New York Times*, February 9, 1959.

GUADALUPE-HIDALGO, TREATY OF (1848), treaty ending the Mexican War. In this treaty, the United States obtained territory south to the Rio Grande River and 32° north latitude and including the port of San Diego for a payment of $15 million plus an additional $3.25 million in assumed American claims against Mexico. The territorial acquisition, known as the Mexican cession, included California and New Mexico and totaled approximately 500,000 square miles. Nicholas P. Trist* was the American negotiator for the treaty, which was signed at the Mexico City suburb of Guadalupe-Hidalgo on February 2, 1848, and ratified by the Senate, 38–14, on March 10, 1848. Merk, Frederick, *The Monroe Doctrine and American Expansionism, 1843–1849* (1966); Pletcher, David, *The Diplomacy of Annexation* (1973); Singletary, Otis, *The Mexican War* (1960).

GUATEMALA ACCORD (1987). See **ESQUIPULAS II (1987).**

GUATEMALAN CRISIS (1954). When the leftist government of Jácobo Arbenz in Guatemala expropriated 234,000 hectares (about 95,000 acres) of United Fruit Company* land as part of a land reform program in 1952, the company protested both the estimated valuation of the land and the method of compensation. United Fruit was economically dominant in Guatemala and was resented for it, and it was no surprise when the U.S. government sided with the company, denouncing the compensation offer and branding Arbenz and his government as Communist dominated. At the Caracas Conference* in March 1954, with the Guatemalan situation in mind, the U.S. delegation pushed reluctant Latin American delegates into passing a sharp anti-Communist resolution, which only Guatemala opposed. Three months later, the Central Intelligence Agency (CIA)* instigated an invasion of Guatemala from Honduras, led by Colonel Carlos Castillo Armas, which successfully precipitated the coup ousting Arbenz. The United States blocked efforts to have the United Nations* Security Council consider the matter, terming it a local dispute for a regional organization to handle. Latin American nations felt that the United States was wrong and that Guatemala should have been able to lay its case before the United Nations. Clearly more concerned with U.S. intervention than Communist penetration, Latin Americans resented this return to a policy thought to have been repudiated by the United States. In Guatemala, the new government, while dictatorial and repressive, was pro–United States, and United Fruit got most of its expropriated land back. The crisis is related to the Bay of Pigs invasion (1961)* in that Cuba's premier, Fidel Castro, studied it to ensure the CIA could not repeat its performance, while the CIA thought that it could. Immerman, Richard H., *The CIA in Guatemala* (1982); Schlesinger, Steven, and Steven Kinzer, *Bitter Fruit* (1982); Schneider, Ronald M., *Communism in Guatemala, 1944–1954* (1958).

GUGGENHEIM, HARRY FRANK (1890–1971). Born in West End, New Jersey, on August 23, 1890, Harry F. Guggenheim attended Yale and graduated from Cambridge in 1913. He was an aviator during World War I before returning to Cambridge for an A.M. degree in 1918. From 1919 to 1923 he was an official and director of several copper companies, and after 1923, he spent much of his time promoting aeronautics through the Daniel Guggenheim Fund, of which he was president. As ambassador to Cuba during the administration of President Herbert Hoover (1929–1933), Guggenheim had to deal with the dictator General Gerardo Machado and blunt the Cuban's penchant for violent political retribution. After his diplomatic career, he wrote *The United States and Cuba* (1934), a study of U.S.-Cuban relations that stops short of his own ambassadorship. Guggenheim was involved in newspaper work during the 1930s and 1940s, founding *Newsday* in 1941, and had mining interests as well, especially in South American nitrate deposits. He was a well-known horseman who played an important role in the establishment of the New York Racing Association and a philanthropist who founded the H. F. Guggenheim Fund, which made grants to a wide variety of charitable causes. Guggenheim was married and divorced twice and died January 22, 1971, in Sands Point, Long Island. *NCAB*, C:48; *New York Times*, January 23, 1971.

GULF OF TONKIN INCIDENTS (1964). A major event of the Vietnam War, this refers to two incidents in early August 1964 wherein North Vietnamese patrol boats reportedly attacked two American destroyers in the Gulf of Tonkin supposedly in international waters off the coast of North Vietnam. The American ships were cooperating with South Vietnamese coastal raiding attacks and may have been within North Vietnamese territorial waters part of the time. Although there were no casualties, President Lyndon B. Johnson ordered retaliatory air raids and sent to Congress a draft resolution, prepared earlier in the year, that would give the president the authority to "take all necessary measures to repel any armed attack against the forces of the United States and to prevent further aggression." Passed by the House of Representatives, 416–0, and by the Senate, 88–2, the Gulf of Tonkin Resolution, as it became known, became the legal authority for U.S. escalation of the war and as such a controversial aspect of this controversial war. In 1970, the U.S. Senate repealed the Gulf of Tonkin Resolution. There is considerable controversy about the actual facts of the incident that triggered the Gulf of Tonkin Resolution. Goulden, Joseph C., *Truth Is the First Casualty* (1969); Karnow, Stanley, *Vietnam: A History* (1983); Poole, Peter A., *The United States and the Indochina from FDR to Nixon* (1973); Senate Committee on Foreign Relations, *The Gulf of Tonkin, 1964 Incidents* (1968) Windchy, Eugene C., *Tonkin Gulf* (1971).

GULICK, SIDNEY LEWIS (1860–1945). The son of a Congregationalist missionary, Sidney Gulick was born April 10, 1860, at Ebon in the Marshall Islands. He received A.B. (1883) and A.M. (1886) degrees from Dartmouth, attended Union Theological Seminary, and was ordained in 1886. The following year he married Cora May Fisher and went to Japan, where he stayed for twenty-six years, taught at Doshisha University in Kyoto and at the Kyoto Imperial University, and wrote *Evolution of the Japanese, Social and Psychic* (1903). Gulick organized the American Peace Society of Japan and was interested in improving U.S.-Japanese relations. This interest continued after his return to the United

States in 1913. He wrote another book, *The American Japanese Problem* (1914), for the Federal Council of Churches of Christ and served as secretary of its Commission on Relations with Japan. Becoming affiliated with other organizations promoting better Japanese-American relations, Gulick emerged in the interwar years as a leading public spokesman on the subject, advocating nondiscriminatory immigration laws and full legal rights for Japanese immigrants. Disappointed in the 1924 immigration act excluding Japanese, he continued to work for goodwill between Japanese and American people while at the same time broadening his interests to include China, the Philippines, and ratification of the Kellogg-Briand Pact (1928).* He retired to Hawaii in 1934 and devoted his time to studying sociology and oriental philosophy and religion. Gulick died December 20, 1945, in Boise, Idaho. *DAB*, Supp. 3:322; *New York Times*, December 24, 1945; Taylor, Sandra C., *Advocate of Understanding: Sidney Gulick and the Search for Peace with Japan* (1984).

GUMMERÉ, SAMUEL RENÉ (1849–1920). Born February 19, 1849, in Trenton, New Jersey, Samuel René Gummeré attended Trenton Academy and Lawrenceville School before graduating from Princeton in 1870. He studied law and was admitted to the bar. From 1881 to 1884, he was secretary to James Birney and William L. Dayton,* U.S. ministers to the Netherlands. A Republican, Gummeré was made consul general* to Morocco by the McKinley administration in 1898; in 1905, he was promoted to minister to Morocco, the result of a dramatic incident that was headline news in late 1904. An allegedly naturalized U.S. citizen and friend of Gummeré, Ion Perdicaris, was kidnapped by a Moroccan bandit named Raisuli, and Gummeré held the Moroccan government responsible for Perdicaris's safety. After a month of futile negotiations, a U.S. ultimatum (made famous by Secretary of State John Hay's* phrase, "Perdicaris alive or Raisuli dead!"), along with the presence of the U.S. Mediterranean and South Atlantic fleets, brought about Perdicaris's release. As minister, Gummeré was a delegate to the Algeciras Conference (1906),* where his extensive knowledge of the local situation was valuable. He resigned in 1909, lived in England, and during World War I worked among the wounded. He died in Wimbledon, a London suburb, on May 28, 1920. Collins, George W., "Mission to Morocco," *New Jersey History* 89 (1971): 37–50; *DAB*, 8:50; Dennis, A. L. P., *Adventures in American Diplomacy, 1896–1906* (1928); *New York Times*, May 29, 1920.

GUNBOAT DIPLOMACY, phrase used to describe a diplomatic policy especially prevalent in the Caribbean and Central American region between 1890 and World War II. Under this policy, U.S. naval vessels were stationed near harbors of Caribbean or Central American countries experiencing internal political instability or the threat of European intervention. The display of naval power was presumed to be sufficient to ameliorate a bad situation and avert actual military intervention, although in practice, there were numerous examples of direct intervention. Challener, Richard D., *Admirals, Generals and American Foreign Policy, 1898–1914* (1973).

GUNTHER, JOHN JOSEPH (1901–1970). A native of Chicago, where he was born August 30, 1901, John Gunther graduated from the University of Chicago in 1922 and by 1925 was a correspondent for the *Chicago Daily News*, covering events in Europe and, after 1930, concentrating on Germany, Austria, and the Balkans. His news dispatches were highly analytical and provided much background on the major personalities of Europe in the decade before World War II. From 1935 to 1939, Gunther divided his time between Europe and the Far East and began publishing the "Inside" books, on which his greatest fame rests: *Inside Europe* (1936, with several revisions in succeeding years); *Inside Asia* (1939, 1942); *Inside Latin America* (1941); and several others after the war. He moved to radio in 1941 as a radio commentator for the NBC Blue Network and worked as special consultant for the U.S. War Department from 1942 to 1944. After the war, he concentrated his efforts on writing, publishing, in addition to "Inside" volumes, several novels and nonfiction works, most notably *Death Be Not Proud* (1949). Gunther was married twice and died in New York City on May 29, 1970. *CB* (1941):356–58; *New York Times*, May 30, 1970; *WWWA*, 6 (1974–1976):172.

GUTHRIE, GEORGE WILKINS (1848–1917). A native of Pittsburgh, George W. Guthrie was born September 5, 1848, and educated at the Western University of Pennsylvania (now the University of Pittsburgh), receiving both A.B. (1866) and A.M. (1868) degrees. He also graduated from Columbia College (now George Washington University) Law School in 1869 and was admitted to the bar the same year. He returned to Pittsburgh and soon became a prominent lawyer, taking part in many important civil cases and becoming involved in Democratic politics, first as secretary of the Democratic National Convention in 1884 and much later as mayor of Pittsburgh, 1906–1909. The Democratic Wilson administration selected him as ambassador to Japan in 1913, and in his four years there he managed somewhat to ease the tense state of relations. Guthrie was successful in persuading the Japanese to distinguish between California, the hotbed of anti-Japanese hostility, and the rest of the United States. After the outbreak of war, Guthrie handled German affairs in Japan. He died suddenly of a stroke in Tokyo on March 8, 1917, and his body was transported to the United States on a Japanese cruiser, a token of high respect. *DAB*, 8:60; *New York Times*, March 9, 1917.

HABIB, PHILIP CHARLES (b. 1920). A native of Brooklyn, where he was born February 25, 1920, Philip Habib received a B.S. degree from the University of Idaho in 1942, served in the army during World War II, and earned a Ph.D. at the University of California at Berkeley in 1952. Married to Marjorie W. Slightam in 1942, he entered the Foreign Service in 1949 and held minor posts in Ottawa, Wellington, Trinidad, and Washington before 1962. He was counselor* for political affairs in Seoul, 1962–1965, and in Saigon, 1965–1967. Except for three years (1971–1974) as ambassador to the Republic of Korea, Habib spent most of the rest of his career at a variety of State Department administrative posts in Washington, although he was a participant under Averell Harriman* in the Paris peace talks on Vietnam in 1968–1969. In 1978, heart problems forced Habib to take early retirement, but he has since been called back frequently as a diplomatic troubleshooter. Between 1981 and 1983, he represented the Reagan administration in various Middle East discussions, and in 1986, he was a special envoy to the Philippines and to Central America. In the Philippines, he investigated the crumbling regime of Ferdinand Marcos and advised Reagan that Marcos could not survive politically, managing to change the president's viewpoint on support of the Philippine dictator. Throughout his career, Habib has maintained a good international reputation and an excellent ability to negotiate and to make independent judgments. When not on diplomatic duty, Habib is associated with the Hoover Institute and the American Enterprise Institute. Rubenberg, Cheryl A., *Israel and the American National Interest* (1986); *New York Times*, May 28, 1981, March 12, 1986; *WWA* (1986–1987):1143–44.

HAGUE PEACE CONFERENCES (1899 and 1907). These international conferences, held at the Hague, Netherlands, dealt principally with the question of arbitration.* The United States worked in concert with Great Britain, usually in opposition to Germany. In 1899, Germany blocked the establishment of a panel of arbitrators to which disputes might be submitted, a proposal of the British and American delegations. The conference did set up a Permanent Court of Arbitration,* to which nations could, if they chose, appeal for arbitration. Eight years later, Germany tried, without success, to exploit Anglo-American differences over neutral rights, a major topic of debate. Additionally, President Theodore Roosevelt supported a general treaty of arbitration to deal with such matters as debt collection, but Germany and seven other European nations opposed compulsory arbitration. As a result, the 1907 conference did little more than improve the procedures for voluntary arbitration established in 1899.

Beale, Howard K., *Theodore Roosevelt and the Rise of America to World Power* (1956); Davis, Calvin DeArmond, *The United States and the First Hague Peace Conference* (1962), and *The United States and the Second Hague Peace Conference: American Diplomacy and International Organization, 1899–1914* (1978); *FR* (1907), 2:1099–1287; Perkins, Bradford, *The Great Rapprochement* (1968); Wank, Solomon, ed., *Doves and Diplomats* (1978).

HAIG, ALEXANDER MEIGS, JR. (b. 1924). President Ronald Reagan's first secretary of state, Alexander Haig was born December 2, 1924, in Philadelphia. He attended Notre Dame but graduated from West Point in 1947 and received an M. A. from Georgetown in 1961. From 1947 to 1973 and 1974 to 1979, Haig was on active army duty, serving in Vietnam, at West Point, and in the White House as President Richard M. Nixon's military adviser and deputy national security assistant from 1969 to 1973. Taking a brief leave from military service, he was Nixon's White House chief of staff in 1973–1974, during the final months of Watergate. From 1974 to 1979, he served as supreme allied commander, SHAPE (Supreme Headquarters, Allied Powers Europe), the head of the North Atlantic Treaty Organization.* Haig left the military in 1979 to become the chief operating officer of United Technologies Corporation but two years later joined the Reagan administration. As secretary of state, he tried without success to center foreign policy authority in the State Department rather than the White House and National Security Council.* He concentrated on combating international terrorism, normalizing relations with the People's Republic of China, and trying to mediate a settlement of the Falkland Islands War* through a variant of shuttle diplomacy. Suspicious of the USSR, he helped put a global cast on the Central American turmoil and to create the contra* movement. Within a year of coming to office, the mercurial Haig was having sharp conflicts with Secretary of Defense Caspar Weinberger and National Security Adviser William P. Clark* over Middle East policy and lines of authority within the administration. In June 1982, Haig resigned his post, founded an international consulting firm, Worldwide Associates, and wrote his memoirs, *Caveat: Realism, Reagan, and Foreign Policy* (1984). Married to Patricia Antoinette Fox in 1950, Haig made an unsuccessful attempt to win the Republican presidential nomination in 1988. Brownstein, Ronald, and Nina Easton, *Reagan's Ruling Class* (1982); *CB* (September 1987): 18:9, 20–23; Honick, Morris, "Haig: The Diplomacy of Command," in Jordan, Robert S., ed., *Generals in International Politics* (1987); Morris, Roger, *Haig, the General's Progress* (1982); *New York Times*, June 26, July 2, 7, 1982, March 24, 1987; *WWA* (1986–1987):1151.

HALE, EDWARD JOSEPH (1839–1922). Born Christmas Day 1839 in Fayetteville, North Carolina, Edward J. Hale graduated from the University of North Carolina in 1860, married Maria Ruett Hill in 1861, served in the Confederate army and was thrice wounded, and after the war worked for the *Fayetteville Observer*, serving as its editor from 1882 to 1913. Active in the Democratic party, Hale was named consul* to Manchester in 1885 and was popular in Britain, especially as a public speaker. When he was replaced as consul in 1889, he went to India as a commissioner for the North of England Trust Company to work on problems with the indigo crop. He served as vice-president of the International Congress on Navigation (1890) and American commissioner for the Manchester Ship Canal (1890–1891) and became an advocate of a U.S.-built Nicaragua Canal. As minister to Costa Rica (1913–1919) during World War I, Hale kept the Germans from getting a concession for a wireless station and gave asylum to overthrown Costa Rican President Alfredo Gonzalez. After his return to the United States, Hale lived in Fayetteville, where he studied and wrote on problems of the Cape Fear River until his death February 15, 1922. *DAB*, 8:100; *NCAB*, 19:200; *New York Times*, February 16, 1922; *WWWA*, 1 (1897–1942):502.

HALE, WILLIAM BAYARD (1869–1924). William Bayard Hale was born in Richmond, Indiana, on April 6, 1869. He attended Boston University and Harvard and was ordained an Episcopal priest in 1893. Hale served as a mission priest at a church in Middleboro, Massachusetts, but soon turned to a career as a writer and lecturer on contemporary issues. He campaigned for William Jennings Bryan* in 1900 and then wrote for *Cosmopolitan, Current Literature*, and the *World*. In 1907, he was Paris correspondent for the *New York Times* and had a controversial interview (suppressed before publication at Hale's request) with Kaiser Wilhelm, in which the German leader harshly criticized Edward VII of Great Britain, Catholics, and the Japanese. In 1913, President Woodrow Wilson sent Hale to Mexico as a special agent, and he recommended not recognizing the Huerta government, the policy that Wilson adopted. When World War I began, Hale went to work for the German Information Service, advising the Germans with regard to propaganda in the United States. For $15,000 a year, paid from Berlin, Hale spoke out for Germany against Britain and tried to halt munitions shipments to the Entente Cordiale.* He was widely denounced in the United States for these pro-German activities, especially after the extent of his involvement with Berlin was revealed in 1918 through intercepted German cables. One specific criticism leveled against him was his editing of the so-called Dernberg speech justifying the sinking of the *Lusitania*.* By the end of the war, bitterly anti-Wilson and despised by his own countrymen, Hale went to Germany and lived out his life in seclusion, dying in Munich on April 10, 1924. Among his published writings are *A Week in the White House with Theodore Roosevelt* (1908); *Woodrow Wilson: The Story of His Life* (1912), a campaign biography; and *The Story of a Style* (1920), an anti-Wilson polemic. *DAB*, 8:112; *New York Times*, April 11, 1924.

HALSEY, THOMAS LLOYD (c. 1776–1855). Born in Providence, Rhode Island, around 1776, Thomas L. Halsey graduated from the College of Rhode Island (now Brown University) in 1793 and entered private business. By 1807, he was engaged in commercial activities in Buenos Aires and probably because of this was appointed U.S. consul* there in 1812 and began to function in that capacity in 1814. The Spanish-American wars for independence were taking place, and Halsey profitably supplied U.S. munitions to the armies of General José de San Martín, guaranteed a $2 million loan to the provinces of the Río de la Plata, which prolonged the government of Juan Martín Pueyrredón. In 1818, however, his recall was requested for aiding José Artígas, an opponent of Pueyrredón. Secretary of State John Quincy Adams* was happy to oblige, since Halsey had also been illegally commissioning privateers against Spain. After his commission had been revoked, Halsey continued in business in Buenos Aires, living a life of opulence and winning distinction for introducing blooded merino sheep into Argentina. He was a trustee of Brown University, 1809–1839, and died in Providence on February 2, 1855. *DAB*, 8:162; Whitaker, Arthur P., *The U.S. and the Independence of Latin America, 1800–1830* (1931).

HAMMOND, OGDEN H. (1869–1956). Born in Louisville, Kentucky, on October 13, 1869, Ogden Hammond attended Phillips Exeter Academy and graduated from Yale in 1893. He went into the real estate business in Superior, Wisconsin, after college but in 1907 opened an insurance agency in New York City. He lived in New Jersey, became involved in Republican politics, served in the state legislature, and attended Republican national conventions in 1916 and 1924. His loyal Republicanism probably influenced his being chosen as minister to Spain in 1925. In Madrid for four years, Hammond negotiated an indefinite extension of a commercial treaty and settled problems arising from the expropriation of American oil companies in Spain. He returned from Spain in 1929 and resumed his business career. Hammond, who survived the sinking of the *Lusitania** in 1915, died in New York City on October 29, 1956. *NCAB*, D:350; *New York Times*, October 30, 1956.

HARE, RAYMOND ARTHUR (b. 1901). Raymond A. Hare was born in Martinsburg, West Virginia, on April 3, 1901, graduated from Grinnell College in 1924, and taught for three years at Robert College in Constantinople. From 1927 to 1944, he held minor posts in the Foreign Service, becoming first secretary at the London embassy in 1944. In that capacity, he attended the Dumbarton Oaks Conference,* the first session of the United Nations* General Assembly in London, 1946, and the Paris Peace Conference, 1946.* Hare worked at the National War College, 1946–1947, and with the Office of Middle East and Indian Affairs, 1947–1950. Beginning in 1950, he served in a succession of ministerial and ambassadorial posts in the Middle East: Saudi Arabia and Yemen, 1950–1953; Lebanon, 1953; Egypt, 1956–1958; United Arab Republic, 1958–1960; Yemen, 1959–1960; and Turkey, 1961–1965. In addition, he was director-general of the Foreign Service, 1954–1956; deputy under secretary of state, 1960–1961; and assistant secretary of state for Near Eastern and South Asian affairs, 1965–1966. Hare was in Egypt during the Suez crisis (1956),* at the time of the U.S. withdrawal of support for the Aswan Dam and the nationalization of the canal. He was involved in negotiations with Egyptian leaders toward a compromise by which Egypt would run the canal as Egyptian property but would grant users certain rights and agree to submit all disputes to the International Court of Justice.* Hare was named a career ambassador in 1965 and retired the following year. He married Julia Cygan in 1932 and since 1966 has been associated with the Middle East Institute as president (1966–1969) and as national chairman (1969–1976). Since 1976, he has been chairman emeritus of the institute. *NCAB* 1:211; *New York Times*, August 15, 1956; *WWA* (1976–1977):1330.

HARRIET **INCIDENT (1831).** This was a diplomatic incident involving the United States that grew out of the long-standing dispute between Argentina and Great Britain over possession of the Falkland Islands. Louis Vernet, the Argentine governor, seized four American fishing vessels, including a schooner, the *Harriet*, and took the ships to Buenos Aires as prizes to demonstrate Argentine authority in the Falklands. Protests by the U.S. consul* in Buenos Aires and the forced deportation of nearly the entire island population by the U.S. Navy produced an impasse. Francis Baylies* was sent as chargé d'affaires* in 1832 to negotiate a treaty acknowledging the right of Americans to fish in the area of the islands, but he and Argentine officials could not reach an agreement. Baylies left late in 1832, and no other American diplomat returned to Argentina until 1844. Meanwhile, Great Britain reoccupied the Falklands in 1833, and the United States chose not to protest what the Argentines saw as a violation of the Monroe Doctrine.* Goebel, Julius L., *The Struggle for the Falkland Islands* (1927); Klafter, Craig Evan, "United States Involvement in the Falkland Islands Crisis of 1831–1833," *Journal of the Early Republic* 4, 4 (Winter 1984):395–402; Peterson, Harold, *Argentina and the United States, 1810–1960* (1964); Rawle, Francis, "Edward Livingston," in Bemis, Samuel F., ed., *American Secretaries of State and their Diplomacy*, vol. 4 (1928).

HARRIMAN, FLORENCE JAFFREY HURST (1870–1967). A member of a wealthy New York family, Florence Jaffrey Hurst was born July 21, 1870, and educated at fashionable Mrs. Lockwood's School. She married J. Borden Harriman in 1889 and pursued a career of social work and suffragism in the early 1900s. She was the manager of the New York State Reformatory for Women (1906–1918) and a member of the Federal Industrial Relations Committee in 1913. During World War I, she worked in France with the Red Cross and after that supported the League of Nations* and worked with the Women's National Democratic Club. A close friend of Frances Perkins, secretary of labor under President Franklin D. Roosevelt, Harriman was chosen minister to Norway in 1937, the second woman to hold that diplomatic rank. In Norway, she dealt at length with a commercial treaty and a dispute over the U.S. duty on whale oil. In 1940, she fled the German invasion and occupation of Oslo and spent the final four months of her tour in Stockholm engaging in refugee relief work. She returned to the United States in August 1940 in the company of members of the Norwegian royal family. She wrote of her Norwegian experience in *Mission to the North* (1941) and retired to a house in Georgetown. Her husband had died in 1914, but she lived to the age of ninety-seven, dying August 31, 1967, in Georgetown. *New York Times*, September 1, 1967; *WWWA*, 4 (1961–1968):408.

HARRIMAN, WILLIAM AVERELL (1891–1986). One of America's most prominent diplomats since World War II, W. Averell Harriman was born November 15, 1891, in New York City. After graduation from Yale in 1913, he worked for the Union Pacific Railroad for four years and then organized the Merchant Shipbuilding Company, which by the mid–1920s claimed the largest American merchant fleet. In 1920, he founded an investment banking firm, W. A. Harriman and Company, which engaged in some early financial dealings with the Soviets and merged with Brown Brothers in 1931. That year, Harriman became chairman of the executive committee of the Illinois Central Railroad, a position he retained until 1942, though he also became chairman of the board of Union Pacific in 1932. Except for a short stint with the National Recovery Administration (1934–1935), Harriman first entered public life in 1940, when he held the first of a series of defense related posts. In 1941–1942, he was Lend-Lease* administrator for Great Britain, serving also as a valuable political liaison between the two governments. He participated in the Atlantic Conference (1941),* undertook a special mission to Moscow in 1941 to arrange Lend-Lease for the Soviet Union, and attended most other wartime conferences. As ambassador to the Soviet Union, 1943–1946, Harriman won the friendship and respect of Premier Joseph Stalin, who trusted him to convey faithfully Roosevelt's policies. A short tour as ambassador to Great Britain in 1946 preceded his appointment as secretary of commerce in the Truman administration. In 1948, Harriman went to Paris as U.S. representative in Europe for the Economic Cooperation Act (Marshall Plan),* serving as chief administrator for that aid program until 1950. Other assignments followed: special assistant to the president, 1950–1951; U.S. representative to the North Atlantic Treaty Organization (NATO),* 1951; and director, Mutual Security Administration,* 1951–1953. Harriman left federal service with the installation of the Eisenhower administration but was elected governor of New York in 1954. In the Kennedy administration, Harriman was an ambassador-at-large and assistant secretary of state (Far Eastern affairs), where his main service was heading the U.S. delegation at the Geneva Conference in Laos.* As under secretary of state (political affairs), 1963–1965, he negotiated the Partial Nuclear Test Ban Treaty, 1963,* which he considered his most important accomplishment. As ambassador-at-large, 1965–1969, he made several trips involving the war in Vietnam; fittingly, he was named chairman of the U.S. delegation at the Paris Peace Conference, 1968–1969, to work out an agreeable settlement for that war. Known for his urbanity and negotiating skills, Harriman fell in line with traditional cold war* thinking after World War II, favoring a strong NATO and an expanded Atlantic community. As containment* became more military and global in orientation, however, he opposed much of it, except in China and Southeast Asia. He strongly opposed Secretary of State John Foster Dulles's* policy of "liberation,"* considering it unrealistic. Twice married, Harriman continued into his nineties as an elder statesman of the Democratic party and was frequently sought for advice on foreign policy matters. He wrote several books on public policy, including *Peace with Russia?* (1959) and *America and Russia in a Changing World* (1971), and donated $10 million to Columbia University for the creation of the Harriman Institute, for the advanced study of the Soviet Union. He died in Yorktown Heights, New York, on July 26, 1986. Burke, Lee H., *Ambassador at Large: Diplomat Extraordinary* (1972); Harriman, W. Averell, and Elie Abel, *Special Envoy to Churchill and Stalin, 1941–1946* (1975); Isaacson, Walter, and Evan Thomas, *The Wise Men: Six Friends and the World They Made* (1986); *NCAB*, G:16; *New York Times*, May 5, 1967, July 27, 1986; *WWA* (1976–1977):1339.

HARRIS, TOWNSEND (1804–1878). The first accredited U.S. minister to Japan, Townsend Harris was born in Sandy Hill, New York, on October 3, 1804. He had little formal education and worked in his family's import business for a number of years. In 1846, he sat on the New York Board of Education and was instrumental in the founding of City College of New York. In 1848, he went to California, and then to the Far East. Appointed consul* at Ningpo, Japan, in 1854, Harris was promoted to consul general for Japan the following year through the influence of his friends William L. Marcy and William H. Seward. In 1859, he was named minister to Japan, remaining at his post until early 1862. Harris is best known for negotiating the first commercial treaty with Japan (1858), sometimes called the Harris Treaty.* He was successful in winning the confidence of the Japanese government and advised it in its dealings with other Western nations. In 1857, while on his way to Japan, he also negotiated a commercial treaty with Siam. After 1862, Harris, who never married, lived in genteel retirement in New York City, maintaining an interest in Christian missions and temperance, until his death February 25, 1878. Harris's journal, edited by Mario Emilio Cossenza, is *The Complete Journal of Townsend Harris, First American Counsul General and Minister to Japan* (1930). *DAB*, 8:324; Dennett, Tyler, *Americans in Eastern Asia* (1922).

HARRIS TREATY (1858), treaty between Japan and the United States. This was a major treaty negotiated by Townsend Harris,* U.S. minister to Japan, and provided for consuls* in Tokyo and all six open ports, with freedom of travel; for the U.S. president to act as mediator in Japanese-European conflicts; for the Japanese right to acquire ships, munitions, and artisans in the United States; for the U.S. Navy to keep supplies in three Japanese ports; and for Americans to enjoy freedom of religion in Japan. The treaty also contained tariff provisions and served as a model for similar treaties between Japan and other Western nations. In general, the terms of this treaty were more liberal than those of the Treaties of Wanghia* and Tientsin* with China, but in Japan the treaty contributed to considerable domestic political turmoil over the next decade, featuring many acts of antiforeignism. Dennett, Tyler, *Americans in Eastern Asia* (1922); Neu, Charles E., *The Troubled Encounter: The United States and Japan* (1975).

HARRISON, LELAND (1883–1951). Born in New York City on April 25, 1883, Leland Harrison graduated from Harvard (1907) and attended Harvard Law School for a short time before becoming private secretary to Thomas J. O'Brien,* U.S. ambassador to Japan, late in 1907. In 1908, he became third secretary of the legation, and for the next ten years, he held similar posts in Peking, London, and Bogotá. Harrison served as diplomatic secretary for the American Peace Commission in 1918–1919 and in 1920 was made counselor* at the Paris embassy. The following year, he returned to the United States to act as an "expert assistant" at the Washington Conference (1921–1922).* From 1922 to 1927, Harrison was assistant secretary of state, handling administrative tasks in Washington, but in 1927 he was appointed to the first of a series of ministries that would take him to four different nations over the next twenty years. Harrison was minister to Sweden (1927–1929), Uruguay (1929–1930), Romania (1935–1937), and Switzerland (1937–1947). Of these, the mission in Switzerland was the most important, for there he served as an observer to the League of Nations,* and, after 1939, he was able to report to the State Department on German activities. In 1945, Harrison transmitted the Japanese surrender note of August 14 to the United States and its allies. After 1949, he was chairman of the U.S. delegation to the International Red Cross Conference in Geneva, which adopted the Geneva Conventions (1949)* on the treatment of prisoners of war and enemy casualties. Harrison married Ann C. Coleman in 1925, was an avid and expert golfer, and died in Washington, D.C., on June 7, 1951. *NCAB*, 38:583; *New York Times*, June 8, 1951; *WWWA*, 3 (1951–1960):375.

HARTMAN, ARTHUR A. (b. 1926). A native of New York City, where he was born March 12, 1926, Arthur A. Hartman graduated from Harvard in 1944 and attended Harvard Law School in 1947–1948. Between 1948 and 1956, he held various positions with the Economic Cooperation Administration, administrators of the Marshall Plan,* and subsequent military aid organizations. Hartman was stationed in Saigon as part of the European Army Conference from 1956 to 1958 and then returned to Washington and the State Department, working with the Bureau of Economic Affairs until 1961. During the Kennedy administration (1961–1963), he was on the staff of the under secretary of state for economic affairs. From 1963 to 1967, he was in the economic section of the U.S. embassy in London. Hartman occupied other bureaucratic posts in the State Department until 1974, when he became assistant secretary of state for European affairs. As such, he negotiated the opening of diplomatic relations with East Germany in 1974, finding agreement on such matters as claims for U.S. victims of the Nazi regime and future consular trade relations. From 1977 to 1981, Hartman was ambassador to France, the first career diplomat to hold that post since Charles Bohlen* in the 1960s. In France, he was well regarded, although his outspokenness on occasion was criticized by leaders of both parties. He did, however, maintain warm relations when Socialist President François Mitterand was elected in 1981, shortly after Ronald Reagan took office as president. Later in 1981, Hartman was transferred to the embassy in Moscow, where he served five years. After his return to the United States, he became embroiled in a controversy regarding security leaks in the Moscow embassy's marine guard delegation; his aloof management style was said to have contributed to the environment that made such security breaches possible. *New York Times*, November 5, 1974, April 26, 30, 1977, August 22, 1981, January 20, 1988; *Washington Post*, February 26, 1988; *WWA* (1978–1979):1407.

HARVEY, GEORGE BRINTON McCLELLAN (1864–1928). One of the most prominent journalists and Republicans in the 1920s, George Harvey was born February 16, 1864, in Peacham, Vermont, and educated at Peacham Academy. He became a reporter at age fifteen and by 1891 had risen to the position of managing editor of the *New York World*. A supporter of Democrat Grover Cleveland for the presidency in 1892, Harvey went on to make a fortune through investments in utilities and street railways between 1893 and 1899 and bought the *North American Review* in 1899. In 1901, he became editor of *Harper's Weekly* as well. Harvey was an early supporter of Woodrow Wilson but by 1913 had broken with the president. He retired from publishing in 1915 and from the Democratic party in 1916 and, soon after, founded a new magazine, *Harvey's Weekly*, specifically to attack Wilson's policies. Stoutly opposed to the Treaty of Versailles,* Harvey became an adviser to the irreconcilables* and other Wilsonian opponents in Congress in 1919–1920. In 1920, he was influential in the Republicans' choice of Warren G. Harding as a presidential candidate, and upon Harding's election, he was rewarded with the ambassadorship to Great Britain. He spent two years (1921–1923) in Britain making controversial speeches critical of the League of Nations,* of the professed war aims of the United States, and of the results of the Washington Conference (1921–1922),* but privately he communicated well with British leaders and improved Anglo-American relations. After his diplomatic service, Harvey became editor of the *Washington Post* (1924–1925), opposed U.S. involvement in the war debts question, and wrote a biography of industrialist Henry Clay Frick (1928). He married Alma Arabella Parker in 1887 and died from a heart attack brought on by asthma on August 20, 1928, at his summer home in Dublin, New Hampshire. *DAB*, 8:372; Johnson, Willis Fletcher, *George Harvey* (1929); *New York Times*, August 21, 1928.

HAVANA CONFERENCE (1928). This meeting, the Sixth International Conference of American States, had an anti-U.S. atmosphere due to renewed intervention in Nicaragua and ongoing problems with Mexico. Latin American delegates tried to strike at U.S. dominance of the Pan-American Union* by means of a resolution excluding that body from political functions, but after heated debate at the conference, the resolution was never ratified subsequently by a sufficient number of states. A draft treaty eschewing intervention drew heated U.S. opposition and was postponed, although a resolution condemning acts of aggression was passed. Other treaties adopted at the conference dealt with matters such as aliens, political asylum, consular agents, and the duties of states in the event of civil strife. It was also agreed to convene a special meeting on arbitration* and conciliation in Washington, D.C., within a year; this was held (December 1928–January 1929) and resulted in a general treaty of arbitration and a general convention on conciliation, which the U.S. Senate approved with the reservation that the Senate must consent to any U.S. action under arbitration treaties. The U.S. delegation to the Havana Conference was headed by former Secretary of State Charles Evans Hughes.* *FR* (1928), 1:527–621; Inman, Samuel Guy, *Inter-American Conferences* (1965); Meacham, J. Lloyd, *A Survey of United States–Latin American Relations* (1965).

HAWAIIAN RECIPROCITY TREATY (1875), commercial treaty between Hawaii and the United States. This treaty evolved out of negotiations between Hawaiian commissioners Elisha Allen* and H. A. P. Carter* and Secretary of State Hamilton Fish.* Initiated by a Hawaiian desire to shore up the islands' sugar-based economy, the treaty permitted the free importation of "grades of sugar heretofore commonly imported from the Hawaiian Islands" and a number of lesser products. In return, Americans were permitted to export freely to Hawaii a long list of important products, nearly all the American goods Hawaiians had any use for. The treaty was ratified by the Senate, 50–12, on March 18, 1875, as many senators foresaw political and strategic advantages stemming from the commercial ties thus created. Stevens, Sylvester K., *American Expansion in Hawaii, 1842–1898* (1945).

HAWLEY-SMOOT TARIFF (1930). See **SMOOT-HAWLEY TARIFF (1930).**

HAY, JOHN MILTON (1838–1905). John Hay had, in reality, two distinct careers a generation apart: secretary to and biographer of Abraham Lincoln and, much later, secretary of state under William McKinley and Theodore Roosevelt. He was born in Salem, Indiana, on October 8, 1838, graduated from Brown University (1858), and was admitted to the bar (1861). He first met Lincoln in 1859 and became the president's assistant private secretary in 1861. From 1865 to 1870, he held legation secretary or chargé* posts in Paris, Vienna, and Madrid. In 1870, however, he exchanged diplomacy for writing and began a twenty-five year career as a writer and traveler, the most notable result of which was the *Life of Lincoln* (10 vols., 1875–1890), written with John Nicolay. In 1897, President William McKinley named Hay ambassador to Great Britain, his first contact with diplomacy since a short stint as assistant secretary of state from 1879 to 1881. Hay was convinced of the importance of maintaining good relations with Britain, and in London he secured British neutrality* toward the United

States in the Spanish-American War. In 1898, McKinley brought him home to replace William R. Day* as secretary of state, and he remained in that post until his death. Among his accomplishments was the Open Door Policy,* formulated in two sets of diplomatic notes (1899–1900), and designed to guarantee freedom of commerce in China and Chinese territorial integrity. In addition, Hay settled several outstanding Anglo-American problems, notably the Alaskan boundary question, resolved through a joint tribunal, the abrogation of the Clayton-Bulwer Treaty (1850),* and the negotiation of its replacement, the Hay-Pauncefote Treaty (1901),* giving the United States the right to construct and fortify an isthmian canal. The canal became a reality after the signing of the Hay–Bunau-Varilla Treaty (1903),* in which newly independent Panama granted the United States the right to a Canal Zone in which to construct the waterway. Hay married Clara L. Stone in 1874 and, after several years of declining health, died in Newbury, New Hampshire, on July 1, 1905. Clymer, Kenton J., *John Hay: The Gentleman as Diplomat* (1975); *DAB*, 8:430; Dennett, Tyler, *John Hay: From Poetry to Politics* (1934); Dennis, A. L. P., *Adventures in American Diplomacy, 1896–1906* (1928); Dulles, Foster Rhea, "John Hay," in Graebner, Norman, ed., *An Uncertain Tradition* (1961); McCullough, David, *The Path Between the Seas* (1977).

HAY-BOND TREATY (1902). The successor to the unratified Blaine-Bond Treaty, this treaty provided for reciprocal reduction of duties between the United States and Newfoundland. However, opposition from New England fishing interests and the influential Senator Henry Cabot Lodge, Sr.* (R., Massachusetts) prevented ratification, much to the distress of Secretary of State John Hay.* Campbell, Charles S., *Anglo-American Understanding, 1898–1903* (1957).

HAY–BUNAU-VARILLA TREATY (1903), treaty between Panama and the United States. Negotiated between Secretary of State John Hay* and Panamanian representative Philippe Bunau-Varilla, this treaty followed closely the independence of Panama and provided for the construction of an isthmian canal across Panama. The United States agreed to guarantee Panama's independence and to pay $10 million immediately and $250,000 per year after nine years for a lease in perpetuity over the Canal Zone, a strip of land ten miles wide through which the canal would pass. The Senate ratified the treaty February 23, 1904. After years of controversy and minor adjustments in the lease payments, Panama and the United States signed two new accords, the Panama Canal Treaties,* in 1977. Anguizola, Gustave A., *Philippe Bunau-Varilla: The Man behind the Panama Canal* (1980); LaFeber, Walter, *The Panama Canal* (1979); Liss, Sheldon, *The Canal* (1976); Miner, Dwight C., *The Fight for the Panama Route* (1940); Weisberger, Bernard A., "The Strange Affair of the Taking of the Panama Canal Zone," *American Heritage* (October 1976): 6–11, 68–77.

HAY-HERRÁN TREATY (1903), proposed treaty between the United States and Colombia. This treaty called for the construction by the United States of an isthmian canal across the Colombian state of Panama. For the canal rights, the

United States would pay $10 million immediately and $250,000 per year after nine years. The U.S. Senate ratified the treaty, which had been negotiated by Secretary of State John Hay* and Colombian chargé d'affaires* Tomás Herrán, rather promptly, but the Colombian senate refused ratification, and the treaty failed. Later in the year, the Panamanians revolted against Colombia, with tacit American support, and a canal treaty, the Hay–Bunau-Varilla Treaty,* was negotiated between the United States and Panama. Calcott, Wilfrid, *The Caribbean Policy of the United States, 1890–1920* (1942); *FR* (1903):132–230; McCullough, David, *The Path between the Seas* (1977); Miner, Dwight, *The Fight for the Panama Route* (1940); LaFeber, Walter, *The Panama Canal* (1979).

HAY-PAUNCEFOTE TREATY (1901), treaty between the United States and Great Britain. This treaty, negotiated by Secretary of State John Hay* and British Ambassador Lord Julian Pauncefote, replaced the Clayton-Bulwer Treaty (1850)* and provided that the United States could build and operate by itself an isthmian canal, open to the commerce of all nations. The earlier Hay-Pauncefote Treaty (1900) had been amended by the Senate on matters concerning fortifications and the adherence of other nations to the treaty in such a way that Britain found the entire treaty unacceptable. The signing and ratification of this treaty indicated Britain's concession that the Caribbean was America's sphere of influence. Campbell, Charles S., *Anglo-American Understanding, 1898–1903* (1957); *FR* (1901), 237–47; McCullough, David, *The Path between the Seas* (1977); Miner, Dwight, *The Fight for the Panama Route* (1940); Mowat, R. B., *The Life of Lord Pauncefote* (1929).

HAYES, CARLETON JOSEPH HUNTLEY (1882–1964). Carleton J. H. Hayes was born May 16, 1882, in Afton, New York, and received A.B. (1904), A.M. (1905), and Ph.D. (1909) degrees in history from Columbia. He taught history at Columbia from 1907 to 1950, when he became a professor emeritus. Specializing in the history of Western Europe, he wrote *British Social Politics* (1913) and a basic history textbook in 1916. During World War I, Hayes served in the army's military intelligence division, and from 1942 to 1945 he was ambassador to Spain, appointed because he was a strong supporter of Franklin D. Roosevelt and a Catholic. He came under criticism for his overly favorable view of Franco-ruled Spain but did succeed in deterring Spain from entering into a full alliance with the Axis powers. Hayes was active in professional organizations, serving as president of the American Historical Association and helping create the National Association of Christians and Jews. Married to Mary Evelyn Carroll, Hayes remained active in academic life until his death in Afton on September 3, 1964. His ambassadorship in Spain is recounted in his *Wartime Mission to Spain* (1945). *New York Times*, September 4, 1964; *WWWA*, vol. 4 (1961–1968):421.

HEATH, DONALD READ (1894–1981). Born in Topeka, Kansas, on August 12, 1894, Donald R. Heath studied at Washburn College and the University of Montpellier in France and served in World War I before entering the Foreign Service in 1920. Between 1921 and 1933, he served in minor posts in Bucharest, Warsaw, Bern, and Port-au-Prince. In 1933, he became assistant chief, Division of Latin American Affairs, remaining at that post until 1937. He then went to Berlin as first secretary, 1938–1941, to Santiago as counselor,* 1941–1944, and back to Germany, attached to the Office of Military Government, 1944–1947. In 1947, he embarked upon a series of ministerial and ambassadorial appointments: minister to Bulgaria, 1947–1950, and Vietnam, Cambodia, and Laos, 1950–1952; and ambassador to Vietnam and Cambodia, 1952–1955, to Lebanon, 1955–1957, and to Saudi Arabia, 1957–1961. Of these, the most important for Heath and the United States was his ministry to Bulgaria. He was the first minister to that country after World War II and the signing of the peace treaty, and he served uneventfully for nearly three years. In January 1950, however, he was accused of meddling in Bulgarian internal affairs and declared persona non grata. Relations between the United States and Bulgaria were broken the following month after Bulgarian allegations of U.S. spying and U.S. protests about the treatment of legation personnel. Heath returned to the United States when relations were severed but was soon appointed the first minister to what was then called the Associated States of Indo-China. There he was involved in talks during June 1952 with U.S. and French representatives reexamining U.S. policy toward Southeast Asia. After his retirement from diplomatic service in 1961, Heath served as vice-president of the Foreign Bondholders Protective Council, 1961–1967; president, 1967–1971; and chairman, 1972. After 1973, Heath lived in New York and worked as a consultant for Foreign Bondholders. Married to Sue Louise Bell in 1920, he died in Orinda, California, on October 16, 1981. *New York Times*, February 22, March 9, June 21, 1950, June 2, 1952, October 17, 1981; *WWA* (1976–1977):1387.

HELM, CHARLES JOHN (1817–1868). The Confederacy's man in Havana, Charles J. Helm was born June 21, 1817, in Harnellsville, New York, studied for the law, and was admitted to the bar in 1842. He practiced law in Newport, Kentucky, where his family had moved when he was a child, served in the Mexican War, and sat in the Kentucky legislature, 1851–1853. Later in the 1850s, Helm was appointed U.S. commercial agent in St. Thomas, where he was successful in obtaining the abolition of some Danish duties. In 1858, he became consul general* in Havana, resigning in 1861 at the outbreak of the Civil War to become a Confederate special agent, also in Havana. There was a good deal of sympathy for the Confederacy in Cuba, and Helm was able to buy arms and supplies and administer blockade*-running activities without interference from the Spanish authorities. He reported on the inefficiency of the Union blockade at New Orleans and Mobile and furnished statistics for the Confederate propagandists in Great Britain. After the war, Helm retired in Toronto, where he died in February 1868. *DAB*, 7:512; Owsley, Frank L., *King Cotton Diplomacy* (1959); *WWWA*, Historical Volume, p. 245.

HELMS, RICHARD McGARRAH (b. 1913). Born March 30, 1913, in St. David's, Pennsylvania, Richard Helms graduated from Williams College in 1935 and went to work as a journalist with United Press in Europe, 1935–1937, and with the *Indianapolis Times*, 1937–1942. He worked in the Office of Strategic Services (OSS) during World War II and joined the Central Intelligence Agency (CIA)* when it was created in 1947. Helms worked for the CIA for twenty-six years, the last seven of which he was its director. In 1973, he was dismissed from this post by President Richard Nixon, who was upset because Helms would not allow the CIA to participate in the Watergate scandal cover-up. As a consolation prize, Helms accepted the ambassadorship to Iran, something quite pleasing to the shah's government, which viewed Helms as an important person with close ties to the White House. In Iran, Helms helped the government set up a sophisticated communications intelligence system. Helms came away from Iran believing the shah was firmly in control; his reports encouraged the Carter administration to criticize Iran's human rights record and encourage reform. His three-year tenure in Iran, however, was frequently interrupted by congressional investigations of the CIA and its involvement in political assassinations and in the overthrow of the Salvador Allende government in Chile. In 1977, he was indicted for perjury for lying to the Senate Foreign Relations Committee about the CIA's role in Chilean affairs; a plea bargain resulted in a $2,000 fine and a two-year suspended sentence. Since 1977, Helms, who has been married twice, has headed Safeer Company, a firm that helps Iranians do business in the United States. Powers, Thomas, *The Man Who Kept the Secrets: Richard Helms and the CIA* (1979); Prados, John, *Presidents' Secret Wars* (1986); Rubin, Barry, *Paved with Good Intentions* (1980); *New York Times*, June 1, November 21–24, 26, 1975, December 13, 1976; *WWA* (1986–1987):1250.

HELSINKI CONFERENCE (1975). Held from July 30 to August 1, 1975, this meeting was for the purpose of ratifying agreements reached by the Conference on Security and Cooperation in Europe (CSCE), which had met periodically since 1973. The document ratified was not a treaty but a "statement of intent," signed by thirty-five nations and containing ten principles related to European security, including guarantees of territorial integrity and inviolability of frontiers, respect for human rights, pledges for the fulfillment of international obligations, and cooperation in the areas of economic policy, science, and environmental matters. U.S. accession to this statement was a recognition of Soviet hegemony in East Europe and a ratification, in a sense, of the changes in postwar U.S. foreign policy made necessary by the pursuit of détente.* According to Gaddis, the significance of the Helsinki agreement may lie in the human rights provision and the fact that it can be used as a standard against which Soviet human rights policy may be measured—an "unintended consequence" potentially beneficial to the United States. To Henry Kissinger,* the Helsinki agreement was significant because it stabilized spheres of influence in Europe and thus stabilized détente in the vortex of the cold war.* Since 1980, the United States has used the human rights provisions as a vehicle by which to criticize the Soviet Union at appropriate times. Criticism intensified for a time after the Moscow Group, organized to monitor human rights progress in the USSR, was disbanded in 1982. General review conferences were held in Belgrade in 1977, in Madrid between 1980 and 1983, in Stockholm in 1984 and 1985, and in Vienna in 1986. The more recent of these conferences have dealt with measures to reduce military tensions in Europe through notification of large-scale military maneuvers and opening them to observers from the other side. Gaddis, John L., *Russia, the Soviet Union and the United States* (1978); Graebner, Norman, *Cold War Diplomacy* (1977); *New York Times*, July 31, 1985; Stoessinger, John G., *Henry Kissinger: The Anguish of Power* (1978).

HENDERSON, LOY WESLEY (1892–1986). One of the most prominent and highly respected U.S. diplomats of the mid–twentieth century, Loy Henderson was born near Rogers, Arkansas, on June 28, 1892, graduated from Northwestern (1915), and attended Denver University Law School. During World War I, he worked with the Red Cross in France, and, in 1918, he became a member of the Interallied Commission to Germany, dealing with repatriation and prison camp inspection. After two more years with the Red Cross, 1919–1921, Henderson joined the diplomatic service in 1922 and served in a succession of minor posts in Dublin, Queenstown (Ireland), Washington, Riga, Kaunas, Tallinn, and Moscow (where he was second secretary, 1934–1936, first secretary, 1936–1938, and chargé d'affaires* intermittently, 1936–1938). From 1938 to 1942, he was assistant chief, Division of East European Affairs, but in the latter year, he returned to Moscow as counselor of the U.S. embassy. He played an important role in wartime Moscow, serving as the U.S. representative at a meeting between Churchill and Stalin in August 1942. He became minister to Iraq in 1943, where he handled U.S. relations with a number of Middle East oil-producing states, but in 1945, he returned to Washington as chief of the Division of Near Eastern and African Affairs. In this position, he went to Greece in August 1947 to facilitate the implementation of aid granted under the Truman Doctrine* by persuading the Greeks to broaden the political base of their government. In addition, he was an adviser to United Nations* Ambassador Warren R. Austin* in working on the Middle East question prior to the creation of the state of Israel. Here, his concern about U.S. access to oil led to criticism that he was too pro-Arab. From 1948 to 1951, Henderson was ambassador to India and minister to Nepal; from 1951 to 1955, he was ambassador to Iran, where he was involved in the takeover of Iranian oil fields by an international consortium. In 1955, he returned to Washington as an assistant secretary of state; later that year, he became deputy under secretary of state. As such, he was a member of the Suez

Commission and attended the First and Second Suez Conferences (1956) and headed a mission to arrange for opening diplomatic relations with a number of newly independent African nations in 1960. He was honored with the title of career ambassador in 1956 and retired from the State Department in 1961. After his retirement, he taught at American University and directed the Washington Institute of Foreign Affairs for a number of years. He married Elise Marie Heinrichson in 1930 and died in Bethesda, Maryland, on March 24, 1986. Baer, George W., ed., *A Question of Trust—the Origins of U.S.-Soviet Diplomacy: The Memoirs of Loy W. Henderson* (1986); *CB* (1948):276–78; Jones, Kenneth Paul, *U.S. Diplomats in Europe, 1919–1941* (1981); *New York Times*, May 10, September 3, 1956, March 26, 1986; *WWA* (1976–1977):1408.

HEPBURN BILL (1902), bill passed January 9, 1902, by the House of Representatives authorizing the construction of an isthmian canal along the Nicaraguan route. It was amended and replaced by the Spooner Act,* which passed both Houses of Congress on June 28, 1902, and changed the route preference from Nicaragua to Panama. Miner, Dwight C., *The Fight for the Panama Route* (1940); Munro, Dana G., *Intervention and Dollar Diplomacy in the Caribbean, 1900–1921* (1964).

HERRICK, MYRON TIMOTHY (1854–1929). Self-styled "Friend of France," Myron T. Herrick twice served as U.S. ambassador to that country. He was born in Huntington, Ohio, on October 9, 1854, attended Oberlin Academy and Ohio Wesleyan College, studied law, and gained admission to the bar in 1878. He practiced law in Cleveland but gradually became involved in banking and Republican politics, serving as president of Cleveland's Society for Saving in 1894, and in politics on the Cleveland City Council (1885–1887) and as governor of Ohio (1903–1905). A close friend of William McKinley and Mark Hanna, Herrick was offered the cabinet post of secretary of the treasury but declined it for business reasons. In 1912, he was named ambassador to France for the first time. In his two years at the Paris embassy, he aided Americans stranded in Paris at the beginning of the war, urged the creation of an American ambulance corps, and calmly stayed in Paris after the French government and most of the rest of the diplomatic corps had left, helping to prevent panic in the city. His second tenure in Paris, 1921–1929, saw him involved in postwar financial settlements, restoring cordial relations, hosting Charles A. Lindbergh after his historic flight, and negotiating for the purchase of land for a new U.S. embassy. When Marshal Foch, the French wartime commander, died in 1929, Herrick was deeply affected, both mentally and physically, and died himself just five days after Foch's funeral, on March 31, 1929. He was married in 1880 to Caroline M. Parmely; she died in 1918. Herrick's biography, *Myron T. Herrick, Friend of France* (1929), by T. Bently Mott, was largely written in consultation with Herrick. *DAB*, 8:587; *New York Times*, April 1, 1929; Willson, Beckles, *America's Ambassadors to France, 1777–1927* (1928).

HERTER, CHRISTIAN ARCHIBALD (1895–1966). Secretary of state during the last year and a half of the Eisenhower presidency (1959–1961), Christian A. Herter was born March 28, 1895, of expatriate artist parents living in Paris, France. He graduated from Harvard (1915) and briefly attended Columbia University's School of Architecture before entering diplomatic service in 1916. He served as an attaché to Ambassador James W. Gerard* in Germany before U.S. entry into World War I, married Mary Caroline Pratt in 1917, later was a staff member on the U.S. delegation at the Paris Peace Conference (1919),* and then became an assistant to Herbert Hoover in the American Relief Administration. From 1921 to 1924, he continued to work for Hoover as assistant secretary of commerce while Hoover was secretary. Out of public life as editor and copublisher of a Boston weekly, the *Independent* (1924–1928), and an instructor at Harvard (1929–1930), Herter began a political career in the Massachusetts legislature in 1931 and moved up to the U.S. House of Representatives in 1943. There for five terms (1943–1953), he was an advocate of the United Nations* and was involved in preliminary work for the Marshall Plan.* From 1953 to 1957, he was governor of Massachusetts. In 1957, he was named under secretary of state; two years later, he became secretary of state upon the death of John Foster Dulles.* As secretary of state, he dealt with the Berlin crisis,* not yet fully blown, mediating differences among European allies over Berlin's security. As U.S. representative at the Geneva Conference of Foreign Ministers, 1959, he became suspicious of Soviet aims toward Berlin and West Germany and adopted, with congressional support, a stronger official stand on the issue. In addition, he defended American U-2 flights during the U-2 incident* in 1960 and helped settle a minor dispute with Panama, in which the Panamanian flag was permitted to fly along with the U.S. flag in the Canal Zone, and a greater amount of aid was given to Panama. Herter advocated restraint toward Castro's Cuba and kept the Congo crisis* a United Nations matter. From 1962 to 1966, he served the Kennedy and Johnson administrations as chief planner and negotiator in foreign trade matters and, in particular, with the European Common Market. Herter died in Washington on December 30, 1966. Herter's diplomacy was marked by efforts at closer Western ties and improved U.S.–Soviet relations, the latter having been thwarted by the U-2 incident. *NCAB*, 1:14; *New York Times*, January 1, 1967; Noble, G. Bernard, "Christian Herter," in Ferrell, Robert H., ed., *American Secretaries of State and Their Diplomacy*, vol. 18 (1970).

HIGGINS, MARGUERITE (1920–1966). The best-known war correspondent of the Korean War (1950–1953), Marguerite Higgins was born of American parents in Hong Kong on September 3, 1920. She graduated from the University of California (B.A., 1941) and Columbia (M.A., 1942) and became a reporter for the *New York Herald Tribune* in 1942. A war correspondent in London in 1944–1945, Higgins was promoted to chief of the Berlin bureau of the *Herald Tribune* in 1945, covering many postwar events in Europe. In 1950, she went to Tokyo and in June of that year moved on to Korea to cover the war there. A controversy arose when Major General Walton H. Walker ordered her to leave the front lines, but after she appealed to General Douglas MacArthur,* the order was rescinded. Her coverage of the war from the front lines won for her the Pulitzer Prize in 1951 and led to a book, *War in Korea: Report of a Woman Combat Correspondent* (1951). Higgins remained in Korea until 1958 and then returned to the United States to work as a diplomatic correspondent based in Washington, making one more trip in the mid-1960s to observe the Vietnam War firsthand. She married William E. Hall, wrote other books, including *Our Vietnam Nightmare* (1965), and died January 3, 1966, in Washington of a rare tropical ailment contracted in Asia. *CB* (1951):274–76; *New York Times*, January 4, 1966; *WWWA*, 4 (1961–1968):438.

HILL, DAVID JAYNE (1850–1932). A man equally prominent in the fields of education and diplomacy, David Jayne Hill was born in Plainfield, New Jersey, on June 10, 1850, and graduated from the University at Lewisburg (Pennsylvania), now Bucknell, in 1874 and received an A.M. degree in 1877. He taught at Bucknell and proved his worth quickly, for he was chosen its president in 1879. In 1888, he moved to the presidency of the University of Rochester, remaining there until 1896. After two years of foreign study, he was named assistant secretary of state in 1898. In this office, he frequently served as acting secretary of state during the illnesses of John Hay.* Additionally, Hill prepared the instructions for the U.S. delegations to the first Hague Conference (1899)* and to the Second International Conference of American States, Mexico City (1902).* In 1903, he was named minister to Switzerland, where his duties were light enough for him to write *History of Diplomacy in the International Development of Europe* (2 vols., 1905–1906). Hill was minister to the Netherlands, 1905–1907; here his routine was broken only by membership on the U.S. delegation to the second Hague Conference (1907).* In 1908, his diplomatic career was capped with appointment as ambassador to Germany. In his three years at the Berlin embassy, Hill faced no major diplomatic problems but rather dealt with minor matters of extradition, expulsion of Mormon missionaries, and the presentation to Germany of a statue of General Friedrich von Steuben of Revolutionary War fame. After some initial tentativeness, Hill and the kaiser formed a good relationship, and there was disappointment in Germany when the ambassador was forced to resign in 1911 for the political convenience of the Republican party. Wilson's policies after 1913 did not please Hill; he argued for preparedness and supported U.S. entry into the war and strongly opposed U.S. entry into the League of Nations* after the war because of the flexibility and vagueness of its covenant and a personal antipathy toward Wilson. During the 1920s, Hill became a leading spokesman for the peace movement but nonetheless opposed the World Court* because he felt it was too closely tied to the league to be a true world court. Hill, who was twice married, died in Washington on March 2, 1932. Among his other writings are biographies of Washington Irving* and William Cullen Bryant, a psychology textbook, books on Christianity and socialism, and volumes on foreign policy, including *Present Problems in Foreign Policy* (1919), *American World Policies* (1920), and *The Problem of a World Court* (1927). *DAB*, Supp. 1:401; Parkman, Aubrey, *David Jayne Hill and the Problem of World Peace* (1975); *New York Times*, March 3, 1932.

HILLENBRAND, MARTIN JOSEPH ANTHONY (b. 1905). A native of Youngstown, Ohio, where he was born August 1, 1915, Martin J. Hillenbrand graduated from the University of Dayton (1937), received advanced degrees from Columbia University (M.A., 1938; Ph.D., 1948), and studied further at Harvard (1949–1950). Entering the Foreign Service in 1939, he had served in minor posts in Zurich, Rangoon, Calcutta, Laurenco Marques, Bremen, and Washington by 1952. From 1952 to 1956, he was first secretary at the Paris embassy. In 1956, he became a political adviser in Berlin, the beginning of a long series of German-related assignments: director, Office of German Affairs, 1958–1962; director, Berlin Task Force, 1962–1963, where he directed the management of the waning Berlin crisis* on a day-to-day basis; and minister and deputy chief of mission, Bonn, 1963–1967. In 1967, Hillenbrand was named ambassador to Hungary, serving there two years before returning to Washington as assistant secretary of state for European affairs, a post he held until 1972. That year, the Nixon administration named him ambassador to Germany. In four rather quiet years there, his main concern was the presence of U.S. troops; in 1974, he signed an agreement by which Germany agreed to provide $2.2 billion over a two-year period to help maintain the American military establishment. He retired from diplomatic service in 1976. From 1977 to 1982, Hillenbrand was director-general of the Institute of International Affairs in Paris, and since 1982, he has been Dean Rusk Professor of International Relations at the University of Georgia. Married to Faith Stewart in 1941, Hillenbrand has written or coauthored three books: *Power and Morals* (1949), *Zwischen Politik und Ethnik* (1968), and *Germany in an Era of Transition* (1983). Ausland, John C., and Col. Hugh C. Richardson, "Crisis in Management: Berlin, Cyprus, Laos," *Foreign Affairs* 44 (January 1966):291–303; *New York Times*, April 26, 1974; *WWA* (1986–1987):1287.

HILSMAN, ROGER, JR. (b. 1919). Born in Waco, Texas, on November 23, 1919, Roger Hilsman graduated from West Point in 1943, served four years in the army, and returned to school, receiving an M.A. (1950) and Ph.D. (1951) from Yale. From 1950 to 1953, he worked in London and Frankfurt on North Atlantic Treaty Organization* planning. From 1953 to 1956, he was a research associate and professor at Princeton. For the next five years, Hilsman was connected with the Library of Congress and Johns Hopkins University as a researcher, writing studies on post–World War II military policy and foreign relations. In 1961, he joined the Kennedy administration as director of the State Department's Bureau of Intelligence and Research. In this position, he traveled to crisis areas and made reports to the secretary of state. For South Vietnam, he recommended techniques to deal with guerrilla warfare and popular support. From 1963 to 1964, Hilsman was assistant secretary of state for Far Eastern affairs, where he continued to be involved with South Vietnam and especially with U.S. relations with President Ngo Dinh Diem. He studied the Sino-Soviet split and recommended "leaving the door open" to altering U.S. policy toward China. In 1968, his article in *Foreign Affairs* recommended deescalating the Vietnam War and implementing the policy that came to be known as Vietnamization.* Since 1964, Hilsman has taught at Columbia University. Married to Eleanor Willis Hoyt in 1946, he is the author of *To Move a Nation* (1967), a study of Kennedy administration foreign policy, as well as *The Politics of Policy Making in Defense and Foreign Affairs* (1971), *The Crouching Future* (1975), *To Govern America* (1979), *The Politics of Governing America* (1985), and *The Politics of Policy Making* (1986). *CB* (1964):194–96; Halbertstam, David, *The Best and the Brightest* (1972); Hilsman, Roger, Jr., "Must We Invade the North?" *Foreign Affairs* 46 (April 1968): 425–41; *WWA* (1986–1987):1289.

HISE, ELIJAH (1801–1867). Born in Allegheny County, Pennsylvania, on Independence Day, 1801, Elijah Hise grew up in Kentucky and received an LL.B. degree from Transylvania College in Lexington in 1823. He became a successful lawyer in Russellville, Kentucky, married Elvira D. Stewart in 1832, and served in the Kentucky legislature. In 1848, he was appointed chargé d'affaires* in Guatemala. At this time, Anglo-American rivalry was quite sharp in Central America, with the United States concerned about British expansion along the east coast of the isthmus. Hise was instructed to gather information about the region to aid the Polk administration in making policy. However, he exceeded his instructions by negotiating treaties of friendship with Nicaragua, Honduras, and Guatemala, hoping to blunt British advances and prevent monopolization of the canal route. He then concluded a canal treaty with Nicaragua (1849), which was never ratified and led to his recall. Returning to Kentucky, he practiced law and served as a judge on the Kentucky Court of Appeals (1851–1854) and a term in the U.S. House of Representatives (1866–1867) before taking his own life in Russellville on May 8, 1867. *DAB*, 9:69; *NCAB*, 12:54; Williams, Mary W., *Anglo-American Isthmian Diplomacy, 1815–1915* (1916).

HITCHCOCK, ETHAN ALLEN (1835–1909). Ethan A. Hitchcock was born September 19, 1835, in Mobile, Alabama, attended an academy in New Haven, Connecticut, and moved to St. Louis in 1851. In 1860, he went to China and engaged in the commission business, becoming a partner in Olyphant and Company of Hong Kong. Twelve years later he was able to retire from this business with a great deal of wealth. He returned to St. Louis and from 1874 to 1897 was involved in a variety of business activities ranging from plate glass to steel. At the same time, he grew active in the Republican party and developed a friendship with William McKinley. When McKinley became president in 1897, Hitchcock was his choice as minister to Russia. In 1897, the legation in St.

Petersburg was upgraded to an embassy, and Hitchcock became America's first ambassador to that country. As ambassador, Hitchcock was successful in increasing American exports to Russia and was useful in keeping the Russians informed about the Spanish-American War and the territorial acquisitions of the United States after the war. He resigned in December 1898 to accept the post of secretary of the interior. Hitchcock remained interior secretary until 1907 and proved a diligent investigator into public land frauds. He married Margaret D. Collier in 1869 and died in Washington on April 9, 1909. *DAB*, 9:73; *NCAB*, 11:16; *New York Times*, April 10, 1909.

HITCHCOCK RESERVATIONS, five mild reservations to the Treaty of Versailles,* acceptable to President Woodrow Wilson (the first four he drafted) and used by Senator G. M. Hitchcock (D., Nebraska) in Senate debate over the treaty, especially in opposition to the Lodge reservations.* Never attached to the treaty, these reservations were interpretive rather than substantive and involved, among other things, requiring the approval of Congress in conjunction with the collective security* obligation of Article X,* and clarifying Article XV, which specified that documents concerning domestic matters did not have to be submitted to the League of Nations*. Bailey, Thomas A., *Woodrow Wilson and the Great Betrayal* (1945); Smith, Daniel M., *The Great Departure* (1965).

HOARE-LAVAL PLAN (1935). This plan was proposed by Sir Samuel Hoare, British foreign secretary, and Pierre Laval, premier of France, as a way to end the Italo-Ethiopian War.* If implemented, the plan would have given Italy 60,000 square miles of territory in Africa and economic control of the southern half of Ethiopia, including the most fertile areas of the country. Ethiopia would have been compensated, in a manner of speaking, with 3,000 square miles of territory elsewhere. Withdrawn after protests from other Western powers, the plan demonstrated the weakness of collective security* measures through the League of Nations* and cost Hoare and Laval their jobs. President Franklin D. Roosevelt and State Department officials publicly declared outrage at what they felt was traditional Old World diplomatic dealing, and U.S. isolationists* were further fueled by this display of European duplicity. Divine, Robert A., *Illusion of Neutrality* (1962); Offner, Arnold A., *The Origins of the Second World War* (1975).

HOFFMAN, PAUL GRAY (1891–1974). Born in Western Springs, Illinois, on April 26, 1891, Paul G. Hoffman studied at the University of Chicago and served in the army during World War I. He was a successful automobile salesman in California as early as 1911 and by 1925 was a district sales manager. That year, he joined Studebaker as a vice-president, rising to president in 1935 and remaining at that post until 1948. After heading a $10 million drive for China relief at the end of World War II, Hoffman was named to the Harriman Committee (on foreign aid) in 1947. Already a strong supporter of the Marshall Plan,* he was appointed its chief administrator in 1948, remaining in the post for over two years and overseeing the disbursement of $10 billion in aid. Perhaps troubled by the increasing militarization of European aid, he left the Marshall Plan in 1950 to head the Ford Foundation. In 1952, he was an enthusiastic supporter of General Dwight D. Eisenhower's quest for the Republican nomination and subsequent election, earning the wrath of conservatives in the process. In 1953, Hoffman returned to the failing Studebaker Corporation as chairman of the board; despite a merger with Packard, its fortunes did not improve, and he resigned in 1956 to accept an appointment to the U.S. delegation at the United Nations.* Two years later, he moved to the United Nations Secretariat as head of the United Nations Special Fund, the organization's principal development agency. In 1966, the Special Fund was merged with the Extended Program for Technical Assistance to form the United Nations Development Fund, and Hoffman assumed the directorship of that, where he tirelessly raised money from industrial nations for use as seed money in development projects of Third World* countries. Throughout his career, he was a strong advocate of foreign aid as a means toward political stability and the growth of free enterprise. Twice married, Hoffman wrote several books, including *Seven Roads to Safety* (1939), *Peace Can Be Won* (1951), and *World without Want* (1962). He died in New York City on October 8, 1974. Raucher, Alan R., *Paul G. Hoffman: Architect of Foreign Aid* (1985); *New York Times*, October 9, 1974; *WWWA*, 6 (1974–1976):196.

HOLCOMBE, CHESTER (1844–1912). Born in Winfield, New York, on October 16, 1844, Chester Holcombe was educated for the ministry, graduating from Union College in 1862, receiving a license to preach in 1867, and being ordained in the Presbyterian church in 1868. In 1869, he went to China as a missionary, ran a boys' school, and wrote religious books in Chinese, including a life of Christ. His knowledge of Chinese led to his becoming an interpreter for the U.S. legation in 1871. From 1876 to 1885 Holcombe was legation secretary and occasionally chargé d'affaires.* In this position he helped draft the U.S.–Chinese treaty (1880) controlling Chinese immigration to the United States. This treaty authorized the United States to regulate or suspend but not prohibit Chinese immigration. Protests from the west coast states led to the Chinese Exclusion Act (1882).* Holcombe also helped negotiate the first treaty between the United States and Korea (1882). After 1885, he remained in China as an adviser to the Chinese government, helping to plan a large loan and a 3,000-mile railway, while hoping in vain, for an appointment as U.S. minister to China. Finally, he returned to the United States, sold Chinese goods, and wrote and lectured on China until his death in Rochester, New York, on April 25, 1912. *DAB*, 9:133; Dennett, Tyler, *Americans in Eastern Asia* (1922); *NCAB*, 3:311.

HOLT, HAMILTON BOWEN (1872–1951). A prominent peace activist, journalist, and educator in the first half of the twentieth century, Hamilton Holt was born in Brooklyn on August 19, 1872, and graduated from Yale in 1894. He went to work for the liberal weekly magazine, the *Independent*, in 1894, becoming managing editor in 1897 and owner in 1912. As owner, he appointed himself editor in 1913 and remained in that position until 1921, consistently supporting various Progressive era reforms. Holt's involvement with the peace movement began in 1903; he supported a world organization and became a leading internationalist before World War I. He attended the second Hague Peace Conference (1907),* founded the World Federalist League in 1910, and was active in other, similar organizations, especially the League to Enforce Peace.* After World War I, Holt attended the Paris Peace Conference* and become a believer in the League of Nations,* which he continued to promote during the early 1920s. In 1925, he rather abruptly changed careers to become president of Rollins College in Florida. There he instituted an innovative curriculum, raised a great deal of money, and built a beautiful campus, but the college never achieved the national prominence he had anticipated. He married Alexina Crawford in 1899; she died in 1936. Holt retired from the presidency of Rollins in 1949 and died in Woodstock, Connecticut, on April 26, 1951. *DAB*, Supp. 5:307–9; Herman, Sondra, *Eleven against War* (1969); Kuehl, Warren F., *Hamilton Holt: Journalist, Internationalist, and Educator* (1960) and *Seeking World Order* (1969); Marchand, C. Ronald, *The American Peace Movement, 1898–1918* (1972); *New York Times*, April 27, 1951.

HOLY ALLIANCE. Created in September 1815 by Czar Alexander, this alliance bound Russia, Prussia, and Austria in a "Christian union of charity, peace, and love." It is frequently confused with the Quadruple Alliance,* of the same era, which also included Great Britain. The Holy Alliance was subsequently endorsed by nearly every monarch in Europe, except those of Great Britain and the Ottoman Empire, but it is generally considered to have had no practical importance. Thomson, David, *Europe since Napoleon* (1960).

HOOVER MORATORIUM (1931). On June 20, 1931, President Herbert Hoover announced a one-year suspension of all intergovernmental payments, including debts and reparations,* subject to the agreement of other nations. France, which stood to lose a considerable amount in reparations payments, balked but finally agreed on July 6. Congress approved the moratorium in December (but made the act of approval retroactive to July 1). Designed to help Germany out of its depression-induced financial crisis, the moratorium resulted in another agreement in July 1931 for a standstill on German short-term debts and led to the Lausanne Conference, June 1932.* Ellis, L. Ethan, *Republican Foreign Policy, 1921–1933* (1968); Ferrell, Robert, *American Diplomacy in the Great Depression* (1957); *FR* (1931), 1:1–249.

HOPKINS, HARRY (1890–1946). Principal aide and adviser to President Franklin D. Roosevelt, Harry Hopkins was born in Sioux City, Iowa, on August 17, 1890, and graduated from Grinnell College in 1912. His early career was directed toward social work. After five years as a New York City social worker,

Hopkins held positions with the Red Cross (1917–1922), the (New York) Association for Improving the Condition of the Poor (1922–1924), and the New York Tuberculosis Association (1924–1933). In 1933, Hopkins joined the Roosevelt administration as director of the Federal Emergency Relief Administration and later the Works Progress Administration, and in 1938, he became secretary of commerce. His next assignment, in 1941, was Lend-Lease* administrator, and after some months at that job, he moved into the White House as an assistant to the president. As Roosevelt's aide, he went to Moscow in July 1941 to make personal contact with Stalin and arrange for Russia's participation in Lend-Lease. He went to the Atlantic Conference (August 1941)* between Roosevelt and Churchill and attended all the other major wartime conferences (except Potsdam), ably advising Roosevelt, accurately representing his views, and winning the high regard of both Churchill and Stalin. After Roosevelt's death, Hopkins continued on as an adviser to Truman, especially on United Nations* matters, went to Moscow (May-June 1945) to plan the Potsdam Conference,* and helped break U.S.-Soviet deadlocks over the United Nations Security Council composition and rules and the Polish question. In late 1945, he retired from government service and became chairman of the Coat and Suit Industry. He died in New York City on January 29, 1946. Hopkins was married three times and wrote a book, *Spending to Save* (1936). *DAB*, Supp. 4:391; Feis, Herbert, *Churchill-Roosevelt-Stalin* (1957); *NCAB*, 42:16; Sherwood, Robert, *Roosevelt and Hopkins* (1948); *New York Times*, January 30, 1946; Tuttle, Dwight W., *Harry L. Hopkins and Anglo-American-Soviet Relations, 1941–1945* (1987).

HORNBECK, STANLEY KUHL (1883–1966). One of the foremost U.S. experts on Far Eastern affairs before World War II, Stanley K. Hornbeck was born in Franklin, Massachusetts, on May 4, 1883, attended the University of Colorado but graduated from the University of Denver in 1903, was a Rhodes scholar at Oxford, 1904–1907, and received a Ph.D. from the University of Wisconsin in 1909, where he was a student of Paul S. Reinsch.* Between 1909 and 1916, he taught at the University of Hangchow and other institutions in China. After service with army ordnance during World War I, Hornbeck became a member of the U.S. delegation at the Paris Peace Conference (1919),* where he worked against a pro-Japanese settlement on the Shantung question.* During the 1920s, he taught at Harvard but in 1928 resumed his career in diplomacy by assuming the post of chief, Division of Far Eastern Affairs, which he held for nearly a decade. In this period, he maintained a sympathetic attitude toward China and took a somewhat stronger stand than most other U.S. officials during the Manchurian crisis (1931),* advocating an embargo against Japan if the moral sanctions of the League of Nations* failed. He aided Secretary of State Henry L. Stimson* in writing an open letter to Senator William E. Borah,* stressing U.S. rights in the Pacific and the sanctity of the Nine-Power Treaty* and implicitly threatening to increase U.S. naval buildup, an embargo on war materiel to Japan, and, later, taking even broader economic sanctions against Japan. By

1941, he was calling for a greater amount of aid to China, in order to tie the Japanese military forces down. Before long, he became a supporter of unlimited aid to Chiang Kai-shek. In 1944, he was rather abruptly removed from Far Eastern concerns and made ambassador to the Netherlands. The Dutch government was still in exile in London; Hornbeck accompanied it back to the Hague and made arrangements for the resumption of normal diplomatic relations there. Feeling that the Dutch mission was a kind of diplomatic exile, Hornbeck left it and the State Department in 1947 and devoted his time to writing books and articles on Far Eastern affairs. He married Virginia Barkalow in 1938 and frequently spoke out in opposition to the recognition of the People's Republic of China and in favor of U.S. efforts in Korea and Vietnam. Hornbeck died in Washington on December 10, 1966. Buhite, Russell, "Stanley K. Hornbeck and American Far Eastern Policy," in Merli, Frank J., and Theodore A. Wilson, eds., *Makers of American Diplomacy*, vol. 2 (1974); Burns, Richard Dean, "Stanley K. Hornbeck: The Diplomacy of the Open Door," in Burns, R. D., and Edward M. Bennett, eds., *Diplomats in Crisis* (1974); Doenecke, Justus D., comp., *The Diplomacy of Frustration* (1981); Ferrell, Robert H., *American Diplomacy in the Great Depression* (1957); *New York Times*, December 12, 1966.

HORTALEZ (RODRIGUE) AND COMPANY, a fictitious company organized in 1776 by Pierre A. C. Beaumarchais, the French poet and secret agent, to deliver a loan to the United States of 1 million livres in the form of munitions. This dummy company served as a conduit through which the United States received considerable quantities of war supplies from France between 1776 and 1778. Payments to this company led to a controversy between Arthur Lee* and Silas Deane,* American diplomats seeking aid from France. Deane accused Lee of enriching himself with government funds. Bemis, Samuel F., *The Diplomacy of the American Revolution* (1935); Stourzh, Gerald, *Benjamin Franklin and American Foreign Policy* (1954).

HOT SPRINGS CONFERENCE (1943). At this meeting, held from May 8 to June 3, 1943, in Hot Springs, Virginia, delegations from several member countries of the United Nations* agreed that a permanent international organization on food and agriculture should be established. The conference resulted in the creation of an Interim Commission of Food and Agriculture, which by August 1944 had written a constitution for the Food and Agriculture Organization (FAO), affiliated with the United Nations organization as basically an advisory body for production, marketing, and technical assistance. McNeill, William H., *America, Britain, and Russia* (1953).

HOTZE, HENRY (1833–1887). A native of Zurich, Switzerland, where he was born September 2, 1833, Henry Hotze moved to the United States and became a citizen after his education at a Jesuit college. By 1855, he was in Alabama working as a journalist on the *Mobile Register*. When the Civil War broke out, Hotze was designated public opinion director in Europe for the Confederacy and instructed to persuade the British that the Confederacy was a viable government that could carry on the war and maintain its independence. In London, he wrote editorials for the *London Post* and other papers and published the *Index*, a "Confederate-British" journal, from 1862 to 1865. By 1863, Hotze favored emancipation of slaves if necessary to win southern independence, and in 1864, after the recall of Edwin De Leon,* he worked in France planting news items in newspapers. Hotze was an accomplished propagandist and, according to Wakelyn, "probably the most talented Confederate in Europe." Hotze lived in Europe after the war and died in Zug, Switzerland, on April 19, 1887. He was married to Ruby Senac. Cullop, Charles P., *Confederate Propaganda in Europe* (1969); Owsley, Frank, *King Cotton Diplomacy* (1959); Wakelyn, Jon L., *Biographical Directory of the Confederacy* (1977).

HOUGHTON, ALANSON BIGELOW (1863–1941). Born into a prominent Boston family on October 10, 1863, Alanson B. Houghton was educated at St. Paul's School in Concord, New Hampshire, and at Harvard, from which he graduated in 1886. He studied further at Göttingen, Berlin, and Paris before joining his father's factory, the Corning Glass Works, Corning, New York, as a clerk. By 1903, he was second vice-president; by 1910, he had become president, and eight years later, he became chairman of the board. A Republican, Houghton was twice a presidential elector and a member of the U.S. House of Representatives (1919–1923). In 1922, the Harding administration selected him ambassador to Germany. He spent three years in the swirl of Weimar Republic affairs and played an important role in convincing German leaders to accept the Dawes Plan (1924).* In 1925, he was transferred to the London embassy, where his calm style and good humor were a marked contrast to the vigorous outspokenness of George Harvey,* ambassador from 1921 to 1923. There were no major diplomatic conflicts between the two nations, and Houghton's cultured demeanor and businesslike attitude blended into the British scene well. He returned to the United States in 1928, made an unsuccessful bid for a U.S. Senate seat from New York, and resumed his post as board chairman of Corning Glass. Houghton married Adelaide Wellington in 1891 and died in South Dartmouth, Massachusetts, on September 16, 1941. Allen, H. C., *Great Britain and the United States* (1969); Jones, Kenneth Paul, *U.S. Diplomats in Europe 1919–1941* (1981); *NCAB*, 13:7; *New York Times*, September 16, 1941.

HOUGHTON, AMORY (1899–1981). Associated with Corning Glass Works since 1921 and chairman of its board for twenty years (1941–1961), Amory Houghton, son of Alanson B. Houghton,* served as ambassador to France during the second term of Dwight D. Eisenhower (1957–1961). Born July 27, 1899, in Corning, New York, Houghton graduated from Harvard in 1921, married Laura DeKay Richardson that year, and joined Corning. During World War II, he held government posts with the War Production Board and spent some time in London with Lend-Lease* and the U.S. Mission for Economic Affairs. In

London, his responsibilities included overseeing the flow of materials to Britain and the front lines in Europe. In France, Houghton enjoyed good relations with President Charles de Gaulle and thought highly of French policy toward its former African colonies. In the main, however, Houghton's mission was socially oriented. After 1961, Houghton continued his association with Corning until his death February 21, 1981, in Charleston, South Carolina. Luce, Clare Boothe, "The Ambassadorial Issue: Professionals or Amateurs?" *Foreign Affairs* 36 (October 1957): 108–9; *New York Times*, February 26, December 14, 1957, January 13, 1961, February 22, 1981; *WWA* (1976–1977):1506.

HOUSE, EDWARD HOWARD (1836–1901). Edward H. House was born in Boston on September 5, 1836, and studied music as a youth. A bank note engraver from 1851 to 1854, he joined the *Boston Courier* as a music and drama critic and moved to the *New York Tribune* in 1858. During the Civil War, he was a special correspondent with Union armies in Virginia and, after the war, managed theaters in New York and London. A return to journalism with the *New York Times* in 1870 was short-lived; in 1871, he was appointed Professor of the English Language and Literature at Nanko University in Tokyo, soon becoming the leading English teacher in Japan. In 1873, at the invitation of the Japanese government, he accompanied an army mission to Formosa, sending dispatches back to the *New York Herald Tribune*. His book, *The Japanese Expedition to Formosa* (1875), detailed this experience. In 1877, he established and published the *Tokyo Times*, an English-language paper, expressing a highly nationalistic viewpoint and criticizing other foreigners in Japan. By 1880, House had offended enough people that the government ended its subsidization of his newspaper, but he continued to express his views favorable to Japanese expansion. He returned to the United States in 1880 but soon traveled on to London, where he suffered a stroke in 1883. He returned to Japan, where the government granted him a pension, and he spent his time writing novels and articles, including *Yone Santo, a Child of Japan* (1889), an antimissionary novel. In 1900, he was appointed director of the Imperial Court Orchestra and conducted the first orchestral concerts given in Japan. House died in Tokyo on December 17, 1901. *DAB*, 9:257; *WWWA*, 1 (1897–1942):591.

HOUSE, EDWARD MANDELL (1858–1938). Born in Houston on September 28, 1858, Col. Edward M. House attended Cornell University and became wealthy as a young man managing the family cotton plantations. In the 1890s, he entered Texas Democratic politics as campaign manager for Governor James Stephen Hogg. By 1911, he was involved in national Democratic party campaigns and in that year met Woodrow Wilson and was influential in securing Texan support for Wilson's nomination for president the following year. After Wilson's election, House became the president's most intimate adviser, especially in foreign affairs. He formed a close relationship with British Foreign Secretary Edward Grey and spent considerable time in Europe from 1914 to 1916 trying to reduce Anglo-German tensions. In December 1917, House served as chief of the American mission to the Interallied Conference* to coordinate the American and Allied war effort. He also worked with Wilson in formulating the structure of the League of Nations* and worked out a pre-Armistice agreement based on the Fourteen Points,* a task considered his greatest diplomatic achievement. At the Paris Peace Conference,* House was Wilson's chief deputy, at which time differences between the two rose over the degree of conciliation to extend to the demands of Britain and France. The final break came when House urged the president to compromise with the Senate over the ratification issue; he never saw Wilson after June 1919. In later life, House traveled frequently to Europe, maintaining his contacts with European leaders, and he advised Franklin D. Roosevelt in the 1932 campaign. House died of pleurisy in Austin, Texas, on March 28, 1938. *DAB*, Supp. 2:310; George, Alexander, and Juliette L. George, *Woodrow Wilson and Colonel House* (1956); May, Ernest, *The World War and American Isolation, 1914–1917* (1959); Seymour, Charles, *The Intimate Papers of Colonel House*, 4 vols. (1926–1928); *New York Times*, March 29, 1938.

HOUSE-GREY MEMORANDUM (1916). This agreement, made on February 22, 1916, between Col. Edward M. House* and Lord Grey, British foreign secretary, stated that the United States should cooperate with the Allies against the Central Powers, with force if necessary, to end the war and create a new world order. The agreement reflected House's pro-British and pro-democratic sentiments, as well as the more general feeling that American security would be threatened by German victory. The memorandum also provided that the United States call an international conference at a time opportune for the Allies; if Germany refused to attend, the United States would consider entering the war against Germany. If the conference were held but produced no results, the United States would join the Allied side. Finally, if Allied fortunes rose soon, the United States would not call a conference. Levin, N. Gordon, Jr., *Woodrow Wilson and World Politics* (1968); Seymour, Charles, *American Diplomacy during the World War* (1934).

HUBBARD, RICHARD BENNETT (1832–1901). Born in Walton County, Georgia, on November 1, 1832, Richard B. Hubbard graduated from Mercer College in Georgia (1851) and from Harvard Law School (1853). He settled in Tyler, Texas, as a lawyer but soon became involved in that state's Democratic party politics, campaigning for James Buchanan* in 1856 and winning renown as an orator ("Demosthenes of Texas") and an appointment as U.S. attorney for the Western District of Texas. After service in the state legislature, 1859–1861, he fought for the Confederacy during the Civil War but returned to law practice and Democratic politics after the war, helping to "redeem" Texas from carpetbag government in the 1870s. Hubbard was elected lieutenant governor in 1873 and governor in 1877. With the return of the Democrats to national power in the presidency of Grover Cleveland, Hubbard was named minister to Japan

(1885–1889). There his main task was working on treaty revision, involving such issues as the tariff, extraterritoriality, and the provision for most-favored-nation treatment* in separate negotiations and at a conference involving all the Western powers (1886–1887). Nothing concrete came from these talks; the treaty revisions were not completed for another decade. In addition, he observed Sino-Japanese rivalry in Korea, complicated by Russian and British intrigues and separate negotiations between France and China, and he dealt with a number of minor cases involving claims and discriminatory treatment against Americans. He did put together what Treat calls "The Incomplete Treaty of 1889," but it was abandoned as unsatisfactory by his successor, John Franklin Swift,* who continued negotiations. After his Japanese mission, Hubbard for the most part retired from public affairs but did lecture occasionally; he published a book, *The United States in the Far East* (1899). Twice married, he died July 12, 1901, in Tyler, Texas. *DAB*, 9:331; Treat, Payson J., *Diplomatic Relations between the United States and Japan, 1853–1895*, 2 vols. (1932); Turner, Martha Anne, *Richard Bennett Hubbard: An American Life* (1979); *WWWA*, 1 (1897–1942):600.

HUDSON'S BAY COMPANY, British fur-trading company. Chartered by King Charles II in 1670, this company originally had a profitable monopoly on trade in the Hudson Bay area. In the Revolutionary War era, the company was active in fur trading north of the Great Lakes, and in 1800 the founding of the North West Company brought about competition. The successful expedition of Alexander MacKenzie to the Pacific Northwest (1789–1793) drew both companies into what came to be known as the Oregon Territory. In 1821, Hudson's Bay Company absorbed the North West Company and became the dominant commercial enterprise in the area. The company built forts from the Columbia River to Alaska and in 1838 established a subsidiary, Puget's Sound Agricultural Company, to begin sheep-grazing operations near the sound. By the 1840s, however, American migration and British commercial decline, among other causes, led to the Oregon Treaty (1846)* and the removal of the company's influence south of 49° north latitude. McInnis, Edgar, *Canada* (1959); Merk, Frederick, *The Oregon Question* (1967); Pletcher, David, *The Diplomacy of Annexation* (1973).

HUGHES, CHARLES EVANS (1862–1948). Secretary of state under Presidents Warren G. Harding and Calvin Coolidge, Charles Evans Hughes was born in Glens Falls, New York, on April 11, 1862, attended Colgate University, and graduated from Brown University (A.B., 1881; A.M., 1884) and from Columbia Law School (1884). Admitted to the bar in 1884, he first tutored and worked as a law clerk and then practiced law in New York City until 1906 except for a two-year stint teaching at Cornell (1891–1893). In 1907, he was elected Republican governor of New York, serving one term and gaining a reputation as a reformer. Between 1910 and 1921, Hughes was an associate justice of the Supreme Court, except in 1916 in his unsuccessful presidential race against incumbent Woodrow Wilson. Hughes was a reservationist* on the League of Nations* but believed in international cooperation, and his four years (1921–1925) as secretary of state contain numerous examples of his efforts to institute a highly legalistic notion of international relations. He supported U.S. affiliation with the World Court* and involved the United States in the Reparations Commission* in 1923, whose work led to the Dawes Plan (1924).* He sponsored the Washington Conference* and succeeded in winning acceptance of a number of treaties aimed at naval arms limitation and stability in the Far East. He upheld the policy of nonrecognition of Soviet Russia and employed the same policy in Mexico until 1923 in order to protect American interests. However, in other areas of Latin America, Hughes moved away from the prevailing policy of military intervention and negotiated a multilateral arbitration* at the Santiago Conference (1923).* He signed a peace treaty (Treaty of Berlin, 1921)* ending World War I with Germany and a treaty giving $25 million to Colombia for Panama. Although legalistic, Hughes was enough of a realist to recognize that the Johnson-Reed Act (1924),* severely limiting immigration into the United States, would have negative consequences and advocated instead a reciprocal immigration treaty. In 1925, he returned to private law practice, occasionally representing the United States at international conferences, but in 1930 he reentered public life as chief justice of the Supreme Court, a position he held until 1941. He was married to Antoinette Carter in 1888, and after several years of retirement in Washington, he died in Osterville, Massachusetts, on August 27, 1948. *DAB*, Supp. 4:403; Glad, Betty, *Charles Evans Hughes and the Illusions of Innocence* (1966); Perkins, Dexter, *Charles Evans Hughes and American Democratic Statesmanship* (1956); Pusey, Merlo J., *Charles Evans Hughes*, 2 vols. (1951); *New York Times*, August 28, 1948; Venson, John Chalmers, "Charles Evans Hughes," in Graebner, N., ed., *An Uncertain Tradition* (1961).

HUGHES, CHRISTOPHER (1786–1849). Born in Baltimore in 1786, Christopher Hughes studied law and entered the diplomatic service at a relatively early age. In 1814, he was legation secretary in London and later that year became secretary of the U.S. peace commission at Ghent, favorably impressing commissioners John Quincy Adams* and Henry Clay.* Two years later he was sent to New Granada as a special envoy to secure the release of some American prisoners; later that year, he was appointed legation secretary in Stockholm, remaining there until 1825 and serving as chargé d'affaires* much of the time. In 1825, Hughes was appointed chargé to the Netherlands, but when the Senate did not approve his appointment as minister in 1828, he remained chargé until 1830. He then went back to Stockholm as chargé, 1830–1842, and once again to the Netherlands as chargé, 1842–1845. He retired in 1845 to Baltimore and died there September 18, 1849. Hughes married Laura Sophia Smith in 1811 and throughout his career was highly regarded for his ability to report news clearly and for his wit and social grace. According to the *NCAB*, Hughes was known around the world for "saying more wise things, strange things, droll things than ever tongue uttered or mind conceived." *DAB*, 9:346; *NCAB*, 7:165.

HUKUANG RAILWAY LOAN (1909). This loan was made to China in June 1909 by a consortium of English, French, and German bankers for the construction of railroads in central and southern China. Willard Straight,* recently resigned from the State Department, represented a group of American bankers, who, after President William Howard Taft personally intervened with the Chinese prince regent, also received a share of the loan. American involvement in this arrangement is considered to be the beginning of dollar diplomacy* in the Far East. Cohen, Warren I., *America's Response to China* (1971); *FR* (1910), 269–292; *FR* (1912), 87–159.

HULL, CORDELL (1871–1955). Secretary of state during nearly all the long presidency of Franklin D. Roosevelt, Cordell Hull spent nearly twelve years in the office, a record matched by no other secretary. Hull was born in Oberton (now Pickett) County, Tennessee, on October 2, 1871, attended National Normal University in Lebanon, Ohio, from 1889 to 1890, and graduated from Cumberland Law School in 1891, gaining admittance to the bar the same year. He lost little time in embarking on a political career, serving in the Tennessee legislature, 1893–1897, and after service in Cuba during the Spanish-American War, becoming a judge in the Fifth Judicial Circuit of Tennessee, 1903–1907. He entered the U.S. House of Representatives in 1907, serving continuously (except for two years, 1921–1922) until 1931, when he was elected to the Senate. In Congress, he was a major author of the federal income tax system (1913) and the federal inheritance act (1916), but he had little connection with foreign affairs except as an advocate of reciprocal trade agreements. Chosen by Roosevelt in 1933 as secretary of state largely because of his power and influence in Congress, Hull concentrated much of his effort on reciprocity and Latin American relations, leaving European and wartime diplomacy to Roosevelt and Harry Hopkins.* In 1934, with Hull's enthusiastic support, Congress passed the Reciprocal Trade Agreements Act,* giving the executive branch broad powers to negotiate bilateral trade agreements based on mutually beneficial tariff reductions. Toward Latin America, Hull did much to demonstrate that the United States had ended its policy of intervention; that he was convincing is shown by the high degree of Western Hemisphere solidarity during World War II. During the war, Hull's effectiveness was damaged by a quarrel with Under Secretary of State Benjamin Sumner Welles* over access to the president; Welles resigned, but Hull's wartime diplomatic activity was confined largely to planning for the United Nations* (he played a major role at the Dumbarton Oaks Conference, 1944*) and ensuring a maximum of bipartisan congressional support for the administration's war policies. For his work in United Nations planning, Hull received the Nobel Peace Prize in 1945. He retired from the State Department in late 1944 and lived in Washington, where he wrote his *Memoirs* (2 vols., 1948) and advised subsequent foreign policy makers. Married in 1917 to Rose Francis Whitney, who died in 1954, Hull himself died in Bethesda, Maryland, on July 23, 1955. Darilek, Richard E., *A Loyal Opposition in Time of War* (1976); Kolko, Gabriel, *The Politics of War* (1968); Pratt, Julius W., "Cordell Hull," in Bemis, S. F., ed., *American Secretaries of State and Their Diplomacy*, vols. 12–13 (1964); *New York Times*, July 24, 1955; Utley, Jonathan G., *Going to War with Japan, 1937–1941* (1985); Woods, Randall B., *The Roosevelt Foreign Policy Establishment and the "Good Neighbor": The United States and Argentina, 1941–1945* (1979); *WWWA*, 3 (1951–1960):428.

HUNT, WILLIAM HENRY (1823–1884). Born in Charleston, South Carolina, on June 12, 1823, William H. Hunt attended Yale, 1839–1841, went to New Orleans, and there read law and was admitted to the bar in 1844. From 1844 to 1878, he was a successful lawyer in New Orleans, maintaining an interest in politics and traveling through the Whig, Know-Nothing, and Constitutional Union parties before settling down as one of the few prominent southern Republicans. He became Louisiana attorney general in 1876 and two years later moved to Washington as a U.S. Court of Claims judge. In 1881, the Garfield administration named Hunt secretary of the navy, but the following year he was moved out of the Navy Department and appointed minister to Russia, an appointment he considered tantamount to exile. In St. Petersburg, his major tasks were dealing with cases of persecution against American Jews and protesting a law banning the American Bible Society's activities in the Caucasus. In early 1884, his health failed from a worsening of a liver condition, and he died in St. Petersburg on February 27. He was married four times. *DAB*, 9:396; Hunt, Thomas, *Life of William H. Hunt* (1922); *NCAB*, 4:244; *New York Times*, February 28, 1884.

HUNTER, ROBERT MERCER TALIAFERRO (1809–1887). Robert M. T. Hunter was born April 21, 1809, in Essex County, Virginia, graduated from the University of Virginia, and began the practice of law in 1830. He served in the Virginia General Assembly and the U.S. House of Representatives, where he was Speaker, 1839–1841, and a follower of John C. Calhoun.* From 1846 to 1861, he represented Virginia in the U.S. Senate. Resigning in 1861 to serve the Confederacy, Hunter was secretary of state from July 1861 to February 1862, during which his most notable achievements were the appointments of James M. Mason* and John Slidell* as commissioners to France and England and Henry Hotze* and Edward De Leon* as publicity agents in Europe for the Confederacy. After resigning as secretary of state, Hunter sat in the Confederate Senate and represented the Confederacy at the Hampton Roads Conference, February 1865, an unsuccessful attempt to work out a negotiated peace. After the war, he remained active in Virginia politics until his death near Lloyds, Virginia, on July 18, 1887. *DAB*, 9: 403; Owsley, Frank, *King Cotton Diplomacy* (1959).

HURLBUT, STEPHEN AUGUSTUS (1815–1882). Born November 29, 1815, in Charleston, South Carolina, Stephen A. Hurlbut had a "liberal and thorough" education and was admitted to the South Carolina bar, practicing law in Charleston until 1845. He moved to Illinois, served in the Illinois legislature, and was a Union general in the Civil War. In 1866, he was appointed minister to Colombia, a post he held for six years without incident. In 1881, he became minister to Peru, where he became involved in the diplomacy of the War of the Pacific.* Hurlbut exceeded his instructions by getting Peru to cede to the United States territory for a coaling station; he also was anxious for American naval intervention in the war and fought against the cession of any territory to Chile. His brusque manner made him unsuitable for a time of delicate negotiations, and William H. Trescot* was sent as a special envoy. Hurlbut died in Lima, Peru, on March 28, 1882, of a heart attack, during Trescot's mission. *DAB*, 9:425; Pletcher, David, *The Awkward Years* (1962); *New York Times*, April 3, 1882.

HURLEY, PATRICK JAY (1883–1963). Born in Choctaw, Indian Territory (Oklahoma), on January 8, 1883, Patrick J. Hurley attended Baptist Indian University (now Bacone Junior College) but graduated from National University in Washington, D.C. (B.A., 1908) and George Washington University (L.L.D., 1913). He returned to Oklahoma, where he practiced law in Tulsa and was the attorney for the Choctaw Nation (1912–1917). He served with the army in France in World War I and returned to law practice after the war until his appointment as secretary of war in the Hoover administration (1929–1933). During the remainder of the 1930s, he worked as a lawyer in Washington, representing, among other matters, American oil companies involved in the Mexican expropriation dispute and contributing to the resolution of the problem in 1940. In 1942, President Roosevelt named him ambassador to New Zealand; there his main task was to assure the people of American aid and support. Hurley returned to Washington later that year to serve as a personal representative of Roosevelt, going to Moscow in 1942, and to the Middle East and the Teheran Conference* in 1943. At Teheran, he drafted the Iran Declaration, granting Iran parity with other Allied nations and extending the principles of the Atlantic Charter* to the Middle East. In 1944, he undertook his most significant mission, traveling to China as the president's personal representative, but becoming ambassador later in the year. In China, his work dealt mainly with military and strategic questions and in helping to keep the Nationalist government and army of Chiang Kai-shek stable and sympathetic to the United States. He initiated talks between the Nationalist and Communist factions in an attempt to end the civil war but resigned in 1945 amid a good deal of controversy surrounding his accusations that "careerists" in the State Department had sabotaged his diplomatic efforts by advocating policies at Yalta* and elsewhere too favorable to the Communists. Much of his frustration found fuller expression later through the China Lobby.* After his resignation, Hurley remained active in Republican politics, running unsuccessfully for a New Mexico Senate seat three times. Married to Ruth Wilson in 1919, he became interested in mining projects, particularly uranium, during the 1950s, and died July 30, 1963, in Santa Fe. Buhite, Russell, *Patrick J. Hurley and United States Foreign Policy* (1973); Kolko, Gabriel, *The Politics of War* (1968); Kolko, Joyce, and Gabriel Kolko, *The Limits of Power* (1972); *NCAB*, 53:21; Rose, Lisle A., *Roots of Tragedy* (1976); *New York Times*, July 31, 1963; *WWWA*, 4 (1961–1968): 476.

IBRD. See **INTERNATIONAL BANK FOR RECONSTRUCTION AND DEVELOPMENT.**

IDB. See **INTER-AMERICAN DEVELOPMENT BANK.**

IDE, HENRY CLAY (1844–1921). Born in Barnet, Vermont, on September 18, 1844, Henry Clay Ide graduated from Dartmouth (1866) and, after reading law, gained admittance to the bar in 1871. He practiced law in St. Johnsbury, Vermont, from 1871 to 1891, serving as state's attorney in Caledonia County (1876–1877) and as a Republican state senator (1882–1886). In 1889, Ide was named land commissioner in Samoa to adjust conflicting claims after the 1889 Berlin Treaty* but served only six months because of family illness. But in 1893, he returned to Samoa for a four-year term as chief justice, a job that also included legislative advisory aspects as well. Between 1900 and 1906, Ide was on the Philippine Commission (1900), secretary of finance and justice for the islands (1901–1904), where he helped draw up the Civil Procedure and Internal Revenue codes, vice-governor (1904), acting governor (1905–1906), and governor-general (1906). A friend of William Howard Taft, Ide was made minister to Spain after Taft became president in 1909. He stayed four uneventful years. He married Mary M. Melcher in 1871 and died in St. Johnsbury on June 13, 1921. *DAB*, 9:458; *NCAB*, 23:29; *New York Times*, June 14, 1921.

IMF. See **INTERNATIONAL MONETARY FUND.**

IMPERIALISM, a concept of international relations describing the dominance of one nation over other nations, territories, or peoples. Imperialism is most traditionally expressed through colonialism,* or the possession of colonies, but it can be effected without actual colonies through overwhelming economic, political, or cultural dominance so that nations, territories, or peoples under that dominance act as though they were colonies. Hartman, Frederick H., *The Relations of Nations* (1962); Healy, David, "Imperialism," in DeConde, Alexander, ed., *Encyclopedia of American Foreign Policy* (1979); Koebner, Richard, and H. D. Schmidt, *Imperialism: The Story and Significance of a Political World, 1840–1860* (1964); Mommsen, Wolfgang J., *Theories of Imperialism* (1982); Thornton, A. P., *The Imperial Idea and Its Enemies* (1959) and *Imperialism in the Twentieth Century* (1977); Williams, William A., *The Tragedy of American Diplomacy* (1959).

IMPRESSMENT (of U.S. sailors). Beginning as early as 1790, this was the British practice of forcibly enlisting alleged British deserters serving on American merchant ships into the British navy. In many cases, the impressed seamen were native-born Americans. Impressment was viewed as a national humiliation by many in America, was strongly defended by many in Britain, and was a contributing cause of the War of 1812. The *Chesapeake* affair (1807),* brought on by impressment, was a major blow to Anglo-American relations and led to the Embargo Act (1807).* The French did not engage in impressment, although American sailors were sometimes harassed in French ports. Egan, Clifford L., *Neither Peace nor War: Franco-American Relations, 1803–1812* (1983); Perkins, Bradford, *Prologue to War* (1961); Zimmerman, James F., *Impressment of American Seamen* (1925).

INF TREATY. See **INTERMEDIATE NUCLEAR FORCE (INF) TREATY.**

INGERSOLL, JOSEPH REED (1786–1868). Joseph R. Ingersoll was born in Philadelphia on June 14, 1786, graduated from Princeton (A.B., 1804; A.M., 1807), studied law, and was admitted to the bar. He practiced law in Philadelphia, served in the U.S. House of Representatives (1835–1837, 1841–1849), and was appointed minister to Great Britain in 1852. He spent about one year at the London post and signed a claims convention (1853), referring all outstanding claims since 1814 to two commissioners, one American and one British. This commission met over the next year and settled the claims satisfactorily. Ingersoll spent the years after 1853 in retirement, devoting his time to writing books such as *Secession a Folly and a Crime* (1861) and *Memoir of Samuel Breck* (1863). He died February 20, 1868, in Philadelphia. One of his outside interests was the Pennsylvania Academy of Fine Arts, of which he was president from 1846 to 1852. *NCAB*, 7:530; Willson, Beckles, *America's Ambassadors to England, 1785–1929* (1929).

INGERSOLL, ROBERT STEPHEN (b. 1914). Robert Ingersoll was born in Galesburg, Illinois, on January 28, 1914, and graduated from Yale in 1937. After working two years for Armco Steel Company he joined Borg-Warner Company, a manufacturer of auto equipment, air-conditioners, chemicals, and plastics, as an engineer, rising through the corporate ranks to become chairman in 1961 and emphasizing the international business of the company. His international business connections and his activity in Illinois Republican politics led to his selection in 1972 as ambassador to Japan, the first businessman-ambassador since before World War II. In his two years in Japan, he was concerned with trade matters and, in particular, the worsening international trade position of the United States. He had to deal with U.S.-Japanese conflicts brought on by intensifying trade and investment problems and by the failure of the United States to notify Japan in advance of a 10 percent import surtax (1971) or of President Richard M. Nixon's China trip (1972). Ingersoll returned to Washington in 1974, serving a brief time as assistant secretary of state, Far Eastern affairs, before becoming deputy secretary of state, a post which he held until his retirement from the State Department in 1976. He married Carolyn Eleanor Reid in 1938 and remains active in the affairs of Yale, the University of Chicago, and the Council on Foreign Relations.* *New York Times*, January 26, 28, 1972; *WWA* (1978–1979):1611.

INTERALLIED CONFERENCE (1917). This conference of eighteen nations met in Paris in late 1917, following preliminary talks in London. The American delegation, led by Colonel Edward M. House*, General Tasker Bliss,* and Bainbridge Colby*, wanted to know the priority of Allied needs and to hear suggestions for a permanent body or procedure to settle major international questions. The United States learned that manpower and shipping were major problems, but distrust between Britain and France prevented consensus on other points. The Americans were important in bringing about what coordination and cooperation there was, as in the creation of a number of interallied councils for transport, food, and petroleum. Seymour states that the conference "marked the decisive crossroads in the path to Allied victory." Seymour, Charles, *American Diplomacy during the World War* (1934), and *The Intimate Papers of Colonel House*, 2 vols. (1926).

INTERALLIED GAMES (1919), an Olympic-type athletic competition for Allied soldiers in France, held in Paris from June 22 to July 6, 1919. Over 1,400 soldier-athletes from eighteen nations competed in twenty-four separate events ranging from golf to hand-grenade throwing. The United States won twelve events and finished second in seven, and France won six and finished second in six. These Interallied Games followed a series of Far Eastern Games that had been held under the auspices of the YMCA as a device for improving Allied relations. They were the inspiration of Elwood S. Brown, a YMCA official, and were strongly supported by General John J. Pershing and the host French government. Members of the American team included 1920 Olympians Charley Paddock and Norman Ross. Wythe, George (comp.), and Capt. Joseph Mills Hanson, eds., *The Interallied Games* (1919).

INTER-AMERICAN DEVELOPMENT BANK (IDB). Inspired by "Operation Pan-America," a developmental plan of Juscelino Kubitschek of Brazil, the IDB was established in December 1959 to facilitate U.S. loans to Latin American nations and serve as a clearinghouse for development capital from Latin American nations themselves. Since 1959, the bank has grown to include forty-four members, twenty-seven from the Western Hemisphere and seventeen from Europe, Asia, and the Middle East. The bank also works to encourage private investment in developmental projects and to provide technical expertise on planning and financing economic development, including efforts at regional and subregional economic integration. Since 1961, the IDB has loaned over $35 billion to finance a wide variety of projects, divided roughly equally among agriculture, energy, and urban development. The bank's headquarters are in Washington, and the United States' share of the capital stock (and, therefore, voting power) is about 35 percent. Banks, Arthur S., ed., *Political Handbook of the World 1987* (1987); Dell, Sidney, *The Inter-American Development Bank: A Study in Development Financing* (1972); White, John A., *Regional Development Banks* (1972).

INTERMEDIATE NUCLEAR FORCE (INF) TREATY (1987). This treaty, the first to provide for a reduction of nuclear weapons, refers to missiles with a range of 300 to about 3,400 miles. Signed at the Washington Summit Conference,* December 8, 1987, the treaty calls for the dismantling of all systems within three years and bans all further production and flight testing of this class of missile. The treaty is noteworthy for including the principle of asymmetrical reduction (the Soviet Union agreed to destroy four times the number of warheads as the United States) and an unprecedentedly intrusive verification procedure. Negotiations for this treaty began in 1981, were suspended in 1983 after the U.S. deployment of cruise missiles* in Western Europe, and resumed in 1985. The treaty represents the success of what the United States had termed a "dual-track" strategy—further deployment simultaneously with negotiating efforts. The Senate ratified the treaty by an overwhelming margin in May 1988, and ratifications were exchanged at the Moscow Summit Conference* later that month. *New York Times*, December 8–11, 1987.

INTERNATIONAL AGREEMENT. International law recognizes several different terms denoting agreements between states, or heads of state, that are legally binding. The most common, and formal, of these terms is *treaty*, signifying any contract between two or more states that is obligatory in character. *Accord* and *agreement* mean nearly the same and refer to arrangements less formal than a treaty. A *convention* is quite similar to a treaty but usually used in reference to agreements made at international conferences by a large number of states. Often conventions are nonpolitical, dealing instead with administrative, legal, or commercial matters. A *protocol* is a less formal and less significant international agreement; it often refers to an amendment or supplement to a formal treaty. The term *pact* is normally used only in a generic or popular sense for any treaty or convention, especially those concerned with peacekeeping. See also executive agreement.* Gamboa, Melquiades J., *Elements of Diplomatic and Consular Practice* (1966); Plischke, Elmer, *Conduct of American Diplomacy* (1967).

INTERNATIONAL BANK FOR RECONSTRUCTION AND DEVELOPMENT (IDRB). Created at the Bretton Woods Conference (1944),* ratified in Washington (December 1945), and brought into operation at a meeting in Savannah, Georgia (March 1946), the IDRB, or World Bank, as it is popularly known, was designed to provide funds for long-range capital improvements, in concert with—not as a replacement for—private foreign investment. The initial capitalization was $7.6 billion, subscribed by member nations of the International Monetary Fund (IMF).* Under the loose supervision of the United Nations* Economic and Social Council as a coordinating body, the first tasks of the IDRB were to supplement the rehabilitation efforts of the United Nations Relief and Rehabilitation Administration (UNRRA)* and to help nations create stable monetary conditions as specified in the International Monetary Fund agreement. In the summer of 1946, the bank was used as a replacement for Lend-Lease* as an expediter of U.S. exports but because of underfunding was insignificant in this role. Beginning in 1958–1959, the World Bank expanded its developmental assistance program to meet the needs of newly independent Third World* nations, increasing its total funding by marketing bonds, both in Europe and in the United States. By this time, the IDRB was more truly an international bank; it supported the International Development Association (IDA), an affiliate created in 1960 to make riskier loans to the poorest of nations. An even more active policy followed the appointment of Robert McNamara as president of the bank in 1969. Under McNamara, the bank favored greatly increased lending, particularly to less developed areas of the world, and involving bank funds in specific welfare problems, hitherto avoided, such as overpopulation, income maldistribution, and disease. In the 1980s the international debt crisis became a matter of concern to the World Bank, which has grown from an original 44 members to 151 members in 1987. Because of the debt crisis and the bank's policy in recent years to target more of its loans to the poorer people in borrower countries, the bank, like the IMF, has begun to pay more attention to the economic policies of those countries and, at times, to demand economic reform. In the mid-1980s, the IBRD and IDA together averaged approximately $14 billion in loans annually, with India, Indonesia, and Brazil ranking as the largest recipients. Eckes, Alfred E., *The Search for Solvency* (1975); Makin, John H., *The Global Debt Crisis* (1984); Solomon, Robert, *The International Monetary System, 1945–1981* (1982).

INTERNATIONAL COURT OF JUSTICE. See PERMANENT COURT OF INTERNATIONAL JUSTICE (WORLD COURT).

INTERNATIONAL DEBT CRISIS. Caused by rising oil prices after 1973, a worldwide recession including a drop in commodity prices, and a tightening of U.S. monetary policies leading to higher interest rates, the international debt crisis first attracted public notice in 1982, when Brazil and Mexico nearly defaulted on their external debt. One estimate is that the cumulative total of medium and long-term debt owed by less developed countries (LDC's) rose from $86 billion in 1971 to $606 billion in 1983. Two-thirds of this debt is held by twenty countries; Brazil and Mexico are the largest debtors. The U.S. government was involved as a lender and then as a provider of emergency assistance and debt rescheduling, while the International Monetary Fund* also played an important role, lending money at low interest rates but demanding internal economic reforms on the part of the borrower. Much of the money loaned came from U.S.

commercial banks, whose financial stability was threatened in the event of defaults. A global economic recovery in 1983–1984 helped ease the crisis, and in October 1985, Secretary of the Treasury James Baker III announced "A Program for Sustained Growth," also known as the Baker Plan, to bring about relief. Under this plan, the International Bank for Reconstruction and Development* and regional development banks, such as the Inter-American Development Bank,* would lend an additional $9 billion to the LDC's over a three-year period in order to facilitate economic reforms, and commercial banks would lend $20 billion to foster the kind of economic growth that would help LDC's to raise themselves out of their financial difficulties. After some initial enthusiasm, support for the Baker Plan dropped off, as banks saw too many risks and debtor nations saw too much U.S. government involvement. Since 1986, some banks have simply been writing off portions of their loans as uncollectible, while others have been experimenting with alternative schemes, such as "debt for equity," in which a debtor nation transfers to the bank title to a government-owned entity, which the bank can then sell. Loomis, Carol J., "Why Baker's Debt Plan Won't Work," *Fortune*, 112 (December 23, 1985); Makin, John, *The Global Debt Crisis* (1984); *New York Times*, May 26, 1987, March 31, 1988; Wellons, Philip A., *Passing the Buck* (1987).

INTERNATIONAL LABOR ORGANIZATION (ILO). Created in the Treaty of Versailles (1919),* the International Labor Organization was intended to promote equitable labor standards on a worldwide basis with each member nation responsible for legislating its own standards. The ILO has its headquarters in Geneva, Switzerland, and holds occasional general conferences. The organization was closely related to but not an integral part of the League of Nations*; as such, the United States did not become a member until 1934. After the creation of the United Nations,* the ILO became an affiliate of that organization. In 1977, amid claims that the ILO had become highly politicized by Communist-bloc and developing nations and was investigating human rights problems on a selective basis, the United States withdrew from the organization. By early 1980, the Carter administration concluded that the ILO had adopted a more balanced view of human rights and announced that the United States would return. Alcock, Anthony, *History of the International Labor Organization* (1971); Franck, Thomas M., *Nation against Nation* (1985); *New York Times*, November 2, 1977, April 16, 1980.

INTERNATIONAL MILITARY TRIBUNAL FOR THE FAR EAST (1946–1948). Established in January 1946 by order of the Supreme Commander in the Pacific, the purpose of this tribunal was the "prompt trial and punishment of the major war criminals in the Far East." The court consisted of six to eleven members and a presiding officer appointed by the supreme commander. The trial of twenty-seven high-ranking Japanese leaders lasted from January 1946 to November 1948; of the twenty-five still living at the end of the trial, seven were sentenced to death and executed in December 1948, sixteen were sentenced to life imprisonment, one to twenty years in prison, and one to seven years in prison. The sentences were reviewed and confirmed by the Far Eastern Commission. The trial testimony, made available to historians, contains a massive amount of documentary material on wartime Japan. Minear, Richard H., *Victor's Justice* (1971); Wheeler-Bennett, John W., and Anthony Nicholls, *The Semblance of Peace* (1972).

INTERNATIONAL MILITARY TRIBUNAL OF NUREMBERG (1945–1946). Based on a memorandum written for President Franklin D. Roosevelt by his legal adviser, Samuel Rosenman, and approved by Secretary of State Edward R. Stettinius,* Secretary of War Henry L. Stimson,* and Attorney General Francis Biddle, this military court was sanctioned by the Soviet Union, Great Britain, and France in May 1945, and its charter was formally signed in August. It assembled in Berlin in October and brought forth a list of twenty-four indictments. The trial began in Nuremberg in November and lasted almost a year, garnering much publicity for its revelations of Nazi infamy. Of the twenty-one defendants who lived through the trial, eighteen were found guilty, and of these, twelve were condemned to death and six were given prison sentences ranging from ten years to life. The Nuremberg Trials, as they are commonly known, were important in setting precedents for international law and providing students with a mountain of documentation on Nazi Germany, although some historians distrust this evidence. Busch, William J., *Judgment on Nuremberg* (1970); Conot, Robert, *Justice at Nuremberg* (1983); Schonfeld, Walter T., "A Record of Horrors," *American History Illustrated* 20 (June 1985): 42–49; Wheeler-Bennett, John W., and Anthony Nicholls, *The Semblance of Peace* (1972).

INTERNATIONAL MONETARY FUND (IMF). Created at the Bretton Woods Conference (1944)* from plans devised by Harry Dexter White,* the IMF grew out of two needs: (1) stability and order with freedom in international exchange in order to facilitate world trade and investment expansion and (2) international monetary cooperation and the mechanism to implement it among member nations. Through its lending policies, the IMF hoped to avoid competition in exchange depreciations and to promote a multilateral system of international payments. To this end, the fund in 1946 established a schedule of par values for exchange rates but failed the test in 1949 when there was a massive international depreciation following the British devaluation of the pound sterling. Weathering that storm, the IMF had by 1958 loaned $4.1 billion to thirty-six countries and had proved important in Europe, particularly after the Marshall Plan* ended, by helping to facilitate the monetary reform known as external convertibility. In the 1960s and 1970s, the United States supported increases in IMF quotas so as to raise the amount of funds available to borrowers. By the 1980s, the IMF had grown to 151 members and become a major force in the international debt crisis, which began in 1982. The fund helps less developed countries experiencing balance-of-payments problems by lending them money at below market rates, subject to economic policy conditionality. *Conditionality* is a term signifying that the IMF requires a debtor nation to make adjustments in its economic policy that will lead to the restoration of its economic well-being. The question of conditionality is controversial because many IMF adjustment plans are quite intrusive and threaten economic dislocation and political instability. Dell, Sidney, *On Being Grandmotherly: The Evolution of IMF Conditionality* (1981); deVries, Margaret G., *The IMF in a Changing World, 1945–1985* (1986); Eckes, Alfred E., *The Search for Solvency* (1975); Solomon, Robert, *The International Monetary System, 1945–1981* (1982).

INTERNATIONAL TRADE ORGANIZATION (ITO) (1947). This proposed organization would have worked toward freer trade policies in a multilateral environment. A draft charter was prepared at the International Trade and Employment Conference in Geneva in the summer of 1947, and a conference was held in November in Havana to approve the charter. Will Clayton,* former under secretary of state for economic affairs, headed the U.S. delegation to this conference, where fifty-four of the fifty-seven participating nations signed the ITO charter. However, the U.S. Senate refused to consider the document because of the complexity of compromises and concessions made in preparing the charter. These changes resulted in an organization that was substantially altered from its original purpose, and despite Clayton's insistence that an imperfect ITO was better than none at all, the organization failed to materialize once U.S. refusal to participate was made clear. Dobney, Frederick J., ed., *Selected Papers of Will Clayton* (1971); Kolko, Joyce, and Gabriel Kolko, *The Limits of Power* (1972).

IRAN-CONTRA SCANDAL (1986). This, the most serious scandal of the Reagan administration, was apparently motivated by the twin desires to get U.S. hostages in the Middle East released and to circumvent the congressional ban on aid to the Nicaraguan contras.* In early 1985, the idea floated to the Reagan administration through Israeli contacts was that if arms were sold to Iranian moderates (who might also be a useful entry into a post-Khomeini regime), there was a good chance to get the hostages freed. In addition, there was an even better chance for those involved to make a great deal of money. Colonel Oliver North, a marine officer attached to the National Security Council (NSC),* was the principal facilitator in this operation, by which arms were shipped to Iran through Israel on several occasions between the summer of 1985 and the fall of 1986. Beginning in April 1986, part of the sizable profits from the arms sales were diverted to the contras. Although there was some discussion of these activities within the administration, National Security Adviser John Poindexter* failed to inform the president fully so that he would have "plausible deniability," and the information provided to Congress was, at best, misleading. In October 1986, a Lebanese publication broke the story, and an avalanche of facts and allegations followed. The president appointed a special investigating committee, headed by former Senator John Tower (R., Texas), to look into the role of the

NSC. House and Senate select committees held joint hearings in the spring and summer of 1987, and a special prosecutor, Lawrence Walsh, investigated the affair from the standpoint of criminal activities, obtaining indictments on North, Poindexter, and two others involved in the sale of arms and diversion of profits. Cohen, William, and George Mitchell, *Men of Zeal* (1988); *New York Times*, October 23, 1986, January 3, 12, February 5, 15, July 9, August 4, November 19, 1987.

IRAN CRISIS (1946). In 1942, the United States, Great Britain, and the USSR agreed to the joint occupation of Iran in order to prevent a German takeover of the oil fields. Although each ally had pledged to withdraw its troops six months after the end of the war (with promises to protect neighboring Soviet interests), Soviet troops still remained in northern Iran in early 1946, using a Communist-inspired revolt in the region as a pretext for keeping troops there but at the same time pressuring the Iranian government for oil concessions. Iran appealed to the United Nations* to induce the Soviets to withdraw their troops; the United States sent a strongly worded note to Moscow; and the troops left Iran in March 1946 with the simultaneous announcement of the formation of an Iranian-Soviet oil company, to be ratified by the Iranian parliament, which later rejected the proposed oil company. The incident was a stepping-stone toward cold war* hostility. *FR* (1946), 7:289–567; *FR* (1947), 5:890–998; Gaddis, John L., *The United States and the Origins of the Cold War* (1972); LaFeber, Walter, *America, Russia, and the Cold War, 1945–1984* (1985).

IRANIAN HOSTAGE CRISIS (1979–1981). Because of U.S. support for the deposed shah, Iranian militants raided the U.S. embassy compound in November 1979 and seized sixty-eight hostages, demanding that the shah, then receiving medical treatment in New York City, be returned to Iran. President Jimmy Carter refused, and the militants, after releasing thirteen women and blacks, reiterated their demands. A series of sanctions against Iran, ranging from the freezing of Iranian assets in the United States to condemnatory resolutions from the United Nations* Security Council, failed to resolve the crisis. The pressure increased; in December, the United States expelled 183 Iranian diplomats, and in April 1980, diplomatic relations were formally terminated. Responding to increasing public frustration, President Carter authorized a military rescue mission in April; it failed utterly, costing eight lives, and brought about the resignation of Secretary of State Cyrus Vance.* Iran threatened to put the hostages on trial and, after the shah died in July 1980, replaced demands for his return with demands for the return of his wealth. In the fall of 1980, the Iran-Iraq war* heated up, and Algeria entered the picture as a negotiating go-between, with Warren Christopher* taking the main role for the United States in these talks. A settlement, agreeing to the lifting of the various U.S. sanctions, was agreed upon in January 1981, and the hostages were freed on the day Ronald Reagan was inaugurated. Jordan, Hamilton, *Crisis: The Last Year of the Carter Presidency* (1982); Kreisberg, Paul H., ed., *American Hostages in Iran: The Conduct of a Crisis* (1985); Scott, Charles W.,

Pieces of the Game: The Human Drama of Americans Held Hostage in Iran (1984); Sick, Gary, *All Fall Down* (1985).

IRAN-IRAQ WAR (1980–). War between these two Middle Eastern neighbors broke out September 22, 1980, and has continued since in an often bloody but irresolute way. There have been frequent land battles along the belligerents' common border, missile attacks on their major cities, and beginning in 1982, a tanker war, perpetrated by aircraft or missiles, in the Persian Gulf designed to hamper international oil trade. U.S. policy has been officially neutral and has generally been to aid both sides when necessary to keep either from winning decisively and to do whatever is necessary to prevent the war from spreading. In practice, this has meant more frequent U.S. assistance to Iraq, the smaller of the adversaries. In 1985 and 1986, however, arms were secretly supplied to Iran in an apparent attempt to free U.S. hostages in the region, an incident that became known as the Iran-contra scandal.* In 1987, to protect Kuwait's gulf shipping, the United States began the practice of reflagging, permitting Kuwaiti ships to display the American flag and enjoy U.S. naval protection. Although there have been several incidents of Iraqi or Iranian attacks on U.S.-flagged ships (and in one case, a U.S. naval vessel), responses have been proportionate, and large-scale involvement of the U.S. military has so far been avoided. In August 1988, both Iran and Iraq accepted UN Security Council Resolution 598, calling for a cease fire in their war. Peace talks began in late August but soon stalemated. Abdulghani, Jasim, *Iraq and Iran: The Years of Crisis* (1984); Axelgard, Frederick W., "Iraq and the War with Iran," *Current History* 86, 517 (February 1987): 61–65, 82, 90–91; Ismael, Tareq Y., *Iraq and Iran: The Roots of Conflict* (1982); Ramazani, R. K., "The Iran-Iraq War and the Persian Gulf Crisis," *Current History* 87, 526 (February 1988): 61–64, 86–88; Renfrew, Nina, "Who Started the War?" *Foreign Policy* 66 (Spring 1987): 98–108.

IRON CURTAIN, pejorative catchword, post-1945. This term was first used by German propaganda minister Joseph Goebbels in diary entries as early as 1944 and was brought into public discourse by British Prime Minister Winston Churchill in May 1945 to describe the division of Europe between the Soviet Union and the West in the context of troop movements and emplacements shortly after V-E Day. The term was elaborated upon and popularized by Churchill in a speech given at Fulton, Missouri, on March 5, 1946. Here he portrayed a Europe divided by an "iron curtain," with the nations of Eastern Europe, behind the curtain, increasingly under Soviet control. Peace, said Churchill, could not be preserved if Moscow were permitted to perpetuate this control. Churchill's speech, according to Gaddis, reflected privately held views of the Truman administration, then moving toward a tougher policy toward the Soviet Union. Gaddis, John L., *The United States and the Origins of the Cold War* (1972); Rees, David, *The Age of Containment* (1968).

IRRECONCILABLES, a term describing a group of fourteen to sixteen U.S. senators who, during the debate on the ratification of the Treaty of Versailles,* were unalterably opposed to ratification, with or without reservations. Different senators had different reasons for their opposition; some felt ratification (and membership in the League of Nations*) would endanger the country; some worked for personal political gain; some felt the nation could best serve the world by setting an example in isolation; some felt great antipathy toward America's wartime allies. Among the irreconcilables were prominent senators such as former Secretary of State Philander C. Knox (R., Pennsylvania),* Albert B. Fall (R., New Mexico), Hiram W. Johnson (R., California), and William E. Borah (R., Idaho).* Bailey, Thomas A., *Woodrow Wilson and the Great Betrayal* (1945); Stone, Ralph A., *The Irreconcilables* (1970).

IRVING, WASHINGTON (1783–1859). One of America's best known-writers of the early nineteenth century, Washington Irving also had a part in U.S. diplomacy as minister to Spain from 1842 to 1846. Born in New York City on April 3, 1783, Irving had only a fragmentary private education but read law and traveled in Europe from 1804 to 1806. Deciding that he did not want a career in the law, he chose instead to be a writer and, beginning in 1806, published a variety of highly regarded works. In 1814, he went to work in a branch of the family business in Liverpool. While in Britain, he met Sir Walter Scott, and his subsequent writing shows the influence of Scott. Irving lived in Britain and on the Continent until 1832, spending the years from 1826 to 1829 in Spain and 1829 to 1832 as legation secretary in London. In 1842, President John Tyler, an admirer of his writing, named Irving minister to Spain. His mission was fairly routine, but his correspondence was informative and analytical during the unsettled early years of the reign of Queen Isabella II and her regent, Espartero. He attended meetings of the Liceo, an aristocratic literary and intellectual circle, and professed great admiration for the adolescent queen. From 1842 to 1844, Irving's legation secretary was Alexander Hamilton, grandson of the treasury secretary and Federalist leader of the 1790s. After his return to the United States, Irving finished his monumental biography of George Washington and lived quietly in New York until his death November 28, 1859, at his estate near Tarrytown. Bowers, Claude G., *The Spanish Adventures of Washington Irving* (1940); *DAB*, 9:505; Irving, Pierre M., *The Life and Letters of Washington Irving*, 3 vols. (1889); Reichert, Walter A., *Washinton Irving and Germany* (1953).

IRWIN, JOHN NICHOL, II (b. 1913). Ambassador to France during the latter years of the Nixon administration, John N. Irwin was born in Keokuk, Iowa, on New Year's Eve 1913 and graduated from Princeton (B.A., 1937), Fordham (LL.B., 1941), and Oxford (B.A., Jurisprudence, 1939; M.A., 1944). After service in World War II, he was admitted to the New York bar (1946) and began a career as a New York lawyer, with intermittent federal government service. He was deputy assistant secretary of defense, 1957–1958, and assistant secretary of defense for security affairs, 1958–1961, acting in this post as a liaison between the Defense and State departments. In addition, Irwin went to Peru as a special envoy to discuss problems arising from seizure of U.S. oil properties and worked in the early stages of Panama Canal treaty* talks. After several years out of public life, Irwin returned to Washington in 1970 as under secretary of state, a title that was changed to deputy secretary of state in 1972. Here he conferred (in January 1971) with Middle East leaders over a threatened world oil crisis and contributed to a satisfactory agreement among twenty-three international oil companies and the five Persian Gulf oil states. In 1972, he contributed $50,500 to the Nixon campaign and the following year was named ambassador to France, where his tour of about a year was uneventful. Irwin returned to his law practice in 1974. Married to Jane Watson from 1949 until her death in 1970 and to Jane German Reimer since 1976, Irwin was for a time chairman of the board of the Union Theological Seminary and is a trustee emeritus of Princeton and a director of IBM. *New York Times*, February 17, 1971, March 17, November 17, 1974, November 19, 1975; *WWA* (1986–1987):1385.

ISOLATIONISM, a term used to indicate a policy of abstaining from an active role in international affairs. In American history, isolationism has been used to characterize diplomacy throughout most of the nineteenth century and, more commonly, to describe the foreign policy of the years between World Wars I and II. In the earlier period of isolationism, the United States was geographically separate and economically and militarily weak, and the term has a literal meaning. In the twentieth century, the use of the word *isolationism* has brought about considerable historical discussion, primarily in the sense of limiting isolationism to the American policy of refusing to join the League of Nations* or other international organizations or a turning away from active response to world crisis and avoiding, for as long as possible, involvement in World War II. Isolationism did not apply to areas such as Latin America, where military intervention continued into the 1930s and economic development grew rapidly, or China, where political and economic influence remained considerable. Adler, Selig, *The Isolationist Impulse* (1957); Guinsberg, Thomas N., *The Pursuit of Isolationism in the United States Senate from Versailles to Pearl Harbor* (1987); Osgood, Robert E., *Ideals and Self-Interest in America's Foreign Relations* (1953); Williams, W. A., *The Tragedy of American Diplomacy* (1959).

ITALO-ETHIOPIAN WAR (1935–1936). The United States responded to this war (in which Italy easily subjugated and annexed Ethopia) by invoking an embargo on arms sales, discouraging trade in other strategic materials, and warning Americans against traveling on belligerent ships. Since Ethiopia's economic contact with the United States was nil, the restrictions were really aimed at expressing American disapproval of Italian aggression. The United States tried to avoid any appearance of open communication with the League of Nations,* which recommended that its member states impose similar sanctions. In practice, the United States (and league) sanctions were largely ineffective, although there was public support for the principle of neutrality* expressed by the sanctions. The U.S. and league sanctions were further damaged by the Hoare-Laval Plan,* which tried to end the war by appeasing Italy with a favorable settlement. In general, the Italo-Ethiopian War illustrated the practical problems of maintaining neutrality. Divine, Robert A., *The Illusion of Neutrality* (1962); Dugan, James, and Laurence Lafore, *Days of Emperor and Clown* (1973); *FR* (1935), 1:594–908; *FR* (1936), 3:34–341; Offner, Arnold A., *The Origins of the Second World War* (1975).

***ITATA* INCIDENT (1891).** This incident concerned a Chilean naval vessel, the *Itata*, captured by rebels in 1891 during a civil war in Chile and taken to San Diego to pick up a shipment of arms. Detained by federal authorities in San Diego on charges of violating neutrality* laws, the crew overpowered an American deputy marshal on board and sailed the *Itata* back to Chile, where it was surrendered to the United States, whose ships had pursued it to Chile. Although the United States released the ship in 1893 after a Supreme Court hearing, the incident damaged U.S.-Chilean relations, especially inasmuch as the rebels won the war with German weapons after being denied U.S. arms. Some of this anti-American feeling carried over to the U.S.S. *Baltimore* affair* later in 1891. Devine, Michael J., *John W. Foster: Politics and Diplomacy in the Imperial Era, 1873–1917* (1981); *FR* (1891):122–32; Hardy, Osgood, "The *Itata* Incident," *Hispanic American Historical Review* 5 (May 1922): 195–226; Meacham, J. Lloyd, *A Survey of United States–Latin American Relations* (1965).

JACKSON, JOHN BRINCKERHOFF (1862–1920). John Brinckerhoff Jackson was born in Newark, New Jersey, on August 19, 1862, and graduated from the U.S. Naval Academy in 1883. On active naval duty until 1886, he then began the study of law, married Florence A. Baird, and gained admittance to the bar in 1889. The following year, he began a diplomatic career with appointment as second secretary of the legation in Berlin. By 1894, he had become legation secretary, serving in that post until 1902, giving the legation continuity and the benefit of his knowledge of local affairs. For twenty months (1898–1900), he was chargé d'affaires*, handling legation matters during the Spanish-American War, the first Hague Peace Conference (1899),* and the Boxer Rebellion (1900)* and winning the respect and friendship of the German Emperor, William II. His good work in Germany led to his selection as minister to Greece (1902–1907) and his accreditation at various times to other Balkan countries. Following his mission in Greece, Jackson served as minister to Persia (1907–1909), Cuba (1909–1911), and Romania, Bulgaria, and Serbia (1911–1913), all relatively uneventful posts. After 1913, he was a special agent in the State Department, stationed in Germany, where his experience proved valuable until the U.S. embassy was withdrawn in 1917. After U.S. entry into World War I, he retired and lived in Switzerland, where he died on December 20, 1920. *DAB*, 9:548; Dennis, A. L. P., *Adventures in American Diplomacy, 1896–1906* (1928); *NCAB*, 12:250; *New York Times*, December 21, 1920.

JAPANESE-KOREAN EXCLUSION LEAGUE (1905–1907), a California-based group founded in 1905 to work for the extension of the Chinese exclusion laws to Japanese and Koreans. The organization supported the San Francisco Board of Education's plan to segregate Japanese students in the city school system. In 1906–1907, the league denounced the diplomatic settlement of the immigration matter and continued to insist on nothing less than exclusion, even after the Gentleman's Agreement* of February 1907. The president of the league was a local labor leader, Olaf Treitmore. Neu, Charles E., *An Uncertain Friendship* (1967).

JAPANESE PEACE TREATY (1951). The notion of a Japanese peace treaty began to find its way into State Department discussions in 1949, amid much controversy over whether there should be such a treaty and, if so, what provisions it should contain. A first draft was completed in October 1949 based on the restoration of Japanese sovereignty. In April 1950, partially to defuse partisan criticism from Republicans, John Foster Dulles* was appointed a State Department consultant with the understanding that his primary responsibility would be the Japanese treaty. In September 1950, the draft treaty was discussed by the Far East Commission, and although the Soviet Union argued that the Council of Foreign Ministers* should prepare the treaty, as it had done with those for defeated European nations, the United States rejected the contention. The United States and Great Britain agreed on the basic components of the treaty in February 1951 and had it approved by other allies in a San Francisco conference authoritatively chaired by Secretary of State Dean Acheson* in July. On September 8, 1951, the formal signing took place. The treaty, in its final form, ended the state of war between the United States and Japan, restored full Japanese sovereignty in political and economic matters, asked for and then excused reparations* from Japan, and gave Japan the right to maintain forces necessary for individual and collective self-defense. The treaty was important in its recognition of Japanese nationalism and in making Japan a cold war* ally and strong friendly outpost in the western Pacific. On the same day, the U.S.-Japanese Security Treaty was signed. Recognizing the fact that a disarmed Japan could not defend itself, this treaty allowed U.S. troops to be stationed on Japanese territory and permitted gradual Japanese rearmanent for an indefinite duration. This treaty was reviewed in 1960 and recast in such a way as to recognize the mutual security obligations of both nations. McLellan, David S., *Dean Acheson: The State Department Years* (1976); Wheeler-Bennett, John W., and Anthony Nicholls, *The Semblance of Peace* (1972).

JARVIS, WILLIAM (1770–1859). William Jarvis was born in Boston on February 2, 1770, and, after schooling at the Bordentown Academy and William Waring's School in Philadelphia, entered business in Boston. He did not prosper until 1797, when he bought a one-third interest in a brig and involved himself with foreign trade. In 1802, he was named consul* and chargé d'affaires* in Portugal, and in eight years there, during which he conducted profitably his private business, he protected American sailors by persuading the government to stop the practice of impressment* in Lisbon. He blocked a proposed high tariff on American flour and obtained modification of a quarantine against yellow fever for northern ships. In addition, he bought 3,500 merino sheep in 1808 when Napoleon took over Spain and shipped them back to the United States, a move that delighted President Thomas Jefferson.* In 1810, he returned to the United States, lived on a Vermont farm and maintained a continuing interest in politics until his death on October 21, 1859. *DAB*, 9:624.

JAY, JOHN (1745–1829). A founding father who was intimately involved in the foreign affairs of the new nation, John Jay was born in New York City on December 12, 1745. A 1764 graduate of King's College (now Columbia), he went on to read law and was admitted to the bar in 1768. He became a successful and socially prominent New York lawyer, married Sarah Van Brugh Livingston in 1774, and was active in the New York Committee of Correspondence before the Revolution. A member of both the First and Second Continental Congresses, Jay served also as chief justice of New York (1776–1779). His first contact with diplomacy came in 1779 when he was named minister to Spain. Although unable to obtain Spanish recognition of U.S. independence, he did secure an under-the-table loan of $170,000. In 1782–1783, he was a peace commissioner with Benjamin Franklin* and John Adams*; he caused some controversy by insisting that British envoys treat with "United States of America" representatives rather than "colonial" representatives, delaying negotiations for some time. Jay became secretary of foreign affairs (1784–1790) under the Articles of Confederation government and was faced with major problems relating to Great Britain's refusal to evacuate northwestern forts and Spain's intransigence over the Mississippi River and disputed territory in the Old Southwest. Jay's diplomacy was unsuccessful, due principally to the weakness of the central government under the Articles. First chief justice of the Supreme Court under George Washington, Jay was dispatched to Britain in 1794 to negotiate the treaty that bears his name. Jay's Treaty* was controversial in its day and bore the strong influence of Alexander Hamilton but was important for maintaining peace. Jay was governor of New York (1795–1801), after which he lived in retirement at his farm in Westchester County, New York. He died in Bedford, New York, on May 17, 1829. Bemis, Samuel F., *The Diplomacy of the American Revolution* (1935), and *Jay's Treaty* (1923); *DAB*, 10:5.

JAY-GARDOQUI TREATY (1786). Negotiated by John Jay,* then secretary for foreign affairs, and Don Diego de Gardoqui, Spanish minister to the United States, this proposed treaty would have required the United States to abandon claims to land east of the Mississippi River and south of the Yazoo River, as well as the right to use the Mississippi River. In return for these concessions, the United States would receive trading privileges with Spain. Violent protests from the South and word of a growing separatist movement in the West convinced Jay to break off negotiations. The one-sidedness of the proposed treaty demonstrated the diplomatic weakness of the United States during the Confederation period. Bemis, Samuel F., *Pinckney's Treaty*, rev. ed. (1960); Van Alstyne, Richard, *The Rising American Empire* (1960); Whitaker, Arthur, *The Spanish Frontier, 1783–1795* (1927).

JAY'S TREATY (1794). Formally known as the Anglo-American Treaty of Amity, Commerce and Navigation, this treaty was the first important agreement signed between the United States and a major European power. In 1793, Great Britain was still controlling forts in the Northwest, in violation of the Peace of Paris (1783),* and encouraging Indians to attack settlers. In addition, ships of the British navy were seizing American merchant vessels bound for France. Relations between the two countries had deteriorated to a point where Republicans in Congress were demanding either an embargo on British trade or war.

To ward off Republican protests and to preserve profitable commerce with Britain, President George Washington named John Jay,* then chief justice of the Supreme Court, as special envoy to work out the differences with the British. In the treaty that resulted, Great Britain agreed to evacuate the Northwest forts and to arrange for commissions on boundary questions and compensation for ships illegally seized. The British, however, did not agree to the principle of free ships, free goods,* or to a commercial treaty allowing American trade in the British West Indies. The treaty was ratified June 24, 1795, by a narrow margin after a highly partisan debate. In retrospect, Jay's Treaty put off a likely war with Great Britain and contributed to the successful conclusion of Pinckney's Treaty (1795).* Bemis, Samuel F., *Jay's Treaty* (1923); Combs, Jerald A., *The Jay Treaty* (1970); Perkins, Bradford, *The First Rapprochement: Britain and the United States, 1795–1805* (1955); Varg, Paul A., *Foreign Policy of the Founding Fathers* (1963).

JCS 1067. Joint Chiefs of Staff recommendation, 1944. JCS 1067 was the file number of a document prepared under the authority of the U.S. Joint Chiefs of Staff in September 1944 concerning the treatment of Germany in the period between surrender and the implementation of postwar occupation programs. According to the report, Germany was to be treated as a defeated nation, with only minimal rehabilitation (enough to prevent disease and disorder). There was to be an extensive "denazification" program, including the arrest of Nazi party members and sympathizers. Many Americans, including Lucius D. Clay* and Robert D. Murphy,* thought the ideas contained in JCS 1067 were unwise and would create unemployment at a time when Europe required the necessities that skilled German workers could produce. Additionally, critics pointed out that JCS 1067 was too insular, dealing with Germany without considering its neighbors. The Potsdam Agreement, in August 1945, revised U.S. policy toward Germany somewhat by allowing administrators more flexibility in economic matters, despite French objection to such liberalities. In July 1947, JCS 1779 replaced JCS 1067; this was a more permissive directive regarding German reconstruction, reflecting a more realistic approach to Germany, and a new set of cold war* attitudes. Gaddis, John L., *The United States and the Origins of the Cold War* (1972); Gimbel, John, *The American Occupation of Germany* (1968); Wheeler-Bennett, John W., and Anthony Nicholls, *The Semblance of Peace* (1972).

JEFFERSON, THOMAS (1743–1826). A founding father, author of the Declaration of Independence, and third president of the United States, Thomas Jefferson also had his hand in early American diplomacy as minister to France (1785–1789) and secretary of state (1789–1793). Born April 24, 1743, in Albemarle County, Virginia, Jefferson was educated by private tutors, graduated from William and Mary (1762), and was admitted to the bar (1767). His political career began in 1769, with election to the Virginia House of Burgesses. In 1775, he was a member of the Second Continental Congress, which put forth the Declaration of Independence. Back in the Virginia legislature from 1776 to 1779, he became governor of Virginia, 1779–1781, and a U.S. congressman (1782–1784) before his selection as minister to France in 1785. In France, Jefferson was somewhat overshadowed by Benjamin Franklin's* reputation and by Lafayette's presence but still managed to negotiate a commercial treaty with Prussia (1785) and a consular convention with France (1788). In general, he brought about improved Franco-American commercial relations and enhanced the image of France in America to reinforce the lingering hostility toward Britain. As secretary of state in the first term of George Washington, Jefferson maintained his pro-French attitude and fell into a sharp conflict with Secretary of the Treasury Alexander Hamilton, well known for his British proclivities. Jefferson favored economic sanctions against Britain to force it from forts on U.S. territory it still occupied; Hamilton undercut Jefferson's letter to British Minister George Hammond detailing U.S. grievances with private assurances to Hammond. The French Revolution and American neutrality* widened the breach, as Jefferson, not as alarmed as many others by the excesses of the revolution or its spread into a general European war, argued against the use of the term *neutrality*. In 1793, he urged Washington to receive French envoy Edmund Gênet and was embarrassed by Gênet's constant indiscretions. He resigned later that year but remained active in public life, opposing Jay's Treaty.* He was vice-president, 1797–1801, under his political foe, John Adams.* As president, 1801–1809, Jefferson was responsible for the Louisiana Purchase,* tried to acquire Florida without success, exacted a settlement from the Barbary pirates* with naval force, and tried to win concessions from the British and French with the Embargo Act (1807).* In retirement at Monticello, his Virginia home, Jefferson devoted himself to correspondence, working for the betterment of Virginia and especially the University of Virginia, chartered in 1819, whose campus he largely designed. Married to Martha Skelton from 1772 to her death in 1782, Jefferson died at Monticello on July 4, 1826, the fiftieth anniversary of the signing of the Declaration of Independence. *DAB*, 10:17; Heald, Morrell, and Lawrence S. Kaplan, *Culture and Diplomacy: The American Experience* (1977); Malone, Dumas, *Jefferson and His Times*, 6 vols. (1948–1981); Willson, Beckles, *America's Ambassadors to France, 1777–1927* (1928); Woolery, William Kirk, *The Relation of Thomas Jefferson to American Foreign Policy, 1783–1793* (1927).

JESSUP, PHILIP CARYL (1897–1986). One of the foremost international lawyers in U.S. history, Philip C. Jessup was born January 5, 1897, in New York City, served in World War I as an enlisted man, and after the war graduated from Hamilton College (1919), Yale Law School (1924), and Columbia University (A.M., 1924; Ph.D., 1927). His contact with the diplomacy of international law began early. In 1925–1926, he was an adviser to Senator Irvine Lenroot (R., Wisconsin) on the Permanent Court of International Justice (World Court)* question. Three years later, he was an assistant to former Secretary of State Elihu Root* on the issue of whether the United States should join the court. In 1930, Jessup was a legal adviser to Ambassador Harry F. Guggenheim* in

Cuba. Except for these brief assignments, however, Jessup spent most of the time between 1925 and 1942 practicing law in New York City and lecturing at Columbia University Law School. In 1942, he was appointed associate director of the Naval School of Military Government and Administration, located at Columbia. From 1947 to 1949, he served on the United Nations* Committee on International Law; the following year, he was U.S. deputy representative to the Interim Committee of the United Nations General Assembly. In 1949, Jessup became the first ambassador-at-large, a post created to permit the secretary of state to remain in Washington yet still have distinguished representation at important meetings and conferences. In this post, he negotiated with Soviet Ambassador Jacob Malik over the lifting of the Berlin blockade,* helped review China policy and prepare the China White Paper,* and accompanied President Harry S Truman in his Wake Island talks with General Douglas MacArthur.* While remaining ambassador-at-large, Jessup was also appointed a member of the U.S. delegation to the United Nations, a controversial appointment because of alleged but unproved Communist ties. From 1961 to 1970, Jessup was a judge on the World Court, where he issued an important dissent in 1966 when the court ruled in favor of South Africa in a case involving the establishment of apartheid in Southwest Africa. He was married to Lois Kellogg in 1921 and wrote much on international law and diplomacy, including *The United States and the World Court* (1929), *International Security* (1935), *Elihu Root* (2 vols., 1938), *A Modern Law of Nations* (1948), *The Price of Justice* (1971), and *The Birth of Nations* (1974). He died January 31, 1986, in Newton, Pennsylvania.

Burke, Lee H., *Ambassador-at-Large: Diplomat Extraordinary* (1972); Fasulo, Linda M., *Representing America: Experiences of U.S. Diplomats at the UN* (1984); McLellan, David S., *Dean Acheson: The State Department Years* (1976); *NCAB*, H:45; *New York Times*, September 23, 1951; *WWA* (1976–1977):1600.

JOHNSON, NELSON TRUSLER (1887–1954). A career diplomat with a special interest in the Far East and a long-time chief of mission* in China, Nelson T. Johnson was born in Washington, D.C., on April 3, 1887, and attended George Washington University, 1906–1907, before going to China as a student interpreter. By 1909, Johnson was in the consular service as vice– and deputy consul general* at Mukden and over the next nine years held various consular posts at different Chinese towns. From 1918 to 1921, he was back in Washington with the Division of Far Eastern Affairs. At the Washington Conference (1921–1922),* he was a special assistant, after which he returned to the Far East as a consul-general-at-large (1922–1925). Among his duties in this assignment was working in earthquake relief and reconstruction at Yokohama in 1923. Chief of the Division of Far Eastern Affairs from 1925 to 1927, Johnson moved up to assistant secretary of state from 1927 to 1929, working on Foreign Service personnel matters. In 1929, he was appointed minister to China, remaining there until 1941 (the legation was raised in status to an embassy, and Johnson became an ambassador in 1935). In China, he served through the Manchurian crisis

(1931–1933)* and played a role in the talks that settled the dispute. He stayed in China after the Japanese invasion in 1937, protecting American interests on his own initiative and moving the embassy with the Chinese government to Hankow and then to Chungking. Retiring from the State Department in 1941, he taught foreign policy to U.S. Department of Agriculture employees and wrote articles on China and Australia. From 1946 to 1952, he was secretary-general of the Far Eastern Commission. Johnson died in Washington on December 3, 1954. He married Jane Thornton Beck in 1931, was interested in Chinese archaeology, and collected Chinese artifacts. Burns, Richard Dean, and Edward M. Bennett, eds., *Diplomats in Crisis* (1974); *NCAB*, 43:241; *New York Times*, December 4, 1954; *WWWA*, 3 (1951–1960): 452.

JOHNSON, REVERDY (1796–1876). One of the most prominent constitutional lawyers of his day, Reverdy Johnson was born May 21, 1796, in Annapolis, Maryland. He graduated from St. John's College in Annapolis in 1811 and was admitted to the bar in 1815. For nearly sixty years, he practiced law in Baltimore, playing prominent roles in cases such as *Dred Scott* v. *Sanford* (1857). From 1845 to 1849 and again from 1863 to 1868 he served in the U.S. Senate, and in 1868 he replaced Charles Francis Adams* as minister to Great Britain. He spent only a year in London, where he was well regarded, and signed a number of agreements with Britain. These included arbitration* over jurisdiction of San Juan Island in Puget Sound, the right of expatriation for British subjects, and, in the Johnson-Clarendon Convention (1869), the settlement of outstanding financial claims. Because of congressional hostility toward President Andrew Johnson, none of these was ratified, but most of the ideas were incorporated into later treaties. After his mission ended in 1869, Johnson returned to his law practice, where, among other cases, he defended many ex-Confederates. He was still active when he died February 10, 1876, in Annapolis from the effects of a fall. *DAB*, 10:112; Steiner, Bernard C., *The Life of Reverdy Johnson* (1914); Willson, Beckles, *America's Ambassadors to England, 1785–1929* (1929).

JOHNSON, URAL ALEXIS (b. 1908). Born October 17, 1908, in Falun, Kansas, U. Alexis Johnson graduated from Occidental College (1931) and attended the Georgetown School of Foreign Service in 1931–1932. He joined the Foreign Service in 1935 and served in a variety of minor posts in Tokyo, Seoul, Tienstin, and Mukden before being interned by the Japanese in 1941. Exchanged the following year, Johnson spent from 1942 to 1944 in Rio de Janeiro and, after a year with the Army Civil Affairs Training School in Chicago, returned to the Far East in 1945 as a consul* in Manila. He moved to Yokohoma later in 1945 and became consul general there in 1947. In 1949, he went to Washington to work in the office of Northeast Asian Affairs; in 1951, he was promoted to deputy assistant secretary of state, a post he held until 1953. That year, he was named ambassador to Czechoslovakia, where his major task was negotiating the release of an American citizen, John Hvasta. In addition, he coordinated the

U.S. delegation to the Geneva Conference (1954)* and held talks with the Chinese Communists at the Geneva Summit Conference (1955).* In 1958, Johnson became ambassador to Thailand, where he simultaneously functioned as U.S. representative to the Southeast Asia Treaty Organization.* The Kennedy administration brought him back to Washington as deputy under secretary of state in 1961, giving him important assignments with regard to crises in Berlin (1961) and Laos (1963). In 1964, the post of deputy ambassador to Vietnam was created for Johnson so he could go the Saigon and assist Ambassador Maxwell Taylor* at a difficult time in the Vietnam War. In 1965, Johnson was made deputy under secretary of state for political affairs; in 1969, he rose to under secretary. Named an ambassador-at-large in 1973, he was chief U.S. delegate in the Strategics Arms Limitation Talks (SALT II)* process until 1977. Married to Patricia Ann Tillman in 1932, Johnson lives in Washington, where he is a State Department consultant. He has published *Memoirs: The Right Hand of Power* (1984). Ausland, John C., and Col. Hugh F. Richardson, "Crisis Management: Berlin, Cyprus, Laos," *Foreign Affairs* 44 (January 1966): 292; *NCAB*, 1:342; *New York Times*, June 24, 1964, July 26, 1966; *WWA* (1978–1979):1673.

JOHNSON, WILLIS FLETCHER (1857–1931). Born October 7, 1857, in New York City and an 1879 graduate of New York University, Willis Fletcher Johnson worked fifty-one years as a journalist with the *New York Tribune*, primarily as a foreign and diplomatic correspondent. In addition, he was a contributing editor to the *North American Review* (1912–1929) and *Harvey's Weekly* (1918). He is best known for his many books dealing with historical and biographical subjects. His *History of the Johnstown Flood* (1889) was a best-seller; he also wrote biographies of James G. Blaine,* General William T. Sherman, Henry Stanley, and his good friend George Harvey.* On foreign affairs, his writings included *A Century of Expansion* (1903), *Four Centuries of the Panama Canal* (1906), and *America's Foreign Relations* (2 vols., 1916). After 1913, he was honorary professor of American foreign relations at New York University. He married Sue Rockhill in 1878 and died in Summit, New Jersey, March 28, 1931. *DAB*, 10:135; *New York Times*, March 29, 1931.

JOHNSON-REED ACT (1924). This act succeeded the Emergency Quota Act (1921), which had limited immigration by assigning quotas to each nonhemispheric nation based on a percentage of foreign-born residents of that nationality in the United States in 1910. The Johnson-Reed Act maintained the same system for assigning quotas but lowered the percentage from 3 percent to 2 percent and changed the applicable census from 1910 to 1890. The effect was to reduce greatly the number of Southern and Eastern European immigrants. A more controversial section of the act prohibited Japanese immigration altogether by denying entrance to any alien ineligible for citizenship, as the Japanese had been since a U.S. Supreme Court ruling in 1922. This measure substantially worsened

Japanese-American relations. Ellis, L. Ethan, *Republican Foreign Policy, 1921–1933* (1968); Neu, Charles E., *The Troubled Encounter* (1975).

JOINT OCCUPATION, a phrase used by British and American diplomats to describe the status of the Oregon Territory by virtue of the Convention of 1818* and the Joint Occupation Treaty (1827).* According to Bemis, the term is misleading because it implies a cooperative governance, when in fact the meaning was that the territory was open for settlement by subjects or citizens of either Britain or the United States. Bemis, Samuel F., *John Quincy Adams and the Foundations of American Foreign Policy* (1949); Merk, Frederick, *The Oregon Question* (1967).

JOINT OCCUPATION TREATY (1827). This treaty was a renewal of the joint occupation* status of Oregon, originally stipulated in the Convention of 1818,* extending such occupation indefinitely and requiring one year's notice for abrogation. The treaty was ultimately superseded by the Oregon Treaty (1846),* but in 1827 it demonstrated the inability of Albert Gallatin,* the American negotiator, and his British counterparts to settle the Oregon question.* Merk, Frederick, *The Oregon Question* (1967); Pletcher, David, *The Diplomacy of Annexation* (1973).

JONES, HILARY POLLARD (1863–1938). A leading advocate of U.S. naval strength in the interwar period, Hilary Jones was born in Hanover County, Virginia, on November 14, 1863, and graduated from the U.S. Naval Academy in 1884. He rose through the ranks in the navy in a succession of ship and shore tours, served in the Spanish-American War, and reached the rank of rear admiral in 1917. During World War I, he was principally on duty in the Atlantic, though by the war's end, he had an administrative post in Newport News, Virginia. Promoted to admiral in 1921, he was commander in chief of the entire U.S. fleet in 1922–1923. His connection with U.S. diplomacy concerns his participation in the 1927 ("Coolidge") Geneva Naval Conference,* where his stalwart insistence on a larger quota of heavy cruisers than the British wanted to allow contributed to the collapse of that conference, and in the 1930 London Naval Conference,* where his renewed assertion for higher American limits was torpedoed by his fellow delegates in a compromise arrangement. Jones married Virginia Lippincott in 1917 and died in Washington, D.C., on New Year's Day, 1938. *DAB*, Supp. 2:351–52; Ferrell, Robert H., *Peace in Their Time* (1952); *New York Times*, January 2, 1938; *WWWA*, 1 (1897–1942):648.

JUDD, NORMAN BUEL (1815–1878). Minister to Prussia during the Civil War, Norman Judd was born in Rome, New York, on January 10, 1815, and educated in local schools. He read law, was admitted to the bar in 1836, and moved to Chicago the same year. There he was city attorney (1837–1838), alderman (1842–1844), and Illinois state senator (1844–1860) while practicing law, specializing in railroad issues. An early convert to the Republican party, he was chairman of the party's committee in Illinois, 1856–1860, and helped arrange the Lincoln-Douglas debates. In 1860, he managed Lincoln's campaign but lost a race for governor and settled instead for an appointment as minister to Prussia. Judd, like other ministers in Europe, capably prevented recognition and undue aid to the Confederacy. After returning to Illinois, Judd was elected to the U.S. House of Representatives (1867–1871) and served as collector of customs in Chicago (1872–1876). He married Adeline Rossiter in 1844 and died in Chicago November 11, 1878. *DAB*, 20:230; Edwards, Arthur, *Sketch of the Life of Norman Judd* (1878); *NCAB*, 11:273.

KALTENBORN, HANS von (1878–1965). H. V. Kaltenborn was born in Milwaukee on July 9, 1878, and graduated from Harvard in 1909, after several years of working in his father's business, serving in the Spanish-American War, being a traveling salesman in France, reporting for the *Brooklyn Eagle*, and tutoring the children of the Astor family. After college, he went back to work for the *Brooklyn Eagle* until 1930, although he also was involved in radio work after 1922. In 1929, he joined CBS, covering, among other events, the London Economic Conference (1933),*other international conferences, and the Spanish Civil War,* in which he was the first radio correspondent to report a live battle. His greatest fame came with his up-to-the-minute broadcast of the 1938 Munich Conference.* Known for his extemporaneous commentary, Kaltenborn was highly regarded by his contemporaries in broadcasting and was the first to show that radio could be useful as a medium of reporting foreign affairs. Politically he was an internationalist, favoring harsh measures against Germany and Japan and earning the wrath of America First.* He continued in radio until his retirement in 1955 and died in New York City on June 14, 1965. Kaltenborn married the Baroness Olga von Nordenflycht in 1910 and was the author of several books, including an autobiography, *Fifty Fabulous Years* (1950). *CB* (1940): 446–48; Culbert, David H., *News for Everyman* (1976); *New York Times*, June 15, 1965; *WWWA*, 4 (1961–1968):510.

KANAGAWA, TREATY OF (1854). This was the first treaty between Japan and a Western nation. In it, Japan promised not to imprison crews of shipwrecked vessels and opened the ports of Shimoda and Hakodate for U.S. ships to obtain wood, water, and other supplies. American consuls* could be stationed at Shimoda and Hakodate, and commerce between the two nations could be conducted strictly on a cash basis, supervised by government officials. The treaty did contain the most-favored-nation* clause but not provisions for extraterritoriality. Additionally, there may have been an unwritten pledge made by Commodore Matthew C. Perry,* who negotiated the treaty for the United States, that the United States would aid Japan in any controversy between Japan and a European power. Dennett, Tyler, *Americans in Eastern Asia* (1922); Dulles, Foster R., *Yankees and Samurai* (1965).

KASSON, JOHN ADAM (1822–1910). John A. Kasson was born January 11, 1822, in Charlotte, Vermont, graduated from the University of Vermont in 1842, read law, and was admitted to the bar in 1845. By 1857, he had moved to Des

Moines, Iowa, where he became involved in Republican party politics. A delegate to the 1860 convention, he drafted much of the platform. He became assistant postmaster-general in 1861, attended the Paris Postal Conference in 1863, and negotiated six postal conventions. Kasson served as a U.S. congressman from 1863 to 1867 and again from 1873 to 1877. From 1877 to 1881, he was minister to Austria-Hungary, where he was popular but faced no important diplomatic issues. In 1884, he was named minister to Germany; he stayed only until 1885, but it was far more productive than his previous ministry. In Germany, he was the American representative at the Berlin Conference (1884–1885)* and was especially active in the treaty deliberations concerning humane treatment of Africans and regional neutrality. In 1889, he represented the United States at the Berlin Conference concerning Samoa, helping negotiate the Tripartite Treaty* with Britain and Germany. Finally, in 1898, Kasson was a member of the Canadian-American Joint High Commission dealing with the Alaska boundary question and as a special commissioner on reciprocity as authorized by the Dingley Tariff (1897). Also a writer and historian, Kasson published a history of the Monroe Doctrine,* a centennial history of the Constitution, and works dealing with the tariff. Kasson, who was never married, died May 18, 1910, in Washington. Buggs, John E., "Iowa and the Diplomatic Service," *Iowa Journal of History and Politics* 19 (1921): 321–65; *DAB*, 10:260; *New York Times*, May 19, 1910; Younger, Edward, *John A. Kasson: Politics and Diplomacy from Lincoln to McKinley* (1955).

KEARNEY, LAWRENCE (1789–1868). A career naval officer, Lawrence Kearney was born in Perth Amboy, New Jersey, on November 30, 1789, and joined the navy in 1807. Appointed a lieutenant in 1813, he commanded various smaller vessels, saw some action in the War of 1812, and was eventually promoted to captain in 1832. In 1840 he was given command of the East India Squadron and went to China, where for several years he played an influential role in the early development of U.S.-Chinese relations. He impressed the Chinese with his declaration that the United States did not sanction opium smuggling or the violation of Chinese trade laws and was able to arrange indemnity payments for American merchants who had lost goods during the Opium War. His talks with the Chinese concerning equal trading rights for the United States helped lead to the Treaty of Wanghia (1844).* Throughout the early 1840s, Kearney transmitted much valuable information to Washington. After his tour in China, Kearney had command duty at various land posts until his retirement from the navy in 1861. Married to Josephine C. Hall in 1834, he died in Perth Amboy on November 29, 1868. His correspondence on China was published by the U.S. Senate (Sen. Doc. No. 139, 29th Cong., 1st. sess.). *DAB*, 10:270; Dennett, Tyler, *Americans in Eastern Asia* (1922).

KEATING, KENNETH BARNARD (1900–1975). Kenneth Keating was born in Lima, New York, on May 18, 1900, and received an A.B. from the University of Rochester (1919) and an LL.B. from Harvard (1923). He practiced law in

Rochester, taught in the Far East as a colonel in the army in World War II, and entered politics after the war. Elected as a Republican to the U.S. House of Representatives in 1946, he served six terms before a successful race for the Senate in 1958. In his one Senate term, he gained national attention by his early warning of Soviet missiles implanted in Cuba—the beginning of the Cuban missile crisis.* Defeated for reelection in 1964, Keating practiced law until his appointment as ambassador to India in 1969. His tour in India (1969–1972) was punctuated by the India-Pakistan dispute, in which Keating was harshly criticized when American aid to India was cut in 1971, his protests for a more positive Indian policy notwithstanding. Named ambassador to Israel in 1973, his role was subordinate to that of Secretary of State Henry Kissinger,* trying in frequent trips to the Middle East to bring about a regional peace settlement. In the spring of 1975 he returned to the United States for health reasons and died May 5 in New York City. *New York Times*, May 6, 1975.

KEITH, MINOR COOPER (1848–1929). Born January 19, 1848, in Brooklyn, Keith went west as a young man and entered the cattle-raising business. In 1872, he began planting bananas in Costa Rica while building a railroad from San José to Limón, completed in 1890. He married Cristina Castro, daughter of José M. Castro, an ex-president of Costa Rica, expanded his banana properties to Panama and Nicaragua, and continued development of a unified Central American railway system. By 1898, Keith was the largest banana grower in Central America. In 1899, he was a cofounder, with Andrew W. Preston, of the United Fruit Company* and for many years was a vice-president and plantation manager for the company. He urged, without success, U.S. financial intervention in Honduras in 1913 and was deeply involved in the international debt problems of Costa Rica and Guatemala, whose governments had borrowed heavily to subsidize his railroad construction. He retired from active plantation management in 1921 and died in Babylon, New York, on June 14, 1929. Adams, F. U., *Conquest of the Tropics* (1914); *DAB*, 10:291; Findling, John E., *Close Neighbors, Distant Friends* (1987); Kepner, C. D., Jr., and J. H. Soothill, *The Banana Empire* (1935); Munro, Dana G., *Intervention and Dollar Diplomacy in the Caribbean, 1900–1921* (1964); *New York Times*, June 15, 1929; Stewart, Watt, *Keith and Costa Rica* (1964).

KELLOGG, FRANK BILLINGS (1856–1937). Secretary of state under President Calvin Coolidge from 1925 to 1929, Frank B. Kellogg was born in Potsdam, New York, on December 22, 1856. His family moved to Minnesota soon after his birth, with the result that he was raised on a farm and received little formal education. However, he read law and was admitted to the bar in 1877. After ten years of law practice and local political involvement, Kellogg joined a large Minneapolis law firm and over the next twenty-five years became one of the country's most prominent lawyers through his involvement in the trust-busting suits of the Theodore Roosevelt era. In 1912, he was elected president of the American Bar Association; in 1917, he was elected to the U.S. Senate as a

Republican. In the Senate, he was a "mild reservationist"* on the League of Nations.* In 1923, after Coolidge assumed the presidency, Kellogg replaced George Harvey* as ambassador to Great Britain. There he participated in the reparations conference that resulted in the Dawes Plan (1924)* and helped mediate differences between French and German representatives. In early 1925, Kellogg was called back to Washington to be secretary of state. As secretary, he signed some eighty treaties, including conciliation treaties with Latin American nations, treaties related to liquor prohibition in the United States, and various arbitration,* commercial, and extradition treaties. He dealt with Chinese recognition and received substantial criticism for renewing intervention in Nicaragua. His most notable achievement was the negotiation of the Kellogg-Briand Pact (1928),* for which he received the Nobel Peace Prize in 1929. After leaving the State Department, Kellogg served a term as a judge on the Permanent Court of International Justice (1930–1935).* Married to Clara M. Cook in 1886, Kellogg died in St. Paul, Minnesota, on December 21, 1937. Bryn-Jones, David, *Frank B. Kellogg: A Biography* (1937); *DAB*, Supp. 2:355; Ellis, L. Ethan, *Republican Foreign Policy, 1921–1933* (1965); Ferrell, Robert, *Peace in Their Time* (1952); *New York Times*, December 22, 1937; Wank, Solomon, ed., *Doves and Diplomats* (1978).

KELLOGG-BRIAND PACT (1928). A multilateral covenant signed by nearly all the nations of the world, the Kellogg-Briand Pact (also known as the Pact of Paris) attempted to outlaw war "as an instrument of national policy." French Premier Aristide Briand first raised the idea in April 1927; he sought a bilateral Franco-American treaty. Secretary of State Frank B. Kellogg* suggested the pact be broadened in scope to include all nations. In this form, it was signed August 27, 1928. On January 15, 1929, the Senate ratified the treaty, 85–1. The Kellogg-Briand Pact was solely dependent on moral suasion and though frequently invoked seems to have had no tangible effect on world events in subsequent years. Doenecke, Justus D., comp., *The Diplomacy of Frustration* (1981); Ellis, L. Ethan, *Republican Foreign Policy, 1921–1933* (1968); Ferrell, Robert H., *Peace in their Time: The Origins of the Kellogg-Briand Pact* (1952); *FR* (1928), 1:1–231.

KENNAN, GEORGE FROST (b. 1904). A leading figure in the diplomacy of Soviet-American relations since World War II and an important foreign policy theorist, George F. Kennan was born in Milwaukee on February 16, 1904, graduated from Princeton in 1925, and joined the Foreign Service the following year. After service in minor posts in Geneva and Hamburg, Kennan studied Russian language and culture in Berlin, 1929–1931, went to Soviet observation posts in the Baltic cities of Tallinn and Riga, and then was a member of the first mission to Moscow, 1933, spending much of the next three years there. Before World War II, he was also posted in Prague (1938–1939) and Berlin, where he was at the beginning of World War II. Interned by the Germans for several months, he was repatriated in 1942 and spent the remainder of the war as a counselor* in Lisbon, 1942–1943, with the European Advisory Committee in

London, 1943–1944, and as minister-counselor in Moscow, 1944–1946. His perceptions about Soviet intentions contributed to his return to Washington for a brief stint with the National War College (1946–1947) and, more important, as director of the Policy Planning Staff of the State Department (1947–1949), where the policy of containment* originated. Kennan developed in these years a view of Soviet Russia as internally insecure but untrustworthy and aggressively expansive and advocated a forceful policy in response. This was the basis for his *Foreign Affairs* article, "The Sources of Soviet Power," signed "Mr. X," outlining containment. To Kennan's later regret, the article also became the basis of a highly militarized global containment policy, something he never intended in the original concept. Later he softened his attitude toward the Soviet Union and urged a policy of disengagement,* based on a neutralized, nonaligned area of Central Europe around and including Germany. In 1952, Kennan was appointed ambassador to the Soviet Union but served only a short while before being declared persona non grata by the Soviets for some unflattering remarks he made in Berlin about Soviet treatment of Western diplomats. A teacher at Princeton and Oxford during the remainder of the 1950s, Kennan returned to diplomatic service in 1961 as the Kennedy administration's ambassador to Yugoslavia. He remained only two years at his post before leaving the diplomatic service out of disgust with the continued cold war* attitudes of the administration. He returned to teaching and writing, describing himself as "sort of neoisolationist" and calling for a gradual withdrawal from Vietnam in 1966. Kennan married Annelise Sorenson in 1931 and has written a number of important books, including *American Diplomacy, 1900–1950* (1951), *Soviet-American Relations, 1917–1920* (2 vols., 1956–1958), *Russia, the Atom, and the West* (1958), *Memoirs, 1925–1950* (1967), *Memoirs, 1950–1963* (1972), *A Cloud of Danger* (1977), and *The Nuclear Delusion* (1982). Feis, Herbert, *From Trust to Terror* (1970); Isaacson, Walter, and Evan Thomas, *The Wise Men: Six Friends and the World They Made* (1986); *NCAB*, 1:308; Paterson, Thomas G., "George F. Kennan and American Foreign Policy," in Merli, Frank, and Theodore A. Wilson, eds., *Makers of American Diplomacy*, vol. 2 (1974); *WWA* (1976–1977):1693; X, Mr., "The Sources of Soviet Power," *Foreign Affairs* 25 (July 1947):566–82; " 'X' Plus 25: Interview with George F. Kennan," *Foreign Policy* 7 (Summer 1972): 5–21.

KENNEDY, JOSEPH PATRICK (1888–1969). Father of President John F. Kennedy, Joseph P. Kennedy made his own mark in U.S. diplomacy. Born in Boston on September 6, 1888, he graduated from Harvard in 1912, married Rose Fitzgerald in 1914, and embarked on a business career that centered around banking and theater operations in the Boston area. In 1926, Kennedy moved to New York and, foreseeing problems in the stock market, sold out before the 1929 crash. A supporter of Franklin D. Roosevelt in 1932, he entered public life with the Roosevelt administration as the first chairman of the Securities and Exchange Commission, 1935–1937. With the end of prohibition, Kennedy also became an important and successful liquor franchiser. In 1938, he was appointed ambassador to Great Britain, a post he held until 1940. In London, he became a close confidant of Prime Minister Neville Chamberlain, agreeing with his policy of appeasement and trying to keep the United States out of European affairs by nurturing cordial German-American relations, which included a plan to take Jewish people out of Germany and resettle them around the world. To the dismay of Roosevelt and the State Department, Kennedy often argued with and tried to alter State Department policies and frequently misled the department concerning his activities. According to Koskoff, he did not comprehend the nature and threat of nazism. After his return to the United States, Kennedy increased his fortune through oil and real estate investments and shepherded the political careers of his sons. He died in Hyannis Port, Massachusetts, on November 18, 1969. Jones, Kenneth Paul, *U.S. Diplomats in Europe, 1919–1941* (1981); Kaufmann, William W., "Two American Ambassadors: Bullitt and Kennedy," in Craig, Gordon, and Felix Gilbert, eds., *The Diplomats* (1953); Koskoff, David E., *Joseph P. Kennedy* (1974); *New York Times*, November 19, 1969.

KENNEDY ROUND, tariff negotiations, 1963–1967. The Kennedy Round was the sixth session of tariff negotiations under the procedures laid down by the General Agreement on Tariffs and Trade (GATT)* in 1947. Former Secretary of State Christian A. Herter* was the chief U.S. negotiator early in the talks; W. Michael Blumenthal and William M. Roth were also important U.S. negotiators. The Kennedy Round was initiated in 1963 at Geneva after the passage of the Trade Expansion Act (1962), legislation resulting from concern over the increasing economic strength of Western Europe and the lack in the United States of substantially forceful negotiating power. In general, the talks attempted to increase U.S. exports to Common Market nations in return for greater access to U.S. markets for European products through the mutual reduction of tariffs. After four years of negotiations among fifty-three nations, the average tariff reduction among major trading nations was in the range of 35 to 39 percent. A total of $40 billion of trade volume was affected by the reductions, although achievements were limited in the areas of textiles and agricultural products and with respect to developing nations. In addition, the delegates to the Kennedy Round concluded a joint agreement to supply 4.5 million tons of wheat per year as food aid and drafted an international code to help standardize antidumping practices. Curtis, Thomas B., and John Robert Vastine, Jr., *The Kennedy Round and the Future of American Trade* (1971); Evans, John W., *The Kennedy Round in American Trade Policy* (1971); Hammond, Paul Y., *Cold War and Détente* (1975); Preeg, Ernest H., *Traders and Diplomats* (1970).

KILPATRICK, HUGH JUDSON (1836–1881). Judson Kilpatrick was born near Deckertown, New Jersey, on January 14, 1836, and was an 1861 graduate of West Point. He fought in Virginia during the Civil War, rising to the rank of brevet major general for gallantry in the campaign in the Carolinas in early 1865. The *Nation* described Kilpatrick at this time as a "harum-scarum cavalry leader.'' Appointed minister to Chile in late 1865, he served four uneventful years in the South American post before returning to the United States and private life in 1870. He returned to Chile as U.S. minister in 1881 and became involved in a controversy with U.S. Minister to Peru Stephen W. Hurlbut* over the question of whether Peru should be compelled to cede territory to Chile as part of the settlement of the War of the Pacific,* which Chile had won. Before the dispute could be resolved, Kilpatrick died of kidney trouble in Santiago, Chile, on December 4, 1881. *DAB*, 10:374; Millington, Herbert, *American Diplomacy in the War of the Pacific* (1948); *NCAB*, 4:273; *New York Times*, December 27, 1881; *WWWA*, Historical Volume, pp. 293–94.

KING, RUFUS (1755–1827). Twice minister to Great Britain (1796–1803, 1825–1826), Rufus King was one of the most prominent members of the Federalist party in the early National period. He was born March 24, 1755, in Scarboro, Maine, graduated from Harvard (1777), and was admitted to the bar in 1780. He was a member of the Confederation Congress, 1784–1786, a delegate to the Constitutional Convention, 1787, where he distinguished himself as an orator, and a U.S. senator from 1789 to 1796. He was the vice-presidential nominee of the Federalist party in 1804 and 1808 and the presidential nominee of the party in 1816, all lost causes. In his first, and most important, ministry to Britain, he dealt with questions arising from the claims commission authorized by Jay's Treaty* and with British public opinion during the quasi-war* with France, and urged the United States to exploit the revolutionary situation in South America. He also negotiated the King-Hawkesbury Convention (1803),* dealing with the U.S.–Canadian boundary. Between his two missions, he was a U.S. senator (1813–1825) and chairman of the Senate Foreign Relations Committee (1822–1823). King was seventy and in fragile health when he embarked on his second ministry to Britain, and it lasted only a year before illness dictated his return to the United States. The mission was as unsuccessful as it was short; King was able to deal only with the matter of slave indemnities from the War of 1812 and could reach no agreeable settlement on this matter. He died in New York City on April 29, 1827, a few months after his return from London. *DAB*, 10:398; Ernst, Robert, *Rufus King, American Federalist* (1968); Willson, Beckles, *America's Ambassadors to England, 1785–1929* (1929).

KING, WILLIAM RUFUS DE VANE (1786–1853). Born in Sampson County, North Carolina, on April 7, 1786, William R. King graduated from the University of North Carolina in 1803, read law, and was admitted to the bar in 1806. He soon embarked on a political career, serving in the U.S. House of Representatives, 1810–1816, and the Senate, 1818–1844 and 1846–1853. From 1844 to 1846, King was minister to France, where his main tasks were to prevent joint Anglo-French intervention into Texas and to procure French acceptance of Texas annexation. By October 1845, King reported that the French would accept annexation. Another French concern was Hawaii, and King assured the government that American interests in the islands were simply to avoid European dominance and not for the purpose of bringing them into the United States. King returned to the Senate, 1846–1853, and, as chairman of the Foreign Relations Committee during this time, played a major role in the ratification of the Clayton-Bulwer Treaty (1850).* Elected vice-president on the Pierce ticket in 1852, King went to Cuba seeking respite from tuberculosis early in 1853 but died April 18, 1853, in Catawba, Alabama, shortly after his return from Cuba. *DAB*, 10:406; *NCAB*, 4:147; Willson, Beckles, *America's Ambassadors to France, 1777–1927* (1928).

KING COTTON DIPLOMACY, phrase used to describe the fundamental diplomacy of the Confederacy during the Civil War, based on the economic strength of cotton. The premise used by Confederate leaders was that because England and France considered southern cotton so vital to their economies, those nations would give recognition and aid to the South and protest the northern blockade in order to regain access to the cotton supply. The South attempted to deny cotton to Europe, first through an embargo and later through reduction (by burning and other means) of the total amount of cotton available. King Cotton Diplomacy failed because of substantial stockpiling of cotton before the war, British fear of war with the North, the development of India as an alternative source of cotton, and profits from other British industries, such as linen, wool, munitions, and merchant shipping. Blumenthal, Henry, "Confederate Diplomacy: Popular Notions and International Realities," *Journal of Southern History* 32 (1966): 1512–71; Crook, D. P., *Diplomacy during the American Civil War* (1975); Owsley, Frank, *King Cotton Diplomacy*, 2d ed. (1959); Warren, Gordon, H., "The King Cotton Theory," in DeConde, Alexander, ed., *Encyclopedia of American Foreign Policy* (1979).

KING-CRANE COMMISSION (1919). More formally known as the American Section of the Interallied Commission on Mandates in Turkey, this commission was appointed by President Woodrow Wilson to gather information about the Middle East and the Ottoman Empire for the purpose of creating a stable peace in the Middle East. The commission—led by Charles R. Crane,* a Chicago industrialist and former minister-designate to China, and Dr. Henry Churchill King, a professor of religion at Oberlin College—was appointed in April 1919 and left Paris near the end of May. After spending two and one-half months in the Middle East, the commission submitted a report and recommendations regarding mandates for Syria and Palestine, Iraq, and Turkey. These recommendations, which included an active American mandatory role in the area, had little impact on U.S. foreign policy (or the Paris Peace Conference)* but, according to Howard, constituted a "constructive and challenging contribution to the technique of peacemaking." *FR* (1919), The Paris Peace Conference, 12:745–866; Howard, Harry N., *The King-Crane Commission* (1963); Stookey, Robert W., *America and the Arab States* (1975).

KING-HAWKESBURY CONVENTION (1803). This proposed convention between the United States and Great Britain would have closed gaps in the northwestern and northeastern boundaries between the United States and Canada. The northwestern boundary would have been fixed by a line drawn from the source of the Mississippi River to the Lake of the Woods; the northeastern, by a mixed commission. The treaty was never ratified by the U.S. Senate, and the boundary questions were settled by the Convention of 1818* and the Webster-Ashburton Treaty (1842).* Bemis, Samuel F., *John Quincy Adams and the Foundations of American Foreign Policy* (1949).

KINNEY, WILLIAM BURNET (1799–1880). An important U.S. diplomatic representative to Italy (then accredited to Sardinia and headquartered at Turin), William B. Kinney was born in Speedwell, New Jersey, on September 4, 1799, attended but did not graduate from West Point, and became a journalist, working first for the *New Jersey Eagle*, a Newark weekly. From 1825 to 1835, he was a literary adviser to Hayser & Brothers, New York publishers, and from 1835 to 1850, he edited the *Newark Daily Advertiser*. In 1850, he was named chargé d'affaires* to Sardinia. There he advised the government in its constitutional reconstruction along more democratic lines and successfully urged provisions for greater religious tolerance. Kinney also advised Secretary of State Daniel Webster* against giving official recognition to Hungarian revolutionary Louis Kossuth during his U.S. tour in 1851 because of adverse European reaction. He resigned in 1853 and lived in Florence, Italy, where he was friendly with the literary Brownings and worked on a history of the Medici family. In the early 1860s, he advised Cavour and other Italian nationalists as they prepared to unify Italy. Kinney returned to Newark in 1865 and involved himself in literary work until his death in New York City on October 21, 1880. He was married twice. *DAB*, 10:417; *NCAB*, 13:156.

KIRK, ALAN GOODRICH (1882–1963). A native of Philadelphia, where he was born October 30, 1888, Alan G. Kirk graduated from the U.S. Naval Academy in 1909 and remained on active duty with the navy until 1946, retiring with the rank of admiral. During his naval career, he graduated from and taught at the Naval War College (1929–1931), was naval attaché at the U.S. embassy in London (1939–1941), and commanded the U.S. naval forces during the invasion of Normandy (1944). Upon his retirement, he entered a diplomatic career that took him as ambassador to Belgium (1946–1949), the Soviet Union (1949–1951), and China (1962–1963). In addition, he served as the U.S. representative on a United Nations* Special Committee on the Balkans (1947–1948) and undertook unofficial missions during the Congo crisis (1961).* Kirk's most important post was in the Soviet Union, where he represented the United States during the Korean War and the height of cold war* tensions. He was able to confer very seldom with Soviet leaders (only once with Premier Joseph Stalin) and instead worked to maintain a high level of embassy morale and traveled as much as possible in the Soviet Union. In China, his main task was dealing with the aging and irascible Chiang Kai-shek. Between his assignments in the Soviet Union and China, Kirk served as head of the American Committee for the Liberation of the People of Russia, working with radio broadcasts and dissident exile groups. In 1961, he was president of the Belgian-American Development Corporation and had close ties with mineral producers in the Katanga province of the Congo. Kirk, who married Lydia S. Chapin in 1918, died in New York City on October 15, 1963. *NCAB*, 50:407–8; *New York Times*, May 5, 1962, October 16, 1963; *WWWA*, 4 (1961–1968):532.

KIRKPATRICK, JEANE DUANE (JORDAN) (b. 1926). Jeane Jordan was born in Duncan, Oklahoma, on November 19, 1926, graduated from Barnard College (A.B., 1948) and Columbia University (M.A., 1950), and married Evron M. Kirkpatrick in 1955. She received a Ph.D. from Columbia in 1967. During the 1950s, she had been a researcher for the State Department, George Washington University, and the Fund for the Republic; in 1962, she began a teaching career at Trinity College in Washington, D.C. Since 1967, she has taught at Georgetown when not engaged in public service. Although she was nominally a Democrat through the 1970s, she attracted the attention of the Reagan administration in 1981 because of her article, "Dictatorships and Double Standards," published in *Commentary* magazine in 1979 and later expanded into a monograph. The article, which attempted to draw a distinction between redeemable authorization dictators of the right and irredeemable totalitarian dictators of the left, led to her appointment as ambassador to the United Nations* in 1981. At the United Nations, she reflected the staunch anti-Communist line of the administration but was criticized for her inflexibility and for a tendency to lecture her colleagues rather than discuss with them. But she effectively prevented the imposition of sanctions against Israel after the bombing of a nuclear power reactor in Iraq. Within the administration, Kirkpatrick developed a reputation as a conservative ideologue and was influential in the formulation of a Central American policy that emphasized the East-West dimension of the conflicts in El Salvador and Nicaragua. Unhappy at being passed over for a more influential position in the administration, Kirkpatrick resigned in 1985 and returned to teaching. In addition to *Dictatorships and Double Standards*, she has written *Political Women* (1974), *Dismantling the Parties* (1978), and *The Reagan Phenomenon* (1982). Brownstein, Ronald, and Nina Easton, *Reagan's Ruling Class* (1982); *CB* (1981):255–59; Ewell, Judith, "Barely in the Inner Circle: Jeane Kirkpatrick," in Crapol, Edward P., *Women and American Foreign Policy* (1987); Fasulo, Linda M., *Representing America: Experiences of U.S. Diplomats at the UN* (1984); Finger, Seymour Maxwell, "Jeane Kirkpatrick at the United Nations," *Foreign Affairs* 62, 2 (Winter 1983–1984): 436–57; *New York Times*, April 28, 1985; *WWA* (1986–1987):1537.

KISSINGER, HENRY ALFRED (b. 1923). One of the most influential secretaries of state in the twentieth century, Henry A. Kissinger was born in the Bavarian town of Fürth on May 27, 1923, immigrated to the United States in

1938, served in World War II and subsequently in occupied Germany until 1946, and then went to Harvard (B.A., 1950; M.A., 1952; Ph.D., 1954). Remaining at Harvard as a faculty member after 1954, Kissinger also held frequent consultative and research appointments. From 1954 to 1956, he was a research director for the Council of Foreign Relations,* his work resulting in *Nuclear Weapons and Foreign Policy* (1957), a book that challenged the prevailing defense policy of massive retaliation* and advocated a flexible response. His next book, *The Necessity of Choice* (1961), developed from a directorship of a Rockefeller Brothers special studies project in 1956–1958. A National Security Council* consultant from 1961 to 1962, he resigned because of his opposition to the formation of a multilateral nuclear force as part of the North Atlantic Treaty Organization,* but returned to government service as a State Department consultant, 1965–1969, where he took part in secret meetings with the North Vietnamese that helped pave the way to the opening of peace talks in 1968. Although Kissinger had little prior acquaintance with President Richard Nixon when the latter began his presidency in 1969, he was named special assistant for national security affairs, a post that allowed him to be executive secretary of the National Security Council. His ideas and style were complementary with those of Nixon, and although the two were not personally close, they forged a harmonious and efficient working relationship and concentrated foreign policy machinery in the White House. Kissinger's foreign policy was based on the idea of balance of power,* a concept emanating from his own historical study of early nineteenth-century Europe and on the belief that Soviet policy was inherently destabilizing. A realist, he believed that the United States should strive for legitimate national interests and not such visionary goals as permanent world peace or the conquest of communism. Hence, under Nixon and Kissinger, the confrontations of the cold war* were replaced by new initiatives directed toward finding areas of cooperation with the USSR and China—a policy known as détente.* In addition, Kissinger worked to stabilize existing problem areas of the world, winning the Nobel Peace Prize in 1973 (with Le Duc Tho) for negotiating the cease-fire agreement that ended the U.S. role in the Vietnam War, attempting to settle the complex Middle East situation after the Yom Kippur War (1973)* by extensive personal diplomacy, and opening the way for Nixon's trip to China in 1972 and the subsequent establishment of limited diplomatic relations with Beijing. Kissinger was also involved in the destabilization of the elected leftist Chilean government in 1973, in covert attempts to influence national elections in Italy in 1972, and in initiating the Strategic Arms Limitation Talks (SALT)* with the Soviet Union. In mid-1973, Kissinger replaced William P. Rogers* as secretary of state and continued in that position during the administration of President Gerald R. Ford (1974–1977). According to Stoessinger, Kissinger's greatest success was his work in the opening of China, made possible by his ability to exploit the Sino-Soviet split. His biggest failure was Vietnam, since, concludes Stoessinger, a similar peace could have been made in 1969, and the Cambodian incursion (1970)* was a bad blunder. Since 1977, Kissinger, who has been married twice, has taught at Georgetown University and has published his memoirs, *The White House Years* (1979), *For the Record* (1981), and *Years of Upheaval* (1982). In 1983, President Ronald Reagan named Kissinger chairman of the National Bipartisan Commission on Central America.* Among his other writings are: *A World Restored: Castlereagh, Metternich, and the Restoration of Peace, 1812–1822* (1957), *The Troubled Partnership* (1965), and *American Foreign Policy* (1974). After leaving public life, Kissinger founded an international consulting group, Kissinger Associates, Inc. *CB* (1972):254–57; Roskin, Michael, "Henry A. Kissinger and the Global Balance of Power," in Merli, Frank G., and Theodore A. Wilson, eds., *Makers of American Diplomacy*, vol. 2 (1974); Starr, Harvey, *Henry Kissinger: Perceptions of International Politics* (1984); Stoessinger, John G., *Henry Kissinger: The Anguish of Power* (1976); Szulc, Tad, *The Illusion of Peace* (1978); *WWA* (1986–1987):1540.

KISSINGER COMMISSION. See **NATIONAL BIPARTISAN COMMISSION ON CENTRAL AMERICA.**

KNOX, PHILANDER CHASE (1853–1921). Best known for his policy of dollar diplomacy,* Philander C. Knox was born in Brownsville, Pennsylvania, on May 6, 1853. He graduated from Mount Union College in Ohio (1872) and was admitted to the bar three years later. He married Lillie Smith in 1880 and soon became a leading corporate lawyer in Pittsburgh and was president of the Pennsylvania Bar Association in 1897. Soon after, Knox played a major role in the creation of the U.S. Steel Corporation, and in 1901 he became attorney general and examined and cleared the title of the New Panama Canal Company* to its property prior to the Hay–Bunau-Varilla Treaty (1903).* From 1904 to 1909, Knox was a U.S. senator from Pennsylvania, and in 1909 incoming President William Howard Taft named him secretary of state. With First Assistant Secretary F. M. Huntington Wilson,* Knox reorganized the State Department on a divisional basis and extended the merit system. But his major interest was in the protection and encouragement to American business abroad—the policy known as dollar diplomacy—especially in China and Latin America. Among other issues Knox faced were the denial to Japan of the purchase of Magdalena Bay in Mexico (Lodge Corollary)* and the settlement of the Bering Sea sealing and North Atlantic fisheries controversies. However, poor relations with Congress scuttled ratification of an arbitration* treaty with Great Britain and financial treaties with Nicaragua, Honduras, and Liberia. Leaving the State Department at the end of Taft's term in 1913, Knox returned to his law practice until 1917, when he was elected again to the Senate. Knox remained in the Senate until his death in Washington on October 12, 1921, and was an "irreconcilable"* during the debate over the ratification of the Treaty of Versailles,* believing that America's joining the League of Nations* under the treaty stipulations would be unconstitutional. *DAB*, 10:478; Scholes, Walter F., "Philander C. Knox," in Graebner, Norman, ed., *An Uncertain Tradition* (1961); *New York Times*, October 13, 1921; Wilson,

F. M. Huntington, *Memoirs of an Ex-diplomat* (1946); Wright, Herbert F., "Philander C. Knox," in Bemis, Samuel F., ed., *American Secretaries of State and Their Diplomacy*, vol. 9 (1929).

KNOX-CASTRILLO CONVENTION (1911). Signed by Secretary of State Philander C. Knox* and Salvatore Castrillo, Nicaraguan minister to the United States, this convention called for a $15 million loan to Nicaragua backed by an American-managed customs collectorship. When the ratification vote was delayed until the 1912 session of Congress, American bankers provided a short-term loan in September 1911. In December, the custom collectorship went into operation, serving both American and foreign bondholders. Despite strong efforts by Taft and Knox to obtain ratification, the convention failed on an unusual tie vote to receive a favorable report from the Foreign Relations Committee in May 1912. The heavy involvement of bankers in Nicaragua in anticipation of favorable treaty action could not be undone, and when a revolution broke out in July, U.S. military intervention was assured. Callcott, Wilfrid H., *The Caribbean Policy of the United States, 1890–1920* (1942); Munro, Dana G., *Intervention and Dollar Diplomacy in the Caribbean, 1900–1921* (1964).

KOHLER, FOY DAVID (b. 1908). A leading post–World War II Soviet expert, Foy D. Kohler was born in Oakwood, Ohio, on February 15, 1908, attended the University of Toledo, and graduated from Ohio State University in 1931, the same year he joined the Foreign Service. Over the next fourteen years, he served in minor posts in Windsor, Bucharest, Belgrade, Athens, Cairo, and Washington. He served on the U.S. delegation at the San Francisco Conference (1945),* was an observer of the Greek elections (1945–1946), and in 1947 became the first secretary and counselor at the U.S. embassy in Moscow, serving there until 1949 and acting as chargé d'affaires* for a time in 1948. From 1949 to 1952, he was chief of the Division of International Broadcasting, operating the Voice of America. After four years as counselor in Ankara (1952–1956), Kohler directed the International Cooperation Administration (ICA) (1956–1958) and was a deputy assistant secretary of state (1958–1959). In 1959, he was promoted to assistant secretary of state for European affairs; three years at this post included the day-to-day management of the Berlin crisis* as director of the Berlin Task Force and led to his most important assignment, ambassador to the Soviet Union. In Moscow, he worked to get talks on Berlin and disarmament moving again, to seek ways of reducing the chances of nuclear war; in general, his experiences reassured him about the likelihood of continued peaceful coexistence.* After a year as deputy under secretary of state for political affairs (1966–1967), Kohler retired from the State Department and taught at the Center for Advanced International Studies at the University of Miami and worked as an occasional consultant for the State and Defense Departments until 1985. He married Phyllis Penn in 1935 and has published a number of books related to the Soviet Union, including *Understanding the Russians* (1970), *The Soviet Union Yesterday, Today, and Tomorrow* (1975), and *SALT II: How Not to Negotiate with the Russians* (1979). Ausland, John C., and Col. Hugh F. Richardson, "Crisis Management: Berlin, Cyprus, Laos," *Foreign Affairs* 44 (January 1966): 292.

L

LADD, WILLIAM (1778–1841). An early peace advocate, William Ladd was born in Exeter, New Hampshire on May 10, 1778, graduated from Harvard in 1798, and married Sophia Ann Augusta Stidolph the following year. From 1798 to 1812, he was a sea captain. After 1812, he was a farmer interested in the cause of international peace, and in 1828 he founded the American Peace Society. He related pacifism to feminism and published *The Duty of Females to Promote the Cause of Peace* (1836), encouraging women to denounce anything militaristic and raise their children with the same attitude. A more important work was *An Essay on a Congress of Nations* (1840), in which Ladd described a model for an international organization consisting of a congress for formulating international law and a world court for adjudicating or arbitrating conflicts under the law. He realized the importance of public opinion and was an effective propagandist for his cause. Many features of Ladd's model were incorporated in subsequent years at the Hague Conferences (1899, 1907)* and in the League of Nations* and Permanent Court of International Justice (World Court).* Ladd died April 9, 1841, in Portsmouth, New Hampshire. Curti, Merle E., *The American Peace Crusade, 1815–1860* (1929), and *Peace or War: The American Struggle, 1636–1936* (1959); *DAB*, 10:527.

LAIRD RAMS, British-built naval vessels. Laird rams, built for the Confederacy in 1863 by Laird's shipbuilding yard, Birkenhead, England, were shallow-draft, quick-turning ironclads armed with an iron spear attached to the bow six or seven feet below the waterline. Their purpose was to sink blockading ships of the Union navy and thereby open southern ports. After some delay caused by Union protest and despite their transfer to French registry, the two Laird rams that had been completed were seized by the British government for violations of the Foreign Enlistment Act.* In 1864, the British government purchased the ships and commissioned them into the Royal Navy. Adams, Ephraim D., *Great Britain and the American Civil War* (1925); *FR* (1864), 1:203–41, 400–30; Merli, Frank J., *Great Britain and the Confederate Navy* (1965).

LAMONT, THOMAS WILLIAM (1870–1948). Thomas W. Lamont was born in Claverack, New York, September 30, 1870, went to Phillips Exeter Academy, and graduated from Harvard in 1892. After working for the *New York Tribune* for two years, he became secretary of Cushman Brothers, a New York marketing firm, which was reorganized in 1898 to Lamont, Collins and Company. In 1903, the successful Lamont became secretary-treasurer of Bankers Trust Company;

in 1909, he moved to the position of vice-president and director of First National Bank. Two years later, he became a partner in J. P. Morgan and Company, where he remained the rest of his life, rising to board chairman in 1943. With Morgan, Lamont became involved in loans to Britain and France after the outbreak of World War I, including the large $500 million Anglo-French loan of October 1915. When the United States joined the war in 1917, Lamont served on Liberty Loan committees and advised Colonel E. M. House* in his efforts to coordinate the U.S. war effort with that of the Allies. At the Paris Peace Conference,* he represented the U.S. Treasury Department, along with Norman Davis,* and was involved in reparations* debates. During the 1920s, Lamont was involved in many international financial dealings, including developmental loans to China, a $100 million recovery loan to Austria (1921), the settlement of Mexico's foreign debt (1923), credits to France and Italy to stabilize their currencies (1924–1925), the drafting of the Dawes Plan (1924)* and Young Plan (1929),* and loans to Japan for earthquake recovery. During the Great Depression, Lamont helped establish the Bank for International Settlements (1931) and was a delegate to the World Economic Conference in London (1933). Lamont married Florence Haskell Corliss in 1895 and maintained an interest in journalism, buying the *New York Post* in 1918 and helping to establish the *Saturday Review* in 1924. He wrote two autobiographical works: *My Boyhood in a Parsonage* (1946) and *Across World Frontiers* (1951). Lamont died in Boca Grande, Florida, on February 2, 1948. Cohen, Warren I., *The Chinese Connection* (1978); *DAB*, Supp. 4:469; Jones, Kenneth Paul, *U.S. Diplomats in Europe, 1919–1941* (1981); *New York Times*, February 3, 1948.

LANE, ARTHUR BLISS (1894–1956). Born in the Long Island community of Bay Ridge on June 16, 1894, Arthur Bliss Lane graduated from Yale in 1916 after further study at the Ecole de l'Isle de France. In 1916, he became private secretary to Ambassador Thomas Nelson Page* in Italy. From 1917 to 1933, he served in minor posts in London, Paris, Bern, Warsaw, and Mexico City. His appointment as minister to Nicaragua in 1933 began a series of ministerial and ambassadorial tours, including minister to Estonia, Latvia, and Lithuania (1936–1937), minister to Yugoslavia (1937–1941), minister to Costa Rica (1941), ambassador to Colombia (1942–1944), and ambassador to Poland (1944–1947). In Yugoslavia, he supported ex–King Peter in an uprising against pro-Fascist Prince Paul and ably safeguarded U.S. citizens after the German bombing and invasion of Belgrade in 1941. In Poland, his most important assignment, he was dismayed by the lack of Soviet and Polish compliance with the terms of the Yalta and Potsdam agreements and requested his recall after the elections of January 1947 had resulted in a pro-Soviet government. He believed that a U.S. policy of appeasement toward Stalin had led to Soviet domination of Poland and recommended faith and humanitarian relief as the best policy toward Poland, inasmuch as geography and the military situation vis-à-vis the Soviet Union made intervention impractical. Upon his return to the United States, Lane became a writer and lecturer in the anti-Communist movement, advocated abandoning the policy of containment,* and urged breaking diplomatic relations with the USSR and adopting the policy of liberation.* Married to Cornelia Thayer Baldwin in 1918, Lane wrote his memoirs, *I Saw Poland Betrayed* (1948), and died in New York City on August 12, 1956. Petrov, Vladimir, *A Study in Diplomacy: The Story of Arthur Bliss Lane* (1971); *New York Times*, August 14, 1956; *WWWA*, 3 (1951–1960): 498.

LANGSTON, JOHN MERCER (1829–1897). One of the relatively few blacks to hold high diplomatic rank in the nineteenth century, John M. Langston was born December 14, 1829, in Louisa County, Virginia. He graduated from Oberlin College in 1849, received a B.D. degree in 1853, and after studying law was admitted to the bar in 1854, the same year he married Caroline M. Wall. From 1855 to 1870, he practiced law in Oberlin, and during the Civil War, he helped recruit black troops. He held local political office in Oberlin after the war until his appointment as inspector general of the Freedmen's Bureau in 1868, followed a year later by his selection as dean of Howard University, where he organized the law school. In 1877, Langston became minister to Haiti. In eight years there, he reorganized the consular service, cleared up some minor hindrances to U.S. trade, and worked to increase trade by advising coffee exporters on new marketing techniques and recommending the importation of American-made denim, which was adopted by the Haitian army for its uniforms. He mediated the settlement of a major political dispute that threatened to bring on a revolution and pressed claims of distressed Americans. Upon his return, Langston sued the U.S. government for $7,666.66 for unpaid salary and won. From 1885 to 1888, he was president of the Virginia Normal and Collegiate Institute; from 1889 to 1891, he was a U.S. Congressman from Virginia. In 1894, he published his self-adulatory, third-person autobiography, *From the Virginia Plantation to the National Capital*. He died in Washington on November 15, 1897. Christopher, Maurine, *Black Americans in Congress* (1976); *DAB*, 10:597; Miller, Jake C., *The Black Presence in American Foreign Affairs* (1978); *NCAB*, 3:328.

LANSING, ROBERT (1864–1928). Woodrow Wilson's second secretary of state (1915–1920), Robert Lansing was born in Watertown, New York, on October 17, 1864, graduated from Amherst (1886), read law, and was admitted to the bar (1889). He began practicing law in 1890 with his father but in 1892 was named associate counsel for the United States in the fur-seal arbitration, the first of many such appointments as counsel or agent in international proceedings. In subsequent years, Lansing was counsel for the Bering Sea Claims Commission (1896–1897), the Alaskan Boundary Tribunal (1903), the North Atlantic Coast Fisheries arbitration (1908–1910), and the American and British claims arbitration (1912). In addition, he was counsel for the Chinese (1894–1895) and Mexican (1900–1901) legations in Washington. In 1914, Lansing, a Democrat, became counselor* for the State Department, where he dealt with the legal complexities brought on by the outbreak of World War I and served as acting secretary of state during the frequent absences of William Jennings Bryan.* When Bryan resigned in 1915, Lansing replaced him and spent the next five years operating largely in the shadow of Wilson and his chief adviser, Colonel Edward M. House.* His greatest influence came in areas apart from the war. In 1916, he signed the treaty for the purchase of the Danish West Indies*; the following year, he negotiated the Lansing-Ishii Agreement* with Japan. He broke with Wilson at the Paris Peace Conference* when his legalistic view of the settlement clashed with Wilson's idealism. He thought Wilson was wrong in combining the peace treaty with the Covenant of the League of Nations* but advocated the ratification of the treaty on the ground that it was better to have this treaty than none at all. In 1920, during Wilson's illness, Lansing convened meetings of the cabinet without the president's permission; when Wilson found out, Lansing's resignation was demanded—a predictable event in the light of their divergent views. During the 1920s Lansing practiced law in Washington and served as counsel for Chile during some of the Tacna-Arica arbitration in 1923 and again in 1925. He was married in 1890 to Eleanor Foster, the daughter of John W. Foster,* a secretary of state, and he died in Washington on October 30, 1928. Lansing wrote a number of personal accounts of his secretaryship: *The Big Four and Others of the Peace Conference* (1921), *The Peace Negotiations: A Personal Narrative* (1921), and *War Memories of Robert Lansing* (1935). *DAB*, 10:609; *New York Times*, October 31, 1928; Pratt, Julius W., "Robert Lansing," in Bemis, Samuel F., ed., *American Secretaries of State and Their Diplomacy*, vol. 9 (1929); Smith Daniel M., *Robert Lansing and American Neutrality* (1972).

LANSING-ISHII AGREEMENT (1917). The result of negotiations between September and November 1917, this agreement indicated U.S. recognition of Japan's special interests in China. However, both nations averred that Chinese territorial sovereignty should be upheld and that the Open Door* principles should be respected. Japan and the United States expressed their mutual opposition to any nation's acquiring any special rights in China that might impair Chinese sovereignty. A secret protocol pledged both nations not to take advantage of the war to obtain special privileges in China. The United States felt that this agreement was an important reaffirmation of Chinese sovereignty and the Root-Takahira Agreement,* and it was well received by European allies. In April 1923, in the aftermath of the Washington Conference on the Limitation of Armaments*, the Lansing-Ishii agreement was abrogated because it was virtually the same as the Nine-Power Treaty.* Curry, Roy Watson, *Woodrow Wilson and Far Eastern Policy, 1913–1921* (1957); Smith, Daniel M., *The Great Departure* (1965).

LAOTIAN CRISIS (1960–1962). This crisis developed after Laos was made nominally independent at the Geneva Conference (1954)*. A rivalry developed between pro-West Prince Souvanna Phouma, who had been given control of the government in 1954, and pro-Communist Prince Souphanouvong, who had close ties with a Communist-dominated liberation movement known as the Pathet Lao. To combat Pathet Lao subversion, the United States funded the Royal Lao Army in the late 1950s. In 1958, Prince Souvanna Phouma resigned, claiming that U.S. pressure prevented him from forming a truly effective coalition government. Restored to power in August 1960, Souvanna Phouma presided over a chaotic political situation that finally broke down into a civil war, causing him to flee to Cambodia in December 1960. The new administration of President John F. Kennedy saw Laos as a testing ground of the cold war* in 1961 and, believing in the domino theory,* first decided to stand by anti-Communist forces in Laos. However, when the weakness of the Laotian military and the unpredictability of Laotian politicians were fully realized, the Kennedy administration chose to go to the negotiating table to work out a cease-fire and a neutralized Laos. This the Geneva Conference (1961–1962)* accomplished. Fall, Bernard B., *Anatomy of a Crisis* (1969); Fall, Bernard B., *Anatomy of a Crisis* (1969); Goldstein, Martin E., *American Policy toward Laos* (1973); Hilsman, Roger, *To Move a Nation* (1967); Poole, Peter A., *The United States and Indochina from FDR to Nixon* (1973); Stevenson, Charles A., *The End of Nowhere* (1972).

LAOTIAN INCURSION (1971). This military operation was launched on February 8, 1971, by South Vietnamese troops with American air and logistical support into the Laotian panhandle. The objective of the incursion was to cut the Ho Chi Minh Trail and interdict supplies coming into South Vietnam. Ostensibly the incursion would make U.S. troop withdrawal more secure and prevent a North Vietnamese buildup that might produce a major offensive in 1972. Within five weeks, the North Vietnamese, fighting more fiercely than anticipated, had driven the South Vietnamese forces out of Laos, bringing about a termination of the operation somewhat earlier than planned. The Laotian incursion showed that the South Vietnamese army (ARVN) was not able to mount an offensive in the war. Although smaller in scale than the Cambodian incursion (1970),* the Laotian operation provoked considerable domestic criticism of the Nixon administration's war policy. According to Karnow, the mission was a ''monumental blunder,'' utilizing too few ARVN troops who fell back before reaching their objective and displayed mainly the fact that they were not a good fighting force. Hersch, Seymour, *The Price of Power: Kissinger in the White House* (1983); Karnow, Stanley, *Vietnam: A History* (1983); Szulc, Tad, *The Illusion of Peace* (1978).

LARKIN, THOMAS OLIVER (1802–1858). Born September 16, 1802, in Charlestown, Massachusetts, and lacking any extensive formal education, Thomas O. Larkin went to Monterey, California, in 1832, setting himself up in the flour-milling business. He married Rachel Holmes in 1833 and soon became a general merchandiser, trading with Mexico and Hawaii, and a land speculator. In 1844, he was made U.S. consul* in California, and two years later he added the duties of confidential agent. During the war with Mexico, he also served as naval agent and storekeeper. In his positions as consul and agent, Larkin aided Americans in California and promoted business; more important, he watched the activities of British and French agents, reported any suspicious moves, and was instructed to warn Californians not to be taken in by British or French advances. He advocated and propagandized for separation from Mexico and annexation to the United States, and the Treaty of Guadalupe-Hidalgo (1848)* did just that. After the war, he returned to private business until his death in Monterey on October 27, 1858. *DAB*, 10:617; Graebner, Norman, *Empire on the Pacific* (1955).

LATANÉ, JOHN HOLLADAY (1869–1932). One of America's first diplomatic historians, John H. Latané was born on April 1, 1869, in Staunton, Virginia. He received an A.B. degree in 1892 and a Ph.D. in 1895, both from Johns Hopkins University. After three years of high school teaching, he took a teaching appointment at Randolph-Macon Woman's College in 1898; this was followed in 1902 by an appointment at Washington and Lee and, in 1913, by a post at Johns Hopkins. In 1931, he joined the research staff of the Walter Hines Page School of International Relations. Latané's first major book was *The Diplomatic Relations of the United States and Spanish America* (1900); several others followed, often dealing with current or recent events. Latané's writing lacked a true historical perspective and denied him access to the best sources, but his writing is clear and reflects good judgment. Among his other works are *America as a World Power, 1897–1907* (1907), *From Isolation to Leadership* (1918), *The United States and Latin America* (1920), and a textbook, *A History of American Foreign Policy* (1927). Latané was an ardent Democrat and supporter of Wilsonian foreign policy during and after World War I. During the 1920s, he was critical of U.S. foreign policy, especially that directed toward Latin America, and continued to advocate joining the League of Nations* and the Permanent Court of International Justice (World Court).* He was married to Elinor Jackson Cox in 1905 and died New Year's Day, 1932, in New Orleans. *DAB*, Supp 1:483; *NCAB*, 23:394; *New York Times*, January 2, 1932.

LAURENS, HENRY (1724–1792). Henry Laurens was born in Charleston, South Carolina, on March 6, 1724, and became wealthy through a career as an import-export merchant and, later, as a plantation manager. He served in the South Carolina Assembly (1757–1776) and the Continental Congress (1777–1779) before launching a diplomatic career as commissioner to the Netherlands in 1779. From October 1780 to December 1781, he was in a British prison, having been caught with an American treaty draft among his papers. He was appointed a peace commissioner in May 1782 and participated in the negotiations and signed the preliminary draft of the Peace of Paris (1783).* Between 1782 and 1784, he served as unofficial minister to Great Britain, conferring with British officials on commercial and political matters. After 1784, he retired to his South Carolina plantation, where he died December 8, 1792. Laurens married

Eleanor Bale in 1750 and was one of the first Americans to be cremated. *DAB*, 11:32; Morris, Richard B., *The Peacemakers* (1965); Wallace, D. D., *Life of Henry Laurens* (1915).

LAUSANNE CONFERENCE (1932). This conference, held in the summer of 1932 simultaneously with the Geneva Disarmament Conference, brought European debtor nations together to seek a solution to the war debt and reparations* problems. The conferees agreed to reduce the total amount Germany owed by about 90 percent (to a figure of $714.6 million) contingent upon the United States's making proportionate reductions in the amount Britain and France owed in war and reconstruction loans. In the United States, the debt question became mired in 1932 campaign politics, and the Hoover administration worked grimly to try to salvage something of the principle of debt repayment in the face of threatened Allied repudiation. In the end, the Great Depression forced the final result: the termination of the debt-reparation question by "one, solid, defaulting phalanx" of debtors against a single creditor. Ellis, L. Ethan, *Republican Foreign Policy, 1921–1933* (1968); Ferrell, Robert H., *American Diplomacy in the Great Depression* (1957); *FR* (1932), 1:636–91; Wilson, Joan Hoff, *American Business and Foreign Policy, 1920–1933* (1971).

LAWRENCE, ABBOTT (1792–1855). Abbott Lawrence was born December 16, 1792, in Groton, Massachusetts. His formal education was limited to attendance at Groton School, and at the age of fifteen, he was apprenticed to his brother Amos, a Boston merchant. In 1814, he was made a partner in the business and for the next forty years ranked among Boston's leading businessmen as an importer of dry goods and Chinese items. Active in the development of New England industry, he helped found the town of Lawrence, Massachusetts. Lawrence was also an early railroad advocate and a U.S. Congressman from Massachusetts (1835–1837, 1839–1841). In 1842, he was named a commissioner to work on the settlement of the northeastern boundary dispute, which was finally resolved by the Webster-Ashburton Treaty (1842).* A Whig, Lawrence was appointed minister to Great Britain by the Taylor administration. In London his main concern was the Anglo-American dispute in Central America over a prospective ship canal; this was settled for the time being by the Clayton-Bulwer Treaty (1850),* with most of the negotiations taking place in Washington. Lawrence also supervised American participation in the Crystal Palace Exhibition (1851), reported on the Irish situation, which was producing massive immigration to the United States, and dealt with postal rate and fisheries questions. Returning from Britain in 1852, Lawrence took up his private business interests in Boston. He married Katherine Bigelow in 1819 and late in life gave money to found Lawrence Scientific School at Harvard. Lawrence died in Boston on August 18, 1855. *DAB*, 11:44; Hill, Hamilton A., *Memoir of Abbott Lawrence* (1884); *NCAB*, 3:62; Willson, Beckles, *America's Ambassadors to England, 1785–1929* (1929).

LEA, HOMER (1876–1912). Born November 17, 1876, in Denver, Homer Lea went to California as a youth and attended the University of the Pacific. As a schoolboy, he became obsessed with the idea of freeing the Chinese people from Manchu rule. In 1900, he joined the forces relieving Peking during the Boxer Rebellion* as an adventurer. After a short trip to California in 1901 to organize the Young China Association, he returned to China, becoming a military general of exceptional renown and an associate of K'ang Yu-wei, a reformer, and later, of Sun Yat-sen during his successful revolution of 1911. Lea wrote several books, including *The Vermilion Pencil* (1908), a novel, as well as *The Valor of Ignorance* (1909) and *The Day of the Saxon* (1912), dealing with the dangers of Oriental attacks on the United States and the British Empire, respectively. A frail person, with some physical deformity, Lea died in Ocean Park, California, on November 1, 1912. *DAB*, 11:69; *New York Times*, November 2, 1912.

LEAGUE FOR AMERICAN NEUTRALITY, political pressure group, 1935–1936. This organization was created in December 1935 by Italian-Americans from New England unhappy with restrictions on U.S. trade with Italy during the Italo-Ethiopian War,* which they considered a "colonial expedition." Despite the Italian connection, the league claimed to represent Americans of all ethnic and religious backgrounds. The group lobbied against the trade quota plan and other proposed features of the Neutrality Act of 1936* that they considered harmful to Italy. The trade quota plan, never enacted, would have given the president discretion to limit trade in raw materials with a belligerent by establishing quotas at trade levels equal to a designated prewar average. With the end of the Italo-Ethiopian War and the defeat of the trade quota plan, the League for American Neutrality faded from public view. Divine, Robert A., *The Illusion of Neutrality* (1962).

LEAGUE OF NATIONS. Created by the Treaty of Versailles (1919),* the League of Nations began operation January 10, 1920, and disbanded formally April 18, 1946 (it met for the final time December 14, 1939). At one time or another, the league included every self-governing nation in the world but the United States, a total of sixty-three; however, league membership hovered around fifty due to resignations and late entries. Most political and military power was concentrated in its European members. Like its successor, the United Nations,* the League of Nations was organized around an assembly, including all member nations, and a council, composed of several permanent and several nonpermanent members. A secretariat administered the organization and directed the affairs of its several nonpolitical agencies, which dealt with matters such as labor and health. The league also included a World Court, the Permanent Court of International Justice.* While never formally a member, the United States usually maintained an observer at the league and on occasion tried to act in cooperation with it, as in the Manchurian crisis (1931)* and in the war debt and reparations* questions. Dexter, Byron, *The Years of Opportunity: The League of Nations, 1920–*

1926 (1967); Doenecke, Justus D., comp., *The Diplomacy of Frustration* (1981); North-ledge, F. S., *The League of Nations: Its Life and Times, 1920–1946* (1986); Walters, F. P., *A History of the League of Nations*, 2 vols. (1952).

LEAGUE TO ENFORCE PEACE, internationalist organization, c. 1915–1920. This internationalist organization was founded in 1915 by Hamilton Holt* and a number of prominent members of the New York Peace Society. Under its first president, William Howard Taft, its aim was to create a world organization to settle peacefully all disputes involving its members through the use of diplomacy, arbitration,* or an international court of justice. The founders believed that the United States should take the lead in creating an international organization, that collective security* measures could be employed if necessary to prevent war, and that periodic conferences should be held to update international law. The League to Enforce Peace strongly supported U.S. membership in the League of Nations* but had little influence on the struggle for ratification of the Treaty of Versailles* (which included the covenant of the League of Nations), especially after its leadership split over the question of reservations to league membership. After the Senate rejection of the Treaty of Versailles, the League to Enforce Peace was never effective, and most of its members found their way into other organizations. Bartlett, Ruhl J., *The League to Enforce Peace* (1944); Divine, Robert A., *Second Chance* (1967); Kuehl, Warren F., *Seeking World Order* (1969).

LEAHY, WILLIAM DANIEL (1875–1959). Best known as a naval commander, William D. Leahy also saw significant service in U.S. diplomacy before and during World War II. He was born in Hampton, Iowa, on May 6, 1875, and graduated from the U.S. Naval Academy in 1897. An active duty career that spanned the forty years from 1899 to 1939 found Leahy serving in the Spanish-American War, the Boxer Rebellion,* the Nicaraguan and Haitian occupations, the Mexican punitive expedition, and World War I. From 1937 to 1939, he was, with the rank of admiral, chief of naval operations. He left naval duty in 1939, and in 1940, he was named ambassador to France, a difficult post at which he remained for two years. Appointed because of his naval background and the expectation that he would get along well with the military leaders of the Vichy government, Marshal Philippe Pétain and Admiral François Darlan, Leahy's main task was to keep France from giving aid to Germany beyond that required by the armistice and to explain that the United States found it necessary to continue aiding Great Britain by all means short of war. He also was concerned with providing food for refugees in unoccupied parts of France, served as an important listening post for the United States, and recommended maintaining relations with the Vichy government at a time when many were urging the severing of relations because of Vichy collaboration with Germany. Leahy resigned in 1942 at the point of political crisis in the Vichy government growing out of a power struggle between Darlan and former Premier Pierre Laval. Appointed chief of staff to President Roosevelt in 1942, with the naval rank of fleet admiral, Leahy became a highly influential senior adviser to Roosevelt at virtually all wartime conferences including Yalta,* and also advised President Harry S Truman at the Potsdam Conference (1945).* Leahy's position assured the U.S. Joint Chiefs of Staff and the Anglo-American Combined Chiefs of Staff a privileged position in wartime decision making. After the war, he continued in this post as chief of staff, playing an important role in organizing the Department of Defense, created by the National Security Act (1947). He retired from the navy in 1949 and died July 20, 1959, in Bethesda, Maryland. Leahy was married to Louise Tennant Harrington in 1904 (she died in France in 1942) and published his memoirs, *I Was There*, in 1950. Adams, Henry H., *Witness to Power: The Life of Fleet Admiral William D. Leahy* (1985); *NCAB*, F:44; *New York Times*, July 2, 1959; *WWWA*, 3 (1951–1960):506.

LEAR, TOBIAS (1762–1816). Son of a prosperous shipmaster and farmer, Tobias Lear was born September 19, 1762, in Portsmouth, New Hampshire, and graduated from Harvard in 1783. After some time spent traveling and studying in Europe, he became George Washington's private secretary in 1786. He held this position, which also included the tutoring of Washington's children, until 1792. From 1793 to 1794, he was in Britain; in 1795, he became president of the Potomac Canal Company. During the quasi-war* with France, 1798–1799, he returned to service with Washington as a military secretary. In 1801, Lear was chosen consul* to Santo Domingo and spent a year there managing the affairs of Americans during the revolution of Toussaint L'Ouverture until forced to leave by the French general Leclerc. From 1803 until 1812, Lear was consul general in Algiers. There he negotiated a treaty with Morocco, maintained peace with Algiers and Tunis, and dealt with Tripoli, where 300 Americans were being held prisoner. In June 1805, he signed an accord with the pasha of Tripoli agreeing to ransom the prisoners. This brought intense criticism from General William Eaton, nearby with an American military force, who believed that Tripoli could have been taken militarily. President Thomas Jefferson* defended the treaty, which was unpopular in the United States and considered unnecessary because of the American military presence nearby. After several more uneventful years, Lear was sent home in 1812 by the dey of Algiers. He returned to Washington and became an accountant in the War Department until his suicide in the capital on October 11, 1816. *DAB*, 11:76; *NCAB*, 13:466.

LEBANESE CIVIL WAR. Lebanon, a Middle Eastern state made independent in 1943, is a mixture of religious sects and political factions, potentially unstable and made more so after 1971 by increasing numbers of Palestinian refugees entering the country. In 1975, the country was sharply divided between Muslims, politically leftist, and Christians, politically right wing, with the Palestinians tending to ally with the Muslims, or so it seemed to the Christians. Syria was also a factor because of its geographical proximity and the fact that the Syrians regarded the Palestinians as their clients, supporting them as a means of extending

Syrian influence into Lebanon. In early 1976, during the war, Syria switched sides and supported the Christian right along with the United States, whose general policy was to restrain neighboring Israel and help keep the war from widening into a general Middle East conflict. At the war's end, late in 1976, Syrian forces occupied Lebanon, 44,000 Lebanese were dead, the Palestinian element was reduced in power, and Lebanon could hardly be considered an independent nation. During this war, the U.S. ambassador to Lebanon, Francis Meloy,* was assassinated, leading to the evacuation of all U.S. citizens from the country. Most Americans had returned by the fall of 1977, but an Israeli invasion in 1978 showed that the trouble in Lebanon still seethed. Another Israeli invasion in 1982 triggered the Lebanon crisis (1982–1984),* which involved a U.S. intervention. Since 1984, Syria remains in effective control of most of Lebanon, and while there may not be a full-scale civil war in progress, there are frequent outbursts of violence, the taking of American or European hostages, and a general sense that a permanent peaceful solution is not likely in the foreseeable future. Bulloch, John, *Death of a Country: The Civil War In Lebanon* (1977); Petran, Tabitha, *The Struggle over Lebanon* (1987); Rabinovich, Itamar, *The War for Lebanon, 1970–1985* (1986).

LEBANON CRISIS (1982–1984). A part of the ongoing Lebanese Civil War,* this crisis began with an Israeli invasion of Lebanon in June 1982 in order to root out Palestinian terrorists who had for several years been raiding northern Israel and Lebanese civilian population centers. By early August, the leaders and forces of the Palestine Liberation Organization (PLO),* the principal organization representing the Palestinian people, found themselves besieged in Beirut; the United States, Italy, and France formed a multinational force (MNF) to evacuate the PLO and bring about a cease-fire in the conflict. Although the PLO forces had been evacuated by September 1, 1982, the situation in Lebanon continued to deteriorate, with a Christian militia massacre of a civilian Shiite Muslim camp in mid-September resulting in 700 deaths and international outrage. The MNF decided to stay in Lebanon as a presence and, it was hoped, a deterrent to further violence, but the U.S. role was never made clear. Since the United States had other interests in the region, it was uncertain whom the marines were supporting or protecting. Late in 1982, they were assigned to protect (and stay at) the Beirut airport, a suitable strategic objective but hopelessly defenseless. By early 1983, the U.S. policy seemed to be tilting toward Israel at the expense of Lebanon (and Syria) and toward the Christian faction as opposed to the various Muslim groups. American forces appeared to rival factions to be increasingly less neutral in the spring and summer of 1983, hostile acts against marines became more frequent, and on October 23, a truck loaded with 12,000 pounds of high explosives drove into the marine barracks at the airport compound, detonating and killing 241 marines. There was much pressure on the Reagan administration to withdraw the marines, but the president, not wanting to show national weakness, called Lebanon a vital interest and held out until February

1984 before "redeploying" the marines out of the country, utilizing naval shelling of suspected Shiite hideouts in retaliation. On March 30, 1984, the United States formally withdrew from the MNF. Gabriel, Richard W., *Military Incompetence* (1985); Hammel, Eric, *The Root: The Marines in Beirut, August 1982-February 1984* (1985).

LEBANON INTERVENTION (1958). Following the Suez crisis (1956),* Arab nationalists and the Soviet Union enjoyed heightened influence in the Middle East. Fearful that such nationalism would play into the hands of Soviet expansionists and endanger U.S. interests in the strategically important region, Congress approved the Eisenhower Doctrine,* offering U.S. aid to threatened nations in that region. In early 1958, the merger of Egypt and Syria into the United Arab Republic was perceived as a threat to U.S. interests, and a bloody coup in Iraq in July was deemed even more serious. Thus, when Lebanon, whose government was not secure, asked for military intervention, the Eisenhower Doctrine was invoked. About 15,000 U.S. troops were landed in mid-July and remained until October 15. Although there were continuing incidents of violence in and around Beirut, where the U.S. troops were stationed, they seldom involved the Americans, who suffered just one casualty. Spiller, Roger J., " 'Not War But Like War': The American Intervention in Lebanon," Combat Studies Institute *Leavenworth Papers* 3 (January 1981).

LEE, ARTHUR (1740–1792). Arthur Lee was born in Westmoreland County, Virginia, on December 21, 1740, studied medicine and law in England, and traveled widely in Europe, learning French, Italian, and Spanish and forming "fairly wide acquaintances." In 1775, he was appointed, along with Benjamin Franklin,* American agent in London, and in 1776, he joined Franklin and Silas Deane* as a member of the commission sent to France to seek aid and recognition. Lee was delegated to go to Spain in February 1777 to seek Spanish support; later that year he undertook a similar mission to Prussia, where he was not received. In that same year, he quarreled sharply with Deane over the manner of payments to Hortalez (Rodrigue) and Company,* through which French aid was reaching America. His allegations that Deane was personally profiting from these payments confirmed the decision by the Continental Congress to recall his rival. After his return to the United States in 1780, he pursued a political career in Virginia until retiring to his estate in 1789, where he died December 12, 1792. Bemis, Samuel F., *The Diplomacy of the American Revolution* (1935); *DAB*, 11:96; Morris, Richard B., *The Peacemakers* (1965); Potts, Lewis W., *Arthur Lee, Virtuous Revolutionary* (1981); Riggs, A. R., *The Nine Lives of Arthur Lee, Virginia Patriot* (1976).

LEE, FITZHUGH (1835–1905). A nephew of the Confederate general Robert E. Lee, Fitzhugh Lee was born in Fairfax County, Virginia, on November 19, 1835, and graduated from West Point in the class of 1856. He taught at West Point during the last year before the Civil War but returned home in 1861 to serve four years with the Confederate army, earning a reputation as an excellent cavalry leader. For twenty years after the war, he was a Virginia farmer, but in 1886 he was elected governor of the state, serving until 1890. In 1896, he was sent to Havana as U.S. consul general.* In his two years there, he gained national prominence by his firm American stand in the immediate prewar period, playing a role in the removal of the Spanish general Valeriano Weyler. He recommended (too late) not sending the U.S.S. *Maine** to Havana in early 1898. During the war, Lee was a major general in charge of volunteers with the Seventh Army Corps and continued on active army duty until his retirement in 1901. In retirement, he helped plan the Jamestown Exposition of 1907 but died in Washington on April 28, 1905. He married Ellen Bernard Fowle in 1871 and published a biography of Robert E. Lee in 1894. *DAB*, 11:103; *NCAB*, 9:1.

LE GENDRE, CHARLES WILLIAM (1830–1899). A native of France, Charles W. Le Gendre was born in Ouillins on August 26, 1830, and educated at the University of Paris. He was married to Clara Victoria Mulock in 1854 and came to the United States a short time later. He served as a Union officer during the Civil War, lost an eye, and was discharged in 1864. In 1866, he was named U.S. consul* at Amoy, China, with his jurisdiction including Formosa. There, he was involved in an incident in 1867 when the crew of a U.S. bark, *Rover*, was massacred by Formosan natives. Le Gendre tried in vain to get the Chinese to search for possible survivors and ultimately led a party on the island himself and successfully established ties with the more important tribes and signed a convention for the protection of those stranded by shipwrecks. In 1872, Le Gendre went to Japan, en route to the United States, but instead became an adviser to the Japanese government, using his knowledge of China and Formosa to assist the Japanese in achieving their objective of conquest. He accompanied the Japanese on a diplomatic expedition to Peking in 1873 and a military expedition to Formosa the following year. Le Gendre remained in Japan as an adviser until 1890, receiving (in 1875) the decoration of second class of merit (Rising Sun), seldom given to foreigners. In 1890, he went to Seoul as an adviser to the king of Korea and died there on September 1, 1899. During his stay in Japan, he wrote *Progressive Japan: A Study of the Political and Social Needs of the Empire* (1878). *DAB*, 11:145; *NCAB*, 25:79; Neumann, William L., *America Encounters Japan* (1963); Presseisen, Ernst L., "Roots of Japanese Imperialism: A Memorandum of Gen. Le Gendre," *Journal of Modern History* 29 (1957):108–11; Thomson, Sandra C., "Filibustering to Formosa: General Charles Le Gendre and the Japanese," *Pacific Historical Review* 40 (November 1971): 442–56.

LEISHMAN, JOHN G. A. (1857–1924). Born in Pittsburgh on March 28, 1857, John G. A. Leishman lived in an orphanage until the age of twelve and then went to work as an office boy in an iron and steel works. He later formed a highly successful iron and steel brokerage with which Andrew Carnegie* did business and, in 1886, went to work for Carnegie, rising to the presidency of

Carnegie Steel Company by the mid-1890s. In 1897, Leishman, a Republican, began a diplomatic career that included appointments as minister to Switzerland (1897–1901), minister and ambassador to Turkey (1901–1909), ambassador to Italy (1909–1911), and ambassador to Germany (1911–1913). Of these missions, the Turkish was the most important, both for Leishman's tenure there and for the problems he encountered. For years, U.S. diplomats had struggled with the problem of Turkish harassment of American schools and missionaries, and Leishman's experience was no different. In 1901, he had to contend with the kidnapping of an American missionary, Miss Stone, by Macedonian revolutionaries; she was released after a $68,200 ransom was paid. Later, after the State Department had decided a show of naval force would be an effective inducement to obtain better treatment from the Turks, Leishman faced the problem of riots in Beirut occasioned by the visit of an American warship. Although his rank was raised from minister to ambassador in 1906, Leishman never could satisfactorily settle all the problems, principally because of the State Department's policy of avoiding deep political entanglements in that region. In 1913, Leishman had a $75,158 judgment laid against him for his improper use of information obtained through his official diplomatic position. He married Julia Crawford in 1880 and died in Nice, France, on March 27, 1924. *DAB*, 11:155; Dennis, A. L. P., *Adventures in American Diplomacy, 1896–1906* (1928); *NCAB*, 13:598; *New York Times*, March 28, 1924.

LEND-LEASE, World War II aid program, 1941–1945. In 1939, with Britain having financial problems and President Franklin D. Roosevelt convinced that Britain needed aid in the interest of U.S. security, the idea of a large-scale program began to germinate. Secretary of the Treasury Henry Morgenthau was important in the early planning of Lend-Lease, which in its final form was passed by Congress in March 1941, with votes of 260–165 in the House of Representatives and 60–31 in the Senate. Lend-Lease provided Allies with war materiel, supposedly to be returned after the war. In reality, the goods were not returned, and after U.S. entry into the war, the program evolved into a system wherein resources were pooled cooperatively for a common end. In the United States, Lend-Lease was first administered by Harry Hopkins,* then by Edward R. Stettinius, Jr.* It was terminated in August 1945, with the United States and Britain (the main Lend-Lease customer) signing an agreement in March 1946 in which Britain agreed to a liability of $650 million for leftover materials. Feis relates the following figures as total Lend-Lease aid from March 1941 to June 1945: Great Britain, $13.5 billion; USSR, $9.1 billion; African, Middle Eastern, and Mediterranean countries, $3.3 billion; China and India, $2.2 billion; others $3.0 billion, for a total of $31.1 billion. Feis, Herbert, *Churchill-Roosevelt-Stalin* (1967); Herring, George C., Jr., *Aid to Russia, 1941–1946* (1973); Kimball, Warren F., *The Most Unsordid Act: Lend-Lease, 1939–1941* (1969); McNeill, William H., *America, Britain, and Russia* (1953); Martel, Leon, *Lend-Lease, Loans and the Coming of the Cold War* (1979); Stettinius, Edward R., Jr., *Lend-Lease: Weapon for Victory* (1944).

LEVERMORE, CHARLES HERBERT (1856–1927). A well-known peace advocate during the 1920s, Charles H. Levermore was born in Mansfield, Connecticut, on October 15, 1856, and graduated from Yale (A.B., 1879) and Johns Hopkins (Ph.D., 1886). He taught history at various schools, including the University of California and the Massachusetts Institute of Technology, until 1893, when he became principal of Adelphi Academy in Brooklyn, a position he retained until 1909. From 1896 to 1912, he was also president of Adelphi College. After two years of teaching at Adelphi, 1912–1914, Levermore retired to devote his full time to the cause of world peace. For the next fourteen years, he was an officer of one or another peace organization: the World Peace Foundation, the New York Peace Society, the World Court and League of Nations Union, the American Association for International Cooperation, and the League of Nations Non-Partisan Association. In February 1924, Levermore reached his greatest fame as a winner of $50,000, half the American Peace Award (given by Edward W. Bok for the best plan for U.S.–world cooperation toward peace). His plan suggested that the United States (1) join the World Court,* (2) consult with the League of Nations* without actually joining, and (3) undertake a review and revision of international law to maintain international justice and define the social rights and responsibilities of nations. After 1924, Levermore went on the public lecture circuit for a time, after which he spent two years in Europe and the Middle East studying international relations. He died in Berkeley, California, on October 20, 1927, not long after his return. Levermore married Mettie Norton Tuttle in 1884 and was the author of several books, including a series of League of Nations yearbooks published by the *Brooklyn Eagle* and a number of hymnals. *DAB*, 11:199; *NCAB*, 33:137; *New York Times*, October 22, 1927.

LEVINSON, SALMON OLIVER (1865–1941). Born in Noblesville, Indiana, on December 29, 1865, Salmon O. Levinson attended the University of Chicago, 1883–1886, but graduated from Yale (1888) and the Chicago College of Law (1891). He practiced law in Chicago, specializing in corporate reorganization, and became wealthy. By World War I, he had virtually abandoned his law practice and had become a peace advocate and the chief sponsor of the idea that war should be illegal. When he failed to get his idea incorporated into the Covenant of the League of Nations,* he became a bitter league and Permanent Court of International Justice (World Court)* opponent. Levinson was also unsuccessful in obtaining approbation of his cause at the Washington Conference (1921–1922)* and organized the American Committee for the Outlawry of War and took his campaign to the public and to various other peace groups. In 1927, he helped bring about a Franco-American proposal to outlaw war; this became reality in the Kellogg-Briand Pact (1928).* Levinson was also interested in the postwar debt and reparations problem and wanted to link it with outlawry. In the late 1930s, he tried to find a way to end the Sino-Japanese War through arbitration. Among those who worked closely with Levinson were former Secretary of State Philander Knox,* who worked out a plan that was presented to the Washington Conference, and Senator William E. Borah,* who may have been more interested in the political dividends of the cause than the cause itself. Levinson was married twice and died February 2, 1941, in Chicago. *DAB*, Supp. 3:456; Ferrell, Robert, *Peace in Their Time: The Origins of the Kellogg-Briand Pact* (1952); *NCAB*, 31:198; Stoner, John E., *S. O. Levinson and the Pact of Paris* (1943).

LEWIS, FULTON, JR. (1903–1966). The best-known conservative news commentator in the years before World War II, Fulton Lewis, Jr., was born in Washington, D.C., on April 30, 1903, and attended the University of Virginia. A reporter and city editor for the *Washington Herald* (1924–1928) and a correspondent for the Universal News Service and International News Service (1928–1937), Lewis achieved some fame by his investigation of irregularities in government airmail contracts between 1931 and 1934. In 1937, he moved to radio as a news commentator for the Mutual Broadcasting System, where he advocated a strong national defense and opposed President Franklin D. Roosevelt's foreign policy. He was involved in a controversy in 1939 over his invitation to Charles A. Lindbergh, a spokesman for isolationism,* to speak on his radio show after war had broken out in Europe. In 1940, Lewis stirred up more controversy by ridiculing the Battle of Britain and accusing photographers of news management by their selective photography. Less influential during the war, Lewis reemerged after 1945 as an avid anti-Communist, attacking people such as Harry Hopkins,* Henry A. Wallace, and David E. Lilienthal and befriending and supporting Senator Joseph R. McCarthy (R., Wisconsin) in his anti-Communist activities. Lewis married Alice Huston in 1930 and died August 21, 1966. *CB* (1942):509–11; Culbert, David H., *News for Everyman* (1976); Herndon, Booton, *Praised and Damned: The Story of Fulton Lewis, Jr.* (1954); *WWWA*, 4 (1961–1968):572.

LEWIS, SAMUEL WINFIELD (b. 1930). Born in Houston, October 1, 1930, and a graduate of Yale (B.A., 1952) and Johns Hopkins (M.A., 1954), Samuel W. Lewis entered diplomatic service in 1954. He served in minor posts in Naples, Florence, and Washington between 1954 and 1958, when he became a senior staff member for Latin American affairs on the National Security Council.* In 1969, Lewis moved to the Bureau of Inter-American Affairs as a special assistant for political planning, and the following year, he was appointed special assistant to the director-general of the Foreign Service. From 1971 to 1974, he was deputy chief of mission and counselor at Kabul, Afghanistan, but he returned to Washington in 1974 to be deputy director of the State Department's Policy Planning Staff. In 1977, the Carter administration appointed Lewis ambassador to Israel, where he established a good relationship with Prime Minister Menachem Begin and was known for his ability to be candid while maintaining diplomatic confidences. In the Egypt-Israeli talks in late 1977, Lewis was useful in providing "messenger service" between Cairo and Tel Aviv. In 1985, Lewis left the State Department and became a diplomat-in-residence at Johns Hopkins. He married

Sallie Kate Smoot in 1953. *New York Times*, January 28, 1978; *WWA* (1986–1987):1690.

"LIBERATION," diplomatic concept, c. 1952–1956. The term *liberation* as applied to U.S. foreign policy was first used by John Foster Dulles* and other Republicans in the 1952 election campaign to provide voters with an alternative to the prevailing policy of containment.* Liberation had the virtues of dynamism, forcefulness, and moral righteousness and provided a contrast to a containment policy described as futile and stagnant. By definition, liberation was a policy that would bring "genuine independence in the nations of Europe and Asia now dominated by Moscow," hopefully peacefully, through a linkage with other current diplomatic concepts such as deterrence and massive retaliation.* In practice, however, nothing was liberated. According to Graebner, liberation ran counter to U.S. security interests or the realities of American power and thus proved unworkable. The real test of liberation and the demonstration of its failure came in Hungary in 1956 when, during a revolutionary movement, the United States did nothing to back up its rhetoric of liberation. Gerson, Louis L., "John Foster Dulles," in Ferrell, Robert H., ed., *American Secretaries of State and Their Diplomacy*, vol. 18 (1967); Graebner, Norman A., *Cold War Diplomacy* (1977).

LIMA CONFERENCE (1938). The Eighth International Conference of American States, as this meeting was formally titled, was held in Lima December 9–27, 1938. Cordell Hull,* the secretary of state, led the U.S. delegation with the objective of strengthening hemispheric solidarity in the face of threats from what were delicately termed "non-American sources." The main conflict was between the United States and Argentina, which opposed a U.S.-sponsored treaty condemning aggression and supporting solidarity in the face of a possible invasion. After much private consultation, the delegates agreed to the Declaration of Lima, a weak statement affirming each nation's right to act individually but calling for consultation at appropriate times by means of ad hoc foreign ministers' meetings. In addition, the Lima Conference confirmed previous approvals of reciprocity and passed the Lima Declaration in Favor of Women's Rights. However, the conferees did not do much substantive work on matters such as peacekeeping and the strengthening of the regional organization. A number of anti-Axis resolutions were adopted, despite noisy street protests of Fascist partisans in Lima. On the whole, however, the seriousness of the European threat was hardly acknowledged, as the Declaration of Lima marked very little progress toward solidarity from the Buenos Aires Consulative Pact (1936). Connell-Smith, Gordon, *The United States and Latin America* (1974); *FR* (1938), 5:1–88; Inman, Samuel Guy, *Inter-American Conferences* (1965); Mecham, J. Lloyd, *A Survey of United States–Latin American Relations* (1965).

LIMITED TEST BAN TREATY (1963). See PARTIAL NUCLEAR TEST BAN TREATY (1963).

LINCOLN, LEVI (1749–1820). Levi Lincoln was born May 15, 1749, in Hingham, Massachusetts, graduated from Harvard in 1772, and served briefly in the American Revolution. After the war, he practiced law in Worcester, Massachusetts, married Martha Waldo in 1781, and became prominent in local affairs and in the development of state government. He served in the Massachusetts legislature, 1796–1799, and in the U.S. House of Representatives, 1800, before being appointed attorney general in 1801. As attorney general, he also served as secretary of state ad interim between March and May 1801, bridging the gap between John Marshall's* departure from the Supreme Court and James Madison's* arrival in Washington. Lincoln left the attorney general's post in 1804 and returned to state politics, serving on the governor's council, 1806 and 1810–1812; as lieutenant governor, 1807–1808; and, briefly, as governor, 1808–1809. He declined an appointment to the Supreme Court in 1812 because of failing eyesight and retired to his farm in Worcester, where he died April 14, 1820. *DAB*, 11:262; *NCAB*, 1:111; Washburn, E., *Memoir of Hon. Levi Lincoln . . .* (1869).

LINCOLN, ROBERT TODD (1843–1926). The eldest son of President Abraham Lincoln, Robert T. Lincoln carved out an important legal and political career in his own right, serving as secretary of war (1881–1885) and minister to Great Britain (1889–1893). Born in Springfield, Illinois, on August 1, 1843, he graduated from Harvard in 1864 and was admitted to the bar in 1867. He married Mary Harlan in 1868 and practiced law in Chicago until 1880. An active Republican and supporter of a third term for U.S. Grant in 1880, he was included in the cabinet of James A. Garfield in 1881. When the Republicans returned to power in 1889, Lincoln was named minister to Great Britain. This was not a time of major Anglo-American problems, but Lincoln did try to augment Secretary of State James G. Blaine's* Pan-Americanism* by working for a settlement of the British dispute with Venezuela, without success. He did some background research on the Bering Sea controversy, helped update the U.S.–British extradition treaty, officially invited the British to participate in the Columbian Exposition in 1893, and surveyed the impact of the McKinley tariff on British exports to the United States. In 1893, he returned to law practice in Chicago. Four years later, he accepted the presidency of the Pullman Company, rising to chairman of the board in 1911. He moved to Washington in 1912, pursued his keen interests in astronomy and golf, and died July 26, 1926, at his summer home in Manchester, Vermont. *DAB*, 11:266; Goff, John S., *Robert Todd Lincoln* (1969); *NCAB*, 21:59; *New York Times*, July 27, 1926.

LISBON AGREEMENTS (1952). Decisions concerning a number of issues related to the North Atlantic Treaty Organization (NATO)* were settled at a council meeting at Lisbon, Portugal, in February 1952. Among these decisions was the creation of a second NATO council, which would include Germany as a member, so that nation could have a voice in NATO affairs without being a formal member of the organization. The Lisbon Agreements also included an affirmation of Anglo-American support for the European Defense Community (EDC),* the reorganization of the German financial contribution to European defense, concurrence as to the extent of Germany military production, and the moving of NATO headquarters to Paris. The main problem faced by the principal negotiators, Secretary of State Dean Acheson* and British Foreign Secretary Anthony Eden, was to counter continuing French opposition to giving Germany anything of military or economic substance. McLellan, David S., *Dean Acheson* (1976).

LITTLE BELT **INCIDENT (1811).** The British sloop H.M.S. *Little Belt* skirmished with the much larger U.S.S. *President*, commanded by Commodore John Rodgers, and was forced to surrender. This May 1811 incident off the Virginia coast heightened public support for a war with Britain and convinced many Americans that the U.S. Navy might well be superior to the Royal Navy. Horsman, Reginald, *The Causes of the War of 1812* (1962); Perkins, Bradford, *Prologue to War* (1961).

LIVINGSTON, EDWARD (1764–1836). The brother of Robert Livingston,* Edward Livingston was born in Columbia County, New York, on May 26, 1764, and graduated from the College of New Jersey (now Princeton) in 1781. Admitted to the bar in 1785, he became a lawyer and a politician, sitting in the U.S. House of Representatives, 1795–1801, and serving as mayor of New York City, 1801–1803. About 1804, Livingston moved to New Orleans, where he practiced law and, for a time, was in considerable financial difficulty. He was an adviser to Andrew Jackson during the Louisiana phase of the War of 1812, went to the Louisiana legislature in 1820 and won wide acclaim for his proposed revision of the state penal code, and was elected to the U.S. House again in 1823 and to the Senate in 1829. In 1831, Andrew Jackson, now president, appointed Livingston secretary of state, where his main concerns were dealing with the French spoliation claims* and drafting the Nullification Proclamation (1832). He resigned in 1833 to accept the U.S. ministry in France, taking his son-in-law, Thomas Barton,* as legation secretary. Livingston went to Paris to secure payments of the spoliations as provided in the treaty, but negotiations to this end were unsuccessful, partly because the French demanded an apology from Jackson for his threat to seize French property if the payments were not made. Finally, in 1836, with the help of British mediation, the settlement was made. But Livingston had left France in 1835 and died May 23, 1836, at Montgomery Place in Dutchess County, New York. He was married twice: to Mary McEvers (1788–1801) and to Louise Moreau de Lassy (1805–1836). *DAB*, 11:309; *NCAB*, 5:293; Rawle, Francis, "Edward Livingston," in Bemis, Samuel F., ed., *American Secretaries of State and Their Diplomacy*, vol. 4 (1928); Willson, Beckles, *America's Ambassadors to France, 1777–1927* (1928).

LIVINGSTON, ROBERT R. (1746–1813). Robert R. Livingston was born in New York City on November 27, 1746, graduated from King's College (now Columbia) in 1765, read law, and was admitted to the bar in 1770. In 1773, he became recorder of New York City, and two years later he was elected to the Continental Congress, serving in 1775–1776, 1779–1781, and 1784–1785. He was on the committee that drafted the Declaration of Independence, although he never signed it. In 1781, Livingston entered office as the first secretary of foreign affairs, the predecessor to the office of secretary of state. He approved the instructions sent to the peace negotiators in Paris and generally favored the Peace of Paris (1783)* although he was displeased with that negotiating done secretly from France. Livingston himself contributed arguments for negotiating purposes on boundaries, fishing rights, and Loyalist affairs. In addition, he made a major contribution in setting up the initial bureaucracy and procedures. He resigned in 1783 because of the poor pay and returned to law practice and, occasionally, service in Congress or as chancellor of New York. In 1803, he was named minister to France, a position he held until 1804. There his object was to prevent the retrocession of Louisiana, to acquire West Florida if retrocession took place, and to press for payment of French spoliation claims. In early 1803, with special envoy James Monroe,* Livingston arranged for the U.S. purchase of Louisiana* for $15 million, including $3.75 million in assumed claims payments. After his return from France in 1804, he retired to his New York estate, Clermont, where he died February 26, 1813. Bonham, M. L., Jr., "Robert Livingston," in Bemis, Samuel F., ed., *American Secretaries of State and Their Diplomacy*, vol. 1 (1927); *DAB*, 11:319; Willson, Beckles, *America's Ambassadors to France, 1777–1927* (1928).

LOCARNO, TREATY OF (1925). The Treaty of Locarno encompassed a set of treaties designed to strengthen French (and general European) security. Included were (1) a treaty guaranteeing the Franco-German and Belgo-German frontiers; (2) arbitration treaties between Germany on one hand and France, Belgium, Czechoslovakia, and Poland on the other hand; and (3) a treaty of mutual guarantee among France, Czechoslovakia, and Poland. The package was signed in London, December 1, 1925. President Calvin Coolidge spoke approvingly of the treaty since it appeared to demonstrate that European nations could settle problems among themselves. At the time, the treaty was hailed as a major step forward in the pursuit of lasting peace; Germany was readmitted to the Council of Great Powers and would enter the League of Nations* the following year. Carr, E. H., *International Relations between the Two World Wars (1919–1939)* (1947); Craig, Gordon A., and Felix Gilbert, eds., *The Diplomats, 1919–1939*, vol. 1 (1965); Jacobsen, Jon, *Locarno Diplomacy: Germany and the West, 1925–1929* (1973).

LODGE, HENRY CABOT, JR. (1902–1985). The grandson of Henry Cabot Lodge, Sr.,* and a native of Nahant, Massachusetts, Henry Cabot Lodge, Jr., was born on July 5, 1902, and graduated from Harvard in 1924. He married

Emily Sears in 1926 and worked as a journalist with the *Boston Evening Transcript* and *New York Herald Tribune* until 1932, when he entered the Massachusetts legislature. In 1936, he was elected as a Republican to the U.S. Senate and served there (except for army service, 1944–1945) until 1953. As a senator, he was an internationalist after 1937 and made an extensive tour of the war fronts in 1943. Defeated for reelection (by John F. Kennedy) in 1952, Lodge was appointed ambassador to the United Nations* in 1953, a post he held until 1960. There he worked for a cease-fire in the Suez crisis* and the dispatching of a United Nations Emergency Force to the Middle East in 1956, defended U.S. intervention in Lebanon* in 1958, and countered criticism of the U-2 incident (1960)* by showing evidence of Soviet spying. He ran unsuccessfully with the Republican presidential candidate, Richard M. Nixon, in 1960 but in 1963 was named ambassador to Vietnam by the Democratic Kennedy administration. Lodge felt that the Vietnam War was a war of territorial aggression, not ideology, but he did not believe that the United States could impose a military solution and was an agent of the U.S. abandonment of the Ngo Dinh Diem regime. He returned from Vietnam in 1964 but was reappointed ambassador in 1965; this tour dealt mainly with efforts to stabilize the South Vietnamese government in Saigon. In 1967, he was appointed ambassador-at-large, but his concerns were still principally with Vietnamese affairs; one task was to advise the U.S. commission observing the 1967 elections in Vietnam. An uneventful tour as ambassador to (West) Germany, 1968–1969, preceded his appointment as head of the U.S. delegation at the Paris peace talks in 1969, where his efforts were in vain because of North Vietnamese intransigence and the tendency of both sides to milk the negotiations for their propaganda value. In 1970, Lodge accepted the less hectic position of special envoy to the Vatican, where he worked on such matters as the international drug traffic and the Vatican's involvement with peace and humanitarian relief projects. Returning from the Vatican in 1975, Lodge lived in Massachusetts and lectured at local colleges. He wrote two autobiographical works, *The Storm Has Many Eyes* (1973) and *As It Was* (1976). He died January 27, 1985, in Beverly, Massachusetts. His brother, John Davis Lodge (1903–1985), served as ambassador to Spain, Argentina, and Switzerland at various times. Burke, Lee H., *Ambassador-at-Large: Diplomat Extraordinary* (1972); Karnow, Stanley, *Vietnam: A History* (1983); *NCAB*, G:97; *New York Times*, February 28, 1985; *WWA* (1976–1977):1926.

LODGE, HENRY CABOT, SR. (1850–1924). A senator for over thirty years and chairman of the Foreign Relations Committee from 1919 to 1924, Henry Cabot Lodge, Sr., is best known for his staunch opposition to President Woodrow Wilson and the League of Nations.* Born in Boston on May 12, 1850, he graduated from Harvard (A.B., 1871; Ph.D., 1876) and Harvard Law School (LL.B., 1874) and worked as an assistant editor of the *North American Review* (1873–1876) and an instructor at Harvard (1876–1879) before embarking on his political career. He served in the Massachusetts legislature (1880–1883) and the

U.S. House of Representatives (1887–1893) before entering the Senate in 1893. Lodge's Senate career was closely tied to the nation's foreign policy. He drafted the Philippine Organic Act, was in charge of the ratification of the second Hay-Pauncefote Treaty (1901),* served on the Alaska Boundary Tribunal (1903), and throughout was a close friend, mentor, and adviser to President Theodore Roosevelt. As chairman of the Foreign Relations Committee, Lodge emerged as a leading reservationist* and Wilsonian opponent, due partly to partisan politics and partly to his concern that membership in the League of Nations would compromise U.S. freedom of action. In the Harding administration, Lodge led the debate over the ratification of the German and Austrian treaties, was a delegate to the Washington Conference (1921–1922),* introduced the Thomson-Urrutia Treaty* giving Colombia $25 million with respect to Panama, and blocked administration efforts to join the Permanent Court of International Justice (World Court).* Lodge died in Cambridge, Massachusetts, on November 9, 1924. He married Anna Cabot Davis in 1871, did much historical writing and editing (biographies of George Washington, Alexander Hamilton, and Daniel Webster,* among other works), and was the grandfather of Henry Cabot Lodge, Jr.,* former ambassador to the United Nations* and South Vietnam. *DAB*, 11:346; Garraty, John, *Henry Cabot Lodge* (1953); Lodge, Henry C., Sr., *The Senate and the League of Nations* (1925); *NCAB*, 19:52; Widenor, William C., *Henry Cabot Lodge and the Search for an American Foreign Policy* (1980).

LODGE COROLLARY (1911). This corollary to the Monroe Doctrine,* named for Senator Henry C. Lodge, Sr.,* developed out of the projected sale of a tract of land in lower California, including Magdalena Bay, by an American syndicate to a group of Japanese investors. The harbor was deemed to have strategic military value. The Lodge Corollary stated that such strategic places could not be sold to a foreign country whose government might make military use of them against the United States. The Senate supported a resolution to this effect on August 2, 1912, by a 51–4 vote, but President William H. Taft opposed it. The sale was never consummated. Wright, Herbert F., "Philander Chase Knox," in Bemis, Samuel F., ed., *American Secretaries of State and Their Diplomacy*, vol. 9 (1928).

LODGE RESERVATIONS, a set of fourteen reservations attached to the Treaty of Versailles (1919)* that, to President Woodrow Wilson, nullified the treaty and caused him to bring pressure to bear against it. The reservations, dealing with the Covenant of the League of Nations,* were named for Senator Henry Cabot Lodge, Sr. (R., Massachusetts),* chairman of the Senate Foreign Relations Committee and Wilson's principal congressional opponent. Of the reservations, the second one, stipulating that an act or joint resolution of Congress be required for any U.S. action under Article X* of the covenant, was the most important because of Wilson's adamant opposition to it. Although the reservations were defeated in November 1919, eight of the fourteen were passed and attached to the treaty in February and March 1920, but the whole treaty, with these reservations, was rejected March 19, 1920. Bailey, Thomas A., *Woodrow Wilson and the Great Betrayal* (1945); Smith, Daniel M., *The Great Departure* (1965).

LOGAN, CORNELIUS AMBROSE (1832–1899). Born in Deerfield, Massachusetts, on August 24, 1832, Cornelius Logan was educated to be a doctor, graduating from Woodward College (Ohio) in 1850 and from Ohio Medical College three years later. He became a doctor, practicing in Cincinnati and Leavenworth, Kansas, before serving as a surgeon in the Union army during the Civil War. After the war, he became the first president of the reorganized Kansas Medical Society in 1866 and was also active in the Odd Fellows fraternal organization. Defeated in an election for the U.S. Senate in 1873, the Republican Logan was appointed minister to Chile, where he arbitrated differences between Chile and Peru in 1874 and attempted to mediate conflicts during the early stages of the Tacna-Arica dispute before leaving his post in 1877. Between 1879 and 1882, Logan was minister to the Central American republics, an uneventful period for that region. In 1882, he was transferred back to Chile, where for a time he played an important role in the negotiations settling the War of the Pacific.* Chile had the upper hand militarily, and Logan wrote a letter urging Peru to cede Tacna-Arica to Chile for $15 million. A great controversy arose when this letter was made public. Logan quarreled with the American minister to Peru, and negotiations from this point were carried on without American participation. Logan returned from Chile in 1885, became literary executor of the estate of his cousin, General John A. Logan of Illinois, and published Logan's book, *The Volunteer Soldier of America* (1887). He was married to Zoe Shaw in 1854 and died in Los Angeles on January 30, 1899. *DAB*, 11:357; Millington, Herbert, *American Diplomacy and the War of the Pacific* (1948); Pletcher, David, *The Awkward Years* (1962); Rogers, Augustus C., *Our Representatives Abroad* (1874).

LOGAN, JAMES ADDISON, JR. (1879–1930). A native of Philadelphia, where he was born November 11, 1879, James A. Logan spent a year at Haverford College before enlisting in the army and eventually rising to the rank of colonel. He served in the Philippines during the Spanish-American War, graduated from the Army War College in 1912, and, because of his knowledge of French, served as an aide to General John J. Pershing during World War I. After the war, he was a deputy of Herbert Hoover in postwar relief work and became an unofficial observer for the United States at many postwar meetings and international conferences. From 1919 to 1923, he sat in on meetings of the Reparations* Commission; his observations contributed greatly to the Dawes Plan (1924).* He was also an adviser to the American Relief Association, 1921–1923, with particular responsibility for Russian relief. In 1922, Logan retired from the army, and, in 1925, he married Esther Tone Griswold and left public service to join the New York banking firm of Dillon, Read and Company. He died October 27, 1930, in Philadelphia. *New York Times*, August 17, 1924, February 8, May 31, 1925, October 28, 1930; *WWWA*, 1 (1897–1942):741.

LOGAN ACT (1799). Dr. George Logan, an American traveling in France in 1798, talked with French Foreign Minister Talleyrand and conveyed to him the impression that most Americans were pro-French and that only the Federalist John Adams* administration stood in the way of cordial Franco-American relations. When news of this reached America, Secretary of State Timothy Pickering* was outraged at this unauthorized diplomacy. Congress passed a law, known as the Logan Act, providing punishment for any citizen who, without authorization, tried to influence the conduct of a foreign government toward the United States during periods of dispute or controversy. Logan was elected to the U.S. Senate from Pennsylvania in 1801. In 1810, in apparent defiance of the act named for him, Logan traveled to England, making speeches and holding conversations with the British ministry. Ford, Henry J., "Timothy Pickering," in Bemis, Samuel F., ed., *American Secretaries of State and Their Diplomacy*, vol. 1 (1928); Smelser, Marshall, *The Democratic Republic, 1801–1815* (1968).

LONDON, DECLARATION OF (1909). This set of rules for the maritime rights of neutrals, drawn up at the London Naval Conference (1909), was based on "generally recognized principles of international law." Among the articles in the declaration was one that attempted to list in detail articles considered to be contraband.* Before World War I, Germany, Austria, and the United States, among others, ratified the declaration, but Britain refused, and it remained inoperative in practice. For the United States, Secretary of State and, later, Senator Elihu Root* played an important role in bringing about American acceptance of the declaration. Burchard, Edwin, and William P. Lage, *Neutrality for the United States* (1937); Coogan, John W., *The End of Neutrality: The United States, Britain, and Maritime Rights, 1899–1915* (1981); *FR* (1914), 2:215–70.

LONDON, TREATY OF (1915), a secret treaty between the Allies (Great Britain and France) and Italy. Italy promised to enter the war on the Allied side in return for promises of territorial spoils, including the German-inhabited South Tyrol, certain areas of the northeast Adriatic coast (but not Fiume), and a small area of present-day Albania surrounding the town of Valona. Bailey criticizes the treaty for its secretiveness and its partial violation of the principle of self-determination* and castigates President Woodrow Wilson for acquiescing in it. Bailey, Thomas A., *Woodrow Wilson and the Lost Peace* (1944); Seymour, Charles, *American Diplomacy during the World War* (1934).

LONDON CONFERENCE (1954). This was a conference of nine European powers (all members of the Brussels Pact*) in which the main subject was the future participation of Germany in European defense matters after the French scuttling of the European Defense Community (EDC).* An agreement worked out at this conference and signed in Paris in October provided for ending German occupation quickly, obtaining German (and Italian) adherence to the Brussels Pact (which would become known as the Western European Union), creating a European arms control agency, and recommending Germany's admission to the

North Atlantic Treaty Organization.* After some balking by the French legislature, ratifications of this agreement were exchanged in December 1954. British Foreign Secretary Anthony Eden was the main architect of this agreement. Wheeler-Bennett, John W., and Anthony Nicholls, *The Semblance of Peace* (1972).

LONDON NAVAL CONFERENCE (1930). Convened at the suggestion of Prime Minister Ramsay McDonald of Great Britain, this conference was another attempt to control the post–World War I naval arms race. The conferees met from January 21 to April 22, 1930, and agreed to limit the numbers of battleships and heavy cruisers and the total fleet tonnage of cruisers, destroyers, and submarines. Japan's ratio was raised from the 10:10:6 stipulated in the Five-Power Treaty (1922)* to 10:10:7, and a clause was included permitting a nation to exceed its limits of naval strength if national security so dictated. On the whole, the treaty resulted in practically no naval arms reduction, but the conference was important in restoring good political relations between the United States and Great Britain. The United States was represented by Secretary of the Navy Charles Francis Adams, Dwight Morrow,* Hugh Gibson,* Admiral Hilary P. Jones,* Senators David A. Reed and James T. Robinson, and Secretary of State Henry L. Stimson.* The Senate ratified the treaty July 21, 1930, and it took effect January 1, 1931. Ellis, L. Ethan, *Republican Foreign Policy, 1921–1933* (1968); Ferrell, Robert H., *American Diplomacy in the Great Depression* (1957); *FR* (1929), 1:112–317; *FR* (1930), 1:1–131; O'Connor, Raymond G., *The United States and the London Naval Conference of 1930* (1962).

LONDON NAVAL CONFERENCE (1935–1936). This conference, which brought together the United States, Great Britain, and Japan, was an unsuccessful attempt to limit still further the sizes of the powers' respective navies. During the meetings, which lasted from December 1935 to March 1936, Japan demanded that the United States and Great Britain set an upper limit on naval growth, but the United States and Britain rejected the demand. Only one agreement was concluded: the United States and Britain would limit the size of their existing battleships to 35,000 tons, arm them with guns no larger than 14 inches, and extend the construction holiday on heavy cruisers and battleships. The main significance of the conference may have been the encouraging signs of Anglo-American harmony. *FR* (1935), 1:64–161; *FR* (1936), 1:22–131; Offner, Arnold A., *The Origins of the Second World War* (1975).

LONG, BOAZ WALTON (1876–1962). Boaz Long was born in Warsaw, Indiana, on September 27, 1876, and attended St. Michael College in Santa Fe, New Mexico. In 1899, he entered the commission business, working in San Francisco, Chicago, and Mexico City until 1913. From 1914 to 1919 he was minister to El Salvador, and from 1919 to 1922 he occupied a similar post in Cuba. During these years, he took part in the Pan-American Scientific Congress (1915), aided in earthquake relief in El Salvador (1917), and mediated the

Guatemalan–El Salvador boundary dispute (1918). Out of government service during the Republican years of the 1920s, Long arranged concessions for ITT in Latin America, 1922–1930, and headed N. W. Ayer's foreign department, 1930–1933. In 1933, he joined the Roosevelt administration as public relations director for the National Recovery Administration, 1933–1934 and deputy administrator for Puerto Rico, 1934–1936. In 1936, he reentered diplomatic service as minister to Nicaragua (1936–1938) and Ecuador (1938–1941) and as ambassador to Ecuador (1942–1943) and Guatemala (1943–1945). His major contribution during these years was his work in founding the American School in Ecuador, 1940, and in bringing about the termination of that country's German schools. A firm believer in close U.S.-Cuban relations, Long was an opponent of the abrogation of the Platt Amendment.* After his retirement in 1945, he directed the Museum of New Mexico, 1948–1956, and was chairman of its School of American Research, 1954–1961. He married Eleanor Lessen in 1930 and died July 30, 1962, in Santa Fe. *NCAB*, 50:613–14; *New York Times*, July 31, 1962; *WWWA*, 4 (1961–1968):582.

LOOMIS, FRANCIS BUTLER (1861–1948). An important and somewhat controversial figure in the State Department during the Theodore Roosevelt years, Francis Loomis was born July 27, 1861, in Marietta, Ohio, and graduated from Marietta College in 1883. He began a career in journalism, working for the *New York Tribune*, 1884–1885, and the *Philadelphia Press*, 1887–1890. A Republican, Loomis also worked as press agent for James G. Blaine* in 1884 and was Ohio State librarian, 1885–1887. In 1890, he became consul* at St. Etienne, France, a post he held for three years before returning to Ohio to edit the *Cincinnati Daily Tribune*. He worked in the McKinley campaign, 1896, and was rewarded with an appointment as minister to Venezuela, 1897–1901, and Portugal, 1901–1902. In Venezuela, Loomis negotiated commercial treaties and parcel post conventions, prevented Spanish ships from leaving port during the Spanish-American War, and traveled up the Orinoco River in 1898 looking for U.S. commercial opportunities. His stay in Portugal was uneventful, but in 1903 he returned to Washington as first assistant secretary of state in time to play an important role in the Panama Canal negotiations. A strong advocate of American business abroad, Loomis was accused of improper relations with the Asphalt Trust, a concern with large Venezuelan investments. President Roosevelt exonerated him with a reprimand in 1905. In 1905, Loomis traveled to France as a special ambassador to receive the remains of John Paul Jones. In 1908, he was special envoy to the Tokyo trade fair, and in 1911–1912 he again was a special envoy, this time to the Turin Exposition and the Berlin Exposition Congress. After 1912, he worked as a foreign trade adviser for Standard Oil Company (California). He married Elizabeth Mast in 1897 and died in Burlingame, California, on August 5, 1948. *NCAB*, 37:38; *New York Times*, August 7, 1948; *WWWA*, 2 (1943–1950):329.

LOUIS, JOHN J., JR., (b. 1925). Born in Evanston, Illinois, on June 10, 1925, John J. Louis served in World War II and attended Northwestern University before graduating from Williams College (B.A., 1947) and Dartmouth (M.B.A., 1949). Successful in private business between 1949 and 1981, he became a major contributor to the Republican party and was rewarded with the appointment as ambassador to Great Britain by the Reagan administration. After two uneventful years in London, Louis was replaced rather abruptly in September 1983 after White House dissatisfaction with his handling of the arrangements for Prime Minister Margaret Thatcher's visit and his management generally after Edward J. Streator, the chargé d'affaires,* went on sick leave. Louis, who married Josephine Peters in 1953, returned to private business. *New York Times*, September 15, 1983; *WWA* (1986–1987):1733.

LOUISIANA PURCHASE (1803). Both the Americans and the French were interested in the Spanish trans-Mississippi territory after 1763, and American interest heightened after Pinckney's Treaty (1795)* opened the Old Southwest area. The French saw Louisiana as a source of food and other supplies, and their Caribbean empire, and had acquired it from Spain in the Treaty of San Ildefonso (1800).* However, a stalemated European war and a difficult insurrection in Haiti convinced Napoleon to accept the purchase offer made by Robert Livingston* and James Monroe* in April 1803. For $11.25 million plus $3.75 million in claims against the French that the United States would assume, the Jefferson administration doubled the size of the country. DeConde, Alexander, *This Affair of Louisiana* (1976); Malone, Dumas, *Jefferson, The President, 1801–1805* (1971); Van Alstyne, Richard W., *The Rising American Empire* (1960); Varg, Paul A., *Foreign Policies of the Founding Fathers* (1963).

LOVETT, ROBERT ABERCROMBIE (1895–1986). Born in Huntsville, Texas, on September 14, 1895, Robert A. Lovett served in World War I, 1917–1918, graduated from Yale in 1918, and attended graduate school at Harvard from 1919 to 1921. After leaving Harvard, he worked in the New York banking industry, mostly for Brown Brothers, Harriman and Company, in which he became a partner. He entered government service in 1940 as a special assistant to the secretary of war; in 1941, he was promoted to assistant secretary of war for air, a position he held for the duration of the war. After two years back in the banking industry, Lovett was called again to public service in 1947 as under secretary of state, succeeding Dean Acheson* in that post. He functioned as chief of staff under Secretary of State George C. Marshall,* was closely involved with the planning and negotiations leading to the North Atlantic Treaty,* 1948–1949, and strongly supported the Berlin airlift, based on his World War II experiences managing the airlift of supplies over the Himalayas to China. Lovett also gave strong backing to the Marshall Plan,* which he saw as the last chance to avert "real trouble" in Europe. He left the State Department in 1949, but the following year, he was named deputy secretary of defense, rising to secretary of defense in 1951, in which position he supported President Truman's dismissal of General Douglas MacArthur* and presided over the U.S. military buildup in the early 1950s. Lovett married Adele Quartley Brown in 1919 and was involved in private business interests until his death in Locust Valley, New York, on May 7, 1986. Feis, Herbert, *From Trust to Terror* (1970); Gimbel, John, *The Origins of the Marshall Plan* (1976); Isaacson, Walter, and Evan Thomas, *The Wise Men: Six Friends and the World They Made* (1977); McLellan, David S., *Dean Acheson: The State Department Years* (1976); *NCAB*, H:15; *New York Times*, May 8, 1986; *WWA* (1976–1977):1947; Yergin, Daniel, *Shattered Peace* (1971).

LOW, FREDERICK FERDINAND (1828–1894). Born June 30, 1828, in Frankfort, Maine, Frederick F. Low attended public schools until 1843 when he was apprenticed to Russell, Sturgis and Company of Boston, a prominent mercantile firm with much China trade. In 1849, Low went to California, married Mollie Creed in 1850, and became a successful San Francisco merchant, involved with steamship and banking operations as well. He served a term in the U.S. House of Representatives, 1862–1863, a year as a collector of the port of San Francisco, 1863, and a term as governor of California, 1864–1868. A Republican, Low was chosen minister to China in 1869 by the Grant administration. He spent four years in Peking, reporting on the Tientsin Revolution (1870), negotiating an abortive U.S.-Korea treaty (1871), and dealing with the audience question controversy (1873) over the right of foreigners to have an audience with the emperor, winning high regard from the Chinese. In 1874, back in California, Low became joint manager of the Anglo-California Bank, second largest on the West Coast. He helped found the University of California and Golden Gate Park before his death in San Francisco on July 21, 1894. Anderson, David L., *Imperialism and Idealism* (1985); *DAB*, 11:445; Dennett, Tyler, *Americans in Eastern Asia* (1922); *WWWA*, Historical Volume, p. 393.

LOW-ROGERS EXPEDITION (1871). Designed to enter Korea as Commodore Matthew C. Perry had entered Japan, this expedition, led by Frederick F. Low* and Admiral John Rogers, with five steamships, arrived near Seoul, Korea, in May 1871. Initial negotiations had just begun when a Korean fort fired on an American survey team, killing two Americans and several Korean workers. When no apology was made, American retaliatory fire destroyed 5 forts and caused 350 casualties. The Koreans still refused to open communications, and Admiral Rogers withdrew his squadron in early July. The failure of the expedition hurt Western relations with the nations of the Far East, especially China. Dennett, Tyler, *Americans in Eastern Asia* (1922).

LOWELL, JAMES RUSSELL (1819–1891). One of a number of American literary notables who also pursued a diplomatic career, James Russell Lowell was born in Cambridge, Massachusetts, on February 22, 1819; he graduated from Harvard in 1838 and from Harvard Law School in 1840. A poet and critic as well as a reformer, particularly interested in abolitionism, Lowell spent his time writing, traveling in Europe, teaching at Harvard (1856–1872, 1874–1877), and editing the *Atlantic Monthly* (1857–1861) and the *North American Review* (1864–1872). Between 1877 and 1885, he was minister to Spain (1877–1880) and to Great Britain (1880–1885). In Spain, his ministry was concerned with matters of court and ceremony, but in Britain, he was involved in a number of important diplomatic issues. He handled the negotiations concerning Irish affairs, including various Fenian disturbances, and was involved in discussions over North American fisheries and modification of the Clayton-Bulwer Treaty (1850).* Lowell liked London and was popular there, but in the United States, he received substantial criticism for his hostility toward the plight of Irish who had become naturalized American citizens, returned to Ireland, been arrested, and were seeking protection from the minister and his legation. A Republican, Lowell was replaced in 1885 by an appointee of the Democratic administration of Grover Cleveland. Lowell married Maria Winte in 1844; after her death in 1853, he married Frances Dunlap in 1857, and she died in 1885. Lowell died in Cambridge on August 12, 1891. *DAB*, 11:458; Duberman, Martin, *James Russell Lowell* (1966); Kaplan, Lawrence S., "The Brahmin as Diplomat in Nineteenth Century America," *Civil War History* 19, 1 (March 1973):5–28; Klibbe, Lawrence H., *James Russell Lowell's Residence in Spain* (1964); Wagenknecht, E. C., *James Russell Lowell: Portrait of a Many-Sided Man* (1971).

LUCE, ANN CLARE BOOTHE (1903–1987). Born in New York City on April 10, 1903, Clare Boothe was educated at private preparatory schools and in 1923 married the wealthy George Tuttle Brokaw. After a divorce in 1929, she went to work as an associate editor of *Vogue* in 1930 and a year later moved to *Vanity Fair* as associate editor, 1931–1932, and managing editor, 1933–1934. In 1935, she married the publisher of *Time*, Henry Robinson Luce. A Republican, she took an active part in the 1940 campaign and was elected to the U.S. House of Representatives in 1942, serving two terms. Luce was active in the anti-Communist movement after World War II and strongly supported the candidacy of General Dwight D. Eisenhower in 1952. After his election, she was named ambassador to Italy, a post she held until 1956. In Rome, she had to deal with the unstable internal political situation and with a demoralized embassy staff harassed by McCarthyite investigations. She made a major contribution to the settlement of the Trieste dispute between Italy and Yugoslavia by initiating discussions between the two nations. Luce also expressed official U.S. concern over Communist strength in Italian labor unions and convinced the government to permit an atomic artillery division to relocate in Italy from Austria and to sign the Status of Forces Treaty. In 1959, she was named ambassador to Brazil but resigned soon after her confirmation because of sharp criticism from opponents such as Senator Wayne Morse of Oregon. After 1959, she pursued interests in painting and writing. She served as a member of the President's Foreign Intelligence Advisory Board under different Republican presidents. Her husband died in 1967, and she died in Washington on October 10, 1987. Hatch, Alden,

Ambassador Extraordinary (1955); *NCAB*, F:435; *New York Times*, October 10, 1987; Shadegg, Stephen, *Clare Boothe Luce* (1970); *WWA* (1986–1987):1741.

LUDLOW AMENDMENT (1938). Named for Congressman Louis Ludlow (D., Indiana), this idea was couched in a proposed constitutional amendment providing for a national vote, or referendum, to be taken before Congress could declare war, except in the instance of a direct attack on the United States, its territories, or another nation of the Western Hemisphere. Originated by Ludlow in 1935, the proposal reached the House of Representatives in December 1937 by means of a discharge petition and was rejected 209–188 on January 10, 1938. According to Divine, the amendment, had it passed, would have severely limited presidential authority in foreign affairs. President Franklin D. Roosevelt said the referendum was not consistent with the principle of representative government and used considerable political pressure to ensure the defeat of the measure. The large vote in favor of the Ludlow Amendment is an indicator of the sizable isolationist* sentiment in the nation. Bolt, Ernest C., *Ballots Before Bullets* (1977); Divine, Robert A., *The Illusion of Neutrality* (1962).

LUGAR, RICHARD G. (b. 1932). Born in Indianapolis on April 4, 1932, Richard Lugar graduated from Denison in 1954 and then, as a Rhodes Scholar, received B.A. and M.S. degrees from Oxford in 1956. After three years in the naval reserves, he became involved in local Republican politics, serving as mayor of Indianapolis from 1968 to 1975. In 1976, he was elected to the U.S. Senate. Reelected in 1982, he became chairman of the Senate Foreign Relations Committee in 1985, replacing Charles Percy of Illinois who had been defeated for reelection. As Foreign Relations Committee chair, Lugar generally stood with the Reagan administration, particularly on the succession of contra* aid bills. In February 1986, he went to Manila to observe the national elections and their aftermath, concluded they were fraudulent, and was influential in persuading the administration to abandon Ferdinand Marcos and support Corazon Aquino in the Philippine crisis (1986).* Not always in step with the administration, Lugar wrote the bill to place economic sanctions against South Africa in 1986 and worked to get the necessary Republican votes to override the president's veto. In January 1987, with the Democrats back in control of the Senate, Lugar lost his chairmanship and then, in a bitter intraparty struggle with Senator Jesse Helms of North Carolina, lost his position as ranking minority member. Now (1988) ranking minority member on the Agriculture Committee, Lugar still serves on the Foreign Relations Committee and frequently opposes Helms. Married in 1956 to Charlene Smeltzer, Lugar has farming interests in Indiana. *Courier-Journal* (Louisville), May 7, 1987; *New York Times*, December 9, 1984, May 26, September 27, 1985.

LUSITANIA, an English luxury liner, sunk May 5, 1915, by German U-boat* *U–20* off the Irish coast, with the loss of 1,198 lives, including 128 Americans. The incident caused a strong nationalistic response in the United States, and

President Woodrow Wilson sent two protests to Germany in the next five weeks, demanding accountability in the sinking of the ship and implying a threat of war. Secretary of State William Jennings Bryan,* who had advocated a less militant response, resigned from his post June 6, 1915, after Wilson rejected his advice. According to May, the *Lusitania* sinking symbolized a change in the United States from "indrawn pacifist reformism" to "Progressive nationalism." It brought America closer to the European conflict and was the first major blow to American prestige and honor. Bailey, Thomas A., and Paul B. Ryan, *The Lusitania Disaster* (1975); *FR, Lansing Papers*, 1:385–465, 488–96, passim; Jonas, Manfred, *The United States and Germany* (1984); May, Ernest, *The World War and American Isolation, 1914–1917* (1959); Simpson, Colin, *The Lusitania* (1972).

LYON, CECIL BURTON (b. 1903). Born on Staten Island, New York, on November 8, 1903, Cecil B. Lyon graduated from Harvard in 1927 and went to work as an investment banker in New York City. He joined the Foreign Service in 1931, serving in minor posts in Havana, Hong Kong, Tokyo, Peking, Santiago, Washington, and Cairo before 1947. That year he became special assistant to the assistant secretary of state for political affairs. From 1948 to 1950, Lyon was counselor* at the Warsaw embassy. The following year he had an assignment at the National War College. In 1951, he became director of the Berlin element of the Office of the U.S. High Commissioner for Germany, where he handled problems caused by a temporary renewal of the Berlin blockade* in 1952. In 1954, he returned to Washington as director of the State Department's German office. After a year in that post, Lyon became deputy assistant secretary of state for inter-American affairs; this post led to his first ambassadorship, to Chile, 1956–1958. He left Chile in 1958 and went to Paris for the next six years as deputy chief of mission and minister at the U.S. embassy there. His last tour was as ambassador to Sri Lanka (Ceylon), 1964–1967; he also represented the United States in the Maldive Islands, 1965–1967. Retiring from the State Department after his return from Sri Lanka, Lyon has since been associated with the International Rescue Committee. Lyon married Elizabeth Sturgis Grew, the daughter of Joseph C. Grew,* in 1933. Department of State *Bulletin*, January 31, 1955, pp. 183–89; *New York Times*, April 3, 1956, March 7, 1958; *WWA* (1986–1987):1754.

LYTTON COMMISSION (1931–1933). This commission of inquiry was appointed in December 1931 by the League of Nations* to investigate the Manchurian crisis* after the Mukden incident.* Japan accepted the commission with the reservation that it not preclude any future Japanese military action. Reporting in October 1932, the commission blamed both China and Japan for the situation but placed more blame on Japan. The commission concluded that Manchuria was rightfully Chinese territory and that Manchukuo, a Japanese puppet empire created in March 1932, should not be recognized. The commission was headed by the earl of Lytton and included a U.S. congressman Major General Frank R. McCoy. Upon the league's acceptance of the report and its recommendations, Japan withdrew from membership in the world organization. However, the response of the United States and Western Europe to the report was favorable. Burns, Richard Dean, and Edward M. Bennett, eds., *Diplomats in Crisis* (1974); Ferrell, Robert H., *American Diplomacy in the Great Depression* (1957); Thorne, Christopher, *The Limits of Foreign Policy* (1972).

M

MacARTHUR, DOUGLAS (1880–1964). A military hero of World War II, Douglas MacArthur has an important place in U.S. diplomacy as supreme commander of the occupation of Japan, 1945–1950. Born on an army post near Little Rock, Arkansas, on January 26, 1880, he graduated from West Point in 1903 and embarked on an active duty career that lasted until 1951, except for a period of retirement from 1937 to 1941. In his career, he served in the Philippine insurrection, in Mexico, with the famous Rainbow Division during World War I, and as superintendent of West Point after the war. Promoted to general in 1930, he led troops in harshly resisting the demands of World War I veterans for a promised bonus in the so-called bonus march in 1932 and was a military adviser in the Philippines, 1935–1937, building up an indigenous defense force in the islands. While retired from the U.S. Army, he was field marshal for the Philippines. In 1941, the Philippine army was merged with the U.S. Army, and MacArthur spent the war as commander in chief of army forces in the Pacific theater, accepting the Japanese surrender in 1945. As occupation forces commander in postwar Japan, MacArthur put a personal touch on Japan; his leadership was strong willed, dignified, austere, and demanding of total loyalty. These traits appealed to the Japanese and, along with MacArthur's flair for the dramatic, gained him great respect and admiration. Under MacArthur, who practically wrote the Japanese constitution by himself, the country established democratic government and achieved economic recovery while repressing any urges toward rearmament. The main problems of occupation, none of them serious, revolved around the complexity of its organization, the need for skilled personnel, and the corruptive influence of the occupation on the occupiers. In 1950, MacArthur took command of United Nations* forces in Korea, but President Harry S Truman, in a controversial affair, removed him from his command in 1951, on the grounds of insubordination when the general publicly lobbied against administration war policy. In 1952, he became chairman of Remington Rand and was the subject of an abortive boomlet for the Republican presidential nomination. Twice married, MacArthur died in Washington on April 5, 1964. James, D. Clayton, *The Years of MacArthur*, 3 vols. (1970–1985); Manchester, William, *American Caesar* (1978); Perry, John Curtis, *Beneath the Eagle's Wings: Americans in Occupied Japan* (1981).

MacARTHUR, DOUGLAS II (b. 1909). A nephew of General Douglas MacArthur* and a native of Bryn Mawr, Pennsylvania, Douglas MacArthur II was born July 5, 1909, and graduated from Yale in 1932. After three years in the Officers' Reserve Corps, he joined the Foreign Service in 1935 and served in minor posts in Vancouver, Naples, Paris, and Lisbon. From 1942 to 1944, he was interned in France. When released he became a political adviser to SHAEF (Supreme Headquarters, Allied Expeditionary Force), followed by four years attached to the U.S. embassy in Paris. In 1949, he became chief of the division, West European Affairs, followed by a stint as deputy director, European Regulatory Affairs, during which he helped establish the North Atlantic Treaty Organization (NATO).* After five years (1951–1956) as a counselor,* two in Paris and three in Washington, MacArthur was appointed ambassador to Japan (1956–1961), ambassador to Belgium (1961–1965), assistant secretary of state for congressional affairs (1965–1967), ambassador to Austria (1967–1969), and ambassador to Iran (1969–1972). Despite the succession of ambassadorial posts, MacArthur's most significant work was in the creation of NATO and in subsequent work with John Foster Dulles* in the Middle East and at the Manila Conference (1954),* establishing regional alliances for those parts of the world. Since 1972, MacArthur has worked as a business consultant and serves as a director of various companies. He married Laura Louise Barkley, daughter of former Vice-President Alben Barkley, in 1934 and lives in Brussels. *CB* (1954), 418–18; *New York Times*, April 26, 1953, November 3, 1971; *WWA* (1976–1977):1972.

McCARTEE, DIVIE BETHUNE (1820–1900). A native of Philadelphia, where he was born January 13, 1820, Divie Bethune McCartee attended Columbia University before graduating from the University of Pennsylvania in 1840. Three years later, he was sent as a Presbyterian missionary to China, settling in Ningpo for many years and serving as U.S. consul* there, 1857–1862 and 1865–1872. McCartee resigned his mission in 1872 to work full time at the consulate as an interpreter and assessor in the mixed court at Shanghai. After only a short while, he was sent to Japan on a special mission by the Chinese government and stayed on to teach at the Imperial University and serve as secretary to the Chinese legation in Japan. In this role, he was involved in the Sino-Japanese dispute (1879) over the Loo Choo Islands. Former President U.S. Grant mediated this controversy, with McCartee's advice, and managed to ameliorate the excessive propaganda on both sides and avert an open break. McCartee returned to the United States in 1880. He was married to Joanna M. Knight in 1853 and died in San Francisco on July 17, 1900. *DAB*, 11:569; *NCAB*, 24:159.

McCONAUGHY, WALTER PATRICK, JR. (b. 1908). Born September 11, 1908, in Montevallo, Alabama, Walter P. McConaughy graduated from Birmingham Southern College (1928), taught high school for two years, and studied further at Duke University before joining the Foreign Service in 1930. He served in minor posts in Tampico, Kobe, Osaka, and Peking before being interned by the Japanese in Peking in 1941. Released in 1942, he went on assignments to La Paz, Rio de Janeiro, and the National War College before being posted in Shanghai in 1948 and earning the distinction of being the last U.S. Foreign

Service officer to leave mainland China after the Communist victory in the civil war. From 1950 to 1952, McConaughy was consul general* at Hong Kong, and from 1952 to 1957, he directed the State Department's Office of Chinese Affairs. In 1957, he began a series of ambassadorial appointments—Burma (1957–1959); Korea (1959–1961); Pakistan (1962–1966); and the Republic of China (Taiwan) (1966–1974)—interrupted by a stint as assistant secretary of state for Far Eastern affairs (1961–1962), where he worked closely with his friend, Secretary of State Dean Rusk.* As ambassador to Taiwan, he stressed the continuing U.S. commitment to military and diplomatic support of the Nationalists, seemingly overlooking the changing U.S. policy toward the People's Republic of China under President Richard M. Nixon. McConaughy married Dorothy Davis in 1973 and retired from the State Department in 1974. *New York Times*, October 6, 1959, November 27, 1961, June 23, 1974; *WWA* (1968–1969):1453.

McCORMICK, ROBERT SANDERSON (1849–1919). Robert McCormick was born July 26, 1849, in Rockbridge County, Virginia, but moved to Illinois at an early age and attended both the University of Chicago and the University of Virginia. Before his entry into the diplomatic service, he was involved in the family reaping-machine business. From 1889 to 1892, he was secretary of the legation in London; there he was resident commissioner for the Columbian Exposition and worked to restore the damage done to commercial relations by the McKinley Tariff of 1890. In 1901, McCormick was appointed minister to Austria-Hungary; a year later the legation was raised in rank to an embassy, and he became the first ambassador to Austria-Hungary. In 1903, he became ambassador to Russia, and in two years there he persuaded the czar to honor U.S. passports given to Jews and secured permission for the Associated Press to report news from Russia. He handled Japanese affairs in Russia during the Russo-Japanese War (1904–1905)* and was honored by Japan for this work. From 1905 to 1907, McCormick was ambassador to France, where business was mainly social, concerned, for example, with making arrangements for the celebration of Benjamin Franklin's* bicentenary in 1906. He married Katherine Van Etta Medill in 1876 and was the father of Senator Medill McCormick (R., Illinois). Well known as a collector of books, Napoleonic biographies, and etchings, McCormick was an advocate of a world court before his death in Hinsdale, Illinois, on April 16, 1919. *DAB*, 11:612; Dennis, A.L.P., *Adventures in American Diplomacy, 1896–1906* (1928); *New York Times*, April 17, 1919; Willson, Beckles, *America's Ambassadors to France, 1777–1927* (1928).

McDONALD, JAMES GROVER (1886–1964). America's first ambassador to Israel, James G. McDonald was born in Coldwater, Ohio, on November 29, 1886, graduated from Indiana University (A.B., 1909; A.M., 1910), and did further graduate work at Harvard from 1911 to 1914. He taught history and political science at Indiana until 1918, when he became president of the Foreign Policy Association,* a position he held until 1933. In that year, he was named high commissioner for refugees from Germany, his first contact with Jewish affairs. In 1936, McDonald joined the *New York Times* editorial staff. Two years later, he returned to academic life as president of the Brooklyn Institute of Arts and Sciences. After two years as news analyst for the Blue (Radio) Network, he was chosen as a member of the Anglo-American Commission in Inquiry on Palestine, 1945–1946. Mcdonald spent the year 1947 studying on his own in Palestine, and the following year, he was appointed special representative to the newly created state of Israel, a job title that changed to ambassador in January 1949, after elections to the Knesset had taken place and the United States granted Israel de jure recognition. In Israel, McDonald concerned himself with the refugee problem, boundaries, and peace; he observed and cooperated with the Palestinian Conciliation Commission in its futile effort to find a solution to that question. He tried to encourage the United States to push for direct negotiations between Israel and the Arabs and to push Israel toward a more flexible stance on the crucial issues concerning the Middle East. After leaving Israel in 1951, he became chairman of the advisory council of the Israel Bond Organization and a consultant on European and Middle East affairs. Married in 1915 to Ruth Stafford, he wrote of his experiences as a diplomat in *My Mission to Israel* (1951) and died in Bronxville, New York, on September 26, 1964. *New York Times*, September 27, 1964; Waldeck, Countess, "The Great New Migration," *Foreign Affairs* 15, 3 (April 1937):543; *WWWA*, 4 (1961–1968):635.

McFARLANE, ROBERT CARL (b. 1937). The son of a Texas congressman, Robert McFarlane was born in Washington, D.C., on July 12, 1937. He graduated from the Naval Academy with the class of 1958 and was a career officer in the marines until 1979, earning an M.S. in strategic studies from the University of Geneva in 1964. During the mid–1970s he was a military assistant on the National Security Council (NSC)* staff. After retirement from the marines in 1979, McFarlane joined the staff of the Senate Armed Services Committee, working for its ranking minority member, Senator John Tower (R., Texas). When the Reagan administration took office in 1981, McFarlane became a counselor* in the State Department and a confidant of Secretary of State Alexander Haig.* After Haig's departure in 1982, McFarlane went to the NSC again, where he was a deputy to William P. Clark,* handling administrative matters while Clark promoted a conservative view of foreign policy within the administration. In addition, he was an effective lobbyist with Congress on such matters as the MX missile development and arms control. In July 1983, President Reagan appointed him his personal representative to the Middle East to work on getting foreign troops out of Lebanon and to pursue an Israeli-Arab settlement. He achieved no results with diplomacy and advocated continuing marine support for the Lebanese government. When the bombing of the marine barracks occurred in October 1983, McFarlane was among those who felt a precipitate withdrawal of American forces would be taken as a sign of weakness. In October 1983, he was named national security adviser, replacing Clark. In this position, he was principally concerned with the Persian Gulf difficulties, the Intermediate Nuclear Forces (INF) Treaty,* and Central American policy. In 1985, he became centrally involved in the Iran-contra scandal,* especially in the decision to sell arms to Iran, and remained so even after his resignation as national security adviser in late 1985, going to Iran in May 1986 to facilitate the deal and working to raise money for the contras* from countries such as Israel and Saudi Arabia. Feeling that he had failed his country after the Iran-contra scandal became public knowledge, McFarlane attempted suicide in February 1987 but recovered and testified in the congressional hearings during the summer of 1987. He married Jonda Riley in 1959 and since 1987 has been engaged in research at Georgetown University's Center for Strategic and International Studies. With R. G. Head and F. W. Short, he wrote *Crisis Resolution: Presidential Decision Making in the "Mayagüez" and Korean Confrontations* (1979). *CB* (1984):265–68; *New York Times*, October 18, 1983, December 5–6, 1985, February 10–12, 1987.

MacGAHAN, JANUARIUS ALOYSIUS (1844–1878). J. A. MacGahan was born in Perry County, Ohio, on June 12, 1844, attended local schools, and during the 1860s worked as a bookkeeper in Huntington, Indiana, and St. Louis. In 1869, he went to Europe to study law, lived in Belgium, France, and Germany briefly, and was appointed a war correspondent for the *New York Herald*, with instructions to cover the Franco-Prussian War (1870). He followed its campaigns until he was jailed briefly, and after his release he traveled around Europe as the Russian correspondent for the *Herald*. MacGahan married Barbara Nicholavna Elagin in 1872, spent much time in Russia, became an intimate of the czar's court, went to the Crimea, and took a fabled ride alone into the desert of Central Asia, which formed the basis for his book, *Campaigning on the Oxus* (1874). In 1874–1875, he traveled in Spain and Cuba, and later in 1875 he accompanied an Arctic voyage searching for the lost crew of explorer Sir John Franklin, prompting another book, *Under the Northern Lights* (1876?). Next, he reported on the so-called Eastern question from Bulgaria for the *London Daily News*, and his letters from Bulgaria helped create the atmosphere that led to war between Russia and Britain. Since one result of this was Bulgarian independence, MacGahan became known there as "The Liberator," but he had scant time to enjoy the accolade, dying of typhus in Constantinople on June 9, 1878. *DAB*, 12:45; *NCAB*, 6:187.

McGHEE, GEORGE CREWS (b. 1912). George C. McGhee was born in Waco, Texas, on March 10, 1912, graduated from the University of Oklahoma in 1933, and, going to Britain as a Rhodes Scholar, received a Ph.D. from Oxford in 1937. He worked as a geologist and geophysicist for various oil companies in the late 1930s before starting his own McGhee Production Company in 1940. During World War II, he was in federal government service with the War Production Board (1941) and the Combined Raw Materials Board (1942) and military service with the U.S. Navy (1943–1945). After the war McGhee became involved in diplomatic work as a special assistant to the under secretary of state for economic affairs (1946), coordinator of aid to Greece and Turkey (1947–1949), and assistant secretary of state for Near Eastern, South Asian and African affairs (1949–1951). In 1951, the Truman administration appointed the experienced bureaucrat ambassador to Turkey, where he helped arrange that nation's membership in the North Atlantic Treaty Organization,* and generally improved the Turkish image in the West. With the incoming Republican administration of Dwight D. Eisenhower in 1953, McGhee returned to private business in Texas. Called back to Washington by the Kennedy administration in 1961, McGhee reentered diplomatic service as a State Department counselor* and chairman of the Policy Planning Staff, moving later that year to the post of under secretary of state for political affairs. From 1963 to 1968, McGhee was ambassador to West Germany, where he traveled frequently around the country, established good relationships with Chancellor Ludwig Erhard and Foreign Minister Gerhard Schroeder, and helped formulate the allied response to Soviet roadblocks on access roads to West Berlin in 1963. A long-time friend of President Lyndon B. Johnson, McGhee returned to Washington in 1968 to serve about a year as ambassador-at-large. He left federal government service in 1969 and has since been involved in Washington, D.C., civic and local governmental affairs. McGhee married Cecilia Jeanne DeGolyer in 1938 and wrote his memoirs, *Envoy to the Middle World: Adventures in Diplomacy* (1983). McGhee, George C., "Turkey Joins the West," *Foreign Affairs* 32 (July 1954): 217–30; *New York Times*, November 27, 1961; *WWA* (1986–1987):1872.

McKINLEY TARIFF ACT (1890). This tariff, named for Ohio Congressman William McKinley, reflected the business orientation of the late nineteenth century. It provided for higher protective rates than ever before, with the major exception of raw sugar, on which the duty was removed. This feature of the act also ended reciprocity with Hawaii, a major sugar producer, badly crippling both the Hawaiian economy and Hawaiian-American relations. However, commercial reciprocity was included in the act through the influence of Secretary of State James G. Blaine,* who was attempting to create closer political and economic ties with Western Hemisphere nations. Reciprocity agreements based on the McKinley Tariff were also signed with Germany and Austria-Hungary, but all such agreements were terminated with the passage of the Wilson-Gorman Tariff Act (1894). Faulkner, Harold U., *Politics, Reform, and Expansion* (1959); LaFeber, Walter, *The New Empire* (1963); Taussig, F. W., *The Tariff History of the United States* 6th ed. (1914).

McLANE, LOUIS (1786–1857). Born in Smyrna, Delaware, on May 28, 1786, Louis McLane served in the navy, 1798–1801, attended Newark College (now the University of Delaware), read law with James A. Bayard, and was admitted to the bar in 1807. He married Catherine Mary Mulligan in 1812 and embarked upon a political career in 1816 with election to the U.S. House of Representatives.

After five terms in the House, McLane moved to the Senate but served only two years before being named minister to Great Britain in 1829. In London, where his legation secretary was Washington Irving,* McLane developed excellent rapport with King William IV and negotiated an important trade agreement (1831) that opened British West Indian ports to U.S. vessels and U.S. ports to British vessels for the first time since 1827. After two years in Britain, McLane returned to serve in President Andrew Jackson's cabinet, first as secretary of the treasury (1831–1833) and then as secretary of state (1833–1834). As secretary of state, he dealt with Mexican claims and boundaries questions, Great Britain and the northeast boundary problem, and the particularly vexing French spoliation claims* matter. Although a spoliation treaty was signed in 1831, the French refused to pay, and McLane ordered reprisals against French shipping, bringing on a clash with Martin Van Buren* and leading to his departure from the State Department. After several years in private life as president of the B&O Railroad, McLane accepted a second appointment as minister to Great Britain in 1845. There his main task was to negotiate the Oregon question,* although to his disappointment the crucial talks took place in Washington. He stayed only a year in London before returning to the United States and the B&O Railroad, which he headed until 1848. During the 1850s, McLane remained active in Democratic politics on both state and national levels until his death in Baltimore on October 7, 1857. *DAB*, 12:113; McCormick, E. I., "Louis McLane," in Bemis, Samuel F., ed., *American Secretaries of State and Their Diplomacy*, vol.4 (1928); Murrell, John A., *Louis McLane: Federalist and Jacksonian* (1973); Willson, Beckles, *America's Ambassadors to England, 1785–1929* (1929).

McLANE, ROBERT MILLIGAN (1815–1898). Robert M. McLane was born June 23, 1815, in Wilmington, Delaware, and was a member of the class of 1837 at West Point. He fought in the Seminole War, 1838, studied law, and was admitted to the Washington, D.C., bar in 1840 and the Maryland bar in 1845. In 1841, he went to Europe to make an engineering study of dikes and drainage, but his future career centered on law and politics. He served in the Maryland legislature, 1845–1847, and the U.S. House of Representatives, 1847–1851, before his first diplomatic assignment as commissioner to China, 1853–1854. There he was unsuccessful in attempts to get the commercial treaty renewed and returned home in late 1854 because of poor health. In 1859, he was minister to Mexico, recognizing the government of Benito Juárez and signing the McLane-Ocampo Treaty* for a Mexican transit route and political and commercial advantages. Because of the impending Civil War, the treaty was never ratified, and McLane returned to his law practice. From 1879 to 1883, he served again in the U.S. House, and from 1883 to 1885 he was Maryland's governor. In 1885, McLane, a Democrat, was chosen minister to France by the Cleveland administration. In four relatively uneventful years, McLane's major concern was protection of the rights of French-born naturalized U.S. citizens who were being drafted into French military service. McLane, who married Georgine Urquhart in 1841, continued to reside in Paris after his ministry and died there on April 16, 1898. *DAB*, 12:15; McLane, Robert, *Reminiscences* (1903, 1972); Willson, Beckles, *America's Ambassadors to France, 1777–1927* (1928).

McLANE-OCAMPO TREATY (1859). This treaty, never ratified, proposed to make Mexico a virtual protectorate of the United States by allowing the United States the right of intervention and police power in Mexico, as well as perpetual right of transit across both the Isthmus of Tehuantepec and northern Mexico. In return, the United States would pay $4 million, half of which would be used to pay American claims against Mexico. The treaty, negotiated by U.S. Minister to Mexico Robert M. McLane* and Melchor Ocampo, the minister of foreign affairs was rejected by the Senate, May 31, 1860, on sectional grounds, northern senators being strongly opposed. Perkins, Dexter, *A History of the Monroe Doctrine*, rev. ed. (1955); Rippy, J. Fred, *The United States and Mexico*, rev. ed. (1931); Roeder, Ralph, *Juarez and His Mexico* (1947).

MACLAY, ROBERT SAMUEL (1824–1907). Robert S. Maclay was born in Concord, Pennsylvania, on February 7, 1824, graduated from Dickinson College in 1845, and was ordained a Methodist minister the following year. In 1847, he was sent to Foochow, China, as a missionary and over the next twenty-five years became "practically the founder of Methodist missions in China" through his work as secretary-treasurer of the Foochow group. In 1872, Maclay was sent to Japan to spread the Methodist work; he stayed there until 1888, making a special trip to Korea, seeking permission to start missions there. In addition, he was involved in educational work. He took a leave from Japan in 1881 to return to Foochow and open the Anglo-Chinese College; two years later, he started the Anglo-Japanese College in Tokyo, serving as its president from 1883 to 1887. Maclay also founded the Philander Smith Bible Institute in Tokyo in 1884. In 1888, he returned to the United States and worked as the dean of Maclay College of Theology until 1893. He was married twice: in 1850 to Henrietta Caroline Sperry, who died in 1879, and in 1882 to Sarah Ann Barr. Retired after 1893, Robert Maclay died on August 18, 1907, in San Fernando, California. *DAB*, 12:121.

MacLEISH, ARCHIBALD (1892–1982). A renowned American poet and playwright, Archibald MacLeish played a constructive diplomatic role at the end of World War II in the planning of the United Nations.* He was born in Glencoe, Illinois, on May 7, 1892, and graduated from Yale (1915) and Harvard Law School (1919). He married Ada Hitchcock in 1916 and during World War I was an ambulance driver and artillery captain. After the war, MacLeish practiced law in Boston, but he moved to Paris in 1923 and joined the band of U.S. literary expatriates there. In 1929, he traveled in Mexico. Upon his return, he became an editor of *Fortune* magazine. From 1939 to 1944, MacLeish was Librarian of Congress. Throughout this period, he remained an active poet and an enthusiastic internationalist and worked for a time in the Office of War Information. In 1944, the Roosevelt administration named him assistant secretary of state for public and cultural relations. He helped plan and publicize the Dumbarton Oaks proposals for the United Nations by sending out speakers and by producing radio broadcasts and a short documentary film. The publicity campaign climaxed at the time of the San Francisco Conference,* April 1945, after which he worked with the organization of the United Nations Educational, Scientific, and Cultural Organization, attending the London conference that drafted its constitution, leading the U.S. delegation to its first general conference in 1946, and serving as a member of its general council. After 1949, MacLeish taught at Harvard and continued writing poetry and plays, among which was the highly acclaimed *J.B.: A Play in Verse* (1958). He worked on the biographical film, *The Eleanor Roosevelt Story* (1966), and died in Boston April 20, 1982. *CB* (November 1959):279–81; Divine, Robert, *Second Chance* (1967); *NCAB*, F:39; *New York Times*, April 21, 1982; *WWWA* 8 (1982–1985):256.

MACON'S BILL NUMBER ONE (November 1809). This bill was an attempt at economic coercion by the United States, wherein American ports would be closed to Britain and France but would open to the power or powers that rescinded their decrees inhibiting U.S. shipping (cf. Berlin Decree,* Milan Decree,* Orders-in-Council (1807), Order-in-Council (1809).* The bill passed the House; an amended version passed the Senate; and in the conference committee, conferees deadlocked, which led to the much weaker Macon's Bill Number Two.* Perkins, Bradford, *Prologue to War* (1961).

MACON'S BILL NUMBER TWO (May 1810). This bill, named for Senate Foreign Relations Committee Chairman Nathaniel Macon, removed all economic sanctions against Great Britain and France but promised to restore them against one if the other rescinded its decrees (the Orders-in-Council* or the Berlin Decree* and Milan Decree*). Generally considered a weak American attempt at economic coercion, Macon's Bill Number Two led to no policy change in Britain and to the insincere Cadore letter* in France. Perkins, Bradford, *Prologue to War* (1961).

MacVEAGH, CHARLES (1860–1931). Charles MacVeagh, born June 6, 1860, in West Chester, Pennsylvania, was the son of Wayne MacVeagh, a former ambassador to Italy and minister to Turkey, and the father of Lincoln Mac-Veagh,* a career Foreign Service officer. He was educated at Phillips Exeter Academy, Harvard (A.B., 1881), and Columbia Law School (LL.B., 1883) and admitted to the bar in 1883. He practiced law in New York City, 1883–1901, and then became an incorporator and solicitor of U.S. Steel, 1901–1925. From 1925 to 1929, MacVeagh was ambassador to Japan. Despite some bad feelings in Japan resulting from the restrictive immigration policies of the United States, MacVeagh enjoyed good relations with the Japanese and made a special effort to understand Japanese culture. During and after World War I, he had done relief work for Japanese orphans and, for this, was decorated by the government. He also worked for Serbian relief and was honored by the Yugoslavian government. After his return from Japan in 1929, MacVeagh was vice-president and secretary of Fatherless Children of France and president of Immediate Relief to Italy Fund. Married to Fanny Davenport Rogers in 1887, he died December 4, 1931, near Santa Barbara, California. *DAB*, Supp. 2:534; *New York Times*, December 5, 1931.

MacVEAGH, LINCOLN (1890–1972). Son of Charles MacVeagh,* U.S. ambassador to Japan in the 1920s, Lincoln MacVeagh was born in Narragansett Pier, Rhode Island, on October 1, 1890. He was a 1913 Harvard graduate and studied further at the University of Paris, 1913–1914. In 1914, he joined U.S. Steel Products Company as a clerk but after a year, moved to Henry Holt & Company, publishers, remaining there until 1923 except for a two-year army tour in World War I. In 1923, he founded and became president of Dial Press, publishers of *Dial Magazine* and numerous noteworthy books of the 1920s. MacVeagh resigned in 1933 upon his appointment as minister to Greece (1933–1941), the first of six ministerial or ambassadorial posts: minister to Iceland (1941–1942), minister to South Africa (1942–1943), ambassador to Greece and Yugoslavia (1943–1948), ambassador to Portugal (1948–1952); and ambassador to Spain (1952–1953). In Greece, he handled the diplomacy of the extradition case of American fugitive Samuel Insull and negotiated a commercial treaty. In Iceland, he coordinated U.S. military arrangements for Iceland's defense during World War II, including negotiations for a U.S. base at Keflavik. He oversaw U.S. wartime agencies in South Africa and studied political movements in the Balkans, making reports that helped in the formulation of the Truman Doctrine.* MacVeagh helped Portugal join the Atlantic Pact. His short mission in Spain was uneventful. He married Margaret Charlton in 1917 and lived in retirement after 1953 until his death in Adelphi, Maryland, on January 15, 1972. With his wife, he wrote a children's book, *Greek Journey* (1937). Iatrides, John O., ed., *Ambassador MacVeagh Reports* (1980); *NCAB*, F:234; *New York Times*, January 17, 1972.

MADISON, JAMES (1751–1836). Secretary of state under President Thomas Jefferson* (1801–1809) and president himself (1809–1817), James Madison was born on March 16, 1751, in Port Conway, Virginia. He graduated from the College of New Jersey (now Princeton) in 1771 and entered politics as a member of the Virginia legislature in 1776. He remained in Virginia politics until 1780 and then became a member of the Continental Congress, serving until 1783. He was again a Virginia state legislator, 1784–1786, and then gained national prominence as a delegate to the Constitutional Convention in 1787, where, despite his relative youth, he exerted a great deal of influence on the writing and subsequent ratification of the Constitution. From 1789 to 1797, he sat in the U.S. House of Representatives. The years 1799–1801 saw Madison once again in the

Virginia legislature, but Jefferson's election as president in 1801 brought him back to national prominence as secretary of state. Jefferson and Madison had been close friends for twenty-five years and saw alike on virtually every political and diplomatic issue. Madison's policies as secretary of state were totally aligned with those of Jefferson with regard to their mutual interest in preserving the peace and in their perception of America's national interests. Although seemingly overshadowed by the president's interest and involvement in foreign policy, Madison was able to exert some influence in the Louisiana Purchase,* overcoming problems caused by the indiscretions of the U.S. minister to France, Robert R. Livingston,* and helping to formulate the Embargo Act (1807).* He carried out the details of Jefferson's foreign policy, launched protests, in vain, against British and French maritime policies, and favored a declaration of war against Britain and France in early 1809. As president, Madison accepted the Cadore letter,* fired the incompetent and intriguing Secretary of State Robert Smith,* replacing him with James Monroe,* and directed the policies that ultimately led to the War of 1812. After his second term ended in 1817, Madison lived in retirement in Virginia. He maintained an interest in the Monroe Doctrine* and the American Colonization Society, of which he was president in 1833. He was married to Dolly Payne Todd in 1794 and died at his Virginia estate, Montpelier, on June 28, 1836. Brant, Irving, *James Madison*, 6 vols. (1941–1961), 1-vol. ed. (1970); *DAB*, 12:184; Egan, Clifford L., *Neither Peace nor War: Franco-American Relations, 1803–1812* (1983); Ketcham, Ralph, *James Madison* (1971); Rutland, Robert A., *James Madison* (1987).

MAGIC. American code designation, World War II. MAGIC was the code name given to the intercepting and diciphering of secret Japanese diplomatic messages, begun in 1940 and continuing through the attack on Pearl Harbor.* MAGIC gave U.S. officials the knowledge that the Japanese planned an attack somewhere in early 1941, but the exact location could not be determined with certainty. Wohlstetter explains that the Pearl Harbor attack was not specifically foreseen, despite MAGIC, because of an abundance of irrelevant messages, the tendency of analysts to attach significance to messages they expected to be significant, and the necessity of secrecy, which often kept U.S. officials from sharing information. Feis, Herbert, *The Road to Pearl Harbor* (1950); Offner, Arnold A., *The Origins of the Second World War* (1975); Wohlstetter, Roberta, *Pearl Harbor: Warning and Decision* (1962).

MAGOON, CHARLES EDWARD (1861–1920). A leading figure in Cuban and Canal Zone history, Charles E. Magoon was born December 5, 1861, in Steele County, Minnesota, attended the University of Nebraska, read law, and gained admittance to the Nebraska bar in 1882. He practiced law in Lincoln, 1882–1899, served as a major and judge advocate in the Nebraska National Guard, and in 1899 went to Washington to work as the legal officer of the Bureau of Insular Affairs. He published two important treatises on legal matters related to the acquisition of territory after the Spanish-American War, and one of these, "The Law of Civil Government Under Military Occupation," attracted the attention of Secretary of War Elihu Root.* This connection helped Magoon become general counsel to the Isthmian Canal Commission, 1904–1905, a commission member, and governor of the Canal Zone, 1905–1906, and, most important, provisional governor of Cuba during the U.S. military occupation from 1906 to 1909. This was a difficult and unstable time in Cuban affairs, yet Magoon was able to bring about great improvements in sanitation on the island, helping to eradicate yellow fever. Magoon, who never married, died January 14, 1920, in Washington, D.C. *DAB*, 12:201; *New York Times*, January 15, 1920; Millett, Allan R., *Politics of Intervention: The Military Occupation of Cuba, 1906–1909* (1968).

MAHAN, ALFRED THAYER (1840–1914). The son of well-known army engineer Dennis Hart Mahan, Alfred Thayer Mahan was born at West Point on September 27, 1840, and graduated from the U.S. Naval Academy in 1859. He served various tours of sea duty between 1859 and 1885 and lectured at the Naval War College from 1885 to 1889 and 1892 to 1893, serving as its president from 1886 to 1889 and from 1892 to 1894. He is better known as a theorist of American expansionism and the writer of numerous books and articles in the 1890s supporting expansion. Of particular significance was *The Influence of Sea Power upon History, 1660–1783* (1890), which attributed the rise of the British empire to a strong navy. His major thesis was that increased production in America created a need for a large merchant marine, which made colonial acquisitions a necessity. Mahan, like historian Frederick Jackson Turner, believed that a new frontier overseas would have to be developed to continue without interruption or disorder the progress of America. Later Mahan played down the importance of a nation's merchant marine and instead emphasized colonies as strategic bases from which to exploit, both commercially and spiritually, the presumed vast markets of Asia and Latin America. His books and theories were influential in the naval growth of Germany and Britain as well as America. Married to Ellen Lyle in 1872, Mahan retired from the navy in 1906 and died in Washington, D.C., on December 1, 1914. LaFeber, Walter, *The New Empire* (1963); Mahan, Alfred T., *The Influence of Sea Power upon History, 1660–1783* (1890); McCullough, David, *The Path between the Seas* (1977); Puleston, W. D., *Mahan: The Life and Work of Captain Alfred Thayer Mahan, U.S.N.* (1939); Seager, Robert, *Alfred Thayer Mahan: The Man and His Letters* (1977).

MAINE, **U.S.S.** This American second-class battleship became an emotional precursor to the Spanish-American War by virtue of its being blown up in Havana harbor on February 15, 1898. The *Maine* had arrived in Havana on January 25, ostensibly on a goodwill visit. The explosion, which killed 260, was a sensation in the American press, and the blame was laid on the Spanish, with whom relations had been bad for some time. Investigations have never conclusively placed the responsibility on any party. Nevertheless, the destruction of the *Maine* accelerated the pace toward war. Cortada, James W.; *Two Nations over Time: Spain and the United States, 1776–1977* (1978); *FR* (1898), 1024–46; Millis, Walter, *The Martial Spirit* (1931); Morgan, H. Wayne, *America's Road to Empire* (1965).

MALTA CONFERENCE (1945). This conference brought together U.S. and British leaders on the eve of the Yalta Conference* to ensure as much Anglo-American unity at Yalta as possible. Secretary of State Edward R. Stettinius,* British Foreign Secretary Anthony Eden, and the Combined Chiefs of Staff met from January 31 to February 2 and discussed a variety of military and political questions. Among military decisions made were to move troops from the Italian peninsula to the western front, as the United States wanted to do, instead of across the Adriatic, as the British desired. Stettinius and Eden agreed to give France an occupation zone in Germany, carved out of the British and American zones, to reject recognition of the Soviet-dominated government in Poland, and to allow the great powers veto rights in the United Nations* Security Council. In addition, there was concurrence on halting Soviet influence in Iran and Eastern Europe and in resisting British and American exclusion from Eastern Europe. President Franklin D. Roosevelt arrived at Malta on February 2 and, with Prime Minister Winston Churchill, approved the decisions that had been made. *FR: The Conferences at Malta and Yalta, 1945*, pp. 459–548; McNeill, William H., *America, Britain, and Russia* (1953); Wheeler-Bennett, John W., and Anthony Nicholls, *The Semblance of Peace* (1972).

MALVINAS ISLANDS WAR (1982). See **FALKLAND ISLANDS WAR (1982).**

MANCHURIAN CRISIS (1931–1933). After the Mukden incident (1931),* Japanese troops swiftly overran all of Manchuria. A Japanese puppet empire known as Manchukuo was created in March 1932, a month after the independence of Manchuria had been declared. American response was cautious, and Secretary of State Henry L. Stimson* and President Herbert Hoover attempted to act in cooperation with the League of Nations,* sending Charles G. Dawes* to Geneva as an American representative. In the end, the league delayed taking action by sending the Lytton Commission* to investigate, and Japanese activities in Manchuria continued unchecked. In January, 1932, Stimson made public a statement known as the Stimson Doctrine,* advocating the nonrecognition of governments created by means of aggression. Although the league approved the Stimson Doctrine in March, it had no impact on the Japanese, who withdrew from the league the next year when the Lytton Commission report concluded that Manchukuo was rightfully Chinese territory. Manchukuo continued to exist until Japan's defeat in World War II and was recognized by a few governments, including El Salvador, the Dominican Republic, Italy, Spain, Germany, Poland, Hungary, and Russia, as well as the Vatican. Ferrell, Robert H., *American Diplomacy in the Great Depression* (1957); *FR* (1931), 2:1–715; *FR* (1932), 3–4: 1–463; *FR*

(1933), 3:1–493; *FR: Japan, 1931–1941*, 1:1–160; Thorne, Christopher, *The Limits of Foreign Policy* (1972).

MANDATES, WORLD WAR I. These resulted from a system by which the former colonies of Germany and the Ottoman Empire were placed under the control, or mandate, of various Allied nations for administration, with the League of Nations* exercising general supervision and title to the areas. President Woodrow Wilson was primarily responsible for the plan, which fit in well with various of his Fourteen Points* and appeared to give the league some important responsibilities. Wilson, however, chose not to have the United States assume any administrative responsibility. Other Allied powers preferred outright annexation; the issue was a divisive one at the peace conference. A similar arrangement after World War II saw colonies of defeated powers administered by the United Nations* as trusteeships. Bailey, Thomas A., *Woodrow Wilson and the Lost Peace* (1944); Bennett, Edward M., "Mandates and Trusteeships," in DeConde, Alexander, ed., *Encyclopedia of American Foreign Policy* (1979); Seymour, Charles, *American Diplomacy during the World War* (1934).

MANIFEST DESTINY, diplomatic catchword, c. 1845–1850. This phrase was originated by John L. O'Sullivan,* the expansionist editor of the *United States Magazine and Diplomatic Review*, in 1845. Manifest Destiny referred to the feeling held by many Americans that there existed some providential destiny for the United States to expand across the continent. Historians since have seen crasser motivations behind Manifest Destiny: economic or commercial advantage, fear of foreign encroachment, feelings of Anglo-Saxon superiority. The phrase found currency primarily during the expansionist administration of James K. Polk. Graebner, Norman, *Empire on the Pacific* (1955); Pletcher, David M., "Manifest Destiny," in DeConde, Alexander, ed., *Encyclopedia of American Foreign Policy* (1979); Weinberg, Albert K., *Manifest Destiny* (1935).

MANILA PACT (1954). Negotiated and signed at the Manila Conference, September 6–8, 1954, this pact is more formally known as the Southeast Asia Collective Defense Treaty and provides for the defense of the South Pacific area (excluding Hong Kong and Formosa) by calling for joint action to meet aggression; an attack on one would be considered an attack on all, and each signatory would meet the crisis according to its constitutional precepts. In addition, the treaty included cooperation in economic and social areas and consultation in the event a signatory was threatened by subversion directed by an outside power. A protocol added Cambodia, Laos, and Vietnam to the protective umbrella of SEATO* (Southeast Asian Treaty Organization), the organization established to administer the details of the treaty. The Manila Pact came about because of Communist advances in Asia, most notably the "loss" of North Vietnam as a result of the Geneva Accords* in July 1954. Secretary of State John Foster Dulles,* who favored a containment* policy based on a system of military alliances, led the U.S. delegation and was the major architect of the treaty. In

February 1955, the U.S. Senate ratified the Manila Pact by an 82–1 vote. Fifield, Russell H., *Americans in Southeast Asia* (1973); Spanier, John A., *American Foreign Policy since World War II* (1977).

MANN, THOMAS CLIFTON (b. 1912). A native of Laredo, Texas, where he was born November 11, 1912, Thomas C. Mann attended the University of Colorado but graduated from Baylor University (B.A., LL.B., 1934) and practiced law in Laredo until 1942. Joining the State Department in that year, he served in various minor posts until 1950, when he became deputy under secretary of state (inter-American affairs), a post he held until 1953. From 1953 to 1955, he was counselor* at the U.S. embassy in Athens. After a short time in the same position in Guatemala City, he was named ambassador to El Salvador. In 1957, Mann became assistant secretary of state (economic affairs). In three years at that assignment and one as assistant secretary of state (inter-American affairs), he represented the United States at many economic conferences, generally advocating an activist policy for the United States with regard to Latin American economic problems. In this way he contributed to the Act of Bogotá (1960), a forerunner of the Alliance for Progress.* In 1961, Mann went to Mexico City as U.S. ambassador to Mexico; there he helped negotiate the Chamizal Treaty concerning disputed territory near El Paso, Texas. Returning to the position of assistant secretary of state (inter-American affairs) in 1964, he became the chief spokesman for the Johnson administration on Latin American relations and negotiated a settlement of the anti-U.S. Panama riots in 1964. He was in charge of the Alliance for Progress and handled the initial stages of the diplomacy of the Dominican intervention (1965),* where his mission to establish an acceptable democratic government failed, leading to substantial press criticism and his replacement by Ellsworth Bunker.* His last State Department post was under secretary of state (economic affairs), 1965–1966. Since that time, Mann has taught at the Johns Hopkins School for Advanced International Studies and has been president of the Automobile Manufacturers Association. He married Nancy Aynesworth in 1933. *CB*, (1964):273–76; Lichtenstein, Nelson, ed., *Political Profiles: The Johnson Years* (1976); *WWA* (1971–1972):2009–10.

MANSFIELD, MICHAEL JOSEPH (b. 1903). Born in New York City on March 16, 1903, Mike Mansfield served in the navy, 1918–1919, the army, 1919–1920, and the Marine Corps, 1920–1922, before becoming a miner and mining engineer in Montana. He married Maureen Hayes in 1932 and attended the Montana School of Mines but graduated from the University of Montana (A.B., 1933; A.M., 1934) and did graduate work at the University of California, during the summers of 1936 and 1937. Between 1933 and 1942, Mansfield taught history at the University of Montana. In the latter year, however, he was elected to the U.S. House of Representatives as a Democrat; after five terms, he moved up to the Senate, where he served for twenty-three years, until 1976. While in Congress, he undertook a number of assignments related to foreign affairs, beginning with a confidential mission to China in 1944 to look into political conditions. He attended the Bogotá Conference (1948),* the Sixth United Nations* General Assembly in Paris (1951–1952), and the Manila Conference (1954)* and completed an assortment of special assignments to Europe, Vietnam, and China. In 1977, President Jimmy Carter named him ambassador to Japan, where one of his concerns was to warn Japan about suspicious trade practices, the dangers of excessive exports to the United States, and the deleterious effects of that trade imbalance on the American economy. Mansfield retired from his post in late 1988. Baldwin, Louis, *Hon. Politician: Mike Mansfield of Montana* (1979); *CB* (January 1978):29–33; *Forbes*, July 10, 1978, 84; *New York Times*, April 8, 1978, November 15, 1988; *Washington Post*, October 5, 1977.

MARCY, WILLIAM LEARNED (1786–1857). Secretary of state under President Franklin Pierce, William L. Marcy was born December 12, 1786, in Sturbridge, Massachusetts, graduated from Brown University in 1808, read law, and was admitted to the bar in 1811. He was an officer in the War of 1812 and adjutant general of New York. After the war, he practiced law and held city offices in Troy, New York, until 1823, when he became state comptroller. A friend of Martin Van Buren,* Marcy was appointed an associate justice of the New York Supreme Court in 1829 but resigned in 1831 to accept a U.S. Senate seat. In 1833, he was elected governor of New York, remaining in the statehouse until 1838. From 1840 to 1842, he showed negotiating skill as a member of the Mexican Claims Commission. Under President James K. Polk, Marcy was secretary of state. In office, his main concerns were opposing British encroachments in Canadian fishing waters and Central America and restraining filibusters* (toward whom critics found him too acquiescent). Marcy negotiated or signed some twenty-four treaties, including the Gadsden Treaty (1853),* the Marcy-Elgin Reciprocity Treaty of 1854* (with Great Britain, over Canadian fisheries), a treaty opening Dutch colonial ports to U.S. ships (1855), and a treaty abolishing the Danish Sound tolls (1857). Marcy also settled the Koszta case with Austria and the *Black Warrior* case* with Spain (1855). Finally, he led U.S. opposition to the Declaration of Paris (1856).* Marcy was married twice and died in Ballston Spa, New York, on July 4, 1857, four months after leaving office. *DAB*, 12:274; Learned, A. B., "William Learned Marcy," in Bemis, Samuel F., ed., *American Secretaries of State and Their Diplomacy*, vol. 7 (1928); Spencer, Ivor Debenham, *Victor and the Spoils, a Life of William Learned Marcy* (1959).

MARCY-ELGIN TREATY (1854). More formally known as the Marcy-Elgin Reciprocity and Fisheries Treaty, this agreement was negotiated by Secretary of State William L. Marcy* and Governor-General Lord Elgin of Canada. It was designed to correct problems arising from provisions regarding fishing rights in the Convention of 1818* and from trade relations since the British repeal of the Corn Laws in 1846. The treaty increased American fishing rights off the Canadian coast and permitted Canadians to fish off the Atlantic coast of the United States south to Norfolk. Free reciprocal trade was allowed on certain items, and agreements were made as to navigation on bodies of water such as Lake Michigan and the St. Lawrence River. According to Learned, "Generally speaking, the new treaty favored the United States: American fishermen, the lumber interests and American manufacturers were the gainers." The treaty was terminated in 1866 due to American anger over the St. Albans raid (1864), in which a band of southerners invaded St. Albans, Vermont, from Canada, killing three people and robbing the banks. Learned, Henry Barrett, "William Learned Marcy," in Bemis, Samuel F., ed., *American Secretaries of State and Their Diplomacy*, vol. 6, (1928); Morton, W. L., *The Kingdom of Canada*, 2d ed. (1969).

MARITIME CANAL COMPANY, isthmian canal company. Two American private enterprises by this name were interested in constructing a Central American isthmian canal. The first Maritime Canal Company was founded in 1879 by Admiral Daniel Ammen, Captain Seth L. Phelps,* and others, as the Provisional Interoceanic Canal Society. Reorganized as the Maritime Canal Company after receiving a concession from Nicaragua, the enterprise planned a canal across Nicaragua, following the San Juan River and crossing Lake Nicaragua. In 1882, Secretary of State Frederick T. Frelinghuysen* and the State Department began to take an active interest in a Nicaraguan canal; ultimately, this resulted in the unratified Frelinghuysen-Zavala Treaty (1884),* providing for a government-built canal. Maritime's promoters could not associate themselves with this project; their concession expired in September 1884, and the company faded away. The second Maritime Canal Company received a concession in 1889 to build an isthmian canal along the Nicaraguan route. After a promising beginning, the company fell victim to the 1893 panic and spent the next six years attempting to obtain federal funding. Maritime's concession expired in 1899, and the company failed to win an extension in an arbitration* procedure. The Maritime Canal Company represented the last serious attempt by private enterprise to build a Central American canal, and the company's failure showed conclusively that the task was beyond private means at this time due to the cost and the economic conditions of the 1890s. Henderson, John B., *American Diplomatic Questions* (1901); LaFeber, Walter, *The New Empire* (1963); Pletcher, David, *The Awkward Years* (1962).

MARSH, GEORGE PERKINS (1801–1882). Born March 15, 1801, in Woodstock, Vermont, George Perkins Marsh graduated from Dartmouth (1820) as a student of languages. To make a living, he became a lawyer in 1825 and practiced law in Vermont from 1825 to 1849 except for two terms in the U.S. House of Representatives (1835–1839). In 1849, he was appointed minister to Turkey, where his language ability served him well during his five-year stay. He worked with the British minister, Sir Stratford Canning, in aiding refugees from the 1848 revolutions in Europe. He arranged for the departure of Lajos Kossuth, the Hungarian nationalist, and his friends on a ship to the United States. In 1852, he went to Athens to investigate the case of the imprisoned American missionary

Jonas King and tried to win his release. The following year, he was involved in the Koszta case, concerning a Hungarian in the process of becoming a naturalized American citizen, who had been captured by an Austrian naval commander. Under diplomatic pressure, the Austrian turned Koszta over to the French, and he was ultimately released. Marsh was in the United States from 1854 to 1861, serving as fish commissioner of Vermont and lecturing at Columbia. In 1861, however, he went to Italy as America's first minister to that country, and spent the rest of his life there, winning high regard as both a diplomat and a scholar. He wrote numerous books on diverse subjects, ranging from the camel to Icelandic grammar and was an early spokesman for conservation. Twice married, Marsh died at Vallambrosa, Italy, on July 23, 1882. *DAB*, 12:297; Lowenthal, David, *George Perkins Marsh, Versatile Vermonter* (1958); *WWWA*, Historical Volume, p. 333.

MARSHALL, GEORGE CATLETT (1880–1959). Secretary of state under President Harry S Truman (1947–1949), George C. Marshall was born on New Year's Eve, 1880, in Uniontown, Pennsylvania, graduated from Virginia Military Institute in 1901, and attended the U.S. Infantry-Calvary School (1907) and the Army War College (1908). On active army duty from 1902 to 1945, Marshall served in World War I, became a general in 1936, and was army chief of staff from 1939 to 1945. He attended various wartime conferences in that position, including Yalta (1945)* and Potsdam (1945).* In late 1945, he was sent to China as a special representative of the president, with ambassadorial rank, in an unsuccessful attempt to mediate the civil war there. Returning from China in early 1947, Marshall was chosen to replace James F. Byrnes* as secretary of state. In this role, he is best known for the Marshall Plan* for European postwar recovery, but, enjoying great respect and trust from Truman, he accomplished much of note in other areas. He created the Policy Planning Staff, first headed by George F. Kennan,* to formulate long-range foreign policies and was known for his firmness toward the Soviet Union and his reliance on military preparedness. Except for support of the Bogotá Pact, which established the Organization of American States,* Marshall overlooked Latin America, and, unlike Truman, he did not favor the immediate recognition of Israel when that state was created in 1948. Although he favored aid to Europe and helped lay the groundwork for the North Atlantic Treaty Organization,* he approved only limited assistance for Chiang Kai-shek in China and was later criticized for not having extended large-scale military assistance. After a year (1949–1950) as president of the American National Red Cross and a year (1950–1951) as secretary of defense, Marshall returned to his home near Pinehurst, North Carolina. Married to Elizabeth Carter Cole in 1902 and, after her death in 1927, to Katherine Boyce Brown in 1930, Marshall won the Nobel Peace Prize in 1953 and died in Washington on October 16, 1959. Beal, John Robinson, *Marshall in China* (1970); DeConde, Alexander, "George C. Marshall," in Graebner, Norman, ed., *An Uncertain Tradition* (1961); Feis, Herbert, *From Trust to Terror* (1970); *New York Times*, October

17, 1959; Pogue, Forrest, C., *George Marshall, Statesman, 1945–1949* (1987); *WWWA*, 3 (1951–1960):555.

MARSHALL, JAMES FOWLE BALDWIN (1819–1891). James F. B. Marshall was born August 8, 1819, in Charlestown, Massachusetts, and attended Harvard but withdrew before graduating because of poor eyesight. In 1838, he went to Hawaii and entered the mercantile business in Honolulu. For many years he was a partner in a large trading firm and served in the Hawaiian legislature, where he advocated protection of native rights and adoption of a land tenure system. In 1843, he was secretly appointed an envoy of the Hawaiian government of King Kamehameha II to England to prevent specious annexation by Lord George Paulet, a British naval captain. According to Marshall's own account, he went through the United States on his way, talked with Secretary of State Daniel Webster,* and received assurances of U.S. support. In London, he met with Lord Aberdeen, who disavowed any possible annexationist move by Paulet. This led to a joint British-French declaration recognizing Hawaiian independence. Marshall returned to Boston around 1859, served as a paymaster to Massachusetts troops during the Civil War, and from 1870 to 1874 was resident trustee and a teacher at Hampton Institute in Virginia. He married Eunice S. Hooper in 1843; after her death, he married Martha A. T. Johnson in 1848. Marshall died in Weston, Massachusetts, on May 6, 1891. *DAB*, 12:312; Marshall, J.F.B., "An Unpublished Chapter of Hawaiian History," *Harper's Magazine* (September 1883); Stevens, Sylvester K., *American Expansion in Hawaii, 1842–1898* (1968).

MARSHALL, JOHN (1755–1835). Best known as America's first chief justice of the Supreme Court, John Marshall also served as secretary of state for ten months in 1800–1801. He was born September 24, 1755, near Germantown, Virginia, educated by private tutors, and after service in the American Revolution read law and was admitted to the bar in 1780. He practiced law in Richmond, married Mary Ambler in 1783, and served several years in the Virginia legislature (1782–1784, 1787). In the 1790s, he emerged as a Federalist leader in the state. As a commissioner to France, 1797, he was involved in the XYZ affair;* and he was a U.S. congressman, 1799–1800. When Timothy Pickering* was dismissed as secretary of state in 1800, Marshall was appointed in his stead and served out the rest of Adams's presidency. As secretary of state, he pushed for acceptance of the Convention of 1800* with France, ensured somewhat unwillingly that the tributes to the Barbary pirates* were paid, protested to Spain concerning violations of American neutrality, dealt with the British over the increasingly troublesome issue of impressment,* and authorized the minister to Britain, Rufus King,* to negotiate a settlement of the controversy of British debts from Americans, dating back to Revolutionary War days, which King did, for £600,000. Just before the end of Adams's term, Marshall was named chief justice, a position he maintained until his death July 6, 1835, in Philadelphia. Marshall also completed the first major biography of George Washington (5 vols., 1804–1807). Baker, Leonard, *John Marshall: A Life in Law* (1974); *DAB*, 12:315; DeConde, Alexander, *The Quasi-War* (1966).

MARSHALL PLAN, post–World War II aid program. The Marshall Plan was a massive economic aid program for sixteen nations in Europe, which grew out of the sentiments of the Truman Doctrine* and Secretary of State George Marshall's* impressions of Soviet ambitions in Europe, noted at the Council of Foreign Ministers* meeting in Moscow in April 1947. George F. Kennan* headed the State Department staff that drew up the basic outline of the plan, insisting that aid be limited but given to all Europe, not just cold war* crisis areas. Will Clayton,* under secretary of state, was also highly influential in planning. The Soviet Union was to be invited to participate, with the foreknowledge that it probably would decline given the government's reluctance to disclose information about its economic system or expose its citizens (or satellites) to such American largesse. First made public by Marshall in a speech at Harvard University in June 1947, the plan had two major aims: (1) to keep Communists out of political power in Western Europe and (2) to stabilize an international economic order in a way favorable to capitalism. As part of the plan, the United States requested that European nations submit a collective recovery plan; this was done during the summer of 1947. The Truman administration then prepared a four-year, $17 billion program for congressional consideration; Congress obliged by appropriating between $13 billion and $14 billion. The principal administrator of the Marshall Plan was Paul G. Hoffman,* a successful entrepreneur; the chief U.S. official for much of the plan's life was W. Averell Harriman.* According to LaFeber, the Marshall Plan was the last attempt by the United States to bring the Western world together by economic rather than military means, but the Berlin blockade,* repression in Czechoslovakia, and Far Eastern events such as the Korean War forced a shift in the nature of the aid, with substantial amounts diverted to military and security-related items. By 1952, over $12 billion had been expended, with over half going to Great Britain, France, and West Germany. In terms of economic recovery, the Marshall Plan was hugely successful, although there were problems of uneven distribution and some balkiness in European economic integration. A political bonus derived from the all-Europe nature of the program was that the likelihood of a revived Germany was easier to accept. Gembel, John, *The Origin of the Marshall Plan* (1976); Hogan, Michael J., *The Marshall Plan: America, Britain, and the Reconstruction of Europe, 1947–1952*, (1987); Jones, Joseph M., *The Fifteen Weeks* (1955); Painter, David S., "Oil and the Marshall Plan," *Business History Review* 58 (Autumn 1984):359–83; Pogue, Forrest C., *George C. Marshall: Statesman, 1945–1959* (1987); Raucher, Alan R., *Paul G. Hoffman: Architect of Foreign Aid* (1985); Wexler, Imanuel, *The Marshall Plan Revisited: The European Recovery in Economic Perspective* (1983).

MARTIN, GRAHAM ANDERSON (b. 1912). Born in Mars Hill, North Carolina, on September 12, 1912, Graham Martin graduated from Wake Forest in 1932 and, after a year as a journalist in Washington, became W. Averell Harriman's* aide in the National Recovery Administration in 1934. An assortment of other bureaucratic positions and four years in the army air force preceded Martin's entrance into the Foreign Service in 1947. For the first eight years, he was posted in Paris as an attaché, counselor,* and assistant chief of mission. From 1955 to 1957, he was attached to the Air War College, and from 1957 to 1959, he was a special assistant to Douglas Dillon,* the under secretary of state for economic affairs. Martin's first ambassadorial post was Thailand (1963–1967), where he successfully restored proposed U.S. military aid cutbacks, persuaded the Thais to permit the U.S. Air Force to use bases in the country, and served as a U.S. representative to the Southeast Asia Treaty Organization.* In Italy as ambassador from 1969 to 1973, Martin helped funnel covert funds to favored political parties and individuals before the 1974 elections. Known for his tough anti-Communist stand, he replaced Ellsworth Bunker* as U.S. ambassador to Vietnam in 1973, where he presided over the denouement of the war in that country (and, according to some, hastened the end by misleading reportage to the State Department), fleeing in April 1975 as the North Vietnamese captured Saigon. After his return from Vietnam, he was a special assistant to Secretary of State Henry Kissinger,* 1975–1976, and worked as a political analyst. Martin married Dorothy Wallace in 1934. Hung, Nguyen Tien, and Jerrold L. Schnecter, *The Palace File* (1986); Snepp, Frank, *Decent Interval* (1977); *New York Times*, April 2, 1973, May 2, August 26, 1976; Szulc, Tad, *The Illusion of Peace* (1978); *WWA* (1978–1979): 2097.

MARYE, GEORGE THOMAS (1849–1933). Born in Baltimore on December 13, 1849, George T. Marye was educated in Europe, studying at several schools before receiving an LL. B. degree from Cambridge in 1872. He joined his family in California, was admitted to the bar in 1875, practiced law, and joined his father in the mining and brokerage business in San Francisco and Virginia City, Nevada. He became involved with Democratic party politics, acting as a presidential elector, 1888, and chairman of the Democratic executive committee in California, 1888–1893. About 1900, he moved to Washington, D.C., where he practiced law and maintained his interest in the Democrats. In 1914, President Woodrow Wilson, who did not know Marye, nonetheless named him ambassador to Russia on the strength of his knowledge of international law and several languages. He arrived after the outbreak of World War I, and much of his work concerned looking after the interests of German and Austrian prisoners of war. He left Russia in 1916 and did not foresee the revolutionary turmoil that would come the next year. In 1920, he wrote of his Russian experience in *Nearing the End in Imperial Russia*. He resumed his law practice in Washington and died there on September 2, 1933. He married Marie Alice Doyle in 1904 and also wrote a biography of his father, *From '49 to '83 in California and Nevada* (1924). *NCAB*, 30:251; *New York Times*, September 3, 1933; *WWWA*, 1 (1897–1942): 785.

MASON, JAMES MURRAY (1798–1871). James M. Mason was born on November 3, 1798, in Georgetown, Washington, D.C., and graduated from the University of Pennsylvania in 1818. He studied law at William and Mary College in Virginia, entering politics in that state as a Democrat in the state legislature (1827–1831) and in congress as a congressman (1837–1839) and a senator (1847–1861). In the Senate, he served for ten years as chairman of the Foreign Relations Committee and wrote the Fugitive Slave Act in 1850. Joining the Confederacy in 1861, he was appointed diplomatic agent to seek recognition and aid from England. He was seized with John Slidell* on the *Trent*.* After his release, he proceeded to England, acted as the center of a propaganda program, and was involved in the Confederate loan secured from Erlanger and Company*. He objected to the original terms that Slidell had negotiated, obtained slightly more favorable ones, and then bought cotton bonds (the loan instrument) on the London market to help sustain their value. In general, he did as well as might be expected. Although he was never received officially, he did cultivate good relations for the Confederacy among the English upper classes. He spent the years from 1866 to 1868 in Canadian exile, returned to the United States after President Andrew Johnson's second proclamation of amnesty, and died near Alexandria, Virginia, on April 28, 1871. *DAB*, 12:364; Owsley, Frank, *King Cotton Diplomacy*, 2d ed. (1959).

MASON, JOHN YOUNG (1799–1859). A native of Greencastle County, Virginia, John Y. Mason was born April 18, 1799, graduated from the University of North Carolina (1816), read law at Litchfield, Connecticut, and was admitted to the Virginia bar in 1819. He soon staked out a political career, serving in the Virginia General Assembly, 1823–1831, before gaining election to the U.S. House of Representatives, where he sat from 1831 to 1837. Mason was a federal judge for the next seven years and then joined President John Tyler's cabinet as secretary of the navy, 1844–1845, as attorney general, 1845–1846, and moving back to the Navy Department for the years 1846–1849. He practiced law during the Whig interim, 1849–1853, but with the arrival of the Pierce administration, Mason was named minister to France, remaining in that post until his death in Paris October 3, 1859. He is best known as one of the three signers (along with James Buchanan* and Pierre Soulé*) of the Ostend Manifesto (1854)*. In addition, Mason upheld U.S. neutrality* during the Crimean War and was involved with the Morey case, concerning an unfortunate American entrepreneur who went to France, wound up in debtors' prison, and was fatally shot by a guard. Mason was able to arrange an indemnity payment for Morey's widow. He married Mary Ann Fort in 1821. *DAB*, 12:369; Ettiger, A. A., *The Mission to Spain of Pierre Soulé, 1853–55* (1932); Willson, Beckles, *America's Ambassadors to France, 1777–1927* (1928).

MASSIVE RETALIATION, diplomatic-military slogan, 1950s. This slogan from the era of Secretary of State John Foster Dulles,* who first used it in early 1954, suggested that the United States would rely on the deterrent power of the huge hydrogen bombs being developed in the early 1950s as a primary means of conducting foreign policy. This was deemed an acceptable alternative to more costly, albeit more responsive, conventional military forces. Such a policy, it was felt, would allow the United States to negotiate from a position of strength and would help the Eisenhower administration achieve its goal of a balanced budget. In practice, charged critics, massive retaliation gravely limited U.S. foreign policy options, leaving little but total war or total inaction. Dulles continued the rhetoric of massive retaliation but limited its application, stating that local wars would not become nuclear holocausts. One alternative policy suggested by foes of massive retaliation was disengagement.* Carleton, William G. *The Revolution in American Foreign Policy* (1963); George, Alexander L., and Richard Smoke, *Deterrence in American Foreign Policy* (1973); Gerson, Louis L., "John Foster Dulles," in Ferrell, Robert H., ed., *American Secretaries of State and Their Diplomacy*, vol. 17 (1967); Graebner, Norman A., *Cold War Diplomacy* (1975).

MATLOCK, JACK FOUST, JR. (b. 1929). President Ronald Reagan's principal Soviet policy adviser, Jack F. Matlock was born October 1, 1929, in Greensboro, North Carolina, and graduated from Duke (A.B., 1950) and Columbia (M.A., 1952). A Russian language major, he taught at Dartmouth, 1953–1956, before joining the Foreign Service. From 1956 to 1971, he served in minor posts in Washington, Vienna, Munich, Moscow, Accra, Zanzibar, and Dar es Salaam. In 1971, he became USSR country director in the State Department, moving to the Moscow embassy as minister-counselor in 1974. During the 1978–1979 academic year, he was diplomat in residence at Vanderbilt University. In 1979–1980, he was the deputy director of the Foreign Service Institute. With the incoming Reagan administration, he spent two years as ambassador to Czechoslovakia and in 1983 joined the National Security Council* staff as a special assistant on European and Soviet affairs. In 1987, he replaced Arthur Hartman as ambassador to the Soviet Union. In Moscow, he lodged a U.S. protest about the implantation of Soviet spy devices in the U.S. embassy then under construction. As a Reagan adviser, Matlock had been involved in the Geneva* and Reykjavik* Summits in 1985–1986; as ambassador, he helped plan the Washington* and Moscow* Summits of 1987–1988. He married Rebecca Burrum in 1949 and edited the *Index to J. V. Stalin's Work* (1971). *New York Times*, January 31, December 8, 1987; *WWA* (1986–1987):1828.

MAYAGÜEZ **INCIDENT (1975).** An American merchant ship, the S. S. *Mayagüez* was captured May 12, 1975, by Cambodian patrol boats sixty miles off the Cambodian coast. The ship and its crew of thirty-nine were taken to Koh Tang Island, thirty miles off the coast, and the crew was then moved to the mainland. Coming in the wake of the fall of Saigon and the end of the Vietnam War, this act of piracy led President Gerald Ford and Secretary of State Henry Kissinger* to respond with a determined show of force. When Cambodia refused to release the ship and crew, a marine rescue force was sent in. The marines captured the ship without resistance, and, unaware that the crew had already been released from the mainland, they launched a fierce attack on Koh Tang Island and met strong resistance from Cambodian troops. The United States lost eighteen men in combat and twenty-three others in an offshore plane crash. Regardless of the military bungling, the Ford administration claimed a victory in the incident, and the American public voiced its strong approval. Gabriel, Richard A., *Military Incompetence* (1985); Head, Richard G., *Crisis Resolution* (1978); Rowan, Roy, *The Four Days of Mayagüez* (1975).

MEIGGS, HENRY (1811–1877). A prominent U.S. entrepreneur in Latin America, Henry Meiggs was born July 7, 1811, in Catskill, New York. He had only a limited formal education before he went to work in the lumber business in Williamsburg, New York. In 1848, he took a load of lumber by ship to San Francisco and there made large profits in the lumber and sawmill business. He overextended himself financially, however, and fled to South America, leaving behind debts of $800,000. In Chile, he became involved in railroad building and in 1861 received a $12 million contract to finish the line from Santiago to Valparaiso. Completing the job in less than two years, Meiggs made a profit of $1.32 million. He then became briefly involved in Bolivian railroads and the guano industry, but in 1868 he went to Peru, where he contracted with the government for the building of over 1,000 miles of railroad. Overriding all competition by clever bribery, he constructed a technologically spectacular railroad through and over the Andes at altitudes up to 15,658 feet but left other planned railroads uncompleted. Peru was bankrupt at this time, and Meiggs accepted as payment a concession to operate the Cerro de Pasco silver mines. He found difficulty marketing Peruvian bonds in London and never was wholly free of financial worry, although over the years he did manage to repay most of his San Francisco debts and contribute a great deal to the beautification of Lima. In 1871 Meiggs received a contract to construct a railroad in Costa Rica, a project taken over by his nephew, Minor Keith,* after Meiggs's death. He was twice married and died in Lima September 29, 1877. *DAB*, 12:501; Findling, John E., *Close Neighbors, Distant Friends* (1987); Rogers, Augustus C., ed., *Our Representatives Abroad* (1874); Stewart, Watt, *Henry Meiggs, Yankee Pizarro* (1946).

MEIN, JOHN GORDON (1913–1968). The first American ambassador to be assassinated at his post, John Gordon Mein was born in Cadiz, Kentucky, on September 10, 1913, and graduated from Georgetown (Kentucky) College (A.B., 1936) and George Washington University Law School (LL.B., 1939). From 1936 to 1941, Mein worked for the Department of Agriculture, but in 1941 he joined the Foreign Service as a junior officer at Rio de Janeiro. Until 1960, he held a succession of junior-level assignments in Washington and at various overseas posts. In 1960, he was appointed minister-counselor at Manila and, three years later, moved to Rio de Janeiro in the same position. Named ambassador to Guatemala in 1965, Mein went to a country that had been troubled by political opposition that often involved the tactics of urban guerrilla forces. He was killed in Guatemala City on August 28, 1968, by members of the political opposition. *NCAB*, 54:528; *New York Times*, August 29, 1968.

MELLON, ANDREW WILLIAM (1855–1937). Much better known as an aluminum magnate and secretary of the treasury (1921–1932) under Presidents Warren G. Harding, Calvin Coolidge, and Herbert Hoover, Andrew Mellon also spent two years as U.S. ambassador to Great Britain (1932–1934). Born in Pittsburgh on March 24, 1855, Mellon attended Western University of Pennsylvania (now the University of Pittsburgh) before entering the family lumber and banking business. In 1886, he and his brother Richard assumed control of the business operations; by this time the Mellon National Bank was one of the largest private financial institutions in the country. Two years later, they capitalized the Aluminum Company of America; the following year, they organized the Union Trust Company and the Union Savings Bank. With all of this and other prudent investments as well, Mellon became very wealthy and politically very conservative, as shown by his policies while secretary of the treasury. In 1931, he did some "roving ambassadorial" work for President Hoover on the issue of the debt moratorium; this led to his appointment as ambassador to Great Britain. Mellon enjoyed his stint in London. Already well known through his business enterprise and Treasury career, he made speeches, added to his art collection, and had no major diplomatic concerns. Nearly eighty when he returned to the United States, he spent the remaining three years of his life involved in a tax evasion case (he was charged but never convicted) and, more important, planning the National Gallery of Art in Washington, with his donation totaling $27 million in cash and art works. He also donated to the Carnegie Institute and Carnegie Library in Pittsburgh, as well as the Pennsylvania College for Women and the Mellon Institute of Industrial Research (founded by the family in 1913). Mellon died August 26, 1937, in Southampton, Long Island. Mellon married Nora McMillen in 1900; they were divorced in 1912. *NCAB*, 28:336; *New York Times*, August 27, 1937.

MELOY, FRANCIS EDWARD, JR. (1917–1976). Born in Washington, D.C., on March 28, 1917, Francis E. Meloy, Jr., graduated from American University (B.A., 1939) and Yale (M.A., 1942) and served in the navy during World War II. In 1946, he joined the Foreign Service and served in minor posts at Dhahran (Saudi Arabia), Washington, Saigon, and Paris and with the North Atlantic Treaty Organization* by 1958. From 1959 to 1960, Meloy was attached to the Imperial War College in London. From 1960 to 1962, he was back in Washington with the State Department, moving to the Office of West European Affairs as director in 1962. In 1964, he was sent to Rome as minister and deputy chief of mission at the U.S. embassy. Meloy's first ambassadorial assignment, the Dominican Republic, came in 1969, and four years later, he was transferred to Guatemala, where he effectively coordinated relief after the February 1976 earthquake. This work led to his appointment as ambassador to Lebanon, then torn by civil war. After just a month in Beirut, Meloy was assassinated, on June 16, 1976, by extremists who were never identified with certainty. *New York Times*, June 17, 1976; *WWA* (1976–1977):2152.

MENOCAL, ANICETO GARCIA (1836–1908). Aniceto G. Menocal was born September 1, 1836, in Cuba but came to the United States for his education and graduated in 1862 from Rensselaer Polytechnic Institute. From 1862 to 1870, he was the engineer in charge of the construction of the Havana waterworks. Returning to the United States to stay in 1870, he worked for the New York City Department of Public Works, 1870–1872. He went to Central America in 1872, making canal surveys in both Panama and Nicaragua and becoming an enthusiastic supporter of the latter route. In 1874, he became an engineer in the U.S. Navy and, in 1880, helped organize the Provisional Interoceanic Canal Society, which later became a part of the Maritime Canal Company.* Throughout the 1880s, Menocal continued to be an important publicist for an isthmian canal, and he was sent to Central America to make another survey of the Nicaraguan route in 1884 in connection with the pending Frelinghuysen-Zavala Treaty.* He retired from the navy in 1898 but continued to serve frequently as an adviser to or consultant on various engineering projects. He married Elvira Marten in 1866 and died in New York City on July 20, 1908. *DAB*, 12:537; Pletcher, David, *The Awkward Years* (1962).

MERRY, WILLIAM LAWRENCE (1842–1911). An important isthmian canal advocate and minister to various Central American republics, William L. Merry was born in New York City on December 27, 1842, and attended the Collegiate Institute of that city. He went to sea at the age of sixteen and in 1863 became an agent of the U.S. Mail Steamship Company. Four years later, he had moved to Nicaragua as general agent for Nicaragua transit for the Central American Transit Company and the North American Steamship Company. In 1874, he moved to San Francisco, where he was president of the North American Navigation Company and consul general* for Nicaragua. He remained in San Francisco until 1897, achieving local prominence in seven years of service as president of the chamber of commerce and through his outspoken advocacy of a Nicaragua canal. In 1897, the McKinley administration, which supported the idea of an isthmian canal, sent Merry to Central America as minister to Nicaragua, Costa Rica, and El Salvador. In 1907, El Salvador was removed from his jurisdiction, and from 1908 to 1911 he was accredited to Costa Rica alone. Much to Merry's disappointment, most of the important canal diplomacy took place in Washington, but Merry remained an important and persistent advocate, writing articles and making speeches. After the decision for Panama was made, Merry's effectiveness was hampered by his increasing inability to get along with Nicaraguan President José Santos Zelaya. He retired in 1911 and died in Battle Creek, Michigan, on December 14 of that year. *DAB*, 12:574; Findling, John E., ''The

Diplomacy of Expediency'' (Ph. D. diss., University of Texas, 1971); *New York Times*, December 16, 1911.

MESSERSMITH, GEORGE STRAUSSER (1883–1960). Born October 3, 1883, in Fleetwood, Pennsylvania, George S. Messersmith completed a two-year course of study at Keystone Normal School in Kutztown, moved to Delaware, and taught and administered in public schools there until 1914. In 1908, he published a civics text, *The Government of Delaware*, and from 1912 to 1914, he was a member of the State Board of Education. In 1914, he married Marnie Mustard and joined the consular service, serving at posts in Fort Erie, Ontario, Curaçao, Antwerp, and Buenos Aires until 1929. After a year as a Foreign Service inspector, Messersmith was named consul general* in Berlin in 1930. In four years there and three more as minister to Austria, he observed the rise of nazism, of which he quickly became highly suspicious. His dispatches from Berlin and Vienna, warning of the impending danger in Central Europe, are models of diplomatic reportage. In 1937, he returned to Washington to be assistant secretary of state for administration, replacing Wilbur J. Carr.* An assertive administrator, he managed to improve the State Department's budget, secure a pension plan, and bring commerical and agricultural attachés under State Department jurisdiction. During World War II, Messersmith was ambassador to Cuba (1940–1941) and Mexico (1941–1946), handling duties related to the wartime alliance. In 1946, he was transferred to the embassy in Buenos Aires, where his assignment was to persuade the Argentine government of Juan Perón to cease continuing pro-Nazi activities and become a cooperative partner in hemispheric affairs before the upcoming conference in Rio de Janeiro at which the Rio Treaty* would be adopted. Messersmith achieved his objective by establishing a warm and cordial relationship with Perón, much to the annoyance of Spruille Braden,* then the assistant secretary of state for inter-American affairs, who believed only the worst of Perón and thought Messersmith was merely an apologist for the controversial Argentine leader. Their feud, which lasted several months, eventually led to their virtually simultaneous forced resignations from the department in 1947. From 1947 to 1954, Messersmith was chairman of the Mexican Light and Power Company. After 1954, he continued to live in Mexico. He died January 29, 1960, in Houston. *DAB*, Supp. 6:450–2; Dallek, Robert, "Beyond Tradition: The Diplomatic Careers of William E. Dodd and George S. Messersmith, 1933–1938," *South Atlantic Quarterly* 66, 2 (Spring 1967): 233–44; Jones, Kenneth Paul, ed., *U.S. Diplomats in Europe, 1919–1941* (1981); *New York Times*, January 30, 1960; Stiller, Jesse H., *George S. Messersmith: Diplomat of Democracy* (1987); *WWWA*, 3 (1951–1960):595.

MESTA, PERLE SKIRVIN (1891?–1975). Born in Sturgis, Michigan, probably in 1891, Perle Skirvin was educated in private schools in Galveston, Texas, studying voice and piano. She married George Mesta in 1917; he died in 1925, leaving her a good deal of wealth to add to that from her father. By the 1930s she had become a well-known hostess in Newport, Rhode Island. In 1941, she moved to Washington and continued her social activities. In addition, she was an advocate of women's rights and a member of the National Women's party, lobbying for the equal rights amendment. A Democrat after 1940, Mesta also worked as a fund raiser for the Democratic National Committee in 1944 and 1948. In 1949, President Harry S Truman appointed her minister to Luxembourg, separating that mission from Belgium for the first time. She was the third woman to hold a ministerial or ambassadorial appointment. The American embassy in Luxembourg became a European social center, as might have been expected, and Mesta's official duties in the trouble-free country consisted of little but routine reporting of political opinion. In 1953, Mesta returned to Washington social life, although she never achieved the limelight that she had during the Roosevelt and Truman years. She died March 16, 1975, in Oklahoma City. Irving Berlin modeled his musical play *Call Me Madam* on the life of Perle Mesta. Mesta, Perle, and Robert Cahn, *Perle: My Story* (1960); *New York Times*, June 22, July 6, December 25, 1949, March 17, 1975.

MEXICO CITY CONFERENCE (1901–1902). This, the Second International Conference of American States, opened in Mexico City on October 22, 1901, and adjourned on January 31, 1902. Henry G. Davis, a former senator from West Virginia, headed the U.S. delegation, which also included William I. Buchanan* and John Barrett.* It was the first inter-American conference held after the United States had achieved recognition as a world power following the Venezuelan crisis (1895)* and the Spanish-American War. Arbitration* was the most contentious topic, with Chile and Brazil opposed to obligatory arbitration; the final treaty called for support of voluntary arbitration, in line with the recommendations of the Hague Conference (1899).* Other resolutions encouraged the development of hemispheric communications, a Pan-American bank, the simplification of customs procedures to stimulate commerce, and measures to improve international sanitation. In addition, a commission was established to codify American international law; extradition was extended to cover anarchists; and the organizational structure of the Bureau of American Republics was strengthened, especially the Commerce Bureau. Generally the conference was marked by cordial exchange, although some of the resolutions were so vague that they tended to mask differences rather than signify agreement. Most of the treaties drafted at the conference were ratified very slowly and never received a sufficient number of ratifications to take effect. For example, only six nations ratified the arbitration treaty. Connell-Smith, Gordon, *The United States and Latin America* (1974); Inman, Samuel Guy, *Inter-American Conferences* (1965); Mecham, J. Lloyd, *A Survey of United States–Latin American Relations* (1965).

MEXICO CITY CONFERENCE (1945). This conference, also called the Chapultepec Conference, brought together all the Western Hemisphere nations that had cooperated in the World War II effort (all but Argentina). Meeting from

February 21 to March 8, 1945, delegates considered the Argentina problem and decided that Argentina's delay in joining the Allies would be forgiven if it accepted the results of the conference (which it did, on March 27). These results included an agreement for a continuing regional security system, the Act of Chapultepec, branding an attack on one nation an attack on all and providing for consultation to agree upon a response. In addition, promises of postwar economic cooperation were made and the United States agreed to curtail only gradually its orders of strategic raw materials from Latin America after the war's end to avoid economic chaos. The Act of Chapultepec, the most important consequence of this conference, was made permanent in the Rio Treaty (1947).*
FR (1945), 9:1–153; Mecham, J. Lloyd, A Survey of United States–Latin American Relations (1965); Thomas, Ann Van Wynen, and A. J. Thomas, Jr., The Organization of American States (1963).

MEYER, ARMIN HENRY (b. 1914). Born in Fort Wayne, Indiana, on January 19, 1914, Armin H. Meyer attended Lincoln College (Illinois) from 1931 to 1933, and graduated from Capital University (Ohio) in 1935. He taught at Capital from 1935 to 1941, received an M.A. degree from Ohio State University in 1941, and was an Office of War Information staff member in Iraq and Egypt during World War II, helping win Egypt's support of the Allied war effort. In 1947–1948, Meyer was a U.S. public affairs officer in Baghdad. Joining the State Department in 1948, he served in mission posts in Washington, Beirut, and Kabul until 1961. In that year, he was named ambassador to Lebanon, where he was influential in guiding the peaceful progress of domestic politics and helping to prevent a crisis similar to that that had brought U.S. intervention in 1958. In 1965, Meyer was appointed ambassador to Iran, where, recognizing the political and economic progress made by the shah, he terminated America's patronizing diplomacy as well as many aid programs. His most important post was ambassador to Japan, 1969–1972. There he dealt with such complex issues as the reversion of Okinawa, the extension of the 1960 Mutual Security Treaty, and an assortment of economic disputes, as well as the impact on Japan of the changing relationship between the United States and the People's Republic of China. In early 1973, Meyer was named head of an American intelligence team to work with Israelis fighting Palestinian guerrillas. In 1974–1975, he taught at American University; since 1975, he has taught at Georgetown University. He married Alice James in 1949 and wrote his memoirs, Assignment Tokyo, an Ambassador's Journal (1974), which contains a careful analysis of modern Japan and its political and economic relationship with the United States. New York Times, April 27, 1969, January 27, 1972, April 14, 1973; WWA (1986–1987):1924–25.

MEYER, GEORGE von LENGERKE (1858–1918). A close friend and adviser of President Theodore Roosevelt, George von Lengerke Meyer was born in Boston on June 24, 1858, and graduated from Harvard in 1879, one year ahead of Roosevelt. He pursued a business and political career in Boston, serving on the Boston Common Council, 1889–1890, as an alderman, 1891, and in the state legislature, 1892–1897. In business, he was a director of several companies including the Amoskeag Manufacturing Company, the Amory Company, the National Bank of Commerce, and the Ames Plow Company (of which he was also president). In 1900, he was named ambassador to Italy. There he became a friend of the king and as such a popular and influential diplomat who formed contacts all over Europe and kept in close contact with Roosevelt and Senator Henry Cabot Lodge, Sr.* He had a particularly good relationship with Kaiser Wilhelm II of Germany, with whom he often vacationed. After five years in Italy, Meyer was transferred to Russia, where he presented Roosevelt's proposal for ending the Russo-Japanese War,* using his friendship with Wilhelm to advantage, since Wilhelm helped persuade Czar Nicholas II to go along with the peace offer. In 1907, Meyer was brought back to Washington to be post-master-general, a position from which he could advise Roosevelt more directly. In the Taft administration, 1909–1913, he was secretary of the navy and an advocate of preparedness and a modern navy. Meyer had a well-publicized street fight with Truxtun Beale* in 1916, over what the press demurely termed, "a long-standing difference." He married Marian Alice Appleton in 1885 and died in Boston on March 9, 1918. *DAB*, 12:587; Dennis, A.L.P., *Adventures in American Diplomacy, 1896–1906* (1928); *New York Times*, January 25, 1916, March 10, 1918; Wiegand, W. G., "Ambassador in Absentia: George Meyer, William II, and Theodore Roosevelt," *Mid-America* 56 (January 1974): 3–15, and *Politician in the Progressive Era* (1987).

MIDDLETON, HENRY (1770–1846). Born in London, England, on September 28, 1770, Henry Middleton was educated in both England and South Carolina and traveled extensively in Europe during the late eighteenth century. By 1801, he had inherited much wealth and property in South Carolina and Rhode Island. He sat in the South Carolina legislature, 1801–1810, was governor, 1810–1812, and a U.S. congressman, 1815–1819. In 1820, Middleton was appointed minister to Russia, presenting his credentials in 1821 and remaining until 1830, by far the longest tenure of any other American minister or ambassador to Russia. In 1824, he negotiated a treaty regulating trade and fishing in the Pacific Northwest, whereby the latitute of 54°40′ was established as a dividing line between Russian and American trading posts but allowing freedom of trade across the dividing line for ten years. Middleton was instructed to urge Russian mediation between Spain and its rebellious colonies and to negotiate a general commercial treaty in 1828 but was not successful in either endeavor. After his diplomatic career, he returned to South Carolina and became a Unionist and political foe of John C. Calhoun.* Middleton married Mary Helen Hering in 1794, died in Charleston, South Carolina, on June 14, 1846, and is remembered as one of the very few American representatives who enjoyed his residence in the forbidding Russian capital of St. Petersburg. *DAB*, 12:600; Kushner, Howard I., *Conflict on the Northwest*

Coast (1975); *NCAB*, 12:163; Thomas, Benjamin P., *Russo-American Relations, 1815–1867* (1930).

MILAN DECREE (December 1807). Part of Napoleon's Continental System,* the Milan Decree expanded and strengthened the effect of the Berlin Decree* by stating that neutral ships that obeyed British regulations, submitted to British searches, sailed to a British port, or paid a British duty would be subject to confiscation as enemy ships. This decree was a response to the British Orders-in-Council,* issued a month earlier. Its effect was to limit further American shipping by increasing the likelihood of capture by the French navy or by French port authorities. Egan, Clifford L., *Neither Peace nor War: Franco-American Relations, 1803–1812* (1983); Horsman, Reginald, *The Causes of the War of 1812* (1962); Perkins, Bradford, *Prologue to War* (1961).

MILLIS, WALTER (1899–1968). A prominent journalist and historian best known for his works on U.S. involvement in the Spanish-American War and World War I, Walter Millis was born on March 16, 1899, in Atlanta and was graduated from Yale in 1920 after service in World War I. In 1924, he began a thirty-year career as an editorialist and staff writer for the *New York Herald-Tribune*. In 1931, he published his first book, *The Martial Spirit*, dealing with the Spanish-American War, and four years later he published *Road to War: America, 1914–1917*, a revisionist account of American diplomacy leading up to World War I. An isolationist* in the early 1930s, he had become an interventionist by 1940 when he wrote *Why Europe Fights*, on the origins of World War II. He blamed the military commanders in Hawaii, in *This Is Pearl!* (1947), for the Japanese attack at Pearl Harbor.* Later Millis edited the diaries of Secretary of Defense James Forrestal and worked as an editor-at-large for the *Saturday Review*. In the early 1950s, he was a vocal opponent of McCarthyism; in the 1960s, he wrote articles opposing American policy toward Vietnam. He was married twice and was an avid sailor, owning several boats over the years. Millis died in New York on March 17, 1968. *New York Times*, March 18, 1968.

MINISTER. See **CHIEF OF MISSION.**

MINISTER-RESIDENT. See **CHIEF OF MISSION.**

MIRAMAR, CONVENTION OF (1864). This was the treaty by which Maximilian accepted the throne in Mexico, with the support of the French emperor Napoleon III and French troops. In return, Maximilian pledged to pay for the intervention and for Mexican debts owed to France. The United States viewed Maximilian's presence unfavorably, and diplomatic pressure on the part of Secretary of State William Henry Seward* after the Civil War brought about the removal of French troops. With his protection gone, Maximilian was captured by the forces of nationalist leader Benito Juárez and executed June 19, 1867. Parkes, Henry B., *A History of Mexico* (1966).

MISSION, American diplomatic catchword, c. 1840s and 1890s. This term, closely associated with *Manifest Destiny*,* was seen in the 1840s as an obligation to regenerate Mexico and the Mexican people. *Mission* was used more prominently in the 1890s to refer to an Anglo-Saxon duty to civilize and Christianize all the world's "lesser" races. Termed by poet Rudyard Kipling the "White Man's Burden," mission as an American ideal faded with the disillusionment of the post–World War I years but returned after World War II as part of a conviction of national superiority and a consequent responsibility to exercise beneficent world leadership. Frederick Merk differentiates between "Manifest Destiny" and "mission" by characterizing the latter as more generous, idealistic, peaceful, responsible, and durable. Merk, Frederick, *Manifest Destiny and Mission in American History* (1963); Weinberg, Albert, *Manifest Destiny* (1935).

MITCHELL, JOHN (1711–1768). The maker of Mitchell's Map was born in Lancaster County, Virginia, on April 13, 1711, and graduated from the University of Edinburgh in 1729. He studied medicine in Edinburgh until 1731 or 1732, when he returned to the United States, and practiced medicine until 1746. He then returned to Britain, where he spent the rest of his life, enjoying prominence as a doctor and botanist. His map-making career was apparently limited to one map, known formally as a "Map of the British and French Dominions in North America. . . . '' It was drawn in the early 1750s for the Board of Trade and Plantations and published in 1755. Drawn to a scale of 1:2 million, the map went through four editions, several different printings, and many plagiarisms. Mitchell's Map was used in the negotiations ending the American Revolution and in settling other boundary disputes existing at the time of its compilation. Its official status was agreed to by the United States and Great Britain in 1827, and it was used many times subsequently. During the Webster-Ashburton Treaty* negotiations (1842), a French map purported to be Mitchell's Map was used to help determine the northeastern boundary. Mitchell died February 29, 1768, probably in London. Bemis, Samuel F., *John Quincy Adams and the Foundations of American Foreign Policy* (1949); Berkeley, Edmund, and Dorothy Smith Berkeley, *Dr. John Mitchell, the Man Who Made the Map of North America* (1974); *DAB*, 13:50.

MOBILE ACT (1804). This congressional act authorized President Thomas Jefferson* to establish a customs district at Mobile, in Spanish West Florida, an area that Americans were claiming as part of the Louisiana Purchase.* After the Spanish minister, Carlos Yrujo, protested vigorously, diplomatic discussions concerning American acquisition of Florida were held, but to no avail. President Jefferson, who strongly favored American acquisition of Florida, was disappointed. Varg, Paul A., *Foreign Policies of the Founding Fathers* (1962).

MOFFAT, JAY PIERREPONT (1896–1943). Jay Pierrepont Moffat was born in Rye, New York, on July 18, 1896. He attended Harvard (1915–1917) but never graduated, going instead to the Netherlands to be private secretary to

Minister John W. Garrett.* Moffat joined the Foreign Service in 1919 and over ten of the next twelve years held various legation secretarial posts in Warsaw, Tokyo, Istanbul, and Bern. From 1925 to 1927, he was protocol officer at the White House; during that time he married Lilla Cabot Grew, the daughter of Joseph C. Grew.* In 1932, Moffat returned to Washington as chief of the West European Division in the State Department, and three years later he went to Sydney, Australia, as consul general.* Perhaps his most important assignment came in 1937 when he was named chief of the Division of European Affairs. In this post, he was instrumental in U.S. policymaking in the years leading up to World War II. He went to Europe in 1940 with Sumner Welles* to discuss a peaceful early settlement of the war; the mission was not successful. Later that same year, Moffat was appointed ambassador to Canada, where he concerned himself principally with coordinating Canadian and U.S. defense preparation and served as the minister to the Luxembourg government-in-exile. His death in Ottawa on January 24, 1943, at the age of forty-six deprived the United States of one of its most talented diplomats. *DAB*, Supp. 3:528; Hooker, Nancy Harrison, ed., *The Moffat Papers: Selections from the Diplomatic Journals of Jay Pierrepont Moffat, 1919–43* (1956); *New York Times*, January 25, 1943.

MONROE, JAMES (1758–1831). Fifth president of the United States (1817–1825), James Monroe engaged in an active diplomatic career before reaching the White House. As minister to both France (1794–1796, 1803) and Great Britain (1803–1807) and secretary of state (1811–1817) under his predecessor, James Madison,* Monroe was in the forefront of American foreign policy for over twenty-five years. He was born in Westmoreland County, Virginia, on April 28, 1758, attended William and Mary College (1774–1776), served in the Revolutionary War, and after the war studied law under Thomas Jefferson.* He married Eliza Kortwright in 1786, when he was a member of the Confederation Congress and a leading opponent of the proposed Jay-Gardoqui Treaty.* He opposed the ratification of the U.S. Constitution, but once it was ratified, he became a U.S. senator from Virginia (1790–1794) before his appointment to France. In Paris, Monroe had a difficult time mollifying French concern over Jay's Treaty* and was recalled in 1796. From 1799 to 1802, he was governor of Virginia. The following year, he was sent back to France on a special mission to assist U.S. Minister to France Robert R. Livingston* with the Louisiana Purchase.* Later that year, he moved to London as minister to Great Britain, a post he held through four increasingly troublesome years. Monroe was snubbed socially in England, a move at least partly in retaliation for President Jefferson's dislike of Anthony Merry, the British minister in America, and partly because of worsening Anglo-American relations. With the help of special envoy William Pinkney,* Monroe tried to shore up those relations in the Monroe-Pinkney Treaty (1806),* which, unfortunately, turned out to be unacceptable to Jefferson and Secretary of State James Madison. As secretary of state, Monroe was unsuccessful in averting through diplomacy the War of 1812. After the War broke out, he supported it and accepted the Treaty of Ghent (1814),* which brought it to an end. During Monroe's presidency, the Monroe Doctrine* was promulgated, although most historians believe that credit for its ideas should go primarily to Monroe's secretary of state, John Quincy Adams.* After 1825, Monroe lived in retirement in Virginia for a few years but moved to his daughter's home in New York City in 1830 and died there July 4, 1831. Ammon, Henry, *James Monroe: The Quest for National Identity* (1971); *DAB*, 13:87; Egan, Clifford L., *Neither Peace nor War: Franco-American Relations, 1803–1812* (1983); Perkins, Bradford, *Prologue to War* (1968).

MONROE DOCTRINE (1823). This policy statement, included in President James Monroe's* annual message to Congress in December 1823, incorporated these principles: (1) that European nations should not establish new colonies in the Western Hemisphere; (2) that European nations should not intervene in the affairs of independent nations of the Western Hemisphere; and (3) that the United States would not interfere in the affairs of European nations. Drafted largely by Secretary of State John Quincy Adams,* the Monroe Doctrine became a fundamental tenet of American diplomacy after a generation and has since been raised as a barrier to European intervention in Latin America, and through the Roosevelt Corollary* from 1904 to 1933, as a vehicle for American intervention. Bemis, Samuel F., *John Quincy Adams and the Foundation of American Foreign Policy* (1949); Cortada, James W., *Two Nations over Time: Spain and the United States, 1776–1977* (1978); May, Ernest R., *The Making of the Monroe Doctrine* (1975); Perkins, Dexter, *The Monroe Doctrine, 1823–1826* (1927); Van Alstyne, Richard W., "The Monroe Doctrine," in DeConde, Alexander, ed., *Encyclopedia of American Foreign Policy* (1979).

MONROE-PINKNEY TREATY (1806). Negotiated for the United States by Minister James Monroe* and special envoy William Pinkney,* this proposed treaty with Great Britain failed to gain concessions on impressment* but did include a liberalization of Britain's reexport trade policy. President Thomas Jefferson* protested strenuously a clause in the treaty stating American objection and resistance to the recently proclaimed Berlin Decree* and refused to submit the treaty to the Senate for ratification. The failure of the treaty has occasioned considerable historiographical debate, with some historians believing a successful treaty at this time might have averted the War of 1812. Perkins, Bradford, *Prologue to War* (1961).

MONTEVIDEO CONFERENCE (1933). In session from December 3 to December 28, 1933, the Seventh International Conference of American States, as it was formally known, met at the height of the Great Depression and amid considerable political instability in Latin America. In contrast with earlier inter-American conferences, the U.S. delegation, led by Secretary of State Cordell Hull,* took a less patronizing and domineering attitude in Montevideo, seeming to reflect the spirit of the Good Neighbor Policy.* Hull outlined his reciprocity plan as a way to improve international commerce, and the delegates approved it in principle. Five separate peacekeeping treaties were debated, including Argentina Foreign Minister Carlos Saavedra Lamas's Anti-War Pact, but despite Hull's strong statement abjuring aggression, no single treaty was agreed upon. The conference did adopt the Convention on the Rights and Duties of States, opposing intervention by one state into the affairs of another. The United States voted for this, with the mild reservation that the convention should not stand in the way of existing treaty obligations and the accepted tenets of international law. After some clarification, the convention was narrowed in scope and understood to pertain only to "armed" intervention. Connell-Smith, Gordon, *The United States and Latin America* (1973); *FR* (1933), 4:1–227; Inman, Samuel Guy, *Inter-American Conferences* (1965); Mecham, J. Lloyd, *A Survey of United States–Latin America Relations* (1965).

MOORE, JOHN BASSETT (1860–1947). Born December 3, 1860, in Smyrna, Delaware, John Bassett Moore attended the University of Virginia (1877–1880), read law, and was admitted to the bar in 1883. He joined the State Department two years later as a clerk for Alvey A. Adee,* then became third assistant secretary (1886–1891), where he received valuable diplomatic training. During this time, he assisted solicitor Francis Wharton in compiling *A Digest of International Law of the United States* (3 vols., 1886). From 1891 to 1924, Moore taught law and diplomacy at Columbia while continuing to do research in the State Department archives and write the books that gained him the reputation as America's foremost authority on international law. In these years, he wrote and compiled works such as *History and Digest of International Arbitration* (6 vols., 1898), *Digest of International Law* (8 vols., 1906), *American Diplomacy: Its Spirit and Achievements* (1905), and *Four Phases of American Development* (1908). He was a realist and an internationalist, advocating U.S. participation in various world legal, cultural, and economic institutions. As assistant secretary of state from April to September 1898, he served as secretary and counsel to the U.S. delegation at the Paris Peace Conference and helped draft the Treaty of Paris (1898).* Later he helped put together the Hay-Pauncefote Treaty (1901)* and provided a legal justification for seizing the isthmus of Panama. In 1912, Moore became a member of the Permanent Court of Arbitration* but resigned early in 1914 out of opposition to Wilson's Mexican policy. After World War I, he opposed the League of Nations,* believing that the idea of collective security* would lead to world war, but he favored the World Court* and served as its first American judge (1921–1928). In retirement after 1928, Moore edited *International Adjudications* (1936). He married Helen Francis Toland in 1890 and died in New York City on November 12, 1947. Borchard, Edwin, et al., *The Collected Papers of John Bassett Moore*, 7 vols. (1944); *DAB*, Supp. 4:597; Megargee, Richard, "Realism in American Foreign Policy: The Diplomacy of John Bassett Moore" (Ph. D. diss., Northwestern University, 1963); *New York Times*, November 13, 1947.

MORAN, BENJAMIN (1820–1886). Benjamin Moran was born August 1, 1820, in Chester County, Pennsylvania, attended public schools, and went to work for a Philadelphia printer. In 1851, he traveled to Great Britain to write and published some volumes of travelers' descriptions. In 1854, he became private secretary to James Buchanan,* U.S. minister to Great Britain, and after Buchanan left, Moran moved to the position of assistant secretary of the legation in 1857. In 1864, he was promoted to legation secretary, holding that post for ten years and serving on several occasions as chargé d'affaires* in the absence of the minister. He kept a detailed journal of his activities and of U.S.-British relations between 1857 and 1874 and, by virtue of his continuity and knowledge, exercised considerable influence on policy. A staunch Unionist, popular with British political leaders, Moran helped prevent British recognition of the Confederacy. In 1874, he was named minister to Portugal, spending two uneventful years as minister and six more as chargé. A stroke felled him in 1882, and he returned to England to live four years more as an invalid before dying in Essex on June 20, 1886. Adams, E. D., *Great Britain and the American Civil War*, 2 vols. (1925); *DAB*, 13:150; *NCAB*, 10:56.

MORGAN, EDWIN VERNON (1865–1934). Born on Washington's birthday, 1865, in Aurora, New York, Edwin V. Morgan received both A.B. (1890) and A.M. (1891) degrees from Harvard and studied further at Berlin and again at Harvard between 1891 and 1895. He taught history at Adelbert College and Western Reserve University, 1895–1898, and in 1899 became secretary to Bartlett Tripp, U.S. delegate to the tripartite commission sent to Samoa; he then was chosen secretary for the commission. Between 1900 and 1904, Morgan held minor posts in Seoul, St. Petersburg, Dairen, and Dalny, Manchuria. In 1905, he received his first ministerial appointment to Korea, but later that year he was sent to Cuba. In four years as minister there, he worked much of the time with the provisional government of Charles E. Magoon.* Short ministerial stints to Paraguay and Uruguay (1910) and Portugal (1911) were followed by appointment as minister to Brazil in 1912, where Morgan remained until 1933, just short of George P. Marsh's* record tenure for U.S. diplomats. In Rio de Janeiro, he worked to improve communication, transportation, and cultural ties between the United States and Brazil and personally cultivated excellent relations with Brazilian leaders. He negotiated coffee and wheat exchange agreements between the two nations and stayed in Brazil after his retirement in 1933. However, Morgan, who never married, died less than a year later, on April 16, 1934, in Petropolis. *DAB*, Supp. 1:563; *New York Times*, April 17, 1934.

MORGAN, JOHN TYLER (1824–1907). The Senate's foremost advocate of an isthmian canal during the 1890s, John Tyler Morgan was born in Athens, Tennessee, on June 20, 1824, read law, and was admitted to the bar in 1845. He practiced law in Calhoun County, Alabama, after 1845, married Cornelia Willis in 1846, and served in the Confederate army during the Civil War, rising to the rank of brigadier general. Morgan was elected to the U.S. Senate in 1876 and remained there until his death in Washington on June 11, 1907. In the Senate, he became best known for his work in the area of foreign relations, serving as chairman of both the Interoceanic Canal and Foreign Relations committees. When the isthmian canal question emerged in the 1890s, Morgan enthusiastically advocated a waterway along the Nicaraguan route but believed any canal would benefit southern commerce. During the late 1890s, he urged intervention in Cuba, and after the Spanish-American War, he supported annexation of and statehood for Cuba and Puerto Rico in order to increase southern power in Congress. Morgan was also known as a staunch Anglophobe,* opposing arbitration* treaties and other measures designed to conciliate matters between the two nations. Described as the "most industrious" senator, Morgan was one of the few southerners of his time who achieved a national reputation. *DAB*, 13:180; Fry, Joseph A., "John Tyler Morgan's Southern Expansionism," *Diplomatic History* 9 (1985):329–46; *New York Times*, June 12, 1907; Pletcher, David C., *The Awkward Years* (1962); Radke, August C., "Senator Morgan and the Nicaraguan Canal," *Alabama Review* 12, 1 (January 1959):5–34.

MORGAN, JUNIUS SPENCER (1813–1890). Father of famous financier J. P. Morgan, Junius Spencer Morgan was a notable international banker in his own right. Born April 14, 1813, in West Springfield, Massachusetts, into a wealthy family, Morgan was privately educated and soon became a partner in a mercantile house, J. M. Beebe, Morgan & Company, in Boston. In 1836, he married Juliet Pierpont and in 1854, moved into banking as a partner in George Peabody & Company. The high point of his international financial career was a $50 million loan to France in 1870 during the Franco-Prussian War, a loan that proved profitable despite French losses and dire warnings from the German prime minister, Bismarck. During the period after the Civil War, most of the substantial amount of British capital invested in the United States went through Morgan's bank. His son gradually took over the management of the bank's affairs in the 1880s, and Morgan died April 8, 1890, in Monte Carlo from injuries received leaping from his carriage after the horses had run wild. Carosso, Vincent P., *The Morgans* (1987); *DAB*, 12:181.

MORGENTHAU PLAN (1944). Drawn up in August 1944 and named for its originator, Secretary of the Treasury Henry Morgenthau, Jr., who believed that an industrialized Germany would always be a threat to world peace, this plan suggested the dismantling of Germany's industrial facilities, closing its mines, and transforming the nation into an agricultural and pastoral land. Closing the heavily industrialized Ruhr District would, furthermore, remove a major competitor to British industry. President Roosevelt and British Prime Minister Winston Churchill discussed the plan at the Quebec Conference (1944),* and Morgenthau won Churchill's acquiescence by offering a large loan to Britain. Roosevelt was initially in favor, although Secretary of State Cordell Hull* and

Secretary of War Henry L. Stimson* were vehemently opposed, and adverse public reaction soon turned Roosevelt against the plan, which reportedly strengthened German resistance during the time the president appeared to favor it. Although a dead issue in a practical sense, the Morgenthau Plan was referred to from time to time until Secretary of State James F. Byrnes* officially killed it in his famous September 1946 speech at Stuttgart reflecting cold war* attitudes and U.S.-Soviet competition over Germany. Its influence and some of its provisions were seen in JCS 1067,* the basic occupation policy document in the early postwar period. Gaddis, John L., *The United States and the Origins of the Cold War* (1972); Kimball, Warren F., *Swords or Ploughshares? The Morgenthau Plan for Defeated Nazi Germany, 1943–1946* (1976); Kolko, Gabriel, *The Politics of War* (1968); McNeill, William H., *America, Britain, and Russia* (1953); Wheeler-Bennett, John W., and Anthony Nicholls, *The Semblance of Peace* (1972).

MORRIS, GOUVERNEUR (1752–1816). Born into the New York aristocracy at Morrisania on January 31, 1752, Gouverneur Morris graduated from King's College (now Columbia) in 1768, read law, and gained admittance to the bar in 1771. Before the American Revolution, he was a conservative aristocrat who had lost a leg in a carriage accident, but he cast his lot with the forces for independence in 1775 and during the next twelve years was closely involved with the politics of New York State and the Continental Congress. In 1789, he went to France on legal business, observed the French Revolution, and became an important American in Paris as a private businessman and an unofficial agent for the United States. In 1790–1791, he undertook an unsuccessful mission to England to negotiate problems left over from the Peace of Paris (1783).* President George Washington named him minister to France in 1792, and he spent two years in the turmoil of Paris before his recall in 1794 at the request of the French and in response to the demanded recall of French envoy Edmund Gênet. Morris was the only foreign representative who remained in Paris during the Reign of Terror, and the U.S. legation became an asylum for political outcasts. He was also involved in an abortive plot to secure Louis XVI's escape; the money left over from this affair made its way to Lafayette, then in a prison in the Netherlands. In addition, he arranged for the final payments of the French loan dating back to the Revolution. Morris's activities were hampered somewhat by his penchant for operating contrary to the instructions of Secretary of State Thomas Jefferson,* and Jefferson's consequent decision to ignore him by not sending any new instructions. After his recall in 1794, Morris traveled four years in Europe before returning to the United States. From 1800 to 1803, he served in the U.S. Senate and then spent the rest of his life in genteel retirement at Morrisania. He married Anne Carey Randolph in 1809, was an advocate of the Erie Canal and chairman of the canal commission, and an extreme opponent of the War of 1812. He died at Morrisania November 5, 1816. *DAB*, 13:209; Kline, Mary-Jo, *Gouverneur Morris and the New Nation, 1775–1788* (1971, 1978); Mintz, Max M., *Gouverneur Morris and the American Revolution* (1970); Roosevelt, Theodore, *Gouverneur Morris* (1898); Whitridge, A., "Gouverneur Morris in France," *History Today* 22 (1972): 759–67; Willson, Beckles, *America's Ambassadors to France, 1777–1927* (1928).

MORRIS, RICHARD VALENTINE (1768–1815). Born at his family estate in Morrisania, New York, on March 8, 1768, Richard Valentine Morris married Anne Walton in 1797 and was commissioned a captain in the United States Navy the following year. In 1802, he was promoted to commodore and placed in command of a naval squadron sent to operate against the Barbary pirates* at Tripoli and to supervise negotiations between the United States and the North African sultanates at Tripoli, Tunis, Algiers, and Morocco, working with consular agent William H. Eaton. After several months of inactivity at Gibraltar and Malta, Morris took his fleet to Tunis, where his political inexperience contributed to the failure of negotiations regarding tribute payments. After a brief skirmish with Moroccan forces and further futile talks in the summer of 1803, Morris was ordered back to Washington, largely on the testimony of Eaton, who had returned earlier, and charged with lacking the "diligence and activity necessary to execute the important duties of his station." He resigned from the navy, wrote a spirited defense of his conduct, and retired to Morrisania, where he engaged in family affairs and private business until his death May 13, 1815. *DAB*, 13:219; Edwards, Samuel, *Barbary General: The Life of William H. Eaton* (1968); Irwin, R. W., *The Diplomatic Relations of the United States with the Barbary Powers* (1931); Morris, R. V., *A Defense of the Conduct of Commodore Morris During His Command in the Mediterranean* (1804).

MORRIS, ROLAND SLETOR (1874–1945). Roland Sletor Morris was born in Olympia, Washington, on March 11, 1874, and received a B.A. from Princeton in 1896 and a law degree from the University of Pennsylvania in 1899. He entered law practice in Philadelphia, married Augusta Twiggs in 1903, and became involved in Pennsylvania Democratic politics, attending several national conventions. A former student of Woodrow Wilson at Princeton, Morris was appointed ambassador to Japan in 1917, during the administration of his former teacher. In Japan, he took part in preliminary discussions regarding the establishment of the New Consortium.* He also negotiated an agreement among the Allies, Russia, and Japan dealing with the operation of the Siberian and Chinese Eastern Railways under Allied military supervision, but the agreement went unrecognized by Japan. In 1921, Morris arranged with the Japanese a treaty revision of the Gentlemen's Agreement (1907),* but it was never submitted to the Senate, and he resigned his post. In general, he is credited with lessening friction and creating goodwill between the two nations. After his diplomatic service, Morris taught law at the University of Pennsylvania and was a prominent Episcopal layman. He died in Philadelphia on November 23, 1945. Curry, Roy Watson, *Woodrow Wilson and Far Eastern Policy, 1913–1921* (1957); Levin, N. Gordon, *Woodrow Wilson and World Politics* (1968); *New York Times*, November 24, 1945.

MORRISON, WILLIAM McCUTCHAN (1867–1918). One of the best-known Congo missionaries, William M. Morrison was born near Lexington, Virginia, on November 10, 1867, and attended Washington and Lee University before graduating from Louisville Presbyterian Theological Seminary in 1896. The following year, he went to Luebo, Congo Free State, as a missionary of the Southern Presbyterian church. There he was engaged in educational work, translating the Bible into native languages and writing a grammar and dictionary of the Buluba-Lulua language. He became politically involved in the Congo, defending native interests against the Free State government and concessionaires in the rubber districts of the country. Morrison worked with the Congo Reform Association in London, compaigned by making speeches and utilizing the press, and ultimately persuaded King Leopold of Belgium to appoint an investigatory commission, which eventually resulted in some reforms. Morrison was married to Bertha Marian Stebbins, who died in the Congo in 1910, and he was twice elected president of the Conference of Protestant Missions in the Congo. He died March 14, 1918, in Luebo. *DAB*, 12:231; Vinson, T. C., *William McCutchan Morrison* (1921).

MORROW, DWIGHT WHITNEY (1873–1931). Born in Huntington, West Virginia, on January 11, 1873, and educated at Amherst College (A.B., 1895) and Columbia Law School (LL. B., 1899), Dwight Morrow married Elizabeth Reeve Cutter in 1903, settled in New Jersey, and practiced law from 1899 to 1914. A corporate law specialist, he helped draft the New Jersey workmen's compensation law (1911) and served in various New Jersey state agencies. In 1914, he joined the Morgan banking interests and remained there until 1927 (except during World War I, when he was a civilian aide in logistics and intelligence to General John J. Pershing). His one diplomatic tour, minister to Mexico, 1927–1930, was a brilliant success. Discreet and tactful, Morrow's negotiations with President Plutarco Calles brought about removal of the 1925 law that threatened retroactive confiscation of American-held oil rights in Mexico. He informally settled divisive problems between the Mexican government and the Catholic church that had caused a substantial amount of violence and gave valuable advice in the matter of Mexico's internal finances. Personally popular, he improved U.S.-Mexico amity even further by arranging for his son-in-law, Charles A. Lindbergh, to make a goodwill flight to Mexico. Morrow was a delegate to the Sixth International Conference of American States in Havana (1928)* and after his Mexican service was over, a delegate to the London Naval Conference (1930),* where his main responsibility was the French delegation. In 1930, he was elected as a Republican to the U.S. Senate representing New Jersey and was widely considered a possible presidential candidate when he died suddenly in Englewood, New Jersey, on October 5, 1931, of a cerebral hemorrhage. *DAB*, 13:234; Nicholson, Harold, *Dwight Morrow* (1935); *New York Times*, October 6, 1931.

MORTEFONTAINE, TREATY OF (1800). See **CONVENTION OF 1800.**

MORTON, LEVI PARSONS (1824–1920). A minister to France (1881–1885) and a vice-president (1889–1893), Levi P. Morton was born in Shoreham, Vermont, on May 16, 1824. He had practically no formal education but entered business at the age of twenty, running a general store in Hanover, New Hampshire. During the 1850s, he was involved in a wholesale business in Boston that failed in 1861, and two years later he began a bank in New York City, Morton, Bliss and Company, with a London branch, Morton, Rose and Company. Unlike his earlier ventures, Morton's bank was exceedingly successful. In 1872, his London branch handled the finances related to claims resulting from the Civil War raids of the C.S.S. *Alabama*,* and in 1875 his bank funded the U.S. national debt and sold bonds. He served a term in the U.S. House of Representatives, 1879–1881, and in 1881 went to Paris as minister to France. Morton's duties there were largely social, although he played a role in the Statue of Liberty gift (1884) and in the pork controversy (failing to obtain remission of the French order banning the importation of U.S. pork). He did, however, succeed in gaining modifications of French commercial regulations so that U.S. businesses could place agencies in France. In 1884, he attempted to mediate a settlement of the war between France and China, but the Chinese government rejected his proposals concerning indemnities and temporary French occupation. In Paris, his protests were successful in getting the address of the recently moved legation changed from Place de la bitche to Place des Etats-Unis. From 1889 to 1893, Morton was vice-president under Benjamin Harrison, where his wealth and dignity served him well; and from 1895 to 1897, he was governor of New York. After 1897, he returned to the banking business until his retirement in 1909. Twice married, Morton was one of America's longest-lived statesmen, dying in Rhinebeck, New York, on his ninety-sixth birthday. *DAB*, 13:258; McElroy, Robert McNutt, *Levi Parsons Morton: Banker, Diplomat and Statesman* (1975); *New York Times*, May 17, 1920; Pletcher, David, *The Awkward Years* (1962); Willson, Beckles, *America's Ambassadors to France, 1777–1927* (1928).

MOSCOW CONFERENCE (1943). At this wartime conference, Soviet Foreign Minister V. M. Molotov, British Foreign Secretary Anthony Eden, Secretary of State Cordell Hull,* General John R. Deane, and Sir Hastings Ismay met to discuss military coordination among the Allies, and postwar planning. The main accomplishment was the Four-Power Declaration on General Security.* In addition, the conferees established the European Advisory Commission and an Advisory Council on Italy to study possible postwar operations in those countries and agreed upon a Declaration on German Atrocities, providing for the punishment of the perpetrators of such atrocities. The conference met from October 18 to October 30, 1943, and served as a prelude to the Teheran Conference.* Gaddis, John L., *The United States and the Origins of the Cold War* (1972); McNeill, William H., *America, Britain, and Russia* (1953); Sainsbury, Keith, *The Turning Point*

(1985); Wheeler-Bennett, John W., and Anthony Nicholls, *The Semblance of Peace* (1972).

MOSCOW CONFERENCE (1944). This conference, from October 9 to October 20, 1944, brought together Joseph Stalin and Winston Churchill, with Ambassador W. Averell Harriman* of the United States as an observer. Churchill's objectives were to settle the Polish question, define the extent of Soviet influence in the Balkans and Central Europe, and do some preliminary work on postwar political settlements. The Polish question, concerning the conflict between rival governments in London and Lublin and the location of the Russo-Polish border, proved insoluble and was put off until the Yalta Conference,* three months later. Churchill agreed to Soviet military predominance in Hungary, Bulgaria, and Romania, with British forces to occupy Greece and both powers to handle Yugoslavia jointly. Gaddis, John L., *The United States and the Orgins of the Cold War* (1972); McNeill, William H., *America, Britain, and Russia* (1953); Wheeler-Bennett, John W., and Anthony Nicholls, *The Semblance of Peace* (1972).

MOSCOW CONFERENCE (1945). Meeting from December 16 to December 26, 1945, the Council of Foreign Ministers*—which included Secretary of State James F. Byrnes,* British Foreign Secretary Ernest Bevin, and Soviet Foreign Minister V. M. Molotov—worked on a number of issues, including planning for the peace settlement in general and for the Paris Peace Conference (1946)* in particular. Britain and Russia agreed to permit the United States to exercise full control over the occupation of Japan. A commission was established to reform the Romanian government along more democratic lines, and the Soviet Union was authorized to carry out similar reforms in Bulgaria. A hazy declaration on the desirability of a unified and democratic China was agreed upon, as was an arrangement whereby the United States and the USSR would share in the postwar occupation of Korea. In Iran, American concern over the presence of Soviet troops in the northern part of the country was discussed but not resolved, although there was general agreement on the idea of a United Nations* Atomic Energy Commission. The matter of atomic energy information, over which the United States still maintained a monopoly, had stirred considerable controversy on the eve of Byrnes's departure for Moscow, when the secretary intimated that he might be willing to discuss atomic matters with the Soviets. Some political leaders, including Senator Arthur Vandenberg (R., Michigan),* understood this to mean that Byrnes would dispense atomic energy information before adequate atomic energy controls had been established through the United Nations. Although the agreements made at Moscow contained no sharing of atomic energy information, Byrnes's handling of this issue helped open a breach between him and President Truman that was never healed. Curry, George, "James F. Byrnes," in Bemis, Samuel F., ed., *American Secretaries of State and Their Diplomacy*, vol. 14 (1965); *FR* (1945), 2:560–826; Kolko, Joyce, and Gabriel Kolko, *The Limits of Power* (1972); McNeill, William H., *America, Britain, and Russia* (1953); Wheeler-Bennett,

John W., and Anthony Nicholls, *The Semblance of Peace* (1972); Yergin, Daniel, *Shattered Peace* (1977).

MOSCOW CONFERENCE (1947). Secretary of State George C. Marshall* traveled to Moscow to meet with Soviet Foreign Minister V. M. Molotov and British Foreign Secretary Ernest Bevin from March 12 to April 24, 1947. By this time, considerable hostility had developed between the United States and the Soviet Union, and the lack of agreement on questions concerning reparations,* German unification, an Austrian peace treaty, and Yugoslavian territorial demands in Carinthia and Styria clearly demonstrated the escalation of the cold war.* The climate of the conference convinced Marshall that U.S. policy would be better served by a firmer stance toward Russia; later in 1947, the policy of containment* reflected the secretary of state's thinking. Feis, Herbert, *From Trust to Terror* (1970); *FR* (1947), 2:139–576; Gaddis, John L., *The United States and the Origins of the Cold War* (1972); Wheeler-Bennett, John W., and Anthony Nicholls, *The Semblance of Peace* (1972); Yergin, Daniel, *Shattered Peace* (1977).

MOSCOW SUMMIT CONFERENCE (1972). This meeting, from May 22 to May 29, 1972, between President Richard M. Nixon and Soviet Premier Leonid Brezhnev took place after preparations made by national security adviser Henry Kissinger* resulted in an increased number of joint committees and activities to minimize chances for a direct and hostile confrontation. Nixon and Brezhnev discussed arms limitation and commercial, scientific, and cultural matters. With respect to arms, the United States and the USSR signed SALT I (Strategic Arms Limitation Talks),* a pact to limit defensive missiles to two sites and, as an interim agreement, to freeze offensive weapons levels in quantity (but not quality) for five years. The summit was held in an atmosphere of some tension, since the Soviet Union was supporting a North Vietnamese offensive in the ongoing Vietnam War, while the United States had recently resumed the bombing of Hanoi and had mined the harbor at Haiphong. Brandon, Henry, *The Retreat of American Power* (1972); Graebner, Norman, *Cold War Diplomacy* (1977); Szulc, Tad, *The Illusion of Power* (1978); Wehlmiller, Gordon R., and Dusko Doder, *U.S.-Soviet Summits* (1986).

MOSCOW SUMMIT CONFERENCE (1974). This conference took place between June 29 and July 3, 1974, and brought President Richard M. Nixon, only five weeks away from his resignation, and Soviet Premier Leonid Brezhnev together for the third time in just over two years. In contrast to their 1972 meeting, this summit saw only limited results. Attempts to work out a new arrangement on the limitation of offensive weapons failed, except for agreements limiting underground nuclear testing and reducing the number of antiballistic missile sites from two to one. Other agreements concerned less controversial matters such as energy, housing, and artifical heart research. Graebner, Norman, *Cold War Diplomacy* (1977); Szulc, Tad, *The Illusion of Power* (1978); Wehlmiller, Gordon R., and Dusko Doder, *U.S.-Soviet Summits* (1986).

MOSCOW SUMMIT CONFERENCE (1988). This was the fourth and final summit conference between President Ronald Reagan and General Secretary Mikhail Gorbachev, held from May 29 to June 2, 1988. There had been hope that a START (Strategic Arms Reduction Talks)* agreement would be signed at this summit, but negotiations slowed; the main event was the formal exchange of Intermediate Nuclear Force (INF) Treaty* ratifications. Seven minor agreements, on such matters as student exchanges and fishing rights, were signed, and START issues were discussed, but no major breakthroughs occurred. Similarly, regional concerns in such places as the Middle East and southern Africa received attention. As with previous summits between these two leaders, each was looking to strengthen his personal position—Reagan for his legacy, Gorbachev for his internal political power. The summit may have been most significant in demonstrating how relatively normal and undramatic these events had become. *Washington Post*, June 2, 1988; *New York Times*, June 3, 5, 1988.

MOSES-LINTHICUM ACT (1931). Passed by Congress on February 23, 1931, this act created a corps of Foreign Service clerical personnel, assured impartiality in determining transfers, assignments, and promotions, and placed other limitations on Foreign Service officers to ensure more qualified and experienced people in high-level positions. The act also reorganized the Board of Foreign Service, modified the classification system, and provided for special living allowances, annual leaves, and automatic salary increases. In general, this act replaced the Rogers Act (1924)* in many respects as the governing document of the Foreign Service. Its principal sponsors were Senator George H. Moses (R., New Hampshire) and Congressman J. Charles Linthicum (R., Maryland). Ilchman, Warren F., *Professional Diplomacy in the United States, 1779–1939* (1961); Plischke, Elmer, *The Conduct of American Diplomacy* (1967).

MOST-FAVORED-NATION TREATMENT, a clause often included in bilateral trade and consular agreements or treaties stating that one (or both) signatories will have the same rights and privileges accorded to any other treaty partner. By equalizing competition, the host nation can avoid conflict among trade competitors and exploitation by any one of them. Plischke notes that this clause provoked a controversy between the United States and Great Britain in the years before World War I, the United States stipulating that it was "conditional" and did not include special conditions given to one particular nation and Great Britain arguing that it was "unconditional." In 1923, the United States accepted the British view. After the United States adopted the unconditional version of the most-favored-nation treatment, it sought to negotiate tariff agreements with the leading suppliers of certain imports and then extend the agreement to other suppliers of those imports. In practice, however, the original agreements were negotiated with nations in competitive decline (such as Great Britain between World War I and World War II), granting the same privileges unconditionally to nations (such as Japan) in the process of developing export industries whose products overwhelmed similar U.S. products in the marketplace. The most-favored-nation treatment principle has largely been abandoned in recent years, since in recent General Agreement on Tariffs and Trade* negotiation rounds, the United States has engaged in multilateral trade negotiations and concerned itself more with nontariff barriers. Plische, Elmer, *Conduct of American Diplomacy* (1967); Renouvin, Pierre, and Jean-Baptiste Duroselle, *Introduction to the History of International Relations* (1964).

MOTLEY, JOHN LOTHROP (1814–1877). One of the several literary notables who have seen major diplomatic service, John Lothrop Motley was born April 15, 1814, in Dorchester, Massachusetts. He was a student of George Bancroft* during his early school days, graduated from Harvard (1831), and studied further in Germany. He was admitted to the bar in 1837 but did not like law practice. In 1841, he was secretary of the legation at St. Petersburg but was there only a short time. By 1847, he had decided on the profession of writing history and spent most of the 1850s in Europe doing research on the history of the Netherlands, which he published as *The History of the United Netherlands* (4 vols., 1860–1867), considered a classic work although biased in favor of William of Orange. From 1861 to 1867, Motley was minister to Austria, where he reported European reactions to the Civil War both to the United States and in influential articles to the *London Times* and continued his historical research. He was also involved in some inconclusive discussions concerning Maximilian's ascendancy in Mexico. His resignation came about after he openly criticized the Andrew Johnson administration. In 1869, Motley, who had a reputation for impulsiveness and indiscretion, went to London as minister to Great Britain. There he negotiated a naturalization treaty but was left out of the major Anglo-American problem, the *Alabama** claims, because those talks were held in Washington. Motley was abruptly recalled in 1870, possibly victimized by the politics of the Grant-Summer feud over the proposed annexation of the Dominican Republic. He married Mary Benjamin in 1837 and spent much time after 1870 in Europe. He died in England May 29, 1877. *DAB*, 13:282; Kaplan, Lawrence S., "The Brahmin as Diplomat in Nineteenth Century America," *Civil War History*, 19, 1 (March 1973):5–28; Nevins, Allan, *Hamilton Fish*, 2 vols. (1957); Rogers, Augustus C., ed., *Our Representatives Abroad* (1874); Willson, Beckles, *America's Ambassadors to England, 1785–1929* (1929).

MOYNIHAN, DANIEL PATRICK (b. 1927). Born in Tulsa, Oklahoma, on March 16, 1927, Daniel Patrick Moynihan attended City College of New York in 1943, served in the navy, 1944–1947, and graduated from Tufts (B.A., 1948) and the Fletcher School of Law and Diplomacy (M.A., 1949; Ph.D., 1961). From 1955 to 1958, he was assistant secretary and then secretary to the governor of New York; from 1959–1960, he served on the New York State Tenure Commission. After finishing his graduate work in 1961, Moynihan went to work for the Department of Labor, holding various high-level assignments until 1965 and winning headlines for his advocacy of "benign neglect" in dealing with urban and racial problems. He began teaching education and urban politics at Harvard in 1966 but took a leave of absence in 1969 to become President Richard M. Nixon's urban affairs adviser. After a year, he returned to Harvard until 1973, when he accepted an appointment as ambassador to India. Sent there to improve relations after U.S. support of Pakistan during the 1971 Indo-Pakistan conflict in what is now Bangladesh, he deplored the official U.S. neglect of India, all the worse since India was a democracy, and recommended more balance in U.S. policy toward India and the People's Republic of China. In India, Moynihan kept to himself, made few public statements, and saw few people, trying to avoid becoming too involved with the charm of the country. Several months after his return from India, he was named ambassador to the United Nations.* There he developed a reputation as a "brawler," raising controversy on such issues as the "Zionism is racism" resolution, December 1975, accusing the Third World* majority in the General Assembly of irresponsible and hypocritical politics, and "verbal overkill." In general, Moynihan advocated increased American activism in the United Nations and other international organizations. He resigned from his ambassadorship in 1976 to make a successful race for the U.S. Senate from New York. He married Elizabeth Therese Brennan in 1955 and has written a number of books, including *Maximum Feasible Misunderstanding* (1969), *Coping: On the Practice of Government* (1974), *A Dangerous Place* (1978), *Family and Nation* (1986), and *Came the Revolution* (1988). Fasulo, Linda M., *Representing America: Experiences of U.S. Diplomats at the UN* (1984); *Nation*, December 20, 1975, pp. 654–58; *New York Times*, December 12, 1972, December 15, 1974, December 7, 1975; *WWA* (1986–1987):2006.

MUHLENBERG, HENRY AUGUSTUS PHILIP (1782–1844). Henry A. P. Muhlenberg was born in Lancaster, Pennsylvania, on May 13, 1782, studied privately for the Lutheran ministry, and was ordained in 1804. From 1803 to 1829, he served as the pastor of Trinity Church in Reading, Pennsylvania, and from 1829 to 1838 he was a member of the U.S. House of Representatives as a Jackson Democrat. In 1838, he was appointed America's first minister to Austria and served until 1840. There he promoted American cotton sales, was on good terms with Prince Metternich, traveled, and spent more than he earned, which prompted his request to come home. In 1844, he ran for governor of Pennsylvania but died on August 11 in Reading during the midst of the campaign. Muhlenberg was married to Mary Elizabeth Hiester in 1805; when she died in 1806, he married her sister Rebecca. *DAB*, 13:309.

MUKDEN INCIDENT (1931). Described as "the most important international event" during the tenure of Secretary of State Henry L. Stimson,* the Mukden incident involved the destruction, in September 1931, of a small section of the South Manchurian Railroad track near the town of Mukden, Manchuria. The railroad was run by the Japanese and protected by Japanese troops who claimed that the Chinese were responsible for the damage. In response, Japan took military countermeasures, which soon resulted in the Japanese occupation of much of Manchuria. The evidence, however, suggests that the Japanese military manufactured the event as a pretext for seizing control of Manchuria. This incident led to the Manchurian crisis (1931–1933)* involving apparent Japanese aggression in Manchuria and displaying the inertia of U.S. and League of Nations* diplomacy in meeting the challenge. Ferrell, Robert H., *American Diplomacy in the Great Depression* (1957); *FR* (1931), 2:10–80; *FR: Japan, 1931–1941*, 1:1–160; Thorne, Christopher, *The Limits of Foreign Policy* (1972).

MUNICH CONFERENCE (1938). This celebrated conference in late September 1938 turned *appeasement* into an ugly word. Neville Chamberlain, the prime minister of Great Britain, and Edouard Daladier, premier of France, appeased Adolf Hitler by consenting to the cession by Czechoslovakia of the Sudetenland to Germany, Teschen to Poland, and parts of southern Slovakia and Ruthenia to Hungary, costing the Czechs one-third of their territory and population and virtually all of the country's defensive and political viability. In return, Hitler promised to expand Germany no further. At the time of the conference, President Franklin D. Roosevelt contemplated offering his services as an arbitrator but resorted to a message to the concerned parties expressing his confidence that all problems could be settled peacefully. After the agreement, the State Department announced that it had brought "a universal sense of relief" but pointedly shied away from making a qualitative judgment on its merits. *FR* (1938), 1:657–739; Langer, William L., and S. Everett Gleason, *The Challenge to Isolation* (1952); Offner, Arnold A., *The Origins of the Second World War* (1975).

MUNRO-BLANCHET TREATY (1932). This treaty, signed by U.S. Minister to Haiti Dana G. Munro and Foreign Minister Albert Blanchet on September 6, 1932, would have returned to Haiti a good measure of control over its fiscal and military operations after years of American occupation. Haitian control of its National Guard was to be finalized by December 31, 1934, with the concomitant withdrawal of U.S. Marines. Haiti was to have a "fiscal representative" from the United States to supervise affairs after 1934 until a bond issue dating back to 1919 was retired. The Haitian National Assembly, however, feeling there were too many strings attached and wishing to embarrass President Stenio Vincent, rejected the treaty September 15. Ellis, L. Ethan, *Republican Foreign Policy, 1921–1933* (1968); Munro, Dana G., *The United States and the Caribbean Republics, 1921–1933* (1974).

MURPHY, DOMINIC IGNATIUS (1847–1930). Born May 31, 1847, and educated in Philadelphia, Dominic Murphy worked as a journalist and lawyer before 1871. In that year, he obtained a position in the U.S. Pension Office and remained there until 1897. From 1896 to 1897, he was commissioner of pensions. After leaving the Pension Office, Murphy practiced law in Washington until 1904, when he became secretary of the Isthmian Canal Commission. A year in this post led to a consular career that took him to Bordeaux (1905–1909), St. Gall, Switzerland (1909–1914), and Amsterdam (1914–1915) as consul,* and to Sofia (1915–1919) and Stockholm (1919–1924) as consul general. In Sofia, he performed valuable service during wartime, inducing Bulgaria to ask the Allies for an armistice and taking care of the interests of British prisoners of war and interned subjects. In Stockholm, Murphy worked effectively to better commercial and cultural relations. He married Bessie Atkinson in 1904 and died in Stockholm on April 13, 1930. *DAB*, 13:347; *NCAB*, 13:599; *New York Times*, April 14, 1930.

MURPHY, RICHARD WILLIAM (b. 1929). Richard W. Murphy was born in Boston on July 29, 1929, and graduated from Harvard (B.A., 1951) and Emanuel College, Cambridge (A.B. 1953). After two years in the army, Murphy married Anne Herrick Cook and joined the State Department in 1955. Until 1970, he served in a succession of minor posts in Africa and the Middle East. In 1970, he became director of Arabian peninsular affairs in the State Department. Between 1971 and 1983, Murphy held a series of ambassadorial posts: Mauritania, 1971–1974; Syria, 1974–1978; Philippines, 1978–1981; and Saudi Arabia, 1981–1983. He was the first U.S. ambassador to Syria after the resumption of relations, which had been broken following the Six-Day War (1967).* In Saudi Arabia, Murphy had to contend with the controversial sale of Airborne Warning and Control System (AWACS) radar surveillance plans, which Israel felt represented a major threat to its security. In 1983, Murphy returned to Washington as assistant secretary of state for Near Eastern and South Asian affairs. In that position, he serves as special envoy for the Middle East, negotiating problems according to need. He was, for example, involved in negotiating the Israeli withdrawal from Lebanon in 1984. In 1985, he was named career ambassador. *International Herald Tribune*, November 17–18, 1984; *New York Times* August 5, 1983; *WWA* (1986–1987):2020.

MURPHY, ROBERT DANIEL (1894–1978). One of the most ubiquitous U.S. diplomats between 1940 and 1970, Robert D. Murphy was born in Milwaukee on October 28, 1894, attended Marquette University, and graduated from George Washington University Law School (LL.B., 1920; LL.M. 1921). Before law school, Murphy had been a clerk in the U.S. legation in Bern, Switzerland; after law school, he embarked on a Foreign Service career that took him to minor posts in Zurich, Munich, Seville, and Washington by 1930. In that year, he went to Paris as a consul* and remained there until 1941, serving as first secretary (1936–1939), counselor* (1939–1941), and chargé d'affaires* (1940). He negotiated an economic pact with the French government in North Africa in 1940 allowing American observers into Axis-controlled areas, which proved helpful during the later North African campaign. In the months before that campaign, Murphy acted as a liaison between French military authorities and the Allied headquarters, winning general French support for the invasion while revealing few details about it to the French before its actual occurrance on November 8, 1942. He was attached to General Dwight D. Eisenhower's headquarters, serving in a variety of assignments and attending various conferences and functioning throughout the war as Eisenhower's chief political adviser. After the war, Murphy was political adviser to the U.S. occupation government in Germany, working closely with General Lucius D. Clay* until 1949, when he became ambassador to Belgium. In Brussels, he worked to implement the Marshall Plan,* advised Minister Perle Mesta* in Luxembourg, and helped negotiate a new agreement for purchasing uranium ore from the Belgian Congo. After three years in Belgium, Murphy was appointed the first ambassador to Japan following the 1951 peace treaty. He had to deal with Communist agitation in Japan, as well as the maintenance of U.S. control over the Bonin Islands, the improvement of Japanese–South Korean relations, and the Korean truce talks. From 1953 to 1959, Murphy was in Washington in a succession of important State Department posts, generally concerning himself with Soviet affairs but helping in the Trieste negotiations, 1954, and serving as a special representative of President Eisenhower in Lebanon during the 1958 U.S. intervention. After arranging the visit of Soviet Premier Nikita Khrushchev to the United States in 1959, Murphy retired from the State Department and was associated with the Corning Glass Works. In 1969, he advised President Richard M. Nixon on his diplomatic appointments, and in 1976 he served on the Foreign Intelligence Advisory Board. He married Mildred Claire Taylor in 1921 (she died in 1974), wrote his memoirs, *Diplomat among Warriors* (1964), and died in New York City on January 9, 1978. *CB* (1958): 294–96; Gimbel, John, *The American Occupation of Germany* (1968); McNeill, William H., *America, Britain, and Russia* (1953); *NCAB*, G:196; *New York Times*, January 10, 1978.

MURRAY, WILLIAM VANS (1760–1803). A native of Cambridge, Maryland, where he was born February 9, 1760, William Vans Murray was privately educated in Maryland but studied law at London's Middle Temple from 1784 to 1787. Admitted to the bar in 1787, he began the practice of law but within a year had embarked on a political career that took him to the Maryland legislature (1788–1790) and the U.S. House of Representatives (1791–1797). In the House, he was a Federalist, an adviser to President George Washington, and a supporter and friend of President John Adams,* who named him minister to the Netherlands (1797–1801). There he got into some trouble by prematurely recognizing a short-lived revolutionary regime in 1798 but, staying at his post, proved valuable as a conduit for communication between France and the United States during the quasi-war.* After French Foreign Minister Charles Maurice de Talleyrand had, through Murray, convinced Adams of the sincerity of his request for renewed negotiations, the president appointed Murray, along with Oliver Ellsworth and William R. Davie, to a new commission to France. It was this commission that negotiated the Convention of 1800.* According to Hill, Murray emphasized the point to his fellow commissioners that ending the hostilities and abrogating the old treaty were more important to the United States than receiving indemnity payments for captured ships. Murray resigned his post in 1801 and retired to his farm in Maryland, dying either there or in Philadelphia on December 11, 1803. He married Charlotte Hughens in 1789 and wrote a political treatise, *Political Sketches*, in 1787, dedicating it to his friend John Adams. *DAB*, 13:368; DeConde, Alexander, *The Quasi-War* (1966); Hill, Peter P., *William Vans Murray, Federalist Diplomat* (1971); *NCAB*, 11:360.

MURROW, EDWARD [EGBERT] ROSCOE (1908–1965). The best-known World War II correspondent, Edward R. Murrow was born April 25, 1908, in Greensboro, North Carolina, and graduated from Washington State College in 1930. After working a short while in the timber industry in the Northwest, Murrow became assistant director of the International Institute of Education, 1932–1935, before joining the Columbia Broadcasting System as a reporter. From 1937 to 1945 Murrow was in Europe for CBS, gaining national fame as a result of his wartime broadcasts from London, especially during the Battle of Britain in 1940. His portrayal of British courage was effective in pushing American opinion toward joining the war on the Allied side; he was also influential in changing British attitudes toward the eventuality of American participation. From December 1940, he urged American military intervention against Germany. After the war, Murrow was a vice-president and director of public affairs for CBS, but tiring of administrative routine in 1947, he returned to the air as a radio and television commentator and host of highly regarded series such as "Person to Person" and "See It Now." As director of the United States Information Agency* from 1961 to 1964, Murrow tried to professionalize the operation and maintain objectivity in the Voice of America, not always successfully. Married in 1934 to Janet Huntington Brewster, Murrow died April 27, 1965, in Pawling, New York. *CB* (1953): 448–50; Culbert, David H., *News for Everyman* (1976); Kendrick, Alexander, *Prime Time: The Life of Edward R. Murrow* (1969); Stott, William, *Documentary Expression and Thirties America* (1973); *New York Times*, April 28, 1965; *WWWA*, 3 (1951–1960): 692.

MUSKIE, EDMUND SIXTUS (b. 1914). Born in Rumford, Maine, on March 28, 1914, Edmund Muskie received a B.A. from Bates College in 1936 and a law degree from Cornell in 1939. Following naval service in World War II, he practiced law in Maine. In 1948, he married Jane Francis Gray and was elected to the Maine House of Representatives. From 1955 to 1958, he served as governor of his home state. In 1959, he began a lengthy career as a U.S. senator, where he was regarded as a political moderate but liberal on social issues and a supporter of President Lyndon B. Johnson's Vietnam policy. In 1968, he joined Hubert Humphrey on the Democratic ticket. When Cyrus Vance* resigned his post as secretary of state in 1980, President Jimmy Carter selected Muskie as Vance's successor. With less than a year left in the administration, Muskie's efforts were concentrated on resolving the Iranian hostage crisis.* After leaving public office in 1981, Muskie joined a Washington law firm, but in 1986 he served on the Tower Commission, which made a preliminary investigation of the Iran-contra affair.* He is the author of *Journeys* (1972) and the coauthor, with McGeorge Bundy,* of *Presidential Promises and Performances* (1980). *New York Times*, February 27, 1987; *WWA* (1986–1987):2025.

MUTUAL AND BALANCED FORCE REDUCTION (MBFR) TALKS. These negotiations concern efforts to reduce conventional force levels in Central Europe as a means to increase political and military stability and reduce tensions. The talks, which began in 1973 and are customarily held in Vienna, involve representatives from the North Atlantic Treaty Organization (NATO)* and Warsaw Pact. A major worry of NATO is the numerical superiority of the Eastern bloc. A proposal, introduced in 1982 by the West, called for agreement on a collective total of 900,000 army and air force personnel for each side, with reductions to that level to be achieved in stages over several years. The principal difficulties in reaching agreement lie in the discrepancy between what the East claims it deploys and what Western intelligence sources conclude is the true total, a difference of 160,000 troops, and in agreeing on verification procedures, wherein the East is reluctant to accept anything involving direct on-site observation or inspection. Some critics of the Intermediate Nuclear Force (INF) Treaty,* which also bears on Central European security, asserted that it would be dangerous to ratify the INF Treaty without an MBFR treaty. Some of the peripheral concerns with conventional forces have been dealt with at the periodic meetings held since the Helsinki Accords (1975).* *New York Times*, January 19, 1984, December 6, 1985, March 21, December 12, 1986.

MUTUAL SECURITY ACT (1951). The passage of the Mutual Security Act in 1951, the first of several annual acts, represented a new approach to foreign aid, reflecting the heightening tensions of the cold war.* In May 1951, President Harry S Truman requested $8.5 billion for what he called the Mutual Security Program, of which $6.3 billion was designated for military assistance, principally to European allies, and $2.2 billion was for economic aid. Congress approved this request in the Mutual Security Act of 1951 (although reducing the amount appropriated to $7.5 billion) and created the Mutual Security Agency (MSA) to administer foreign aid. The MSA was changed to the Foreign Operations Administration (FOA) in 1953, and the FOA was changed to the International Cooperation Administration (ICA) in 1955, but functionally it was the same agency. A consistent point of controversy was whether foreign assistance should be distributed in the form of grants or loans, with loans gradually increasing as a proportion of the total aid amount. The total foreign aid budget during the 1950s declined in most years, however, as Congress chose to emphasize assistance to U.S. private investment abroad. The Mutual Security Act was replaced in 1961 by the Foreign Assistance Act,* but during the 1950s, about $18 billion had been disbursed, mainly to recipient nations on the periphery of the Communist bloc. Foreign aid in the 1950s became an important component of the global policy of containment.* Pastor, Robert A., *Congress and the Politics of U.S. Foreign Economic Policy, 1929–1976* (1980).

NAMIBIA. Formerly known as Southwest Africa, this territory is important to the United States for its deposits of strategic minerals. Its geographic location between South Africa and Angola gives it importance in the geopolitics of southern Africa. While there is much sentiment internationally for Namibian independence (the United Nations* passed a resolution supporting independence in 1978), U.S. policy has been to oppose South African attempts to annex the land but not to oppose South African occupation. Under the policy of constructive engagement,* the United States hoped to link a settlement to the Namibian question with an end to the Angolan civil war,* with the help of a cooperative South Africa. In December 1988, Angola, Cuba, and South Africa signed an agreement providing for the independence of Namibia and the gradual withdrawal of Cuban troops from Angola. The accord was facilitated by U.S. and Soviet diplomatic mediation. The agreement, however, did not deal with the Angolan civil war. Baker, Pauline H., "United States Policy in Southern Africa," *Current History* 86, 520 (May 1987):193–96, 225–27; Bissell, Richard E., *South Africa and the United States* (1982); Cooper, Allan D., *U.S. Economic Power and Political Influence in Namibia, 1700–1982* (1982); *New York Times,* December 14, 1988.

NANKING, TREATY OF (1842). This treaty ended the so-called Opium War (1839–1842) between Britain, whose merchants carried on trade in opium, and China, whose government wanted to stop it. The treaty restored peace and gave Britain an unrestricted right to trade at five south China ports, as well as the possession of Hong Kong. This was the first treaty between China and a Western nation and set an example that Americans followed in the Treaty of Wang-hsia (1844).* Dennett, Tyler, *Americans in Eastern Asia* (1922); Goetzmann, William H., *When the Eagle Screamed* (1966).

NANKING INCIDENT (1927). In March 1927, Nationalist Chinese forces entered Nanking and attacked the foreign community, killing one American and five Europeans. American, British, and Japanese diplomats proposed that Chiang Kai-shek be sent an ultimatum demanding that amends be made lest sanctions be imposed. The State Department hesitated, fearing to make threats it had no desire to back up. A split in internal Chinese affairs between Chiang and the Communists encouraged Secretary of State Frank B. Kellogg* to continue the policy of inaction, much to the unhappiness of American ambassador J.V.A. McMurray, who favored more resolute action. In the end, the Allies undertook no concerted measures against Chiang and the Nationalists. Cohen, Warren I.,

America's Response to China (1971); Ellis, L. Ethan, *Republican Foreign Policy, 1921–1933* (1968).

NATIONAL BIPARTISAN COMMISSION ON CENTRAL AMERICA.
Appointed by the Reagan administration in July 1983, this twelve-member panel headed by former Secretary of State Henry Kissinger* was instructed to find a "long-term, unified national approach" toward U.S. policy in Central America. With Jeane Kirkpatrick* as President Reagan's personal representative on the commission and none of the members known opponents of administration policy, it was not surprising that the commission's report, issued in January 1984, substantially supported the administration's current actions. The report confirmed that vital interests of the United States were at stake in Central America and recommended an $8 billion, five-year economic aid program to redress socio-economic problems that had deep roots in the region's history. The idea behind the commission was to win public support for U.S. policy in Central America, but critics questioned whether the security threat from the region was serious, whether it was appropriate (as the commission did) to employ the domino theory,* and whether the huge economic aid package would buy peace and stability. Within a short time, interest in the Kissinger Commission (as it was commonly known) report died down, and administration policy continued its course. Findling, John E., *Close Neighbors, Distant Friends* (1987); LeoGrande, William M., "Through the Looking Glass: The Kissinger Report on Central America," *World Policy Journal* 1, 2 (Winter 1984): 251–84; *The Report of the President's National Bipartisan Commission on Central America* (1984); *New York Times*, January 17–18, February 20, 1984.

NATIONAL DEFENSE ACT (1940). Of particular significance was Section 6 of this act, passed July 2, 1940, providing for the control of exports deemed necessary for national security. Although the Treasury Department wanted to exercise this control, the act gave that power to the president, who appointed a special administrator, Russell L. Maxwell, responsible directly to the White House and the State Department. Beginning in mid-1940, soon after passage of the act, Section 6 was applied to Japan and intensified in stages, so that more and more of the raw materials and supplies Japan considered essential were cut off, including metals, chemicals, machine tools, and industrial parts. In May 1941, Section 6 was applied to all territories of the United States, including the Philippines. The economic restrictions that Section 6 placed on Japan were a factor in its decision for war. Divine, Robert A., *The Reluctant Belligerent* (1965); Feis, Herbert, *The Road to Pearl Harbor* (1950); Langer, William L., and S. Everett Gleason, *The Challenge to Isolation* (1952).

NATIONAL SECURITY COUNCIL (NSC), presidential advisory body, 1947– . World War II created a need for an agency to coordinate diplomatic and defense interests. In 1944, therefore, the ad hoc State-War-Navy Coordinating Committee (SWNCC) was created. With the passage of the National

Security Act (1974), this committee became the State-Army-Navy-Air Force Coordinating Committee (SANACC), but this was soon superseded by the present National Security Council, created in the National Security Act (1947). This body consists of the president, vice-president, the secretaries of state and defense, and the director of the Office of Emergency Planning as regular members. Its general function is to advise the president on the integration of foreign, military, and domestic policies related to national security. An administrative organization, headed by the national security adviser and headquartered in the White House, it has evolved to a point where it makes investigations and recommendations, one of the most important of which was NSC-68.* Although Presidents John F. Kennedy and Lyndon B. Johnson made comparatively limited use of the NSC, President Richard M. Nixon and his national security adviser, Henry Kissinger,* elevated the NSC to the major foreign policymaking body of the federal government, bypassing the State Department almost entirely. In more recent years, considerable rivalry has developed between the national security adviser and the secretary of state over who has the more influential role in foreign policymaking. Problems developed between Cyrus Vance* and Zbigniew Brzezinski* in the Carter administration, and between Alexander Haig* and William Clark* in the Reagan administration. In 1985–1986, operatives attached to the NSC became deeply involved in the Iran-contra scandal,* causing many observers to suggest that the NSC had evolved well beyond what its creators intended it to be. Johnson, Richard A., *The Administration of the United States Foreign Policy* (1971); Nelson, Anna Kasten, "President Truman and the Evolution of the National Security Council," *Journal of American History* 72, 2 (September 1985): 360–78; Plischke, Elmer, *The Conduct of American Diplomacy* (1967); Szulc, Tad, *The Illusion of Peace* (1978).

NATO. See NORTH ATLANTIC TREATY ORGANIZATION.

NAZI-SOVIET NON-AGGRESSION PACT (1939). This German-Russian treaty provided that if one country went to war, the other would remain neutral in the conflict. A secret clause provided further that if war did come, Germany and Russia would divide Poland between them. In addition, Germany asserted a sphere of influence in Lithuania, the Soviets in the other Baltic states and Finland. The treaty was to remain in force for ten years but was terminated abruptly by the German attack on Russia in June 1941. American officials were disappointed when this treaty was concluded but were not surprised, and many correctly felt it could not be maintained very long. *FR* (1939), 1:312–50; Gaddis, John L., *Russia, the Soviet Union and the United States* (1978); Offner, Arnold A., *The Origins of the Second World War* (1975).

NEGROPONTE, JOHN DIMITRI (b. 1939). Born in London, England, on July 21, 1939, John D. Negroponte received a B.A. degree from Yale University in 1950 and joined the foreign service the same year. After a stint as vice-consul in Hong Kong, 1961–1963, he spent four years in Saigon at the height of the

Vietnam War, working as political officer in the U.S. embassy. In 1968–1969, he was a member of the U.S. delegation to the Paris peace talks, and from 1970 to 1973, he was on the staff of the National Security Council,* where he played a key role in communicating the proposed Paris Peace Agreement (1973)* to South Vietnamese President Nguyen Van Thieu in 1972 and then advising National Security Adviser Henry Kissinger,* the chief negotiator, that Thieu would, in all likelihood, not accept it. In 1973, Negroponte was assigned to Quito as a political counselor*; two years later he went to Thessaloniki as consul general.* He married Diana Mary Villiers in 1976 and returned to Washington in 1977 as deputy assistant secretary of state for oceans and fisheries affairs, followed in 1981 by a parallel move to the office of East Asian and Pacific Affairs. In 1981, the incoming Reagan administration, aware of his experience in Saigon, named Negroponte ambassador to Honduras. There he was instrumental in orchestrating much of the U.S. effort to aid the contras,* while keeping on excellent terms with the Honduran military establishment and civilian government leaders, to the point where his influence seemed to dominate national affairs in Honduras. In 1985, in what was called a routine rotation, Negroponte was brought back to Washington, where he served as assistant secretary of state for the international environment and scientific bureau. Findling, John E., *Close Neighbors, Distant Friends* (1987); Hersch, Seymour M., *The Price of Power: Kissinger in the Nixon White House* (1983); *New York Times*, April 3, 1983, July 22, 1984.

NEOISOLATIONISM. A term current in the late 1960s and 1970s "neoisolationism" describes a policy related to U.S. withdrawal from Vietnam and involving, in general, reduced commitments, particularly military, in other parts of the world. George F. Kennan* applied the term to his own thinking at this time, suggesting a less visible role abroad for the United States (particularly in Southeast Asia) and more concern with domestic problems. Neoisolationists would assert that the United States no longer has the capability nor should feel the obligation to police the rest of the world. Neoisolationism was seen in a practical sense in matters such as Senator Michael J. Mansfield's* call in 1969 for major troop withdrawals from Europe. Brandon, Henry, *The Retreat of American Power* (1972); Patterson, Thomas G., "George F. Kennan and American Foreign Policy," in Merli, Frank G., and Theodore A. Wilson, *Makers of American Diplomacy*, vol. 2 (1974).

NEUTRALITY, diplomatic principal. Neutrality is the state of abstaining from a war (or an alliance) and remaining on friendly terms with belligerents on either side. The concept of neutrality, though known in the Middle Ages, became significant with the development of the nation-state system around the sixteenth century. Neutrals have the obligation to remain strictly impartial in a conflict; in return, belligerents abstain from attacking or provoking the neutral. From the sixteenth century, rules for neutrals have slowly evolved but are tenuous and not always consistent or universally accepted. Several international conferences have produced declarations or treaties attempting to define precisely neutrals' rights (Declaration of Paris, 1856*; Declaration of London, 1909*), but these treaties have not received universal approbation. Burchard, Edwin, and William Potter Lage, *Neutrality for the United States* (1937).

NEUTRALITY ACT (1935). Passed by Congress and signed by President Franklin D. Roosevelt in August 1935, this act authorized the president to identify belligerents publicly and suspend exports of war materiel to them. The act also created the National Munitions Control Board to regulate the arms traffic and prohibited American shippers from transporting munitions to belligerents or to neutrals for transshipment to belligerents. The president was given discretionary power to ban the shipment of war-related goods to belligerent ships, to ban belligerent submarines from American waters, and to prevent Americans from traveling on belligerent ships except at their own risk. The administration, especially Secretary of State Cordell Hull,* had misgivings about the impartial nature of the arms embargo, feeling that the president ought to be able to distinguish between an aggressor nation and its victim. The public generally supported the act as necessary to keep the United States out of war. The act was temporary; the arms embargo clause expired on February 29, 1936. Adler, Selig, *The Isolationist Impulse* (1957); Divine, Robert A., *The Illusion of Neutrality* (1962).

NEUTRALITY ACT (1936). A successor to the Neutrality Act (1935),* this act was signed by President Franklin D. Roosevelt on February 29, 1936, and extended the arms embargo feature of the previous act. In addition, the new act banned virtually all loans to belligerents, giving credence to the Nye Committee's* conclusion that bankers had helped bring the United States into World War I. This act also limited the President's discretion in implementing the arms embargo and in restricting trade in raw materials. Although not entirely happy with the new limitations placed on his power, Roosevelt signed the act, possibly because 1936 was an election year or because of the intensive lobbying activities of concerned groups such as Italian-Americans, who were determined to weaken the bill's overall impact. Also, Roosevelt wanted some leverage to be able to work actively with other nations to restrain aggression. A temporary measure like its predecessor, the Neutrality Act of 1936 had an expiration date of May 1, 1937. According to Adler, this act reflected American unwillingness to cooperate even tacitly with the League of Nations* in implementing the principle of collective security.* Adler, Selig, *The Isolationist Impulse* (1957); Divine, Robert A., *The Illusion of Neutrality* (1962).

NEUTRALITY ACT (1937). Third in the series of Neutrality Acts, this received President Roosevelt's signature on May 1, 1937, and fulfilled the goals of those seeking permanent neutrality legislation. Upon the outbreak of war deemed threatening to U.S. security, this act provided automatically for an arms embargo, a loan prohibition, a ban on passenger travel on belligerent ships, and a prohibition on the arming of U.S. merchant ships. The act also included a cash-and-carry* plan, for a two-year period, requiring belligerents trading in noncontraband goods with the United States to pay cash for the goods and carry them away in foreign ships, an idea originally suggested by Bernard Baruch* in 1935 as a way to preserve safely some of the profits of neutral trade in a time of war. According to Divine, this hybrid act did not satisfy anyone completely. Adler, Selig, *The Isolationist Impulse* (1957); Divine, Robert A., *The Illusion of Neutrality* (1962); Porter, David L., *The Seventy-sixth Congress and World War II, 1939–1940* (1979).

NEUTRALITY ACT (1939). Passed by Congress in November 1939, after the outbreak of war in Europe, and influenced by sympathy toward beleaguered Britain and France, this act did away with the impartial arms embargo feature of earlier neutrality legislation and replaced it with general cash-and-carry* provisions. In addition, American ships were not to enter a war zone, as defined around Northern Europe, or any belligerent port anywhere in Europe. Restrictions on loans and passenger travel were continued as in the Neutrality Act (1937).* Greatly pleasing to Britain and France, the act was a substantial blow to isolationists* who believed in the fundamental evil of munitions sales. In November 1941, the act was amended to permit the travel of U.S. merchant ships through the war zone to British ports, a move that would inevitably have led to war with Germany, had the attack on Pearl Harbor* not occurred. Adler, Selig, *The Isolationist Impulse* (1957); Divine, Robert A., *The Illusion of Neutrality* (1962); Porter, David L., *The Seventy-sixth Congress and World War II, 1939–1940* (1979).

NEUTRALITY PROCLAMATION (1793). Issued by President George Washington, this proclamation announced America's neutrality in the Anglo-French War without using the word *neutrality*. It required Americans to "conduct themselves in a friendly and impartial" manner toward all belligerents. Americans were not to carry contraband* "by the modern usage of nations." The proclamation stemmed from debate within the Washington administration over the validity of the Franco-American Treaty (1778).* Ritcheson, Charles R., *Aftermath of Revolution: British Policy Toward the United States, (1783–1795* (1969); Sears, Louis M., *George Washington and the French Revolution* (1960).

NEW CONSORTIUM. In 1917, European bankers, members of the 1911 consortium that had made loans to China, appealed for U.S. assistance to contain Japanese financial advances in northern China and Manchuria. The threat of excessive Japanese financial influence in China was increased that year when China sought a large new loan. In July 1918, the United States, which had withdrawn from the earlier consortium, invited Japan, France, and Great Britain to join in a new consortium, requiring members to consider as consortium loans any individual loans they now held. Japan, not surprisingly, objected to this requirement but after lengthy negotiations entered the consortium in May 1920. Although the new consortium never made any loans, it did deter further Japanese financial control in China. Curry, Roy Watson, *Woodrow Wilson and Far Eastern Policy, 1913–1921* (1957); Parrini, Carl P., *Heir to Empire* (1969).

NEW MANIFEST DESTINY, diplomatic catchphrase, c. 1890s. *New Manifest Destiny* describes a revival of the spirit of American expansionism of the 1840s, bolstered by a belief in Anglo-Saxon racial superiority and an obligation to civilize and Christianize "lesser" peoples of the world. Unlike the earlier Manifest Destiny,* expansion was no longer continental but transoceanic, with expansionist efforts directed primarily at Latin America and the Far East. New Manifest Destiny, like its predecessor, was to some a rationalization for crasser concerns of economic exploitation, a way to escape the depression of the 1890s, and a matter of keeping up with Great Britain and Germany, the other great Anglo-Saxon nations. Healy, David, *US Expansionism* (1970); Weinberg, Albert, *Manifest Destiny* (1935).

NEW NAVY, catchphrase, c. 1880s–1890s. This term was applied to the rebuilding and modernization of the U.S. Navy beginning in 1883 and continuing through the 1890s, and encompassing the building of steel ships, the opening in 1884 of the Naval War College, and increasing congressional awareness that ever-widening American interests required the protection of a navy comparable to European navies. Under Secretary of the Navy Benjamin Tracy (1889–1893), battleships were first commissioned, and the navy rapidly grew in strength. This growth continued during the second Cleveland administration (1893–1897), in which five battleships were commissioned and six more authorized. LaFeber, Walter, *The New Empire* (1963); Plesur, Milton, *America's Outward Thrust* (1971).

NEW PANAMA CANAL COMPANY, a French company (Compagnie nouvelle du canal de Panama) that took over a defunct concession in Panama for an isthmian canal. Its American counsel, William Nelson Cromwell,* and a French diplomat and engineer with long experience in Panama, Philippe Bunau-Varilla, worked hard between 1899 and 1902 to swing congressional opinion in favor of the Panamanian route as opposed to the Nicaraguan route. Successful in their lobbying for the route, they also managed to sell for $40 million the interests and property of the New Panama Canal Company to the United States. Later Bunau-Varilla was closely intertwined in the Panama Revolution (November 1903), subsequently became Panamanian minister to the United States, and signed the Hay–Bunau-Varilla Treaty* for the construction of an American isthmian canal across Panama. Bunau-Varilla, Philippe, *Panama: The Creation, Destruction, and Resurrection* (1914); Miner, Dwight C., *The Fight for the Panama Route* (1940); Munro, Dana G., *Intervention and Dollar Diplomacy in the Caribbean, 1900–1921* (1964).

NINE-POWER TREATY (1921). This treaty, signed February 6, 1922, by nine nations at the Washington Conference,* marked agreement on a set of principles with regard to China. The powers stated their willingness to respect

Chinese independence, aid Chinese efforts toward governmental stability, support equal commercial opportunity in China, and refrain from taking advantage of China's instability to gain special privileges. The last principle was a public statement of the Lansing-Ishii Agreement (1917).* In general, the Nine-Power Treaty was a public international affirmation of the Open Door policy.* The U.S. Senate ratified the treaty in March 1922. Buckley, Thomas H., *The United States and the Washington Conference, 1921–1922* (1970); Doenecke, Justus D., comp., *The Diplomacy of Frustration* (1981); Sadao, Asada, "Japan's Special Interests and the Washington Conference, 1921–1922," *American Historical Review* 67, 1 (1961–1962): 62–70.

NINTH INTERNATIONAL CONFERENCE OF AMERICAN STATES (1948). See **BOGOTÁ CONFERENCE (1948).**

NITZE, PAUL HENRY (b. 1907). One of the most prominent arms control negotiators of the 1970s and 1980s, Paul Nitze was born in Amherst, Massachusetts, on January 16, 1907, and graduated from Harvard in 1928. He joined the investment banking firm of Dillon, Read and Company in 1928, remaining there until World War II, when he held a number of federal governmental positions. After the war, he began to focus on international affairs, serving as deputy director of the Office of International Trade Policy and deputy to the assistant secretary of state for economic affairs before 1950. In that year, he was named director of the Policy Planning Staff, a position he held until 1953, when he became president of the Foreign Service Education Foundation. During the Kennedy and Johnson administrations, 1961–1969, Nitze held defense-related positions, and in 1969, he was named to head the negotiating team for the Strategic Arms Limitation Talks (SALT).* Under his direction, SALT I was successfully concluded in 1972, and he stayed on for the beginning stages of SALT II but left government service in 1974. Late in the 1970s, he emerged as a leading critic of SALT II, endearing him to the new Reagan administration, which in 1981 lured him out of retirement to head once again the arms control negotiation team in the Geneva arms talks. In 1984, Nitze stepped down from the hectic pace of negotiation to become a special adviser on arms limitation to President Reagan. Despite his dislike of SALT II, he recommended that the administration continue its informal adherence to it while other arms talks went on. In the mid-1980s, he was involved in the Intermediate Nuclear Force (INF) Treaty* process, particularly with respect to verification matters, and he accompanied the president to the Reykjavik Summit (1986)* as an adviser. Nitze, who married Phyllis Pratt in 1932, is the author of *U.S. Foreign Policy, 1945–1955* (1956). Talbott, Strobe, *Deadly Gambits* (1984); *New York Times*, December 5, 6, 8, 1984, March 14, 1986, August 7, 12, October 10, 1986; *WWA* (1986–1987):2071.

NIXON DOCTRINE (1969). A response to Vietnam War criticism, to budgetary squeezes, and to a wave of neoisolationism,* the Nixon Doctrine was revealed by President Richard M. Nixon in a talk with newsmen on Guam on July 25,

1969, and reiterated during his subsequent Far Eastern tour. The Nixon Doctrine provided for the maintenance of the U.S. nuclear umbrella, as well as continuing air and naval power to defend Southeast Asia and Japan but stated that Asian troops, rather than U.S. troops, would have to fight any land war. The policy was to become effective only after the end of the Vietnam War and was not intended to abrogate any standing treaty commitments connected with the Southeast Asia Treaty Organization,* ANZUS,* or bilateral pacts with Japan, South Korea, the Philippines, or Taiwan. In 1971, the Nixon Doctrine was applied to Iran to justify increased economic and military aid to that country. Ravenal, criticizing the Nixon Doctrine, asserts that it presupposes the continuation of the policy of the containment* but makes the United States more dependent on its Asian allies without absolutely assuring that U.S. military involvement could be avoided. Rather, he concludes, the United States should review and not be afraid to revise containment to obviate as far as possible the likelihood of a military response to an Asian crisis. Brandon, Henry, *The Retreat of American Power* (1972); Etzold, Thomas H., "The Nixon Doctrine," in DeConde, Alexander, ed., *Encyclopedia of American Foreign Policy* (1979); George, Alexander L., and Richard Smoke, *Deterrence in American Foreign Policy* (1974); LaFeber, Walter, *America, Russia, and the Cold War, 1945–1984* (1985); Ravenal, Earl C., "The Nixon Doctrine and Our Asian Commitments," *Foreign Affairs* 49 (January 1971):201–17; Szulc, Tad, *The Illusion of Peace* (1978).

NOLTING, FREDERICK ERNEST (b. 1911). Born August 24, 1911, in Richmond, Virginia, Frederick E. Nolting graduated from the University of Virginia (B.A., 1933; M.A., 1934; Ph.D., 1942) and also received an M.A. from Harvard in 1941. While in school, he worked for an investment firm in Richmond. After navy service, 1942–1946, Nolting joined the State Department and served in a succession of minor posts until 1955, when he became a member of the U.S. delegation to the North Atlantic Treaty Organization.* In 1957, he was made the alternate U.S. permanent representative to the North Atlantic Council. In 1961, Nolting was appointed ambassador to Vietnam, with instructions to reestablish cordial relations with President Ngo Dinh Diem. He generally (and increasingly, during his tour there) supported Diem and his policies, tried to honor his requests for U.S. aid, and reassured him of continued U.S. backing. In 1963, Nolting was replaced by Henry Cabot Lodge, Jr.,* less sympathetic to and emotionally involved with Diem, representing similar views by the Kennedy administration. Later Nolting was criticized for his weak reports and poor information about changing conditions in Vietnam. Leaving the State Department, Nolting went to work as a vice-president of Morgan Guaranty Trust Company, remaining with that firm until 1973, when he began teaching at the University of Virginia. In 1975, he became director of the White Burkett Miller Center for Public Affairs. He married Olivia Lindsay Crumpler in 1940. Halberstam, David, *The Best and the Brightest* (1972); Karnow, Stanley, *Vietnam: A History* (1983); Walton, Richard J., *Cold War and Counterrevolution* (1972); WWA (1978–1979):2336.

NONCOLONIZATION, DOCTRINE OF (1823). A major principle enunciated in the Monroe Doctrine,* the doctrine of noncolonization emerged as a response to Russian and British moves to establish new colonies on the northwest coast of North America. John Quincy Adams,* secretary of state, was the originator of this principle, which stated that the United States would look with disfavor on any attempt to establish new colonies in the Western Hemisphere, that the hemisphere was "closed" to further colonization. Bemis, Samuel F., *John Quincy Adams and the Foundations of American Foreign Policy* (1949); Merk, Frederick, *The Oregon Question* (1967); Perkins, Dexter, *The Monroe Doctrine, 1823–1826* (1927).

NON-IMPORTATION ACT (1806). This act was the first of a series of American measures designed to end impressment* and British commercial restrictions by economic coercion. It prohibited the importation from England of certain articles, including beer, leather goods, glass, and silverware. Passed by Congress in April 1806, the act was not implemented until December 1807, as the Jefferson administration awaited the outcome of the Monroe-Pinkney Treaty* negotiations. In practice, the act had much less effect on imports than the Embargo Act* had on exports. The policy of nonimportation continued in nominal force throughout the whole prewar period. Horsman, Reginald, *The Causes of the War of 1812* (1962); Perkins, Bradford, *Prologue to War* (1961).

NON-INTERCOURSE ACT (1809). This act, which replaced the Embargo Act* in March 1809, closed export and import trade with both Britain and France, prohibited the entry of armed ships of those nations to American ports, and authorized the president to reopen trade with any power that revoked its decrees and respected America's neutral rights. Trade was permitted with areas outside the British Empire and those controlled by Napoleon. Weaker than the Embargo Act, the Non-Intercourse Act had no real power of economic coercion, and any effect it might have had was overshadowed by the events surrounding the Erskine Agreements* affair. American trade continued to suffer, and Congress replaced Non-Intercourse with Macon's Bill Number Two* in May 1810. Perkins, Bradford, *Prologue to War* (1961).

NONINTERVENTION, DOCTRINE OF (1823). Stated in the Monroe Doctrine,* the doctrine of nonintervention set forth America's objection to European intervention in the affairs of independent Western Hemisphere nations. This doctrine grew out of American suspicions of European plans to mount an expedition to recapture and recolonize Latin America for Spain. The Roosevelt Corollary (1904)* prescribed U.S. intervention in Latin America to ward off European intervention. Bemis, Samuel F., *John Quincy Adams and the Foundations of American Foreign Policy* (1949); Perkins, Dexter, *The Monroe Doctrine, 1823–1826* (1927).

NON-PROLIFERATION TREATY (1968). This treaty, which is designed to prevent the spread of nuclear weapons, continue efforts toward nuclear disarmament, and encourage peaceful uses of atomic energy, was drafted by the United States and the Soviet Union on May 31, 1968, and given the approval of the United Nations* General Assembly on June 12 by a vote of 95–4. Although twenty-one countries abstained from voting, it was signed later in the summer by over fifty nations, including the United States, Great Britain, and the USSR, and went into force on March 5, 1970, after ratification by the Big Three and forty other states. The treaty evolved over a period of some seven years through initiatives by several nonnuclear states and discussions in an Eighteen-Nation Disarmament Committee (established by joint agreement of the United States and the Soviet Union, this consisted of five North Atlantic Treaty Organization* members, five Warsaw Pact nations, and nonaligned nations); its main provisions include the prohibition of nuclear proliferation through transfer by a nuclear power to a nonnuclear power or through manufacture with other means of acquisition by nonnuclear powers and a pledge by nuclear states to pursue further disarmament talks. By July 1985, over 125 nations had ratified the treaty, but several countries with nuclear programs had not, including Argentina, Brazil, India, North Korea, Pakistan, and South Africa. Epstein, William, *The Last Chance* (1976); Shaker, Mohamed I., *The Nuclear Non-Proliferation Treaty: Origin and Implementation, 1959–1979*, 3 vols. (1980); Willrich, Mason, *Non-Proliferation Treaty* (1969).

NOOTKA SOUND AFFAIR, Anglo-Spanish conflict, 1790. Spain and Great Britain clashed over rival claims to a trading site on Vancouver Island, and war threatened. If war came, U.S. security would be involved by the likelihood of Spanish Florida's involvement, as well as a probable British request to send troops across American territory. There were suggestions that, as a price for American neutrality,* Britain would give up forts it still held in the Northwest. The crisis, however, passed without war. Burt, A. L., *The United States, Great Britain, and British North America* (1940); Darling, Arthur B., *Our Rising Empire* (1940); Manning, W. R., "The Nootka Sound Controversy," in *Annual Report of the American Historical Association, 1904*, pp. 279–333.

NORTH ATLANTIC TREATY (1949). This treaty was an outgrowth of the Brussels Pact* (1948) and was signed on April 4, 1949, by the five signatories of that treaty along with the United States, Canada, Denmark, Iceland, Italy, Portugal, and Norway. The treaty provided for mutual support in the event of an attack, in line with the right of collective self-defense recognized by Article 51 of the United Nations* Charter. The North Atlantic Treaty Organization (NATO)* was established to implement the treaty provisions. The U.S. Senate ratified the treaty in July 1949, and Greece (1952), Turkey (1952), and West Germany (1955) were later adherents. The principal Soviet response to the creation of NATO was the Warsaw Pact (1955), which formed a Soviet–Eastern European alliance known as the Warsaw Treaty Organization. Graebner, Norman

H., *Cold War Diplomacy* (1977); Heald, Morrell, and Lawrence S. Kaplan, *Culture and Diplomacy: The American Experience* (1977); Plano, Jack C., and Roy Olton, *The International Relations Dictionary* (1969).

NORTH ATLANTIC TREATY ORGANIZATION (NATO). An important step in the evolution of the policy of containment,* NATO was created by the North Atlantic Treaty (1949)* and came into existence in August 1949. The U.S. Congress approved the Organization, the first U.S. peacetime military alliance outside the hemisphere, with the idea that it would serve as deterrent to Soviet expansion and heighten Western European morale; Senator Arthur H. Vandenberg (R., Michigan)* considered it an extension of the Monroe Doctrine.* Administered by a body known as the North Atlantic Council, NATO features an integrated military force in Europe under the Supreme Allied Commander for Europe (SACEUR) and the Supreme Headquarters of the Allied Powers in Europe (SHAPE). The Korean War encouraged the formation of this standing military force, on duty by December 1950, with the popular General Dwight D. Eisenhower as commander. The main problems were the cost, both economically and politically, of rearmament in Europe and the additional demands made on the United States for increased aid. Much was accomplished by a special committee, composed of U.S., British, and French representatives, created in October 1951, to devise a fair way of spreading the burden fairly among the member nations. In 1954, NATO first included tactical nuclear weapons in its strategy due partly to shortfalls in raising conventional troops, partly as a response to the Soviet nuclear program, and partly to the influence of the Eisenhower-Dulles notion of massive retaliation.* An early and major point of controversy was the participation in NATO of German troops. This happened in 1952 as part of an integrated European command structure, the European Defense Community (EDC).* The EDC treaty was scuttled by the suspicious French in 1954, however, and was replaced by the West European Union, a similar plan. In 1966, the headquarters of NATO was moved from Paris to Brussels, and French troops were removed from NATO command because of French President Charles de Gaulle's desire to pursue a more independent foreign policy, particularly with respect to the Soviet Union. NATO remains an important factor in U.S. diplomacy and is the rationale for the maintenance of approximately 300,000 U.S. troops in Europe. Twelve nations were the original signatories of the North Atlantic Treaty: the United States, Canada, Iceland, the United Kingdom, France, Belgium, the Netherlands, Luxembourg, Denmark, Norway, Portugal, and Italy. Since 1949, West Germany, Greece, Turkey, and Spain have become members. By 1988, the question of defense burden sharing, intensified by high U.S. budget and balance-of-payments deficits, became an issue of contention. Although the alliance had cooperated on the development of cruise missiles* in the early 1980s and generally supported the Intermediate Nuclear Force (INF) Treaty (1987)* removing them, there were those who worried about the sincerity of the U.S. commitment to its NATO partners. Ireland, Timothy P., *Creating the Entangling Alliance* (1981); Kaplan, Lawrence S., *NATO and the United States: The Enduring Alliance* (1988); Rubenstein, Richard L., ed., *The Dissolving Alliance* (1987).

NORTH PACIFIC SEALING CONVENTION (1911). Designed to resolve the long-festering controversy over pelagic sealing in the Bering Sea, this treaty pledged its signatories to prohibit their nationals from the practice. In return, the United States agreed to give Japan and Canada each 15 percent of the skins taken from the seals harvested on the Pribilof islands. The arrangement was revised somewhat in a new convention in 1957. Bailey, Thomas A., "The North Pacific Sealing Convention of 1911," *Pacific Historical Review* 4 (1935):1–14; Tansill, C. C., *Canadian-American Relations, 1875–1911* (1943).

NO-TRANSFER PRINCIPLE AND RESOLUTION (1811). This was the first statement of American objection to the transfer of a Western Hemisphere colony from one European nation to another, lest a strong power acquire colonies enough to endanger American security. The 1811 resolution was directed specifically toward the Floridas and the possibility that a weak Spain might try to rid itself of an indefensible colony. The no-transfer principle is associated in American diplomatic history with the principles of the Monroe Doctrine* and was officially tied thereto by Secretary of State Hamilton Fish* in 1870. Bemis, Samuel F., *John Quincy Adams and the Foundations of American Foreign Policy* (1949); Perkins, Dexter, *The Monroe Doctrine, 1867–1907* (1937).

NOYES, EDWARD FOLLENSBEE (1832–1890). Edward F. Noyes was born October 3, 1832, in Haverhill, Massachusetts, and graduated from Dartmouth in 1857. He moved to Ohio, received a law degree from Cincinnati College (1858), and staked out a career in Ohio Republican politics. He was a Union officer in the Civil War and lost his left foot in battle. In 1865, he became a probate judge in Hamilton County and served six years. From 1872 to 1874, he was governor of Ohio but was defeated for reelection. Chairman of the Ohio delegation to the 1876 Republican convention, Noyes placed Rutherford B. Hayes's name in nomination and upon Hayes's election was rewarded with the appointment of minister to France. He was in France for four years, and although there were no major diplomatic crises, he was active in a number of minor matters. He assisted in an international monetary conference (1878) and secured American participation in the Paris Exposition of the same year. He was successful in quelling French fears about an American protectorate in Liberia and traveled to Africa on behalf of American commerce. In 1880, he was a delegate to the Paris Conference on Industrial Property. After his return to Ohio, he practiced law in Cincinnati and in 1889 was elected to the superior court of Ohio. He married Margaret Wilson Proctor in 1863 and was known for his oratorical abilities. Noyes died September 4, 1890, in Cincinnati. *DAB*, 13:587; *NCAB*, 3:142; Willson, Beckles, *America's Ambassadors to France, 1777–1927* (1928).

NSC-68, National Security Council* document, 1950. One of the foundations of cold war* defense and diplomacy, this National Security Council report asserted the bipolarity of world power between the United States and the Soviet Union and outlined Soviet efforts at world domination. Its policy recommendations were based on a perception of what the USSR was capable of doing rather than what it was likely to do. NSC-68 recommended that the United States stand up to the Soviet Union by imposing order in the non-Communist world, using military power to deter Soviet expansionism, and fighting limited wars if necessary. The report advised against negotiations with Moscow and urged instead the development of the hydrogen bomb, the buildup of conventional military forces (paid for by a large tax increase), the mobilization of American society to the anti-Communist cause, the creation of a strong U.S.-directed military alliance system, and the effective use of propaganda to win over the hearts of the Russian people. The outbreak of the Korean War in June 1950 seemed to confirm many of the assumptions of NSC-68 and made its implementation, in the form of greatly increased defense spending, feasible. *FR*, (1950), 1:126 passim; Gaddis, John L., *Russia, the Soviet Union and the United States* (1978); LaFeber, Walter, *America, Russia, and the Cold War 1945–1984* (1985).

NUCLEAR TEST BAN TREATY (1963). See **PARTIAL NUCLEAR TEST BAN TREATY (1963).**

NYE COMMITTEE, Senate investigating committee, 1934–1936. Formally known as the Special Committee Investigating the Munitions Industry, this committee was chaired by Senator Gerald P. Nye (R., North Dakota) and first met in September 1934. The committee continued to meet intermittently until February 1936, looking into collusion in the shipbuilding, armaments, powder, and chemical industries in the 1914–1917 period, before U.S. entry into World War I. In 1935, President Franklin D. Roosevelt requested the Nye Committee to look into the question of neutrality* and draw up legislative proposals for American neutrality during a European war, perhaps to divert the committee from its more sensational munitions investigations. Since the first Neutrality Act* was passed in August 1935, most historians have identified a close relationship between the committee's work and legislated neutrality, although Wiltz believes the committee's role has been exaggerated. Divine, Robert A., *The Illusion of Neutrality* (1962); *FR* (1934), 1:427–48; *FR* (1935), 1:316–73; Wiltz, John E., *In Search of Peace: The Senate Munitions Inquiry, 1934–1936* (1963).

O

O'BRIEN, THOMAS JAMES (1842–1933). A Michigan lawyer, Thomas J. O'Brien was born July 30, 1842, in Jackson County, Michigan, and went to the University of Michigan Law School, graduated with the class of 1865, and gained admittance to the bar the same year. He practiced law in Marshall, Michigan (1865–1871), and Grand Rapids (after 1871), married Delia Howard in 1873, took an active part in Republican politics, and was involved in the iron business. In 1905, he began an eight-year diplomatic career, which included appointments as minister to Denmark (1905–1907), ambassador to Japan (1907–1911, and ambassador to Italy (1911–1913). In Denmark, O'Brien initiated formal discussions that, in 1917, resulted in the purchase of the Danish West Indies. His stint in Japan was clouded by strained relations resulting from the anti-Japanese difficulties in California, but he did negotiate a successful commercial agreement assisting U.S. business in Japan and Korea and was influential in talks leading up to the Gentlemen's Agreement* by obtaining prior assurances that Japan would halt the emigration of laborers to the United States. During his Italian ambassadorship, O'Brien helped settle a dispute between Italy and Turkey that had flared into a short war before his arrival in 1911. He returned to his law practice in Grand Rapids in 1913 and died there on May 19, 1933. *DAB*, Supp. 1:578; *New York Times*, May 20, 1933.

O'DWYER, WILLIAM (1890–1964). Born July 11, 1890, in County Mayo, Ireland, William O'Dwyer studied at the University of Salamanca (Spain), came to the United States in 1910, and graduated from Fordham University Law School in 1923. He practiced law in New York City after 1923, served as county court judge, Kings County, 1938–1939, and Kings County district attorney, 1939–1942, and won national attention for smashing Murder, Inc., the Brooklyn chapter of a national organized crime syndicate that had special disciplinary enforcement responsibilities. During World War II, O'Dwyer was an officer in the army air force with assignments in materiel and investigations divisions. He became mayor of New York City in 1946, having previously lost a race for the position in 1941. His four years as mayor were controversial; he resigned in 1950 for health reasons but was later implicated in protection racket schemes during the Kefauver hearings. In 1950, he was named ambassador to Mexico, serving two years at that post. His duties were largely social in nature, and he achieved popularity through his gala multinational Fourth of July parties and his visits to every part of Mexico. He became well versed in Mexican affairs, however, and after resigning as ambassador practiced law in Mexico City until 1960. That year he returned to New York, where he lived largely in retirement until his death November 24, 1964. *New York Times*, November 25, 1964; *WWWA*, 4 (1961–1968): 715.

OLNEY, RICHARD (1835–1917). Richard Olney, who became secretary of state upon the death of Walter Q. Gresham* in 1895, was born in Oxford, Massachusetts, on September 15, 1835. A graduate of Brown University (A.M., 1856) and Harvard Law School (LL.B., 1858), he was admitted to the bar in 1859, married Agnes Park Thomas in 1861, and entered corporate law practice in Boston. He served a term in the Massachusetts legislature in 1874 but was quite unknown to the public in 1893 when President Grover Cleveland named him attorney general. And although he lacked foreign experience altogether, he became secretary of state about the time the Venezuelan crisis* reached a critical juncture. In this controversy, Olney was instrumental in pushing the British toward arbitration* by invoking the Monroe Doctrine* in a challenging diplomatic note. Among other diplomatic questions faced by Olney was the Mora claim from Spain, a long-standing problem finally settled with Enrique Dupuy de Lome, the Spanish minister to the United States, in such a way that there was a temporary improvement in Spanish-American relations over Cuba. In Cuba, Olney tried, without notable success, to convince the Spanish to institute reforms and appointed the expansionist-minded Fitzhugh Lee* as consul general* in Havana. In China, however, Olney was less interested in expansion; he blunted U.S. Minister Charles Denby's* attempts to promote American business. In general, according to Eggert, Olney naively believed that directness and determination would compensate for his lack of diplomatic experience. The fact that no harm came from his tenure as secretary of state may be less due to him than to the state of world affairs at the time. After 1897, Olney returned to his Boston law practice and did not reenter politics, although he was from time to time mentioned for political office. He died in Boston on April 8, 1917. *DAB*, 14:32; Eggert, Gerald G., *Richard Olney* (1974); *New York Times*, April 10, 1917.

OLNEY-PAUNCEFOTE CONVENTION (1897). Negotiated by Secretary of State Richard Olney* and British Minister to the United States Sir Julian Pauncefote, this general arbitration* treaty provided different arbitration procedures for different categories of claims: (1) less than £100,000; (2) greater than £100,000; and (3) territorial, "principle of grave importance," or "national rights." The treaty was rejected by the Senate in May 1897, 43–26, although it had been ratified by Britain. The U.S. rejection was due to the unpopularity of President Grover Cleveland, residual anti-British feelings of various senators, and senatorial jealousy of its prerogatives in treaty making. Eggert, Gerald G., *Richard Olney* (1974); Perkins, Bradford, *The Great Rapprochement* (1968).

ONTARIO, U.S.S., EXPEDITION (1817–1818). President James Monroe* sent the *Ontario*, commanded by Capt. James Biddle, to the Pacific Northwest to stake an American claim at the mouth of the Columbia River, which was done in August 1818. British Prime Minister Lord Castlereagh and Parliament acquiesced in this episode, although the British had claims in the same area. Bemis, Samuel F., *John Quincy Adams and the Foundations of American Foreign Policy* (1949); Perkins, Bradford, *Castlereagh and Adams* (1964).

OPEC. See **ORGANIZATION OF PETROLEUM EXPORTING COUNTRIES.**

OPEN DIPLOMACY, a diplomatic concept, the substance of Point I of Woodrow Wilson's Fourteen Points.* Open diplomacy meant not that discussions and negotiations leading up to a treaty should be public, as the American public believed in 1919, but rather that once a treaty was made, it should be exposed to public scrutiny. Hence there was disillusionment among the American public upon learning of the secret negotiations and arrangements that had been made at the Paris Peace Conference.* The League of Nations* Covenant called for the registration of all treaties, which was open diplomacy in the sense Wilson meant. Bailey, Thomas A., *Woodrow Wilson and the Lost Peace* (1944); Smith, Daniel, *The Great Departure* (1965).

OPEN DOOR POLICY, American diplomatic principle, 1899–1900. The Open Door policy developed from two sets of notes—Open Door Notes—written by Secretary of State John Hay* and Assistant Secretary of State W. W. Rockhill.* These notes requested that foreign powers operating in China give equal treatment to all commercial interests within their spheres of influence* and that all foreign powers respect Chinese territorial and administrative integrity. The policy had strong commercial overtones, and one diplomatic historian, W. A. Williams, has concluded that the Open Door principle is the foundation of all twentieth-century American diplomacy. Crane, David M., and Thomas A. Breslin, *An Ordinary Relationship* (1986); Fairbank, John K., *The United States and China*, rev. ed. (1958); McCormick, Thomas J., *China Market* (1967); Van Alstyne, Richard W., "The Open Door Policy," in DeConde, Alexander, ed., *Encyclopedia of American Foreign Policy* (1979); Williams, W. A., *The Tragedy of American Diplomacy* (1959).

ORDER-IN-COUNCIL (April 1809). This British order slightly relaxed the stipulations of the Orders-in-Council of November 1807.* The order declared a general blockade against Napoleon's France and its immediate satellites but opened Germany and the Baltic area to American and other properly licensed neutral ships. The order also reduced the duties on goods transshipped through Britain to Europe. Designed to help British merchants and placate Americans, the order's effectiveness was blunted by the difficulties surrounding the Erskine Agreement* affair, and Americans were subsequently discriminated against in the licensing procedure. Horsman, Reginald, *The Causes of the War of 1812* (1962); Perkins, Bradford, *Prologue to War* (1961).

ORDERS-IN-COUNCIL (November 1807). A British maritime regulation designed to deprive Britain's enemies of foreign supplies, the Orders-in-Council of November 1807 set up a virtual blockade on all countries at war with Great Britain. Neutrals could trade with enemy colonies and ship their products to "free ports" in British possessions, where they would then be shipped to Britain. Neutrals could also ship British goods to enemy ports, and if a British duty were paid, they could ship foreign goods out of Britain as well. The Orders-in-Council led to Napoleon's Milan Decree,* as well as to various U.S. measures designed to try to force an end to the commercial restrictions of Britain and France. These Orders-in-Council were revised by the Order-in-Council of April 1809.* Horsman, Reginald, *The Causes of the War of 1812* (1962); Perkins, Bradford, *Prologue to War* (1961).

OREGON QUESTION, Anglo-American diplomatic problem, 1818–1846. Historians apply this term to the matter of the status of the territory north of 42° north latitude, west of the Rocky Mountains, and south of 54° 40' north latitude, claimed by both Great Britain and the United States. This territory was commonly known as the Oregon Territory and was the subject of occasional diplomatic agreements from 1818 until its final disposition in the Oregon Treaty (1846).* Bemis, Samuel F., *John Quincy Adams and the Foundations of American Diplomacy* (1949); Merk, Frederick, *The Oregon Question* (1967); Pletcher, David, *The Diplomacy of Annexation* (1973).

OREGON TREATY (1846). Also known as the Buchanan-Pakenham Treaty, this agreement marked the final settlement of the Oregon question.* The treaty extended the U.S.-Canadian boundary line of 49° north latitude west to the Straits of San Juan de Fuca, then south around Vancouver Island. The British were granted navigation rights on the Columbia River, most of which now lay within American territory. At worst an even compromise, at best an American diplomatic victory, the Oregon Treaty gave the United States more territory by far than that "lost" in the highly criticized Webster-Ashburton Treaty (1842).* The treaty was negotiated by Secretary of State James Buchanan* and British Minister to the United States Richard Pakenham. Merk, Frederick, *The Oregon Question* (1967); Pletcher, David, *The Diplomacy of Annexation* (1973).

ORGANIZATION OF AMERICAN STATES (OAS). The idea for this regional organization for collective security* was conceived at the Mexico City Conference (1945)*; the organization itself was created at the Bogotá Conference (1948),* at which the charter of the OAS was adopted, formalizing the inter-American defense structure and integrating it into the United Nations* under the authority of Article 51 of the United Nations Charter. Using the mandate of the Rio Treaty (1947),* providing for hemispheric collective security, the OAS has managed to settle numerous minor disputes in Latin America since 1948, to take sanctions against Castro's Cuba and suspend that nation from the organization, and to play a secondary role in the Dominican crisis (1965).* In the 1980s, the

OAS has been principally concerned with the Falkland Islands War (1982),* in the aftermath of which the organization has called for renewed negotiations, and with U.S. policy in Central America, where it has been unable to do much more than constitute a forum in which the contending parties can debate their viewpoints and over which a division has developed between English-speaking and Spanish-speaking members, a division deepened by the Grenada intervention (1983).* In 1988, the OAS consisted of thirty-one active members and Cuba, whose participation remained suspended. In addition twenty other nations have been accorded permanent observer status. The organization includes the Inter-American Conference, which meets every five years, the OAS Council, which meets and consults more frequently, and an assortment of subsidiary social, cultural, and economic agencies. Slater argues that U.S. policy toward the OAS has varied from (1) internal collective security, where it has been effective, to (2) anticommunism, to (3) antidictatorship, where it has been divisive. Ball, M. Margaret, *The OAS in Transition* (1969); Drier, John C., *The Organization of American States and the Hemisphere Crisis* (1962); Slater, Jerome, *The OAS and United States Foreign Policy* (1967); Stoetzer, O. C., *The Organization of American States: An Introduction* (1965).

ORGANIZATION OF PETROLEUM EXPORTING COUNTRIES (OPEC). OPEC was founded in September 1960 in response to arbitrary price-cutting policies of the multinational oil companies. The organization was the formalization of efforts dating back to 1945 and the work of the Arab League, a permanent intergovernmental organization functioning in accordance with Article 102 of the United Nations* Charter. Initially composed of Iran, Iraq, Kuwait, Saudi Arabia, and Venezuela, OPEC has added Qatar, Libya, Indonesia, the United Arab Emirates, Algeria, Nigeria, Ecuador, and Gabon (an associate member) to its ranks since 1960. The founding of OPEC reflected the dissatisfaction with which oil-rich nations regarded what they considered to be inequitable concession agreements. Although they had fifty-fifty profit-sharing agreements with the oil companies, which gave them a stake in the prevailing price of oil, they had no participation in setting that price before 1960. Ineffective during the 1960s, OPEC, under the pushing of radicalized Libya, began to unite more determinedly in the early 1970s to raise oil prices (through means of taxation) and to nationalize foreign-owned oil facilities. Their collective efforts climaxed in 1973–1974, when, as a result of the Yom Kippur War* and greater awareness of the industrialized nations' dependence on imported oil, OPEC members implemented an oil embargo followed by a massive price increase. Because of U.S. need for imported oil, OPEC has taken on increased importance in U.S. foreign policy, causing vastly increased arms sales to OPEC members and tentative efforts of consumer nations to act collectively against OPEC. The 1980s saw OPEC members in conflict over production quotas first imposed in 1981 because of a global economic recession and an oil glut. Violations of their quotas by various members created discord and contributed to a fall in oil prices.

In the mid-1980s, OPEC's influence appeared to have abated with the continuing surplus, the regional discord caused by the Iran-Iraq War,* and sharp policy disagreements among OPEC members. Ahavi, Mohammed E., *OPEC: The Failing Giant* (1986); Kubbach, Abdul Amir Q., *OPEC: Past and Present* (1974); Rustow, Dankwart A., and John F. Mungo, *OPEC: Success and Prospects* (1976); Shwadran, Benjamin, *Middle East Oil Crises Since 1973* (1986).

OSBORN, THOMAS ANDREW (1836–1898). Thomas A. Osborn was born in Meadville, Pennsylvania, on October 26, 1836, attended Allegheny College (1855–1857), and was admitted to the bar in 1857. He moved to Kansas, practiced law, and served as a Republican in the state senate (1859–1862), as lieutenant governor (1862–1864), as a U.S. marshal (1864–1867), and as governor (1873–1877). After his defeat for a U.S. Senate seat in 1876, Osborn was consoled with appointments as minister to Chile (1877–1881) and to Brazil (1881–1885). In Chile, he was one of several American diplomatic representatives who were unsuccessful in efforts to end the War of the Pacific,* although he did find a successful solution to the Patagonian boundary dispute, with the help of the U.S. minister to Argentina, Thomas Ogden Osborn* (no relation). Osborn's four years in Brazil were uneventful but apparently cordial; he received the Grand Cross of the Order of the Rose, Brazil's highest civilian honor to a foreigner. After his return to Kansas, he served four years (1889–1893) in the state senate and engaged in private business. He married Julia Delahay in 1870 and died in Meadville, Pennsylvania, on February 4, 1898. *DAB*, 14:74; *NCAB*, 8:344.

OSBORN, THOMAS OGDEN (1832–1904). Born in Jersey, Ohio, on August 11, 1832, Thomas Ogden Osborn graduated from Ohio University (1854) and read law with General "Lew" Wallace,* gaining admittance to the bar in 1856. He practiced law in Chicago, 1858–1861, fought and was wounded in the Civil War, and was treasurer of Cook County, 1867–1869. In 1873–1874, he investigated Texas boundary "depredations," after which he was named minister to Argentina. He served eleven years (1874–1885) and achieved success in ending a civil war between the national government and the province of Buenos Aires and in settling the Patagonian boundary dispute with Chile in 1881, accomplished in cooperation with Thomas Andrew Osborn* (no relation), U.S. minister to Chile. The final treaty was ratified by telegraph and is known as the "Osborn Telegraph Treaty." Argentina honored Osborn's work toward this treaty by presenting him with a $70,000 artistic shield, created by Gustave Doré. After resigning as minister, Osborn remained in South America and was involved with railroad projects until 1890, when he retired to Chicago. Never married, he died March 27, 1904, in Washington, D.C. *DAB*, 14:71; *NCAB*, 10:146.

O'SHAUGHNESSY, NELSON JARVIS WATERBURY (1876–1932). Nelson O'Shaughnessy was born on Lincoln's birthday, 1876, and was educated for a diplomatic career. He attended Georgetown University, 1892–1893, graduated from St. John's College, Oxford (A.B., 1899), and studied international law in London and languages on the Continent, 1899–1904. He entered the Foreign Service in 1904 and in the next seven years held various legation secretaryships in Copenhagen, Berlin, St. Petersburg, Vienna, and Bucharest. In 1911, he was appointed second secretary of the legation in Mexico City and was promoted to first secretary in 1913, remaining until 1914. Here his most significant service occurred. A friend of Mexican dictator Victoriano Huerta, whom President Wilson would not recognize, O'Shaughnessy tried to conciliate the United States and Mexico after the arrest of several U.S. sailors in Tampico but could not prevent the American occupation of Veracruz. As chargé d'affaires* after the departure of U.S. Minister Henry Lane Wilson,* he worked at cross-purposes with special commissioner John Lind and finally left Mexico to become a special diplomatic agent in Vienna, 1914–1916. Later O'Shaughnessy testified against Wilson's Mexico policy, terming it "preposterous, . . . brutal, unwarranted and stupid." After 1916, he represented Western Union in South America, acquiring cable concessions, and then moved to Europe and represented American bondholders in Yugoslavia. He died in Vienna on July 25, 1932. His wife, Edith Louise Coues, whom he had married in 1901, achieved some distinction by publishing several books about diplomatic life, notably *A Diplomat's Wife in Mexico* (1916). *DAB*, Supp 1:589; *New York Times*, July 27, 1932.

OSTEND MANIFESTO (1854). Pierre Soulé,* James Buchanan,* and John Y. Mason* were American ministers to Spain, Great Britain, and France, respectively, and together they issued this public statement in October 1854 from Ostend, Belgium, urging that the United States forcibly take Cuba from Spain should Spain not agree to sell the island. Interest in Cuba was high because of its potential for slave expansion and also because of rumors that Spain was about to free Cuban slaves. The Ostend Manifesto represents emotional American expansionism but had little practical value in its time. President Franklin Pierce disavowed the statement because of uproar from Whigs in Congress and from Spain. Van Alstyne, Richard W., *The Rising American Empire* (1960); Weinberg, Albert K., *Manifest Destiny* (1935).

O'SULLIVAN, JOHN LOUIS (1813–1895). Born on a British warship at Gibraltar, probably in November 1813, John L. O'Sullivan went to military school in France and Westminster School, England, before graduating from Columbia College (A.B., 1831; A.M., 1834). He was admitted to the bar and practiced law in New York City, 1835–1839, and founded and edited the *U.S. Magazine and Democratic Review* between 1837 and 1846. In the pages of the *Democratic Review*, as it was known, O'Sullivan emerged as a leading publicist of nationalism and expansionism in the 1840s. In an 1845 editorial, he first used the phrase "Manifest Destiny,"* which soon became virtually synonymous with America's territorial growth. In late 1849, O'Sullivan gained some notoriety for his support of the Narciso López filibustering* expedition to Cuba and subsequently was indicted twice for violating neutrality* laws in connection with Cuban adventures. Never convicted, O'Sullivan in 1854 was named chargé d'affaires* and then minister to Portugal, holding the post until 1858. There he remained interested in Cuban annexation and was admonished for associating with a European revolutionary named Frondé. During the Civil War he had pro-southern views and lived in Europe; he did not return to New York until the 1870s. All but forgotten, O'Sullivan died in New York City on March 24, 1895. *DAB*, 14:89; *NCAB*, 12:337; Pratt, Julius W., ''John L. O'Sullivan and Manifest Destiny,'' *New York History* 14, 3 (July 1933):213–34.

OWEN, RUTH BRYAN (1885–1954). See ROHDE, RUTH BRYAN OWEN.

P

PACIFIC MAIL STEAMSHIP COMPANY. Established before the Civil War with government subsidies, this company had regular connections with the Far East and Hawaii. When a congressional investigation in 1874 showed that the company president had been accepting bribes, subsidies were ended. Nevertheless, the company continued operating until the early 1880s, when rival British lines began providing faster service. Pletcher, David, *The Awkward Years* (1962).

PACT. See **INTERNATIONAL AGREEMENT.**

PACT OF PARIS (1928). See **KELLOGG-BRIAND PACT (1928).**

PAGE, THOMAS NELSON (1853–1922). A popular American writer of the 1890s whose books most often dealt with the South, Thomas Nelson Page was born in Hanover County, Virginia, on April 23, 1853, attended Washington and Lee College (1869–1872), and received a law degree from the University of Virginia (1874). He practiced law in Virginia until 1893, while writing stories, novels, travel books, and essays and making lecture tours. A Democrat, Page was an early supporter of Woodrow Wilson. When Wilson took office in 1913, Page was rewarded with the appointment as ambassador to Italy, particularly pleasing to him because of his love of Italian art and literature. He aided Americans stranded in Europe when the war began and helped them return home, he supported Italian aspirations at the Paris Peace Conference (1919),* most notably with regard to Fiume, where his pro-Italian view sharply contrasted with Wilson's, and he wrote a sympathetic account of Italy's role in the war. Page returned to the United States in 1919 and resumed his literary career in the face of declining health. He was married to Anne Sedden Bruce in 1886. After her death in 1888, he married Florence Lathrop Field in 1893; she died in 1921. A "worthy and representative member of the Virginia aristocracy," Page died in Richmond on November 1, 1922. *DAB*, 14:141; *New York Times*, November 2, 1922.

PAGE, WALTER HINES (1855–1918). The American ambassador to Great Britain during World War I, Walter Hines Page was born August 15, 1855, in Cary, North Carolina, attended Trinity College (now Duke) from 1871 to 1873, and graduated from Randolph-Macon College in 1876. After further study at Johns Hopkins (1876–1878), Page became a reporter for the *St. Joseph* (Missouri) *Gazette* in 1880, the same year he married Willia Alice Page. From 1881 to 1883, he was a roving reporter for the *New York World*, following which he had a number of other journalistic positions, including the editorship of *Forum* magazine (1887–1895) and *Atlantic Monthly* (after 1898). His friendship with Woodrow Wilson brought him his appointment to Great Britain in 1913. Before the outbreak of World War I, Page worked for Anglo-American harmony in matters such as the Mexican recognition policy and the Panama tolls controversy.* When the war came, however, Page took over German, Austrian, and Turkish affairs, worked well with British Foreign Minister Earl Grey on matters of mutual interest, and played an important role in coordinating relief supplies to Europe and financial aid to Britain and France. Page heartily disagreed with Wilson's neutrality* policy and felt that the United States should intervene to meet the great challenge of Germany to democracy, and that Anglo-American unity was necessary in this crisis to save world civilization. His views were strong enough to cause his biographer (Gregory) to describe him as "a more enthusiastic exponent of idealistic missionary nationalism than Wilson." In general, Page followed his instructions though was not as effective as he might have been because of his obvious biases toward Britain and against the State Department and U.S. policy. The work of the wartime embassy wore Page's health down, and he returned to the United States in October 1918, a very ill man. He died December 21, 1918, in Pinehurst, North Carolina. Page's letters, which were edited by Burton J. Hendrick in a popular publication of the 1920s, are described as "rich in literary and human quality and so full of whimsical humor." Page also wrote a semiautobiographical novel, *The Southerner* (1909), under the pseudonym Nicholas Worth. *DAB*, 14:142; Grattan, C. Hartley, "The Walter Hines Page Legend," *American Mercury* 6 (September 1925):39–51; Gregory, Ross, *Walter Hines Page: Ambassador to the Court of St. James* (1970); *New York Times*, December 23, 1918; Willson, Beckles, *America's Ambassadors to England, 1785–1929* (1929).

PALESTINE LIBERATION ORGANIZATION (PLO). At an Arab summit meeting in January 1964, the Palestine Liberation Organization was established to represent the interests of the Palestinian people. PLO representatives wrote the National Covenant and General Principles of a Fundamental Law to serve as a constitution for a government in exile. Originally the PLO was founded for the purpose of destroying Israel and liberating the Palestinian people and their land under Israeli control. The PLO first rose to prominence after the Six-Day War (1967)* and by 1974 was generally accepted as the legitimate representative of the Palestinians, with the United States and Israel prominent among those nations refusing to accord the PLO recognition. In the mid-1970s, moderate elements within the PLO began to pursue a strategy based on a "two-state solution," acknowledging the existence of Israel but demanding a separate Palestinian state. When Israel remained intransigent toward the PLO, radical elements came to dominate the organization. The PLO denounced the Camp David Accords (1978)* because it did not include a solution for the Palestinian question, and PLO guerrillas in southern Lebanon increased their raids into northern Israel, helping to precipitate the Israeli invasion of 1982 and the Lebanon crisis (1982–1984).* After years of hostility toward the PLO, the United States announced in December 1988 that the organization had met three conditions—acceptance of UN Security Council Resolution 242,* recognition of Israel's right to exist, and renunciation of terrorism—that had previously prevented U.S. willingness to negotiate with it. Preliminary talks between U.S. diplomats and representatives of Yasir Arafat, principal leader of the PLO since 1969, began before the end of the year. Becker, Jillian, *The PLO: The Rise and Fall of the Palestine Liberation Organization* (1984); Blitzer, Wolf, *Between Washington and Jerusalem: A Reporter's Notebook* (1985); *New York Times*, December 15, 1988; Rubenberg, Cheryl A., *Israel and the American National Interest* (1986).

PANAMA CANAL TREATIES (1977). Negotiations on a new or revised Panama Canal treaty began in 1964 after a series of anti-American riots in Panama had resulted in twenty-four deaths. Although discussions were held sporadically between 1964 and 1977, little of substance was accomplished until early 1977, when Ellsworth Bunker* and Sol M. Linowitz, the American negotiators, and Romulo Escobar Betancourt, Edwin Elias Fabrega Velarde, and Aristides Royo, the Panamanian team, resumed the talks with new optimism and intensity. The final treaty drafts were signed in Washington on September 7, 1977. There were two treaties. The Panama Canal Treaty revoked the Hay-Bunau-Varilla Treaty (1903)* and provided that after its expiration on December 31, 1999, complete control of the canal and the canal zone would transfer to Panama. The treaty also provided for the joint U.S.-Panama defense of the canal and for U.S. payment to Panama of $40 million to $50 million per year out of toll collections, $10 million per year for operating the canal, and an additional $10 million per year if the toll receipts justified the bonus. In addition, there were provisions for U.S. loans and loan guarantees directed toward the economic development of Panama. The second treaty, the Treaty Concerning the Permanent Neutrality and Operation of the Panama Canal, included Panamanian pledges for the neutrality* of the canal, for nondiscrimination among users, and for the efficient operation and maintenance of the waterway. The United States guaranteed to help maintain the canal's neutrality and received preferential treatment for naval vessels in emergencies. An added protocol allowed other nations to agree to the permanent neutrality of the canal. In October 1977 the people of Panama ratified the treaties by a plebiscite. After long and often rancorous debate, the U.S. Senate ratified each treaty by a 68–32 vote in March and April 1978. Hogan, J. Michael, *The Panama Canal in American Politics* (1986); Jordan, William J., *Panama Odyssey* (1986); Moffett, George D., III, *The Limits of Victory: The Ratification of the Panama Canal Treaties* (1985); *New York Times*, May 29, September 7, 8, 15, October 21, 1977, March 17, April 19, 1978.

PANAMA CONGRESS (1826). An idea of Simon Bolívar, the Panama Congress was to be an attempt to fulfill his dream of a United Hispanic America. President John Quincy Adams* and Secretary of State Henry Clay* accepted an invitation and appointed delegates (Richard C. Anderson* and John Sergeant) to go to the congress and promote commercial relations and agreements on freedom of the seas and noncolonization. But Anderson died en route, and Sergeant arrived after the conference had adjourned in July 1826. The failure of American participation enabled the British agent, Edward J. Dawkins, to advance British interests in Latin America without American competition. Bemis, Samuel F., *John Quincy Adams and the Foundations of American Foreign Policy* (1949); Whitaker, Arthur, *The United States and the Independence of Latin America, 1800–1830* (1941).

PANAMA TOLLS CONTROVERSY (1911–1914). This controversy revolved around the tolls to be charged to Panama Canal users once the canal had been completed. The British insisted that tolls charged to their ships be equal to tolls charged U.S. ships, based on their interpretation of the Hay-Pauncefote Treaty (1901),* but many Americans thought U.S. ships engaged in coastal trade should be exempt from tolls. Some authorities suggested arbitration,* but President William H. Taft, among others, felt that since most of the world sided with the British, it would be hard to get an objective judgment. Meanwhile, in 1912, Congress passed the Panama Canal Act, with a discriminatory tolls schedule, and Taft, overcoming his own objections, signed it. Woodrow Wilson, who succeeded Taft as President in 1913, believed that the British were right and that the act should be repealed or the matter put to arbitration. With the help of former Secretary of State Elihu Root,* who had assisted in the Hay-Pauncefote Treaty negotiations, in June 1914, Wilson was able to induce Congress to repeal the clause exempting U.S. ships from canal tolls. In addition to solving this annoying problem with the British, Wilson was able to win British support of U.S. policy toward the Mexican Revolution. Callcott, Wilfrid H., *The Caribbean Policy of the United States, 1890–1920* (1940); *FR* (1912), 467–89; *FR* (1914), 317–18; Mecham, J. Lloyd, *A Survey of United States–Latin American Relations* (1965).

PAN-AMERICAN CONFERENCE. See under the name of city where the conference was held.

PAN-AMERICAN UNION, hemispheric organization. Established formally at the Buenos Aires Conference, or Fourth International Conference of American States (1910),* the Pan-American Union was to facilitate a great variety of inter-American activities, political, economic, cultural, and humanitarian in nature. Andrew Carnegie* donated the headquarters building, located in Washington, D.C. The Pan-American Union had its roots in the purely commercial Bureau of American Republics,* created in 1890, and now serves as the Secretariat of the Organization of American States.* Much of the constructive early work of the Pan-American Union was due to the efforts of its first director-general, John Barrett.* Bemis, Samuel F., *The Latin American Policy of the United States* (1943); Mecham, J. Lloyd, *A Survey of United States–Latin American Relations* (1965).

PAN-AMERICANISM, American diplomatic concept, c. 1880s. Pan-Americanism was an idea, promoted in the 1880s by Secretary of State James G. Blaine,* of hemispheric unity in the interests of lasting peace and mutual commercial advantage. Pan-Americanism had a symbolic inauguration with the First International Conference of American States,* originally scheduled to be held in Washington in 1882 but postponed until 1889. Out of this conference came the establishment of the Bureau of American Republics,* a predecessor of the Pan-American Union.* The spirit of Pan-Americanism seemed to foreshadow the Good Neighbor Policy* of the 1930s, but in practice the idea was replaced around 1909 by dollar diplomacy* and found currency only in a series of inter-American conferences held in Mexico City (1901),* Rio de Janeiro (1906),* Buenos Aires (1910),* Santiago (1923),* and Havana (1928).* Mecham, J. Lloyd, *A Survey of United States–Latin American Relations* (1965); Plesur, Milton, *America's Outward Thrust* (1968).

PANAY **EPISODE (1937).** The *Panay* was a U.S. gunboat that, on December 12, 1937, was sunk on the Yangtze River near Nanking during a Japanese air assault on that city. Two Americans were killed; several were injured; and a number of other British and American vessels nearby were damaged. The United States demanded an indemnity and apology from the Japanese, and the suspicion lingered that the sinking of the *Panay* was not accidental. In Washington, there were several days of intensive discussions concerning the possibility of imposing sanctions on Japan, but the furor died down when the official apology arrived from Tokyo on December 24. In general, the incident tended to heighten sympathy for the Chinese and hostility toward Japan, but Borg points out that while the *Panay* episode may have shocked the American public, it brought practically no change in U.S. policy toward Japan. President Roosevelt did not want to go to war with Japan and took no measures that would lead to war. Borg, Dorothy, *The United States and the Far Eastern Crisis of 1933–1938* (1964); *FR* (1937), 4:485–520; Offner, Arnold A., *The Origins of the Second World War* (1975).

PARIS, DECLARATION OF (1856). This multilateral agreement abolished privateering, providing for protection of enemy goods (except contraband)* on neutral ships and for neutral goods on enemy ships, and stating that blockades* must be effective to be recognized. Secretary of State William L. Marcy* refused American compliance with the agreement without an amendment protecting private property from capture at sea by a belligerent. Marcy was also opposed to the antiprivateering clause because, he claimed, it tended to leave naval domination to the greatest naval powers. During the Civil War, Secretary of State William H. Seward* moved toward adherence to the declaration in order to strike against Confederate privateering but was unable to bring about U.S. compliance. Learned, Henry B., "William Learned Marcy," in Bemis, Samuel F., ed., *American Secretaries of State and Their Diplomacy*, vol.6 (1928); Van Deusen, Glyndon, *William Henry Seward* (1967).

PARIS, TREATY OF (1783). See **PEACE OF PARIS (1783).**

PARIS, TREATY OF (1898), treaty between the United States and Spain. Between October and December 1898, American and Spanish representatives met at a Paris Peace Conference to negotiate a treaty ending the Spanish-American War. The American commission included *New York Tribune* editor Whitelaw Reid,* Senator George Gray (D., Delaware), Judge W. R. Day,* Senator William P. Frye (R., Maine), and Senator Cushman K. Davis (R., Minnesota), with John Bassett Moore* serving as secretary. The main concern for the American delegation was the fate of the Philippines; late in October, it was decided to keep the islands and to pay Spain $20 million for them. Additionally, the United States gained Puerto Rico, Guam, and a protectorate over Cuba and released Spain from all further indemnity claims. The treaty was ratified by a bare majority of one in the Senate (57–27) on February 6, 1899, as opponents raised serious doubts about the desirability of an American commitment in the Far East. Cortada, James W. *Two Nations over Time: Spain and the United States, 1776–1977* (1978); *FR* (1898), 819–41, 904–66; Millis, Walter, *The Martial Spirit* (1931); Morgan, H. Wayne, *America's Road to Empire* (1965).

PARIS CONFERENCE (1947). This sixteen-nation conference was called at the request of the United States to plan collectively economic needs to be funded under the Marshall Plan.* The actual planning was done by the Committee on European Economic Cooperation. As a result, the U.S. Congress in April 1948 appropriated some $13 billion for European recovery and reconstruction, and in the same month the Organization for European Economic Cooperation was created to implement the plan. The Paris Conference contributed, in a sense, to cold war* tensions because the Soviet Union, after walking out of the conference, responded by creating Cominform (Communist Information Bureau) in October 1947 and scuttled the democratic Czech government in February 1948. The sixteen nations represented at the Paris Conference were Austria, Belgium, Denmark, France, Greece, Iceland, Ireland, Italy, Luxembourg, the Netherlands, Norway, Portugal, Sweden, Switzerland, Turkey, and the United Kingdom. The conference lasted from July 12 to September 22, 1947. Gimbel, John, *The Origins of the Marshall Plan* (1968); Wheeler-Bennett, John W., and Anthony Nicholls, *The Semblance of Peace* (1972).

PARIS CONFERENCE (1954). This nine-power meeting, September 28–October 23, 1954, followed French rejection of the European Defense Community* and resulted in a set of agreements known as the Paris Agreements, concerning European defense. The conferees agreed that the occupation of Germany should end as soon as possible, that Germany and Italy should sign the Brussels Pact (1948),* to be renamed the Western European Union, that a European arms control agency should be created, and that Germany should join the North Atlantic Treaty Organization.* The main stumbling block to these agreements was France, ever fearful of a rearmed Germany; but after pressure from British Foreign Secretary Anthony Eden, the French Assembly ratified the agreements in December 1954. The United States was represented at this conference by Secretary of State John Foster Dulles.* Other nations at the conference were Great Britain, Canada, France, West Germany, Italy, Belgium, the Netherlands, and Luxembourg. Wheeler-Bennett, John W., and Anthony Nicholls, *The Semblance of Peace* (1972).

PARIS PEACE AGREEMENT (1973). This agreement, which terminated U.S. involvement in the Vietnam War, was negotiated by National Security Adviser Henry Kissinger* and North Vietnamese envoy Le Duc Tho in secret talks begun in 1969. Formally known as the Agreement on Ending the War and Restoring Peace in Vietnam, it was signed January 27, 1973, and specified that a cease-fire would become effective January 28, 1973; that U.S. personnel would be evacuated within sixty days; that U.S. bases would be dismantled and U.S. mines cleared from Haiphong harbor and other rivers and harbors in North Vietnam; that prisoners of war on both sides would be released; that North Vietnamese troops in South Vietnam could stay but not be reinforced; that all foreign troops would be withdrawn from Laos and Cambodia; that the demilitarized zone at the seventeenth parallel would remain the provisional dividing line, although Vietnam was acknowledged to be a single state; and that a 160-member International Commission of Control and Supervision, composed of representatives from Canada, Hungary, Indonesia, and Poland, would supervise the release of prisoners of war, troop withdrawal, and national elections, with the present South Vietnamese government remaining in power until the elections were held. The agreement was similar to one made in October 1972, which collapsed, leading to another round of intensive U.S. bombing, apparently for no gain, a point of controversy among historians and political analysts. However, the agreement did achieve the long-sought goals of extracting the United States from Vietnam and freeing the prisoners of war. Kissinger and Le Duc Tho were awarded the Nobel Peace Prize in 1973 for this agreement. Kolko, Gabriel, *Anatomy of a War* (1985); Kurland, Gerald, ed., *The United States in Vietnam* (1974); Poole, Peter A., *The United States and Indochina from FDR to Nixon* (1973); Szulc, Tad, *The Illusion of Peace* (1978).

PARIS PEACE CONFERENCE (1919). At this conference, the Treaty of Versailles* was concluded, ending World War I. The conference began January 12, 1919, and ended with the signing of the treaty on June 28, 1919. The main participants were those who comprised the Council of Four*: Woodrow Wilson, David Lloyd George, Georges Clemenceau, and Vittorio Orlando, although there were in all thirty-two nations represented, with thousands of participants and over sixty commissions dealing with specific problems. Bailey, Thomas A., *Woodrow Wilson and the Lost Peace* (1944); Birdsall, Paul, *Versailles Twenty Years After* (1941); FR, *Paris Peace Conference, 1919*, 13 vols. (1942–1947); Smith, Daniel M.,

The Great Departure (1965); Walworth, Arthur, *Wilson and His Peacemakers: American Diplomacy at the Paris Peace Conference* (1986).

PARIS PEACE CONFERENCE (1946). This conference, planned at the Moscow Conference (1945),* brought representatives from twenty-one Allied countries together to write peace treaties with the defeated minor nations—Italy, Romania, Bulgaria, Hungary, and Finland. The conferees set about their tasks amid some acrimony, as cold war* tensions were rising, and managed to accomplish much of what they set out to do, although the final texts of the draft treaties were left for a Council of Foreign Ministers* meeting in New York in November 1946. Among the substantive matters discussed were the border conflict between Italy and Yugoslavia, control of Trieste, Italian reparations,* and Danube River navigation. The conference opened on July 29, 1946, and adjourned October 15, 1946. Feis, Herbert, *From Trust to Terror* (1970); *FR* (1946), vols. 3–4; Gaddis, John L., *The United States and the Origins of the Cold War* (1972); McNeill, William H., *America, Britain, and Russia* (1953); Wheeler-Bennett, John W., and Anthony Nicholls, *The Semblance of Peace* (1972).

PARKER, EDWARD BENNINGTON (1868–1929). A University of Texas law graduate (1889), Edward B. Parker was born on September 7, 1868, in Shelbina, Missouri. He worked for the Missouri, Kansas, and Texas Railroad, 1889–1893, before beginning his Houston law practice. By 1913, he was prominent in his field, and during the war, he helped organize and was a member of the War Industries Board, serving as its priorities commissioner and, in 1919, as chairman of its Liquidation Commission. Among Parker's wartime duties was handling claims arising from the sinking of the *Lusitania*.* From 1919 to 1923, he was general counsel for Texaco. In 1923, however, he was appointed umpire of the Mixed Claims Commission for the United States and Germany, and over the next six years he adjudicated 12,400 claims, many of which were new to international law, concerning damage by airplanes, poison gas, and submarines. His opinions in these pathbreaking cases have been highly regarded by international lawyers. He was also chairman of the Tripartite Claims Commission, which considered American war-related claims against Austria and Hungary. In 1928, Parker was named arbiter for claims from Germans and Austrians owning ships seized in U.S. harbors at the time of America's entry to the war. Before much of this task could be completed, however, Parker died in Washington on October 30, 1929. In 1894, he married Katherine Putman Blunt, and, at his death, he bequeathed money for a school of international affairs to be established at Columbia University. *DAB*, 14:216. *New York Times*, October 31, 1929.

PARKER, PETER (1804–1888). Peter Parker was born June 18, 1804, in Framingham, Massachusetts. He attended Amherst College (1827–1830) before graduating from Yale in 1831 and receiving a medical degree there in 1834. As an adolescent, he had strong religious feelings and decided he wanted to be a foreign missionary. Accordingly, the Presbyterian church sent him to China in 1834, the first Protestant medical missionary to that nation. Parker opened a hospital in Canton in 1835 and soon established a highly respected medical practice as a surgeon and taught medicine to Chinese students. In 1838, he organized the Medical Missionary Society in China, and from 1840 to 1842 he was in the United States, where he married Harriet Colby Webster. In 1844, back in China, he became secretary to envoy Caleb Cushing. From 1845 to 1855, he was legation secretary and occasionally chargé d'affaires*; and from 1855 to 1857 he was American commissioner and minister to China. These were the years just before the second Anglo-Chinese War, and Parker incurred considerable criticism by his advocacy of a stronger U.S. policy than approved of in Washington, suggesting that U.S. troops occupy Formosa to force a desired revision in the Treaty of Wang-hsia (1844)* and work in concert with British and French troops to extract other concessions from the Chinese. This controversy contributed to his recall in 1857, and from then until his death January 19, 1888, he lived in genteel retirement on Lafayette Square in Washington. *DAB*, 14:234; Gulick, Edward V., *Peter Parker and the Opening of China* (1973); Hunt, Michael H., *The Making of a Special Relationship: The United States and China to 1914* (1983); Stevens, George B., *Life, Letters and Journals of the Rev. and Hon. Peter Parker* (1896, 1972).

PARTIAL NUCLEAR TEST BAN TREATY (1963). The idea for such a treaty was first seriously proposed in the United Nations* General Assembly in 1955, partially in response to an aroused public opinion. Negotiations had been in progress since 1958 but had deadlocked over inspection problems and an atmosphere of mutual suspicion between the United States and the Soviet Union. However, in April 1963, after the Cuban missile crisis* and in the midst of the widening Sino-Soviet breach, the Soviets responded favorably to President John F. Kennedy's request to reopen the talks but limit them to nuclear tests that contaminated the atmosphere. Negotiations resumed in late July, and the treaty was signed August 5 by the United States, the USSR, and Great Britain. It placed a ban on nuclear testing in outer space, in the atmosphere, and underwater and on helping others so test. The Joint Chiefs of Staff, initially dubious, supported the treaty after Secretary of Defense Robert McNamara pointed out persuasively that the United States could continue underground testing, be ready to resume atmospheric testing, continue laboratory research, and improve its ability to detect violations. Ratified by the Senate, 80-19, in September 1963, the treaty went into force on October 10, 1963. By the mid-1980s, over 110 nations had adhered to the treaty, although France and the People's Republic of China, both nuclear powers, were not among them. This was the first agreement to limit nuclear development, made possible by the fact that violations could be detected from outside the Soviet Union, thus avoiding the earlier problems related to verification. According to Epstein, however, the treaty's effectiveness in limiting nuclear development has been weakened by the fact that permitting underground testing was more of a loophole than had been assumed. W. Averell Harriman* was the principal negotiator for the United States in the making of this treaty. Epstien, William, *The Last Chance* (1976); Gaddis, John L., *Russia, the Soviet Union, and the United States* (1978); Hammond, Paul Y., *Cold War and Detente* (1975); Seaborg, Glenn T., et al., *Kennedy, Khrushchev, and the Test Ban* (1981); Taylor, Maxwell D., *Swords and Plowshares* (1972).

PARTRIDGE, JAMES RUDOLPH (1823–1884). Born in 1823 in Baltimore, James Partridge received both A.B. (1841) and LL.B. (1843) degrees from Harvard. He returned to Baltimore to practice law, married Mary Baltzell in 1847, and in 1856 was elected to the Maryland legislature. Two years later, he became Maryland's secretary of state and became known as a strong Unionist who helped keep his state loyal. A diplomatic career was inaugurated in 1862 with Partridge's appointment as commissioner to the Exhibition of the Industries of All the Nations, London (1862). Later in 1862, he became minister to Honduras, and from 1863 to 1866 he was accredited to El Salvador. Partridge was also minister to Venezuela (1869–1870), to Brazil (1871–1877), and to Peru (1882–1883). In Honduras, Partridge failed both in securing ratification of an 1860 treaty and in preventing a war between El Salvador and Guatemala. In Venezuela, however, he was successful in persuading the government to make payments as determined by a mixed claims commission. His longest mission, in Brazil, was highlighted by his work with the Italian minister in arbitrating a British claim against Brazil. Partridge's mission to Peru was his most important; the region was embroiled in the War of the Pacific,* and the United States was attempting through diplomacy to effect a settlement. Unfortunately, Partridge's partiality toward Peru relegated him to a position of little consequence compared with the minister to Chile, Cornelius Logan.* The two ministers quarreled, and ultimately the Treaty of Ancon (1883) ending the war was negotiated without U.S. involvement. Partridge was recalled after circulating to the diplomatic community an unauthorized note recommending joint intervention on the side of Peru. An unhappy man, he committed suicide February 24, 1884, in Alicante, Spain. *DAB*, 14:282; Millington, Herbert, *American Diplomacy and the War of the Pacific* (1948); Pletcher, David, *The Awkward Years* (1962).

PEACE CORPS. The idea for this organization, which sends volunteers to developing nations to perform public service tasks, had floated around in Congress since 1957 but emerged publicly during the 1960 presidential campaign of John F. Kennedy. The Peace Corps was formally established by executive order on March 1, 1961, with Kennedy's brother-in-law, Sargent Shriver, as the first director. The first volunteers were sent to Ghana in the fall of 1961. In September 1961, Congress passed the Peace Corps Act, formally authorizing (and funding) the organization. Since that time, volunteers have worked on community and economic development projects, in the health and nutrition area, and with the basics of food production and elementary education. In addition, they have also been instruments of propaganda in countering the prevalent image of the United States as a greedy capitalist exploiter of the Third World.* By 1988, the Peace Corps had over 6,000 volunteers in fifty-nine countries and an annual budget of approximately $150 million. Redmon, Coates, *Come as You Are: The Peace Corps Story* (1986); Rice, Gerard, T., *The Bold Experiment: JFK's Peace Corps* (1985); Shriver, Sargent, "Two Years of the Peace Corps," *Foreign Affairs* 41, 2 (October 1963): 694–707.

PEACE OF PARIS (1783). This treaty formally ended the American Revolution and confirmed the fact of American independence. American negotiators were John Jay,* John Adams,* Benjamin Franklin,* and Henry Laurens.* The nine-article agreement signed September 3, 1783, set boundaries for the United States, granted fishing rights off Newfoundland to Americans, provided for British creditors, encouraged restitution of confiscated Loyalist property, prohibited future confiscations and persecutions of Loyalists, and permitted both nations to use the Mississippi River. In addition, Britain exchanged other territories in the Caribbean, West Africa, and the Mediterranean with France and Spain. Bemis, Samuel F., *The Diplomatic History of the American Revolution* (1935); Morris, Richard B., *The Peacemakers* (1965).

PEARL HARBOR, ATTACK ON (1941). On Sunday morning, December 7, 1941, Japanese carrier-launched planes attacked the U.S. naval base at Pearl Harbor, Hawaii, destroying or disabling eight battleships and eleven other naval vessels and 120 planes, and resulting in 2,403 military and civilian deaths and 1,178 wounded. The attack catapulted the United States into World War II. According to Rose, Japan's attack was a desperately risky maneuver since it did not have the resources to wage a major war with America although such a war had been inevitable since July 1941, when Japan moved into Indochina. This move created a situation in which war could be avoided only if Japan retreated or if America continued to supply strategic materials to a blatant aggressor. Neither of these was a realistic possibility. The attack provoked a storm of controversy over who, if anyone, was to blame for the disaster, and an official investigation, directed by Supreme Court Justice Owen D. Roberts, found Admiral Husband E. Kimmel and Major General Walter C. Short, the local commanders at Pearl Harbor, to have been negligent; their resignations were forced in February 1942. For a number of years after Pearl Harbor, anti-Roosevelt revisionist historians arraigned the administration for its role in the Pearl Harbor tragedy, claiming that it knew from broken Japanese codes that the attack was coming but failed to warn the Hawaiian commanders so that the disaster would be so immense as to galvanize American public opinion in support of entry into the war. Historical writing on the Pearl Harbor attack is immense. Among the noteworthy books are Melosi, Martin V., *The Shadow of Pearl Harbor* (1977); Pelz, Stephen E., *Race to Pearl Harbor* (1974); Rose, Lisle, *The Long Shadow* (1978); Tansill, C. C., *Back Door to War* (1952); Wohlstetter, Roberta, *Pearl Harbor: Warning and Decision*, (1962).

PEARL HARBOR TREATY (1887), Hawaiian-American treaty. Originating in Senate debate over the renewal of the Hawaiian Reciprocity Treaty (1875),* this treaty was written as an amendment to grant the United States the exclusive right to use Pearl Harbor as a coaling and repair station. Although President Grover Cleveland and Secretary of State Thomas F. Bayard* initially opposed the amendment, the Senate adopted it in January 1887. Hawaiian moves in the direction of Germany and Great Britain later that year, however, changed administration opinion, and after assurances that Hawaiian sovereignty would not be affected, Cleveland and Bayard supported the treaty, and ratifications were exchanged in Hawaii in November 1887. Stevens, Sylvester K., *American Expansion in Hawaii, 1842–1898* (1945); Tansill, C. C., *The Foreign Policy of Thomas F. Bayard, 1885–1897* (1940).

PEIRCE, HENRY AUGUSTUS (1808–1885). Born in Dorchester, Massachusetts, on December 15, 1808, Henry A. Peirce went to sea at the age of fifteen on the ship *Griffon*, captained by his brother. For five years he cruised in the Pacific between Hawaii, Alaska, and Mexico. In 1828, he settled in Honolulu, found work as a clerk until 1830 when he became a partner in a local mercantile firm that engaged in a profitable China trade, allowing him to retire in 1843. He was involved in the shipping business in Boston from 1843 to 1866 and then failed in an attempt to be a Mississippi planter, after having lost much of his shipping fortune to Confederate privateers. In 1869, he was appointed minister to Hawaii. In his eight years at that post, his most notable achievement was helping to negotiate the Hawaiian Reciprocity Treaty (1875).* In 1877, he returned to Hawaii and became minister for foreign affairs, a position he held only four months before disputes with the king brought on his resignation. Peirce, who had married Susan Thompson in 1838, retired in San Francisco, where he died July 29, 1885. *DAB*, 14:404; Rigby, Barry, "American Expansion in Hawaii: The Contribution of Henry A. Peirce," *Diplomatic History*, 4, 4 (Fall 1980): 353–69; Rogers, Augustus C., ed., *Our Representatives Abroad* (1874).

PEIXOTTO, BENJAMIN FRANKLIN (1834–1890). Benjamin F. Peixotto was born November 13, 1834, in New York City. He moved to Cleveland in 1847, worked as an editor for the *Cleveland Plain Dealer*, and from 1863 to 1866 was grand master of the B'nai Brith. In 1869, Peixotto continued westward to San Francisco, where he practiced law. The following year, he was named U.S. consul* at Bucharest, a post he held for six years. There he did much to quell Jewish persecutions in Romania and blunt the anti-Semitic campaign, working through official channels, as well as through a German-language newspaper he established. One important consequence of his efforts was the inclusion of clauses protecting minorities in the Treaty of Berlin (1876). After a stint as consul in Lyons, France, Peixotto returned to New York, where, in 1886, he founded the *Menorah*, the only English-language Jewish monthly in the United States. He edited it until his death in New York on September 18, 1890. Peixotto was married to Hannah Strauss of Louisville in 1858. *DAB*, 14:406; Rogers, Augustus C., *Our Representatives Abroad* (1874).

PENDLETON, GEORGE HUNT (1825–1889). Born in Cincinnati on July 29, 1825, George H. Pendleton attended Cincinnati College and studied abroad, 1844–1847, spending some time at the University of Heidelberg. He was admitted to the bar in 1847 and began practicing law in his home town. In 1854, he was elected as a Democrat to the Ohio State Senate; two years later, he moved to the U.S. House of Representatives, where he stayed through the Civil War. He was General George B. McClellan's running mate on the Democratic ticket in 1864 and was mentioned for the Democratic presidential nomination in 1868. From 1869 to 1879, Pendleton was president of the Kentucky Central Railroad, and from 1877 to 1885 he was a U.S. senator. In 1885, the Cleveland administration appointed him minister to Germany; he remained there until 1889. His tenure in Germany was marred by the death in 1886 of his wife, Alice Key (the daughter of Francis Scott Key), whom he had married in 1846. Pendleton took an active part in the Samoan negotiations prior to the Berlin Treaty (1889).* On November 24, 1889, he died from a stroke in Brussels. *DAB*, 14:419; *New York Times*, November 26, 1889; WWWA, Historical Volume, p. 403.

PENFIELD, FREDERIC COURTLAND (1855–1922). Born in East Haddam, Connecticut, on April 23, 1855, Frederic C. Penfield received an A.M. degree from Princeton about 1878 and studied further in Britain and Germany. From 1880 to 1885, he worked for the *Hartford Courant* and in 1885 entered the Foreign Service as vice–consul general* in London. Penfield went to Cairo as diplomat agent and consul general, 1893–1897, and then spent sixteen years traveling and writing books such as *Present Day Egypt* (1899) and *East of Suez* (1907). In 1913, President Wilson appointed Penfield, a Democrat, minister to Austria, and he remained in Vienna until the United States entered World War I in 1917. There he helped Americans caught in the midst of the war, reported on conditions in Austria, and capably dealt with Austrian complaints about U.S. arms sales to Britain and its allies. Penfield also handled British and French interests in Austria after 1914. He was successful in muting press criticisms of American policy but failed in efforts to drive a wedge between Austria and its ally Germany. After his return to the United States, Penfield lived in retirement in New York, where he died June 19, 1922, of "congestion of the brain." He was married twice: to Katherine Alberta McMurdy (1892–1905) and to Anne Walker (1908–1922). *DAB*, 14:425; *New York Times*, June 20, 1922.

PERMANENT COURT OF ARBITRATION (HAGUE TRIBUNAL). Established at the first Hague Peace Conference (1899)* and reviewed and revised at the second Hague Peace Conference (1907),* the Hague Tribunal consisted originally of a panel of a hundred international figures to whom nations could appeal for the peaceful settlement of disputes. Now, each of the seventy-six members may nominate up to four persons to the panel. By 1921, the court had dealt with eighteen cases involving sixteen nations, mostly European. During the early years of the World Court,* the members of the Hague Tribunal designated the candidates for justices on the World Court in an attempt to keep the Court depoliticized. Structurally, the Hague Tribunal consists only of the registrar and bureau, where a panel of judges is maintained from which selections are made to arbitrate a particular dispute. The U.S. Senate approved American affiliation with the tribunal with the reservation that the United States would not relinquish the Monroe Doctrine.* Between 1910 and 1932, the United States used the Permanent Court of Arbitration on at least five occasions in disputes with Great Britain, Venezuela, the Netherlands, Norway, and Sweden. Since that time, the Permanent Court of Arbitration has become less important in the peaceful conciliation of international disputes. One Commission of Enquiry, three cases of conciliation, and one arbitration* comprise the activity of the tribunal since World War II. In the wake of the Iran hostage crisis,* the court facilitated the work of the Iran-United States Claims Tribunal, which settled American claims against Iranian assets in the United States that had been frozen during the crisis. Banks, Arthur S., ed., *Political Handbook of the World, 1988* (1988); Hudson, Manley O., "The United States and the New International Court," *Foreign Affairs* 1 (December 1922): 71, 74; Plischke, Elmer, *The Conduct of American Diplomacy* (1967); Politis, Nicholas, "How the World Court Has Functioned," *Foreign Affairs* 4 (April 1926):443–45.

PERMANENT COURT OF INTERNATIONAL JUSTICE (WORLD COURT). Authorized by Article XIV of the Covenant of the League of Nations,* the court was formally established in October 1921 by the league's first assembly. Between 1921 and 1931, the court successfully adjudicated a significant number of cases brought by minor powers. Although the United States was not a member of the League of Nations, American internationalists made efforts during the 1920s to associate the United States with the World Court, but Congress never passed a bill to that effect in a form acceptable to member nations, and as a result, the United States did not participate in the court until after World War II when the United Nations* Charter made it an integral part of that world organization. For most of its postwar existence, the World Court has attracted little attention, but a controversy arose in 1984 when Nicaragua brought suit against the United States for various alleged violations of its sovereignity, and the Reagan administration responded by declaring it would not accept or abide by the court's verdict. Although the court found in favor of Nicaragua, it had no means of enforcing its decision. Dexter, Byron, *The Years of Opportunity: The League of Nations, 1920–1926* (1967); Fleming, Denna F., *The United States and the World Court* (1945); *New York Times*, October 7–8, 1985.

PERRY, MATTHEW CALBRAITH (1794–1858). Perry was born on April 10, 1794, in Newport, Rhode Island, entered the navy at age fifteen and saw his first action in the *Little Belt* incident (1811).* He continued on active duty, helping to establish the Naval Academy in 1845 and becoming known as an early advocate of steam power. In the 1840s, he commanded a squadron sent to suppress the African slave trade and was active in the Mexican War off Mexico's east coast. He is best known, however, for commanding a four-ship squadron to Japan, where he arrived in July 1853 to negotiate a treaty with the Japanese. The result was the Treaty of Kanagawa (1854).* The expedition to Japan resulted from the imprisonment of shipwrecked American sailors, commercial pressures to open up Japan for trade, missionary desires to Christianize Japan, and, perhaps, an expression of Manifest Destiny.* After his return to the United States, Perry wrote a long three-volume report of his voyages, *Narrative of the Expedition of an American Squadron to the China Seas and Japan* (1856). Married to Jane Slidell, the sister of John Slidell,* in 1814, Perry died in New York City on March 4, 1858. *DAB*, 14:486; Dulles, Foster R., *Yankees and Samurai* (1965); Morison, Samuel E., *"Old Bruin": Commodore Matthew C. Perry, 1794–1858* (1967); Walworth, Arthur C., *Black Ships off Japan* (1946).

PEURIFOY, JOHN EMIL (1907–1955). Born August 9, 1907, in Walterboro, South Carolina, John Peurifoy studied at West Point, George Washington University, and American University but never received a degree. He worked in the banking and insurance business from 1928 to 1934 and held a variety of federal positions from 1934 to 1938. In that year, he joined the State Department, where he spent the rest of his career except for two years (1942–1944) with the War Production Board. In 1945, he was a special assistant to the secretary-general at the San Francisco Conference,* doing logistical work for the delegates. From 1946 to 1950, he held various administrative State Department positions in Washington. In 1950, he was appointed ambassador to Greece, where he assisted the Athens government in reestablishing stability after a civil war and also ended dissension in the U.S. embassy. In 1953, Peurifoy was sent to Guatemala as ambassador; there he was a central figure in the Guatemala crisis (1954)* involving the overthrow of the Jácobo Arbenz government directed by the Central Intelligency Agency.* Late in 1954, he was named ambassador to Thailand and worked to implement the Manila Pact* and the Southeast Asia Treaty Organization.* Married to Betty Jane Cox in 1936, Peurifoy was killed in an automobile accident near Hua Hin, Thailand, on August 12, 1955. Immerman, Richard, *The CIA in Guatemala* (1982); *New York Times*, August 12, 1955; *WWWA*, 3 (1951–1960):682.

PHELPS, EDWARD JOHN (1822–1900). Edward J. Phelps was born on July 11, 1822, in Middlebury, Vermont, and graduated from Middlebury College in 1840. He attended Yale Law School, 1841–1842, was admitted to the bar the following year, and married Mary L. Maight in 1845. Between 1843 and 1885, he practiced law in Vermont, running unsuccessful races as a Democrat for the U.S. Senate and for governor. Phelps was comptroller for the Treasury Department, 1851–1853, and was the first president of the Vermont Bar Association in 1880. In 1885, with the election of the Democrat Grover Cleveland, Phelps was rewarded with the position of minister to Great Britain. Despite his lack of foreign experience, Phelps's mission was successful in a period where the most pressing problems were the North Atlantic fisheries and the Bering Sea dispute* concerning fur sealing. Although no solutions were forthcoming to these problems during his four years in London, he carried on discussions capably. Through Phelps, the United States offered to mediate the boundary dispute between Venezuela and Great Britain, which in 1895 became the Venezuelan crisis,* but was turned down. After 1889, Phelps taught law at Yale. He died March 9, 1900, in New Haven, Connecticut. *DAB*, 14:528; Parsons, Frances, *Six Men of Yale* (1939, 1971); *New York Times*, March 10, 1900; Willson, Beckles, *America's Ambassadors to England, 1785–1928* (1929).

PHELPS, PHELPS (1897–1981). A native of Bonn, (West) Germany, where he was born May 4, 1897, Phelps Phelps came to the United States in 1899, was naturalized in 1910, served in the Canadian Royal Flying Corps in World War I, and studied at Yale but received a B.A. degree from Williams in 1922 and a law degree from Fordham in 1925. During the 1920s and 1930s, he served in the New York Assembly as both a Republican (1924–1928) and a Democrat (1937–1938). From time to time, he was a radio commentator. During the 1930s, he published two books: *Our Defenses Within and Without* (1932) and *America on Trial* (1933). In 1951, he became the civilian governor of American Samoa, a post he held for a year until he was named ambassador to the Dominican Republic. While his single year at that post was quiet, Phelps later became a critic of the Dwight D. Eisenhower administration's placing Point Four* programs under the Mutual Security Administration, asserting that it diverted Point Four away from its original goal of improving the standard of living in developing countries and toward a linkage with military strategy and political ends. Phelps, who never married, died in Wildwood, New Jersey, on June 11, 1981. *New York Times*, June 21, 1952, October 7, 1953, June 12, 1981; *WWA* (1958–1959):2181.

PHELPS, SETH LEDYARD (1824–1885). Born January 13, 1824, in Parkman, Ohio, and a navy midshipman at age seventeen, Seth Ledyard Phelps served with the South Pacific squadron off Chile and Peru during the Civil War, rising to the rank of lieutenant commander. After the war, he became a vice-president of the Pacific Mail Steamship Company,* helping it to establish service to China, Japan, and Mexico. With Daniel Ammon, Phelps founded the Provisional Interoceanic Canal Society, acquired a concession from Nicaragua in 1879, and, after reorganizing the company into the Maritime Canal Company,* spent several years attempting without success to bring about the construction of an isthmian canal. In 1883, he was named minister to Peru, where his main involvement was in the settlement of the War of the Pacific* along the lines of a proposal by Secretary of State Frederick R. Frelinghuysen.* Phelps died at his post in Lima on June 24, 1885; his canal project had died the year before with the failure of the Senate to ratify the Frelinghuysen-Zavala Treaty.* *NCAB*, 12:358; *New York Times*, June 23, 1883, June 25, 1885; Pletcher, David, *The Awkward Years* (1962).

PHELPS, WILLIAM WALTER (1839–1894). Born August 24, 1839, in Dundaff, Pennsylvania, William W. Phelps graduated from Yale in 1860 and from Columbia Law School in 1863. He practiced law in New York City after 1863, served as a Republican in the U.S. House of Representatives, 1873–1875, and supported James G. Blaine* for the Republican nomination for president in 1880. In 1881, when Blaine became secretary of state, Phelps was named minister to Austria. He served one uneventful year there and was elected again to the House in 1882. In 1889, he resigned from Congress to accept appointment as a commissioner to the Berlin Conference on Samoa. Later that year, he was chosen minister to Germany. In four years, his most significant achievement was settling the so-called pork dispute by persuading the German government to remove its prohibition on the importation of U.S. pork products. A good public speaker, Phelps was popular among the German people. After his return from Berlin, he was a justice on the New Jersey Court of Errors and Appeals. Phelps was married to Ellen Maria Sheffield in 1860 and died of tuberculosis in Teaneck, New Jersey, on June 17, 1894. *DAB*, 14:533; *NCAB*, 7:451.

PHILIP, HOFFMAN (1872–1951). Born in Washington, D.C., on July 13, 1872, Hoffman Philip attended Magdalene College, Cambridge University (1892–1894), and graduated from Columbia University Law School (1896). He was a Rough Rider under his close friend Theodore Roosevelt during the Spanish-American War and began a diplomatic career as vice-consul at Tangiers in 1901. Before he left there in 1908, he had become consul general* and legation secretary. In 1908, he was a member of the Mixed Claims Commission meeting in Casablanca and later that year was minister to Abyssinia (Ethiopia), a post he held only a year. Between 1909 and 1916, he was stationed in Rio de Janeiro (until 1910) and Constantinople as embassy secretary, counselor,*or chargé d'affaires. In Constantinople, he represented the interests of various powers at war with Turkey and directed the delivery of relief supplies to Syria. Philip went to Colombia as minister in 1917; there he exchanged ratification of the Thompson-Urrutia Treaty (1921),* in which the United States paid Colombia $25 million over the Panama question. Other relatively uneventful missions followed: minister to Uruguay (1922–1925), minister to Persia (1925–1928), minister to Norway (1930–1935) and ambassador to Chile (1935–1937). Throughout this time, Philip attended inaugurations and coronations as the official U.S. representative, was the chairman of the U.S. delegation to the American states' International Labor Organization (ILO)* meeting in Santiago (1935), and represented Haiti in the arbitration of its claims against the Dominican Republic. Philip, who married Josephine Roberts in 1925, retired in 1937, wrote *Abyssinian Memories*

(1948), and died in Santa Barbara, California, on October 31, 1951. *NCAB*, 44:410; *New York Times*, November 1, 1951.

PHILIPPINE CRISIS (1986). The crisis that ended the twenty-year dictatorship of Ferdinand Marcos began in August 1983 with the assassination of opposition leader Benigno Aquino upon his return from self-imposed exile in the United States. Over the next two years, the growth of domestic political opposition and a nettlesome leftist guerrilla conflict combined to make Marcos's rule even more despotic. Under pressure from the United States, Marcos agreed to hold presidential elections in February 1986. His principal opposition, after a good deal of quarreling among rival groups, was Corazon Aquino, the widow of Benigno Aquino. In the election, Marcos was the apparent winner, but nearly all observers, including a team of Americans headed by Senator Richard Lugar (R., Indiana),* chairman of the Senate Foreign Relations Committee, declared the election was fraudulent. With the credibility of the election destroyed, the opposition, including some elements of the military, coalesced around Aquino and declared her the winner. When the United States indicated its assent to this, Marcos fled to Hawaii. Aquino entered onto a shaky rule in Manila but one that benefited from the warm and lucrative support of the United States. Bonner, Raymond, *Waltzing with a Dictator* (1987); Bresnan, John, ed., *Crisis in the Philippines: The Marcos Era and Beyond* (1986); Gregor, A. James, *Crisis in the Philippines: A Threat to U.S. Interests* (1984); *New York Times*, March 30, 1986.

PHILLIPS, WILLIAM (1878–1968). A career diplomat well known for his administrative skills, William Phillips was born May 30, 1878, in Beverly, Massachusetts, and graduated from Harvard in 1900. After attending Harvard Law School, 1900–1903, he became private secretary to U.S. Ambassador to Great Britain Joseph H. Choate.* A regular Foreign Service appointment followed, and after service in Tienstin and a stint in Washington as third assistant secretary of state, Phillips found himself back in London as first secretary of the U.S. embassy in 1909, the same year he married Caroline Astor Drayton. From 1912 to 1914, he was secretary of the corporation of Harvard College, but in the latter year he returned to diplomacy again as third assistant secretary of state. Three years later, he had become assistant secretary, and in 1920 he received the first of four ministerial and ambassadorial appointments as minister to the Netherlands and Luxembourg. In 1922, he was back in Washington as under secretary of state, but in 1924 he was sent to Europe again with a joint appointment as ambassador to Belgium and minister to Luxembourg. The year 1927 saw Phillips move to Canada as the first U.S. minister accredited in Ottawa; two years later, he left the State Department for private business activity. In 1933, he returned as under secretary of state, and in 1936 he went to Rome as U.S. ambassador to Italy, his most important post. He left Italy in 1941 shortly before the U.S. entry into the war and spent 1942 in London directing the office of strategic services. Phillips was President Roosevelt's personal representative in

India, 1942–1943, and a political adviser to General Dwight Eisenhower, 1943–1944. In 1945, he was a special assistant to Secretary of State Edward R. Stettinius*; in 1946, he served on the Anglo-American Committee on Palestine, and in 1947, he chaired the International Commission on the Siam-Indochina boundary question, his last public service assignment. In Canada, Phillips was charged with initiating diplomatic procedures and familiarizing Canadian officials with them. He traveled throughout the country and dealt with problems concerning liquor smuggling and the development of the St. Lawrence Seaway. His mission in Italy on the eve of World War II involved the handling of diplomatic problems arising from Italy's conquest of Ethiopia and transmitting appeals from Roosevelt to Mussolini to stay out of an alliance with Germany and Japan. Interested in India, whose independence from Britain he favored, Phillips was president of the India Institute after 1947 while writing his memoirs, *Ventures in Diplomacy* (1952). He died in Sarasota, Florida, on February 23, 1968. *New York Times*, February 24, 1968.

PICKENS, FRANCIS WILKINS (1805–1869). Born in the Colleton District, South Carolina, on April 7, 1805, Francis Pickens attended Franklin College (Georgia) and South Carolina College, read law, and was admitted to the bar in 1828. Using inherited wealth, he built a large estate, Edgewood, at Edgefield in his native state and entered politics, serving in both houses of the state legislature (1832–1834; 1844–1856) and the U.S. House of Representatives (1834–1843). After being defeated for a seat in the U.S. Senate in 1857, Pickens was appointed minister to Russia and held the post from 1858 to 1860. No special distinction attached to his mission. Although talks were being conducted in Washington relative to the purchase of Alaska, Pickens evidently did little or nothing with the subject in St. Petersburg. He returned home on the eve of the secession crisis, was governor of South Carolina, 1860–1862, and was the official who demanded the surrender of Fort Sumter in 1861. After the expiration of his term as governor, Pickens retired to his plantation, where he died January 25, 1869. He was married three times. *DAB*, 14:559; *NCAB*, 12:173; Thomas, Benjamin P., *Russo-American Relations, 1815–1867* (1930).

PICKERING, THOMAS REEVE (b. 1931). Thomas R. Pickering was born in Orange, New Jersey, on November 5, 1931, graduated from Bowdoin (A.B., 1953) and the Fletcher School of Law and Diplomacy (M.A., 1954), and received a second M.A. from the University of Melbourne in 1956. After three years of service in the navy, he joined the Foreign Service in 1959 and held minor posts until 1962, when he was political adviser to the U.S. delegation at the Eighteen-Nation Disarmament Conference. From 1965 to 1967, he was a consul in Zanzibar; from 1967 to 1969, he moved to mainland Africa to be counselor* and deputy chief of mission at Dar es Salaam, Tanzania. Back in Washington from 1969 to 1973, Pickering was deputy director of the State Department's Bureau of Politico-Military Affairs. In 1973, he was appointed special assistant to the secretary of state and executive secretary of the State Department, where he was responsible for the dissemination of information from the secretary of state to other State Department agencies and foreign embassies. In 1974, he began a four-year tour as ambassador to Jordan. There he dealt with Jordanian discrimination against U.S. exporters that had Jewish members on their boards of directors and with working out a compromise over conditions attached to the U.S. sale to Jordan of Hawk antiaircraft missiles. In 1978, he returned to Washington to become assistant secretary of state for oceans and international environmental and scientific affairs. In the administration of Ronald Reagan, Pickering served as ambassador to Nigeria (1981–1983), El Salvador (1983–1985), and Israel (1986–89). Known as a highly professional career diplomat, Pickering was sent to Central America to reflect more consistently the strong anti-Communist policy of the administration. In December 1988 he was nominated to be ambassador to the United Nations in the incoming Bush administration. Pickering married Alice J. Stover in 1955 and is a member of the Council on Foreign Relations.* *New York Times*, January 30, 1974, June 3, 1983, December 7, 1988; Department of State *Newsletter* (October 1978):18; *WWA* (1986–1987):2213.

PICKERING, TIMOTHY (1745–1829). Secretary of state under President John Adams,* Timothy Pickering was born July 17, 1745, in Salem, Massachusetts, graduated from Harvard (A.B. 1763; M.A., 1766), studied law, and was admitted to the Massachusetts bar in 1768. During the Revolutionary War years, he was a pamphleteer, newspaper writer, and, evidently, only a mediocre lawyer. He married Rebecca White in 1776, served in the Massachusetts militia, and became its quartermaster general (1780–1785). In 1787, he moved to the Wyoming Valley area in Pennsylvania, became involved in the Federalist politics, and was appointed postmaster general in 1791. Named secretary of war in 1795, he supported ratification of Jay's Treaty* because of the benefits it would bring to New England's commerce. Later in 1795, he succeeded Edmund Randolph* as secretary of state, holding that post until 1800. As secretary of state, Pickering clashed with President Adams in 1798 over U.S. policy toward France. He aligned himself, as he often did on other issues, with Alexander Hamilton's faction of the party in advocating war with France and an alliance with Great Britain. After Adams steadfastly refused to declare war on France, Pickering involved himself in partisan machinations and plotting against the president's policies and was fired in May 1800. Clarfield describes Pickering as a "provincial with a narrow view of America's role in international politics" and the "the first to use a moral yardstick." Because Adams was able to maintain control of his foreign policy, Pickering's influence was relatively slight, but he did have significant impact as an independent-minded administrator. After his dismissal in 1800, Pickering spent two years as a Massachusetts judge before going to the U.S. Senate (1803–1811) where he was a persistent opponent of President Thomas Jefferson* and James Madison* and heartily opposed to the War of 1812. Service on the executive council of Massachusetts (1812–1813) and the

U.S. House of Representatives (1813–1817) concluded his public career. He retired to his Massachusetts farm, did some historical and polemical writing, and died in Salem on January 29, 1829. Clarfield, Gerard H., *Timothy Pickering and American Diplomacy, 1795–1800* (1969); *DAB*, 14:565; DeConde, Alexander, *The Quasi-War* (1966).

PICKETT, JOHN T. (c. 1825–c. 1890s). John T. Pickett was born in Maysville, Kentucky, around 1825. He attended West Point and studied law at Lexington (Kentucky) Law School before 1850. In that year, he went with the Lopez expedition to Cuba, and from 1853 to 1861, he was a U.S. consul,* first at Turks Island, in the Caribbean, and then at Veracruz, where he knew Benito Juárez and other Mexican liberals but gained a reputation for hot-headedness. In 1861, he cast his lot with the Confederacy and was named diplomatic commissioner to Mexico, with instructions to go to Mexico City and establish diplomatic relations with the Juárez government. Pickett went far beyond his instructions when he suggested that support of the Confederacy might win for Mexico a retrocession of the land the United States had acquired in the Treaty of Guadalupe-Hidalgo (1848).* Then, to add to his woes, he was jailed for courting favor with the conservative faction in Mexico while the Juárez government was still in power. He won his release and left Mexico City on December 31, 1861, although he did return briefly in 1865 as a special envoy extraordinary. In 1870, Pickett sold his diplomatic correspondence, the Pickett Papers, to the U.S. government for $75,000. He practiced law in Washington until his death sometime in the 1890s. Owsley, Frank L., *King Cotton Diplomacy* (1959); Wakelyn, Jon L., *Biographical Dictionary of the Confederacy* (1977).

PIERREPONT, EDWARDS (1817–1892). Born March 4, 1817, in North Haven, Connecticut, and an 1837 Yale graduate, Edwards Pierrepont went on to study law and was admitted to the bar in 1840. He practiced law in Columbus, Ohio (1841–1846), and New York City (1846–1857) before becoming a superior court judge in New York in 1857. During the Civil War, Pierrepont was a member of the Union Defense Committee and an active supporter of Lincoln in 1864. He favored Grant's election in 1868 and in 1875 was appointed attorney general in Grant's cabinet. The following year he became minister to Great Britain, a post he held for about a year. In London, Pierrepont's major task was to explain the U.S. currency policy to the British and bear the brunt of their criticism. In 1877, he obtained for visiting ex-President Grant the same amenities in London that had recently been granted to the ex-ruler of France. The Hayes administration would have continued Pierrepont's mission in Britain, but he asked to be replaced because of the financial burdens of the post. Returning to New York, he resumed law practice and died there March 6, 1892. In 1846, he had married Margaretta Willoughby. *DAB*, 14:587; *NCAB*, 4:21; Willson, Beckles, *America's Ambassadors to England, 1785–1929* (1929).

PINCKNEY, CHARLES (1757–1824). The second cousin of Charles Coatesworth Pinckney* and Thomas Pinckney,* Charles Pinckney was born in Charleston, South Carolina, on October 26, 1757. He was privately educated in Charleston and was admitted to the bar shortly before going off to fight in the American Revolution. He served a term in the South Carolina legislature (1779–1780), was a prisoner of war (1780–1781), and then served in the Confederation Congress (1784–1787), where he led the opposition to the Jay-Gardoqui Treaty (1786).* He married Mary Eleanor Laurens in 1788, was twice governor of South Carolina (1789–1792, 1796–1798), and a U.S. senator (1788–1801) before his appointment as minister to Spain in 1801. In four years, Pinckney concerned himself with three major problems. First, he arranged a joint tribunal to settle Spanish spoliation claims resulting from attacks on U.S. shipping; this was never ratified because of the entanglements over the Louisiana Purchase.* Second, Pinckney had to secure Spanish assent to that purchase and was successful in doing so. Third, he tried to persuade Spain to sell Florida to the United States but was not successful in this endeavor. He returned to South Carolina in 1805 and reentered politics, serving another term as governor (1806–1808), as well as terms in the state legislature (1810–1814) and U.S. House of Representatives (1819–1821). Pinckney died in Charleston on October 29, 1824. Bethea, Andrew J., *The Contribution of Charles Pinckney to the Formation of the American Union* (1937); *DAB*, 14:611.

PINCKNEY, CHARLES COTESWORTH (1745–1825). The brother of Thomas Pinckney,* C. C. Pinckney was born on Valentine's Day 1745, in Charleston, South Carolina, and was educated in England at Oxford and Middle Temple, winning entrance to the English bar in 1769 and the South Carolina bar in 1770. He practiced law in South Carolina, served in the provincial congress (1775) and the state legislature (1778–1782), and fought in the American Revolution. A delegate to the Constitutional Convention in 1787, Pinckney declined several offers of political office under President Washington before accepting appointment as minister to France in 1796. Upon his arrival in France in December 1776, Pinckney found that the Directory, the French governing unit, refused to recognize his status and ordered him to leave the country. He went to Amsterdam and later joined Elbridge Gerry and John Marshall* in the special mission that provoked the XYZ affair* in 1797. Pinckney returned to the United States and his law practice, managed his country estate near Charleston, and was closely involved with the Society of Cincinnati as its president-general, 1805–1825, and with the Charleston Library Society. He was married twice and died in Charleston on August 16, 1825. *DAB*, 14:614, Willson, Beckles, *America's Ambassadors to France, 1777–1927* (1928); Zahniser, Marvin R., *Charles Cotesworth Pinckney, Founding Father* (1967).

PINCKNEY, THOMAS (1750–1828). Thomas Pinckney was the brother of C. C. Pinckney* and the second cousin of Charles Pinckney,* all from Charleston, South Carolina. He was born on October 23, 1750, graduated from Christ

Church College, Oxford, in 1768, and was admitted to the bar in both England and South Carolina in 1774. He served in the South Carolina militia during the American Revolution and was severely wounded in 1780. After the war, he practiced law (1782–1787) and was governor of South Carolina (1787–1789). A Federalist, Pinckney became minister to Great Britain in 1792 and held that post for four years. He instituted a functioning consular system, kept the State Department informed about British attitudes toward the French Revolution, and dutifully, if not very productively, protested British violations of American neutrality.* In addition, he cooperated closely with John Jay in the negotiation of Jay's Treaty (1794).* In 1795, he was sent to Spain as a special commissioner; there he negotiated the highly successful Pinckney's Treaty (1795),* which settled a variety of Spanish-U.S. problems dating back to the Revolution. After his return to the United States, he was the Federalist vice-presidential candidate in 1796, losing to Thomas Jefferson,* and then served a term in the U.S. House of Representatives (1797–1799). Much of the remainder of his life was spent in South Carolina, where he was a scientific planter, interested in irrigation and reclamation, and wrote articles for the *Southern Agriculturist*. He was married to Elizabeth Molte (1779–1796) and her sister, Frances Molte Middleton (1797–1828). Thomas Pinckney died in Charleston on November 2, 1828. Bemis, Samuel F., *Pinckney's Treaty* (1926); Cross, Jack Lee, *London Mission: The First Critical Years* (1968); *DAB*, 14:617.

PINCKNEY'S TREATY (1795), Spanish-American treaty. Also known as the Treaty of San Lorenzo, this treaty, negotiated by American envoy Thomas Pinckney,* settled a number of outstanding problems between the two nations and is generally considered a major diplomatic victory for the United States. In the treaty, the United States gained navigation rights on the Mississippi River, achieved full claim to the territory of the Old Southwest south to 31° north latitude, and was granted the right of deposit at the port of New Orleans. In addition, the treaty provided for a mixed commission to judge the question of spoliations. Spain's capitulation has occasioned some historical controversy. Bemis attributes it to Spanish ignorance of the terms of Jay's Treaty,* whereas Whitaker cites Spain's weak hold on the area under dispute. Bemis, Samuel F., *Pinckney's Treaty*, rev. ed. (1960); Whitaker, Arthur P., *The Spanish-American Frontier 1763–1795* (1927).

PINKNEY, WILLIAM (1764–1822). William Pinkney was born in Annapolis, Maryland, on March 17, 1764; he had little formal education but read law and was admitted to the bar in 1786. He opposed the ratification of the U.S. Constitution at the Maryland convention and served in the Maryland legislature (1788–1792) and on the state executive council (1792–1795). From 1796 to 1804, he was in Britain as a special commissioner to adjust claims according to stipulations in Jay's Treaty.* From 1805 to 1806, Pinkney was Maryland's attorney general. In 1806, he was sent to Britain again, this time to join Minister

James Monroe* in negotiating the Monroe-Pinkney Treaty (1806),* which was rejected by President Thomas Jefferson.* He stayed on as minister to Great Britain (1808–1811) after Monroe's recall, handling affairs in a state of high tension caused by the *Chesapeake** affair and the consequent Embargo Act (1807).* Pinkney was unsuccessful in his efforts to get Foreign Minister George Canning to repeal the Orders-in-Council,* even after the French had reportedly repealed the Berlin Decree* and Milan Decree* in 1810. Finally, he left London in early 1811, some weeks after the British minister to the United States had left Washington. While U.S. attorney general (1811–1814), Pinkney fought and was wounded in the War of 1812. In addition, from 1816 to 1818, he was minister to Russia, where he secured the recall of every Russian diplomatic officer in the United States after the arrest of one named Kosloff. Although he failed to negotiate a commercial treaty, he did improve the cordiality of U.S.-Russian relations. He served in the U.S. House of Representatives (1815–1816) and Senate (1819–1822) and argued important cases (*McCulloch* v. *Maryland*) before the Supreme Court. Pinkney married Ann Maria Rogers in 1789 and died in Washington on February 25, 1822. *DAB*, 14:525; Ireland, Robert M., *The Legal Career of William Pinkney, 1764–1822* (1986); Perkins, Bradford, *Prologue to War* (1968); Pinkney, William, *Life of William Pinkney* (1853); Willson, Beckles, *America's Ambassadors to England, 1785–1929* (1929).

PITTMAN, KEY (1872–1940). A native of Vicksburg, Mississippi, where he was born September 19, 1872, Key Pittman (a namesake of his ancestor, Francis Scott Key) studied at Southwestern Presbyterian University in Clarksville, Tennessee, read law, and was admitted to the bar in Seattle in 1892. He worked as a miner and lawyer during the Klondike gold rush in the Yukon, 1897–1899, moved to Nome, Alaska, in 1899, married Mimosa Jane Gates in 1900, and moved to Nevada the next year, where he acquired mining property. Elected to the Senate in 1912, he quickly became known for his fealty to the silver interests and the mining industry and his skills as a congressional parliamentarian. An internationalist in the 1920s, Pittman became chairman of the Senate Foreign Relations Committee in 1933. In that post, he was generally cooperative with President Franklin D. Roosevelt but more vocal in his denunciation of dictators and his feeling that Congress should chart a foreign policy course for the executive branch to follow. Pittman was a strong backer of 1930s neutrality* legislation and played a major role in the development of the cash-and-carry* principle to favor the British. Later in the 1930s, as age and alcoholism diminished his skills, he became less effective as a Senate leader and less cooperative with the administration. In 1940, he was openly critical of the administration's conciliatory policy toward British violations of American neutrality. Pittman died on November 10, 1940, in Reno, Nevada, a few days after winning a sixth Senate term. *DAB*, Supp. 2:530–32; Glad, Betty, *Key Pittman* (1986); Israel, Fred L., *Nevada's Key Pittman* (1963); *New York Times*, November 11, 1940.

PLAN OF 1776, draft or model treaty. Also known as the "Plan of Treaties," this was the model to be proposed to France. Worked out by John Adams,* the Plan of 1776 stipulated that only the United States should have the privilege of conquest in North America and required that France (as the likely ally) agree to the principle of "free ships, free goods"* for neutrals (excepting only a narrow list of contraband*—arms, ammunition, and armor). The draft further requested French assent to full reciprocity in its territory for American ships and citizens. In the Treaty of Amity and Commerce* with France in 1778, "full reciprocity" was altered to most-favored-nation treatment,* and many of the other principles enumerated in the Plan of 1776 were repeated in Jay's instructions prior to Jay's Treaty (1794)* and in Washington's Farewell Address (1796).* Bemis, Samuel F., *John Quincy Adams and the Foundations of American Foreign Policy* (1949); Darling, Arthur B., *Our Rising Empire* (1940).

PLATT, ORVILLE HITCHCOCK (1827–1905). Orville H. Platt was born July 19, 1827, in Washington, Connecticut, and was privately tutored by Frederick W. Gunn at the so-called Gunnery Academy. He read law, was admitted to the bar in 1850, and practiced law in Meriden, Connecticut. From 1864 to 1879, Platt served in the Connecticut House of Representatives; from 1879 to 1905, he was a Republican U.S. senator. Platt's major identification with foreign affairs came late in his career, when he was chairman of the committee on Cuban affairs. He had tried to find a way to avert the Spanish-American War but became an expansionist after the war, favoring the annexation of Hawaii and the Philippines. In February 1901 he introduced the measure known as the Platt Amendment,* to require U.S. intervention in Cuba when deemed advisable and to limit rather strictly Cuba's freedom of action in foreign policy. These provisions were written into the Cuban constitution as well. Platt also favored the reciprocity treaty with Cuba (1902) and worked to secure its ratification. He was married to Annie Bull in 1850 and died April 21, 1905, in Meriden. Coolidge, Louis A., *An Old-Fashioned Senator* (1971); *DAB*, 15:2; Dennis, A.L.P., *Adventures in American Diplomacy* (1928); Munro, Dana G., *Intervention and Dollar Diplomacy in the Caribbean, 1900–1921* (1964).

PLATT AMENDMENT (1901), amendment to the Cuban constitution. Written by Secretary of War Elihu Root* and named for Senator Orville Platt (R., Connecticut),* this amendment granted the United States the right to intervene in Cuba to protect lives and property, preserve Cuban independence, or facilitate American security needs. Under its provisions, the United States intervened several times in Cuban affairs, most notably in 1906–1909, before the amendment was eliminated through a new United States–Cuban treaty signed May 29, 1934, and ratified by the Senate two days later. Bemis, Samuel F., *The Latin American Policy of the United States* (1943); Hitchman, James H., "The Platt Amendment Revisited: A Bibliographical Survey," *Americas* 23 (1967): 343–69; Perez Louis A., *Cuba under the Platt Amendment, 1902–1934* (1986).

P.L. 480. See **AGRICULTURE TRADE DEVELOPMENT AND ASSIS-TANCE ACT (1954).**

PLO. See **PALESTINE LIBERATION ORGANIZATION.**

POINDEXTER, JOHN MARLAN (b. 1936). A career navy officer who be-came a central figure in the Iran-contra scandal,* John Poindexter was born August 12, 1936, in Washington, Indiana, and graduated first in his class from the Naval Academy in 1958, the same year he married Linda A. Goodwin. He received a Ph. D. in nuclear physics from Cal Tech in 1964. From 1958 to 1981, Poindexter had a successful but relatively typical active duty career as a naval officer, alternating between sea duty and shore assignments of increasing re-sponsibility. In 1981, the year he was promoted to rear admiral, he joined the National Security Council (NSC)* as a military adviser to Richard V. Allen* and William P. Clark.* In this position, he generally recommended a greater reliance on military options to achieve foreign policy goals. When Robert McFarlane* became national security adviser in 1983, Poindexter became his chief deputy, working on regional issues, such as the Grenada intervention,* and crisis management, rather than arms control. He improved staff organization and became known as a good administrator who played a low-key role in pol-icymaking. When the more highly visible McFarlane resigned in late 1985, Poindexter was an obvious choice as his replacement in an administration that sought to keep the NSC out of the headlines. Poindexter's tenure as national security adviser lasted slightly less than a year; he resigned when the Iran-contra scandal became public knowledge, and in the hearings that followed, it was revealed that he had made many key decisions on the affair but had withheld them from President Reagan in order to provide the president with future "plau-sible deniability." In the Senate hearings, Poindexter defended his actions as in the best long-term interests of the United States. In mid-1988, he had requested but not been granted his resignation from the navy and was working in a Pentagon planning job while awaiting trial. *CB* (1987):435–39; *New York Times*, December 5, 1985, January 27, November 26, 1986.

POINSETT, JOEL ROBERTS (1779–1851). Born March 2, 1779, in Charles-ton, South Carolina, Joel R. Poinsett was educated privately, as well as at a medical school in Edinburgh and a military academy in Woolwich, England. He traveled in Europe and western Asia from 1801 to 1804 and again from 1806 to 1808, and in 1810, he was sent as a special agent to Río de la Plata (Argentina) and Chile, where he advised various revolutionary leaders. Returning to Charles-ton in 1815, he declined an appointment as a special commissioner to South America in 1817 and instead served in the South Carolina legislature (1816–1820) and the U.S. House of Representatives (1821–1825), except during 1822 when he served as special agent to Mexico. In 1825, Poinsett was named the first U.S. minister to Mexico, a choice seemingly wise because of his experience, knowledge of Spanish, and persuasive, charming manner. In Mexico, he negotiated a commercial treaty in 1828 (never ratified by the Mexican senate) and a Texas boundary treaty (likewise unratified) but became embroiled in a conflict with the British chargé d'affaires* in Mexico that, in the end, destroyed his effectiveness as a diplomatic representative. Because of his rivalry with the British envoy and his strong belief in spreading the blessing of American democracy southward, Poinsett became hopelessly embroiled in internal Mexican politics, principally through his alliance with the York Rite Masons, and finally left the country in 1829 at the request of the government. He returned to South Carolina, became a Unionist leader, married Mary Izard Pringle in 1833, and served as secretary of war under President Martin Van Buren (1837–1841). Late in life, he opposed the Mexican War and the early secessionist movement. A horticulturalist, Poinsett is credited with introducing the poinsettia, developed from a Mexican flower, into the United States. He died near Statesburg, South Carolina, on December 12, 1851. *DAB*, 15:30; Manning, W. R., *Early Diplomatic Relations between the U.S. and Mexico* (1916); Poinsett, J. R., *Notes on Mexico Made in 1822 . . .* (1824); Rippy, J. Fred, *Joel R. Poinsett, Versatile American* (1935, 1970).

POINT FOUR (TECHNICAL COOPERATION ADMINISTRATION), technical aid program, 1949–1953. Named for the fourth point in President Harry S Truman's 1949 inaugural address, Point Four was a technical assistance program directed mainly to Latin America by means of agreements signed between 1951 and 1953 with all nations except Argentina under the provisions of the Mutual Security Act (1951). Mecham notes that the program had roots in the World War II work of the Institute of Inter-American Affairs in education, health, and agriculture. Ideally, Point Four was to be multilateral, administered by the United Nations,* and of low cost to the United States, with the private sector providing large amounts of investment capital. The Truman administration considered it an alternative to ensuring peace through military power; however, the program never reached its full potential before being phased out during the 1950s and is significant mainly for demonstrating how much more potentially could have been done in technical and economic assistance at this time. Amuzeger, Jahangir, "Point Four: Performance and Prospect," *Political Science Quarterly* 73 (December 1958): 530–46; Daniels, Walter M., *The Point Four Program* (1951); Mecham, J. Lloyd, *A Survey of United States–Latin American Relations* (1965); Rockefeller, Nelson A., "Widening Boundaries of National Interest," *Foreign Affairs* 29 (July 1951): 523–38.

POLIGNAC MEMORANDUM (1823), diplomatic note, France to England. This note from Prince de Polignac, French ambassador to Great Britain, to Foreign Secretary George Canning, stipulated that France did not believe Spanish America would be restored to Spain, that France had no plans to acquire any former Spanish American colonies, and that France opposed using force against the colonies in any case. The note cooled Canning's ardor for a joint Anglo-

American caveat against European intervention in Spanish America and in that way contributed to the unilateral Monroe Doctrine.* Bemis, Samuel F., *John Quincy Adams and the Foundations of American Foreign Policy* (1949); Perkins, Dexter, *The Monroe Doctrine, 1823–1826* (1927).

POLK, FRANK LYON (1871–1943). Born in New York City on September 13, 1871, Frank L. Polk graduated from Yale (1894) and Columbia Law School (1897) and was admitted to the bar in 1897. He joined the prestigious New York law firm of Evarts, Choate and Beman, served in Puerto Rico during the Spanish-American War, and after the war, in 1900, formed his own law firm, Alexander, Watkins and Polk. He prospered in the law, became involved in civic affairs as a Democrat and a reformer, and was corporation counsel for New York City (1914–1915). In 1915, Polk joined the State Department as counselor* after former Counselor Robert Lansing* had become secretary of state. In this position, he handled the diplomacy brought on by Pershing's punitive expedition against Pancho Villa, advised Wilson on neutrality* problems, and served as acting secretary of state (December 1918–July 1919) while Lansing was at the Paris Peace Conference.* In 1919, Polk became the first official to hold the position of under secretary of state and later that year went to Paris and headed the U.S. delegation during the last months of the peace conference. Out of office in 1920, he established a new law firm, served as a director of several banks, and remained active in Democratic politics. He married Elizabeth Sturgis in 1908 and died in New York City on February 7, 1943. *DAB*, Supp. 3:605; *New York Times*, February 8, 1943.

POLK-STOCKTON INTRIGUE (1845). According to this theory, there was a conspiracy in the Polk administration wherein Commodore Richard F. Stockton,* commanding the Texas militia, would capture the Mexican port of Matamoros, before Texas annexation was completed. This would cause war between Texas and Mexico, and upon the annexation of Texas, the war would be transferred from Texas to the United States. All of this would be done with the foreknowledge of President James K. Polk, whose intentions toward Mexico were clearly acquisitory and warlike. The intrigue was reported by Anson Jones, then president of the Republic of Texas and opposed to the scheme. The theory was first propounded in 1935 by Richard R. Stenberg and later amplified by Glenn R. Price, but it is not taken too seriously by most historians, at least with regard to the direct involvement of Polk. Pletcher, David, *The Diplomacy of Annexation* (1973); Price, Glenn R., *The Origins of the War with Mexico* (1967); Stenberg, Richard R., "The Failure of Polk's Mexican War Intrigue of 1845," *Pacific Historical Review* 4 (1935).

***POLLY* DECISION (1800),** British Admiralty Court decision. This granted ships in the American reexport trade "almost complete immunity from seizure" as long as the goods were landed and duty paid on them in America. This trade involved carrying goods from a foreign colony to a home port of the mother country and, during the Napoleonic Wars, made up a substantial part of American foreign commerce. The *Polly* decision was replaced in 1805 by the far more restrictive *Essex* decision,* which invoked the Rule of the War of 1756.* Perkins, Bradford, *Prologue to War* (1961).

PORTER, HORACE (1837–1921). Son of a Pennsylvania governor, Horace Porter was born April 15, 1837, in Huntingdon, Pennsylvania, and was an 1860 graduate of West Point. He fought in the Civil War, winning the Congressional Medal of Honor for valor at Chickamauga, and became aide-de-camp to General Ulysses S. Grant. From 1869 to 1872, when Grant was president, Porter was his military secretary. Between the 1870s and 1890s, he was active in a number of private business ventures, as well as in the Sons of the American Revolution. In 1897, Porter was named ambassador to France by the McKinley administration and spent eight years in Paris. As ambassador, he allayed French fears regarding American ambitions in the Spanish-American War, worked to get French acquiescence in the Open Door Policy,* found the burial place of John Paul Jones, and arranged for the transfer of the body to Annapolis, paying many of the costs out of his own pocket. Believing that hard liquor was poisonous, Porter tried to get tariff reductions on French wines imported into the United States. In 1907, he was a delegate to the second Hague Conference;* there he was responsible for the acceptance of a variation of the Drago Doctrine,* rejecting the use of force by nations in collecting contracted debts. From 1909 to 1915, he was president of the Navy League. Prior to World War I, he advocated preparedness, and, after the war, he opposed U.S. entry into the League of Nations.* He headed a drive to raise money for Grant's tomb and was the last survivor of Grant's staff. Porter also invented the ticket chopper, a device to mutilate elevated-train tickets to prevent their re-use. He was married to Sophie McHarg in 1863 and died in New York City on May 29, 1921. *DAB*, 15:92; Mende, Elsie Porter, and H. G. Pearson, *An American Soldier and Diplomat* (1927); *New York Times*, May 30, 1921; Willson, Beckles, *America's Ambassadors to France, 1777–1927* (1928).

PORTSMOUTH, TREATY OF (1905). This treaty settled the Russo-Japanese War (1904–1905)* and was the result of a six-week conference held at Portsmouth, New Hampshire, and directed by President Theodore Roosevelt. Japan, having the military edge, forced Russia to agree to withdraw from Korea and to surrender certain interests in Manchuria, including control of Port Arthur. In addition, other, more difficult, negotiations resulted in the partition of Sakhalin, an island north of Japan, and the withdrawal of Japanese demands for an indemnity. The treaty meant for Roosevelt a Nobel Peace Prize and greater international prestige, but the Japanese felt resentment toward the United States for not receiving a full share of the spoils of war. According to Beale, Roosevelt sought an end to the war because he wanted to establish a balance of power in the Far East in order to strenghten American commerce in Manchuria and guarantee a peaceful region in the future. Beale, Howard K., *Theodore Roosevelt and* *the Rise of America to World Power* (1956); Esthus, Raymond A., *Double Eagle and the Rising Sun: The Russians and Japanese at Portsmouth in 1905* (1988); May, Ernest R., "The Far Eastern Policy of the United States in the Period of Russo-Japanese War: A Russian View," *American Historical Review* 62 (1957):345–51; Trani, Eugene P., *The Treaty of Portsmouth* (1969); White, John Albert, *The Diplomacy of the Russo-Japanese War* (1964).

POTSDAM CONFERENCE (1945). This, the last of the Big Three war time conferences, brought together President Harry S Truman, Premier Joseph Stalin, and Prime Minister Winston Churchill, who was replaced midway through the conference by newly elected Clement Attlee. In addition, Secretary of State James F. Byrnes,* British Foreign Secretary Anthony Eden (replaced by Ernest Bevin), and Soviet Foreign Minister V. M. Molotov attended. The meeting lasted from July 17 to August 2, 1945, and except for military details of the Soviet entry into the Pacific war, it dealt with political questions and German occupation matters. The Soviets wanted to maximize reparations* and freedom of action in their own zone and transfer the territory east of the Oder-Neisse line from Germany to Poland. The United States was mainly interested in obtaining Russian aid in the Far East at no greater cost than agreed to at the Yalta Conference (1945),* but was also angry at the failure of the Declaration on Liberated Europe,* signed at Yalta, to be effective in its aim of bringing democracy to Eastern European nations. According to some historians, however, democracy in Eastern Europe was less important to the United States than increasing its economic and political influence in Soviet-occupied areas. The Soviets were granted the right to transfer freely 10 percent of the industrial equipment from the western zones as reparations and to take a further 15 percent in exchange for food and raw materials from the Soviet zone. In another area, the Potsdam conferees created the Council of Foreign Ministers* to work on peace treaties with Germany and its allies, agreeing that an Italian peace treaty would be the item of highest priority. The Allied Control Council,* composed of the four Allied occupation force commanders, was established to administer Germany. The conference also included the Potsdam Declaration (July 26), demanding that Japan surrender unconditionally or be destroyed. News of the successful testing of the atomic bomb on July 16 reached Truman at Potsdam and, according to Churchill, created in the president a new mood of assertiveness at the conference and impatience that the conference reach an end. A point of contention among diplomatic historians is that Truman's assertiveness derived from the administration's aim to use its atomic monopoly as a diplomatic lever against the Soviet Union. Alperovitz, Gar, *Atomic Diplomacy* (1965); Feis, Herbert, *Between War and Peace: The Potsdam Conference* (1960); *FR, Berlin*, vols. 1 and 2, passim; Gaddis, John L., *The United States and the Origins of the Cold War* (1972); Kolko, Gabriel, *The Politics of War* (1968); Mee, Charles L., Jr., *Meeting at Potsdam* (1975); Wheeler-Bennett, John W., and Anthony Nicholls, *The Semblance of Peace* (1972); Yergin, Daniel, *Shattered Peace* (1977).

PRESTON, WILLIAM, (1816–1887). A Kentuckian, Preston was born near Louisville on October 16, 1816, received a law degree from Harvard in 1838, and returned to his native state to practice law. Entering politics after service in the Mexican War, he served in both the Kentucky and national legislatures before his appointment in 1858 as minister to Spain. In Madrid, he opposed Spanish designs at Samaná Bay, a part of the Dominican Republic thought to be of strategic importance to the United States. He resigned in 1861 to join the Confederacy, was made brigadier general, and fought in several major battles. In January 1864, Preston was appointed special envoy to Mexico to negotiate a treaty of amity and commerce. However, he never went to Mexico; instead, he interviewed the Mexican ministers to Britain and France in Europe and was unbable to convince them that southern independence was important to the success of Maximilian in Mexico. After the war, he settled in Lexington, served another term in the state legislature, and remained interested in Democratic party politics until his death on September 21, 1887. *DAB*, 15:206; Owsley, Frank, *King Cotton Diplomacy*, rev. ed. (1959).

PRICE, CHARLES H., II (b. 1931). A native of Kansas City, Missouri, where he was born April 1, 1931, Charles H. Price graduated from the University of Missouri in 1953 and entered private business. In 1960, he became president of Linwood Securities Company, Kansas City; by 1981, he was also chairman of American Bank and Trust and the American Mortgage Company of Kansas City. A major Republican contributor, Price was appointed ambassador to Belgium by President Ronald Reagan in 1981; two years later, he was elevated to the embassy in London. As ambassador to Great Britain, Price has principally social and ceremonial duties, but he does relay administration policies to the British government and criticize the British Labour party's anti-nuclear policy. *Times* (London), September 25, December 15, 1983; *WWA* (1986–1987):2257.

PROTOCOL. See INTERNATIONAL AGREEMENT.

PRUYN, ROBERT HEWSON (1815–1882). Born in Albany, New York, on February 14, 1815, Robert H. Pruyn graduated from Rutgers (A.B., 1833; A.M., 1836) and served on Albany's municipal council (1839). He was judge advocate general (1841–1846, 1851–1854) and adjutant general (1855–1857) of the state militia, and also served in the state legislature (1848–1850, 1854–1855). In 1862, Pruyn succeeded Townsend Harris* as minister to Japan. Arriving in Japan in May, during a period of antiforeignism (but not anti-Americanism), he worked to restrain his European colleagues from overly harsh reactions and by 1863 had negotiated the Shimonoseki indemnity of $3 million, which satisfied a major European complaint, and forestalled intervention or similar action that would have threatened Japan's political stability. Part of the success of his negotiations stemmed from a joint naval demonstration attempting to induce other changes in Japanese policy; this resulted in the sinking of several Japanese ships and the destruction of a large part of the town of Kagoshima. He negotiated a convention (1864) reducing tariff rates in return for a speedier opening of closed Japanese ports and returned home in 1865. After 1865, he was president of the Albany National Commercial Bank. Pruyn married Jane Anne Lansing in 1841 and died in Albany on February 26, 1882. *DAB*, 15:254; Dennett, Tyler, *Americans in Eastern Asia* (1922); *NCAB*, 13:439; Treat, Payson J., *Early Relations Between the United States and Japan, 1853–65* (1917).

PUEBLO INCIDENT (1968). In January 1968, the U.S.S. *Pueblo*, an intelligence-gathering naval vessel disguised as an oceanographic research ship, was operating in international waters off the North Korean coast when it was approached by the North Koreans and forced into the port of Wonsan. Eighty-two crewmen (one had been killed at sea during the seizure of the ship) were taken prisoner and endured harsh treatment over the next several months. The Johnson administration, concluding that the most important goal was to secure the safe return of the crew and realizing that the Vietnam War made direct retaliation a difficult option to employ, chose not to react militarily, but rather to solve the problem through diplomatic overtures. Efforts were made in the United Nations* Security Council and in contacts with the Soviet Union, but to no avail. Finally, a breakthrough was achieved when the North Koreans agreed to private talks at Panmunjon, and after several months of difficult negotiations, Major General Gilbert H. Woodward, the chief U.S. negotiator, signed a document, which he had previously repudiated, admitting that the *Pueblo* had been engaged in espionage acts in North Korean territorial waters. With the signing of this "confession," the crew of the *Pueblo* was released in December 1968, after eleven months of captivity. Armbrister, Trevor, *A Matter of Accountability* (1970); Bucher, Lloyd M., *Bucher: My Story* (1970).

PUNTA DEL ESTE MEETING (1962). More formally known as the Eighth Meeting of Consultation of Ministers of Foreign Affairs, this conference dealt with Cuba, now firmly led by Fidel Castro and in the Communist orbit. The delegates, including Secretary of State Dean Rusk,* voted to exclude Castro's Cuba from the inter-American system and to apply limited sanctions against the island. The United States had wanted more severe sanctions, but Brazil advocated a milder approach in order to prevent Cuba from sailing even further into Communist waters; this viewpoint carried the day. Other decisions made at the Uruguayan resort halted arms sales to Cuba and excluded it from the Inter-American Defense Board. The conference opened on January 22 and adjourned on January 31. Mecham, J. Lloyd, *A Survey of United States–Latin American Relations* (1965).

Q

QUADRIPARTITE AGREEMENT ON BERLIN (1971). See **BERLIN, TREATY OF (QUADRIPARTITE AGREEMENT ON BERLIN, 1971).**

QUADRUPLE ALLIANCE (1815–1818). The four nations in this alliance— Great Britain, Prussia, Russia, and Austria—agreed to maintain the peace treaties made at Chaumont, Vienna, and Paris for twenty years. Thus was created the Concert of Europe, so called because of the sweeping nature of their pact and the commitment of its members to hold periodic meetings. In 1818, at the Congress of Aix-la-Chapelle,* France was added, and the alliance became known as the Quintuple Alliance. Great Britain, however, had serious reservations regarding the degree to which it would defend Louis XVIII of France and over the question of intervening in European revolutions. By 1822, Britain had withdrawn from the alliance. Thomson, David, *Europe since Napoleon* (1960); Webb, Robert K., *Modern England* (1968); Woodward, Sir Llewellyn, *The Age of Reform, 1815–1870* (1962).

QUASI-WAR. This is the name given to the state of undeclared war between France and the United States from 1797 to 1800, and including the XYZ affair,* some naval engagements, and an angry partisan debate in the United States. Federalists argued for a broader war, while Republicans urged restraint. In March 1800, the Adams administration responded to the conciliatory offer from France to resume negotiations and a lifting of orders to attack U.S. shipping by sending a negotiating team of William Vans Murray,* Oliver Ellsworth, and William R. Davie to Paris. The result was the Convention of 1800.* Bowman, A. H., *The Struggle for Neutrality: Franco-American Diplomacy during the Federalist Era* (1974); DeConde, Alexander, *The Quasi-War* (1966); Hill, Peter P., *William Vans Murray, Federalist Diplomat* (1971).

QUEBEC CONFERENCE (1943). Known also as QUADRANT, its code name, this August 1943 conference involved President Franklin D. Roosevelt and British Prime Minister Winston Churchill in discussions involving military operations in Italy and Burma, as well as the cross-channel invasion and the Southeast Asia command. Roosevelt and Churchill agreed to mount a cross-channel invasion of twenty-nine divisions on May 1, 1944, depending on the military situation at that time. Code-named OVERLORD, the invasion received the highest military priority from this time on. Discussions on the Pacific war included plans for naval, air, and amphibian operations against various Japanese-held Pacific islands and for expanded operations in China. Feis, Herbert, *Churchill-Roosevelt-Stalin* (1967); *FR: Conferences at Washington and Quebec, 1943*, pp. 391–1172; McNeill, William H., *America, Britain, and Russia* (1953); Sainsbury, Keith, *The Turning Point* (1985).

QUEBEC CONFERENCE (1944). Code-named OCTAGON, this conference brought together President Franklin D. Roosevelt and British Prime Minister Winston Churchill to discuss postwar plans for Germany and military plans for the Pacific war. Secretary of the Treasury Henry Morgenthau was there to present his Morgenthau Plan* for postwar Germany, and Roosevelt and Churchill gave initial approval to the plan. By September 1944, when this meeting took place, the military outlook in Europe was bright, and there was no trouble deciding to push on into Germany from the western front. In the Pacific, where the military situation was more complex, it was decided to capture the Philippines, make landings on Formosa and, possibly, on mainland China, and then undertake an invasion into the heart of industrial Japan. Simultaneously, the Allies would carry on the Battle of Burma and continue to supply the Soviet Union and its armies with the hope that it eventually would enter the war in the Pacific. Feis, Herbert, *Churchill-Roosevelt-Stalin* (1967); *FR: The Conference at Quebec, 1944*; McNeill, William H., *America, Britain, and Russia* (1953).

QUEMOY-MATSU CRISES (1954–1955, 1958). This crises began in September 1954 when Communist Chinese batteries shelled the offshore island of Quemoy, killing two Americans, and raising the threat of an invasion. The Eisenhower administration debated whether to employ the policy of massive retaliation* and bomb mainland China and if so, what the consequences might be, including the likelihood of Soviet involvement. The decision was made not to bomb but to let the United Nations* deal with the incident and to sign a mutual defense treaty with Nationalist China (done in December 1954). In January 1955, the shelling of Quemoy (as well as a nearby island, Matsu) intensified. This led to the Formosa Resolution, passed by the Senate, which authorized the president to do whatever was necessary to protect Formosa and the Pescadores (but not Quemoy and Matsu) against attack. The resolution, however, did not satisfy either the American public or Great Britain, which urged stronger action, but President Eisenhower was now determined to avoid the risk of nuclear war over Quemoy and Matsu, to the great dismay of Nationalist Chinese leader Chiang Kai-shek. The crisis waned in April 1955 when Chou En-lai, premier of the People's Republic of China, suggested that his nation was willing to abandon aggression in the straits between mainland China and Formosa. Trouble over Quemoy and Matsu flared anew in 1958 when the islands were shelled again. The United States swiftly responded by sending the Seventh Fleet to the area; it proved an effective deterrent, and the hostility eased. George, Alexander L., and Richard Smoke, *Deterrence in American Foreign Policy* (1974); Gerson, Louis L. "John Foster Dulles," in Ferrell, Robert H., ed., *American Secretaries of State and Their Diplomacy*, vol. 17 (1967).

QUINTERO, JUAN A. (?–?). There is no record of the birth or death of Juan A. Quintero. He was born in Havana, Cuba, and, after living some years in Mexico, became a U.S. citizen in 1853. In 1861, he became a Confederate diplomatic agent to the Mexican border states of Nuevo León, Coahuila, and Tamaulipas, with instructions to obtain an agreement on border security from Santiago Vidaurri, the local political leader of this region. It was the aim of Confederate diplomacy to curry favor with Vidaurri and use his territory as a conduit for supplies. To this end, the Confederate government was willing to support Vidaurri's efforts toward independence from Mexico. Quintero was initially successful, securing promises of supplies, but by 1862 much of the diplomacy with Vidaurri was in a shambles because of border raids and disagreements over tariff rates, all climaxed in December 1863 by Vidaurri's seizure of $16 million in Confederate funds. After the war, Quintero was, for a time, in charge of the land office in Austin, Texas. Owsley, Frank L., *King Cotton Diplomacy* (1959); Wakelyn, Jon L., *Biographical Dictionary of the Confederacy* (1977).

RAMBOUILLET, DECREE OF (March 1810). Promulgated by Napoleon, the Decree of Rambouillet was occasioned by the pro-British impact of the Non-Intercourse Act (1809)* and by difficulties in dealing with the American minister to France, John Armstrong.* The decree ordered all American ships in French-controlled ports seized, regardless of whether they had violated the Berlin Decree* and Milan Decree.* The Cadore letter* of August 1810 ostensibly replaced the intent of this decree by promising the revocation of the Berlin and Milan decrees in November 1810. But American ships and cargoes worth $10 million were seized in the meantime, and American ability to cope with the European situation was at its lowest point. Horsman, Reginald, *The Causes of the War of 1812* (1962); Perkins, Bradford, *Prologue to War* (1961).

RANDOLPH, EDMUND JENNINGS (1753–1813). Secretary of state (1794–1795) under President George Washington, Edmund Randolph was born near Williamsburg, Virginia, on August 10, 1753, attended William and Mary College, 1770–1771, studied law with his father, and was admitted to the bar in 1774. In 1775, he served as an aide to General Washington, newly in command of American forces. The following year, he returned to Virginia to serve as attorney general and to marry Elizabeth Nichols. Other political offices followed: mayor of Williamsburg, member of the Second Continental Congress, governor of Virginia, delegate to the Constitutional Convention, and U.S. attorney general (1789–1794). In 1794, he replaced Thomas Jefferson* as secretary of state. In that office, he had to contend with Alexander Hamilton, who liked to involve himself in foreign affairs. More substantively, he forced the recall of Edmund Genêt as French minister to the United States but protected him by granting political asylum. He recalled Minister Gouveneur Morris* from France and replaced him with James Monroe.* In addition, Randolph opposed the appointment of John Jay* as special envoy to Great Britain because of Jay's position as chief justice; but once Jay had been named, the secretary worked with Hamilton to draw up the instructions for Jay's mission, favored the treaty the envoy brought home, and tried to convince France that the treaty did not violate existing treaty obligations with the French. Under Randolph's tenure, negotiations for Pinckney's Treaty* were initiated. Before they could be concluded, however, Randolph's retirement was forced by allegations of illicit dealings between him and French Minister Joseph Fauchet. In retirement, Randolph published *A Vindication of Mr. Randolph's Resignation* (1795), which, according to Reardon, did not vindicate its author. He practiced law in Richmond and wrote a *History of*

Virginia (1811) before his death in Clarke County, Virginia, on September 12, 1813. Anderson, D. F., "Edmund Randolph," in Bemis, Samuel F., ed., *American Secretaries of State and Their Diplomacy*, vol. 2 (1927); *DAB*, 15:353; Reardon, John J., *Edmund Randolph: A Biography* (1974).

RAPALLO, TREATY OF (1922). This treaty of friendship between Germany and the Soviet Union was signed April 17, 1922, and represented the first recognition of the Soviet Union by a major Western nation. The treaty also marked Germany's first effort since the Treaty of Versailles (1919)* to conduct an independent foreign policy. The Treaty of Rapallo made the Allied powers unhappy but led to cordial German-Russian relations for the next ten years. In substance, the treaty restored diplomatic and consular relations between the two nations and renounced financial claims held by each against the other. The treaty also helped legitimize German-Russian cooperation in military affairs, begun in the fall of 1921 with the creation of jointly staffed schools for tank warfare and flight training. In addition, the Russians let contracts to German manufacturers for weapons and other war supplies. Carr, E. H., *International Relations between the Two World Wars [1919–1939]* (1947); Offner, Arnold A., *The Origins of the Second World War* (1975); Wheeler-Bennett, John W., *The Nemesis of Power* (1964).

RAPIDAN CONFERENCE (1929). President Herbert Hoover and British Prime Minister Ramsay MacDonald met in October 1929 to discuss naval matters. MacDonald wanted to reduce the maximum size of battleships from 35,000 tons to 25,000 tons; Hoover wanted to reduce the number of such ships. In addition, Hoover wanted a strongly protective policy for neutrals and hinted at a British withdrawal from its Western Hemisphere bases. None of these specific points was reconciled at the Rapidan Conference, but the meeting did enhance goodwill between the two countries and served as a stepping-stone to the London Naval Conference (1930). Ellis, L. Ethan, *Republican Foreign Policy, 1921–1933* (1968); Ferrell, Robert H., *American Diplomacy in the Great Depression* (1957); *FR* (1929), 3:1–37.

READ, JOHN MEREDITH (1837–1896). John M. Read was born in Philadelphia on February 21, 1837, graduated from Brown University (M.A., 1858) and Albany Law School (LL.B., 1859), and was admitted to the bar in 1859. He practiced law in Albany, 1859–1860, and in the Civil War was adjutant general of the New York militia. In 1869, he became the first consul general* in Paris, where, with Minister Elihu Washburne,* he protected the interests of German subjects during the Franco-Prussian War. In 1873, Read, a Republican, was named minister to Greece, a post he held until Congress closed it for reasons of economy in 1878. Diplomatically, Read's problems in Greece were minor; he won a revocation of an order prohibiting the sale of English-language Bibles and worked to secure advantages for U.S. grain exporters during the Russo-Turkish War (1877–1878). He also investigated and reported on various archaeological discoveries in Greece. After his mission ended, he toured Europe until 1881 as a representative of the Greek government advocating various territorial claims. From 1881 until his death on November 27, 1896, Read lived in Paris, collecting manuscripts and engaging in historical research and writing. Among other subjects, he wrote on British-Russian relations and a life of Henry Hudson. Read was married to Delphine Marie Pumpelly. *DAB*, 15:428; Rogers, Augustus, C., ed., *Our Representatives Abroad* (1874).

REAGAN DOCTRINE. A major focus of foreign policy during the Reagan administration, the Reagan Doctrine was essentially a commitment to support guerrillas and other opposition forces fighting Soviet-backed Marxist regimes in Africa, Asia, and Latin America. The doctrine emerged from Reagan's speeches during the 1980 campaign, as well as articles by those who supported him, and was confirmed by the administration's early decision to create the contra* force to challenge the Sandinista government in Nicaragua. The doctrine is also related to the sense that there is a ''democratic revolution'' in process in much of the world that deserves active U.S. support. Unlike other presidential ''doctrines,'' there is no single definitive statement of the Reagan Doctrine. It was developed out of a series of individual cases involving various levels of assistance, ranging from full-fledged intervention, as in Grenada, to relatively modest levels of financial aid, as in Cambodia or Ethiopia. At times, the doctrine functions overtly; at other times, covert operations are utilized. Bode, William R., ''The Reagan Doctrine,'' *Strategic Review* (Winter 1986): 23–24; *New York Times* March 14–15, April 3, 9, 1986.

RECIPROCAL TRADE AGREEMENTS ACT (1934). This act marked the success of a crusade by Secretary of State Cordell Hull* to facilitate bilateral trade agreements based on the reciprocal reduction of tariff rates, so that U.S. exports would recover. By 1933, U.S. general exports had fallen in volume by about a third, but because of the decline in price, this represented a drop of over two-thirds in value. The act passed the House of Representatives in March 1934 by a 274–111 vote and the Senate in June by a 57–33 vote. Written as an amendment to the Smoot-Hawley Tariff (1930),* the act authorized the president to make reciprocal trade agreements with other nations without specific congressional approval and to raise or lower tariff rate in the agreements by up to 50 percent of Smoot-Hawley levels. The Reciprocal Trade Agreements Act was reviewed by Congress in 1937, 1940, 1943, and 1945, by which time the United States had made agreements with thirty-seven nations. Pearson concluded that after eight years, the program had been effective without being a spectacular success. By that time, twenty-four agreements had been signed, including such major trading partners as France, Great Britain, and Argentina, resulting in an improved position for U.S. exports and the acquisition of valuable new markets for U.S. products. In general, the United States had better trade relations with reciprocity partners than with nations with which there was no reciprocity. Hull,

Cordell, *Memoirs*, 2 vols. (1948); Pearson, James C., *The Reciprocal Trade Agreements Program: The Policy of the United States and Its Effectiveness* (1942); Wood, Bryce, *The Making of the Good Neighbor Policy* (1961).

REED, WILLIAM BRADFORD (1806–1876). Born in Philadelphia on June 30, 1806, William Bradford Reed graduated from the University of Pennsylvania in 1822, read law, and was admitted to the bar in 1826. That same year, he accompanied his uncle, John Sergeant, on his unsuccessful mission to the Panama Congress* and in 1827 began law practice in Philadelphia. In 1834, he entered politics as a member of the Pennsylvania legislature, moving on to the post of state attorney general (1838–1839) and state senator (1841–1842). Reed began teaching American history at the University of Pennsylvania in 1850, the same year he became district attorney in Philadelphia. Both of these careers ended with his appointment as minister to China (1857–1858). His main concern in China was with some unsatisfactory aspects of the treaties China had made with the United States in the 1840s. Reed negotiated a new Treaty of Tientsin (1858),* in which the United States was granted privileges similar to those given to European nations. This treaty, along with two additional agreements signed later in 1858, opened two new Chinese ports to U.S. ships, eased tonnage restrictions on coastal trade, provided greater religious toleration, and contained arrangements for the adjustment of American claims. After his return to America, Reed, a Whig turned Democrat, became a bitter opponent of the Civil War. His law practice declined, and he earned a living by writing for the *New York World*. He was married twice and died in New York City on February 18, 1876. *DAB*, 15:461; Dennett, Tyler, *Americans in Eastern Asia* (1922).

REID, GILBERT (1857–1927). A missionary in China for many years, Gilbert Reid was born November 29, 1857, in Laurel, New York, graduated from Hamilton College (1879) and Union Theological Seminary (1882), and was ordained a Presbyterian minister in 1882. He went immediately to China, serving as a Presbyterian missionary from 1882 to 1892 and as an independent missionary after 1894. He founded and was the director in chief of the International Institute of China (Peking) in 1894. This was an organization to promote international peace and religious goodwill among Chinese intellectuals. Reid traveled to the United States in 1897–1898, to promote the IIC, opening a U.S. library and museum, issuing publications and holding forums. During this trip, he married Sallie B. Reynolds. He returned to Peking in 1898, was wounded during the Boxer Rebellion (1900),* and lived in Shanghai from 1903 until 1910. His work was slowed when he fell afoul of the Chinese revolutionary leadership in 1911 and again during World War I. During the war, he took over the editorship of the English-language *Peking Post*, in the pages of which he criticized the U.S. government and opposed Chinese entry into the war. For this alleged pro-Germanism, Reid found himself deported and his papers confiscated. He returned to the United States in 1918 and wrote two books on China and religious missions.

In 1921, he made one last trip to China to try to revive the IIC, but because of China's political instability and his own failing health, he was unsuccessful. Reid died September 30, 1927, in Shanghai. *DAB*, 15:476; *FR* (1890), 155ff.; *New York Times*, October 1, 1927.

REID, WHITELAW (1837–1912). Owner and editor of the *New York Tribune* from 1872 to 1905, Whitelaw Reid was not only a leading American journalist but also became a highly influential Republican. As such, he filled the two most important diplomatic posts of his day: minister to France (1889–1892) and ambassador to Great Britain (1905–1912). Reid was born near Xenia, Ohio, on October 27, 1837, was graduated from Miami University (Ohio) in 1856, and moved immediately into a journalism career with the *Xenia News*. After working for the *Cincinnati Times* and the *Cincinnati Gazette* during the early years of the Civil War, holding the position of librarian of the U.S. House of Representatives from 1863 to 1866, and trying his luck as a farmer in the South, Reid joined the *Tribune* in 1868 and rose to control of the paper four years later. His loyal Republicanism and friendship with James G. Blaine* produced his mission to France in 1889. There his most notable achievement was the negotiation of a reciprocity treaty that included the remission of the pork embargo, but it was never approved by the French legislature. In 1892, he was the Republican vice-presidential candidate, and in 1898 he was a member of the U.S. delegation to the peace conference with Spain. By this time, he had moved away from the position of diplomatic nonentanglement he had advocated in the 1880s and toward the mainstream of American imperialistic thought, as seen by his advocating the retention of all of the Philippines. Close politically and socially with John Hay* and Theodore Roosevelt, Reid was chosen ambassador to Great Britain in 1905. The major diplomatic problem was Newfoundland and its problems with American fishing interests; Reid negotiated a modus vivendi that temporarily settled the matter. Apart from that, Reid's mission was primarily social in nature; his wealth and close ties with British leaders, including King Edward VII, paved the way to close Anglo-American relations before World War I. Reid married Elizabeth Mills in 1881 and died at his post in London on December 15, 1912. Reid wrote on diplomacy in works such as *Our New Interests* (1900) and *Problems of Expansion* (1900). *DAB*, 15:482; Duncan, Bingham, *Whitelaw Reid: Journalist, Politician, Diplomat* (1975); *New York Times*, December 16, 1912.

REINHARDT, GEORGE FREDERICK (1911–1971). Born in Berkeley, California, on October 21, 1911, George F. Reinhardt graduated from the University of California (B.A., 1933) and Cornell University (A.M., 1935) and attended the Cesare Alfien Institute of Diplomacy in Florence, Italy, in 1937. That year he was appointed a Foreign Service officer, holding minor appointments in Austria, Latvia, Estonia, and the Soviet Union before World War II. During the war, he served as a political adviser to various military staffs, including that of General Dwight D. Eisenhower. From 1945 to 1948, Reinhardt was first secretary and consul general* in Moscow, and from 1948 to 1955 he held various assignments in Washington. His first ambassadorial post was to Vietnam (1955–1957), where his reputation as a Soviet expert proved useful in the cold war* context of Indochina. After Saigon, Reinhardt went briefly to the United Arab Republic and Yemen as ambassador and minister, respectively, from 1960 to 1961. From 1961 to 1968, he served as ambassador to Italy; there he was critical of White House interference in Italian affairs during the Kennedy administration, particularly the efforts of Arthur Schlesinger, Jr., to win U.S. support for a center-left coalition government in Italy. Retiring from the State Department in 1968, Reinhardt joined the Stanford Research Institute in Geneva, Switzerland. He was married to Lillian Larke Tootle and died in Geneva on February 22, 1971. *New York Times*, April 8, 1955, February 24, 1971.

REINSCH, PAUL SAMUEL (1869–1923). American minister to China during World War I, Paul S. Reinsch was born June 10, 1869, in Milwaukee and graduated from the University of Wisconsin (B.A., 1892; LL.B., 1894; Ph.D., 1898). He taught political science at Wisconsin, 1898–1913 (except for a year at the University of Berlin and Leipzig, 1911–1912), became a specialist in Far Eastern affairs, and was a co-organizer of the American Political Science Association in 1904. In 1913, the Wilson administration named Reinsch minister to China, and in his six years there, he developed considerable sympathy for the Chinese people and used his political science expertise to advise government officials. He tried to secure Red Cross assistance for the Huai River project and worked to persuade China to join in World War I against Germany, arguing that through successful participation in the war effort, China's international treaty status might improve. However, the Shantung question* (awarding the province to the Japanese in the Treaty of Versailles*) dashed these hopes and contributed to Reinsch's resignation in 1919. Back in the United States, Reinsch practiced law, wrote his memoirs, *An American Diplomat in China* (1922), continued to advise the Chinese government, and was a special adviser at the Washington Conference (1921–1922).* He married Alma Marie Moser in 1900 and died in Shanghai on January 24, 1923. *DAB*, 15:491; *New York Times*, August 28, 1919, January 26, 1923; Pugach, Noel H., *Paul S. Reinsch: Open Door Diplomat in Action* (1979); Reinsch, Paul S., *Intellectual and Political Currents in the Far East* (1911, 1971).

REISCHAUER, EDWIN OLDFATHER (b. 1910). Probably the most highly respected U.S. authority on modern Japan, Edwin O. Reischauer was born of missionary parents in Tokyo on October 15, 1910, graduated from Oberlin College (B.A., 1931) and Harvard (M.A., 1933, Ph.D., 1939), and also studied at the University of Paris (1933–1935) and in Japan and China (1935–1938). He married Adrienne Danton in 1935; after her death, he married Haru Matsukata in 1956. Reischauer began a teaching career at Harvard in 1938 but was involved frequently in research and consultative activities. During World War II, he was a research analyst on the Far East for the State Department and a military intelligence officer. From 1945 to 1946, he was a special assistant to the Office of Far Eastern Affairs in the State Department. In 1948–1949, he went to Japan as a member of a cultural and scientific mission. He directed Harvard's Yenching Institute from 1956 to 1961; it was from that post that he was called to be ambassador to Japan. An article he wrote for *Foreign Affairs* (October 1960) regarding a "broken dialogue" between the United States and Japan may have been influential in his appointment. Reischauer spent five years (1961–1966) in Japan and during that time was able to bring about marked improvement in U.S.-Japanese relations and in Japanese relations with other Far Eastern nations. Highly respected for his scholarship and diplomacy, he restored much of the "broken dialogue," influenced Japanese press coverage of the Vietnam War toward greater objectivity, and encouraged better relations between Japan and South Korea. He advised the Japanese government to assert more regional leadership and, as a result, in April 1966 Japan hosted a conference on Southeast Asian economic affairs, the first ministerial-level meeting held at Japan's initiative. After his return to the United States, Reischauer taught Far Eastern Studies at Harvard until 1981 and continued his research and writing. Among his books are *The United States and Japan* (1950; rev. eds., 1957, 1965); *Japan: The Story of a Nation* (1970; rev. ed., 1981); *Beyond Vietnam* (1967); *Toward the 21st Century: Education for a Changing World* (1973); *The Japanese* (1977); and his memoirs, *My Life between Japan and America* (1986). New York Times, March 25, 1962, July 26, July 17, 1966; WWA (1986–1987):2317.

REORGANIZATION ACT (1939). This act concerned the organization of the State Department and was made necessary by the increasing specialization of Foreign Service personnel, particularly since the Rogers Act (1924).* By the terms of the Reorganization Act, 114 officers from the Commerce and Agriculture departments were placed in the State Department hierarchy, and representatives from those departments were included on the Foreign Service administrative boards. The object of the act was to prevent interdepartmental conflict and place the diplomacy of overseas commerce within the purview of a single department. Ilchman, Warren F., *Professional Diplomacy in the United States, 1779–1939* (1961).

REPARATIONS, WORLD WAR I, payments imposed on the loser of a war by the winner to "repair" the damages of the conflict and repay the winner's costs. Reparations were a major issue at the Paris Peace Conference (1919),* as the Allies demanded huge payments from the defeated Germans and linked the reparations question to that of the war debts most Allies owed the United States. The Reparations Commission, established at the conference and included in the Treaty of Versailles,* had powers to fix and collect reparations from Germany. The American delegation hoped, by its presence on the commission, to exercise restraint on the Allies, but when the Senate refused to ratify the treaty, the United States lost its place on the commission. In 1921, the commission decided to include Allied pensions in the total amount of reparations, thus raising the German bill from about $10 billion to $33 billion, a clearly unmanageable sum. Such reparations also, according to Bailey, seemed to violate Wilson's Fourteen Points,* which prohibited "punitive damages." Later, in the Young Plan (1929),* reparations were scaled down to about $8 billion. In July 1931, the Hoover moratorium* suspended reparations payments for one year. The Lausanne Conference (1932)* would have reduced the total of reparations payments by about 90 percent, but the United States did not consent. Finally, in 1933, Adolf Hitler repudiated all further reparations payments. Bailey, Thomas A., *Woodrow Wilson and the Lost Peace* (1954); Burnett, Philip Mason, *Reparations at the Paris Peace Conference from the Standpoint of the American Delegation* (1940); *FR* (1919) The Paris Peace Conference, 13:380–525; FR (1923), 2:46–110; Keynes, John M., *The Economic Consequences of the Peace* (1921); Offner, Arnold A., *The Origins of the Second World War* (1975).

REPARATIONS, WORLD WAR II. Reparations were first seriously discussed at the Yalta Conference (1945),* when the Soviets proposed a total of $20 billion, half to go to themselves. The United States and Great Britain were not ready to make commitments but agreed to the Soviet figure as a basis for further discussion. At the Potsdam Conference (1945),* the topic became a point of controversy when the United States insisted that reparations should be paid only when Germany had recovered a minimally functional national economy. Furthermore, the United States asserted that reparations preferably should be based on exchanges between occupation zones or taken only from the zone of the recipient. Ultimately the conferees reluctantly agreed at Potsdam that the Soviet Union could remove 10 percent of the industrial capacity of the western zones freely and have another 15 percent in exchange for food and raw materials from the Soviet zone. According to Nettl, Soviet reparations taken from Germany (not including "military trophies") included, first, coal mine installations, railway repair shops, and power stations. After the spring of 1946, reparations for the Soviets were confined to their own zone because of the poor rate of economic recovery in the western zones and Soviet reluctance to cooperate in economic unification programs. Other Soviet reparations included removal from current inventories or production of livestock, food, timber, industrial goods, and consumer goods for reexport. There were even some reparations in the form of labor, used either in the Soviet Union or Germany. Reparations constituted a great economic success for the USSR; they were helpful in the Soviet Union's domestic reconstruction but at the cost of Allied goodwill and German public opinion. By 1951, reparations had greatly diminished. Nettl cites a Soviet estimate of the total value of reparations as over $3 billion, but most Western sources place the total much higher. Jones, Manfred, *The United States and Germany* (1984); Kuklick, Bruce, *American Policy and the Division of Germany* (1972); Maddox, Robert, "Reparations and the Origins of the Cold War," *Mid-America* 67, 3 (October 1985):125–35; McLellan, David S., *Dean Acheson: The State Department Years* (1976); Nettl, Peter, "German Reparations in the Soviet Empire," *Foreign Affairs* 29 (January, 1951):300–307; Yergin, Daniel, *Shattered Peace* (1977).

RESERVATIONISTS. This term was applied to those U.S. senators who, in the debate over the ratification of the Treaty of Versailles* in 1919–1920, favored the addition of amendments or reservations to the treaty. Most of the proposed reservations concerned U.S. participation in the League of Nations* and affiliated organizations. Senate reservationists insisted, for example, on the right of Congress to approve participation in collective security* actions or in the arbitration* or inquiry of any matter that involved the Monroe Doctrine.* Bailey distinguishes between "strong" reservationists and "mild" reservationists. Strong reservationists, about twenty in number, followed the lead of Senator Henry Cabot Lodge, Sr.* (R., Massachusetts) and supported the Lodge Reservations.* Their number included Senators Warren G. Harding (R., Ohio) and Charles C. Curtis (R., Kansas). Mild reservationists, some twelve in number, including future Secretary of State Frank B. Kellogg,* were generally in favor of the league but supported reservations that clarified America's basic interests while still maintaining the basic integrity of the league's covenant. Bailey, Thomas A., *Woodrow Wilson and the Great Betrayal* (1945); Garraty John A., *Henry Cabot Lodge, a Biography* (1953).

RESOLUTION 242. In November 1967, following the Six-Day War,* the United Nations* Security Council passed this resolution, unanimously calling for Israel to withdraw from occupied areas and for all states to recognize the sovereignty and security of all other states in the region. Gunnar Jarring was named United Nations special representative for the Middle East to try to win acceptance of the resolution, while U.S. Ambassador Arthur Goldberg, who led the debate on this resolution, was praised for his success in obtaining the consent of Egypt, Israel, and the Soviet Union. An effort was made to implement the resolution in the Rogers Plan (1969),* and Israel seemed to accept the principle of withdrawal in 1970, but no practical results were achieved. During the 1973 Yom Kippur War* and its aftermath, an opportunity for a comprehensive Middle East peace incorporating Resolution 242 never materialized. The Camp David Accords (1978)* were based on Resolution 242 but did not explicitly require Israeli withdrawal from the West Bank and Gaza, the two most sensitive areas under occupation. Another complicating factor is the existence of the Palestine Liberation Organization (PLO),* which Israel does not recognize. The PLO, which maintains that it is the legitimate representative of the Palentinian people, will not subscribe to Resolution 242 until Israel accords it recognition. During the Reagan administration, Resolution 242 was again brought up with reference to the West Bank and Gaza; to date, the problem has not been resolved. A new wave of Israeli-Palestinian violence in Gaza in 1988 pointed up the continuing difficulty. Bailey, Sydney D., *The Making of Resolution 242* (1985); Blitzer, Wolf, *Between Washington and Jerusalem: A Reporter's Notebook* (1985); Fasulo, Linda M., *Representing America: Experiences of U.S. Diplomats at the UN* (1984); *Washington Post*, April 10, 1988; Rubenberg, Cheryl A., *Israel and the American National Interest* (1986).

REYKJAVIK SUMMIT CONFERENCE (1986). At this, the second summit conference between President Ronald Reagan and General Secretary Mikhail Gorbachev of the Soviet Union, the main topic of discussion was the Strategic Arms Reduction Talks (START).* The two leaders reached an agreement in principle to reduce strategic offensive weapons by 50 percent within five years. President Reagan promised that there would be no Strategic Defense Initiative (SDI)* deployment for ten years, but the fact that he would not make further concessions on SDI contributed to the conference's ending on a note of discord. Another controversial aspect concerned a report that the two leaders agreed to eliminate all nuclear weapons in ten years, but subsequently a difference in interpretation was made public. The Soviets claimed, and the Americans eventually concurred, that the president had agreed to eliminate nuclear weapons in a decade but that what he meant was all nuclear ballistic weapons (sparing bombers, cruise missiles, and tactical nuclear weapons). In addition to arms reduction, the conferees discussed human rights, regional conflicts, and bilateral contacts and communications without arriving at any significant new agreements. Planned without much time for preparation, the summit was held October 11–12, 1986, in Iceland, dates chosen in part because it was hoped the meeting would have a positive impact for Republicans in the November mid-term elections. Mandlebaum, Michael, and Strobe Talbott, "Reykjavik and Beyond," *Foreign Affairs* 65, 3 (Spring 1987):426–46; *New York Times*, October 14, 19, 1986.

RICHARDS, WILLIAM (1793–1847). A leader in mid-nineteenth-century Hawaiian affairs, William Richards was born in Plainfield, Massachusetts, on August 22, 1793. He graduated from Williams College in 1819 and from Andover Theological Seminary in 1822, the same year he married Clarissa Lyman and went to Hawaii as a missionary. For thirteen years, he was successful in his religious work, becoming a political adviser to the native government, which instituted, under his tutelage, a republican form of government and a bill of rights in 1839 and a constitution in 1840. In the early 1840s, he was sent on a diplomatic mission to the United States, Great Britain, and France to secure recognition of Hawaiian independence and favorable commercial treaties; he was successful in the former objective but not the latter. Richards also sponsored a controversial and speculative project involving the use of foreign capital to foster agricultural development in Hawaii. When the venture failed, Richards was severely criticized. Still, in 1846, he was made minister of public education and president of a board of commissioners to resolve disputes over land titles. He translated many English-language books into Hawaiian and wrote Hawaiian school textbooks. Richards died in Honolulu on November 7, 1847. *DAB*, 15:500; Daws, Gavan, *Shoal of Time* (1968).

RICHARDSON, ELLIOT LEE (b. 1920). Born in Boston on July 20, Elliot Richardson graduated from Harvard (A.B., 1941; LL.B., 1947) and was admitted to the Massachusetts bar in 1949. His schooling was interrupted by army service during World War II. In 1949, he became a lawyer in Boston and in 1952 married Anne Francis Hazard. Entering Republican politics in 1953, Richardson became an aide to Senator Leverett Saltonstall. In 1957, he joined the Eisenhower administration as an assistant secretary of health, education and welfare. Two years later, he was named U.S. attorney for the Massachusetts District. After private law practice from 1961 to 1964, Richardson was elected lieutenant governor of Massachusetts, serving from 1965 to 1967, and then became state attorney general from 1967 to 1969. The Nixon administration named him under secretary of state in 1969, the first of several high-level appointments in that administration. Cabinet appointments followed: secretary of health, education and welfare (1970–1973), secretary of defense (1973), and attorney general (1973). In October 1973, while serving as attorney general, he was fired by President Nixon for failing to dismiss Watergate prosecutor Archibald Cox and returned to private law practice. President Gerald Ford named Richardson ambassador to Great Britain in 1975. There his main function was to serve as an advance man for Secretary of State Henry Kissinger,* a function made more meaningful by the probability that he would succeed Kissinger in a future Republican administration. In London, Richardson dealt with such matters as long-range economic and energy planning, North Atlantic Treaty Organization* strategy and relations with Warsaw Pact nations, and relations between the United States and the European Economic Community. He was in Britain less than a year, however, before returning to Washington to be secretary of commerce, a post he held until the end of the Ford administration in 1977. From 1978 to 1982, Richardson served as chief U.S. negotiator for the Law of the Sea treaty. He has written *The Creative Balance* (1976) and *The Uses and Limitations of Law* (1982). Fasulo, Linda M., *Representing America: Experiences of U.S. Diplomats at the UN* (1984); *New York Times*, March 2, November 4, 1975; *WWA* (1976–1977):2624.

RIDDLE, JOHN WALLACE (1864–1941). John Wallace Riddle was born July 12, 1864, in Philadelphia, graduated from Harvard (1886), and studied at Columbia Law School (1888–1890) and the Ecole des sciences politiques, Paris (1891–1893). Having been trained for diplomacy, he entered that service in 1893 as legation secretary in Turkey, where he stayed until 1900. There he was particularly concerned with the restrictions that limited the activities of American teachers and missionaries working in that Muslim country. He served as legation secretary and occasional chargé in St. Petersburg (1901–1903), presenting a petition to the government from American Jews protesting the brutal treatment of Jews during the Kishineff pogram, a very delicate maneuver. From 1903 to 1905, Riddle was agent and consul general* in Egypt; from 1905 to 1906 he was minister to Romania and Serbia. After these uneventful missions, he became minister to Russia (1906–1909) and secured permission for American Jews to visit relatives there. A Republican, Riddle was out of the diplomatic service until 1921, when he was named minister to Argentina, where he worked to improve trade relations with the United States. Riddle married Theodate Pope in 1916 and in his retirement after 1925 served as honorary chairman of Avon Old Farms, a private school. He died in Farmington, Connecticut, on December 8, 1941. *NCAB*, 30:288; *New York Times*, December 9, 1941.

RIO de JANEIRO CONFERENCE (1906). This was formally known as the Third International Conference of American States and involved all the republics of the Western Hemisphere except Haiti and Venezuela. Secretary of State Elihu Root* led the U.S. delegation, and Brazilian Foreign Minister Joaquim Nabuco was president of the conference, which lasted from July 25 to August 27. Recent U.S. intervention in the Caribbean posed potentially disruptive problems for the delegates, but Root's sympathy for Latin America prevailed and brought harmony. The Drago Doctrine, *named for Argentine Foreign Minister Luís María Drago, was the main topic of debate. The United States spoke against this doctrine, which opposed forceful intervention to collect debts, and offered instead the Porter Resolution, which opposed forceful debt collection unless arbitration* was refused by the debtor nation. It was decided to let the second Hague Peace Conference,* scheduled to meet the following year, examine the whole matter of forceful debt collection. (It did and adopted, over Latin American objections, the essentials of the Porter Resolution.) In addition, the Rio de Janeiro Conference reorganized the Bureau of American Republics,* which was made a "permanent committee of the International American Conferences" to make studies and reports on subjects designated at the periodic conferences. Connell-Smith, Gordon, *The United States and Latin America* (1974); *FR*, (1906), 2:1565–1625; Inman, Samuel Guy, *Inter-American Conferences* (1965); Mecham, J. Lloyd, *A Survey of United States– Latin American Relations* (1965).

RIO de JANEIRO CONFERENCE (1942). At this, the Third Meeting of Consultation of American Foreign Ministers, the U.S. objective was a declaration in which all hemispheric nations would pledge to sever relations with the Axis. (At this time, January 1942, ten had already declared war, but eleven others were neutral.) Because of objections from Chile and Argentina, the U.S.-sponsored declaration was discarded and replaced by a milder resolution containing a recommendation that relations with the Axis be severed. Chile feared the Axis because of its coastal vulnerability, while Argentina had a long tradition of cordial relations with both Germany and Italy. Also adopted at this conference were resolutions to establish the Inter-American Defense Board and the Emergency Advisory Committee for Political Defense, the former to give Latin Americans a sense of participation in hemispheric defense matters, the latter (which turned out to be more active) to control pro-Axis subversion. The information gathered by the Emergency Advisory Committee helped persuade Chile to break diplomatic relations with the Axis in 1943. Connell-Smith, Gordon, *The United States and Latin America* (1974); Mecham, J. Lloyd, *A Survey of United States–Latin American Relations* (1965).

RIO TREATY (1947). Known formally as the Inter-American Treaty of Reciprocal Assistance, the Rio Treaty contains the provisions of the Act of Chapultepec (1945) concerning inter-American security and provides that any attack on an American nation will be considered an attack on all and will be met by collective sanctions, political, economic, and/or military, in line with Article 51 of the United Nations* Charter. The area covered by the treaty includes Canada and the remaining European dependencies in the Western Hemisphere. Validated in December 1948, when Costa Rica became the fourteenth nation to ratify, the Rio Treaty is implemented by the Organization of American States (OAS)* through its meetings of Consultation of Ministers of Foreign Affairs. Broadly defining *attack* to include subversion, the OAS invoked the treaty against Cuba (with sanctions and expulsion from the OAS) in 1962 and in the Dominican crisis (1965).* The Rio Treaty served as a model for the North Atlantic Treaty (1949)* and the Manila Pact (1954).* Connell-Smith, Gordon, *The United States and Latin America* (1974); *FR* (1947), 8:1–93; Mecham, J. Lloyd, *A Survey of United States–Latin American Relations* (1965); Plano, Jack C., and Roy Olton, *The International Relations Dictionary* (1969).

RIVES, WILLIAM CABELL (1793–1868). Born in Amherst County, Virginia, on May 4, 1793, William C. Rives attended Hampden-Sydney College, graduated from William and Mary College (1809), and studied law with Thomas Jefferson.* In 1817, he entered politics as a Virginia state representative (1817–1823) and then served as a member of the U.S. House of Representatives (1823–1829). In 1829, he began the first of his two separate stints as minister to France. There he was involved with the aged Lafayette in the politics of the 1830 revolution and the accession of Louis Philippe. He also participated in talks leading to the settlement of the French spoliations claims,* a dispute in which the United States received 25 million francs in six annual installments, a treaty never ratified during Rives's ministry. His good relations with the French royal family were demonstrated when Queen Amelie became godmother to his daughter. After his return from France in 1832, Rives served in the U.S. Senate from 1832 to 1834 and from 1836 to 1845. In 1849, Rives was sent to France as minister for the second time. In this relatively uneventful mission, Rives was impressed with the rise to power of Louis-Napoleon, and the civil turmoil in Europe almost made him a Unionist during the U.S. Civil War, although he eventually served in the Confederate congress. He returned to Virginia in 1853 and wrote the three-volume *History of the Life and Times of James Madison* (1859–1868). Rives married Judith Page Walker in 1819 and died in Albermarle County, Virginia, on April 25, 1868. *DAB* 15:635; *NCAB*, 6:215; Willson, Beckles, *America's Ambassadors to France, 1777–1927* (1928).

ROBINSON, CHRISTOPHER (1806–1889). A native of Providence, Rhode Island, Christopher Robinson was born May 15, 1806, and graduated from Brown University in 1825. He taught school, read law, and was admitted to the bar in

1833. Except for a term as Rhode Island attorney general (1853–1854) and a term as a U.S. congressman (1859–1861), Robinson was engaged in law practice until his appointment as minister to Peru (1861–1865). In Lima, Robinson faced two major problems. First, Peru had many Confederate supporters; Robinson, however, swung the government to the Union side by noting the dangers of European intervention and the Spanish seizure of the Chincha Islands in 1864. Second, Americans had lodged a number of claims against the Peruvian government; Robinson settled most by means of a mixed claims commission and arranged for two to be settled by arbitration* (which apparently never happened). After his return, Robinson settled back into his law practice. Retirement in Woonsocket, Rhode Island, preceded his death there on January 16, 1889. He was married three times. *DAB*, 16:38; *NCAB*, 12:117.

ROCKEFELLER, NELSON ALDRICH (1908–1979). A grandson of John D. Rockefeller, Nelson A. Rockefeller was born into this wealthy family on July 8, 1908, in Bar Harbor, Maine. He graduated from Dartmouth (1930) and after a year of travel went to work for Chase National Bank. Later in 1931, he joined Rockefeller Center, rising to the position of chairman of the board (1945–1953, 1956–1958). In addition, he was a director in part of the family oil interests, the Creole Petroleum Corporation, the Venezuelan subsidiary of Standard Oil of New Jersey. From 1940 to 1944, Rockefeller was with the State Department as director of the Office of Inter-American Affairs, where he knit economic ties in the hemisphere by obtaining U.S. markets for Latin American goods formerly sold to Europe and by blacklisting pro-Axis businesses and individuals. In 1944, he became assistant secretary of state (American Republic affairs), in which capacity he signed the Act of Chapultepec for the United States in 1945. President Harry S Truman named him chairman of the International Development Advisory Board, and, as such, he played a part in the administration of the Point Four* program. From the 1950s, Rockefeller was involved in New York State politics as governor, 1958–1973, and in national politics as a frequent contender for his party's presidential nomination and as vice-president, 1974–1977. Leaving politics in 1977, Rockefeller promoted fine art reproductions until his death in New York City on January 26, 1979. Twice married, he was the author of *Unity, Freedom, and Peace* (1968). Connery, Robert H., *Rockefeller of New York* (1979); Mecham, J. Lloyd, *The United States and Inter-American Security, 1889–1960* (1961); *NCAB*, 1:196; Persico, Joseph E., *The Imperial Rockefeller* (1982); *New York Times*, January 27–28, 1979; Woods, Randall B., *The Roosevelt Foreign Policy Establishment and the "Good Neighbor": The United States and Argentina, 1941–1945* (1979).

ROCKHILL, WILLIAM WOODVILLE (1854–1914). A turn-of-the-century diplomat with vast knowledge of and experience in the Far East, W. W. Rockhill was born in Philadelphia in April 1854. He graduated from a military school in St. Ayr, France, in 1873, where he had become interested in Far Eastern studies. After a stint as a lieutenant in the French army, stationed in Algiers, Rockhill joined the Foreign Service and held a series of minor posts in Peking and Seoul between 1884 and 1888. Over the next five years (1888–1893), he pursued Eastern studies for the Smithsonian Institution, traveling to Mongolia and Tibet (he was the third white man to visit Tibet). He returned to the State Department in 1893 as chief clerk (1893–1894), rising to third assistant secretary of state (1894–1895) and assistant secretary (1896–1897). From 1897–1899, he was minister to Greece, Romania, and Serbia. In 1899, he returned to Washington as director of the International Bureau of American Republics,* a post he held until 1905, except for a leave in 1900–1901, when he went to China as a special agent to mitigate the international response and indemnity demands to the Boxer Rebellion* and sign the final protocol for the United States. Rockhill, who advocated a generally benevolent China policy, made his most significant diplomatic contribution on the Open Door Policy (1899–1900), in which Secretary of State John Hay* used Rockhill's ideas as expressed in a State Department memorandum of August 1899. From 1905 to 1909, Rockhill was minister to China; this mission was followed by appointments as minister to Russia (1910–1911) and Turkey (1911–1913). His mission to Russia was especially fortuitous because of Russia's activities in the Far East and Rockhill's knowledge of the area. After his retirement from the State Department in 1913, Rockhill was invited to become an adviser to Chinese President Yuan Shih-kai, but he died in Honolulu on December 8, 1914, en route to China. Rockhill was married to Caroline Adams in 1876; after her death, he married Edith Howell Perkins in 1900. *DAB*, 16:55; Dennis, A.L.P., *Adventures in American Diplomacy, 1896–1906* (1928); Hunt, Michael H., *The Making of a Special Relationship: The United States and China to 1914* (1983); McKee, Delber L., *Chinese Exclusion and the Open Door* (1971); *New York Times*, December 9, 1914; Varg, Paul A., *Open Door Diplomat: The Life of W. W. Rockhill* (1952).

RODGERS, JOE M. (b. 1933). Born in Bay Minette, Alabama, on November 12, 1933, Joe Rodgers graduated with a civil engineering degree from the University of Alabama in 1956. After three years in the Coast Guard, Rodgers became chief engineer for Burgess, Inc. (1959–1963) and manager of sales and products for the Dixie Concrete Pipe Line Company (1963–1966) before founding and serving as chairman of his own company, Rodgers Construction International. In 1976, he founded JMR Investments of Nashville, Tennessee, and in 1979, he became chairman of American Constructors, Inc. Active in the highest circles of Republican party politics since the late 1970s, Rodgers was appointed U.S. commissioner-general to the 1982 World's Fair in Knoxville, Tennessee. In 1984, he worked as the finance chairman for the Reagan-Bush reelection campaign; the following year, he was named ambassador to France. *WWA* (1986–1987):2366.

ROGERS, WILLIAM PIERCE (b. 1913). President Richard M. Nixon's first secretary of state (1969–1973), William P. Rogers was born in Norfolk, New York, on June 23, 1913, graduated from Colgate (1934) and Cornell Law School

(1937), and was admitted to the bar in 1937. From 1938 to 1942, he served as an assistant district attorney in New York under Thomas E. Dewey. After four years of naval duty during World War II (1942–1946), Rogers went to work for the U.S. Senate as a special counsel (1947–1948) and as chief counsel for a subcommittee of the Senate Investigations Committee (1948–1950). He practiced law in Washington from 1950 to 1953 but was closely involved in Nixon's campaign for the vice-presidency in 1952 and as a result was named deputy attorney general in the Eisenhower administration in 1953. Four years later he rose to attorney general, where his main concern was in enforcing civil rights legislation. In private law practice from 1961 to 1969, Rogers emerged again in 1969 with the Republicans' recapture of the White House. His lack of experience in foreign affairs made his appointment as secretary of state something of a surprise, but he was a long-time friend, whom Nixon trusted and who would let Nixon be, in effect, his own secretary of state. In addition Rogers was considered to have negotiating skills and judgment sufficient to cope with foreign leaders and to have the ability to get along with both Congress and the press. Because Nixon and his adviser on national security affairs, Henry Kissinger,* reserved much of the major areas of diplomacy to themselves, Rogers's activities were limited to the more peripheral concerns of U.S. foreign policy. He participated in early attempts to settle the Middle East turmoil (Rogers Plan),* worked on preparations for a European security conference, and participated in talks on mutual balanced force reduction* between Eastern and Western Europe, but played little part in Vietnamese peace negotiations or Strategic Arms Limitation Talks (SALT).* Rogers resigned at Nixon's request in 1973 so that Kissinger could become secretary of state. Rogers married Adele Langston in 1936 and since 1973 has practiced law in New York City and Washington. In 1986, he headed the commission that investigated the space shuttle *Challenger* disaster. Brandon, Henry, *The Retreat of American Power* (1972); *CB* (1969):372–75; Szulc, Tad, *The Illusion of Peace* (1978); *New York Times*, December 1, 1972, February 4, 1986; *WWA* (1986–1987):2373.

ROGERS ACT (1924). This important act created the modern Foreign Service by combining the diplomatic service, responsible for the political functions of the legation or embassy, and the consular service, responsible for the legal function, into a single entity. The act established career conditions for Foreign Service officers, creating titles and grades, providing for entrance by examination, requiring the keeping of efficiency records, and setting up a retirement system—all free from political influence. The Rogers Act also secured for Foreign Service personnel higher salaries than other civil service officers of similar rank and seniority were receiving. The Foreign Service Act of 1946* built upon the Rogers Act, further clarifying and professionalizing the Foreign Service. In a practical sense, notes Plischke, the main result of the Rogers Act was not only to combine diplomatic and consular services but also to permit the interchange of personnel between the two. The act was named for its congressional sponsor,

Congressman John J. Rogers (R., Massachusetts), but Wilbur J. Carr,* a State Department official, was also instrumental in its development. Harr, John E., *The Professional Diplomat* (1960); Ilchman, Warren F., *Professional Diplomacy in the United States, 1779–1939* (1961); Plischke, Elmer, *The Conduct of American Diplomacy* (1967).

ROGERS PLAN, proposal for Middle East peace, 1969. Secretary of State William P. Rogers* combined proposals for Israeli-Egyptian peace and Israeli-Jordanian peace in this plan for a general Middle East settlement. In its simplest form, the Rogers Plan called for Arab consent to a permanent peace based on the assurance to Israel of territorial integrity under the provisions of Security Council Resolution 242,* following which Israel would withdraw from territory occupied since the Six-Day War* in June 1967. (Security Council Resolution 242, adopted in November 1967, called for the evacuation of Israeli-occupied territory and satisfaction of Palestinian rights but also recognized Israel's need for security, peace, and free access to regional waterways, including the Suez Canal.) Rogers hoped to work out the settlement through cooperation with the Soviet Union, but neither Israel nor the Arab states found the plan acceptable. Brandon, Henry A., *The Retreat of American Power* (1972); Stookey, Robert W., *America and the Arab States* (1975); Szulc, Tad, *The Illusion of Peace* (1978).

ROHDE, RUTH BRYAN OWEN (1885–1954). A daughter of William Jennings Bryan,* Ruth Bryan was born in Jacksonville, Illinois, on October 2, 1885. She attended public schools in Lincoln, Nebraska, and the University of Nebraska and traveled in Europe and the Caribbean. An early marriage to William Homer Leavitt ended in divorce in 1909, and the following year she married Reginald Altham Owen, a British military officer. During World War I, she worked as a nurse in the Middle East and was a member of the executive committee of the American Women's War Relief Fund. After the war, she lectured on the Chautauqua circuit and taught at the University of Miami (Florida) before her election as a Democrat in 1928 to the U.S. House of Representatives. An enthusiastic advocate of women in politics, she was defeated for reelection in 1932. The following year she was appointed minister to Denmark, the first American woman to hold ministerial rank. Her three-year mission in Copenhagen was mainly social, although a minor controversy arose in 1934 when she used a Coast Guard cutter to travel to the United States from Greenland, a trip described as an "extravagant junket" by congressional opponents. She wrote two books related to her travels and diplomatic service, *Leaves from a Greenland Diary* (1935) and *Denmark Caravan* (1936). In later years, she lived in Ossining, New York, wrote, and lectured, emerging into public life in 1945 to serve as a special assistant for public liaison at the San Francisco Conference* and in 1949 as an alternate delegate to the United Nations* General Assembly. Reginald Owen died in 1927, and she married Borge Rohde in 1936. She died in Copenhagen on July 26, 1954. *CB* (1944): 522–525; *NCAB*, A:368; *New York Times*, July 27, 1954.

ROOSEVELT, ANNA ELEANOR (1884–1962). The wife of President Franklin D. Roosevelt and a woman active in U.S. foreign policy in her own right, Eleanor Roosevelt was born October 11, 1884, in New York City. Her family, distantly related to Franklin Roosevelt's, was wealthy and socially prominent; she was educated in England and by travel in Europe. She married in 1905 and took a more independent and public role as First Lady than most other presidential wives, emerging as a spokswoman on a large number of issues of concern to women. After the death of her husband, Eleanor Roosevelt was appointed a member of the U.S. delegation to the United Nations,* a post she held from 1945 to 1953 and again in 1961. There she opposed the U.S. arms embargo to Israel in 1948, favored the partition of Palestine into Jewish and Arab states, and advocated negotiating an end to the cold war,* ending nuclear testing, and recognizing the People's Republic of China. Her most prominent UN assignment was that of chairman of the Commission on Human Rights, part of the UN Educational, Scientific, and Cultural Organization, from 1946 to 1951. Her views were considered idealistic, but she won the admiration of old political foes such as John Foster Dulles* and Senator Arthur Vandenberg* (R., Michigan) as she supervised the drafting of a Covenant on Human Rights, accepted by the U.S. Congress. In 1953, she resigned when the Republican Eisenhower administration came into office. After 1953, she traveled frequently, wrote her autobiography, and was active in the American Association for the United Nations. She died in New York City on November 7, 1962. Cook, Blanche Wiesen, "Eleanor Roosevelt and Human Rights: The Battle for Peace and Planetary Decency," in Crapol, Edward P., *Women and American Foreign Policy* (1987); Lash, Joseph, *Eleanor: The Years Alone* (1972); *NCAB*, 57:601; Roosevelt, Eleanor, "The Promise of Human Rights," *Foreign Affairs* 26 (April 1948): 470–77, and *Autobiography* (1961); *New York Times*, November 8, 1962; Youngs, J. William T., *Eleanor Roosevelt: A Personal and Public Life* (1985).

ROOSEVELT COROLLARY (1904), statement of diplomatic policy. An extension of the Monroe Doctrine (1823),* the Roosevelt Corollary asserted the right of the United States to intervene in a Latin American nation in order to prevent intervention by a European nation. At this time, a number of Caribbean and Central American nations were deeply in debt to various European powers, which were threatening to intervene to collect what was owed them. The United States regarded such interventions, especially in the area of the proposed Panama Canal, as threats to its security. Moreover, it was feared that these interventions could become roadblocks to American economic hegemony in Latin America. The corollary was first made public December 6, 1904, by President Theodore Roosevelt in his annual message to Congress and implemented the following February by means of a protocol to the Senate. Over the next several years, the corollary was utilized on a number of occasions to justify intervention, particularly in instances when Caribbean or Central American nations had defaulted on payments of debts to European creditors. In 1928, the *Memorandum on the Monroe Doctrine*, by Under Secretary of State J. Reuben Clark,* repudiated the

Roosevelt Corollary. Bemis, Samuel F., *The Latin American Policy of the United States; FR* (1905), 298–391; Perkins, Dexter, *The Monroe Doctrine, 1867–1907* (1937).

ROOSEVELT-KONOYE MEETING (1941). In August 1941, Japanese Prime Minister Prince Fumimaro Konoye, trying to find a way to avoid war with the United States while still saving face in the light of harsher economic sanctions, proposed that he and President Franklin D. Roosevelt meet, possibly in Alaska. American Ambassador to Japan Joseph Grew* urged careful consideration of the proposal, noting that the military elements in Japanese politics would seize the nation's destiny should the meeting fail. Secretary of State Cordell Hull,* however, felt that Konoye was not powerful enough in Tokyo to be trusted, that MAGIC* confirmed this reality of Japanese politics, and that the idea was a Japanese stall to allow more time to prepare for a surprise military move. Roosevelt hesitated for several weeks before concurring with Hull that the meeting should not take place, at least not until Japan had nullified the Tripartite Pact* and withdrawn from China as preconditions. The failure of the Roosevelt administration to agree to the meeting has occasioned controversy; some observers and historians, including Grew, believe it was a mistake to have passed up this chance to break a diplomatic deadlock. Divine, Robert A., *The Reluctant Belligerent* (1965); Feis, Herbert, *The Road to Pearl Harbor* (1950).

ROOSEVELT-LITVINOV AGREEMENTS (1933). After the Russian Revolution of 1917, the United States chose not to establish diplomatic relations with the Soviet Union, feeling that the Communist experiment would soon be replaced by a more democratic government. But in the early 1930s, when the Soviet government seemed more cooperative with the West, the United States saw potential economic gain from recognizing Moscow, and these factors brought Soviet Foreign Minister Maxim Litvinov to Washington, where, on November 16, 1933, he signed the Roosevelt-Litvinov Agreements with President Franklin D. Roosevelt. In return for the establishment of full diplomatic relations, the Soviet Union agreed to protect the religious liberty of Americans in Russia, to prevent the formation of organizations dedicated to the overthrow of the U.S. government, and to pay at least $75 million additional interest on loans for Soviet purchases in the United States (as compensation for older debts). Although often sharp and not entirely cordial, the negotiations were successful in their purpose of establishing diplomatic ties. According to Bishop, the Soviet government did not live up to the pledges made in the Roosevelt-Litvinov Agreements, contributing to the widely believed notion that "you can't trust the Russians." The failure to pay acknowledged debts and to stop the activities of the Comintern and its connections with the U.S. Communist party were the most glaring broken pledges, causing some Americans to advocate severing diplomatic relations in the mid-1930s, an advocacy not shared by the Roosevelt administration. Bennett, Edward M., *Franklin D. Roosevelt and the Search for Security: American Soviet Relations, 1933–1939* (1985); Bishop, Donald G., *The Roosevelt-Litvinov Agreements: The*

American View (1965); *FR* (1933), 2:778–840; *FR: Soviet Union 1933–1939*, pp. 1–62; Gaddis, John L., *Russia, the Soviet Union and the United States* (1978).

"ROOSTOOK WAR" (1838), U.S.–Canadian conflict. In late 1838, in the Aroostook Valley, an area of boundary dispute between Great Britain and the United States, residents of Maine and Canada clashed when the Canadians cut timber in Maine and then seized an agent sent by the Maine governor. Troops expelled the Canadians, but tensions escalated. Gen. Winfield Scott arrived to work out a temporary settlement, which was accomplished in an agreement signed by the governors of Maine and Nova Scotia. In 1842, the Webster-Ashburton Treaty* brought about a permanent settlement of this northeastern boundary dispute. Jones, Howard, *To the Webster-Ashburton Treaty* (1977); McCormac, Eugene I., "John Forsyth," in Bemis, Samuel F., ed., *American Secretaries of State and Their Diplomacy*, vol. 4 (1928); Pletcher, David, *The Diplomacy of Annexation* (1973).

ROOT, ELIHU (1845–1937). Secretary of state (1905–1909) under President Theodore Roosevelt, Elihu Root was involved in foreign policy matters for much of his long life. Born February 15, 1845, in Clinton, New York, he graduated from Hamilton College (B.A., 1864; M.A., 1867) and the New York University Law School (1867). After gaining admission to the bar in 1867, he began a law partnership with J. A. Strahan in 1868 in New York City and soon became extremely successful in corporate law, to a point where he was the "acknowledged leader of the American bar." A Republican, Root joined the Union League Club but confined his involvement to local politics until 1899, when he became a friend and adviser to New York politician Theodore Roosevelt. In 1899, he became secretary of war, a position that brought him his first major contact with foreign affairs. He helped with the supervision of the newly acquired territories of Cuba, Puerto Rico, and the Philippines, directed the anti-insurrection campaign in the Philippines, and wrote the island's Organic Act (1902), setting up a colonial administration. In 1905, Root moved to the State Department, where his main contribution was in Latin American relations. He toured South America in 1906, helping to improve the U.S. image and making contacts with various Latin American diplomats. He called the Washington Conference (1907)* to settle affairs in troublesome Central America; this meeting resulted in the founding of a Central American Court* to settle isthmian differences. Root tried also to build friendly relations with Japan through the Gentlemen's Agreement (1907)* and the Root-Takahira Agreement (1908).* He was involved in trying to solve the fisheries problems with Canada and after leaving office was U.S. counsel in the North American Fisheries Arbitration (1910). In addition, he negotiated arbitration* treaties with twenty-four nations, secured the ratification of over forty-five treaties, settled many outstanding but minor disputes, and reorganized the U.S. diplomatic and consular services. Root was elected to the Senate after leaving the State Department and was active in the Panama Canal tolls controversy,* believing that U.S. ships should pay tolls like other nations.

In 1917, he headed a special mission to Russia, hoping to keep that nation in the war. After the failure of this venture, his relations with Wilson declined. Root was a reservationist* in the League of Nations* debate, served on the committee that wrote the statute for the Permanent Court of International Justice,* and advocated U.S. membership on the court without league membership. In 1921–1922, he was a delegate at the Washington Conference,* where his main responsibility was drafting the Five-Power Treaty.* In 1929, he was the unofficial U.S. representative to the League of Nations. Married to Clara Frances Wales in 1878, Elihu Root died in New York City on February 7, 1937. He received the Nobel Peace Prize in 1912 in recognition of his work in the Western Hemisphere, with Japan, and in the conclusion of the arbitration treaties. He was also deeply involved in the work of the Carnegie Endowment for International Peace,* serving as its president from 1910 to 1925. *DAB*, Supp. 2:577; Jessup, Philip C., *Elihu Root*, 2 vols. (1938); Leopold, Richard W., *Elihu Root and the Conservative Tradition* (1954); *New York Times*, February 8, 1937.

ROOT, JOSEPH POMEROY (1826–1885). Born in Greenwich, Massachusetts, on April 23, 1826, Joseph P. Root was graduated from Berkshire Medical College in 1851, moved to Connecticut, and began a medical practice. He served a term in the Connecticut legislature (1855–1856) before emigrating to Kansas, where he was politically active in the abolitionist faction as a state senator (1857–1859) and lieutenant governor (1861–1863). During the Civil War, he was an army surgeon, and after the war he returned to Kansas and Republican party politics. In 1870, the Grant administration appointed Root minister to Chile. He stayed three years at the post, traveling a good deal and reporting to the State Department on the advisability of U.S. shipping lines working the Chilean coast, the causes of earthquakes, and the status of Indians in Chile. During a severe smallpox epidemic in Santiago (1872), Root provided useful medical service. He returned to Kansas in 1873, resumed the practice of medicine, and involved himself with causes such as temperance, greenbackism, and the Kansas Historical Society. From 1877 to 1879, he lived in Clifton Springs, New York. Root, who married Francis Evaline Alden in 1851, died in Wyandotte, Kansas, on July 20, 1885. *DAB*, 16:150; *NCAB*, 13:309.

ROOT-TAKAHIRA AGREEMENT (1908). After the successful visit of the Great White Fleet* and preliminary talks carried on in Japan by President Theodore Roosevelt's friend, newspaperman John C. O'Laughlin, Secretary of State Elihu Root,* and Japanese Ambassador Kogoro Takahira in November 1908 exchanged a set of notes known as the Root-Takahira Agreement. By its terms, neither country would seek absolute control of the Pacific; each country would recognize the status quo in the area; and neither would disrupt the territorial integrity of China. According to Neu, Roosevelt's objectives were to ease tensions with the Japanese and to clarify the status quo and the vital interests of each in the Far East. Some historians have criticized the agreement as a surrender of the Open Door* principles, whereas others have felt it was a realistic rec-ognition of Japan's position of strength in the region. Esthus, however, concludes that the main significance of the agreement was to mollify public opinion, ruffled by the hostility of the past two years. Bailey, Thomas A., "The Root-Takahira Agreement of 1908," *Pacific Historical Review* 9 (March 1940): 19–35; Esthus, Raymond A., *Theodore Roosevelt and Japan* (1966); Neu, Charles E., *An Uncertain Friendship* (1967).

ROSECRANS, WILLIAM STARKE (1819–1898). A notable Union Civil War general, William S. Rosecrans was born September 6, 1819, in Delaware County, Ohio, and was an 1842 graduate of West Point. He married Ann Eliza Hegeman shortly after his graduation and taught at West Point until 1847, when he moved on to other army assignments. He left active service in 1854 and worked as an engineer and architect in Cincinnati, where he also managed an oil refinery. When the Civil War broke out, he was a volunteer who, rising quickly to the rank of general, saw much successful battle action until losing at the Battle of Chickamauga in September 1863. In 1868, he was named minister to Mexico, and in his six months there (December 1868-June 1869), he encouraged railway construction and helped bring about greater political stability. His experience in Mexico was personally important, for it led to his involvement in various Mexican railroad and industrial ventures, including the Tehuantepec isthmian railway project, between 1869 and 1881. In 1872, he wrote a short book on Mexico's need to attract foreign capital for railroad construction, published in Spanish. From 1881 to 1885, Rosecrans was a U.S. representative from California; from 1885 to 1893, he was register of the Treasury Department. After 1893, he retired to his ranch at Redondo, California, where he grew fruit until his death March 11, 1898. *DAB*, 16:163; *NCAB*, 4:162; *New York Times*, March 12, 1898.

ROSTOW, EUGENE VICTOR DEBS (b. 1913). Born in Brooklyn on August 25, 1913, Eugene Rostow graduated from Yale (B.A., 1933; LL.B., 1937; M.A., 1944) and was admitted to the New York bar in 1937. He practiced law in New York City for a year before joining the Yale Law School faculty in 1938. He maintained his teaching post until 1961 but took time out to serve as general counsel for Lend-Lease* (1942–1944), as director of economic operations, North African theater (1944–1945), and as assistant executive secretary of the United Nations* Economic Commission for Europe (1949–1950). In 1955, he became dean of Yale Law School, a post he held until 1965, a year after he resumed teaching. Rostow became under secretary of state (political affairs) in 1966, the third-ranking post in the State Department. In this office, he supervised economic activities, including assistance programs, especially those directed to India, In-donesia, and Pakistan. In addition he had a hand in Middle East problems, chaired the Interdepartmental Task Force on Telecommunications Policy, and worked on various abortive peace initiatives to end the Vietnam War. Rostow thought U.S. policy in Vietnam was flawed by tentativeness, indirection, and the influence of misinformed public opinion. He advocated closer alliances with European and Asian friends to contain Soviet and Chinese expansion and greater coordination of international monetary and economic policies among allies. Rostow left the State Department in 1969 and returned to teaching, at Oxford (1969–1970) and Yale (1970–1981, 1983–1984). In 1981, he joined the Reagan administration as director of the Arms Control and Disarmament Agency, a post he held until 1983. An emeritus professor at Yale since 1984, Rostow has also taught at the National Defense University and has been president of the Atlantic Treaty Assocation. Rostow, who married Edna Berman Greenberg in 1933, is the author of, among others, *Planning for Freedom* (1959), *A National Policy for the Oil Industry* (1947), *Law, Power, and the Pursuit of Peace* (1968), and *Peace in the Balance* (1972). Brownstein, Ronald, and Nina Easton, *Reagan's Ruling Class* (1982); *CB* (1961):393–95; *WWA* (1986–1987):2397.

ROSTOW, WALT WHITMAN (b. 1916). An important White House foreign policy adviser during the 1960s, and the brother of Eugene Rostow,* Walt W. Rostow was born in New York City on October 7, 1916 and graduated from Yale (B.A., 1936; Ph.D., 1940), spending two years at Oxford as a Rhodes Scholar in the process. After a year's teaching at Columbia. Rostow worked for the Office of Strategic Services (OSS), attached to the British Air Ministry during World War II, and was the assistant chief of the State Department's Germany-Austria economic division for a year after the war. He taught at Oxford, 1946–1947, and then had a two-year stint with the Economic Commission for Europe before settling into teaching and writing on a regular basis at Cambridge (1949–1960). During this time he wrote *British Economy of the Nineteenth Century* (1948), the highly influential *The Stages of Economic Growth* (1960), and *The United States in the World Arena* (1960). He began to advise John F. Kennedy in 1957 and, upon Kennedy's election as president in 1961, became deputy special assistant for national security affairs and chairman of the Policy Planning Council. He continued in the post under President Lyndon B. Johnson until 1966, when he became a special assistant to the president, serving until 1969. A positive-thinking cold warrior,* Rostow was a believer in the policy of containing Soviet and Chinese expansion, which he saw occurring in wars of "national liberation," such as Vietnam, and which had to be forestalled. He went on the Taylor-Rostow Mission (1961)* to Vietnam, which recommended the sending of combat troops to the war and later became a great believer in the efficacy of bombing and perhaps the most loyal supporter of the Johnson administration's war policy. So loyal was he that others in the administration criticized him for his inflexibility in foreign policy thinking and his inability to adapt to changed situations, such as that wrought by the Sino-Soviet split in the 1960s. Rostow also helped plan the Alliance for Progress* and served from 1964 to 1966 on the alliance's Inter-American Conference. He married Elspeth Vaughan Davies in 1947 and since 1969 has taught at the University of Texas. He has written a memoir, *The Diffusion of Power* (1972); a summing up of much of his economic thought, *The World Economy: History and Prospect* (1978); and a number of other books, including *Eisenhower, Kennedy and Foreign Aid* (1985) and *The United States and the Regional Organizations of Asia and the Pacific* (1986). *CB* (1961):395–97; Garraty, John, ed., *Encyclopedia of American Biography* (1974); Halberstam, David, *The Best and the Brightest* (1972); *WWA* (1986–1987):2397–98.

ROWE, LEO STANTON (1871–1946). Leo S. Rowe was born in McGregor, Iowa, on September 17, 1871, graduated from the Wharton School of Finance and Commerce (University of Pennsylvania) in 1890, and received a Ph.D. from the University of Halle in 1892 and an LL.B. from the University of Pennsylvania Law School in 1895. Although he was admitted to the bar in 1895, he chose to teach instead and taught classes in political science and law at Penn from 1895 to 1917. During his teaching career, he undertook occasional special assignments for the government, including service on the Commission to Revise and Compile the Laws of Porto [*sic*] Rico (1900–1902), the Insular Code Commission (1902), the Third International Conference of American States (1906),* and several other conferences dealing with inter-American affairs. In 1917, he became assistant secretary of the treasury; there his duties included supervision of Latin American affairs and international loans. Two years later, he moved to the post of chief of the Latin American Division in the State Department, where he began the process of ending the U.S. policy of intervention. In 1920, Rowe was chosen director-general of the Pan-American Union,* a post he held the rest of his life. He strengthened the role of his office and that of the organization in harmonizing hemispheric relations, especially during the era of the Good Neighbor Policy.* He traveled widely in Latin America, encouraged cultural exchanges and educational improvements, and attended virtually every conference between 1920 and 1945. Never married, Rowe was killed in a traffic accident in Washington on December 5, 1946. Pan American Union *Bulletin* (April 1947); *DAB*, Supp. 4:705; *New York Times*, December 6, 1946.

RULE OF THE WAR OF 1756, British maritime policy. This "Rule of '56," as it was often known, became a maritime policy in the Seven Years' War, stipulating that trade prohibited to neutrals in peacetime must also be closed to them in wartime. Although the *Polly* decision (1800)* virtually nullified the Rule of '56, the *Essex* decision (1805)* restored its limitations on American (and other neutral) commerce in the years before the War of 1812. Perkins, Bradford, *Prologue to War* (1961).

RUSH, DAVID KENNETH (b. 1910). Kenneth Rush was born in Walla Walla, Washington, on January 17, 1910, and graduated from the University of Tennessee (A.B., 1930) and Yale (J.D., 1932). He practiced law in New York City from 1932 to 1936, taught law at Duke University, 1936–1937, where one of his students was Richard M. Nixon, and then joined Union Carbide, where he remained until 1969, serving as president from 1966 to 1969. A Republican, Rush was appointed ambassador to West Germany by his former law student in 1969. There for three years, he signed the Quadripartite Agreement on Berlin, 1971,* guaranteeing Western access to the city, and proved himself a firm but tactful negotiator in the process. In 1972, he returned to Washington as deputy secretary of defense but the following year moved back to the State Department as deputy secretary, in which position he functioned as acting secretary of state between the terms of William P. Rogers* and Henry Kissinger.* At the end of the Nixon administration in 1974, Rush was briefly a counselor to the president for economic policy. Later that year, under President Gerald R. Ford, he became ambassador to France. In Paris, he arranged the meeting in Martinique between Ford and French President Giscard D'Estaing and forged good relations with French Foreign Minister Jean Sauvagnargues during a time when inflation and oil policies were potentially disruptive issues. Rush married Jane Gilbert Smith in 1937, is an avid golfer, and has been active in the Foreign Policy Association,* serving as its director from 1964 to 1969. He also serves on the board of the Alliance to Save Energy and was chairman of the President's Committee for the German American Tricentennial, 1983–1984. *CB* (1975):366–68; *New York Times*, January 26, 1972, May 28, September 5, 1974; *WWA* (1986–1987):2418.

RUSH, RICHARD (1780–1859). A native of Philadelphia, where he was born on August 29, 1780, Richard Rush graduated from the College of New Jersey, read law, and was admitted to the bar in 1800. He practiced law in Philadelphia, 1800–1811, before entering politics as state attorney general (1811–1812), comptroller of the Treasury Department (1812–1814) and U.S. Attorney General (1814–1817). From March until September 1817, between the tenures of James Monroe* and John Quincy Adams,* Rush was Secretary of State ad interim. In this post he negotiated the Rush-Bagot Agreement,* one of the basic Anglo-American settlements following the War of 1812. Late in 1817, he was named minister to Great Britain, a mission that lasted eight years. In London, he handled a variety of problems remaining from the war, including fisheries, the northwestern boundary, and America's share in the West India trade. He negotiated the arrangement provided for joint occupation of Oregon* and discussed the delicate problem of the Ambrister and Arbuthnot Affair (1818),* Andrew Jackson's execution of two British subjects during his celebrated raid into Spanish Florida. Rush's most widely known role in diplomacy perhaps is his transmitting the suggestion of George Canning for a joint declaration of restraint toward Latin America, a suggestion that ultimately developed into the Monroe Doctrine.* Rush returned to the United States in 1825, spent four years as secretary of the treasury, and retired to private life, writing *Memoranda of a Residence at the Court of London* (1833; 1845). In 1847, Rush was called again into diplomatic service, this time as minister to France. His two years in Paris were filled with the events and aftermath of the February (1848) revolution, and Rush recognized the new French

Republic without waiting for instructions from Washington, an action that won subsequent praise. Rush was married to Catherine E. Murray and died in Philadelphia on July 30, 1859. *DAB*, 16:231; Powell, John Harvey, *Richard Rush: Republican Diplomat* (1942); Willson, Beckles, *America's Ambassadors to England 1785–1929* (1929), and *America's Ambassadors to France, 1777–1927* (1928).

RUSH-BAGOT AGREEMENT (1817), Anglo-American diplomatic agreement. Naval engagements on the Great Lakes during the War of 1812 and postwar arms buildups in the area prompted British Minister to the United States Charles Bagot and Secretary of State James Monroe* to negotiate toward an arms limitation agreement. Although an atmosphere of mutual suspicion and doubt hung over the talks, formal agreement was reached in April 1817 by Bagot and Richard Rush,* then acting secretary of state. The Senate approved the arrangement a year later. By its terms, each side limited its naval forces to one ship on Lake Ontario, one on Lake Champlain, and two on the upper lakes, to be used only to enforce revenue laws. The Rush-Bagot Agreement was the first instance of reciprocal naval disarmament in the history of international relations and, according to Bemis, an "advantageous arrangement" for the United States. Bemis, Samuel F., *John Quincy Adams and the Foundations of American Foreign Policy* (1949); Perkins, Bradford, *Castlereagh and Adams* (1964).

RUSK, DAVID DEAN (b. 1909). Secretary of state (1961–1969) under Presidents John F. Kennedy and Lyndon B. Johnson, Dean Rusk was born February 9, 1909, in Cherokee County, Georgia, graduated from Davidson (B.A., 1931) and Oxford (B.S., 1933; M.A., 1934), and taught at Mills College from 1934 to 1938. In 1937, he began studying law at the University of California, maintaining his position at Mills; in 1938, he became dean of faculty at the college. Rusk left both Mills and his law study in 1940 to join the army, where he served in the China-Burma-India theater during World War II. After his discharge in 1946, he held positions with the War Department, 1946–1947, before moving to the State Department as director of the Office of Special Political Affairs (later renamed Office of United Nations Affairs), helping to develop the policy of containment.* In 1949, he was promoted to assistant secretary of state (United Nations affairs); later that year he rose to deputy under secretary of state, the third-ranking post in the State Department hierarchy. In 1950, however, he was granted his wish to step down a rung and become assistant secretary of state (Far Eastern affairs) in order to deal more directly with Chinese, Korean, and Japanese matters. During this time he won the admiration of Secretary of State Dean Acheson* and John Foster Dulles,* whom he helped negotiate the Japanese Peace Treaty (1951).* In 1952, he left the State Department to become president of the Rockefeller Foundation; in nine years, he did much to expand the foundation's international activities. Upon the recommendation of Acheson and Robert A. Lovett,* Rusk was named secretary of state in 1961. Somewhat to Kennedy's disappointment, he stayed in the background and seldom was a strong advocate of administration policy. Highly self-controlled and knowledgeable, he was known as an excellent administrator but not given to innovative policy-making. His Vietnam policy was hawkish, based on his high regard for the military and his strong antipathy to the People's Republic of China, acquired in World War II and Korea. Under President Lyndon B. Johnson, to whom he related more easily, Rusk concentrated his attention on Vietnam and containment and took little note of Third World* problems, diplomatic administration, or long-range planning. Throughout his tenure, he enjoyed excellent relations with Congress and especially with southern committee chairmen. Rusk married Virginia Foisie in 1937 and since 1970 has taught international law at the University of Georgia. Cohen, Warren I., "Dean Rusk," in Ferrell, Robert H., ed., *American Secretaries of State and Their Diplomacy* (1980); Halberstam, David, *The Best and the Brightest* (1972); Hilsman, Roger, *To Move a Nation* (1967); *NCAB*, J:22; Schoenbaum, Thomas J., *Waging Peace and War: Dean Rusk in the Truman, Kennedy, and Johnson Years* (1988); *WWA* (1986–1987):2418.

RUSSELL, CHARLES WELLS (1856–1927). Born March 16, 1856, in Wheeling, West Virginia, Charles W. Russell graduated from Georgetown Law School (LL.B., 1883; LL.M., 1884) and went to work for the Justice Department. He investigated the French spoliation claims, 1886–1893, and conditions in Cuba, 1897. After the Treaty of Paris (1898),* he handled claims before the U.S.–Spanish Claims Commission. In 1902, as a special assistant to the attorney general, Russell investigated the French Panama Canal Company title, found it sound, and arranged for the transfer of the company's property to the United States. From 1902 to 1905, he was in charge of insular matters for the Justice Department, and from 1905 to 1909 he was assistant attorney general. Under the Taft administration, Russell was minister to Persia (1909–1914), handling U.S. affairs during a period in which Persian sovereignty was threatened by European-supported revolutionary organizations. When Persia, possibly upon Russell's suggestion, asked for U.S. financial advice, the minister escorted the Shuster mission (May–December 1911), headed by W. Morgan Shuster, around the country. In the end, Persian sovereignty was preserved. After 1914, Russell lived in Washington, writing poetry and editing the *Memoirs of Col. John S. Mosby* (1917). Married twice, first to Lucy Floyd Mosby, and after her death, to her sister, Lelia James Mosby, Russell died April 5, 1927, in Washington, D.C. *DAB*, 16:241; McDaniel, Robert A., *The Shuster Mission and the Persian Constitutional Revolution* (1974); Shuster, W. Morgan, *The Strangling of Persia* (1912).

RUSSELL, JONATHAN (1771–1832). Jonathan Russell was born in Providence, Rhode Island, on February 27, 1771, and graduated from Rhode Island College (now Brown University) in 1791. He became a successful merchant, a well-known orator, and a prominent Jeffersonian Republican. In 1810, he was made chargé d'affaires in Paris; the next year, he moved to London in the same post, remaining there until 1814. Part of the U.S. delegation that negotiated the Treaty of Ghent (1814),* Russell opposed conceding the free navigation of the

Mississippi River in exchange for rights in the northeastern fishing areas but otherwise played less of a role in the negotiations than the others in the delegation. A U.S. representative from 1821 to 1823, Russell's political career was undone because of a bitter quarrel he had with John Quincy Adams* over the Mississippi River fisheries controversy. When Russell tried to discredit Adams in 1822 by means of a falsified document from the Ghent negotiations, Adams used the press to disprove Russell's allegations one by one to a point where, according to Engleman, the phrase "to jonathanrussell" someone (meaning to destroy him publicly) became commonplace. The disgraced Russell, who was married twice, died in Milton, Massachusetts, on February 17, 1832. *DAB*, 16:254; Egan, Clifford L., *Neither Peace nor War: Franco-American Relations, 1803–1812* (1983); Engleman, Fred L., *The Peace of Christmas Eve* (1960); *NCAB*, 8:57.

RUSSELL, WILLIAM WORTHINGTON (1859–1944). Born in Washington, D.C., on December 3, 1859, W. W. Russell graduated in 1881 from the U.S. Naval Academy and became a civil engineer. He helped survey rail routes in South America and the United States, including the proposed route for the Tehuantepec ship-railway project of James B. Eads.* From 1895 to 1904, Russell was legation secretary in Caracas, Venezuela, but was recalled when the State Department broke off relations after the Venezuelan government had canceled several important American concessions. In 1904, Russell was sent to Panama as U.S. chargé d'affaires*; he was America's first accredited diplomatic representative there. Later in 1904, he moved to Bogotá as minister to Colombia, where he was involved in some tentative efforts to restore cordial relations after the Panamanian revolution. Russell had other diplomatic posts: minister to Venezuela (1905–1908), minister to the Dominican Republic (1910–1913, 1915–1925), and minister to Siam (1925–1927). In the Dominican Republic, Russell was minister during the U.S. armed intervention and assumption of financial control in 1916; his recommendations, based on the local situation, helped shape State Department policy. Following his last post, Russell lived in retirement in Washington, D.C., until his death on March 11, 1944. He married Grace C. Lidstone in 1905. Munro, Dana G., *Intervention and Dollar Diplomacy in the Caribbean, 1900–1921* (1964); *NCAB*, 15:58; *Washington Post*, March 13, 1944; *WWWA*, 4 (1961–1968):821.

RUSSIAN-AMERICAN COMPANY, Russian fur-trading company, c. 1750–1824. Founded in the mid-eighteenth century, the Russian-American Company was headquartered after 1799 at Sitka and monopolized hunting and trapping over a wide, undefined area of northwest North America south to 55° north latitude, where it came into conflict with various British, Spanish, and American claims. A more direct conflict arose in 1820–1821, with increased American interest in the region clashing with a Russian ukase claiming territorial exclusivity south to 51° north latitude. This conflict formed the basis for the noncolonization doctrine,* spelled out in the Monroe Doctrine (1823).* A convention, April 17, 1824, fixed the Russian southern boundary at 54° 40′, included an agreement on the principle of freedom of the seas,* and granted Americans the right to trade on unsettled parts of the northwest coast for a period of at least ten years. This convention was negotiated by Henry Middleton* for the United States and Count Nesselrode for Russia. Bemis, Samuel F., *John Quincy Adams and the Foundations of American Foreign Policy* (1949).

RUSSO-JAPANESE WAR (1904–1905). This Far Eastern conflict grew out of Japan's long-standing distrust of Russian moves in Manchuria and Korea, a threat to Japanese security, as well as the emergence of a younger, more confidently optimistic generation of Japanese political leaders. The war began in February 1904 with a Japanese naval attack on the Russian fleet and continued for over a year, with Japan generally having the upper hand militarily. In July 1905, delegations from the two sides entered peace negotiations, directed by President Theodore Roosevelt. These resulted in the Treaty of Portsmouth (1905).* U.S. policy was to prevent either side from gaining a decisive victory, which would threaten China, upset the balance of power in the Far East, and adversely affect American commerce in Manchuria. Beale, Howard K., *Theodore Roosevelt and the Rise of America to World Power* (1956); May, Ernest R., "The Far Eastern Policy of the United States in the Period of the Russo-Japanese War: A Russian View," *American Historical Review* 62 (1957):345–51; Neu, Charles E., *The Troubled Encounter* (1975); White, John Albert, *The Diplomacy of the Russo-Japanese War* (1964).

SACKETT, FREDERIC MOSELEY (1868–1941). A native of Providence, Rhode Island, where he was born December 17, 1868, Frederic M. Sackett graduated from Brown in 1890 and from Harvard Law School in 1893 and began the practice of law, gradually moving westward from Columbus, Ohio (1893–1897), to Cincinnati (1897–1898), to Louisville, Kentucky, where he made his permanent home after 1898. In 1907, he entered the business world as president of the Louisville Gas Company and the Louisville Lighting Company, remaining until 1913, when he assumed the presidency of Black Star Coal Company. In 1917, he became federal food administrator for Kentucky and formed a close friendship with Herbert Hoover, then the director of the Food Administration in Washington. In 1924, Sackett was elected as a Republican to the U.S. Senate from Kentucky, serving one term before being appointed ambassador to Germany in 1930. In that depression-wracked country, he worked with Chancellor Dr. Heinrich Brüning to revive the economy and made an emergency trip to Washington to transmit President Paul von Hindenberg's personal plea for U.S. aid; this led to President Herbert Hoover's one-year debt moratorium.* Sackett tried to save the Brüning government (and the Weimar Republic) from collapse, but the Hoover administration, preoccupied with domestic problems, was uninterested until the moratorium, which came too late. He left Germany in 1932 to go to London to help organize an upcoming economic conference and to the United States to campaign for Hoover. Back in Germany in early 1933, he observed the Nazi rise to power and then returned to his business interests in Kentucky. He married Olive Speed in 1898 and died in Baltimore on May 18, 1941. Burke, Bernard V., "American Economic Diplomacy and the Weimar Republic," *Mid-America* 54 (October 1972):211–33, and "Senator and Diplomat: The Public Career of Frederic M. Sackett," *Filson Club Historical Quarterly* 61, 2 (April 1987):185–216; *NCAB*, E:95; *New York Times*, May 19, 1941.

SAFER, MORLEY (b. 1931). Born November 8, 1931, in Toronto, Morley Safer attended the University of Western Ontario, worked briefly for Reuters in London in 1955, and then became a correspondent and producer for the Canadian Broadcasting Corporation (CBC), for which he covered the Algerian revolution. In 1961, he went to London for the CBC and in 1964 joined the Columbia Broadcasting System (CBS). His first major assignment for CBS was as a correspondent in Vietnam, and there he came to prominence as the first network reporter to portray American involvement in that war critically. Although his reporting outraged President Lyndon B. Johnson, it won several awards, encouraged other reporters to probe more deeply into the war, and gained for Safer a reputation among journalists as one of the best television reporters of the war. His coverage of Vietnam culminated with a one-hour special, "Morley Safer's Vietnam: A Personal View" (1967). From 1967 to 1970, he was a London correspondent for CBS, and early in 1971, he became a co-host of "60 Minutes," his current assignment. Gates, Gary Paul, *Air Time: The Inside Story of CBS News* (1978); *WWA* (1986–1987):2432.

ST. GERMAIN, TREATY OF (1919). Signed September 10, 1919, at St. Germain-en-Laye, a Paris suburb, this treaty ended World War I for Austria. Non-Germanic areas of Austria were detached and ceded to Italy and Czechoslovakia; minorities remaining in Austria were afforded special protection. Austria was disarmed, deprived of foreign investments, and charged with substantial reparations.* Because the treaty incorporated the Covenant of the League of Nations,* the United States refused to ratify it and on August 24, 1921, made a separate peace with Austria, which was ratified on October 18, 1921. *FR* (1921) 1:270–81; Hyamson, A. M., *A Dictionary of International Affairs* (1947); Low, Alfred D., *The Anschluss Movement, 1918–1919, and the Paris Peace Conference* (1974).

SALT. See STRATEGIC ARMS LIMITATION TALKS.

SAMOAN TREATY (1878). This treaty, made between Samoan native chiefs and Commander Richard W. Meade for the United States, offered the Samoans the good offices of the United States in disputes between the chiefs and other governments in return for American use of the harbor at Pago Pago. The treaty was concluded in 1872 but not ratified by the Senate until 1878 and reflects the increasing interest in the islands during the 1870s by several different U.S. commercial enterprises. Around the same time, Great Britain and Germany obtained similar treaties, setting up a rivalry that was later resolved by the Treaty of Berlin (1889)* and the Convention of 1899.* LaFeber, Walter, *The New Empire* (1963); Pletcher, David, *The Awkward Years* (1962); Ryden, George H., *The Foreign Policy of the United States in Relation to Samoa* (1933).

SAN DOMINGO IMPROVEMENT COMPANY, a New York company that built a railroad in Haiti in the 1880s and early 1890s. In 1893, at the suggestion of Secretary of State John W. Foster,* the company took over bond marketing and customs collections so that French or German interests would not assume them. New bond issues were floated and more railroad track was laid, all amid a good deal of inefficiency and competition. When a new government came into power in 1899, the company lost political favor, and the Haitian congress refused to pass a bill extending the financial privileges of the company, which, accordingly, complained to the State Department. Lengthy negotiations led to arbitration,* which ended in a $4.5 million award to the company. The company's claim, however, became intertwined with other financial problems of Haiti and contributed to the establishment of a U.S. customs receivership in 1907. *FR* (1904), 270–86; Munro, Dana G., *Intervention and Dollar Diplomacy in the Caribbean, 1900–1921* (1964).

SAN FRANCISCO CONFERENCE (1945). More formally known as the United Nations* Conference on International Organization, this meeting, from April 25 to June 26, 1945, brought together delegates from fifty nations to write the United Nations Charter based on draft proposals prepared at the Dumbarton Oaks Conference.* The main point of contention was the extent of the veto power of the permanent Security Council members. After some acrimonious discussion, and communication with Soviet Premier Joseph Stalin in Moscow, the "Yalta formula" for the veto, providing for the veto on council action but not topics of debate, was adopted. One major point of contention concerned the manner in which regional organizations should relate to the Security Council, as the United States and other Western Hemisphere nations wanted to settle inter-American disputes among themselves. This was resolved in Article 51 of the charter, which permitted "individual or collective self-defense against armed attack, until the Security Council has taken the [necessary] measures." Other major decisions concerned the General Assembly, which was given more authority to make recommendations to the Security Council, and the Economic and Social Council, which was made more important by giving it supervisory power over the International Labor Organization (ILO),* the World Health Organization (WHO), United Nations Educational, Social, and Cultural Organization (UNESCO), and other specialized agencies. A new International Court of Justice* was created, similar in structure to its predecessor, an affiliate of the League of Nations,* but different in that this new court was an integral part of the United Nations. Finally, a Trusteeship Council was created to administer affairs of colonies and mandates of defeated Axis nations and other non-self-governing territories. The U.S. delegation was notable for its bipartisanship, consisting as it did, of Secretary of State Edward R. Stettinius,* Senator Tom Connally (D., Texas), and Senator Arthur Vandenberg (R., Michigan)*; John Foster Dulles* was an adviser to the U.S. delegation. *FR, 1945.* vol. 1; Gaddis, John L., *The United States and the Origins of the Cold War* (1972); McNeill, William H., *America, Britain, and Russia* (1953); Nicholas, H. G., *The United Nations as a Political Institution* (1963); Wheeler-Bennett, John W., and Anthony Nicholls, *The Semblance of Peace* (1972).

SAN ILDEFONSO, TREATY OF (1800), Franco-Spanish treaty. In this treaty, France regained the Louisiana Territory from Spain, to which it had lost the area by virtue of the Treaty of Paris (1763). This transfer of territory was a matter of concern to the United States, which considered France a much greater security threat than Spain, and efforts to purchase Louisiana were undertaken with new vigor. Montague, Andrew J., "John Marshall," in Bemis, Samuel F., ed., *American Secretaries of State and Their Diplomacy*, vol. 2 (1928); Van Alstyne, Richard W., *The Rising American Empire* (1960).

SAN JOSÉ, TREATIES OF (1906). The Marblehead Treaty, which settled the 1906 war between Guatemala and El Salvador, called for a general conference of all Central American nations to be held within two months at San José, Costa Rica. The conference was held, with all the republics but Nicaragua in attendance, and the treaties that resulted provided affirmations of peace, a mutual commitment to outside arbitration* of differences, and the establishment of an international Central American bureau in Guatemala and a Central American school in San José. The agreements did not bring permanent peace to the region but did provide a foundation for the Washington Conference* the following year. Hill, Howard C., *Roosevelt and the Caribbean* (1927); Munro, Dana G., *Intervention and Dollar Diplomacy in the Caribbean, 1900–1921* (1964).

SAN REMO CONFERENCE (1920). This was a meeting of the Allied Supreme Council (Britain, France, Italy) on April 24, 1920, at which mandates for the Middle East were discussed. The council offered mandates to France for Syria and Lebanon and to Britain for Palestine, replacing Turkey in those areas. The sultan of Constantinople was to be left in power, and Turkish sovereignty was to be preserved. Turkish assent to the terms of this agreement was supposedly secured with the Treaty of Sèvres (1920), but Turkish nationalist leaders then in power never formally recognized its provisions. The Treaty of Lausanne (1923) finally confirmed British and French mandates. The rejection of the Treaty of Versailles* by the U.S. Senate deprived the United States of any role in this part of the world. Howard, Harry N., *The King-Crane Commission* (1963); Stookey, Robert W., *America and the Arab States* (1975).

SANFORD, HENRY SHELTON (1823–1891). Born June 15, 1823, in Woodbury, Connecticut, Henry S. Sanford attended Washington College in Hartford in 1841 and six years later became an attaché to the U.S. mission at St. Petersburg. In 1848, he was acting legation secretary in Frankfurt; the following year, he went to Paris as legation secretary, remaining until 1854. In 1861, the Republican Sanford was appointed minister to Belgium, where, apart from preventing Confederate recognition, he signed a number of significant agreements, including the Scheldt Treaties, concerning import duties and the capitalization of the Scheldt dues (1863), a naturalization treaty, and a consular convention including a trademark article supplemental to the commercial treaty of 1858. In addition, Sanford coordinated northern secret service operations during the Civil War, arranged for the purchase of war materiels for the Union, and delivered a message from Secretary of State William H. Seward* to Guiseppe Garibaldi, offering the Italian patriot a Union command. After the termination of his mission in 1869, Sanford settled in Florida, founded the town of Sanford in 1870, and involved himself with Florida railroad development. In 1876, he became a member of the executive committee of the International Association for the Exploration and Civilization of Central Africa and played a major role in obtaining U.S. recognition of the association as a "friendly government." Sanford's interest in Africa led to his selection as a delegate to the Berlin Conference on the Congo (1884–1885),* and in 1890, he signed for the United States a multinational treaty to suppress the African slave trade and restrict traffic in firearms and liquors. Sanford, who married Gertrude E. Dupuy in 1864, died in Healing Springs, Virginia, on May 21, 1891. *DAB*, 16:348; Fry, Joseph A., *Henry S. Sanford* (1982); Sanford, C. E., *Thomas Sanford*, 2 vols. (1911).

SANTIAGO CONFERENCE (1923). Also known as the Fifth International Conference of American States, this meeting convened in Santiago on March 25, 1923, after a great influx of American banks and business into Latin America following World War I, in which there had been a fair degree of solidarity although only eight nations had declared war on Germany. Most hemispheric nations favored the League of Nations,* and the U.S. rejection of the league was a divisive issue at Santiago, where Latin American delegations on the whole were more politicized and more candid than at previous conferences. Among major achievements at this conference was the approval of the Gondra Treaty, named for Dr. Manuel Gondra of Paraguay, which provided for the settlement of conflicts by committees of investigations (two were established: one in Montevideo, one in Washington), which would make a report, the disputants agreeing to avoid warfare during the investigation. There was some sympathy for the creation of an "American League of Nations," as a "regional understanding" under Article XXI of the League of Nations, but the United States wanted no connection whatsoever with the league and would not even discuss the proposal, maintaining that in the absence of any tangible threat to hemispheric security, no entangling alliances were needed. Another sharp controversy concerned delegates to the Pan-American Union* in Washington from countries not diplomatically recognized by the United States. Latin American nations disputed the U.S. contention that only envoys accredited to the United States could be accredited to the PAU, and finally won their point, so that countries without diplomatic ties to the United States could send a special representative to the PAU. Henry P. Fletcher* headed the U.S. delegation to this conference, which adjourned May 3, 1923. Mexico, Bolivia, and Chile were not represented. Connell-Smith, Gordon, *The United States and Latin America* (1974); *FR* (1923), 1:286–320; Inman, Samuel Guy, *Inter-American Conferences* (1965); Mecham, J. Lloyd, *A Survey of United States–Latin American Relations* (1965).

SCHENCK, ROBERT CUMMING (1809–1890). A prominent Ohio politician, Robert C. Schenck was born in Franklin, Ohio, on October 4, 1809, graduated from Miami (Ohio) University in 1827, read law, and was admitted to the bar about 1830. He practiced law in Dayton until his election to the Ohio legislature in 1841; after a term there, he went to the U.S. House of Representatives (1843–1851). During the Civil War, he was a brigadier general and was wounded at the Second Battle of Bull Run. His injury caused him to leave the service, and he returned to the House of Representatives for eight more years

(1863–1871). Schenck was a member of the Joint High Commission between the United States and Great Britain and signed the Treaty of Washington (1871).* Later in 1871, he was named minister to Great Britain, a post he occupied until 1876. In London, he handled matters related to the Treaty of Washington and the arbitration* of the *Alabama** claims, and was particularly concerned with the U.S. demand for payment of indirect claims, to which the British strongly objected. In other matters, he failed to negotiate an acceptable consular convention or get British support for U.S. demands that Spain modify its Cuba policy. Schenck resigned in 1876 amid controversy arising from a congressional investigation of his allegedly shady dealings with the stock of a British-managed silver mine in the United States. Schenck also earned some criticism for his introduction of draw poker into British government circles; he was reputedly the best poker player in the United States and in 1880 published *Draw Poker*. Schenck married Rennelche W. Smith in 1834 and died in Washington on March 23, 1890. *DAB*, 16:427; Keller, John W., *The Game of Draw Poker* (1887); Rogers, Augustus C., ed., *Our Representatives Abroad* (1874); *New York Times*, March 24, 1890; Willson, Beckles, *America's Ambassadors to England, 1785–1929* (1929).

SCHURMAN, JACOB GOULD (1854–1942). Born in Freetown, Prince Edward Island, Canada, on May 22, 1854, Jacob G. Schurman graduated from the Universities of London (B.A., 1877; M.A., 1878) and Edinburgh (Sc.D., 1878) and also studied in Paris, Germany, Italy, and Switzerland. From 1880 to 1886, he taught in Canadian universities, and in 1884 he married Barbara Forrest Munro. Schurman joined the faculty of Cornell University in 1886, and six years later he was chosen president of the university, a post he occupied until 1920. In 1899, President William McKinley asked him to head the First Philippine Commission, which became known as the Schurman Commission.* In 1912, he was appointed minister to Greece and Montenegro but left the uneventful post in 1913. A Republican, Schurman served as minister to China (1921–1925) and ambassador to Germany (1925–1930) during the Harding, Coolidge, and Hoover administrations. In China, he supported Chinese nationalism and opposed foreign intervention but felt that the instability of Chinese politics precluded the United States from surrendering its privileged treaty rights, such as extraterritoriality. He reported faithfully and accurately on the shifting fortunes of Sun Yat-sen and the development of Sino-Russian ties. Schurman had been an early advocate of postwar aid for Germany and for German membership in the League of Nations.* He was a popular minister in Germany but could do little to prevent the collapse of the Weimar Republic, which he foresaw. During his German mission, he raised $500,000 to erect a new building at the University of Heidelberg; when dedicated in 1931, it was named Schurman Hall. Retired after 1930, Schurman advocated preparedness in the face of German and Japanese expansion and supported Republican candidates Alf Landon and Wendell Willkie. He died in New York City on August 12, 1942. Schurman wrote a large number of articles on philosophy and current events, as well as *Philippine Affairs—a Retrospect* *and an Outlook* (1902), based on his commission experience. Cohen, Warren I., *America's Response to China* (1971); *NCAB*, 40:491; *New York Times*, August 13, 1942.

SCHURMAN COMMISSION, U.S. commission to the Philippines, 1899. Led by Jacob G. Schurman,* president of Cornell University, this commission was appointed early in 1899 to investigate the situation in the insurrection-ridden Philippines and make policy recommendations. In the islands, the commission was unable to convince rebel leader Emilio Aguinaldo to accept a colonial government. The members split on the question of whether the fighting should continue, with a majority feeling that it should. Schurman also raised a good deal of controversy with his suggestion that only one Protestant denomination should proselytize in the Philippines so that the inhabitants would have a clear choice between that denomination and Catholicism. The final report of the commission, submitted in November 1899, supported the McKinley administration's policy and argued that an independent Philippines was possible only after a period of American occupation following the crushing of the insurrection. Healy, David, *US Expansionism* (1970).

SCHURZ, CARL (1829–1906). Born in Liblar, Germany, on March 2, 1829, Carl Schurz attended the University of Bonn from 1846 to 1849. He was involved in the revolutionary movements of 1848–1849, escaped to Switzerland, and came to the United States in 1852. Before the Civil War, he lived and practiced law in Philadelphia and Wisconsin, became a Republican, and campaigned for Abraham Lincoln in 1860. Accordingly, he was named minister to Spain when the Lincoln administration entered office. He stayed in Madrid less than a year, protecting Union sentiment and studying military strategy and tactics before returning home in early 1862 to join the army. His decision to return was probably also made out of his conviction that Spain was a backward place, rife with political corruption. Schurz won military distinction during the war, served in the Senate from 1869 to 1877, beginning there a long career as an anti-imperialist by opposing plans to annex the Dominican Republic, and was interior secretary under President Rutherford B. Hayes (1877–1881). He wrote for the *New York Post*, the *Nation*, and *Harper's Weekly* after 1881 and during the Spanish-American War was a leading opponent of territorial annexation, fearing the costs involved and the dangers to American security inherent in the managing of distant colonies. Schurz was married to Margarethe Meyer in 1852. He died in New York City on May 14, 1906. He wrote his autobiography, *Reminiscences of Carl Schurz*, 2 vols. (1907–1908). *DAB*, 16:466; Easum, C. V., *The Americanization of Carl Schurz* (1929); Fuess, C. M., *Carl Schurz, Reformer* (1932); *New York Times*, May 15, 1906; Trefousse, Hans, *Carl Schurz, a Biography* (1982).

SCHUYLER, EUGENE (1840–1890). Eugene Schuyler was born in Ithaca, New York, on February 26, 1840, graduated from Yale (A.B., 1859; Ph.D., 1861) and Columbia Law School (1863), and was admitted to the bar. He practiced law in New York City until a diplomatic career beckoned in 1867. From 1867 to 1869, he was consul* in Moscow; over the next several years, he served as consul in Revel (now Tallinn) and Estonia and as legation secretary in St. Petersburg. By 1876, he was legation secretary and consul general in Constantinople. There he published a report on Turkish atrocities in the war with Bulgaria that received wide distribution and may have been significant in bringing Britain closer to Russia in the diplomacy of the affair, thus increasing Turkish wrath. Nonetheless, Schuyler remained in Turkey until 1880, when he became U.S. diplomatic representative to Romania; two years later, he was named minister to Greece, Rumania, and Serbia, the first accredited U.S. minister to Rumania and Serbia. He negotiated and signed commercial treaties with both nations before returning to the United States in 1884. For the next two years, he lectured at Johns Hopkins University, and from 1886 to 1889 he lived in retirement in Alassio, Italy, where he continued a lifelong interest in literary work, translating Russian works, writing a travel book about Russia and a biography of Peter the Great, and analyzing American foreign policy in *American Diplomacy and the Furtherance of Commerce* (1886). He married Gertrude Wallace King in 1877, was nominated but not confirmed for the office of assistant secretary of state in 1889, and spent a brief time as agent and consul general in Egypt (1889–1890) before his death in Italy on July 16, 1890. Schuyler's Turkish report is published in J. A. MacGahan, *The Turkish Atrocities in Belgium* . . . (1876). *DAB*, 16:471.

SCOTT, JAMES BROWN (1866–1943). A prominent legal scholar with close ties to American diplomacy, James Brown Scott was born June 3, 1866, in Kincardine, Ontario. His family moved to Philadelphia in 1876, and he graduated from Harvard (A.B., 1890; A.M., 1891) and the University of Heidelberg (1894). He began the practice of law in Los Angeles in 1894 but two years later organized the Los Angeles Law School and became its dean (1896–1899). In 1899, he was named dean of the University of Illinois College of Law, and in 1903, he accepted a law professorship at Columbia University. His only State Department post was solicitor (1906–1911), during which time he attended the second Hague Peace Conference (1907)* and wrote *The Hague Peace Conferences of 1899 and 1907* (1909). After 1911, Scott attended numerous international conferences as a delegate or adviser, including the Paris Peace Conference (1919),* the Washington Conference (1921–1922),* and the Sixth International Conference of American States (1928).* He was also an adviser to the 1920 conference that established the Permanent Court of International Justice.* He gained even greater prominence from his extensive writing and editing of works relating to international law and history. Among his works are a biography, *Robert Bacon* (1923), and an edition of James Madison's *Notes of Debates in the Federal Convention of 1787* (1918). Throughout the period from 1911 to his death, Scott continued to lecture on international law at George Washington University, Johns Hopkins University, and Georgetown University and was active in the affairs of the Carnegie Endowment for International Peace.* He married Adele Cooper Reed in 1901 and died June 25, 1943, in Wardour, Maryland. Coogan, John W., *The End of Neutrality: The United States, Britain and Maritime Rights, 1899–1915* (1981); *DAB*, 3:699; *New York Times*, June 27, 1943.

SCRUGGS, WILLIAM LINDSAY (1836–1912). William L. Scruggs was born near Knoxville, Tennessee, on September 14, 1836, attended Strawberry Plains College (Tennessee), and married Judith Ann Potts in 1858. That year, he became principal of Hamilton Male Academy, but in 1861 he moved to Georgia, read law, and was admitted to the bar. Combining law with journalism, Scruggs edited the *Columbus* (Georgia) *Daily Sun* (1862–1865) and the *Atlanta Daily New Era* (1870–1872). From 1873 to 1876, he was minister to Colombia, where he arbitrated a British-Colombian claims dispute and settled the Montejo case, a maritime matter. Between 1876 and 1882, he served as consul* in Chin-kiang and Canton, China, returning to Colombia as minister (1882–1885). In 1885, he was successful in preventing the Colombian government from hiking customs duties on goods transported across the Panamanian isthmus. His last post was Venezuela, where he was minister from 1889 to 1893. There he was involved with the Venezuelan crisis,* supporting the Venezuelan claim and representing Venezuela as a special agent in the matter from 1894 to 1898. He unsuccessfully sought support for Venezuela from Secretary of State Walter Q. Gresham* and President Grover Cleveland, and while he approved of Secretary of State Richard Olney's* controversial note to Great Britain, he was apparently not the inspiration for it, as has been claimed. During the crisis, he wrote a polemical analysis of the matter and later wrote histories of Colombia and Venezuela and several other works on international relations. Scruggs died on July 18, 1912, in Atlanta. *DAB*, 16:520; Eggert, Gerald, *Richard Olney* (1974); Grenville, John A. S., and George B. Young, *Politics, Strategy, and American Diplomacy: Studies in Foreign Policy, 1873–1917* (1966).

SDI. See **STRATEGIC DEFENSE INITIATIVE (SDI).**

SEATO. See **SOUTHEAST ASIA TREATY ORGANIZATION.**

SECOND FRONT. Allied military-diplomatic issue, 1941–1944. A second front was the main objective of the Russians early in World War II—an invasion of Western Europe to create for the Axis a second front that would relieve the military pressure on the Russian front. First requested by the Russians in July 1941, the second front did not occur until June 1944 with OVERLORD, the cross-channel or Normandy invasion. The long delay was due to the lack of sufficient numbers of troops and quantities of supplies to ensure success, as well as to British and American differences over the location of the front. The British were reluctant to go into France because of their World War I experience and preferred instead a Mediterranean-Balkan strategy, which would have had the potential political advantage of denying large parts of Eastern Europe to Soviet military occupation. The United States, less concerned about who controlled the Balkans, favored the cross-channel invasion because of the shorter distance and simpler logistics. Stoler emphasizes the political considerations in the second-front decision, pointing out that the cross-channel invasion, far from possible territorial conflict with the Soviets, was necessary to ensure continued Soviet participation in the European war and future Soviet aid in the Pacific theater. Another factor in the decision was that a Normandy invasion would allow enough U.S. troops to land in Europe to give the United States more bargaining power at the peace conference most Americans presumed would take place. However, while the second front was established and was successful in its military objective, Premier Joseph Stalin believed the delay in decision making was deliberate, done to let the Soviets take greater losses. This suspicion of his allies never deserted Stalin and helped create frictions in the Grand Alliance that contributed to the development of the cold war.* Gaddis, John L., *Russia, the Soviet Union and the United States* (1978); Herring, George C., Jr., *Aid to Russia, 1941–1946* (1973); Stoler, Mark A., *The Politics of the Second Front* (1977); McNeill, William H., *America, Britain, and Russia* (1953).

SECOND INTERNATIONAL CONFERENCE OF AMERICAN STATES (1901–1902). See **MEXICO CITY CONFERENCE (1901–1902).**

SECRET TREATIES. These were controversial pacts, such as the Treaty of London (1915), which the Allies in World War I made to divide the spoils of war. They were the antithesis of Wilson's idealistic diplomacy and a source of considerable disillusionment for the American public in the years after the war, although, in reality, such treaties had for many years been an accepted fixture of international relations. Bailey, Thomas A., *Woodrow Wilson and the Lost Peace* (1944); Seymour, Charles, *American Diplomacy during the World War* (1934).

SELF-DETERMINATION, a principle espoused by Woodrow Wilson and others during World War I and at the Paris Peace Conference,* wherein so-called submerged minorities would be given the opportunity, through a plebiscite or other means, to determine the government under which they wanted to live. Many of the territorial settlements at the peace conference honored the principle of self-determination; some, like the settlement dealing with Germans in Austria, did not. In a later period, the principle of self-determination was occasionally used by U.S. leaders as a justification for American involvement in the Vietnam War. In this sense, the South Vietnamese were presumed to be under attack by the North Vietnamese, who were denying them the right to determine the government under which they desired to live. Bailey, Thomas A., *Woodrow Wilson and the Lost Peace* (1944); Fitzgerald, Frances, *Fire in the Lake* (1972).

SEVAREID, ARNOLD ERIC (b. 1912). Born November 12, 1912, in Velva, North Dakota, Eric Sevareid graduated from the University of Minnesota in 1935 and went to work as a reporter for the *Minneapolis Star*. In 1937, he went to

Paris as a reporter and city editor for the Paris edition of the *New York Herald Tribune*. Two years later, after a stint as a United Press editor, Sevareid was hired by Edward R. Murrow* as a European correspondent for the Columbia Broadcasting System (CBS). During the early years of World War II, he reported the fall of France and broadcast from London with Murrow. In 1941, he returned to the United States to work for CBS in Washington but in 1943 went to the Pacific theater and reported from the China-Burma-Indian theater. In 1944–1945, he was again covering the European war. After the war, he covered the San Francisco Conference (1945)* and other special domestic and foreign assignments for CBS. From 1964 to his retirement in 1977, Sevareid was a correspondent and commentator for CBS television news, where he gained a nickname ("The Gray Eminence") and a reputation for serious, thoughtful, politically moderate news analysis. Twice married, Sevareid has written several books, including *Not So Wild a Dream* (1946) and *This Is Eric Sevareid* (1964), and is a consultant for CBS. *CB* (1966):363–66; Gates, Gary Paul, *Air Time: The Inside Story of CBS News* (1978); *WWA* (1986–1987):2522.

SEVENTH INTERNATIONAL CONFERENCE OF AMERICAN STATES (1933). See **MONTEVIDEO CONFERENCE (1933).**

SEWALL, HAROLD MARSH (1860–1924). Born in Bath, Maine, on January 3, 1860, Harold M. Sewall graduated from Harvard (A.B., 1882; LL.B., 1885) and became a vice-consul in Liverpool. In 1887, he was named consul general* at Apia, Samoa, where he had to contend with German and British representatives and resist a German coup d'état. However, his zeal was excessive, and Secretary of State Thomas F. Bayard* had to request his resignation in January 1889. Sewell participated in the negotiation of the Berlin Treaty (1889),* which led to the system of tripartite control over Samoa. From 1890 to 1892, Sewall was back in Samoa as U.S. consul general and secured for the United States a naval station at Pago Pago. As minister to Hawaii (1897–1898), he formally received the transfer of the islands after their annexation in 1898. He remained in Hawaii until 1900 as a special diplomatic agent. Sewall, who came from a wealthy family, lived in Bath after 1900, serving in the Maine legislature (1903–1909) as a Republican and sitting on the Advisory Committee for the Washington Conference (1921–1922).* He married Camilla Loyall Ashe in 1893 and died in New York City on October 28, 1924. *DAB*, 16:606; *New York Times*, October 29, 1924; Ryden, G. H., *The Foreign Policy of the United States in Relation to Samoa* (1933).

SEWARD, FREDERICK WILLIAM (1830–1915). The son of Lincoln's secretary of state, William H. Seward,* Frederick W. Seward played a role of his own in U.S. foreign policy. Born July 8, 1830, in Auburn, New York, he graduated from Union College in 1849 and was admitted to the bar in 1851. For the next ten years, he worked on the staff of the *Albany Evening Journal*. When his father became secretary of state in 1861, Frederick became assistant secretary of state. In this assignment, he was mainly responsible for sending and receiving consular dispatches, but in 1866, he undertook a special mission to the Dominican Republic to inspect Samana Bay for possible lease or purchase, and he also took part in the negotiations for the purchase of Alaska (1867)* and the Burlingame Treaty (1868)* with China. When his father was injured in a carriage accident in early 1865, he became acting secretary; in April of that year, he was injured in the Lincoln assassination plot, aimed also at his father. Leaving the State Department in 1869, Seward became editor and part-owner of the *Albany Evening Journal* and edited the papers of Thurlow Weed as well as his father's book, *Travels Around the World* (1872). In 1875–1876, he ran unsuccessfully for New York secretary of state and for the state senate. President Rutherford B. Hayes appointed him assistant secretary of state in 1877, however, and in this second stint he was responsible for U.S. policy regarding the recognition of Mexican president Porfirio Díaz and for negotiating a lease on Pago Pago harbor in Samoa. After 1881, he devoted his time to newspaper work and writing, completing a biography of Andrew Johnson (1890) and of his father, *Life and Letters of William H. Seward* (1891), and his own *Reminiscences of a War-Time Statesman and Diplomat* (1916). Seward married Anna M. Wharton in 1854 and died in Auburn on April 25, 1915. *DAB*, 16:612; *New York Times*, April 26, 1915.

SEWARD, WILLIAM HENRY (1801–1872). Secretary of state under Presidents Abraham Lincoln and Andrew Johnson (1861–1869), William H. Seward was born May 16, 1801, in Florida, New York. He graduated from Union College in 1820, read law, and was admitted to the bar in 1822. He began law practice in Auburn, New York, that year, married Frances Miller in 1824, and gradually became involved in state politics, sitting in the state senate from 1830 to 1834, losing a race for governor in 1834, but winning four years later and serving as governor from 1838 to 1842. A Whig by this time, Seward favored public schools and the abolition of slavery and carried his political career to the U.S. Senate in 1849. Seward remained in the Senate until 1861, emerging as a national leader in the new Republican party and an outspoken opponent of slavery. His extreme views on slavery helped cost him the presidential nomination of his party in 1860, but, upon Lincoln's election, he joined the administration as secretary of state. Early on, he advocated war with Europe as a means to reunite the American people, but apart from this unfortunate suggestion, he administered his office well and with firmness in matters such as the *Trent* affair (1861),* European recognition of the Confederacy, Confederate ship-outfitting activities in British ports, and the French intervention in Mexico. After the Civil War, he remained in office under President Johnson and successfully arranged for the Alaska purchase (1867)* but unsuccessfully tried to obtain part of the Danish West Indies and to annex Hawaii. According to Van Duesen, Seward compiled an excellent record as secretary of state by his appointments to Britain and France and his excellent rapport with foreign representatives at a time when personal relationships were important. Interested in practical results, he sometimes used international law loosely but always directed his policy toward the main purpose of preventing any foreign recognition of the South. After his retirement in 1869, he traveled widely and wrote the *Autobiography of William H. Seward . . . ,* which was edited by his son, Frederick Seward, and published in 1877. Seward died October 10, 1872, in Auburn, New York. Adams, Ephraim D., *Great Britain and the American Civil War*, 2 vols., (1925); *DAB*, 16:615; Van Duesen, Glyndon G., *William Henry Seward* (1967); Kushner, Howard I., *Conflict on the Northwest Coast* (1975), Paolino, Ernest N., *The Foundations of the American Empire* (1973).

SHANGHAI INCIDENT (1932). Following a Chinese boycott of Japanese goods entering Shanghai, Japanese marines entered the city on January 28, 1932, and met resistance from Chinese troops. Japanese planes fire-bombed the Chinese positions, causing many civilian deaths and shocking the Western world. Secretary of State Henry L. Stimson* attempted without success to rally Britain and other Western powers in support of supervised Sino-Japanese negotiations or an international conference and then made a unilateral statement in an open letter sent February 23 to Senator William E. Borah,* chairman of the Foreign Relations Committee. The Borah letter was similar to the Stimson note of January 1932, outlining the doctrine of nonrecognition but added an emphasis on the Nine-Power Treaty (1922)* and hinted that the United States might have to fortify further Guam and the Philippines. Stimson thought his letter to Borah was important, but it had no significant effect on Japan (or Great Britain, for that matter), and the tenor of President Herbert Hoover's speeches in the following months discounted the implied threats in the letter. Meanwhile, on their own, Japan and China signed an armistice on May 5, 1932. Current, Richard N., *Secretary Stimson* (1954), Ferrell, Robert H., *American Diplomacy in the Great Depression* (1957); *FR: Japan, 1931–1941*, 1:161–222.

SHANTUNG QUESTION, the major Far Eastern issue dealt with at the Paris Peace Conference (1919).* In Shantung, a province in northeastern China, Germany had its sphere of influence, with corresponding economic privileges. Japan coveted these railroad and mining properties and the leasehold at the port of Kiaochow and, indeed, had been promised these rights by the Chinese, British, and French in various secret treaties made during the war. At the peace conference, Japan pressed the matter with diligence, pledging to bolt both the conference and the League of Nations* if not given satisfaction. In the end, the Japanese were given the German holdings in Shantung in return for the withdrawal of their troops from the province and the promise to uphold full Chinese sovereignty there. This decision earned President Woodrow Wilson much criticism in the United States and was a major factor in the rejection of the Treaty of Versailles.* Bailey, Thomas A., *Woodrow Wilson and the Lost Peace* (1944); Fifield, Russell, H., *Woodrow Wilson and the Far East: The Diplomacy of the Shantung Question* (1952), *FR* (1919), 1:686–724; *FR: Lansing Papers*, 2:455–58; Smith, Daniel, *The Great Departure* (1965).

SHARP, WILLIAM GRAVES (1859–1922). America's ambassador to France during World War I, William G. Sharp was born March 14, 1859, in Mount Gilead, Ohio, and graduated from the University of Michigan (LL.B., 1881). After college, he edited a newspaper in Fargo, North Dakota, for a brief period but moved to Elyria, Ohio, in 1884, set up a law practice, and was elected prosecuting attorney (1885–1888). Sharp then moved into manufacturing, making a fortune with the Lake Superior Iron and Coal Company over the next twenty years. From 1909 to 1914, he served in the U.S. House of Representatives as a Democrat and was a member of the Foreign Affairs Committee. He was nominated ambassador to Russia, but, because of his vote to end the commercial treaty with Russia, the Russian government found him unacceptable. He then was appointed ambassador to France, serving from 1914 to 1919. In Paris, he managed German, Austrian, and Turkish affairs, visited prison camps, and engaged in relief work but did not play much of a role in major policy matters, since these were handled in Washington. He did send President Wilson important information on the sinking of the *Sussex** that helped prompt Wilson to make an unusually strong protest to the German government. Interested in aviation, Sharp visited airfields and training camps. He took part in the Paris Peace Conference (1919)* and was a staunch advocate of the League of Nations.* An amateur astronomer, he married Hattie M. Clough in 1895 and died in Elyria on November 17, 1922. *DAB*, 17:25; *NCAB*, 19:299; *New York Times*, November 18, 1922; Sharp, William G., *The War Memories of William Graves Sharp* (1931); Willson, Beckles, *America's Ambassadors to France, 1777–1927* (1928).

SHERMAN, JOHN (1823–1900). President William McKinley's first secretary of state (1897–1898) and one of the oldest to hold that position, John Sherman was born in Lancester, Ohio, on May 10, 1823, attended various schools but was not a college graduate, read law, and was admitted to the bar in 1844. In 1854, he began a long congressional career with election to the U.S. House of Representatives as a Republican. Over the next forty-two years, Sherman served in the House (1855–1861), the Senate (1861–1877, 1881–1897), and as secretary of the treasury (1877–1881). As senator, he opposed Chinese exclusion for a time but modified his stand, supported the protective tariff policy of his party, and was interested in an American-built isthmian canal. Upon William McKinley's election in 1896, the aging Sherman was given the appointment of secretary of state to compliment his Republican loyalty and to clear a Senate seat for Mark Hanna, McKinley's astute campaign manager and close friend. At a time of national crisis and impending war, he was not equipped to handle the duties of the office, despite the excellent assistance of First Assistant Secretary of State William R. Day,* Second Assistant Alvey A. Adee,* John Bassett Moore,* and former Secretary of State John W. Foster.* When the Spanish-American War broke out, Sherman's failing health and antiexpansionist feelings dictated his resignation. He wrote his memoirs, *Reminiscences of Forty Years (1895, 1896)* and lived in retirement in Washington until his death on October

22, 1900, shortly after that of his wife, Margaret Steward, whom he had married in 1848. Burton, Theodore F., *John Sherman* (1906, 1972); *DAB*, 17:84; Sears, L. M., "John Sherman," in Bemis, Samuel F., ed., *American Secretaries of State and Their Diplomacy*, vol. 9 (1929).

SHIMODA, CONVENTION OF (1857). The first convention negotiated by Townsend Harris,* this improved the position of Americans in Japan in a number of ways. Nagasaki was opened as a port of call, and the United States was granted the right to have a vice-consul at Hakodate and extraterritoriality and residential rights at Shimoda and Hakodate. Visiting American ships were given bartering rights, and Americans benefited from a new monetary exchange rate. The convention of Shimoda also abrogated the clause in the Treaty of Kanagawa* that had placed all trade under government supervision and, finally, gave Harris himself greater personal freedom of travel. Dennett, Tyler, *Americans in Eastern Asia* (1922).

SHORT, WILLIAM (1759–1849). One of the longest-lived Revolutionary-era statesmen, William Short was born in Surry County, Virginia, on September 30, 1759, and graduated from William and Mary College in 1779. He served on the Virginia executive council, 1783–1784, before becoming private secretary to Thomas Jefferson,* then U.S. minister in France, 1785–1789. From 1789 to 1791, Short was chargé d'affaires* in France, where he worked on a commercial treaty and then became overly sympathetic to the French Revolution. Moved to the Netherlands as U.S. minister, 1792–1793, he faced no major diplomatic issues. Later in 1793, he was sent to Spain as a joint commissioner and was raised to the position of minister the following year. There he did preliminary work on what became known as Pinckney's Treaty,* cooperating with special envoy Thomas Pinckney* after his arrival in 1795. Resigning his ministry in 1795, Short lived in France, 1795–1802, before returning to the United States, where he went into private business and acquired a large fortune before his death in Philadelphia on December 5, 1849. Bemis, Samuel F., *Pinckney's Treaty* (1926); *DAB*, 17:128.

SHRIVER, ROBERT SARGENT, JR. (b. 1915). Sargent Shriver was born November 9, 1915, in Westminister, Maryland, graduated from Yale (A.B., 1938; LL.B., 1941), served in the navy during World War II, and after a year with *Newsweek* went to work at the Merchandise Mart in Chicago, where he was assistant general manager from 1948 to 1960. In 1953, he married Eunice Kennedy, sister of U.S. Senator John F. Kennedy and daughter of Joseph P. Kennedy,* owner of the Merchandise Mart and former ambassador to Great Britain. Shriver was a campaign adviser to Kennedy in 1960, became a recruiter for the incoming Democratic administration, and in 1961 was named to organize and direct the Peace Corps.* Remaining with the Peace Corps until 1965, he became director of the Office of Economic Opportunity and a special assistant to President Lyndon B. Johnson. From 1968 to 1970, he was ambassador to France, where he generally improved Franco-American relations, impressing his staff with his energy, candor, and informality. In a time free of major diplomatic crises, Shriver worked to develop cooperation in scientific and technological areas, including oceanography, space science, and medicine. He became well known for his frequent contact with the people of France and for arranging visits to the United States for French authorities. Since 1971, he has practiced law in Washington, New York, and London. He was the Democratic candidate for vice-president in 1972, running with Senator George McGovern (D., South Dakota). Shriver's book, *Point of the Lance* (1964), deals with the first three years of the Peace Corps. *NCAB*, J:62; *New York Times*, March 23, 1970; *WWA* (1986–1987):2558.

SHUFELDT, ROBERT WILSON (1822–1895). Born in Red Hook, New York, on February 21, 1822, Robert W. Shufeldt studied one year at the Philadelphia Naval School before entering the navy in 1839. He spent several years both in the navy and commercial shipping before his appointment as consul general* of Cuba in 1861. He rejoined the navy in 1863 for the duration of the Civil War. In 1878, as an exponent of commercial expansion, Shufeldt visited the West African coast and Madagascar and reported favorably on the possibility of trade with native Africans. From 1878 to 1880, he commanded the U.S.S. *Ticonderoga* on a world cruise, with specific instructions to visit Korea and explore its commercial potential. In April 1880, he arrived in Japan but was unable to deal with Korea through Japanese officials, who exercised control in Korea. The next year he was in Tientsin, China, to deal with Viceroy Li Hung Chang, who also claimed hegemony over Korea. In China, Shufeldt complained of bad treatment but nonetheless worked out a treaty acknowledging Korean dependency upon China. Korean authorities assented in May 1882, opening Korea for the first time to foreign commercial penetration. Upon his return, he became president of the Naval Advisory Board and a rear admiral before his retirement in 1884. Shufeldt married Sara Abercrombie in 1847 and died November 7, 1895, in Washington. *DAB*, 17:139; Dennett, Tyler, *Americans in Far Eastern Asia* (1922); Drake, F. C., *The Empire of the Seas* (1984); Hunt, Michael H., *The Making of a Special Relationship: The United States and China to 1914* (1983); Kwak, Tae-hwan, et al., eds., *U.S.-Korean Relations, 1882–1887* (1982); *New York Times*, November 8, 1895; Plesur, Milton, *America's Outward Thrust* (1971); Pletcher, David, *The Awkward Years* (1962).

SHULTZ, GEORGE PRATT (b. 1920). President Ronald Reagan's second secretary of state, George Shultz was born December 13, 1920, in New York City. He earned a B.A. at Princeton in 1942, served in the marines during World War II, and returned to school after the war, receiving a Ph.D. in industrial economics from MIT in 1949. For the next nineteen years, he taught at MIT and the University of Chicago and gained a reputation as a skilled arbitrator of labor-management disputes. After a year as a fellow at the Center for Advanced

Studies in Behavioral Sciences, 1968–1969, Shultz joined the Nixon administration as secretary of labor. In 1970, he became director of the Office of
Management and Budget, where he was involved in Nixon's New Economic
Policy, the program of wage and price controls, abandonment of the gold standard, and import surcharges devised to cure an ailing economy in 1971. From
1972 to 1974, he was secretary of the treasury and was the president's chief
economic adviser. Spared the shame of Watergate, Shultz left government in
1974 to become executive vice-president of the Bechtel Corporation, a huge
international construction and engineering firm. He became president of Bechtel
in 1975 and president of the Bechtel Group in 1981. In June 1982, President
Ronald Reagan named Shultz secretary of state, following the resignation of
Alexander Haig.* Known for his calm demeanor and effectiveness as a mediator,
he presented a sharp contrast in style to the confrontational Haig. Shultz's experience with Bechtel made him something of an expert on Middle East affairs,
and he sought to improve U.S.-Arab relations and worked to shape a new "land
for peace" policy for Israel and its neighbors, a policy that led to the contribution
of U.S. troops to Lebanon during the Lebanon crisis (1982–1984).* After the
attack on the marine barracks in Beirut, Shultz became much more outspoken
on the issue of international terrorism. He opposed the deals that led to the Iran-
contra scandal* and was suitably horrified when he learned of the breadth of the
scandal and that national security adviser John Poindexter* had kept him unin-
formed about the affair. Despite his embarrassment and suggestions that he
resign, Shultz stayed on at the State Department because of his hope to conclude
an arms reduction treaty. In 1987, he succeeded with the Intermediate Nuclear
Force (INF) Treaty.* Shultz married Helena O'Brien in 1946 and is the author
of several books on economics. *CB* (April 1988): 46–52; *New York Times*, June 26,
July 16, 1982, August 1, 1983, May 17, 1985, January 11, July 24, 1987; *WWA* (1986–
1987):2560.

SIBERIAN INTERVENTION (1918–1920). During and after World War I,
Siberia presented a complex problem to the United States. In early 1918, Bolshevik leaders took Russia out of the war with the signing of the Treaty of Brest-
Litovsk.* The advent of bolshevism was perceived as a blow to the legitimate
forces of democratic liberalism in Russia, and the capitulation of these forces
seemed to open Russia to German exploitation. Former German and Austrian
prisoners were armed, posing a threat to Czech troops, who had been fighting
Germans in Russia and were withdrawing to the east. Japan, meanwhile, was
desirous of expanding its influence into Siberia, a move that the United States
did not approve. After some months of interdepartmental deliberation, the United
States intervened in Siberia in August 1918 with about 7,000 troops, in collaboration with a larger number of Japanese troops, for the stated purpose of assisting
the Czechs. American troops stayed until April 1920, serving as a deterrent after
the war's end to Japanese ambitions in Siberia. Japan removed its troops in 1922
as part of the agreements of the Washington Conference.* Curry, Roy Watson,

Woodrow Wilson and Far Eastern Policy, 1913–1920 (1957); Kennan, George F., *The Decision to Intervene* (1958) and *Russia Leaves the War* (1956); Levin, N. Gordon, Jr., *Woodrow Wilson and World Politics* (1968).

SICKLES, DANIEL EDGAR (1819–1914). "Dan" Sickles, as he was commonly known, was born in New York City on October 20, 1819, attended the University of the City of New York, studied law, and was admitted to the bar in 1846. He served in the New York legislature (1847) and as corporation counsel of New York City (1853) before his first brief diplomatic experience as legation secretary in London, 1853–1855. Terms in the New York State Senate (1856–1857) and the U.S. House of Representatives (1857–1861) followed. Sickles became a nationally known figure in 1859 when he shot his wife's lover dead in the streets of Washington. During the Civil War, he rose to the rank of major general and lost a leg at the Battle of Gettysburg. Secretary of State William H. Seward* sent him on a confidential mission to South America in 1865 to negotiate a transit treaty with Colombia. In 1869, Sickles was appointed minister to Spain, his most important diplomatic assignment. In Madrid from 1869 to 1874, he dealt, not very well, with Cuban problems, including the *Virginius* episode,* over which he resigned. He achieved far more notoriety by virtue of his affair with ex–Queen Isabella, which earned him the nickname "Yankee King of Spain." Ultimately, he married Carmelita Creagh, the queen's lady-in-waiting, in a match known to be a *mariage de covenance*. Sickles lived in Europe until 1880. Returning to New York, he served as chairman of the New York State Monument Commission, 1886–1912, and one more term in the U.S. House, 1893–1895. Later in life, he was beset by financial problems. Sickles died in New York City on May 3, 1914. *DAB*, 17:150; Nevins, Allan, *Hamilton Fish*, 2 vols. (1957); *New York Times*, May 4, 1914; Pinchon, Edgcumb, *Dan Sickles* (1945).

SINO-JAPANESE WAR (1894–1895). In 1894, Chinese troops were sent to Korea, ostensibly to stop a rebellion. Japan opposed this intervention, claiming that it violated treaty rights, and sent its own troops to Korea. Although the Korean rebellion was quickly subdued, neither Japan nor China withdrew its troops. Meanwhile, the Korean government requested American intervention, and Secretary of State Water Q. Gresham* offered the good offices of the United States. Japan, which most Americans favored, claimed it sought no territory but insisted on political reforms in Korea. China, on the other hand, was edging toward total national collapse, and there were fears of European partition of the country. Ultimately, Russian, German, and French intervention forced Japan to return captured Korean territory. Chaikin, Nathan, *The Sino-Japanese War* (1983); Cohen, Warren I., *America's Response to China* (1971); *FR* (1894), Appendix 1:5–106; Hunt, Michael H., *The Making of a Special Relationship: The United States and China to 1914* (1983); Schuyler, Montgomery, "Walter Quintin Gresham," in Bemis, Samuel F., ed., *American Secretaries of State and Their Diplomacy*, vol. 8 (1928).

SIX-DAY WAR (1967). In this, the third Middle East War between Israel and its Arab neighbors, Egypt and Syria, since 1948, Israel captured control of the Golan Heights on the Syrian frontier and large areas of the Sinai peninsula; it was the Israeli contention that control of these areas was necessary for national security. In addition, Israel took control of areas on the west bank of the Jordan River and the city of Jerusalem. Another consequence of the war was the increased number of Palestinian refugees and the heightening of Palestinian nationalism, toward whom and which Israel remained implacably unsympathetic. According to Stookey, the war represented a failure of U.S. policy, which had strived to keep the area peaceful. In addition, the war resulted in the closing of the Suez Canal, a temporary oil embargo on the United States, increased Soviet influence among the defeated Arab states, and the termination of U.S. diplomatic relations with Egypt, Syria, and several other Arab states. Dupuy, Trevor N., *Elusive Victory: The Arab-Israeli Wars, 1947–1974* (1978); Hammond, Paul Y., *Cold War and Detente* (1975); Rubenberg Cheryl A., *Israel and the American National Interest* (1986); Stookey, Robert W., *America and the Arab States* (1975).

SIX-NATION CONFERENCE ON GERMANY (1948). This conference, which met in London from February 23 to March 5 and again from April 20 to June 2, 1948, included Great Britain, France, the United States, Belgium, the Netherlands, and Luxembourg in discussions concerning long-range plans for Germany. The London Agreements that emerged from this meeting recommended the formation of a federal government for West Germany out of the British, American, and French zones, with a constitution to be ratified by the German people. In addition, Germany was to participate in the Marshall Plan.* Another topic dealt with at the conference was the industrial Ruhr area, which was to remain under Allied economic control but not be politically separated from Germany. The conference confirmed the inclusion of the Benelux countries in German policy determinations and the exclusion of the Soviet Union from those determinations. Soviet objections to the London Agreements were seen in the Berlin blockade* and the dissolution of the Allied Control Council.*Feis, Herbert, *From Trust to Terror* (1970); Gimbel, John, *The American Occupation of Germany* (1968); Wheeler-Bennett, John W., and Anthony Nicholls, *The Semblance of Peace* (1972).

SIXTH INTERNATIONAL CONFERENCE OF AMERICAN STATES (1928). See **HAVANA CONFERENCE (1928).**

SLIDELL, JOHN (1793–1871). One of a number of Confederate diplomats who had seen U.S. diplomatic service prior to the Civil War, John Slidell was born sometime in 1793 in New York City and graduated from Columbia College in 1810. He was in the mercantile business from 1810 to 1812, but the War of 1812 ruined him financially, and he moved to New Orleans, became a lawyer, and married Mathilde Deslonde in 1835. He ran several unsuccessful races for Congress before winning a seat in the U.S. House of Representatives in 1843.

Two years later, he was named minister to Mexico. Slidell went to Mexico in 1845, hoping to adjust the Texas boundary problem and purchase New Mexico and California, but, because of the instability and hostility of the Mexican government, he never presented his credentials. The failure of his mission was a major step toward the war with Mexico in 1846. In 1853, the Pierce administration offered him the post of minister to Central America, but he declined it and went to London to sell railroad bonds. During the Civil War, Slidell was the Confederate representative in France. Captured in the *Trent* affair,* he eventually got to Paris, where he enjoyed cordial relations with Louis-Napoleon but never attained diplomatic recognition. He remained in Europe after the war and died in Cowes, Isle of Wight, on June 29, 1871. *DAB*, 17:209; Owsley, Frank L., *King Cotton Diplomacy* (1959); Sears, R. M., *John Slidell* (1925); Willson, Beckles, *John Slidell and the Confederates in Paris* (1932).

SMITH, CHARLES EMORY (1842–1908). Born February 18, 1842, in Mansfield, Connecticut, Charles E. Smith graduated from Union College in 1861 and served as a military secretary to General John F. Rathbone during the Civil War's first years. In 1862, he became an instructor at Albany Academy; shortly after, he turned to a journalism career, writing for the *Albany Express* and editing the *Albany Evening Journal*. In the 1880s, he was editor of the *Philadelphia Press*. A Republican, Smith became minister to Russia (1890–1892) during the Harrison administration. He won acclaim there for his efficient distribution of famine relief funds but was unsuccessful in mitigating the so-called May Laws, which discriminated against Russian Jews. He returned to journalism after 1892 but from 1898 to 1901 served as postmaster general and was a close adviser to President William McKinley. He resigned in 1901 to attend to private business interests. Smith was married twice and died in Philadelphia on January 19, 1908. *DAB*, 17:246; *NCAB*, 11:17.

SMITH, EARL E. T. (b. 1903). Born in Newport, Rhode Island, in 1903, Earl E. T. Smith attended Yale in the mid-1920s. He became a stockbroker and a member of the New York Stock Exchange in 1926 and served in the army air force during World War II. Successful in his business, he developed Republican political connections and in 1957 was appointed ambassador to Cuba by the Eisenhower administration. Leaving Cuba in 1959 after the rise to power of Fidel Castro, Smith condemned both Castro and Fulgencio Batista's anti-Castro policy. He had hoped Batista could arrange an orderly transfer of power in 1958, and he later claimed that Castro succeeded because of an indecisive U.S. policy and the work of the State Department bureaucrats sympathetic to Castro's aspirations. Smith has been married three times and from 1971 to 1977 was mayor of Palm Beach, Florida. Langley, Lester D., *The Cuban Policy of the United States* (1968); Smith, Earl E. T., *The Fourth Floor: An Account of the Castro Communist Revolution* (1962); Welch, Richard E., *Response to Revolution: The United States and the Cuban Revolution, 1959–1967* (1983); *WWA* (1986–1987):2601–2.

SMITH, ROBERT (1757–1842). Secretary of state from 1809 to 1811 under President James Madison,* Robert Smith was born in Lancaster, Pennsylvania, on November 3, 1757, graduated from the College of New Jersey in 1781, and subsequently was admitted to the bar. Married to Margaret Smith in 1790, he practiced law in Maryland and began his political career upon election to the Maryland State Senate in 1793. From 1976 to 1800, he sat in the Maryland House of Delegates; part of that time, he was also serving on the Baltimore City Council. In 1801, he was named secretary of the navy, an appointment that may have reflected his legal specialty, admiralty cases. Smith's tenure as secretary of state was rendered ineffective by sharp clashes with both President Madison, who thought he was inefficient, and Treasury Secretary Albert Gallatin,* whose Senate opponents were friends of Smith. According to Egan, Smith was inadequate in carrying on diplomatic correspondence and prone to intrigues with the British and French ministers. In 1811, Gallatin's opponents demanded his resignation; Madison refused to accept it, called Smith in, accused him of disloyalty, and requested his resignation. Smith's major diplomatic endeavor was negotiating the abortive Erskine Agreements (1809).* Smith returned to private life, wrote a pamphlet, "Address to the People of the United States" (1811) defending his reputation, and lived the rest of his life in Baltimore, where he died on November 26, 1842. Brant, Irving, *James Madison*, 1 vol. (1971); *DAB*, 17:337; Egan, Clifford L., *Neither Peace nor War: Franco-American Relations, 1803–1812* (1983); Tansill, C. C., "Robert Smith," in Bemis, Samuel F., ed., *American Secretaries of State and Their Diplomacy*, vol. 3 (1927).

SMITH, WALTER BEDELL (1895–1961). A native of Indianapolis, W. Bedell "Beetle" Smith was born October 5, 1895, served in the state National Guard from 1910 to 1915, married Mary Eleanor Cline in 1917, and embarked on a career in the U.S. army in 1918, fighting in France during World War I and eventually rising to the rank of lieutenant general. During World War II, he served on General Dwight D. Eisenhower's staff in Europe and was Eisenhower's chief of staff in the North African campaign. After the war, he was named ambassador to the Soviet Union (1946–1949), where he dealt with tensions caused by the Soviet presence in northern Iran in 1946, participated in the Paris Peace Conference (1946),* attended the Council of Foreign Ministers meetings in Moscow (1947)* and London (1947),* and attempted to end the Berlin blockade* diplomatically, negotiating with Premier Joseph Stalin and Foreign Minister V. M. Molotov. From 1950 to 1953, Smith was director of the Central Intelligence Agency,* and in 1953, when Eisenhower became president, he was named under secretary of state. In that latter capacity, he headed the Psychological Strategy Board, which evaluated the international impact of U.S. policy decisions, and was chairman of the U.S. delegation to the Geneva Conference (1954),* dealing with Korea and Indochina. After 1954, Smith was vice-chairman of American Machine and Foundry Company and an occasional State Department adviser. He wrote of his ambassadorial experience in *My Three Years* *in Moscow* (1950) and of Eisenhower, *Eisenhower's Six Great Decisions* (1956), before his death in Washington on August 9, 1961. *New York Times*, August 27, 1950, January 8, 1953, August 10, 1961; Poole, Peter A., *The United States and Indochina from FDR to Nixon* (1973); *WWWA*, 4 (1961–1968):880.

SMOOT-HAWLEY TARIFF (1930). This tariff was devised in early 1929 as a means of helping U.S. agriculture, which had endured hard times during most of the 1920s. By June 1930, however, the intent of the tariff had been greatly broadened in response to other sectors of the economy that had been hit hard in the aftermath of the October 1929 stock market crash. As passed by Congress, the Smoot-Hawley Tariff raised rates on many imported products, both agricultural and manufactured. By 1932, U.S. imports and exports had both declined by about 69 percent. Recent research suggests that the tariff was not as important in causing this decline as formerly believed. First, the rate hikes were relatively small, since the Fordney-McCumber Tariff (1922) had already set high rates. Second, many goods still entered the United States duty free. Third, imports had suffered a substantial decline even before the tariff took effect. Despite these mitigating factors, the tariff still made its contribution to the Great Depression. Economic historians do not agree on the degree of this contribution. Galbraith, John K., *The Great Crash 1929* (1961); Jones, Joseph M., Jr., *Tariff Retaliation: Repercussions of the Hawley-Smoot Bill* (1934); Wanniski, Jude, *The Way the World Works* (1978).

SMYTH, JOHN HENRY (1844–1908). Born in Richmond, Virginia, on July 14, 1844, John Henry Smyth attended Quaker schools in Philadelphia until 1857, spent a year at the Pennsylvania Academy of Fine Arts, and graduated from the Institute for Colored Youth in Philadelphia (1862) and Harvard Law School (1872). From 1862 to 1865, he taught school in Philadelphia, and from 1865 to 1869 he studied drama in England. He never took up a career in theater, however, and after law school he practiced law in Raleigh, North Carolina, and campaigned in 1876 for the Republican Rutherford B. Hayes. In 1878, he was appointed minister to Liberia, remaining at that post until 1885 except for one brief interruption. A competent diplomat and reporter, he described conditions in Liberia well and represented German and Belgian interests there for a period of time. After his return to the United States, Smyth was in the real estate business in Washington, edited the *Reformer*, a Richmond newspaper, and, in 1897, founded the Virginia Manual Labor School, serving as its director until his death on September 5, 1908, in Hanover, Virginia. Smyth married Fannie E. Shippen in 1870. *DAB*, 17:375; *NCAB*, 12:526.

SOCIAL DARWINISM. Social Darwinism refers to the application of Darwinian thought to society, in place of species, by thinkers and writers such as Herbert Spencer and William Graham Sumner. In the United States, social Darwinism was current in the late nineteenth century and was often used in combination with prevailing anthropological and biological thought to justify a belief in Anglo-Saxon racial superiority. This racism was basic to arguments explaining or vindicating American expansionism and imperialism in the late nineteenth century. Among popular exponents of social Darwinism and expansion were Reverend Josiah Strong, John Fiske,* Senator Albert Beveridge (R., Indiana),* and Theodore Roosevelt. Hofstadter, Richard, *Social Darwinism in American Thought* (1944).

SOULÉ, PIERRE (1801–1870). A native of France, Pierre Soulé was born in Castillon-en-Couserans on August 31, 1801, studied law in Bordeaux, and, in the political turmoil of the early 1820s, found himself on the wrong side, and went to Haiti in 1825. The same year he moved on to the United States, and after a short stay in Baltimore, he settled in New Orleans, where he practiced law and married Armantine Mercier in 1828. He achieved wealth and prominence as a lawyer, orator, and financier, sat in the Louisiana State Senate (1846), and served a term in the U.S. Senate (1847–1853). A campaigner for Pierce in 1852, Soulé was rewarded with appointment as minister to Spain, an illogical post because of his French heritage but logical because of his ardent desire for Cuban annexation, a prime objective of the Pierce administration. His appointment was not popular in Spain and was made less so by his efforts to obtain Cuba and his undiplomatic behavior in the *Black Warrior* affair (1854)* and in aiding assorted European revolutionaries. Soulé is best known for his collaboration with James Buchanan,* minister to Great Britain, and John Y. Mason,* minister to France, in the Ostend Manifesto (1854).* Resigning after the repudiation of the manifesto by Pierce, Soulé returned to private law practice (one of his clients was William Walker,* the noted filibuster), supported the development of transit routes across the Mexican isthmus of Tehuantepec, but, because of the hostility of Jefferson Davis, held only minor posts on the Confederacy. He died in New Orleans on March 26, 1870. *DAB*, 17:405; Ettlinger, A. A., *The Mission to Spain of Pierre Soulé, 1853–55* (1932).

SOUTHEAST ASIA TREATY ORGANIZATION (SEATO). Created in the Manila Pact (1954)* for South Pacific defense, this organization administered the details of the pact and was similar in some respects to the North Atlantic Treaty Organization (NATO)* and the Central Treaty Organization.* Unlike NATO, however, SEATO did not include a unified military command or joint military forces but only provided for consultation in the event of an emergency. Ratified by the Senate, 82–1, shortly after its creation in September 1954, SEATO formed an important link in the global containment* policy pursued by John Foster Dulles,* who played a major role in the Manila Pact discussions. SEATO was used as justification for the U.S. involvement in Vietnam, and President Richard M. Nixon, in announcing the Nixon Doctrine (1969),* was careful to note that the doctrine did not alter U.S. commitments to the region contained in SEATO. LaFeber notes that SEATO vastly increased the stake the United

States considered it had in Asia, suggesting that the Monroe Doctrine* was being extended across the Pacific. SEATO's membership consisted of the United States, the Philippines, Great Britain, France, Australia, New Zealand, Pakistan, and Thailand; a basic weakness in the organization was the absence of India, Burma, and Indonesia from membership. Thus virtually all of the organization's strength came from powers outside the geographical area. In addition, the dispute between India and Pakistan was exacerbated because India was not a member and Pakistan was. The organization was formally dissolved in 1977. Armstrong, Hamilton Fish, "Thoughts along the Chinese Border," *Foreign Affairs* 38 (January 1960): 238–50; LaFeber, Walter, *America, Russia, and the Cold War, 1945–1984* (1985); Poole, Peter A., *The United States and Indochina from FDR to Nixon* (1973); Spanier, John A., *American Foreign Policy since World War II* (1988).

SPANISH CIVIL WAR (1936–1939). In July 1936, army units rebelled against the Spanish republican government, and the resulting national conflict became a preview of World War II. Germany and Italy aided the rebels, and the Soviet Union helped the Loyalists, as those who supported the government were known. American policy was to impose a "moral embargo," refrain from any interference, and discourage private trade with either side (the impartial arms embargo of the Neutrality Act of 1936* did not apply to civil wars). The moral embargo held up for nearly six months. Then a breach caused Congress to enact legislation extending the arms embargo to civil wars; the effect was to help the rebel side, which was being amply supplied by its allies. An effort by congressional liberals to repeal the arms embargo failed in 1938 but brought about some serious rethinking of the whole matter of U.S. neutrality* and the difficulties inherent in isolationism,* all of which contributed to the general repeal of the arms embargo in the Neutrality Act of 1939.* Some historians have criticized U.S. policy as inadvertently helping to instill fascism of a sort in Spain and thus denying the United States a potential World War II ally. Others claim, however, that lifting the arms embargo might have triggered a general European war and brought about a Communist Spain, both of which were anathema to U.S. policy makers at that time. Cortada, James W., *Two Nations over Time: Spain and the United States, 1776–1977* (1978); Divine, Robert A., *The Illusion of Neutrality* (1962); Flynn, George Q., *Roosevelt and Romanism* (1976); *FR* (1936), 2:437–784; *FR* (1937), 1:245–604; *FR* (1938), 1:149–383; *FR* (1939), 2:715–819; Wiltz, John E., *From Isolation to War, 1931–1941* (1968).

SPHERE OF INFLUENCE. This phrase refers to an arrangement, usually amicable and informal, by which rival nations agree to contain their political and economic activities within a certain area or region of the country in which the rivalry exists. These areas or regions are known as spheres of influence. The practice reached its height in China in the last years of the nineteenth century when several European powers and Japan had fairly well-defined spheres of influence in various parts of China. The fact that the United States did not have such a sphere and was thus closed out of much of the "China market" was a factor in the development of the Open Door policy* of John Hay.* The term has been used in a more general sense and applied to larger areas with respect to mid-twentieth-century international affairs, wherein Latin America may be said to comprise a U.S. sphere of influence and Eastern Europe a Soviet sphere of influence. McCormick, Thomas J., *China Market* (1967); Renouvin, Pierre, and Jean-Baptiste Duroselle, *Introduction to the History of International Relations* (1967).

SPOONER ACT (1902). Offered as an amendment to the Hepburn Bill,* this authorized the president to adopt the Panama route for an isthmian canal if authentic title could be obtained from the New Panama Canal Company* and if satisfactory terms could be made with Colombia. If not, then the president was directed to proceed with the canal along the Nicaragua route. The act was named for Senator John C. Spooner (R., Wisconsin) and was a major victory for the Panama advocates. McCullough, David, *The Path Between the Seas* (1977); Miner, Dwight C., *The Fight for the Panama Route* (1940); Munro, Dana G., *Intervention and Dollar Diplomacy in the Caribbean, 1900–1921* (1964).

SQUIER, EPHRAIM GEORGE (1821–1888). Born June 17, 1821, in Bethlehem, New York, Ephraim G. Squier was self-educated and began a career in journalism before becoming clerk of the Ohio House of Representatives in 1847. In 1849, he was appointed chargé d'affaires* to Central America; there he signed an isthmian canal agreement with Nicaragua that was never ratified but nonetheless nearly torpedoed the pending Clayton-Bulwer Treaty (1850),* which specified that any canal would be a joint Anglo-American project. Squier returned to the United States in 1850, but three years later he was in Central America again, this time in his capacity as secretary of the Honduras Interoceanic Railway Company. He made surveys in Honduras for a rail project that never got off the ground. In 1863, he was named a U.S. commissioner to Peru, where he worked on financial claims matters and explored Inca sites. His last direct contact with diplomacy was service as Honduran consul general* in New York in 1868. In 1871, Squier became the first president of the Anthropological Institute of New York, an organization that later merged with the American Ethnological Society. One concrete result of Squier's missions to Central and South America was a prolific amount of writing on the archaeology and current conditions of those places: *Nicaragua: Its People, Scenery, Monuments and the Proposed Interoceanic Canal* (1852), *Notes on Central America* (1854), *Waikua, or Adventures on the Mosquito Shore* (1855), *The States of Central America* (1857; rev. ed., 1870), *Honduras* (1870), and *Peru: Incidents of Travel and Exploration in the Land of the Incas* (1897). Squier died in Brooklyn on April 17, 1888, after a long illness. *DAB*, 17:489; *NCAB*, 4:79; *New York Times*, April 18, 1888.

SQUIERS, HERBERT GOLDSMITH (1859–1911). Born April 20, 1859, in Madoc, Ontario, Herbert G. Squiers graduated from the Minnesota Military Academy in 1877 and the U.S. Artillery School in 1880 and followed a career in the army until 1891. In 1894, he joined the diplomatic service as second secretary in Berlin; in 1898, he became legation secretary at Peking, where he served well during the Boxer Rebellion* as chief of staff. He left China in 1902 to become minister to Cuba, a position he held until 1905. In Cuba, Squiers was a strong U.S. representative, insisting on dealing directly with the president of Cuba and urging Cuba to remain stable, solvent, sanitary, and pro-American. From 1906 to 1910, he was minister to Panama, where he received considerable criticism for his involvement in local political affairs. Twice married, Squiers died October 19, 1911, in London. *DAB*, 17:490; Dennis, A.L.P., *Adventures in American Diplomacy, 1896–1906* (1928); *NCAB*, 12:333; *New York Times*, October 24, 1911.

STANDLEY, WILLIAM HARRISON (1872–1963). An admiral in the U.S. Navy who became a World War II–era ambassador to the Soviet Union, William H. Standley was born December 18, 1872, in Ukiah, California, and graduated from the Naval Academy in 1895. His active duty saw service in the Philippine insurrection and terms as assistant chief of naval operations (1927–1933) and chief of naval operations (1933–1937) before retirement and work as a director of and consultant to the Electric Boat Company (1939–1941). Recalled to active duty in 1941, Standley served in the military throughout World War II except for his stint as ambassador to the Soviet Union (1942–1943). Among his wartime duties was membership on the board investigating the attack on Pearl Harbor.* As ambassador, his main objective was to create maximum cooperation in the war effort; his forthright diplomacy was respected by the Soviets, but he was criticized in the United States for stating that the Russian people were not being adequately informed about U.S. aid. In his book, *Admiral Ambassador to Russia* (1955), however, Standley expressed resentment at the limitations placed on his conduct as ambassador by the government and at being bypassed in such matters as Lend-Lease.* After World War II, Standley lived in San Diego, California, and participated in anti-Communist, conservative political organizations such as Ten Million Americans Mobilizing for Justice. He married Evelyn C. Curtis in 1898 and died in San Diego on October 25, 1963. Chadwin, Mark L., *The Warhawks* (1968); *DAB*, Supp. 7:713–14; Eubank, Keith, *Summit at Teheran* (1985); Gaddis, John L., *The United States and the Origins of the Cold War* (1972); Herring, George C., Jr., *Aid to Russia, 1941–1946* (1973); *New York Times*, October 26, 1963; *WWWA*, 4 (1961–1968):895.

"STAR WARS." See **STRATEGIC DEFENSE INITIATIVE (SDI).**

START. See **STRATEGIC ARMS REDUCTION TALKS (START).**

STEINHARDT, LAWRENCE ADOLPH (1892–1950). Lawrence A. Steinhardt was born October 6, 1892, in New York City, graduated from Columbia (B.A., 1913; M.A., 1915; LL.B., 1915), and served in World War I. After the war, he practiced law in New York City, married Dulcie Yates Hofman in 1923, and became a friend of Franklin D. Roosevelt. He served on the Democratic national campaign committee in 1932 and was rewarded with diplomatic appointments as minister to Sweden (1933–1937) and Peru (1937–1939) and ambassador to the Soviet Union (1939–1942), Turkey (1942–1944), Czechoslovakia (1944–1948), and Canada (1948–1950). In Sweden, Steinhardt negotiated a new trade treaty, but his primary function was keeping a watch on Soviet affairs. In Peru, he was a delegate to the Lima Conference (1938).* His mission in the Soviet Union was highlighted by his handling of Lend-Lease* arrangements in that nation and helping to end the Russo-Finnish War in 1940. Steinhardt worked to keep Turkey from joining the Axis and arranged Lend-Lease there as well. Life in Czechoslovakia was difficult after the Communist coup in 1948, and Steinhardt's Canadian mission was uneventful. He and his wife were killed in a plane crash near Ramsayville, Ontario, on March 28, 1950. Kolko, Joyce, and Gabriel Kolko, *The Limits of Power* (1972); Langer, William L., and S. Everett Gleason, *The Challenge to Isolation, 1937–1940* (1952); *NCAB*, 40:70; *New York Times*, March 29, 1950; Ullman, Walter, *The United States in Prague, 1945–1948* (1978).

STEPHENS, JOHN LLOYD (1805–1852). More famous for his travel narratives of Central America than for his diplomacy there, John Lloyd Stephens was born November 28, 1805, in Shrewsbury, New Jersey. He graduated from Columbia College (1822), attended the law school in Litchfield, Connecticut, and was admitted to the bar in 1826. After eight years as a lawyer, Stephens took an extended trip to the Mediterranean and Eastern Europe (1834–1836), publishing in 1838 an account of his journey that earned him the nickname "the American traveler." In 1839, he was sent to Central America as a confidential agent but, because of the political instability in the area, could practice little actual diplomacy. Stephens used the opportunity to travel throughout the region with an English artist, Frederick Catherwood, visiting Mayan ruins. Out of these trips came two popular two-volume books, *Incidents of Travel in Central America, Chiapas and Yucatan* (1841) and *Incidents of Travel in Yucatan* (1843). In 1847, Stephens became a director of the Ocean Steam Navigation Company (a line between the United States and Germany) and was also involved with the development of the transisthmian Panama railroad. He negotiated a transit agreement with the government of New Granada and surveyed the route in 1849 and oversaw the construction in 1850–1851. Debilitated by this Panama experience, Stephens died in New York City on October 12, 1852. *DAB*, 17:579; *NCAB*, 5:424.

STETTINIUS, EDWARD REILLY, JR. (1900–1949). Secretary of state at the end of World War II, Edward R. Stettinius, Jr., was born October 22, 1900, in Chicago. He attended the University of Virginia and began a business career with General Motors in 1924. In 1930, he became assistant to its president, Alfred P. Sloan, Jr.; the following year, he joined U.S. Steel as vice-president for industrial and public relations. In 1934, Stettinius was made chairman of the finance committee, and four years later, at only thirty-seven, he became chairman of the board. He served in the New Deal as a member of the Industrial Advisory Board (1933–1935), chairman of the War Resources Board (1939–1940), and member of the National Defense Advisory Commission (1940–1941). In 1941, he was named director of priorities in the Office of Production Management; later that year he took over administration of Lend-Lease,* demonstrating a talent for administration. Stettinius joined the State Department in 1943 as under secretary of state with instructions to reorganize the department administratively and improve its public relations operation. On December 1, 1944, he replaced Cordell Hull* as secretary of state, although his influence on policy was minimal because of President Roosevelt's proclivity to make the major decisions. Stettinius's major role was in relation to the United Nations.* He headed the U.S. delegation to the Dumbarton Oaks Conference (1944),* accompanied Roosevelt to Yalta (1945),* attended the Mexico City Conference (1945),* and signed the Act of Chapultepec, and led the U.S. delegation at the San Francisco Conference (1945),* which set the United Nations* in motion. At San Francisco, Stettinius played a major role in conciliating differences among the powers and ensuring a successful conference. He left the post of secretary of state in July 1945 and became chairman of the U.S. delegation to the United Nations Preparatory Commission and subsequently chairman of the first U.S. delegation to the United Nations itself (1946). After 1946, Stettinius retired to private life; he was a rector of the University of Virginia and was interested in the development of Liberia. Stettinius married Virginia Graham Wallace in 1926 and died of a coronary thrombosis on October 31, 1949, in Greenwich, Connecticut. Herring, George C., Jr., *Aid to Russia, 1941–1946* (1973); Johnson, Walter S., "Edward R. Stettinius," in Graebner, Norman E., ed., *An Uncertain Tradition* (1961); *New York Times*, November 1, 1949; Stettinius, E. R., Jr., *Lend-Lease: Weapon for Victory* (1944), and (with Walter S. Johnson), *Roosevelt and the Russians: The Yalta Conference* (1949).

STEVENS, JOHN LEAVITT (1820–1895). Born August 1, 1820, in Mt. Vernon, Maine, John L. Stevens attended Maine Wesleyan Seminary and Waterville Liberal Institute and became a Universalist minister in 1845. After ten years in the ministry, he embarked on a career in journalism, editing and owning (with James G. Blaine* until 1858) the *Kennebec Journal* (Augusta) between 1855 and 1869. Active in Republican party politics, Stevens served in the Maine legislature and on the party's state committee; as a delegate to the 1860 convention, he supported William H. Seward* for the presidential nomination. In 1870, he was named minister to Paraguay and Uruguay and mediated a conflict between Uruguay and Argentina. From 1877 to 1883, he was minister to Norway and Sweden, an uneventful mission. In 1889, Stevens was appointed minister to Hawaii and was there in early 1893 when the provisional government led by Sanford B. Dole forcibly replaced Queen Liliuokalani and sought annexation by the United States. Stevens recognized the Dole government and supported its desire for annexation and in so doing exceeded his authority as a diplomatic representative. He was recalled, accused of conspiring with the revolutionaries, and investigated by the Senate in 1894 but never found officially guilty of misconduct. After 1894, Stevens lived in retirement in Augusta until his death on February 8, 1895. *DAB*, 17:618; Devine, Michael J., *John W. Foster: Politics and Diplomacy in the Imperial Era, 1873–1917* (1981); Rogers, Augustus C., ed., *Our Representatives Abroad* (1874); Stevens, Sylvester K., *American Expansion in Hawaii, 1842–1898* (1945).

STEVENSON, ADLAI EWING II (1900–1965). The grandson of former Vice-President Adlai Stevenson, Adlai E. Stevenson II was born February 5, 1900, in Los Angeles. He graduated from Princeton (1922) and attended Harvard Law School before graduating from Northwestern (1926). Admitted in 1926 to the Illinois bar, he practiced law in Chicago before joining the New Deal in 1933 as a special counsel to the Agricultural Adjustment Administration, 1933–1935. Stevenson was in private practice from 1935 to 1941, when he returned to Washington as counsel for Secretary of the Navy Frank Knox until 1943. In 1945, he became an assistant to Secretaries of State Edward R. Stettinius, Jr.,* and James F. Byrnes,* a representative at the San Francisco Conference* on the United Nations* and, from 1945 to 1947, an aide to the U.S. delegation to the United Nations. Elected Democratic governor of Illinois in 1948, he served one term and then was his party's presidential nominee in 1952 and again in 1956, losing both times to Dwight Eisenhower. In 1961, President John F. Kennedy named Stevenson U.S. ambassador to the United Nations, a position he held until his death in London on July 14, 1965. At the United Nations, he found himself somewhat isolated from official policymaking. He was embarrassed by not being informed about the Bay of Pigs invasion* and was never entirely satisfied with his role. Still, he was an excellent speaker and a patient negotiator and represented U.S. policy well on such issues as the Congo crisis,* the Cuban missile crisis,* the Vietnam War, and the Dominican crisis.* He wrote several books, including *What I Think* (1956) and *Looking Outward* (1963), and was married in 1928 in Ellen Borden; they were divorced in 1949. A son, Adlai E. Stevenson III, served as U.S. senator from Illinois. Martin, John Bartlow, *Adlai Stevenson and the World* (1977); *New York Times*, July 15, 1965; *WWWA*, 4 (1961–1968):904.

STEVENSON, ANDREW (1784–1857). Andrew Stevenson was born January 21, 1784, in Culpeper County, Virginia, attended William and Mary College in the late 1790s, read law, and was admitted to the bar in 1805. From 1809 to 1821 (except 1817), he sat in the Virginia legislature. In 1821, Stevenson was elected to the U.S. House of Representatives, where he remained until 1835, serving as Speaker of the House the last seven years. As Speaker, he was the first to appoint members to House committees strictly on the basis of party. He was also a director of the Richmond branch of the Bank of the United States. In 1836, he became U.S. minister to Great Britain, a post he held until 1841.

Instructed to press for indemnification of liberated slaves, he was generally successful; with the regulation of the slave trade involving the unwanted right of search of American ships, he was not. Stevenson worked for the improvement of British markets for American tobacco and rice, dealt with the long-standing northeastern boundary question (which remained unsettled until 1842), and helped Texas envoy James Hamilton obtain British recognition of Texas independence in 1840. After his diplomatic career, he returned home and became rector of the University of Virginia. Stevenson, who was married three times, died at his home, Blenheim, in Albemarle County, Virginia, on January 18, 1857. *DAB*, 17:630; Wayland, Francis Fry, *Andrew Stevenson: Democrat and Diplomat, 1785–1857* (1949); Willson, Beckles, *America's Ambassadors to England, 1785–1929* (1929).

STIMSON, HENRY LEWIS (1867–1950). Secretary of state in the administration of President Herbert Hoover (1929–1933), Henry L. Stimson was born September 21, 1867, in New York City, graduated from Yale (A.B., 1888) and Harvard (A.M., 1889; LL.B. 1890), and was admitted to the New York bar in 1891. From 1891 to 1899, he practiced law with Elihu Root*; in 1899, he founded his own firm. He became U.S. attorney for the Southern District of New York in 1906 and earned a reputation as a trustbuster in railroad rebate cases. A Republican, Stimson lost a race for New York governor in 1910 but was named secretary of war in the Taft administration the following year. During World War I, he was a colonel in command of an artillery regiment. After the war, he returned to law practice and remained out of public life until 1926, when he represented the U.S. government in the Tacna-Arica dispute. The following year, he traveled to Nicaragua at the request of President Calvin Coolidge and arranged the Peace of Tipitapa (1927)* between warring factions. In 1928–1929, he was governor-general of the Philippines and played an important role in stabilizing the economy and restoring the confidence of the people. Named secretary of state by President Herbert Hoover in 1929, Stimson had to contend with problems caused by the Great Depression. He extended the moratorium on debt payments and in the London Naval Conference (1930)* tried to move further in the area of international arms limitation. His major crisis was Manchuria, where in 1931 after the Mukden incident,* the Japanese swiftly took control. In an open letter to Senator William E. Borah,* Stimson proposed the imposition of economic sanctions. When this proved unfeasible, he proposed what is sometimes known as the Stimson Doctrine*: nonrecognition of conquests by aggression. Although this policy was adopted by the League of Nations,* the Japanese ignored it, and Stimson's policies earned substantial criticism from those who saw unchecked Japanese expansion as a U.S. defeat. At the end of Hoover's administration, he served as a liaison between Hoover and the incoming president, Franklin D. Roosevelt, and retired to private life. In 1940, however, he was appointed secretary of war in an effort to give the Roosevelt administration bipartisan unity in the face of another world war. Stimson served until 1945 and made the decisive recommendation to use the atomic bomb. In retirement after 1945, Stimson lived on Long Island and enjoyed an active outdoor life. He married Mable Wellington White in 1893 and died in Huntington, Long Island, on October 20, 1950. Current, Richard N., *Secretary Stimson* (1954); *DAB*, Supp. 4:784; Doenecke, Justus D., comp., *The Diplomacy of Frustration* (1981); Morrison, Elting E., *Turmoil and Tradition* (1960); *New York Times*, October 21, 1950; Stimson, Henry L., *The Far Eastern Crisis* (1936), Stimson, Henry L., and McGeorge Bundy, *On Active Service in Peace and War* (1948).

STIMSON DOCTRINE (1932), a statement of the doctrine of nonrecognition, expressed by Secretary of State Henry L. Stimson* in January 1932 by means of a diplomatic note to China and Japan. Stimson's note stated that the United States could not recognize any treaty or any de facto government that impaired U.S. treaty rights with China or the provisions of the Nine-Power Treaty* or any situation brought about in violation of the Kellogg-Briand Pact.* Aimed specifically at Japanese actions in Manchuria after the Mukden incident,* the Stimson Doctrine was approved by the League of Nations* in March, and most member nations refused to recognize the puppet state of Manchukuo, created that month by Japan in what had been Manchuria. Although Stimson claimed his was an original statement, its concept, according to Ferrell, had ample precedent in U.S. diplomacy. Current, Richard N., *Secretary Stimson* (1954); Ferrell, Robert H., *American Diplomacy in the Great Depression* (1957); Morison, Elting E., *Turmoil and Tradition* (1960).

STOCKTON, ROBERT FIELD (1795–1866). Robert F. Stockton was born in Princeton, New Jersey, on August 20, 1795, attended Princeton University briefly, and entered the U.S. Navy in 1811. He rose to the rank of commodore and in 1845 had command of the American squadron at Galveston, Texas. An ardent nationalist, Stockton was allegedly involved in what is known as the Polk-Stockton intrigue,* involving Stockton's conspiring with Texas to provoke Mexico into a war. Although proof is elusive, it does appear that Stockton at least encouraged Texans to stand and fight if Mexican troops entered the disputed territory between the Nueces River and the Rio Grande. Later in 1845, he was directed to the California coast to join with the squadron of John D. Sloat, and he prepared for war. He took command on the California coast in June 1846, issued a nationalistic proclamation calling for the expulsion of the Mexicans, and participated in the U.S. occupation of California, completed in early 1847. In 1850, he resigned his commission. Stockton served in the U.S. Senate, 1851–1853, resigning to become president of the Delaware and Raritan Canal. He died in Princeton on October 7, 1866. *Biographical Congressional Dictionary, 1774–1911* (1911); Pletcher, David, *The Diplomacy of Annexation* (1973).

STOESSEL, WALTER JOHN, JR. (1920–1986). A native of Manhattan, Kansas, where he was born January 24, 1920, Walter J. Stoessel, Jr., was a 1941 graduate of Stanford and joined the Foreign Service in 1942. He served as a vice-consul in Caracas before joining the navy in 1944. After his discharge in 1946, he married Mary Ann Ferrandou and reentered the Foreign Service, holding minor posts in Washington, Moscow, and Bad Nauheim (West Germany) before 1952. That year he became chief of the Division of Soviet and East European Affairs, attending several high-level meetings, including the Geneva Conference (1954),* in that capacity. Other assignments followed: adviser to the White House, 1956; attaché to the Paris embassy, 1956–1959; aide to Secretary of State Dean Rusk,* 1961; again in Paris, 1961–1963; deputy chief of mission, Moscow, 1963–1965; and deputy assistant secretary of state, 1965–1968. In 1968, Stoessel was appointed ambassador to Poland, where he carried on talks with representatives of the People's Republic of China at the beginning of the process that led to U.S. recognition of China in 1972. From 1972 to 1974, he was back in Washington as assistant secretary of state for European affairs. His most important assignment, ambassador to the Soviet Union, came in 1974, where détente* diplomacy brought about relaxation of tensions, increased trade, and optimism about increased normalization of U.S.-soviet relations. In 1976, Stoessel moved to Bonn as ambassador to West Germany, where he remained until 1981. His final assignments were in Washington as under secretary of state for political affairs, 1981–1982, and deputy secretary of state, 1982–1986. Stoessel died in Washington, D.C., on December 9, 1986. Brownstein, Ronald, and Nina Easton, *Reagan's Ruling Class* (1982); *New York Times*, August 17, September 12, 1976, December 11, 1986; *WWA* (1986–1987):2694.

STONE-FLOOD ACT (1915). A step forward in the professionalization of the U.S. diplomatic service, this act provided for the establishment of a Board of Examiners and an examination system for prospective diplomatic and consular personnel, for the keeping and reporting of efficiency records, and for the creation of a new personnel classification system to put promotions squarely on a merit basis, and for the appointment of secretaries to classes in a graded system rather than to specific posts, thus facilitating their transfer to posts where their services were more urgently needed. This act is named for Senator William S. Stone (D. Missouri) and Congressman Henry D. Flood (D. Virginia). Ilchman, Warren F., *Professional Diplomacy in the United States, 1779–1939* (1961); Plischke, Elmer, *The Conduct of American Diplomacy* (1967).

STRAIGHT, WILLARD DICKERMAN (1880–1918). Willard Straight was born January 31, 1880, in Oswego, New York, learned fluent Japanese and Chinese as a child when his father became a missionary in Japan, graduated from Cornell in 1901, and embarked on a career in the Far East working for the Chinese Imperial Maritime Customs Service. In 1905, he entered the consular service and served in Seoul and Mukden before becoming chief of the Division of Far Eastern Affairs in 1909. Straight was pro-Chinese and worried about increasing Japanese influence in Manchuria. In 1909, he became a representative for a group of American banking interests, working to implement dollar diplomacy* in China in order to expand American trade and strengthen China at the expense of Japan. Principally, this was to be done through obtaining American participation in the Hukuang railway loan* and, later, through the internationalization of all Manchurian railroads, including the Japanese-owned South Manchurian railroad. However, both Japan and Russia opposed this latter plan; other Western powers did not actively support it, and it was never undertaken. After the collapse of dollar diplomacy in China in 1911, Straight worked for the J. P. Morgan banking interests and for American International Corporation, remaining interested in the development, with American capital, of Chinese and other foreign railroads. During the war, he headed an overseas branch of soldiers' insurance operations before dying December 1, 1918, of pneumonia. Cohen, Warren I., *America's Response to China* (1971); Crane, Daniel M., and Thomas A. Breslin, *An Ordinary Relationship* (1986); Croly, H. D., *Willard Straight* (1924); *DAB*, 18:121; *New York Times*, December 2, 1918.

STRATEGIC ARMS LIMITATION TALKS (SALT). At the time of the signing of the Non-Proliferation Treaty (1968),* both the United States and the Soviet Union expressed a desire to enter negotiations to limit strategic weapons systems. The repression of the Czechoslovakian government of Alexander Dubcek in late 1968 delayed the beginning of SALT until 1969, but the first round of negotiations, known as SALT I, resulted in the Anti-Ballistic Missile (ABM) Treaty, the Interim Agreement on strategic offensive weapons, the Accident Measures Agreement, and the revised Hot-Line Agreement—all signed by President Richard M. Nixon and Premier Leonid Brezhnev at Moscow in May 1972. SALT II began in November 1972 with efforts to limit strategic offensive weapons within the five-year period specified in the Interim Agreement. In 1974, both parties agreed that the five-year deadline could not be met, but in November of that year, President Gerald R. Ford and Brezhnev signed the Vladivostok Agreement, a tentative outline of SALT II goals in overall levels of strategic offensive weapons and multiple independently targeted reentry vehicle launchers. After Vladivostok, talks continued. By late 1977, further tentative decisions had been reached on SALT II. At last President Jimmy Carter and Brezhnev signed the SALT II treaty in Vienna in July 1979. The agreement specified numerical limits on a variety of offensive weapons, but it did not alter the Soviet monopoly on heavy intercontinental ballistic missiles, which they claimed offset the U.S. forward-based systems in Western Europe. The treaty, controversial from the time it was signed, never had a very good chance at being ratified, but the unpopularity of Carter, combined with the Soviet invasion of Afghanistan in December 1979, prevented it from being brought to a vote in the Senate. Nevertheless, both the Reagan administration and post-Brezhnev regimes in Moscow generally observed the terms of SALT II in the 1980s, while pursuing arms reduction measures such as the Intermediate Nuclear Force (INF) Treaty* and Strategic Arms Reduction Talks.* Kintner, William R., and Robert L. Pfaltzgraff,

Jr., eds., *SALT: Implications for Arms Control in the 1970's* (1973); Kohler, Foy, *SALT II: How Not to Negotiate with the Soviets* (1979); Szulc, Tad, *The Illusion of Peace* (1978); Talbott, Strobe, *Deadly Gambits* (1985); Willrich, Mason, and John B. Rhinelander, eds., *SALT: The Moscow Agreements and Beyond* (1974); Wolfe, Thomas W., *The SALT Experience* (1979).

STRATEGIC ARMS REDUCTION TALKS (START). START evolved from the conviction in the Reagan administration that arms reduction was preferable to arms limitation, which had formed the basis of SALT (Strategic Arms Limitation Talks) I and SALT II.* Thus the talks focused on reduction of the number of intercontinental ballistic missile warheads, since warheads were thought to be more inherently destabilizing to the strategic balance of power. The START process began with a speech by President Reagan at Eureka College in May 1982. Negotiations took place until late 1983 when they were broken off by the Soviets because of the deployment in Europe of Pershing II and cruise missiles.* In 1985, talks resumed as part of a multifaceted set of negotiations in Geneva that included intermediate nuclear forces and space-based weapons. The process was boosted by an agreement in principle at the Reykjavik Summit (1986)* to reduce strategic offensive weapons by 50 percent over five years (later changed to seven years). This would allow each side 1,600 delivery vehicles and approximately 6,000 warheads, a figure that was reduced to 4,900 at the Washington Summit (1987).* Progress on START has been delayed by an impasse over the Strategic Defense Initiative (SDI)* program; the United States insists on continuing research, development and testing, while the Soviet Union wants to limit severely what the United States can do with SDI. Talbott, Strobe, *Deadly Gambits* (1984).

STRATEGIC DEFENSE INITIATIVE (SDI). First announced by President Ronald Reagan in March 1983, the Strategic Defense Initiative (SDI), or "Star Wars," as the press quickly came to call it, is a program designed to create a space-based defense against a ballistic missile attack using laser beams or antimissile missiles. SDI would protect civilian population centers or missile sites or both against a Soviet intercontinental ballistic missile assault; to develop it, the Reagan administration asked for $26 billion over five years. Some critics believe that the program violates the ABM Treaty (part of SALT I*), while others are convinced that the technology is not perfectible and, moreover, the USSR would ultimately be able to devise ways to counteract the system. North Atlantic Treaty Organization (NATO)* allies have expressed concern about a "Fortress America" mentality, which would leave them vulnerable, although the United States has promised an SDI umbrella for Europe, and several NATO members are participating in SDI research. The Soviet Union has repeatedly pressed the United States in various arms negotiations for limitations on SDI research and/or deployment as part of any arms reduction treaty. In 1987, the Reagan administration proposed a "broad interpretation" of the ABM Treaty that would allow SDI testing in space. This prompted a heated debate between the administration and Congress over whether a treaty could be reinterpreted after it had been ratified. Meanwhile, SDI research continued on into 1988, although Congress had appropriated less money than the administration had requested. Brzezinski, Zbigniew, ed., *Promise or Peril: The Strategic Defense Initiative* (1986); Haug, C. James, ed., *The Strategic Defense Initiative: An International Perspective* (1987); Miller, Steven E., and Stephen Van Evera, eds., *The Star Wars Controversy* (1986).

STRAUS, JESSE ISIDOR (1872–1936). A native of New York City, where he was born June 25, 1872, Jesse I. Straus graduated from Harvard in 1893 and worked briefly for the Hanover National Bank and Abraham & Straus before joining R. H. Macy & Company in 1896. He rose steadily in that firm's hierarchy until he became president in 1919. A Democrat, Straus actively supported Franklin D. Roosevelt in his 1928 campaign for governor of New York and again in his 1932 presidential campaign. In 1931, Governor Roosevelt named Straus head of the New York Temporary Emergency Relief Administration, and in 1933 President Roosevelt appointed him ambassador to France. In Paris, he negotiated an end to the double taxation of U.S. companies with French branches and discussed a new commercial agreement that involved the removal of trade barriers. The U.S. embassy was a social center in Paris, and Straus's ambassadorship was a pleasing one because of Straus's prior business ties with France and the fact that he spoke French well. In July 1936, he became ill in Paris; he resigned in August and died in New York City on October 4. Straus married Irma Nathan in 1895 and was active in Harvard affairs through donations and service on its Board of Overseers. *DAB*, Supp. 2:635; Kauffman, Reginald W., *Jesse Isidor Straus* (1973); *New York Times*, October 5, 1936.

STRAUS, OSCAR S. (1850–1926). Three times U.S. chief of mission in Turkey, Oscar S. Straus also enjoyed a prominent political and business career in the United States. Born in Otterburg, Rhenish Bavaria (now Germany), on December 23, 1850, Straus emigrated with his family to the United States in 1854, and graduated from Columbia (A.B., 1871; LL.B., 1873). He practiced law until 1881, when he became a partner in L. Straus & Sons, china and glassware merchants. Between 1887 and 1889, he served his first Turkish ministry and was successful in getting American schools reopened for the first time in six years and in securing permission for the American Bible Society to distribute Bibles. He enjoyed good relations with the sultan and arbitrated a major railroad dispute for him. In Straus's second Turkish mission, 1898–1900, he was principally concerned with the protection of American missionaries during a period of violence directed against Armenians. After 1900, he became an adviser to Theodore Roosevelt, and in 1902, he was chosen a member of the Permanent Court of Arbitration* in the Hague and reappointed in 1908. In 1909, however, President William H. Taft named Straus ambassador to Turkey, and he went there for a third time. During this mission, he achieved even greater benefits for American schools and missionaries, freeing them from much of the oppressive Turkish supervision and winning for them the right to own land. He opposed the State Department's policy of actively encouraging U.S. commercial enterprise in Turkey, however, which contributed to his resignation from his post in 1910. Straus ran unsuccessfully for governor in New York in 1912, was active in the affairs of the League to Enforce Peace,* attending the Paris Peace Conference* as its chairman in 1919, and involved himself in Jewish concerns. He married Sarah Laranburg in 1882 and was a writer of nonfiction, including his own memoirs, *Under Four Administrations: From Cleveland to Taft* (1922). Straus died in New York City on May 3, 1926. Cohen, Naomi Wiener, *A Dual Heritage: The Public Career of Oscar S. Straus* (1969); *DAB*, 18:130; Howard, W. W., *Oscar Straus in Turkey* (1912); *New York Times*, May 4, 1926.

STROBEL, EDWARD HENRY (1855–1908). Born in Charleston, South Carolina, on December 7, 1855, Edward H. Strobel graduated from Harvard (1877) and Harvard Law School (1882) and was admitted to the New York bar in 1883. He practiced law in New York City after 1883 and actively opposed James G. Blaine* in the 1884 campaign, writing a tract, *Mr. Blaine and His Foreign Policy*. In 1885, he began a diplomatic career as legation secretary in Madrid, serving until 1890. In 1893–1894, he was third assistant secretary of state. Late in 1894, he spent several months as minister to Ecuador; in early 1895, he was appointed minister to Chile. In Santiago until 1897, Strobel was concerned with the currency question and published *Resumption of Special Payments in Chile* (1896). He also arbitrated the Frérant claims between France and Chile. In 1903, Strobel was sent to Siam as a general adviser, a position bearing ministerial rank. There he did much to improve the government through the establishment of systems of land taxes, import duties, and harbor regulations. He reorganized the postal service, brought about railroad extension, and revised the penal code. For all of this he received the Grand Cross of the Order of the White Elephant, Siam's highest honor. Fatally ill in 1907, he negotiated a treaty between France and Siam. Strobel died in Bangkok on January 15, 1908. *DAB*, 18:140; *NCAB*, 12:324.

STRONG, JOSIAH (1847–1916). Strong was born January 19, 1897, in Naperville, Illinois, and received his doctor of divinity degree from Walnut Hills Seminary in Cincinnati in 1886. He occupied Congregational pulpits in several different churches but became nationally known after the publication of his book, *Our Country: Its Possible Future and Its Present Crisis* (1885), in which he postulated a strong synthesis of social Darwinism,* evangelical Protestantism, and expansionism. His faith in economic progress was based on his conviction that Anglo-Saxons alone were the true bearers of pure Christianity and that Americans were superior to other Anglo-Saxons. Additionally, Strong enthusiastically advocated city life, opposed the "back-to-the-country" movement, and wrote many other books on society and life in the city. *DAB*, 18:150; Hofstadter, Richard, *Social Darwinism in American Thought* (1955); *New York Times*, April 29, 1916.

STUART, JOHN LEIGHTON (1876–1962). Born of missionary parents in Hangchow, China, on June 24, 1876, John Leighton Stuart graduated from Hampton-Sydney College in 1896 and studied further at the Union Theological Seminary and Princeton. Stuart married Olive Hardy in 1904 and went to China the same year. He taught at Nanking Theological Seminary from 1908 to 1919 and then became president of Yenching University, a post he held until 1946. He was highly respected among the Chinese as a man of principle; perhaps because of this, the Japanese interned him for thirty-nine months during World War II. In 1946, the Truman administration chose him to be ambassador to China after the Communist faction had rejected the proposed appointment of General Albert Wedemeyer. As ambassador, he maintained cordial relations with leaders on both sides of the Chinese civil was but was unable to bring about a settlement, either on his own or in collaboration with the mission of General George C. Marshall.* Stuart left China in 1949 when the Communists finally prevailed in the war. His later years were spent in Greek biblical scholarship and writing his memoirs, *Fifty Years in China* (1954). He died in Washington on September 19, 1962. *NCAB* G:370; *New York Times*, September 20, 1962; Rea, Kenneth, and John C. Brewer, eds., *The Forgotten Ambassador: The Reports of John Leighton Stuart, 1946–1949* (1981); Stueck, William, *The Wedemeyer Mission: American Politics and Foreign Policy during the Cold War* (1984).

SUEZ CRISIS (1956). The crisis developed in July 1956 when President Gamal Abdel Nasser of Egypt nationalized the Suez Canal, following the cancellation of U.S., British, and French pledges of aid to Egypt for the Aswan Dam project. Since the Soviet Union was also reluctant to finance the project, Nasser seized the canal partly to use the income to pay for the dam. Britain and France, both large stockholders in the canal company, plotted with Israel, which feared the consequence of a recent Egyptian arms purchase from Czecholovakia and the USSR and wanted to strike first to retake the canal. The plan called for Israel to launch its attack, after which the British and French would intervene as peacemakers. Prime Minister Anthony Eden, who remembered well the consequences of appeasement before World War II, was ready to use force to bring the canal back under international control, and, consequently, U.S. efforts to prevent British-French-Israeli military action by attempting to produce a negotiated settlement in August failed. The scenario plotted by the British, French, and Israelis was played out in October 1956, but when Egypt would not accept the British-French ultimatum to stop fighting (Nasser was determined to hold fast when he learned the United States would not join the military intervention), the United Nations* intervened. A United Nations Emergency Force, supported by both the United States and the Soviet Union, engineered a cease-fire, and amid the complex of subsequent events, the British and French were humiliated, lost all stature in the Middle East, and were resentful toward the United States; Egypt maintained control of the canal. Feis contends that U.S. action in this crisis, seemingly so embarrassing to Britain and France, actually saved those nations from what would have been a difficult military and political situation, preserved British economic interests in the rest of the Middle East, and possibly prevented a much broader war. Aldrich, Winthrop W., "The Suez Crisis: A Footnote to History," *Foreign Affairs* 45 (April 1967): 541–52; Dupuy, Trevor N., *Elusive Victory: The Arab-Israeli Wars, 1947–1974* (1978); Feis, Herbert, "Suez Scenario: A Lamentable Tale," *Foreign Affairs* 38 (July 1960): 598–612; Gerson, Louis L., "John Foster Dulles," in Ferrell, Robert H., ed., *American Secretaries of State and Their Diplomacy*, vol. 17 (1967); Rubenberg, Cheryl A., *Israel and the American National Interest* (1986); Stookey, Robert W., *America and the Arab States* (1975).

SULLIVAN PRINCIPLES (1977). Devised by the Reverend Leon Sullivan, a black American from Philadelphia and the first black director of General Motors, these principles constituted a set of voluntary guidelines to encourage racial justice in the employment practices of U.S. firms working in South Africa. The principles included nonsegregation at the workplace, equal pay for equal work, special training programs for prospective black supervisors and administrators, and the acceleration of black promotions. The Sullivan principles were endorsed by the Carter administration and a small group of corporations in 1977; by 1985, over 150 companies had subscribed. In practice, the principles have not noticeably improved the status of black workers; there are no enforcement provisions, and verification is a problem. Politically, the principles have been used to justify a continued presence in South Africa and to avoid divestment, an antiapartheid strategy that attracted much attention in the mid-1980s, when academic and civil rights groups urged U.S. firms to divest themselves of then South African affiliates and U.S. investors to divest themselves of stock in companies doing business in or with South Africa. Bissell, Richard E., *South Africa and the United States* (1982); Siedman, Ann, *The Roots of Crisis in Southern Africa* (1985).

SUMNER, CHARLES (1811–1874). Charles Sumner was born on January 6, 1811, in Boston and educated at Harvard, receiving an A.B. degree in 1830 and a law degree in 1833. He entered the Senate in 1851 as a Republican and served until his death. Outspoken on many issues of the day, Sumner supported the emancipation of slaves and took an antislavery stand on related issues. In 1861, he began ten years of service as chairman of the Senate Foreign Relations Committee, where he suppressed measures that might have led to war with Britain or France, and opposed President Grant's expansionary plans in Santo Domingo, which ultimately cost him his chairmanship. Married briefly to Alice Mason Hooper (1866–1867), Sumner died in Washington on March 11, 1874. *DAB* 18:208; Donald, David, *Charles Sumner and the Rights of Man* (1973); *New York Times*, March 12, 1874.

SUSSEX **PLEDGE (1916).** The sinking of the British channel steamer *Sussex* in March 1916, with the loss of American lives, caused President Woodrow Wilson, in mid-April, to deliver an ultimatum of sorts to Germany, threatening to sever relations unless Germany stopped its U-boat* attacks on merchant and passenger ships. The German government, after difficult internal deliberation, responded with the so-called *Sussex* pledge in early May, promising that U-boats would not sink ships in or out of the war zone without adequate warning and without attempting to save lives. The pledge averted, for the time being, war with the United States. *FR* (1916), 2:214ff.; *FR: Lansing Papers*, 1:537–62; May, Ernest, *The World War and American Isolation, 1914–1917* (1959); Smith, Daniel M., *The Great Departure* (1965).

SWIFT, JOHN FRANKLIN (1829–1891). John F. Swift was born on February 28, 1829, in Bowling Green, Missouri, had only a limited education, and was apprenticed to be a tinsmith. He moved to San Francisco in 1852, was a produce merchant, and read law, gaining admittance to the bar in 1857. Successful as a lawyer, Swift became involved in Republican politics, served three terms in the state legislature, and was register of the San Francisco land office. He campaigned for General Ulysses S. Grant in the 1868 presidential election, continued to practice law, and became known for his opposition to monopolies and Chinese immigration. In 1880, he went to China on a mission with James B. Angell* and William H. Trescot* to modify the Burlingame Treaty,* and in 1889 the Harrison administration rewarded Swift for his years of Republican loyalty by naming him minister to Japan. His ministry was tainted by his prejudice against Orientals generally, and especially Chinese, typical of the California attitude of the day. In Japan, his main work was in furthering treaty revisions begun under his predecessor, suggesting the dangers of unlimited Japanese immigration, and dealing with problems of Americans caught in the complexities of the Japanese court system. Swift was a frequent and lengthy correspondent, whose dispatches were distinguished in a literary sense and helped harden State Department attitudes toward Japan in a political sense. He died in Tokyo on March 10, 1891, while still minister. Swift was the author of two books, *Going to Jericho* (1868) and *Robert Greathouse* (1870), and was a regent of the University of California from 1872 to 1888. *DAB*, 18:246; Treat, Payson J., *Diplomatic Relations Between the United States and Japan, 1853–1895*, 2 vols. (1932).

SWING, RAYMOND GRAM (1887–1968). One of America's best-known radio news commentators prior to and during World War II, Raymond Swing was born in Cortland, New York, on March 25, 1887. He attended Oberlin College and began a journalism career in 1905, working for various small-town papers until 1913, when he went to Berlin as a correspondent for the *Chicago Daily News*. During World War I, Swing was an examiner for the War Labor Board, and, after the war, he returned to newspaper work with the *New York Herald* (1919–1922), the *Wall Street Journal* (1922–1924), and as a London correspondent for several papers (1924–1934). From 1934 to 1936, Swing was on the editorial board of the *Nation;* from 1936 to 1937, he was a New York correspondent for the *London News Chronicle*. In 1935, he began radio broadcasts for the British Broadcasting Corporation and for the Columbia Broadcasting System. His greatest acclaim came in the 1936–1942 years when he was a commentator for the Mutual Broadcasting System. He was known for his "steady disciplined analysis" and was highly regarded by both President Franklin D. Roosevelt and Winston Churchill. His sympathy with Roosevelt's policies caused him to be considered an unofficial spokesman for the administration. Taken seriously by the Roosevelt administration and by internationalists, Swing was attacking isolationism* as early as 1938, and with H. V. Kaltenborn* reporting from Europe, was the only major news analyst broadcasting regularly in America in 1939. After the war, Swing advocated a world government to prevent nuclear war and was chairman of the board of Americans United for World Government. During the 1950s, Swing was a political commentator for the Voice of America. He was married twice, wrote several books, including his memoirs, *Good Evening: A Professional Memoir* (1964), and died on December 22, 1968, in Washington, D.C. *CB* (1940):782–83; Culbert, David H., *News for Everyman* (1976); *New York Times*, December 24, 1968; *WWWA*, 4 (1969–1973):710.

TAFT, ALPHONSO (1810–1891). Born November 5, 1810, in Townshend, Vermont, Alphonso Taft graduated from Yale (1833) and, after studying law, was admitted to the Connecticut bar in 1838. He moved to Cincinnati, established a highly successful law practice, and was interested in railroad development. From 1865 to 1872, he sat on the bench as a superior court judge in Cincinnati and, in 1876, became secretary of war, moving to the attorney general's post later that year. In 1882 he was appointed minister to Austria-Hungary, and in 1884 he moved to the post of minister to Russia. There were no major diplomatic problems in either mission, but in Russia he suffered from pneumonia, the subsequent complications from which led to a trip to Chile for his health in 1890–1891. Returning from this trip, Taft died in San Diego, California, on May 21, 1891. Taft was married twice: to Fanny Phelps in 1841, who died in 1852, and to Louisa Torrey, whom he married the next year. *DAB*, 18:264; *NCAB*, 4:24.

TAFT AGREEMENT (1904). Worked out by Secretary of War William Howard Taft and William Nelson Cromwell,* this agreement attempted to resolve Panamanian complaints about the opening of commerce in the Canal Zone, where Americans would be exempt from Panamanian taxes and duties. The Taft Agreement provided that imports into the zone would be restricted to items for the canal itself or for sale to ships in transit. No private businesses competing with Panamanian business would be established. In addition, commissaries would not be open to the general public, and zone post offices would use surcharged Panamanian stamps. All of these measures served to protect Panama's economy and assuage its national pride. The agreement remained in effect until 1924. Dean, Arthur H., *William Nelson Cromwell, 1854–1948* (1957); Munro, Dana G., *Intervention and Dollar Diplomacy in the Caribbean, 1900–1921* (1964).

TAFT-KATSURA AGREEMENT (1905). Sometimes termed an "agreed memorandum," this resulted from Secretary of War William Howard Taft's visit to Tokyo in 1905 and his talks with Japan's foreign minister, Count Taro Katsura. In the agreement, the United States informally signaled its willingness to join the Anglo-Japanese Alliance (1902)* and condoned the Japanese dominion over Korea. Japan, for its part, recognized American hegemony in the Philippines. The agreement formed part of President Theodore Roosevelt's policy of maintaining good Japanese-American relations. Esthus, Raymond A., "The Taft-Katsura Agreement—Reality or Myth," *Journal of Modern History* 32 (March 1959):46–51; Neu, Charles E., *The Troubled Encounter* (1975).

TAYLOR, BAYARD (1825–1878). A popular writer and poet in his day, Bayard Taylor was born in Kennett Square, Pennsylvania, on January 22, 1825. He attended Bolmar's Academy in West Chester, Pennsylvania, and Unionville Academy before being apprenticed to a printer in 1842. He began writing soon after this, traveled in Europe, 1844–1846, and in 1848 joined the staff of the *New York Tribune*. He went to and wrote about the California gold rush, traveled in the Near East and Africa, 1851–1853, and became a lyceum lecturer upon his return. In 1860, he settled down at a Vermont estate and continued to publish verse and novels of little lasting merit. Taylor was legation secretary at St. Petersburg in 1862–1863 and worked with Minister Cassius M. Clay* to keep Russia sympathetic to the Union during the Civil War. From 1870 to 1877, he lectured at Cornell University, and in 1878 the Hayes administration sent him to Europe as minister to Germany, a pleasing appointment to Taylor, who planned to write a biography of Goethe. In Germany, Taylor handled problems relating to naturalized German-Americans who had returned to Germany and gotten into legal trouble, often, according to the minister, of their own making. He escorted ex-president Ulysses S. Grant during his visit to Germany and attended meetings of the Berlin Congress (1878). He fell ill toward the end of 1878 and died in Berlin of "constipation of the liver" and dropsy on December 19, 1878. Bayard Taylor was twice married and at the time of his death was a renowned poet, best known for his translation of Goethe's *Faust*. Beatty, Richmond Croom, *Bayard Taylor, Laureate of the Gilded Age* (1936); *DAB*, 18:314; Smyth, A. H., *Bayard Taylor* (1896); Wermuth, P. G., *Bayard Taylor* (1973).

TAYLOR, HANNIS (1851–1922). Hannis Taylor was born in New Bern, North Carolina, on September 12, 1851, attended the University of North Carolina in 1867–1868, studied law, and was admitted to the bar in 1870. He settled in Mobile, Alabama, married Leonore LeBaron in 1878, and practiced law. In 1893, the Cleveland administration named him minister to Spain, and he remained in Madrid until 1897. These were years of difficult relations between the United States and Spain, and Taylor's duties including negotiating various minor treaties, obtaining preferential treatment for American exports to Cuba and Puerto Rico, and protesting arrests of Americans and confiscation of their property in Cuba after the outbreak of war there in 1895. After his return from Madrid, Taylor lectured on political science at various Washington-area universities. Among his scholarly writings are *The Origin and Growth of the English Constitution* (1892) and *International Public Law* (1902). In 1902, he was special counsel for the United States before the Spanish Treaty Claims Commission and the junior American counsel before the Alaska Boundary Counsel in the Alaska boundary dispute.* Taylor continued to practice law until his death on December 26, 1922, in Washington, D.C. *DAB*, 18:326; McWilliams, Tennant S., *Hannis Taylor: The New Southerner as an American* (1978); *NCAB*, 8:118; *New York Times*, December 27, 1922.

TAYLOR, MAXWELL DAVENPORT (1901–1987). A career military officer who played an important diplomatic role during the Vietnam War, Maxwell D. Taylor was born August 26, 1901, in Keynesville, Missouri, graduated from West Point in 1922, attended various specialty schools, and married Lydia Gardner Hopper in 1925. His active duty career included both teaching at West Point (1927–1932) and serving as its superintendent (1945–1949). From 1955 to 1959, he was chief of staff of the army and an ardent advocate of the flexible response doctrine. In the latter year he left active duty to be president of Lincoln Center in New York City (1959–1960). In 1961–1962, he was President John F. Kennedy's special military representative, during which time he led the Taylor-Rostow mission* to Vietnam to evaluate the military and political situation there and make policy recommendations. He also headed an investigation of the Bay of Pigs invasion* and recommended that the Central Intelligence Agency* avoid such major operations. After two years as chairman of the Joint Chiefs of Staff (1962–1964), Taylor was named ambassador to Vietnam, chosen to bolster South Vietnamese morale and help resolve political-military disputes in the conduct of the war. In addition, Taylor's prestige was intended as a signal of the importance the United States attached to Vietnam. His tour was made difficult by the chaotic instability of the Saigon government; after initial misgivings, he recommended bombing North Vietnam and keeping U.S. troop levels under control. According to Halberstam, he gradually lost influence to General William C. Westmoreland and the military commanders who favored large increases in the number of troops. After about a year in Vietnam, Taylor returned to Washington to work as a special counselor to President Lyndon B. Johnson (1965–1969) and, at the same time, as president of the Institute of Defense Analysis (1966–1969), where he wrote *Responsibility and Response* (1967). After 1969, he served as chairman of the Foreign Intelligence Advisory Board and wrote three more books: *An Uncertain Trumpet* (1970), *Swords and Plowshares* (1972), and *Precarious Security* (1976). On April 19, 1987, he died in Washington, D.C. Halberstam, David, *The Best and the Brightest* (1972); Karnow, Stanley, *Vietnam: A History* (1983); *New York Times*, June 24, 1964; *WWA* (1976–1977):3103.

TAYLOR-ROSTOW MISSION, investigative mission to Vietnam, 1961. In October 1961, the Kennedy administration dispatched a high-level team led by General Maxwell D. Taylor*, with Walt W. Rostow* as his chief deputy, to South Vietnam to look into the political and military situation. There they found morale very low, with President Ngo Dinh Diem's political effectiveness questionable and the quality of political and military intelligence poor. There was a "crisis of confidence" in Vietnam because of the neutrality* of Laos and obvious evidence of a Vietcong buildup. Determining that South Vietnam needed "room to breathe," Taylor and Rostow recommended U.S. aid to local government administration and intelligence, increased numbers of military advisers and training personnel, and the dispatch of an 8,000-man "logistical task force" fit for either combat or flood relief, the last measure being one that would also raise national morale. The nature of the recommendations indicated their feeling that the situation was critical but not hopeless. The recommendations, except for the task force, were followed, marking an important step in the progress toward a full-scale U.S. commitment to this war. At this time, Taylor did not think it likely that the United States would become involved in a major land war; Hanoi was too vulnerable to American bombing. Halberstam, David, *The Best and the Brightest* (1972); Hammond, Paul Y., *Cold War and Détente* (1975); Rostow, Walt W., *The Diffusion of Power* (1972); Taylor, Maxwell D., *Swords and Plowshares* (1972).

TEHERAN (TEHRAN) CONFERENCE (1943). Code named EUREKA, the Teheran Conference lasted from November 28 to December 1, 1943, and marked the first meeting of the Big Three: President Franklin D. Roosevelt, Prime Minister Winston Churchill, and Premier Joseph Stalin. Most of the discussions concerned military planning, as the OVERLORD (cross-channel) and ANVIL (southern France) invasions were agreed upon. The Allies also agreed to try to convince Turkey to join in the war and to split Finland away from the Axis. What political questions there were found no solutions. There were discussions about the ''Four Policeman''* concept and a future world organization, about Soviet territorial demands in both Europe and the Far East, and about postwar Germany, where complete surrender would be demanded, followed by postwar occupation and a realignment of the German states. Another topic of debate was Poland, whose boundaries and future government were already a problem. Decisions on Poland, as well as other political matters, were postponed, giving the conference an air of exceptional cordiality. According to McNeill, however, Teheran showed that the Grand Alliance hung together solely on military exigencies and that postwar political issues would not likely find harmonious solutions. Feis, Herbert, *Churchill-Roosevelt-Stalin* (1967); Gaddis, John L., *The United States and the Origins of the Cold War* (1972); McNeill, William H., *America, Britain, and Russia* (1953); Sainsbury, Keith, *The Turning Point: Roosevelt, Stalin, Churchill and Chaing Kai-shek, 1943* (1985).

TELLER, HENRY MOORE (1830–1914). A senator best known for his involvement in the free-silver question, Henry Teller was also the person for whom the Teller Amendment* was named. He was born in Allegheny County, New York, on May 23, 1830, was educated at public schools and Alfred University, and was admitted to the New York bar in 1858. He practiced law in Illinois (1858–1861) before moving to Colorado. There he married Harriet M. Bruce in 1862, developed a successful law practice, and in 1872 became president of the Colorado Central Railroad. From 1876 to 1909, Teller was a U.S. senator, except for the 1882–1885 period when he sat in the cabinet as secretary of the interior. The Teller Amendment (1898), his one major link with foreign affairs, guaranteed at the beginning of the war with Spain that the United States would not annex Cuba. Later, Teller also opposed the Roosevelt administration's policy toward the Philippine insurrection and the U.S. role in the Panama revolution of 1903. In 1902, Teller changed his party affiliation from Republican to Democrat because of the currency question. After 1909, Teller lived in retirement in Denver, where he died on February 23, 1914. *DAB*, 18:362; *New York Times*, February 24, 1914.

TELLER AMENDMENT (1898). Named for Senator Henry M. Teller* (R., Colorado), this was added to the joint resolution for war with Spain. The amendment declared that the United States disclaimed any intention of exercising sovereignty over Cuba except in a pacification role and promised to leave Cuba as soon as the war was over. Although the amendment was accepted in the Senate without debate, American troops remained in Cuba long after the war was ended, and Cuba's future remained uncertain, all the more so after the Platt Amendment (1901)* was appended to the Cuban constitution. Bemis, Samuel F., *The Latin American Policy of the United States* (1943).

TEN YEARS' WAR (1868–1878), Cuban-Spanish war. A Cuban insurrection, supported by a New York–based Cuban junta, this conflict began with the *pronunciamento* of Yara (October 9–10, 1868) and continued over the next ten years as irregular guerrilla warfare on the island. Although the United States disliked Spain's repressive means of quelling the revolt, the Grant administration refrained from active intervention, even at the time of the *Virginius* episode (1873).* Finally, in 1876, with the coronation of Alfonso XII in Spain and new stability in Spanish politics, the insurrection faltered and ended with the Pact of Zanjón (1878).* Langley, Lester D., *The Cuban Policy of the United States* (1968); Millis, Walter, *The Martial Spirit* (1931).

TENNEY, CHARLES DANIEL (1857–1930). Born in Boston on June 29, 1857, Charles D. Tenney graduated from Dartmouth (1878) and Oberlin Theological Seminary (1882). The son of a minister, Tenney married Anna Runcie Jerrell in 1882 and went to China as a Congregationalist missionary. In 1886, he became a tutor to the sons of the Chinese viceroy Li Huang-chang, and in 1895 he was chosen first president of the Imperial Chinese University in Tientsin, a post he held until 1906. His first contact with American diplomacy came with a stint as vice-consul, in Tientsin (1894–1896), but from 1908 to 1912 and 1914 to 1921, he was secretary of the American legation in Peking. During the Boxer Rebellion (1900),* he worked on relief projects with Herbert Hoover, and following the rebellion he was Chinese secretary to the provisional Tientsin government. After 1906, he served as director of Chinese government students in the United States. His long experience in China was helpful in the progress toward amicable U.S.–Chinese relations. After his retirement in 1921, he lived in Palo Alto, California, until his death March 14, 1930. *DAB*, 18:371.

TENTH INTERNATIONAL CONFERENCE OF AMERICAN STATES (1954). See **CARACAS CONFERENCE (1954).**

TERRELL, EDWIN HOLLAND (1848–1910). Edwin H. Terrell was born in Brookville, Indiana, on November 21, 1848, the son of a Methodist minister. He graduated from Asbury University (later DePauw) in 1871 and Harvard Law School in 1873. From 1874 to 1877, he practiced law in Indianapolis. In 1877, however, he moved to San Antonio, where he became a prominent lawyer and leading Republican, representing Texas in the 1880 and 1888 conventions and seconding the nomination of Benjamin Harrison. After Harrison's election, Terrell became minister to Belgium, a post he held until 1893. This was a busy time diplomatically, largely because of Belgian involvement in the Congo. Terrell represented the United States at the Brussels International Slave Trade Conference (1889–1890), dealing with the suppression of the African slave trade. He attended the Brussels Customs and Tariffs Conference (1890), and he negotiated with King Leopold a treaty of amity and commerce between the United States and the Congo Free State (1891). Terrell was also successful in obtaining better treatment for U.S. livestock imported into Belgium, and he was U.S. commissioner at the International Monetary Conference in 1892. After his return from Belgium, he lived in San Antonio, where he remained active in civic, political, and business affairs until his death by suicide July 1, 1910. Terrell was married first to Mary Maverick in 1874; after her death in 1891, he married Lois Lasater in 1895. *DAB*, 18:377; *NCAB*, 1:387; *New York Times*, July 3, 1910.

TEST BAN TREATY (1963). See **PARTIAL NUCLEAR TEST BAN TREATY (1963).**

TEXAS, JOINT RESOLUTION ON (1845). Following the rejection of a treaty of annexation in June 1844, this joint resolution of Congress admitted Texas to the Union while postponing a disputed boundary with Mexico for later settlement and leaving the problems of debt and public lands to the Texans themselves. The resolution also provided for the possible future division of Texas into several states. Texans, in a convention, voted to join the Union in July 1845. The annexation of Texas added 250,000 square miles of territory to the United States and helped precipitate the Mexican War. Merk, Frederick, *The Monroe Doctrine and American Expansion* (1966); Pletcher, David, *The Diplomacy of Annexation* (1973).

THIRD INTERNATIONAL CONFERENCE OF AMERICAN STATES (1906). See **RIO de JANEIRO CONFERENCE (1906).**

THIRD WORLD, a term referring to those countries, many of which received their independence between 1946 and 1960, classified as developing or underdeveloped nations. They are largely nonwhite, nonindustrialized, and located in the Southern Hemisphere; however, they are rich in natural resources and represent potentially good markets for industrial producers and investors. Politically, Third World nations are not aligned with either the Western or Soviet bloc, and an important aspect of the cold war* was the effort by both sides to win the allegiance of Third World nations. Nationalism and the advantages to be gained by playing one side off against the other proved to be formidable barriers to these efforts, and the Third World remains a sizable political bloc. Nations such as India, Indonesia, Nigeria, and Egypt may be said to belong to the Third World. Moynihan, Daniel P., *A Dangerous Place* (1978); Patterson, Thomas G., *American Foreign Policy: A History* (1978); Spanier, John, *American Foreign Policy since World War II* (1988); Thompson, W. Scott, ed., *The Third World: Illusions and Realities* (1978).

THOMAS, WILLIAM WIDGERY, JR. (1839–1927). A lifelong resident of Portland, Maine, where he was born August 26, 1839, W. W. Thomas, Jr., graduated from Bowdoin College (B.A., 1860; M.A., 1865) and attended Harvard Law School in 1866. During the Civil War, he left college to serve as a diplomatic courier (1862) and in various consular posts (1862–1865). After finishing his law studies, he practiced law in Portland and served as a Republican in the Maine legislature (1869–1875, 1879) and as public lands commissioner (1869). Between 1883 and 1905, Thomas served three separate stints as minister to Sweden and Norway (1883–1885, 1889–1894, 1897–1905). While consul* in Göteborg, Sweden, in the 1860s, he had first developed a high regard for Sweden and its people, and during the 1870s he was active in efforts to promote Swedish immigration to the United States and especially to Maine. To facilitate this, he founded New Sweden in northern Maine, a settlement numbering some 2,000 by 1920. As minister, he continued his efforts in Swedish immigration to the United States, worked to get Swedish jurists appointed to international tribunals, and helped the Swedish government prepare an impressive exhibit for the Columbian Exposition in 1893. After his final mission, Thomas lived in Portland and maintained a keen interest in Swedish-American affairs. He was married twice, to sisters: Dagmar Tönnebladh (1887–1912) and Aina Tönnebladh (after 1915). He died in Portland on April 25, 1927. Thomas wrote *Sweden and the Swedes* (1892), a partly autobiographical account of the country. *DAB*, 18:447; *NCAB*, 2:132; *New York Times*, April 26, 1927.

THOMAS AMENDMENT (1939). A proposed amendment to the Neutrality Act (1939),* this would have granted the president the discretionary authority to ban exports of war supplies and raw materials to belligerents and permit such exports to victims of aggression, subject to congressional approval. Thus the United States could legally aid friends while blocking assistance to hostile nations. The measure (formally called Senate Joint Resolution 67) was the product of a variety of internationalist organizations and peace societies desirous of revamping existing neutrality* policy and won strong support from the *New York Times* and former Secretary of State Henry L. Stimson,* among others. The amendment, named for Senator Elbert D. Thomas (D., Utah), was not passed in its original form, but its principle was incorporated into the final form of the Neutrality Act (1939) with the removal of the impartial arms embargo feature of earlier neutrality legislation. Divine, Robert A., *Illusion of Neutrality* (1962).

THOMPSON, LLEWELLYN E., JR. (1904–1972). One of the most highly respected ambassadors to the Soviet Union in the post–World War II period, Llewellyn Thompson was born in Las Animas, Colorado, on August 24, 1904, graduated from the University of Colorado in 1928, and, after attending Foreign Service School, joined the Foreign Service in 1929. After service in a variety of minor and consular posts from 1929 to 1940, Thompson went to Moscow in 1941 as second secretary and consul.* Three years later, he moved to a similar assignment in London. From 1946 to 1950, Thompson worked on the staff of the European Affairs Division in the State Department, and from 1950 to 1952 he was counselor* at the U.S. embassy in Rome. In 1952, he was named high commissioner to Austria, becoming ambassador there after the signing of the Austrian State Treaty (1955),* which he helped negotiate. His work on that treaty and on the Trieste settlement between Italy and Yugoslavia at about the same time earned him a reputation as a careful behind-the-scenes negotiator. His most important assignment, ambassador to the Soviet Union, occupied the years from 1957 to 1962. In Moscow, he urged that Premier Nikita Khrushchev be invited to the United States; Khrushchev's visit in 1959 was a popular, if not a diplomatic, success. Later, he helped plan the abortive Paris summit conference of 1960 and the Vienna summit conference of 1961 between Khrushchev and President John F. Kennedy. In 1962, Thompson returned to Washington to serve as ambassador-at-large, where he was involved in the Cuban missile crisis,* the Partial Nuclear Test Ban Treaty (1963),* United Nations* activities, and East-West trade matters. From 1966 to 1969, he took on a second ambassadorial tour to the Soviet Union, during which the complications of the Vietnam War isolated him somewhat from Soviet leadership. His last assignment, from 1969 to 1971, was as a delegate to the early stages of SALT I.* In general, Thompson enjoyed good relations with Soviet leaders, who trusted his integrity and liked the fact that he was fluent in Russian. Thompson was married to Jane Monroe Goelet in 1948 and died in Washington, D.C., on February 6, 1972. Burke, Lee H., *Ambassador at Large: Diplomat Extraordinary* (1972); *NCAB*, 1:326; *New York Times*, March 11, 1962, February 7, 1972.

THOMPSON, WADDY, JR. (1798–1868). An important minister to Mexico shortly before the American war with that country, Waddy Thompson, Jr., was born in Pickensville, South Carolina, on September 8, 1798, graduated from South Carolina College (now the University of South Carolina) in 1814, studied law, and was admitted to the bar in 1819. From 1819 to 1826, he practiced law. In the latter year, he entered politics, serving four years in the South Carolina legislature. After five more years in private law practice, Thompson was a member of the U.S. House of Representatives from 1835 to 1841. In 1842, the Tyler administration named him minister to Mexico. Thompson held the post for two years, obtaining the release of 300 prisoners from the ill-fated Santa Fe expedition, working out adjustments to claims settlements to enable Mexico to meet the payments, and persuading the Mexican government to continue allowing U.S. immigrants into California. He began what appeared for a while to be successful negotiations for the acquisition of California. Thompson was personally popular in Mexico and reciprocated by showing sympathy for Mexico's aspirations. After his diplomatic career, he became a successful real estate entrepreneur in the South but lost his fortune during the Civil War. He spent his last years living on a plantation in Madison, Florida. Twice married, Thompson died in Tallahassee on November 23, 1868. He wrote about his Mexican experience in *Recollections* (1846). *DAB*, 18:473; Thompson, H. T., *Waddy Thompson, Jr.* (1929).

THOMSON-URRUTIA TREATY (1921). In this treaty, the United States paid Colombia $25 million, considered to be recompense for U.S. involvement in the Panamanian revolution of 1903, although no specific apology was made. Additionally, U.S. business was given oil concessions in Colombia, a feature of the treaty that made its ratification much easier. The treaty was negotiated by U.S. Minister to Colombia Thaddeus A. Thomson and Colombian Foreign Minister Francisco José Urrutia and signed April 6, 1914. Friends of Theodore Roosevelt managed to delay ratification until 1921. Connell-Smith, Gordon, *The United States and Latin America* (1974); *FR* (1914): 146–70; Parks, E. Taylor, *Colombia and the United States, 1765–1934* (1935, 1968).

TIENTSIN, TREATIES OF (1858). These treaties, virtually dictated to the Chinese by the United States, Great Britain, Russia, and France, brought about the opening of eleven new treaty ports, granted foreigners freedom to travel anywhere in the interior of China, fixed the tariff at 5 percent, and legalized the opium trade. All foreign diplomats were to be stationed in Peking. According to Cohen, the provisions of these treaties opened the way for the commercial exploitation and potential cultural subjugation of China. Anderson, David L., *Imperialism and Idealism* (1985); Cohen, Warren I., *America's Response to China* (1971); Gabard, William M., "John Elliott and the Treaty of Tientsin," *West Georgia College Studies in the Social Sciences* 2 (June 1972): 26–44.

TIPITAPA, PEACE OF (1927). This treaty emerged from a peace conference in May 1927 and ended civil strife between Liberals and Conservatives in Nicaragua. Special envoy Henry L. Stimson* orchestrated the treaty, using the presence of American troops as a threat to force rebellious Liberals into line. The agreement called for U.S.-supervised elections in 1928, the establishment of U.S.-trained "constabulary," a general amnesty, and a program wherein the government would pay soldiers of both sides to surrender their weapons. Denny,

Harold N., *Dollars for Bullets* (1929); *FR* (1927), 3:285–406; Kammen, William, *A Search for Stability* (1968).

TOOMBS, ROBERT AUGUSTUS (1810–1885). Born July 2, 1810, and raised in Wilkes County, Georgia, Robert Toombs graduated from Union College in 1828 and was admitted to the bar two years later. After three terms in the Georgia legislature, he went to the U.S. House of Representatives in 1844 and to the Senate in 1853, resigning in 1861. He was named the Confederacy's first secretary of state in February 1861, a recognition on the part of Jefferson Davis of the fire-eater element in the South. As secretary of state, Toombs appointed William L. Yancey,* Pierre A. Rost, and Ambrose Dudley Mann as the first Confederate diplomatic mission in March 1861, instructing them to seek recognition and aid, first from Britain, then from France, Russia, and Belgium. Toombs soon became contemptuous of Davis's leadership; he resigned from the cabinet in July 1861 and served in the army most of the rest of the war. After exile in London from 1865 to 1867, Toombs returned to law practice in Georgia until his death December 15, 1885, in Washington, Georgia. *DAB*, 13:590; Owsley, Frank, *King Cotton Diplomacy*, 2d ed. (1959); Phillips, Ulrich B., *The Life of Robert Toombs* (1913); Thompson, William Y., *Robert Toombs of Georgia* (1966).

TOON, MALCOLM (b. 1916). Born on Independence Day, 1916, in Troy, New York, Malcolm Toon graduated from Tufts University (A.B., 1937) and the Fletcher School of Law and Diplomacy (M.A., 1939). After naval service from 1942 to 1946, and marriage to Elizabeth Hane Taylor in 1943, Toon entered the Foreign Service, serving in minor posts in Warsaw, Budapest, Berlin, Washington, and London before 1963. From 1963 to 1965, he was counselor* and political affairs officer in Moscow, and there he was falsely accused of being the head of a U.S. spy ring. Returning to Washington soon after this incident, Toon headed the Office of Soviet Affairs and was acting deputy assistant secretary of state (East European affairs) before his first ambassadorial appointment, an uneventful tour in Czechoslovakia, 1969–1971. In 1971, he was transferred to Yugoslavia, where he negotiated an agreement by which the Overseas Private Investment Corporation, a government agency, would underwrite U.S. investors involved in U.S.-Yugoslavia joint ventures. Toon replaced Kenneth Keating* as ambassador to Israel in 1975. In that post, he played a larger role in U.S.-Israel relations than his predecessors, who had often been bypassed by the personal diplomacy of Henry Kissinger.* Toon was criticized for statements that speculated on possible U.S. policy in the future and that criticized Israel for doing nothing to solve its economic problems before requesting more U.S. aid. Regarded as the State Department's foremost active Soviet expert, Toon was appointed ambassador to the Soviet Union in 1976, but Moscow delayed its official approval of the appointment because of lingering distrust dating back to the 1965 spy ring incident. However, Soviet wishes for the withdrawal of Toon's appointment were not granted, and he finally assumed his duties in 1977. In two years at the Moscow post, Toon's major involvement was as a member of the SALT II (Strategic Arms Limitation Talks)* delegation. Since his retirement from the Foreign Service, Toon has taught at various universities. *CB* (July 1978):37–40; *New York Times*, May 8, 1975, November 2, 1976, April 26, 1977, June 23, 1979; *WWA* (1986–1987):2798.

TOWER, CHARLEMAGNE (1848–1923). Born into a prominent Philadelphia family on April 17, 1848, Charlemagne Tower graduated from Harvard (1872), traveled and studied in Europe and the Middle East (1872–1876), read law, and was admitted to the bar (1878). After four years of law practice, he went to Duluth, Minnesota, and joined his father's business, the Minnesota Iron Company, becoming president of a subsidiary, the Duluth and Iron Range Railroad. In 1887, however, he returned to Philadelphia to pursue his legal and business interests there. He married Helen Smith in 1888 and, in 1897, received the first of three important diplomatic appointments, minister to Austria-Hungary. There he worked to exempt from military service Austrians who had become naturalized American citizens. In 1899, he was transferred to Russia, and in his three years as ambassador there he strove to elevate the U.S. embassy to equal status with those of the European powers in display as well as diplomacy, most obviously by ordering uniforms for the embassy staff, thus marking a sharp departure from U.S. diplomatic tradition. In addition, Tower's mission in Russia included the negotiation of an arbitration* agreement over the seizures of vessels in the Bering Sea and his advocacy of the Open Door policy* for Manchuria, where Russian influence was strong. From 1902 to 1908, Tower was U.S. ambassador to Germany. He protested the German blockade of Venezuelan ports and other forceful measures taken to induce the payment of debts; ultimately the matter ended up at the Permanent Court of International Arbitration* in the Hague. Venezuela aside, Tower enjoyed a cordial relationship with the kaiser and a lavish social life in Berlin. He retired from the diplomatic service in 1908 and returned to his business affairs. Tower was a writer and author of *The Marquis de Lafayette in the American Revolution*, (2 vols., 1894, reprinted 1971) and was at one time president of the Historical Society of Pennsylvania. He died in Philadelphia on February 24, 1923. *DAB*, 18:607; Dennis, A.L.P., *Adventures in American Diplomacy, 1896–1906* (1928); *New York Times*, February 25, 1923.

TRANSCONTINENTAL TREATY (1819). See **ADAMS-ONÍS TREATY (1819).**

TREATY. See **INTERNATIONAL AGREEMENT.**

TREATY OF AMITY AND COMMERCE, FRANCO-AMERICAN (1778). The first major diplomatic agreement after the Declaration of Independence, this treaty permitted commercial relations between France and the United States and committed each nation not to make a separate peace. France was to continue the war until the United States had achieved independence but was not to regain any North American territory held before 1763. For its part, the United States agreed to uphold present French possessions in the Western Hemisphere, as well as any new ones it might acquire in the war. Ratified by Congress May 4, 1778, the Franco-American Treaty was of great help to the United States during the American Revolution but a burden once independence had been achieved, leading to a state of quasi-war* between the two nations in the late 1790s before its abrogation in the Convention of 1800.* Bemis, Samuel F., *The Diplomacy of the American Revolution* (1935); Stinchcombe, William C., *The American Revolution and the French Alliance* (1969); Varg, Paul A., *Foreign Policies of the Founding Fathers* (1963).

TRENT **AFFAIR (1861).** This incident was precipitated by the capture in November 1861 of Confederate diplomatic agents James Mason* and John Slidell* and their removal from the British mail packet *Trent* by Charles Wilkes, commanding the U.S.S. *San Jacinto.* Britain strongly protested this action, and war seemed a possibility, but Prince Albert toned down British belligerency, and Secretary of State William Seward* found a way to release Mason and Slidell without appearing to cave in to British demands. Adams, Ephraim D., *Great Britain and the American Civil War* (1924); Ferris, Norman B., *The Trent Affair: A Diplomatic Crisis* (1977); Van Deusen, Glyndon, *William Henry Seward* (1967); Warren, Gordon H., *Fountain of Discontent: The Trent Affair and Freedom of the Seas* (1981).

TRESCOT, WILLIAM HENRY (1822–1898). William H. Trescot was born November 10, 1822, in Charleston, South Carolina, graduated from the College of Charleston in 1841, and two years later was admitted to the bar. He practiced law and studied U.S. diplomacy from 1843 to 1852, served as legation secretary in London, 1852–1854, and returned to diplomatic study and writing, 1854–1860. Out of this period came *Diplomatic History of the Administrations of Washington and Adams* (1857). He served briefly as an assistant secretary of state in 1860 but resigned before the end of the year to serve South Carolina and the Confederacy during the Civil War. He represented the Confederacy in discussions with Britain and France regarding Confederate adherence to the Declaration of Paris (1856).* Out of public life for a number of years following the war, Trescot was sent to China in 1880 to help negotiate changes in the Burlingame Treaty.* The following year saw him in South America, negotiating a treaty with Colombia regarding U.S. rights in Panama and, as a special envoy to Peru, Bolivia, and Chile, trying to bring an end to the War of the Pacific.* His mission was cut short, however, by Secretary of State James G. Blaine's* resignation and subsequent changes in his instructions. In 1882, Trescot concluded a commercial treaty with Mexico. In 1889, he was a delegate to the First International Conference of American States* held in Washington. He was married to Eliza Natalie Cuthbert, and he died in Pendleton, South Carolina, on May 4, 1898. *DAB*, 18:639; Pletcher, David, *The Awkward Years* (1962).

TRESCOT-SANTODOMINGO PROTOCOL (1881). Designed to clarify the Bidlack Treaty (1846), this protocol at first called for American approval of any isthmian canal project in Panama and for U.S. fortification and garrisoning of the canal route. Colombia refused; a revised protocol eliminated the approval clause and called for shared fortification. This protocol was signed by the Colombian minister to the United States, Rafael Santodomingo Vila, on February 17, 1881, but the Bogotá government repudiated it in a fit of anti-Americanism, during which the Bidlack Treaty itself was in danger of abrogation. *FR* (1881), 361–87; Parks, E. Taylor, *Colombia and the United States, 1765–1934* (1935); Pletcher, David, *The Awkward Years* (1962).

TRIANON, TREATY OF (1920). This treaty, signed at the Trianon Palace, Versailles, on June 4, 1920, ended World War I for Hungary. In the treaty, Hungary's area was reduced by half, and its population fell from 21 million to 7 million. The treaty left Hungary landlocked in Central Europe and in other respects was similar to the Treaty of Versailles (1919),* except that Hungary was allowed a 35,000-man army. Because of the inclusion of the Covenant of the League of Nations,* the United States did not ratify this treaty; instead, a separate peace treaty was signed on August 29, 1921, and ratified on October 18, 1921. *FR* (1921), 2:249–63; Hyamson, A. M., *A Dictionary of International Affairs* (1947); Macartney, C. A., *Hungary: A Short History* (1962).

TRIDENT CONFERENCE (1943). President Franklin D. Roosevelt, Prime Minister Winston Churchill, and the Combined Chiefs of Staff met from May 12 to May 25, 1943, in Washington, D.C., for the purpose of military planning and coordination. Churchill proposed a campaign to take Italy out of the war; the U.S. inclination was to stop after the capture of Sicily due to the ruggedness of the Italian terrain. In the end, the matter was compromised. The Allies would invade Italy only to the extent that forces needed for the OVERLORD (cross-channel) invasion, scheduled for May 1, 1944, would not be jeopardized. It was also agreed that the offensive against Japan across the Pacific islands would be accelerated and that additional supplies would be sent to the Burma theater. Feis, Herbert, *Churchill—Roosevelt—Stalin* (1967); McNeill, William H., *America, Britain, and Russia* (1953).

TRIPARTITE PACT (1940). This is the treaty that created the alliance popularly known as the Axis. In it, Japan recognized Germany and Italy as leaders of a New Order in Europe and Germany and Italy similarly recognized Japan's dominance in East Asia. The signatories agreed to come to one another's aid should one be attacked by a power not currently engaged in war in either Europe or China (that is, the United States). The treaty was not to affect relations between any of the signatories and the Soviet Union. The hope of the Axis was that the United States would choose not to fight both Germany and Japan. In the United States, news of the treaty did not come as a surprise; policymakers saw it as a formalization of an existing situation, an act to try to force the United States to end aid to Britain. It had much the opposite effect. The treaty was signed September 27, 1940. Feis, Herbert, *The Road to Pearl Harbor* (1950); *FR* (1940), 1:647–69; Offner, Arnold A., *The Origins of the Second World War* (1975); Rose, Lisle A., *The Long Shadow* (1978).

TRIST, NICHOLAS PHILIP (1800–1874). A Virginian, born June 2, 1800, in Charlottesville, Nicholas Trist attended West Point and married a granddaughter of Thomas Jefferson.* He entered the State Department in 1829, where he spent four years as a clerk and eight years as consul* in Cuba before a four-year respite from 1841 to 1845. In the Polk administration (1845–1849) he was appointed chief clerk, and in 1847 he was sent to Mexico as temporary peace commissioner to present a draft treaty; a full-fledged commission would replace him should Mexico wish to negotiate. After his arrival in Mexico City in the spring of 1847, he became friendly with General Winfield Scott, a Whig and Polk's chief political rival, and made little headway in the peace talks until August. Polk lost patience and recalled Trist in November, but the envoy chose to remain in Mexico, where he concluded the negotiations resulting in the Treaty of Guadalupe-Hidalgo,* in February 1848, ending the Mexican War. After the Mexican War, Trist practiced law without particular success in Virginia, opposed secession, voted for Lincoln, and was rewarded in 1870 with an appointment as postmaster in Alexandria. He died in Alexandria on February 11, 1874. Pletcher, David, *The Diplomacy of Annexation* (1973); Sears, Louis, "Nicholas P. Trist, a Diplomat with Ideals," *Mississippi Valley Historical Review* 11 (1928):85–98.

TRUMAN DOCTRINE (1947). The announcement of the Truman Doctrine on March 12, 1947, triggered by the departure of British troops from Greece during a civil war there and by evidence of Communist-inspired political instability in other areas of the eastern Mediterranean region, marked a new departure in traditional American foreign policy. The Truman Doctrine recognized the reality of the cold war* and called for an immediate $400 million aid program to Greece and Turkey to protect them against the threat of internal subversion or external aggression. Although the doctrine referred specifically to Greece and Turkey, the principle of protecting friendly nations from subversion or aggression was open-ended; it was extended to all of Western Europe with the Marshall Plan* and the North Atlantic Treaty Organization* and subsequently, by extension of the policy known as containment,* made global. Gaddis notes that Truman's March 12 speech was designed more for the American public than for world opinion—to convince Americans that in a sense the war was not yet over. Feis, Herbert, *From Trust to Terror* (1970); Gaddis, John L., *The United States and the Origins of the Cold War* (1972); LaFeber, Walter, "The Truman Doctrine," in DeConde, Alexander, ed., *Encyclopedia of American Foreign Policy* (1979); McLellan, David S., *Dean Acheson* (1976); Wittner, Lawrence S., *American Intervention in Greece, 1943–1949* (1982).

TRUSTEESHIP COUNCIL (UNITED NATIONS). Provisions for international trusteeships over dependent colonies were included in the United Nations* Charter and were to be supervised by a United Nations Trusteeship Council. Trusteeships were thought to be the best way to protect the interests of the inhabitants and encourage progressive development toward self-government or independence appropriate to the circumstances of each colony. The U.S. position was to support trusteeships over former League of Nations* mandates* and former Axis territories but not to demand transfer of existing European colonial empires. The United States also favored the maintenance of military establishments on certain territories deemed strategic (in particular, certain Pacific islands formerly in Japanese control). McNeill, William H., *America, Britain, and Russia* (1953).

TURNER, JAMES MILTON (1840–1915). Born a slave in St. Louis County, Missouri, on May 16, 1840, James Milton Turner was bought into freedom by his father and attended Oberlin College. During the Civil War, he was a servant to a Union officer and was injured at the Battle of Shiloh. Turner was prominently involved in black education after the war and helped found what is now known as Lincoln University in Jefferson City, Missouri. In 1871, he was the first black to join the diplomatic corps by virtue of his selection as minister to Liberia. Turner occupied the post until 1878 and kept the State Department well informed on Liberian affairs, often complex and unstable, advised against resettling American blacks in Liberia because of the climate, and urged U.S. aid for the native tribes of Liberia and for Christian missionary efforts. He toured Europe on his way home and was highly acclaimed by blacks when he reached the United States. In later years, Turner was interested in the career of Dred Scott, in Indian affairs, and in freedmen's lands and rights. He was married to Ella De Burton and died on November 1, 1915, in Ardmore, Oklahoma. *DAB*, 19:66; Dillard, Irving, "James Milton Turner, a Little Known Benefactor of His People," *Journal of Negro History* 19 (October 1934):372–412; *New York Times*, November 2, 1915.

TWENTY-ONE DEMANDS (1915). Made by Japan on China in January 1915, these demands were divided into five groups. The first four groups concerned Japanese moves to strengthen their interests in different areas of China, including Shantung, where Japanese troops had recently overrun German interests. The fifth group of demands specified the inclusion of Japanese advisers into key positions within the Chinese government, a serious threat to Chinese sovereignty. The U.S. ambassador to China, Paul S. Reinsch,* urged strong American resistance, and after some months of temporizing, the Wilson administration issued a statement backing American interests in China and the principle of Chinese sovereignty. Britain made a protest and internal opposition to the demands developed in Japan; all of these helped induce Japan to drop the fifth group of demands. The tensions created in the matter were somewhat alleviated by the Lansing-Ishii Agreement (1917).* Cohen, Warren I., *America's Response to China* (1971); Crane, Daniel M., and Thomas A. Breslin, *An Ordinary Relationship* (1986); Neu, Charles E., *The Troubled Encounter* (1975).

U-2 INCIDENT (1960). For the United States, this was an embarrassing diplomatic episode in which an American surveillance plane, a U-2, was shot down over the Soviet Union in May 1960. The Soviet government released details of the flight and displayed the pilot, who had been captured alive, which made the official U.S. explanation a patent lie and forced President Dwight D. Eisenhower to make a full disclosure of the spy flights and accept responsibility for them. The incident caused the cancellation of a planned summit conference between Eisenhower and Soviet Premier Nikita Khrushchev in Paris later in May, and Khrushchev reacted angrily, exploiting the incident for its propaganda value and putting the United States on the defensive. The U-2 flights were terminated but were soon replaced by more effective satellite surveillance. According to Gaddis, however, Khrushchev was anxious to have the summit take place, gave Eisenhower every opportunity to dismiss the U-2 incident, and became upset only when the president was forthright in his acceptance of responsibility. Gaddis, John L., *Russia, the Soviet Union, and the United States* (1978); Hammond, Paul Y., *Cold War and Détente* (1975).

U-BOATS, GERMAN. Chance sinkings of British ships by German U-boats in the fall of 1914 at a time when these submarines were regarded as experimental led German naval leaders to demand a full-scale compaign as a way to end the British blockade of Germany and damage Allied commerce. In February 1915 the Germans declared the waters around Britain and Ireland a war zone, with any ship found there subject to attack. The sinking of the luxury liner *Lusitania** in May directly involved the United States and led to the first of two temporary suspensions of submarine warfare. The sinking of the channel steamer *Sussex** in March 1916 produced a second suspension, but in January 1917 the German government decided on full and unrestricted submarine warfare, reflecting its willingness to risk American entry into the war, which occurred in April 1917. May, Ernest, *The World War and American Isolation, 1914–1917* (1959); Smith, Daniel M., *The Great Departure* (1965).

UHL, EDWIN FULLER (1841–1901). Born August 14, 1841, in Rush, New York, Edwin F. Uhl graduated from the University of Michigan in 1862 and was admitted to the Michigan bar in 1864. He practiced law in Ypsilanti from 1864 to 1876 and in Grand Rapids from 1876 to 1890. In 1890, he was elected Democratic mayor of Grand Rapids, and in 1893 the Cleveland administration appointed him assistant secretary of state, a post he held until 1896. Because of the illness of Secretary of State Walter Q. Gresham,* Uhl's responsibilities were larger than usual. He arbitrated, in Cleveland's name, a long-standing boundary dispute between Brazil and Argentina in 1895 and tended to many of the day-to-day affairs of the department. In 1896, he became minister to Germany, spending an uneventful year there before being replaced by the appointee of the new McKinley administration, Andrew D. White.* After 1897, Uhl practiced law in Grand Rapids and Chicago for a short time before retiring to a country home near Grand Rapids. He married Alice Follett in 1865 and died at his home on May 17, 1901. *NCAB*, 15:100.

UNITED FRUIT COMPANY. This company, the most important American business enterprise in the history of U.S.–Latin American relations, was founded March 20, 1899, by a merger of several smaller banana companies under the aegis of Andrew Preston, of the Boston Fruit Company, and Minor C. Keith,* a banana grower and railroad builder in Central America since the 1870s. The combination of Boston Fruit's shipping and selling of bananas and Keith's extensive properties proved successful as United Fruit absorbed other banana companies and became the largest American corporation in Central America, growing and shipping not only bananas but also cocoa and sugar cane. In 1930, a merger with Cuyamel Fruit Company made Samuel Zemurray* United's largest stockholder. When the leftist government of Jácobo Arbenz in Guatemala expropriated 234,000 acres of United Fruit Company land in 1953 without adequate compensation, it set in motion the chain of events leading to the ouster of Arbenz, supported by the Central Intelligence Agency.* In 1972, United Fruit was absorbed into United Brands, a large conglomerate. Three years later, Eli Black, the chairman of United Brands, committed suicide after it was revealed that he had paid a $1.25 million bribe to Honduras in order to obtain a 50 percent reduction in the banana export tax. Adams, Frederick Upham, *Conquest of the Tropics* (1914); Barnet, Richard J., *Intervention and Revolution* (1968); Findling, John E., *Close Neighbors, Distant Friends* (1987); Wilson, Charles Morrow, *Empire in Green and Gold* (1947).

UNITED NATIONS. Planned at the Dumbarton Oaks Conference (1944)* and formally established at the San Francisco Conference (1945),* the United Nations was initially perceived by many Americans as a chance to ensure world peace through an international organization based on the principle of collective security.* But to be effective, the United Nations needed to have the lasting cooperation of its major powers. With the onset of the cold war* shortly after World War II, the original purpose of the UN was shattered, and the organization became an instrument in the foreign policy of each major power, to be used as national interests dictated. The United States, contributing the largest share of the budget and having majority support in the General Assembly until the mid-1950s, was able to use the UN to promote such causes as multilateral aid and the Declaration of Human Rights. But peacekeeping has been confined to areas where the United States and the Soviet Union have tacitly agreed to avoid a direct cold war confrontation, as in the Congo (1960–1961) and with the Cyprus dispute (1964).* The United States, on the other hand has effectively blocked UN activity in the Guatemalan crisis (1954),* the Lebanese intervention (1958),* and during the entire war in Vietnam. Similarly, the Soviet Union did not permit UN involvement in the Hungarian (1956) and Czechoslovakian (1968) crises. Bypassing the United Nations' major foreign policy issues has led to public ridicule and serious demands for U.S. withdrawal, but most American leaders recognize the usefulness of the organization as a forum for debate and as a source of considerable worthwhile humanitarian and developmental work. Campbell, Thomas M., *Masquerade Peace: America's UN Policy, 1944–1945* (1973); Eichelbeiger, Clark M., *UN: The First Twenty-Five Years* (1970); Franch, Thomas M., *Nation against Nation* (1985); Gati, Toby Trister, ed., *The U.S., the UN and the Management of Global Change* (1983); Stoessinger, John G., *The United Nations and the Superpowers* (1973); Stromberg, Roland N., *Collective Security and American Foreign Policy* (1963).

UNITED NATIONS DECLARATION (1942). Worked out at the Arcadia Conference,* this document pledged each of its signatories to "employ its full resources" against the members of the Tripartite Pact* and not to make a separate peace. Formally promulgated on January 1, 1942, the United Nations Declaration was signed that day by representatives of the Big Four—the United States, Great Britain, the Soviet Union, and China—and later by twenty-two other nations named as joint declarers. Still other nations signed the declaration as they joined the war against the Axis. For the United States, the declaration symbolized the new internationalism in its diplomacy, a sharp break from past tradition. In addition, its highly principled moral tone had a good psychological effect on the American people. The declaration marked the first official use of the term *United Nations* and, notably, placed the Big Four on a level above other member nations, a priority to be followed in the drafting of the United Nations Charter. Feis, Herbert, *Churchill—Roosevelt—Stalin* (1967); *FR* (1942), 1:1–38; McNeill, William H., *America, Britain, and Russia* (1953); Russell, Ruth B., *A History of the United Nations Charter* (1958).

UNITED NATIONS RELIEF AND REHABILITATION ADMINISTRA-TION (UNRRA). Formally created on November 9, 1943, UNRRA grew out of various suggestions from the United States, Britain, and the Soviet Union on the need for a postwar relief organization. A preliminary constitution was prepared in May 1943 and sent to smaller nations for their consideration. The final draft was signed in Washington in November, and the first session of the UNRRA Council met in Atlantic City, New Jersey, from November 10 to December 1, 1943, with forty-four nations represented. The council elected Herbert Lehman, a former U.S. senator from New York, as director-general, settled budgetary questions, and agreed on procedures of working with military authorities and nations that could not pay. Originally meant for relief to liberated nations, UNRRA was later broadened to include help to displaced persons from Axis countries such as Italy, Austria, and Hungary. Large-scale operations did not get under way until 1946 and lasted until mid-1947, when the pressures of the cold war* and objections to U.S. aid going to Eastern Europe hastened the termination of UNRRA activities. During its lifetime, UNRRA dispensed over $4 billion of commodities to seventeen nations and functioned with political neutrality. In many ways, it was a forerunner of the Marshall Plan.* Darilek, Richard E., *A Loyal Opposition in Time of War* (1976); Herring, George C., Jr., *Aid to Russia, 1941–1946* (1973); McNeill, William H., *America, Britain, and Russia* (1953); Woodbridge, George, *UNRRA: The History of the United Nations Relief and Rehabilitation Administration*, 3 vols. (1950).

UNITED STATES INFORMATION AGENCY (USIA). The USIA is the information (or propaganda) service of the federal government. In 1953, as part of an executive branch reorganization undertaken by the Dwight D. Eisenhower administration, the USIA was created to consolidate programs formerly run by the International Information Administration, the Mutual Security Agency, the Technical Cooperation Administration, and the U.S. occupation authorities in Germany and Austria. Since 1953, the USIA has operated information services, most notably the Voice of America (VOA), as well as a wide variety of cultural and educational exchanges. It is funded independently of the Department of State but works closely on policy coordination with the department, and many of its functions are handled at U.S. embassies. The first director of the USIA was Theodore C. Streibert, the former chairman of the Mutual Broadcasting System, but one of the most important directors was George V. Allen* (1958–1961), who took over the agency at a time of considerable disarray caused by its inability to portray well the civil rights movement in the United States or to respond persuasively to the dramatic Sputnik voyage of the USSR. Under Allen, the USIA initiated a policy of gentle persuasion in information programming and renewed U.S.-USSR cultural exchanges. Although the USIA still participates in a wide variety of activities, the VOA is probably its best-known outlet; in 1986, the VOA transmitted over 1,200 hours per week in English and forty-one other languages to an estimated 120 million listeners. Elder, Robert E., *The Information Machine; The United States Information Agency and American Foreign Policy* (1968); Sorensen, Thomas C., *The Word War: The Story of American Propaganda* (1968).

UPSHUR, ABEL PARKER (1790–1844). One of three men who served as secretary of state under President John Tyler, Abel P. Upshur was born June 17, 1790, in Northampton County, Virginia, attended both the College of New Jersey and Yale but did not graduate, read law, and was admitted to the bar in 1810. Until 1824, he practiced law in Richmond, and in 1826 he became a justice of the Virginia Supreme Court. In 1841, he was named secretary of the navy, and two years later he replaced Daniel Webster* as secretary of state. In that office, he strongly supported Texas annexation, which he felt necessary for southern security, and opened negotiations with Britain on the Oregon question.*

On most political questions, Upshur adopted a conservative, antidemocratic, states' rights, and pro-slavery stance. Upshur completed a draft of a Texas annexation treaty just one day before he was tragically killed in an explosion aboard the U.S.S. *Princeton* on the Potomac River, February 28, 1844. Upshur was married twice, the second time to his cousin, Elizabeth Upshur. Adams, R. G., ''Abel Parker Upshur,'' in Bemis, Samuel F., ed., *American Secretaries of State and Their Diplomacy*, vol. 5 (1928); *DAB*, 19:127; Hall, Claude H., *Abel Parker Upshur, Conservative Virginian, 1790–1844* (1963); *NCAB*, 6:8.

UTI POSSIDETIS, diplomatic-military term. Associated with a truce, this phrase refers to the armies of each belligerent remaining in possession of the territory it controls at the time of the truce. In the American Revolution, this was a point advanced in the Spanish and Russian mediation offers of 1779 and 1781, but it was not acceptable to the United States, since in 1781 the British still controlled vital parts of the country. Bemis, Samuel F., *The Diplomacy of the American Revolution* (1935); Morris, Richard B., *The Peacemakers* (1965); Stinchcombe, William C., *The American Revolution and the French Alliance* (1969).

VAIL, AARON (1796–1878). The son of an American commercial agent, Aaron Vail was born in Lorient, France, on October 24, 1796; he did not come to the United States until 1815 and never lived in the United States for any extended period of time. He was legation secretary in London, 1831–1832, and chargé d'affaires* there, 1832–1836, following the Senate's refusal to confirm Martin Van Buren* as minister to Great Britain. As chargé, he acted in the capacity of a minister, got along well with principal British leaders, among them the duke of Wellington and Lord Palmerston, and was primarily involved with handling U.S. claims concerning slaves released from U.S. ships forced to land in the West Indies during the era of the Napoleonic Wars. Vail succeeded in getting the cases referred to the Privy Council, but, at this time, no actual settlement was made. He also organized and filed the legation records—a task of considerable magnitude—and reported capably on British politics and the Reform Bill of 1832 and on European politics from London's perspective. In 1838, Vail went to Canada as a special agent, where he looked into the cases of Americans thought to be held illegally for alleged crimes committed during the 1837 rebellion. He found that the Canadians had proceeded properly. From 1838 to 1840 he was chief clerk in the State Department, and from 1840 to 1842 he was chargé at Madrid, but both of these assignments were uneventful. After his diplomatic career, Vail, who never married, lived in Europe. He died in Paris on November 4, 1878. Beckles, Willson, *America's Ambassadors to England, 1785–1929* (1928); *DAB*, 19:136.

VAN BUREN, MARTIN (1782–1862). Secretary of state under President Andrew Jackson and president from 1837 to 1841, Martin Van Buren was born December 5, 1782, in Kinderhook, New York, was educated in village schools, became a law clerk at age fourteen, and, after reading law, gained admittance to the bar in 1803. He soon became involved in New York Republican politics and was elected to the state senate in 1812. In 1816, he became state attorney general and from 1821 to 1828, he served in the U.S. Senate. Elected governor of New York in 1828, he served only a short time before Andrew Jackson, whom Van Buren had strongly supported for the presidency, appointed him secretary of state. Van Buren introduced the spoils system into the State Department, settled a West Indies trade dispute, and negotiated a satisfactory French claims settlement and a commercial treaty with Turkey for Black Sea access but failed in an attempt to purchase Texas. Resigning in 1821 because of the Jackson–John C. Calhoun* split, Van Buren was named minister to Great Britain the same year. Although Calhoun's influence in the Senate blocked confirmation of his nomination, Van Buren did spend the period from September 1821 to March 1832 in Britain as acting minister, devoting much of his time arranging for U.S. consulates in the important British manufacturing towns. Vice-president during Jackson's second term (1833–1837), Van Buren succeeded to the presidency. After 1841, he was out of public office but was mentioned as a possible Democratic presidential candidate in 1844. However, his opposition to the annexation of Texas spoiled his chances. In 1848, Van Buren was the presidential candidate of the Free Soil party. Married to Hannah Hoes from 1807 to 1819, Van Buren was a widower much of his life and died in Kinderhook on July 24, 1862. Bennett, J. S., "Martin Van Buren," in Bemis, Samuel F., ed., *American Secretaries of State and Their Diplomacy*, vol. 4 (1928); Cole, Donald B., *Martin Van Buren and the American Political System* (1984); Curtis, James C., *The Fox at Bay* (1970); *DAB*, 19:152; Raybeck, Joseph G., *Martin Van Buren* (1982); Willson, Beckles, *America's Ambassadors to England, 1785–1929* (1929); Wilson, Major L., *The Presidency of Martin Van Buren* (1984).

VANCE, CYRUS ROBERTS (b. 1917). Secretary of state (1977–1980) under President Jimmy Carter, Cyrus Vance was born March 27, 1917, in Clarksburg, West Virginia, graduated from Yale (A.B., 1939; LL.B., 1942), served in the navy during World War II, and was admitted to the bar in 1947. From 1947 to 1961 and again from 1969 to 1976, Vance practiced law in New York City. In the Kennedy administration, he was general counsel for the Defense Department in 1961–1962 and secretary of the army in 1961–1963. A close friend of Lyndon B. Johnson, Vance became deputy secretary of defense (1964–1967) during the Johnson presidency, touring Vietnam in 1966 and defending the administration's Vietnam policy until 1968. From 1968 to 1969, he was the U.S. negotiator at the Paris peace talks on Vietnam. In addition, Vance served on a peacemaking team sent to Panama in 1964 after a series of anti-American riots, and he played a role in the Dominican crisis* in 1965. Vance returned to public service in 1977 as Carter's secretary of state. Chosen because of his talents as an adviser and negotiator, Vance developed a reputation as a competent administrator rather than an innovative policymaker or inspiring leader. He supported the Strategic Arms Limitation Talks (SALT)* process, the Panama Canal treaties (1977),* human rights, and global economic development, although he scaled down the president's commitment toward human rights, making it coordinate more closely with other facets of America's national interests. Vance, who frequently clashed with the mercurial Zbigniew Brzezinski,* the national security adviser, resigned in April 1980 because of his opposition to the failed attempt to rescue American hostages in Iran. He returned to law practice in New York City and wrote his memoirs, *Hard Choices* (1983). He married Grace Elsie Sloane in 1947 and has been active in the United Nations Association and the Council on Foreign Relations.* *CB* (1977): 405–11; McLellan, David S., "Cyrus Vance," in Ferrell, R. H., ed., *American Secretaries of State and Their Diplomacy*, vol. 20 (1985); *New York Times*, December 4, 1976, February 13, 1977, April 29, 1980; *WWA* (1986–1987):2842.

VANDENBERG, ARTHUR HENDRICK (1884–1951). Born in Grand Rapids, Michigan, on March 22, 1884, Arthur H. Vandenberg was educated in local public schools and spent a year at the University of Michigan law school but had to leave for financial reasons. He worked in a cracker factory before joining the *Grand Rapids Herald* in 1900, becoming its editor in 1906 and remaining with the paper until 1928, when he was appointed U.S. senator, an appointment resulting from long service with the Republican state party organization. He remained in the Senate for the rest of his life, taking fairly typical midwestern Republican stands against the New Deal and for isolationism.* By 1943, however, he had come to the conviction that the United States had to play a leadership role in world affairs. Thus, during the war, he supported the Connally Resolution* and the establishment of the United Nations Relief and Rehabilitation Administration (UNRRA),* helped win public favor for the United Nations,* and was a delegate to the San Francisco Conference (1945).* An early cold warrior* after World War II, Vandenberg advised Secretaries of State James F. Byrnes* and George C. Marshall,* and as chairman of the Senate Foreign Relations Committee (1947–1949), he advocated a bipartisan foreign policy and was instrumental in persuading Republicans to back the Truman Doctrine,* the Marshall Plan,* and military aid to allies linked to the United States by international alliances. He strongly favored the North Atlantic Treaty (1949)* as a deterrent to aggression and war, and as a member of the Senate-House Atomic Energy Committee, he favored nuclear disarmament if the Soviet Union would agree to effective international controls. Vandenberg was married twice: to Elizabeth Watson (1907–1916) and to Hazel Whittaker (1918–1950). He died in Grand Rapids on April 18, 1951. Darilek, Richard E., *A Loyal Opposition in Time of War* (1976); McLellan, David S., *Dean Acheson: The State Department Years* (1976); *New York Times*, April 19, 1951; Tompkins, C. David, *Senator Arthur H. Vandenberg: The Evolution of a Modern Republican, 1884–1945* (1970); Vandenberg, Arthur H., Jr., ed., *The Private Papers of Senator Vandenberg* (1952).

VANDERBILT, CORNELIUS (1794–1877). Born May 17, 1794, in Port Richmond, New York, Cornelius Vanderbilt had only a scanty education and became involved in the shipping business early in life, working first for Thomas Gibbons and then on his own. By the 1840s he had become a millionaire. In U.S. diplomacy, the name of Cornelius Vanderbilt is attached to the Nicaragua transit route to California during gold rush days. He established the American Atlantic and Pacific Ship-Canal Company (which operated on the isthmus as the Accessory Transit Company)* in 1850, and was successful in providing a service to California that was two days faster than that going through Panama. When William Walker* obtained control of the Nicaraguan government in 1855, he suborned two of Vanderbilt's associates and arbitrarily cancelled Accessory's concession for violation of its terms; in return, the outraged Vanderbilt contributed to Walker's downfall in 1857. He then sold out his Nicaragua line to the operators of the Panama route. Later, Vanderbilt was involved in the Atlantic shipping trade and, during and after the Civil War, in the railroad industry, gaining control of the New York Central line in 1867. Vanderbilt was married twice, and when he died in New York City on January 4, 1877, he left a fortune estimated at over $100 million. Brown, Charles H., *Agents of Manifest Destiny* (1980); *DAB*, 19:169; Folkman, David I., Jr., *The Nicaragua Route* (1972); Smith, Arthur D. H., *Commodore Vanderbilt: An Epic of American Achievement* (1927).

VAUGHN, JACK HOOD (b. 1920). Born August 18, 1920, in Columbus, Montana, Jack Hood Vaughn graduated from the University of Michigan (B.A., 1943; M.A., 1947), majoring in Latin American studies. A professional boxer in college, Vaughn served in the U.S. Marine Corps from 1943 to 1946 and, after 1947, taught at the University of Pennsylvania. In 1949, he became a United States Information Agency* center director in La Paz, Bolivia; two years later, he moved to San José, Costa Rica, in the same position. Between 1952 and 1961, Vaughn served in a variety of places as an official for the International Cooperation Administration. Upon the establishment of the Peace Corps* in 1961, he became Latin American regional director, leaving the corps in 1964 for a tour as ambassador to Panama. He arrived in Panama after a seven-month diplomatic rupture and did much to heal wounds by traveling throughout the countryside and beginning negotiations on a new Panama Canal treaty. In 1965, he returned to Washington as assistant secretary of state (inter-American affairs), where he coordinated the Alliance for Progress* and many other agencies dealing with Latin America and made an extensive tour of the hemisphere. From 1966 to 1969, Vaughn was director of the Peace Corps*; from 1969 to 1970, he had an uneventful tour as ambassador to Colombia. Fluent in Spanish, Vaughn was an effective diplomat and was highly regarded by Latin American leaders. He left diplomatic service in 1970 and became president of the National Urban Coalition. In 1972, he was appointed dean of international affairs at Florida International University and director of foreign development for Children's Television Workshop. In 1975, he became president of Planned Parenthood. Vaughn married Joanne Cordes Smith in 1946. *CB* (1966):415; *New York Times*, February 13, 1965; *WWA* (1976–1977):3224.

VENEZUELAN CRISIS (1895), Anglo-Venezuelan boundary dispute. Under dispute was the boundary between Venezuela and British Guiana in the area of the Orinoco River. Britain's increasingly extravagant claims appeared to challenge the Monroe Doctrine,* and in February 1895 Congress passed a joint resolution recommending arbitration* of the matter. Secretary of State Richard Olney's* note to Britain, June 20, 1895, demanding to know whether it would submit to arbitration, made a strong and undiplomatic reference to American power behind the Monroe Doctrine. Eventually Britain did agree to arbitration, and in October 1899 an award was made, granting Britain most of what it claimed, though leaving the mouth of the Orinoco in Venezuelan control. Eggert, Gerald

G., *Richard Olney* (1974); *FR* (1895), 1:542–576; 2:1480–90; *FR* (1896), 240–53; Perkins, Bradford, *The Great Rapprochement* (1968).

VENEZUELAN DISPUTE (1902–1903). This crisis revolved around Venezuelan dictator Cipriano Castro and his failure to pay his country's debts or treat with justice nationals of several European nations. In December 1902, Germany, Great Britain, and Italy forcibly intervened, sinking part of the Venezuelan navy and blockading major ports. Castro appealed for arbitration,* and at the urging of the United States, the intervening nations agreed. Mixed claims commissions adjudicated the various Venezuelan debts, and the question of intervention as a criterion for first claim on payment was submitted to the Hague Permanent Court of Arbitration.* The incident spurred Dr. Luis M. Drago to postulate the Drago Doctrine (1903),* opposing intervention for purposes of debt collection. On February 22, 1904, the Hague Court decided that Germany, Britain, and Italy did have preferential rights to the first Venezuelan payments. This decision, which appeared to encourage foreign intervention, helped bring about the Roosevelt Corollary,* justifying American intervention in the Western Hemisphere as a means of preventing European or other foreign intervention. Beale, Howard K., *Theodore Roosevelt and the Rise of America to World Power* (1956); Bemis, Samuel F., *The Latin American Policy of the United States* (1943); Holbo, Paul S., "Perilous Obscurity: Public Diplomacy and the Press in the Venezuelan Crisis, 1902–1903," *Historian* 32 (1970): 428–48; Jonas, Manfred, *The United States and Germany* (1984); Munro, Dana G., *Intervention and Dollar Diplomacy in the Caribbean, 1900–1921* (1964).

VERSAILLES, TREATY OF (1919). This treaty, signed June 28, 1919, ended World War I. It consisted of 440 articles, most of them noncontroversial and technical in nature. However, the treaty included the Covenant of the League of Nations,* a war-guilt clause blaming the Germans for the war, some territorial changes in Central Europe (which cost Germany one-eighth of its territory), and the disposition of former Central Power colonies through a system of mandates.* The U.S. Senate refused to ratify the treaty, mainly because of the League of Nations question, and signed a separate peace treaty with Germany in 1921. Ambrosius, Lloyd E., *Woodrow Wilson and the American Diplomatic Tradition* (1987); Bailey, Thomas A., *Woodrow Wilson and the Lost Peace* (1944); *FR, The Paris Peace Conference* (1919), 13:57–756; Mayer, Arno J., *Politics and Diplomacy of Peacemaking: Containment and Counterrevolution at Versailles, 1918–1919* (1967); Walworth, Arthur C., *America's Moment, 1918: American Diplomacy at the End of World War I* (1977) and *Wilson and His Peacemakers: American Diplomacy at the Paris Peace Conference* (1986).

VICE-CONSUL. See **CONSUL.**

VIETNAMIZATION, Vietnam War policy, 1969–1973. *Vietnamization* is the term used to describe the process, begun under President Richard M. Nixon in 1969, of transferring more and more of the combat burden in the Vietnam War to South Vietnamese troops while maintaining U.S. air and logistical support and gradually withdrawing U.S. combat troops. The initial notion may have come from a 1968 article in *Foreign Affairs*, "Must We Invade the North?" written by Roger Hilsman.* Over four years, 540,000 U.S. troops were withdrawn, and casualties declined correspondingly. Some critics attacked the pace of withdrawal as unnecessarily slow and meant to allow the administration to cling as long as possible to the hope of military victory. The Cambodian incursion (1970)* and Laotian incursion (1971)* were ostensibly undertaken to facilitate the smooth functioning of Vietnamization, or "de-Americanization," as it is sometimes termed. Hung, Nguyen Tien, and Jerrold L. Schecter, *The Palace File* (1986); Kolko, Gabriel, *Anatomy of a War* (1985); Poole, Peter A., *The United States and Indochina from FDR to Nixon* (1973); Szulc, Tad, *The Illusion of Peace* (1978).

VIGNAUD, HENRY (1830–1922). A fixture at the U.S. mission in Paris for nearly fifty years, Henry Vignaud was born in New Orleans, Louisiana, on November 27, 1830. His education was limited to city schools in New Orleans, and from 1852 to 1856 he taught school there. In 1857, he became editor of the Thibodoux weekly, *L'Union de la fourche*, and in 1860 he moved to a weekly cultural review, *La Renaissance louisianaise*. During the Civil War, Vignaud served in the Confederate army, was captured, escaped, went to Paris, and never returned to the United States. He worked for Confederate envoy John Slidell* in Paris and in 1869 became secretary of the Romanian legation. He returned to U.S. service in 1872 as a translator in the *Alabama** claims arbitration,* and in 1875 he was appointed second secretary of the U.S. legation in Paris. Ten years later, he was promoted to first secretary, and in 1909 he received the title of honorary counselor.* Vignaud was on active duty in the legation, often serving as chargé d'affaires* and providing an important sense of continuity to the execution of U.S. policy in France. His long association with the French government earned him the honorific title of Grand Officier in the Legion of Honor. He married Louise Compte in 1879 and late in life achieved distinction of sorts as a historian specializing in Christopher Columbus and his era, coming to certain conclusions about Columbus that have not found acceptance among other historians. Vignaud died in Paris on September 16, 1922. *DAB*, 19:268; *New York Times*, September 19, 1922.

VINCENT, JOHN CARTER (1900–1972). A native of Seneca, Kansas, where he was born on August 19, 1900, John Carter Vincent served in the army during World War I and received a B.A. degree from Mercer College in 1923. In 1925, he began a career in the Foreign Service, soon developing into a specialist on China. He learned to speak fluent Chinese and served in numerous minor posts throughout China during the 1920s and 1930s. From 1942 to 1945, he was counselor* at the relocated U.S. embassy in Chungking. At the war's end, he returned to Washington as director of the Bureau of Far Eastern Affairs. Named a career minister in 1946, Vincent accompanied the mission to China headed by

General George C. Marshall* seeking a settlement of the civil war. Upon his return, he spent four years (1947–1951) as minister to Switzerland and one year as diplomatic agent in Tangier. In 1952, however, he was forced to resign from the Foreign Service because of allegations concerning his loyalty dating back to the Marshall mission. Vincent was brought under suspicion during the McCarthy era because of his belief that, without much greater demands put on Chiang Kai-shek, the Nationalist Chinese would surely lose the war; therefore, it made no sense to give the Nationalists large amounts of aid. Although he was cleared by the Senate Internal Security Subcommittee and the State Department Loyalty Board, the Civil Service Loyalty Board concluded there was some question about his loyalty. Secretary of State John Foster Dulles* requested Vincent's resignation, declaring him loyal but stating that he did not meet State Department standards. After 1953, Vincent was associated with the East Asian Research Center at Harvard until his death in Cambridge, Massachusetts, on December 3, 1972. Daniel, Barry M., The "Loss" of China and American Politics (1982); Kahn, E. J., Jr., The China Hands (1972); Lauren, Paul Gordon, ed., The China Hands' Legacy (1987); May, Gary, China Scapegoat (1979); New York Times, December 5, 1972.

VIRGIN ISLANDS, ACQUISITION OF (1917). See **DANISH WEST INDIES, ACQUISITION OF (1917).**

VIRGINIUS **AFFAIR (1873).** In 1871, Venezuela had nearly come to war with several European nations, including Spain, over various financial matters. The *Virginius*, an American steamer, had aided Venezuela in this conflict and, as a result, was captured by the Spanish in October 1873. Taken to Cuba, the captain and thirty-six of the crew of the ship were executed the following month. This prompted a diplomatic crisis between the United States and Spain, with Secretary of State Hamilton Fish* and Spanish minister Admiral Polo de Bernabe agreeing late in November that the *Virginius* and surviving crew members would be released on the condition that U.S. authorities conduct an investigation and prosecute any who had violated American laws. During its return to New York, the *Virginius* was wrecked, and on December 22, 1873, investigators concluded that the ship had been under the control of Cuban revolutionaries and that therefore its registration as an American ship was fraudulent. On May 5, 1875, Spain paid an indemnity of $80,000 for the deaths and mistreatment of Americans in the incident. Daniel Sickles,* the U.S. minister in Spain, handled negotiations in Madrid, but the agreement was reached in Washington. Bradford, Richard H., The Virginius Affair (1980); Fuller, Joseph V., "Hamilton Fish," in Bemis, Samuel F., ed. American Secretaries of State and Their Diplomacy, vol. 7 (1928); Nevins, Allan, Hamilton Fish, rev. ed. (1957).

VOPICKA, CHARLES JOSEPH (1857–1935). Charles J. Vopicka was born November 3, 1857, in Dolni Hbity, Bohemia, and attended schools in Pribam and Prague. He emigrated to the United States in 1880 and worked as a bookkeeper in Racine, Wisconsin, for a year before moving to Chicago. There he was successful in real estate and banking ventures, founded the Bohemian Brewing Company in 1891 (renamed the Atlas Brewing Company in 1896), and took an active part in Democratic party politics. In 1913, with the entrance of the Wilson administration into power, Vopicka was named minister to Romania, Serbia, and Bulgaria. Headquartered in Bucharest, Vopicka represented the interests of nearly all the belligerents during the early years of the war and was particularly involved in prisoner-of-war affairs. In early 1917, he left Bucharest under German pressure, returned to the United States, and urged U.S. entry into the war. Later that year, he went to Jassy, the temporary Romanian capital, and resumed his diplomatic functions. He went to the Russian front in a vain attempt to persuade the Bolshevik government to stay in the war. Resigning his post in 1920, Vopicka returned to his business and civic interests in Chicago, serving as chairman of the Atlas Brewing Company and as a member of the Board of Education. He went to Latvia in 1925 and received authority to raise a $10 million loan in the United States on behalf of the Latvian government. In 1921, he published his memoirs, *Secrets of the Balkans: Seven Years of a Diplomatist's Life in the Storm Center of Europe*. Vopicka married Victoria Kubin in 1881 and died in Chicago on September 3, 1935. *DAB*, Supp. 1:694; *New York Times*, September 5, 1935.

VORYS AMENDMENT (1939). Named for Congressman John N. Vorys (R., Ohio), this amendment was introduced during the debate on the Neutrality Act (1939).* It called for a limited embargo including arms and ammunition but excluding "implements of war," such as planes. Offered as a compromise to an administration measure to repeal the arms embargo altogether, the Vorys amendment passed the House of Representatives on June 30, 1939, and contributed to the delay of total arms embargo repeal (embodied in the Neutrality Act that ultimately passed) until November 30, 1939, two months after the outbreak of war in Europe. Divine, Robert A., *The Illusion of Neutrality* (1962).

W

WALKER, WILLIAM (1824–1860). Born May 8, 1824, in Nashville, Tennessee, William Walker graduated from the University of Nashville in 1838 and later received both an M.D. and admittance to the bar (in Louisiana) but principally followed a career in journalism, editing a newspaper in New Orleans in the late 1840s. In 1850, he moved to California and three years later headed an unsuccessful expedition to Mexico to colonize Sonora and Lower California. In 1855, at the invitation of the Liberal party of León, Nicaragua, Walker led an expedition there, with the assistance of the Accessory Transit Company.* His forces captured the important Nicaraguan town of Granada in late 1855, and Walker proclaimed himself president in May 1856, remaining in power for a year. Walker hoped for U.S. recognition, and possibly annexation, and U.S. Minister to Central America John Hill Wheeler* recognized his regime. However, the Pierce administration, under pressure from northern antislavery forces, and from the Cornelius Vanderbilt* empire, which was allied with Walker's opposition in Nicaragua, disavowed Wheeler's recognition. In 1860, Walker was captured and executed (on September 12) during another filibustering* expedition in Honduras. Walker was a good writer, and his autobiographical account, *The War in Nicaragua* (1860), is considered one of the most accurate and impartial sources of the whole affair. Brown, Charles H., *Agents of Manifest Destiny* (1980); Carr, Albert Z., *The World and William Walker* (1963); Gerson, Noel B., *Sad Swashbuckler* (1976); Parker, Franklin D., *The Central American Republics* (1964); Williams, Mary W., *Anglo-American Isthmian Diplomacy, 1815–1915* (1916).

WALLACE, HUGH CAMPBELL (1863–1931). Born February 10, 1863, in Lexington, Missouri, Hugh Campbell Wallace attended local schools, moved to the West, and became receiver of public monies in Salt Lake City in 1885. In 1887, he went to Tacoma, Washington, where he organized a bank with his brother, formed the Washington and Alaska Steamship Company, which served prospectors during the Klondike gold rush, invested in real estate, and became an important financial leader in the Northwest. An active Democrat, Wallace served on the party's national committee, 1892–1896 and 1916–1920, and was frequently active in political campaigns. When Woodrow Wilson became president in 1913, Wallace turned down an offer to be secretary of war but remained a close, unofficial adviser to the president and was sometimes referred to as a "second Colonel [Edward M.] House."* In 1919, he was named ambassador to France, where his main task was to maintain Franco-American amity in the aftermath of war. He visited war-torn parts of France, worked on a new commercial treaty, and had heavy social obligations because of the ongoing Paris Peace Conference.* Wallace served as the U.S. representative on the Supreme Allied Council and the Council of Ambassadors at Paris and was influential despite having only observer status. After the peace conference, he signed a treaty concerning Spitzbergen (1920) and the Treaty of Trianon (1920).* He remained at his post until July 1921. In later years, Wallace spent considerable time in France and served as the U.S. representative to the International Academy of Diplomacy there in 1927. Wallace married Mildred Fuller, the daughter of Chief Justice Melville W. Fuller, in 1891, collected books on Franco-American relations (later given to the U.S. embassy in Paris), and died in Washington, D.C., on New Year's Day, 1931. *DAB*, 19:371; *New York Times*, January 2, 1931; Willson, Beckles, *America's Ambassadors to France, 1777–1927* (1928).

WALLACE, LEWIS ("LEW") (1827–1905). Better known as the author of *Ben Hur* (1880) and as a Union general in the Civil War, Lew Wallace was also U.S. minister at the difficult mission in Turkey. He was born April 10, 1827, in Brookville, Indiana, and when he was ten, his father was elected governor of Indiana. His formal schooling was limited, and he worked as a clerk and legislative reporter while studying law, gaining admission to the bar in 1849. He practiced law in Indianapolis, Covington, and Crawfordsville, married Susan Arnold in 1852, and won a seat in the state senate in 1856. When the Civil War broke out, he became adjutant general of Indiana, raising troops for the war. In 1862, he was promoted to major general and saw much active duty. After the war, he spent some time in Mexico helping the forces of Benito Juárez, and in 1878 he was appointed territorial governor of New Mexico. From 1881 to 1885, Wallace was minister to Turkey. There he was highly successful in winning the confidence of the sultan but able to accomplish little else. His main concern was Turkish depredations on American missionaries, and he was instructed to demand that murderers be executed, that lesser criminals be justly punished, and that indemnities be paid to victims. But wily Turkish diplomats outmaneuvered Wallace and won the point that American cases be tried under Turkish law, which forbid testimony of a non-Muslim to be used against a Muslim. Thus it was virtually impossible for Americans to receive justice, and Wallace was unable to do anything about this. After 1885, Wallace lived in Indiana and continued his career as a writer. He died February 14, 1905, in Crawfordsville. His memoirs, *Lew Wallace, An Autobiography* (1906), were completed by his wife and Mary H. Krout. *DAB* 19:375; Morsberger, Robert E., and Katherine Morsberger, *Lew Wallace: Militant Romantic* (1980); *NCAB*, 4:363; Pletcher, David, *The Awkward Years* (1962).

WALTERS, VERNON ANTHONY (b. 1917). A native of New York City, where he was born January 3, 1917, Vernon Walters lived in Europe during much of his youth, studying at schools in France and England and learning French, German, and Spanish. During the 1930s, he worked for his father as an insurance adjuster and, in 1941, began a thirty-five year army career, retiring in 1976 with the rank of lieutenant general. Because of his linguistic ability, he spent much of his career as a translator or aide to prominent military and civilian leaders, including Dwight Eisenhower, George C. Marshall,* and Averell Harriman.* Walters accompanied Eisenhower on most of the foreign trips he made during his presidency and was with Richard Nixon in 1958 when the vice-president made his disastrous trip to Latin America. From 1962 to 1964, Walters was U.S. military attaché in Rio de Janeiro, Brazil, and his easy familiarity with the military officers who overthrew the government of João Goulart in 1964 raised suspicions that the United States had underwritten the coup. From 1967 to 1972, he was defense attaché in Paris and was responsible for spiriting Henry Kissinger* in and out of the city while he was engaging in secret talks to end the Vietnam War. Between 1972 and 1976, Walters was deputy director for the Central Intelligence Agency; here his major task was in liaison work with various foreign intelligence services. In retirement from 1977 to 1981, Walters wrote his memoirs, *Silent Missions* (1978), and returned to public service in 1981 as an ambassador-at-large in the Reagan administration. In this post, he utilized his military background to further U.S. interests among the military dictatorships of Latin America. In addition, he worked with friendly nations in North Africa to isolate Libya and helped in the attempt to implement the policy of constructive engagement* in South Africa. When Jeane Kirkpatrick* resigned as United Nations* ambassador in 1985, Walters was chosen as her replacement. In that organization, he has worked principally on the Iran-Iraq war,* and on international terrorism and has put forth his cold war* attitudes less confrontationally than his predecessor. *CB* (February, 1988):54–57; Massing, Michael, "America's Top Messenger Boy," *New Republic*, September 16–23, 1987, pp. 21–25; *New York Times*, May 31, July 9, 1985; *WWA* (1986–1987):2896.

WAMBAUGH, SARAH (1882–1955). Born in Cincinnati on March 6, 1882, Sarah Wambaugh graduated from Radcliffe (B.A., 1902; M.A., 1917) and studied further at London and Oxford after teaching at Radcliffe (1902–1906). She worked in the Women's Educational and Industrial Union in Boston from 1906 to 1916 and was active in the Women's Peace party during World War I, where she first became interested in plebiscites—a process wherein the electorate of an area votes for or against attachment to or detachment from a particular state. After the war, Wambaugh taught for a year at the Academy of International Law at the Hague and wrote *A Monograph on Plebiscites* (1920), which brought her an immediate international reputation as an expert on the subject. She then became a League of Nations* secretariat staff member, studying postwar plebiscites (1922–1924) and serving as a technical adviser and commissioner for others held during the interwar period, including the Tacna-Arica dispute (1925–1926) and the Saar plebiscite (1934–1935). During the 1930s, she opposed the neutrality* policy of the United States and defended the League of Nations, believing that its work in managing plebiscites had been worthwhile. In the

United States during World War II, she worked for the creation of the United Nations* and advocated a postwar international peace force to curtail armed aggression. She was a technical adviser on the U.S. team sent to observe the Greek elections (1945–1946) and worked on the United Nations Plebiscite Commission in Jammu (India) and Kashmir in 1949. Never married, Wambaugh wrote *Plebiscites since the World War* (1933) and *The Saar Plebiscite* (1940, 1971) and died in Cambridge, Massachusetts, on November 12, 1955. *CB* (1946): 619–20; *DAB*, Supp. 5:723; *New York Times*, February 17, 1946, November 13, 1955.

WANG-HSIA (WANGHIA), TREATY OF (1844). Negotiated by U.S. Minister Caleb Cushing and Chinese official Ch'i-ying, the Treaty of Wang-hsia was closely modeled upon the Treaty of Nanking (1842).* It provided for American consuls* and trade in five Chinese ports and included rights of extraterritoriality.* The treaty ports were Canton, Amoy, Ningpo, Foochow, and Shanghai; all were usable on terms equal to those granted the British. The United States acquired no Chinese territory in this treaty, the first commercial treaty between the two countries. Cohen, Warren I., *America's Response to China* (1971); Dennett, Tyler, *Americans in Eastern Asia* (1922); Goetzmann, William H., *When the Eagle Screamed* (1966).

WAR HAWKS, group of American congressmen, 1810–1812. This name was applied to a group of younger members of the Twelfth Congress elected in 1810–1811, who emerged in Congress as the war party in the impending conflict with Britain. They were led by Speaker of the House Henry Clay* and were most concerned with maritime matters as they concerned American honor, feeling that continued submission to impressment* and commercial restrictions was a humiliation. The War Hawks wanted war to restore national honor, since no one believed Britain would change its policies by any other means. The motivations of the War Hawks (as well as their cohesiveness and influence as a group) have been a matter of considerable historiographical debate. Horsman, Reginald, *The Causes of the War of 1812* (1962); Perkins, Bradford, *Prologue to War* (1961).

WAR OF THE PACIFIC (1879–1881), Chilean-Bolivian war. This war concerned sovereignty over an unsettled area between Chile and Bolivia rich in nitrates and other natural resources. Chile easily triumphed over Bolivia and its ally, Peru. Secretary of State James G. Blaine* in 1881 saw a chance to implement Pan-Americanism* and attempted mediation of the conflict, first through resident American ministers and then through a special envoy, the experienced diplomat William Henry Trescot.* At that point, Blaine was replaced by Frederick T. Frelinghuysen*, who recalled Trescot and turned mediation efforts over to the new minister to Chile, Cornelius A. Logan.* The peace negotiations resulted at last in the Treaty of Ancon, October 20, 1883, in which the Peruvian provinces of Tacna and Arica were to be occupied by Chile for ten years, with a plebiscite to follow. American interventive diplomacy had proved contradictory and ineffective; but many years later, in 1929, with the plebiscite never having been held, U.S. arbitration* led to Tacna's being given to Peru and Arica to Chile. Brown, Philip M., "Frederick T. Frelinghuysen," in Bemis, Samuel F. ed., *American Secretaries of State and Their Diplomacy*, vol. 8 (1928); Lockney, Joseph B., "James Gillespie Blaine," in Bemis, Samuel F. ed., *American Secretaries of State and Their Diplomacy*, vol. 7 (1928); Millington, Herbert A., *American Diplomacy and the War of the Pacific* (1948); Stuart, Graham A., *Latin America and the United States* (1955).

WAR POWERS RESOLUTION (1973). This joint congressional resolution, passed November 7, 1973, over President Richard Nixon's veto, represented the determination of Congress to reassert control over foreign policy following the Vietnam War. The resolution was designed to limit the power of the president to commit U.S. forces to combat without totally paralyzing the president's ability to react to a crisis. The resolution requires the president to report to Congress any utilization of armed forces in hostile situations and to withdraw such forces within sixty days unless Congress authorizes otherwise. Another part of the resolution gives Congress the power to force the withdrawal of troops at any time by passage of a concurrent resolution to that effect, although the constitutionality of this has been called into question. In practice, all presidents since Nixon have opposed the War Powers Resolution as unnecessarily (and perhaps unconstitutionally) constraining on their power to conduct foreign policy and act as commander in chief of the armed forces. Nevertheless, presidents have submitted reports under the provision of the resolution on such occasions as the rescue mission during the the Iran hostage crisis* and the Grenada intervention.* In other instances, such as the sending of military advisers to El Salvador, the president has not reported. In 1983, during the Lebanon crisis,* Congress invoked the resolution when the president did not, but allowed troops to stay up to eighteen months rather than sixty days. The War Powers Resolution remains a point of controversy between the president and Congress, and various amendments or revisions have frequently been suggested. Holt, Pat M., *The War Powers Resolution: The Role of Congress in U.S. Armed Intervention* (1978); Reveley, W. Taylor, *War Powers of the President and Congress* (1981); Turner, Robert F., *The War Powers Resolution: Its Implementation in Theory and Practice* (1983).

WARNKE, PAUL CULLITON (b. 1920). A native of Webster, Massachusetts, where he was born January 31, 1920, Paul Warnke graduated from Yale (1941), served in the Coast Guard during World War II, and, after his discharge, returned to school, earning a law degree from Columbia (1948). Admitted to the bar that year, he practiced law in Washington until 1966, when he became general counsel for the Defense Department (1966–1967) and then assistant secretary of defense for international security affairs (1967–1969). During this time, he came to oppose the Vietnam War, believing that the United States was overcommitted in a war that neither side could win militarily. He worked with the Democratic National Committee and was a prominent spokesman against the war and against the rapid pace of new weapons development. Out of government during the Nixon and Ford administrations (1969–1977), Warnke returned in 1977 as director of the Arms Control and Disarmament Agency and chief negotiator at the Strategic Arms Limitation Talks (SALT II).* His appointment was controversial; critics alleged that he favored unilateral arms reduction and would be too lenient in dealing with the Soviet Union and too keen to cut the defense budget, since he had opposed such projects as the B-1 bomber and the Trident nuclear submarine. Warnke, however, asserted that both the United States and the Soviet Union had sufficient armaments to destroy one another and that further weapons systems were a block to fruitful disarmament talks. Believing that the United States did not need to maintain "cosmetic" military superiority, he argued for a less global U.S. military establishment and noted that military intervention is generally unwanted and counterproductive. In March 1977, Warnke began talks to revise the provisional SALT II agreement reached at Valdivostok by President Gerald R. Ford and Soviet Premier Leonid Brezhnev in 1974. After an initial Soviet rejection of a U.S. proposal, talks resumed in may 1977 and had moved close to a SALT II agreement in October 1978, when Warnke resigned. From 1978 to 1981, he was a special consultant to the secretary of state. Married to Jean Farjeon Rowe in 1948, Warnke practices law in Washington and has been a member and director of the Council on Foreign Relations.* *CB* (1977):427–30; *New York Times*, February 3, 1977; Warnke, Paul, "Apes on a Treadmill," *Foreign Policy* 18 (Spring 1975): 12–30; *WWA* (1986–1987): 2905.

WASHBURN, ALBERT HENRY (1866–1930). Albert H. Washburn was born in Middleboro, Massachusetts, on April 11, 1866, graduated from Cornell (1889), and entered the consular service, serving in Magdeberg, Germany, 1890–1893. From 1893 to 1896, he was private secretary to Senator Henry Cabot Lodge, Sr.,* while at the same time attending Georgetown Law School. He received his law degree in 1895 and was an assistant U.S. attorney for Massachusetts from 1897 to 1901 and a U.S. Treasury Department lawyer specializing in tariff problems from 1901 to 1904. Between 1904 and 1922, Washburn was in private law practice, continuing to specialize in customs matters and teaching international law at Dartmouth, 1919–1921. In 1922, he was named minister to Austria, the first since World War I. His reports to the State Department on conditions in Central and Eastern Europe were particularly useful, and he was of considerable value to the Austrian government as a financial adviser. He was president of a mixed commission adjudicating Austrian-Yugoslavian problems (1923–1925) and negotiated a U.S.-Austrian treaty of friendship and commerce (1928). While still serving as minister, Washburn died in Vienna on April 2, 1930, of erysipelas resulting from a scratch on the leg. He married Florence B. Lincoln in 1906. *DAB*, 19:494; *New York Times*, April 3, 1930.

WASHBURNE, ELIHU BENJAMIN (1816–1887). A prominent Civil War–era politician, Elihu Washburne was minister to France during the two terms of President Ulysses S. Grant. Born in Livermore, Maine, on September 23, 1816, he was a printer's apprentice and then a printer before studying law at Harvard and gaining admittance to the bar in 1840. That year he moved to Illinois, where he practiced law, married Adele Gratiot in 1845, and was elected to the U.S. House of Representatives as a Whig in 1852. He became a Republican upon the founding of that party and gained a reputation in the House as the "Watch-dog of the Treasury." An adviser to Lincoln and a recruiter during the Civil War, Washburne was a member of the Joint Committee of Reconstruction and an opponent of President Andrew Johnson after the war. When Grant, a long-time friend, was elected president in 1869, Washburne was given a courtesy appointment as secretary of state from March 5 to March 16, a move designed to give him prestige as minister to France. Although he spent eight years in Paris, the most exciting period came early in his tenure, during the Franco-Prussian War (1870) and the regime of the radical Commune the following year. The only foreign representative to remain in Paris during this time, Washburne proved an excellent observer and successfully maintained U.S. neutrality.* He represented German interests and dealt with some 30,000 refugees and prisoners during the days of the Commune, although he opposed the political philosophy of its leaders. After his return from France in 1877, he supported Grant's 1880 presidential bid and was president of the Chicago Historical Society from 1844 to 1887, writing and editing material on Illinois history. Washburne wrote his memoirs, *Recollections of a Minister to France, 1869–1877* (1877), and died in Chicago on October 23, 1887. Clifford, Dale, "Elihu Benjamin Washburne: An American Diplomat in Paris, 1870–1871," *Prologue* 2 (Winter 1970):161–74; *DAB*, 19:504; Nevins, Allan, *Hamilton Fish*, 2 vols. (1957); Willson, Beckles, *America's Ambassadors to France, 1777–1927* (1928).

WASHINGTON, TREATY OF (1871). This treaty settled problems stemming from British construction of Confederate raiders during the Civil War, as well as a number of other less consequential matters. A five-man arbitration* board was established to rule on questions concerning the *Alabama** claims. The arbitration was held at Geneva between December 1871 and July 1872 and resulted in a $15.5 million award to the United States for damages caused by the *Alabama* and other British-built Confederate raiders. American claims for compensation for indirect damages were dismissed. In addition, the Treaty of Washington expressed Britain's regret for Confederate depredations. *FR* (1871), 495–530; *FR* (1872), 2: vols. 1–5; Nevins, Allan, *Hamilton Fish*, rev. ed. (1957); Robson, Maureen M., "The Alabama Claims and the Anglo-American Reconciliation, 1865–1871," *Canadian Historical Review* 43 (March 1961).

WASHINGTON CONFERENCE (1889). Secretary of State James G. Blaine* first proposed this conference in 1882 but soon left office, and the conference was delayed until October 1889, after Blaine had returned to the State Department. Although praised in the press, the conference accomplished little of a concrete nature besides an arbitration* plan and the creation of an inter-American organization, the Bureau of American Republics,* later known as the Pan-American Union,* to deal with customs barriers and other commercial matters. The Conference, formally known as the First International Conference of American states, symbolized Blaine's devotion to Pan-Americanism.* Connell-Smith, Gordon, *The United States and Latin America* (1974); Mecham, J. Lloyd, *A Survey of United States–Latin American Relations* (1965); Plesur, Milton, *America's Outward Thrust* (1971).

WASHINGTON CONFERENCE (1907). In August 1907, President Theodore Roosevelt and Mexican President Porfirio Díaz called a Central American conference to settle the various ongoing disputes plaguing the isthmus, and in November delegates from the five republics, Guatemala, Honduras, El Salvador, Nicaragua, and Costa Rica, met in Washington and, under the supervision of Secretary of State Elihu Root,* negotiated a number of treaties. The most important of these was the General Treaty of Peace and Amity, which established the Permanent Central American Court of Justice to settle future disputes. In addition, Honduras was made permanently neutral, and signatories pledged that their territory would not be used as a base for revolutionary movements against other states. Other conventions and treaties sought closer economic and cultural ties. The treaties were not effective in pacifying the region, and ultimately American military and financial intervention occurred. *FR* (1907), 2:606–727; Hill, Howard C., *Roosevelt and the Caribbean* (1927); Munro, Dana G., *Intervention and Dollar Diplomacy in the Caribbean, 1900–1921* (1964).

WASHINGTON CONFERENCE ON THE LIMITATION OF ARMAMENTS (WASHINGTON NAVAL CONFERENCE 1921–1922). Concerned with naval arms limitations, this conference began in November 1921 and ended in February 1922. Three major treaties were concluded: the Four-Power Treaty,* respecting the status quo in the Pacific; the Five-Power Treaty,* on naval arms apportionment; and the Nine-Power Treaty,* guaranteeing the territorial and administrative integrity of China. Participants in the conference were the United States, Great Britain, Japan, France, Italy, Portugal, the Netherlands, Belgium, and China. The United States, represented by Secretary of State Charles Evans Hughes,* achieved its objectives of ending the naval arms race, breaking the Anglo-Japanese alliance,* and obtaining international approbation of the Open Door policy.* Buckley, Thomas H., *The United States and the Washington Conference, 1921–1922* (1970); Buell, Raymond Leslie, *The Washington Conference* (1922); *FR* (1921), 1–18–87; *FR* (1922), 1:1–384.

WASHINGTON SUMMIT CONFERENCE (1987). The highlight of this summit, held December 7–9, 1987, in Washington, D.C., was the signing of the Intermediate Nuclear Force (INF) Treaty,* a matter of grand ceremony but no substance. Serious talks took place with respect to the Strategic Arms Reduction Talks (START)*; President Ronald Reagan and General Secretary Mikhail Gorbachev agreed on a limit of 4,900 strategic offensive missile warheads. In addition, the Soviets announced that their missile throwweight (lifting) capacity would be reduced by 50 percent and the number of SS-18s would also be cut in half. In return, the United States agreed to limits to sea-launched cruise missiles (SLCM) without specifying numbers or manner of verification. The INF Treaty verification procedures were to be worked into a START agreement. The two sides failed to agree on limits for land-based missile warheads—the United States proposing 3,300, the Soviets rejecting that figure unless the United States agreed to limit its SLCM warheads to 3,300, which was unacceptable to the Americans. This issue was deferred, as was the question of the interpretation of the Anti-Ballistic Missile Treaty or the length of time each side would guarantee to observe that treaty. Other proposals were introduced into the conference: an agreement on the need to work out a method for counting air-launched cruise missiles and a Soviet idea on verifying SCLMs through the use of special devices mounted on helicopters. This summit was also important to President Reagan with respect to his domestic standing (as it was also for Gorbachev) and for his historical legacy. *New York Times*, December 10–11, 1987.

WATSON, ARTHUR KITTREDGE (1919–1974). Arthur K. Watson was born April 23, 1919, in Summit, New Jersey, graduated from Yale (1942), and, after service in World War II, joined his father's company, IBM, in 1947. After becoming a director and vice-president in 1949, he moved to the position of President of IBM World Trade Corporation, a subsidiary, in 1954 and board chairman in 1963, responsible for IBM's manufacturing and marketing operations abroad. During the 1960s, Watson fought the protectionist movement and served on various advisory panels seeking ways to increase U.S. foreign trade. A Republican, he was named ambassador to France in 1970 by the Nixon administration. In Paris, he handled the first official contacts between the People's Republic of China and the United States and enjoyed a cordial relationship with China's ambassador to France. Watson also maintained close ties with French President Georges Pompidou and German Prime Minister Willy Brandt. He returned to the United States and IBM in 1972 and died July 26, 1974, in Norwalk, Connecticut. *CB* (1971):434–36; *New York Times*, August 30, 1972, July 27, 1974.

WATSON, THOMAS J., JR. (b. 1914). The long-time head of International Business Machines (IBM), Thomas J. Watson was born in Dayton, Ohio, on January 8, 1914 and graduated from Brown in 1937. Except for service in the air force during World War II, Watson worked for IBM from his graduation until 1979, climbing up the corporate ladder to become chief executive officer, 1956–1971; chairman, 1961–1971; and chairman of the executive committee, 1971–1979. In 1979, Watson accepted the appointment of his good friend, President Jimmy Carter, and went to Moscow as ambassador to the Soviet Union. He was the first political appointee to be posted there in twenty-seven years, a fact that dismayed some career diplomats, such as Malcolm Toon,* his predecessor, and many more observers after the Soviet invasion of Afghanistan in December 1979 and the subsequent cooling of U.S.-Soviet relations. Watson, who had thought his mission would be highly social in nature, now had to deal with sensitive geopolitical issues. Although he was almost totally unfamiliar with Soviet affairs and the Russian language, his common sense and close ties with the president served him well, and he remained in Moscow until the end of Carter's term. After his return to the United States, Watson became chairman emeritus of IBM. He married Olive Field Cawley in 1941 and is an active director of various educational, cultural, and environmental organizations. *Newsweek*, February 11, 1980; *New York Times*, June 23, 1979, February 9, 1981; *WWA*, (1986–1987):2913.

WEBB, JAMES WATSON (1802–1884). Born February 8, 1802, in Claverack, New York, James Watson Webb was orphaned at an early age, joined the army at age seventeen, and received a commission as a second lieutenant. He served on the frontier, 1821–1827, and then resigned his commission and embarked on a career in journalism in New York City. Acquiring the *Morning Courier* in 1827, he merged it two years later with the *New York Enquirer* and continued as owner-editor until 1861, when he sold out to the *New York World*. A Republican, Webb was appointed minister to Brazil in 1861 by the Lincoln administration. He went to Brazil by way of Paris, and in an interview with his longtime friend, Louis-Napoleon, he received a pledge of French withdrawal from Mexico. In Brazil, Webb protested aid given to Confederate raiders, competed with British rivals, including a particularly hostile British minister who was eventually recalled, and protected American interests during the Paraguayan War. Leaving Brazil in 1869, he traveled in Europe until 1871 and lived in retirement in New York City until his death on June 7, 1884. He was married twice: to Helen Lispenand Stewart (1823–1848) and to Laura Virginia Cram (after 1849). *DAB*, 19:574; *NCAB*, 3:30.

WEBB-POMERENE ACT (1918). Sponsored by Sen. Atlee Pomerene (D., Ohio) and Rep. Edwin Webb (D., North Carolina), this act was designed to enable American corporations to compete more effectively in international markets with British or German cartels. The act removed antitrust provisions from foreign commerce, allowing American companies to divide foreign markets or to make vertical combinations to facilitate trade. The Paris Economic Conference (1916), at which Britain, France, and their allies agreed to cooperate in postwar foreign commerce, provided the inspiration for the Webb-Pomerene Act. A corollary act, the Edge Act, was passed December 24, 1919, to permit banks to combine their capital available for foreign operators to aid in the financing of American foreign commerce. The Edge Act also allowed the chartering of corporations to furnish long-term loans to foreign governments and businesses. Parrini, Carl, *Heir to Empire: United States Economic Diplomacy, 1916–1923* (1969).

WEBSTER, DANIEL (1782–1852). Twice secretary of state (1841–1943, 1850–1852), Daniel Webster is better known as a prominent senator and orator. Born January 18, 1782, in Salisbury, New Hampshire, he graduated from Dartmouth College in 1801, read law, and was admitted to the bar in 1805. Early on he developed a reputation as an orator, but he also taught and practiced law in Portsmouth, New Hampshire, until winning election to the House of Representatives in 1813. He served two terms and then moved to Boston in 1817, while at the same time becoming a prominent lawyer involved in various landmark Supreme Court decisions. From 1823 to 1841, he served in the House (1823–1827) and Senate (1827–1841), a spokesman against states' rights and nullification. His first stint as secretary of state, under Presidents William Henry Harrison and John Tyler, was highlighted by the Webster-Ashburton Treaty (1842),* settling the long-standing Maine boundary dispute. He was also involved in efforts to control the African slave trade and in preliminary discussions in regard to a treaty with China. Webster resigned in 1843 because of personal financial problems and opposition to Tyler's desire to annex Texas. He continued to oppose Texas annexation, as a senator, 1845–1850, and returned to the State Department under President Millard Fillmore. Here he defended the principles of American government in the Hulsemann letter, described by Fuess as "bluster and bombast," and spent a good deal of time defending the Compromise of 1850 and the Fugitive Slave Law. He did conduct negotiations with Spain (apologizing for the Lopez filibustering* expedition to Cuba and arranging for release of the prisoners), with Mexico (concerning a Tehuantepec transit treaty), and with Great Britain (over problems emanating from the Clayton-Bulwer Treaty, 1850).* He was still secretary of state when he died October 24, 1852, in Marshfield, Massachusetts. Webster was married twice: to Grace Fletcher (1808–1828) and to Carolina le Roy (1829–1852). Baxter, Maurice G., *One and Inseparable: Daniel Webster and the Union* (1984); Brown, Norman D., *Daniel Webster and the Politics of Availability* (1969); *DAB*, 19:585; Dalzell, Robert F., *Daniel Webster and the Trial of American Nationalism* (1973); Fuess, Claude M., *Daniel Webster*, 2 vols. (1930, 1968); Peterson, Merrill D., *The Great Triumvirate: Webster, Clay, and Calhoun* (1987); Shewmaker, Kenneth E., "Daniel Webster and the Politics of Foreign Policy, 1850–52," *Journal of American History* 63 (September 1976): 303–15; "Forging the 'Great Chain': Daniel Webster and the Origins of American Foreign Policy toward East Asia and the Pacific, 1841–1852," *Proceedings of the American Philosophical Society* 129 (September 1985): 225–59.

WEBSTER-ASHBURTON TREATY (1842). Daniel Webster,* secretary of state, and Lord Ashburton, British minister of the United States, negotiated this settlement of the northeast boundary dispute. Anxious to please the British and using what was averred to be a Mitchell Map* with a line drawn to indicate a boundary agreed to in 1782 (but what was really an irrelevant French map), Webster agreed to the British claims and ceded much of the disputed territory, although the United States retained 7,000 of the 12,000 square miles. The treaty also contained provisions for extradition. The Webster-Ashburton Treaty was much criticized in America but was important in maintaining Anglo-American harmony. Bemis, Samuel F., *John Quincy Adams and the Foundations of American Foreign Policy* (1949); Jones, Howard, *To the Webster-Ashburton Treaty* (1977); Pletcher, David, *The Politics of Annexation* (1973).

WEDDELL, ALEXANDER WILBOURNE (1876–1948). Ambassador to Argentina during the Great Depression and to Spain during the early years of World War II, Alexander W. Weddell was born in Richmond, Virginia, on April 6, 1876, attended local schools, and went to work at the age of sixteen. In 1904, he was a clerk at the Library of Congress while attending George Washington Law School, from which he received a degree in 1908. From 1907 to 1910, he was private secretary to the U.S. minister to Denmark, Francis Egan. Weddell entered the consular service in 1910 and, over the next eighteen years, served as consul* or consul general in Zanzibar, Catania (Italy), Athens, Calcutta, and Mexico City. Between 1928 and 1933, he devoted his time to philanthropic and civic affairs, but in 1933 the Roosevelt administration named him ambassador to Argentina. In six years there, he represented the United States at several international conferences, including the Montevideo Conference (1933)* and the Chaco Peace Conference (1935). He also spread the Good Neighbor Policy* into Argentina social life by introducing mint juleps at cocktail parties. In 1939, he was transferred to Spain, where his main function was to ensure the continued neutrality* of the Franco government. He tried to do this with promises of American aid. When Secretary of State Cordell Hull* squelched that idea, Weddell's relations with Spanish Foreign Minister Serrano Suñer broke down, and his effectiveness declined, bringing about his resignation in 1942. He returned to private life with his wife, Virginia Chase Steedman, whom he had married in 1923. On New Year's Day, 1948, Weddell and his wife were killed in a rail accident near Sedalia, Missouri. *DAB*, Supp. 4:863; Halstead, Charles R., "Diligent Diplomat: Alexander W. Weddell as American Ambassador to Spain, 1939–42," *Virginia Magazine of History and Biography* (January 1974): 3–38; *New York Times*, January 2, 1948; Weddell, Alexander W., *Introduction to Argentina* (1939).

WELLES, BENJAMIN SUMNER (1892–1961). A career diplomat who figured prominently in Latin American and World War II policymaking, Sumner Welles was born in New York City on October 14, 1892, and graduated from Harvard in 1914. Entering the State Department in 1915, he held minor posts in Tokyo, Buenos Aires, and Washington before 1922 and was a delegate or special representative on several international commissions during the 1920s. In 1933, President Franklin D. Roosevelt named Welles assistant secretary of state, a position he held until 1937 except for the period of April to December 1933, when he was ambassador to Cuba. This was a stormy period in Cuban politics, and Welles, who believed in the principle of friendly intervention, was instructed to help stabilize the situation and thus enhance U.S.-Cuban trade relations. During his short tenure, Welles saw one government overthrown and replaced by a distinctly anti-American one, which ultimately forced his departure from the island. He recommended armed intervention and encouraged other Cuban factions to bring about a new government. Returning to Washington as assistant secretary of state and, in 1937, under secretary of state, Welles continued to be involved deeply in hemispheric affairs and is credited with originating the phrase *Good Neighbor Policy.** He coordinated the flow of information during the Munich Conference (1938),* headed the U.S. delegation to the Panama Conference (1939) on inter-American security, made an exploratory mission to several European capitals (1940), meeting with Adolf Hitler, Benito Mussolini, and Neville Chamberlain, and accompanied Roosevelt to the Arcadia Conference* with Winston Churchill (1941). Because of disagreements with Secretary of State Cordell Hull* over access to the president and, possibly, attitudes toward the Soviet Union, Welles resigned in September 1943 amid a good deal of controversy in the press. Most of his time after 1943 was devoted to writing about foreign affairs in such books as *The Time for Decision* (1944), *Where Are We Heading* (1946), *We Need Not Fail* (1948), and *Seven Decisions That Shaped History* (1950). Thrice married, Welles died in Bernardsville, New Jersey, on September 24, 1961. *New York Times*, February 10, 1940, September 25, 1961; Pratt, Julius W., "Cordell Hull," in Bemis, Samuel F., ed., *American Secretaries of State and Their Diplomacy*, vol. 13 (1964); Ronning, Neale C., and Albert P. Vannucci, eds., *Ambassadors in Foreign Policy* (1987); Smith, Robert F., *The United States and Cuba, Business and Diplomacy, 1917–1960* (1960); Woods, Randall B., *The Roosevelt Foreign Policy Establishment and the "Good Neighbor": The United States and Argentina, 1941–1945* (1979); *WWWA*, 4 (1961–1968):995.

WELSH, JOHN (1805–1886). A native of Philadelphia, where he was born November 9, 1805, John Welsh was educated privately and entered business at an early age. He became a commission merchant in partnership with his brothers and became wealthy from the West Indies trade. He was chairman of the Board of Finance for the Centennial Exposition in Philadelphia, 1873–1877, and, because he was a Republican, he was named minister to Great Britain in 1877. He stayed two years in London, reporting on financial and business conditions there, a matter of particular concern because of the general economic decline of the 1870s in both the United States and Britain, and securing the release of several Americans imprisoned for Fenian-related crimes. Welsh, past seventy at the time of his appointment, found the British climate unhealthful and returned to Philadelphia in 1879. There he was active in hospital and Episcopal church affairs and founded a chair of history and English literature at the University of Pennsylvania. He died in Philadelphia on April 19, 1886. *NCAB*, 3:412; Willson, Beckles, *America's Ambassadors to England, 1785–1929* (1929).

WHEATON, HENRY (1785–1848). Born in Providence, Rhode Island, on November 27, 1785, Henry Wheaton graduated from Rhode Island College (now Brown University) in 1802, read law, and was admitted to the bar in 1805. After a study trip to Europe, 1805–1806, he practiced law in Providence until 1812 and then became editor of the *National Advocate* (New York City), a Republican political paper. Between 1814 and 1827 Wheaton held posts related to the judiciary, including that of Supreme Court reporter (1816–1827), in which he published the annual volumes of court decisions. His diplomatic career began in 1827 with appointment as chargé d'affaires* to Denmark. There until 1835, he negotiated a highly successful settlement in 1830 compensating Americans claiming violations of neutral rights. His success was due in part to his interest in Scandinavia and knowledge of Danish; he spent time in Denmark studying and writing about Scandinavian law. In 1835, he was transferred to Berlin, the first American representative there since 1797, and two years later he was appointed minister to Prussia, a post he held until 1846. In Prussia, he successfully negotiated a commercial treaty with the German *Zollverein* and an extradition treaty, but neither was ratified while he was minister. Another treaty, to remove special taxes laid against German emigrants to America and their property, was successfully ratified. After a year of travel in Europe, Wheaton returned to the United States to teach international law, but failing health intervened, and he died on March 11, 1848, in Dorchester, Massachusetts. Although Wheaton's diplomatic career was generally constructive, his fame rests on his legal scholarship: *Elements of International Law* (1836) and *History of the Law of Nations in Europe and America . . .* (1842) are considered classics. Baker, Elizabeth F., *Henry Wheaton, 1785–1848* (1937, 1971); *DAB*, 20:39.

WHEELER, JOHN HILL (1806–1882). Born in Murfreesboro, Tennessee, on August 2, 1806, John Hill Wheeler graduated from Columbian College (now George Washington University) in 1826 and received an M.A. degree from the University of North Carolina in 1828, a year after he was licensed to practice law. From 1827 to 1830, he sat in the North Carolina legislature. In 1832, Wheeler was secretary of the French spoliations claims* commission, and from 1837 to 1841 he served as superintendent of the Charlotte (North Carolina) branch of the U.S. mint. He was state treasurer of North Carolina, 1842–1844, and spent the next several years writing *Historical Sketches of North Carolina* (1845–1851). After another term in the state legislature (1852–1853), Wheeler was named minister to Nicaragua in 1854. His three years in the Central American nation were highlighted by William Walker's* filibustering* expedition, and Wheeler was censured by Secretary of State William L. Marcy* for recognizing a Walker-supported government in Nicaragua before he was instructed to do so. In May 1856 he contravened his instructions by recognizing Walker as president of Nicaragua, thinking this recognition best for the country's political stability. This action led to his forced resignation in 1857. After his diplomatic career, Wheeler spent his time engaged in historical and journalistic work, completing two more books on North Carolina. He was married twice and died in Washington on December 7, 1882. *DAB*, 20:50; *NCAB*, 6:485; Scroggs, W. O., *Filibusters and Financiers* (1916); Wheeler, John Hill, *Diario de John Hill Wheeler* (1974), translated from an unpublished manuscript in the Library of Congress.

WHITE, ANDREW DICKSON (1832–1918). Andrew D. White, long-time president of Cornell University and ambassador to Germany, was born November 7, 1832, in Homer, New York, attended Hobart College, and graduated from Yale in 1853. He traveled and studied in Europe and was an attaché at the U.S. legation in St. Petersburg (1854–1855). From 1857 to 1864 he taught history at the University of Michigan, returning to New York to take a seat in the state senate. Through this office, he helped found Cornell in 1865 and then became its first president, serving from 1867 to 1885, except for two years (1879–1881) he spent as minister to Germany, where his duties were routine. From 1885 to 1889 he traveled in Europe to recover his health, and from 1889 to 1892, he held teaching posts in various places. In 1892 he was named minister to Russia, where even ordinary diplomatic functioning was hampered by the small size and limited budget of the legation. He left Russia in 1894 and three years later received his most important assignment as ambassador to Germany (1897–1902). In Berlin, White got along well with Foreign Minister Prince Bernhard Von Bülow despite serious policy differences over Samoa, commerce, and the Spanish-American War. Additionally, he led the U.S. delegation at the first Hague Conference (1899).* In retirement after 1902, White wrote his *Autobiography of Andrew Dickson White* (2 vols., 1905), served as a Smithsonian Institution regent, and lived in Ithaca, New York. He was twice married and in 1884 helped establish the American Historical Association and was its first president. He died November 4, 1918, in Ithaca. Altschuler, Glenn C., *Andrew D. White, Educator, Historian, Diplomat* (1979); *DAB*, 20:28; Dennis, A.L.P., *Adventures in American Diplomacy, 1896–1906* (1928); *New York Times*, November 5, 1918.

WHITE, HARRY DEXTER (1892–1948). Born in Boston on October 29, 1892, Harry Dexter White graduated from Stanford (B.A., 1924; M.A., 1925) and Harvard (A. D., 1930) after service in World War I and two years as director of an American Expeditionary Forces orphanage. From 1929 to 1934, he taught at Harvard and Lawrence (Wisconsin) colleges. Joining the Treasury Department in 1934, White became director of monetary research in 1938 and was an adviser to Secretary of the Treasury Henry Morgenthau on international monetary matters. In 1941–1942, he was instrumental in early planning for the United Nations,* especially with respect to international monetary problems. He devised a plan in 1943, proposing an interallied stabilization fund, later called a United Nations stabilization fund, which, combined with a Bank for Reconstruction and Development, would amount to a kind of central bank for the world and would be capitalized at $5 billion. Much of the substance of this plan was adopted at the Bretton Woods Conference (1944)* as the International Monetary Fund

(IMF).* White served as U.S. director of the IMF from 1946 to 1947. However, his career was clouded by a House Committee on Un-American Activities investigation in 1948, during which it was alleged that he had used his influence to place employees with Communist sympathies in key Treasury Department positions with access to secret information. White denied the charges but died a short time later on August 16, 1948, in Fitzwilliam, New Hampshire. Eckes concludes that White liked the economic planning of the Soviet Union and hoped for postwar U.S.-Soviet collaboration but was too independent to have accepted the discipline required of a Communist party member. Eckes, Alfred E., *The Search for Solvency* (1975); *New York Times*, August 18, 1948; White, Harry Dexter, "The Monetary Fund: Some Criticism Examined," *Foreign Affairs* 23 (January 1945): 195–210.

WHITE, HENRY (1850–1927). An important figure in Anglo-American diplomacy from the 1880s until 1905, Henry White was born into a wealthy Baltimore family on March 29, 1850. By the time he was thirty, he had spent more than half his life in Europe, studying under private tutors, learning languages and politics, and making social contacts. In 1883, he became legation secretary in Vienna; the same year, he moved to London as second secretary. He served ten years as second, and then first, secretary, providing valuable assistance to a succession of U.S. ministers. In 1893, White, a Republican, was replaced for political reasons, but in 1897, with the return of his party to the White House, he went back to London as first secretary and remained there for eight important years. His role was crucial because of his excellent rapport with Presidents William McKinley and Theodore Roosevelt, their secretaries of state, various ambassadors, and British political leaders. His work in London facilitated the Hay-Pauncefote Treaty,* the Alaskan boundary settlement, and the Venezuelan dispute (1902–1903).* White worked with Secretary of State John Hay* on the Open Door policy* and in general contributed much to the Anglo-American rapprochement of those years. Two ambassadorial posts followed his tenure in London: ambassador to Italy (1905–1907) and ambassador to France (1907–1909), but both missions were less eventful, although White did represent the United States at the Algeciras Conference (1906)* and at the International Conference on Agriculture, held in Rome. A minor controversy arose soon after his arrival in France when he requested the wearing of formal uniforms at his first reception, giving the affair the look of a comic opera and the aroma of mothballs. His recall by President William Howard Taft in 1909 was for "personal reasons," and it contributed to the split between Taft and Theodore Roosevelt that divided the Republican party. President Woodrow Wilson appointed White to the U.S. delegation to the Paris Peace Conference,* the only Republican so named. At the conference, White's major concerns were Fiume,* Shantung,* and Balkan problems, and although he became a firm advocate of the League of Nations,* his overall influence on Wilson or within the delegation was limited. White was married twice, and he died in Lenox, Massachusetts, on July 15, 1927. *DAB*,

20:102; Nevins, Allan, *Henry White: Thirty Years of American Diplomacy* (1930); *New York Times*, July 16, 1927; Wilson, Beckles, *America's Ambassadors to France, 1777–1927* (1928).

WHITLOCK, BRAND (1869–1934). America's minister to Belgium during World War I, Brand Whitlock also achieved fame as the Progressive era mayor of Toledo, Ohio. He was born in Urbana, Ohio, on March 4, 1869, graduated from high school in Toledo, and later studied law, gaining admittance to the Illinois bar in 1894 and the Ohio bar three years later. He worked as a journalist in Toledo (1887–1890) and in Chicago (1891–1893) and as a clerk in the office of the Illinois secretary of state (1893–1897) before settling in Toledo as a lawyer in 1897. There he became friends with Mayor Sam Jones, working as his legal adviser and, in 1905, succeeding him as mayor. After eight years as mayor, Whitlock accepted appointment as minister to Belgium, where he hoped he could do some writing. He served until 1919, when the legation was raised in status to an embassy, making him an ambassador. Only his first year was relaxed; he began writing a novel, and his duties were mainly social. After the outbreak of World War I and the German sweep through Belgium, Whitlock stayed at his post, urging resistance fighters and providing relief through the Committee for the Relief of Belgium, organized by Herbert Hoover to bring food and other supplies to Belgians. He also repatriated Germans caught in Belgium by the war and persuaded the Germans to stop sending Belgians to work camps in Germany. He made an effort to save the life of Edith Cavell, the British nurse convicted and executed for collaborative activities. Whitlock, who became a hero to the Belgians, resigned his post in 1921 but spent a good deal of time in Belgium and France in later years. He did some more writing, including *Belgium: A Personal Record* (2 vols., 1919) and a number of novels, and died in Cannes, France, on May 24, 1934. Whitlock was married twice. Crunden, Robert, *A Hero in Spite of Himself* (1969); *DAB*, 20:137; *New York Times*, May 25, 27, 1934.

WHITNEY, JOHN HAY (1904–1982). Grandson of Secretary of State John Hay* and born August 17, 1904, in Ellsworth, Maine, John Hay Whitney graduated from Yale (1926), studied a year at Oxford, and entered the film industry. He founded Pioneer Pictures, the first to produce Technicolor feature films, and from 1936 to 1940, he was chairman of Selznick International Pictures. He served in the army air force during World War II, and in 1949, he created the John Hay Whitney Foundation, which sponsored educational programs directed toward minorities. A Republican, Whitney was appointed in 1953 by President Dwight D. Eisenhower to the Presidential Commission on Foreign Economic Policy, investigating trade and tariff programs. In 1957, he replaced Winthrop W. Aldrich* as ambassador to Great Britain, amid allegations, denied by the State Department, that Aldrich's reporting of the Suez crisis (1956)* had been deficient. His four years in Great Britain were primarily social (Whitney was a prominent "turfman" and polo enthusiast) and diplomatically uneventful. In 1957, Whitney became publisher of the *New York Herald Tribune*; upon his return from Britain in 1961, he became the paper's editor in chief as well and eventually spent almost $40 million in an unsuccessful effort to save the paper in 1966. Whitney was married twice and was active in the affairs of Yale University and the Carnegie Endowment for International Peace.* He was an art collector of significance and a trustee of the New York Racing Association for many years before his death in Manhasset, New York, on February 8, 1982. Kahn, E. J., *Jock, The Life and Times of John Hay Whitney* (1981); *New York Times*, December 28, 1956, February 9, 1982; *WWWA*, 8 (1982–1985):425.

WILLARD, JOSEPH EDWARD (1865–1924). Joseph E. Willard, whose father owned the famous Willard Hotel in Washington, was born there May 1, 1865. He graduated from Virginia Military Institute in 1886, studied law briefly at the University of Virginia and then privately, and became a prominent and wealthy Richmond lawyer. In the Spanish-American War, he was acting aide-de-camp to General Fitzhugh Lee.* Later, he organized a company of volunteers from Fairfax County, Virginia, for service in the Philippines and paid them himself. A Democrat, Willard served in the Virginia House of Delegates from 1894 to 1902 and as lieutenant governor from 1902 to 1906. He was state corporation commissioner, 1906–1910. In 1913, Willard was chosen as minister to Spain; later that year, the legation was upgraded to an embassy, making him an ambassador. Remaining in Madrid throughout Wilson's two terms, he was instructed to turn down offers to joint Spanish-American mediation to the belligerents in 1914 and again in 1916 and tried without success to facilitate cooperation in the face of German U-boat* practices. Also, Willard negotiated an agreement by which the United States exported goods to Spain and Spain supplied war materiel needed in France. After his return to the United States, Willard practiced law in Richmond, Washington, and New York City. His daughter married Theodore Roosevelt's son Kermit. Willard himself married Belle Layton Wyatt in 1891 and died in New York City on April 4, 1924. *DAB*, 20:236; *New York Times*, April 5, 1924.

WILLIAMS, EDWARD THOMAS (1854–1944). Born October 17, 1854, in Columbus, Ohio, Edward T. Williams graduated from Bethany College, West Virginia, in 1875 and was ordained a minister of the Disciples of Christ. Between 1875 and 1887, he held pastorates in Springfield, Illinois; Denver; Brooklyn; and Cincinnati. In 1887, he went to China as a missionary, remaining nine years before leaving the ministry in 1896. In 1897, he was U.S. vice–consul general* in Shanghai; the next year he became a translator for the Chinese government. In 1901, he returned to the U.S. diplomacy as a Chinese secretary in the American legation at Peking; after seven years, he moved to Tientsin as consul general. From 1909 to 1911, he was in Washington as assistant chief in the Division of Far Eastern Affairs, returning to China in the latter year to be first secretary and in charge of the American legation at Peking, where he urged recognition of the

Yuan government. As chief of the Far Eastern Division in the State Department, 1914–1918, Williams handled the response to the Twenty-one Demands* of Japan (1915) and was involved in the preparation of the Lansing-Ishii Agreement (1917).* In 1919, he went to the Paris Peace Conference* as an adviser on Far Eastern affairs. From 1918 to 1927, except for his time in Paris, he taught at the University of California and wrote *China Yesterday and Today* (1923) and *A Short History of China* (1928). Twice married, Williams died in Berkeley, California, on January 27, 1944. Crane, Daniel M., and Thomas A. Breslin, *An Ordinary Relationship* (1986); *DAB*, Supp. 3:825; Li, Tien-yi, *Woodrow Wilson's China Policy, 1913–1917* (1952).

WILLIAMS, JAMES (1796–1869). Little is known of James Williams's early life except that he was born in Grainger County, Tennessee, on July 1, 1796, and had some military experience as a young man. In 1841, he founded the *Knoxville Post* and was its editor for several years; in 1843, he served in the Tennessee legislature. Around 1850, he moved to Nashville, published essays, and continued to be active in public issues and Democratic politics. He became minister to Turkey in 1858. There for two years, he tried to secure consular jurisdiction for Americans involved in civil litigation and traveled around the Middle East working for laws or regulations that would better protect American missionaries. Williams returned to the United States as the Civil War threatened and during the war was a diplomatic agent for the Confederacy, working with Henry Hotze* in his publicity and propaganda efforts. He was especially effective in describing clearly the slavery issue in a number of British newspaper articles. Additionally, he was involved with Maximilian, the Austrian ruling Mexico under French supervision. He urged Maximilian to ally Mexico with the Confederacy, or at least recognize it, and he kept in close contact with James M. Mason* and John Slidell* concerning Maximilian, who might actually have recognized the Confederacy had Louis-Napoleon given him the choice. After the war, Williams remained in Europe, dying in Graz, Austria, on April 10, 1869. He was married to Lucy Jane Graham. *DAB*, 20:267; Owsley, Frank L., *King Cotton Diplomacy*, rev. ed. (1959).

WILLIS, ALBERT SHELBY (1843–1897). Born in Shelbyville, Kentucky, on January 22, 1843, Albert S. Willis graduated from the Louisville Law School in 1863 and practiced law in Louisville from 1864 to 1874. In 1874, he became county attorney in Jefferson County, Kentucky, and three years later entered the U.S. House of Representatives, serving until 1887. In private law practice from 1887 to 1893, Willis, a Democrat, was called to public service with the return of Grover Cleveland to the White House. Appointed minister to Hawaii, he arrived soon after the Provisional Government, headed by Sanford B. Dole, had ousted Queen Liliuokalani and assumed power. He was instructed to persuade the government to dissolve itself and restore power to the queen, who would in turn grant amnesty. While Willis was able to persuade the queen to pledge amnesty, the Provisional Government leaders refused to yield, and the restoration plan failed. When annexation also failed, Willis continued as minister and managed to win respect and goodwill in a hostile environment. He died in Honolulu on January 6, 1897. In 1878, he married Florence Dulaney and was the founder and president of the Sun Life Insurance Company. *DAB*, 20:304, *FR* (1894), Appx. 2:95–97.

WILSON, FRANCIS MAIRS HUNTINGTON (1875–1946). F. M. Huntington Wilson was born in Chicago on December 15, 1875, graduated from Yale in 1897, and entered the Foreign Service in the same year. He was sent to Tokyo as second secretary of the legation, was promoted to first secretary in 1900, and remained until 1906, frequently acting as chargé d'affaires.* During a home leave in 1904 he married Lucy Wortham James. In 1906, he became third assistant secretary of state. In 1909, under the new administration of President William Howard Taft, he was chosen assistant secretary of state. Under Secretary of State Elihu Root* (1906–1908), Wilson handled Far Eastern affairs and was chairman of the Board of Examiners, Consular and Diplomatic Service. More constructive work came under Secretary of State Philander C. Knox* (1909–1913), as Wilson was instrumental in the major bureaucratic reorganization that was carried out. More (geographical) area desks were created, and the Division of Information was established to serve the press and diplomatic corps. Foreign service applicants were given stringent exams, and if they passed, more rigorous training, since a major objective was to create a more career-oriented service. Wilson's diplomatic career ended at the age of thirty-eight when he resigned in 1913 because of President Woodrow Wilson's China policy, which he regarded as a repudiation of his and Knox's policy. For a while, Wilson traveled and lived a rather aimless life, divorcing his wife in 1915 and working short stints for two Philadelphia newspapers and a New York bank. From 1927 to 1935, he was president of the M&H Manufacturing Company, which made signal devices, and from 1928 to 1932, he was director of the Philadelphia Commercial Museum. He married Hope Butler in 1925 and continued a career as a professional writer, which had begun in 1914 with *Stultitia*, a play pleading for pre–World War I preparedness. Wilson died New Year's Eve 1946 in New Haven, Connecticut. Crane, Daniel M., and Thomas A. Breslin, *An Ordinary Relationship* (1986); *NCAB*, 38:482; *New York Times*, January 1, 1947; Wilson, F. M. Huntington, *Memoirs of an Ex-Diplomat* (1945).

WILSON, HENRY LANE (1857–1932). Son of a U.S. minister to Venezuela, Henry Lane Wilson was born in Crawfordsville, Indiana, on November 3, 1857, graduated from Wabash College in 1879, and studied law in the office of Benjamin Harrison. From 1882 to 1885, he was the owner-editor of the *Lafayette Journal*, but in the latter year he went to Spokane, Washington, to practice law and involve himself in banking and real estate. He declined appointment as minister to Venezuela in 1889, when Harrison became president, but in 1897, having been badly hurt by the depression of the 1890s, Wilson went to Chile as U.S. minister. His service there, 1897–1904, was uneventful, although he took part in efforts to avert a war between Chile and Argentina. From 1905 to 1909, he was minister to Belgium, where he represented the United States at a conference revising the General Act of Brussels (1890) and at King Leopold's coronation (1909). His most noteworthy post was Mexico, where he was ambassador from 1909 to 1913. There he defended U.S. interests in the early years of the revolution, played a significant and interventionist role in the coup that led to the assassination of Francisco Madero and the rise of Victoriano Huerta, and urged, in vain, the recognition of Huerta. Ultimately President Wilson accepted his resignation in August 1913. During World War I, Wilson was involved in organizations such as the World Court League, the Security League, and the League to Enforce Peace.* In 1927, he published *Diplomatic Episodes in Mexico, Belgium, and Chile*, defending his conduct in Mexico and his relationship with Huerta. Wilson married Alice Vajer in 1884 and died in Indianapolis on December 22, 1932. *DAB*, 20:325; *FR* (1913), 692–867; Haley, P. Edward, *Revolution and Intervention: The Diplomacy of Taft and Wilson with Mexico, 1910–1917* (1970); *New York Times*, December 23, 1932.

WILSON, HUGH ROBERT (1885–1946). Born January 29, 1885, in Evanston, Illinois, Hugh R. Wilson graduated from Yale (1906) and entered the family clothing business in Chicago. Deciding to prepare himself for a career in diplomacy, he studied in Paris, 1910–1911, and worked for a time as private secretary to Edwin Morgan,* U.S. minister to Portugal. Wilson entered the Foreign Service in 1912 and held various minor posts in Guatemala City, Buenos Aires, and Bern until 1919. In 1920, he became counselor* in Berlin; in 1921, he moved to the same post in Tokyo. Wilson returned to Washington in 1924 as chief of the State Department's Division of Current Information and received his first ministerial post in 1927 with appointment as minister to Switzerland. A Republican, Wilson had favored U.S. entry into World War I on Britian's side but was disappointed by Woodrow Wilson's zealous idealism and the vindictiveness he saw in the Treaty of Versailles.* He opposed U.S. entry into the League of Nations,* but, ironically, in his ten years as minister to Switzerland (1927–1937), he came as close to being a League of Nations delegate as the United States ever had. He reported on league activities, worked closely in securing league approval of the Stimson Doctrine,* and was a delegate to the World Disarmament Conference (1932–1934).* From 1937 to 1939, he was ambassador to Germany, one of the first career diplomats to gain that rank. In Berlin, he aligned himself with the appeasers in defending the Austrian *Anschluss* and the Munich agreement.* He returned to the United States in 1939 and, during World War II, worked with the Office of Strategic Services. Wilson, who married Katherine Bogle in 1914, died in Bennington, Vermont, on December 29, 1946. He wrote extensive memoirs: *The Education of a Diplomat* (1938); *Diplomat between Wars* (1941), and *A Career Diplomat* (1960; 1973). *DAB*, Supp. 4:897;

Offner, Arnold, *American Appeasement: U.S. Foreign Policy and Germany, 1933–38* (1969).

WILSON PLAN (1914). Named for its designer, President Woodrow Wilson, this plan was brought to the Dominican Republic in 1914 by the first of the Fort Missions* in order to settle a civil war. Opposing factions were to select a provisional president and hold elections under U.S. observation. If the elections were carried out satisfactorily, American support would follow; otherwise new elections would have to be held. The Fort Mission was to brook no argument, and a show of military force accompanied the mission. Thought was given to employing the same plan in Haiti the following year, but the political system lacked organized parties and was handicapped further by a politically ignorant and indifferent populace. Munro, Dana G., *Intervention and Dollar Diplomacy in the Caribbean, 1900–1921* (1964).

WINANT, JOHN GILBERT (1889–1947). John G. Winant was born in New York City on February 23, 1889, and graduated from Princeton (M.A., 1925), having also attended Dartmouth. While still a college student, Winant began a political career as a Republican in New Hampshire state politics, serving in the state house (1917, 1922–1924), the state senate (1921–1923), and as governor (1925–1926, 1931–1935). Between 1926 and 1931, he had been the assistant director of the International Labor Organization (ILO)*; he returned to that organization in 1937 after a stint as head of the Social Security Board (1935–1936) and was ILO's director in 1939–1940. That year, President Franklin D. Roosevelt appointed Winant ambassador to Great Britain, a position he held throughout World War II until 1946. Although he did not play an important role in wartime Anglo-American diplomacy, Winant served well as a symbol of U.S. commitment to the people of Britain. He had exceptional rapport with Britain trade unions, with whose goals he sympathized. He helped plan the Moscow Conference (1943)* and served on the European Advisory Commission, helping plan the future of liberated Europe and the occupation of Germany. Returning to the United States in 1946, Winant helped create the United Nations Economic and Social Commission and served as the U.S. representative to the United Nations Educational, Scientific, and Cultural Organization before his death November 3, 1947, in Concord, New Hampshire. He married Constance Rivington Russell in 1919 and wrote an account of his experience in London, *Letter from Grosvenor Square* (1947). Bellush, Bernard, *He Walked Alone: A Biography of John G. Winant* (1968); *DAB*, Supp. 4:899; Gaddis, John L., *The United States and the Origins of the Cold War* (1972); *New York Times*, September 15, November 4, 1947.

WOMEN'S INTERNATIONAL LEAGUE FOR PEACE AND FREEDOM (WILPF). This pacifist organization was founded in 1915 as the International Congress of Women and met at the Hague. Jane Addams led the U.S. delegation and remained active in the organization for twenty years. The present name was adopted in 1919 and the headquarters moved to Geneva to be near the League of Nations,* inasmuch as the first goal of the WILPF was to make the league an effective organization in working toward the removal of the causes of war through disarmament and whatever was necessary to create a reconciled Europe. The U.S. committee, led by Dorothy Detzer and Emily Greene Balch after Jane Addam's death, worked for an arms embargo on Japan after the Manchurian crisis (1931)* and after the outbreak of general war in China in 1937. The WILPF in the United States supported neutrality* legislation and urged that it include a prohibition on the sale of raw materials to belligerents. Detzer was influential in the creation of the Nye Committee* and its investigation of the causes of World War I. The group continued to oppose U.S. entry into World War II until the attack on Pearl Harbor.* After the war, the WILPF was involved with refugee aid and in its own survival, which was marginal for several years. The U.S. committee gave support to the agencies of the United Nations* and supported the admission of the People's Republic of China to the UN. Headquartered in Geneva, Switzerland, the WILPF has national organizations in twenty-two countries and is active in a wide range of issues related to peace, human rights, and disarmament. Bussey, Gertrude Carman, and Margaret Tims, *The Women's International League for Peace and Freedom, 1915–1965* (1965); Divine, Robert A., *The Illusion of Neutrality* (1962); Schapsmeier, Edward L., and Frederick H. Schapsmeier, *Political Parties and Civic Action Groups* (1981).

WOOD, LEONARD (1860–1927). Leonard Wood, whose long military career was closely tied to U.S. diplomacy, was born on October 9, 1860, in Winchester, New Hampshire. He attended local schools, graduated from Harvard Medical School in 1884, and joined the army. In 1890 he married Louisa A. Condit Smith, and, by 1891, having served in the Indian wars against Geronimo, he had risen to the rank of captain. He was President William McKinley's personal physician and a close friend of Theodore Roosevelt, cooperating with Roosevelt in the formation of the Rough Riders and serving as the organization's military commander. After the Spanish-American War, he was first military governor of Santiago, Cuba, but, by 1899, had become military governor of the whole island, serving until 1902 and effectively stabilizing politics and finances, establishing or improving schools and police, and in general working toward a smooth transition to an elected Cuban government. In 1903, Wood held a similar position in Moro Province in the Philippines. Here, however, he had to pacify the area and, according to some critics, did so ruthlessly. By this time, he was a major general. From 1910 to 1914, he was army chief of staff. As World War I drew near, Wood advocated preparedness and civilian military training, but in the war itself, he saw no active duty, a source of controversy. By 1920, Wood's fame as a military man and his Republicanism made him a logical contender for the presidential nomination, but the effort failed. In 1921, he was sent on a special investigatory mission to the Philippines; this mission led to his appointment as governor-general of the islands, where he built up the power of the office and blocked Philippine moves toward independence. He died in Boston on August 7, 1927, following surgery for a brain tumor. *DAB*, 20:467; Hagedorn, Herman, *Leonard Wood*, 2 vols. (1931); Hitchman, James H., *Leonard Wood and Cuban Independence, 1898–1902* (1971); Lane, Jack C., *Armed Progressive* (1978); *New York Times*, August 7, 1927; Onorato, Michael P., *Leonard Wood as Governor-General* (1969).

WOOD, THOMAS BOND (1844–1922). A missionary and educator who played a prominent role in Argentine and Peruvian life for over forty years, Thomas B. Wood was born in Lafayette, Indiana, on March 17, 1844, and graduated from Asbury University (1863) and Wesleyan College (1864). He taught at Wesleyan for three years while undergoing Methodist ministerial training and was ordained in 1867, the same year he married Ellen Dow. From 1867 to 1869, he was president of Valparaiso (Indiana) University; in 1869, he was sent to Argentina as a missionary. His life in Argentina was rich and varied. He was chairman of the Rosario board of school examiners, president of the national educational commission, a U.S. consul* (1873–1878), and a lawyer (admitted to practice, 1875). He spent four years (1877–1881) in Montevideo editing a religious newspaper, *La Evangelista*, and from 1879 to 1887 he was the superintendent of all Methodist missions in South America. Wood founded the Methodist Seminary in Buenos Aires in 1889. He spent years from 1891 to 1913 principally in Peru, where he was engaged in a struggle to remove constitutional restrictions on religious liberty while continuing the same kind of educational and religious activities he had done in Argentina. In 1913, Wood returned to the United States and two years later he retired. In addition to his religious interests, he was an amateur astronomer of some note, proficient enough to teach the subject at the national university in Argentina. He died in Tacoma, Washington, on December 18, 1922. *DAB*, 20:473; *New York Times*, December 19, 1922.

WOODFORD, STEWART LYNDON (1835–1913). Born in New York City on September 3, 1835, Stewart L. Woodford graduated from Columbia College in 1854, studied law, and was admitted to the bar in 1857. He practiced law in New York City and became active in Republican party politics well before the Civil War. During the war, he was a lieutenant colonel in a New York volunteer brigade and after the war was the first military governor of Charleston, South Carolina. From 1867 to 1869, he was lieutenant governor of New York, but he lost a race for governor in 1870. Woodford served a term in Congress (1873–1874) and then became federal district attorney for the Southern District of New York (1877–1883). Between 1883 and 1897, he was once again in private law practice. In 1897, the McKinley administration named him minister to Spain. He tried to shore up the deteriorating U.S.-Spanish relationship over Cuba and persuaded the Spanish government to accede to U.S. demands, but war came nevertheless. In an unprecedented diplomatic move, he authorized the Spanish government to publish all the negotiations he had conducted with it. After his mission, which terminated with the outbreak of war, Woodford practiced law in New York City and was a director and general counsel of the Metropolitan Life Insurance Company and a trustee or director of several other organizations. In 1909, he was president of the Hudson-Fulton Celebration Commission. Twice married, Woodford died in New York on February 14, 1913. *DAB*, 20:489; Dennis, A.L.P., *Adventures in American Diplomacy, 1896–1906* (1928); *NCAB*, 9:2; *New York Times*, February 15, 1913.

WORLD BANK. See **INTERNATIONAL BANK FOR RECONSTRUCTION AND DEVELOPMENT.**

WORLD COURT. See **PERMANENT COURT OF INTERNATIONAL JUSTICE.**

WORLD DISARMAMENT CONFERENCE (1932–1934). The largest international conference ever held up to that time, the World Disarmament Conference opened February 2, 1932, with delegations from fifty-nine countries attempting to do for land armaments what the Washington Conference (1921–1922)* and London Conference (1930)* had done for naval armaments. The first year's session was full of problems, ranging from Franco-German rivalry to the de facto state of war in Manchuria to a realization of the complexity of the task. The U.S. delegation—led by Norman Davis,* and including Hugh Gibson,* Senator Claude Swanson (D., Virginia), Hugh Wilson,* and Dr. Mary E. Woolley, president of Mount Holyoke College—stayed generally aloof but collaborated on matters of real importance. The chances for an effective disarmament treaty were virtually ended by Germany's unilateral decision in October 1933 to rearm and increase the size of its army irrespective of the limitations imposed by the Treaty of Versailles (1919).* The World Disarmament Conference met in annual session through 1934 but without any tangible results. The Women's International League for Peace and Freedom* was significant in bringing this conference about by means of a massive petition drive. Dulles, Allen W., "Progress Toward Disarmament," *Foreign Affairs* 10 (October 1932): 54–65; Ferrell, Robert H., *American Diplomacy in the Great Depression* (1957); *FR* (1932), 1:1–574; *FR* (1933), 1:1–356; *FR* (1934), 1:1–216; *FR* (1935), 1:1–61; Offner, Arnold A., *The Origins of the Second World War* (1975).

WRIGHT, JOSEPH ALBERT (1810–1867). Born in Washington, Pennsylvania, on April 17, 1810, Joseph Wright moved to Indiana with his family around 1820, spent two years at the state seminary (later Indiana University), read law, and was admitted to the bar in 1829. He entered law practice in Rockville, Indiana, married Louisa Cook (1831), served two terms in the state legislature (1833, 1836), and advanced to the state senate (1839), the U.S. House of Representatives (1843–1845), and, finally, to the state house in Indianapolis (1849–1857), where, as governor, he worked to improve the farmers' lot by creating the State Board of Agriculture and the State Agricultural Society. In

1857, the administration of President James Buchanan* named him minister to Prussia. He served until 1861 and, in 1865, was reappointed to the same post, serving until his death May 11, 1867, in Berlin. In Prussia, he worked to prevent German-Americans from being inducted into Prussian military service, to acquire German agricultural literature for U.S. farmers and agricultural societies, and to arrange for the exchange of German and American seeds. Between his two missions in Prussia, Wright served in the U.S. Senate by appointment, 1862–1863. *DAB*, 20:559; *NCAB*, 13:269.

WRIGHT, JOSHUA BUTLER (1877–1939). A career diplomat who joined the State Department in 1909 at the age of thirty-two and died as ambassador to Cuba in 1939, Joshua Butler Wright was born October 18, 1877, in Irvington-on-Hudson, New York. An 1899 graduate of Princeton, Wright was a banker (1899–1906) and a rancher (1907–1908) before entering the diplomatic ranks. From 1909 to 1923, he served in minor posts in Tegucigalpa, Honduras, Washington, D.C., Brussels, Rio de Janeiro, Petrograd, and London. In 1923, he became third assistant secretary of state; the following year, he was promoted to assistant secretary. In 1927, he was appointed to the first of a series of ministries and ambassadorships: Hungary (1927–1930), Uruguay (1930–1934), Czechoslovakia (1934–1937), and Cuba (1937–1939). Of these missions, the appointment to Cuba was the most significant. Wright was committed to a policy of nonintervention and noninterference, as opposed to Jefferson Caffery,* his predecessor, and tried to end the practice of the American ambassador's acting as a domestic policy adviser to the Cuban government. Unlike Caffery, he adopted a rather formal relationship with Fulgencio Batista, the Cuban dictator, and tried to deal with the problems of Cuban debts and American creditors. Wright, who was married twice, died in Havana on December 4, 1939. Gellman, Irwin F., *Roosevelt and Batista* (1973); *NCAB* 30:196; *New York Times*, December 5, 1939.

WRIGHT, LUKE EDWARD (1846–1922). Son of a chief justice of the Tennessee Supreme Court, Luke Edward Wright was born in Giles County, Tennessee, on August 29, 1846, served in the Confederate army, 1861–1865, attended the University of Mississippi, 1867–1868, read law, and was admitted to the bar in 1868. He married Katherine Middleton Semmes, daughter of Confederate naval hero Raphael Semmes, in 1869, and settled into law practice in Memphis. Wright won some acclaim for supervising relief work in Memphis during a yellow fever epidemic in 1878–1879 and introducing new hygienic measures in the city. In 1896, he left the Democratic party, and in 1900 he was named a member of the Second Philippine Commission. He remained in the Philippines as vice-governor 1901–1904, governor in 1904, and governor-general 1905–1906, and provided the islands with strong, rigid rule. Wright's tenure in the Philippines was marked by the first census, the first election, agricultural promotion, and highway construction. In 1906, he was appointed the first U.S. ambassador to Japan, but his year in Tokyo was uneventful, coming just prior to the anti-Japanese problems in California. Wright was secretary of war, 1908–1909, after which he lived in Memphis until his death on November 17, 1922. *DAB*, 20:561; *NCAB*, 26:94; *New York Times*, November 18, 1922.

WRISTON REPORT (1954). In 1954, Secretary of State John Foster Dulles* appointed the Public Committee on Personnel, headed by Dr. Henry M. Wriston, to investigate organizational problems in the State Department subsequent to the Foreign Service Act (1946).* Popularly known as the Wriston Report, the published finding of the committee (*Toward a Stronger Foreign Service*) recommended that State Department and Foreign Service personnel be integrated into a single administrative system, and this was carried out between 1954 and 1956. A more important recommendation was that qualified individuals from outside the Foreign Service be allowed to enter the middle ranks of the service, a process termed "lateral entry," or "Wristonization." This greatly enlarged the size of the Foreign Service and created something of a morale problem for veteran careerists. Etzold, Thomas J., *The Conduct of American Foreign Relations: The Other Side of Diplomacy* (1977); Plischke, Elmer, *Conduct of American Diplomacy* (1967).

XYZ AFFAIR (1797–1798), Franco-American diplomatic incident. In 1797, an American delegation—consisting of John Marshall,* Charles Cotesworth Pinckney,* and Elbridge Gerry—was sent to France to try to settle existing problems. Before French Foreign Minister Charles Maurice de Talleyrand would receive them, the three Americans were approached by three French agents, who attempted to extort a bribe. This incident delayed negotiations and worsened relations between France and America. When President John Adams* released the diplomatic correspondence concerning the affair to Congress in April 1798, he designated the French agents as X, Y, and Z. Public knowledge of the affair produced a hostile reaction toward the French and led to a state of quasi-war* between the two nations until the Convention of 1800* settled matters. Clarfield, Gerald H., *Timothy Pickering and American Diplomacy, 1795–1800* (1969); DeConde, Alexander, *The Quasi-War* (1966).

YALTA CONFERENCE (1945). This was the second and most controversial meeting of the wartime Grand Alliance leaders: President Franklin D. Roosevelt, Prime Minister Winston Churchill, and Premier Joseph Stalin. Meeting from February 4 to February 11 at the Crimean resort of Yalta, the Big Three dealt with the question of who should govern Poland, the nature of Security Council voting in the United Nations,* the status of postwar Germany, including reparations,* and the conditions of Soviet entry into the war in the Pacific. The Soviets agreed that in Poland, the pro-Communist Lublin government would be reorganized along more democratic lines, with elections to be held in the near future. In addition, the Soviet-Polish border was moved westward to the Curzon Line (a frontier proclaimed by Lord Curzon, an Englishman, after World War I), with Poland promised additional territory on its western front in compensation. Although some American policymakers had urged the creation of an Emergency High Commission for Europe to ensure joint Allied occupation of Eastern Europe, Roosevelt opted for a high-sounding Declaration on Liberated Europe,* in which the Allies pledged to work toward the establishment of representative governments by means of free elections in the nations liberated from the Axis. With regard to the Security Council, the permanent members were given the right to veto substantive resolutions inimical to their national interests and, in certain situations, even the discussion of those matters, thus ensuring paralysis of the United Nations in any dispute concerning two or more of the permanent members. (At the San Francisco Conference,* the veto was limited to Security Council action alone.) Little was agreed upon with respect to Germany except that the country would be divided into four zones of occupation, with the French receiving the fourth zone. The Soviets were insistent in their demands for substantial reparations to be paid by Germany for both compensatory and punitive reasons; the British and Americans, on the other hand, recalled the economic nightmare that reparations had caused after World War I. After some heated debate, the conferees agreed to let a reparations commission determine the amount of reparations, using the Soviet figure of $20 million "as a basis for discussion." In a secret U.S.-Soviet agreement, Stalin pledged to join the Far Eastern war two or three months after the German surrender in return for the cession of the Kuril Islands, lower Sakhalin, leaseholds at Port Arthur and Dairen, control of the main Manchurian railroads, and recognition of Outer Mongolia's independence from China. The Yalta Conference was the subject of intensive public criticism in the United States for a number of years after World War II on the grounds that it was a sellout of Eastern Europe and mainland China to the Soviet Union, but, according to Gaddis, Roosevelt gave away nothing not already under Soviet control or potentially so. Alperovitz, Gar, *Atomic Diplomacy* (1965); Clemens, Diane, *Yalta* (1970); Davis, Lynn Etheridge, *The Cold War Begins* (1974); *FR, The Conferences of Malta and Yalta, 1945*, pp. 549–998; Gaddis, John L., *The United States and the Origins of the Cold War* (1972); Kolko, Gabriel, *The Politics of War* (1968); McNeill, William H., *America, Britain, and Russia* (1953); Theoharis, Athon, *The Yalta Myths* (1970); Wheeler-Bennett, John W., and Anthony Nicholls, *The Semblance of Peace* (1972); Yergin, Daniel, *Shattered Peace* (1977).

YANCEY, WILLIAM LOWNDES (1814–1863). A well-known champion of slavery, William L. Yancey was born August 10, 1814, in Warren County, Georgia, and attended Williams College. He became a lawyer in 1833, practicing in Greenville, South Carolina, while editing the *Greenville Mountaineer*. In 1836, he moved to Alabama and entered politics, serving in the Alabama legislature from 1841 to 1844 and in the U.S. Congress from 1844 to 1846. He practiced law from 1848 to 1860 and achieved fame as a poised and dignified orator. After the outbreak of the Civil War, he was appointed a Confederate diplomatic commissioner in the first mission abroad. With Pierre A. Rost, Yancey interviewed Napoleon III and found him willing to follow Britain's lead in the question of Confederate recognition. Yancey also protested the Union blockade and the *Trent* affair* before resigning in September 1861. He served in the Confederate Senate from 1862 to 1863 and died in Montgomery on July 27, 1863. *DAB*, 20:592; Dubose, John W., *The Life and Times of William Lowndes Yancey* (1892); Owsley, Frank L., *King Cotton Diplomacy*, 2d ed. (1959).

YOM KIPPUR WAR (1973). Although Israel had gained considerable territory in the Six-Day War (1967),* the government still felt besieged, and an arms buildup in the Middle East continued. American diplomatic efforts failed to ease the tension, and in October 1973, during the Yom Kippur religious holiday, Egypt and Syria attacked Israel by surprise. After about two weeks of inconclusive fighting, both sides accepted a United Nations* Security Council cease-fire on October 22, which became effective after another week of fighting. The aftermath of the war saw strenuous personal diplomatic efforts, "shuttle diplomacy," by Secretary of State Henry A. Kissinger* that failed to produce any permanent Middle East peace treaty. Kissinger's work did, however, lead to the restoration of U.S.-Egyptian diplomatic relations, Israeli and Egyptian pledges to enter into further peace talks, and increased amounts of U.S. aid to both Israel and the Arab states. The war tended to elevate Anwar Sadat of Egypt as the preeminent Arab leader and contributed to the decision by the Arab members of the Organization of Petroleum Exporting Countries* to institute an oil embargo on the United States, Western Europe, and Japan, which lasted from November 1973 to March 1974. Dupuy, Trevor N., *Elusive Victory: The Arab-Israei Wars, 1947–1974* (1978); Hammond, Paul Y., *Cold War and Detente* (1975); *London Sunday Times* Insight Team, *The Yom Kippur War* (1974); Rubenberg, Cheryl A., *Israel and the American National Interest* (1986); Stookey, Robert W., *America, and the Arab States* (1975); Szulc, Tad, *The Illusion of Peace* (1978).

YOST, CHARLES WOODRUFF (1907–1981). Born November 6, 1907, in Watertown, New York, Charles W. Yost graduated from Princeton in 1928 and studied a year at the University of Paris before joining the Foreign Service in 1930. After service in minor posts in Alexandria and Warsaw, Yost resigned in 1933 and became a freelance journalist. He married Irena Oldakowska in 1934. He rejoined the State Department in 1935, and worked in arms and munitions control under the Neutrality Acts* until 1941 and held other minor State Department positions during World War II. His first prominent assignment was as secretary-general of the U.S. delegation to the Potsdam Conference (1945),* after which he was chargé d'affaires* to Siam (1945–1946); counselor* in Prague (1946–1947) and Vienna (1947–1949); director of the Office of European Affairs (1949–1950); minister-counselor in Athens (1950–1953); and deputy high commissioner to Austria (1953–1954). In 1954, Yost was named minister to Laos, the first of several appointments as chief of mission. He was the first U.S. minister of Laos, which had been granted sovereignty under the Geneva Accords (1954),* and his mission was raised to ambassadorial level in 1955 in response to a perceived Communist threat. After Laos, Yost served as ambassador to Syria (1957) and Morocco (1958–1961). In Morocco, he negotiated an agreement whereby U.S. military forces would be gradually withdrawn, easing a politically troublesome issue. In 1961–1966 and again in 1969–1971, Yost's diplomatic service was with the U.S. delegation to the United Nations.* In between, he was a senior fellow with the Council on Foreign Relations.* After 1971, Yost taught at Columbia University (1971–1973), served as president of the National Commission on U.S.-China Relations (1973–1975), and was a senior fellow at the Brookings Institution (1975–1981). He wrote *The Insecurity of Nations* (1968), *The Conduct and Misconduct of Foreign Affairs* (1972), and *History* *and Memory* (1980). He died in Washington, D.C., on May 22, 1981. *CB* (1959):492–94; *New York Times*, May 23, 1981; *WWWA* 8 (1982–1985):438.

YOUNG, ANDREW JACKSON, JR. (b. 1932). A controversial ambassador to the United Nations* (1977–1979), Andrew Young was born in New Orleans on March 12, 1932, attended Dillard University (1947–1948), and graduated from Howard University (B.D., 1955). Married to Jean Childs in 1954 and ordained in 1955, he became engaged in church and social work until 1961, when he became a staff member and officer of the Southern Christian Leadership Conference, serving as its executive director from 1964 to 1968 and vice-president from 1968–1970. In 1972, Young, a Democrat, was elected to the U.S. House of Respresentatives from an Atlanta, Georgia, district, after two years as chairman of the Atlanta Community Relations Commission. He served two terms in the House, and after working for Jimmy Carter in the 1976 campaign, he was named ambassador to the United Nations upon Carter's entrance into the White House. Young occasioned considerable controversy with his outspokenness and sympathetic attitude toward black nationalist movements in Africa, which he considered appropriate forms of self-determination.* He resigned from his United Nations post in August 1979 in the aftermath of even greater controversy regarding unauthorized talks he had with representatives of the Palestine Liberation Organization.* Returning to Atlanta, Young was elected mayor in October 1981 and reelected in October 1985. Bryant, Ira B., *Andrew Jackson Young: Mr. Ambassador* (1979); *CB* (1977):449–52; Fasulo, Linda M., *Representing America: Experiences of U.S. Diplomats at the UN* (1984); Gardner, Carl, *Andrew Young* (1978); *New York Times*, December 17, 1976, February 6, 1977, August 19, 1979, October 13, 1985.

YOUNG, JOHN RUSSELL (1840–1899). John Russell Young was born in Tyrone County, Ireland, on November 20, 1840, but his family emigrated to the United States in the next year, settled in Philadelphia for a decade, and then moved to New Orleans in 1851. Young graduated from high school in New Orleans, worked as an assistant proofreader there, and then went back to Philadelphia, where he obtained a job with the *Philadelphia Press*, first as a copy boy and later as a reporter. As a war correspondent, Young was the first to report on the Battle of Bull Run, 1861. In 1862, he became managing editor of the *Press*; four years later, he moved to the same job with the *New York Tribune*. In 1870 and 1871, he made two trips to Europe as a special agent for the Treasury and State Departments, respectively. From 1872 to 1877, he worked for the *New York Herald*, and, from 1877 to 1879, he accompanied ex-President Ulysses S. Grant on his lengthy journey abroad and wrote about it in *Around the World with General Grant* (1879). The Arthur administration appointed Young minister to China in 1882, and there he was successful in cultivating sufficient goodwill to settle all outstanding U.S. claims against China. He was unsuccessful, however, in mediating a conflict between France and China over the disputed provinces of Annam and Tong King. In 1885, he returned to his work at the *New*

York Herald, retiring in 1890. From 1897 to 1899, Young was Librarian of Congress. He died January 17, 1899, in Washington, D.C. Young's memoirs, *Men and Memories*, were edited by Mary D. Russell Young and published posthumously in 1901. Anderson, David L., *Imperialism and Idealism* (1985); *DAB* 20:630; Hunt, Michael H., *The Making of a Special Relationship: The United States and China to 1914* (1983); *New York Times*, January 18, 1899.

YOUNG, OWEN D. (1874–1962). A successful corporate executive and lawyer who played a central role in U.S. foreign policy in the 1920s, Owen D. Young was born October 27, 1874, in Van Hornesville, New York, and graduated from St. Lawrence University (1894) and Harvard Law School (1896). He lectured at Boston Law School (1896–1903) and practiced law (1903–1913) before becoming general counsel for General Electric (GE) in 1913. By 1922, he had risen to be chairman of the board, a position he held until 1939. In 1919, he organized the Radio Corporation of America (RCA) to protect U.S. patents and promote a U.S. role in international communications, and he remained chairman of RCA until 1929 when a court order forced him to choose between GE and RCA. He also was involved in the establishment of the National Broadcasting Company (NBC) in the mid-1920s. Meanwhile, he emerged in the early 1920s as a leading Democratic spokesman on foreign policy issues, and as a result, he was appointed, along with Charles G. Dawes,* to the Allied Reparations Commission in 1923. On that commission, he was a principal author of the Dawes Plan* and then an influential mediator in winning its acceptance by other governments. In 1929, Young presided over a reparations conference in Paris, out of which emerged the Young Plan,* his handiwork. He devised the Bank for International Settlements (BIS), part of the Young Plan, as a clearinghouse for international financial transactions. On the whole, Europeans were impressed with his fairness and ability. Young was mentioned as a possible Democratic presidential nominee in 1932 but declined consideration because of his wife's poor health. Early in Franklin D. Roosevelt's administration, he was an economic adviser, but his close Wall Street and public utility ties made him suspect to many New Dealers. After retiring from GE in 1939 (only to return from 1942–1944), he reentered public life one more time, as an adviser for the Marshall Plan* in 1947. Otherwise he lived on the family farm in Van Hornesville with Louise Powis Clark, his second wife (his first wife, Josephine Shelden Edmunds, died in 1935), and worked on community matters, dairy farming, and educational issues. Young died in St. Augustine, Florida, on July 11, 1962. Case, Everett, and Josephine Young Case, *Owen D. Young and American Enterprise* (1982); *DAB*, Supp. 7:808–10; Jones, Kenneth P., *U.S. Diplomats in Europe, 1919–1941* (1981); Leffler, Melvyn, P., *The Elusive Quest* (1979); *New York Times*, July 12, 1962.

YOUNG AMERICA. This term refers to the heightened spirit of nationalism in America in the 1850s, following the Mexican War. It was spurred by the 1848 revolutions in Europe and the large numbers of recent Irish and German

immigrants at this time. One goal of their enthusiasm was the push for intervention against the despotisms still controlling much of Europe. A main target
was the Hungarian revolution, led by Louis Kossuth, that had been harshly
suppressed by Austria, with help from Russia. In 1851, Kossuth came to the
United States and received a hero's welcome and a substantial amount of money
for his cause but, to his great disappointment, no move toward intervention. The
concept of Manifest Destiny* and the activities of filibusters* are also linked to
Young America. Curti, Merle, "Young America," *American Historical Review* 32
(1926): 34–55; Riegel, Robert E., *Young America, 1830–1850* (1949, 1973); Spencer,
Donald S., *Louis Kossuth and Young America* (1977).

YOUNG PLAN (1929). This plan was a further refinement of the World War
I reparations* question and was worked out by a committee led by Owen D.
Young,* an American financial expert. The committee recommended that Germany pay thirty-seven annuities averaging £100 million (less than the £125
million stipulated in the Dawes Plan*), followed by twenty-two smaller payments
equal in toto to war debts owed the United States. The German government
would be responsible for transferring the money into currencies of the creditor
nations. Two-thirds of each annuity could be delayed a maximum of two years
in the event of financial exigencies, and a Bank of International Settlements was
to be created to receive and distribute reparations payments. Adoption of the
plan was complicated somewhat by conflict between Britain and France over the
percentage of payments each was to receive. Finally, the plan was approved by
Britain, France, Germany, and twelve other nations at a conference January 20,
1930, and put into effect May 17, 1930. However definitive the plan might have
appeared as a solution to the reparations issue, it did not survive long after the
onset of the Great Depression, as payments were suspended by the Hoover
moratorium* in 1931 and, to all practical intent, terminated at the Lausanne
Conference (1932).* Carr, E. H., *International Relations between the Two World Wars
[1919–1939]* (1947); Davis, Joseph S., *The World between the Wars, 1919–39: An
Economist's View* (1975); Ellis, L. Ethan, *Republican Foreign Policy, 1921–1933* (1968);
FR (1929), 2:1025–83.

ZANJON, PACT OF (1878), Cuban-Spanish treaty. This treaty ended the Ten Years' War between Spain and Cuban insurgents, who had not been able to win U.S. support of their cause. The treaty ended the insurgency through the granting of amnesty and the promise for Cuba of a government modeled on the one in Puerto Rico, although neither side knew just what kind of government Puerto Rico had. Emigrant rebels from this war came to the United States and helped lay the groundwork for the public sympathy toward Cuba at the time of the Spanish-American War. Cortada, James W., *Two Nations over Time: Spain and the United States, 1776–1977* (1978); Millis, Walter, *The Martial Spirit* (1931).

ZEMURRAY, SAMUEL (1877–1961). A native of Bessarabia, where he was born sometime in 1877, Samuel Zemurray came to the United States in 1892 and settled in Louisiana. He was part owner of the Hubbard-Zemurray Steamship Company, a major banana producer in Honduras and, after 1899, a subsidiary of United Fruit.* In 1910, he supported a successful revolution in Honduras, led by Manuel Bonilla and American adventurer Lee Christmas but officially opposed by the U.S. government. Bonilla, who became president of Honduras, tried to obtain a loan from Zemurray rather than take one from the J. P. Morgan interests under U.S. government supervision, but when the Senate Foreign Relations Committee quashed a proposed treaty for a customs collectorship, all loan arrangements collapsed. In the 1920s, Zemurray owned the Cuyamel Fruit Company, a major competitor of United. When he sold Cuyamel to United in 1930, he emerged as United's largest stockholder. During the mid-1930s, he improved United's fortunes as chief of operations and rose to the presidency of the company in 1938, an office he held every year but one until 1951. He was known for his philanthropy and his opposition to Huey Long in Louisiana politics. Zemurray died November 30, 1961, in New Orleans. Munro, Dana G., *Intervention and Dollar Diplomacy in the Caribbean, 1900–1921* (1964); *New York Times*, December 2, 1961.

ZIMMERMANN TELEGRAM (1917). This telegram, purportedly written January 16, 1917, by German Under Secretary of State Arthur Zimmermann and sent to the German minister in Mexico, Heinrich von Eckhardt, proposed that should the United States join the war against Germany, a German-Mexican alliance should be forged, with Mexico receiving financial aid and restitution of the Mexican cession in return for its aid to Germany against the United States. The telegram was intercepted by British intelligence and passed on to the United

States, where it had a great effect on the Woodrow Wilson administration, as the president was convinced of German treachery. Made public on February 28, the telegram aroused hostility toward Germany and accelerated U.S. entrance into the war. Some historians believe that the telegram was a hoax perpetrated by the British to push the United States into the war on their side. Tuchmann, Barbara, *The Zimmermann Telegram* (1966); Zeman, Z.A.B., *The Gentlemen Negotiators* (1971).

CHRONOLOGY OF AMERICAN DIPLOMATIC HISTORY

This appendix lists in chronological order major events in American diplomatic history between 1775 and 1988. Items that are entries in the main body of this volume are indicated by an asterisk. Wherever possible, as precise a date as can be determined has been given; important sources for this information are Richard B. Morris (ed.), *Encyclopedia of American History* (1953 and 1976 eds.), William L. Langer (ed.), *An Encyclopedia of World History* (1948), and Richard Dougall and Mary Patricia Chapman, *United States Chiefs of Mission, 1778–1973* (1973).

1776	(Sept. 17)	Plan of 1776,* model treaty, devised by John Adams.*
	(Sept. 26)	Diplomatic commission appointed by Continental Congress to seek treaties in the European nations.
1778	(Feb. 6)	Franco-American Alliance* signed.
1779	(Apr. 12)	Treaty of Aranjuez* concluded between Spain and France.
1781	(June 14)	U.S. peace commission appointed by Congress.
	(Aug. 10)	Robert Livingston* named first secretary of foreign affairs by Congress.
1783	(Apr. 15)	Peace of Paris,* in provisional form, ratified by Congress.
	(Sept. 3)	Peace of Paris,* ending the American Revolution and securing U.S. independence, signed by the United States and Great Britain.
1784	(May 7)	John Jay* appointed secretary of foreign affairs by Congress.
	(Aug. 30)	Opening of China trade with arrival of *Empress of China* in Canton.
1785	(June 1)	Beginning of diplomatic relations with Great Britain.
1786	(Aug. 29)	Jay-Gardoqui Treaty* negotiations broken off.
1791	(May 13)	Beginning of diplomatic relations with Portugal.
1793	(Apr. 22)	Neutrality Proclamation* issued by President Washington.
	(Aug. 2)	Recall of French envoy "Citizen" Gênet demanded by the Washington administration.
1794	(Nov. 19)	Jay's Treaty* with Great Britain signed in London.
1795	(Aug. 3)	Treaty of Greenville,* adjusting the northwest boundary, signed by the United States and several Indian tribes under British protection.
	(Oct. 27)	Pinckney's Treaty* signed by the United States and Spain.
1796	(Sept. 19)	Washington's Farewell Address* published.
1797	(Dec. 5)	Beginning of diplomatic relations with Prussia (Germany).
1798	(Apr.)	XYZ affair* made public by President John Adams.*
	(Nov.-Sept. 30, 1800)	Undeclared naval war (quasi-war)* with France.

1800	(Sept. 30)	Convention of 1800* signed, ending quasi-war between the United States and France.
	(Oct. 1)	Louisiana given back to France by Spain in Treaty of San Ildefonso.*
1802	(Apr. 18)	Treaty of Amiens* signed, bringing about a short-lived truce in Napoleonic Wars.
1803		U.S. expedition against Barbary pirates* brought release of American prisoners and stability to Mediterranean area by 1805.
	(Apr. 30)	Treaty signed by the United States and France providing for Louisiana Purchase.*
1805	(July 23)	*Essex* decision* announced, prohibiting U.S. practice of "continuous voyage."
1806	(Apr. 18)	Non-Importation Act,* prohibiting import of certain British goods, passed by Congress.
	(Nov. 21)	Berlin Decree* announced by Napoleon, placing Great Britain under blockade* and forbidding trade in British goods.
	(Dec. 31)	Abortive Monroe-Pinkney Treaty* signed in London.
1807	(June 22)	U.S.S. *Chesapeake* fired upon and boarded by H.M.S. *Leopard* in incident known as *Chesapeake* affair.*
	(Nov. 11)	Orders-in-Council,* blockading France, issued by Great Britain.
	(Dec. 17)	Milan Decree* made public by Napoleon.
	(Dec. 22)	Embargo Act* signed; cut off virtually all U.S. trade.
1809	(Mar. 1)	Non-Intercourse Act* passed by Congress.
	(Apr. 18-19)	Erskine Agreements* exchanged between the United States and Great Britain.
	(July 21)	Erskine Agreements* repudiated by Great Britain.
	(Nov. 5)	Beginning of diplomatic relations with Russia.
1810	(March)	Decree of Rambouillet* announced by France.
	(May 1)	Macon's Bill No. 2* passed by Congress.
	(Aug. 5)	Cadore letter,* suggesting French repeal of Berlin* and Milan* decrees, delivered to the United States.
1812	(June 16)	British Orders-in-Council* suspended.
	(June 18)	War declared on Great Britain.
1814	(Sept.-June 1815)	Congress of Vienna, major European diplomatic conference, held.
	(Dec. 24)	Treaty of Ghent,* ending War of 1812, signed by the United States and Great Britain.
1817	(Apr. 28-29)	Rush-Bagot Agreement,* demilitarizing the Great Lakes, signed by the United States and Great Britain.
1818	(Sept.)	Congress of Aix-la-Chapelle* held; discussion held on European recapture of rebellious Spanish American colonies.
	(Oct. 20)	Convention of 1818* signed by the United States and Great Britain, setting several boundary and other problems.
1819	(Feb. 22)	Adams-Onís Treaty* signed by the United States and Spain.
1822	(Mar. 28)	Recognition of newly independent Latin American nations urged by House resolution.

1823	(Dec. 2)	Monroe Doctrine* spelled out in president's annual message to Congress.
1825	(Feb. 18)	Anglo-Russian Convention* signed, adjusting Russian-Canadian boundary.
1826	(June 22-July 15)	Panama Congress* met without U.S. representation.
1829	(Dec.)	U.S. Minister Joel R. Poinsett* recalled from Mexico because of involvement in internal political affairs.
1831	(July 4)	French spoliation claims* treaty signed.
1832	(Aug.-Sept.)	U.S.S. *Lexington* raided Falkland Islands, creating U.S.-Argentine diplomatic conflict under chargé d'affaires Francis Baylies.*
1837	(Dec.)	*Caroline* incident,* involving the United States and Canada.
1838	(Jan.-Mar.)	Roostook War* between Maine and Nova Scotia.
	(Nov. 7)	Beginning of diplomatic relations with Austria.
1839		*Amistad* affair,* diplomatic conflict between the United States and Spain.
1840	(Sept. 15)	Beginning of diplomatic relations with Sardinia (Italy after 1861).
1841	(Nov.)	*Creole* affair* begun by slave mutiny on U.S.S. *Creole*.
1842	(Aug. 9)	Webster-Ashburton Treaty* signed by the United States and Great Britain, settling northeast boundary issue.
	(Aug. 29)	Treaty of Nanking* signed by Great Britain and China.
1844	(Feb. 28)	Secretary of State Abel P. Upshur* killed by explosion aboard U.S.S. *Princeton*.*
	(July 3)	Treaty of Wang-hsia* signed by the United States and China.
1845	(Feb. 28)	Joint Resolution on Texas* passed by Congress, paving way for annexation.
	(Mar. 28)	United States-Mexican relations suspended by Mexico.
	(Nov. 7-Mar. 12, 1846)	Diplomatic mission to Mexico of John Slidell.*
	(Dec. 27)	Phrase Manifest Destiny* used in *The United States Magazine and Democratic Review* editorial.
1846		Yucatán caste war,* prompting U.S. thoughts of intervention and annexation.
	(May)	Bear Flag revolt* of Americans against Mexican rule in California.
	(May 13)	War declared on Mexico.
	(June 15)	Oregon Treaty* signed by the United States and Great Britain.
	(Dec. 12)	Bidlack Treaty signed with New Granada.
1848	(Feb. 2)	Treaty of Guadalupe-Hidalgo,* ending Mexican War, signed.
1849	(Mar. 17)	Beginning of diplomatic relations with Egypt.
1850	(Apr. 19)	Clayton-Bulwer Treaty* signed by the United States and Great Britain.
1853	(June 29)	Beginning of diplomatic relations with Switzerland.
	(July)	Visit to Japan of Commodore Matthew C. Perry.*
	(Dec. 30)	Gadsden Purchase* made.

1854   (Feb. 28)   U.S. steamer *Black Warrior** seized by Spain.
        (Mar. 31)   Treaty of Kanagawa* signed by the United States and Japan.
        (June 5)   Marcy-Elgin Treaty,* on U.S.-Canadian fishing and trade mat-
                      ters, signed.
        (July 13)   Greytown, Nicaragua, destroyed by U.S.S. *Cyane*, in incident
                      related to Accessory Transit Company.*
        (Oct. 18)   Ostend Manifesto* issued as public statement by U.S. ministers
                      to Great Britain, France, Spain.
1858   (June 26-29) Treaties of Tientsin* signed by China with the United States,
                      Great Britain, Russia, and France.
        (July)   Shimoda Convention* negotiated with Japan by Townsend
                      Harris.*
1861   *Foreign Relations** first published by State Department.
        (Nov. 8-   *Trent* affair,* diplomatic crisis with Great Britain over capture
        Dec. 25)   of Confederate agents.
1862   (Apr. 7)   African Slave Trade Treaty* signed by the United States and
                      Great Britain.
1863   (Feb.)   Mediation of Civil War proposed by France's Napoleon III.
1864   (Apr. 10)   Maximilian made emperor of Mexico by French intervention.
1866   (May 31)   Fenian uprising between Irish-Americans and Canadian troops.
1867   (Mar. 30)   Alaska purchase* made by the United States in treaty with
                      Russia.
        (June 19)   Maximilian executed by Mexican nationalists under Benito
                      Juárez.
1868   (July 28)   Burlingame Treaty* signed by the United States and China,
                      clarifying U.S. rights in China and reaffirming Chinese
                      sovereignty.
1870   (Jan.-July)   Failure of Grant administration efforts to annex Santo Domingo.
1871   (Mar. 1)   James Milton Turner* named minister to Liberia; first black to
                      serve at ministerial rank.
        (May)   U.S.-Korean conflict upon arrival of Low-Rogers Expedition.*
        (May 8)   Treaty of Washington* signed by the United States and Great
                      Britain, settling Confederate raider claims.
1873   (Oct. 31)   *Virginius* episode,* sparked by Spanish capture of the American
                      steamer *Virginius*.
1874   (Sept.-Oct.) Bern Conference* held; Universal Postal Union established.
1875   (Mar. 18)   Hawaiian Reciprocity Treaty* ratified by Senate.
1876   African International Association* founded by King Leopold II
                      of Belgium to encourage exploration and colonization of sub-
                      Saharan Africa.
        (Jan. 17)   Samoan Treaty,* giving the United States the right to use har-
                      bor at Pago Pago, ratified by Senate.
1882   (May 6)   Chinese Exclusion Act* passed, restricting Chinese immigration
                      into the United States for ten years.
        (May 22)   U.S.-Korean treaty signed, recognizing independence of Korea.
1883   (June 11)   Beginning of diplomatic relations with Persia (Iran).
1884   (Nov. 15-   Berlin Conference* on questions concerning the Congo held.
        Feb. 26,
        1885)

1887	(Nov.)	Ratifications of Pearl Harbor Treaty* exchanged, granting the United States the right to use Pearl Harbor as a coaling and repair station.
1889	(June 14)	Berlin Treaty* signed, providing tripartite (U.S., British, and German) control over Samoa.
	(Oct. 2-Apr. 19, 1890)	Washington Conference,* first Pan-American Conference, held; Bureau of American Republics* created.
1890	(Oct. 15-Mar. 31, 1891)	Diplomatic dispute with Italy following lynching of eleven Italians in New Orleans.
1891	(May 5)	Chilean vessel *Itata*★ detained by U.S. authorities in San Diego.
	(Oct. 16)	U.S.S. *Baltimore* incident* in Valparaiso, Chile.
1892	(Feb. 29)	Anglo-American arbitration* treaty signed, referring Bering Sea dispute* to mixed international tribunal.
1893		Rank of ambassador first used by the United States for missions in Great Britain, France, Italy, and Germany.
	(Mar. 11)	James H. Blount* sent to Hawaii to investigate overthrow of Queen Lilioukalani by annexationist faction.
1894	Aug.-Apr. 1895)	Sino-Japanese War* over Korea.
	(Aug. 7)	Republic of Hawaii recognized by Cleveland administration.
1895	(July 20)	Venezuelan crisis* climaxed with assertive note of Secretary of State Richard Olney.*
1898	(Jan.)	American Asiatic Association* created to encourage a more active U.S. policy toward Asia.
	(Feb. 9)	De Lome letter* criticizing President McKinley published.
	(Feb. 15)	U.S.S. *Maine*★ sunk at Havana.
	(Apr. 20)	War declared on Spain; Teller Amendment* added to resolution declaring war on Spain.
	(July)	Anglo-American League* founded to encourage closer and more cordial relations between the two nations.
	(July 7)	Hawaii formally annexed by the United States.
	(Nov. 19)	Anti-Imperialist League* founded to combat America's colonial policy.
	(Dec. 10)	Treaty of Paris,* ending Spanish-American War, signed by the United States and Spain.
1899	(Jan. 20)	Schurman Commission* appointed to investigate political situation in Philippines.
	(Feb. 4-mid-1902)	Philippine insurrection against U.S. rule.
	(Mar. 20)	United Fruit Company* founded.
	(May 18-July 29)	First Hague Peace Conference* held; Permanent Court of International Arbitration* established.
	(Sept. 6)	First set of notes comprising Open Door policy* circulated by John Hay.*
	(Dec. 2)	Convention of 1899* signed by the United States, Great Britain, and Germany, partitioning Samoa.
1900	(June-Aug.)	Siege of foreign compound in Peking during Boxer Rebellion.*

(Feb. 5)	First Hay-Pauncefote Treaty* signed by the United States and Great Britain.
(July 3)	Second set of notes comprising Open Door policy* circulated by John Hay.*
1901 (Mar.)	First Hay-Pauncefote Treaty* rejected by British.
(Mar. 2)	Platt Amendment,* allowing U.S. intervention in Cuba, adopted by Senate.
(Oct. 22-Jan. 31, 1902)	Mexico City Conference,* on inter-American affairs.
(Nov. 18)	Hay-Pauncefote Treaty,* abrogating Clayton-Bulwer Treaty,* signed by the United States and Great Britain.
1902 (Jan. 9)	Hepburn Bill,* authorizing a Nicaraguan canal, passed by House of Representatives.
(Jan. 30)	Anglo-Japanese alliance* made by treaty.
(June 28)	Spooner Act* passed by Congress, deciding on Panama route for isthmian canal.
1902 (Dec.)	Venezuelan dispute* over European debts set off by naval intervention of Germany, Great Britain, and Italy.
(Dec. 11)	Cuban Reciprocity Treaty signed, providing U.S. market for Cuban sugar and Cuban market for U.S. goods.
1903 (Jan. 22)	Hay-Herrán Treaty,* for isthmian canal, signed by the United States and Colombia.
(Jan. 24)	Hay-Herbert Treaty,* fixing Alaska-Canada boundary, signed.
(Aug. 12)	Hay-Herrán Treaty* rejected by Colombian Senate.
(Oct.)	Alaska Arbitral Tribunal announces settlement of Alaska boundary dispute* between the United States and Canada.
(Nov. 3)	Revolt of Panama against Colombia successfully accomplished.
(Nov. 18)	Hay-Bunau-Varilla Treaty,* giving the United States the right to build Panama Canal, signed.
1905 (Feb. 15)	Roosevelt Corollary* to Monroe Doctrine* made public.
(July 29)	Taft-Katsura Agreement* made, recognizing territorial status quo in Far East.
(Sept. 5)	Treaty of Portsmouth* signed by Russia and Japan after negotiations coordinated by Theodore Roosevelt.
1906 (Jan.-Mar.)	Algeciras Conference* to settle Franco-German conflict over Morocco.
(July 25-Aug. 27)	Rio de Janeiro Conference*; forceful means of collecting international debts considered.
1907 (Feb. 24)	Gentlemen's Agreement,* to ease U.S.-Japanese tensions, concluded.
(July 15-Oct. 15)	Second Hague Peace Conference.*
(Nov.-Dec.)	Treaties of Washington signed by nations of Central America at conference in Washington.
(Dec. 16-Feb. 22, 1909)	Great White Fleet* sent on world cruise to show U.S. naval power.

1908	(Nov. 30)	Root-Takahira Agreement* made between the United States and Japan to ease mutual tensions.
1909	(June)	Hukuang Railway loan* made to China; U.S. participation signified policy of dollar diplomacy.*
1910		Carnegie Endowment for International Peace* founded.
	(July 12- Aug. 30)	Buenos Aires Conference.*
1911	(July 7)	North Pacific Sealing Convention* signed, resolving pelagic-sealing dispute.
1912	(Aug. 2)	Lodge Corollary* to Monroe Doctrine supported by Senate resolution.
	(Aug. 14)	U.S. Marine intervention in Nicaragua.
	(Aug. 24)	Panama Canal Act passed, favoring the United States with preferential tolls.
1913	(Apr.)	"Cooling-off" treaties of William Jennings Bryan* negotiated.
1914	(Apr. 21)	Veracruz, Mexico, bombarded by U.S. naval forces.
	(May 20- June 30)	ABC mediation,* to settle U.S.-Mexican dispute, held.
	(June 15)	Preferential tolls for U.S. ships ended with repeal of that clause in Panama Canal Act (1912).
	(Aug. 5)	Bryan-Chamorro Treaty* signed, giving the United States the right to build a canal across Nicaragua.
	(Aug. 19)	Neutrality proclamation issued by Wilson after outbreak (Aug. 1) of World War I in Europe.
1915		League to Enforce Peace* founded.
		Women's International League for Peace and Freedom* founded.
	(May 5)	Luxury liner *Lusitania** sunk off Irish coast.
	(July 29)	U.S. Marine intervention in Haiti.
1916	(Feb. 22)	U.S. aid to Allies against Central Powers pledged in House-Grey Memorandum.*
	(May 4)	*Sussex* pledge* made by Germany.
	(Nov. 29)	U.S. Marine intervention in the Dominican Republic.
1917	(Jan. 7)	Treaty to purchase Virgin Islands* ratified by Senate.
	(Feb. 28)	Zimmermann Telegram,* from Germany to Mexico, made public.
	(Apr. 6)	War declared on Germany.
	(Nov. 2)	Lansing-Ishii Agreement,* stabilizing Far Eastern affairs, signed.
	(Nov. 7)	Interruption of diplomatic relations with Russia.
	(Dec. 7)	War declared on Austria-Hungary.
1918	(Jan. 8)	Fourteen Points* presented by Wilson to Congress.
	(Mar. 3)	Treaty of Brest-Litovsk* signed, ending hostilities between the Central Powers with Russia.
	(Apr. 10)	Webb-Pomerene Act* passed, enabling U.S. businesses to compete abroad on more favorable terms.
	(Aug.-Apr. 1920)	U.S. intervention in Siberia.

1919	(Jan. 12- June 28)	Paris Peace Conference* held, resulting in the Treaty of Versailles* ending World War I.
	(Jan. 25- Feb. 14)	Covenant of the League of Nations* drafted.
	(Apr.)	King-Crane Commission,* to investigate postwar conditions in Middle East, appointed.
	(June 28)	Treaty of Versailles* signed, ending World War I.
	(Nov. 19)	First negative Senate vote on Treaty of Versailles.*
1920	(Jan. 10)	First meeting of League of Nations.*
	(Mar. 19)	Second and final negative Senate vote on Treaty of Versailles.*
1921		Council on Foreign Relations* created.
	(Apr.)	Thomson-Urrutia Treaty* ratified, providing $25 million to Colombia over the Panama issue.
	(May 19)	Emergency Quota Act* passed, limiting immigration into the United States.
	(Aug. 25)	Berlin Treaty* signed by the United States and Germany, formally ending World War I between the two nations.
	(Oct.)	Permanent Court of International Justice (World Court)* formally established under the authority of the League of Nations.*
	(Nov. 12- Feb. 6, 1922)	Washington Conference on the Limitation of Armaments* held.
	(Dec. 13)	Four-Power Treaty* approved at Washington Naval Conference.*
1922	(Feb. 6)	Five-Power Treaty* approved at Washington Naval Conference.*
	(Feb. 6)	Nine-Power Treaty* signed at the Washington Naval Conference.*
1923	(Mar. 25- May 3)	Santiago Conference* held; Gondra Treaty, on peaceful settlement of inter-American disputes, approved.
	(Aug. 31)	U.S.-Mexican diplomatic relations reestablished after signing of Bucareli Agreement.*
1924	(Apr. 9)	Dawes Plan,* on German reparations* payments, reported.
	(May 24)	Rogers Act,* reorganizing and professionalizing Foreign Service, passed.
	(May 26)	Johnson-Reed Act* passed, severely restricting immigration into the United States.
	(July)	Termination of Dominican Republic intervention.
1925	(Dec. 1)	Treaty of Locarno* signed, enhancing European security.
1927	(May)	Peace of Tipitapa* signed, ending Nicaraguan civil war.
	(June 1)	Beginning of direct diplomatic relations with Canada
	(June 20- Aug. 4)	Geneva Naval Conference* held in attempt to bring about further naval disarmament.
1928	(Jan. 16- Feb. 18)	Havana Conference,* on U.S.-Latin American matters.
	(June)	Anglo-French Naval Agreement* signed.
	(Aug. 27)	Kellogg-Briand Pact,* outlawing war, signed.

	(Dec. 17)	Clark Memorandum, repudiating Roosevelt Corollary,* prepared by J. Reuben Clark.*
1929	(June 17)	Young Plan,* rearranging German reparations* payments, agreed upon.
	(Oct. 4-6)	Rapidan Conference* between the United States and Great Britain; naval disarmament discussed.
1930	(Jan. 21-Apr. 22)	Further naval disarmament discussed at London Naval Conference.*
1931	(June 20)	Reparations* payments suspended by Hoover moratorium.*
	(Sept. 30)	Part of South Manchurian railway destroyed in Mukden incident.*
1932	(Jan. 7)	Stimson Doctrine,* on nonrecognition of governments created by aggression, pronounced.
	(Jan. 28)	Far Eastern situation worsened by Shanghai incident.*
	(Feb. 2)	World Disarmament Conference* convened in Geneva.
	(Oct. 4)	Lytton Commission* report, on Manchuria, made public.
1933	(Jan.)	Termination of U.S. intervention in Nicaragua.
	(Mar. 4)	Good Neighbor Policy* emphasized in Roosevelt's inauguration address.
	(Apr. 13)	Ruth Bryan Owen* appointed minister to Denmark, first woman to hold ministerial rank in U.S. diplomacy.
	(June 12-July 27)	London Economic Conference; no progress in international economic cooperation.
	(Nov. 16)	Roosevelt-Litvinov Agreements* signed, establishing diplomatic ties between the United States and the USSR.
	(Dec. 3-29)	Montevideo Conference.*
1934	(Mar.)	Export-Import Bank* created.
	(June 12)	Reciprocal Trade Agreements Act* signed into law.
	(Aug. 6)	Termination of U.S. intervention in Haiti.
	(Sept.)	First meeting of Nye Committee,* investigating causes of U.S. entry into World War I, held.
1935	(May)	Outbreak of the Italo-Ethiopian War.*
	(Aug. 31)	Neutrality Act (1935)* signed into law.
	(Dec.-Mar. 1936)	Second London Naval Conference* held.
1936	(Feb. 29)	U.S. neutrality* extended by Neutrality Act (1936).*
	(July 18-1939)	Spanish Civil War.*
	(Nov.)	Anti-Cominterm Pact* signed by Germany and Japan, with Italy joining the following year.
	(Dec. 1-23)	Buenos Aires Conference,* on hemispheric peace and solidarity, held.
1937	(May 1)	U.S. neutrality* extended and broadened in Neutrality Act (1937).*
	(Oct. 5)	International "quarantine" of aggressors suggested by Roosevelt in Chicago speech.
	(Nov.)	Delegates from various Western nations met at the Brussels Conference* and discussed possible responses to Japan's invasion of China.

	(Dec. 12)	U.S.S. *Panay** sunk in Yangtze River by Japanese planes.
1938	(Jan. 10)	Ludlow Amendment* proposal rejected by House of Representatives.
	(Mar. 18)	Expropriation of U.S. and British oil properties carried out by Mexican government.
	(Sept. 29)	Hitler appeased at Munich Conference.*
	(Dec. 9-27)	Lima Conference,* on hemispheric solidarity, held.
1939	(Aug. 23)	Nazi-Soviet Non-Aggression Pact* signed.
	(Sept. 1)	Beginning of World War II in Europe; invasion of Poland by Germany.
	(Sept. 5)	Neutrality* proclamation issued by Roosevelt.
	(Oct. 3)	Declaration of Panama made, creating sea safety zones around Western Hemisphere.
	(Nov. 4)	U.S. neutrality* altered by Neutrality Act (1939).*
	(Dec. 14)	Final meeting of League of Nations.*
1940	(May)	Committee to Defend America by Aiding the Allies (CDAAA)* established.
	(June)	America First,* major noninterventionist group, created.
	(July)	Century Group,* pro-interventionist group, created.
	(July 30)	Act of Havana approved, providing hemispheric guardianship for territories of European states conquered by Axis.
	(Sept. 27)	Tripartite Pact* signed, creating Axis.
1941	(Mar. 11)	Lend-Lease* Act passed by Congress.
	(Apr.)	Fight for Freedom Committee,* interventionist organization, founded.
	(Aug. 12)	Atlantic Charter,* a set of principles to guide Allies in World War II, signed in Newfoundland at Atlantic Conference.*
	(Nov. 19)	Mexican expropriation controversy settled in U.S.-Mexican agreement.
	(Dec. 7)	Japanese attack on Pearl Harbor.*
	(Dec. 22-Jan. 14, 1942)	Arcadia Conference* held, concerning U.S.-British military strategy.
1942	(Jan. 1)	United Nations Declaration,* for Allied unity against Axis, signed.
	(Jan. 15-28)	Rio de Janeiro Conference* on wartime hemispheric solidarity against Axis.
	(Aug. 12-15)	Moscow Conference on joint military planning.
1943	(Jan. 14-25)	Casablanca Conference,* on U.S.-British military planning.
	(May 8-June 3)	Food and Agricultural Organization planned at Hot Springs Conference.*
	(May 12-25)	TRIDENT Conference* in Washington; U.S.-British military planning.
	(May 29-June 3)	Algiers Conference,* concerning U.S.-British joint military planning in Mediterranean theater of World War II.
	(Aug. 11-24)	Quebec Conference* between the United States and Great Britain, concerning military planning, including cross-channel invasion.

	(Oct. 18-30)	Allied military coordination and postwar planning discussed at Moscow Conference.*
	(Oct. 30)	Four-Power Declaration on General Security* approved at Moscow Conference.*
	(Nov. 4)	Connally Resolution,* pledging postwar cooperation by the United States in an international organization, passed by Senate.
	(Nov. 9)	United Nations Relief and Rehabilitation Administration (UN-RRA)* created.
	(Nov. 22-26)	Cairo Conference,* concerning Far Eastern strategy in World War II.
	(Nov. 28-Dec. 1)	Teheran Conference,* first wartime Big Three meeting.
1944	(July 1-22)	Bretton Woods Conference* held; the International Monetary Fund (IMF)* and the International Bank for Reconstruction and Development (IBRD)* created.
	(Aug.)	Morgenthau Plan,* on policy for defeated Germany, drawn up.
	(Aug. 21-Oct. 7)	Dumbarton Oaks Conference,* on United Nations* planning, held.
	(Sept. 11-16)	Quebec Conference,* between the United States and Great Britain concerning postwar plans for Germany and military strategy in the Pacific.
	(Sept. 23)	JCS 1067,* dealing with postwar Germany, completed.
	(Oct. 9-20)	Polish question and other wartime issues discussed by Great Britain and USSR at Moscow Conference.*
1945	(Jan. 31-Feb. 2)	Preparations for Yalta Conference* made by Americans and British at Malta Conference.*
	(Feb. 4-11)	Yalta Conference,* on postwar matters; second wartime Big Three meeting.
	(Feb. 21-Mar. 8)	Mexico City Conference,* on regional security.
	(Apr. 25-June 26)	San Francisco Conference,* creating United Nations.*
	(June 5)	First meeting of Allied Control Council,* supervising body for German affairs after World War II.
	(July 17-Aug. 2)	Potsdam Conference,* concerning postwar issues in Europe; final wartime Big Three meeting.
	(Aug. 2)	Council of Foreign Ministers* confirmed in Potsdam Prolocol.
	(Aug. 21)	Lend-Lease* aid terminated.
	(Nov. 20-Oct. 1, 1946)	German war crimes trials conducted by International Military Tribunal of Nuremberg.*
	(Dec. 16-26)	World War II peace settlement discussed by Allied Foreign Ministers at Moscow Conference.*
1946	(Jan.-Apr.)	Iran crisis* brought on by presence of Soviet troops.
	(Mar. 5)	"Iron curtain"* publicized in Churchill's speech, Fulton, Missouri.
	(May)	Acheson-Lilienthal Plan* for international atomic energy control made public.

(June 3- Nov. 12, 1948)	Japanese war crimes trials conducted by International Military Tribunal for the Far East.*	
(June 14)	Baruch Plan on international control of atomic energy presented to the United Nations* by Bernard M. Baruch.*	
(July 29- Oct. 15)	Paris Conference* held to draft treaties with defeated minor nations of Axis.	
(Dec. 2)	Financial merger of U.S. and British occupation zones formalized in Bevin-Byrnes Bizonal Fusion Agreement, creating entity known as Bizonia.*	

1947   (Mar. 12)   Truman Doctrine* announced in speech requesting aid for Greece and Turkey.

(Mar. 12-
Apr. 14)   Various postwar matters disputed by Allied Foreign Ministers at Moscow Conference.*

(June 4)   Marshall Plan* outlined by Secretary of State George Marshall* in speech at Harvard.

(July)   Publication of George F. Kennan's* *Foreign Affairs* article outlining containment.*

(July 12-
Sept. 22)   Paris Conference* held for European nations to plan uses of Marshall Plan* aid.

(July 26)   National Security Act passed by Congress, creating the Central Intelligence Agency (CIA)* and the National Security Council.*

(Sept. 2)   Rio Treaty* signed, providing inter-American security guarantees.

(Oct. 30)   General Agreement on Tariffs and Trade (GATT)* concluded.

1948   (Feb. 23)   Six-Nation Conference on Germany* convened.

(Mar. 17)   Brussels Pact* signed by Great Britain, France, the Netherlands, Belgium, and Luxembourg, creates a defensive alliance in Western Europe.

(Mar. 30-
May 2)   Bogotá Conference*; Organization of American States* created.

(Apr. 30)   Charter of Organization of American States* adopted.

(June 24)   Berlin blockade* imposed.

1949   (Jan. 20)   Point Four,* technical assistance program, outlined in Truman's inaugural address.

(Feb.)   U.S. Ambassador Selden Chapin* declared *persona non grata* by Hungary.

(Mar. 2)   Post of ambassador-at-large created; Philip C. Jessup* first appointee.

(Apr. 4)   North Atlantic Treaty,* creating the North Atlantic Treaty Organization (NATO),* signed.

(May 4)   Berlin blockade* lifted.

(June 21)   Central Intelligence Agency Act signed into law, giving CIA* authority to work in secret.

(Aug.)   China White Paper* published by State Department.

(Dec. 8)   Flight of Nationalist Chinese to Formosa; end of civil war in China.

1950	(Jan.)	U.S. Minister Donald R. Heath* declared *persona non grata* by Bulgaria.
	(Jan.-Apr.)	NSC-68* drawn up by National Security Council.*
	(June 25)	Beginning of Korean War.
	(Oct. 22)	Beginning of diplomatic relations with (South) Vietnam.
1951	(Apr. 11)	Gen. Douglas MacArthur* removed from United Nations Command in Korea.
	(Sept. 1)	ANZUS Treaty* signed by the United States, Australia, and New Zealand.
	(Sept. 8)	Japanese Peace Treaty* signed, ending state of war and U.S. occupation of Japan; U.S.-Japanese Security Treaty signed.
1952	(May 26)	Bonn Conventions* signed by the United States, Great Britain, France, and West Germany, proclaiming German sovereignty in most matters.
1953	(July 27)	Effective date of Korean truce, concluding Korean War.
	(Oct. 1)	Mutual defense treaty signed by the United States and South Korea.
	(Dec. 4-8)	Bermuda Conference,* held by the United States, Great Britain, and France, concerning European defense matters.
1954	(Jan. 25-Feb. 18)	Berlin Conference,* dealing with German reunification, Austrian treaty, and Asian problems.
	(Mar. 1-28)	Caracas Conference,* on anticommunism in Latin America.
	(Apr.)	Domino theory* spelled out by President Eisenhower.
	(Apr. 26-July 21)	Geneva Conference,* on Korea and Indochina.
	(June)	Guatemalan crisis*; government of Jacobo Árbenz ousted by CIA-inspired coup.
	(July 21)	Geneva Accords,* concerning political and military affairs in Indochina, signed.
	(Sept.-Apr. 1955)	Quemoy-Matsu crisis*; massive retaliation* considered by the United States.
	(Sept. 8)	Manila Pact,* creating Southeast Asia Treaty Organization (SEATO),* signed.
	(Sept. 28-Oct. 23)	Paris Conference* on European defense matters; Western European Union created.
	(Dec. 2)	Mutual defense treaty signed by the United States and the Republic of China (Nationalist China).
1955	(May 15)	Austrian State Treaty* signed by the United States, Great Britain, France, the USSR, and Austria.
	(July 18-23)	Geneva Summit Conference,* on German reunification and European security.
	(Nov. 21)	Middle East Treaty Organization, outgrowth of Baghdad Pact,* created to extend containment* to that part of the world.
1956	(July-Oct.)	Suez crisis,* following nationalization by Egypt of Suez Canal.
	(Nov. 4)	Hungarian revolt crushed by the Soviet Union.
1957	(Mar. 7)	Eisenhower Doctrine* passed as joint resolution of Congress.
	(Oct. 4)	*Sputnik* launched by Soviet Union.

1958   (Nov.)   Insistence by USSR on end of four-power occupation of Berlin;
                     Berlin crisis (1958–1962)* inaugurated.
1959   (Jan. 1)   Beginning of the Fidel Castro regime in Cuba.
       (Mar.)   Central Treaty Organization (CENTO)* formed.
       (Apr. 9)   Inter-American Development Bank* chartered.
1960   (May 5)   U-2 incident,* involving the United States and the Soviet
                     Union.
       (Sept.)   Organization of Petroleum Exporting Countries (OPEC)*
                     created.
1961   (Apr. 15)   Bay of Pigs invasion* launched against Cuba.
       (May-July,   Geneva Conference,* on Laotian crisis, held.
       1962)
       (June 3-4)   Summit meeting of President Kennedy and Premier Khrusch-
                     chev in Vienna.
       (Aug. 13)   Berlin Wall constructed.
       (Aug. 17)   Alliance for Progress* created at Punta del Este, Uruguay.
       (Oct.)   Taylor-Rostow mission* sent to investigate conditions in
                     Vietnam.
1962   (Jan. 22-31) Limited economic and political sanctions placed on Cuba at
                     Punda del Este meeting* of foreign ministers of the Organiza-
                     tion of American States (OAS).*
       (Oct. 22-28) Cuban missile crisis* played out.
1963   (Aug. 5)   Partial Nuclear Test Ban Treaty* signed by the United States,
                     the USSR, and Great Britain.
1964   (Aug. 2-4)   U.S. naval vessels allegedly attacked in Gulf of Tonkin
                     incident.*
1965   (Feb. 7)   Bombing of North Vietnam begun after Vietcong attack on U.S.
                     base at Pleiku.
       (Apr. 28)   Intervention of U.S. Marines in Dominican (Republic) crisis.*
1967   (June 5-10)   Six-Day War* between Israel and Arab states Egypt and Syria.
       (June 23-25) Meeting between President Lyndon Johnson and Soviet Premier
                     Aleksei Kosygin in Glassboro, New Jersey.
1968   (Jan. 23-   *Pueblo* incident*; crew of U.S.S. *Pueblo* held by North
       Dec. 22)   Koreans.
       (Jan. 30-   Tet offensive in Vietnam War.
       Feb. 24)
       (June 12)   Non-Proliferation Treaty* approved by United Nations General
                     Assembly.
       (Aug. 28)   U.S. Ambassador John Gordon Mein* assassinated in Guate-
                     mala City.
1969   (June)   Process of Vietnamization* begun by President Richard M.
                     Nixon.
       (July 25)   Nixon Doctrine* announced in Guam.
1970   (Apr. 29-   Cambodian incursion,* aspect of Vietnam War, undertaken.
       June 30)
1971   (Feb.-Mar.)   Laotian incursion* undertaken as part of U.S. policy in Vietnam
                     War.

	(Sept. 3)	Berlin Treaty* signed, guaranteeing access to Berlin and resolving other East-West problems relating to Germany.
1972	(Feb. 21-28)	Visit of President Nixon to People's Republic of China.
	(May 22-29)	SALT I (Strategic Arms Limitation Talks*) signed by the United States and the USSR at Moscow Summit Conference.*
	(Dec. 21)	Accord signed between East and West Germany, each virtually recognizing the permanent division of Germany.
1973	(Jan. 27)	Paris Peace Agreement,* signed by the United States and North Vietnam, terminating U.S. involvement in the Vietnam War.
	(June 17-25)	Meeting of President Nixon and Soviet party leader Brezhnev in Washington.
	(Sept. 11)	Chilean President Salvador Allende overthrown by CIA-inspired military coup.
	(Oct. 6-Nov. 11)	Yom Kippur War,* with Israel fighting Egypt and Syria.
1974	(June 29-July 3)	Second Moscow Summit Conference* between Nixon and Brezhnev held.
	(Sept. 19)	John Sherman Cooper* appointed first U.S. ambassador to East Germany.
1975	(Apr. 29)	Surrender of Saigon government to North Vietnamese and Vietcong; end of Vietnam War.
	(July 30-Aug. 1)	Helsinki Conference,* on European security.
1976	(Jan. 27)	Congress disapproved further funding of pro-West faction in Angolan civil war.*
	(June 16)	U.S. Ambassador to Lebanon Francis E. Meloy, Jr.,* assassinated in Beirut.
1977	(Sept. 7)	Panama Canal Treaties* signed by the United States and Panama.
1978	(Oct.)	Camp David Accords,* between Egypt and Israel, mediated by President Carter.
1979	(Feb. 14)	U.S. Ambassador Adolph Dubs* assassinated in Kabul, Afghanistan.
	(May 4)	Margaret Thatcher becomes first female prime minister of Great Britain.
	(June 18)	President Carter and Brezhnev sign SALT II (Strategic Arms Limitation Talks)* Treaty in Vienna.
	(July 19)	Sandinistas take control of Nicaragua.
	(Nov. 4)	Beginning of Iranian hostage crisis* as Iranian militants seize hostages at U.S. embassy in Tehran.
	(Dec. 27)	Soviet troops invade Afghanistan.
1980	(Jan. 23)	President Carter announces Carter Doctrine* (the United States will defend its interests in the Persian Gulf).
	(Feb. 18)	United States resumes membership in International Labor Organization.*
	(Apr. 29)	Military mission to rescue hostages in Iran fails.
1981	(Jan. 20)	Iran frees U.S. hostages.

	(Oct. 6)	Egyptian President Anwar Sadat assassinated in Cairo.
	(Nov. 30)	Intermediate Nuclear Force (INF)* talks begin in Geneva.
1982	(Mar. 25- July 12)	Falkland Islands War* between Argentina and Great Britain.
	(June 6)	Israeli troops invade Lebanon.
	(June 29)	Strategic Arms Reduction Talks (START)* begin in Geneva.
	(July 6)	United States makes commitment to participate in multinational peacekeeping force in Lebanon.
1983	(Aug. 21)	Philippine political opposition leader Benigno Aquino assassinated in Manila.
	(Sept. 1)	USSR shoots down Korean airliner in Soviet airspace near Japan.
	(Oct. 9-15)	Kissinger Commission* tours Central America.
	(Oct. 23)	Suicide truck-bomb attack kills 241 U.S. military personnel at Beirut airport.
	(Oct. 25)	United States intervenes with military force in Grenada invasion.*
1984	(Jan. 11)	Kissinger Commission report on Central America released.
	(Feb. 26)	U.S. troops complete withdrawal from Lebanon.
	(Oct. 31)	Indian Prime Minister Indira Gandhi assassinated by Sikh extremists.
1985	(Mar. 12)	The United States and USSR resume arms talks in Geneva.
	(Sept. 9)	Reagan administration places limited sanctions on South Africa.
	(Oct. 7-9)	*Achille Lauro*, cruise ship, hijacked by Palestinian radicals.
	(Oct. 7-11)	Baker Plan to relieve international debt crisis* revealed.
	(Nov. 19- 21)	Reagan-Gorbachev summit in Geneva.
1986	(Feb. 7)	Fraudulent elections mark end of Marcos dictatorship in Philippines.
	(Feb. 18)	Angolan rebel Jonas Savimbi of UNITA receives $15 million in covert aid.
	(Apr. 15)	United States launches air strike against Libya.
	(Oct. 11-12)	Reykjavik Summit Conference* between President Reagan and Gorbachev.
	(Oct. 17)	Congress approves $100 million in aid to contras.*
	(Nov. 3)	Lebanese magazine *Al Shiraa* breaks story of Iran-contra scandal.*
1987	(Feb. 26)	Tower commission releases report on National Security Council* and Iran-contra scandal.*
	(May 17)	U.S. frigate *Stark* hit by Iraqi missile in Persian Gulf.
	(Aug. 7)	Esquipulas II* signed in Guatemala City.
	(Nov. 18)	House and Senate select committees release report on Iran-contra scandal.*
	(Dec. 7-10)	Reagan-Gorbachev summit in Washington.
1988	(May 29- June 2)	Reagan-Gorbachev summit in Moscow.
	(July 3)	U.S. cruiser *Vincennes* shoots down Iranian airliner.

KEY DIPLOMATIC PERSONNEL LISTED BY PRESIDENTIAL ADMINISTRATION

This appendix is a listing of the most important persons in American diplomatic history ordered by presidential administration. Arranged in tabular form, the appendix includes for each administration the president, secretary of state, chairman of the Senate Foreign Relations Committee, and chiefs of mission to Great Britain, France, and various other countries, depending on the time period. An asterisk indicates that the person is the subject of an entry in the main body of this volume. Principal sources for this information are Richardson Dougall and Mary Patricia Chapman, *United States Chiefs of Mission, 1778–1973* (1973), and Thomas G. Patterson et al., *American Foreign Policy: A History* (1978).

Key Diplomatic Personnel Listed by Presidential Administration

PRESIDENT	SECRETARY OF STATE	CHAIRMAN, SENATE FOREIGN RELATIONS COMMITTEE	MINISTER/ AMBASSADOR TO GREAT BRITAIN	MINISTER/ AMBASSADOR TO FRANCE	MINISTER/ AMBASSADOR TO OTHER NATIONS
George Washington (1789-1797)	Thomas Jefferson* (1789-1793) Edmund Randolph* (1794-1795) Timothy Pickering* (1795-1800)		Thomas Pinckney* (1792-1796)	Thomas Jefferson* (1789) William Short* (1790-1792) Gouverneur Morris* (1792-1794) James Monroe* (1794-1796)	John Quincy Adams* Netherlands (1794-1797)
John Adams* (1797-1801)	Timothy Pickering* (1795-1800) John Marshall* (1800-1801)		Rufus King* (1796-1803)		William Vans Murray* Netherlands (1797-1801) John Quincy Adams* Prussia (1797-1801)
Thomas Jefferson* (1801-1809)	James Madison* (1801-1809)		Rufus King* (1796-1803) James Monroe* (1803-1807) William Pinkney* (1808-1811)	Robert R. Livingston* (1801-1804) John Armstrong* (1804-1810)	Charles Pinckney* Spain (1802-1805)

PRESIDENT	SECRETARY OF STATE	CHAIRMAN, SENATE FOREIGN RELATIONS COMMITTEE	MINISTER/ AMBASSADOR TO GREAT BRITAIN	MINISTER/ AMBASSADOR TO FRANCE	MINISTER/ AMBASSADOR TO OTHER NATIONS
James Madison* (1809-1817)	Robert Smith* (1809-1811) James Monroe* (1811-1817)	James Barbour* (1816-1818)	William Pinkney* (1808-1811) Jonathan Russell* (1811-1812) John Quincy Adams* (1815-1817)	William H. Crawford* (1813-1815) Albert Gallatin* (1816-1823)	William Eustis Netherlands (1815-1818) John Quincy Adams* Russia (1809-1814)
James Monroe* (1817-1825)	John Quincy Adams* (1817-1825)	James Barbour* (1816-1818) Nathaniel Macon (1818-1819) James Brown* (1819-1820) James Barbour* (1820-1821) Rufus King* (1821-1822) James Barbour* (1822-1825)	Richard Rush* (1817-1825)	Albert Gallatin* (1816-1823)	William Pinkney* Russia (1817-1818) Henry Middleton* Russia (1820-1830) John Forsyth* Spain (1819-1823)
John Quincy Adams* (1825-1829)	Henry Clay* (1825-1829)	Nathaniel Macon (1825-1826) Nathan Sanford (1826-1827) Nathaniel Macon (1827-1828) Littleton W. Tazewell (1828-1832)	Rufus King* (1825-1826) Albert Gallatin* (1826-1827) James Barbour* (1828-1829)	James Brown* (1823-1829)	Henry Middleton* Russia (1820-1830) Henry Wheaton* Denmark (1827-1835) Joel R. Poinsett* Mexico (1825-1829)

PRESIDENT	SECRETARY OF STATE	CHAIRMAN, SENATE FOREIGN RELATIONS COMMITTEE	MINISTER/ AMBASSADOR TO GREAT BRITAIN	MINISTER/ AMBASSADOR TO FRANCE	MINISTER/ AMBASSADOR TO OTHER NATIONS
Andrew Jackson (1829-1837)	Martin Van Buren* (1829-1831)	Littleton W. Tazewell (1828-1832)	Louis McLane* (1829-1831)	William C. Rives* (1829-1832)	Anthony Butler Mexico (1830-1835)
	Edward Livingston* (1831-1833)	John Forsyth* (1832-1833)	Martin Van Buren* (1831-1832)	Edward Livingston* (1833-1835)	Henry Wheaton* Prussia (1835-1846)
	Louis McLane* (1833-1834)	William Wilkins (1833-1834)	Aaron Vail* (chargé) (1832-1836)	Lewis Cass* (1836-1842)	James Buchanan* Russia (1832-1833)
	John Forsyth* (1834-1841)	Henry Clay* (1834-1836)	Andrew Stevenson* (1836-1841)		
		James Buchanan* (1836-1841)			
Martin Van Buren* (1837-1841)	John Forsyth* (1834-1841)	James Buchanan* (1836-1841)	Andrew Stevenson* (1836-1841)	Lewis Cass* (1836-1842)	George M. Dallas* Russia (1837-1839)
					John H. Eaton Spain (1837-1840)
William Henry Harrison (1841)	Daniel Webster* (1841-1843)	William C. Rives* (1841-1842)	Andrew Stevenson* (1836-1841)	Lewis Cass* (1836-1842)	Aaron Vail* (chargé) Spain (1840-1842)
John Tyler (1841-1845)	Daniel Webster* (1841-1843)	William C. Rives* (1841-1842)	Edward Everett* (1841-1845)	Lewis Cass* (1836-1842)	Washington Irving* Spain (1842-1846)
	Abel P. Upshur* (1843-1844)	William S. Archer (1842-1845)		William R. King* (1844-1846)	Charles S. Todd Russia (1844-1846)
	John C. Calhoun* (1844-1845)				Henry Wheaton* Prussia (1835-1846)
James K. Polk (1845-1849)	James Buchanan* (1845-1849)	William Allen (1845-1846)	Louis McLane* (1845-1846)	William R. King* (1844-1846)	Andrew J. Donelson* Prussia (1846-1849)
			George Bancroft* (1846-1849)	Richard Rush* (1847-1849)	Washington Irving* Spain (1842-1846)

PRESIDENT	SECRETARY OF STATE	CHAIRMAN, SENATE FOREIGN RELATIONS COMMITTEE	MINISTER/ AMBASSADOR TO GREAT BRITAIN	MINISTER/ AMBASSADOR TO FRANCE	MINISTER/ AMBASSADOR TO OTHER NATIONS
Zachary Taylor (1849-1850) Millard Fillmore (1850-1853)	John M. Clayton* (1849-1850) Daniel Webster* (1850-1852) Edward Everett* (1852-1853)	William R. King* (1849-1850) Henry S. Foote (1850-1851) James M. Mason* (1851-1861)	Abbott Lawrence* (1849-1852) Abbott Lawrence* (1849-1852) Joseph R. Ingersoll* (1852-1853)	William C. Rives* (1849-1853) William C. Rives* (1849-1853)	George P. Marsh* Turkey (1849-1853) Daniel D. Barnard* Prussia (1850-1853)
Franklin Pierce (1853-1857)	William L. Marcy* (1853-1857)	James M. Mason* (1851-1861)	James Buchanan* (1853-1856) George M. Dallas* (1856-1861)	John Y. Mason* (1854-1859)	James Gadsden* Mexico (1853-1856) August Belmont* Netherlands (1854-1857) Pierre Soulé* Spain (1853-1855)
James Buchanan* (1857-1861)	Lewis Cass* (1857-1860) Jeremiah S. Black* (1860-1861)	James M. Mason* (1851-1861)	George M. Dallas* (1856-1861)	John Y. Mason* (1854-1859) Charles J. Faulkner* (1860-1861)	Joseph A. Wright* Prussia (1857-1861) Townsend Harris* Japan (1859-1862)
Abraham Lincoln (1861-1865)	William H. Seward* (1861-1869)	Charles Sumner* (1861-1871)	Charles F. Adams* (1861-1868)	William L. Dayton* (1861-1864)	Cassius M. Clay* Russia (1861-1862; 1863-1869) Thomas Corwin* Mexico (1861-1864) Norman B. Judd* Prussia (1861-1865) George P. Marsh* Italy (1861-1882)

PRESIDENT	SECRETARY OF STATE	CHAIRMAN, SENATE FOREIGN RELATIONS COMMITTEE	MINISTER/ AMBASSADOR TO GREAT BRITAIN	MINISTER/ AMBASSADOR TO FRANCE	MINISTER/ AMBASSADOR TO OTHER NATIONS
Andrew Johnson (1865-1869)	William H. Seward* (1861-1869)	Charles Sumner* (1861-1871)	Charles F. Adams* (1861-1868)	John Bigelow* (1865-1866) John A. Dix* (1866-1869)	Cassius M. Clay* Russia (1863-1869) William S. Rosecrans* Mexico (1868-1869)
Ulysses S. Grant (1869-1877)	Elihu B. Washburne* (1869) Hamilton Fish* (1869-1877)	Charles Sumner* (1861-1871) Simon Cameron* (1871-1877)	John Lothrop Motley* (1869-1870) Robert C. Schenck* (1870-1876) Edwards Pierrepont* (1876-1877)	Elihu B. Washburne* (1869-1877)	Daniel E. Sickles* Spain (1869-1874) John W. Foster* Mexico (1873-1880) J. Milton Turner* Liberia (1871-1878) John A. Bingham* Japan (1873-1885)
Rutherford B. Hayes (1877-1881)	William M. Evarts* (1877-1881)	Hannibal Hamlin (1877-1879) William W. Eaton (1879-1881)	John Welsh* (1877-1879) James Russell Lowell* (1880-1885)	Edward F. Noyes* (1877-1881)	James Russel Lowell* Spain (1877-1880) John A. Kasson* Austria (1877-1881)
James A. Garfield (1881)	James G. Blaine* (1881)	Ambrose E. Burnside (1881) George F. Edmunds (1881)	James Russell Lowell* (1880-1885)	Levi P. Morton* (1881-1885)	Stephen A. Hurlbut* Peru (1881) Judson Kilpatrick* Chile (1881)
Chester A. Arthur (1881-1885)	Frederick T. Frelinghuysen* (1881-1885)	William Windon (1881-1883)	James Russell Lowell* (1880-1885)	Levi P. Morton* (1881-1885)	Seth L. Phelps* Peru (1883-1885)

PRESIDENT	SECRETARY OF STATE	CHAIRMAN, SENATE FOREIGN RELATIONS COMMITTEE	MINISTER/ AMBASSADOR TO GREAT BRITAIN	MINISTER/ AMBASSADOR TO FRANCE	MINISTER/ AMBASSADOR TO OTHER NATIONS
		John F. Miller (1883-1887)			John A. Kasson* Germany (1884-1885) Cornelius A. Logan* Chile (1882-1885)
Grover Cleveland (1885-1889)	Thomas F. Bayard* (1885-1889)	John F. Miller (1883-1887) John Sherman* (1887-1893)	Edward J. Phelps* (1885-1889)	Robert M. McLane* (1885-1889)	Charles Denby* China (1885-1898) Richard B. Hubbard* Japan (1885-1889)
Benjamin Harrison (1889-1893)	James G. Blaine* (1889-1892) John W. Foster* (1892-1893)	John Sherman* (1887-1893)	Robert T. Lincoln* (1889-1893)	Whitelaw Reid* (1889-1892) T. Jefferson Coolidge* (1892-1893)	John F. Swift* Japan (1889-1891) Frank L. Coombs* Japan (1892-1893) Charles Denby* China (1885-1898)
Grover Cleveland (1893-1897)	Walter Q. Gresham* (1893-1895) Richard Olney* (1895-1897)	John T. Morgan* (1893-1895) John Sherman* (1895-1897)	Thomas F. Bayard* (1893-1897)	James B. Eustis* (1893-1897)	Charles Denby* China (1885-1898) Edwin Dun* Japan (1893-1897) Allen Thomas Venezuela (1895-1897)

PRESIDENT	SECRETARY OF STATE	CHAIRMAN, SENATE FOREIGN RELATIONS COMMITTEE	MINISTER/ AMBASSADOR TO GREAT BRITAIN	MINISTER/ AMBASSADOR TO FRANCE	MINISTER/ AMBASSADOR TO OTHER NATIONS
William McKinley (1897-1901)	John Sherman* (1897-1898) William R. Day* (1898) John Hay* (1898-1905)	William P. Frye (1897) Cushman K. Davis (1897-1901)	John Hay* (1897-1898) Joseph H. Choate* (1899-1905)	Horace Porter* (1897-1905)	Stewart L. Woodford* Spain (1897-1898) Andrew D. White* Germany (1897-1902) Edwin H. Conger* China (1898-1905)
Theodore Roosevelt (1901-1909)	John Hay* (1898-1905) Elihu Root* (1905-1909) Robert Bacon* (1909)	Shelby M. Cullom (1901-1913)	Joseph H. Choate* (1899-1905) Whitelaw Reid* (1905-1912)	Horace Porter* (1897-1905) Robert S. McCormick* (1905-1907) Henry White* (1907-1909)	Charlemagne Tower* Germany (1902-1908) John G. A. Leishman* Turkey (1901-1909) Herbert W. Bowen* Venezuela (1901-1905)
William Howard Taft (1909-1913)	Philander C. Knox* (1909-1913)	Shelby M. Cullom (1901-1913)	Whitelaw Reid* (1905-1912)	Robert Bacon* (1909-1912) Myron T. Herrick* (1912-1914)	Henry Lane Wilson* Mexico (1910-1913) David Jayne Hill* Germany (1908-1911) William James Calhoun* China (1909-1912)
Woodrow Wilson (1913-1921)	William Jennings Bryan* (1913-1915)	Augustus O. Bacon (1913-1915)	Walter Hines Page* (1913-1918)	Myron T. Herrick* (1912-1914)	Henry P. Fletcher* Mexico (1917-1919)

PRESIDENT	SECRETARY OF STATE	CHAIRMAN, SENATE FOREIGN RELATIONS COMMITTEE	MINISTER/ AMBASSADOR TO GREAT BRITAIN	MINISTER/ AMBASSADOR TO FRANCE	MINISTER/ AMBASSADOR TO OTHER NATIONS
	Robert Lansing* (1915-1920) Bainbridge Colby* (1920-1921)	William J. Stone (1915-1919) Henry Cabot Lodge, Sr.* (1919-1924)	John W. Davis* (1918-1921)	William G. Sharp* (1914-1919) Hugh Campbell Wallace* (1919-1921)	Thomas Nelson Page* Italy (1913-1919) James W. Gerard* Germany (1913-1917) Paul S. Reinsch* China (1913-1919)
Warren G. Harding (1921-1923)	Charles E. Hughes* (1921-1925)	Henry Cabot Lodge, Sr.* (1919-1924)	George Harvey* (1921-1923)	Myron T. Herrick* (1921-1929)	Richard Washburn Child* Italy (1921-1924) Jacob Gould Schurman* China (1921-1925)
Calvin Coolidge (1923-1929)	Charles E. Hughes* (1921-1925) Frank B. Kellogg* (1925-1929)	Henry Cabot Lodge, Sr.* (1919-1924) William E. Borah* (1925-1933)	Frank B. Kellogg* (1924-1925) Alanson B. Houghton* (1925-1929)	Myron T. Herrick* (1921-1929)	Jacob Gould Schurman* Germany (1925-1930) Charles McVeagh* Japan (1925-1928) Dwight W. Morrow* Mexico (1927-1930)
Herbert Hoover (1929-1933)	Henry L. Stimson* (1929-1933)	William E. Borah* (1925-1933)	Charles G. Dawes* (1929-1931) Andrew W. Mellon* (1932-1933)	Walter E. Edge* (1929-1933)	Jacob Gould Schurman* Germany (1925-1930) Frederic M. Sackett* Germany (1930-1933) Nelson T. Johnson* China (1930-1941) Joseph W. Grew* (1932-1941)

PRESIDENT	SECRETARY OF STATE	CHAIRMAN, SENATE FOREIGN RELATIONS COMMITTEE	MINISTER/ AMBASSADOR TO GREAT BRITAIN	MINISTER/ AMBASSADOR TO FRANCE	MINISTER/ AMBASSADOR TO OTHER NATIONS
Franklin D. Roosevelt (1933-1945)	Cordell Hull* (1933-1944) Edward R. Stettinius, Jr.* (1944-1945)	Key Pittman (1933-1941) Walter F. George (1941) Tom Connally (1941-1947)	Robert W. Bingham* (1933-1937) Joseph P. Kennedy* (1938-1940) John G. Winant* (1941-1946)	Jesse Isidor Straus* (1933-1936) William C. Bullitt* (1936-1940) William D. Leahy* (1941-1942) Jefferson Caffrey* (1944-1949)	William E. Dodd* Germany (1933-1937) Hugh R. Wilson* Germany (1937-1938) Joseph W. Grew* Japan (1932-1941) Nelson T. Johnson* China (1930-1941) William C. Bullitt* USSR (1933-1936) Joseph E. Davies* USSR (1937-1938) Lawrence A. Steinhardt* USSR (1939-1941) William H. Standley* USSR (1942-1943) W. Averell Harriman* USSR (1943-1946)
Harry S Truman (1945-1953)	Edward R. Stettinius, Jr.* (1944-1945) James F. Byrnes* (1945-1947)	Tom Connally (1941-1947) Arthur H. Vandenberg* (1947-1949)	John G. Winant* (1941-1946) W. Averell Harriman* (1946)	Jefferson Caffrey* (1944-1949) David K. E. Bruce* (1949-1952)	W. Averell Harriman* USSR (1943-1946) W. Bedell Smith* USSR (1946-1948)

PRESIDENT	SECRETARY OF STATE	CHAIRMAN, SENATE FOREIGN RELATIONS COMMITTEE	MINISTER/ AMBASSADOR TO GREAT BRITAIN	MINISTER/ AMBASSADOR TO FRANCE	MINISTER/ AMBASSADOR TO OTHER NATIONS
	George C. Marshall* (1947-1949) Dean G. Acheson* (1949-1953)	Tom Connally (1949-1953)	Lewis W. Douglas* (1947-1950) Walter S. Gifford* (1950-1953)	James Clement Dunn (1952-1953)	Alan G. Kirk* USSR (1949-1951) George F. Kennan* USSR (1952) John Leighton Stuart* China (1946-1949) Warren R. Austin* United Nations (1947-1953)
Dwight D. Eisenhower (1953-1961)	John Foster Dulles* (1953-1959) Christian A. Herter* (1959-1961)	Alexander Wiley (1953-1955) Walter F. George (1955-1957) Theodore F. Green (1957-1959) J. William Fulbright* (1959-1974)	Winthrop W. Aldrich* (1953-1957) John Hay Whitney* (1957-1961)	C. Douglas Dillon* (1953-1957) Amory Houghton* (1957-1961)	Walter C. Dowling* Germany (1959-1963) Charles E. Bohlen* USSR (1953-1957) Llewellyn E. Thompson* USSR (1957-1962) Henry Cabot Lodge, Jr.* United Nations (1953-1960)
John F. Kennedy (1961-1963)	Dean Rusk* (1961-1969)	J. William Fulbright* (1959-1974)	David K. E. Bruce* (1961-1969)	James M. Gavin* (1961-1962) Charles E. Bohlen* (1962-1968)	Llewellyn E. Thompson* USSR (1957-1962) Foy D. Kohler* USSR (1962-1966) Walter C. Dowling* Germany (1959-1963)

PRESIDENT	SECRETARY OF STATE	CHAIRMAN, SENATE FOREIGN RELATIONS COMMITTEE	MINISTER/ AMBASSADOR TO GREAT BRITAIN	MINISTER/ AMBASSADOR TO FRANCE	MINISTER/ AMBASSADOR TO OTHER NATIONS
Lyndon B. Johnson (1963-1969)	Dean Rusk* (1961-1969)	J. William Fulbright* (1959-1974)	David K. E. Bruce* (1961-1969)	Charles E. Bohlen* (1962-1968) R. Sargent Shriver, Jr.* (1968-1970)	Frederick E. Nolting, Jr.* Vietnam (1961-1963) Henry Cabot Lodge, Jr.* Vietnam (1963-1964) Adlai E. Stevenson* United Nations (1961-1965) Foy D. Kohler* USSR (1962-1966) Llewellyn E. Thompson* USSR (1967-1969) Henry Cabot Lodge, Jr.* Vietnam (1963-1964) Maxwell D. Taylor* Vietnam (1964-1965) Henry Cabot Lodge, Jr.* Vietnam (1965-1967) Ellsworth Bunker* Vietnam (1967-1973)

PRESIDENT	SECRETARY OF STATE	CHAIRMAN, SENATE FOREIGN RELATIONS COMMITTEE	MINISTER/ AMBASSADOR TO GREAT BRITAIN	MINISTER/ AMBASSADOR TO FRANCE	MINISTER/ AMBASSADOR TO OTHER NATIONS
Richard M. Nixon (1969-1974)	William P. Rogers* (1969-1973) Henry A. Kissinger* (1973-1977)	J. William Fulbright* (1959-1974)	Walter H. Annenberg* (1969-1974)	R. Sargent Shriver, Jr.* (1968-1970) Arthur K. Watson* (1970-1972) John N. Irwin II* (1973-1974)	Jacob D. Beam* USSR (1969-1973) Walter J. Stoessel, Jr.* USSR (1974-1976) Ellsworth Bunker* Vietnam (1967-1973) Graham A. Martin* Vietnam (1973-1975)
Gerald R. Ford (1974-1977)	Henry A. Kissinger* (1973-1977)	J. William Fulbright* (1959-1974) John Sparkman (1975-1979)	Elliott L. Richardson* (1975-1976) Anne L. Armstrong* (1976-1977)	Kenneth Rush* (1974-1977)	Walter J. Stoessel, Jr.* USSR (1974-1976) Graham A. Martin* Vietnam (1973-1975) Daniel P. Moynihan* United Nations (1975-1976)
Jimmy Carter (1977-1981)	Cyrus A. Vance* (1977-1980) Edmund S. Muskie* (1980-1981)	John Sparkman (1975-1979) Frank Church (1979-1981)	Kingman Brewster, Jr.* (1977-1981)	Arthur A. Hartman* (1977-1981)	Malcolm Toon* USSR (1977-1979) Andrew J. Young* United Nations (1977-1979) Thomas J. Watson, Jr. USSR (1979-1981)

PRESIDENT	SECRETARY OF STATE	CHAIRMAN, SENATE FOREIGN RELATIONS COMMITTEE	MINISTER/ AMBASSADOR TO GREAT BRITAIN	MINISTER/ AMBASSADOR TO FRANCE	MINISTER/ AMBASSADOR TO OTHER NATIONS
Ronald W. Reagan (1981–1989)	Alexander M. Haig, Jr.* (1981–1982) George P. Schultz (1982–1989)	Charles Percy (1981–1985) Richard Lugar* (1985–1987) Claiborne Pell (1987–)	John J. Louis, Jr.* (1981–1983) Charles H. Price II* (1983–1989)	Evan G. Galbraith* (1981–1985) Joe M. Rodgers* (1985–1989)	Arthur A. Hartman* USSR (1981–1986) Jack F. Matlock, Jr.* USSR (1986–1989) Jeane Kirkpatrick* United Nations (1981–1985) Vernon A. Walters* United Nations (1985–1989)

INITIATION, SUSPENSION, AND TERMINATION OF DIPLOMATIC RELATIONS

This appendix lists every country with which the United States has had or currently has formal diplomatic relations. Indicated for each country is the year in which diplomatic relations were begun, the year, if any, during which relations were suspended for extraordinary causes, and the year in which relations were terminated. Delays between the resignation of one minister or ambassador and the appointment of his successor have, on occasion, been quite lengthy. Since these delays are generally the result of bureaucratic procedures or domestic political necessities, they do not represent a real interruption of formal diplomatic relations and have not generally been included in the suspension column. Termination dates include recent occasions (for example, Libya, 1980) in which relations have been suspended but not resumed as of July 1988, as well as cases in which the country involved no longer exists as an independent entity (for example, the Kingdom of the Two Sicilies, 1858). The sources for this appendix are U.S. Department of State, *Principal Officers of the Department of State and United States Chiefs of Mission, 1778–1986* (1986); Arthur S. Banks, ed., *Political Handbook of the World 1987* (1987); and *New York Times*.

Initiation, Suspension, and Termination of Diplomatic Relations

COUNTRY	INITIATION	SUSPENSION	TERMINATION
Afghanistan	1935	—	
Albania	1922	—	1939
Algeria	1962	1967–1974	—
Antigua and Barbuda	1981	—	—
Argentina	1823	1832–1844	—
		1944–1945	—
Australia	1940	—	—
Austria	1838	1917–1921	—
		1938–1946	—
Bahamas	1973	—	—
Bahrain	1971	—	—
Bangladesh	1972	—	—
Barbados	1967	—	—
Belgium	1832	—	—
Benin	1960	—	—
Bolivia	1848	1943–1944	—
Botswana	1971	—	—

COUNTRY	INITIATION	SUSPENSION	TERMINATION
Brazil	1825	—	—
Brunei	1984	—	—
Bulgaria	1901	1918–1921	—
		1941–1947	—
		1950–1960	—
Burkina Faso (Upper Volta)	1960	—	—
Burma	1947	—	—
Burundi	1962	1966–1968	—
Cameroon	1960	—	—
Canada	1927	—	—
Cape Verde Islands	1976	—	—
Chad	1960	—	—
Chile	1823	—	—
China, People's Republic of	1979	—	—
China, Republic of (Taiwan)	1843	1912–1913	—
		1949–1953	1979
Colombia	1823	—	—
Comoro Islands	1982	—	—
Congo (Brazzaville)	1960	1965–1979	—
Costa Rica	1858[1]	1917–1922	—
Cuba	1902	1933–1934	1961
Cyprus	1960	—	—
Czechoslovakia	1919	1939–1941	—
Denmark	1827	—	—
Djibouti	1980	—	—
Dominica	1979	—	—
Dominican Republic	1883	1960–1962	—
Ecuador	1848	1963–1964	—
Egypt	1848	1967–1974	—
El Salvador	1863[2]	1931–1934	—
Equatorial Guinea	1968	1976–1979	—
Estonia	1922	—	1940
Ethiopia	1908	1910–1927	—
		1936–1943	—
Fiji	1972	—	—
Finland	1920	1942–1946	—
France	1778	1796–1801	—
Gabon	1960	—	—
Gambia	1965	—	—

COUNTRY	INITIATION	SUSPENSION	TERMINATION
Germany	1797	1801–1835	1941
		1917–1921	—
Germany, Democratic Republic of	1974	—	—
Germany, Federal Republic of	1955	—	—
Ghana	1957	—	—
Greece	1868	1920–1924	—
Grenada	1974	1981–1984	—
Guatemala	1825	1826–1883	—
		1839–1849	—
		1849–1855	—
		1921–1922	—
Guinea	1959	—	—
Guinea-Bissau	1977	—	—
Guyana	1966	—	—
Haiti	1862	1921–1930	—
		1963	—
Hawaii	1853	—	1898
Honduras	1858[3]	1919–1922	—
Hungary	1921	1941–1946	—
		1957–1967	—
Iceland	1941	—	—
India	1947	—	—
Indonesia	1949	—	—
Iran	1883	—	1980
Iraq	1931	1967–1984	—
Ireland	1927	—	—
Israel	1949	—	—
Italy	1840	1941–1944	—
Ivory Coast	1960	—	—
Jamaica	1962	—	—
Japan	1859	1941–1952	—
Jordan	1950	—	—
Kampuchea (Cambodia)	1950	1965–1970	1975
Kenya	1964	—	—
Kiribati	1980	—	—
Korea	1883	—	1905
Korea, Republic of	1949	—	—
Kuwait	1961	—	—
Laos	1950	—	1975[4]
Latvia	1922	—	1940

COUNTRY	INITIATION	SUSPENSION	TERMINATION
Lebanon	1942	—	—
Lesotho	1971	—	—
Liberia	1863	—	—
Libya	1952	—	1980
Lithuania	1922	—	1940
Luxembourg	1903	—	—
Madagascar	1960	—	—
Malawi	1964	—	—
Malaysia	1957	—	—
Maldives	1965	—	—
Mali	1960	—	—
Malta	1965	—	—
Mauritania	1960	1967–1970	—
Mauritius	1968	—	—
Mexico	1825[5]	1845–1848	—
		1858–1859	—
		1913–1916	—
		1919–1924	—
Montenegro	1905	—	1918
Morocco	1905	—	—
Mozambique	1975	—	—
Nauru	1974	—	—
Nepal	1948	—	—
Netherlands	1781	—	—
New Zealand	1942	—	—
Nicaragua	1851	1909–1911	—
Niger	1960	—	—
Nigeria	1960	—	—
Norway	1905	—	—
Oman	1972	—	—
Pakistan	1947	—	—
Panama	1903	1964	—
Papal States[6]	1848	—	1867
Papua New Guinea	1975	—	—
Paraguay	1861	—	—
Peru	1826	1860–1861	—
		1865–1866	—
		1881–1883	—
		1962–1963	—
Philippines	1946	—	—
Poland	1919	—	—

COUNTRY	INITIATION	SUSPENSION	TERMINATION
Portugal	1791	1910–1911	—
Qatar	1971	—	—
Romania	1880	1941–1947	—
Rwanda	1962	—	—
St. Christopher and Nevis	1984	—	—
St. Lucia	1979	—	—
St. Vincent	1981	—	—
São Tome e Principe	1975	—	—
Saudi Arabia	1939	—	—
Senegal	1960	—	—
Seychelles	1976	—	—
Sierra Leone	1961	—	—
Singapore	1966	—	—
Solomon Islands	1978	—	—
Somalia	1960	—	—
South Africa	1929	—	—
Southern Yemen (People's Democratic Republic of Yemen)	1967	—	1969
Spain	1790[7]	1805–1816	—
Sri Lanka (Ceylon)	1948	1898–1899	—
Sudan	1956	1967–1972	—
Surinam	1975	—	—
Swaziland	1968	—	—
Sweden	1814[8]	—	—
Switzerland	1853	—	—
Syria	1942	1967–1974	—
Tanzania	1961	—	—
Texas	1837	—	1845
Thailand	1882	1942–1945	—
Togo	1960	—	—
Tonga	1972	—	—
Trinidad and Tobago	1962	—	—
Tunisia	1956	—	—
Turkey	1831	1917–1927	—
Tuvalu	1979	—	—
Two Sicilies	1832	—	1858
Uganda	1963	1973	—

COUNTRY	INITIATION	SUSPENSION	TERMINATION
Union of Soviet Socialist Republics (Russia)	1809[9]	1917–1933	—
United Arab Emirates	1972	—	—
United Kingdom	1785	1812–1815	—
Uruguay	1867	—	—
Vatican City	1941	1944–1984	—
Venezuela	1835	1908–1909	—
Vietnam, Republic of	1950	—	1975
Western Samoa	1971	—	—
Yemen Arab Republic	1946	1962–1972	—
Yugoslavia	1882	—	—
Zaire	1960	—	—
Zambia	1964	—	—
Zimbabwe	1980	—	—

Initiation, Suspension, and Termination of Diplomatic Relations With International Organizations

ORGANIZATION	INITIATION	SUSPENSION	TERMINATION
European Communities	1959	—	—
International Atomic Energy Agency	1957	—	—
International Civil Aviation Organization	1947	—	—
North Atlantic Treaty Organization	1952	—	—
Organization for Economic Cooperation and Development	1961	—	—
Organization of American States	1948	—	—
Southeast Asia Treaty Organization	1954	—	1977
United Nations	1946	—	—
United Nations Agencies for Food and Agriculture	1983	—	—

ORGANIZATION	INITIATION	SUSPENSION	TERMINATION
United Nations Educational, Scientific, and Cultural Organization	1961	—	—
United Nations European Office	1958	—	—
United Nations Industrial Development Organization	1969	—	—
United Nations Office, Vienna	1983	—	—
U.S. Office for Arms Reduction Negotiations	1985	—	—

Notes

1. The first diplomatic official was commissioned to Costa Rica in 1853; however, none presented credentials until 1858.

2. The first diplomatic official was commissioned to El Salvador in 1853; however, none presented credentials until 1863.

3. The first diplomatic official was commissioned to Honduras in 1853; however, none presented credentials until 1858.

4. Although relations have not been formally terminated, the United States has not had an ambassador in Laos since 1975.

5. The first diplomatic official was commissioned to Mexico in 1853; however, none presented credentials until 1825.

6. See also Vatican City.

7. The first diplomatic official was commissioned to Russia in 1780; however, none presented credentials until 1809.

8. The first diplomatic official was commissioned to Spain in 1779; however, none presented credentials until approximately 1790.

9. Benjamin Franklin was accredited also to France and never went to Sweden; Jonathan Russell was the first American to present credentials in Sweden in 1814.

PLACE OF BIRTH

This appendix is divided into three sections: United States, Foreign, and Unknown. The first section lists each person who is a subject of a biographical entry in this volume by state of birth. Asterisks indicate those persons who did not hold regular diplomatic or consular appointments from the Continental Congress, Articles of Confederation Congress, or Department of State. The abbreviation "n.a." means that the information was not ascertainable.

United States

NAME	BIRTHDATE	CITY OR COUNTY
Alabama		
Hitchcock, Ethan A.	September 19, 1835	Mobile
McConaughy, Walter P. J.	September 11, 1908	Montevallo
Rodgers, Joe M.	November 12, 1933	Bay Minette
Arizona		
Douglas, Lewis W.	July 2, 1894	Bisbee
Arkansas		
Henderson, Loy W.	June 28, 1892	near Rogers
MacArthur, Douglas	January 26, 1880	near Little Rock
California		
*Bailey, Thomas A.	December 14, 1902	San José
Beale, Truxtun	March 6, 1856	San Francisco
Black, Shirley Temple	April 23, 1928	Santa Monica
Clark, William P.	October 23, 1931	Oxnard
Coombs, Frank L.	December 27, 1853	Napa
Durbrow, Elbridge	September 21, 1903	San Francisco
Gibson, Hugh S.	August 16, 1883	Los Angeles
Grady, Henry F.	February 12, 1882	San Francisco
Reinhardt, George F.	October 21, 1911	Berkeley
Standley, William H.	December 18, 1872	Ukiah
Stevenson, Adlai	February 5, 1900	Los Angeles

NAME	BIRTHDATE	CITY OR COUNTY

Colorado

| *Lea, Homer | November 17, 1876 | Denver |
| Thompson, Llewellyn E., Jr. | August 24, 1904 | Las Animas |

Connecticut

*Abbott, Willis John	March 16, 1863	New Haven
Acheson, Dean G.	April 11, 1893	Middletown
Barlow, Joel	March 24, 1754	Redding
Barnard, Daniel D.	July 16, 1797	East Hartford
Bassett, Ebenezer	October 16, 1833	Litchfield
Blatchford, Richard M.	April 23, 1798	Stratford
Bradley, Charles W.	June 27, 1807	New Haven
Deane, Silas	December 24, 1737	Groton
Donnelly, Walter J.	January 9, 1896	New Haven
Enders, Thomas O.	November 28, 1931	Hartford
*Fiske, John	March 30, 1842	Hartford
*Levermore, Charles H.	October 15, 1856	Mansfield
Penfield, Frederic C.	April 23, 1855	East Haddam
Pierrepont, Edwards	March 4, 1817	North Haven
*Platt, Orville Hitchcock	July 19, 1827	Washington
Sanford, Henry S.	June 15, 1823	Woodbury
Smith, Charles E.	February 18, 1842	Mansfield

Delaware

Bayard, Thomas F.	October 29, 1828	Wilmington
Clayton, John M.	July 24, 1796	Dogsborough
McLane, Louis	May 1786	Smyrna
McLane, Robert M.	June 23, 1815	Wilmington
Moore, John Bassett	December 3, 1860	Smyrna

District of Columbia

Beale, Edward Fitzgerald	February 4, 1822	D.C.
Dulles, John Foster	February 25, 1888	D.C.
Gauss, Clarence E.	January 12, 1887	D.C.
Johnson, Nelson T.	April 3, 1887	D.C.
*Lewis, Fulton, Jr.	April 30, 1903	D.C.
Mason, James M.	November 3, 1798	Georgetown
McFarlane, Robert	July 12, 1937	D.C.
Meloy, Francis E., Jr.	March 28, 1917	D.C.
Phillip, Hoffman	July 13, 1872	D.C.

NAME	BIRTHDATE	CITY OR COUNTY
Russell, William W.	December 3, 1859	D.C.
Willard, Joseph E.	May 1, 1865	D.C.

Georgia

Battle, Lucius D.	June 1, 1918	Dawson
Bennett, W. Tapley, Jr.	April 1, 1917	Griffin
Blount, James H.	September 12, 1837	Jones Co.
*Clay, Lucius D.	April 23, 1897	Marietta
Dowling, Walter C.	August 4, 1905	Atkinson
Hubbard, Richard B.	November 1, 1832	Walton Co.
*Millis, Walter	March 16, 1899	Atlanta
Rusk, Dean	February 9, 1909	Cherokee Co.
*Toombs, Robert A.	July 2, 1810	Wilkes Co.
*Yancey, William L.	August 10, 1814	Warren Co.

Hawaii

*Carter, Henry A. P.	August 7, 1837	Honolulu
Castle, William R., Jr.	June 19, 1878	Honolulu

Illinois

Bancroft, Edgar A.	November 20, 1857	Galesburg
Beaupré, Arthur M.	July 29, 1853	Kendall Co.
Blair, William McC., Jr.	October 24, 1916	Chicago
*Borah, William E.	June 29, 1865	near Fairfield
Bryan, William Jennings	March 19, 1860	Salem
Conger, Edwin E.	March 7, 1843	near Galesburg
Crane, Charles R.	August 7, 1843	Chicago
Dubs, Adolph	August 4, 1920	Chicago
Gunther, John J.	August 30, 1903	Chicago
Hoffman, Paul G.	April 26, 1891	Western Springs
Ingersoll, Robert S.	January 28, 1914	Galesburg
Lincoln, Robert T.	August 1, 1843	Springfield
Louis, John J., Jr.	June 10, 1925	Evanston
MacLeish, Archibald	May 7, 1892	Glencoe
Owen, Ruth Bryan	October 2, 1885	Jacksonville
Stettinius, Edward R., Jr	October 22, 1900	Chicago
*Strong, Josiah	January 19, 1847	Naperville
Wilson, F. M. Huntington	December 15, 1875	Chicago
Wilson, Hugh R.	January 29, 1885	Evanston

NAME	BIRTHDATE	CITY OR COUNTY
Indiana		
*Beard, Charles A.	November 27, 1874	near Knightstown
Berry, Burton Yost	August 31, 1901	Fowler
Bowers, Claude G.	November 20, 1878	Hamilton Co.
Byroade, Henry A.	July 24, 1913	Allen Co.
*Davis, Elmer H.	January 13, 1890	Aurora
Davis, Monnett Bain	August 13, 1893	Greencastle
Denby, Charles, II	November 14, 1861	Evansville
Eads, James B.	May 23, 1820	Lawrenceburg
Foster, John W.	March 2, 1836	Pike Co.
Gresham, Walter Q.	March 17, 1832	near Lanesville
*Hale, William B.	April 6, 1869	Richmond
Hay, John M.	October 8, 1838	Salem
*Levinson, Salmon O.	December 29, 1865	Noblesville
Long, Boaz	September 27, 1876	Warsaw
*Lugar, Richard G.	April 4, 1933	Indianapolis
Meyer, Armin H.	January 19, 1914	Fort Wayne
*Poindexter, John M.	August 12, 1936	Washington
Smith, Walter Bedell	October 5, 1895	Indianapolis
Terrell, Edwin Holland	November 21, 1848	Brookville
Wallace, Lew	April 10, 1827	Brookville
Wilson, Henry Lane	November 3, 1857	Crawfordsville
*Wood, Thomas Bond	March 17, 1844	Lafayette
Iowa		
*Adams, Ephraim D.	December 18, 1865	Decorah
*Hopkins, Harry	August 17, 1890	Sioux City
Irwin, John N., II	December 31, 1913	Keokuk
Leahy, William D.	May 6, 1875	Hampton
Rowe, Leo Stanton	September 17, 1871	McGregor
Kansas		
Allison, John M.	April 7, 1905	Holton
Eberhardt, Charles C.	July 27, 1871	Salina
Eisenhower, Milton S.	September 15, 1899	Abilene
Heath, Donald R.	August 12, 1894	Topeka
Johnson, U. Alexis	October 17, 1908	Falun
Stoessel, Walter J., Jr.	January 24, 1920	Manhattan
Vincent, John Carter	August 19, 1900	Seneca
Kentucky		
Anderson, Richard C.	August 4, 1788	Jefferson Co.

NAME	BIRTHDATE	CITY OR COUNTY
Baker, Jehu	November 4, 1822	Fayette Co.
Clay, Cassius M.	October 19, 1810	Madison Co.
Cooper, John Sherman	August 23, 1901	Somerset
Corwin, Thomas	July 29, 1794	Bourbon Co.
Francis, Davis R.	October 1, 1850	Richmond
Green, Benjamin E.	February 5, 1822	Elkton
Hammond, Ogden H.	October 13, 1869	Louisville
Mein, John Gordon	September 10, 1913	Cadiz
*Pickett, John T.	c. 1825	Maysville
*Preston, William	October 16, 1816	near Louisville
Willis, Albert S.	January 22, 1843	Shelbyville

Louisiana

Armstrong, Anne L.	December 27, 1927	New Orleans
Bailly-Blanchard, Arthur	October 1, 1855	New Orleans
Caffery, Jefferson	December 1, 1886	Lafayette
Dimitry, Alexander	February 7, 1805	New Orleans
Eustis, James B.	August 21, 1834	New Orleans
Vignaud, Henry	November 27, 1830	New Orleans
Young, Andrew J., Jr.	March 12, 1932	New Orleans

Maine

*Andrews, Israel	May, 1813	near Eastport
King, Rufus	March 24, 1755	Scarboro
Low, Frederick	June 30, 1828	Frankfort
Muskie, Edmund S.	March 28, 1914	Rumford
Rockefeller, Nelson A.	July 8, 1908	Bar Harbor
Sewall, Harold M.	January 3, 1860	Bath
Stevens, John L.	August 1, 1820	Mt. Vernon
Thomas, William W., Jr.	August 26, 1839	Portland
Washburne, Elihu B.	September 23, 1816	Livermore
Whitney, John Hay	August 17, 1904	Ellsworth

Maryland

Bruce, David K. E.	February 12, 1898	Baltimore
Douglass, Frederick	February, 1817	Tuckahoe
Garrett, John W.	May 19, 1872	Baltimore
Hughes, Christopher	1786	Baltimore
Johnson, Reverdy	May 21, 1796	Annapolis
Marye, George T.	December 13, 1857	Baltimore
Murray, William Vans	February 9, 1760	Cambridge

NAME	BIRTHDATE	CITY OR COUNTY
Partridge, James R.	1823	Baltimore
Pinkney, William	March 17, 1764	Annapolis
Shriver, R. Sargent	November 9, 1915	Westminster
White, Henry	March 29, 1850	Baltimore

Massachusetts

*Adams, Brooks	June 24, 1848	Quincy
Adams, Charles Francis	August 18, 1807	Boston
Adams, John	October 19, 1735	Braintree
Adams, John Quincy	July 11, 1767	Braintree
*Allen, Elisha Hunt	January 28, 1804	New Salem
Bacon, Robert	July 5, 1860	Jamaica Plain
Bancroft, George	October 3, 1800	Worcester
Barbour, Walworth	June 4, 1908	Cambridge
Baylies, Francis	October 16, 1783	Taunton
*Bemis, Samuel F.	October 20, 1891	Worcester
Berle, Adolf A., Jr.	January 29, 1895	Boston
Bowles, Chester	April 5, 1901	Springfield
Brewster, Kingman, Jr.	June 17, 1919	Longmeadow
Briggs, Ellis O.	December 1, 1899	Watertown
*Bundy, McGeorge	March 30, 1919	Boston
Bush, George	June 12, 1924	Milton
Cabot, John M.	December 11, 1901	Cambridge
Child, Richard W.	August 5, 1881	Worcester
Choate, Joseph H.	January 24, 1832	Salem
Conant, James B.	March 26, 1893	Dorchester
Coolidge, T. Jefferson	August 26, 1831	Boston
Davis, John C. B.	December 29, 1822	Worcester
Davis, Nathaniel	April 12, 1925	Boston
Dodge, Henry P.	January 18, 1870	Boston
Dresel, Ellis L.	November 28, 1865	Boston
Evarts, William M.	February 6, 1818	Boston
Everett, Edward	April 11, 1794	Dorchester
Franklin, Benjamin	January 17, 1706	Boston
Gifford, Walter S.	January 10, 1885	Salem
Green, Marshall	January 27, 1916	Holyoke
Grew, Joseph C.	May 27, 1880	Boston
Griffis, Stanton	May 2, 1887	Boston
Hornbeck, Stanley K.	May 4, 1883	Franklin
Houghton, Alanson B.	October 10, 1863	Cambridge
*House, Edward H.	September 5, 1836	Boston

NAME	BIRTHDATE	CITY OR COUNTY
Jarvis, William	February 2, 1770	Boston
Kennedy, Joseph P.	September 6, 1888	Boston
Larkin, Thomas O.	September 16, 1802	Charlestown
Lawrence, Abbott	December 16, 1792	Groton
Lincoln, Levi	May 15, 1749	Hingham
Lodge, Henry Cabot, Jr.	July 5, 1902	Nahant
*Lodge, Henry Cabot, Sr.	May 12, 1850	Boston
Logan, Cornelius A.	August 24, 1832	Deerfield
Lowell, James Russell	February 22, 1819	Cambridge
Marcy, William L.	December 12, 1786	Sturbridge
*Marshall, James F. B.	August 8, 1819	Charlestown
Meyer, George von L.	June 24, 1858	Boston
*Morgan, Junius Spencer	April 14, 1813	W. Springfield
Motley, John Lothrop	April 15, 1814	Dorchester
Murphy, Richard W.	July 29, 1929	Boston
Nitze, Paul	January 16, 1907	Amherst
Noyes, Edward F.	October 3, 1832	Haverhill
Olney, Richard	September 15, 1835	Oxford
*Parker, Peter	June 18, 1804	Framingham
Peirce, Henry A.	December 15, 1808	Dorchester
Phillips, William	May 30, 1878	Beverly
Pickering, Timothy	July 17, 1745	Salem
*Richards, William	August 22, 1793	Plainfield
Richardson, Elliot Lee	July 20, 1920	Boston
Root, Joseph P.	April 23, 1826	Greenwich
*Sumner, Charles	January 6, 1811	Boston
Tenney, Charles D.	June 29, 1857	Boston
*Warnke, Paul C.	January 31, 1920	Webster
Washburn, Albert H.	April 11, 1866	Middleboro
*White, Harry Dexter	October 29, 1892	Boston

Michigan

Brentano, Theodore	March 29, 1854	Kalamazoo
Bunche, Ralph J.	August 7, 1904	Detroit
Mesta, Perle	c. 1891	Sturgis
O'Brien, Thomas J.	July 30, 1842	Jackson Co.
*Vandenberg, Arthur H.	March 22, 1884	Grand Rapids

Minnesota

Dawson, William, Jr.	August 11, 1885	St. Paul
Magoon, Charles E.	December 5, 1861	Steele Co.

NAME	BIRTHDATE	CITY OR COUNTY
Mississippi		
Clayton, Will	February 7, 1880	near Tupelo
*Pittman, Key	September 19, 1872	Vicksburg
Missouri		
Blake, Maxwell	November 15, 1877	Kansas City
Bliss, Robert Woods	August 5, 1875	St. Louis
Colby, Bainbridge	December 22, 1869	St. Louis
*Cronkite, Walter	November 4, 1916	St. Joseph
Crowder, Enoch H.	April 11, 1859	Edinburgh
Davis, Roy Tasco	June 24, 1889	Ewing
Dodge, Augustus C.	January 2, 1812	Ste. Genevieve
*Fulbright, J. William	April 8, 1905	Sumner
*Parker, Edwin B.	September 7, 1868	Shelbina
Price, Charles H., II	April 1, 1931	Kansas City
Swift, John F.	February 28, 1829	Bowling Green
Taylor, Maxwell	August 26, 1901	Keytesville
Turner, James M.	May 16, 1840	St. Louis Co.
Wallace, Hugh C.	February 10, 1863	Lexington
Montana		
Braden, Spruille	March 13, 1894	Elkhorn
Vaughn, Jack Hood	August 18, 1920	Columbus
New Hampshire		
Cass, Lewis	October 9, 1792	Exeter
Dix, John A.	July 24, 1798	Boscawen
Ladd, William	May 10, 1778	Exeter
Lear, Tobias	September 9, 1762	Portsmouth
Webster, Daniel	January 18, 1782	Salisbury
*Wood, Leonard	October 9, 1860	Winchester
New Jersey		
Allen, Richard V.	January 1, 1936	Collingswood
Beam, Jacob D.	March 24, 1908	Princeton
Birch, Thomas H.	September 5, 1875	Burlington
*Bristol, Mark L.	April 17, 1868	Glassboro
Dayton, William L.	February 17, 1807	Basking Ridge
*Fort, John F.	March 20, 1852	Pemberton
Frelinghuysen, Frederick T.	August 4, 1817	Millstone

NAME	BIRTHDATE	CITY OR COUNTY
*Gilbert, Parker	October 13, 1892	Bloomfield
*Green, John Cleve	April 4, 1800	Maidenhead
Griscom, Lloyd C.	November 4, 1872	Riverton
Guggenheim, Harry F.	August 23, 1890	West End
Gummeré, Samuel R.	February 19, 1848	Trenton
Hill, David Jayne	June 10, 1850	Plainfield
Jackson, John B.	August 19, 1862	Newark
*Kearney, Lawrence	November 30, 1789	Perth Amboy
Kilpatrick, Hugh J.	January 14, 1836	near Deckertown
Kinney, William B.	September 4, 1789	Speedwell
Pickering, Thomas R.	November 5, 1931	Orange
Stephens, John Lloyd	November 28, 1805	Shrewsburg
*Stockton, Robert F.	August 20, 1795	Princeton
Watson, Arthur K.	April 23, 1919	Summit

New York

NAME	BIRTHDATE	CITY OR COUNTY
Abrams, Elliott	January 24, 1948	New York City
Adee, Alvey A.	November 27, 1842	Astoria
Agar, Herbert	September 29, 1897	New Rochelle
Bartlett, Joseph Jackson	November 4, 1834	Binghamton
Batcheller, George S.	July 25, 1837	Batchellerville
Belcher, Taylor G.	July 1, 1920	Staten Island
Bell, Isaac, Jr.	November 6, 1846	New York City
Belmont, Perry	December 28, 1851	New York City
Berger, Samuel D.	December 6, 1911	New York City
Bidlack, Benjamin A.	September 8, 1804	Paris
Bigelow, John	November 25, 1817	Madden
Bohlen, Charles E.	August 30, 1904	Clayton
Bonsal, Philip W.	May 22, 1903	New York City
Bowen, Herbert W.	February 29, 1856	Brooklyn
Bunker, Ellsworth	May 11, 1894	Yonkers
Christiancy, Isaac	March 12, 1812	Johnstown
*Cromwell, William N.	1854	Brooklyn
Draper, William H., Jr.	August 10, 1894	New York City
Einstein, Lewis D.	March 15, 1877	New York City
Feis, Herbert	June 7, 1893	New York City
Fish, Hamilton	August 3, 1808	New York City
Gallman, Waldemar	April 27, 1899	Wellsville
Gavin, James M.	March 22, 1907	Brooklyn
Gerard, James W.	August 25, 1867	Geneseo
Habib, Philip	February 25, 1920	Brooklyn

NAME	BIRTHDATE	CITY OR COUNTY
Harriman, Florence J.	July 21, 1870	New York City
Harriman, W. Averell	November 15, 1891	New York City
Harris, Townsend	October 13, 1804	Sandy Hill
Harrison, Leland	April 25, 1883	New York City
Hartman, Arthur A.	March 12, 1926	New York City
Hayes, Carleton J. H.	May 16, 1882	Afton
Helm, Charles J.	June 25, 1817	Hornellsville
Holcombe, Chester	October 16, 1844	Winfield
*Holt, Hamilton	August 19, 1872	Brooklyn
Houghton, Amory	July 27, 1899	Corning
Hughes, Charles E.	April 11, 1862	Glens Falls
Irving, Washington	April 3, 1783	New York City
Jay, John	December 12, 1745	New York City
Jessup, Philip C.	January 5, 1897	New York City
*Johnson, Willis F.	October 7, 1857	New York City
Judd, Norman B.	January 10, 1815	Rome
Keating, Kenneth	May 18, 1900	Lima
*Keith, Minor C.	January 19, 1848	Brooklyn
Kellogg, Frank B.	December 22, 1856	Potsdam
*Lamont, Thomas W.	September 30, 1870	Claverack
Lane, Arthur Bliss	June 16, 1894	Bayridge
Lansing, Robert	October 17, 1864	Watertown
Livingston, Edward	May 26, 1764	Columbia Co.
Livingston, Robert R.	November 27, 1746	New York City
Luce, Clare Boothe	April 10, 1903	New York City
Lyon, Cecil B.	November 8, 1903	Staten Island
*Mahan, Alfred Thayer	September 27, 1840	West Point
Mansfield, Michael J.	March 16, 1903	New York City
*Meiggs, Henry	July 7, 1811	Catskill
Merry, William L.	December 27, 1842	New York City
Moffat, Jay Pierrepont	July 18, 1896	Rye
Morgan, Edwin	February 22, 1865	Aurora
Morris, Gouverneur	January 31, 1752	Morrisania
*Morris, Richard V.	March 8, 1768	Morrisania
O'Shaughnessy, Nelson	February 12, 1876	New York City
Peixotto, Benjamin F.	November 13, 1834	New York City
Polk, Frank L.	September 13, 1871	New York City
Pruyn, Robert H.	February 14, 1815	Albany
*Reid, Gilbert	November 29, 1857	Laurel
Rogers, William P.	June 23, 1913	Norfolk
Roosevelt, Eleanor	October 11, 1884	New York City

NAME	BIRTHDATE	CITY OR COUNTY
Root, Elihu	February 15, 1845	Clinton
*Rostow, Eugene	August 25, 1913	Brooklyn
Schuyler, Eugene	February 26, 1840	Ithaca
Seward, Frederick W.	July 8, 1830	Auburn
Seward, William H.	May 16, 1801	Florida
*Shufeldt, Robert W.	February 21, 1822	Red Hook
Shultz, George	December 13, 1920	New York City
Sickles, Daniel E.	October 29, 1819	New York City
Slidell, John	1793	New York City
Squier, Ephraim G.	June 17, 1821	Bethlehem
Steinhardt, Laurence	October 6, 1892	New York City
Stimson, Henry L.	September 21, 1867	New York City
Straight, Willard	January 31, 1880	Oswego
Straus, Jesse I.	June 25, 1872	New York City
*Swing, Raymond	March 25, 1887	Cortland
*Teller, Henry Moore	May 23, 1830	Allegany Co.
Toon, Malcolm	July 4, 1916	Troy
Uhl, Edwin F.	August 14, 1841	Rush
Van Buren, Martin	December 5, 1782	Kinderhook
*Vanderbilt, Cornelius	May 27, 1794	Port Richmond
Walters, Vernon	January 3, 1917	New York City
Webb, James W.	February 8, 1802	Claverack
Welles, Sumner	October 14, 1892	New York City
White, Andrew D.	November 7, 1832	Homer
Winant, John G.	February 23, 1889	New York City
Woodford, Steward L.	September 3, 1835	New York City
Wright, Joshua B.	October 18, 1877	Irvington-on-Hudson
Yost, Charles W.	November 6, 1907	Watertown
Young, Owen D.	October 27, 1874	Van Hornesville

North Carolina

Allen, George V.	November 3, 1903	Durham
Barringer, Daniel M.	July 30, 1806	Poplar Grove
Bingham, Robert W.	November 8, 1871	Orange Co.
Daniels, Josephus, Jr.	May 18, 1862	Washington
Dodd, William E.	October 27, 1869	near Clayton
Hale, Edward J.	December 25, 1839	Fayetteville
King, William Rufus	April 7, 1786	Sampson Co.
Martin, Graham A.	September 12, 1912	Mars Hill
Matlock, Jack F., Jr.	October 1, 1929	Greensboro
*Murrow, Edward R.	April 25, 1908	Greensboro

NAME	BIRTHDATE	CITY OR COUNTY
Page, Walter Hines	August 15, 1855	Camden
Taylor, Hannis	September 12, 1851	New Bern
Wheeler, John H.	August 2, 1806	Murfreesboro

North Dakota

Christopher, Warren M.	October 27, 1925	Scranton
*Sevareid, Arnold Eric	November 12, 1912	Velva

Ohio

*Beveridge, Albert J.	October 6, 1862	Highland Co.
Brown, John Porter	August 17, 1814	Chillicothe
Buchanan, William I.	September 10, 1852	near Covington
Campbell, Lewis D.	August 9, 1811	Franklin
Carr, Wilbur J.	October 31, 1870	near Taylorsville
Cox, Samuel S.	September 30, 1824	Zanesville
Dawes, Charles G.	August 27, 1865	Marietta
Day, William R.	April 17, 1849	Ravenna
Dun, Edwin	July 1848	Chillicothe
Galbraith, Evan	July 2, 1928	Toledo
Herrick, Myron T.	October 9, 1854	Huntington
Hillenbrand, Martin	August 1, 1915	Youngstown
Kohler, Foy D.	February 15, 1908	Oakwood
Loomis, Francis	July 27, 1861	Marietta
McDonald, James G.	November 29, 1886	Coldwater
*MacGahan, Januarius	June 12, 1844	Perry Co.
Osborn, Thomas O.	August 11, 1832	Jersey
Pendleton, George H.	July 29, 1825	Cincinnati
Phelps, Seth L.	January 13, 1824	Parkman
Reid, Whitelaw	October 27, 1837	near Xenia
Rosecrans, Williams S.	September 6, 1819	Delaware Co.
Schenck, Robert C.	October 4, 1809	Franklin
Sharp, William G.	March 14, 1859	Mt. Gilead
Sherman, John	May 10, 1823	Lancaster
Wambaugh, Sarah	March 6, 1882	Cincinnati
Watson, Thomas	January 8, 1914	Dayton
Whitlock, Brand	March 4, 1869	Urbana
*Williams, Edward T.	October 17, 1854	Columbus

Oklahoma (Indian Territory)

Hurley, Patrick Jay	January 8, 1883	Choctaw Res.
Kirkpatrick, Jeane J.	November 19, 1926	Duncan

NAME	BIRTHDATE	CITY OR COUNTY
Moynihan, Daniel P.	March 16, 1927	Tulsa

Pennsylvania

NAME	BIRTHDATE	CITY OR COUNTY
Armstrong, John	November 25, 1755	Carlisle
Atherton, Alfred	November 22, 1921	Pittsburgh
Barton, Thomas P.	1803	Philadelphia
Biddle, A.J.D., Jr.	December 17, 1897	Philadelphia
*Biddle, James	February 18, 1783	Philadelphia
Bingham, John A.	January 21, 1815	Mercer
Black, Jeremiah S.	January 10, 1810	Somerset Co.
Blaine, James G.	January 31, 1830	West Brownsville
Blancké, Wilton W.	June 29, 1908	Philadelphia
Bliss, Tasker H.	December 31, 1853	Lewisburg
Boker, George H.	October 6, 1823	Philadelphia
Buchanan, James	April 23, 1791	near Mercersburg
Bullitt, William C.	January 25, 1891	Philadelphia
Calhoun, William J.	October 5, 1848	Pittsburgh
Cameron, Simon	March 8, 1799	Lancaster Co.
Carlucci, Frank	October 18, 1930	Scranton
Chapin, Selden	September 19, 1899	Erie
Dallas, George M.	July 10, 1792	Philadelphia
*Davis, Richard Harding	April 18, 1864	Philadelphia
Edge, Walter E.	November 20, 1873	Philadelphia
Fletcher, Henry P.	April 10, 1873	Greencastle
Guthrie, George W.	September 5, 1848	Pittsburgh
Haig, Alexander M., Jr.	December 2, 1924	Philadelphia
Helms, Richard	March 30, 1913	St. David
Hise, Elijah	July 4, 1801	Allegheny Co.
Ingersoll, Joseph R.	June 14, 1786	Philadelphia
Kirk, Alan G.	October 30, 1888	Philadelphia
Knox, Philander C.	May 6, 1853	Brownsville
Leishman, John G. A.	March 28, 1857	Pittsburgh
*Logan, James A.	November 11, 1879	Philadelphia
MacArthur, Douglas, II	July 5, 1909	Bryn Mawr
*McCartee, Divie B.	January 13, 1820	Philadelphia
*Maclay, Robert S.	February 7, 1824	Concord
MacVeagh, Charles	June 6, 1860	West Chester
Marshall, George	December 31, 1880	Uniontown
Mellon, Andrew W.	March 24, 1855	Pittsburgh
Messersmith, George	October 3, 1883	Fleetwood
Moran, Benjamin	August 1, 1820	Chester Co.

NAME	BIRTHDATE	CITY OR COUNTY
Muhlenberg, Henry A. P.	May 13, 1782	Lancaster
Murphy, Dominic I.	May 31, 1847	Philadelphia
Osborn, Thomas A.	October 26, 1836	Meadville
Phelps, William W.	August 24, 1839	Dundaff
Porter, Horace	April 15, 1837	Huntingdon
Read, John Meredith	February 21, 1837	Philadelphia
Reed, William B.	June 30, 1806	Philadelphia
Riddle, John W.	July 12, 1864	Philadelphia
Rockhill, William W.	April 1854	Philadelphia
Rush, Richard	August 29, 1780	Philadelphia
Smith, Robert	November 3, 1757	Lancaster
Taylor, Bayard	January 11, 1825	Kennett Square
Tower, Charlemagne	April 17, 1848	Philadelphia
Welsh, John	November 9, 1805	Philadelphia
Wright, Joseph A.	April 17, 1810	Washington

Rhode Island

Aldrich, Winthrop W.	November 2, 1885	Providence
Angell, James B.	January 7, 1829	near Scituate
Beaulac, Willard L.	July 25, 1899	Pawtucket
Halsey, Thomas L.	c. 1776	Providence
MacVeagh, Lincoln	October 1, 1890	Narragansett Pier
Perry, Matthew C.	April 10, 1794	Newport
Robinson, Christopher	May 15, 1806	Providence
Russell, Jonathan	February 27, 1771	Providence
Sackett, Frederic M.	December 17, 1868	Providence
Smith, Earl E. T.	1903	Newport
Wheaton, Henry	November 27, 1785	Providence

South Carolina

Baker, James M.	August 18, 1861	Lowndesville
Baruch, Bernard M.	August 19, 1870	Camden
Byrnes, James F.	May 2, 1879	Charleston
Calhoun, John C.	March 18, 1782	Abbeville Co.
DeLeon, Edwin	May 4, 1818	Columbia
Gadsden, James	May 15, 1788	Charleston
Hunt, William H.	June 12, 1823	Charleston
Hurlbut, Stephen A.	November 29, 1815	Charleston
Laurens, Henry	March 6, 1724	Charleston
Peurifoy, John E.	August 9, 1907	Walterboro
Pickens, Francis	April 7, 1805	Colleton District

NAME	BIRTHDATE	CITY OR COUNTY
Pinckney, Charles	October 26, 1757	Charleston
Pinckney, Charles Cotesworth	February 14, 1745	Charleston
Pinckney, Thomas	October 23, 1750	Charleston
Poinsett, Joel Roberts	March 2, 1779	Charleston
Strobel, Edward H.	December 7, 1885	Charleston
Thompson, Waddy, Jr.	September 8, 1798	Pickensville
Trescot, William H.	November 10, 1822	Charleston

Tennessee

Davis, Norman H.	August 9, 1878	Normandy
Donelson, Andrew J.	August 25, 1799	near Nashville
Hull, Cordell	October 2, 1871	Overton (now Pickett) Co.
*Morgan, John Tyler	June 20, 1824	Athens
Scruggs, William L.	September 14, 1836	near Knoxville
*Walker, William	May 8, 1824	Nashville
Williams, James	July 1, 1796	Grainger Co.
Wright, Luke E.	August 29, 1846	Giles Co.

Texas

Hilsman, Roger	November 23, 1919	Waco
House, Edward M.	September 28, 1858	Houston
Lewis, Samuel W.	October 1, 1930	Houston
Lovett, Robert A.	September 14, 1895	Huntsville
McGhee, George C.	March 10, 1912	Waco
Mann, Thomas C.	November 11, 1912	Laredo

Utah

Cannon, Cavendish	February 1, 1895	Salt Lake City
Clark, Joshua R., Jr.	September 1, 1871	Grantsville

Vermont

Austin, Warren R.	November 12, 1877	Highgate
Barrett, John	November 28, 1866	Grafton
Barton, James L.	September 23, 1855	Charlotte
*Dewey, George B.	December 26, 1837	Montpelier
Harvey, George	February 16, 1864	Peacham
Ide, Henry Clay	September 18, 1844	Barnet
Kasson, John A.	January 11, 1822	Charlotte
Marsh, George P.	March 15, 1801	Woodstock

NAME	BIRTHDATE	CITY OR COUNTY
Morton, Levi P.	May 16, 1824	Shoreham
Phelps, Edward J.	July 11, 1822	Middlebury
Taft, Alphonso	November 5, 1810	Townshend

Virginia

Bagby, Arthur P.	1794	Louisa Co.
Barbour, James	June 10, 1775	Barbourville
Blow, Henry T.	July 15, 1817	Southampton Co.
Borland, Solon	September 21, 1808	Suffolk
Bowlin, James	January 16, 1804	Fredericksburg
Brown, James	September 11, 1766	near Staunton
Clay, Henry	April 12, 1777	Hanover Co.
Crawford, William H.	February 24, 1772	Amherst Co.
Denby, Charles	June 16, 1830	Mount Joy
Faulkner, Charles J.	July 6, 1806	Martinsburg (now in West Virginia)
Forsyth, John	October 22, 1780	Fredericksburgh
Graham, John	1774	Dumfries
*Hunter, Robert M. T.	April 21, 1809	Essex Co.
Jefferson, Thomas	April 13, 1743	Albemarle Co.
Jones, Hilary P.	November 14, 1863	Hanover Co.
Langston, John M.	December 14, 1829	Louisa Co.
*Latané, John H.	April 1, 1869	Staunton
Lee, Arthur	December 21, 1740	Westmoreland Co.
Lee, Charles	July 1758	Fauquier Co.
Lee, Fitzhugh	November 19, 1835	Fairfax Co.
McCormick, Robert S.	July 26, 1849	Rockbridge Co.
Madison, James	March 16, 1751	Port Conway
Marshall, John	September 24, 1755	near Germantown
Mason, John Y.	April 18, 1799	Greencastle Co.
*Mitchell, John	April 13, 1711	Lancaster Co.
Monroe, James	April 28, 1758	Westmoreland Co.
Morrison, William McC.	November 10, 1867	near Lexington
Nolting, Frederick E.	August 24, 1911	Richmond
Page, Thomas Nelson	April 23, 1853	Hanover Co.
Randolph, Edmund J.	August 10, 1753	near Williamsburg
Rives, William C.	May 4, 1793	Amherst
Short, William	September 30, 1759	Surry Co.
Smyth, John H.	July 14, 1844	Richmond
Stevenson, Andrew	January 21, 1784	Culpeper Co.
Trist, Nicholas P.	June 2, 1800	Charlottesville

NAME	BIRTHDATE	CITY OR COUNTY
Upshur, Abel P.	June 17, 1790	Northampton Co.
Weddell, Alexander W.	April 6, 1877	Richmond

Washington

Morris, Roland Sletor	March 11, 1874	Olympia
Rush, David Kenneth	January 17, 1919	Walla Walla

West Virginia

Davis, John W.	April 13, 1873	Clarksburg
Hare, Raymond	April 3, 1901	Martinsburg
Morrow, Dwight	January 11, 1873	Huntington
Russell, Charles W.	March 16, 1856	Wheeling
Vance, Cyrus R.	March 27, 1917	Clarksburg

Wisconsin

Annenberg, Walter H.	March 13, 1908	Milwaukee
Davies, Joseph E.	November 29, 1876	Watertown
Dawson, Thomas C.	July 30, 1865	Hudson
*Dennett, Tyler	June 13, 1883	Spencer
Droppers, Garrett A.	April 12, 1860	Milwaukee
*Kaltenborn, H. V.	July 9, 1878	Milwaukee
Kennan, George F.	February 16, 1904	Milwaukee
Murphy, Robert D.	October 28, 1894	Milwaukee
Reinsch, Paul S.	June 10, 1869	Milwaukee

Foreign

NAME	BIRTH DATE	CITY AND/OR COUNTRY
Armour, Norman	November 4, 1887	Brighton, England
Belmont, August	December 2, 1816	Alzei, Rhenish Palatinate
*Benjamin, Judah P.	August 6, 1811	St. Thomas, British West Indies
Benjamin, Samuel G. W.	February 13, 1837	Argos, Greece
Bernstein, Herman	September 21, 1876	Neustadt-Scherwindt, Russia
Boal, Pierre	1895	France
Booth, Ralph H.	September 29, 1873	Toronto
*Brzezinski, Zbigniew	March 28, 1928	Warsaw, Poland

NAME	BIRTH DATE	CITY AND/OR COUNTRY
Burns, Arthur F.	April 27, 1904	Stanislaw, Austria
Burt, Richard R.	February 3, 1942	Sewell, Chile
*Carnegie, Andrew	November 25, 1836	Dumferline, Scotland
*Carter, Boake	September 15/28 1903	Baku, South Russia
Davies, John Paton, Jr.	April 6, 1908	Kiating, China
*Dennis, A.L.P.	May 21, 1874	Beirut
Dillon, C. Douglas	August 21, 1909	Geneva, Switzerland
Egan, Patrick	August 13, 1841	Ballymahon, Ireland
Eilts, Herman F.	March 23, 1922	Weissenfels Saale, Germany
Engert, Cornelius	December 31, 1887	Vienna, Austria
Galbraith, J. Kenneth	October 15, 1908	near Iona Station, Ontario
Gallatin, Albert	January 29, 1761	Geneva, Switzerland
*Grace, William R.	May 10, 1832	Queenstown, Ireland
*Gulick, Sidney L.	April 10, 1860	Ebon, Marshall Islands
Herter, Christian A.	March 28, 1895	Paris, France
*Higgins, Marguerite	September 3, 1920	Hong Kong
Hotze, Henry	September 2, 1883	Zurich, Switzerland
Kissinger, Henry A.	May 27, 1923	Furth, Bavaria, Germany
LeGendre, Charles W.	August 26, 1830	Ouillins, France
*Menocal, Aniceto G.	September 1, 1836	Cuba
Middletown, Henry	September 28, 1770	London, England
Negroponte, John	July 21, 1939	London, England
O'Dwyer, William	July 11, 1890	County Mayo, Ireland
O'Sullivan, John L.	November 1813	at sea, near Gibraltar
Phelps, Phelps	May 4, 1897	Bonn, Germany
Quintero, Juan A.	n.a.	Havana, Cuba
Reischauer, Edwin O.	October 15, 1910	Tokyo
Safer, Morley	November 8, 1931	Toronto
Schurman, Jacob G.	May 22, 1854	Freetown, Prince Edward Island
Schurz, Carl	March 2, 1829	Liblar, Germany
Scott, James Brown	June 3, 1866	Kincardine, Ontario
Soulé, Pierre	August 31, 1801	Castillon-en-Couserans, France
Squiers, Herbert	April 20, 1859	Madoc, Ontario
Straus, Oscar S.	December 23, 1850	Otterburg, Rhenish Bavaria
Stuart, John Leighton	June 24, 1876	Hanchow, China
Vail, Aaron	October 24, 1796	Lorient, France
Vopicka, Charles J.	November 3, 1857	Dolni Hbity, Bohemia

NAME	BIRTH DATE	CITY AND/OR COUNTRY
Young, John Russell	November 20, 1840	Tyrone County, Ireland
Zemurray, Samuel	1877	Bessarabia

Unknown

De Long, Charles	c. 1831	—
Hall, Henry	c. 1820	—

LOCATIONS OF MANUSCRIPT COLLECTIONS AND ORAL HISTORIES

The first part of this appendix lists persons and diplomatic events for whom or which manuscript collections exist and the location or locations of significant collections. The appendix does not attempt to list papers of an individual or event contained in a collection ascribed to another individual or event (for example, papers of James Madison located in a Thomas Jefferson collection). The appendix also avoids listing collections smaller than a few hundred pieces, although exceptions have been made when a small collection seems particularly valuable or is all that exists for a particular individual.

With the development of oral-history techniques since World War II, a number of individuals prominent in American diplomatic history have recorded their experiences. Important collections of these recordings are housed at Columbia and Princeton universities and at the various presidential libraries. The second part of this appendix lists the location of oral-history recordings by those persons who are subjects of biographical entries in this volume. In addition, a few Columbia University oral-history special projects of interest to students of diplomatic history are noted.

The major sources for the information contained in this appendix are: Philip M. Hammer, *Guide to Archives and Manuscript Collections in the United States (1960); National Union Catalog of Manuscript Collections* (1959–); Columbia University, *The Oral History Collection* (1973); and material provided by the various presidential libraries, usually in a publication titled *Historical Materials in the . . .* , which contain listings and brief descriptions of manuscript and oral history holdings, along with information regarding their accessibility and guidelines for their use.

These standard abbreviations have been used to designate major respositories:

LC—Library of Congress
NYPL—New York Public Library
HCH Lib.—Herbert Hoover Presidential Library
FDR Lib.—Franklin D. Roosevelt Presidential Library
HST Lib.—Harry S Truman Presidential Library
DDE Lib.–Dwight D. Eisenhower Presidential Library
JFK Lib.–John F. Kennedy Presidential Library
LBJ Lib.–Lyndon B. Johnson Presidential Library
GRF Lib.–Gerald R. Ford Presidential Library

Locations of Manuscript Collections

PERSON AND/OR EVENT	MANUSCRIPT COLLECTION AND LOCATION
Acheson, Dean	HST Lib.
Adams, Brooks	Harvard
Adams, Charles Francis	Mass. Hist. Soc.; Adams Nat. Hist. Site
Adams, John	LC; Mass. Hist. Soc.; Adams Nat. Hist. Site
Adams, John Quincy	LC; Mass. Hist. Soc.; N.Y. Hist. Soc.
Adee, Alvey A.	LC
Alabama, U.S.S.	Hist. Soc. of Pa.
Alaska Commercial Company	Cal. Hist. Soc.; Stanford
Aldrich, Winthrop	Harvard
Allen, Elisha Hunt	LC
Allen, George V.	HST Lib.
America First Committee	Stanford
Anderson, Richard C.	Filson Club (Ky.); Va. St. Lib.; Huntington Lib. (Calif.)
Angell, James	Univ. of Mich.
Armstrong, Anne	GRF Lib.
Armstrong, John	LC; Dickinson Coll. Lib.; Ind. Hist. Soc.
Austin, Warren R.	Univ. of Vt.
Bancroft, Edgar A.	Knox Coll. (Ill.)
Bancroft, George	LC; Mass. Hist. Soc.; Cornell; NYPL
Barbour, James	NYPL; Univ. of Va.; Va. St. Lib.
Barlow, Joel	Harvard; N.Y. Hist. Soc.
Barnard, Daniel D.	N.Y. St. Lib.; LC
Barrett, John	LC
Barringer, Daniel M.	Univ. of N.C.
Barton, Thomas Pennant	Boston Pub. Lib.
Baruch, Bernard M.	Princeton
Batcheller, George S.	N.Y. St. Lib.
Bayard, Thomas F.	LC
Baylies, Francis	Old Colony Hist. Soc.; LC
Beale, Edward Fitzgerald	LC
Beale, Truxtun	LC
Beard, Charles A.	DePauw Univ. (Ind.)
Belmont, August	NYPL
Belmont, Perry	LC
Berle, Adolf A., Jr.	FDR Lib.
Berry, B. Y.	Ind. Univ.
Beveridge, Albert J.	LC; Ind. Hist. Soc.
Bigelow, John	N.Y. Pub. Lib.; LC
Bingham, John A.	Ohio Hist. Soc.
Bingham, Robert W.	LC
Black, Jeremiah Sullivan	LC
Blaine, James G.	LC

PERSON AND/OR EVENT	MANUSCRIPT COLLECTION AND LOCATION
Blair, Francis P.	LC; Princeton
Blake, Maxwell	Univ. of Mo.
Bliss, Tasker H.	LC
Bohlen, Charles E.	LC
Boker, George H.	Princeton
Borah, William E.	LC; Idaho Hist. Soc.; Wash. St. Univ.
Bowles, Chester	JFK Lib.; Yale
Bristol, Mark L.	LC
Brown, James	LC
Bruce, David K. E.	FDR Lib.
Bryan, William Jennings	LC
Buchanan, James	LC; Hist. Soc. of Pa.
Bunche, Ralph J.	UCLA
Bundy, McGeorge	JFK Lib.
Burns, Arthur	GRF Lib.
Byrnes, James F.	Clemson
Cabot, John M.	JFK Lib.
Calhoun, John C.	LC; Univ. of S.C.; Clemson
Cameron, Simon	LC; Hist. Soc. of Dauphin Co. (Pa.)
Carnegie, Andrew	LC
Carnegie Endowment for International Peace	Columbia
Carr, Wilbur J.	LC
Cass, Lewis	Univ. of Mich.; Detroit Pub. Lib.; LC
Castle, William R.	HCH Lib.; Harvard
Child, Richard W.	LC
Choate, Joseph H.	LC
Clark, J. Reuben	Brigham Young Univ.
Clay, Cassius M.	Filson Club (Ky.); Lincoln Univ. (Tenn.); LC
Clay, Henry	LC; Ohio Hist. Soc.; Univ. of Ky.
Clay, Lucius D.	JFK Lib.
Clayton, John M.	LC
Clayton, Will	HST Lib.; Rice Univ.
Colby, Bainbridge	LC
Committee to Defend America by Aiding the Allies	Yale; Princeton
Coolidge, Thomas Jefferson	Mass. Hist. Soc.
Corwin, Thomas	LC
Crawford, William H.	LC
Dallas, George M.	Hist. Soc. of Pa.; Univ. of Pa.
Daniels, Josephus	LC
Davies, Joseph E.	LC

PERSON AND/OR EVENT	MANUSCRIPT COLLECTION AND LOCATION
Davis, Elmer	LC
Davis, J. C. Bancroft	LC
Davis, Nathaniel P.	HST Lib.
Davis, Norman H.	LC
Davis, Roy Tasco	LC; HCH Lib.
Dawes, Charles G.	Northwestern Univ.
Day, William R.	LC
Dayton, William L.	Princeton
Deane, Silas	LC; Conn. Hist. Soc.
DeLeon, Edwin	Univ. of S.C.; LC
Dennett, Tyler	LC
Dewey, George	LC
Dimitry, Alexander	Tulane Univ.
Dix, John A.	Columbia; N.Y. St. Lib.
Dodd, William E.	LC; Randolph-Macon Coll.
Dodge, Augustus Caesar	St. Hist. Soc. of Iowa
Donelson, Andrew J.	LC
Douglass, Frederick	Frederick Douglass Mem. Home
Draper, William H.	DDE Lib.
Dresel, Ellis L.	Harvard
Dulles, John Foster	Princeton; DDE Lib.
Eads, James B.	Mo. Hist. Soc.
Einstein, Lewis	Univ. of Wyo.
Eisenhower, Milton	DDE Lib.
Eustis, William	LC; Mass. Hist. Soc.
Evarts, William M.	LC
Everett, Edward	LC; Mass. Hist. Soc.
Faulkner, Charles J.	Univ. of N.C.; Univ. of Va.
Feis, Herbert	LC
Fight for Freedom	Princeton
Fish, Hamilton	LC; Columbia
Fiske, John	LC; Huntington Lib. (Calif.)
Fletcher, Henry P.	LC
Forsyth, John	LC
Foster, John W.	LC
Francis, David R.	Mo. Hist. Soc.
Franklin, Benjamin	LC; Yale; Univ. of Pa.; Am. Phil. Soc.; Hist. Soc. of Pa.
Frelinghuysen, Frederick T.	LC
Fulbright, J. William	Univ. of Ark.; JFK Lib.
Galbraith, John K.	JFK Lib.
Gallatin, Albert	LC; N.Y. Hist. Soc.
Garrett, John Work	LC
Ghent, Treaty of	NYPL

PERSON AND/OR EVENT	MANUSCRIPT COLLECTION AND LOCATION
Gibson, Hugh	Stanford; HCH Lib.
Grady, Henry F.	HST Lib.
Gresham, Walter Q.	LC
Grew, Joseph C.	Harvard
Griffis, Stanton	HST Lib.
Griscom, Lloyd C.	LC
Guggenheim, Harry F.	LC
Gulick, Sidney L.	Harvard
Hale, Edward J.	Univ. of N.C.
Hare, Raymond	JFK Lib.
Harriman, Florence J.	LC
Harriman, W. Averell	LC
Harris, Townsend	City Coll. of N.Y.; NYPL; LC
Harrison, Leland	LC
Harvey, George	Univ. of N.C.
Hay, John M.	LC; Ill. St. Hist. Lib.; Brown Univ.
Henderson, Loy W.	LC
Herrick, Myron T.	Western Reserve Hist. Soc.; Ohio Hist. Soc.; LC
Herter, Christian A.	DDE Lib.; JFK Lib.
Hill, David Jayne	Univ. of Rochester; Bucknell Coll.
Hilsman, Roger	JFK Lib.
Hoffman, Paul G.	HST Lib.
Hopkins, Harry	FDR Lib.
Hornbeck, Stanley K.	HCH Lib.; Stanford
Hotze, Henry	LC
House, Edward M.	LC; Yale
Hughes, Charles E.	LC
Hughes, Christopher	Univ. of Mich.
Hull, Cordell	LC
Hunter, Robert M. T.	Univ. of Va.
Hurley, Patrick J.	Univ. of Okla.
International Tribunal, Far East	Stanford
International Tribunal, Nuremberg	Stanford
Irving, Washington	NYPL
Jarvis, William	Mass. Hist. Soc.
Jay, John	LC; N.Y. St. Lib.; Columbia; N.Y. Hist. Soc.
Jefferson, Thomas	LC; Univ. of Va.; Mass. Hist. Soc.
Jessup, Philip C.	LC
Johnson, Nelson T.	LC
Johnson, Reverdy	LC; Md. Hist. Soc.
Johnson, U. Alexis	GRF Lib.

PERSON AND/OR EVENT	MANUSCRIPT COLLECTION AND LOCATION
Jones, Hilary P.	LC
Kaltenborn, H. V.	St. Hist. Soc. of Wisc.
Kasson, John A.	Iowa St. Dept. of Hist. and Arch.
Kearney, Lawrence	N.J. Hist. Soc.
Kellogg, Frank B.	Minn. Hist. Soc.; LC
Kennan, George F.	Princeton
Kennedy, Joseph P.	JFK Lib.
King, Rufus	LC; Huntington Lib. (Calif.); N.Y. Hist. Soc.
King, William Rufus	Ala. Dept. of Arch. and Hist.
Kirk, Alan	LC
Kissinger, Henry A.	LC
Knox, Philander C.	LC
Ladd, William	LC; Swarthmore Coll.
Lamont, Thomas	Harvard
Lane, Arthur Bliss	Yale
Lansing, Robert	LC
Larkin, Thomas O.	Univ. of Calif. (Berkeley)
Laurens, Henry	Univ. of S.C.; LC
Lawrence, Abbott	Harvard
Lea, Homer	Stanford
League of Nations	United Nations Arch.
Leahy, William D.	LC; Wis. St. Hist. Soc.
Lear, Tobias	LC
Lee, Arthur	Harvard; Univ. of Va.
Le Gendre, Charles W.	LC; Waseda Univ. (Tokyo)
Levinson, Salmon O.	Univ. of Chicago
Lewis, Fulton, Jr.	Syracuse Univ.
Lincoln, Levi	Am. Antiq. Soc.
Lincoln, Robert T.	LC; Ill. St. Hist. Soc.
Livingston, Robert R.	LC; N.Y. Hist. Soc.
Lodge, Henry Cabot, Sr.	Mass. Hist. Soc.
Loomis, Francis B.	Stanford
Louisiana Purchase	La. Hist. Soc.; Chicago Hist. Soc.; Bibliotheca Parsoniana (La.)
Lowell, James Russell	Harvard; LC
Luce, Henry R.	LC
MacArthur, Douglas	MacArthur Mem. Arch. (Va.)
McDonald, James G.	Columbia
McGhee, George C.	HST Lib.
McLane, Louis	Del. Hist. Soc.; LC
Madison, James	LC; Hist. Soc. of Pa.
Mahan, Alfred T.	LC
Marcy, William L.	LC; N.Y. St. Lib.

PERSON AND/OR EVENT	MANUSCRIPT COLLECTION AND LOCATION
Marsh, George P.	Dartmouth
Marshall, George C.	G.C. Marshall Research Center (Va.)
Marshall, John	LC
Mason, James M.	LC
Mason, John Y.	LC
Messersmith, George S.	Univ. of Del.
Meyer, George von L.	LC; Mass. Hist. Soc.
Moffat, Jay Pierrepont	Harvard
Monroe, James	LC; NYPL; James Monroe Mem. Foundation (Va.)
Moore, John Bassett	LC
Moran, Benjamin	LC
Morgan, John T.	LC
Morris, Gouverneur	LC
Morris, Roland S.	LC
Morton, Levi P.	Syracuse
Motley, John Lothrop	Harvard
Murray, William Vans	LC
Murrow, Edward R.	Tufts Univ.
National Council for the Prevention of War	Stanford
Olney, Richard	LC
O'Shaughnessy, Nelson	N.Y. Hist. Soc.
Pacific Mail Steamship Company	Huntington Lib. (Calif.)
Page, Thomas Nelson	Duke Univ.
Page, Walter Hines	LC; Harvard
Paris Peace Conference (1919)	LC; Stanford
Peixotto, Benjamin F.	Am. Jewish Arch. (Ohio)
Perry, Matthew C.	LC
Phelps, Seth L.	Mo. Hist. Soc.
Phelps, William W.	Huntington Lib. (Calif.)
Philip, Hoffman	N.Y. Hist. Soc.
Phillips, William	Harvard
Pickering, Timothy	LC; Mass. Hist. Soc.; Essex Inst. (Mass.)
Pickett, John	LC
Pierrepont, Edwards	Yale; LC
Pinckney, Charles	LC
Pinckney, Charles Cotesworth	LC; Duke Univ.
Pinckney, Thomas	LC; Duke Univ.; S.C. Hist. Soc.
Pinkney, William	Md. Hist. Soc.; Harvard
Pittman, Key	LC
Platt, Orville H.	Conn. St. Lib.
Poinsett, Joel R.	LC; Hist. Soc. of Pa.

| | MANUSCRIPT COLLECTION |
PERSON AND/OR EVENT	AND LOCATION
Polk, Frank L.	Yale
Porter, Horace	LC
Randolph, Edmund	LC; Va. Hist. Soc.
Read, John Meredith	Hist. Soc. of Pa.; Lib. Co. of Philadelphia
Reed, William B.	LC
Reid, Whitelaw	LC; Yale
Reinsch, Paul S.	St. Hist. Soc. of Wis.
Reparations Commission	Stanford
Richardson, Elliot	LC
Rives, William C.	LC; Univ. of Va.
Rockhill, William W.	LC; Harvard
Rogers, William P.	DDE Lib.
Roosevelt, Eleanor	FDR Lib.
Root, Elihu	LC
Rosecrans, William S.	UCLA
Rostow, Eugene, V. D.	LBJ Lib.
Rostow, Walt	JFK Lib.
Rowe, Leo Stanton	Pan American Union Lib. (Washington, D.C.)
Rush, Richard	LC; Hist. Soc. of Pa.
Rusk, Dean	JFK Lib.
Russell, Jonathan	Brown Univ.; Mass. Hist. Soc.
San Francisco Conference (1945)	United Nations Arch.
Sanford, Henry	Sanford Mem. Lib. (Fla.)
Schurz, Carl	LC
Schuyler, Eugene	LC
Scott, James Brown	Georgetown Univ.
Scruggs, William W.	LC
Service, John S.	HST Lib.
Seward, William H.	LC; Univ. of Rochester
Sherman, John	LC
Short, William	LC; Am. Phil. Soc.
Shotwell, James T.	Columbia
Shufeldt, Robert W.	LC
Sickles, Daniel E.	LC; N.Y. Hist. Soc.
Slidell, John	Tulane
Smith, Robert	LC
Smith, W. Bedell	DDE Lib.
Squier, Ephraim G.	LC; Huntington Lib. (Calif.); N.Y. Hist. Soc.
Standley, William H.	LC; Univ. of S. Calif.
Steinhardt, Laurence A.	LC
Stettinius, Edward R., Jr.	Univ. of Va.

PERSON AND/OR EVENT	MANUSCRIPT COLLECTION AND LOCATION
Stevenson, Adlai	Princeton
Stevenson, Andrew	LC
Stimson, Henry L.	Yale
Stockton, Robert F.	Princeton
Straight, Willard	Cornell
Straus, Oscar S.	LC
Sumner, Charles	Harvard
Swing, Raymond	LC
Taft, Alphonso	LC
Taylor, Bayard	Harvard; Cornell
Teller, Henry	Denver Pub. Lib.; St. Hist. Soc. of Colo.
Thompson, Waddy, Jr.	Univ. of Texas; LC
Tower, Charlemagne	Columbia
Trescot, William H.	LC; Univ. of S.C.
Trist, Nicholas P.	LC; Duke Univ.
United Nations	United Nations Arch.
United Nations Relief and Rehabilitation Administration	United Nations Arch.
United States Mail Steamship Company	N.Y.Hist. Soc.
Vail, Aaron	N.Y. St. Lib.
Van Buren, Martin	LC
Vandenberg, Arthur H.	Univ. of Mich.
Vignaud, Henry	La. St. Arch.; Univ. of Mich.; Hamilton Coll. (N.Y.)
Walker, William	Tulane
Wallace, Lew	Ind. Univ.; Ind. Hist. Soc.
Washburne, Elihu B.	LC; Chicago Pub. Lib.
Webb, James Watson	Yale
Webster, Daniel	LC; Dartmouth; N.H. Hist. Soc.
Weddell, Alexander	Va. Hist. Soc.
Welsh, John	Hist. Soc. of Pa.
Wheaton, Henry	Mass. Hist. Soc.
Wheeler, John H.	LC
White, Andrew D.	Cornell
White, Harry Dexter	Princeton
White, Henry	LC; Columbia
Whitlock, Brand	LC; Stanford
Williams, Edward T.	Univ. of Calif. (Berkeley)
Willis, Albert Shelby	Filson Club (Ky.)
Wilson, F. M. Huntington	Ursinius Coll.
Wilson, Hugh R.	HCH Lib.
Winant, John G.	FDR Lib.
Wood, Leonard	LC
Woodford, Stewart L.	LC

PERSON AND/OR EVENT	MANUSCRIPT COLLECTION AND LOCATION
Wright, Joseph A.	Ind. St. Lib.
Young, John Russell	LC
Young, Owen D.	Van Hornsville (N.Y.) Comm. Corp.

Locations of Oral-History Interviews

COLUMBIA UNIVERSITY ORAL HISTORY COLLECTION

Aldrich, Winthrop
Allen, George V.
Berle, Adolf A.
Blair, William McC.
Bohlen, Charles E.
Bowers, Claude G.
Bowles, Chester
Braden, Spruille
Briggs, Ellis O.
Burns, Arthur E.
Clay, Lucius D.
Davis, Elmer H.
Davis, John W.
Dillon, C. Douglas
Douglas, Lewis
Eisenhower, Milton S.
Fulbright, J. William
Gavin, James M.
Gerard, James W.
Griscom, Lloyd C.
Hare, Raymond A.
Harriman, Florence J.
Harriman, W. Averell
Henderson, Loy W.
Houghton, Amory
Jessup, Philip C.
Johnson, Nelson T.
Keating, Kenneth B.
Kirk, Alan G.
Lovett, Robert
Luce, Clare Booth
Mann, Thomas C.
Murphy, Robert D.
O'Dwyer, William

Phillips, William
Rockefeller, Nelson A.
Rogers, William P.
San Francisco Conference (1945)
Sevareid, Eric
Shotwell, James T.
Stimson, Henry L.

Special Projects at Columbia

Adlai E. Stevenson
Eisenhower Administration
International Negotiations
League of Nations
Marshall Plan
The Occupation of Japan
World Bank

HOOVER LIBRARY ORAL HISTORY COLLECTION

Clay, Lucius D.

TRUMAN LIBRARY ORAL HISTORY COLLECTION

Acheson, Dean
Battle, Lucius D.
Blair, William McC.
Bruce, David K. E.
Cabot, John M.
Clay, Lucius D.
Draper, William H.
Durbrow, Elbridge
Harriman, W. Averell
Henderson, Loy W.
Hoffman, Paul G.
Johnson, U. Alexis
Lovett, Robert A.
McGhee, George C.
Mann, Thomas C.
Nolting, Frederick E.
Service, John S.

EISENHOWER LIBRARY ORAL HISTORY COLLECTION

Mann, Thomas C.
Walters, Vernon

In addition, the Eisenhower Library, which has done a Special Project on the Eisenhower Administration, contains copies of all relevant interviews from the Columbia University Oral History Collection.

KENNEDY LIBRARY ORAL HISTORY COLLECTION

Acheson, Dean
Bohlen, Charles E.
Bowles, Chester
Bruce, David K. E.
Bundy, McGeorge
Cabot, John M.
Clay, Lucius D.
Fulbright, J. William
Hare, Raymond
Harriman, W. Averell
Helms, Richard M.
Hillenbrand, Martin
Hilsman, Roger
Johnson, U. Alexis
Kennan, George F.
Kirk, Alan
Kohler, Foy
Lodge, Jr., Henry Cabot
Lovett, Robert A.
McGhee, George C.
Mann, Thomas C.
Mansfield, Mike
Muskie, Edmund S.
Nitze, Paul H.
Reischauer, Edwin O.
Rostow, Walt W.
Rusk, Dean
Taylor, Maxwell

JOHNSON LIBRARY ORAL HISTORY COLLECTION

Battle, Lucius D.
Bohlen, Charles E.
Bowles, Chester
Bruce, David K. E.
Brzezinski, Zbigniew
Bundy, McGeorge
Bunker, Ellsworth
Cabot, John M.
Christopher, Warren M.

Cooper, John Sherman
Durbrow, Elbridge
Eisenhower, Milton S.
Harriman, W. Averell
Helms, Richard M.
Hilsman, Roger
Johnson, U. Alexis
Martin, John Bartlow
Nitze, Paul H.
Nolting, Frederick
Reischauer, Edwin O.
Richardson, Elliot
Rockefeller, Nelson
Rostow, Eugene V.
Rostow, Walt W.
Rusk, Dean
Shriver, Sargent
Vance, Cyrus
Vaughn, Jack Hood
Warnke, Paul C.
Young, Andrew J., Jr.

PRINCETON UNIVERSITY, DULLES ORAL HISTORY COLLECTION

Bohlen, Charles E.
Bruce, David K. E.
Byrnes, James F.
Clay, Lucius D.
Cooper, John Sherman
Dillon, C. Douglas
Eisenhower, Milton S.
Harriman, W. Averell
Henderson, Loy W.
Herter, Christian
Johnson, U. Alexis
Kennan, George F.
Lodge, Henry Cabot, Jr.,
MacArthur II, Douglas
Mann, Thomas C.
Mansfield, Michael C.
Nolting, Frederick E.
Reinhardt, George F.
Taylor, Maxwell
Thompson, Llewellyn
Yost, Charles W.

INDEX

The page numbers set in **boldface** indicate the location of the main entry.

Abbott, Willis J., **3**
ABC mediation, **3**
ABC–1 Staff Agreement (1941), **3–4**
Abrams, Elliott, **4–5**
Accessory Transit Company, **5**, 21, 524, 530
Accord. *See* International Agreement
Acheson, Dean G., **5–6**, 45–46, 91, 115, 121–22, 133, 158–59, 308–9, 457–58; and Cold War, 317–18; and Good Neighbor Policy, 208
Acheson-Lilienthal Report (1946), **6**, 43–44
Adams, Brooks, **6–7**
Adams, Charles Francis, **7–8**, 273
Adams, Ephraim D., **8**
Adams, John, **8–9**, 9, 10, 192, 270–71; and American Revolution, 407, 421; and quasi-war with France, 314, 371–72, 416–17, 429
Adams, John Quincy, 7, **9**, 40, 47, 99, 222–23, 268–69, 335–56; and Adams-Onis Treaty (1819), 10; and Latin America, 399–400; and Monroe Doctrine, 356, 384; and War of 1812, 206, 249–50, 458–59
"Adams formula," **9–10**
Adams-Onis Treaty, 9, **10**, 20, 189
Addams, Jane, 551–52, 557
Adee, Alvey A., **10**, 151, 474–75
Adenauer, Konrad, 83–84, 125
Afghanistan, 10–11, 95–96, 167, 176; and Soviet invasion of, 106
Afghanistan crisis (1979), **10–11**, 156, 493–94, 538
African Development Bank, **11**
African International Association, **11–12**
African National Congress, 127–28

African Slave Trade Treaty (1862), **12**
Agar, Herbert, **12**, 111
Agency for International Development, 187
Agriculture Trade and Development Act (1954), **12–13**
Aguinaldo, Emilio, 467
Airborne Warning and Control System (AWACS), 370
Aix-la-Chapelle, Congress of, **13**, 113
Alabama, C.S.S., 6, **13**, 363, 367, 465–66, 527, 536; claims and arbitration concerning, 29–30, 185
Alaska Arbitral Tribunal, 13
Alaska boundary dispute (1898–1903), 13, 116, 132, 190, 229–30, 277–78, 293–94, 311–12, 502, 545
Alaska Commercial Company, **14**
Alaska Purchase (1867), **14**, 118–19, 415, 471–72, 472–73
Albania, 60, 314
Aldrich, Winthrop W., **14–15**, 546–47
Algeciras Conference, **15**, 172–73, 218, 545–46
Algeria, 393–94
Algiers Conference, **15**
Alien and Sedition Acts (1798), **15–16**
Allen, Elisha Hunt, **16**, 229
Allen, George V., **16–17**, 520
Allen, Richard V., **17–18**, 118, 422
Allende, Salvador, 114
Alliance for Progress, **18**, 56, 157–58, 161–62, 337, 454–55, 525
Allied Control Council, 18–19, 426, 479
Allison, John M., **19**
"All-of-Mexico" movement, **20**
"All-Oregon," **20**
Ambassador. *See* Chief of Mission

Ambrister, Robert C. and Arbuthnot, Alexander, affair of, **20**, 196, 456–57

America First Committee, **20–21**, 49, 277

American Asiatic Association, **21**

American Atlantic and Pacific Ship-Canal Company, 5, **21**, 524

American China Development Company, **22**

American Foreign Service Association, **22**

American Peace Award (1924), 305

American Peace Society, 291

American Relief Administration, 206–7, 236, 313

American Revolution, 244, 354, 521; diplomatic representatives, U.S., during, 152, 192, 302, 511; treaties concerning, 29, 30, 407, 419, 421

Amiens, Treaty of (1802), **22**

Amistad affair, **22**

Ammer, Daniel, 170, 339

Ancon, Treaty of (1883), 406, 533–34

Anderson, Richard C., **22–23**, 399–400

Andrews, Israel DeWolf, **23**

Angell, James B., **23–24**, 499

Anglo-American Arbitration Treaty (1911), **24**

Anglo-American League, **24**

Anglo-American Northeastern Fisheries Commission, **23–24**

Anglo-French Naval Agreement (1928), **24–25**

Anglo-Japanese Alliance (1902), **25**, 191, 501, 537

Anglophobia, **25**, 60–61, 358–59

Anglo-Russian Convention (1825), 13, **25**

Anglo-Russian Treaty (1942), **25**

Angola, 26, 127–28, 180–81

Angolan Civil War (1974–), **26**, 146–47, 375

Annenberg, Walter H., **26–27**

Anti-Ballistic Missile (ABM) Treaty (1972), 493–94, 494–95, 537–38

Anti-Comitern Pact (1936), **27**

Anti-imperialism, **27–28**, 467

Anti-Imperialist League, **28**, 103–4

ANZUS Treaty (1951), **28**, 382–83

Appeasement, 240, 265–66, 281–82, 292–93, 550–51

Aquino, Corazon, 414

Arab-American Oil Company, **28–29**

Arabic, sinking of, **29**

Arafat, Yasir, 398–99

ARAMCO. *See* Arab-American Oil Company

Aranjuez, Treaty of (1779), **29**

Arbenz, Jacobo, 31, 518

Arbitration, **29–30**, 88, 104, 357, 358–59, 400, 440, 511; diplomatic representatives concerned with, 444–45, 451–52; discussed at international conferences, 220–21, 228–29, 350, 443, 465–66; disputes resolved by, 38–39, 55–56, 339, 390, 525, 526, 533–34, 536; treaties providing for, 24, 390, 464; and Permanent Court of Arbitration, 409–10

Arcadia Conference, **30**, 519, 541–42

Argentina Conference. *See* Atlantic Conference (1941)

Argentina, 3, 182, 224, 307, 385; diplomatic representatives, U.S., in (before 1900), 47, 88, 222–23, 394; diplomatic representatives, U.S., in (since 1900), 31, 41–42, 50, 50–51, 68–69, 79, 91–92, 199, 214–15, 349, 442–43, 541; hemispheric conferences and, 350–51, 443

Arias, Oscar, 177

Arias Plan. *See* Esquipulas II

Armed Neutrality, League of, **30**

Armour, Norman, **31**

Arms Control and Disarmament Agency, 534–35

Arms limitation, 373, 453–54, 494; nuclear arms limitation treaties, 257, 385, 405–6, 493–94

Armstrong, Anne Legendre, **31**

Armstrong, John, **31–32**, 97, 432

Arthur, Chester administration, 58, 115–16. *See also* Frelinghuysen, Frederick T.; *names of U.S. diplomatic representatives*

Article X, **32**, 124, 240, 312–13

Article 51, United Nations Charter, 385–86, 392–93, **444**, 463

Ashburton, Lord (Alexander Baring), 137–38

Asian Development Bank, **32**

Associated States of Indo-China, 232

Atherton, Alfred L., Jr., **32–33**

Atkinson, Edward, 27–28, 28

Atlantic Charter, 25, **33**, 252–53

Atlantic Conference (1941), **33–34**, 242–43

Atomic energy, 43–44, 364–65

Atomic Energy Commission, United Nations, 34, 43–44, 364–65

Austin, Warren R., **34**, 234–35

Australia, 28, 199–200, 483–84

Austria, 13, 20, 242, 291–92, 328, 402, 429, 462; diplomatic representatives, U.S., in (before 1870), 367, 368; di-plo-matic representatives, U.S., in (since 1920), 163, 164–65, 323–24, 349, 508, 535, 559–60

Austria-Hungary diplomatic representatives, U.S., in, 47–48, 277–78, 325, 409, 413, 501, 511, 519–20

Austrian State Treaty (1955), **35**, 134–35, 204, 365, 508

Axis, 513–14

Bacon, Robert, **36**, 468–69

Bagby, Arthur P., **36**

Baghdad Pact (1955), **36–37**, 111, 129, 146, 167–68, 172, 198–99

Bahamas, 137–38

Bailey, Thomas A., **37**

Bailly-Blanchard, Arthur, **37–38**

Baker, James, III, 258–59

Baker, James M., **38**

Baker Plan, 258–59

Balance of power, **38**, 286–88

Baltimore affair, **38–39**, 66–67, 171–72, 190, **266**

Bancroft, Edgar A., **39**

Bancroft, George, **39**, 159, 367

Bangladesh, 367–68

Bank of International Settlements, 207–8, 291–92, 561, 562

Banks, multinational, 11, 32, 256–57, 257–58

Barbary pirates, relations with, **39–40**, 61–62, 270–71, 300, 341–42, 361

Barbour, James, **40**

Barbour, Walworth, **40–41**

Barlow, Joel, **41**

Barnard, Daniel D., **41**

Barrett, John, **41–42**, 350, 400

Barringer, Daniel M., **42**

Bartlett, Joseph J., **42**

Barton, James L., **42–43**

Barton, Thomas P., **43**, 309

Baruch, Bernard, 6, **43–44**, 379–80, 380

Bassett, Ebenezer Don Carlos, **44**

Batcheller, George S., **44–45**

Batista, Fulgencio, 79, 98, 480, 555

Battle, Lucius D., **45–46**

Bay of Pigs invasion, **46**, 110, 140, 216, 489, 503

Bayard, James A., 206

Bayard, Thomas F., **46**, 46–47, 215, 408, 471

Bayard-Chamberlain Treaty (1888), **46–47**

Baylies, Frances, **47**, 224

Beale, Edward Fitzgerald, **47–48**

Beale, Truxtun, **48**, 351–52

Beam, Jacob D., **48–49**

Beard, Charles A., **49**, 188

Bear Flag Revolt, **49–50**

Beaulac, Willard L., **50**

Beaumarchais, Pierre A. C., 244

Beaupré, Arthur M., **50–51**

Belcher, Taylor G., **51**

Belgian Relief Commission, 8

Belgium, 11–12, 301, 386–87, 402, 402–3, 479, 537; diplomatic representatives, U.S., in (before 1920), 464–65, 506, 546, 549–50; diplomatic representatives, U.S., in (since 1920), 143–44, 186–87, 206–7, 285–86, 323–24, 414–15, 427. *See also* Leopold II (King of the Belgians)

Belly, Felix, 108

Belmont, August, **52**

Belmont, Perry, **52**

Bemis, Samuel F., 9, **52–53**

Benjamin, Judah P., **53**

Benjamin, Samuel G. W., **53–54**

Bennett, W. Tapley, Jr., **54**, 161–62

Berger, Samuel D., **55**

Bering Sea dispute, 46, **55–56**, 213–14, 288–89, 293–94, 308, 411–12

Berle, Adolf A., Jr., **56**

Berlin, Treaty of (1876), 408–9

Berlin, Treaty of (1889), **56–57**, 132, 254, 409, 462, 471

Berlin, Treaty of (1921), **57**, 166, 248–49

Berlin, Treaty of (Quadripartite Agreement on Berlin, 1971), **57**, 455–56

Berlin blockade (1948–1949), **57–58**, 95–96, 120, 271–72, 317–18, 321, 342, 479

Berlin Conference (1884–1885), 11–12, **58**, 277–78, 464–65

Berlin Congress (1878), 502

Berlin crisis (1958–1962), **58–59**, 120, 164–65, 236, 238, 273–74, 289–90

Berlin Debt Conference, 167–68

Berlin Decree (1806), 41, **59**, 69–70, 97, 129–30, 198, 331, 356, 419–20, 432. *See also* Milan Decree; War of 1812

Bermuda Conference (1953), **59**

Bern Conference (1874), **59**

Bernstein, Herman, **60**

Berry, Burton Y., **60**

Beveridge, Albert J., **60–61**, 482–83

Bevin, Ernest, 364–65, 365, 426

Bevin-Byrnes Bizonal Fusion Agreement (1946), 65

Biddle, Anthony J. D., Jr., **61**

Biddle, James, **61–62**, 390–91

Bidlack, Benjamin A., **62**

Bidlack Treaty (1846), 62, 513

Bigelow, John, **63**, 151–52

Big Four, **62**, 135, 519

"Big Four," **62–63**

"Big Three," 62–63

Bingham, John A., **63–64**

Bingham, Robert W., **64**

Birch, Thomas H., **64–65**

Birney, James, 218

Bizonia, **65**

Black, Jeremiah S., **65**

Black, Shirley Temple, **65–66**

Black Warrior, affair of, **66**, 160, 338, 483

Blaine, James G., 48, 52, **66–67**, 109–10, 116–17, 193, 274, 308, 316, 328, 413, 436, 488–89, 512–13, 533–34, 536; and Latin American affairs, 171–72, 401, 536

Blair, William McCormick, Jr., **67**

Blake, Maxwell, **67–68**

Blancké, Wilton W., **68**

Bland, Theodorick, 210

Blatchford, Richard M., **68–69**

Bliss, Robert Woods, **69**

Bliss, Tasker H., **69–70**, 256

Blockade, 40, **70**, 140, 193, 401; in War of 1812, 391, 392

Blount, James H., **70**, 213–14

Blow, Henry T., **71**

Blumenthal, W. Michael, **282**

Boal, Pierre de Lagarde, **71**

Boer War (1899–1902), **71–72**, 147–48

Bogotá, Act of (1960), 337

Bogotá, Conference (1948), 50, **72**, 337–38, 392–93

Bohlen, Charles E., **72–73**, 227–28

Boker, George H., **73**

Boland, Edward P., 73

Boland Amendment, **73**

Bolivar, Simon, 399–400

Bolivia, 111–12, 533–34. *See also* War of the Pacific; Chaco War

Bonn Conventions (1952), **74**

Bonsal, Philip W., **74**

Booth, Ralph H., **74–75**

Borah, William E., **75**, 243–44, 264, 305–6, 473, 490–91

Borland, Solon, 5, **75–76**

Borton, Hugh, 76

Borton Drafts (1947), 76

Bowen, Herbert W., **76–77**

Bowers, Claude G., **77**

Bowles, Chester B., **77–78**

Bowlin, James B., **78**

Boxer rebellion (1900), 10, **78–79**, 125–26, 155, 267, 298, 299–300, 435–36, 445–46, 505; and American legation in

Peking, 125–26, 485–86. *See also* Open Door Policy

Braden, Spruille, **79**, 81–82, 111–12, 349

Bradley, Charles W., **79–80**

Brazil, 3, 257–58, 258–59, 319–20, 385; diplomatic representatives, U.S., in (before 1900), 71–72, 125–26, 394, 406, 539; diplomatic representatives, U.S., in (since 1900), 56, 81–82, 97, 98, 206–7, 215, 358

Brentano, Theodore, **80**

Brest-Litovsk, Treaty of (1917), **80**, 477–78

Bretton Woods Conference (1944), **80–81**, 257–58, 260–61, 544–45

Brewster, Kingman, Jr., **81**

Brezhnev, Leonid, 365, 365–66, 493–94, 534–35

Briand, Aristide, 280

Briggs, Ellis O., **81–82**

Brinkmanship, **82**, 167–68

Bristol, Mark L., **82–83**

British Northwest Company, **83**

Broadcasters, Vietnam War, 138–39, 461–62; World War II, 138–39, 144–45, 277, 306, 372, 470–71, 499–500

Brown, James, **83**

Brown, John Porter, **83–84**

Bruce, David K. E., **84–85**, 94, 164–65

Brussels Conference (1937), 27, **85**, 147

Brussels Pact (1948), **85**, 314–15, 385–86, 402–3

Bryan, William Jennings, 27–28, 64–65, **85–86**, 143, 191–92, 222, 293–94, 320–21, 448

Bryan-Chamorro Treaty (1916), **86**, 109, 112

Brzezinski, Zbigniew, 17–18, **86–87**, 376–77, 523

Bucareli Agreement (1923), **87**, 123

Buchanan, James, 65, **87–88**, 107–8, 162–63, 182–83, 247–48, 344, 358, 392, 395, 483. *See also* Cass, Lewis; *names of U.S. diplomatic representatives*

Buchanan, William I., **88**, 350

Buchanan-Pakenham Treaty (1846). *See* Oregon Treaty (1846)

Buenos Aires Conference (1910), **88–89**, 215, 400, 401

Buenos Aires Conference (1936), **89**, 111–12

Bulgaria, 95, 134–35, 146–47, 172–73, 267, 327, 364, 364–65, 369–70, 404, 467–68, 528–29

Bullitt, William C., **89–90**

Bunau-Varilla, Philippe, 138, 381

Bunche, Ralph J., **90–91**

Bundy, McGeorge, **91**, 372–73

Bunker, Ellsworth, **91–92**, 161–62, 337, 342–43, 399

Bureau of American Republics, 66–67, 88–89, **92**, 400, 401, 443, 445, 536

Burlingame, Anson, 92–93

Burlingame Treaty (1868), **92–93**, 115–16, 471–72, 499, 512–13

Burma, 95–96, 324–25, 483–84

Burns, Arthur F., **93**

Burt, Richard R., **93–94**

Burton, Theordore, 202

Bush, George H. W., **94**, 110

Butler, Nicholas Murray, **94–95**, 104

Butterworth, W. Walton, 115

Byrnes, James F., 43–44, **95**, 120, 340–41, 359–60, 364–65, 426, 489, 524

Byroade, Henry A., **95–96**

Cabot, John M., **97**

Cadore letter (1810), 31–32, **97**, 331, 332–33, 432

Caffery, Jefferson, **98**, 163, 555

Cairo Conference (1943), **98–99**

Calhoun, John C., **99**, 352–53, 522–23

Calhoun, William J., **99–100**

California, acquisition of, 49–50, 215–16, 295–96, 508–9; anti-Oriental agitation, 219

Cambodia, 100, 175–76, 203, 336–37, 345–46, 403, 434. *See also* Cambodian incursion (1970)

Cambodian incursion (1970), **100**, 286–88, 295, 526

Cameron, Simon, **100–101**, 118–19

Camp David Accords (1978), 32–33, **101**, 398–99, 440

Campbell, Lewis D., **101–2**

Canada, 104, 522; Alaska boundary question and, 13, 25; Cold War and, 202, 203, 385–86, 386–87, 402–3, 403; diplomatic representatives, U.S., in, 31, 175–76, 354–55, 414–15, 486–87; fishing and sealing disputes, 14, 46–47, 55–56, 338, 338–39; Northeastern boundary question, 451; reciprocity and, 23, 338–39

Canadian-American Deep Waterways Commission, 23–24

Canadian-American Joint High Commission, 277–78

Cannon, Cavendish W., **102**

Caracas Conference (1954), **102**, 216

Carlucci, Frank, **102–3**

Carnegie, Andrew, 27–28, 28, **103–4**, 104, 303–4, 400

Carnegie Endowment for International Peace, 94–95, 103–4, 104, 452, 468–69, 546–47

Caroline affair (1837), **104**, 180

Carr, Wilbur J., **104–5**, 349, 447–48

Carter, Boake (Harold Thomas Henry), **105**

Carter, H. A. P., **105–6**, 229

Carter, Jimmy, 86–87, 101, 399; diplomacy during presidential administration of (1977–1981), 10–11, 32–33, 101, 106, 262–63, 399, 493–94, 523, 560. *See also* Vance, Cyrus R.; *names of U.S. diplomatic representatives*

Carter Doctrine, 10–11, **106**

Casablanca Conference (1943), **106–7**

Casey, William J., 110

"Cash-and-carry," **107**, 378–80, 420

Cass, Lewis, 65, **107–8**

Cass-Yrissari Treaty (1857), **108**

Caste war, Yucatán, **108**

Castle, William R., **108–9**

Castro, Fidel, 18, 216, 480

Catherwood, Frederick, 487

Cavell, Edith, 206–7

Centennial Exposition (1876), 73, 542

CENTO. *See* Central Treaty Organization

Central African Republic, 68

Central America, 128–29, 142, 161, 175–76, 184–85, 218–19, 376, 518, 563; diplomatic representatives, U.S., in 75–76, 239, 313, 487; treaties among nations of, 177, 464, 537. *See also* Costa Rica; El Salvador; Guatemala; Honduras; Nicaragua; *related topics under Panama*

Central American Court of Justice, 86, **109**, 451–52, 537

Central American Treaty (1923), **109**

Central American Union, **109–10**

Central Intelligence Agency (CIA), 73, 94, 102–3, **110**, 114, 146–47, 167–68, 196–97, 216, 232, 411, 481–82, 503, 518, 531–32

Central Powers, 80, **110**, 130, 247

Central Treaty Organization (CENTO), 36–37, **111**, 172, 483–84

Century Group, **111**, 121–22, 125, 144–45, 184

Chaco Peace Conference (1935–1938), 79, 541

Chaco War, 89, **111–12**, 206–7

Chad, 68

Chamizal Treaty, 337

Chamorro, Emiliano, 112

Chamorro-Weitzel Treaty (1913), 86, **112**

Chapin, Seldin, **112**

Chapultepec, Act of (1945), 34, 56, 350–51, 444, 445, 487–88

Chargé d'affaires, **112–13**

Chesapeake Affair (1807), **113**, 174–75, 255, 419–20

Chiang Kai-Shek, 98–99, 114–15, 199–200, 285–86, 375–76, 430, 527

Chief of mission, **113**

Child, Richard W., **113–14**

Chile, 3, 66–67, 114, 266, 346, 533–34; *Baltimore* Affair and, 38–39, 66–67, 171–72; diplomatic representatives, U.S., in (before 1900), 171–72, 282–83, 313, 394, 452, 496, 549–50; diplomatic representatives, U.S., in (since 1900), 31, 50, 77, 146–47, 150, 186–87, 321, 413–14, 549–50; War of the Pacific and, 66–67, 282–83, 313, 394,

533–34; World War II and, 77, 350–51, 443

Chilean Intervention (1973), 110, **114**, 146–47, 233, 286–88

China, 63–64, 78–79, 161, 265, 294, 298, 375–76, 478–79; Chinese civil war (to 1949) and, 114–15, 144, 340–41, 497; Cold War (to 1949) and, 114–15, 340–41; diplomatic representatives, U.S., in (1840–1900), 23–24, 79–80, 125, 154–55, 303, 318, 324, 329–30, 404–5, 435, 499, 560; diplomatic representatives, U.S, in (1900–1949), 94, 95–96, 97, 99–100, 136–37, 144, 155, 199–200, 252–53, 272, 285–86, 324–25, 340–41, 437, 445–46, 466–67, 497, 527, 547; immigration problems and, 23–24, 92–93, 115–16, 179, 201–2, 241, 474–75, 499; international conferences and, 98–99, 537; interwar period, Manchurian crisis and, 321–22, 368–69, 473, 491; missionaries and traders in, 241, 278, 324, 330, 404–5, 435–36, 505, 547; Open Door Policy and, 229–30, 381–82, 391, 484–85; treaties and agreements with other nations: 375, 509; treaties and agreements with U.S., 92–93, 381–82, 509, 533; U.S. economic interest in, 21–22, 127, 211, 221, 250, 380–81, 492–93; World War I and, 473, 515–16; World War II and, 62–63, 210–11 252–53, 364–65. *See also* China, People's Republic of; China, Republic of; Chiang Kai-Shek

China, People's Republic of, 32, 97, 117, 286–88, 367–68, 551–52; Chinese civil war (to 1949) and, 144, 340–41, 497; Cold War and, 48–49, 203, 430, 457–58; diplomatic representatives in, 84–85; normalization of relations with, 351, 491–92

China, Republic of, 32, 324–25, 382–83

China Lobby, **114–15**, 144, 252–53

China White Paper (1949), 114–15, **115**, 271–72

Chinese Exclusion Act (1882), 92–93, **115–16**, 179, 201, 241

Choate, Joseph H., **116**, 414–15

Christiancy, Isaac P., **116–17**

Christopher, Warren M., **117**, 262–63

Churchill, Winston S., 33, 59, 98–99, 204–5, 242–43, 263, 359–60, 504, 557–58; World War II conferences and, 30, 33–34, 106–7, 364, 426, 429–30, 430, 513

Civil War, 7, 65, 472–73; diplomatic representatives to European legations during: Austria, 367; Belgium, 464–65; France, 151–52; Great Britain, 6–7, 358; Italy, 275–76, 339–40; Prussia, 275–76; Russia, 100–101 118–19, 502; Spain, 52, 467; diplomatic representatives to Latin American legations during: Brazil, 539; Mexico, 134; Peru, 444–45; maritime issues and, 130, 187–88, 401; *See also* Alabama, C.S.S.; Confederate diplomacy; Laird rams; *Trent* Affair (1961); Washington, Treaty of (1871)

Clarendon, Lord (George W. F. Villiers), 142

Clark, J. Reuben, Jr., **117–18**, 449–50

Clark, William P., **118**, 175–76, 221, 326–27, 376–77, 422

Clark Memorandum, 117–18

Clay, Cassius M., **118–19**, 502

Clay, Henry, **119**, 134, 206, 249–50, 399–400, 533

Clay, Lucius D., 18–19, 57–58, **120**, 163–64, 270, 370–71

Clayton, John M., **120–21**

Clayton, Will, **121–22**, 201–2, 261, 342

Clayton-Bulwer Treaty (1850), 21, 39, 120–21, **122**, 145, 485, 540; efforts to alter or abrogate, 116, 193, 229–30, 231, 318–19; problems of implementation, 87–88, 142, 283, 297. *See also* Isthmian canal question

Clemenceau, Georges, 135, 403–4

Cleveland, Grover, 69–70; diplomacy during presidential administrations of (1893–1897; 1885–1889), 46, 390. *See also* Bayard, Thomas F.; Gresham, Walter Q.; Olney, Richard; *names of U.S. diplomatic representatives*

Cluseret case, 159

Coexistence, peaceful, **122**

Colby, Bainbridge, **123**, 256

Cold War, 57–58, 65, **123–24**, 262, 373–74, 469–70, 506–7, 514–15, 519–20; diplomatic representatives and statesmen during (1945–1953), 5–6, 34, 60, 84–85, 120, 121–22, 163–64, 225–26, 280–81, 285–86, 292–93, 317–18, 327–28, 340–41, 370–71; diplomatic representatives and statesmen during (since 1953), 72–73, 167–68, 236, 240–41, 310–11, 319–20, 411, 436–37, 453–54, 454–55; international conferences during, 59, 134–35, 314–15, 402, 404; international organizations concerned with, 386–87, 518; papers and documents illustrative of, 76, 152–53, 270, 359–60, 388; terms and slogans, 122, 124, 129, 158–59, 162, 174, 263, 280–81, 307, 344–45; treaties and agreements during, 35, 36–37, 178, 233–34, 336–37, 342. *See also names of specific crises and incidents; names of statesmen and diplomatic representatives*

Collective security, 75, **124**, 240, 299, 357, 392; League of Nations and, 240, 379, 440; United Nations and, 194–95, 518–19

Colombia: diplomatic representatives, U.S., in (before 1920), 22–23, 41–42, 50–51, 150, 252, 459, 469; diplomatic representatives, U.S., in (since 1920), 50, 74, 79, 97, 98, 150, 292–93, 413–14, 525; treaties and agreements with, 230–31, 509, 512–13, 513

Colonialism, **124**, 254

Commission on Human Rights, UNESCO, 449

Committee for Foreign Affairs. *See* Committee of Secret Correspondence

Committee of One Million, 114–15

Committee of Secret Correspondence, **124**, 152

Committee to Defend America by Aiding the Allies (CDAAA), 111, **125**, 184

Communist Information Bureau (COMINFORM), 402

Conant, James B., **125**, 164–65

Confederate diplomacy, 176–77, 284; Confederate secretaries of state and, 53, 251, 510; diplomatic agents and publicists, 153, 232–33, 244–45, 343–44, 417, 427, 431, 479–80, 512–13, 527, 548, 558; naval matters, 13, 68–69, 151–52, 187–88, 401. *See also* Civil War; *Trent* Affair; Washington, Treaty of (1871)

Conger, Edwin H., **125–26**

Congo, Belgian, 11–12, 58, 126–27, 362, 370–71, 506. *See also* Leopold II (King of the Belgians)

Congo (Brazzaville), 68

Congo crisis (1960), 90–91, 102–3, **126–27**, 236, 285–86, 489, 518–19

Connally, Tom, 127, 463

Connally Resolution, **127**, 191, 524

Consortium Loan to China (1911–1913), **127**

Constructive engagement, 26, **127–28**, 375, 531–32

Consul, **128**

Consul-general. *See* Consul

Consular agent. *See* Consul

Contadora Group, **128–29**, 177

Containment, **129**, 194–95, 292–93, 307; development of (before 1953), 5, 280–81, 342, 365, 373–74, 386–87; development of (since 1953), 36–37, 167–68, 336–37, 382–83, 457–58, 483–84, 514–15

Continental System, **129–30**, 353

"Continuous voyage" doctrine, **130**

Contras, 4, 73, 110, 128–29, **130–31**, 177, 221, 261–62, 320, 326–27, 377–78, 434

Contraband, 40, **130**, 193, 314, 380, 401, 421

Convention. *See* International agreement

Convention of 1800, **131**, 341–42, 371–72, 429, 511–12, 557

Convention of 1818, 9, 10, 83, **131–32**, 198, 206, 275, 285, 338–39

Convention of 1866, 63–64

Convention of 1899, 56–57, **132**, 462

Convention on the Rights and Duties of States (1933), 208

Coolidge, Calvin, 94–95; diplomacy during presidential adminis—tration of (1925–1929), 202, 204, 279–80, 310, 509. *See also* Kellogg, Frank B.; *names of U.S. diplomatic representatives*

Coolidge, Thomas Jefferson, **132**, 178–79

Coombs, Frank L., **133**

Cooper, John Sherman, **133–34**

Corwin, Thomas, **134**

Costa Rica, 279, 346, 537; diplomatic representatives, U.S., in (before 1900), 158; diplomatic representatives, U.S., in (since 1900), 148, 163, 170, 172–73, 221–22, 292–93, 348–49. *See also* Central America

Council of Foreign Ministers, 60, 95, **134–35**; and post-war conferences, 364–65, 404, 426; and post-war treaties and agreements, 35

Council of Four, 62, **135**, 403–4

Council of Ten, 62, **135**

Council on Foreign Relations, 91, 121–22, **135–36**, 147, 164–65, 183–84, 286–88, 415–16, 523, 584–85, 559–60

Counselor, **136**

Cox, Samuel S., **136**

Crane, Charles R. **136–37**, 284

Crawford, William H., **137**

Creole Affair (1841–1842), 53, 137–38

Crimean War, 344

Crocker, Chester, 127–28

Croly, Herbert, 188

Cromwell, William Nelson, **138**, 381, 501

Cronkite, Walter L., Jr., **138–39**

Crowder, Enoch H., **139**

Cruise Missiles, deployment of, **139–40**, 257, 386–87, 494

Crystal Palace Exhibition (1851), 297

Cuba, 174, 185, 232–33, 315–16, 505, 521 diplomatic representatives, U.S., in (1900–1930): 50–51, 69–70, 139, 267, 358, 485–86; diplomatic represen- tatives, U.S., in (1930–1960), 50–74, 79, 98, 216–17, 349, 480, 541–42, 555; efforts toward acquisition of (c. 1850–1860): 42, 87–88, 160, 180, 211, 395, 483; relations since 1960, U.S. and, 46, 140, 212–13, 375, 392–93, 428, 444; Spanish-American War and, 302–3, 334–35, 358–59, 390, 402, 421, 502, 505; Ten Years War (1868–1878) and, 563; treaties and agreements with, 140, 180–81; U.S. occupation (1900–1902; 1906–1909) and, 69–70, 140, 333–34, 421, 552. *See also* Batista, Fulgencio; Castro, Fidel

Cuban missile crisis (1962), 18, 69–70, **140**, 278–79, 405–6, 508; Kennedy administration and, 489

Cuban Reciprocity Treaty (1902), 69–70, **140**

Curtis, William E., 92

Cushing, Caleb, 404–5

Cuyamel Fruit Company, 518, 563

Cyane, U.S.S., 75–76

Cyprus, 51, 90–91

Cyprus dispute (1964), 90–91, 518–19

Cyprus question (1974–1976), **141**, 518–19

Czechoslovakia, 310, 342, 402; diplomatic representatives, U.S., in (before 1948), 104–5, 172–73, 486–87, 555; diplomatic representatives, U.S., in (since 1948), 19, 48–49, 81–82, 273–74, 345, 510–11; World War II and, 61, 104–5, 280–81, 369

Czechoslovakian crisis (1968), 493–94, 518–19

Dallas, George M., **142**

Dallas–Clarendon Convention, **142**

Daniels, Josephus, Jr., **143**

Danish West Indies, acquisition of (1917), **143**, 293–94, 389

Davie, William R., 131, 371–72, 429

Davies, John Paton, Jr., **143–44**

Davies, Joseph E., **144**

Davis, Elmer H., **144–45**

Davis, John C. B., **145**

Davis, John W., **145–46**

Davis, Monnett Bain, **146**

Davis, Nathaniel, 114, **146–47**

Davis, Norman H., 85, **147**, 291–92, 554

Davis, Richard H., **147–48**, 215

Davis, Roy Tasco, **148**

Dawes, Charles G., **148–49**, 149, 335–36, 561

Dawes Plan (1924), 148–49, **149**, 159–60, 207–8, 248–49, 279–80, 291–92, 313, 561, 562

Dawson, Thomas C., **150**

Dawson, William, Jr., **150**

Dawson Agreements, **150–51**

Day, William R., **151**, 229–30, 402, 474–75

Dayton, William L., 63, **151–52**, 182–83, 218

Deane, Silas, **152**, 192, 244, 302

Declaration of Lima (1938), 307

Declaration of London (1909), 130

Declaration on Liberated Europe, **152–53**, 426, 557

DeGaulle, Charles, 106–7, 200–201, 245–46, 386–87

DeLeon, Edwin, **153**, 244–45, 251

De Lome letter (1898), **153–54**

De Long, Charles E., **154**

Denby, Charles, **154–55**, 169, 390

Denby, Charle, II, **155**

Dennett, Tyler W. **155–56**

Denmark, 30, 143, 160–61, 385–86, 386–87, 402; diplomatic representatives, U.S., in (before 1900), 543; diplomatic representatives, U.S., in (since (1900), 67, 74–75, 146, 214, 389, 448

Dennis, Alfred L. P., **156**

Destroyers-bases exchange plan (1940), 111, 125

Détente, 123–24, **156**, 96–97, 233–34, 286–88, 491–92

Dewey, George B., **157**

Diaz, Adolfo, 150–51

Diem, Ngo Dinh, 169, 238–39, 310–11, 383, 503–4

Dillon C. Douglas, **157–58**, 342–43

Dimitry, Alexander, **158**

Dingley Tariff Act (1897), 277–78

Disengagement, **158–59**, 280–81, 344–45

Dix, John A., **159**

Dodd, William E., **159–60**

Dodge, Augustus C., **160**

Dodge, Henry P., **160–61**

Dole, Sanford B., 488–89, 548–49

Dollar Diplomacy, 99–100, **161**, 250, 288–89, 380–81, 401, 492–93

Dominican crisis (1965), 54, 91–92, **161–62**, 337, 392–93, 444, 489, 523

Dominican Republic, 54, 81–82, 150, 300, 335–36, 347–48, 412, 413–14, 427, 459; attempts to annex (c. 1870), 44, 185, 211, 467, 471–72, 498; U. S. intervention in, 161, 189–90, 551. *See also* Dominican crisis (1965)

Domino theory, **162**, 294–95, 376

Donelson, Andrew J., **162–63**

Donnelly, Walter J., **163**

Douglas, Lewis W., 111, **163–64**

Douglass, Frederick (Frederick Augustus Washington Baily), **164**

Dowling, Walter C., **164–65**

Drago, Luis, 165

Drago Doctrine (1903), **165**, 425, 443, 526

Draper, William H., Jr., **165–66**

Draw poker, 465–66

Dresel, Ellis L., **166**

Droppers, Garrett A., **166**

Dubs, Adolph, **167**

Dulles, Allen W., 110, 133, 167–68

Dulles, John Foster, 5–6, 48–49, 102, 129, 138, 157–59, 167–68, 190, 225–26, 236, 307, 323–24, 449, 457–458, 483–84, 527; conferences attended, 59, 402–3, 463; terms and catchphrases popularized, 82, 174, 344–45; treaties and agreements arranged, 178, 336–37

Dumbarton Oaks Conference (1944), 18–19, 34, 90–91, **168–69**, 223- 24, 250–51, 463, 487–88, 518–19

Dun, Edwin, **169**

Durbrow, Elbridge, **169**

Eads, James B., 71–72, **170**, 459

Eaton, John H., 361

Eaton, William H., 300

Eberhardt, Charles C., **170**

Economic Cooperation Administration (ECA), 163, 225–26, 227–28. *See also* Marshall Plan

Ecuador, 150, 315–16, 393–94, 496

EDC. *See* European Defense Community

Eden, Anthony, 25, 308–9, 314–15, 335, 363–64, 402–3, 426, 497–98

Edge, Walter E., **171**

Edge Amendment, 171

Egan, Maurice F., 143

Egan, Patrick, 38–39, **171–72**

Egypt, 32–33, 44–45, 45–46, 95–96, 98, 172, 214–15, 223–24, 302, 409, 558–59; Arab-Israeli dispute, 101, 172, 479, 497–98

Eichelberger, Clark, 125

Eighteen–Nation Disarmament Committee, 385

Eighth International Conference of American States (1938). *See* Lima Conference (1938)

Eilts, Herman F., **172**

Einstein, Lewis D., **172–73**

Eisenhower, Dwight D., 15, 18–19, 59, 302, 370–71; diplomacy during presidential administration of (1953–1961), 84–85, 133–34, 157–58, 162, 167–68, 173, 204–5, 344–45, 517. *See also* Dulles, John F.; Herter, Christian A.; *names of U.S. diplomatic representatives*

Eisenhower, Milton S., **173**

Eisenhower Doctrine, 167–68, **174**

El Salvador, 286, 335–36, 534, 537; diplomatic representatives, U.S., in, 98, 160–61, 315, 337, 348–49, 406, 415–16

El Salvador civil war (1979–), **174**

Ellsworth, Oliver, 131, 371–72, 429

Embargo Act (1807), 113, **174–75**, 255, 332–33, 384, 419–20

Embargo Act (1812), **175**, 270–71

Emergency Quota Act (1921), **175**

Emory, Frederic, 92

Enders, Thomas O., **175–76**

Engert, Cornelius, **176**

Entente Cordiale, **176**, 191–92, 222

Erlanger and Company, **176–77**

Erlanger loan, 343–44

Erskine agreements (1809), **177**, 384, 391, 481

Esquipulas II (1987), 128–29, 130–31, **177**

Essex decision (1805), 130, **178**, 424–25, 455

Estonia, 292–93

Estrada, Juan J., 150–51

Ethiopia, 176, 240, 265–66, 413–14, 434

European Advisory Commission, 18–19, 551

European Coal and Steel Community, 84–85

European Coal Organization, 55

European Common Market, 236, 282

European Defense Community (EDC), 84–85, 157–58, **178**, 308–9, 314–15, 386–87, 402–3

Eustis, James B., **178–79**

Evarts, William M., 68–69, 116–17, **179**

Everett, Edward, **180**

Executive agreement, **180**, 257

Export–Import Bank, 121–22, **180–81**, 199–200

Exterritoriality, 181

Extraterritoriality, **181**, 247–48, 533

Falkland Islands, 47, 224

Falkland Islands War (1982), **182**, 221, 392–93

Far Eastern Commission, 267, 272

Farewell Address (George Washington), **182**, 421

Faulkner, Charles J., **182–83**

Feis, Herbert, **183–84**

Feland, Logan, 170

Fenian controversy, 318–19, 542

FFF. *See* Fight for Freedom Committee

Fifth International Conference of American States (1923). *See* Santiago Conference (1923)

"Fifty-four Forty or Fight!" 20, **184**

Fight for Freedom Committee, 125, **184**

Filibuster, 5, 108, 120–21, **184–85**, 395–96, 530, 540, 561–62

Fillmore, Millard, 134. *See also* Webster,

Daniel; Everett, Edward; *names of U.S. diplomatic representatives*
Finland, 95, 134–35, 377, 404
First Hague Peace Conference (1899). *See* Hague Peace Conferences (1899 and 1907)
First International Conference of American States (1889). *See* Washington Conference (1889)
First Philippine Commission. *See* Schurman Commission
Fish, Hamilton, **185**, 229, 387, 528
Fiske, John, **185–86**, 482–83
Fiume problem, **186**, 397, 545–46
Five-Power Treaty (1922), **186**, 315, 451–52, 537
Fletcher, Henry P., 168–69, **186–87**, 465
Florida, 10, 20, 31–32, 310, 354, 387, 418
Food and Agriculture Organization (FAO), 244
"Food for Peace." *See* Agricultural Development and Trade Act (1954)
Ford, Gerald, 534–35; diplomacy during presidential administration of (1974–1977), 233–34, 286–88, 345–46; 493–94. *See also* Kissinger, Henry A.; *names of U.S. diplomatic representatives*
Fordney-McCumber Tariff (1922), 482
Foreign Assistance Act (1961), **187**, 373–74
Foreign Enlistment Act, **187–88**, 291
Foreign Operations Administration, 373–74
Foreign Policy Association, **188**, 325–26, 455–56
Foreign Relations of the United States: Diplomatic Papers, **188**
Foreign Service, U.S., organization and professionalization of, 556; congressional acts relating to, 366, 438, 492; individuals concerned with, 104–5, 112, 288–89, 549
Foreign Service Act (1946), 104–5, **188–89**, 447–48, 556
Foreign Service Institute, 188–89
Formosa Resolution, 430

Formosa Straits crises (1954–1955; 1958). *See* Quemoy-Matsu crises
Forsyth, John, **189**
Fort Missions, **189–90**, 551
Foster, John W., 167–68, **190**, 293–94, 462–63, 474–75
"Four Policeman," **190–91**, 504
Four Power Declaration on General Security (1943), 127, **191**, 363–64
Four-Power Treaty, 25, **191**, 537
Fourteen Points, 80, **191**, 246–47, 336, 391, 438–39
Fourth International Conference of American States (1910). *See* Buenos Aires Conference (1910)
France, 176, 291–92, 301–2; American Revolution and; 9, 29, 152, 192, 244, 302; Cold War and; 57, 178, 497–98; diplomatic representatives, U.S., in (1778–1850), 31–32, 41, 83, 107–8, 137, 192, 198, 270–71, 283–84, 309, 310, 341–42, 355–56, 360–61, 418, 444, 456–57, 475; diplomatic representatives, U.S., in (1850–1900), 63, 132, 159, 178–79, 182–83, 329–30, 344, 363, 387, 425, 436, 527, 536; diplomatic representatives, U.S., in (1900–1940), 36, 89–90, 171, 235, 299–300, 316, 325, 370–71, 425, 474, 495, 530–31, 545–46; diplomatic representatives, U.S., in (1940–1988), 61, 72, 84–85, 98, 157–58, 196–97, 200–201, 227–28, 245–46, 264–65, 321, 446, 455–56, 475–76, 538; international conferences and (before 1941), 13, 15, 369, 537; international conferences and (since 1941), 203, 204–5, 402, 402–3, 479; international organizations and: 386–87, 483–84; Napoleonic Wars and; 22, 31–32, 59, 331, 353, 432; "quasi-war" (1798–1800) and; 9, 314, 341–42, 371–72, 429, 557; treaties and agreements with other nations, 22, 24–25, 29, 310, 314, 353, 423–24, 429, 463, 509; treaties and agreements with U.S. (before 1900), 131, 194, 317; treaties and agreements with U.S.

(since 1900), 24, 35, 57, 186, 191, 242, 280, 511–12, 519; World War I and, 135, 256, 464; World War II and, 18–19, 260–61, 299–300, 370–71. *See also* Clemenceau, Georges; DeGaulle, Charles; Napoleon, Louis

Francis, David R., **191–92**

Franco-American alliance. *See* Treaty of Amity and Commerce, Franco-American (1778)

Franco-Prussian War (1870), 327, 359, 433–34, 536

Franklin, Benjamin, 152, **192**, 268–69, 270–71, 302, 325, 407

"Free ships, free goods," **193**, 269–70, 421

"Freedom of the seas," **193**, 399–400, 459–60

Frelinghuysen, Frederick T., 145, **193**, 194, 339, 412–13, 533–34

Frelinghuysen-Zavala Treaty (1884), 193, **194**, 339, 348, 412–13

French Revolution, 270–71, 360–61, 429, 475. *See also related topics under* France

French spoliation claims, 43, 83, 137, 189, **194**, 198, 309, 310, 328–29, 444, 543

Frerant claims, 496

Fulbright, J. William, 127, **194–95**

Fulbright Resolution, 191, 194–95

Gabon, 68, 393–94

Gadsden, James, **196**

Gadsden Purchase, **196**, 338

Galbraith, Evan G., **196–97**

Galbraith, J. Kenneth, 77–78, **197–98**

Gallatin, Albert, 131–32, 142, **198**, 206, 275, 481

Gallman, Waldemar J., **198–99**

Garfield, James, 66–67

Garrett, John W., **199**, 354–55

GATT. *See* General Agreement on Tariffs and Trade

Gauss, Clarence E., **199–200**

Gavin, James M., **200–201**

Geary Act (1892), **201**

General Agreement on Tariffs and Trade (GATT), 121–22, **201–2**, 282, 366–67

Gênet, Edmund, 270–71, 360–61, 432–33

Geneva Accords (1954), **202**, 336–37

Geneva Arms Convention (1925), **202**, 203

Geneva Conference (1954), 74, 202, **203**, 273–74, 294–95, 481–82, 491–92

Geneva Conference (1961–1962), **203**, 225–26, 294–95

Geneva Conventions (1949), **203**, 227

Geneva Disarmament Conference (1932), 297

Geneva Economic Conference (1927), 147

Geneva Foreign Ministers Conference, 164–65

Geneva Naval Conference (1927), **204**, 206–7, 275

Geneva Protocol (1924), **204**

Geneva Summit Conference (1955), **204–5**, 273–74

Geneva Summit Conference (1985), **205**, 345

Gentlemen's Agreement (1907), **205**, 267, 361, 389, 451–52

Gerard, James W., **205–6**, 236

Germany, 526; colonial expansion (1871–1914) and, 56–57, 58, 277–78, 381, 462; diplomatic representatives, U.S., in (before 1900), 39, 145, 408, 413, 502, 517–18, 544; diplomatic representatives, U.S., in (1900–1941), 159–60, 205–6, 237–38, 245, 267, 303–4, 461, 466–67, 511, 550–51; international conferences and (before 1941), 15, 220–21, 369; interwar period and, 149, 159–60, 242, 335–36, 369, 438–39, 554; treaties and agreements with other nations, 27, 310, 377, 433, 513–14; treaties and agreements with U.S., 56–57, 132, 328; World War I and, 57, 166, 222, 247, 320, 499, 517, 563–64; World II and, 3–4, 27, 107, 260, 426, 430, 493, 504, 513–14, 557–58. *See also* Adenauer, Konrad; Germany, Democratic Republic of, Germany,

Federal Republic of; Hitler, Adolf; Weimar Republic; Wilhelm, Kaiser

Germany, Democratic Republic of (East Germany), 57, 58–59, 133–34, 227–28

Germany, Federal Republic of (West Germany), 310–11; Cold War and, 5, 57–58, 58–59, 178, 314–15, 385–86; diplomatic representatives, U.S., in (1955–1988), 125, 163–64, 321; diplomatic representatives, U.S, in (1955–1988), 84–85, 93–94, 125, 163–64, 238, 327–28, 455–56, 491–92; European defense and, 5, 386–87; international conferences and, 204–5, 402–3, 479; international organizations and, 308–9, 386–87; post-World War II reconstruction and, 18–19, 65, 120, 133–34, 165–66, 270–71, 370–71. *See also* Adenauer, Konrad; Germany; Germany, Democratic Republic of

Gerry, Elbridge, 418, 557

Ghana, 65–66

Ghent, Treaty of (1814), 9, 119, 142, 198, **206**, 355–56, 458–59

Gibson, Hugh S., 202, **206–7**, 315, 554

Gifford, Walter S., **207**

Gilbert, Parker, **207–8**

Giraud, Henri, 106–7

Glass, Carter, 184

Godkin, E. L., 27–28, 28

Goldberg, Arthur, 440

Gondra Treaty (1923), 465

Good Neighbor Policy, 56, 161–62, **208**, 356–57, 401, 455, 541, 541–42

Gorbachev Mikhail, 123–24, 129, 205, 366, 441, 537–38

Gore, Thomas, 208–9

Gore-McLemore Resolutions (1915–1916), **208–9**

Grace, William R., **209**

Grady, Henry F., **209–10**

Graham, John, **210**

Grand Alliance, 469–70. *See also* "Big Four" (World War II)

Grant, Ulysses S., 324, 499; diplomacy during presidential administration of (1869–1877), 73, 185, 229, 498. *See also* Fish, Hamilton; *names of U.S. and diplomatic representatives*

Great Britain, 20, 24, 25, 47, 55–56, 71–72, 176, 182, 224, 366–67, 381, 385, 525, 526; acts of Parliament and orders of Privy Council, 187–88, 391, 392; admiralty decisions and policies, 178, 424–25, 452; American Revolution and, 8–9, 192, 296–97, 407; Civil War and, 244–45, 343–44, 512; Cold War and, 57, 74, 111, 152–53, 203, 204–5, 262, 342, 365, 402, 479, 497–98; diplomatic representatives, U.S., in (1785–1850), 8–9, 9, 39, 40, 180, 198, 296–97, 328–29, 355–56, 418–19, 419–20, 456–57, 489–90, 522; diplomatic representatives, U.S., in (1850–1900), 6–7, 46, 87–88, 116, 142, 229–30, 255, 273, 283, 297, 308, 318–19, 411–12, 417, 465–66, 542, 545–6; diplomatic representatives, U.S., in (1900–1945), 64, 148–49, 228, 229–30, 245, 279–80, 281–82, 347, 397–98, 436, 545–46, 551; diplomatic representatives, U.S., in (since 1945), 14–15, 26–27, 31, 81–82, 163–64, 207, 225–26, 317, 427, 441–42, 546–47; international conferences and (before 1941): 13, 204, 220–21, 315, 369, 433, 537; international conferences and (since 1941), 203, 204–5, 335, 402, 402–3, 426, 479, 557–58; international organizations and, 111, 386–87, 409–10, 410, 483–84, 518–19, 519–20; Isthmian canal question and, 21, 66–67, 142, 239, 297; Napoleonic Wars and, 59, 255, 269–70, 353, 355–56; Northeastern boundary question and, 328–29, 451, 540; Oregon question and, 328–29, 392; treaties and agreements with other nations, 22, 24–25, 25, 36–37, 314, 375, 423–24, 429, 509; treaties and agreements with U.S. (before 1900), 12, 122, 131–32, 142, 206, 212, 269–70, 277, 285, 328–29, 356, 390, 536, 540; treaties and agreements with U.S. (since 1900), 3–4, 24, 35, 46–47, 56–57, 57,

186, 191, 231, 405–6, 519; War of
1812 and, 9, 331, 356, 384, 391, 392,
424–25; World War I and, 29, 135,
247, 256, 314, 397–98, 464, 563–64;
World War II and, 3–4, 15, 62–63,
107, 125, 184, 225–26, 260 262, 304,
335, 364, 364–65, 369, 430, 504, 519,
551, 557–58; See also Attlee, Clement;
Bevin, Ernest; Churchill, Winston;
Eden, Anthony; Lloyd George, David
Great White Fleet (1907–1908), **210**,
452–53
Greater East Asia Co-Prosperity Sphere,
210–11
Greece: Cold War and, 60, 385–86, 386–
87, 402, 445–46, 466–67, 514–15;
diplomatic representatives, U.S., in
(before 1900), 48, 433–34, 467–68;
diplomatic representatives, U.S., in
(since 1900), 16–17, 81–82, 166, 209–
10, 267, 332, 411
Green, Benjamin E., **211**
Green, John C., **211**
Green, Marshall, **212**
Greenville, Treaty of (1795), 212
Grenada, 212–13
Grenada Intervention (1983), **212–13**,
392–93, 422, 434, 534
Gresham, Walter Q., **213–14**, 390, 469,
478–79, 517–18
Grew, Joseph C., 212, **214**, 321, 354–
55, 450
Griffis, Stanton, **214–15**
Griscom, Lloyd C., 147–48, 215
Guadalupe-Hidalgo, Treaty of (1848),
108, 211, **215–16**, 295–96, 417, 514
Guam, **4**, 382–83, 402
Guantanamo Naval Base, Cuba, 50–51
Guatemala, 31, 146–47, 148, 239, 279,
315–16, 346–47, 411, 537. *See also*
Central America; Guatemalan crisis
(1954)
Guatemala Accord (1987). *See* Esquipu-
las II
Guatemalan crisis (1954), 31, 102, 110,
216, 411, 518, 518–19
Guggenheim, Harry F., **216–17**, 271–72

Gulf of Tonkin incidents (1964), 217.
See also Vietnam War
Gulf of Tonkin Resolution (1964), 194–
95, **217**
Gulick, Sidney L., **218**
Gummeré, Samuel René, **218**
"Gunboat diplomacy," **218–19**
Gunther, John, **219**
Guthrie, George W., **219**

Habib, Philip, **220**
Hague Peace Conferences (1899 and
1907), **220–21**, 291, 409–410; First
(1899) Conference, 29–30, 237–38,
267, 350, 544; Second (1907) Conference, 116, 165, 167–68, 237–38, 241–
42, 425, 443, 468–69
Haig, Alexander M., Jr., 17–18, 118,
182, **221**, 326–27, 376–77, 476–77
Haiti, 413–14, 551; diplomatic representatives, U.S., in (before 1900), 44,
148, 164, 293; diplomatic representatives, U.S., in (since 1900), 31, 37–
38; U.S. intervention in, 37–38, 161,
189–90, 369, 462–63
Hale, William B., **222**
Halsey, Thomas L., **222–23**
Hamilton, Alexander, 9, 182, 268–69,
270–71, 311–12, 416–17, 432–33
Hammond, Ogden H., **223**
Harding, Warren G., 440; diplomacy
during presidential administration of
(1921–1923), 57, 175, 537. *See also*
Hughes, Charles Evans; *names of U.S.
diplomatic representatives*
Hare, Raymond A., 45–46, 95–96, **223–
24**
Harriet incident (1831), 47, **224**
Harriman, Florence J., **224–25**
Harriman, W. Averell, 33, 74, 220, **225–
26**, 342, 342–43, 364, 405–6, 531–32
Harris, Townsend, **226**, 226–27, 427–28,
475
Harris Treaty (1858), **226–27**
Harrison, Benjamin, 506; diplomacy dur-
ing presidential administration of
(1889–1892), 164, 171–72. *See also*
Blaine, James G.; Foster, John W.;

*names of U.S. diplomatic
representatives*
Harrison, Leland, **227**
Harrison, William Henry. *See* Webster,
Daniel
Hartman, Arthur A., **227–28**, 345
Harvey, George B. McC., **228**, 245,
274, 279–80
Havana Conference (1928), **228–29**, 362,
401, 468–69
Hawaii, 193, 283–84, 397, 408; annexa-
tion of, 27–28, 69–70, 190, 213–14,
471, 472–73, 488–89, 548–49; diplo-
matic representatives of, 16, 341, 408,
441; trade and reciprocity, 105–6, 185,
229, 328; World War II and, 3–4, 407
Hawaiian Reciprocity Treaty (1875), 16,
105–6, **229**, 408
Hawley-Smoot Tariff (1930). *See* Smoot-
Hawley Tariff (1930)
Hay, John M., 116, 156, 218, **229–30**,
237–38, 391, 436, 445–46, 484–85,
545–46; treaties negotiated by, 230,
230–31, 231
Hay-Bond Treaty (1902), **230**
Hay-Bunau-Varilla Treaty (1903), **229–
30**, 230–231, 288–89, 381, 399
Hay-Herbert Treaty (1903), 13, 25
Hay-Herrán Treaty (1903), 50–51, **230–
31**
Hay-Pauncefote Treaty (1901), 122, 229–
30, **231**, 311–12, 357, 400, 545–46
Hayes, Carleton J. H., **231**
Hayes, Rutherford B., 115–16. *See also*
Evarts, William M.; *names of U.S.
diplomatic representatives*
Heath, Donald R., **232**
Helm, Charles J., **232–33**
Helms, Richard McG., **233**
Helsinki Conference (1975), **233–34**, 373
Henderson, Loy W., **234–35**
Hepburn bill (1902), **235**, 485
Herrick, Myron T., **235**
Herter, Christian A., **236**, 282
Hickenlooper Amendment, 187
Higgins, Marguerite, **236–37**
Hill, David Jayne, **237–38**
Hillenbrand, Martin J. A., **238**

Hilsman, Roger, Jr., **238–39**, 526
Hise, Elijah, **239**
Historians, diplomatic, 36–37, 49, 52–
53, 155–56, 190, 274, 296, 353
Hitchcock, Ethan A., **239–40**
Hitchcock, G. M., 240
Hitchcock Reservations, **240**
Hitler, Adolf, 27, 369, 438–39
Hoare-Laval Plan, **240**, 265–66
Hobson, Henry W., 111, 184
Hoffman, Paul G., **240–41**, 342
Holcombe, Chester, **241**
Holt, Hamilton, 104, **241–42**, 299
Holy Alliance, **242**
Honduras, 160–61, 239, 279, 377–78,
406, 485, 505, 537, 563. *See also*
Central America
Hong Kong, 324–25, 375
Hoover, Herbert, 8, 205–6, 206–7, 236,
313, 546; diplomacy during presiden-
tial administration of (1929–1933),
208, 242, 433, 461, 473. *See also*
Stimson, Henry L.; *names of U.S. dip-
lomatic representatives*
Hoover moratorium (1931), 108–9, 148–
49, **242**, 347, 438–39, 461, 562
Hopkins, Harry, 30, 33, 33–34, **242–43**,
250–51, 304, 306
Hornbeck, Stanley K., 144–45, **243–44**
Hortalez (Rodrigue) and Company, **244**,
302
"Hot pursuit," 179
Hot Springs Conference (1943), **244**
Hotze, Henry, 153, **244–45**, 251, 548
Houghton, Alanson B., **245**
Houghton, Amory, **245–46**
House, Edward Howard, 29, **246**, 191–
92
House, Edward Mandell, **246–47**, 247,
256, 293–94, 530–31
House-Grey Memorandum, **247**
Huai River project, 437
Hubbard, Richard B., **247–48**
Hudson's Bay Company, **248**
Huerta, Victoriano, 394–95, 549–50
Hughes, Charles Evans, 149, 204, **248–
49**, 537
Hughes, Christopher, **249–50**

Hukuang Railway Loan, **250**, 492–93
Hull, Cordell, 64, 113–14, **250–51**, 379, 434–35, 541, 541–42; and Latin American affairs, 72, 89, 208, 228–29, 303, 356–57; and World War II, 102, 191, 359–60, 363–64, 450, 487–88
Hungarian revolt (1956), 518–19
Hungary, 95, 134–35, 307, 335–36, 364, 403, 404, 513, 519–20; diplomatic representatives, U.S., in, 80, 112, 238, 555
Hunt, William H., **251**
Hunter, Robert M. T., **251**
Hurlbut, Stephen A., **252**, 282–83
Hurley, Patrick J., 144, 199–200, **252–53**

IBRD. *See* International Bank for Reconstruction and Development
Iceland, 332, 385–86, 386–87, 402
IDB. *See* Inter-American Development Bank
Ide, Henry Clay, **254**
IMF. *See* International Monetary Fund
Immigration, 248–49, 507; exclusion of Chinese, 23–24, 92–93, 115–16, 179, 201–2, 241, 474–75, 499; exclusion of Japanese, 39, 205, 217–18, 267, 274–75, 499; acts of Congress affecting, 115–16, 175, 274–75
Imperialism, 124, **254**
Impressment, 40, 113, 131–32, **255**, 341–42, 356, 384, 533
India, 202, 203, 257–58, 385, 414–15, 453–54, 483–84; diplomatic representatives, U.S., in, 16–17, 77–78, 91–92, 133–34, 197–98, 209–10, 234–35, 278–79, 367–68
Indochina, 202, 203. *See also* Cambodia; Laos; Vietnam, Demo—cratic Republic of (North Vietnam); Vietnam, Republic of (South Vietnam); Vietnam War
Indonesia, 19, 91–92, 257–58, 393–94, 403, 453–54, 483–84
INF Treaty (1987). *See* Intermediate Nuclear Force Treaty (1987)
Ingersoll, Joseph R., **255**
Ingersoll, Robert S., **255–56**
Inonu, Ismet, 98–99

Interallied Conference (1917), 246–47, **256**
Interallied Council, 123
Interallied Games (1919), **256**
Inter-American Defense Board, 443
Inter-American Development Bank (IDB), 157–58, **256–57**, 258–59
Inter-American Treaty of Reciprocal Assistance (1947). *See* Rio Treaty (1947)
Intermediate Nuclear Force Treaty (1987), 93–94, 123–24, 129, 139–40, 257, 326–27, 366, 373, 382, 386–87, 476–77, 493–94, 538
International agreement, **257**
International Bank for Reconstruction and Development (IBRD), 5, 80–81, 176, **257–58**
International Colonial Exposition, Paris (1931), 171
International Congress of Navigation, 221–22
International Control Commission, 203
International Cooperation Administration, 289–90, 373–74
International Court of Justice. *See* Permanent Court of International Justice, 168–69
International debt crisis (1982-   ), 257–58, **258–59**
International Development Association, 257–58
International Famine Relief Committee, 136–37
International Information Administration, 520
International Labor Organization (ILO), 183–84, **259**, 413–14, 463, 551
International Military Tribunal for the Far East, **259–60**
International Military Tribunal of Nuremberg, **260**
International Monetary Conference (1881), 179
International Monetary Fund (IMF), 5, 80–81, 257–58, 258–59, **260–61**, 544
International Planned Parenthood, 163–64
International Red Cross Conference (1949), 203, 227

International Sugar Conference (1937), 147

International Supervisory Commission, 203

International Trade and Employment Conference (1947), 261

International Trade Organization (ITO), 121–22, 201–2, **261**

Intervention, U.S., 165, 356–57; in Cuba, 69–70, 140, 333–34, 421, 552; in Dominican Republic, 161, 161–62, 189–90, 551; in Guatemala, 216; in Haiti, 37–38, 161, 189–90, 369, 462–63; in Lebanon, 302; and Monroe Doctrine, 356, 449–50; in Nicaragua, 150, 161, 170, 279–80, 289, 490–91, 509–10; in Siberia, 477–78; in Venezuela, 525, 525–26

Iran, 36–37, 261–62, 262, 262–63, 263, 326–27, 364–65, 393–94; diplomatic representatives, U.S., in, 16–17, 112, 209–10, 233, 234–35, 323–24, 351. See also Iran crisis (1946); Persia

Iran-contra scandal (1986), 4, 73, 94, 102–3, 110, 118, **261–62**, 263, 372–73, 376–77, 422, 476–77

Iran crisis (1946), 16–17, 95, **262**

Iranian hostage crisis (1979–1981), 117, **262–63**, 372–73, 409–10, 523, 534

Iran-Iraq War (1980-   ), 262–63, **263**, 393–94, 531–32

Iraq, 36–37, 60, 174, 198–99, 234–35, 263, 284, 302, 393–94

Ireland, 318–19, 402

"Iron curtain," **263**

"Irreconcilables," 75, 228, **264**, 288–89

Irving, Washington, 237–38, **264**, 328–29

Irwin, John N., **264–65**

Isolationism, 85, 105, 111, 182, **265**, 320, 484, 499–500; supporters of, U.S., 49, 306, 353, 380, 524

Israel, 234–35, 301–2, 340–41; Arab-Israeli dispute, 101, 325–26, 351, 398–99, 440, 448, 476–77, 479, 497–98, 558–59; diplomatic representatives, U.S., in, 40–41, 146, 278–79, 306–7, 325–26, 326–27, 415–16, 510–11

Isthmian Canal Commission, 333–34, 369–70

Isthmian canal question, 122, 185, 221–22, 297, 474–75; and Clayton-Bulwer Treaty, 66–67, 122, 193, 194, 239, 485; and early transit routes, 21, 62, 330, 487; and final choice of Panama route, 138, 229–30, 230, 230–31, 316, 358–59, 381, 458, 485; and proposed Nicaragua canal, 209, 235, 339, 348, 348–49, 412–13. See also Tehuantepec transit project

Italo-Ethiopian War (1935–1936), 176, 240, **265–66**, 298

Italy, 95, 134–35, 186, 285, 291–92, 301–2, 335–36, 386–87, 436, 519–20, 526, 537; diplomatic representatives, U.S., in (before 1920), 215, 339–40, 351–52, 389, 397, 545–46; diplomatic representatives, U.S., in (since 1920), 91–92, 113–14, 186–87, 199, 303–4, 319–20, 342–43, 414–15; international conferences and, 402, 402–3, 404; treaties and agreements, with other nations, 27, 314, 513–14; treaties and agreements, with U.S., 186, 385–86. See also Fiume problem; Italo-Ethiopian War; Orlando, Vittorio

Itata incident (1891), **266**

Ivory Coast, 11

Jackson, Andrew, 99; diplomacy during presidential administration of (1829–1837), 47, 309, 328–29. See also Livingston, Edward; McLane, Louis; Van Buren, Martin; *names of U.S. diplomatic representatives*

Jackson, John B., **267**

Jamestown Exposition (1907), 302–3

Japan, 32, 61–62, 136–37, 210, 246, 291–92, 303, 324; Cold War and, 382–83; diplomatic representatives, U.S., in (before 1900), 63–64, 133, 154, 169, 226, 247–48, 410–11, 427–28, 499; diplomatic representatives, U.S., in (1900–1941), 39, 214, 215, 219, 331–32, 361, 389, 555; diplomatic representatives, U.S., in (since

1945), 19, 255–56, 323–24, 337–38,
351, 370–71, 437–38; foreign wars,
460, 478; immigration problems and,
133, 267; international conferences
and, 314, 537; interwar period, Manchurian crisis, and, 243–44, 321–22,
335–36, 368–69, 473, 491; missionaries, U.S., in, 217–18, 324, 330; postwar reconstruction and, 76, 323, 364–
65; treaties and agreements, with other
nations, 25, 57, 425, 513–14; treaties
and agreements, with U.S., (before
1900), 226–27, 277, 475; treaties and
agreements, with U.S. (since 1900),
186, 191, 205, 294, 380–81, 452, 501;
World War I and, 135, 473, 515–16;
World War II and, 3–4, 210–11, 214,
259–60, 333, 376, 401, 407
Japanese-Korean Exclusion League
(1905–1907), **267**
Japanese Peace Treaty (1951), 28, 167–
68, **267**, 457–58
Japanese Security Treaty, 267
Jarvis, William, 268
Jay, John, **268–69**, 269, 407, 432–33
Jay-Gardoqui Treaty (1786), **269**, 355–
56, 418
Jay's Treaty (1794), 29–30, 268–69,
269–70, 270–71, 283, 355–56, 416–
17, 418–19, 419–20, 421; consequences of, 212, 419; ratification of,
270–71, 416–17
JCS 1067, 120, **270**, 359–60
JCS 1779, 270
Jefferson, Thomas, 198, 268, **270–71**,
300, 355–56, 360–61, 416–17, 432–
33; diplomacy during presidential
administration of (1801–1809), 22, 39–
40, 113, 174–75, 317, 332–33, 354,
356, 419–20; as Minister to France,
192; as Secretary of State, 418–19,
475. *See also* Madison, James; *names
of U.S. diplomatic representatives*;
War of 1812
Jessup, Philip C., 115, **271–72**
Johnson, Andrew, 179, 193, 367; diplomacy during presidential administration
of (1865–1869), 14, 92–93. *See also*

Seward, William H.; *names of U.S.
diplomatic representatives*
Johnson, Hiram W., 264
Johnson, Lyndon B., 6, 91, 138–39; di-
plomacy during presidential administra-
tion of (1963–1969), 54, 161–62, 217,
238–39, 327–28, 428, 453–54. *See
also* Rusk, Dean; *names of U.S. diplo-
matic representatives*; Vietnam War
Johnson, Nelson T., **272**
Johnson, Reverdy, **273**
Johnson, U. Alexis, **273–74**
Johnson, Willis Fletcher, **274**
Johnson-Clarendon Convention (1869),
273
Johnson-Reed Act (1924), 98, 175, 205,
248–49, **274–75**
"Joint occupation," **275**
Joint Occupation Treaty (1827), **275**
Jones, Hilary P., **275**, 315
Jordan, 174, 415–16
Journalists and correspondents: nineteenth
century, 246, 327, 395–96; World War
I, 3; World War II, 12, 219, 236–37;
Korean War, 236–37. *See also* Broad-
casters; Historians, diplomatic
Juárez, Benito, 101–2, 417
Judd, Norman B., **275–76**
Judd, Walter, 114–15

Kaltenborn, Hans von, **277**, 499–500
Kampuchea, 100. *See also* Cambodia
Kanagawa, Treaty of (1854), **277**, 410–
11, 475
Kasson, John A., 58, **277–78**
Katanga, 126–27
Kearney, Lawrence, **278**
Keating, Kenneth B., **278–79**
Keith, Minor C., **279**, 346, 518
Kellogg, Frank B., **279–80**, 280, 375–
76, 440
Kellogg-Briand Pact (1928), 94–95, 217–
18, 279–80, **280**, 305–6, 491
Kennan, George F., 71–72, 122, 129,
158–59, **280–81**, 340–41, 342, 378
Kennedy, John F., 6, 91, 238–39, 281–
82, 454–55, 475–76; diplomacy during
presidential administration of (1961–

1963), 18, 58–59, 77–78, 91, 126–27, 140, 238–39, 294–95, 405–6, 406–7, 454–55, 475–76, 489, 503–4. *See also* Rusk, Dean; *names of U.S. diplomatic representatives*; Vietnam War
Kennedy, Joseph P., **281–82**, 475–76
Kennedy Round, 201–2, **282**
Khrushchev, Nikita, 58–59, 140, 164–65, 508, 517
Kilpatrick, Hugh J., **282–83**
King, Henry Churchill, 136–37, **284**
King, Rufus, 198, **283**, 341–42
King, William R., **283–84**
King Cotton diplomacy, 284. *See also* Confederate diplomacy
King-Crane Commission (1919), 136–37, **284**
King-Hawkesbury Convention (1803), 283, **285**
Kingdom of the Serbs, Croats and Slovenes, 160–61
Kinney, William B., **285**
Kirk, Alan G., 91, **285–86**
Kirkpatrick, Jeane J., 118, 175–76, **286**, 376, 531–32
Kishineff pogrom, 442–43
Kissinger, Henry A., 38, 86–87, **286–88**, 342–43, 441–42, 446–47, 455–56, 510–11, 531–32, 558–59; as National Security adviser, 156, 365, 376–77, 377–78, 403; as Secretary of State, 26, 31, 102–3, 113, 141, 146–47, 172, 233–34, 278–79, 345–46
Kissinger Commission. *See* National Bipartisan Commission on Central America
Knox, Philander C., 161, 264, **288–89**, 289, 305–6, 549
Knox-Castrillo Convention (1911), **289**
Knoxville World's Fair (1982), 446
Kohlberg, Alfred, 114–15
Kohler, Foy D., **289–90**
Korea, 63–64, 81–82, 241, 267, 303, 318, 358, 476, 478–79. *See also* Korea, Democratic Republic of (North Korea); Korea, Republic of (South Korea); Korean War

Korea, Democratic Republic of (North Korea), 385, 428
Korea, Republic of (South Korea), 55, 164–65, 203, 220, 324–25, 382–83, 437–38
Korean War, 5, 34, 82, 342; and U.S. policy, 81–82, 124, 323, 370–71, 388
Kossuth, Louis, 285, 561–62
Koszta affair, 83–84, 338, 339–40
Kubitschek, Juscelino, 18, 256–57
Kuwait, 393–94

Ladd, William, **291**
Laird rams, 7, 187–88, **291**
Lamont, Thomas W., **291–92**
Lane, Arthur B., **292–93**
Langston, John M., 44, **293**
Lansing, Robert, **44**, 123, 143, 167–68, 191–92, **293–94**, 424
Lansing-Ishii Agreement (1917), 180, **294**, 381–82, 515–16, 547
Laos, 203, 232, 295, 336–37, 403, 503–4, 559–60. *See also* Laotian crisis (1960–1962); Laotian incursion (1971)
Laotian crisis (1960–1962), 203, 273–74, **294–95**
Laotian incursion (1971), **295**, 526
Larkin, Thomas O., **295–96**
Latane, John H., **296**
Latin America, 41–42, 88, 150, 250–51, 296, 444, 445, 451–52, 455; hemispheric conferences, 72, 88–89, 102, 307, 350, 356–57, 399–400, 443, 465, 536; hemispheric organizations, 92, 180–81, 256–57, 392–93, 400; U.S. policies toward, 18, 117–18, 161, 208, 356, 401, 449–50. *See also names of individual countries*
Latvia, 292–93, 528–29
Laurens, Henry, **296–97**, 407
Lausanne Conference (1922), 82–83, 113, 214, 464
Lausanne Conference (1932), 242, **297**, 438–39, 562
Law of the Sea treaty, 441–42
Lawrence, Abbott, **297**
Lazare claim, 44
Lea, Homer, **298**

League for American Neutrality, **298**
League of Armed Neutrality, 193
League of Free Nations Association, 188
League of Nations, 75, 85, 89, 104, 148–49, 168–69, 188, 206–7, 214, 227, 243–44, 259, 265, 291, **298–99**, 310, 379, 465, 490–91, 513, 526, 550–51; creation of, 191, 246–47, 496; crises and incidents handled by, 265–66, 321–22, 335–36, 368–69, 473; opponents of, in U.S., 60–61, 186–87, 228, 237–38, 248–49, 264, 279–80, 288–89, 305–6, 311–12, 357, 425, 451–52; partisans of, in U.S., 3, 64, 123, 147, 205–6, 224–25, 241–42, 293–94, 296, 299, 305, 474, 532–33, 545–46, 551–52; principles involved in, 32, 124, 204, 240, 391, 491; rejection of, by U.S. Senate, 32, 240, 264, 312–13, 440, 526; treaties and agreements arranged through, 240, 336, 410, 462
League to Enforce Peace, 241–42, **299**, 495–96, 549–50
Leahy, William D., **299–300**
Lear, Tobias, **300**
Lebanese civil war, **300–301**, 301–2, 347–48
Lebanon, 176, 223–24, 232, 348, 351; U.S. intervention in, 174
Lebanon Crisis (1982–1984), 300–301, **301–2**, 326, 370, 398–99, 476–77, 534
Lebanon intervention (1958), 174, **302**, 310–11, 370–71, 518–19
Lee, Arthur, 124, 152, 192, 244, **302**
Lee, Fitzhugh, **302–3**, 390, 547
Le Gendre, Charles W., 154, **303**
Leishman, John G. A., **303–4**
Lend-Lease, 20–21, 55, 121–22, 125, 257–58, **304**; administrators of, 5, 225–26, 242–43, 245–46, 453–54, 486–87, 487–88
Leopold II (King of the Belgians), 11–12, 58, 362, 506
Levermore, Charles H., **305**
Levinson, Salmon O., **305–6**
Lewis, Fulton, Jr., **306**
Lewis, Samuel W., **306–7**

"Liberation," 167–68, 225–26, 292–93, **307**
Liberia, 387, 482, 515
Libya, 393–94, 531–32
Lilienthal, David E., 6
Liliuokalani, Queen of Hawaii, 488–89, 548–49
Lima Conference (1938), **307**, 486–87
Limited Nuclear Test Ban Treaty (1963). *See* Partial Nuclear Test Ban Treaty (1963)
Lincoln, Abraham, 23–24, 100–101, 229–30, 308; diplomacy during presidential administration of (1861–1865), 12, 353, 512. *See also* Seward, William H.; *names of U.S. diplomatic representatives*; Civil War; Confederate diplomacy
Lincoln, Levi, **308**
Lincoln, Robert T., **308**
Lind, John, 394–95
Lindbergh, Charles A., 235, 306–7, 362
Linowitz, Sol M., 399
Lisbon Agreements (1952), **308–9**
Lithuania, 292–93, 377
Little Belt incident (1811), **309**, 410–11
Livingston, Edward, 31–32, 43, **309**
Livingston, Robert R., 31–32, **310**, 317, 332–33, 355–56
Lloyd George, David, 135, 403–4
Locarno, Treaty of (1925), **310**
Lodge, Henry Cabot, Jr., 34, **310–11**, 311–12, 312, 383
Lodge, Henry Cabot, Sr., 230, 310–11, **311–12**, 312–13, 351–52, 440, 535
Lodge, John Davis, 310–11
Lodge Corollary, 288–89, **312**
Lodge Reservations, 32, 240, **312–13**, 440
Logan, Cornelius A., **313**, 406, 533–34
Logan, George, 314
Logan, James A., Jr., **313**
Logan Act (1799), **314**
London, Declaration of (1909), **314**, 378–79
London, Treaty of (1915), **314**, 470
London Agreements (1948), 479
London Conference (1954), **314–15**

London Economic Conference (World
  Economic Conference in London),
  183, 277, 291–92
London International Exhibition (1862),
  406
London Naval Conference (1909), 314,
  554
London Naval Conference (1930), 108–9,
  148, 171, 186, 204, 206–7, 275, **315**,
  362, 433
London Naval Conference (1935–1936),
  147, **315**
Long, Boaz Walton, **315–16**
Lon Nol, 100
Loomis, Francis B., **316**
Louis, John J., Jr., **317**
Louisiana Purchase (1803), 131, 270–71,
  310, **317**, 332–33, 354, 355–56, 418;
  treaties and agreements related to, 22,
  463
Louisiana Purchase Exposition, St. Louis
  (1904), 191–92
Lovett, Robert A., **317–18**, 457–58
Low, Frederick F., **318**
Low-Rogers Expedition, **318**
Lowell, James Russell, **318–19**
Luce, Clare Boothe, 169, **319–20**
Luce, Henry R., 114–15
Ludlow Amendment, **320**
Lugar, Richard G., 320, 414
Lumumba, Patrice, 126–27
Lusitania, 29, 85, 147–48, 222–23, **320–
  21**, 404, 517
Luxembourg, 50–51, 143–44, 186–87,
  199, 206–7, 349–50, 386–87, 402,
  402–3, 413–14, 479
Lyon, Cecil B., **321**
Lytton Commission, 321–22, 335–36

MacArthur, Douglas, 236–37, 271–72,
  317–18, **323**, 323–24
MacArthur, Douglas II, **323–24**
McCartee, Divie B., **324**
McCarthy, Joseph R., 114–15, 306
McConaughy, Walter P., Jr., **324–25**
McCormick, Robert S., **325**
MacDonald, Ramsay, 433
McDonald, James G., **325–26**

McFarlane, Robert C., **326–27**, 422
MacGahan, Januarius, **327**
McGhee, George C., **327–28**
McKinley, William, 328, 480, 552–53;
  diplomacy during presidential adminis-
  tration of (1897–1901), 78–79, 132,
  151, 153–54, 220–21, 231, 350, 391,
  467. *See also* Day, W. R.; Hay, John
  M.; Sherman, John; *names of U.S.
  diplomatic representatives*; Isthmian
  canal question; Spanish-American War
McKinley Tariff Act (1890), 325, **328**
McLane, Louis, **328–29**
McLane, Robert M., **329–30** 330
McLane-Ocampo Treaty (1859), 329–30,
  330
MacLeish, Archibald, **330–31**
McLemore, Jeff, 208–9
McMurray, J.V.A., 375–76
McNamara, Robert S., 257–58, 405–6
MacVeagh, Charles, **331–32**
MacVeagh, Lincoln, 331–32, **332**
Maclay, Robert S., **330**
Macon, Nathaniel, 331
Macon's Bill Number One, **331**
Macon's Bill Number Two, **331**, 384
Madagascar, 476
Madison, James, 41, 97, 198, 210, 308,
  332–33, 416–17, 481; diplomacy dur-
  ing presidential administration of
  (1809–1817), 175; as Secretary of
  State, 39–40, 300, 317, 354. *See also*
  Jefferson, Thomas; Monroe, James;
  Smith, Robert; *names of U.S. diplo-
  matic representatives*; War of 1812
MAGIC, **333**, 450
Magoon, Charles E., **333–34**, 358
Mahan, Alfred Thayer, **334**
Maine, U.S.S., 302–3, 334–35
Maldives, 321
Malta, 335
Malta Conference (1945), **335**
Malvinas Islands War (1982). *See* Falk-
  land Islands War (1982)
Manchester Ship Canal, 221–22
Manchukuo, 321–22, 335–36, 491
Manchurian crisis (1931–1933), 148–49,
  243–44, 272, **335–36**, 368–69, 490–

91, 491, 551–52; League of Nations and, 298–99, 321–22

Mandates, World War I, 284, **336**, 464, 515, 526

Manifest Destiny, 185–86, **336**, 354, 381, 395–96, 410–11, 561–62

Manila Conference (1954), 323–24, 336–37, 337–38

Manila Pact (1954), **336–37**, 411, 444, 483–84

Mann, Ambrose Dudley, 510

Mann, Thomas C., **337**

Mansfield, Michael J., **337–38**, 378

Marblehead Treaty (1906), 464

Marcos, Ferdinand, 220, 414

Marcy, William L., 87–88, 226, **338**, 338–39, 401, 543–44

Marcy-Elgin Treaty (1854), 23, 338, **338–39**

Maritime Canal Company, 170, **339**, 348, 412–13

Marsh, George P., **339–40**

Marshall, George C., 5, 15, 85, 95–96, 134–35, 317–18, **340–41**, 524, 531–32; and Cold War diplomacy, 342, 365, 497, 526–27

Marshall, James F. B., **341**

Marshall, John, 308, **341–42**, 418, 557

Marshall Plan, 14–15, 134–35, 157–58, 187, **342**, 514–15, 524, 561; administrators and diplomats concerned with, 5, 71–72, 74, 84–85, 121–22, 163–64, 209–10, 225–26, 227–28, 236, 240–41, 317–18, 340–41, 370–71; conferences concerned with, 402, 479; treaties, agreements, and agencies concerned with, 201–2, 260–61, 519–20. *See also* Cold War

Martin, Graham A., **342–43**

Martin, John Bartlow, 54

Marye, George T., **343**

Mason, James M., 176–77, 251, **343–44**, 512, 548

Mason, John Y., 87–88, **344**, 395, 483

Massive retaliation, 5–6, 167–68, 200–201, 286–88, 307, **344–45**, 386–87, 430

Matlock, Jack F., Jr., **345**

Mauritania, 370

Maximilian (emperor of Mexico), 47–48, 63, 134, 353, 367, 427, 548

Maxwell, Russell L., 376

Mayagüez incident (1975), **345–46**

MBFR Talks. *See* Mutual and Balanced Force Reduction Talks

Meiggs, Henry, **346**

Mein, John Gordon, **346–47**

Mellon, Andrew W., 171, **347**

Meloy, Francis E., Jr., 300–301, **347–48**

Menocal, Aniceto G., **348**

Merry, William L., **348–49**

Messersmith, George S., 79, 349

Mesta, Perle S., **349–50**, 370–71

Mexican cession, 62. *See also* Guadalupe-Hidalgo, Treaty of (1848)

Mexican-Guatemalan boundary dispute, 193

Mexican War, 9, 20, 119, 215–16, 424, 479–80, 506, 514; in California, 49–50, 491

Mexico, 108, 170, 179, 208, 258–59, 291–92, 471–72, 563–64; Civil War, French intervention, and, 353, 417, 431, 548; diplomatic representatives, U.S., in (1825–1860), 196, 211, 329–30, 422–23, 479–80, 508–9; diplomatic representatives, U.S., in (1860–1916), 101–2, 125, 134, 186–87, 190, 222, 394–95, 453, 549–50; diplomatic representatives, U.S., in (since 1924), 117–18, 143, 349, 362, 389–90; international conferences and, 102, 228–29, 350, 350–51; Mexican revolution (1910–1917) and, 394–95, 400, 549–50; recognition questions and, 87; Texas question and, 215–16, 506; treaties and agreements, with U.S., 196, 215–16, 330, 512–13. *See also* Huerta, Victoriano; Juarez, Benito; Mexican War; Tehuantepec transit project; Texas

Mexico City Conference (1901–1902), 88, 237–38, **350**, 401

Mexico City Conference (1945), 34, 56, 121–22, **350–51**, 392–93, 487–88

Meyer, Armin H., **351**

Meyer, George von L., **351–52**

Middle East, 28–29, 36–37, 101, 106, 111, 174, 300–301, 301–2, 302, 325–26, 326–27, 370, 393–94, 440, 448, 476–77, 497–98. *See also names of specific countries*

Middle East Treaty Organization, 36–37

Middleton, Henry, **352–53**

Milan Decree (1807), 41, 59, 69–70, 97, 129, 198, 331, **353**, 392, 419–20, 432

Miller, Francis P., 111

Millis, Walter, **353**

Minister. *See* Chief of mission

Minister-resident. *See* Chief of mission

Miramar, Convention of (1864), **353**

Mission, **354**. *See also* Manifest Destiny; New Manifest Destiny

Missionaries: in Argentina, 553; in China, 241, 324, 330, 404–5, 435–36; in the Congo, 362; in Hawaii, 441; in Japan, 217–18, 324, 330; in Persia, 48, 53–54; in Peru, 553; in Turkey, 42–43, 303–4, 442–43, 495–96, 531, 548

Mitchell, John, **354**, 540–41

Mitchell's Map, 354

Mixed Claims Commission for the United States and Germany (1923–1929), 404

Mobile Act (1804), **354**

Moffat, Jay Pierrepont, **354–55**

Molotov, V. M., 25, 363–64, 364–65, 365, 426, 481–82

Monroe, James, 9, 210, 310, 317, 332–33, **355–56**, 356, 419–20, 432–33, 456–57; diplomacy during presidential administration of (1817–1825), 10, 25, 131–32, 210, 356, 390–91, 457. *See also* Adams, John Quincy; Rush, Richard; *names of U.S. diplomatic representatives*

Monroe Doctrine, 46, 58, 87–89, 277–78, 332–33, **356**, 386–87, 390, 423–24, 456–57, 460, 483–84; corollaries, 312, 449–50; creators of, 9, 355–56; principles behind, 117–18, 384, 387

Monroe-Pinkney Treaty (1806), 59, **355–56**, 384, 419–20

Montenegro, 166, 466–67

Montevideo Conference (1933), 79, 89, **356–57**, 541

Moore, John Bassett, 88–89, 151, **357**, 402, 474–75

Moran, Benjamin, **358**

Morgan, Edward V., **358**

Morgan, John Tyler, **358–59**

Morgan, Junius S., **359**

Morgenthau, Henry, Jr., 80–81, 304, 359–60, 544–45

Morgenthau Plan (1944), **359–60**, 430

Morocco, 15, 67–68, 74, 102, 160–61, 218, 559–60

Morris, Gouverneur, **360–61**, 432–33

Morris, Richard V., **361**

Morris, Roland Sletor, **361**

Morrison, William McC., **362**

Morrow, Dwight W., 87, 117–18, 315, **362**

Mortefontaine, Treaty of (1800). *See* Convention of 1800

Morton, Levi P., **363**

Moscow Conference (1943), 18–19, 102, 127, 191, **363–64**, 551

Moscow Conference (1944), **364**

Moscow Conference (1945), **364–65**, 404

Moscow Conference (1947), **365**, 481–82

Moscow Memorandum (1955), 35

Moscow Summit Conference (1972), **365**, 493–94

Moscow Summit Conference (1974), **365–66**

Moscow Summit Conference (1988), 345, **366**

Moses-Linthicum Act (1931), **366**

"Most-favored-nation" treatment, 92–93, 247–48, 277, 366–67, 421

Motley, John Lothrop, **367**

Moynihan, Daniel Patrick, **367–68**

Muhlenberg, Henry A. P., **368**

Mukden incident (1931), 321–22, 335–36, **368–69**, 490–91, 491

Munich Conference (1938), 277, **369**, 541–42, 550–51

Munro, Dana G., 369

Munro-Blanchet Treaty (1932), **369**

Murphy, Dominic I., **369–70**

Murphy, Richard W., **370**
Murphy, Robert D., 270, **370–71**
Murray, William Vans, 131, **371–72**, 429
Murrow, Edward R., **372**, 470–71
Muskie, Edmund S., 117, **372–73**
Mussolini, Benito, 113–14, 186–87
Mutual Balanced Force Reduction
    (MBFR) Talks, **373**, 446–47
Mutual Security Act (1951), 187, **373–
    74**, 423
Mutual Security Agency, 165–66, 225–
    26, 373–74, 412, 520

Namibia, 127–28, **375**
Nanking, Treaty of (1842), **375**, 533
Nanking incident (1927), **375–76**
Napoleon, Louis, 151–52, 539, 548. *See
    also* Confederate diplomacy; Maximi-
    lian (emperor of Mexico)
Nasser, Gamal Abdel, 95–96, 497–98
National Bipartisan Commission on Cen-
    tral America, 286–88, **376**
National Defense Act (1940), **376**
National Munitions Control Board, 202,
    379
National Security Act (1947), 110, 299–
    300, 376–77
National Security Council (NSC), 17–18,
    73, 86–87, 110, 146–47, 261–62, 286–
    88, 306–7, 326–27, **376–77**, 377–78,
    388, 422
NATO. *See* North Atlantic Treaty
    Organization
Nazi-Soviet Non-Aggression Pact (1939),
    27, **377**
Near East Relief, 42–43
Negroponte, John D., **377–78**
Nehru, Jawaharlal, 77–78, 91–92
"Neo-isolationism," 280–81, **378**, 382
Nepal, 16–17, 91–92, 209–10, 234–35
Netherlands, 8–9, 30, 91–92, 386–87,
    402, 402–3, 479, 537; diplomatic rep-
    resentatives, U.S., in (before 1900), 9,
    51–52, 371–72, 475; diplomatic repre-
    sentatives, U.S., in (since 1900), 50–
    51, 112, 199, 243–44, 414–15
Neutrality, 29–30, 35, 111–12, 187–88,
    193, 203, 265–66, 344, **378–79**, 385,

395–96, 399; in Napoleonic Wars,
    130, 270–71, 418–19, 455; before
    World War I, 85, 130, 424; before
    World War II, 89, 107, 379, 379–80,
    380, 388, 420, 484, 507–8, 529, 551–
    52
Neutrality Act (1794), **379**
Neutrality Act (1935), 20–21, 27, **379**,
    388
Neutrality Act (1936), 20–21, 27, 298,
    379, 484
Neutrality Act (1937), 20–21, 27, 107,
    379–80, 380
Neutrality Act (1939), 107, **380**, 484,
    507–8, 529
Neutrality Proclamation (1793), **380**
New Consortium, 361, **380–81**
New Granada, 62, 78, 249–50. *See also*
    Colombia
"New look" (military-diplomatic policy),
    200–201
New Manifest Destiny, **381**
"New Navy," **381**
New Panama Canal Company, 138, 288–
    89, **381**, 485
New York Agreement, 57–58
New Zealand, 28, 252–53, 483–84
Newfoundland, 230
Nicaragua, 130–31, 174, 212–13, 213–
    14, 286, 410, 434, 530, 537; diplo-
    matic representatives, U.S., in (before
    1900), 158, 239, 543–44; diplomatic
    representatives, U.S., in (since 1900),
    71–72, 170, 292–93, 315–16, 348–49;
    Isthmian transit question, 21, 86, 108,
    112, 194, 339; U.S. intervention in,
    150, 161, 170, 279–80, 289, 490–91,
    509–10
Nigeria, 415–16
Nine-Power Treaty (1922), 85, 243–44,
    294, **381–82**, 473, 491, 537
Ninth International Conference of Ameri-
    can States (1948). *See* Bogota Confer-
    ence (1948)
Nitze, Paul H., **382**
Nixon, Richard M., 31, 50, 55, 310–11,
    455–56, 531–32; diplomacy during
    presidential administration of, 100,

156, 365, 365–66, 382–83, 493–94, 526–27. *See also* Kissinger, Henry A.; Rogers, William P.; *names of U.S. diplomatic representatives*; Vietnam War

Nixon Doctrine (1969), **382–83**

Nobel Peace Prize, 90–91, 94–95, 148–49, 177, 250–51, 279–80, 286–88, 340–41, 403, 425–26

Nolting, Frederick E., Jr., 169, **383**

Non-colonization, doctrine of (1823), **384**, 399–400, 459–60

Non-Importation Act (1806), **384**

Non-Intercourse Act (1809), 174–75, **384**, 432

Non-intervention, doctrine of (1823), **384**

Non-Proliferation Treaty (1968), **385**, 493–94

Nootka Sound Affair (1790), **385**

North, Oliver, 261–62

North Atlantic Council, 386–87

North Atlantic Treaty, 28, 85, 317–18, **385–86**, 386–87, 524

North Atlantic Treaty Organization (NATO), 74, 85, 141, 156, 178, 194–95, 202, 385–86, **386–87**, 444, 483–84; diplomats concerned with (before 1953), 5, 34, 54, 102, 139–40, 163–64, 200–201, 225–26, 340–41; diplomats concerned with (since 1953), 45–46, 84–85, 221, 286–88, 323–24, 327–28, 347–48, 383, 441–42; international conferences related to, 204–5, 308–9, 314–15, 373, 402–3; U. S. diplomatic policy and, 57–58, 129, 139–40, 212–13, 494–95, 514–15

North Pacific Sealing Convention (1911), 55–56, **387**

Norway, 42, 61, 224–25, 385–86, 386–87, 402, 413–14, 488–89, 507

No-Transfer Principle and Resolution (1811), **387**

Noyes, Edward F., **387**

NSC–68, 376–77, **388**

Nuclear Test Ban Treaty (1963). *See* Partial Nuclear Test Ban Treaty (1963)

Nuremberg trials. *See* International Military Tribunal of Nuremberg

Nye Committee, 379, **388**, 551–52

OAS. *See* Organization of American States

O'Brien, Thomas J., **389**

OCTAGON Conference. *See* Quebec Conference (1944)

O'Dwyer, William, **389**

Office of Strategic Services (OSS), 110, 454–55, 550–51

Oil, 28–29, 262, 263, 264–65, 393–94, 479, 558–59

Olney, Richard, 46, 213–14, **390**, 469, 525–26

Olney-Pauncefote Convention (1897), **390**

Ontario, U.S.S., expedition (1817–1818), **390–91**

OPEC. *See* Organization of Petroleum Exporting Countries

"Open diplomacy," **391**

Open Door Policy, 67–68, 78–79, 113–14, 116, 125–26, **391**, 425, 484–85, 537; diplomats concerned with, 229–30, 445–46, 511, 545–46; treaties and agreements related to, 25, 294, 381–82, 452–53

"Open skies," 204–5

Opium War (1839–1842), 278, 375

Order-in-Council (April 1809), 177, 331, 353, **391**, 392, 419–20

Orders-in-Council (1807), 59, 129–30, 177, 331, 353, **392**, 419–20

Oregon Question, 20, 25, 184, 275, 390–91, **392**; diplomats concerned with, 328–29, 456–57, 520–21; trading companies concerned with, 83, 248, 459–60; treaties and agreements related to, 10, 131–32, 275

Oregon Treaty (1846), 87–88, 99, 184, 248, 275, **392**

Organization for European Economic Co-operation (OEEC), 157–58

Organization of African Unity, 146–47

Organization of American States (OAS), 161–62, 177, 212–13, **392–93**, 400, 444; diplomats concerned with, 91–92, 150, 340–41; international conferences related to, 72, 102

Organization of Eastern Caribbean States, 212–13
Organization of Petroleum Exporting Countries (OPEC), 28–29, **393–94**
Orlando, Vittorio, 135, 186, 403–4
Osborn, Thomas A., **394**
Osborn, Thomas O., **394**
O'Shaughnessy, Nelson J. W., **394–95**
Ostend Manifesto, 66, 87–88, 344, **395**, 483
O'Sullivan, John L., 336, **395–96**
Oum, Boun (Laotian prince), 203
Owen, Ruth Bryan. *See* Rohde, Ruth Bryan Owen

Pacific Mail Steamship Company, **397**, 412–13
Pact. *See* International agreement
Pact of Paris (1928). *See* Kellogg-Briand Pact (1928)
Page, Thomas Nelson, 292–93, **397**
Page, Walter Hines, **397–98**
Pakistan, 36–37, 95–96, 324–25, 385, 453–54, 483–84
Palestine, 284, 464
Palestine Liberation Organization (PLO), 101, 301–2, **398–99**, 440, 560
Palestinian question, 101, 300–301, 301–2, 398–99, 448, 479
Panama, 62, 230–31, 236, 357, 381, 399, 509, 513; diplomatic representatives, U.S., in (1903–1939), 41–42, 148, 150, 160, 459, 485–86; diplomatic representatives, U.S., in (since 1939), 112, 146, 150, 337, 525; treaties and agreements with U.S., 230, 399, 523. *See also* Isthmian canal question; Panama Canal Treaties (1977); Panama Tolls controversy; Colombia
Panama Canal Treaties (1977), 91–92, 117, 230, 264–65, **399**, 523, 525
Panama Canal Zone, 333–34, 501
Panama Conference (1939), 541–42
Panama Congress (1826), 22–23, 119, **399–400**, 435
Panama Tolls Controversy, 397–98, **400**, 451–52

Pan-American Conference. *See under name of city where conference was held*
Pan-American Union, 41–42, 88–89, 92, 103–4, 150, 168–69, **400**, 401, 455; conferences related to, 228–29, 465, 536
Pan-Americanism, 41–42, 66–67, 103–4, 109–10, 147, 308, **401**, 533–34, 536
Panay episode (1937), **401**
Paraguay, 50, 78, 111–12, 358
Paris, Declaration of (1856), 7, 130, 338, 378–79, **401**, 512–13
Paris, Treaty of (1763), 463
Paris, Treaty of (1783). *See* Peace of Paris (1783)
Paris, Treaty of (1898), 151, 357, **402**, 458
Paris Conference (1947), **402**
Paris Conference (1954), **402–3**
Paris Economic Conference (1916), 539–40
Paris Peace Agreement (1973), 286–88, 377–78, **403**
Paris Peace Conference (1898), 357, 402, 436
Paris Peace Conference (1919), 62, 69–70, 89–90, 135, 166, 188, 403–4; principal U.S. delegates at, 246–27, 424, 474, 545–46; problems and issues dealt with, at, 186, 391, 438–39, 470, 473; treaties and agreements related to, 284, 526; U.S. advisers and consultants, 43–44, 67–68, 143–44, 145, 167–68, 191–92, 214, 227, 236, 241–42, 243–44, 291, 397, 468–69, 495–96, 530–31
Paris Peace Conference (1946), 95, 134–35, 223–24, 364–65, **404**, 481–82
Paris Peace Conference (1968–1969), 225–26, 310–11, 523
Paris Postal Conference (1863), 277–78
Paris Universal Expositions: (1867), 159; (1878), 387
Parker, Edward B., **404**
Parker, Peter, **404–5**
Partial Nuclear Test Ban Treaty, 225–26, **405–6**, 508

Partridge, James R., **406**

Pathet Lao, 203, 294–95

Peace Corps, 146–47, **406–7**, 475–76, 525

Peace of Paris (1783), 8, 192, 269–70, 296–97, 310, 360–61, **407**

"Peaceful coexistence," 298–90

Pearl Harbor, attack on (1941), 20–21, 30, 49, 184, 214, 333, 353, 380, **407**, 486, 551–52

Pearl Harbor Treaty (1887), 105–6, 193, **408**

Peirce, Henry A., **408**

Peixotto, Benjamin F., **408–9**

Pelagic sealing, 14, 387

Pendleton, George H., **409**

Penfield, Frederic C., **409**

Perdicaris, Ian, 218

Permanent Court of Arbitration (Hague Tribunal), **409–10**, 495–96, 511, 526

Permanent Court of International Justice (World Court), 204, 237 38, 248–49, 291, 296, 298–99, 305, 305–6, 311–12, 357, **410**, 468–69; International Court of Justice, 168–69, 223–24, 271–72, 463; U.S. judges, 271–72, 279–80, 451–52

Perón, Juan D., 50, 79, 91–92, 214–15, 349

Perry, Matthew C., 120–21, 277, **410–11**

Persia, 48, 53–54, 76–77, 215, 267, 413–14, 458, 553. *See also* Iran

Peru, 264–65, 346, 485; diplomatic representatives, U.S., in (before 1900), 116–17, 252, 406, 412–13, 444–45; diplomatic representatives, U.S., in (since 1900), 51, 81–82, 112, 486–87; entrepreneurs in 209, 346; War of the Pacific and, 116–17, 252, 406, 412–13, 533–34

Peurifoy, John E., **411**

Phelps, Edward J., **411–12**

Phelps, Phelps, **412**

Phelps, Seth L., 170, 339, **412–13**

Phelps, William W., **413**

Philip, Hoffman **413–14**

Philippine Crisis (1986), 220, 320, **414**

Philippines, 3–4, 67, 72, 95–96, 220, 323, 370, 382–83, 483–84; U.S. occupation of, 139, 157, 254, 402, 451–52, 467, 552–53, 555–56. *See also* Spanish-American War

Phillips, William, **414–15**

Pickens, Francis W., **415**

Pickering, Thomas R., **415–16**

Pickering, Timothy, 314, 341–42, **416–17**

Pickett, John T., 134, 417

Pierce, Franklin: diplomacy during presidential administration of (1853–1857), 5, 19, 66, 75–76, 196, 277, 338–39, 395, 410–11. *See also* Marcy, William L.; *names of U.S. diplomatic representatives*

Pierrepont, Edwards, **417**

Pinckney, Charles, **418**, 418–19

Pinckney, Charles Cotesworth, **418**, 418–19, 557

Pinckney, Thomas, **418–19**, 419, 475

Pinckney's Treaty (1795), 269–70, 317, 418–19, **419**, 432–33, 475

Pinkney, William, 355–56, 356, **419–20**

Pittman, Key, **420**

Plan of 1776, 193, **421**

Plan of Treaties. *See* Plan of 1776

Platt, Orville H., **421**

Platt Amendment (1901), 139, 170, 315–16, **421**, 505

Plebiscite, 470, 532–33, 533–34

Pleven Plan, 178

Poindexter, John M., 261–62, **422**, 476–77

Poinsett, Joel R., **422–23**

Point Four (Technical Cooperation Administration), 60, 77–78, 412, **423**, 445

Poland, 202, 203, 310, 335–36, 377, 403; diplomatic representatives, U.S., in, 48–49, 61, 97, 198–99, 206–7, 214–15, 292–93, 491–92. *See also* Polish question, World War II

Policy Planning Staff (State Department), 86–87, 183–84, 280–81, 306–7, 327–28, 340–41, 382

Polignac Memorandum (1823), **423–24**

Polish question, World War II, 364, 504, 557–58
Polk, Frank L., **424**
Polk, James J., 424; diplomacy during presidential administration of (1845–1849), 336, 338, 514. *See also* Buchanan, James; *names of U.S. diplomatic representatives*; Mexican War
Polk-Stockton intrigue (1845), **424**, 491
Polly decision (1800), 178, **424–25** 455
Pork controversy, 363, 413, 436
Porter, Horace, **425**
Porter Resolution, 443
Portsmouth, Treaty of (1905), **425–26**, 460
Portugal, 30, 120–21, 385–86, 386–87, 402, 537; diplomatic representa-tives, U.S., in (before 1900), 44–45, 210, 268, 358, 395–96; diplomatic representatives, U.S., in (since 1900), 54, 64–65, 102–3, 316, 332, 358
Potsdam Agreement (1945), 270
Potsdam Conference (1945), 134–35, 143–44, **426**, 439; U.S. delegates and advisers, 95, 102, 121–22, 299–300, 340–41
Potsdam Declaration (1945), **426**
President, U.S.S., 309
Preston, Andrew W., 279
Preston, William, **427**
Price, Charles H., **427**
Protocol. *See* International agreement
Prussia, 9, 30, 39, 41, 162–63, 242, 270–71, 275–76, 302, 429, 543, 554–55. *See also* Germany
Pruyn, Robert H., **427–28**
Pueblo incident (1968), 428
Puerto Rico, 315, 402, 502, 563
Punta del Este Conference (1961), 157–58, **428**

Qatar, 393–94
QUADRANT Conference (1943). *See* Quebec Conference (1943)
Quadripartite Agreement on Berlin (1971). *See* Berlin Treaty (1971)
Quadruple Alliance (1815–1818), 242, **429**

"Quasi-war" with France (1798–1800), 15–16, 131, **429**, 511–12, 557; diplomats involved in, 8–9, 283, 300, 341–42, 371–72, 416–17
Quebec Conference (1943), **429–30**
Quebec Conference (1944), 359–60, **430**
Quemoy-Matsu crises (1954–1955; 1958), 82, **430**
Quintero, Juan A., **431**
Quintuple Alliance, 429
Quitman, John A., 184–85

Rambouillet, Decree of, **432**
Randolph, Edmund J., 416–17, **432–33**
Rapallo, Treaty of (1922), **433**
Rapidan Conference (1929), 24–25, **433**
Read, John Meredith, **433–34**
Reader, Ella Rawls, 138
Reagan, Ronald, 4, 123–24, 261–62; diplomacy during presidential administration of: diplomatic advisers, 17–18, 175–76, 196–97, 220, 286, 326–27, 370, 377–78, 415–16, 422; Africa, 26, 127–8, 498; Central America, 73, 128–19, 130–31, 162, 174, 177, 376, 410; Soviet Union, 10–11, 205, 355, 441, 537–38; other areas, 106, 182, 212–13, 301–2, 320, 414. *See also* Haig, Alexander; Shultz, George; *names of U.S. diplomatic representatives*
Reagan Doctrine, 26, **434**
Reciprocal Trade Agreement Act (1934), 250–52, **434–35**
Reciprocity, 98, 140, 250–51
Reed, William B., **435**
Reid, Gilbert, **435–36**
Reid, Whitelaw, 24, 402, **436**
Reinhardt, George F., **436–37**
Reinsch, Paul S., 88–89, **437**, 515–16
Reischauer, Edwin O., **437–38**
Reorganization Act (1939), **438**
Reparations, World War I, 108–9, 148–49, 207–8, 242, 297, 299, **438–39**, 462, 562
Reparations, World War II, 18–19, 121–22, 365, 404, 426, **439**, 557–58
Reparations Commission, 167–68, 248–49, 313

Reservationists, 248–49, 279–80, 311–12, **440**, 451–52

Resolution 242 (United Nations), 398–99, **440**, 448

Reykjavik Summit Conference (1986), 345, 382, **441**, 494

Rhodesia, 81

Richards, William, **441**

Richardson, Elliot, **441–42**

Riddle, John W., **442–43**

Rio de Janeiro Conference (1906), 88, 401, **443**, 455

Rio de Janeiro Conference (1942), **443**

Rio Treaty (1947), 85, 102, 163, 214–15, 349, 350–51, 392–93, **444**

Rives, William C., 194, **444**

Robinson, Christopher, **444–45**

Rockefeller, Nelson A., 14–15, 121–22, **445**

Rockhill, William W., 92, 391, **445–46**

Rodgers, Joe M., **446**

Rodney, Caesar, 210

Rogers, John, 318

Rogers, William P., 286–88, **446–47**, 448, 455–56

Rogers Act (1924), 22, 104–5, 188–89, 366, 438, **447–48**

Rogers Plan (1969), 440, 446–47, **448**

Rohde, Ruth Bryan Owen, **448**

Romania, 95, 134–35, 364, 364–65, 404; diplomatic representatives, U.S., in (before 1900), 48, 408–9, 467–68; diplomatic representatives, U.S., in (since 1900), 60, 227, 267, 442–43, 445–46, 528–29

Roosevelt, Eleanor, 330–31, **449**

Roosevelt, Franklin D., 30, 33, 33–34, 64, 98–99, 449, 450, 450–51; diplomacy during presidential administration of, (1933–1945) (Latin America), 56, 111–12, 208, 434–35; diplomacy during presidential administration of (neutrality), 320, 379, 379–80, 380, 420, 484; diplomatic advisers, 72–73, 89–90, 147, 242–43, 299–300, 429–30, 430, 504, 513, 557–58. *See also* Hull, Cordell; Stettinius, Edward J., Jr.;

names of U.S. diplomatic representatives; World War II; United Nations

Roosevelt, Theodore, 15, 147–48, 351–52, 482–83, 495–96, 509, 552–53; diplomacy during presidential administration of, (1901–1909) (Far East), 21–22, 210, 421, 425–26, 436, 460; diplomacy during presidential administration of, (Latin America), 76–77, 449–50, 504–5, 526. *See also* Hay, John M.; Root, Elihu; *names of U.S. diplomatic representatives*

Roosevelt Corollary (1904), 161–62, 356, 384, **449–50**

Roosevelt-Konoye meeting (1941), **450**

Roosevelt-Litvinov Agreements (1933), 89–90, **450–51**

"Roostook" War (1838), **451**

Root, Elihu, 36, 104, 109, 215, 271–72, 333–34, 400, 421, 443, **451–52**, 537, 549; treaties and agreements negotiated, 205, 314, 452–53

Root, Joseph Pomeroy, **452**

Root-Takahira Agreement (1908), 180, 294, 451–52, 452–53

Rosecrans, William S., **453**

Rost, Pierre A., 510, 558

Rostow, Eugene V. D., **453–54**, 454–55

Rostow, Walt W., 91, **454–55**, 503–4

Roth, William M., 282

Rover, U.S.S., 303

Rowe, Leo Stanton, **455**

Rule of the War of 1756, 130, 178, 424–25, **455**

Rush, Kenneth, **455–56**

Rush, Richard, 131–32, 198, **456–57**, 457

Rush-Bagot Agreement (1817), 180, 206, 456–57, **457**

Rusk, Dean, 91, 197–98, 324–25, 428, **457–58**, 491–92

Russell, Charles W., **458**

Russell, Jonathan, 206, **458–59**

Russell, William W., **459**

Russia, 13, 42, 176, 474; diplomatic representatives, U.S., in (before 1850), 9, 36, 87–88, 352–53; diplomatic representatives, U.S., in (1850–1900), 73,

100–101, 190, 239–40, 251, 480, 501, 544; diplomatic representatives, U.S., in (1900–1918), 118, 191–92, 325, 343, 351–52, 442–43, 445–46, 511; Far Eastern involvements of, 25, 477–78; treaties and agreements made by, 25, 30, 80, 242, 425–26, 429, 509. *See also* Soviet Union
Russian-American Company, 459–60
Russo-Japanese War (1905), 10, 139, 147–48, 215, 325, 351–52, 425–26, **460**

Sackett, Frederick M., **461**
Sadat, Anwar, 172, 558–59
Safer, Morley, **461–62**
St. Germain, Treaty of (1919), **462**
SALT. *See* Strategic Arms Limitation Talks
Samoa, 46, 56–57, 132, 254, 358, 412, 462, 471, 471–72, 544
Samoan Treaty (1876), **462**
San Domingo Improvement Company, **462–63**
San Francisco Conference (1945), 90–91, **463**, 470–71, 518–19, 557–58; U.S. delegates at, 16–17, 167–68, 289–90, 330–31, 411, 448, 487–88, 489, 524
San Idlefonso, Treaty of (1800), 317, **463**
San José, Treaties of (1906), **464**
San Lorenzo, Treaty of (1795). *See* Pinckney's Treaty (1795)
San Remo Conference (1920), **464**
Sandinistas, 130–31
Sanford, Henry S., 11–12, **464–65**
Santiago Conference (1923), 248–49, 401, **465**
Santo Domingo. *See* Dominican Republic
Sardinia, 285. *See also* Italy
Saudi Arabia, 28–29, 172, 223–24, 232, 326–27, 370
Savimbi, Jonas, 26
Scheldt Treaties, 464–65
Schenck, Robert C., **465–66**
Schmidt, Helmut, 93
Schurman, Jacob G., **466–67**
Schurman Commission, 466–67, **467**

Schurz, Carl, 24, 27–28, 28, **467**
Schuyler, Eugene, **467–68**
Scott, James Brown, 104, **468–69**
Scott, Winfield, 104, 514
Scruggs, William L., **469**
SEATO. *See* Southeast Asian Treaty Organization
Second Front, **469–70**
Second Hague Peace Conference (1907). *See* Hague Peace Conferences (1899 and 1907)
Second International Conference of American States (1901–1902). *See* Mexico City Conference (1901–1902)
Security Council Resolution 242. *See* Resolution 242 (United Nations)
"Secret treaties," **470**
Self-determination, 33, 91, **470**, 560
SDI. *See* Strategic Defense Initiative
Serbia, 48, 267, 442–43, 445–46, 467–68, 528–29
Sergeant, John, 435
Sevareid, Eric, **470–71**
Seventh International Conference of American States (1933). *See* Montevideo Conference (1933)
Sévres, Treaty of (1920), 464
Sewall, Harold M., **471**
Seward, Frederick W., **471–72**
Seward, William Henry, 7, 12, 14, 101–2, 151–52, 226, 353, 401, 471–72, **472–73**, 478, 488–89, 512. *See also* Civil War
"Seward's Folly," 14
SEXTANT Conference (1943). *See* Cairo Conference (1943)
Shanghai incident (1932), **473**
Shantung question, 243–44, 437, **473**, 545–46
Sharp, William G., **474**
Shepherdson, Whitney, 111
75
Shimoda, Convention of (1857), **475**
Shimonoseki indemnity (1863), 427–28
Ships: British, 29, 309, 320–21, 499, 512; Chilean, 266; Confederate, 13, 291; German, 517; United States', 38–

39, 66, 224, 303, 334–35, 345–46,
    390–91, 401, 428, 528; other, 22
Short, William, **475**
Shriver, Sargent, 406–7, **475–76**
Shufeldt, Robert W., **476**
Shultz, George, 4, **476–77**
Shuster mission, 458
"Shuttle diplomacy," 172, 221, 558–59
Siam, 38, 41–42, 226, 459, 496. *See
    also* Thailand
Siberian intervention, **477–78**
Sickles, Daniel E., 10, **478**, 528
Sino-Japanese War (1894–1895), 21,
    154–55, 169, 213–14, **478–79**
Six-Day War (1967), 398–99, 448, **479**,
    558–59
Six-Nation Conference on Germany
    (1948), 163–64, **479**
Sixth International Conference of Ameri-
    can States (1928). *See* Havana Confer-
    ence (1928)
Slave trade issue, 12, 489–90, 506, 540
Slidell, John, 151–52, 153, 176–77, 178–
    79, 251, 343–44, 410–11, **479–80**,
    512, 527, 548
Slogans and catchwords, 25, 107, 218,
    506; of the Cold War, 12–13, 82, 114–
    15, 122, 263, 289–90, 307, 344–45,
    378, 494–95, 558–59; of U.S. expan-
    sionism, 14, 20, 184, 218–29, 336,
    354, 381, 561–62; of World War II,
    62–63, 107, 190–91
Smith, Charles E., **480**
Smith, Earl E. T., **480**
Smith, Robert, 177, 332–33, **481**
Smith, W. Bedell, 110, 203, **481–82**
Smoot-Hawley Tariff (1930), 171, 434–
    35, **482**
Smyth, John H., **482**
Social Darwinism, 185–86, **482–83**, 496–
    97. *See also* New Manifest Destiny
Somoza, Anastasio, Jr., 130–31
Soulé, Pierre, 66, 87–88, 160, 344, 395,
    483
Souphanouvong (Laotian prince), 203,
    294–95
South Africa, 26, 95–96, 127–28, 198–

99, 271–72, 320, 332, 375, 385, 498,
    531–32
Southampton, Treaty of (1625), 130
Southeast Asia Treaty Organization
    (SEATO), 129, 167–68, 202, 203,
    273–74, 336–37, 342–43, 382–83,
    411, **483–84**
Souvanna Phouma (Laotian prince), 203,
    294–95
Soviet Union, 335–36, 477–78; arms lim-
    itation and, 385, 405–6, 441, 493–94,
    494, 494–95; Cold War and (before
    1953), 57–58, 123–24, 129, 262, 263,
    388, 402; Cold War and (since 1953),
    10, 57, 72–73, 122, 129, 517; detente
    and, 123–24, 156 , 233–34; diplomatic
    representatives, U.S., in (1933–1953),
    89–90, 143, 225–26, 234–35, 280–81,
    285–86, 481–82, 486, 486–87; diplo-
    matic representatives, U.S., in (since
    1953), 48–49, 72–73, 227–28, 289–90,
    345, 491–92, 508, 510–11; interna-
    tional conferences, World War II, 363–
    64, 364, 364–65; international confer-
    ences (1945–1953), 365, 426, 557–58;
    international conferences (since 1953),
    203, 204–5, 205, 233–34, 365, 365–
    66, 441, 538–39; international organi-
    zations and, 127, 134–35, 518–19,
    519–20; recognition of, 108–9, 450–
    51; treaties and agreements, with other
    nations, 25, 377 433; treaties and
    agreements, with U.S. (before 1953),
    5–6, 450–51, 519; treaties and agree-
    ments, with U.S. (since 1953), 35, 57,
    257, 385, 405–6, 493–94; World War
    II and, 5, 62–63, 260, 439, 469–70,
    504, 557–58. *See also* Brezhnev, Leo-
    nid; Gorbachev, Mikhail; Khrushchev,
    Nikita; Stalin, Joseph; World War II;
    Cold War
Spain, 13, 15, 20, 22, 66, 334–35, 335–
    36, 385, 484, 505, 528; American
    Revolution and, 29, 302; diplomatic
    representatives, U.S., in (1779–1850),
    42, 189, 264, 268–69, 418, 475; dip-
    lomatic representatives, U.S., in
    (1850–1900), 52, 160, 190, 318–19,

427, 467, 478, 483, 502, 553–54; diplomatic representatives, U.S., in (since
1900), 31, 61, 77, 175–76, 214–15,
223, 231, 254, 332, 541, 547; territorial expansion, U.S., and, 395; treaties
and agreements, with U.S., 10, 269,
386–87, 419; treaties and agreements
with other nations, 29, 463, 563
Spanish-American War (1898), 147–48,
153–54, 155, 157, 350, 504–5, 505;
causes of, 153–54, 334–35; diplomatic
representatives, U.S., during, 23–24,
99–100, 178–79, 229–30, 239–40,
302–3, 316, 425, 544, 553–54; peacemaking and subsequent problems, 27–
28, 103–4, 151, 402, 467
Spanish civil war (1936–1939), 77, 277,
484
Spencer, Herbert, 185–86, 482–83
"Sphere of influence," 391, **484–85**
Spooner Act (1902), 235, **485**
Squier, Ephraim G., 21, **485**
Squiers, Herbert G., **485–86**
Sri Lanka (Ceylon), 321
Stalin, Joseph, 25, 48–49, 152–53, 225–
26, 242–43, 364, 463, 469–70, 481–
82, 504, 557–58
Standley, William H., 111, **486**
"Star Wars." *See* Strategic Defense
Initiative
START. *See* Strategic Arms Reduction
Talks
State-Army-Navy-Air Force Coordinating
Committee (SANACC), 376–77
State-War-Navy Coordinating Committee
(SWNCC), 376–77
Steinhardt, Lawrence A., **486–87**
Stephens, John Lloyd, **487**
Stettinius, Edward R., Jr., 168–69, 260,
304, 335, 414–15, 463, **487–88**, 489
Stevens, John L., **488–89**
Stevenson, Adlai E., II, 67, 209–10, **489**
Stevenson, Andrew, **498–90**
Stilwell, Joseph, 144, 199–200
Stimson, Henry L., 91, 170, 243–44,
315, 473, **490–91**; and Latin America,
509–10; and Manchurian crisis, 335–
36, 368–69, 491; and World War II,

260, 359–60, 507–8. *See also* Stimson
Doctrine
Stimson Doctrine (1932), 108–9, 335–36,
490–91, **491**, 550–51
Stockton, Robert F., 49–50, 151–52, **491**
Stoessel, Walter J., Jr., **491–92**
Stone, William J., 492
Stone-Flood Act (1915), **492**
Straight, Willard D., 161, 250, **492–93**
Strategic Arms Limitation Talks (SALT),
10–11, 156, 273–74, 286–88, 365,
382, 446–47, **493–94**, 508, 510–11,
512, 534–35
Strategic Arms Reduction Talks
(START), 366, 441, 493–94, **494**, 538
Strategic Defense Initiative (SDI), 205,
441, 494, **494–95**
Straus, Jesse I., **495**
Straus, Oscar S., **495–96**
Strobel, Edward H., **496**
Strong, Josiah, 482–83, **496–97**
Stuart, John Leighton, **497**
Suez crisis (1956), 36–37, 90–91, 167–
68, 174, 302, **497–98**; U.S. diplomats
concerned with, 14–15, 95–96, 223–
24, 310–11, 546–47
Sullivan, Leon, 498
Sullivan Principles, **498**
Sumner, Charles, **498**
Sun Yat-Sen, 298, 466–67
Sussex pledge (1916), 474, **499**, 517
Swanson, Claude, 554
Sweden, 30, 42, 68–69, 97, 227, 402,
486–87, 488–89, 507
Swift, John F., 23–24, 133, 247–48, **499**
Swing, Raymond Gram, **499–500**
Switzerland, 146–47, 206–7, 214, 227,
237–38, 303–4, 402, 527–28, 550–51
Syria, 102, 284, 300–301, 301–2, 370,
464, 479, 558–59, 559–60

Tacna-Arica dispute, 313, 490–91, 532–
33, 533–34
Taft, Alphonso, **501**
Taft, William Howard, 24, 138, 299,
501; diplomacy during presidential
administration of (1909–1913), 161,

312, 400, 492–93, 549. *See also*
Knox, Philander C.; *names of U.S.
diplomatic representatives*
Taft Agreement (1904), 138, **501**
Taft-Katsura Agreement (1905), **501**
Taylor, Bayard, **502**
Taylor, Hannis, **502**
Taylor, Maxwell D., 273–74, **503**, 503–4
Taylor, Zachary: diplomacy during presidential administration of (1849–1850),
122. *See also* Clayton, John M.; *names
of U.S. diplomatic representatives*
Taylor-Rostow Mission, 454–55, 503,
503–4
Technical Cooperation Administration.
See Point Four
Teheran Conference (1943), 72–73, 98–
99, 143–44, 190–91, 252–53, 363–64,
504
Tehuantepec transit projects, 170, 330,
453, 459, 483, 540
Teller, Henry M., **504–5**, 505
Teller Amendment (1898), 504, **504–5**
Ten Years' War (1868–1878), **505**
Tenney, Charles D., 505
Tenth International Conference of American States (1954). *See* Caracas Conference (1954)
Terrell, Edwin H., **506**
Territorial acquisitions, U.S.: Alaska,
334; Canal Zone, 229–30; Danish West
Indies, 143; Florida, 10; Gadsden Purchase, 196; Guam, 402; Louisiana Purchase, 317; Mexican cession, 215–16;
Oregon, 392; Puerto Rico, 402; Texas,
506; Webster-Ashburton Treaty, 540–
41
Texas, 9, 10, 36, 99, 119, 162–63, 189,
211, 283, 424, 498–90, 506, 520–21,
522–23, 540
Texas, Joint Resolution on (1845), **506**
Thailand, 273–74, 342–43, 411, 483–84.
See also Siam
Third International Conference of American States (1906). *See* Rio de Janeiro
Conference (1906)
"Third World," 240–41, 257–58, 367–
68, 406–7, 457–58, **506–7**

Thomas, William W., Jr., **507**
Thomas Amendment, **507–8**
Thompson, Llewellyn, **508**
Thompson, Waddy, Jr., **508–9**
Thomson-Urrutia Treaty (1921), 311–12,
413–14, **509**
Tientsin, Treaties of (1858), 92–93, 226–
27, 435, **509**
Tipitapa, Peace of (1927), 170, 490–91,
509–10
Tokyo Round, 201–2
Tonkin Gulf Resolution (1964). *See* Gulf
of Tonkin Resolution (1964)
Toombs, Robert A., **510**
Toon, Malcolm, **510–11**, 538–39
Tower, Charlemagne, **511**
Tower, John, 261–62, 326–27
Tracy, Benjamin, 381
Transcontinental Treaty (1819). *See* Adams-Onis Treaty (1819)
Treaty. *See* International agreement
Treaty of Amity and Commerce, Franco-
American (1778), 131, 192, 380, 421,
511–12
Trent affair (1861), 136, 343–44, 472–
73, 479–80, **512**, 558
Trescot, William H., 23–24, 252, 499,
512–13, 533–34
Trescot-Santodomingo Protocol (1881),
513
Trianon, Treaty of (1920), 80, **513**, 530–
31
TRIDENT Conference, 15, **513**
Trieste question, 204–5, 319–20, 370–71,
404, 508
Trilateral Commission, 86–87
Tripartite Claims Commission, 404
Tripartite Pact (1940), 450, **513–14**, 519
Tripartite Treaty (1889). *See* Berlin
Treaty (1889)
Trist, Nicholas P., 215–16, **514**
Truman, Harry S, 271–72, 299–300; diplomacy during presidential administration of (1945–1953), 72, 77–78, 129,
342, 364–65, 423, 426, 439, 514–15.
See also Byrnes, James F.; Marshall,
George C.; Acheson, Dean G.; *names
of U.S. diplomatic representatives*;

Cold War; Korean War; Truman Doctrine

Truman Doctrine (1947), 5–6, 60, 234–35, 332, 342, **514–15**, 524

Trusteeship Council (United Nations), 90–91, 463, **515**

Tshombe, Moise, 126–27

Turkey, 42–43, 141, 522–23; and Cold War, 36–37, 385–86, 386–87, 402, 514–15; diplomatic representatives, U.S., in (before 1900), 23–24, 61–62, 73, 83, 136, 339–40, 467–68, 495–96, 531, 548; diplomatic representatives, U.S., in (since 1900), 82–83, 172–73, 214, 223–24, 303–4, 327–28, 413–14, 445–46, 486–87, 495–96; and World War I, 284, 464; and World War II, 98–99

Turner, James M., **515**

Twenty-One Demands, 85–86, **515–16**, 547

Two Sicilies, 30

Tyler, John: diplomacy during presidential administration of (1841–1845), 137–38, 375, 506, 533, 540–41. *See also* Cal-houn, John C.; Upshur, Abel P.; Webster, Daniel; *names of U.S. diplomatic representatives*

U–2 incident (1960), 58–59, 236, 310–11, **517**

U-boats, German, 29, 208–9, 320–21, 499, **517**

Uhl, Edwin F., **517–18**

United Arab Emirates, 393–94

United Arab Republic, 45–46, 223–24, 302, 436–37

United Fruit Company, 216, 279, **518**, 563

United Nations, 35, 76, 104, 114–15, 127–28, 187, 194–95, 216, 298–99, 336, **518–19**, 532–33; atomic energy and, 5–6; auxiliary organizations and, 80–81, 259, 410, 423, 515; creation of, 34, 124, 127, 135–36, 168–69, 190–91, 223–24, 242–43, 244, 250–51, 330–31, 463, 487–88, 524, 544–45, 557–58; crises and incidents in-volving, 26, 126–27, 182, 262, 262–63, 375, 428, 430, 440, 497–98, 558–59; diplomatic representatives, U.S., to (before 1960), 34, 90–91, 133–34, 167–68, 271–72, 285–86, 310–11, 448, 449, 453–54, 487–88, 489; diplomatic representatives, U.S., to (since 1960), 54, 65–66, 94, 240–41, 286, 367–68, 489, 531–32, 559–60, 560; public organizations in support of, 188, 551–52; regional organizations and, 392–93, 393–94, 398–99

United Nations Declaration (1942), 30, 62–63, 127, **519**

United Nations Development Fund, 240–41

United Nations Economic and Social Commission (ECOSOC), 551

United Nations Educational, Social, and Cultural Organization (UNESCO), 65–66, 173, 194–95, 330–31, 449–50, 463, 551

United Nations Emergency Force (UNEF), 310–11, 497–98

United Nations Population Commission, 165–66

United Nations Relief and Rehabilitation Administration (UNRRA), 5, 21–11, 176, 257–58, **519–20**, 524

United States Information Agency (USIA), 16–17, 102, 372, **520**, 525

United States Mail Steamship Company, 348–49

Universal Postal Union, 59

Upshur, Abel P., 99, **520–21**

Uruguay, 81–82, 150, 227, 358, 413–14, 488–89, 555; international conferences in, 356–57, 428

Uruguay Round, 201–2

USIA. *See* United States Information Agency

"Uti possidetis," **521**

Vail, Aaron, **522**

Van Buren, Martin, 104, 338, **522–23**; diplomacy during presidential administration of (1837–1841), 328–29, 522.

See also Forsyth, John; Jackson, Andrew

Vance, Cyrus R., 86–87, 117, 262–63, 372–73, 376–77, **523**

Vandenberg, Arthur H., 364–65, 386–87, 449, 463, **524**

Vandenberg Resolution, 85

Vanderbilt, Cornelius, 5, **524–25**, 530

Vargas, Getulio, 98

Vatican City, 310–11, 335–36

Vaughn, Jack Hood, **525**

Venezuela, 88, 393–94, 525–26, 526; diplomatic representatives, U.S., in (before 1900), 76–77, 316, 406, 469; diplomatic representatives, U.S., in (since 1900), 31, 99–100, 163, 199, 459. *See also* Venezuelan crisis (1895); Venezuelan dispute (1902–1903)

Venezuelan crisis (1895), 46, 350, 390, 411–12, 469, **525–26**

Venezuelan dispute (1902–1903), 76–77, 165, 511, **526**, 545–46

Versailles, Treaty of (1919), 69–70, 89–90, 124, 144–45, 228, 299, 437, 438–39, **526**, 550–51; conferences and treaties related to, 57, 403–4, 433, 464, 513, 554; controversial sections of, 32, 473; organizations created by, 259, 298–99; ratification of, by U.S. Senate, opponents, 264, 288–89, 312–13, 440; ratification of, supporters, 188, 240. *See also* Wilson, Woodrow; Paris Peace Conference (1919); World War I

Vice-consul. *See* Consul

Vienna, Second Congress of, 113

Vienna Summit Conference (1961), 508

Vietnam, Democratic Republic of (North Vietnam), 202, 203

Vietnam, Republic of (South Vietnam), 202, 203, 336–37; diplomatic representatives, U.S., in (before 1963), 169, 232, 383, 436–37; diplomatic representatives, U.S., in (1963–1975), 91–92, 310–11, 342–43, 503. *See also* Vietnam War

Vietnam War, 365, 403; diplomats, U.S., concerned with conduct of, 55, 91–92, 220, 238–39, 273–74, 310–11, 342–

43, 377–78, 383, 454–55, 489, 503; diplomats, U.S., concerned with peacemaking, 84–85, 91–92, 220, 225–26, 286–88, 310–11, 377–78, 453–54; incidents related to, 100, 110, 217, 295, 503–4; opponents of, 138–39, 194–95, 378, 461–62, 534–35; principles involved in, 162, 382–83, 470, 526–27; supporters of, 372–73. *See also* Vietnam, Republic of (South Vietnam)

Vietnamization, 91–92, 238–39, **526–27**

Vignaud, Henry, 178–79, **527**

Vincent, John Carter, **527–28**

Virgin Islands, acquisition of (1917). *See* Danish West Indies, acquisition of (1917)

Virginius episode (1873), 185, 478, 505, **528**

Vladivostok Agreement (1974), 493–94, 534–35

Voice of America (VOA), 520

Vopicka, Charles J., 172–73, **528–29**

Vorys amendment (1939), 529

Wake Island, 4

Walker, William, 5, 108, 184–85, 483, 524–25, **530**, 543–44

Wallace, Hugh Campbell, **530–31**

Wallace, Lew, **531**

Walters, Vernon, **531–32**

Wambaugh, Sarah, **532–33**

Wang-hsia, Treaty of (1844), 61–62, 226–27, 278, 375, 404–5, **533**

"War Hawks," **533**

War of 1812, 9, 25, 97, 177, 356, 360–61; British violations of U.S. neutrality, 113, 178, 255, 391, 392; diplomatic representatives concerned with, 31–32, 41, 137, 198, 355–56; French violations of U.S. neutrality, 59, 129–30, 353, 432; peace settlements, 119, 130–31, 206, 249–50, 457; U.S. responses to violations of neutrality, 174–75, 175, 309, 331, 384, 533. *See also* Jefferson, Thomas; Madison, James

War of the Pacific (1879–1883), 116–17,

179, 193, 209, **533–34**; diplomatic representatives, U.S., concerned with, 66–67, 252, 282–83, 313, 394, 406, 412–13, 512–13

War Powers Resolution (1973), **534**

Warnke, Paul C., **534–35**

Wars, foreign: before 1900, 71–72, 478–79, 505, 533–34; since 1900, 460, 479, 533–34, 558–59

Warsaw Pact (1955), 373, 385, 385–86, 441–42

Washburn, Albert H., **535**

Washburne, Elihu B., 433–34, **536**

Washington, George, 182, 311–12, 341–42; diplomacy during presidential administration of (1789–1797), 270–71, 380. *See also* Jefferson, Thomas; Randolph, Edmund

Washington, Treaty of (1871), 7–8, 13, 145, 179, 185, 465–66, **536**

Washington Conference (1889), 66–67, 92, 103–4, 132, 401, 512–13, **536**

Washington Conference (1907), 10, 88, 109–10, 451–52, 464, **537**

Washington Conference on the Limitation of Naval Armaments (1921–1922), 68–69, 75, 117–18, 123, 155–56, 294, 305–6, 477–78, **537**; diplomatic representatives concerned with, 199, 227, 228, 248–49, 272, 311–12, 437, 451–52, 468–69, 471; other conferences related to, 204, 554; treaties concluded, 186, 191, 381–82

Washington Summit Conference (1987), 257, 345, 494, **538**

Water Witch, affair of (1858), 78

Watson, Arthur K., **538**

Watson, Thomas J., Jr., **538–39**

Webb, James Watson, 539

Webb-Pomerene Act (1918), **539–40**

Webster, Daniel, 7, 107–8, 137–38, 180, 285, 311–12, 341, 520–21, **540**, 540–41

Webster-Ashburton Treaty (1842), 16, 137–38, 285, 354, 392, 451, 540, **540–41**; diplomatic representatives, U.S., concerned with, 107–8, 180, 297

Weddell, Alexander W., **541**

Wedemeyer, Albert C., 497

Weimar Republic, 461, 466–67

Weitzel, George T., 112

Welles, Sumner, 250–51, 354–55, **541–42**

Welsh, John, **542**

Western European Union (WEU), 178, 314–15, 386–87, 402–3

Westphalia, Treaty of (1648), 38

Wheaton, Henry, **543**

Wheeler, John H., 530, **543–44**

White, Andrew D., 517–18, **544**

White, Harry Dexter, 80–81, 260–61, **544–45**

White, Henry, 88–89, **545**

White, William Allen, 125

"White man's burden," 354

Whitlock, Brand, 206–7, **546**

Whitney, John Hay, **546–47**

Wilhelm, Kaiser (William II), 267, 351–52

Willard, Joseph E., **547**

Williams, Edward T., **547**

Williams, James, **548**

Willis, Albert S., **548–49**

WILPF. *See* Women's International League for Peace and Freedom

Wilson, F.M. Huntington, 288–89, **549**

Wilson, Henry Lane, 394–95, **549–50**

Wilson, Hugh R., **550–51**, 554

Wilson, Woodrow, 135, 136–37, 336, 391, 397, 470, 551; diplomacy during presidential administration of (1913–1921), 85–86, 127, 246–47, 361, 397–98, 400, 403–4. *See also* Bryan, William Jennings; Colby, Bainbridge; Lansing, Robert; *names of U.S. diplomatic representatives*; Paris Peace Conference (1919); Versailles, Treaty of (1919); World War I

Wilson Plan (1914), **551**

Wilson-Gorman Tariff (1894), 328

Winant, John G., 12, **551**

Women's International League for Peace and Freedom (WILPF), **551–52**, 554

Wood, Leonard, **552–53**

Wood, Thomas B., **553**

Woodford, Stewart L., **553–54**

Wooley, Mary E., 551–52
World Bank. *See* International Bank for Reconstruction and Development
World Court. *See* Permanent Court of International Justice
World Disarmament Conference (1932–1934), 147, 206–7, 550–51, **554**World Health Organization (WHO), 463
World War I, 69–70, 110, 176, 191, 256, 403–4, 470; controversy over intervention in, 147–48, 388; diplomatic representatives concerned with, 160–61, 166, 172–73, 199, 205–6 221–22, 235, 343, 361, 369–70, 397, 397–98, 409, 437, 474, 528–29, 546, 547; incidents leading to U.S. intervention in, 29, 80, 208–9, 247, 291–92, 320–21, 499, 517, 563–64; State Department officials and advisers concerned with, 145–46, 246–47, 284; treaties subsequent to, 57, 462, 513, 526. *See also* Paris Peace Conference (1919); Versailles, Treaty of (1919)
World War II, 62–63, 259–60, 260, 323, 376, 407, 450, 469–70; broadcasters and correspondents, 138–39, 144–45, 277, 306, 372, 470–71, 499–500; conferences, Allied military and strategic, 15, 30, 98–99, 106–7, 335, 363–64, 429–30, 430, 443, 504, 513, 519; conferences, international, non-military, 168–69, 335, 364, 364–65, 404, 426, 430, 557–58; Congressional acts and resolutions, 127, 376; major diplomatic representatives, U.S., during, 60, 61, 77, 79, 199–200, 225–26, 227, 231, 234–35, 242–43, 252–53, 299–300, 332, 349, 354–55, 370–71, 414–15, 486, 551; organizations, internationalist, 104, 111, 125, 184, 188; organizations, isolationist, 20–21; post-war planning and reconstruction, 65, 152–53, 168–69, 178, 190–91, 359–60, 439, 519–20, 557–58; State Depart-

ment officials and advisers, 95, 143–44, 147, 183–84, 209–10, 243–44; treaties and agreements, among other nations, 25, 27, 377, 513–14; treaties and agreements, with U.S., 33, 304. *See also* Cold War; France; Germany; Great Britain; Japan; Soviet Union; United Nations
World's Columbian Exposition, Chicago (1893), 48, 88, 308, 325, 507
Wright, Joseph A., **554–55**
Wright, Joshua B., **555**
Wright, Luke E., **555–56**
Wriston, Henry, 556
Wriston Report, **556**

XYZ Affair, 341–42, 418, 429, 557

Yalta Conference (1945), 134–35, 180, 252–53, **557–58**; agreements made, 18–19, 152–53, 439; other conferences related to, 168–69, 335, 364, 426; U.S. delegates to, 95, 299–300, 340–41, 487–88
Yancey, William L., 510, **558**
Yemen Arab Republic, 90–91, 223–24, 436–37
Yom Kippur War (1973), 286–88, 393–94, 440, **558–59**
Yost, Charles W., **559–60**
Young, Andrew J., Jr., **560**
Young, John R., **560–61**
Young, Owen D., **561**, 562
Young America, **561–62**
Young Plan (1929), 149, 159–60, 207–8, 291–92, 438–39, 510–11, 561, **562**
Yucatan caste war. *See* Caste war, Yucatan
Yugoslavia, 16–17, 102, 186, 280–81, 319–20, 332, 365, 404, 535

Zanjon, Pact of (1878), 505, **563**
Zelaya, Jose Santos, 348–49
Zemurray, Samuel, 518, **563**
Zimmerman Telegram, 186–87, **563–64**

ABOUT THE AUTHOR

John E. Findling is professor of history at Indiana University Southeast in New Albany, Indiana. He is the author of the original *Dictionary of American Diplomatic History* (Greenwood Press, 1980), *Close Neighbors, Distant Friends: United States-Central American Relations* (Greenwood Press, 1987), and articles appearing in several scholarly publications. Mr. Findling is presently working on a historical dictionary of world's fairs.